CONTENTS

KU-745-728

The English Tourist Board
The Board is a statutory body created by the Development of Tourism Act 1969, to develop and market England's tourism. Its main objectives are to provide a welcome for people visiting England; to encourage people living in England to take their holidays there; and to encourage the provision and improvement of tourist amenities and facilities in England. The Board has a statutory duty to advise the Government on tourism matters relating to England and administers the official voluntary registration scheme approved and supported by the Government. This scheme provides information needed for the planning and development of tourist facilities in the future. Through Where to Stay, it also gives hoteliers and other providers of tourist accommodation the chance to tell you, the customer, what they have to offer during 1989.

Important: The information contained in this guide has been published in good faith on the basis of information submitted to the English Tourist Board by the proprietors of the premises listed, who have paid for their entries to appear. The English Tourist Board cannot guarantee the accuracy of the information in this guide and accepts no responsibility for any error or misrepresentation. All liability for loss, disappointment, negligence or other damage caused by reliance on the information contained in this guide, or in the event of bankruptcy, or liquidation, or cessation of trade of any company, individual or firm mentioned, is hereby excluded.

Published by:
English Tourist Board, Thames Tower, Black's Road, Hammersmith, London W6 9EL
Internal Reference Number ETB/213/89
AS/1128/47.5M/88

Managing Editor: Sally Marshall
Design & Production: Guide Associates, Croydon
Colour Photography: Glyn Williams and 'Britain on View'
Regional Maps: Colin Earl Cartography
Cartography: ESR Ltd, West Byfleet
Typesetting: SB Datagraphics Ltd, Colchester, and Guide Associates, Croydon
Printing & Binding: Bemrose Security Printing, Derby
Advertisement Department: James of Fleet Street Ltd, 184 Fleet Street, London EC4A 2HD
Telephone: 01-242 0101

© English Tourist Board.

KINGSTON UPON THAMES
PUBLIC LIBRARIES

B33957

ALL	CLASS	
HR	914.2	
CAT	REFS	
P 4.95	BNB	

There is one holiday country that appeals to all — whatever your age, whatever your tastes, whatever the weather. That country is England. Sandy beaches, quiet coves and wild headlands...mountains, moors, lakes and rivers...old-world villages, historic cities and mellow market towns...castles, cathedrals, stately homes and museums...theme parks, animal kingdoms and grand gardens. England has them all.

Add to that mix better standards of accommodation...new all-weather facilities and leisure attractions...a renaissance of English cooking...ease of travel...no language problems...and the appeal of England as a holiday destination is complete.

With the help of this 'Where to Stay' guide, you can put together your own perfect holiday package and discover again the real appeal of England.

The appeal of England also rests in the sheer diversity of its accommodation for tourists. There are old-world village inns; bed & breakfasts in town and on the coast; low-cost hostels and university accommodation, particularly suitable for young people and groups; and working farms which offer a more informal style of hospitality. They're all ready with a warm welcome for you.

Each accommodation entry in this guide has a short description to help you get the 'feel' of the place, an indication of prices and a set of symbols to show the facilities and services available. There is a key to the symbols inside the back cover.

Spend a little time with this guide and whichever part of the country you're planning to visit, you're sure to find accommodation that's right at a price that's right for you.

Tourist
Information

INFORMATION

There are over 550 Tourist Information Centres throughout England offering advice and information to the tourist. The centres are staffed by people who understand that there is more to tourist information than simply handing out brochures — people who can help with the sort of inside information that makes a holiday a success.

Services offered include all or many of the following:

IDEAS FOR PLACES TO VISIT AND THINGS TO DO

HOW TO GET THERE BY CAR OR PUBLIC TRANSPORT

TICKET BOOKINGS FOR TRAVEL AND ATTRACTIONS

BROCHURES, PAMPHLETS, MAPS AND GUIDES, BOTH FREE AND FOR SALE

FINDING A PLACE TO STAY, FROM A FARMHOUSE TO A 5 CROWN HOTEL

ON-THE-SPOT SHOPPING FOR SOUVENIRS, LOCAL GOODS AND CRAFTS

To get the best from your holiday, follow the $\boxed{i}$ sign for advice and information that's friendly and free.

Look out also for the $\boxed{i}$ sign at Tourist Information Points in the form of displays in town centres, car parks, lay-bys and picnic sites.

Tourist Information Centres are listed in the regional information sections of this 'Where to Stay' guide. A national directory of centres is available free of charge from Tourist Information Centres themselves or by post from the English Tourist Board.

When you see the Crown or Listed sign at a hotel, guesthouse, farmhouse, inn or B&B in England you'll know you have found accommodation you can check into with confidence. Every establishment displaying the sign is checked out regularly by inspectors from the Tourist Board and is given a classification — from 'Listed' up to '5 Crowns' — to indicate the level of facilities and services provided. Brief explanations of the six classifications are given opposite while a fuller explanation

CONFIDENCE

Listed Clean and comfortable accommodation, although the range of facilities and services may be limited.

Accommodation with additional facilities, including washbasins in all bedrooms, a lounge area and use of a telephone.

Accommodation with a wider range of facilities and services, including morning tea/coffee and calls, bedside lights in all bedrooms, colour TV in lounge or bedrooms, assistance with luggage.

Accommodation with at least one-third of the bedrooms with en suite WC and bath or shower, plus easy chair and full-length mirror in all bedrooms, shoe cleaning facilities and hairdryers available, and a separate quiet lounge.

Accommodation with at least three-quarters of the bedrooms with en suite WC and bath or shower plus colour TV, radio and telephone in all bedrooms, 24-hour access and lounge service until midnight.

Accommodation with all bedrooms having WC, bath and shower en suite, trouser press (or valet service), plus a wide range of facilities and services, including room service, all-night lounge service and laundry service.

The classifications which appear in the entries in this guide were correct at the time the entries were accepted. Establishments which do not show a classification may have been inspected and classified since the publishing deadline for the guide.

All establishments featured in this guide are registered with the English Tourist Board and undertake to meet or exceed the Board's minimum standards and to observe the Tourist Boards' Code of Conduct.

of the national Crown Classification Scheme is given at the back of this guide.

A lower classification does not imply lower standards; although the range of facilities and services may be less extensive, they may be provided to a high standard.

There are minimum requirements for each classification. However, all classified accommodation is likely to have some of the facilities and services of a higher classification.

This 'Where to Stay' guide will make it easy for you to find accommodation in England to suit your mood and your pocket. The content has been structured to enable you to find a place to stay even if you have only a general idea of the area you are planning to visit. Just follow the notes below and you'll soon find accommodation that's right for you.

WHAT IT CONTAINS

The main body of this guide is divided into 12 sections corresponding with England's tourist regions (illustrated in the map on page 12).

Each regional section begins with a location map and an introduction with details of major attractions and events for 1989, followed by a list of Tourist Information Centres.

The region's cities, towns and villages with their accommodation are then listed alphabetically. Accompanying each place name is a map reference which refers to the colour maps towards the back of the guide. This enables you to pinpoint the exact location.

There is a complete index at the end of the guide which lists cities, towns and villages with accommodation featured in the guide.

FINDING ACCOMMODATION

If you already know the name of the city, town or village in which you wish to stay, simply use the index at the end of the guide to find the relevant page number.

If you are touring or only know the general area in which you wish to stay,

look at the colour maps (which pinpoint all the places with accommodation listed in the guide) to locate particular place names, and then refer to the index of place names.

DESCRIPTIONS OF ACCOMMODATION

Accommodation information published in this guide has been provided by the proprietors of the establishments. Some of the information is represented by symbols and you will find a key to these inside the back cover flap.

BEFORE BOOKING

We advise you to read the 'Further Information' section at the back of this guide before making a booking, particularly the section on 'Cancellations'. You should always check prices and other details with the establishment at the time of booking to avoid misunderstandings.

MAKING ENQUIRIES

Two types of enquiry coupon are included at the back of the guide. One is to help you when contacting establishments about accommodation; the other can be used to request information from any of the advertisers in the guide.

England is divided into 12 tourist regions, each of which has its own section in this guide. The regions are shown on the map above and also listed opposite together with an index which identifies the region in which each county is located.

Counties

Regions

Colour maps showing all the places with accommodation listed in this 'Where to Stay' guide and an index to place names can be found towards the back. More detailed information on how to get the best out of this guide can be found on pages 10 and 11.

London

If you're thinking of one place in England which seems to have most of everything, you must have London on your mind.

It has all the variety and vitality you'd expect of a capital city: top-line shopping in the West End and Knightsbridge; museums and art galleries catering for every interest; restaurants offering every conceivable type of cooking; pubs, both traditional and modern. There are visitor attractions of all kinds, historic houses and churches, major sporting and leisure facilities, 'Theatreland', the Royal parks and gardens. In fact, the list is almost endless.

And then there are the newer places of interest. Sample Covent Garden, with its Continental-style restaurants and shopping; Docklands, now in the throes of an impressive revitalisation programme; and the Barbican entertainments complex in the City.

But don't forget that the London tourist region is not just Central London. It stretches from Heathrow in the west to Romford in the east, from Hadley Wood in the north to Purley in the south. So when you've seen enough of the centre, why not step out a little further and see what else London has to offer?

Now, that's a capital idea!

FIND OUT MORE

Further information about holidays and attractions in the London tourist region is available from:
London Tourist Board and Convention Bureau,
26 Grosvenor Gardens, London SW1W 0DU. ☎ 01-730 3488.

These publications are available from the London Tourist Board and Convention Bureau (prices include postage and packing):
Exploring Central London £2.45
Exploring Outer London £2.25
Children's London £2.60
Traditional London £2.60
London Made Easy £2.60
Shopping in London £1.00

WHERE TO GO, WHAT TO SEE

Cabinet War Rooms
Clive Steps, King Charles Street, London SW1A 2AQ ☎ 01-930 6961
The underground base of Winston Churchill, the War Cabinet and Chiefs of Staff of Britain's Armed Forces during the second world war. Churchill made some of his most memorable wartime broadcasts from here.
Admission charge.

Camden Lock
off Chalk Farm Road, London NW1
Converted 19th C stables and warehouses beside the Regent's Canal, now housing eating-places, workshops and studios for craftsmen, designers and artists in all spheres. Craft and antique market each weekend.

Chessington World of Adventures
Leatherhead Road, Chessington, Surrey KT9 2NE ☎ (037 27) 27227
See Circus World and the Tamara Coco Circus, the Zoological Gardens, Safari Skyway and themed rides including the Fifth Dimension and the Runaway Mine Train.
Admission charge.

Freud Museum
20 Maresfield Gardens, Hampstead, London NW3 5SX ☎ 01-435 2002
Former home of Sigmund Freud, containing his library, consulting room and famous couch.
Admission charge.

HAMPTON COURT PALACE

Britain on View

Hampton Court Palace
East Molesey, Surrey KT8 9AU
☎ 01-977 8441
The oldest Tudor palace in England, home of King Henry VIII. Tudor kitchens, tennis court, maze and State Apartments.
Admission charge.

International Shakespeare Globe Centre
Bear Gardens, Bankside, London SE1 9EB ☎ 01-928 6342
Museum depicting Elizabethan theatre history 1550 – 1642 with models and replicas of the 'Globe' and 'Cockpit' playhouses.
Admission charge.

Museum of the Moving Image
National Film Theatre, London SE1
Museum charting developments in film and TV history with 'hands-on' exhibits and over 50 exhibition areas including a TV studio with cameras.
Admission charge.

ROYAL BOTANIC GARDENS

Britain on View

Royal Botanic Gardens
Kew, Richmond, Surrey TW9 3AB
☎ 01-940 1171
300 acres, formerly owned by the royal family, containing living collections of over 25,000 plant species and varieties. Glasshouses include the most recently opened Princess of Wales glasshouse.
Admission charge.

Royal Britain
Barbican, London EC2
The story of 1,000 years of royal history brought to life by audio-visual techniques.
Admission charge.

3001 – Space Adventure
Tooley Street, London SE1
A flight simulator gives a futuristic ride to Mars via the moon.
Admission charge.

Syon House
Brentford, Middlesex TW8 8JG
☎ 01-560 0881
London home of the Duke of Northumberland. Interiors designed by Adam with gardens laid out by 'Capability' Brown. In Syon Park, London Butterfly Centre, Heritage Motor Museum, art centre and garden centre.
Admission charge.

Tobacco Dock
Wapping, London E1
'Leisure shopping village', with a wide selection of shops and restaurants as well as special themed events and a daily programme of street theatre and entertainment.

MAKE A DATE FOR...

Crufts Dog Show
Earl's Court Exhibition Centre, Warwick Road, London SW5 *9 – 12 February*

Daily Mail Ideal Home Exhibition
Earl's Court Exhibition Centre, Warwick Road, London SW5 *7 March – 2 April*

Easter Parade
Battersea Park, London SW11
26 March *

London Marathon
Greenwich Park, London SE10, to Westminster Bridge, London SW1
23 April

F.A. Challenge Cup Final
Wembley Stadium, Wembley, London
20 May

Chelsea Flower Show
Royal Hospital, Chelsea, London SW3
23 – 26 May (members only on 23 and 24 May)

Trooping the Colour – the Queen's Official Birthday Parade
Horse Guards' Parade, Whitehall, London SW1 *17 June*

Lawn Tennis Championships
All England Lawn Tennis and Croquet Club, Wimbledon, London SW19
26 June – 9 July

Lord Mayor's Show
The City, London *11 November*

Royal Smithfield Show and Agricultural Machinery Exhibition
Earl's Court Exhibition Centre, Warwick Road, London SW5 *3 – 7 December*

* Provisional date only

CRUFTS DOG SHOW

Lee Crocker

WHICH PART OF LONDON?

The majority of tourist accommodation is situated in Central London and is therefore very convenient for most of the city's attractions and night life.

However, there are many hotels in Outer London which provide other advantages, such as easier parking. We have divided London into two main areas — Central London and Outer London — as shown on colour maps 6 and 7 at the back of this guide.

These areas are further subdivided as shown below.

CENTRAL 1
(see page 20)
Covering West End, Piccadilly, Soho, Regent Street, Mayfair, Park Lane, Westminster, Victoria, Elephant and Castle, Whitehall.

CENTRAL 2
(see page 20)
Covering Knightsbridge, South Kensington, Chelsea, Earl's Court, Fulham.

CENTRAL 3
(see page 21)
Covering High Street Kensington, West Kensington, Holland Park, Notting Hill, Olympia, Hammersmith.

CENTRAL 4
(see page 21)
Covering Bayswater, Paddington, Maida Vale.

CENTRAL 5
(see page 22)
Covering King's Cross, St. Pancras, Euston, Bloomsbury, Kingsway, Marylebone, Regents Park, Leicester Square, Strand, Charing Cross, Fleet Street, Holborn, City.

EAST LONDON
(see page 22)
Covering the London boroughs of Barking, Hackney, Havering, Newham, Redbridge, Tower Hamlets, Waltham Forest.

NORTH LONDON
(see page 22)
Covering the London boroughs of Barnet, Brent, Camden, Enfield, Haringey, Harrow, Islington

SOUTH EAST LONDON
(see page 23)
Covering the London boroughs of Bexley, Bromley, Croydon, Greenwich, Lewisham, Southwark.

SOUTH WEST LONDON
(see page 24)
Covering the London boroughs of Kingston upon Thames, Lambeth, Merton, Richmond, Sutton, Wandsworth.

WEST LONDON
(see page 24)
Covering the London boroughs of Ealing, Hammersmith, Hillingdon, Hounslow, also London Airport (Heathrow).

Tourist Information

Tourist and leisure information can be obtained from Tourist Information Centres throughout England. Details of centres and other information services in Greater London are listed below. The symbol 🛏 means that an accommodation booking service is provided. Centres marked with a ✳ are open during the summer months only.

TOURIST INFORMATION CENTRES

CENTRAL LONDON

British Travel Centre 🛏
12 Regent Street, Piccadilly Circus, SW1 ☎ 01-730 3400
Monday-Friday: 0900-1830.
Saturday: 0900-1700 (reduced winter opening). Sunday: 1000-1600 (personal callers only).
Information on travel, accommodation, events and entertainment in England, Scotland, Wales and Northern Ireland. Booking service for rail, air, coach and car travel, sightseeing tours, theatre tickets and accommodation. Bureau de change, bookshop and gift shop.

Victoria Station, Forecourt, SW1 🛏
The information centre on the station forecourt provides tourist information, offers a hotel accommodation booking service, stocks free and saleable

publications on Britain and London and sells theatre tickets, tourist tickets for bus and underground and tickets for sightseeing tours.
November-March: Monday-Saturday: 0900-1900. Sunday: 0900-1700. Easter-October: daily 0900-2030.

Tower of London 🖵 *
West Gate, HM Tower of London, EC3
April-October: daily: 1000-1800.
This centre offers information, sells tourist tickets and publications on London and provides an accommodation booking service.

Selfridges 🖵
Oxford Street, W1 (Basement Services Arcade) and
Harrods 🖵
Knightsbridge, SW1 (on 4th floor)
Open during normal store hours, these centres supply tourist information, leaflets, useful publications, tourist tickets for bus and underground and sightseeing tours and provide an accommodation booking service.

Clerkenwell Heritage (Islington Visitor) Centre
35 St. John's Square, EC1M 4DN
☎ 01-250 1039
April-September: Monday-Friday: 0900-1730.
October-March: Monday-Friday: 1000-1700
Information on Clerkenwell and the London Borough of Islington.

GREATER LONDON

Heathrow Terminals 1,2,3 Underground Station Concourse (Heathrow Airport) 🖵
This centre provides tourist information, stocks free and saleable publications, and offers a hotel accommodation booking service.
Open daily 0900-1800.

Heathrow Terminal 2, Arrivals Concourse (Heathrow Airport)
Daily: 0900-1900.
This centre provides tourist information and stocks free and saleable publications.

Croydon Tourist Information Centre
Katharine Street, Croydon, Surrey, CR9 1ET
☎ 01-760 5630 (direct line) or 01-760 5400 ext. 2984/5
Monday: 0930-1900. Tuesday-Friday: 0930-1800. Saturday: 0900-1700.
Information and advice on places of interest, events and activities in Croydon and the surrounding area.

Greenwich Tourist Information Centre 🖵
46 Greenwich Church Street, SE10 ☎ 01-858 6376
May-September: Daily 1000-1800. October-April: Daily 1000-1700.
Information on places of historic interest in Greenwich.

Harrow Tourist Information Centre
Civic Centre, Station Road, Harrow, Middlesex HA1 2UH
☎ 01-863 5611 ext. 2100/2/3
Monday-Friday: 0900-1700.
Information and advice on places of interest, events and activities in the Borough of Harrow and the surrounding area.

Hillingdon Tourist Information Centre
Central Library, High Street, Uxbridge, Middlesex
☎ (0895) 50706
Monday-Friday: 0930-2000. Saturday: 0930-1700.
Information on places of interest and events in the Borough of Hillingdon and the surrounding area.

Kingston upon Thames Tourist Information Centre
Heritage Centre, Wheatfield Way, Kingston upon Thames, Surrey KT1 2PS
☎ 01-546 5386
Monday-Saturday: 1000-1700.
Information on places of interest and events in Kingston upon Thames and the surrounding area.

Lewisham Tourist Information Centre
Lewisham Library, Lewisham High Street, SE13 6LG
☎ 01-690 8325
Saturday and Monday: 0930-1700. Tuesday-Thursday: 0930-2000. Friday: 0930-1300.
Information on places of interest and events in Lewisham.

▶

Richmond Tourist Information Centre 🏠

Old Town Hall, Whittaker Avenue, Richmond, Surrey

☎ 01-940 9125

Monday, Tuesday, Thursday, Friday: 1000-1800. Wednesday: 1000-2000. Saturday: 1000-1700. Sunday and Bank Holidays: 1015-1515.

Information on places of interest and events in the Borough of Richmond upon Thames.

Tower Hamlets Tourist Information Centre

Mayfield House, Cambridge Heath Road, E2 9LL

☎ 01-980 4831 ext. 5313/5

Monday-Friday: 0900-1700

Information on places of interest and events in the Borough of Tower Hamlets.

Twickenham Tourist Information Centre

District Library, Garfield Road, Twickenham, Middlesex

☎ 01-892 0032

Monday-Saturday: 1000-1700.

Information on places of interest and events in the Twickenham area.

TELEPHONE INFORMATION SERVICE

A telephone information service is provided on Greater London from Monday to Friday, 0900-1800, on 01-730 3488 (an automatic queueing system is in operation). A Riverboat Information Service operates on 01-730 4812.

HOTEL ACCOMMODATION SERVICE

The London Tourist Board and Convention Bureau helps visitors to find and book accommodation at a wide range of prices in hotels and guesthouses, including budget accommodation, within 20 miles of Central London. Reservations are made with hotels which are members of LTB denoted in this guide with the symbol **AA** by their name.

Reservations on arrival are handled at the Tourist Information centres operated by LTB at Victoria Station forecourt, Heathrow Terminals 1,2,3 Underground Station Concourse, HM Tower of London, Harrods and Selfridges. Go to any of them **on the day** when you need accommodation. A communication charge and a refundable deposit are payable when making a reservation.

Advance bookings are handled by letter. Please write to the Accommodation Services advance booking department at LTB's head office at 26 Grosvenor Gardens, London SW1W ODU at least six weeks before you intend to arrive. The Board acts as an introductory agency and will make a provisional reservation on your behalf. Unless the booking is confirmed with the hotel direct and a copy sent to LTB the reservation will be cancelled.

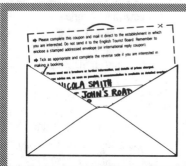

When enquiring about accommodation you may find it helpful to use the booking enquiry coupons which can be found towards the end of the guide. These should be cut out and mailed direct to the establishments in which you are interested. Remember to include your name and address and please enclose a stamped addressed envelope (or an international reply coupon if writing from outside Britain).

London Index

If you are looking for accommodation in a particular establishment in London and you know its name, this index will give you the page number of the full entry in the guide. London establishments which are separately listed in the special Group & Youth Section (pages 346 – 357) are not indexed below.

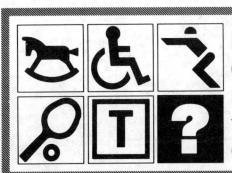

KEY TO SYMBOLS

Open out the flap inside the back cover of this guide and the key to symbols will be easy to use.

Entries in this regional section are listed under 5 Central London areas and 5 Outer London areas — shown on colour maps 6 and 7 towards the end of this guide. If you want to look up a particular establishment, use the index to establishments to find the page number.

Telephone numbers include the 01- London prefix. Remember not to use this prefix if dialling from inside the London area.

The Crown Classifications are explained on pages 8 and 9, and the key to symbols is on the flap inside the back cover — keep it open for easy reference.

CENTRAL LONDON 1

Covering West End, Piccadilly, Soho, Regent Street, Mayfair, Park Lane, Westminster, Victoria, Elephant and Castle, Whitehall. See map 6.

Blandford Hotel
80 Chiltern St., London
W1M 1PS
☎ 01-486 3103
Convenient for Baker Street underground station.
Bedrooms: 9 single, 9 double & 9 twin, 6 family rooms.
Bathrooms: 33 private.
Bed & breakfast: from £45.95 single, from £57.45 double.
Credit: Access, Visa, Diners, Amex.
🛏 🛆 📞 🖵 🖅 📺 ◑ 🎬 🍽 🐾 T

Elizabeth Hotel ₼
😃
37 Eccleston Sq., London
SW1V 1PB
☎ 01-828 6812
Friendly, quiet hotel overlooking lovely gardens of stately residential square (c. 1835). Close to Belgravia and within 5 minutes' walk of Victoria.
Bedrooms: 11 single, 4 double & 4 twin, 6 family rooms.
Bathrooms: 3 private, 6 public; 4 private showers.
Bed & breakfast: max. £26 single, £40-£57 double.
🛏 🛆 📞 ✂ 📺 🎬 🖼 🛆 🐾 ❄ 🍽 ᴅᴀᴘ T

Enrico Guest House
77-79 Warwick Way, London
SW1V 1QP
☎ 01-834 9538
Small hotel convenient for Victoria station.
Bedrooms: 4 single, 13 double & 9 twin.

Bathrooms: 5 public; 8 private showers.
Bed & breakfast: £20-£22 single, £30-£36 double.
🛏 🛆 🖅 ᵁᴸ 🖅 📺 🎬 🛆 🍽 🐾

Jubilee Bed and Breakfast
31 Eccleston Sq., London
SW1V 1NZ
☎ 01-834 0873 & 0845
Eccleston Square is ideally situated only a few minutes from Victoria coach and railway stations and within walking distance of Westminster and Buckingham Palace.
Bedrooms: 2 single, 7 double & 6 twin, 9 family rooms.
Bathrooms: 1 private, 4 public; 10 private showers.
Bed & breakfast: £16-£22 single, £26-£34 double.
🛏 🛆 ᵁᴸ ᶜᴮ 🖅 📺 ◑ 🛆 🐾 🍽 T

Sidney Hotel ₼
😃😃
76 Belgrave Rd., London
SW1V 4LU
☎ 01-834 2738 & 2860
Friendly establishment, a few minutes' walk from Victoria rail and coach stations.
Bedrooms: 7 single, 7 double & 5 twin, 4 family rooms.
Bathrooms: 15 private, 3 public; 2 private showers.
Bed & breakfast: £21.50-£28.50 single, £34-£42 double.
Credit: Access, Visa, Diners, Amex.
🛏 🛆 📞 ⑨ 🖵 ᵁᴸ 🖅 📺 ◑ 🎬 🛆 🍽 ᴅᴀᴘ ꜱᴘ T

Westminster House Hotel
96 Ebury St., London
SW1W 9QD
☎ 01-730 4302
Bedrooms: 3 single, 3 double & 4 twin, 2 family rooms.

Bathrooms: 2 private, 3 public.
Bed & breakfast: from £26 single, £36-£42 double.
🛏 🛆 🖵 ✪ ᵁᴸ 🖅 🛆 🍽 ꜱᴘ T

Windermere Hotel ₼
😃😃😃
142 Warwick Way, London
SW1V 4JE
☎ 01-834 5163 & 5480
Telex 94017182 WIREG
A small bed and breakfast hotel near Victoria coach and railway stations, with many of the amenities of a large hotel.
Bedrooms: 1 single, 2 double & 3 twin, 3 family rooms.
Bathrooms: 9 private, 1 public.
Bed & breakfast: £30-£38 single, £44-£54 double.
Credit: Visa.
🛏 😃6 🛆 📞 🖵 ᵁᴸ 🌡 ◑ 🎬 🛆 🍽 ᴅᴀᴘ ꜱᴘ T

CENTRAL LONDON 2

Covering Knightsbridge, South Kensington, Chelsea, Earl's Court, Fulham. See map 6.

Beaver Hotel ₼
😃😃
57-59 Philbeach Gdns., London SW5 9ED
☎ 01-373 4553
In a quiet, tree-lined crescent of late Victorian terraced houses, close to Earl's Court Exhibition Centre and 10 minutes from the West End.
Bedrooms: 18 single, 6 double & 9 twin, 5 family rooms.
Bathrooms: 17 private, 12 public.
Bed & breakfast: £20-£32 single, £30-£42 double.
Parking for 23.
Credit: Visa.
🛏 🛆 📞 ⑨ 🖅 📺 🎬 🛆 T

Flaxman House ₼
ʟɪꜱᴛᴇᴅ
104-105 Oakley St., London
SW3 5NT
☎ 01-352 0187
Chelsea guesthouse with a country atmosphere close to the Kings Road.
Bedrooms: 8 single, 8 double & 4 twin, 1 family room.
Bathrooms: 6 public.
Bed & breakfast: max. £20 single, max. £35 double.
Credit: Access, Visa, Diners, Amex.
🛏 🛆 ᵁᴸ ᶜᴮ 🛆 🍽 🐾 🖼 📻 T

Merlyn Court Hotel ₼
😃😃
2 Barkston Gdns., London
SW5 0EN
☎ 01-370 1640
Well-established, quiet family-run hotel, close to Earl's Court and Olympia, with direct underground link to Heathrow and West End.
Bedrooms: 4 single, 4 double & 4 twin, 5 family rooms.
Bathrooms: 6 public; 2 private showers.
Bed & breakfast: £18-£22 single, £24-£29 double.
🛏 🛆 🖵 🍴 🖅 📺 🛆 ᴅᴀᴘ 🐾 ꜱᴘ

Hotel Oliver ₼
😃😃😃
198 Cromwell Rd., London
SW5 0SN
☎ 01-370 6881
Telex 918325 OLIVER G
Completely modernised, centrally heated hotel with lift service to all floors.
Bedrooms: 22 single, 12 double & 11 twin, 5 family rooms.
Bathrooms: 50 private.
Bed & breakfast: from £32 single, from £42.50 double.
Credit: Access, Visa, Diners, Amex.
🛏 🛆 📞 ⑨ 🖵 ᵁᴸ ✂ 🖅 📺 ◑ 🌡 🎬 🛆 🍴 🍽 ꜱᴘ T

Oliver Plaza Hotel ₼
😃😃
33 Trebovir Rd., London
SW5 0LR
☎ 01-373 7183 & 2058
A small hotel with emphasis on efficiency of service and comfort for guests.
Bedrooms: 20 single, 3 double & 5 twin, 7 family rooms.
Bathrooms: 11 private; 24 private showers.
Bed & breakfast: £25-£27.50 single, £32.50-£35 double.
Parking for 7.
Credit: Access, Visa, Diners, Amex.
🛏 🛆 📞 🖵 ᵁᴸ ᶜᴮ 🖅 📺 ◑ 🌡 🎬 🛆 🍽 🐾 ꜱᴘ T

Hotel Plaza Continental ₼
😃😃
9 Knaresborough Pl., London
SW5 0TP
☎ 01-370 3246
Small bed and breakfast hotel off Cromwell Road with easy access to Earl's Court, Knightsbridge, West End and Heathrow Airport by bus and underground.
Bedrooms: 8 single, 5 double & 5 twin, 2 family rooms.
Bathrooms: 16 private, 2 public.

Bed & breakfast: £34.50-£38 single, £48.30-£55 double.
Credit: Access, Visa, Amex.

Windsor House M
Listed
12 Penywern Rd., London
SW5 9ST
☎ 01-373 9087
Budget-priced bed and breakfast establishment in Earl's Court. Easily reached from airports and motorway. The West End is minutes away by underground.
Bedrooms: 2 single, 5 double & 3 twin, 5 family rooms.
Bathrooms: 4 public;
1 private shower.
Bed & breakfast: £16-£19 single, £25-£28 double.

CENTRAL LONDON 3

Covering High Street Kensington, West Kensington, Holland Park, Notting Hill, Olympia, Hammersmith. See map 6.

B and B Flatlets M
72 Holland Park Ave.,
London W11 3QZ
☎ 01-229 9233
Clean, family-run guesthouses offering budget rates. Centrally located, very close to public transport. All rooms have cooking facilities and full English breakfast is served in room. Minimum stay 3 nights.
Bedrooms: 5 twin.
Bathrooms: 2 public.
Bed & breakfast: £14-£17 single, £18-£25 double.

Observatory House Hotel M
≋≋≋
Observatory Gdns., London
W8 7NS
☎ 01-937 1577 & 6353
Telex 914972 OBSERV
Period mansion built on the site of the old observatory, after the death of Sir James South, the astronomer who owned the estate.
Bedrooms: 8 single, 8 double & 5 twin, 5 family rooms.
Bathrooms: 24 private,
1 public.
Bed & breakfast: £35-£48 single, £55-£70 double.
Credit: Access, Visa, Diners, Amex.

Mrs L. Stephan
152 Kensington Park Rd.,
London W11 2EP
☎ 01-727 7174
Pleasantly situated Victorian terrace house, close to all amenities. Clients receive individual attention in homely and friendly surroundings.
Bedrooms: 2 double, 1 family room.
Bathrooms: 3 private,
1 public.
Bed & breakfast: £14-£17 double.

Mrs. Jean Thompson
☎
57 St. Dunstan's Rd., Barons Court, London W6 8RE
☎ 01-748 8004
Friendly English family home, some French and German spoken. Quiet street near Barons Court underground station and buses. Parking available.
Bedrooms: 1 single, 1 double & 1 twin.
Bathrooms: 1 public.
Bed & breakfast: £9 single, £18 double.

Topaz Hotel M
☎
15 Lexham Gdns., London
W8 5JJ
☎ 01-373 3466
Small moderately-priced bed and breakfast.
Bedrooms: 4 single, 4 double & 4 twin, 3 family rooms.
Bathrooms: 5 public.
Bed & breakfast: £18 single, £26-£30 double.

CENTRAL LONDON 4

Covering Bayswater, Paddington, Maida Vale. See map 6.

Abbey Court Hotel M
Listed
174 Sussex Gdns., London
W2 1TP
☎ 01-402 0704
Budget hotel near Hyde Park and with easy reach of the West End. 2 minutes' walk from Lancaster Gate and Paddington underground stations.
Bedrooms: 1 single, 16 double & 20 twin, 8 family rooms.
Bathrooms: 8 private,
3 public; 20 private showers.

Bed & breakfast: from £18 single, from £24 double.
Parking for 12.
Credit: Access, Visa, C.Bl., Diners, Amex.

Andrews House Hotel M
Listed
12 Westbourne St., Hyde Park, London W2 2TZ
☎ 01-723 5365 & 4514
Family-run bed and breakfast within walking distance of Marble Arch and Oxford Street. Near Lancaster Gate and Paddington underground stations. Hebrew and other languages spoken.
Bedrooms: 1 single, 6 double & 4 twin, 6 family rooms.
Bathrooms: 1 private,
3 public; 9 private showers.
Bed & breakfast: £25-£30 single, £28-£35 double.

Barry House Hotel
Listed
12 Sussex Pl., London
W2 2TP
☎ 01-723 7340
Bedrooms: 4 single, 8 double & 3 twin, 3 family rooms.
Bathrooms: 18 private,
4 public.
Bed & breakfast: £18-£22 single, £30-£35 double.
Credit: Visa, Amex.

Beverley House Hotel M
≋≋≋
142 Sussex Gdns., London
W2 1UB
☎ 01-723 4615
Close to Oxford Street and Hyde Park.
Bedrooms: 4 single, 13 twin, 3 family rooms.
Bathrooms: 16 private,
1 public; 3 private showers.
Bed & breakfast: £24-£42 single, £28-£49 double.
Parking for 2.
Credit: Access, Visa, Diners, Amex.

Coburg Hotel M
≋≋≋≋
129 Bayswater Rd., London
W2 4RJ
☎ 01-229 3654 Telex 268235
Traditional British hotel offering a warm welcome to both business and holiday travellers. Conveniently situated.
Bedrooms: 59 single, 5 double & 53 twin, 8 family rooms.

Bathrooms: 84 private,
18 public.
Bed & breakfast: from £59 single, from £77 double.
Lunch available.
Evening meal 6.30pm (l.o. 9.30pm).
Credit: Access, Visa, C.Bl., Diners, Amex.

Picton House Hotel
122 Sussex Gdns., London
W2 1UB
☎ 01-723 5498
Bedrooms: 1 single, 4 double & 2 twin, 8 family rooms.
Bathrooms: 5 private,
3 public; 3 private showers.
Bed & breakfast: £20-£25 single, £28-£38 double.
Credit: Access, Visa, Diners, Amex.

Royal Norfolk Hotel M
≋≋
25 London St., London
W2 1HH
☎ 01-402 5221 & 01-723 3386 Telex 266059
Immediate access to mainline and underground stations and close to Oxford Street.
Bedrooms: 5 single, 20 double & 20 twin, 20 family rooms.
Bathrooms: 5 private,
20 public; 9 private showers.
Bed & breakfast: £25-£39.50 single, £44-£50 double.
Half board: £35-£49.50 daily.
Lunch available.
Evening meal 6pm (l.o. 10pm).
Credit: Access, Visa, C.Bl., Diners, Amex.

Sass House Hotel M
Listed
11 Craven Ter., London
W2 3QD
☎ 01-262 2325
Budget accommodation, convenient for central London, Hyde Park and the West End. Paddington and Lancaster Gate underground stations nearby. Free car parking.
Bedrooms: 2 single, 4 double & 6 twin, 6 family rooms.
Bathrooms: 3 public.
Bed & breakfast: from £15 single, from £22 double.
Parking for 4.
Credit: Access, Visa, C.Bl., Diners, Amex.

CENTRAL LONDON 4
Continued

Springfield Hotel
154 Sussex Gdns., London
W2 1UD
☎ 01-723 9898
Bedrooms: 3 single, 3 double
& 2 twin, 9 family rooms.
Bathrooms: 8 private,
3 public; 3 private showers.
Bed & breakfast: £18-£20
single, £28-£32 double.
Parking for 2.

Hotel Tria M
35-37 St. Stephen's Gdns.,
London W2 5NA
☎ 01-221 0450 & 01-723
3386
Telex 266059 STY-AL G
*In the heart of Portobello
antique market, within walking
distance of local shopping
centre, bus and underground
stations.*
Bedrooms: 5 single, 15 double
& 15 twin, 7 family rooms.
Bathrooms: 42 private.
Bed & breakfast: £39.50-£45
single, £50-£55 double.
Half board: £49.50-£55 daily.
Evening meal 7pm (l.o.
10pm).
Credit: Access, Visa, C.Bl.,
Diners, Amex.

Westpoint Hotel M
170-172 Sussex Gdns.,
London W2 1TP
☎ 01-402 0281
*Budget accommodation,
convenient for central London,
Hyde Park, West End.
Paddington and Lancaster
Gate underground stations
nearby. Car parking available.*
Bedrooms: 5 single, 7 double
& 8 twin, 5 family rooms.
Bathrooms: 19 private,
3 public.
Bed & breakfast: from £15
single, from £22 double.
Parking for 8.
Credit: Access, Visa, C.Bl.,
Diners, Amex.

**PLEASE CHECK
PRICES AND OTHER
DETAILS AT THE
TIME OF BOOKING.**

CENTRAL LONDON 5

Covering King's Cross,
St. Pancras, Euston,
Bloomsbury, Kingsway,
Marylebone, Regent's
Park, Leicester Square,
The Strand, Charing
Cross, Fleet Street,
Holborn, City. See map 6.

Alhambra Hotel
17-20 Argyle St., London
WC1H 8EJ
☎ 01-837 9575 & 9836
*Family-run bed and breakfast
with colour TV in all rooms. 1
minute's walk from 3 main line
stations, bus stop and
underground.*
Bedrooms: 21 single, 2 double
& 9 twin, 5 family rooms.
Bathrooms: 8 public;
8 private showers.
Bed & breakfast: £18-£22
single, £26-£30 double.

Crescent Hotel M
49-50 Cartwright Gdns.,
London WC1H 9EL
☎ 01-387 1515
*In a quiet period crescent, with
private gardens and tennis
courts. Comfortable and
central. Colour TV lounge.*
Bedrooms: 12 single, 5 double
& 5 twin, 7 family rooms.
Bathrooms: 1 private,
6 public; 3 private showers.
Bed & breakfast: £23-£25
single, £37-£41 double.
Credit: Visa.

Museum Inn
27 Montague St., London
WC1
☎ 01-580 5360
*A small quiet establishment
suitable for young and old.
Convenient for many places of
interest in central London.*
Bedrooms: 1 single, 2 double
& 6 twin, 2 family rooms.
Bathrooms: 5 public.
Bed & breakfast: £17-£20
single, £26-£30 double.
Credit: Access, Visa.

St. Athan's Hotel M
20 Tavistock Pl., Russell Sq.,
London WC1H 9RE
☎ 01-837 9140 & 9627
Small family-run hotel.
Bedrooms: 16 single, 5 double
& 5 twin, 6 family rooms.

Bathrooms: 2 private,
8 public.
Bed & breakfast: £22-£28
single, £30-£38 double.
Half board: £145-£170
weekly.
Credit: Access, Visa, Diners,
Amex.

**Hotel Strand
Continental M**
143 The Strand, London
WC2R 1JA
☎ 01-836 4880
*Small hotel with friendly
atmosphere, near theatres and
famous London landmarks.*
Bedrooms: 10 single, 7 double
& 2 twin, 3 family rooms.
Bathrooms: 6 public.
Bed & breakfast: £16-£20
single, £22-£26 double.

Thanet Hotel.
8 Bedford Pl., London
WC1B 5JA
☎ 01-636 2869 & 01-580
3377
*Comfortable, family-run hotel,
with colour television in all
rooms.*
Bedrooms: 2 single, 4 double
& 5 twin, 3 family rooms.
Bathrooms: 3 private,
4 public.
Bed & breakfast: £25-£28.50
single, £35-£45 double.
Credit: Visa.

EAST LONDON

Covering the boroughs of
Barking, Hackney,
Havering, Newham,
Redbridge, Tower
Hamlets, Waltham Forest.
See map 7.

**Grangewood Lodge
Hotel M**
104 Clova Rd., Forest Gate,
London E7 9AF
☎ 01-534 0637
*Comfortable budget
accommodation in a quiet road,
pleasant garden. Easy access
to central London.*
Bedrooms: 10 single, 8 twin,
1 family room.
Bathrooms: 3 public.
Bed & breakfast: £11-£13
single, £18-£19 double.

Sans Souci House
11 Chelmsford Rd.,
Leytonstone, London
E11 1BT
☎ 01-539 1367
Bedrooms: 5 twin, 1 family
room.
Bathrooms: 2 public.
Bed & breakfast: £13-£16
single, £24-£30 double.
Parking for 4.

Westbury Guest House
8 Westbury Rd., Forest Gate,
London E7 8BU
☎ 01-472 9848
*Victorian family house with all
modern amenities and close to
travel facilities.*
Bedrooms: 1 single, 1 double
& 2 twin.
Bathrooms: 1 public.
Bed & breakfast: £12.50-£15
single, £25-£30 double.
Parking for 2.

NORTH LONDON

Covering the boroughs of
Barnet, Brent, Camden,
Enfield, Haringey,
Harrow, Islington. See
map 7.

Byron Villa
147 Bounds Green Rd., New
Southgate, London N11 2ED
☎ 01-888 1278
*Victorian character family
home, 15 minutes from central
London. Self catering facilities
available.*
Bedrooms: 1 double, 2 family
rooms.
Bathrooms: 1 public.
Bed & breakfast: £10-£12
single, £18-£24 double.
Parking for 4.

Capital Homes M
200 Chase Side, London
N14 4PH
☎ 01-441 7378 & 01-440
7535
*Friendly guest house close to
Southgate underground station.
Garden available to guests.
Also agency offering wide
variety of accommodation.*
Bedrooms: 2 single, 2 twin,
3 family rooms.
Bathrooms: 1 private,
1 public.
Bed & breakfast: £15-£24
single, £25-£34 double.
Half board: £20-£29 daily,
from £140 weekly.
Lunch available.

Evening meal 6pm (l.o. 9pm).
Parking for 4.
Credit: Access, Visa.

Central Hotel
☺☺
6 Hindes Rd., Harrow,
Middlesex HA1 1SJ
☎ 01-427 0893
*Comfortable family-run hotel.
20 minutes by underground
from central London. Wembley
complex 5 minutes away, close
to M1 and M25.*
Bedrooms: 3 single, 6 double,
1 family room.
Bathrooms: 3 private,
3 public.
Bed & breakfast: £20-£30
single, £30-£40 double.
Parking for 8.
Credit: Access, Visa, Diners,
Amex.

Chumleigh Lodge
Hotel ᴍ
☺☺
226-228 Nether St., Finchley,
London N3 1HU
☎ 01-346 1614 & 0059
*Large Victorian house in a
residential area. Close to parks
and shopping centre, with easy
access to the West End.*
Bedrooms: 8 single, 4 double
& 2 twin, 5 family rooms.
Bathrooms: 4 private,
4 public; 2 private showers.
Bed & breakfast: £21-£39
single, £30-£39 double.
Parking for 8.
Credit: Access, Visa.

Five King's Guest
House ᴍ
☺
59 Anson Rd., Tufnell Park,
London N7 0AR
☎ 01-607 3996
*A well-maintained friendly
guesthouse offering personal
service. Easily accessible by
underground and buses. 15
minutes from the West End.*
Bedrooms: 8 single, 3 double
& 3 twin, 2 family rooms.
Bathrooms: 3 public.
Bed & breakfast: £12-£15
single, £22-£26 double.

Four Seasons
70 Netherlands Rd., New
Barnet, Hertfordshire
EN5 1BP
☎ 01-440 9075 & 01-449
7664

*Family house 3 minutes from
Oakleigh Park station. Central
London 25 minutes away.
Close to buses and
underground.*
Bedrooms: 1 single, 1 double
& 1 twin, 1 family room.
Bathrooms: 2 private,
2 public; 1 private shower.
Bed & breakfast: max. £12
single, max. £20 double.
Parking for 4.

Mrs M. Herbert
88 Charteris Rd., Kilburn,
London NW6 7EX
☎ 01-328 0584
*Modernised, Victorian,
terraced house with off-street
parking. On bus route to
Oxford Street.*
Bedrooms: 2 double.
Bathrooms: 1 public.
Bed & breakfast: £13 single,
£26 double.

J & T Guest House
98 Park Avenue North,
Willesden Green, London
NW10 1JY
☎ 01-452 4085
*Small guesthouse in north
London close to underground.*
Bedrooms: 1 single, 1 twin,
1 family room.
Bathrooms: 1 private,
2 public.
Bed & breakfast: £11-12.50
single, £22-£25 double.
Parking for 2.

Kandara Annexe
65 Ockendon Rd., London
N1 3NN
☎ 01-226 5721 & 3379
*Small family-run guesthouse
close to West End and public
transport.*
Bedrooms: 1 single, 1 double
& 2 twin, 1 family room.
Bathrooms: 2 public.
Bed & breakfast: £14-£16
single, £20-£26 double.

Kandara Guest House
68 Ockendon Rd., London
N1 3NW
☎ 01-226 5721 & 3379
*Small family-run guesthouse
close to West End and public
transport.*
Bedrooms: 4 single, 2 double
& 1 twin.
Bathrooms: 2 public.
Bed & breakfast: £14-£16
single, £20-£26 double.

Majestic Hotel ᴍ
Listed
394 Seven Sisters Rd.,
London N4 2PQ
☎ 01-800 2022
*Comfortable and economically
priced accommodation in a
convenient location for the
centre of London. Opposite
Finsbury Park.*
Bedrooms: 10 double &
18 twin, 4 family rooms.
Bathrooms: 10 public.
Bed & breakfast: £25-£30
single, £33-£36.30 double.
Parking for 40.
Credit: Access, Visa, C.Bl.,
Diners, Amex.

Pane Residence
154 Boundary Rd., Wood
Green, London N22 5AE
☎ 01-889 3735
*In a pleasant location 6
minutes' walk from Turnpike
Lane underground station.*
Bedrooms: 1 single, 1 double
& 1 twin.
Bathrooms: 1 public.
Bed & breakfast: from £11
single, from £14.50 double.

White Lodge ᴍ
☺
1 Church Lane, Hornsey,
London N8 7BU
☎ 01-348 9765
*Small, friendly family hotel
offering personal service.
Extended and refurbished in
1986. Easy access to all
transport.*
Bedrooms: 6 single, 6 double
& 2 twin, 4 family rooms.
Bathrooms: 4 private,
3 public.
Bed & breakfast: £12-£14
single, £24-£26 double.
Credit: Access.

SOUTH EAST LONDON

Covering the boroughs of
Bexley, Bromley,
Croydon, Greenwich,
Lewisham, Southwark.
See map 7.

Bern House
293A Hither Green Lane,
Lewisham, London
SE13 6TH
☎ 01-852 1698
*Good train and bus connections
to Central London.*
Bedrooms: 1 single, 2 double.
Bathrooms: 1 public.

Bed & breakfast: £45-£65
single, £65-£70 double.
Half board: £85-£90 daily,
£150-£175 weekly.

Conifer's
41 Peaks Hill, Purley, Surrey
CR2 3JJ
☎ 01-660 6902
*Detached house 15 miles from
central London. Golf, tennis,
cricket clubs 10-20 minutes'
walk away.*
Bedrooms: 1 single, 1 double.
Bathrooms: 1 private,
2 public.
Bed & breakfast: £15.50-
£17.50 single, £25-£30 double.
Parking for 4.

Fairview Guest House
Listed
85 Brigstock Rd., Thornton
Heath, Croydon, Surrey
CR4 7JL
☎ 01-683 2779
*Friendly bed and breakfast
near Croydon. Close to British
Rail and bus routes.*
Bedrooms: 4 single, 1 double
& 4 twin, 1 family rooms.
Bathrooms: 2 public.
Bed & breakfast: £18-£19
single, £30-£32 double.

Godolphin House
62 Glengarry Rd., East
Dulwich, London SE22 8QD
☎ 01-693 6089
*Family-run guesthouse within
walking distance of public
transport.*
Bedrooms: 2 single, 1 double
& 2 twin, 1 family room.
Bathrooms: 1 public;
5 private showers.
Bed & breakfast: £12-£14
single, £22-£25 double.

Ipplepen
☺☺☺
50 Upper Selsdon Rd.,
Selsdon, South Croydon,
Surrey CR2 8DE
☎ 01-657 2543
*Convenient for London, the
South Coast and M25.
Chauffeured trips by
arrangement, free transfer East
Croydon station.*
Bedrooms: 1 twin.
Bathrooms: 1 private.
Bed & breakfast: £24-£28
single, £26-£28 double.

SOUTH EAST LONDON

Continued

Half board: £22-£38 daily.
Evening meal 7pm.
Parking for 1.
⊞ 🖵 ⊘ ⓤ ▯ 🛡 Ⓥ 📼 ⛶
▱ ✿ ⅔ 🗡

Iverna

1 Annandale Rd.,
Addiscombe, Croydon,
Surrey CR0 7HP
☎ 01-654 8639
*Large house in a quiet road.
Close to East Croydon British
Rail station, Victoria 15
minutes away.*
Bedrooms: 1 single, 2 twin,
1 family room.
Bathrooms: 1 public.
Bed & breakfast: £12-£18
single, £24-£32 double.
🐾 🛡 ⊞ 🖵 ⊘ ⓤ Ⓥ ⛶
▱ 🗡

James Lodge ⋀
Listed

116 Barry Rd., Dulwich,
London SE22 0HP
☎ 01-693 7744
*Conveniently located for
central London.*
Bedrooms: 1 single, 4 double,
1 family room.
Bathrooms: 2 public.
Bed & breakfast: £15-£18
single, £30-£35 double.
🛡 ⓤ 📼 ⛶ ▱ 🗡 ⃞

49 Ling's Coppice

Croxted Rd., West Dulwich,
London SE21
☎ 01-670 4021
*Convenient for Crystal Palace
Sports Centre and near the bus
route to Oxford Circus.*
Bedrooms: 2 single, 2 twin.
Bathrooms: 1 public.
Bed & breakfast: £11-£13
single, £22-£26 double.
Parking for 1.
🐾14 🛡 🖵 ⊘ ⓤ ⛶ ▱ ↻
🗡 🚲

Meadow Croft Lodge ⋀
⚉

96-98 Southwood Rd., New
Eltham, London SE9 3QS
☎ 01-859 1488
*Spacious rooms and warm
friendly atmosphere. Between
A2 and A20, near New Eltham
station with easy access to
London.*
Bedrooms: 4 single, 3 double
& 9 twin, 1 family room.
Bathrooms: 1 private,
4 public; 8 private showers.
Bed & breakfast: £18-£20
single, £30-£35 double.
Parking for 10.
🐾 ⓤ 📼 ⛶ ▱ 🗡 🚲

Penrith

21 York Rd., Selsdon, South
Croydon, Surrey CR2 8NR
☎ 01-657 5023
*Bus service every 20 minutes to
East Croydon. 400 yards from
shops. 50 miles from the
nearest coast.*
Bedrooms: 1 twin.
Bathrooms: 1 public.
Bed & breakfast: £10-£11
single, £20 double.
Parking for 2.
Open February-November.

Shirwin House

33 Bargery Rd., Catford,
London SE6 2LJ
☎ 01-698 6381
*Victorian semi in tree lined
road. Convenient for Catford
town centre.*
Bedrooms: 1 single, 1 double
& 2 twin, 1 family room.
Bathrooms: 1 public.
Bed & breakfast: from £13
single, from £20 double.
🐾5 🛡 ⊞ 🖵 ⊘ ⓤ ▯ ⅔ 📼
⛶ ▱ 🗡 🚲

Mrs. J. Stock
Listed

51 Selcroft Rd., Purley,
Surrey CR2 1AJ
☎ 01-660 3054
*Central London 20 minutes by
train, convenient for M25.*
Bedrooms: 2 twin.
Bathrooms: 1 public.
Bed & breakfast: £12 single,
£24 double.
Open January-November.
🐾 🛡 ⚲ ⓤ 🛡 📼 ⛶ ▱ 🐾

SOUTH WEST LONDON

Covering the boroughs of
Kingston upon Thames,
Lambeth, Merton,
Richmond, Sutton,
Wandsworth. See map 7.

Alnwick
Listed

27 Roehampton Lane,
Putney, London SW15 5LS
☎ 01-878 9449
*Homely accommodation close
to Richmond Park. Central
London easily accessible by bus
and train.*
Bedrooms: 1 single, 1 family
room.
Bathrooms: 1 private,
1 public.
Bed & breakfast: £12-£14
single, max. £24 double.
Parking for 1.
🐾 ⚲ ⓤ ⃝ 📼 ⛶ 🗡 🚲

Mrs. L. Catterall
Listed

12 Avarn Rd., Tooting,
London SW17 9HA
☎ 01-767 0584
*Family home near
underground station and buses.
All rooms have refrigerator
and a pay-phone is available
for guests.*
Bedrooms: 1 single, 1 twin,
1 family room.
Bathrooms: 1 public.
Bed & breakfast: £9-£11
single, £18-£22 double.
🐾 🛡 🖵 ⊘ ⓤ ⛶ ▱ 🗡 🚲

Mrs J. Dixon
Listed

17 Osmond Gdns.,
Wallington, Surrey SM6 8SX
☎ 01-647 1943
*Comfortable family home
welcomes guests. Easy rail
access to London and Gatwick,
and local bus to Windsor and
Hampton Court.*
Bedrooms: 1 double, 1 family
room.
Bathrooms: 1 public;
1 private shower.
Bed & breakfast: £28-£30
double.
Parking for 1.
🐾 🛡 ⓡ 🖵 ⊘ ⓤ ⛶ ▱ 🗡 🚲

Hobart Hall
⚉⚉

43-47 Petersham Rd.,
Richmond upon Thames,
Surrey TW10 6UL
☎ 01-940 0435 Telex 265451
MONRET Ref:72 MAG
3510Z
*Built circa 1690 with 1752
additions. Past tenants include
the Earl of Buckinghamshire,
the Hon. Henry Hobart and
the Duke of Clarence (King
William IV).*
Bedrooms: 11 single, 4 double
& 3 twin.
Bathrooms: 18 private,
1 public.
Bed & breakfast: £25-£35
single, £35-£45 double.
Half board: £31.50-£41.50
daily.
Parking for 10.
Credit: Access, Visa, Amex.
🐾5 ⚲ 📠 ⓡ 🖵 ⓤ 📼 ⛶
▱ ✿ ⃞ 🦮 🏍 ⃞

**THERE IS A SPECIAL
SECTION IN THIS
GUIDE LISTING
ACCOMMODATION
ESPECIALLY
SUITABLE FOR
GROUPS AND
YOUNG PEOPLE.**

WEST LONDON

Covering the boroughs of
Ealing, Hammersmith,
Hillingdon, Hounslow,
also London Airport
(Heathrow). See map 7.

Ashleigh

22 Lingwood Gdns., Osterley,
Middlesex TW7 5LZ
☎ 01-568 3800
*In quiet cul-de-sac, close to
Osterley underground station
and National Trust house and
parkland. Convenient for
Heathrow Airport.*
Bedrooms: 1 single, 1 twin,
2 family rooms.
Bathrooms: 1 public.
Bed & breakfast: £12-£14
single, £20-£22 double.
Parking for 2.
🐾3 ▯ 🛡 Ⓥ ⛶ 🗡 🚲

Badger House

1 Airedale Ave., Chiswick,
London W4 2NW
☎ 01-995 9754
*In a quiet, pleasant location
with small car park and free
street parking, 20 minutes from
central London and Heathrow
Airport.*
Bedrooms: 3 single, 4 twin,
2 family rooms.
Bathrooms: 3 public.
Bed & breakfast: from £16
single, from £28 double.
🐾6 🖵 ⊘ ⓤ 🅒🅑 📼 ⛶ ▱ 🗡
🚲 ⃞

Corfton Guest House
⚉⚉

42 Corfton Rd., Ealing,
London W5 2HT
☎ 01-998 1120
*Close to Ealing Broadway
station, in a quiet residential
area of considerable character.*
Bedrooms: 3 single, 4 double
& 2 twin, 2 family rooms.
Bathrooms: 4 private,
2 public.
Bed & breakfast: £12-£20
single, £20-£28 double.
Parking for 6.
🐾 ⚲ ⓤ ▯ 📼 ⛶ ▱ 🗡 🚲

Gresham Hotel
Listed

10 Hanger Lane, Ealing,
London W5 3HH
☎ 01-992 0801
Telex 923421 WEMSEC G
*Conveniently located family-
run bed and breakfast.*
Bedrooms: 4 single, 2 double
& 4 twin, 3 family rooms.
Bathrooms: 2 public.
Bed & breakfast: from £20
single, from £32 double.

Half board: from £28 daily.
Evening meal 6.20pm.
Parking for 10.
Credit: Access, Visa.

Lampton Guesthouse
4 Lampton Park Rd.,
Hounslow, Middlesex
TW3 4HS
☎ 01-572 8622
*Detached property with garden
at rear. Convenient for the high
street, underground station and
Heathrow Airport.*
Bedrooms: 4 single, 3 twin.
Bathrooms: 1 public;
1 private shower.
Bed & breakfast: £15-£17
single, £25-£27 double.
Parking for 6.

Mrs. Josephine Clements
17 Madeley Rd., London
W5 2LA
☎ 01-998 5222
*Detached Victorian home,
beautifully renovated, with
spacious rooms. Full English
breakfast. Non-smokers
preferred. 3 minutes from the
underground, with easy access
to central London, Heathrow
Airport, Hampton Court, Kew
Gardens and Windsor.
Riverside walks. Minimum
stay 2 nights.*
Bedrooms: 1 single, 1 double
& 1 twin, 1 family room.
Bathrooms: 2 private,
2 public.
Bed & breakfast: £22 single,
£44 double.

KEY TO SYMBOLS
Open out the flap inside the
back cover of this guide and
the key to symbols will be
easy to use.

FOLLOW THE SIGN
It leads to over 550 Tourist Information Centres throughout England offering friendly help with accommodation and holiday ideas as well as suggestions of places to visit and

Tourist information

things to do. In your home town there may be a centre which can help you before you set out. If not, why not send for the Directory of Tourist Information Centres in Great Britain? It is available free from English Tourist Board, Department D, Bromells Road, Clapham, London SW4 0BJ.

ACCOMMODATION

Central London

Budget Prices

WESTPOINT HOTEL

170 Sussex Gardens, Hyde Park,
London W2 1PT. Tel: 01-402 0281 (Reservations)
Open all year. Central heating.
Most rooms with private shower & toilet, radio/intercom
& colour. T.V. Children welcome. TV lounge

This hotel has long been a popular choice amongst tourists because of its central location, being near to Hyde Park and only 2 minutes from Paddington and Lancaster Gate tube stations. The West End's tourist attractions, including theatres, museums and Oxford Street stores are within easy reach. Individuals, families and groups are all welcome.

* PRIVATE CAR PARK *

RATES:– Low Season
    Singles from £14 per person.
    Doubles from £11 per person.
    Family rooms from £9.50 per person.

– High Season
    Singles from £21 per person.
    Doubles from £12.50 per person.
    Family Rooms from £11 per person.

ABBEY COURT HOTEL

174 Sussex Gardens, Hyde Park
London W2 1TP Tel: 01-402 0704

Open all year. Radio/Intercom in every room. Children welcome. Most rooms with private shower, toilet and colour TV.

* CAR PARKING *

This Hotel has long been popular with tourists because of its central location near to Hyde Park and two minutes from Paddington and Lancaster Gate tube stations. The tourist attractions of the West End including theatres, museums and Oxford Street are within easy reach. Individuals, families, school parties and groups are all welcome and group tours can be arranged.

TERMS per person:
High season: Single from £20.00, double from £15.00 p.p., family £10.00 p.p.
Low season: Single from £15.00, double from £12.50 p.p., family from £9.00p.p

Special Prices
SASS HOUSE HOTEL

*11 Craven Terrace,
Hyde Park, London, W2 3QD. Tel: 01-262 2325*

★ Centrally located—within easy reach of London's most famous tourist attractions ★ Nearest underground Paddington and Lancaster Gate. ★ Served by a network of bus routes. ★ Colour television lounge. ★ Centrally heated. ★ Radio and intercom in all rooms. ★ Special group and party booking rates ★ Parking facilities available.

RATES per person: single room from £12.00
Double room from £9.00 p.p. and family room or party booking rate from £8.00 p.p. inc bed & breakfast

👑 ELIZABETH HOTEL
CENTRAL LONDON SW1

Intimate, friendly, private Hotel ideally located for all parts of the Capital

37 Eccleston Square, VICTORIA, London SWIV 1PB.
Telephone: 01-828 6812/3

★ 1986 Winner of the ★
British Tourist Authority's
London Bed and Breakfast Award

Situated in stately garden square (c. 1835), close to Belgravia and a few doors from one of the residences of the late Sir Winston Churchill. Within two minutes' walk of Victoria Station/Coach Station/Air Terminals. Parking nearby.
Comfortable single, twin, double and family rooms.
Attractive Lounge and pleasant Breakfast Room.
Good ENGLISH BREAKFAST, or Continental breakfast at any time for EARLY DEPARTURES.
MODERATE PRICES include accommodation, breakfast and Tax.
FREE COLOUR BROCHURE AVAILABLE

When requesting brochures or further information from advertisers in this guide, you may find it helpful to use the advertisement enquiry coupons which can be found towards the end of the guide. These should be cut out and mailed direct to the companies in which you are interested. Remember to include your name and address and enclose a stamped and addressed envelope or stamps if requested by the advertiser.

PLEASE NOTE

Individual establishments who have a display advertisement have a line listing under the appropriate town heading

FOLLOW THE SIGN

It leads to over 550 Tourist Information Centres throughout England offering friendly help with accommodation and holiday ideas as well as suggestions of places to visit and

things to do. In your home town there may be a centre which can help you before you set out. If not, why not send for the Directory of Tourist Information Centres in Great Britain? It is available free from English Tourist Board, Department D, Bromells Road, Clapham, London SW4 0BJ.

Cumbria

Although only the one county of Cumbria makes up the Cumbria tourist region, what a county!

It's best known for the Lake District — that wonderful collection of water playgrounds, ranging from busy Windermere and Ullswater to the lesser-known Wast Water.

In Cumbria, you'll find some of the finest cooking in England — which will be featured throughout 1989 in the Celebration of British Food and Farming — together with some of the finest landscapes.

Towering peaks and plunging valleys, fells and crags, lakes and tarns offer the climber, the hill walker

LAKE WINDERMERE

Britain on View

and the watersports enthusiast a wealth of holiday opportunities.

But Cumbria is not just the Lakes. There are 150 miles of undeveloped coastline, stretching from Morecambe Bay up to the lonely Solway Firth, offering spectacular vistas of sea and sand.

To the north of the county is historic Carlisle, with its 12thC castle and cathedral, and there's Hadrian's Wall which here begins its long march across the Pennines to the other side of England.

And everywhere in Cumbria you'll find pretty villages (like Ravenglass and Holmrook) and old towns (like Maryport and Whitehaven) which extend a warm and homely welcome to visitors from afar.

FIND OUT MORE

Further information about holidays and attractions in the Cumbria tourist region is available from: **Cumbria Tourist Board,** Ashleigh, Holly Road, Windermere, Cumbria LA23 2AQ. ☎ (096 62) 4444.

These publications are available from the Cumbria Tourist Board (post free):
Cumbria English Lake District Touring Map (including tourist information and touring caravan and camping parks) £1.95
Places to Visit and Things to Do in Cumbria English Lake District (over 150 ideas for a great day out) 60p
Wordsworth's Lake District (an illustrated guide and map) 25p

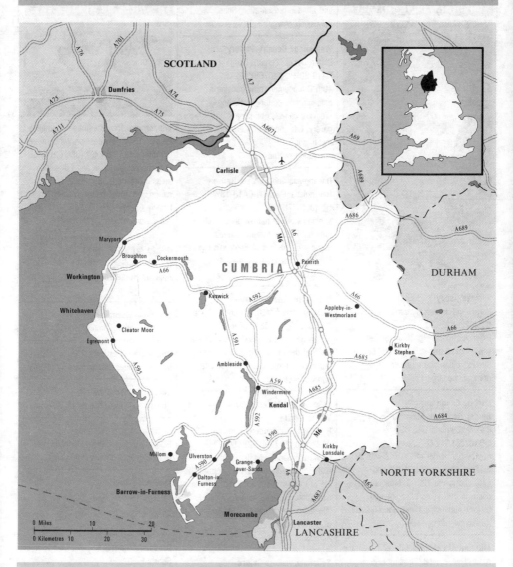

WHERE TO GO, WHAT TO SEE

Appleby Castle Conservation Centre
Appleby-in-Westmorland, Cumbria
CA16 6XH ☎ (076 83) 51402
Riverside setting for rare breeds of
British farm animals and birds. Fine
11th C Norman keep. Nature trail,

Tarzan trail, tea rooms, shop.
Admission charge.

**Dove Cottage and
Wordsworth Museum**
Grasmere, Cumbria LA22 9SG

☎ (096 65) 544/547
Wordsworth's home from 1799 – 1808,
the cottage remains almost as it was in
his time and contains some of his
furniture and personal belongings.
Admission charge. ▶

Britain on View

Furness Abbey
Barrow-in-Furness, Cumbria LA13 0TJ
☎ (0229) 23420
Extensive remains of dramatic red sandstone abbey in a beautiful setting. Site exhibition and museum.
Admission charge.

Carlisle Castle and Border Regiment Museum
Carlisle, Cumbria CA3 8UR
☎ (0228) 31777
Impressive border stronghold with a massive keep, built in 1092 and extended in the 12th C. Museum contains 300 years of regimental history, audio-visual and video displays.
Admission charge.

Museum of Lakeland Life and Industry
Abbot Hall, Kendal, Cumbria LA9 5AL
☎ (0539) 22464
Reconstructions of workshops and farmhouse rooms, agricultural exhibits, craft shop.
Admission charge.

Cumberland Pencil Museum
Southey Hill Works, Keswick, Cumbria CA12 5NG ☎ (076 87) 73626
The pencil story, from the discovery of graphite to present-day methods of pencil manufacture, told with exhibitions and a video presentation. Shop.
Admission charge.

Wetheriggs Country Pottery
Clifton Dykes, Penrith, Cumbria CA10 2DH ☎ (0768) 62946
19th C monument now housing a museum and pottery workshop. Weavers can also be seen in the gallery. Gift shop and licensed restaurant.
Admission charge.

Ravenglass and Eskdale Railway
Ravenglass, Cumbria CA18 1SW
☎ (065 77) 226
England's oldest narrow-gauge railway runs for 7 miles through glorious scenery to the foot of England's highest hills. Most trains steam-hauled.
Admission charge.

South Tynedale Railway
Railway Station, Alston, Cumbria CA9 3JB ☎ (0498) 81696
2ft gauge railway following part of the route of the former Alston-Haltwhistle branch line through South Tynedale.
Admission charge.

Lake District National Park Visitor Centre
Brockhole, Windermere, Cumbria LA23 1LJ ☎ (096 62) 6601
Living Lakeland exhibition, daily talks and film shows on many aspects of the life of the National Park. Beatrix Potter exhibition. Beautiful gardens and lakeshore walks, nature trails and places to picnic.
Admission charge.

Sellafield Visitors Centre
Seascale, Cumbria CA20 1PG
☎ (0940) 28333
Including displays describing the nuclear power industry, British Nuclear Fuels and the particular function of Sellafield. Computer games, video presentations, working models.
Admission free.

Britain on View

Windermere Iron Steamboat Company
Rayrigg Road, Bowness-on-Windermere, Cumbria LA23 1BN ☎ (096 62) 5565
Collection of Victorian and Edwardian steamboats from 1850 to 1911; early sailing and motor boats. Trips on steam launch 'Osprey'.
Admission charge.

MAKE A DATE FOR...

Appleby Horse Fair
Appleby *14 June*

Musgrave Rushbearing
Great Musgrave, Brough *1 July*

Windermere Festival
Various venues, Windermere *1 – 9 July*

Lakeland Rose Show
County Showfield, Kendal *15 – 16 July*

Cumbria Steam Gathering
Flookburgh Aerodrome, Flookburgh, Grange-over-Sands *29 – 30 July*

Ambleside Sports
Rydal Park, Rydal, Ambleside
3 August

Grasmere Sports
Sports Field, Grasmere *17 August*

Carlisle Great Fair
Carlisle *26 August – 5 September*

Patterdale Sheep Dog Trials
Ullswater *27 August*

Egremont Crab Fair
Baybarrow, Egremont *16 September*

Tourist Information

Tourist and leisure information can be obtained from Tourist Information Centres throughout England. Details of centres in the Cumbria region are listed below. The symbol 🛏 means that an accommodation booking service is provided. Centres marked with a ✱ are open during the summer months only. In the following pages, towns which have a Tourist Information Centre are indicated with the symbol *i* .

Alston 🛏
Railway Station
☎ (0498) 81696

Ambleside 🛏 ✱
The Old Courthouse, Church Street
☎ (053 94) 32582

Appleby-in-Westmorland 🛏
Moot Hall, Boroughgate
☎ (076 83) 51177

Barrow-in-Furness 🛏
Civic Halls, Duke Street
☎ (0229) 25795

Bowness-on-Windermere 🛏 ✱
The Glebe, Bowness Bay
☎ (096 62) 2895 or 5602
(accommodation service)

Brampton ✱
Moot Hall, Market Square
☎ (069 77) 3433

Brough 🛏
The 'One Stop Shop'
☎ (093 04) 260

Carlisle 🛏
Old Town Hall, Green Market
☎ (0228) 25517

Cockermouth 🛏 ✱
Riverside Car Park, Market Street
☎ (0900) 822634

Coniston 🛏 ✱
16 Yewdale Road
☎ (053 94) 41533

Egremont 🛏
Lowes Court Gallery,
12 Main Street
☎ (0946) 820693

Gosforth 🛏 ✱
Car Park
☎ (094 05) 285

Grange-over-Sands 🛏 ✱
Victoria Hall, Main Street
☎ (053 95) 54026

Grasmere 🛏 ✱
Red Bank Road
☎ (096 65) 245

Hawkshead 🛏 ✱
Car Park
☎ (096 66) 525

Kendal 🛏
Town Hall, Highgate
☎ (0539) 25758

Keswick 🛏
Summer —
The Moot Hall, Market Square
Winter —
Council Offices, 50 Main Square
☎ (076 87) 72645

Killington Lake 🛏 ✱
Motorway Service Area,
M6 Southbound
☎ Sedbergh (053 96) 20138

Kirkby Lonsdale 🛏
The Art Store, 18 Main Street
☎ (0468) 71603

Kirkby Stephen 🛏 ✱
Market Place
☎ (0930) 71199

Longtown 🛏
21 Swan Street
☎ (0228) 791201

Maryport 🛏
Maritime Museum,
1 Senhouse Street
☎ (0900) 813738

▶

BOWNESS-ON-WINDERMERE

Britain on View

Millom 🛏 ✳
Millom Folk Museum,
St. George's Road
☎ (0657) 2555

Penrith 🛏
Robinson's School, Middlegate
☎ (0768) 67466

Pooley Bridge 🛏 ✳
The Square
☎ (085 36) 530

Ravenglass 🛏 ✳
The Car Park, Ravenglass &
Eskdale Railway Station
☎ (065 77) 278

Seatoller 🛏 ✳
Seatoller Barn
☎ (059 684) 294

Sedbergh 🛏 ✳
72 Main Street
☎ (053 96) 20125

Silloth 🛏 ✳
Eden Street
☎ (0965) 31944

Southwaite 🛏
M6 Service Area, Southwaite,
Nr. Carlisle
☎ (069 74) 73445/73446

Ullswater 🛏 ✳
Main Car Park, Glenridding
☎ (085 32) 414

Ulverston 🛏
Coronation Hall, County Square
☎ (0229) 57120

Waterhead 🛏 ✳
Waterhead Car Park
☎ (053 94) 32729

Whitehaven 🛏
St. Nicholas Tower,
Lowther Street
☎ (0946) 695678

Windermere 🛏
Victoria Street
☎ (096 62) 6499

When enquiring about accommodation you may find it helpful to use the booking enquiry coupons which can be found towards the end of the guide. These should be cut out and mailed direct to the establishments in which you are interested. Remember to include your name and address and please enclose a stamped addressed envelope (or an international reply coupon if writing from outside Britain).

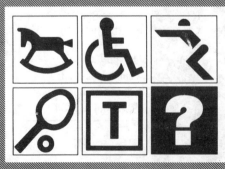

KEY TO SYMBOLS
Open out the flap inside the back cover of this guide and the key to symbols will be easy to use.

John Hillaby's
WALKING IN BRITAIN

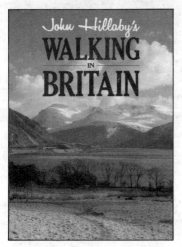

A comprehensive and inspirational guide to the great walks and finest walking country of Britain. With contributions from 20 leading writers and walking enthusiasts such as Hunter Davies, Richard Mabey and Adam Nicolson.

Beautifully illustrated with over 150 colour photographs and stunning watercolours by David Bellamy.

Published in association with the English Tourist Board.

£14.95   Available from all good bookshops

Collins    English Tourist Board

---

• HISTORIC HOUSES ASSOCIATION •
THE COUNTRY HOUSE GUIDE
• FAMILY HOMES IN THE H.H.A. •
Anna Sproule

Fully illustrated with over 100 colour and 150 black and white photographs. Published by Century in association with the English Tourist Board and the Historic Houses Association

Hardback, price £16.95
Available from all good bookshops.

 English Tourist Board

Entries in this regional section are listed in alphabetical order of place name, and then in alphabetical order of establishment. County names are not normally repeated in each establishment entry, but please use the full postal address when writing.

The map references refer to the colour maps towards the end of this guide. The first number is the number of the map, and it is followed by the grid reference.

The Crown Classifications are explained on pages 8 and 9, and the key to symbols is on the flap inside the back cover — keep it open for easy reference.

AINSTABLE
Cumbria
Map ref 5B2

11m NE. Penrith

Basco-Dyke Head Farm
Listed
Ainstable, Carlisle, CA4 9QP
☎ Croglin (076 886) 254
250-acre dairy farm. 17th C. ale house. Ideal countryside for nature walks and touring, with sport activity nearby. Close to the Scottish Borders, Lakes and Roman Wall.
Bedrooms: 1 single, 2 double.
Bathrooms: 1 public.
Bed & breakfast: £7-£10.50 single, £14-£21 double.
Half board: £12.50-£16.50 daily, £95-£103 weekly.
Evening meal 7pm (l.o. 6pm).
Parking for 12.
�ph> ⚫ ↻ ⁂ ✗ ⒟ ⚑ ⚲ ⊞ ⌦

ALSTON
Cumbria
Map ref 5B2

Market town amongst the highest fells of the Pennines and close to the Pennine Way in an Area of Outstanding Natural Beauty. ⓘ

Alston Moor Trekking Centre
Listed
Low Lee House, Garrigill, Alston, CA9 3DH
☎ (0498) 81105
Small trekking centre with a friendly atmosphere. Everyone welcome, children can come unaccompanied. Riding includes long treks over the North Pennines.
Bedrooms: 1 single, 1 twin, 1 family room.
Bathrooms: 2 public.

Bed & breakfast: from £9 single, from £18 double.
Half board: from £14 daily, from £98 weekly.
Evening meal 7.30pm (l.o. 9pm).
Open April-December.
Credit: Access, Visa.

Clarghyll House, Bed & Breakfast M
Alston CA9 3NF
☎ Alston (0498) 81949
17th C. toll house in lovely county of Cumbria. Ideal for touring the Lake District and Eden Valley.
Bedrooms: 1 double & 1 twin, 1 family room.
Bathrooms: 1 public.
Bed & breakfast: £9-£10 single, £18-£20 double.
Half board: £15-£16 daily, £100-£105 weekly.
Evening meal 6.30pm (l.o. 9pm).
Parking for 3.

AMBLESIDE
Cumbria
Map ref 5A3

4m NW. Windermere
At the head of Lake Windermere and surrounded by fells. Good centre for touring, walking and sailing. ⓘ

Brantfell Guest House M
Listed
Kelsick Rd., Ambleside, LA22 0BZ
☎ (053 94) 32239
A traditional Victorian house in the centre of Ambleside with views towards the fells.
Bedrooms: 1 single, 3 double & 1 twin, 1 family room.
Bathrooms: 2 public.

Bed & breakfast: from £11 single, from £22 double.
Parking for 2.

Brantholme Guest House M
Millans Park, Ambleside, LA22 9AG
☎ (053 94) 32034
In a quiet part of Ambleside, 3 minutes' walk from the village, with commanding views of Loughrigg Fell and Fairfield. Honeymoon suite with four-poster bed available.
Bedrooms: 4 double & 1 twin, 2 family rooms.
Bathrooms: 7 private, 2 public.
Bed & breakfast: £13.50-£17 single, £27-£34 double.
Parking for 7.

Claremont House M
Compston Rd., Ambleside, LA22 9DJ
☎ (053 94) 33448
Comfortable accommodation within easy reach of all amenities.
Bedrooms: 1 single, 4 double & 1 twin, 1 family room.
Bathrooms: 2 private, 1 public; 2 private showers.
Bed & breakfast: £11-£13 single, £22-£28 double.
Half board: £18.50-£21.50 daily, £120-£140 weekly.
Evening meal 6.30pm (l.o. 10pm).
Parking for 3.

Crow How Hotel M
Rydal Rd., Ambleside, LA22 9PN
☎ (053 94) 32193
Victorian country house in a quiet location, with two acres of grounds. Only one mile from the centre of Ambleside.
Bedrooms: 6 double & 1 twin, 2 family rooms.
Bathrooms: 9 private.
Bed & breakfast: £15-£17.60 single, £36-£41.80 double.
Half board: £24-£29.90 daily, £151-£176.50 weekly.
Evening meal 7.30pm (l.o. 7.30pm).
Parking for 12.

Fisherbeck Farmhouse M
Old Lake Rd., Ambleside, LA22 0DH
☎ (053 94) 32523
Off the main road, a few minutes' level walk from the centre of Ambleside. Not a working farm.
Bedrooms: 2 double & 1 twin.
Bathrooms: 1 public.
Bed & breakfast: £10.50-£12.50 single, £21-£25 double.
Half board: £17.50-£19.50 daily, £120-£135 weekly.
Parking for 3.
Open March-November.

The Howes M
1 Gale Crescent, Lower Gale, Ambleside, LA22 0BD
☎ (053 94) 33373
In a quiet, commanding position overlooking the fells and town, 3 minutes' walk from the centre. Central for touring and ideal for a relaxing holiday. Bunk house accommodation also available. A warm welcome awaits you.
Bedrooms: 2 single, 2 double & 1 twin, 3 family rooms.
Bathrooms: 2 private, 2 public.
Bed & breakfast: £12-£14.50 single, £24-£29 double.
Half board: £19-£23.50 daily, £129-£136 weekly.
Evening meal 7pm (l.o. 7.30pm).
Parking for 8.
Credit: Diners.

Lattendale Hotel M
Compston Rd., Ambleside, LA22 9DJ
☎ (053 94) 32368
Traditional Lakeland hotel, in the heart of Ambleside. A good base for many pursuits, offering interesting food and wines in a comfortable and relaxed atmosphere.
Bedrooms: 3 single, 2 double & 1 twin, 2 family rooms.
Bathrooms: 3 private, 1 public; 1 private shower.
Bed & breakfast: £12-£13.50 single, £24-£29 double.
Half board: £18.50-£21 daily, £115-£135 weekly.
Evening meal 7pm (l.o. 7.30pm).
Open February-December.
Credit: Access, Visa.

Lyndhurst Guesthouse M
Listed

Wansfell Rd., Ambleside,
LA22 0EG
☎ (053 94) 32421
*Attractive Lakeland stone
house in own gardens, in a
quiet position. Lovely rooms,
warm and friendly service.*
Bedrooms: 3 double & 1 twin,
2 family rooms.
Bathrooms: 3 private,
1 public; 1 private shower.
Bed & breakfast: £20-£28
double.
Half board: £16.50-£20.50
daily, £115-£140 weekly.
Evening meal 6.30pm (l.o.
8pm).
Parking for 6.
Open February-December.
🛏 📠 🖪 🕯 💷 ♿ 🎱 🎺 🖵 📺 🛋
🎀 📠 🐾 ⅏

Old Fisherbeck
Old Lake Rd., Ambleside,
LA22 0DH
☎ (053 94) 33540
*18th C. cottage in tiny garden,
near lake and town centre. On
quiet road with quick access to
fells. Log fires, informal and
peaceful. Non-smoking
establishment. Evening meals
available on request.*
Bedrooms: 1 double & 2 twin.
Bathrooms: 1 public.
Bed & breakfast: £9-£11
single, £18-£22 double.
Half board: £14-£16 daily,
£98-£112 weekly.
Parking for 3.
Open February-November.
🛏 🎱 ⅏ ⎙ 🕯 🖪 🖵 📺 🛋
🖭 🎀 📠 ⅏

Riverside Hotel M
👑👑👑

Under Loughrigg, Nr.
Rothay Bridge, Ambleside,
LA22 9LJ
☎ (053 94) 32395
*Small country hotel in a
peaceful setting over-looking
the river; with extensive
grounds and direct access on to
the Fells.*
Bedrooms: 6 double & 2 twin,
2 family rooms.
Bathrooms: 10 private.
Half board: £30-£40 daily,
£168-£260 weekly.
Evening meal 7pm (l.o. 8pm).
Parking for 20.
Open February-November.
Credit: Access, Visa.
🛏 📠 ⅏ ⎙ 🕯 🖪 🗡 🖵 📺 🛋
🖭 🎺 🎶 🖫 ✳ 🎀 📠 🆂🅿

```
THE SYMBOLS ARE
EXPLAINED ON THE
FLAP INSIDE THE
BACK COVER.
```

Rose Cottage M
Rydal Rd., Ambleside,
LA22 9AN
☎ (053 94) 33917
*Small, friendly "home from
home" house for non-smokers,
centrally located. Guaranteed
to satisfy.*
Bedrooms: 2 double & 1 twin.
Bathrooms: 1 private,
1 public.
Bed & breakfast: £10-£12.50
single, £20-£24 double.
🛏 🖵 ♿ 🖪 🗡 🖫 🖭 📠 🐾
📠

Thorneyfield Guest
House M
👑👑

Compston Rd., Ambleside,
LA22 9DJ
☎ (053 94) 32464
*Cosy family-run guesthouse in
the town centre with friendly
and helpful service. Close to
the park, miniature golf, tennis
and lake.*
Bedrooms: 1 single, 1 double
& 1 twin, 3 family rooms.
Bathrooms: 1 public.
Bed & breakfast: £9-£10
single, £19-£20 double.
Parking for 3.
🛏 ♿ 🖪 🖫 📺 🖵 🛋 📠

Tock How Farm
High Wray, Ambleside,
LA22 0JF
☎ Hawkshead (096 66) 481
*300-acre mixed dairy farm. A
working farmhouse with
panoramic views of Ambleside
and Lake Windermere. Home-
made jam.*
Bedrooms: 2 double, 1 family
room.
Bathrooms: 1 public.
Bed & breakfast: £12-£14
single, £20-£22 double.
Parking for 10.
🛏 ♿ 🖪 ⎙ 🕯 🖵 📺 🛋 📠
📠

Windlehurst
Guesthouse M
👑👑👑

Millans Park, Ambleside,
LA22 9AG
☎ (053 94) 33137
*Elegant Victorian house on a
peaceful road in Ambleside,
within easy walking distance of
shops and amenities.*
Bedrooms: 1 single, 2 double
& 1 twin, 1 family room.
Bathrooms: 2 public.
Bed & breakfast: £10-£13
single, £20-£26 double.
Parking for 6.
🛏 ♿ 🖪 ⎙ 🕯 📺 🛋 🛋 📠

Fox & Pheasant Inn M
Armathwaite, Carlisle,
CA4 9PY
☎ (069 92) 400
*17th C. coaching inn, 2.5 miles
off the A6 between Penrith and
Carlisle, with character and
atmosphere. In a tranquil
setting opposite fields and
River Eden.*
Bedrooms: 2 single, 4 double
& 1 twin, 1 family room.
Bathrooms: 4 private,
1 public; 1 private shower.
Bed & breakfast: £16-£18.50
single, £32-£37 double.
Half board: £26.50-£29 daily,
£175.50-£193 weekly.
Lunch available.
Evening meal 6.30pm (l.o.
9.30pm).
Parking for 40.
Credit: Access, Visa.
🛏 📠 ⅏ ♿ 🕯 🖪 🖭 🖵 📺 🛋
🛋 🎺 🎶 ✳ 🎀 🆂🅿 📠

7m NW. Millom
Ancient village lying close
to bracken-clad fells
where the River Annas
flows by the roadside.

Foldgate Farm
Listed

Coney, Bootle, Millom,
LA19 5TN
☎ (065 78) 660
*100-acre mixed farm. This
19th C. farm is on a scenic
route between Ravenglass and
Broughton.*
Bedrooms: 2 double, 1 family
room.
Bathrooms: 1 public.
Bed & breakfast: £9.50-£10
single, £19-£20 double.
Half board: £14-£15 daily,
£98-£105 weekly.
Evening meal 6pm.
Parking for 8.
🛏 🎱 🖪 🖵 📺 🛋 🐾 📠

Lying south of
Derwentwater in the heart
of the Lake District, the
valley is backed by
towering fells and
mountains. Good centre
for walking and climbing.

The Grange M
💷

Grange-in-Borrowdale,
Keswick, CA12 5UQ
☎ (059 684) 251
*A Georgian house with charm
and character. Ideal for
climbing and for exploring the
Borrowdale Valley.*
Bedrooms: 1 single, 3 double
& 2 twin, 1 family room.
Bathrooms: 1 private,
3 public; 1 private shower.
Bed & breakfast: from £11
single, from £22 double.
Parking for 8.
Open March-November.
🛏 ♿ 🖪 🕯 🖵 🛋 🛋 🐾

At the entry to Whinlatter
Pass, the starting-point
for climbing Grisedale
Pike.

Coledale Inn M
👑👑👑

Braithwaite, Keswick,
CA12 5TN
☎ (059 682) 272
*Victorian country house hotel
and Georgian Inn is on a peaceful
hillside position away from
traffic, with superb mountain
views.*
Bedrooms: 1 single, 2 double
& 1 twin, 4 family rooms.
Bathrooms: 8 private.
Bed & breakfast: £14.50-
£16.50 single, £29-£35 double.
Half board: £20-£23 daily,
£140-£161 weekly.
Lunch available.
Evening meal 7pm (l.o. 9pm).
Parking for 15.
Credit: Access.
🛏 🖵 ♿ 🕯 🗡 🖵 🛋 🛋 🎺
✳ 🎀 📠 🐾 🆂🅿 📠

```
GROUPS, CONSORTIA AND AGENCIES
SPECIALISING IN FARM AND COUNTRY
HOLIDAYS ARE LISTED IN A SPECIAL
SECTION OF THIS GUIDE.
```

BRAMPTON

Cumbria
Map ref 5B2

9m NE. Carlisle
Pleasant market town and
a good centre from which
to explore Hadrian's Wall.
Lanercost Priory is 2
miles away. ℹ

Cracrop Farm ♏
🏅🏅🏅

Kirkcambeck, Brampton,
CA8 2BW
☎ Roadhead (069 78) 245
*425-acre mixed farm. A busy
working farm with a large
dairy herd of Pedigree
Ayrshire cows. Evening meal
by arrangement.*
Bedrooms: 1 twin, 2 family
rooms.
Bathrooms: 3 private,
1 public.
Bed & breakfast: £20-£24
double.
Half board: £70-£84 weekly.
Evening meal 6pm (l.o. 1pm).
Parking for 4.
🛇🅿💷🌱🛡📺
🍽🟥🚶⛔✱🎇

High Nook Farm
Listed

Low Row, Brampton,
CA8 2LU
☎ Hallbankgate (069 76) 273
*100-acre stock rearing farm.
Quiet location in the beautiful
Irthing Valley, near the Roman
Wall, convenient for
Northumberland, Scottish
Borders and the Lake District.
Good hourly bus service.*
Bedrooms: 1 double, 1 family
room.
Bathrooms: 1 public.
Bed & breakfast: £6.50-£7.50
single, £13-£15 double.
Half board: £10-£11 daily,
£68-£73 weekly.
Evening meal 6pm (l.o. 5pm).
Parking for 3.
Open April-October.
🛇🅺💷🛡🚶♉🎇

High Rigg Farm ♏
Listed

Walton, Brampton, Carlisle,
CA8 2AZ
☎ (069 77) 2117
*202-acre mixed farm. Only 1
mile from a riding school, 4
from a swimming pool. Talkin
Tarn Country Park and the
Roman Wall are nearby.*
Bedrooms: 1 double, 1 family
room.
Bathrooms: 1 public.
Bed & breakfast: £8-£8.50
single, £16-£17 double.

Half board: £13-£14 daily,
£85-£90 weekly.
Evening meal 6pm (l.o. 8pm).
Parking for 4.
🛇🅺🅿🌱💷🛡📺
🍽🔌🚶♉✱🎇🐾🗝🏨

Hullerbank ♏
Listed

Talkin, Brampton, CA8 1LB
☎ Hallbankgate (069 76) 668
*14-acre mixed farm. Georgian
farmhouse, part dated 1635
and 1751, near Talkin village.
9 miles from M6 junction 43
and 3 miles from Brampton.*
Bedrooms: 1 double & 2 twin.
Bathrooms: 1 public.
Bed & breakfast: £11-£12
single, £19-£21 double.
Half board: £15-£16 daily,
£95-£100 weekly.
Evening meal 6.30pm (l.o.
8pm).
Parking for 6.
🛇🅺💷🛡🛡💷🛡📺🍽
✱🗝🎇🔵

Kirby Moor
🏅🏅

Longtown Rd., Brampton,
CA8 2AB
☎ (069 77) 2021
*A detached house on the
A6071 well back from the road
with ample parking and
extensive views. 6 miles from
Hadrian's Wall.*
Bedrooms: 1 twin, 2 family
rooms.
Bathrooms: 2 public.
Bed & breakfast: £11-£13
single, £22-£26 double.
Parking for 8.
Open April-October.
🛇🛡📺🍽🔌♉✱🗝🎇
🔵

Oakwood House ♏
🏅🏅

Longtown Rd., Brampton,
CA8 2AP
☎ (069 77) 2436
*Secluded Victorian country
house set in 10 acres of
parkland. Spacious and elegant
rooms. Friendly, personal
attention.*
Bedrooms: 1 double & 2 twin,
1 family room.
Bathrooms: 1 private,
1 public.
Bed & breakfast: £17.50-£21
single, £27-£32 double.
Half board: £25.50-£29 daily,
£170-£195 weekly.
Evening meal 7.30pm (l.o.
6pm).
Parking for 6.
Open March-November.
🛇🛡🛡🛡📺🍽🔌🌿✱
🎇🐾🔵

BROUGHTON-IN-
FURNESS

Cumbria
Map ref 5A3

Old market village whose
historic charter is still
proclaimed every year on
the first day of August in
the market square, when
coins are distributed.
Good centre for touring
the Duddon Valley.

Broom Hill

Broughton-in-Furness,
LA20 6JD
☎ (065 76) 358
*Large manor house on edge of
historic village with fine views
and country walks starting at
our gates.*
Bedrooms: 5 double & 1 twin.
Bathrooms: 2 private,
2 public; 1 private shower.
Bed & breakfast: £11.50
single, £23 double.
Parking for 8.
Open March-November.
🛇🖵💷🛡🛡📺🛡♉
✱🎇🔵

CALDBECK

Cumbria
Map ref 5A2

Quaint limestone village
lying at the northern edge
of the Lake District
National Park. John Peel,
the famous huntsman
who is immortalised in
song, is buried in the
churchyard.

Friar Hall ♏
Listed

Caldbeck, Wigton, CA7 8DS
☎ (069 98) 633
*140-acre mixed farm. In the
lovely village of Caldbeck
overlooking the river and the
church. Ideal for touring the
Lakes, Scottish Borders and
Roman Wall.*
Bedrooms: 2 double, 1 family
room.
Bathrooms: 1 public.
Bed & breakfast: £12-£13
single, £22-£23 double.
Evening meal 6pm.
Parking for 3.
Open April-October.
🛇🛡💷🛡📺🗝🎇

Swaledale Watch

Whelpo, Caldbeck, Wigton,
CA7 8HQ
☎ (069 98) 409

*300-acre mixed farm. Near
fells, surrounded by lovely
countryside with peaceful
walks. Situated within
National Park. Guests
welcome to see farm animals.*
Bedrooms: 1 double & 1 twin,
1 family room.
Bathrooms: 1 public.
Bed & breakfast: £8.50
single, £17 double.
Half board: £14 daily, £98
weekly.
Evening meal 7pm (l.o. 2pm).
Parking for 10.
🛇🔌🌱💷🛡📺🚶🛡📺
🍽🔌✱🗝🎇

CARLISLE

Cumbria
Map ref 5A2

Near the border with
Scotland, this cathedral
city suffered years of
strife through the
centuries, often changing
hands between England
and Scotland. The red
sandstone cathedral with
its beautiful east window
is the second smallest
cathedral in England. The
Castle was founded in
1092 and later enlarged.
The Keep now houses a
museum of the history of
the Border Regiment. ℹ

Corner House ♏
🏅🏅

87 Petteril St., Carlisle,
CA1 2AW
☎ (0228) 41942
*On the main access road to the
city centre from M6 junction
43. 10 minutes' walk to the
town centre, golfing, fishing
and the parks.*
Bedrooms: 2 twin.
Bathrooms: 2 public.
Bed & breakfast: £10-£12.50
single, £20-£25 double.
Parking for 3.
🛇🖵🌱💷🛡📺🍽🔌🚶
🎇

The Gill Farm ♏
Listed

Blackford, Carlisle, CA6 4EL
☎ Kirklinton (022 875) 326
*124-acre farm. An ideal
halfway stopping place or a
good base for touring
Cumbria's beauty spots. In
peaceful countryside, 3 miles
from the M6 junction 44. From
Carlisle go north to Blackford,
fork right at sign for
Kirklinton, 100yds turn right,
half a mile turn left, Gill Farm
on left on this road.*
Bedrooms: 1 double & 1 twin,
1 family room.
Bathrooms: 2 public.

Bed & breakfast: £9.50-£10.50 single, £19-£21 double.
Half board: £15-£16 daily, £100-£110 weekly.
Evening meal 5pm (l.o. 7pm).
Parking for 4.

6 Hartington Place M

Carlisle, CA1 1HL
☎ (0228) 27443
Pleasant Victorian family house a few minutes' walk to city centre and all amenities. Easy access from M6 junction 43. Bus and railway stations nearby.
Bedrooms: 1 single, 1 twin, 1 family room.
Bathrooms: 1 public.
Bed & breakfast: £10-£12 single, £18-£22 double.

Howard House M

27 Howard Place, Carlisle, CA1 1HR
☎ (0228) 29159
Spacious Victorian family-run establishment in quiet residential road, with park, rail and bus stations, castle and cathedral nearby. Family historians welcome.
Bedrooms: 2 single, 2 double & 2 twin.
Bathrooms: 2 public; 2 private showers.
Bed & breakfast: £12-£13 single, £19-£21 double.
Half board: £14-£16 daily, £95-£100 weekly.
Evening meal 6pm (l.o. 10am).

New Pallyards M

Hethersgill, Carlisle, CA6 6HZ
☎ Nicholforest (022 877) 308
65-acre mixed farm. 18th C. farmhouse, recently modernised to a good standard. We offer a warm welcome in peaceful surroundings.
Bedrooms: 1 single, 2 double & 1 twin, 1 family room.
Bathrooms: 3 private, 2 public.
Bed & breakfast: £9-£11 single, £18-£22 double.
Half board: £17-£28 daily, £95-£110 weekly.
Lunch available.

Evening meal 6pm (l.o. 7.30pm).
Parking for 7.

Cumbria
Map ref 5A3

A picturesque conserved village based on a 12th C priory with a well preserved church and gatehouse. Just over 3 miles north of Morecambe Bay and 8 miles from the south tip of Lake Windermere. A peaceful base for fell walking, with historic houses and beautiful scenery.

Bank House M
Listed

125 Station Rd., Cark-in-Cartmel, Nr. Cartmel, LA11 7NY
☎ Flookburgh (044 853) 302
Warm and comfortable accommodation in a quiet village surrounded by lovely countryside. Convenient for the Lakes, country walks and public transport.
Bedrooms: 2 double & 1 twin.
Bathrooms: 1 private, 1 public.
Bed & breakfast: £9.50-£11 single, £19-£22 double.

Eeabank House
Listed

123 Station Rd., Cark-in-Cartmel, Grange-over-Sands, LA11 7NY
☎ Flookburgh (044 853) 8818
Period house in the centre of an old world village. A quarter of a mile from Holker Hall and gardens.
Bedrooms: 3 double.
Bathrooms: 1 public.
Bed & breakfast: max. £10.50 single, max. £21 double.
Half board: max. £16 daily, max. £98 weekly.
Credit: Access.

Cumbria
Map ref 5A2

Market town at the confluence of the Rivers Cocker and Derwent, and the birthplace of William Wordsworth, the Lakeland poet, in 1770. The house where he was born stands at one end of the town's broad tree-lined main street and is now owned by the National Trust. Good base for motoring tours into the Lake District.

Beech Hill Farm

Mosser, Cockermouth, CA13 0SS
☎ (0900) 826985
92-acre beef & sheep farm. Quiet, friendly farm, two miles off the A5086. Home cooking, comfortable lounge with log fire. Loweswater three miles, Cockermouth five miles.
Bedrooms: 2 single, 1 double, 1 family room.
Bathrooms: 1 public.
Bed & breakfast: £8.50 single, max. £17 double.
Half board: max. £12.50 daily, £85 weekly.
Evening meal 6pm (l.o. midday).
Parking for 4.
Open February-November.

Crag End Farm
Listed

Rogerscale, Cockermouth, CA13 0RG
☎ (090 085) 658
250-acre mixed farm. Good home cooking in a typical farmhouse family establishment.
Bedrooms: 1 single, 2 double & 1 twin, 2 family rooms.
Bathrooms: 2 public.
Bed & breakfast: £9.50 single, £19 double.
Half board: £14 daily, £98 weekly.
Evening meal 6.50pm.
Parking for 10.

High Side Farm M

Embleton, Cockermouth, CA13 9TN
☎ (059 681) 351

260-acre mixed hill farm. In pleasant and peaceful countryside 3 miles from Bassenthwaite Lake. This traditionally furnished farmhouse with log fires offers home-made food. No smoking facilities.
Bedrooms: 3 double & 1 twin.
Bathrooms: 1 private, 2 public.
Bed & breakfast: £9-£10 single, £18-£20 double.
Half board: £28-£32 daily, £98-£114 weekly.
Evening meal 7pm.
Parking for 6.
Open April-October.

Low Hall Country Guesthouse M

Brandlingill, Lorton Vale, Nr. Cockermouth, CA13 0RE
☎ (0900) 826654
Secluded 17th C. former farmhouse overlooking Lorton Fells, near Wordsworth's birthplace and the quiet fells and lakes.
Bedrooms: 5 double & 1 twin.
Bathrooms: 3 private; 3 private showers.
Bed & breakfast: £15.50-£18 single, £31-£36 double.
Half board: £24.50-£27 daily, £164.50-£182 weekly.
Evening meal 7pm (l.o. 7.30pm).
Parking for 10.
Open March-November.
Credit: Access, Visa.

Mrs. D.E. Richardson

Pardshaw Hall, Cockermouth, CA13 0SP
☎ (0900) 822607
5-acre mixed farm. Well placed for touring the Lakes, with lovely views and walks, large garden and home cooking.
Bedrooms: 2 single, 1 double & 1 twin, 1 family room.
Bathrooms: 1 public.
Bed & breakfast: from £9 single, from £18 double.
Half board: from £13 daily, from £90 weekly.
Evening meal 6pm (l.o. 6.30pm).
Parking for 4.

THERE IS A SPECIAL SECTION IN THIS GUIDE LISTING ACCOMMODATION ESPECIALLY SUITABLE FOR GROUPS AND YOUNG PEOPLE.

CONISTON

Cumbria
Map ref 5A3

Village lying at the north end of Coniston Water. Along the NW of the village run the Coniston Fells, dominated by Coniston Old Man. Fine centre for walkers. John Ruskin, the Victorian critic, is buried beneath a splendidly carved cross in the churchyard. ℹ

Black Beck Cottage
East Side of the Lake, Coniston, LA21 8AB
☎ (053 94) 41607
A warm welcome is offered along with comfortable accommodation. All the bedrooms have views of the mountains and the lake.
Bedrooms: 4 double & 1 twin.
Bathrooms: 2 private, 1 public.
Bed & breakfast: £20-£30 double.
Parking for 6.
🕭 ⅍ 👜 ⓤ 🗎 ⅍ 🛏 ⊡ 🎞 🖃
🖾 ⊁ 🐾 🖾

How Head Cottage ⋒
East of Lake Coniston, Coniston, LA21 8AA
☎ (053 94) 41594
Detached cottage in own grounds, overlooking lake and surrounding fells. Comfortable accommodation.
Bedrooms: 3 double & 1 twin.
Bathrooms: 2 private, 1 public.
Bed & breakfast: £11.50-£15 single, £23-£25 double.
Half board: £19-£22.50 daily.
Evening meal 7pm.
Parking for 6.
Open March-November.
🕭6 ⓤ 🗎 ⓥ ⅍ 🛏 ⊡ 🎞 ⮾
🐾 🖾

CROOKLANDS

Cumbria
Map ref 5B3

6m SE. Kendal
A village set amidst the rolling fields, hedges and hills of England's largest drumlin belt.

Milton House Barn ⋒
Listed
Milton, Crooklands, Milnthorpe, LA7 7NL
☎ (044 87) 628

Traditional converted Westmorland barn in a rural hamlet. Half a mile from Crooklands (over Lancaster-Kendal canal, first left). Non-smoking establishment.
Bedrooms: 1 single, 1 double & 1 twin.
Bathrooms: 2 public.
Bed & breakfast: from £11 single, from £22 double.
Half board: from £16.50 daily, from £108 weekly.
Evening meal 6.30pm (l.o. 6.30pm).
Parking for 3.
🕭10 ⅍ 👜 👜 ⓤ 🗎 ⓥ ⓣ 🎞
🖾 🖾 ᴰᴬᴾ ˢᴾ 🖾

DENT

Cumbria
Map ref 5B3

Picturesque village with narrow cobbled streets lying in the valley of the River Dee in the Yorkshire Dales National Park.

Sun Inn ⋒
Main St., Dent, Sedbergh, LA10 5QL
☎ (058 75) 208
A 17th C. inn with original beams, in an outstanding conservation area.
Bedrooms: 1 double & 1 twin, 1 family room.
Bathrooms: 1 public.
Bed & breakfast: £15-£25 double.
Evening meal 6.30pm (l.o. 8.30pm).
Parking for 20.
🕭5 🖵 ⅍ 🗎 ⓥ 🎞 🔍 🖾 ᴰᴬᴾ
ˢᴾ 🖾

ELTERWATER

Cumbria
Map ref 5A3

Attractive village in the Langdale Valley, with a small green as its focal point. A nearby bridge spans Great Langdale Beck, which flows into Elterwater, one of the smallest lakes in the area. Gunpowder was once manufactured here.

Britannia Inn ⋒
🏰
Elterwater, Nr. Ambleside, LA22 9HP
☎ Langdale (096 67) 210 & 382 Telex 8950511 G Ref: 14219001

A 400-year-old traditional Lake District inn on a village green in the beautiful Langdale Valley. A warm welcome to all. TV available in bedrooms on request.
Bedrooms: 1 single, 6 double & 2 twin, 1 family room.
Bathrooms: 4 private, 2 public.
Bed & breakfast: £17.75-£19.75 single, £35.50-£39.50 double.
Half board: £28.75-£30.75 daily, £194.25-£208.25 weekly.
Lunch available.
Evening meal 7.30pm (l.o. 7.30pm).
Parking for 10.
Credit: Access, Visa.
🕭 🖵 ⅍ 🗎 ⓥ 🖾 🛏 🎞 🖾 🖾
🖾 ˢᴾ 🖾 ⓣ

Fellside
Lane Ends, Elterwater, Nr. Ambleside, LA22 9HN
☎ Langdale (096 67) 678
In the heart of the Langdales, ideal for fell walking and peaceful holidays.
Bedrooms: 2 single, 1 double & 1 twin.
Bathrooms: 2 public.
Bed & breakfast: £10 single, £20 double.
Evening meal 7pm.
Parking for 4.
🕭6 ⅍ 👜 🗎 🐾 ⅍ 🖾 🖾 🖾

Meadow Bank
Elterwater, Ambleside
☎ Langdale (096 67) 278
Traditional, stone-built house in its own grounds. Home cooking.
Bedrooms: 2 double & 1 twin.
Bathrooms: 2 public.
Bed & breakfast: £10-£11 double.
Half board: £17-£18 daily, £105-£110 weekly.
Evening meal 6.50pm (l.o. 6.50pm).
Parking for 3.
🖵 ⅍ 👜 ⓤ ⓥ ⅍ 🛏 ⓣ 🎞 ❁ ⅍
🖾

FRIZINGTON

Cumbria
Map ref 5A3

Daleside
49 Rowrah Rd., Rowrah, Frizington, CA26 3XJ
☎ Lamplugh (0946) 861536
Bedrooms: 1 single, 1 double, 1 family room.
Bathrooms: 2 public.
Bed & breakfast: £7.50 single, £15 double.

Half board: from £10.50 daily, from £70 weekly.
Evening meal 5pm (l.o. 8pm).
Parking for 4.
🕭 ⅍ ⓤ 🗎 ⅍ ⓣ 🎞 🖾 ᴸ ♨
🖾 ᴰᴬᴾ

GRANGE-OVER-SANDS

Cumbria
Map ref 5A3

Sheltered seaside resort overlooking Morecambe Bay. Pleasant sea-front walks and beautiful gardens. The bay attracts many species of wading birds. Large sea-water swimming pool. ℹ

High Bank
Methven Rd., Grange-over-Sands, LA11 7DU
☎ (044 84) 2902
Friendly service, in a spacious Victorian house with an attractive, interesting garden and sea views. Close to all amenities.
Bedrooms: 1 single, 1 double & 1 twin.
Bathrooms: 1 public.
Bed & breakfast: £9 single, £18 double.
Parking for 2.
🕭5 ⅍ ⅍ ⓤ ⓣ 🎞 ⊁ 🖾 ˢᴾ

GRASMERE

Cumbria
Map ref 5A3

Described by William Wordsworth as 'the loveliest spot that man hath ever found', this village is in a beautiful setting by-passed by the main road and overlooked by Helm Crag. Wordsworth lived at Dove Cottage for 9 years and the cottage and museum are now open to the public. Grasmere gingerbread is made in the old school to a traditional village recipe. Good centre for touring and walking. ℹ

Craigside House ⋒
🏰
Grasmere, Nr. Ambleside, LA22 9SG
☎ (096 65) 292
Delightfully furnished Victorian house on the edge of the village near Dove Cottage. In a large, peaceful garden overlooking the lake and hills.
Bedrooms: 2 double & 1 twin.
Bathrooms: 3 private.

MAP REFERENCES APPLY TO THE COLOUR MAPS TOWARDS THE END OF THIS GUIDE.

Bed & breakfast: £16.50-£38 single, £33-£41 double.
Parking for 6.
📺🞠🗣🞛 ▯ ⚲ 🞠 📶 🞠 ✻
🞠 🞠 🞠

Oak Bank Hotel M
☺☺☺

Broadgate, Grasmere,
LA22 9TA
☎ (096 65) 217 & 501 & 685
Traditionally built 100 years ago in Lakeland stone and now modernised throughout.
Bedrooms: 1 single, 7 double & 5 twin, 1 family room.
Bathrooms: 14 private.
Bed & breakfast: £20-£26 single, £40-£52 double.
Half board: £25-£66 daily, £200-£220 weekly.
Lunch available.
Evening meal 7pm (l.o. 8pm).
Parking for 14.
Open February-December.
Credit: Access, Visa.
🞠 🞠 📞 🞠 🞠 🞠 ▯ 📶 📺
🞠 🞠 🞠 ✻ 🞠 🞠 🞠

Roundhill M
Easedale, Grasmere,
LA22 9QT
☎ Grasmere (096 65) 233
Peaceful situation in Easedale, 1 mile from village centre. Detached house in landscaped garden, with spectacular views. True Lakeland atmosphere.
Bedrooms: 1 double & 1 twin, 1 family room.
Bathrooms: 1 public.
Bed & breakfast: £22-£26 double.
Parking for 3.
Open April-October.
🞠3 🞠 🞠 ▯ 🞠 🞠 🞠 🞠 🞠

Woodland Crag Guest House M
☺☺

Howe Head Lane, Grasmere,
LA22 9SG
☎ (096 65) 351
Charming Victorian residence in landscaped gardens. Well-furnished rooms with lake and fell views. Dove Cottage is nearby. Dinner available out of season. Peace and comfort assured.
Bedrooms: 4 double & 1 twin.
Bathrooms: 3 private, 1 public.
Bed & breakfast: £26-£31 double.
Half board: £20-£22.50 daily, £130-£147 weekly.
Evening meal 7pm (l.o. 3pm).
Parking for 5.
🞠 🞠 🞠 ▯ 🞠 📺 🞠 🞠 ✻
🞠 🞠 🞠

Set in the Levens Valley south-west of Newby Bridge. Headquarters of the Lakeside and Haverthwaite Railway Company. Many craft workshops.

Broad Oaks
☺☺

Haverthwaite, Nr. Ulverston,
LA12 8AL
☎ Newby Bridge
(053 95) 31756
An unusual modern building in a woodland setting with elevated public rooms giving views at tree-top level.
Bedrooms: 1 double & 1 twin.
Bathrooms: 2 private.
Bed & breakfast: £14-£18 single, £25-£30 double.
Half board: £21.50-£24.50 daily, £125-£145 weekly.
Evening meal 7pm.
Parking for 4.
🞠3 🞠 🞠 🞠 ▯ 🞠 🞠 🞠
✻ 🞠 🞠 🞠 🞠

Lying near Esthwaite Water, this village has great charm and character. Its small squares are linked by flagged or cobbled alleys and the main square is dominated by the Market House or Shambles where the butchers had their stalls in days gone by. 🞠

High Grassings M
Sunny Brow, Outgate, Nr.
Hawkshead, LA22 0PU
☎ (096 66) 484
In 7 acres of garden with magnificent mountain views. Log fire. 3 minutes from Hawkshead on the Drunken Duck to Tarn Hows road.
Bedrooms: 3 double & 2 twin, 1 family room.
Bathrooms: 3 private, 1 public.
Bed & breakfast: from £15 single, £22-£26 double.
Parking for 8.
🞠4 🞠 🞠 🞠 ▯ 🞠 🞠 📺 🞠
🞠 ✻ 🞠 🞠

Kings Arms Hotel M
The Square, Hawkshead, Nr.
Ambleside, LA22 0NZ
☎ (096 66) 372

Cosy old world inn overlooking the square. Oak beams, open fire, real ale. Lakeland cottage annexe. Happy, informal atmosphere.
Bedrooms: 6 double & 1 twin, 2 family rooms.
Bathrooms: 5 private, 1 public.
Bed & breakfast: £18-£21 single, £29-£36 double.
Half board: £22-£28 daily, £154-£196 weekly.
Lunch available.
Evening meal 6pm (l.o. 9.30pm).
🞠 🞠 🞠 ▯ 🞠 🞠 🞠 🞠
🞠 🞠

Red Lion Inn M
☺☺☺

The Square, Hawkshead, Nr.
Ambleside, LA22 0NS
☎ (096 66) 213
14th C. coaching inn in the centre of Hawkshead, a uniquely beautiful village in England's most beautiful corner.
Bedrooms: 1 single, 6 double & 2 twin.
Bathrooms: 9 private.
Bed & breakfast: £20 single, £37.50 double.
Half board: £27 daily, £180 weekly.
Lunch available.
Evening meal 7pm (l.o. 9pm).
Parking for 9.
Credit: Access, Visa.
🞠 ▯ 🞠 🞠 🞠 🞠 🞠 🞠 🞠 🞠
🞠 🞠 🞠

Walker Ground Manor M
Hawkshead, LA22 0PD
☎ (096 66) 219
17.5-acre mixed farm. 450-year-old private house, in picturesque and peaceful country setting. Informal, relaxing, log fires. No smoking establishment.
Bedrooms: 2 double & 1 twin.
Bathrooms: 2 private, 2 public.
Bed & breakfast: £15-£25 single, £30 double.
Half board: £23-£35 daily.
Evening meal 7pm.
Parking for 6.
🞠 🞠 🞠 ▯ 🞠 🞠 🞠 📺 🞠 🞠
🞠 🞠 🞠 🞠 🞠

5m NW. Brampton

Hethergrove Byre
☺☺

Hethersgill, Brampton
☎ Kirklinton (022 875) 346

Converted and extended stone byre in small farming community. Ideal for Borders, Hadrian's Wall, southern Scotland. Hethersgill is 2 miles off the Carlisle/Newcastle Road.
Bedrooms: 3 twin.
Bathrooms: 1 public.
Bed & breakfast: £10-£15 single, £20-£25 double.
Half board: £16-£21 daily, £110-£140 weekly.
Evening meal 7pm.
Parking for 8.
🞠 🞠 🞠 ▯ 🞠 📺 🞠 🞠

A pretty village north of Ravenglass with good views and easy walks. Very popular with anglers for fishing the River Irt.

Carleton Green M
☺☺

Saltcoats Rd., Holmrook,
CA19 1YX
☎ (094 04) 608
Spacious Georgian guesthouse in its own peaceful grounds, close to the Eskdale and Wasdale Valleys and near the coast.
Bedrooms: 2 single, 2 double & 1 twin, 2 family rooms.
Bathrooms: 3 private, 1 public.
Bed & breakfast: max. £12 single, max. £20 double.
Half board: max. £18 daily.
Lunch available.
Evening meal 7pm.
Parking for 7.
Open April-October.
🞠 🞠 🞠 ▯ 🞠 📺 🞠 🞠 ✻
🞠 🞠

INDIVIDUAL PROPRIETORS HAVE SUPPLIED ALL DETAILS OF ACCOMMODATION. ALTHOUGH WE DO CHECK FOR ACCURACY, WE ADVISE YOU TO CONFIRM PRICES AND OTHER INFORMATION AT THE TIME OF BOOKING.

KENDAL

Cumbria
Map ref 5B3

The 'Auld Grey Town', so called because of its many grey limestone buildings, lies in the valley of the River Kent with a backcloth of limestone fells on 3 sides. Situated just outside the Lake District National Park, a good centre from which to tour the Lakes and surrounding countryside. The ruined Norman castle was the birthplace of Catherine Parr, Henry VIII's sixth wife. 🖎

Bridge House
🏚

Garnett Bridge, Kendal, LA8 9AZ
☎ Selside (053 983) 288
3-acre smallholding. An old mill house in the hamlet of Garnett Bridge, offering food and accommodation at sensible prices. Ideal for touring the Lakes.
Bedrooms: 1 single, 1 double, 1 family room.
Bathrooms: 1 public; 1 private shower.
Bed & breakfast: £10-£12 single, £20-£24 double.
Half board: £17-£18 daily, £115-£120 weekly.
Evening meal 7pm (l.o. 5pm).
Parking for 8.
🛏 🕏 📺 Ⓥ 🖾 📺 🞐 ⅃ ❅ 🖾 📵 SP 🎬

Castle View 🅜
27 Sedbergh Rd., Kendal, LA9 6AD
☎ (0539) 29327
Comfortable family house, 5 minutes from the centre of Kendal, offering a full English breakfast. On the main A684, 5 miles from the M6.
Bedrooms: 3 twin.
Bathrooms: 1 public.
Bed & breakfast: £8-£9 single, £16-£18 double.
Open April-September.
🛏 10 ⑩ 🕏 📺 🖾 📺 🗙 🖾

Mrs. O. M. Knowles
Cragg Farm, New Hutton, Nr. Kendal, LA8 0BA
☎ (0539) 21760
260-acre working farm. Tastefully modernised but retaining its old world charm. 4 miles from Kendal, 3 miles from M6 junction 37.
Bedrooms: 1 double, 1 family room.
Bathrooms: 1 public.
Bed & breakfast: £19-£21 double.

Half board: £13-£15 daily.
Evening meal 6.30pm (l.o. 6.30pm).
Parking for 3.
Open March-October.
🛏 🎮 🕏 📺 Ⓥ 📺 🞐 🖾 📵 🎬

Fairhaven 🅜
🏚

Sedgwick Rd., Natland, Kendal, LA9 7QQ
☎ Sedgwick (053 95) 60647 & 60732
A modern house providing home cooking, in an attractive and quiet village 2 miles south of Kendal.
Bedrooms: 2 double & 1 twin.
Bathrooms: 3 private.
Bed & breakfast: £15-£20 single, £25-£30 double.
Parking for 6.
🛏 🖵 🕏 📺 Ⓥ 🖾 📺 🞐 🗙 🖾

Fell View Guesthouse 🅜
🏚

12A, Danes Rd., Staveley, Kendal, LA8 9PW
☎ (0539) 821209
A stone house in Staveley, 3 miles from Windermere on the A591. Danes Road is set back from the main road.
Bedrooms: 1 single, 1 double, 1 family room.
Bathrooms: 1 public.
Bed & breakfast: from £11 single, from £22 double.
Half board: from £16.50 daily, from £100 weekly.
Evening meal 7pm (l.o. 10am).
Parking for 3.
🛏 🖵 🕏 📺 🖥 Ⓥ 🖾 📺 🞐 🖾 🗙 SP

Garnett House Farm 🅜
🏚

Burneside, Kendal, LA9 5SF
☎ (0539) 24542
270-acre mixed farm. Just off the A591 Kendal to Windermere road, overlooking tennis courts in Burneside village.
Bedrooms: 2 double & 1 twin, 2 family rooms.
Bathrooms: 2 public.
Bed & breakfast: £18-£20 double.
Half board: £13.25-£14.25 daily.
Evening meal 6.30pm (l.o. 5.30pm).
Parking for 6.
🛏 🖵 🕏 📺 🖾 📺 🞐 🖻 🗙 🖾 🎬

Gateside Farm
🏚

Burneside, Kendal, LA9 5SE
☎ (0539) 22036

300-acre dairy and sheep farm. A traditional Lakeland farm easily accessible from the motorway and on the main tourist route through Lakeland. One night and short stays are welcomed.
Bedrooms: 2 double & 1 twin, 1 family room.
Bathrooms: 2 public.
Bed & breakfast: £19-£20 double.
Half board: £14.50-£15 daily, £93-£95 weekly.
Evening meal (l.o. 5pm).
Parking for 7.
🛏 🖵 🕏 📺 🖾 📺 🞐 🖾 SP

Great Eskirgg End 🅜
Listed

Old Hutton, Nr. Kendal, LA8 0NU
☎ (0539) 24833
9-acre smallholding. Large family farmhouse, formerly a barn, set in open countryside. Ideal for Lakes and Dales. Non-smoking establishment.
Bedrooms: 1 double & 1 twin.
Bathrooms: 1 public.
Bed & breakfast: max. £7 single, max. £14 double.
Half board: max. £10 daily, max. £70 weekly.
Evening meal 6pm.
Parking for 4.
Open March-November.
🛏 🕏 📺 🖥 🖾 📺 🞐 🖻 ∪ ❅ 🗙 🖾

Low Hundhowe Farm 🅜
🏚

Burneside, Kendal, LA8 9AB
☎ (0539) 22060
235-acre mixed farm. In a peaceful area 4 miles from Kendal and 5 miles from Windermere. Family run, offering a varied menu and home-cooking.
Bedrooms: 3 double.
Bathrooms: 1 public.
Bed & breakfast: £18.50-£19.50 double.
Half board: £13-£14 daily.
Evening meal 6.30pm (l.o. 4.30pm).
Parking for 3.
🛏 🕏 📺 🖥 Ⓥ 🖾 📺 ⅃ 🗙 🖾 SP 🎬

Lyndhurst 🅜
🏚

8 South Rd., Kendal, LA9 5QH
☎ (0539) 27281
Terraced house providing comfortable accommodation, in a quiet area with river view. 10 minutes' walk from the town.
Bedrooms: 2 single, 1 double & 1 twin, 1 family room.

Bathrooms: 2 public.
Bed & breakfast: £12-£13 single, £20-£24 double.
Parking for 4.
🛏 🕏 📺 🖾 📺 🞐 🖻 🞓 🖾

Meadow Bank Guest House
Meadow Bank, Shap Rd., Kendal, LA9 6NY
☎ (0539) 21926
1.5 miles from the town centre. Spacious residence in beautiful 1-acre garden. Peaceful and quiet.
Bedrooms: 1 single, 1 double & 2 twin, 2 family rooms.
Bathrooms: 2 public.
Bed & breakfast: £10-£11 single, £20-£22 double.
Parking for 7.
🛏 📺 🖾 📺 🞐 🖻 ❊ 🖾

Newalls 🅜
Listed

Skelsmergh, Kendal, LA9 6NU
☎ (0539) 23202
500-acre dairy farm. Modernised farmhouse on the edge of Lakeland, with private entrance into a large garden. Near the main A6.
Bedrooms: 1 double, 1 family room.
Bathrooms: 1 public.
Bed & breakfast: from £8.50 single, from £17 double.
Half board: from £12.50 daily, from £87.50 weekly.
Evening meal 6pm.
Parking for 3.
Open April-October.
🛏 8 🞐 📺 🖾 📺 🞐 🖻 ❊ 🗙 🖾 🎬

Sonata
19, Burneside Rd., Kendal, LA9 4RL
☎ (0539) 32290
Three-storey, six-bedroomed house within easy walking distance of all facilities. Located off Windermere Road, Kendal.
Bedrooms: 1 double & 1 twin, 2 family rooms.
Bathrooms: 2 public.
Bed & breakfast: £19 double.
Evening meal 5pm (l.o. 7pm).
🛏 3 🕏 📺 📺 🗙 🖾

Stock Bridge Farm
🏚

Kendal Rd., Staveley, Kendal, LA8 9LP
☎ (0539) 821580
6-acre mixed farm. Comfortable well-appointed 17th C. farmhouse on edge of village midway between Kendal and Windermere. Central heating. Full English breakfast. Friendly personal attention.

Bedrooms: 1 single, 4 double,
1 family room.
Bathrooms: 1 public.
Bed & breakfast: £9.50-£10
single, £18-£19 double.
Parking for 6.
Open March-October.

Talisker
Listed
24 Calder Drive, Kendal,
LA9 6LR
☎ (0539) 24355
*A modern, private house with
pleasant gardens and
comfortable furnishings, at the
end of a cul-de-sac overlooking
fields.*
Bedrooms: 1 single, 1 double
& 1 twin.
Bathrooms: 1 public.
Bed & breakfast: £9 single,
£18 double.
Half board: £16.50 daily,
£109.20 weekly.
Evening meal 7pm (l.o.
10am).
Parking for 3.

7 Thorny Hills
Kendal, LA9 7AL
☎ (0539) 20207
*In a quiet, private road close to
all amenities. We offer
wholesome, well-cooked food.
Non-smoking establishment.*
Bedrooms: 2 double & 1 twin.
Bathrooms: 1 private,
2 public.
Bed & breakfast: from £11
single, from £19 double.
Half board: from £16 daily.
Evening meal 6pm.
Parking for 3.
Open February-November.

Wattsfield Farmhouse
Listed
Wattsfield Lane, Kendal
☎ (0539) 27767
*2-acre horse farm. A 17th C.
Westmorland farmhouse with
oak beam and other features of
historic interest; on a bank of
the River Kent, 1 mile from
Kendal town centre.*
Bedrooms: 1 single, 1 family
room.
Bathrooms: 1 private,
1 public.
Bed & breakfast: £12-£15
single, £24-£30 double.
Parking for 4.

**PLEASE MENTION
THIS GUIDE WHEN
MAKING A BOOKING.**

KESWICK
Cumbria
Map ref 5A3

*Attractive town in a
beautiful position beside
Derwentwater and below
the mountains of Skiddaw
and Saddleback. A
natural convergence of
roads makes it a good
base for touring. Motor-
launches operate on
Derwentwater and motor
boats and rowing boats
can be hired.*

Foye House
23 Eskin St., Keswick,
CA12 4DQ
☎ (076 87) 73288
*Established guesthouse offering
comfort and home cooking.
Residential area, 4 minutes'
walk from all amenities.*
Bedrooms: 3 single, 1 double
& 1 twin, 1 family room.
Bathrooms: 2 public.
Bed & breakfast: £10.50-£11
single, £21-£22 double.
Half board: £16.50-£17 daily,
£112 weekly.
Evening meal 7pm (l.o. 5pm).

Greystoke House
9 Leonard St., Keswick,
CA12 4EL
☎ (076 87) 72603
*Traditional 19th C. town house
offering warm, friendly
accommodation with home
cooking. Central for all
amenities.*
Bedrooms: 2 single, 2 double
& 1 twin, 1 family room.
Bathrooms: 2 public.
Bed & breakfast: £10-£10.50
single, £20-£21 double.
Half board: £15-£15.50 daily,
£98-£100 weekly.
Evening meal 6.30pm (l.o.
5pm).
Parking for 4.

Hazeldene Hotel (incorporating Burleigh Mead Hotel)
The Heads, Keswick,
CA12 5ER
☎ (076 87) 72750 & 72106
*Beautiful and central with open
views over Derwentwater to
Borrowdale and the Newlands
Valley. Close to the town
centre and shops.*
Bedrooms: 5 single, 9 double
& 4 twin, 5 family rooms.

Bathrooms: 18 private,
3 public.
Bed & breakfast: £12.80-
£16.90 single, £25.60-£33.80
double.
Half board: £20.30-£24.40
daily, £134-£164 weekly.
Evening meal 6.30pm (l.o.
4pm).
Parking for 18.
Open March-November.

Hazelgrove
4 Ratcliffe Place, Keswick,
CA12 4DZ
☎ (076 87) 73391
*A comfortable guesthouse,
convenient for the shops, park
and lake. Home cooking under
supervision of the owner.*
Bedrooms: 1 single, 2 double
& 1 twin, 1 family room.
Bathrooms: 1 public.
Bed & breakfast: £9-£10
single, £18-£21 double.
Half board: £14.50-£15.50
daily, £95-£105 weekly.
Evening meal 6.30pm (l.o.
6.30pm).
Open March-October.

Hazelmere
Crosthwaite Rd., Keswick,
CA12 5PG
☎ (076 87) 72445
*Comfortable, larger than
average Victorian semi-
detached house on outskirts of
Keswick, easy level walk to
town centre and park. Good
views of fells; private parking
behind house.*
Bedrooms: 1 single, 1 double,
2 family rooms.
Bathrooms: 1 public.
Bed & breakfast: £9.50-
£10.50 single.
Parking for 6.

Holmwood House
The Heads, Keswick,
CA12 5ER
☎ (076 87) 73301
*A well-appointed guesthouse
with magnificent views of Lake
Derwentwater and the
surrounding mountains. Close
to the town centre, the parks
and the lake.*
Bedrooms: 1 single, 3 double
& 2 twin, 1 family room.
Bathrooms: 1 public;
7 private showers.
Bed & breakfast: £12.50-
£13.50 single, £25-£27 double.

Half board: £18.50-£19.50
daily, £126.50 weekly.
Evening meal 7pm (l.o. 2pm).
Open March-November.

Jenkin Hill Cottage
Thornthwaite, Keswick,
CA12 5SG
☎ Braithwaite (059 682) 443
*Located in a village at the edge
of a forest, the cottage has very
quiet, lovely gardens. 4 miles
from town.*
Bedrooms: 2 double, 1 family
room.
Bathrooms: 2 public.
Bed & breakfast: £19-£22
double.
Parking for 4.

Littletown Farm
Newlands, Keswick,
CA12 5TU
☎ Braithwaite (059 682) 353
*150-acre farm. In the
beautiful, unspoilt Newlands
Valley. Comfortable residents'
lounge, dining room and cosy
bar. Traditional 4-course
dinner 6 nights a week.*
Bedrooms: 1 single, 4 double
& 2 twin, 2 family rooms.
Bathrooms: 5 private,
2 public.
Bed & breakfast: £15-£18
single, £30-£36 double.
Half board: £20-£23 daily,
£130-£150 weekly.
Evening meal 7pm.
Parking for 10.
Open April-October.

Mrs. M.E. Thompson
Low Grove Farm, Millbeck,
Keswick, CA12 4PS
☎ (076 87) 72103
*140-acre mixed farm.
Comfortable farmhouse
nestling at the foot of Skiddaw,
2 miles north of Keswick and
just off the main A591 road.
Panoramic views.*
Bedrooms: 1 double, 1 family
room.
Bathrooms: 1 public.
Bed & breakfast: £9-£10
single, £18-£20 double.
Parking for 6.

Pitcairn House
7 Blencathra St., Keswick,
CA12 4HW
☎ (076 87) 72453
Continued ▶

KESWICK

Continued

*Family-run establishment in
the town, with access to rooms
and a large comfortable lounge
all day. Choice of breakfast
menus.*
Bedrooms: 3 double & 1 twin,
3 family rooms.
Bathrooms: 2 public.
Bed & breakfast: £8-£9
single, £16-£18 double.
Half board: £51-£58 weekly.
➷3 ⦿ ⛾ 🆄🅻 ꭍ 🆅 ✂ ꙳ 🆃🆅 ▥
🛆 ✕ 🅳🅰🅿 🐾 🆂🅿

Ravensworth Hotel ⋔
😀😀
Station St., Keswick,
CA12 5HH
☎ (076 87) 72476
*A pleasant, family-run licensed
hotel where you can be at your
ease, adjacent to Fitz Park
and the town centre.*
Bedrooms: 1 single, 5 double
& 2 twin, 1 family room.
Bathrooms: 4 private,
1 public.
Bed & breakfast: £12.50-
£18.50 single, £22-£30 double.
Half board: £17.90-£21.90
daily, £110-£139 weekly.
Evening meal 7pm (l.o. 7pm).
Parking for 5.
Credit: Access, Visa, Diners,
Amex.
➷ ⛾ ⦿ 🅸 🆅 ꭍ 🆃🆅 ▥ 🛆 ⚓
✕ 🐾 🆂🅿 🆃

Rickerby Grange ⋔
😀😀😀
Portinscale, Keswick,
CA12 5RH
☎ (076 87) 72344
*Detached country house in its
own gardens, in a quiet village
on the outskirts of Keswick.
Provides imaginative home
cooking, a bar and TV lounge.*
Bedrooms: 2 single, 6 double
& 4 twin, 2 family rooms.
Bathrooms: 11 private,
2 public; 1 private shower.
Bed & breakfast: £33-£39.50
double.
Half board: £25-£28.50 daily,
£106-£226 weekly.
Evening meal 7pm (l.o. 6pm).
Parking for 13.
➷ ⛳ ⦿ 📞 🅸 🆅 ꭍ 🆃🆅 ▥
🛆 ✿ 🐾 🆂🅿

Rooking House ⋔
😀😀
Portinscale, Keswick,
CA12 5RD
☎ (076 87) 72506
*A fine Edwardian house with
superb views of Lake
Derwentwater and hills.
Friendly atmosphere.*
Bedrooms: 2 double & 3 twin.
Bathrooms: 5 private.

Bed & breakfast: from £15
single, from £30 double.
Half board: from £23 daily,
from £145 weekly.
Evening meal 7.30pm (l.o.
6pm).
Parking for 6.
➷ ⦿10 ⬜ ⛾ 🅸 🆅 ꭍ 🆃🆅 ▥
🛆 ✕ 🐾 🆂🅿

Watendlath Guest
House ⋔
Listed
15 Acorn St., Keswick,
CA12 4EA
☎ (076 87) 74165
*Within easy walking distance
of the lake, hills and town
centre. We offer a warm and
friendly welcome and
traditional English breakfast.*
Bedrooms: 2 double & 1 twin.
Bathrooms: 2 public.
Bed & breakfast: £18-£19
double.
Open March-October.
➷ ⛾ ⦿ ꭍ 🆃🆅 ▥ 🛆 ✕ 🐾

Whitehouse Guest
House
😀😀
15 Ambleside Rd., Keswick,
CA12 4DL
☎ (076 87) 73176
*Small friendly guesthouse 5
minutes' walk from the town
centre. Colour TV, electric
blankets.*
Bedrooms: 2 double, 2 family
rooms.
Bathrooms: 1 private,
1 public.
Bed & breakfast: £18-£21
double.
Half board: £119-£140
weekly.
Parking for 3.
Open April-October.
➷3 ⬜ ⛾ 🆄🅻 ꭍ 🆃🆅 ▥ 🛆 ✕
🐾

KIRKBY LONSDALE

Cumbria
Map ref 5B3

Charming old town of
narrow streets and
Georgian buildings. The
Devil's Bridge over the
River Lune is probably
13th C. ℹ

Barnfield Farm
Tunstall, Nr. Kirkby
Lonsdale, Carnforth,
LA6 2QP
☎ (046 834) 284
*200-acre mixed farm. The
farmhouse was built in 1702
and has been in the same
family for 4 generations. It has
an oak staircase with oak
beams.*
Bedrooms: 1 double, 1 family
room.

Bathrooms: 1 public.
Bed & breakfast: £10 single,
£20 double.
➷ ⛳ ⛾ 🆄🅻 🅸 ꭍ 🆃🆅 ▥ 🛆
✕ 🐾 🆂🅿 🅰

The Courtyard
Fairbank, Kirkby Lonsdale,
LA6 2AZ
☎ (052 42) 71613
*Large Georgian town house
furnished with antiques. Large
private garden, extensive views.
Good shopping nearby.*
Bedrooms: 1 single, 1 double
& 2 twin.
Bathrooms: 1 private,
1 public.
Bed & breakfast: £11-£15
single, £25-£30 double.
Parking for 4.
➷ ⦿10 🅸 ⛾ 🆄🅻 ꭍ 🆃🆅 ◉ ▥
🛆 ⋃ ✿ ✕ 🐾 🐕

Hipping Hall ⋔
Cowan Bridge, Kirkby
Lonsdale, LA6 2JJ
☎ (0468) 71187
*17th C. country estate in
picturesque countryside near
Kirkby Lonsdale. Ideal for the
Lakes and Dales.*
Bedrooms: 2 double & 2 twin.
Bathrooms: 4 private.
Bed & breakfast: £32.50
single, £45-£55 double.
Half board: £34.50-£44.50
daily.
Evening meal 8pm (l.o.
8.30pm).
Parking for 13.
Open March-November.
➷12 ⦿ ⬜ 🆅 ꭍ 🆃🆅 ▥
🛆 ⋃ ✿ 🐾 🆂🅿 🐕 🆃

KIRKBY STEPHEN

Cumbria
Map ref 5B3

Old picturesque market
town on the River Eden.
Good centre for exploring
the Eden Valley. ℹ

Croglin Castle Hotel
South Rd., Kirkby Stephen,
CA17 4SY
☎ (0930) 71389
*A family-run inn with 6 letting
rooms, lounge bar, saloon bar
and games room. Excellent
views and friendly atmosphere.*
Bedrooms: 1 single, 2 double
& 2 twin, 1 family room.
Bathrooms: 1 public.
Bed & breakfast: £12 single,
£24 double.
Half board: £18 daily, £126
weekly.
Evening meal 6.30pm (l.o.
9pm).
Parking for 12.
➷4 ⛾ 🅸 🆅 🆃🆅 ♣ ✕ 🐾 🆂🅿

KIRKBY-IN-
FURNESS

Cumbria
Map ref 5A3

The Hill Farm ⋔
Heathwaite, Grizebeck,
Kirkby-in-Furness
☎ (022 989) 706
*A beautiful oak-beamed
farmhouse, fully modernised
set in unspoilt Lake District
valley with magnificent views.
Peaceful. Between Coniston
and Broughton-in-Furness.
Home-baked bread. TV on
request.*
Bedrooms: 1 double & 1 twin,
1 family room.
Bathrooms: 1 private,
1 public.
Bed & breakfast: £24-£36
double.
Parking for 6.
Open March-November.
➷ ⛾ 🆄🅻 🅸 🆅 ꭍ ▥ 🛆 ✿
✕ 🐾

KIRKSANTON

Cumbria
Map ref 5A3

6m SE. Bootle

Croft Cottage ⋔
Listed
Kirksanton, Millom,
LA18 4NW
☎ (0657) 2582
*A converted coach house in a
quiet village 1 mile from the
beach. Within easy reach of
the Lakes and offering
splendid views of the fells.
Home cooking.*
Bedrooms: 1 double & 4 twin,
1 family room.
Bathrooms: 2 public.
Bed & breakfast: from £8
single, from £16 double.
Half board: from £13 daily,
from £85 weekly.
Evening meal 6pm (l.o.
11pm).
Parking for 5.
➷ ⛳ 🆄🅻 ꭍ 🆃🆅 ✕ 🐾

**GROUPS, CONSORTIA
AND AGENCIES
SPECIALISING
IN FARM AND
COUNTRY HOLIDAYS
ARE LISTED IN A
SPECIAL SECTION
OF THIS GUIDE.**

LAKESIDE
Cumbria
Map ref 5A3

10m NE. Ulverston
There is a pier at
Lakeside for the lake
steamer service on
Windermere and steam
trains run from here along
the 3 mile track to
Haverthwaite during the
summer.

Landing Cottage M
😑😑
Lakeside, Nr. Newby Bridge,
Ulverston, LA12 8AS
☎ (053 95) 31719
*19th C. Lakeland stone
cottage, 100 yards from the
shores of Lake Windermere
and close to the steamer boat
terminal and the
Lakeside/Haverthwaite
pleasure steam train.*
Bedrooms: 3 double, 2 family
rooms.
Bathrooms: 2 private,
2 public.
Bed & breakfast: £22-£25
double.
Half board: £17.50-£19 daily,
£110-£120 weekly.
Evening meal 7pm (l.o.
4.30pm).
Parking for 6.
🛇 🕮 🕈 🛆 🗑 📺 🖚 ✕
📮 SP

LANGDALE
Cumbria
Map ref 5A3

The 2 Langdale valleys
(Great Langdale and Little
Langdale) lie in the heart
of beautiful mountain
scenery. The craggy
Langdale Pikes are
almost 2500 ft high. An
ideal walking and
climbing area.

Inglewood
Chapel Stile, Gt. Langdale,
Nr. Ambleside, LA22 9JG
☎ (096 67) 341
*Traditional 18th C. Lakeland
stone cottage. Turn right after
Chapel Stile Post Office.
Inglewood signed on right 50
yards past church.*
Bedrooms: 1 single, 1 double
& 1 twin.
Bathrooms: 1 public.
Bed & breakfast: £11 single,
£22 double.
Half board: £18.50 daily,
£119-£129.50 weekly.
Evening meal 6.30pm (l.o.
8.30pm).
🛇 🕮 🕈 🛆 🖩 V 🖚 📺 🛆
📮 DAP 🛇

Long House M
😑😑
Great Langdale, Nr.
Ambleside, LA22 9JS
☎ (096 67) 222
*17th C. cottage enjoying a
peaceful position near the foot
of the Langdale Pikes. Beamed
ceilings, original slate floors,
stained glass windows.*
Bedrooms: 2 double & 1 twin.
Bathrooms: 3 private.
Bed & breakfast: £15-£16
single, £30-£32 double.
Half board: £22.50-£23.50
daily, £150-£155 weekly.
Evening meal 6.30pm (l.o.
5pm).
Parking for 5.
Open February-November.
🛇 9 🕮 🛆 V 🖚 📺 🛆 ❄
🐾 📮 SP 🖩

LEVENS
Cumbria
Map ref 5B3

Just outside this village is
Levens Hall, an
Elizabethan mansion with
topiary gardens open to
the public.

Birslack Grange M
Levens, LA8 8PA
☎ Sedgwick (053 95) 60989
*Converted stone barn with
panoramic views over the Lyth
Valley. Ideal for touring the
Lake District.*
Bedrooms: 2 single, 1 double
& 4 twin, 2 family rooms.
Bathrooms: 2 private,
3 public.
Bed & breakfast: £12 single,
£22-£26 double.
Half board: £17 daily, £110
weekly.
Evening meal 7pm (l.o. 9pm).
Parking for 8.
🛇 🕮 🕈 🕈 🕮 ⅙ 📺
🖩 🛆 🍴 ⌖ ❄ ✕ 🖩

LORTON
Cumbria
Map ref 5A3

High and Low Lorton are
set in a beautiful vale
north of Crummock
Water. Church of St.
Cuthbert well worth a
visit.

Hope Farm
Listed
Lorton, Cockermouth,
CA13 9UD
☎ (090 085) 226

*168-acre mixed hill farm.
Country-kitchen cooking, log
fires and magnificent views
over the Lorton Valley.*
Bedrooms: 1 single, 1 double
& 1 twin.
Bathrooms: 2 public.
Bed & breakfast: £9.50
single, £19 double.
Half board: £14.50 daily, £99
weekly.
Evening meal 7pm.
Parking for 4.
🛇 🕮 🕈 🕈 🕮 V 🖚 📺 🛆 🖩

LOWESWATER
Cumbria
Map ref 5A3

This village lies between
Loweswater, one of the
smaller lakes of the Lake
District, and Crummock
Water. Several mountains
lie beyond the village.

Mrs. A. Hayton
😑
Brook Farm, Thackthwaite,
Loweswater, Cockermouth,
CA13 0RP
☎ Lorton (090 085) 606
*180-acre hill farm. In quiet
surroundings and a good
walking area, 5 miles from
Cockermouth. Carrying sheep
and suckler cows.*
Bedrooms: 1 double & 1 twin.
Bathrooms: 1 public.
Bed & breakfast: £9-£10
single, £18-£20 double.
Half board: £14-£15 daily,
£94.50-£98 weekly.
Evening meal 7pm.
Parking for 3.
Open May-October.
🛇 🕮 🛆 🖚 📺 🖩

Graythwaite
Listed
Loweswater, Cockermouth,
CA13 0SU
☎ Lamplugh (0946) 861555
*12-acre smallholding. At the
western end of Loweswater. No
smoking in bedrooms.*
Bedrooms: 1 double & 1 twin.
Bathrooms: 1 public.
Bed & breakfast: from £17
double.
Half board: from £12.50
daily, from £82 weekly.
Evening meal 6.30pm.
Parking for 2.
Open March-November.
🛇 🕈 🕮 📺 🖩 🛆 ❄ ✕ 🖩
SP

Kirkstile Inn M
😑😑
Loweswater, Cockermouth,
CA13 0RU
☎ Lorton (090 085) 219
*A 16th C. inn near an oak-
fringed beck running between
Loweswater and Crummock
Water lakes, surrounded by
fells.*
Bedrooms: 5 double & 2 twin,
3 family rooms.
Bathrooms: 8 private,
2 public.
Bed & breakfast: £22-£29
single, £29-£36 double.
Half board: £32-£39 daily,
£224-£273 weekly.
Lunch available.
Evening meal 6.30pm (l.o.
9pm).
Parking for 40.
Credit: Access.
🛇 🕮 V 🖚 📺 🖩 🛆 🕿 🕗
❄ 🖩 🖩

MUNGRISDALE
Cumbria
Map ref 5A2

The simple, white church
in this hamlet has a 3-
decker pulpit and box
pews.

High Beckside Farm M
Listed
Mungrisdale, Penrith,
CA11 0XR
☎ Threlkeld (059 683) 636
*150-acre mixed farm. In an
ideal walking area and within
easy reach of the lakes.*
Bedrooms: 1 double, 1 family
room.
Bathrooms: 1 public.
Bed & breakfast: £18-£20
double.
Half board: £14-£15 daily,
max. £98 weekly.
Evening meal 6.30pm.
Parking for 2.
Open April-October.
🛇 🕈 🕮 📺 🖩 ✕ 🖩

The Mill Inn M
😑😑
Mungrisdale, Penrith,
CA11 0XR
☎ Threlkeld (059 683) 632
*A refurbished and privately-
owned, 16th C. inn in an
unspoilt Lakeland village.
Ideal for touring the Lakes,
coast and Scottish borders.*
Bedrooms: 1 single, 3 double
& 3 twin.
Bathrooms: 3 private,
1 public; 1 private shower.
Bed & breakfast: £13.50-
£14.50 single, £27-£34 double.
Half board: £20.50-£24.50
daily, £136.50-£168 weekly.
Continued ▶

THE SYMBOLS ARE EXPLAINED ON THE FLAP
INSIDE THE BACK COVER.

MUNGRISDALE

Continued

Evening meal 7pm (l.o. 7pm).
Parking for 25.
Open February-December.
🏠 🎱 Ⅴ ⛽ 📺 ▥ ⌚ ∪ ♪
▶ ❀ 🏠 SP 🏠

Near Howe Farm Hotel 🏠
😊😊

Mungrisdale, Troutbeck,
CA11 0SH
☎ (059 683) 678
*350-acre mixed farm.
Farmhouse in quiet
surroundings 1 mile from
Mungrisdale, half a mile from
the A66 and within easy reach
of all the Lakes.*
Bedrooms: 3 double & 1 twin,
3 family rooms.
Bathrooms: 5 private,
1 public.
Bed & breakfast: £9-£11
single, £18-£22 double.
Half board: £14-£17 daily.
Evening meal 7pm (l.o. 5pm).
Parking for 12.
Open April-October.
🏠 ❄ 🎱 Ⅴ ⛽ 📺 ▥ ⌚ ♨
❀ 🏠

Wham-Head Farm
🄻🄸🅂🅃🄴🄳

Hutton Roof, Mungrisdale,
Penrith, CA11 0XS
☎ Skelton (085 34) 289
*130-acre mixed farm. Peaceful
hamlet 30 minutes' car ride
from the Lakes. 1000ft above
sea level with easy access to
Fells (special interest to
geologists). Golf, heated
swimming pool and pony
trekking in the area.*
Bedrooms: 2 double, 2 family
rooms.
Bathrooms: 1 public.
Bed & breakfast: £8-£10
single, £16-£20 double.
Half board: £13-£15 daily,
from £85 weekly.
Evening meal 6pm (l.o. 4pm).
Parking for 10.
Open March-October.
🏠 ❄ ⓤ 🎱 Ⅴ ⛽ 📺 ⌚ ❀
🏠 🏠

THERE IS A SPECIAL
SECTION IN THIS
GUIDE LISTING
ACCOMMODATION
ESPECIALLY
SUITABLE FOR
GROUPS AND
YOUNG PEOPLE.

PENRITH

Cumbria
Map ref 5B2

This ancient and historic
market town is the
northern gateway to the
Lake District. Penrith
Castle was built as a
defence against the
Scots. Its ruins, open to
the public, stand in the
public park. High above
the town is the famous
Penrith Beacon. ⓘ

Brandelhow Guest House

1 Portland Place, Penrith,
CA11 7QN
☎ (0768) 64470
*Family-run guesthouse just off
the A6 and close to the town
centre.*
Bedrooms: 2 double, 4 family
rooms.
Bathrooms: 2 public.
Bed & breakfast: £10-£14
single, £16-£20 double.
Half board: £13-£15 daily.
Evening meal 6.30pm (l.o.
6pm).
Parking for 4.
🏠 ❏ ⓤ 🎱 Ⅴ ⛽ 📺 ▥
⌚ CAP

Bridge End Farm 🏠
😊😊

Hutton, Hutton John,
Penrith, CA11 0LZ
☎ Greystoke (085 33) 273
*14-acre mixed farm.
Modernised 17th C.
farmhouse, with the original
oak beams and door, in its own
quiet grounds with Lakeland
fell views. 5 miles west of M6.*
Bedrooms: 1 single, 2 double
& 1 twin, 1 family room.
Bathrooms: 1 public.
Bed & breakfast: £9.50-
£10.50 single, £19-£21 double.
Half board: £13.50-£14.50
daily, £92-£98 weekly.
Evening meal 6.30pm (l.o.
5pm).
Parking for 6.
Open April-October.
🏠6 ⓤ Ⅴ ⛽ 📺 ▥ ❀ ✕ 🏠
🏠

Fellside 🏠
🄻🄸🅂🅃🄴🄳

Hartsop, Patterdale, Nr.
Penrith, CA11 0NZ
☎ Glenridding (085 32) 532
*A 17th C. Cumbrian
farmhouse at the foot of
Kirkstone Pass, perfect for
fellwalkers; artists also
welcome. Magnificent scenery,
overlooking Brotherswater.*
Bedrooms: 1 single, 1 double
& 1 twin.
Bathrooms: 2 public.

Bed & breakfast: £8-£10
single, £16-£20 double.
Parking for 3.
🏠 ❄ ⓤ 🎱 Ⅴ ⛽ 📺 ▥ ⌚
❀ 🏠 🏠

The Gales

Stainton, Penrith, CA11 0EE
☎ (0768) 64831
*Modern 2-storey detached
dwelling. Attractive village at
crossing of A66 and M6. At
boundary of Lake District.
Meals on request. No smoking
in bedrooms.*
Bedrooms: 3 single, 2 double.
Bathrooms: 2 public.
Bed & breakfast: max. £9.50
single, max. £17 double.
Half board: £80-£90 weekly.
Evening meal 6.30pm (l.o.
2pm).
Parking for 2.
🏠 ⓤ 🎱 Ⅴ ⛽ 📺 ⌚ ✕ 🏠

George Hotel 🏠
😊😊😊😊

Penrith, CA11 7SU
☎ (0768) 62696
*A 300-year-old, famous
coaching inn providing modern
facilities, in the centre of
Penrith. Privately owned and
managed.*
Bedrooms: 12 single,
10 double & 9 twin.
Bathrooms: 30 private,
1 public.
Bed & breakfast: £30-£31.50
single, £40-£42 double.
Half board: £39.55-£40.25
daily.
Lunch available.
Evening meal 7pm (l.o.
8.30pm).
Parking for 30.
Credit: Access, Visa.
🏠 ☎ 🅟 🎱 ⌚ ⛽ ● ▥
🍴 SP

Mosedale House

Mosedale, Nr. Penrith,
CA11 0XQ
☎ Threlkeld (059 683) 371
*A former working farm with
many outbuildings and some
animals, with direct access to
the Fells and the river.*
Bedrooms: 1 single, 2 double
& 1 twin.
Bathrooms: 1 public;
2 private showers.
Bed & breakfast: £11.50-
£13.50 single, £19-£23 double.
Half board: £17.50-£19.50
daily.
Evening meal 6.30pm (l.o.
8pm).
Parking for 8.
🏠 ❄ ⓤ 🎱 Ⅴ ⌚ ❀ 🏠 🏠

Norcroft Guesthouse

Graham St., Penrith,
CA11 9LQ
☎ (0768) 62365

*Spacious Victorian house with
large comfortable rooms. In a
quiet residential area near the
town centre.*
Bedrooms: 1 single, 2 double
& 4 twin, 2 family rooms.
Bathrooms: 9 private.
Bed & breakfast: £11.50-
£13.50 single, £22-£27 double.
Half board: £15.50-£19 daily,
£100-£125 weekly.
Evening meal 7pm (l.o.
8.30pm).
Parking for 10.
🏠 ❄ ❄ ⓤ 🎱 ⛽ 📺 ⌚ ♨
✕ 🏠

The Old Vicarage 🏠

Eden Hall, Penrith,
CA11 8SX
☎ Langwathby (076 881) 329
*Grade II listed, elegant,
Georgian house extended in the
Victorian period. In three
quarters of an acre of land, in
a peaceful village with easy
access to the Pennines and
Lakes.*
Bedrooms: 1 double & 1 twin,
1 family room.
Bathrooms: 1 private,
1 public.
Bed & breakfast: £10-£12
single, £18-£20 double.
Parking for 2.
Open March-December.
🏠 ❄ ❄ ⓤ ⛽ 📺 ▥ ♨ 🏠
🏠

The Old Vicarage

Mungrisdale, Penrith
CA11 0XR
☎ Threlkeld (059 683) 274
*Spacious Victorian house of
extreme charm and character
nestling at the foot of the
northern Fells. Midway
between Keswick and Penrith,
2 miles north of the A66.*
Bedrooms: 1 single, 1 double
& 1 twin, 1 family room.
Bathrooms: 2 public.
Bed & breakfast: £25-£26
double.
Parking for 6.
🏠 ❄ ⓤ 🎱 Ⅴ ▥ ✕ 🏠
🏠

Tymparon Hall

Newbiggin, Stainton, Nr.
Penrith, CA11 0HS
☎ Greystoke (085 33) 236
*200-acre mixed farm.
Excellent base for visiting
Hadrian's Wall and touring the
Lake District and Yorkshire
Dales. Only 3.5 miles from the
M6 exit 40.*
Bedrooms: 1 double & 1 twin,
1 family room.
Bathrooms: 1 private,
2 public.
Bed & breakfast: £10-£11.50
single, £20-£23 double.
Half board: £16-£17 daily,
£110 weekly.

Evening meal 7pm (l.o. 5pm).
Parking for 4.
Open April-October.

🐄 ♨ Ⓤ 🕯 📺 📠 ❀ ✈
🏨 ᴰᴬᴾ

Wreay Farm Guest House ▲
Listed
Watermillock, Nr. Ullswater,
Penrith, Cumbria. CA11 0LT
☎ (085 36) 296
*Comfortable guesthouse in
beautiful area, overlooking
Lake Ullswater.*
Bedrooms: 7 double, 3 family
rooms.
Bathrooms: 3 public.
Bed & breakfast: £10.50-
£11.50 single, £20-£23 double.
Half board: £16.50-£17.50
daily, max. £108.50 weekly.
Evening meal 7.30pm.
Parking for 12.
Open March-November.

🐄 🍳 ♨ 🕯 Ⓥ 🍽 📺 ▥ &
🅿 🏨

RAVENSTONEDALE
Cumbria
Map ref 5B3

Set below Ash Fell, this
village has a fine church
with an unusual interior,
as sections of the
congregation sit facing
each other and there is a
3-decker pulpit.

Sandbed ▲
Ravenstonedale, CA17 4LP
☎ Newbiggin on Lune
(058 73) 262
*20-acre hill stock rearing farm.
16th C. Westmorland
farmhouse, with oak beams,
open fire and other features.
On A683 between Sedbergh
and Kirkby Stephen.*
Bedrooms: 2 double & 1 twin.
Bathrooms: 1 private;
2 private showers.
Bed & breakfast: £12.50
single, £20 double.
Half board: £15-£20 daily,
from £105 weekly.
Lunch available.
Evening meal 6pm (l.o. 9pm).
Parking for 10.

🐄 ♨ Ⓤ 🕯 Ⓥ 🍽 📺 ▥ 📠
🏨 ᴰᴬᴾ

ROADHEAD
Cumbria
Map ref 5B2

Roadhead, in the parish
of Bewcastle, is set in
dramatic open
countryside, with much
evidence of centuries of
Border conflict in its
castles and castellated
farmhouses.

Bank End Farm
⬛⬛⬛
Bewcastle, Roadhead,
Carlisle, CA6 6NU
☎ Roadhead (069 78) 644
*20-acre hill sheep smallholding.
Private suite for 2 with twin
bedroom, bathroom and sitting
room, in 200-year-old
farmhouse overlooking river
and fells. Close to the Scottish
border. 20 minutes from the
M6.*
Bedrooms: 1 twin.
Bathrooms: 1 private.
Bed & breakfast: £25 double.
Half board: £19.50-£21 daily,
£129-£139 weekly.
Evening meal 6pm (l.o. 2pm).
Parking for 10.

🐄 📠 🍳 Ⓤ 🕯 ⚲ 🍽 📺
▥ 📠 Ʊ ♂ ❀ ✈ 🏨 🏨 SP 🏨
Ⓣ

RYDAL
Cumbria
Map ref 5A3

Hamlet at the east end of
Rydal Water, a small,
beautiful lake sheltered
by Rydal Fell. A good
centre for touring and
walking.

Foxghyll ▲
⬛⬛⬛
Under Loughrigg, Rydal,
Ambleside, LA22 9LL
☎ Ambleside (053 94) 33292
*A family house, steeped in
historic interest : poet Thomas
de Quincey lived here. Ideal
for guests who seek privacy.*
Bedrooms: 2 double & 1 twin.
Bathrooms: 2 private,
1 public.
Bed & breakfast: £21-£27
double.
Parking for 7.

🐄 🍳 ⑤ ♨ 🍽 📺 ▥ 📠 ♪
❀ 🏨 🏨

ST BEES
Cumbria
Map ref 5A3

Small coastal resort with
a good beach. The cliffs
at nearby St. Bees Head
are a sanctuary for
nesting sea birds. Home
of a public school which
was founded in the 16th
C.

Kinder How
Listed
Egremont Road, St. Bees,
CA27 0AS
☎ Egremont (0946) 822376
*Modern bungalow with 2
lounges, one with panoramic
view of Irish Sea to Isle of
Man.*
Bedrooms: 2 double & 1 twin.
Bathrooms: 1 public.
Bed & breakfast: max. £10
single, max. £18 double.
Half board: max. £14.50
daily, max. £91.35 weekly.
Evening meal 6.30pm (l.o.
8pm).
Open March-September.

🐄 📠 🍳 ♨ Ⓤ 🕯 Ⓥ 🍽 📺
▥ 📠 Ʊ ♂ ✈ 🏨

SAWREY
Cumbria
Map ref 5A3

Far Sawrey and Near
Sawrey lie near Esthwaite
Water. Both villages are
small but Near Sawrey is
famous for Hill Top Farm,
home of Beatrix Potter,
now owned by the
National Trust and open
to the public.

Ees Wyke Country House ▲
⬛⬛⬛
Nr. Sawrey, Ambleside,
LA22 0JZ
☎ Hawkshead (096 66) 393
*Ees Wyke is a charming
Georgian country house
overlooking the peaceful and
beautiful Esthwaite Water.
Fine views of the lake,
mountains and Fells.*
Bedrooms: 3 double & 2 twin.
Bathrooms: 5 private.
Bed & breakfast: £34 double.
Lunch available.
Evening meal 7pm (l.o.
7.30pm).
Parking for 11.
Open March-December.

🐄 📠 🍳 🕯 Ⓥ 🍽 📺 Ʊ ❀
✈ 🏨 ⬛ SP 🏨

Tower Bank Arms
Nr. Sawrey, Hawkshead,
LA22 0LF
☎ Hawkshead (096 66) 334
*Tower Bank Arms is next door
to Hill Top, the former home of
Beatrix Potter. It features in
the tale of Jemima
Puddleduck.*
Bedrooms: 2 double & 1 twin.
Bathrooms: 3 private.
Bed & breakfast: from £22
single, from £33 double.
Lunch available.
Evening meal 7pm (l.o. 9pm).
Parking for 8.
Credit: Access, Visa.

🐄 📠 ♨ 🕯 ▥ ♪ 🏨 🏨

SEBERGHAM
Cumbria
Map ref 5A2

10m SSW. Carlisle
Large but scattered
village set in what was
once a great royal hunting
forest - Inglewood Forest.
Now all enclosed as
agricultural land, open fell
extends to the south from
nearby Caldbeck.

Bustabeck ▲
Listed
Sebergham, Carlisle,
CA5 7DX
☎ Raughton Head
(069 96) 339
*72-acre mixed dairy farm.
Built in 1684. Peaceful
location, ideal for touring the
Lakes, Solway Firth, Scottish
Borders and the Roman Wall.*
Bedrooms: 2 double & 1 twin.
Bathrooms: 2 public.
Bed & breakfast: from £9.50
single, from £19 double.
Half board: from £13.50
daily.
Evening meal 6pm (l.o.
midday).
Parking for 5.
Open May-September.

🐄 📠 🍳 🕯 ✈ 📺 📠 ❀ 🏨 🏨

**GROUPS, CONSORTIA AND AGENCIES
SPECIALISING IN FARM AND COUNTRY
HOLIDAYS ARE LISTED IN A SPECIAL
SECTION OF THIS GUIDE.**

**PLEASE CHECK
PRICES AND OTHER
DETAILS AT THE
TIME OF BOOKING.**

SEDBERGH

Cumbria
Map ref 5B3

This busy market town set below the Howgill Fells is an excellent centre for walkers. The noted boys' school was founded in 1525. ℹ

Hole House Farm
Garsdale, Sedbergh
LA10 5NX
☎ (053 96) 20398
30-acre dairy and sheep farm. Situated in National Park land enjoying panoramic views of Garsdale and the Howgill Fells.
Bedrooms: 3 double.
Bathrooms: 1 public.
Bed & breakfast: £10-£12.50 single, £20-£25 double.
Half board: £17.50-£20 daily, £100-£120 weekly.
Parking for 4.
🏠 ▣ ⑩ Ⓤ 📺 ▥ ☕ ♨ ✿ ✕
🐾

The Moss
🏠🏠
Garsdale Road, Sedbergh,
LA10 5JL
☎ (053 96) 20940
Originally built as a farmhouse, extended in 1700. In the National Park, 1 mile from Sedbergh on the A684.
Bedrooms: 1 double & 1 twin, 1 family room.
Bathrooms: 1 public.
Bed & breakfast: £11 single, £22 double.
Half board: £17 daily, £100 weekly.
Evening meal 6pm (l.o. 9pm).
Parking for 5.
Open April-October.
Ⓤ Ⓥ ⁙ 📺 ▥ ✿ ✕ ✕ ⊞

Randall Hill ⋒
🏠🏠
Station Rd., Sedbergh,
LA10 5HJ
☎ (053 96) 20633
Spacious country house in 3 acres of grounds. Quiet, with lovely views.
Bedrooms: 1 double & 2 twin.
Bathrooms: 1 public.
Bed & breakfast: £10-£12 single, £20 double.
Parking for 6.
🏠 ⛽ ♨ Ⓤ 🔋 Ⓥ ⁙
✿ ✕ ⊞

**MAP REFERENCES
APPLY TO COLOUR
MAPS NEAR THE
BACK OF THE GUIDE.**

SEDGWICK

Cumbria
Map ref 5B3

Low Sizergh Farm
🏠🏠
Sizergh, Nr. Kendal,
LA8 8AE
☎ Sedgwick (053 95) 60426
270-acre dairy farm. This spacious and oak-beamed 18th C. farmhouse with its 17th C. buildings is adjacent to Sizergh Castle and 10 minutes' drive from the M6 junction 36.
Bedrooms: 1 double & 2 twin.
Bathrooms: 2 public.
Bed & breakfast: £19-£21 double.
Parking for 10.
Open April-October.
🏠 ♨ Ⓤ ⁙ 📺 ▥ ☕ ✕ ⊞

SELSIDE

Cumbria
Map ref 5B3

4m N. Kendal

Selside Hall Farm ⋒
Selside, Kendal, LA8 9LB
☎ (053 983) 228
300-acre mixed farm. A family-run 14th C. farmhouse and working farm, 5 miles north of Kendal on the A6.
Bedrooms: 2 family rooms.
Bathrooms: 1 public.
Bed & breakfast: £8.50-£10 single, £17-£20 double.
Half board: £13.50-£15.50 daily, £94.50-£108.50 weekly.
Evening meal 6pm (l.o. 6.30pm).
Parking for 4.
Open April-October.
🏠 Ⓤ ⁙ 📺 ▥ ✕ ⊞

SHAP

Cumbria
Map ref 5B3

Village lying nearly 1000 ft above sea-level. Shap Abbey, open to the public, is hidden in a valley nearby. Most of the ruins date from the early 13th C, but the tower is 16th C.

Brookfield
Shap, Penrith, CA10 3PZ
☎ (093 16) 397
Only 2 minutes' drive from the M6 junction 39. Offering home cooking, a large dining room, well-appointed bedrooms and a bar.
Bedrooms: 1 single, 4 double, 2 family rooms.
Bathrooms: 1 public.
Bed & breakfast: £11.50-£12.50 single, £21-£23 double.

Half board: £19.50-£21 daily, from £130 weekly.
Evening meal 7.30pm (l.o. 8.15pm).
Parking for 30.
Open February-December.
🏠 ▣ ⅋ Ⓥ ▥ 📺 ▥ ♨ ✕ ✕
⊞

Kings Arms Hotel ⋒
Main St., Shap, Penrith,
CA10 3NU
☎ (093 16) 277
Comfortable friendly accommodation on the fringe of the Lake District. Directly on the coast walk near M6 junction 39.
Bedrooms: 2 double & 2 twin, 2 family rooms.
Bathrooms: 2 public; 2 private showers.
Bed & breakfast: from £15 single, from £26 double.
Lunch available.
Evening meal 7pm (l.o. 10pm).
Parking for 15.
Credit: Access.
🏠 ♨ ⊞ ▢ ♨ Ⓥ ⚓ ♨ ✿
⊞

THIRLMERE

Cumbria
Map ref 5A3

In Wordsworth's day, this area comprised 2 natural lakes which were almost joined. In the later 19th C Thirlmere became a reservoir. Two paths up Helvellyn, the third highest Lakeland peak, start from Wythburn and Thirlspot.

Stybeck Farm ⋒
Listed
Thirlmere, Keswick,
CA12 4TN
☎ Keswick (076 87) 73232
165-acre mixed farm. At the foot of the Helvellyn range of mountains, in the beautiful Thirlmere Valley. Fishing on Lake Thirlmere and deer stalking nearby.
Bedrooms: 2 double & 1 twin.
Bathrooms: 2 public.
Bed & breakfast: £12-£13.50 single, £24-£26 double.
Half board: £36-£38 daily, £126-£128 weekly.
Evening meal 7pm (l.o. 7pm).
Parking for 3.
🏠 ♨ ♨ Ⓤ 🔋 Ⓥ ▥ 📺 ▥ ☕
✕ ⊞

**THE SYMBOLS ARE
EXPLAINED ON THE
FLAP INSIDE THE
BACK COVER.**

THORNTHWAITE

Cumbria
Map ref 5A3

3m NW. Keswick
Small village, west of Keswick, at the southern tip of Bassenthwaite Lake. Forest trails in Thornthwaite Forest.

Beckstones Farm ⋒
🏠🏠
Thornthwaite, Keswick,
CA12 5SQ
☎ Braithwaite (059 682) 510
4-acre smallholding. In a typical Lakeland setting, with extensive views of the mountains and Thornthwaite Forest.
Bedrooms: 2 double & 1 twin, 1 family room.
Bathrooms: 1 private, 1 public.
Bed & breakfast: £10-£12 single, £20-£24 double.
Half board: £15-£17 daily.
Evening meal 6.30pm.
Parking for 8.
🏠 ♨ Ⓤ 🔋 ▥ 📺 ▥ ✿ ✕
⊞

THRELKELD

Cumbria
Map ref 5A3

This village is a centre for climbing the Saddleback range of mountains, which tower high above it.

Scales Farm
Scales, Threlkeld, Nr.
Keswick, CA12 4SY
☎ Threlkeld (059 683) 660
17th C. farmhouse, convenient for Keswick and the M6. Direct access to Blencathra. Friendly, personal service from the proprietors.
Bedrooms: 1 double & 1 twin, 1 family room.
Bathrooms: 3 private.
Bed & breakfast: £22-£26 double.
Parking for 6.
🏠 ♨ ♨ Ⓤ 🔋 Ⓥ ⚓ ⚓
☕ ▸ ✿ ✕ ▧ ⑤⑨

TROUTBECK PENRITH

Cumbria
Map ref 5B2

Netherdene Guest House ⋒
🏠🏠
Troutbeck, Penrith,
CA11 0SJ
☎ Greystoke (085 33) 475

Delightful country house in a peaceful garden, overlooking the Saddleback Range of mountains. Well-appointed rooms, personal attention.
Bedrooms: 2 double, 2 family rooms.
Bathrooms: 2 public.
Bed & breakfast: £9.50-£11 single, £19-£22 double.
Half board: £14.50-£16.50 daily, £98-£112 weekly.
Evening meal 6.30pm.
Parking for 6.
Open March-November.

Troutbeck Hotel M

Troutbeck, Penrith, CA11 0SJ
☎ Greystoke (085 33) 243
Small country inn half-way between Keswick and Penrith. Approximately 6 miles from the M6 and ideal for all Lakeland activities. Petrol, bar meals and morning coffee available.
Bedrooms: 2 double, 3 family rooms.
Bathrooms: 1 public; 5 private showers.
Bed & breakfast: £10-£10.50 single, £20-£21 double.
Parking for 50.

ULLSWATER
Cumbria
Map ref 5A3

This beautiful lake, which is over 7m long, runs from Patterdale to Pooley Bridge. Lofty peaks ranging round the lake make an impressive background. A steamer service operates along the lake between Pooley Bridge and Glenridding in the summer. ℹ️

Highgate Farm M

Penrith, CA11 0SE
☎ Greystoke (085 33) 339
400-acre mixed farm. This stone-built farmhouse dates back to 1730 and is delightfully decorated throughout, with old beams and brasses. Personal attention is assured.
Bedrooms: 1 single, 1 double & 1 twin, 1 family room.
Bathrooms: 2 public.
Bed & breakfast: £11-£12 single, £22-£24 double.

Half board: £17-£18 daily, £100-£105 weekly.
Evening meal 6pm (l.o. 4pm).
Parking for 4.
Open February-November.

Under Mell House M

Thackthwaite, Dacre, Penrith, CA11 0ND
☎ Pooley Bridge (085 36) 397
18th C. farm cottage with modern extension, in 2 acres of land. On minor road, Dacre - Sparket - Thackthwaite.
Bedrooms: 1 double & 1 twin.
Bathrooms: 1 public.
Bed & breakfast: £10 single, £20 double.
Parking for 10.

White Lion Inn M
Listed

Patterdale, Nr. Penrith, CA11 0NW
☎ Glenridding (085 32) 214
Old world country inn on Lake Ullswater near Helvellyn, with a friendly atmosphere. An ideal centre for walking, fishing and sailing. Traditional beer.
Bedrooms: 1 single, 2 double & 2 twin, 1 family room.
Bathrooms: 1 public.
Bed & breakfast: £14-£15 single, £28-£30 double.
Lunch available.
Evening meal 6.30pm (l.o. 10pm).
Parking for 50.

ULPHA
Cumbria
Map ref 5A3

Oakbank Guest House M

Ulpha, Duddon Valley, Broughton-in-Furness, LA20 6DZ
☎ (065 76) 393
Friendly and informal guesthouse in peaceful valley setting, 4 miles from Broughton in Furness.
Bedrooms: 2 double, 2 family rooms.
Bathrooms: 2 public.
Bed & breakfast: £10 single, £20 double.
Evening meal 6pm.
Parking for 8.
Open January-November.

ULVERSTON
Cumbria
Map ref 5A3

Market town lying between green fells and the sea. The lighthouse on The Hoad is a monument to Sir John Barrow, founder of the Royal Geographical Society. ℹ️

Canal Tavern M

Canal Head, Ulverston, LA12 2JZ
☎ (0229) 57093
On main A590 road at the top of the canal. Home-cooked meals or a choice of food from "special" menu.
Bedrooms: 6 twin, 2 family rooms.
Bathrooms: 1 public.
Bed & breakfast: £12 single, £19 double.
Half board: £14.50 daily, from £94.50 weekly.
Lunch available.
Evening meal 7pm (l.o. 9pm).
Parking for 8.

WINDERMERE
Cumbria
Map ref 5A3

This tourist centre was once a tiny hamlet before the introduction of the railway in 1847. The town adjoins Bowness which is on the lakeside. It is an inland water centre for sailing and boating. A scenic way of seeing the lake is to take a trip on a passenger steamer. Windermere Steamboat Museum has a fine collection of old steamboats. ℹ️

Almeria

17 Broad St., Windermere, LA23 2AB
☎ (096 62) 3026
Homely accommodation with a pleasant atmosphere, close to all amenities.
Bedrooms: 1 single, 1 double, 1 family room.
Bathrooms: 1 public.
Bed & breakfast: £9-£10 single, £18-£20 double.
Half board: £14.50-£16 daily, £101-£110 weekly.
Evening meal 6pm (l.o. 7pm).
Open February-October.

Ashleigh M

11 College Rd., Windermere, LA23 1BU
☎ (096 62) 2292
Small, central, family-run guesthouse with panoramic views, offering home cooking. A non-smoking establishment.
Bedrooms: 1 single, 2 double & 2 twin.
Bathrooms: 2 public.
Bed & breakfast: £10-£11 single, £20-£22 double.
Half board: £15-£16.50 daily, £101.50-£112 weekly.
Evening meal 7pm.

Bannerigg Farm

Windermere, LA23 1JL
☎ (096 62) 3362
150-acre mixed farm. Comfortable farmhouse on the A591, 1 mile from Windermere. Separate dining/lounge area. Extensive views. Central position for touring.
Bedrooms: 2 double & 1 twin, 1 family room.
Bathrooms: 1 public.
Bed & breakfast: £20-£21 double.
Parking for 4.
Open April-October.

Beech House M
Listed

11 Woodland Terrace, Windermere, LA23 2AN
☎ (096 62) 6303
Friendly welcome by local couple to clean and tastefully decorated establishment. Hearty breakfast provided. 5 minutes' walk from station and near all amenities.
Bedrooms: 2 double & 1 twin, 1 family room.
Bathrooms: 1 public.
Bed & breakfast: £10-£12 single, £20-£24 double.
Open April-October.

Blenheim Lodge M

Brantfell Rd., Bowness-on-Windermere, LA23 3AE
☎ (096 62) 3440
Beautiful Lakeland guesthouse with lake and mountain views. Near lake and shops. Quiet and peaceful, friendly atmosphere, home-cooking.
Bedrooms: 3 single, 2 double & 2 twin, 3 family rooms.
Bathrooms: 6 private, 2 public.

Continued ▶

WE ADVISE YOU TO CONFIRM YOUR BOOKING IN WRITING.

WINDERMERE
Continued

Bed & breakfast: £11-£12 single, £22-£32 double.
Half board: £18.50-£23.50 daily, £70-£155 weekly.
Evening meal 7pm (l.o. 4pm).
Parking for 12.

Broadlands Guest House M
19 Broad St., Windermere, LA23 2AB
☎ (096 62) 6532
Centrally situated offering comfortable accommodation, convenient for all facilities. An ideal base for viewing the Lake District.
Bedrooms: 1 single, 5 double & 1 twin, 1 family room.
Bathrooms: 2 public.
Bed & breakfast: £8.50-£11 single, £17-£22 double.
Half board: £12.50-£16 daily.
Evening meal 6.30pm (l.o. 4pm).

Clifton Guest House M
28 Ellerthwaite Rd., Windermere, LA23 2AH
☎ (096 62) 4968
A small friendly guesthouse in a very quiet part of the village, about 4 minutes' walk from the shops and restaurants.
Bedrooms: 2 single, 3 double, 1 family room.
Bathrooms: 1 private, 1 public; 3 private showers.
Bed & breakfast: £9-£14 single, £18-£25 double.
Parking for 4.

The Common Farm
Windermere, LA23 1JQ
☎ (096 62) 3433
160-acre dairy farm. Picturesque and homely 17th C. farmhouse in peaceful surroundings less than a mile from Windermere village.
Bedrooms: 2 double, 1 family room.
Bathrooms: 1 public.
Bed & breakfast: £18-£22 double.
Parking for 4.

Dalegarth Private Hotel M
Lake Rd., Windermere, LA23 2EQ
☎ (096 62) 5052/6702

Family-run hotel built in traditional Lakeland manner. Overlooking Claife Heights, and midway between Bowness and Windermere. Private car park.
Bedrooms: 1 single, 10 double & 1 twin, 1 family room.
Bathrooms: 13 private.
Bed & breakfast: £14.50-£27.50 single, £25-£55 double.
Half board: £23.50-£45 daily, £164-£300 weekly.
Evening meal 7pm (l.o. 8.30pm).
Parking for 14.
Credit: Access, Visa.

Fairfield Country House Hotel M
Brantfell Rd., Bowness-on-Windermere, LA23 3AE
☎ (096 62) 6565 & 6566
A small friendly 200-year-old country house with a half acre of peaceful, secluded gardens. 2 minutes' walk from Lake Windermere and village. Clay pigeon shooting available.
Bedrooms: 1 single, 3 double & 1 twin, 3 family rooms.
Bathrooms: 8 private, 1 public.
Bed & breakfast: £23.50-£33 single, £43-£51 double.
Half board: £34-£38 daily, £215-£225 weekly.
Lunch available.
Evening meal 7pm (l.o. 9.30pm).
Parking for 14.
Credit: Access, Visa, Diners, Amex.

Glenburn M
New Rd., Windermere, LA23 2EE
☎ (096 62) 2649
A well-appointed house offering comfort, cleanliness and service. Located between Windermere and the lake.
Bedrooms: 3 single, 6 double & 1 twin, 4 family rooms.
Bathrooms: 12 private, 1 public.
Bed & breakfast: £13-£17 single, £26-£38 double.
Half board: £22-£28 daily, £135-£175 weekly.
Evening meal 6.30pm (l.o. 4pm).
Parking for 15.
Credit: Access, Visa.

Green Gables Guest House M
37 Broad St., Windermere, LA23 2AB
☎ (096 62) 3886
Family-run guesthouse providing home cooking. Excellent holiday touring base.
Bedrooms: 3 double & 1 twin, 2 family rooms.
Bathrooms: 2 public.
Bed & breakfast: £12-£13 single, £20-£21 double.
Half board: £16-£19 daily, £108.50-£115 weekly.
Evening meal 6pm (l.o. 4pm).

Holly Lodge M
6 College Rd., Windermere, LA23 1BX
☎ (096 62) 3873
Traditional Lakeland stone guesthouse, built in 1854. In a quiet area off the main road, close to the village centre, buses, railway station and all amenities.
Bedrooms: 4 double & 4 twin, 2 family rooms.
Bathrooms: 3 public.
Bed & breakfast: £9-£11 single, £18-£22 double.
Half board: £15-£17 daily, £101.50-£115.50 weekly.
Parking for 6.

Holly Park House M
1 Park Rd., Windermere, LA23 2AW
☎ (096 62) 2107
Handsome stone-built Victorian guesthouse with spacious rooms. Quiet area, convenient for village shops and coach/rail services.
Bedrooms: 5 double & 1 twin.
Bathrooms: 6 private.
Bed & breakfast: £23-£30 double.
Evening meal 7pm (l.o. 9.30am).
Open March-October.

Langdale View Guest House M
114 Craig Walk, Off Helm Rd., Bowness-on-Windermere, LA23 3AX
☎ (096 62) 4076

PLEASE MENTION THIS GUIDE WHEN MAKING A BOOKING.

Traditional, family-run Lakeland guesthouse with home cooking, and lake and mountain views. Within 5 minutes of Lake Windermere. We collect you from the station.
Bedrooms: 1 single, 2 double & 1 twin, 1 family room.
Bathrooms: 2 private, 2 public.
Bed & breakfast: £12-£13 single, £21-£27 double.
Half board: £17.25-£20.25 daily, £116-£130 weekly.
Evening meal 6pm (l.o. 4pm).
Parking for 8.

Osborne Guest House
3 High St., Windermere, LA23 1AF
☎ (096 62) 6452
Stone-built end-terraced house, close to rail station, offering comfortable, clean accommodation and full English breakfast. Close to all activities.
Bedrooms: 3 double.
Bed & breakfast: £9-£12.50 single, £18-£25 double.

Park Beck Guest House M
3 Park Rd., Windermere, LA23 2AW
☎ (096 62) 4025
Ideally situated Lakeland stone guesthouse, close to all facilities. En suite rooms with colour TV.
Bedrooms: 1 single, 3 double, 1 family room.
Bathrooms: 5 private.
Bed & breakfast: £13-£15 single, £24-£28 double.
Half board: £19.50-£21.50 daily, £133-£147 weekly.
Lunch available.
Open February-December.

Rocklands M
Queen's Drive, Windermere, LA23 2EL
☎ (096 62) 3039
A delightful, detached Victorian residence in its own grounds midway between Windermere and Bowness. For a small charge guests have use of facilities at nearby Parklands Country Club - indoor pool, spa, steam room, sauna, solarium, squash, badminton, snooker, indoor bowls, climbing wall.
Bedrooms: 2 double & 1 twin.
Bathrooms: 1 public.

Bed & breakfast: £11-£14 single, £22-£28 double.
Parking for 4.
Open March-November.

🛏 🖵 📺 ⓤ 🛉 Ⓥ 🍴 🎞 ⌂
♪ ✕ 🎯 DAP SP T

Sunny-Bec M
😊

Thornbarrow Rd.,
Windermere, LA23 2EN
☎ (096 62) 2103
*Spacious, detached Lakeland
guesthouse, a short walk from
the lake and shops. Quiet, with
a friendly atmosphere.*
Bedrooms: 1 single, 1 double
& 1 twin, 1 family room.
Bathrooms: 1 public.
Bed & breakfast: £10.50-£12
single, £20-£23 double.
Half board: £17-£18 daily,
£118-£125 weekly.
Evening meal 6pm.
Parking for 5.
Open March-October.

🛏5 📺 ⓤ 🛉 Ⓥ 🍴 📺 🎞 ⌂
❄ ✕ 🎯 SP

Westlake M
😊😊😊

Lake Rd., Windermere,
LA23 2EQ
☎ (096 62) 3020
*Family-run, private hotel
between Windermere and
Bowness. Colour TV in all
rooms. Brochure on request.*
Bedrooms: 4 double & 1 twin,
2 family rooms.
Bathrooms: 7 private.
Bed & breakfast: £12.50-£18
single, £25-£36 double.
Half board: £20.50-£26 daily,
£133-£167 weekly.
Evening meal 7pm (l.o. 5pm).
Parking for 7.

🛏4 🏃 🎯 🖵 📺 🛉 Ⓥ 🍴 🎞
⌂ ✕ 🎯 DAP 🔌 SP

A deep-water port on the
Solway Firth. There are
the ruins of the 14th C
Workington Hall, where
Mary Queen of Scots
stayed in 1568.

Boston Guesthouse

1, St. Michael's Rd.,
Workington, CA14 5EZ
☎ (0900) 3435
*Built 1890. The bricks were
shipped from Boston,
Massachusetts; plenty of
character, especially for visitors
from the USA.*
Bedrooms: 2 twin, 2 family
rooms.
Bathrooms: 1 private,
2 public.
Bed & breakfast: £13-£14
single, £17-£18 double.
Half board: £16-£17 daily,
£112-£119 weekly.
Evening meal 4.45pm (l.o.
6.30pm).
Parking for 3.

🛏2 🏃 🍽 🖵 📺 ⓤ 🛉 🔪 🍴
📺 🎞 ⌂ 🎯 DAP 🔌 SP 📻

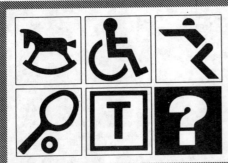

KEY TO SYMBOLS
Open out the flap inside the
back cover of this guide and
the key to symbols will be
easy to use.

When enquiring about accommodation you
may find it helpful to use the booking
enquiry coupons which can be found
towards the end of the guide. These should
be cut out and mailed direct to the establishments in
which you are interested. Remember to include your
name and address and please enclose a stamped
addressed envelope (or an international reply coupon if
writing from outside Britain).

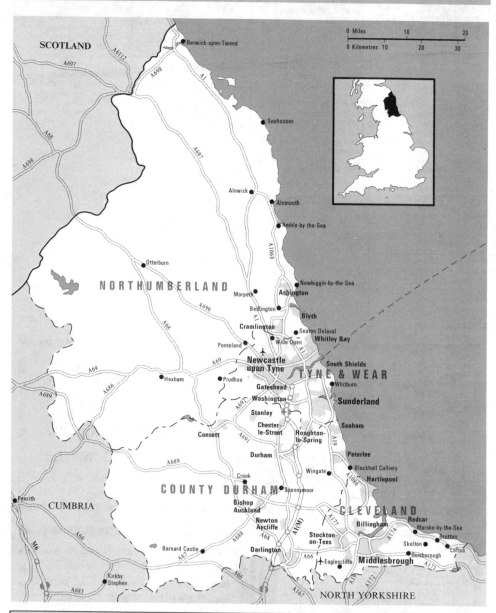

SCOTLAND

0 Miles 10 20
0 Kilometres 10 20 30

Berwick-upon-Tweed

Seahouses

Alnwick
Alnmouth

Amble-by-the-Sea

Otterburn

NORTHUMBERLAND

Newbiggin-by-the-Sea
Morpeth
Ashington
Bedlington
Blyth
Cramlington
Seaton Delaval
Ponteland
Wide Open
Whitley Bay

Newcastle
upon Tyne
South Shields
Hexham
Prudhoe
TYNE & WEAR
Gateshead
Whitburn
Washington
Sunderland
Stanley
Chester-
le-Street
Seaham
Consett
Houghton-
le-Spring
Durham
Peterlee
Crook
Wingate
Blackhall Colliery
Hartlepool
Spennymoor

COUNTY DURHAM

Penrith

CUMBRIA

Bishop
Auckland
CLEVELAND
Newton
Aycliffe
Redcar
Billingham
Marske-by-the-Sea
Barnard Castle
Stockton-
on-Tees
Brotton
Skelton
Darlington
Guisborough
Loftus
Eaglescliffe
Middlesbrough
Kirkby
Stephen

NORTH YORKSHIRE

FIND OUT MORE

Further information about holidays
and attractions in the Northumbria
tourist region is available from:

Northumbria Tourist Board,
Aykley Heads, Durham DH1 5UX.
☎ 091-384 6905.

The 1989 Northumbria Holiday Guide
is available free of charge from the
Northumbria Tourist Board.

Northumbria

The four contrasting counties of Cleveland, Durham, Northumberland and Tyne & Wear comprise the Northumbria tourist region — and between them they can offer the visitor a holiday to remember.

England's most northerly region — between Yorkshire and the Scottish borders — Northumbria is one of those rare holiday destinations: unspoilt and always beautiful.

There's a wonderful variety of scenery in this historic kingdom which has changed little over the years.

Britain on View

BERWICK-UPON-TWEED

Take the hill country areas of the Northumberland National Park and the High Pennines, the fine coastline of Northumberland, Cleveland's coast with its high cliffs; add sparkling rivers, tumbling waterfalls and seemingly endless stretches of golden, sandy beaches; then mix in quiet fishing villages and historic market towns. Now you begin to get the picture of Northumbria.

The region's ties with the past are everywhere to be seen. There are castles, such as Alnwick, Bamburgh and Raby, and the fortifications of Hadrian's Wall. There's the Christian heritage enshrined in abbeys and cathedrals — notably those in Durham and Hexham — and, of course, on Holy Island itself. And there's the industrial heritage, well illustrated in railway and mining centres and in the 'living' museums such as the renowned Beamish Open Air Museum.

WHERE TO GO, WHAT TO SEE

Captain Cook Museum
Stewart Park, Marton, Middlesbrough, Cleveland TS7 8AS ☎ (0642) 311211
Early life and voyages of Captain Cook.
Admission charge.

Preston Hall Museum
Yarm Road, Stockton-on-Tees, Cleveland TS18 8RH ☎ (0642) 781184
Social history museum with period

BEAMISH OPEN AIR MUSEUM

street and rooms, working craftsmen, arms, armour and transport.
Admission charge.

Beamish Open Air Museum
Beamish, Nr. Chester-le-Street, Co. Durham DH9 0RG
☎ (0207) 231811
A living museum vividly showing Northern life around the turn of the ▶

METROCENTRE SHOPPING AND LEISURE COMPLEX

Paul Anscomb

MetroCentre
Gateshead, Tyne & Wear
☎ 091-493 2040
Largest shopping and leisure complex in Western Europe. Free parking for 7,000 cars. Glass-roofed malls with superb decor, arts & crafts and antique centres, most major retailers. Extensive catering facilities.
Admission free.

MAKE A DATE FOR...

▶ century. Five completely reconstructed main areas — 1920s town street; colliery and 'drift' mine; railway station; working farm; transport collection. 'Museum of the Year' 1986.
Admission charge.

Durham Cathedral
Durham, Co. Durham ☎ 091-386 2367
Durham Cathedral and precincts are probably the finest example of a Norman church in England. Tombs of St. Cuthbert and the Venerable Bede.
Admission free.

Raby Castle
Staindrop, Co. Durham DL2 3AH
☎ (0833) 60202
Medieval castle in 200-acre park. 600-year-old kitchen, carriage collection, walled gardens.
Admission charge.

Bowes Museum
Barnard Castle, Co. Durham DL12 8NP
☎ (0833) 690606
Fine and decorative art collections of 15th and 19th C. Paintings, furniture, ceramics and textiles from Britain and Western Europe.
Admission charge.

Alnwick Castle
Alnwick, Northumberland NE66 1NQ
☎ (0665) 602207
Home of the Duke and Duchess of Northumberland. Magnificent border fortress dating back to the 11th C. Main restoration done by Salvin in 19th C.
Admission charge.

Housesteads Roman Fort
Bardon Mill, Northumberland
☎ (049 84) 363
5-acre fort, taking in part of Roman Wall. Best preserved of the Roman forts.   *Admission charge.*

Vindolanda Trust
Bardon Mill, Northumberland NE47 7JN
☎ (049 84) 277
Visitors may wander through the excavations to the superb museum set in ornamental gardens.
Admission charge.

Cragside House and Country Park
Cragside, Rothbury, Morpeth, Northumberland NE65 7PX
☎ (0669) 20333
House built 1879 – 95 for first Lord Armstrong, Tyneside industrialist.
Admission charge.

Morpeth Chantry Bagpipe Museum
The Chantry, Bridge Street, Morpeth, Northumberland NE61 1PJ
☎ (0670) 519466
One of the most extensive collections of its kind in the world. Northumbrian small pipes, Scottish and Irish pipes, Border half-longs and many foreign bagpipes. Unique infra-red sound system.   *Admission charge.*

Lindisfarne Castle
Holy Island, Northumberland
☎ (0289) 89244
Built about 1550. Sir Edwin Lutyens' inspired restoration (1903) provided a comfortable home totally in character.
Admission charge.

Northumbrian Gathering
Various venues, Morpeth, Northumberland *31 March – 2 April*

Riding the Bands
Berwick-upon-Tweed, Northumberland *1 May*

The Hoppings
Town Moor, Newcastle upon Tyne, Tyne & Wear *16 – 24 June*

Wallington Festival
Wallington Hall, Cambo, Northumberland *24 June – 2 July*

Cookson Country Mardi Gras
Various venues, South Shields, Tyne & Wear *24 June – 28 August*

Alnwick Fair
Various venues, Alnwick, Northumberland *25 June – 2 July*

Europa Cup Athletics Festival
Gateshead Stadium, Gateshead, Tyne & Wear *5 – 6 August*

Saltburn Victorian Festival
Various venues, Saltburn, Cleveland *6 – 13 August*

Sunderland Illuminations
Roker and Seaburn, Sunderland, Tyne & Wear *25 August – 5 November* *

Allendale Baal Fire
Market Place, Allendale, Northumberland *31 December*

* Provisional dates only

Tourist Information

Tourist and leisure information can be obtained from Tourist Information Centres throughout England. Details of centres in the Northumbria region are listed below. The symbol 🏠 means that an accommodation booking service is provided. Centres marked with a ✳ are open during the summer months only. In the following pages, towns which have a Tourist Information Centre are indicated with the symbol *i*.

Alnwick
Northumberland 🏠
The Shambles
☎ (0665) 603129

Amble
Northumberland 🏠 ✳
Council Sub Offices,
Dilston Terrace
☎ Alnwick (0665) 712313

Barnard Castle
Co. Durham 🏠
43 Galgate
☎ Teesdale (0833) 690000/
690909 (Sat-Sun)

Belford
Northumberland 🏠
2 & 3 Market Place
☎ (066 83) 888

Bellingham
Northumberland 🏠 ✳
Main Street
☎ (0660) 20616

Berwick-upon-Tweed
Northumberland 🏠
Castlegate Car Park
☎ (0289) 307187

Corbridge
Northumberland 🏠 ✳
The Vicar's Pele, Market Place
☎ (043 471) 2815

Darlington
Co. Durham 🏠
Darlington District Library,
Crown Street
☎ (0325) 469858

Durham City
Co. Durham 🏠
Market Place
☎ 091-384 3720

Gateshead
Tyne & Wear 🏠
Central Library,
Prince Consort Road
☎ 091-477 3478

Guisborough
Cleveland 🏠
Fountain Street
☎ (0287) 33801

Haltwhistle
Northumberland 🏠 ✳
Tynedale District Sub Office,
Sycamore Street
☎ (0498) 20351

Hartlepool
Cleveland 🏠
Leisure and Amenities
Department, Civic Centre,
Victoria Road
☎ (0429) 266522

Hexham
Northumberland 🏠
Manor Office, Hallgates
☎ (0434) 605225

Jarrow
Tyne & Wear 🏠
Jarrow Hall, Church Bank
☎ 091-489 2106

Kielder
Northumberland 🏠
Tower Knowe, Falstone,
Hexham
☎ Bellingham (0660) 40398

Middlesbrough
Cleveland 🏠
125 Albert Road
☎ (0642) 245432 ext. 3580
or (0642) 243425

Morpeth
Northumberland 🏠
The Chantry, Bridge Street
☎ (0670) 511323

Newcastle upon Tyne
Tyne & Wear
City Information Service, Central
Library, Princess Square 🏠
☎ 091-261 0691

Blackfriars Tourist Centre,
Monk Street 🏠
☎ 091-261 5367

Newcastle Airport, Woolsington 🏠
☎ 091-271 1929

North Shields
Tyne & Wear 🏠 ✳
Tyne Commission Quay,
North Shields Ferry Terminal
☎ 091-257 9800

▶

Peterlee
Co. Durham 🛏
20 The Upper Chare
☎ 091-586 4450

Redcar
Cleveland 🛏 ✴
Regent Cinema Building,
Newcomen Terrace
☎ (0642) 471921

Saltburn
Cleveland 🛏
4 Station Buildings,
Station Square
☎ (0287) 22422

Seahouses
Northumberland 🛏 ✴
16 Main Street
☎ (0665) 720424

Shotley Bridge
Co. Durham 🛏
10 Front Street
☎ Consett (0207) 590370

SEAHOUSES, NORTHUMBERLAND

Britain on View

South Shields
Tyne & Wear
South Foreshore 🛏 ✴
☎ 091-455 7411

South Shields Museum,
Ocean Road 🛏
☎ 091-454 6612

Sunderland
Tyne & Wear 🛏
Crowtree Leisure Centre,
Crowtree Road
☎ (0783) 650960/650990

Whitley Bay
Tyne & Wear 🛏 ✴
The Promenade
☎ 091-252 4494

Wooler
Northumberland 🛏 ✴
High Street Car Park
☎ (0668) 81602

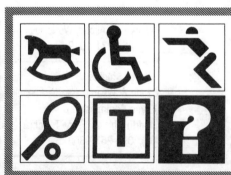

KEY TO SYMBOLS
Open out the flap inside the
back cover of this guide and
the key to symbols will be
easy to use.

Entries in this regional section are listed in alphabetical order of place name, and then in alphabetical order of establishment. County names are not repeated in each establishment entry, but please use the full postal address when writing.

The map references refer to the colour maps towards the end of this guide. The first number is the number of the map, and it is followed by the grid reference.

The Crown Classifications are explained on pages 8 and 9, and the key to symbols is on the flap inside the back cover — keep it open for easy reference.

ACOMB
Northumberland
Map ref 5B2

See also Hexham.
Village on Fallowfield Fell midway between Hexham and Wall, formerly a mining village but now residential. Some attractive 18th C houses surround the village square, and the church of St. John Lee is of great interest.

Acomb House
wwww
Acomb, Hexham, NE46 4PH
☎ (0434) 602596
Village manor with large garden. Drive entrance halfway up hill above turn by southern 30 limit on main road (A6079).
Bedrooms: 1 family room.
Bathrooms: 1 private.
Bed & breakfast: £12.50-£15 single, £25-£30 double.
Half board: £17.50-£21.50 daily, £105-£129.50 weekly.
Credit: Visa.
❧ ⓑ ☐ ♥ Ⓤ ⓒⒷ Ⓥ ⊨ ▱
⚜ ♨ ✿ 🐾 🎠

ALLENDALE
Northumberland
Map ref 5B2

Attractive small town set amongst moors 10 miles south west of Hexham and claimed to be the geographical centre of Britain. Surrounded by unspoilt walking country, with many well-signposted walks along the East and West Allen Rivers. On New Year's Eve the Allendale Fire is a spectacular traditional event.

The Old Hostel
1 Allen View, Catton, Nr. Allendale, NE47 9QQ
☎ (043 483) 780
3-storey house with lovely views from all rooms. First house on left coming out of Catton, towards Allendale. Run by 2 ex-youth hostelers June and Eric Dobbing.
Bedrooms: 2 single, 2 double, 1 family room.
Bathrooms: 2 public.
Bed & breakfast: £8-£11 single, £16-£20 double.
Half board: £12.50-£14.50 daily.
Parking for 4.
❧5 ☒ ☐ ♥ Ⓤ 📞 ▥ ▱ ✆ ✿
🐾 ⒹⒶⓅ 🔌 🆂🅿 🎠

THERE IS A SPECIAL SECTION IN THIS GUIDE LISTING ACCOMMODATION ESPECIALLY SUITABLE FOR GROUPS AND YOUNG PEOPLE.

GROUPS, CONSORTIA AND AGENCIES SPECIALISING IN FARM AND COUNTRY HOLIDAYS ARE LISTED IN A SPECIAL SECTION OF THIS GUIDE.

ALNMOUTH
Northumberland
Map ref 5C1

4m SE. Alnwick
Quiet village with pleasant old buildings at the mouth of the River Aln where extensive dunes and sands stretch along Alnmouth Bay. Old 18th C granaries, some converted to dwellings, still stand.

Blue Dolphins ♏
wwww
Riverside Road, Alnmouth, Alnwick, NE66 2RS
☎ (0665) 830893
Edwardian house with views over the mouth of the River Aln and sea. Opposite sandy beach.
Bedrooms: 4 double & 1 twin.
Bathrooms: 5 private.
Bed & breakfast: £15-£18 single, £25.95-£27 double.
Half board: £85-£95 weekly.
Parking for 5.
❧ ♨ ☐ ♥ Ⓤ Ⓥ ⊨ ▱
✿ 🎠 🆂🅿

The Grange
wwww
Northumberland St., Alnmouth, Alnwick, NE66 2RJ
☎ (0665) 830401
Located in the heart of this unspoilt village. 200-year-old former granary in secluded gardens, with views over the River Aln.
Bedrooms: 1 single, 3 double & 1 twin.
Bathrooms: 2 private, 1 public.
Bed & breakfast: £12.50-£13.50 single, £25-£32 double.
Parking for 8.
☐ ☐ ♥ Ⓤ Ⓥ ⊨ ▱ ✆ ✿
✕ 🎠 🎠

Mrs Janice Edwards, Westlea Guest House ♏
wwww
29 Riverside Rd., Alnmouth, Alnwick, NE66 2SD
☎ (0665) 830730
Newly-built, superior accommodation with panoramic views of the Aln Estuary. Home cooking. 1 minute from the beach. Warm and welcoming atmosphere.
Bedrooms: 1 single, 2 double & 2 twin, 1 family room.
Bathrooms: 3 private, 2 public.
Bed & breakfast: £11-£13 single, £22-£26 double.

Half board: £17.50-£19.50 daily, £122.50-£136.50 weekly.
Evening meal 7pm (l.o. 6pm).
Parking for 8.
❧2 ♨ ☐ ♥ Ⓤ 📞 ▤ ⊨ Ⓣⓥ ▥
▱ ✆ Ⓣ ⚓ 🎠 🆂🅿

ALNWICK
Northumberland
Map ref 5C1

17m N. Morpeth
Ancient and historic market town, entered from the south through the Hotspur Tower, an original gate in the town walls. Dominated by the medieval castle, the seat of the Dukes of Northumberland, which was restored from ruin in the 18th C. It stands in 7 acres of grounds landscaped by Capability Brown. The castle's Italianate interiors contrast with its powerful exterior. Fishing enthusiasts will enjoy the House of Hardy Museum. ℹ

Norfolk ♏
wwww
41 Blakelaw Rd., Alnwick, NE66 1BA
☎ (0665) 602892
Private detached house in quiet area. Tastefully furnished. Comfort and cleanliness assured. Home cooking using own garden produce.
Bedrooms: 1 double & 1 twin.
Bathrooms: 1 public.
Bed & breakfast: max. £10.50 single, max. £21 double.
Half board: max. £16.50 daily, max. £112 weekly.
Evening meal 6.30pm (l.o. 6.30pm).
Parking for 2.
Open April-October.
❧ ♥ Ⓤ ⊨ Ⓣⓥ ▥ ⚓ ✕ 🎠
ⒹⒶⓅ 🆂🅿 Ⓣ

Queens Head Hotel ♏
wwww
Market St., Alnwick, NE66 1SS
☎ (0665) 602442
An old coaching inn in the centre of historic Alnwick near the market place. Ideal for touring Northumberland and Scottish borders.
Bedrooms: 2 single, 1 double & 1 twin, 1 family room.
Bathrooms: 1 public.
Bed & breakfast: £10.50-£12 single, £21-£24 double.
Lunch available.
Evening meal 7pm (l.o. 9pm).
Parking for 20.
❧ ☐ ♥ 📞 Ⓥ ▥ ⚓ ✆ 🐾 🎠

AMBLE-BY-THE-SEA

Northumberland
Map ref 5C1

Small fishing town at the mouth of the River Coquet with fine quiet sandy beaches to north and south. The harbour and estuary are popular for sailing and bird-watching. Coquet Island lies 1 mile offshore. A new marina opened in 1987. *i*

The Granary Hotel M
Links Road, Amble, Morpeth, NE65 0SD
☎ (0665) 710872
Converted from the Links Farm Old Granary buildings to provide accommodation overlooking the sea.
Bedrooms: 2 single, 2 double & 8 twin, 1 family room.
Bathrooms: 13 private.
Bed & breakfast: £16.75-£20.75 single, £32.75-£54.95 double.
Half board: £21.75-£25.75 daily.
Lunch available.
Evening meal 7pm (l.o. 10pm).
Parking for 200.
Credit: Access, Visa.
🏃 ♨ 🕭 ✆ 🖵 🖕 🔲
📺 🛋 🍴 ⚲ 🅿 🐾 SP
T

BAMBURGH

Northumberland
Map ref 5C1

Greystone village with a spectacular red sandstone castle standing 150 ft above the sea. On the village green the magnificent Norman church stands opposite a museum containing mementoes of the heroine Grace Darling.

Greenhill Farm Guest House M
😀😀
Bamburgh, NE69 7AU
☎ (066 84) 265
300-acre mixed farm. An 18th C. farm guesthouse, 300 yards from the beach, with fine views of the Farne Islands and Cheviot Hills.
Bedrooms: 1 double, 4 family rooms.
Bathrooms: 2 public.
Bed & breakfast: £10-£13 single, £20-£26 double.
Half board: £18-£20 daily, £125-£135 weekly.

Evening meal 6.30pm (l.o. midday).
Parking for 5.
Open April-October.
🏃 🕭 Ⓥ 🖕 📺 🔲 ⚛ 🍴

BARNARD CASTLE

Co. Durham
Map ref 5B3

See also Boldron.
High over the Tees, a thriving market town with a busy market square. Bernard Baliol's 12th C castle (now ruins) stands nearby. The Bowes Museum, housed in a grand 19th C French chateau, holds fine paintings and furniture. Nearby are the magnificent Raby Castle, Boose Castle, Rokeby Hall and Egglestone Abbey. *i*

Bowfield Farm
Scargill, Barnard Castle, DL12 9SU
☎ Teesdale (0833) 38636
127-acre mixed farm. A 17th C. stone-built farmhouse overlooking Stang Ridge Forest, 4 miles from Barnard Castle off the A66. We also have a comfortable caravan for holiday letting.
Bedrooms: 1 single, 1 double & 1 twin.
Bathrooms: 1 public.
Bed & breakfast: £7-£8 single, £14-£16 double.
Evening meal 6pm (l.o. 4pm).
Parking for 4.
🏃 🐾 UL 🕭 📺 🛋 ⚛ 🍴
🍴 🛖

Commercial Hotel
Galgate, Barnard Castle, DL12 8BG
☎ Teesdale (0833) 37942
Situated in a market town close to the Yorkshire Dales and many places of historic interest.
Bedrooms: 1 single, 2 double & 1 twin, 1 family room.
Bathrooms: 1 public.
Bed & breakfast: £9.50-£10 single, £19-£20 double.
Lunch available.
🏃 M 🖵 ⚲ 🕭 🖕 📺 🛋 🍴
🅿

George & Dragon Inn
Boldron, Barnard Castle, DL12 9RF
☎ Teesdale (0833) 38215
Attractive inn in beautiful Teesdale, offering comfortable accommodation and friendly hospitality.
Bedrooms: 1 double & 1 twin.
Bathrooms: 1 public.

Bed & breakfast: £9-£9.50 single, £18-£19 double.
Half board: £13-£13.50 daily, £90-£93 weekly.
Lunch available.
Evening meal 7pm (l.o. 5.30pm).
Parking for 20.
🏃 🖵 ♨ 🕭 🖕 📺 🔲 🍴

BEADNELL

Northumberland
Map ref 5C1

Charming fishing village on Beadnell Bay. Seashore lime kilns (National Trust), dating from the 18th C, recall busier days as a coal and lime port and a pub is built on to a medieval pele tower which survives from days of the border wars.

South Swinhoe Farm M
Listed
Beadnell, Chathill, NE67 5AA
☎ (066 589) 226
250-acre mixed farm. A south facing house near sea, within easy reach of many castles, golf courses, Holy Island and the Farnes. Mainline train to Newcastle and Edinburgh.
Bedrooms: 1 single, 1 double & 1 twin, 1 family room.
Bathrooms: 1 public.
Bed & breakfast: £10-£12 single, £20-£24 double.
Parking for 6.
Open April-October.
🏃 ♨ 🕭 📺 🔲 🛋 ⚛ ⚓
🎵 🍴 🍴

BEDLINGTON

Northumberland
Map ref 5C2

See also Morpeth.
Old stone town close to the head of the Blyth estuary, with a wide tree-lined street leading down to the river. Bedlington terriers were first bred here for badger-baiting.

Anglers Arms
Sheepwash Bank, Guide Post, Choppington, Bedlington, NE62 5NB
☎ (0670) 827584 & 822300
Small, friendly residential inn by the River Wansbeck, between Morpeth and Bedlington.
Bedrooms: 5 twin, 1 family room.
Bathrooms: 1 public.

Bed & breakfast: £13 single, £26 double.
Half board: £14.50-£22 daily.
Evening meal 6pm.
Parking for 30.
🏃 ♨ 🕭 🖕 📺 🔲 🍴 🍴

BELFORD

Northumberland
Map ref 5B1

Small market town on the old coaching road, close to the coast, the Scottish border and the north east flank of the Cheviots. Mostly built in stone and very peaceful now that the A1 has by-passed the town, Belford makes an ideal centre for excursions to the moors and to the beautiful unspoilt coastline around Holy Island. *i*

Blue Bell Farm M
😀😀😀
West Street, Belford, Berwick-upon-Tweed, NE70 7QE
☎ (066 83) 362
5-acre working farm. Located just off A1, take Wooler Road 150 yards on right. Well placed for Cheviots, Holy Island, Farne Islands and country walks.
Bedrooms: 1 single, 2 double & 1 twin, 1 family room.
Bathrooms: 2 private, 1 public.
Bed & breakfast: from £12 single, from £24 double.
Half board: from £18 daily.
Evening meal 6pm (l.o. 8pm).
Parking for 20.
🏃 ♨ 🖵 🕭 UL 🖕 📺
🔲 🛋 ♨ ⚲ 🍴 🍴 🅿 SP

BELLINGHAM

Northumberland
Map ref 5B2

Set in the beautiful valley of the North Tyne, small border town close to the Kielder Forest, Kielder Water and lonely moorland below the Cheviots. The church which stands close to the river and to St. Cuthbert's Well has an ancient stone wagon roof fortified in the 18th C. with buttresses. *i*

The Cheviot M
😀😀😀
Bellingham, Hexham, NE48 2AU
☎ (0660) 20216

In the town centre, this old country inn features traditional open fireplaces in the lounge and bar, and a large selection of whiskies.
Bedrooms: 1 single, 2 double & 3 twin.
Bathrooms: 6 private.
Bed & breakfast: £15-£18 single, £30-£36 double.
Half board: £25-£28 daily, £170-£190 weekly.
Lunch available.
Evening meal 7pm (l.o. 9.30pm).
Parking for 10.
Credit: Access, Visa.

Lyndale M
⌂⌂

Bellingham, Hexham, NE48 2AW
☎ (0660) 20361
Attractive dormer bungalow in pleasant village amid moors. Close to the river and ideal for touring Roman Wall and Kielder Water.
Bedrooms: 2 single, 1 double & 1 twin.
Bathrooms: 2 public.
Bed & breakfast: £10 single, £20 double.
Half board: £16 daily, £112 weekly.
Evening meal 6pm (l.o. 7pm).
Parking for 4.

The Moorcock Inn M
⌂⌂⌂

Tarset, Bellingham, NE48 1LF
☎ (0660) 40269
A small rural, family-run inn, 4 miles from Bellingham on the road to Kielder Water.
Bedrooms: 1 double & 2 twin, 1 family room.
Bathrooms: 2 private, 1 public.
Bed & breakfast: £16-£18 single, £30-£35 double.
Half board: £20-£22 daily, £180-£210 weekly.
Lunch available.
Evening meal 7pm (l.o. 9pm).
Parking for 15.
Open May-December.

MAP REFERENCES APPLY TO THE COLOUR MAPS TOWARDS THE END OF THIS GUIDE.

BERWICK-UPON-TWEED

Northumberland
Map ref 5B1

Guarding the mouth of the Tweed, England's northernmost town with the best 16th C city walls in Europe. The handsome Guildhall and Barracks date from the 18th C. The church, unusually, was completed by the Puritans. Three bridges cross to Tweedmouth, the oldest built in 1634. The Barracks holds the regimental museum, town museum and part of the Burrell Art Collection. *i*

Ancroft South Moor

Berwick-upon-Tweed, TD15 2TD
☎ (0289) 87254
400-acre mixed farm. Pleasant farmhouse 5 miles from Berwick, off the B6354.
Bedrooms: 1 double.
Bathrooms: 1 public.
Bed & breakfast: max. £19 double.
Parking for 1.
Open May-September.

Dervaig

1 North Road, Berwick-upon-Tweed, TD15 1PW
☎ (0289) 307378
Beautiful Victorian house, tastefully furnished, with spacious garden. 1 minute from train station, 4 minutes from centre of town. Free indoor and outdoor parking.
Bedrooms: 1 single, 1 double & 1 twin, 1 family room.
Bathrooms: 1 private, 1 public.
Bed & breakfast: £12.50-£20 single, £25-£40 double.
Evening meal 6.30pm (l.o. 7pm).
Parking for 8.

The Estate House M
Listed

Ford, Berwick-upon-Tweed, TD15 2QG
☎ Crookham (089 082) 297
Victorian country house with its own grounds, in a peaceful village. Walking, fishing, gliding, riding by arrangement.
Bedrooms: 2 twin.
Bathrooms: 1 public.
Bed & breakfast: from £11 single, from £22 double.
Half board: from £17.50 daily.

Evening meal 7pm.
Parking for 2.
Open April-October.

The Old Vicarage Guest House M
⌂⌂⌂

24, Church Road, Tweedmouth, Berwick-upon Tweed, TD15 2RW
☎ (0289) 306909
Spacious, detached 19th C. vicarage, recently refurbished to a high standard. 10 minutes' walk from town centre and beautiful beaches.
Bedrooms: 1 single, 2 double & 2 twin, 3 family rooms.
Bathrooms: 4 private, 1 public.
Bed & breakfast: £10 single, £19-£28 double.
Evening meal 6pm (l.o. 6.30pm).

The Roxburgh M
⌂⌂

117 Main St., Spittal, Berwick-upon-Tweed, TD15 1RP
☎ (0289) 306266
Licensed guesthouse ideal for the beach and amusements and within easy reach of Berwick town centre.
Bedrooms: 4 double & 2 twin.
Bathrooms: 2 public; 2 private showers.
Bed & breakfast: £11-£14 single, £22-£25 double.
Half board: £14-£17 daily, £88-£100 weekly.
Lunch available.
Evening meal 6.30pm (l.o. 9.30pm).
Parking for 16.

The Steading

Low Cocklaw, Berwick-upon-Tweed, TD15 1UY
☎ (0289) 86214
Conversion of stone farm steading. In hamlet 2 miles off A1 Berwick bypass (signposted); panoramic views of Cheviots.
Bedrooms: 1 double, 1 family room.
Bathrooms: 1 private, 1 public.
Bed & breakfast: £20-£24 double.
Parking for 3.
Open April-October.

The Walls Guest House
⌂⌂⌂

8 Quay Walls, Berwick-upon-Tweed, TD15 1HB
☎ (0289) 308320
Walls House has been tastefully modernised to provide accommodation on the ancient town walls of Berwick, overlooking the bridges and River Tweed.
Bedrooms: 3 double & 1 twin, 2 family rooms.
Bathrooms: 3 public.
Bed & breakfast: £11-£15 single, £22-£30 double.
Half board: £19.50-£23.50 daily, £136.50-£164.50 weekly.
Evening meal 6.30pm (l.o. 7.15pm).

BISHOP AUCKLAND

Co. Durham
Map ref 5C2

See also Hamsterley Forest.
Busy market town on the bank of the Wear. The Palace, a castellated Norman manor house altered in the 18th C, stands in beautiful gardens. Open to the public and entered from the market square by a handsome 18th C gatehouse, the park is a peaceful retreat of trees and streams.

Breckon Hill Farm M

Westgate-in-Weardale, Bishop Auckland, DL13 1DP
☎ (0388) 517228
Restored Georgian farmhouse with views of Weardale. Close to Wear Valley Way footpath. Ideal touring centre.
Bedrooms: 1 double & 2 twin.
Bathrooms: 3 private.
Bed & breakfast: £13.50-£16.50 single, £24.50-£27 double.
Half board: £18.50-£21.50 daily, £120-£145 weekly.
Evening meal 6pm (l.o. 3pm).
Parking for 6.
Open March-December.

PLEASE CHECK PRICES AND OTHER DETAILS AT THE TIME OF BOOKING.

BISHOP AUCKLAND
Continued

Butsfield Abbey Farm
Satley, Bishop Auckland,
DL13 4JD
☎ (0388) 730509
*176-acre mixed farm.
Farmhouse cottage in a quiet
rural setting. One mile from
A68 and four miles from
Castleside.*
Bedrooms: 2 double.
Bathrooms: 1 public.
Bed & breakfast: £10 single,
£20 double.
Parking for 2.
♿ ☒ ♨ Ⓤ ☐ ⓉⓋ ▥ ⌂ ☖

Oak Lodge
Wind Mill, Nr. Hamsterley,
Bishop Auckland, DL14 0PT
☎ (0388) 718623
*6-acre smallholding. From
West Auckland take the
Corbridge road (A68) through
Toft Hill. Turn left towards
Hamsterley. Left again at the
cross roads. 1 mile to the
hamlet of Windmill. At the
second house on right, turn
right. Oak Lodge set back 20
yards off road.*
Bedrooms: 1 double & 1 twin,
1 family room.
Bathrooms: 1 public.
Bed & breakfast: £12.50-£15
single, £21-£24 double.
Half board: £15.50-£18 daily,
£115-£125 weekly.
Evening meal 6pm (l.o.
8.30pm).
Parking for 6.
♿ ☒ ♨ Ⓤ 🛆 Ⓥ ⌂ ⓉⓋ ▥
⌂ Ὠ ☀ ♞

Rookhope Inn
Rookhope, Weardale, Bishop
Auckland, DL13 2BG
☎ (0388) 517215
*Situated in Weardale in the
village of Rookhope. Excellent
walking country.*
Bedrooms: 1 double, 1 family
room.
Bathrooms: 1 public.
Bed & breakfast: £10 single,
£20 double.
Half board: £13 daily, £80
weekly.
Lunch available.
Evening meal 7pm (l.o.
10.30pm).
Parking for 20.
♿ ♨ 🛆 Ⓥ ⓉⓋ ▥ ⌂ ♣ ♞
♞ ⏟

**THE SYMBOLS ARE
EXPLAINED ON THE
FLAP INSIDE THE
BACK COVER.**

BLANCHLAND
Northumberland
Map ref 5B2

Beautiful medieval village
rebuilt in the 18th C. with
stone from its ruined
abbey, for lead-miners
working on the
surrounding wild moors.
The village is approached
over a stone bridge
across the Derwent or,
from the north, through
the ancient gatehouse.

Winnows Hill Farm
Blanchland, Consett, Co.
Durham. DH8 9PQ
☎ (043 475) 226
*500-acre mixed farm. Friendly
hospitality offered at this
delightful farmhouse with
panoramic views over the
Derwent Reservoir. Ideal for
walking, fishing and sailing
holidays.*
Bedrooms: 1 single, 1 double
& 1 twin.
Bathrooms: 1 public.
Bed & breakfast: £10-£12
single, £20-£24 double.
Half board: £16-£18 daily,
£100-£120 weekly.
Evening meal 6pm (l.o.
8.30pm).
Parking for 4.
♿ ☒ ♨ 🛆 Ⓤ 🛆 Ⓥ ⌂ ⓉⓋ
▥ ⌂ ☀ ♞ ⒮ₚ ⏟

BOLDRON
Co. Durham
Map ref 5B3

See also Barnard Castle.

West Roods 🏠
😊
West Roods Farm, Boldron,
Barnard Castle, DL12 9SW
☎ Teesside (0833) 690116
*58-acre dairy and mixed farm.
In Teesdale area, south of
Barnard Castle, 2.5 miles east
of Bowes. Third farm on right
(north) from Boldron T-junction
travelling west on A66. Water
dowsing and art activity
holidays available. Home
cooking.*
Bedrooms: 1 single, 1 double,
1 family room.
Bathrooms: 1 private,
2 public.
Bed & breakfast: £12-£15
single, £30-£40 double.
Half board: £23-£28 daily,
£161-£196 weekly.
Evening meal 5pm (l.o.
6.30pm).
Parking for 6.
Open March-December.
♿ ♨ 🛆 Ⓤ 🛆 Ⓥ ⓉⓋ ▥ ⌂
♞ ⏟

BRANCEPETH
Co. Durham
Map ref 5C2

See also Durham City.
Pretty village 4 miles west
of Durham City, with a
picturesque church and a
dramatic castle with
massive Norman gate
towers. The castle
overlooks an attractive
golf course.

Stockley Farm 🏠
Ⓛⓘⓢⓣⓔⓓ
Oakenshaw, Crook,
DL15 0TJ
☎ Bishop Auckland
(0388) 746443
*230-acre mixed farm. Family-
run, with pleasant farmland
views from all windows. Set in
ideal walking and touring
country close to Brancepeth,
Durham and the Dales.*
Bedrooms: 1 single, 1 double
& 1 twin.
Bathrooms: 1 public.
Bed & breakfast: £10-£11
single, £20-£22 double.
Parking for 10.
♿ ☒ ☐ ♨ Ⓤ ▥ ⌂ ☖ ▸
☀ ♞ ♞

CHATHILL
Northumberland
Map ref 5C1

See also Tantobie.
Rural hamlet with main
line station. Preston
Tower, a border pele
tower, is nearby.

Doxford Farm 🏠
😊😊
Chathill, NE67 5DY
☎ Charlton Mires
(066 579) 235
*400-acre mixed farm. Georgian
farmhouse set in wooded
grounds. Coast and moorland
are within easy reach.*
Bedrooms: 1 double & 1 twin,
1 family room.
Bathrooms: 1 public.
Bed & breakfast: £10-£15
single, £20-£24 double.
Half board: £15-£20 daily.
Evening meal 7pm (l.o. 5pm).
Parking for 8.
♿② ♨ Ⓤ 🛆 ✂ ⌂ ⓉⓋ ⌂ ☖
♣ ♞ ⏎ Ὠ ⏟ ☀ ♞

**MAP REFERENCES
APPLY TO COLOUR
MAPS NEAR THE
BACK OF THE GUIDE.**

CHESTER-LE-STREET
Co. Durham
Map ref 5C2

Originally a Roman
military site, town with
modern commerce and
light industry on the River
Wear. The ancient church
replaced a wooden
sanctuary which
sheltered the remains of
St. Cuthbert for 113
years. The Anker's house
beside the church is now
a museum.

Waldridge Hall Farm 🏠
Ⓛⓘⓢⓣⓔⓓ
Old Waldridge, Chester-le-
Street, DH2 3SL
☎ (091) 3884210
*160-acre arable farm. A stone-
built Georgian farmhouse with
views over park and farmland.
Betweem Durham City and
Beamish Museum.*
Bedrooms: 1 double, 1 family
room.
Bathrooms: 1 public.
Bed & breakfast: £13-£14
single, £24-£26 double.
Parking for 4.
♿⑤ ☒ ☐ ♨ Ⓤ 🛆 ⌂ ⓉⓋ ▥
⌂ ☀ ♞ ♞ ♞

CONSETT
Co. Durham
Map ref 5B2

See also Tantobie.
Former steel town on the
edge of rolling moors.
Modern development
includes the shopping
centre and a handsome
Roman Catholic church,
designed by a local
architect. To the west, the
Derwent Reservoir
provides water sports
and pleasant walks.

Bee Cottage Farm
Ⓛⓘⓢⓣⓔⓓ
Castleside, Consett,
DH8 9HW
☎ (0207) 508224
*64-acre livestock farm. A
working farm 1.5 miles west of
the A68, between Castleside
and Tow Law. Unspoilt views.
Ideally located for Beamish
Museum and Durham.*
Bedrooms: 1 single, 2 twin,
2 family rooms.
Bathrooms: 1 public.
Bed & breakfast: £12 single,
£24 double.

Half board: £18 daily, £120-£126 weekly.
Lunch available.
Evening meal 5pm (l.o. 8.30pm).
Parking for 26.
⌖ ⚿ ⊎ 📞 ▮ ⊲ 📺 ▥ ⌂ 🍴

Castlenook Guest House ⋒
♔♔

18/20 Front Street, Castleside, Consett, DH8 9AR
☎ (0207) 506634
On the A68 within easy reach of Durham City, Hadrian's Wall, Beamish Museum and Metro Centre. Views over the North Pennines and countless country walks through the Derwent Valley.
Bedrooms: 1 double & 2 twin.
Bathrooms: 3 private.
Bed & breakfast: £10-£14 single, £20-£22 double.
Half board: £14-£18 daily, £86-£90 weekly.
Evening meal 6pm (l.o. 8pm).
Parking for 5.
Credit: Access, Visa.
⌖ ♥ ⊎ 📞 ▮ ⊲ 📺 ▥ ⌂ 🍴 🐾 🏠

CORBRIDGE
Northumberland
Map ref 5B2

Small town on the River Tyne. Close by are extensive remains of the Roman military town Corstopitum, with a museum housing important discoveries from excavations. The town itself is attractive with shady trees, a 17th C bridge and interesting old buildings, notably a 14th C fortified vicarage and a pele tower house about 200 years older. ℹ

Clive House ⋒
♔♔♔

Appletree Lane, Corbridge, NE45 5DN
☎ (043 471) 2617
Old village school (1840) converted to dwelling house; tasteful decor throughout, exposed beams, gallery, and a log fire in breakfast room. Good eating places nearby.
Bedrooms: 2 double & 1 twin.
Bathrooms: 3 private.
Bed & breakfast: £25 single, £35 double.
Parking for 3.
Credit: Access, Visa.
⌖ 12 ⊞ 📞 ♥ 📞 ▮ ⊎ 📺 ▥ ⌂ 🍴 🏠 SP 🏠

Low Barns ⋒
♛

Thornbrough, Corbridge, NE45 5LX
☎ (043 471) 2408
A Northumbrian stone-built farmhouse, recently modernised, in beautiful countryside one mile east of Corbridge.
Bedrooms: 1 double, 1 family room.
Bathrooms: 1 private, 2 public.
Bed & breakfast: £15-£20 single, £24-£30 double.
Half board: £21-£26 daily, £130-£160 weekly.
Evening meal 7pm (l.o. 6.30pm).
Parking for 6.
⌖ 1 ⊞ 📞 ♥ ▮ ▮ ⊲ ▥ ⌂ 🐾 🏠

Low Riding ⋒

Aydon Rd., Corbridge, NE45 5EJ
☎ (043 471) 2340
Attractive detached house with large garden, in a suburban part of the village on the B6321. An ideal touring centre for Northumbria and the Roman Wall.
Bedrooms: 1 single, 1 double & 1 twin.
Bathrooms: 1 public.
Bed & breakfast: from £12 single, from £24 double.
Parking for 4.
⌖ 8 ♥ ⊎ ▥ 🍴 🏠

Wallhouses ⋒
Listed

Wallhouses Farm, Military Road, Corbridge, NE45 5PU
☎ Great Whittington (043 472) 226
300-acre mixed farm. Situated on Roman Wall, its garden being the Roman Ditch.
Bedrooms: 1 double, 1 family room.
Bathrooms: 1 public.
Bed & breakfast: £11 single, £22 double.
Parking for 11.
Open May-October.
⌖ ⚿ ⊎ ▥ 🍴 🏠

GROUPS, CONSORTIA AND AGENCIES SPECIALISING IN FARM AND COUNTRY HOLIDAYS ARE LISTED IN A SPECIAL SECTION OF THIS GUIDE.

CRASTER
Northumberland
Map ref 5C1

Small fishing village with a fine northward view of Dunstanburgh Castle. Fishing cobles in the tiny harbour, stone cottages at the water's edge and a kippering shed where Craster's famous delicacy is produced give the village its unspoilt charm.

Cottage Inn

Dunstan Village, Craster, Alnwick, NE66 3ZS
☎ Embleton (066 576) 658
Old stone building with walled garden, half a mile from the sea. Winter weekend breaks are available from November to April.
Bedrooms: 2 double & 14 twin, 1 family room.
Bathrooms: 10 private, 2 public.
Bed & breakfast: £14-£24 single, £28-£48 double.
Half board: £22.50-£32.50 daily, £135-£195 weekly.
Lunch available.
Evening meal 6pm (l.o. 9.30pm).
Parking for 30.
⌖ ♥ ⊎ 📺 ▥ ⌂ 🐾 🍴 SP

CROOK
Co. Durham
Map ref 5C2

5m NW. Bishop Auckland
Pleasant market town sometimes referred to as 'the gateway to Weardale'. The town's shopping centre surrounds a large open green attractively laid out with lawns and flowerbeds around the Devil's Stone, a relic from the Ice Age.

Greenhead Country House Hotel ⋒
♔♔♔

Fir Tree, Crook, DL15 8BL
☎ Bishop Auckland (0388) 763143
Newly established enterprise with well appointed bedrooms overlooking secluded fields and wooded area. Lounge with sandstone arches, log fire and oak beams.
Bedrooms: 4 double & 1 twin, 1 family room.
Bathrooms: 8 private, 1 public.
Bed & breakfast: £15-£17 single, £25-£28 double.

Half board: £19-£23 daily, £133-£161 weekly.
Evening meal 6pm (l.o. 5pm).
Parking for 18.
Credit: Access, Visa.
⌖ 13 ⚿ ⊞ 📞 ♥ ▮ ⊲ 📺 ▥ ⌂ 🍴 🐾 🍴 DAP ⚲ SP 🏠 T

DALTON
Tyne & Wear
Map ref 5C2

See also Ponteland.

Dalton House

Dalton, Ponteland, Newcastle upon Tyne, Tyne & Wear NE18 0AA
☎ Stamfordham (066 16) 225
Attractive Georgian house in its own grounds, on the site of a 12th C. monastery and once part of the Collingwood estate. Near small villages and country pubs.
Bedrooms: 2 single, 2 twin.
Bathrooms: 2 private, 3 public.
Bed & breakfast: £10-£12 single, £20-£24 double.
Half board: £15-£17 daily, £105-£120 weekly.
Evening meal 6pm (l.o. 7pm).
Parking for 4.
Open April-October.
♥ ⊎ ▮ ⊲ 📺 ▥ ⌂ 🐾 🍴 🏠 🏠

DARLINGTON
Co. Durham
Map ref 5C3

See also Heighington
Industrial town on the River Skerne, home of the earliest passenger railway which first ran to Stockton in 1825. Now the home of a railway museum. Originally a prosperous market town occupying the site of an Anglo-Saxon settlement, with a busy industrial complex, it still holds an open market in the square. ℹ

Woodland Guest House ⋒
♔♔

63, Woodland Road, Darlington, DL3 7BQ
☎ (0325) 461908
Large Victorian house on the main A68. A warm and comfortable atmosphere is assured.
Bedrooms: 2 single, 2 double & 2 twin, 2 family rooms.
Bathrooms: 2 public.
Bed & breakfast: £11-£13 single, £20-£22 double.
⌖ ⊎ ▮ ⊲ 📺 ▥ ⌂

DURHAM CITY

Co. Durham
Map ref 5C2

See also Brancepeth.
Ancient city with its
Norman castle and
cathedral set on a bluff
high over the Wear, a
market and university
town and regional centre,
spreading beyond the
Market Place on both
banks of the river. July
Miners' Gala is a
celebrated Durham
tradition.

Bankside Guest House ⋔

38 Wearside Drive, The
Sands, Durham City,
DH1 1LE
☎ 091-384 2920
*A cosy and comfortable city
home of a professional couple,
only a few minutes' walk from
the market place.*
Bedrooms: 1 single, 2 twin.
Bathrooms: 1 private,
1 public.
Bed & breakfast: £12-£15
single, £24-£32 double.
Evening meal 6pm (l.o.
10am).
Parking for 2.

Bay Horse Inn ⋔

Brandon Village, Durham
City, DH7 8ST.
☎ 091-378 0498
*Stone-built chalets 3 miles
from Durham city centre.*
Bedrooms: 4 twin.
Bathrooms: 4 private.
Bed & breakfast: £24 single,
£32 double.
Half board: £26.50-£28 daily.
Lunch available.
Evening meal 7pm (l.o.
10pm).
Parking for 15.
Credit: Access.

Castle View Guest House ⋔

4 Crossgate, Durham City,
DH1 4PS
☎ 091-386 8852
*A 250-year-old, listed building
in the heart of the old city with
woodland and riverside walks,
and a magnificent view of the
cathedral and castle.*
Bedrooms: 2 single, 1 double
& 2 twin, 1 family room.

Bathrooms: 2 private,
2 public; 1 private shower.
Bed & breakfast: £12-£15
single, £24-£30 double.

Castledene
Listed
37 Nevilledale Terrace,
Durham City, DH1 4QG
☎ 091-384 8386
*An Edwardian end-of-terrace
house half a mile east of the
market place. Within walking
distance of the riverside,
cathedral and castle.*
Bedrooms: 1 single, 2 twin.
Bathrooms: 1 public.
Bed & breakfast: £10.50-£11
single, £20-£22 double.
Parking for 2.

Colebrick ⋔
Listed
21 Crossgate, Durham City,
DH1 4PS
☎ 091-384 9585
*Near the city centre, railway
and bus stations, with
magnificent views of the
cathedral and castle. Dinner
available by prior arrangement.*
Bedrooms: 1 double & 1 twin,
1 family room.
Bathrooms: 1 public.
Bed & breakfast: max. £20
single, £25-£30 double.
Evening meal 6pm (l.o. 7pm).
Parking for 5.

The Gables Hotel
Haswell Plough, Durham
City, DH6 2EW
☎ 091-526 2982
*Small family-run hotel 6 miles
from Durham City on the
B1283. Traditional after-
dinner entertainment.
Horsedrawn wagon tours of
Durham City.*
Bedrooms: 2 double & 2 twin,
1 family room.
Bathrooms: 2 public.
Bed & breakfast: £17.50-
£18.50 single, from £27
double.
Half board: £25-£30 daily,
£140-£150 weekly.
Lunch available.
Evening meal 7pm (l.o.
10pm).
Parking for 30.

Gilesgate Lodge
169 Gilesgate, Durham City,
DH1 1QH
☎ 091-384 1671
Centrally located new house.
Bedrooms: 1 single, 1 double
& 2 twin.

Bathrooms: 1 public.
Bed & breakfast: max. £11
single, max. £22 double.
Half board: max. £16 daily,
max. £100 weekly.
Parking for 2.

Lothlorien ⋔
Listed
Front St., Witton Gilbert,
Durham City, DH7 6SY
☎ 091-371 0067
*Country cottage only 5 minutes
by car from Durham city
centre and on a direct route to
Hadrian's Wall. A good centre
for touring.*
Bedrooms: 2 single, 1 double
& 1 twin.
Bathrooms: 1 public.
Bed & breakfast: from £12
single, from £24 double.
Half board: from £17 daily,
from £119 weekly.
Evening meal 6pm (l.o. 9pm).
Parking for 4.

5, Mowbray Street ⋔
Durham City, DH1 4BH
☎ 091-386 3108
*Early Victorian terraced house
with original features. Near the
town centre, bus and rail
stations.*
Bedrooms: 1 single, 2 double.
Bathrooms: 1 private,
1 public.
Bed & breakfast: £8-£16
single, £16-£24 double.
Half board: £12.50-£21 daily,
£86-£145 weekly.
Evening meal 7.30pm (l.o.
6pm).
Parking for 2.

Northolme
21 Hallgarth Street, Durham
City, DH1 3AT
☎ 091-386 9956
*Georgian terraced house 4
minutes' walk from the
cathedral.*
Bedrooms: 1 single, 1 double,
1 family room.
Bathrooms: 1 public.
Bed & breakfast: £11-£13
single, £22-£24 double.
Parking for 3.

Weardale House
Sherburn Village, Durham
City, DH6 1HB
☎ 091-372 0685
*Modernised detached separate
from main house in a quarter
acre of garden.*
Bedrooms: 1 double.

Bathrooms: 1 private.
Bed & breakfast: from £13.50
single, from £27 double.
Evening meal 6pm (l.o. 5pm).
Parking for 3.

EDMUNDBYERS

Co. Durham
Map ref 5B2

Small village in hilly
country beneath
Muggleswick Common. A
winding, man-made lake
on the River Derwent just
north complements
smaller reservoirs
southward across the
common, traditionally
offering fishing and picnic
places.

Redwell Hall Farm ⋔

Edmundbyers, Shotley Bridge
DH8 9TS
☎ (0207) 55216
*113-acre mixed farm.
Traditional stone-built farm on
the edge of moorland and close
to beautiful Derwent Reservoir.
Accommodation is in
farmhouse and annexe. Ideal
for visiting Durham, Hexham,
Tynedale and the North
Pennines. Weekend embroidery
courses can be arranged.
Conversational German courses
available.*
Bedrooms: 1 double & 1 twin,
1 family room.
Bathrooms: 2 public.
Bed & breakfast: £12-£14
single, £21-£23 double.
Half board: £18-£20 daily,
£119-£125 weekly.
Parking for 10.

FALSTONE

Northumberland
Map ref 5B2

Remote village on the
edge of Kielder Forest
where it spreads beneath
the heathery slopes of the
south west Cheviots
along the valley of the
North Tyne. Just a mile
west lies Kielder Water, a
vast man-made lake
which adds boating and
fishing to forest
recreations.

The Pheasant Inn ⋔

Stannersburn, Falstone,
Hexham, NE48 1DD
☎ Bellingham (0660) 40382

This historic inn is close to Kielder Water. Fishing, riding and all water sports are nearby.
Bedrooms: 5 single, 2 double & 3 twin, 1 family room.
Bathrooms: 2 private, 2 public.
Bed & breakfast: £14-£16 single, £26-£32 double.
Half board: £22-£26 daily, £138.60-£163.80 weekly.
Lunch available.
Evening meal 7pm (l.o. 9pm).
Parking for 30.
Credit: Access, Visa.

FOREST-IN-TEESDALE

Co. Durham
Map ref 5B2

See also Middleton-in-Teesdale.
An area of Upper Teesdale of widely dispersed farmsteads set in wild but beautiful scenery with High Force Waterfall and Cauldron Snout. Once the hunting park of the Earls of Darlington.

Langdon Beck Hotel
Listed
Forest-in-Teesdale, Barnard Castle, DL12 0XP
☎ Teesdale (0833) 22267
A pleasant inn in the magnificent area of Upper Teesdale where a friendly welcome and home cooking are assured. Ideal for walkers and nature lovers.
Bedrooms: 3 single, 2 double & 1 twin, 1 family room.
Bathrooms: 2 public.
Bed & breakfast: from £12 single, from £24 double.
Half board: from £18 daily, from £120 weekly.
Lunch available.
Evening meal 6.30pm (l.o. 7pm).
Parking for 15.

GATESHEAD

Tyne & Wear

See Newcastle upon Tyne, Rowlands Gill.

PLEASE MENTION THIS GUIDE WHEN MAKING A BOOKING.

GREENHEAD

Northumberland
Map ref 5A2

Small hamlet, overlooked by the ruins of Thirlwall Castle, at the junction of the A69 and the B6318 which runs alongside Hadrian's Wall. Some of the finest sections of the wall and the Carvoran Roman Military Museum are nearby.

Burnt Walls M
Listed
Greenhead, Carlisle, Cumbria. CA6 7HX
☎ Gilsland (069 72) 272
Farmhouse with panoramic views in a rural setting. Near Hadrian's Wall and the Pennine Way; between Greenhead and Gilsland.
Bedrooms: 1 double & 1 twin, 1 family room.
Bathrooms: 2 public.
Bed & breakfast: £10-£17 single, £20-£24 double.
Half board: £13.25-£24.50 daily, £85.75-£164.50 weekly.
Evening meal 5.30pm (l.o. 8pm).
Parking for 5.

HALTWHISTLE

Northumberland
Map ref 5B2

Small market town with a tree-shaded early English church. Around Hadrian's Wall, situated just north of it, are numerous Roman sites; further south along the river stands Featherstone Castle, a medieval pele tower with a Jacobean mansion built on.

Broomshaw Hill Farm M
Haltwhistle, NE49 9NP
☎ (0498) 20866
5-acre grazing farm. Attractive 18th C. stone-built farmhouse which has been modernised. On conjunction of bridleway and footpath, both leading to Hadrian's Wall 1 mile away.
Bedrooms: 2 twin, 1 family room.
Bathrooms: 1 public.
Bed & breakfast: max. £12 single, £20-£22 double.
Half board: £15-£16 daily, £100-£105 weekly.

Evening meal 6.30pm (l.o. 9am).
Parking for 8.
Open April-October.

Hall Meadows
Main Street, Haltwhistle, NE49 0AZ
☎ (0498) 21021
Built in 1888, a large family house with large pleasant garden in the centre of Haltwhistle.
Bedrooms: 1 single, 1 twin, 1 family room.
Bathrooms: 1 public.
Bed & breakfast: £10.50 single, £21 double.
Parking for 3.

Oaky Knowe Farm
Haltwhistle, NE49 0NB
☎ (0498) 20648
300-acre stockrearing farm. Overlooking the Tyne Valley, within walking distance of Haltwhistle and the Roman Wall, this comfortable farmhouse offers friendly family holidays.
Bedrooms: 1 twin, 2 family rooms.
Bathrooms: 1 public.
Bed & breakfast: £10-£11 single, £20 double.
Half board: £15 daily, £90 weekly.
Evening meal 5pm (l.o. 6.30pm).
Parking for 8.

Park Burnfoot Farm
Featherstone Park, Haltwhistle, NE49 0JP
☎ (0498) 20378
220-acre stockrearing and dairy farm. Listed 18th C. farmhouse on the banks of the South Tyne. 3 miles from the Roman Wall, 1 mile from Featherstone Castle and 100 yards from woodland walks. Colour TV, log fires.
Bedrooms: 1 double, 1 family room.
Bathrooms: 1 public.
Bed & breakfast: £10 single, £18-£19 double.
Half board: £12.50-£13 daily, £84-£90 weekly.
Parking for 3.
Open April-October.

WE ADVISE YOU TO CONFIRM YOUR BOOKING IN WRITING.

HAMSTERLEY FOREST

Co. Durham
Map ref 5B2

See also Bishop Auckland.
5500 acres of forest offering a forest drive, nature trail, forest walk and stream-side picnic spot. David Bellamy's country.

Grove House
Listed
Redford, Hamsterley Forest, Bishop Auckland, DL13 3NL
☎ Witton-le-Wear (038 888) 203
Country house in the heart of Hamsterley Forest with fishing, walking and birdwatching close at hand. Ideal for families to enjoy tranquil countryside.
Bedrooms: 1 double & 2 twin.
Bathrooms: 1 public.
Bed & breakfast: £14.50 single, £29 double.
Half board: £22 daily, £144 weekly.
Evening meal 6pm (l.o. 9pm).
Parking for 20.

HAYDON BRIDGE

Northumberland
Map ref 5B2

Small town on the banks of the South Tyne with an ancient church, built of stone from sites just along the Roman Wall just north. Ideally situated for exploring Hadrian's Wall and the Border country.

Anchor Hotel M
John Martin St., Haydon Bridge, Hexham, NE47 6AB
☎ (043 484) 227
Riverside inn, in a village close to the Roman Wall. Ideal centre for touring the North Pennines and Northumberland National Park.
Bedrooms: 1 single, 5 double & 4 twin, 2 family rooms.
Bathrooms: 10 private, 1 public.
Bed & breakfast: £21-£26 single, £32-£37 double.
Half board: £134-£159 weekly.
Lunch available.
Evening meal 7pm (l.o. 9pm).
Parking for 20.

Continued ▶

HAYDON BRIDGE

Continued

Credit: Access, Visa, Diners, Amex.

HEIGHINGTON

Co. Durham
Map ref 5C3

See also Darlington.

Eldon House ♨

East Green, Heighington,
Darlington, DL5 6PP
☎ Aycliffe (0325) 312270
A 17th C. manor house with large garden and tennis court overlooking the village green. Large comfortable, well-appointed rooms.
Bedrooms: 1 twin, 1 family room.
Bathrooms: 2 public.
Bed & breakfast: £14 single, £20 double.
Parking for 6.

HEXHAM

Northumberland
Map ref 5B2

See also Slaley.
Old coaching and market town near Hadrian's Wall, lively social and commercial centre for the fertile Tyne Valley. A weekly market has been held in the centre with its market place and abbey park since pre-Norman times, and the richly furnished 12th C abbey church has a superb Anglo-Saxon crypt. There is a racecourse at High Yarridge.

Ausma

23 Leazes Crescent, Hexham,
NE46 3JZ
☎ (0434) 603182
Comfortable, high standard accommodation in large Victorian house. Ideal for Northumbrian country-side and all local amenities.
Bedrooms: 1 single, 1 double & 1 twin, 1 family room.
Bathrooms: 1 public.
Bed & breakfast: £10.75-£12.25 single, £21.50-£24.50 double.

Belle Vue ♨
Listed

Causey Hill, Hexham,
NE46 1JF
☎ (0434) 602328
A comfortable farmhouse style period house overlooking historic Hexham, with a relaxed atmosphere and a warm welcome. Close to Hadrian's Wall.
Bedrooms: 1 double & 1 twin, 1 family room.
Bathrooms: 1 public.
Bed & breakfast: from £14 single, £23-£25 double.
Parking for 4.

Kalnis

2 Woodlands, Hexham,
NE46 1HT
☎ (0434) 602148
An attractive Edwardian house close to all amenities, on the Corbridge side of Hexham.
Bedrooms: 2 single, 2 double.
Bathrooms: 1 public.
Bed & breakfast: £10.50-£11.75 single, £21-£23.50 double.
Half board: £16-£18 daily, £105-£110 weekly.

21 Kern Green

Stonehaugh, Wark, Hexham,
NE48 3DZ
☎ (0660) 30677
Country house in a well-known forest beauty area on the Pennine Way. Ideal for touring and walking. Ample parking.
Bedrooms: 1 single, 2 double.
Bathrooms: 1 public.
Bed & breakfast: £9 single, £17.50 double.
Half board: £13.50 daily, £85 weekly.
Evening meal 6pm (l.o. 7pm).
Parking for 2.
Open March-October.

THERE IS A SPECIAL SECTION IN THIS GUIDE LISTING ACCOMMODATION ESPECIALLY SUITABLE FOR GROUPS AND YOUNG PEOPLE.

GROUPS, CONSORTIA AND AGENCIES SPECIALISING IN FARM AND COUNTRY HOLIDAYS ARE LISTED IN A SPECIAL SECTION OF THIS GUIDE.

Kitty Frisk House ♨♨

Corbridge Rd., Hexham,
NE46 1UN
☎ (0434) 606850
An attractive Victorian house with beautifully furnished large rooms. Set in 3 acres of garden and woodland, which is secluded and peaceful. Warm welcome assured.
Bedrooms: 1 double & 1 twin, 1 family room.
Bathrooms: 1 private, 2 public.
Bed & breakfast: £15-£18 single, £25-£30 double.
Parking for 4.
Open April-October.

Mount Pleasant Farm ♨
♨♨

Sandhoe, Hexham,
NE46 4LX
☎ (0434) 603070
140-acre mixed farm. Traditional farmhouse with a comfortable sun lounge and extensive views of the Tyne Valley. 1 mile north of Corbridge and 1 mile from the A68.
Bedrooms: 1 double, 1 family room.
Bathrooms: 2 public.
Bed & breakfast: £12.50-£15 single, £25-£30 double.
Parking for 4.
Open April-October.

Queens Arms Hotel ♨
♨♨

Main Street, Acomb,
Hexham, NE46 4PT
☎ (0434) 602176
Traditional village inn 2 miles north of Hexham. All bedrooms have colour TV. Beautiful countryside, steeped in Roman and Border history.
Bedrooms: 1 single, 2 double & 2 twin.

Bathrooms: 2 private, 3 public.
Bed & breakfast: £15-£20 single, £25-£30 double.
Half board: £17-£25 daily, £110-£130 weekly.
Evening meal 6pm (l.o. 7.30pm).
Parking for 8.

Queensgate House ♨♨

Cockshaw, Hexham,
NE46 3QU
☎ (0434) 605592
Family-run, converted Victorian house within 300 yards of the Abbey and market square.
Bedrooms: 2 single, 1 double & 1 twin, 1 family room.
Bathrooms: 3 private, 1 public.
Bed & breakfast: £11-£13 single, £22-£26 double.
Half board: £16-£18 daily, £100-£126 weekly.
Evening meal 6pm (l.o. 8pm).
Parking for 5.

32 Shaws Park

Hexham, NE46 3BJ
☎ (0434) 602779
Ground floor bedroom and shower room in family home on quiet modern estate opposite golf course.
Bedrooms: 1 double.
Bathrooms: 1 private.
Bed & breakfast: £21-£22 double.
Parking for 2.

Stotsfold Hall

Steel, Hexham, NE47 0HP
☎ Slaley (043 473) 270
A beautiful house surrounded by 15 acres of gardens and woodland with streams and flowers. Six miles south of Hexham.
Bedrooms: 2 single, 1 double & 1 twin.
Bathrooms: 3 public.
Bed & breakfast: £10 single, £20 double.
Parking for 6.

Topsy Turvy

9 Leazes Lane, Hexham,
NE46 3BA
☎ Hexham (0434) 603152
Pretty, chalet-type house in quiet lane at west end of Hexham. Evening meal optional.
Bedrooms: 2 double.

Bathrooms: 1 private,
1 public.
Bed & breakfast: £10-£11
single, £20-£22 double.
Half board: £15 daily, £105
weekly.
Parking for 3.

2 Tynedale Terrace
Hexham, NE46 3JE
☎ (0434) 602 343
*Victorian house in the west end
of Hexham, 5 minutes' easy
walk from the centre of town.*
Bedrooms: 2 single, 1 double
1 family room.
Bathrooms: 1 public.
Bed & breakfast: £11-£12.50
single, £22-£25 double.

West Close House
⊛⊛
Hextol Terrace, Hexham,
NE46 2AD
☎ (0434) 603307
*Delightful detached 1920's
residence, tastefully
refurbished, set in pretty,
secluded, prize-winning
gardens, in a quiet cul-de-sac.
First left off Allendale Road
(B6305). A warm welcome
awaits you.*
Bedrooms: 2 single, 1 double
& 1 twin.
Bathrooms: 1 private,
1 public.
Bed & breakfast: £10.75-£12
single, £21.50-£29 double.
Evening meal 7pm (l.o. 8pm).
Parking for 3.

KIELDER
Northumberland

See Falstone.

MICKLETON
Co. Durham
Map ref 5B3

Low Green
Mickleton, Barnard Castle,
DL12 OJR
☎ Teesdale (0833) 40425
*7-acre mixed farm. Stone
farmhouse, approximately 200
years old, in 7 acres with views
over Teesdale.*
Bedrooms: 1 double & 1 twin,
1 family room.
Bathrooms: 2 private,
1 public.
Bed & breakfast: £10-£14
single, £20-£25 double.

Half board: £17-£21 daily,
£110-£130 weekly.
Evening meal 7pm.
Parking for 7.

MIDDLETON-IN-TEESDALE
Co. Durham
Map ref 5B3

*See also Forest-in-
Teesdale.*
Small stone town of
hillside terraces
overlooking the river,
developed by the London
Lead Company in the
18th C. There is a
handsome Victorian
fountain and the company
headquarters is now a
shooting lodge. Five miles
up-river is the spectacular
70 ft waterfall, High
Force. *i*

Wythes Hill Farm
Listed
Lunedale, Middleton-in-
Teesdale, Barnard Castle,
DL12 0NX
☎ Teesdale (0833) 40349
*550-acre stockrearing hill
farm. Farmhouse with
panoramic views on the
Pennine Way in lovely walking
area. Peace and quiet,
friendliness and comfort are
guaranteed. Farmhouse
cooking.*
Bedrooms: 1 double & 1 twin,
1 family room.
Bathrooms: 2 public.
Bed & breakfast: £8-£9
single, £16-£18 double.
Half board: £12-£13 daily,
max. £84 weekly.
Evening meal 6pm (l.o.
7.30pm).
Parking for 3.
Open April-October.

MORPETH
Northumberland
Map ref 5C2

See also Bedlington.
Market town on the River
Wansbeck. Vanbrugh's
Town Hall was rebuilt in
1870 and there are other
interesting Victorian
buildings. There are
charming gardens and
parks, among them
Carlisle Park which lies
close to the ancient
remains of Morpeth
Castle. The 14th C. parish
church contains some
fine medieval glass. The
Chantry building houses
the Northumbrian Craft
Centre and the new
Bagpipe Museum. *i*

Anglers Arms Inn ⋈
Weldon Bridge, Morpeth,
NE65 8AX
☎ Longframlington
(066 570) 655 & 271
*Attractive 18th C. former
coaching inn by the lovely
River Coquet; just off the
A697 north of Morpeth.*
Bedrooms: 1 single, 3 double.
Bathrooms: 3 private,
1 public.
Bed & breakfast: max. £25
single, £35-£40 double.
Half board: £42-£47 daily,
from £240 weekly.
Lunch available.
Evening meal 7pm (l.o.
10pm).
Parking for 50.
Credit: Access, Visa, Diners,
Amex.

Gorfen Letch Farm
Gorfen Letch, Morpeth,
NE61 3DW
☎ (0670) 512624
*300-acre mixed farm. Large
farmhouse approximately 4
miles north of Morpeth on the
A697, signposted off roadside.*
Bedrooms: 1 double & 1 twin,
1 family room.
Bathrooms: 1 public.
Bed & breakfast: from £12
single, from £24 double.
Half board: £18-£25 daily.
Open April-October.

---

39 Howard Terrace ⋈
Morpeth, NE61 1JJ
☎ (0670) 519562
*A large family house near
Morpeth's attractive shops,
cinema and riverside parks.
We make children very
welcome.*
Bedrooms: 1 double, 2 family
rooms.
Bathrooms: 1 public.
Bed & breakfast: £10-£13
single, £18-£22 double.

The Retreat
41 Main Street, Felton,
Morpeth, NE65 9PP
☎ (0670) 87831
*Comfortable guesthouse in
quiet location. Within easy
access of local attractions and
restaurants.*
Bedrooms: 1 double, 2 family
rooms.
Bathrooms: 1 public;
1 private shower.
Bed & breakfast: £20-£30
double.

The Shieling
2 Manor Farm, Ulgham, Nr.
Morpeth
☎ (0670) 790317
*Old stone-built farm building
converted into a bungalow. In a
quiet village 5 miles from
Morpeth, on the B1337.*
Bedrooms: 2 twin.
Bathrooms: 2 public.
Bed & breakfast: £10-£12
single, £20 double.
Half board: £15-£17 daily.
Parking for 3.

INDIVIDUAL
PROPRIETORS HAVE
SUPPLIED ALL
DETAILS OF
ACCOMMODATION.
ALTHOUGH WE DO
CHECK FOR
ACCURACY, WE
ADVISE YOU TO
CONFIRM PRICES
AND OTHER
INFORMATION AT
THE TIME OF
BOOKING.

**MAP REFERENCES APPLY TO THE COLOUR
MAPS TOWARDS THE END OF THIS GUIDE.**

NEWCASTLE UPON TYNE

Tyne & Wear
Map ref 5C2

Commercial and cultural centre of the north east, with a large indoor shopping centre, Quayside market, museums and theatres which offer an annual 6 week season by the Royal Shakespeare Company. The Norman castle keep and the town's medieval alleys are near the river with its 6 bridges, old Guildhall and timbered merchants' houses. *ℹ*

Bywell
Listed
54 Holly Avenue, Jesmond, Newcastle upon Tyne, NE2 2QA
☎ 091-281 7615
Victorian town house in a quiet residential cul-de-sac, close to city centre and all amenities.
Bedrooms: 1 double & 2 twin.
Bathrooms: 1 public.
Bed & breakfast: max. £12 single, max. £22 double.

Dunromyn Airport Guest House
4 Main Rd., Kenton Bank Foot, Newcastle upon Tyne, NE13 8AB
☎ 091-286 0377
Guesthouse on the A696 to Newcastle Airport facing Bank Foot metro station. A useful overnight stop for ferry and airport passengers.
Bedrooms: 1 single, 1 twin, 2 family rooms.
Bathrooms: 1 public.
Bed & breakfast: £14-£18 single, £22-£24 double.
Parking for 10.

GROUPS, CONSORTIA AND AGENCIES SPECIALISING IN FARM AND COUNTRY HOLIDAYS ARE LISTED IN A SPECIAL SECTION OF THIS GUIDE.

NORHAM

Northumberland
Map ref 5B1

Border village on the salmon-rich Tweed dominated by its dramatic castle ruin. Stone houses line grassy spaces between castle and river. Near Castle Street is the church, like the castle destroyed after the Battle of Flodden, but rebuilt. Norham Station Railway Museum is just outside the town.

Dromore House
12 Pedwell Way, Norham, Berwick-upon-Tweed, TD15 2LD
☎ (0289) 82313
Guesthouse in a small village on the River Tweed, between the Cheviot and Lammermuir Hills. Quiet beaches are within easy reach.
Bedrooms: 2 double, 1 family room.
Bathrooms: 1 public.
Bed & breakfast: from £8 single, from £16 double.
Half board: from £12 daily, from £84 weekly.
Evening meal 5pm (l.o. 7pm).
Parking for 3.

OTTERBURN

Northumberland
Map ref 5B1

Small village set at the meeting of the River Rede with Otter Burn, the site of the battle of Otterburn in 1388. A peaceful tradition continues in the sale of Otterburn tweeds which is ideal for exploring the border country and the Cheviots. *ℹ*

Blakehopeburnhaugh Farm
Otterburn, Nr. Byrness, Newcastle upon Tyne, Tyne & Wear NE19 1SW
☎ (0830) 20267
150-acre stock rearing farm. Traditional stone farmhouse in a peaceful setting in Redesdale Forest, just off the A68 and 12 miles from Kielder Water.
Bedrooms: 1 single, 1 double, 1 family room.
Bathrooms: 1 public.
Bed & breakfast: £12 single, £20 double.

Half board: £15.50 daily, £100 weekly.
Evening meal 6pm (l.o. 2pm).
Parking for 4.

PONTELAND

Northumberland
Map ref 5C2

See also Dalston.
A place of great antiquity, now a dormitory town for Newcastle. The fine Norman church, fortified rectory, Vicar's Pele and old inn, formerly a 17th C manor house, make this town particularly interesting.

The Gables ♨
Ogle, Ponteland, Newcastle upon Tyne, Tyne & Wear NE20 0AU
☎ Whalton (067 075) 392
A ranch-style bungalow in a small hamlet 15 miles from the city centre and 7 miles from the airport. Own transport essential. Non smoking residence.
Bedrooms: 2 single, 2 family rooms.
Bathrooms: 2 private, 1 public.
Bed & breakfast: £14-£20 single, £25-£30 double.
Parking for 5.

Ye Olde Waggon Inn ♨
Higham Dykes, Belsay Rd., Ponteland, Newcastle-upon-Tyne, NE20 0DH
☎ Belsay (0661) 81286/81666
18th C. old coaching inn on the A696 Newcastle to Jedburgh road.
Bedrooms: 1 twin, 2 family rooms.
Bathrooms: 2 public.
Bed & breakfast: £19.50 single, £25-£29 double.
Lunch available.
Evening meal 6pm (l.o. 7.30pm).
Parking for 150.

THE SYMBOLS ARE EXPLAINED ON THE FLAP INSIDE THE BACK COVER.

REDCAR

Cleveland
Map ref 5C3

Lively holiday resort near Teesside with broad sandy beaches, a fine racecourse, a large indoor funfair at Coatham and other seaside amusements. Britain's oldest existing lifeboat can be seen at the Zetland Museum. *ℹ*

2 St. Anne's Rd.
New Marske, Redcar
☎ (0642) 486849
Large private house with patio.
Bedrooms: 1 double, 1 family room.
Bathrooms: 1 public.
Bed & breakfast: from £7.50 single, from £15 double.
Half board: from £10 daily, from £68 weekly.
Evening meal 6pm (l.o. 8pm).
Parking for 1.

Sunnyside House ♨
22 Station Road, Redcar, TS10 1AQ
☎ (0642) 477531
Centrally situated property close to town centre and beach.
Bedrooms: 1 single, 3 double, 1 family room.
Bathrooms: 2 public.
Bed & breakfast: £9.50 single, £19 double.
Half board: £13 daily, £84.50 weekly.
Evening meal 5pm (l.o. 8pm).

RIDING MILL

Northumberland
Map ref 5B2

A small village on the south bank of the River Tyne near historic Corbridge and the Thomas Bewick Musuem.

Morningside
♨
Riding Mill, NE44 6HL
☎ (043 482) 350
Old stone-built blacksmith's house in a quiet country setting, close to Hadrian's Wall and the beautiful River Tyne.
Bedrooms: 2 single, 2 twin, 1 family room.
Bathrooms: 1 public.
Bed & breakfast: £9-£12 single, £18-£20 double.

Half board: £12-£19 daily, £80-£120 weekly. Evening meal 6pm (l.o. 9pm). Parking for 5.

ROTHBURY

Northumberland
Map ref 5C2

Old market town on the River Coquet near the Simonside Hills. With its leafy, sloping main street, attractive green and lovely views of river and hills it makes an ideal centre for walking and fishing or for exploring all this beautiful area from the coast to the Cheviots. Cragside House and Gardens (National Trust) are open to the public.

Westhills Farm

Rothbury, Morpeth,
NE65 7YT
☎ (0669) 20284
165-acre mixed farm. Attractive farmhouse near Rothbury with splendid views overlooking Coquetdale. Ideal for touring and walking. Comfort assured.
Bedrooms: 2 double & 1 twin.
Bathrooms: 1 public.
Bed & breakfast: £16-£17 double.
Half board: from £16 daily, from £110 weekly.
Evening meal 7pm (l.o. 3pm).
Parking for 6.
Open April-September.

ROWLANDS GILL

Tyne & Wear
Map ref 5C2

Adjacent to the Derwent Walk Country Park on the side of the River Derwent opposite the National Trust Gibside Chapel.

Chopwell Wood House ⚑

Chopwell Woods, Rowlands Gill, NE39 1LT
☎ (0207) 542765
A large, attractive house in 600 acres of woodland in the Derwent Valley, within easy reach of Newcastle, Durham and Hexham. Near to Metro Centre.
Bedrooms: 1 double & 1 twin, 1 family room.
Bathrooms: 1 public.
Bed & breakfast: from £10.50 single, £19-£21 double.

Half board: from £15.50 daily, from £95 weekly.
Evening meal 6pm (l.o. 9pm).
Parking for 6.

ST JOHN'S CHAPEL

Co. Durham
Map ref 5B2

Peaceful village in Upper Weardale. Pubs, village shops and cottages are set around a small market square. Nearby Harthope Burn has an attractive waterfall.

Golden Lion ⚑

St. John's Chapel, Bishop Auckland, DL13 1QF
☎ (0388) 537231
This comfortable inn is a converted 18th C. farmhouse in the heart of unspoilt Weardale.
Bedrooms: 5 family rooms.
Bathrooms: 5 private.
Bed & breakfast: £14.50-£16.50 single, £27-£29 double.
Half board: £21.50-£23.50 daily, £175-£195 weekly.
Lunch available.
Evening meal 7.30pm (l.o. 10pm).
Parking for 40.

Low Chesters ⚑

St. John's Chapel, Weardale, Bishop Auckland
☎ Weardale (0388) 537406
Stone built, 16th C. farmhouse which has all modern conveniences but retains its old world character.
Bedrooms: 5 twin, 1 family room.
Bathrooms: 2 public.
Bed & breakfast: £9-£13 single, £18 double.
Half board: £14-£18 daily, £90-£120 weekly.
Lunch available.
Evening meal 6pm (l.o. 7pm).
Parking for 7.

SEAHOUSES

Northumberland
Map ref 5C1

See also Chathill.
Small modern resort developed around a 19th C herring port. Just offshore, and reached by boat from here, are the rocky Farne Islands (National Trust) where there is an important bird reserve. The bird observatory occupies a medieval pele tower. ℹ

Longstone Guest House ⚑

Main Street, Seahouses,
NE68 7RF
☎ (0665) 720212
In the centre of this fishing village, a friendly, family-run guesthouse with spacious dining room and lounge with colour TV.
Bedrooms: 4 single, 4 double & 2 twin, 2 family rooms.
Bathrooms: 2 private, 2 public.
Bed & breakfast: £11-£14 single, £22-£24 double.
Half board: £17-£17.50 daily, £112 weekly.
Evening meal 6.30pm (l.o. 6.30pm).
Parking for 12.
Open March-October.

Southfield House

143 Main St., Seahouses,
NE68 7TT
☎ (0665) 720059
Stone-built house adjoining the Masonic Lodge with views over farmland towards the Farne Islands. 5 minutes' walk from the harbour and beach.
Bedrooms: 1 single, 2 family rooms.
Bathrooms: 1 public.
Bed & breakfast: £9-£10 single, £18-£20 double.
Half board: £14-£15 daily, £98-£105 weekly.
Evening meal 6pm (l.o. midday).
Parking for 4.
Open April-September.

SLALEY

Northumberland
Map ref 5B2

See also Hexham.
Small hamlet, presently being developed as a major golfing venue, south of Corbridge near to the Derwent Reservoir.

Rye Hill Farm ⚑

Slaley, Nr Hexham,
NE47 0AH
☎ (0434) 73259
30-acre livestock/sheep farm. A warm and comfortable barn conversion where you can enjoy the peace of rural life. Hexham and Hadrian's Wall country are about 15 minutes' drive away.
Bedrooms: 1 single, 2 double & 1 twin, 2 family rooms.
Bathrooms: 3 private, 1 public.
Bed & breakfast: £12-£14 single, £24-£28 double.
Half board: £19-£21 daily, £119-£133 weekly.
Evening meal 7pm (l.o. 7pm).
Parking for 6.

SPENNYMOOR

Co. Durham
Map ref 5C2

Booming coal and iron town from the 18th C until early in the present century when traditional industry gave way to lighter manufacturing and trading estates were built. On the moors south of the town there are fine views of the Wear Valley.

Idsley House ⚑
Listed

4 Green Lane, Spennymoor,
DL16 6HD
☎ Bishop Auckland
(0388) 814237
Spacious family guesthouse 6 miles south of Durham City on A167. Ideal for touring Dales or visiting Durham City.
Bedrooms: 1 single, 3 twin, 1 family room.
Bathrooms: 1 public.
Bed & breakfast: £10.50 single, £21 double.
Half board: £14.50 daily.
Evening meal 6pm (l.o. 8pm).
Parking for 8.

INDIVIDUAL PROPRIETORS HAVE SUPPLIED ALL DETAILS OF ACCOMMODATION. ALTHOUGH WE DO CHECK FOR ACCURACY, WE ADVISE YOU TO CONFIRM PRICES AND OTHER INFORMATION AT THE TIME OF BOOKING.

STOCKSFIELD
Northumberland
Map ref 5B2

Pretty rural village in Tyne Valley in area of good agricultural land. Bywell Hall, the home of Lord Allendale, is nearby as well as Cherryburn the birthplace of Thomas Bewick, where a Musuem dedicated to the life and works of this famous local engraver can be found.

The Dene ₥
😊😊😊
11 Cadehill Rd., Stocksfield, NE43 7PB
☎ (0661) 842025
Large country house in 2 acres of beautiful, quiet garden and woodland, 15 miles from Newcastle upon Tyne.
Bedrooms: 3 twin.
Bathrooms: 1 private, 2 public.
Bed & breakfast: £11-£15 single, £22-£30 double.
Half board: £19-£23 daily, £125-£150 weekly.
Evening meal 7pm (l.o. 7.30pm).
Parking for 3.
🛏 ⓓ ⌨ ✿ ☺ Ⓤ ᵈ 🅿 💷 📺 ❄ 🐾 SP

Wheelbirks Jersey Farm
😊😊😊
Stocksfield-on-Tyne, NE43 7HY
☎ (0661) 843378
340-acre dairy and mixed farm. Victorian farmhouse in the Tyne Valley, close to the Roman Wall country. 12 miles west of Newcastle and 8 miles east of Hexham. An evening meal can be provided on request.
Bedrooms: 2 twin.
Bathrooms: 1 public.
Bed & breakfast: max. £24 double.
Evening meal 6pm (l.o. 8pm).
Parking for 5.
Open April-October.
🛏7 ✿ Ⓤ 💷 ✂ 🅿 📺 💻 🐾 ❄ ✕ 🐕 🏠

THERE IS A SPECIAL SECTION IN THIS GUIDE LISTING ACCOMMODATION ESPECIALLY SUITABLE FOR GROUPS AND YOUNG PEOPLE.

SUNDERLAND
Tyne & Wear
Map ref 5C2

Ancient coal and shipbuilding port on Wearside, with important glassworks since the 17th C. Today's industrial complex dates from the 19th C; modern building includes the Civic Centre. North across the Wear, Monkwearmouth has a historic church with an Anglo-Saxon tower and a grand Victorian railway station preserved as a museum. Nearby are the twin resorts of Roker and Seaburn. *ℹ*

Felicitations
94 Ewesley Road, High Barnes, Sunderland, SR4 7RJ
☎ 091-522 0960
Large rooms with full central heating convenient for bus routes, town centre and Empire Theatre.
Bedrooms: 1 single, 1 double, 1 family room.
Bathrooms: 1 public.
Bed & breakfast: £8-£11 single, £12-£16 double.
Half board: £11-£15 daily, £70-£90 weekly.
Evening meal 6pm (l.o. 6.30pm).
🛏5 💷 Ⓤ 🅿 📺 🐾 ✕ 🐕 ᴰᴬᴾ

25 Park Parade
Roker, Sunderland, SR6 9LU
☎ 091-567 6642
Large terraced house opposite a park. Use of tennis courts, putting, crazy golf and bowling. 5 minutes from beach.
Bedrooms: 1 double, 1 family room.
Bathrooms: 1 public.
Half board: £9-£12 daily.
Evening meal 6pm (l.o. 7pm).
🛏2 💷 Ⓤ 🅿 📺 🐾 ✕ 🐕 ᴰᴬᴾ

TANTOBIE
Co. Durham
Map ref 5C2

See also Consett. North west Durham village. Nearby are Beamish Museum, the restored Tanfield Railway and the oldest existing railway bridge in the world, the Causey Arch.

Oak Tree Cottage ₥
Tantobie, Stanley, DH9 9RF
☎ (0207) 235445
Comfortable stone-built cottage close to Oak Tree Inn where all facilities are available, including restaurant.

Bedrooms: 2 single, 1 twin, 1 family room.
Bathrooms: 1 private, 1 public.
Bed & breakfast: £10-£13 single, £20-£26 double.
Half board: £15-£18 daily, £95-£120 weekly.
Lunch available.
Evening meal 7pm (l.o. 10.30pm).
Parking for 2.
Credit: Access, Amex.
🛏 🔥 ⌨ ✿ ☺ 💷 ✂ 🅿 💻 ♿ 🐾 ⚘ 🅿 💷 📺 ᴰᴬᴾ 🐕 SP 🍽

Oak Tree Inn ₥
😊😊😊
Tantobie, Stanley, DH9 9RF
☎ (0207) 235445
Victorian inn furnished with antiques and four-poster beds. French and English food. Near Beamish Museum, Roman Wall, Metro Centre and Durham.
Bedrooms: 1 single, 2 double & 1 twin, 1 family room.
Bathrooms: 4 private, 1 public; 1 private shower.
Bed & breakfast: £19 single, £28-£32 double.
Half board: £22-£24 daily, £125-£140 weekly.
Lunch available.
Evening meal 7pm (l.o. 10.30pm).
Parking for 10.
Credit: Access, Visa, Amex.
🛏 🔥 ⌨ ✿ ☺ 💷 ✂ 🅿 📺 💻 ♿ ⚘ 🅿 🅿 💷 📺 ᴰᴬᴾ SP 🏠 🍽

WARKWORTH
Northumberland
Map ref 5C1

A pretty village overlooked by its medieval castle. A 14th C fortified bridge across the wooded Coquet gives a superb view of 18th C terraces climbing to the castle. Fishing on the river, sandy beaches on the coast. Upstream is a curious 14th C Hermitage and in the market square is the Norman church of St. Lawrence.

Birling West Cottage
Warkworth, Morpeth, NE65 0XS
☎ Alnwick (0665) 711653
Country cottage set in half an acre of terraced gardens with stream. First cottage on the right entering Warkworth from Alnwick.

Bedrooms: 1 double & 1 twin, 1 family room.
Bathrooms: 1 public.
Bed & breakfast: £19-£20 double.
Parking for 4.
🛏 ⓓ ⌨ ✿ ☺ Ⓤ 💷 📺 📺 💻 ⚘ ❄ 🐕 ᴰᴬᴾ SP

Castlebridge House ₥
Bridge Street, Warkworth, Morpeth, NE65 0XA
☎ Alnwick (0665) 712444
Pleasant 18th C. family accommodation close to Warkworth Castle, River Coquet and seashore. Ideal centre for Northumberland tours.
Bedrooms: 1 double & 1 twin.
Bathrooms: 1 public.
Bed & breakfast: max. £18 double.
Half board: max. £60 weekly.
Evening meal 6pm (l.o. 8pm).
Credit: Visa.
🛏 ⓓ ⌨ ✿ ☺ 💷 📺 💻 ⚘ 🐕 ᴰᴬᴾ

North Cottage ₥
Listed
Birling, Warkworth, Morpeth, NE65 0XS
☎ Alnwick (0665) 711263
Attractive cottage on the outskirts of historic Warkworth.
Bedrooms: 1 single, 1 double & 1 twin, 1 family room.
Bathrooms: 1 public.
Bed & breakfast: £8.50-£9.50 single, £17-£19 double.
Parking for 8.
🛏 ⌨ 🔥 ✿ ☺ Ⓤ 💷 📺 📺 💻 ⚘ ❄ 🏠

Roxbro House
Listed
5 Castle Terrace, Warkworth, Morpeth, NE65 0UP
☎ Alnwick (0665) 711416
Small family guesthouse overlooked by historic Warkworth Castle. Half a mile from sandy beach, in a designated area of outstanding natural beauty.
Bedrooms: 1 double & 1 twin, 1 family room.
Bathrooms: 1 public; 1 private shower.
Bed & breakfast: £18-£20 double.
Parking for 3.
🛏 Ⓤ 📺 💻 ✕ 🐕

PLEASE CHECK PRICES AND OTHER DETAILS AT THE TIME OF BOOKING.

WEST WOODBURN

Northumberland
Map ref 5B2

Small hamlet on the River
Rede in rolling moorland
country.

Bay Horse Inn M
☺☺

West Woodburn, Hexham,
NE48 2RX
☎ Bellingham (0660) 70218
*On A68 between Corbridge
and Otterburn, beside stone
bridge over River Rede.*
Bedrooms: 2 twin, 3 family
rooms.
Bathrooms: 2 public;
1 private shower.
Bed & breakfast: £18-£20
single, £30-£35 double.
Half board: from £22 daily,
from £150 weekly.
Lunch available.
Evening meal 7pm (l.o.
9.30pm).
Parking for 50.
Credit: Access, Visa.

WOOLER

Northumberland
Map ref 5B1

Old greystone town,
marketplace for foresters
and hill farmers, set at the
edge of the north east
Cheviots. This makes a
good base for excursions
to Northumberland's
loveliest coastline, or for
angling and walking in the
Border lands.

Loreto Guest House
☺☺

1 Ryecroft Way, Wooler,
NE71 6BW
☎ (0668) 81350
*Family-run early Georgian
house with spacious grounds in
the lovely Cheviot village of
Wooler, central for touring and
walking.*
Bedrooms: 1 single, 2 double
& 2 twin, 2 family rooms.
Bathrooms: 2 private,
2 public.
Bed & breakfast: £11-£12
single, £22-£24 double.
Half board: £14.50-£16 daily,
£95-£102 weekly.
Evening meal 6.30pm (l.o.
7pm).
Parking for 12.

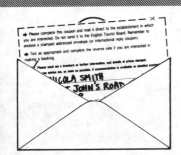

When enquiring about accommodation you may find it helpful to use the booking enquiry coupons which can be found towards the end of the guide. These should be cut out and mailed direct to the establishments in which you are interested. Remember to include your name and address and please enclose a stamped addressed envelope (or an international reply coupon if writing from outside Britain).

INFORMATION

Put Cheshire, Greater Manchester, Lancashire and Merseyside together and what have you got? The answer is the lively, hospitable and surprisingly different tourist region of the North West.

Although that may not have been the first answer that came to mind, just take a look at what makes up the North West of England.

Miles of sand and well-loved resorts to match — like Morecambe, Southport  and that veritable jewel of the north, Blackpool. Historic cities — like Chester, with its medieval buildings, Roman remains and unique shopping 'Rows'. Industrial cities — like Liverpool, now rejuvenated with art galleries, museums and visitor facilities which bear comparison with anywhere else in England.

Away from the coast and the cities you'll find scenic areas like Lancashire's Red Rose Country with the wooded Lune Valley, the solitary Forest of Bowland, the beautiful Ribble Valley and the Rossendale Way. There's the rich Cheshire Plain with its characteristic black and white, half-timbered houses. And on the edge of the Plain, suddenly, towering ridges signal the start of the wild moorlands and rugged hill country of the Peak District National Park.

Jane Noble

KNOWSLEY SAFARI PARK

FIND OUT MORE

Further information about holidays and attractions in the North West tourist region is available from:
North West Tourist Board,
The Last Drop Village, Bromley Cross, Bolton, Lancashire BL7 9PZ.
☎ (0204) 591511.

These publications are available free from the North West Tourist Board (please add 25p to cover postage and packing):

England's North West Holiday Guide

Discover England's North West (map)

WHERE TO GO, WHAT TO SEE

Port Sunlight Village
Port Sunlight, Merseyside
☎ 051-644 6466
Purpose-built village created by Lord Leverhulme at the turn of the century to house his workers. Unique setting also houses the Lady Lever Art Gallery and Interpretation/Information Centre.
Admission free.

Bridgemere Garden World
Bridgemere, Nantwich, Cheshire
CW5 7QB
☎ (093 65) 381
One of the largest garden centres in England with 2 acres of display

gardens, tropical and indoor plants. Large collection of heathers, alpines and herbs, garden shop, Egon Ronay recommended coffee shop.
Admission free.

Dunham Massey Hall
Altrincham, Greater Manchester
WA14 4SJ
☎ 061-941 1025
200-acre formal park with fallow deer. Historic house with outstanding collections of 18th C furniture, silver and portraits.
Admission charge. ▶

Lewis Textile Museum
3 Exchange Street, Blackburn,
Lancashire BB1 7AH
☎ (0254) 667130
Working examples of Hargreaves
Spinning Jenny, Kays Flying Shuttle,
Cromptons Mule, spinning wheel and
hand loom. Art Gallery.
Admission free.

Sandcastle
Promenade, South Shore, Blackpool,
Lancashire FY4 1BB
☎ (0253) 404013
Leisure pool, wave pool, giant slides,
amusements, live entertainment,
snooker, pool, nightclub, children's
playland.
Admission charge.

Paul Jones

THE WILDFOWL TRUST

The Wildfowl Trust
Martin Mere, Burscough, Nr. Ormskirk,
Lancashire L40 0TA ☎ (0704) 895181
Superb natural setting for 1,600 ducks,
geese, swans and flamingos from all
over the world. Acres of wild marshland
are home to many wild birds each
winter.
Admission charge.

Kingdom of Camelot Theme Park
Park Hall Road, Charnock Richard,
Chorley, Lancashire PR7 5LP
☎ (0257) 453044
Family theme park with over 80 rides
and attractions.
Admission charge.

Tatton Park
Knutsford, Cheshire WA16 6QN
☎ (0565) 54822
Georgian mansion with 60-acre garden
and 1,000-acre deer park. Medieval Old
Hall, 1930s farm, shop, restaurant.
Admission charge.

Lancaster Maritime Museum
Customs House, St. George's Quay,
Lancaster, Lancashire LA1 1RB
☎ (0524) 64637
Building of 1764, former Custom House
with displays illustrating 18th C trade
with West Indies and the fishing
communities of Morecambe Bay.
Admission charge.

Albert Dock
Liverpool, Merseyside L3 4AA
☎ 051-709 7373
Britain's largest grade 1 listed historic
building. Restored 4-sided dock, including
shops, wine bars, entertainment, marina
and Maritime Museum.
*Admission free, but charge for museum
entrance.*

Fletcher Moss Museum
Wilmslow Road, Didsbury, Manchester,
Greater Manchester M20 8AU
☎ 061-236 9422
History of Manchester, old maps and
views. Furniture, glass, clocks, paintings.
Admission free.

Frontierland
Marine Road, Morecambe, Lancashire
LA4 4DG ☎ (0524) 410024
Over 30 thrill rides, including Texas
Tornado and Stampede Roller Coaster,
in Wild West theme park.
Admission charge.

Knowsley Safari Park
Prescot, Merseyside L34 4AN
☎ 051-430 9009
5-mile drive through game reserves, set
in 400 acres of parkland containing
lions, tigers, elephants, rhinos, etc.
Picnic areas and children's amusement
park.
Admission charge.

Wigan Pier
Wallgate, Wigan, Greater Manchester
WN3 4EU ☎ (0942) 323666
Heritage Centre, The Way We Were
1900, world's largest steam engine,
schools centre, water buses, picnic
areas.
Admission charge.

Boat Museum
Dock Yard Road, Ellesmere Port,
Cheshire L65 4EF ☎ 051-355 5017
Over 50 historic craft, largest floating
collection in Europe. Craft workshops.
Exhibitions in restored warehouses,
19th C steam engines.
Admission charge.

MAKE A DATE FOR...

Horse racing: Grand National meeting
Aintree Racecourse, Aintree, Liverpool,
Merseyside *6 — 8 April*

World Dinghy Sailing Championships
Marine Lake, West Kirkby, Merseyside
13 — 14 May

Spring Boat Festival
Boat Museum, Ellesmere Port, Cheshire
27 — 29 May

Jane Noble

Cheshire Agricultural Show
Tatton Park, Knutsford, Cheshire
20 — 21 June

Chester Summer Music Festival
Various venues, Chester, Cheshire
14 — 22 July

Royal Lancashire Show
Astley Park, Chorley, Lancashire
28 — 30 July

Morecambe Illuminations
The Promenade, Morecambe, Lancashire
9 August-31 October

Bolton Festival
Various venues, Bolton, Lancashire
25 — 28 August

Blackpool Illuminations
The Promenade, Blackpool, Lancashire
1 September — 29 October

Tourist Information

Tourist and leisure information can be obtained from Tourist Information Centres throughout England. Details of centres in the North West region are listed below. The symbol 🛏 means that an accommodation booking service is provided. Centres marked with a ✳ are open during the summer months only. In the following pages, towns which have a Tourist Information Centre are indicated with the symbol *i* .

Altrincham
Greater Manchester 🛏
Stamford New Road
☎ 061-941 7337

Birkenhead
Merseyside
Central Library, Borough Road
☎ 051-652 6106

Blackburn
Lancashire 🛏
Town Hall
☎ (0254) 53277

Blackpool
Lancashire
1 Clifton Street 🛏
☎ (0253) 21623 & 25212

87a Coronation Street 🛏
☎ (0253) 21891

Blackpool Airport
Squires Gate Lane 🛏
☎ (0253) 43061

Bolton
Lancashire 🛏
Town Hall
☎ (0204) 22311 or (0204) 384174

Bramhall
Cheshire
13 Bramhall Lane South
☎ 061-440 8400

Burnley
Lancashire 🛏
Burnley Mechanics,
Manchester Road
☎ (0282) 30055

Charnock Richard
Lancashire 🛏
Motorway Service Area,
M6 Northbound
☎ Coppull (0257) 793773

Cheadle Hulme
Cheshire
6 Station Road
☎ 061-486 0283

Chester
Cheshire
Information Centre, Town Hall, Northgate Street 🛏
☎ (0244) 40144 or (0244) 49026 evenings and weekends.

Chester Visitor Centre,
Vicars Lane 🛏
☎ (0244) 351609

Clitheroe
Lancashire 🛏
Council Offices, Church Walk
☎ (0200) 25566

Congleton
Cheshire 🛏
Town Hall, High Street
☎ (0260) 271095

Crewe
Cheshire 🛏
Market Hall, Earle Street
☎ (0270) 583191

Fleetwood
Lancashire ✳
Marine Hall, Esplanade
☎ (039 17) 71141

Forton
Lancashire 🛏 ✳
Motorway Service Area,
M6 Northbound
☎ (0524) 792181

Hazel Grove
Cheshire
Civic Hall, 202 London Road
☎ 061-456 4195

Huyton
Merseyside
Municipal Buildings,
Archway Road
☎ 051-443 3400

Kirkby
Merseyside
Municipal Buildings,
Cherryfield Drive
☎ 051-443 4025

Knutsford
Cheshire 🛏
Council Offices, Toft Road
☎ (0565) 2611

▶

Lancaster
Lancashire 🛏
7 Dalton Square
☎ (0524) 32878

Liverpool
Merseyside
29 Lime Street 🛏
☎ 051-709 3631
Atlantic Pavilion, Albert Dock 🛏
☎ 051-708 8854

Lytham St. Annes
Lancashire
The Square,
St. Annes Road West
☎ (0253) 725610/721222

Macclesfield
Cheshire 🛏
Town Hall, Market Place
☎ (0625) 21955

Manchester
Greater Manchester
Town Hall Extension,
Lloyd Street 🛏
☎ 061-234 3157
Manchester International Airport,
Arrivals Hall 🛏
☎ 061-436 3344

Morecambe
Lancashire 🛏
Marine Road Central
☎ (0524) 414110

Nantwich
Cheshire 🛏
Council Offices, Beam Street
☎ (0270) 623914

Nelson
Lancashire
20a Scotland Road
☎ (0282) 692890

New Brighton
Merseyside 🛏
Bathing Pool, Marine Promenade
☎ 051-638 7144

Oldham
Greater Manchester 🛏
Local Studies Library,
84 Union Street
☎ 061-678 4654

Preston
Lancashire 🛏
Guild Hall, Lancaster Road
☎ (0772) 53731

Rawtenstall
Lancashire 🛏
41 — 45 Kay Street
☎ Rossendale (0706) 217777
or (0706) 226590 Saturday a.m.
only.

Rochdale
Greater Manchester
The Clock Tower, Town Hall
☎ (0706) 356592

Runcorn
Cheshire
57 — 61 Church Street
☎ (092 85) 76776/69656

Saddleworth
Greater Manchester
High Street, Upper Mill
☎ (045 77) 4093

Salford
Greater Manchester 🛏
The Crescent
☎ 061-736 3353

Sandbach
Cheshire 🛏
Motorway Service Area,
M6 Northbound
☎ (0270) 760460

Southport
Merseyside 🛏
Lord Street
☎ (0704) 33133/40404

Stockport
Cheshire
9 Princes Street
☎ 061-480 0315

Thornton Cleveleys
Lancashire ✳
Brighton Avenue
☎ Cleveleys (0253) 853378

Warrington
Cheshire
80 Sankey Street
☎ (0925) 36501

Widnes
Cheshire
Municipal Buildings, Kingsway
☎ 051-424 2061

Wigan
Greater Manchester
Trencherfield Mill, Wigan Pier
☎ (0942) 323666 or (0942)
44888 weekends only.

Entries in this regional section are listed in alphabetical order of place name, and then in alphabetical order of establishment. County names are not normally repeated in each establishment entry, but please use the full postal address when writing.

The map references refer to the colour maps towards the end of this guide. The first number is the number of the map, and it is followed by the grid reference.

The Crown Classifications are explained on pages 8 and 9, and the key to symbols is on the flap inside the back cover — keep it open for easy reference.

ASHTON-UNDER-LYNE

Gtr. Manchester
Map ref 4B1

6m E. Manchester
Now part of the borough of Tameside this old market town lies on the north bank of the River Tame. The Assheton family who owned the manor of Ashton from the 14th C are portrayed in the stained glass windows of St. Michael's Church.

Lynwood Hotel
😄

3 Richmond Street, Ashton-under-Lyne, OL6 7TX
☎ 061-330 5358
Small, comfortable, family-run hotel in quiet position. Convenient for shops, theatre, cinema, station and buses. Direct bus service to Manchester.
Bedrooms: 1 single, 1 double & 2 twin.
Bathrooms: 1 private, 1 public; 1 private shower.
Bed & breakfast: £15 single, £26-£30 double.
Parking for 4.
🏠🕯🎁 🖳 ♨ 🛏 📺 ⅢⅢ 🍴
🕷 🎿 SP

BARLEY

Lancashire
Map ref 4B1

3m NW. Nelson

Barley Green Farmhouse ⋒
😄😄

Barley, Nr. Burnley, BB12 9JU
☎ Nelson (0282) 693438

Beautiful 200-year-old house offering friendly, personal service and home-cooked food. Near the village hall in Barley. Closed over the Christmas and New Year period.
Bedrooms: 2 double & 1 twin.
Bathrooms: 1 public.
Bed & breakfast: £12.50-£15 single, £25-£30 double.
Half board: £19-£21.50 daily, £115-£130 weekly.
Evening meal 6pm (l.o. 8pm).
Parking for 6.
🛏🕯🎁 🖳 🍴 ✂ 🛏 📺 ⅢⅢ
🍴 🎿 🚗

BLACKBURN

Lancashire
Map ref 4A1

Once a thriving cotton town, and models of the old machinery may be seen in Lewis Textile Museum. Relics of the Roman occupation in Blackburn Museum. 19th C cathedral, Victorian landscaped Corporation Park. ⓘ

Rose Cottage ⋒
Listed

Longsight Road, Clayton-le-Dale, Nr. Blackburn, BB1 9EX
☎ Mellor (025 481) 3223
100-year-old cottage, on A59, at the gateway to the Ribble Valley, 5 miles from M6 junction 31.
Bedrooms: 1 twin, 1 family room.
Bathrooms: 1 public.
Bed & breakfast: £12-£15 single, £20-£25 double.
Parking for 2.
🛏 ⊙ 🖵 🕯 🖳 🍴 ⅢⅢ 🚗

THERE IS A SPECIAL SECTION IN THIS GUIDE LISTING ACCOMMODATION ESPECIALLY SUITABLE FOR GROUPS AND YOUNG PEOPLE.

BLACKPOOL

Lancashire
Map ref 4A1

See also Singleton.
Largest fun resort in the north with every entertainment including amusement parks, piers, tram-rides along the promenade, sandy beaches and the famous Tower. Among its annual events are the 'Milk Race', the Veteran Car Run and the spectacular autumn illuminations. ⓘ

Alberts, Ramsden Arms Hotel ⋒
Listed

204 Talbot Road, Blackpool, FY1 3AZ
☎ (0253) 23215
Country style public house on fringe of town centre. Adjacent to bus and railway stations and theatres, promenade and beach.
Bedrooms: 3 twin.
Bathrooms: 2 public.
Bed & breakfast: £12-£15 single, £24 double.
Parking for 10.
🛏 🔺 🕯🎁 🖳 🛏 📺 ⅢⅢ 🚗 🍴
🍴 🎿 🚗 SP 🚃

Sunray Hotel ⋒
😄😄😄

42 Knowle Avenue, Blackpool, FY2 9TQ
☎ (0253) 51937
All-round service and care at modest prices, especially in low season. British Tourist Authority commended.
Bedrooms: 3 single, 2 double & 2 twin, 2 family rooms.
Bathrooms: 9 private, 1 public.
Bed & breakfast: £16-£21 single, £32-£38 double.
Half board: £23-£30 daily.
Evening meal 5pm (l.o. 3pm).
Parking for 6.
Open January-November.
🛏 🕿 📞 🖵 🕯 🖳 🖳 🛏 📺
ⅢⅢ 🚗 🎿 OAP SP T

BOLTON-LE-SANDS

Lancashire
Map ref 5B3

5m N. Lancaster Exit 35 M6 to A65
😄😄
The village is on the main A6 trunk road with the picturesque Lancaster Canal passing through it. An ideal touring base.

Thwaite End Farm ⋒
😄😄😄

A6 Road, Bolton-le-Sands, Nr. Carnforth, LA5 9TN
☎ Carnforth (0524) 732551
20-acre beef and sheep farm. 17th C. farmhouse in an ideal area for breaking your journey to and from Scotland. Well placed for touring the Lake District and Lancashire. Self-catering cottage also available.
Bedrooms: 1 single, 1 double & 1 twin.
Bathrooms: 1 private, 2 public.
Bed & breakfast: £12-£13 single, £22-£30 double.
Parking for 4.
🕯 🖳 🛏 📺 ⅢⅢ 🚗 ✿ 🍴 🚗

BURNLEY

Lancashire
Map ref 4B1

See also Barley, Colne, Trawden.
Once the largest cotton-weaving centre in the world but now dominated by engineering. 14th C Towneley Hall has fine period rooms and the entrance hall houses an art gallery and museum. The Kay-Shuttleworth collection of lace and embroidery can be seen at Gawthorpe Hall (National Trust). ⓘ

Starkie Arms Hotel
1 Church Street, Padiham, Burnley, BB12 8HF
☎ Padiham (0282) 72075
Lovely old 16th C. coaching inn on main road, with cobbled road to one side. Ask us about the many famous guests who have stayed here.
Bedrooms: 3 double & 5 twin, 1 family room.
Bathrooms: 2 public.
Bed & breakfast: £12-£15 single, £18-£20 double.
Lunch available.
Parking for 14.
🛏 🎿 🛏 📺 🍴 🎿 🚗 🚃

BURY

Gtr. Manchester
Map ref 4B1

Birthplace of Sir Robert
Peel, Prime Minister and
founder of police force,
commemorated by statue
in Market Place.
Transport Museum
contains items connected
with steam railways.

Loe Farm Livery Stables M
⬛⬛⬛

Redisher Lane, Hawkshaw,
Bury, BL8 4HX
☎ Tottington (020 488) 3668
*19-acre livery stables. Only 5
miles from M62, M61 and
M66. All bedrooms have
private facilities, radio, T.V.
and tea/ coffee making
facilities.*
Bedrooms: 4 double & 2 twin.
Bathrooms: 6 private.
Bed & breakfast: from £15
single, from £25 double.
Half board: from £21.50
daily.
Evening meal 6pm (l.o. 8pm).
Parking for 8.

CHESTER

Cheshire
Map ref 4A2

*See also Malpas,
Tattenhall.*
Interesting Roman and
medieval walled city rich
in architectural and
archaeological treasures.
Fine timber-framed and
plaster buildings.
Shopping in the Rows
(galleried arcades
reached by steps from
the street). Grosvenor
Museum (Roman
remains), 14th C
cathedral, castle and zoo.
ℹ

Aplas Guest House M
Listed

106 Brook Street, Chester,
CH1 3DU
☎ (0244) 312401
*Family-run guesthouse offering
a warm and friendly service. 5
minutes from city centre, 2
minutes from railway station.*
Bedrooms: 1 single, 3 double
& 2 twin, 1 family room.
Bathrooms: 5 private,
1 public.
Bed & breakfast: £12-£15
single, £20-£24 double.

Eaton House M
⬛⬛

36 Eaton Road, Handbridge,
Chester, CH4 7EN
☎ (0244) 671346
*130-year-old Victorian house
with all modern facilities, in
pleasant conservation area,
near river and town centre.*
Bedrooms: 3 family rooms.
Bathrooms: 1 public.
Bed & breakfast: £20 double.
Parking for 5.

Grove Villa M

18 The Groves, Chester,
CH1 1SD
☎ (0244) 49713
*Small friendly Victorian
guesthouse on the banks of the
Dee. 5 minutes from town
centre. Honeymoon suite
available.*
Bedrooms: 1 double & 1 twin,
1 family room.
Bathrooms: 3 private,
1 public.
Bed & breakfast: £22-£25
double.
Parking for 5.

Hatton Hall M
⬛⬛

Hatton Heath, Nr. Chester,
CH3 9AP
☎ Tattenhall (0829) 70601
*250-acre dairy farm. Elegant
Georgian farmhouse within
Norman Moat, with fine
facilities. 5 miles from Chester,
1 mile off the A41.*
Bedrooms: 1 family room.
Bathrooms: 1 private.
Bed & breakfast: £18 single,
£32 double.
Parking for 5.

Holly House

41 Liverpool Road, Chester,
CH2 1AB
☎ (0244) 383484
*Peaceful, elegant, Victorian
townhouse on A5116 offering
warm welcome. Ten minutes'
walk to city centre. Hearty
breakfast, own keys.*
Bedrooms: 1 single, 2 double
& 1 twin.
Bathrooms: 1 private,
1 public; 1 private shower.
Bed & breakfast: £15-£17.50
single, £25-£30 double.
Evening meal 7pm (l.o.
7.30pm).
Parking for 4.

Malvern Guest House

21 Victoria Road, Chester,
CH2 2AX
☎ (0244) 380865
*Victorian terraced town house
comprising 2 storeys, within 8
minutes' walk of the cathedral
and adjacent to a leisure
centre.*
Bedrooms: 1 single, 1 double
& 2 twin, 2 family rooms.
Bathrooms: 2 public.
Bed & breakfast: £9-£12
single, £18-£24 double.
Half board: £12.50-£15.50
daily.
Evening meal 6pm (l.o. 5pm).

Ormonde Guest House

126 Brook Street, Chester,
CH1 3DU
☎ (0244) 28816
*This 18th C. Tudor style
building was frequented by a
former Duke of Westminster
whose horse was named
Ormonde, hence giving us our
name. We are 2 minutes from
the railway station.*
Bedrooms: 2 single, 3 double
& 5 twin, 2 family rooms.
Bathrooms: 8 private,
1 public.
Bed & breakfast: £12-£15
single, £23-£25 double.
Parking for 1.

Roslyn Guest House M
⬛⬛

8 Chester Street, Nr. Saltney,
Chester, CH4 8BJ
☎ (0244) 682306
*Traditional guesthouse offering
comfortable accommodation
and home-cooked meals. Well
placed for exploring Chester,
Liverpool, Cheshire and North
Wales.*
Bedrooms: 3 single, 3 double
& 2 twin, 2 family rooms.
Bathrooms: 2 public;
1 private shower.
Bed & breakfast: £9.50
single, £18 double.
Half board: £14-£14.50 daily,
£91.70-£94.85 weekly.
Evening meal 6.30pm (l.o.
2pm).
Parking for 6.
Credit: Access, Amex.

MAP REFERENCES
APPLY TO THE
COLOUR MAPS
TOWARDS THE END
OF THIS GUIDE.

Tickeridge House M
⬛⬛

Whitchurch Road, Milton
Green, Chester, CH3 9DS
☎ Tattenhall (0829) 70443
*Set in 3.5 acres of gardens
with beautiful views of
Bolesworth Castle. Convenient
for Peckforton, Beeston Castle
and Cheshire Workshops. 6
miles from Chester.*
Bedrooms: 1 single, 1 double,
1 family room.
Bathrooms: 2 public.
Bed & breakfast: £8.50-
£10.50 single, £17-£25 double.
Parking for 3.

CHIPPING

Lancashire
Map ref 4A1

Dairy Farm M
Listed

Goose Lane, Chipping, Nr.
Preston, PR3 2QB
☎ (099 56) 285
*300-year-old farmhouse with
oak beams and log fire. Sauna
due for completion during
1989.*
Bedrooms: 1 single, 1 double
& 2 twin.
Bathrooms: 2 private,
1 public.
Bed & breakfast: £10-£12
single, £20-£24 double.
Half board: £28-£32 daily,
£98-£120 weekly.
Evening meal 6pm (l.o. 8pm).
Parking for 8.

Hough Clough Farmhouse M
⬛⬛

Hough Clough Lane,
Chipping, PR3 2NT
☎ Chipping (099 56) 272
*Hough Clough is a traditional
stone-built Victorian farmhouse
next to Bleasdale Moors near
Chipping and Beacon Fell, in
one of the nation's first
Country Parks. Ideal for
touring both on wheel and on
foot.*
Bedrooms: 1 double & 1 twin,
2 family rooms.
Bathrooms: 4 private.
Bed & breakfast: max. £25
double.
Half board: max. £19 daily,
max. £122.50 weekly.
Evening meal 6.30pm (l.o.
7.30pm).
Parking for 5.

CHORLEY

Lancashire
Map ref 4A1

10m NW. Bolton
Despite its cotton-weaving background, Chorley has a busy market town atmosphere. Jacobean Astley Hall, set in extensive parkland, has fine furniture and long gallery with shovel-board table.

Swifts House Farm M
Listed
Bentley Lane, Heskin, Eccleston, Nr. Chorley, PR7 5PY
☎ Eccleston (0257) 451490
150-acre mixed beef and arable farm. Easy access to the M6 exit 27, 30 minutes from Southport and convenient for the Lake District, Manchester, Liverpool and Blackpool.
Bedrooms: 1 single, 1 double & 1 twin.
Bathrooms: 2 public.
Bed & breakfast: £10-£12 single, £19-£23 double.
Half board: £15-£18 daily, £100-£120 weekly.
Evening meal 6pm (l.o. 8pm).
Parking for 4.
🛪 ⌇ ⑭ 🛢 🛏 ⊡ Ⅲ ▱ ▶
✦ ❀ 🎪

CLITHEROE

Lancashire
Map ref 4A1

See also Newton-in-Bowland, Slaidburn, Whitewell.
Intriguing town with the castle, set in lovely gardens, as its chief attraction. The castle and keep crown the bold limestone rock in the centre of the town and house a museum with special features including an exhibition relating to the Salthill Geology Trail. The Edisford Recreation area with pitch and putt, picnic area and Ribblesdale Pool, and the unique Civic Hall cinema are further attractions. There is a country market on Tuesdays and Saturdays. *i*

Brooklyn M
⌂⌂⌂
32 Pimlico Road, Clitheroe, BB7 2AH
☎ (0200) 28268
Elegant Victorian town house, close to the town centre.

Bedrooms: 1 single, 3 twin.
Bathrooms: 2 private, 1 public.
Bed & breakfast: £10-£11 single, £22-£25 double.
🛪 ⌶ ⌇ ⑭ 🛏 ⊡ Ⅲ ▱ ✕
🎪

Lower Standen Farm M
⌂⌂⌂
Whalley Road, Clitheroe, BB7 1PP
☎ (0200) 24176
140-acre dairy farm. 17th C. farmhouse. Excellent for walking holidays.
Bedrooms: 1 twin, 2 family rooms.
Bathrooms: 1 public; 2 private showers.
Bed & breakfast: £10 single, £20 double.
🛪 ⌇ ⑭ 🛏 ⊡ Ⅲ ▱ 🎪

Manor House Cottage M
Listed
28 Bridge Road, Chatburn, Nr. Clitheroe, BB7 4AW
☎ (0200) 41547
In the centre of Chatburn village, just off the A59. 17th C. guesthouse.
Bedrooms: 1 single, 2 double & 1 family room.
Bathrooms: 2 public.
Bed & breakfast: £11.50-£13.50 single, £23-£27 double.
Half board: £21.50-£27 daily, £100-£150 weekly.
Evening meal 7pm.
Parking for 4.
Credit: Visa.
🛪 ⌥ ⑭ 🛢 ▯ Ⅴ 🛏 ⊡ Ⅲ ▱
🎪 ⊻ SP ⊞

COLNE

Lancashire
Map ref 4B1

Old market town with mixed industries bordering the moorland Bronte country. Nearby are the ruins of Wycoller House, featured in Charlotte Bronte's 'Jane Eyre' as Ferndean Manor.

Higher Wanless Farm M
⌂⌂⌂
Red Lane, Barrowford, Colne, BB8 7JP
☎ (0282) 865301
25-acre breeding shire horses/sheep farm. Delightful farmhouse with oak beams and log fires, tastefully furnished. Convenient for Pendle Witch, Bronte Country and Yorkshire Dales. Evening meal on request.

Bedrooms: 1 single, 1 twin, 1 family room.
Bathrooms: 2 public.
Bed & breakfast: £12.50-£16.50 single, £26-£30 double.
Half board: £18.50-£22.50 daily.
Parking for 4.
Open January-November.
🛪 3 ⌇ ⑭ ▯ 🛏 ⊡ Ⅲ ▱ ∪
✦ ✕ 🎪

CONGLETON

Cheshire
Map ref 4B2

Important cattle market and silk town on the River Dane, now concerned with general textiles. Nearby are Little Moreton Hall, a Tudor house surrounded by a moat, the Bridestones, a chambered tomb, and Mow Cop, topped by a folly. *i*

Cuttleford Farm
Listed
Astbury, Congleton, CW12 4SD
☎ (0260) 272499
135-acre mixed farm. Easy access to the M6. There are 8 golf courses within a 10-mile radius. Reduction for 3 or more nights.
Bedrooms: 2 double & 1 twin.
Bathrooms: 1 private, 1 public.
Bed & breakfast: from £11 single, from £24 double.
Parking for 3.
🛪 ⌇ ⑭ 🛏 ⊡ Ⅲ ▱ ⌖ ❀ 🎪

CREWE

Cheshire
Map ref 4A2

See also Middlewich, Nantwich.
Famous for its railway junction. The railway reached Crewe in 1837 when the Warrington-Birmingham line passed through here transforming this small market town into the first great railway town. *i*

Green Farm
Listed
Deans Lane, Balterley, Nr. Crewe, CW2 5QJ
☎ (0270) 820214
145-acre dairy and arable farm. Lovely old Cheshire farmhouse on quiet country lane off A52 Crewe/Stoke road. Within easy reach of junction 16 M6.

Bedrooms: 1 single, 1 twin, 1 family room.
Bathrooms: 1 public.
Bed & breakfast: from £10 single, from £18 double.
Parking for 3.
🛪 ⌗ ▱ ⌇ ⑭ ▯ Ⅴ 🛏 ⊡
▱ ⌗ ❀ 🎪

DUTTON

Lancashire
Map ref 4A1

Entirely surrounded by agricultural land, Dutton lies on the south-eastern side of Longridge Fell.

Smithy Farm
Huntingdonhall Lane, Dutton, Nr. Longridge, Preston, PR3 2ZT
☎ Ribchester (025 484) 250
14-acre mixed farm. Set in the beautiful Ribble Valley 20 minutes from the M6. Homely atmosphere, children half price.
Bedrooms: 1 double & 1 twin, 1 family room.
Bathrooms: 1 public.
Bed & breakfast: £8 single, £16 double.
Half board: £12 daily, £84 weekly.
Evening meal 7pm (l.o. 9.30pm).
Parking for 4.
🛪 ⑭ 🛢 ▯ Ⅴ 🛏 ⊡ ▱ ❀ 🎪

GARSTANG

Lancashire
Map ref 4A1

10m N. Preston
Garstang is in the east of the borough and is a picturesque country market town. Regarded as the gateway to the fells, it stands on the Lancaster Canal and is popular as a cruising centre. Close by are the remains of Greenhalgh Castle and the Bleasdale Circle.

Castleview M
Bonds Lane, Garstang, PR3 1ZB
☎ (099 52) 2022
Small, pleasant guesthouse close to main A6. Convenient for touring Lake District and North Lancashire.
Bedrooms: 1 single, 1 double & 3 twin.
Bathrooms: 2 public.
Bed & breakfast: from £10 single, from £20 double.
Parking for 12.
🛪 ⑭ 🛏 ⊡ ▱ 🎪

GARSTANG

Continued

Sandbriggs M
☺☺

Lancaster Road, Garstang,
Preston, PR3 1JA
☎ (099 52) 3080
*Comfortable, centrally-heated,
independent accommodation 5
minutes' walk to market and
town centre. Half an hour to
Blackpool, 1 hour to Lake
District/Yorkshire Dales.*
Bedrooms: 2 double & 1 twin.
Bathrooms: 1 private,
3 public.
Bed & breakfast: £10-£12
single, £18-£22 double.
Parking for 10.
☒♨▥UL▣▦⊡□⊿∪▸
❋☒

Stirzakers Farm M
Listed

Barnacre, Garstang,
PR3 1GE
☎ (099 52) 3335
*130-acre dairy farm. Old
stone, beamed farmhouse,
within easy reach of Lake
District, Yorkshire Dales and
coast.*
Bedrooms: 1 single, 1 double,
1 family room.
Bathrooms: 1 public.
Bed & breakfast: £9-£10
single, £18-£20 double.
Parking for 6.
☒☒▥UL◻⊡□⊿⊿
☒☒OAP

HELSBY

Cheshire
Map ref 4A2

8m NE. Chester
Residential village with its
own industries. Helsby
Hill rises to 460 feet with
fine views over the
Helsby estuary. Attractive
hilly countryside to the
south.

Spring Lodge Hotel M
172 Chester Road, Helsby,
WA6 0AR
☎ (092 82) 5959
*Friendly welcome to a
Georgian detached house in
attractive garden. Village
centre on A56, 2 miles from
M56 exit 14 and 7 miles from
Chester.*
Bedrooms: 1 single, 2 double
& 4 twin, 1 family room.
Bathrooms: 3 private,
2 public.
Bed & breakfast: £22-£35
single, £34-£45 double.
Parking for 25.
☒▥♨⊡▥UL◻ⵜ▣⊿⊡
⊿⚲∪▸✕

HEST BANK

Lancashire
Map ref 4A1

Tennessee M
☺☺

62 Coastal Road, Hest Bank,
Nr. Lancaster, LA2 6HQ
☎ (0524) 822741
*Set in a delightful country
area, on main road,
overlooking Morecambe Bay.*
Bedrooms: 2 double & 1 twin,
1 family room.
Bathrooms: 1 public.
Bed & breakfast: £17-£19
double.
Parking for 5.
Open April-October.
☒♨▥UL▣▦⊿⊡□⊿✕☒

HOLMES CHAPEL

Cheshire
Map ref 4A2

4m E. Middlewich
Large village with some
interesting 18th C
buildings, and St. Luke's
church encased in brick
hiding the 15th C original.

Tiree M
Listed

5 Middlewich Road,
Cranage, Holmes Chapel,
CW4 8HG
☎ (0477) 33716
*Modern house set in open
country 3 miles from the M6
junction 18 and close to the
A50, 2 miles north of Holmes
Chapel.*
Bedrooms: 1 single, 1 twin,
1 family room.
Bathrooms: 1 public.
Bed & breakfast: £12 single,
£22 double.
Parking for 4.
☒☒⊡♨▥⚱▣□⊿✕
☒

**INDIVIDUAL
PROPRIETORS HAVE
SUPPLIED ALL
DETAILS OF
ACCOMMODATION.
ALTHOUGH WE DO
CHECK FOR
ACCURACY, WE
ADVISE YOU TO
CONFIRM PRICES
AND OTHER
INFORMATION AT
THE TIME OF
BOOKING.**

HORNBY

Lancashire
Map ref 5B3

The most notable feature
of this village in the Lune
Valley is the Norman
castle, whose Eagle
Tower was added by Sir
Edward Stanley, who
successfully led the
Lancashire men-at-arms
against the Scots at the
Battle of Flodden Field.

Lane Head M
☺☺☺

Millhouses, Wray, Nr.
Hornby, LA2 8NF
☎ (052 42) 21148
*Lane Head dates back to the
1700s and has been extensively
renovated to a high standard.
An ideal base for touring the
Lake District, Yorkshire Dales
and Trough of Bowland.*
Bedrooms: 1 double & 2 twin,
1 family room.
Bathrooms: 4 private.
Bed & breakfast: £19-£25
single, £28-£35 double.
Half board: from £25 daily,
from £175 weekly.
Lunch available.
Evening meal 7pm (l.o.
9.30pm).
Parking for 19.
☒♨4⊡▣⚱▣⊿⚲∪▸✕❋☒OAP
☒▦⊡

HYDE

Gtr. Manchester
Map ref 4B2

Needhams Farm M
☺☺☺

Uplands Road, Werneth
Low, Gee Cross, Nr. Hyde,
Cheshire SK14 3AQ
☎ 061-368 4610
*30-acre beef and suckling cows
farm. 500-year-old farmhouse
with exposed beams in all
rooms and an open fire in
dining/bar room. Surrounded
by excellent views. Well placed
for Manchester and airport.*
Bedrooms: 1 single, 2 double
& 1 twin, 1 family room.
Bathrooms: 3 private,
1 public.
Bed & breakfast: £10-£12
single, £20-£24 double.
Half board: £15-£20 daily,
£100-£130 weekly.
Lunch available.
Evening meal 7pm (l.o.
9.30pm).
Parking for 6.
☒▥⚿▤⊡♨⚱▣⊿✕
⊿⊡□⊿⊿∪▸❋☒☒OAP
☒☒▦

Shire Cottage M
☺☺☺

Benches Lane, Chisworth,
Broadbottom, Hyde,
Cheshire SK14 6RY
☎ 061-427 2377 & Glossop
(045 74) 66536
*180-acre mixed farm. On the
A626 Stockport to Glossop
road, close to the Peak
District, Buxton, Derwent Dam
and Kinder Scout. 20 minutes
from the airport, 16 miles from
Manchester city centre.
Swimming, horse riding, fishing
and boating nearby.*
Bedrooms: 1 single, 1 double,
1 family room.
Bathrooms: 1 private,
1 public.
Bed & breakfast: £12-£16
single, £24-£30 double.
Half board: £18-£21 daily,
£120-£140 weekly.
Evening meal 6pm (l.o. 7pm).
Parking for 7.
☒⚿⊡▥UL▣⊿⊡□
⊿⚲❋☒OAP☒SP

KNOWSLEY

Merseyside
Map ref 4A2

7m NE Liverpool

Knowsley Cottage Guest
House M
☺☺☺

Knowsley Lane, Knowsley
Village, Prescot, Liverpool,
L34 7HF
☎ 051-548 6621
*Large rambling cottage of
historic interest in 2 acres of
secluded gardens and
woodland. 3 minutes from
Knowsley Safari Park and
motorway system, 8 miles from
Liverpool city centre and
Albert Dock complex.*
Bedrooms: 4 single, 1 double.
Bathrooms: 2 public.
Bed & breakfast: from £14
single, from £22 double.
Parking for 7.
☒⚱▥UL▣⚱⚲⊿⊡▥
⊿ⵜ∪▸❋☒OAP▦⊡

**GROUPS, CONSORTIA
AND AGENCIES
SPECIALISING
IN FARM AND
COUNTRY HOLIDAYS
ARE LISTED IN A
SPECIAL SECTION
OF THIS GUIDE.**

KNUTSFORD

Cheshire
Map ref 4A2

6m W. Wilmslow
Derives its name from
Canute, King of the
Danes, said to have
forded the local stream.
Ancient and colourful May
Day celebrations. Nearby
is the Georgian mansion
of Tatton Park. ℹ

Longview Hotel ♨
😀😀

Manchester Road,
Knutsford, WA16 0LX
☎ (0565) 2119 Telex 61556
*A family-run hotel close to the
M6 and M56. Convenient for
business in the North West and
Manchester Airport. Closed
over the Christmas period.*
Bedrooms: 6 single, 8 double
& 9 twin, 1 family room.
Bathrooms: 12 private,
2 public; 6 private showers.
Bed & breakfast: £19-£33
single, £30-£39 double.
Half board: £28-£42 daily.
Evening meal 7pm (l.o.
8.15pm).
Parking for 17.
😀🛗🖵🗢🎨🎍📺⊞🛄

Toft Dairy Farm Guest House ♨
[Listed]

Toft Road, Knutsford,
WA16 9EH
☎ (0565) 3470 Telex 667441
*A delightful Cheshire cottage
style farmhouse on the main
A50. Close to the M6 and
three-quarters of a mile outside
Knutsford. Non-smokers
welcomed.*
Bedrooms: 2 single, 2 double
& 1 twin, 1 family room.
Bathrooms: 1 public.
Bed & breakfast: from £14
single, from £24 double.
Parking for 20.
😀10🖴🛄🎨✂📺⊞❄
🎍🎍🏠

**THERE IS A SPECIAL
SECTION IN THIS
GUIDE LISTING
ACCOMMODATION
ESPECIALLY
SUITABLE FOR
GROUPS AND
YOUNG PEOPLE.**

LANCASTER

Lancashire
Map ref 5B8

*See also Garstang,
Hornby.*
Interesting old county
town on the River Lune
with history dating back
to Roman times. Norman
castle, St. Mary's Church,
Customs House, Town
Hall (Regimental Museum
and Lancaster Museum). ℹ

Edenbreck House ♨
😀😀😀

Sunnyside Lane, Lancaster,
LA1 5ED
☎ (0524) 32464
*Large detached residence in
rural area, yet convenient for
town centre and rail station.
All rooms en-suite, with jacuzzi
available.*
Bedrooms: 2 double & 2 twin,
1 family room.
Bathrooms: 5 private.
Bed & breakfast: £25-£30
double.
Parking for 6.
😀🛗🖵🗢🛄🎨📺⊞
🏠❄🎍

Elsinore House ♨
😀😀

76 Scotforth Road, Lancaster,
LA1 4SF
☎ (0524) 65088
*Large detached house on
outskirts of city, adjacent A6, 3
miles north of M6 junction 33.*
Bedrooms: 2 double & 1 twin.
Bathrooms: 1 public;
1 private shower.
Bed & breakfast: £18-£21
double.
Parking for 3.
😀11🗢🛄🎨🎍📺⊞
🏠🎍

The Old Mill House

Waggon Rd., Lower
Dolphinholme, Nr.
Lancaster, LA2 9AX
☎ Forton (0524) 791855
*17th C mill house with extensive
landscaped gardens on River
Wyre. Private woodland and
ponds, adjacent to Forest of
Bowland. Five minutes from
junction 33 of M6.*
Bedrooms: 1 double & 1 twin,
1 family room.
Bathrooms: 1 public;
1 private shower.
Bed & breakfast: max. £17.50
single, from £25 double.
Half board: £17.50-£20 daily,
£110.25-£126 weekly.
Evening meal 7pm (l.o. 9pm).
Parking for 5.
😀🅱🗢🛄🎨📺⊞🏠❄
🎍SP🎍

LIVERPOOL

Merseyside
Map ref 4A2

Shipping and the sugar
and slave trades
transformed Liverpool
into a major port in the
18th C. Landmarks
include 2 cathedrals
(Anglican and Roman
Catholic), Town Hall,
Walker Art Gallery,
Merseyside Maritime
Museum. Excellent
shopping centre,
entertainment and sports
facilities (Aintree
Racecourse). Speke Hall
(National Trust). ℹ

Anna's

65 Dudlow Lane,
Calderstones, Liverpool,
L18 2EY
☎ 051-722 3708
*Large family house with
friendly atmosphere, in select
residential area close to all
amenities. Direct transport
routes to city centre. 1 mile
from end of M62 motorway.*
Bedrooms: 1 double & 2 twin,
1 family room.
Bathrooms: 1 public.
Bed & breakfast: £10-£11.50
single, £22-£25 double.
Evening meal 6pm (l.o.
midday).
Parking for 6.
😀🗢🛄🎨📺⊞🏠
🎍

LONGRIDGE

Lancashire
Map ref 4A1

Exit 32 M6
Comprises the parishes
of Alston and Dilworth
and serves as the
shopping and social
centre for the
surrounding farming
districts.

Carrside Farm

Chipping, Longridge,
PR2 2TS
☎ (099 56) 590
*150-acre dairy farm. Family-
run dairy farm within walking
distance of the quaint village of
Chipping, in the Forest of
Bowland. Splendid views.
Convienient for coast and Lake
District. 20 minutes from the
motorway.*
Bedrooms: 1 double & 1 twin,
1 family room.
Bathrooms: 1 private,
1 public.

Bed & breakfast: £10-£16
single, £18-£25 double.
Parking for 6.
Open March-October.
😀3🐾🗢🛄🎨📺⊞🏠🎍

MACCLESFIELD

Cheshire
Map ref 4B2

See also Wincle.
Former silk-
manufacturing town with
cobbled streets and
picturesque cottages
overlooking Bollin Valley.
West Park Museum and
Art Gallery and
Gawsworth Hall are
places of interest. ℹ

Barnswood Farm

Rushton Spencer,
Macclesfield, SK11 0RA
☎ Rushton Spencer
(0260) 226261
*100-acre dairy farm. All rooms
have lovely views of the
Rudyard Lake. Alton Towers,
the Peak District and the
potteries are all within a 15-
mile radius.*
Bedrooms: 1 single, 2 double,
1 family room.
Bathrooms: 1 public.
Bed & breakfast: max. £10
single, max. £18 double.
Parking for 5.
😀🐾🗢🛄🎨📺⊞🎍🎍

Sandpit Farm ♨
[Listed]

Messuage Lane, Marton,
Macclesfield, SK11 9HS
☎ (026 04) 254 From April
1989 (0260) 224254
*210-acre arable farm. Hot and
cold water in twin and double
rooms. Convenient for stately
homes and National Trust
properties. Easy access to the
Peak District, Chester and
Manchester Airport. 4 miles
north of Congleton and 1 mile
west of the A34.*
Bedrooms: 1 single, 1 double
& 1 twin.
Bathrooms: 1 public.
Bed & breakfast: from £10
single, from £20 double.
Parking for 4.
😀5🖴🗢🛄🎨📺⊞🏠🎍
🎯

MALPAS

Cheshire
Map ref 4A2

Bell Farm ♨
😀

Tushingham, Whitchurch,
Shropshire SY13 4QS
☎ Whitchurch (0948) 2074
Continued ▶

MALPAS

Continued

112-acre dairy farm. 200-year-old farmhouse 100 yards off the A41. Most rooms have genuine oak beams.
Bedrooms: 2 double, 1 family room.
Bathrooms: 1 public.
Bed & breakfast: from £8.50 single, from £17 double.
Half board: from £13 daily, from £89 weekly.
Evening meal 6.30pm (l.o. 4pm).
Parking for 6.

Millhey Farm M

Barton, Malpas, SY14 7HY
☎ (082 925) 431
160-acre mixed beef farm. Typical, lovely Cheshire black and white part-timbered farmhouse in conservation area, 9 miles from Chester, close to Welsh Border country. On A534, just off A41. Evening meal on request.
Bedrooms: 1 double & 1 twin, 1 family room.
Bathrooms: 1 public.
Bed & breakfast: £8 single, £16 double.
Parking for 2.

Red Lion Hotel

1 Old Hall Street, Malpas, SY14 8NE
☎ Whitchurch (0948) 860368
Old coaching inn in the centre of Malpas, with old oak panelling and Jacobean style staircase. Originally built around 14th C. but modified through time.
Bedrooms: 2 single, 2 double & 1 twin.
Bathrooms: 5 private, 1 public.
Bed & breakfast: £16.95-£18.95 single, £32.95-£34.95 double.
Half board: £22.95-£24.95 daily, £138-£148 weekly.
Lunch available.
Evening meal 7.15pm (l.o. 9.30pm).
Parking for 43.

THE SYMBOLS ARE EXPLAINED ON THE FLAP INSIDE THE BACK COVER.

Tilston Lodge

Tilston, Nr. Malpas, SY14 7DR
☎ (082 98) 223
20-acre mixed farm. Large Victorian farmhouse in landscaped gardens in rural South Cheshire. 13 miles south of Chester. Many tourist attractions in the area. Lunch and evening meal served on request.
Bedrooms: 1 single, 1 double & 1 twin, 2 family rooms.
Bathrooms: 1 private, 1 public.
Bed & breakfast: £10-£12 single, £20-£24 double.
Half board: £15-£18 daily, £95-£100 weekly.
Lunch available.
Evening meal 6.30pm (l.o. 9.30pm).
Parking for 12.

MANCHESTER

Gtr. Manchester

See Ashton-under-Lyne, Bury, Hyde.

MIDDLEWICH

Cheshire
Map ref 4A2

Exit 18 M6
Old Cheshire salt town thriving on an industry begun in Roman times. Stone age tools and weapons and Roman pottery recently found in the area are on display in the town. Was one of the last outposts of bear-baiting in the country.

Forge Mill Farm M

Warmingham, Middlewich, CW10 OHQ
☎ Warmingham (027 077) 204
140-acre beef and sheep farm. Spacious country house in peaceful location. Friendly welcome, comfort and hospitality assured. Good position for Manchester Airport and touring the North West. Close to exits 17 and 18 on the M6.
Bedrooms: 1 double & 1 twin.
Bathrooms: 1 public.
Bed & breakfast: £12.50-£14 single, £25-£28 double.
Parking for 9.

NANTWICH

Cheshire
Map ref 4A2

Pleasant old market town on the River Weaver made prosperous in Roman times by salt springs. Fire destroyed the town in 1583 and many fine buildings were rebuilt in Elizabethan style. ℹ

Burland Farm M

Wrexham Road, Burland, Nr. Nantwich, CW5 8ND
☎ Faddiley (027 074) 210
205-acre dairy and wheat farm. Beautiful Victorian farmhouse with comfortable rooms and period furnishings. Country cooking with home-made bread and local produce. Meals provided with pleasure.
Bedrooms: 2 double & 1 twin.
Bathrooms: 3 private, 1 public.
Bed & breakfast: £15-£20 single, £30-£35 double.
Half board: £22.50-£30 daily, £137-£182 weekly.
Evening meal 7pm.
Parking for 5.

Poole Bank Farm

Poole, Nantwich, CW5 6AL
☎ (0270) 625169
240-acre dairy farm. 17th C. timbered farmhouse in delightful Cheshire countryside, close to the historic town of Nantwich.
Bedrooms: 1 twin, 1 family room.
Bathrooms: 2 public.
Bed & breakfast: £11 single, £22 double.
Parking for 10.
Open April-October.

Stoke Grange Farm

Chester Road, Nantwich, CW5 6BT
☎ (0270) 625525
120-acre dairy farm. Modern and comfortable farmhouse with balcony views of canal, just off the A51 between Nantwich and Chester.
Bedrooms: 1 double & 1 twin, 1 family room.
Bathrooms: 2 public.
Bed & breakfast: £12.50-£17 single, £20-£30 double.
Parking for 6.

NELSON

Lancashire
Map ref 4B1

See also Barley, Colne, Trawden.

Lovett House

6 Howard St., Whitefield, Nelson, BB9 7SZ
☎ (0282) 697352
Victorian terraced house in quiet location within 400 metres of town centre, M65, park, bowling green and canal. Pleasant, friendly accommodation.
Bedrooms: 1 double & 1 twin.
Bathrooms: 1 public.
Bed & breakfast: max. £9.95 single, max. £18 double.
Half board: max. £13.50 daily, max. £87.50 weekly.
Evening meal 6pm (l.o. 11pm).

NEWTON-IN-BOWLAND

Lancashire
Map ref 4A1

Parker's Arms Hotel M

Newton-in-Bowland, Clitheroe, BB7 3DY
☎ Slaidburn (020 06) 236
Country inn in the delightful Forest of Bowland, with accent on food.
Bedrooms: 1 double & 1 twin, 1 family room.
Bathrooms: 1 public.
Bed & breakfast: from £16 single, from £30 double.
Lunch available.
Evening meal 7pm (l.o. 10pm).
Parking for 40.

Salisbury Hall Farm & Cottage

Salisbury Hall Farm, Newton-in-Bowland, Clitheroe, BB7 3DZ
☎ Slaidburn (020 06) 259
90-acre cattle-rearing and sheep farm. In the centre of the village in the picturesque Hodder Valley and Forest of Bowland. Self-catering flat for 4 people also available.
Bedrooms: 1 double & 1 twin, 1 family room.
Bathrooms: 2 public.
Bed & breakfast: £10 single, £20 double.
Half board: from £16 daily.
Continued ▶

NEWTON-IN BOWLAND

Continued

Evening meal 6pm (l.o. 7pm).
Parking for 3.
Open March-October.

NORTHWICH

Cheshire
Map ref 4A2

An important salt-producing town since Roman times, Northwich has been replanned with a modern shopping centre and a number of black and white buildings. Unique Anderton boat-lift on northern outskirts of town.

Springfield Guest House **M**
Listed

Chester Road, Oakmere, Northwich, CW8 2HB
☎ Sandiway (0606) 882538
Family guesthouse erected in 1863. On A556 close to Delamere Forest, Sandstone Trail and Oulton Park Racetrack. Manchester Airport 25 minutes' drive.
Bedrooms: 3 single, 2 double & 1 twin, 1 family room.
Bathrooms: 2 private, 1 public.
Bed & breakfast: £14.50 single, £23 double.
Half board: £19.50 daily, £136 weekly.
Evening meal 6pm (l.o. 8pm).
Parking for 10.

Wincham Hall **M**
☺☺☺

Hall Lane, Wincham, Northwich, CW9 6DG
☎ (0606) 43453
Family-run, country hotel in pleasant surroundings. Personal attention and friendly atmosphere.
Bedrooms: 2 single, 2 double & 5 twin, 1 family room.
Bathrooms: 5 private, 4 public.
Bed & breakfast: £15-£30 single, £24-£40 double.
Half board: £20-£35 daily, £140-£160 weekly.
Lunch available.
Evening meal 5.30pm (l.o. 8.30pm).
Parking for 200.
Credit: Access, Visa.

OLDHAM

Gtr. Manchester
Map ref 4B1

Large important textile town boosted in 19th C by Arkwright's spinning-frame and Watt's steam engine. Outstanding watercolours in Art Gallery and impressive neo-classical Town Hall.
i

Globe Farm Guest House
Listed

Huddersfield Road, Delph, Nr. Oldham, OL3 5LU
☎ Saddleworth (045 77) 3040
18-acre mixed farm. Quarter of a mile from the Pennine Way and high walking country. Bed and breakfast accommodation with independent hostel and camping site.
Bedrooms: 1 double, 1 family room.
Bathrooms: 1 public.
Bed & breakfast: £10 single, £20 double.
Half board: max. £14 daily, max. £95 weekly.
Evening meal 6pm (l.o. 9.30pm).
Parking for 7.

ORMSKIRK

Lancashire
Map ref 4A1

7m SE. Southport Market town with interesting Parish Church of St. Peter and St. Paul containing bells brought from nearby Burscough Priory after its dissolution; half-timbered medieval manor houses, museum of Lancashire folk life and Martinmere Wildfowl Centre.

Martin Inn **M**
☺☺☺

Martin Lane, Burscough, Nr. Ormskirk, L40 0RT
☎ (0704) 892302
Country inn in the heart of west Lancashire, 5 minutes from Martin Mere Wildfowl Trust. Southport is 15 minutes away.
Bedrooms: 3 single, 4 double & 3 twin.
Bathrooms: 10 private.
Bed & breakfast: £15-£20 single, £30-£40 double.
Half board: £20.45-£24 daily, £143-£168 weekly.

Lunch available.
Evening meal 6pm (l.o. 10pm).
Parking for 150.
Credit: Access, Visa, Amex.

PENDLE

Lancashire

See Barley, Colne.

PRESTON

Lancashire
Map ref 4A1

See also Chipping, Garstang, Longridge, St. Michael's on Wyre. Scene of decisive Royalist defeat by Cromwell in the Civil War and later of riots in the Industrial Revolution. Local history exhibited in Harris Museum. *i*

Ashfield House Hotel **M**
☺☺

Lea Road, Lea, Preston, PR2 1TP
☎ (0772) 720201
Detached property set in 2 acres of grounds. 3 miles from the M6 and M55, 7 minutes' drive from Preston centre.
Bedrooms: 2 double & 1 twin.
Bathrooms: 1 public.
Bed & breakfast: £17-£25 single, £34-£39 double.
Half board: £22-£30 daily, £154-£238 weekly.
Lunch available.
Evening meal 6pm (l.o. 8pm).
Parking for 8.
Credit: Access, Visa.

Olde Duncombe House **M**
Listed

Garstang Road, Bilsborrow, Nr. Preston, PR3 0RE
☎ (0995) 40336
In the beautiful Ribble Valley next to the Lancaster Canal, convenient for canal boat enthusiasts. 4 miles north of the M6 junction 32.
Bedrooms: 2 single, 3 double & 1 twin, 2 family rooms.
Bathrooms: 2 private, 2 public.
Bed & breakfast: £15-£17.50 single, £25 double.
Parking for 12.
Credit: Access, Visa.

RIBBLE VALLEY

See Clitheroe, Newton-in-Bowland, Slaidburn, Whitewell.

ROCHDALE

Gtr. Manchester
Map ref 4B1

Old Pennine mill town made prosperous by wool and later cotton-spinning, famous for the Co-operative Movement started in 1844 by a group of Rochdale working men. Birthplace of John Bright (Corn Law opponent) and more recently Gracie Fields. Roman and Bronze Age antiquities in Museum.

Leaches Farm **M**
Listed

Ashworth Valley, Rochdale, OL11 5UN
☎ (0706) 41116 & 228520
140-acre stockrearing hill farm. 18th C. Pennine hill farmhouse with panoramic views and moorland walks. 10 minutes from the M62/M66.
Bedrooms: 1 single, 1 double & 1 twin.
Bathrooms: 1 public.
Bed & breakfast: £10-£12.50 single.
Parking for 4.

ST MICHAEL'S ON WYRE

Lancashire
Map ref 4A1

4m SW. Garstang Village near Blackpool with interesting 13th C Church of St. Michael containing medieval stained glass window depicting sheep shearing, and clock tower bell made in 1548.

Compton House

Garstang Road, St. Michael's on Wyre, Nr. Preston, PR3 0TE
☎ (099 58) 378
Near M6 and 40 minutes from Lake District. Well-furnished country house in own grounds in a picturesque village. Fishing in the Wyre. Antique restoration/reproduction of furniture undertaken on the premises.
Bedrooms: 1 single, 1 double & 2 twin.

Continued ▶

ST MICHAEL'S ON WYRE

Continued

Bathrooms: 2 public.
Bed & breakfast: from £10 single, from £20 double.
Parking for 6.

SALE

Gtr. Manchester
Map ref 4A2

Residential district of Manchester which grew up as a result of the opening of the railway between Altrincham and Manchester in 1849.

Cornerstones ♨

230 Washway Road, Sale, M33 4RA
☎ 061-962 6909
Built at the turn of the century, set in a garden with beautiful mature beech trees. Tastefully decorated yet homely. Central for Sale and Manchester.
Bedrooms: 2 single, 1 double & 2 twin.
Bathrooms: 1 public; 3 private showers.
Bed & breakfast: max. £15 single, max. £25 double.
Half board: from £21 daily.
Parking for 6.

SANDBACH

Cheshire

See Middlewich.

SINGLETON

Lancashire
Map ref 4A1

Ancient parish dating from 1175, mentioned in Domesday Book. Chapel and day school dating back to 1865. Mainly rural area to the north of St. Anne's.

Old Castle Farm ♨

Garstang Road, Singleton, Nr. Blackpool, FY6 8ND
☎ (0253) 883839
Take junction 3 off M55, follow Fleetwood sign to first traffic lights. Turn right, travel 200 yards on A586 to bungalow.
Bedrooms: 1 double & 1 twin, 1 family room.
Bathrooms: 1 public.
Bed & breakfast: £10-£12 single, £18-£20 double.

Half board: £12.50-£14.50 daily, £84-£86 weekly.
Parking for 20.
Open April-October.

SLAIDBURN

Lancashire
Map ref 4A1

7m NNW. Clitheroe
Picturesque greystone village set in moorland region of the Forest of Bowland, with 13th C church, old grammar school, village green and war memorial.

Gold Hill Country House Hotel ♨

Woodhouse Lane, Slaidburn, Clitheroe, BB7 3AH
☎ (020 06) 202
Family-run 16th C. country house with log fires, minstrels gallery and accent on cooking. Set in 150 acres with breathtaking views and sporting rights. 1 mile from Slaidburn. Liquor licence applied for.
Bedrooms: 3 double & 1 twin, 2 family rooms.
Bathrooms: 5 private, 1 public.
Bed & breakfast: from £15 single, from £30 double.
Half board: from £20.50 daily, from £145 weekly.
Lunch available.
Evening meal 7pm.
Parking for 20.
Credit: Access, Visa.

SOUTHPORT

Merseyside
Map ref 4A1

Pleasant resort noted for its gardens, long sandy beach and many golf courses, particularly Royal Birkdale. Southport Flower Show is an annual event. Lord Street is a tree-lined boulevard with fine shops. Atkinson Art Gallery and Steamport Transport Museum are attractions. ℹ

Atlantic Hotel ♨

17 Bath Street, Southport, PR9 0QT
☎ (0704) 30344
Centrally situated close to all entertainments and Lord Street shopping area. Homely atmosphere and home cooking. Comfortably furnished. 24-hour access.

Bedrooms: 4 double & 4 twin, 2 family rooms.
Bathrooms: 3 private, 2 public.
Bed & breakfast: £10-£14 single, £20-£26 double.
Evening meal 5.30pm (l.o. 6.30pm).
Parking for 6.

TATTENHALL

Cheshire
Map ref 4A2

7m SE. Chester

The Pheasant Inn ♨

Burwardsley, Nr. Tattenhall, CH3 9PF
☎ Tattenhall (0829) 70434
300 half-timber and sandstone construction, nestling on the top of the Peckforton Hills. Guest rooms in delightfully converted barn affording pleasant view to Chester.
Bedrooms: 4 double & 2 twin.
Bathrooms: 6 private.
Bed & breakfast: £20-£30 single, £35-£40 double.
Half board: £28-£38 daily, max. £200 weekly.
Lunch available.
Evening meal 7.30pm (l.o. 10pm).
Parking for 60.
Credit: Access, Visa, Diners, Amex.

TRAWDEN

Lancashire
Map ref 4B1

2m SE. Colne

Will o'th Moor Farm

Burnley Road, Trawden, Nr. Colne, BB8 8PW
☎ Colne (0282) 864955
1-acre farm. Homely establishment on the edge of Bronte country with superb views. Well-behaved pets accepted. Non-smokers only. 15 minutes from the M65.
Bedrooms: 1 double.
Bathrooms: 1 private.
Bed & breakfast: £20-£25 double.
Half board: £15-£17 daily.
Evening meal 6pm.
Parking for 6.
Open April-December.

WARRINGTON

Cheshire

See Helsby.

WHITEWELL

Lancashire
Map ref 4A1

Locally known as "Little Switzerland" for the beauty of the wooded valley of the River Hodder.

Inn at Whitewell ♨

Forest of Bowland, Whitewell, Nr. Clitheroe, BB7 3AT
☎ Dunsop Bridge (020 08) 222
Property dating back in part to 14th C. in beautiful river setting. Furnished with genuine antiques. Log fires.
Bedrooms: 6 double & 4 twin.
Bathrooms: 6 private, 2 public.
Bed & breakfast: £28-£32 single, £39-£43 double.
Half board: £34-£52 daily.
Lunch available.
Evening meal 7.30pm (l.o. 9.30pm).
Parking for 50.
Credit: Access, Visa, Diners, Amex.

WINCLE

Cheshire
Map ref 4B2

5m SE. Macclesfield
The sign on the Ship Inn at this remote hamlet high up in the Peak District depicts the 'Nimrod', the vessel in which the local Sir Philip Brocklehurst accompanied Shackleton to the Antarctic.

Fourways Diner Motel ♨

Cleulow Cross, Wincle, Nr. Macclesfield, SK11 0QU
☎ (0260) 227228
Small family-run motel and licensed restaurant with panoramic views, in the Peak National Park overlooking Dane Valley and Roaches.
Bedrooms: 2 double & 2 twin, 3 family rooms.
Bathrooms: 7 private.
Bed & breakfast: £20-£24 single, £30-£36 double.
Half board: £26-£30 daily.
Lunch available.
Evening meal 5.50pm (l.o. 8pm).
Parking for 40.
Credit: Access, Visa.

THE LITTLE MILL INN Rowarth, Via Marple Bridge
Telephone 0663 43178

DERBYSHIRE BELLE Pullman Hotel

Original 1932 Pullman carriage has now been converted
into three double en suite rooms. All wood panelling and
brass fixtures retained. Rowarth is a little village set in the
beautiful foothills of the Peak District with wild trout
stream, horse riding and clay pigeon shooting available.
We also have 2 self catering holiday cottages.

Carvery Restaurant

ETB ♔ ♔ ♔

**Higher Burwardsley,
Tattenhall, Cheshire
Telephone: (0829) 70434**

The Pheasant is a three hundred year old Inn,
nestling on the top of the Peckforton Hills just
10 miles from Chester. All bedrooms have
central heating, colour TV, radio/alarm and
en suite facilities plus panoramic views over
the Cheshire plain. Bistro and bar snack menu
available 7 days. Fully licensed. Large car
park. An ideal centre for touring Cheshire.
Under personal management.

When requesting brochures or further information from advertisers in this guide, you may
find it helpful to use the advertisement
enquiry coupons which can be found
towards the end of the guide. These should be cut out
and mailed direct to the companies in which you are
interested. Remember to include your name and address
and enclose a stamped and addressed envelope or
stamps if requested by the advertiser.

P L E A S E   N O T E
Individual establishments who have a display
advertisement have a line listing under the
appropriate town heading

Yorkshire & Humberside

The three parts of Yorkshire — North, South and West — join with Humberside to make up this tourist region which has come to the fore in recent years thanks to the 'box'.

'Emmerdale Farm' — filmed in Yorkshire; 'Last of the Summer Wine' (and, more recently, 'First of the Summer Wine') — filmed in Yorkshire; 'All Creatures Great and Small' — filmed in Yorkshire in what has now come to be known as 'Herriot Country'. But even before TV, Yorkshire was brought to the fore by just three girls. Inspired by the

NATIONAL RAILWAY MUSEUM, YORK

wild and windy moors, Charlotte, Emily and Anne Brontë wrote their powerful novels. And the visitor can enjoy the same spirit of Yorkshire — in the North York Moors National Park, a walker's paradise; and in the western Yorkshire Dales National Park, where no two dales are the same.

But the region is not just 'big country'. There are the popular resorts of Scarborough, Whitby, Filey and Bridlington; the old industrial cities of Sheffield, Bradford, Halifax and Leeds; and the treasure house of York, a medieval city and a Roman site, with its Minster, city walls, cobbled streets and imaginative museums.

FIND OUT MORE

Further information about holidays and attractions in the Yorkshire & Humberside tourist region is available from: **Yorkshire & Humberside Tourist Board**, 312 Tadcaster Road, York, North Yorkshire YO2 2HF.
☎ (0904) 707961.
Please contact the board for details of publications available.

WHERE TO GO, WHAT TO SEE

Abbeydale Industrial Hamlet
Abbeydale Road South, Sheffield,
S. Yorkshire S7 2QW
☎ (0742) 367731
Late 18th/early 19th C crucible steel and scythe works. Four water wheels, worker's cottage, manager's house and office, museum.
Admission charge.

Castle Howard
Malton, N. Yorkshire YO6 7BZ
☎ (065 384) 333
Paintings, furniture, porcelain, original 18th–20th C period costume, rose gardens.
Admission charge.

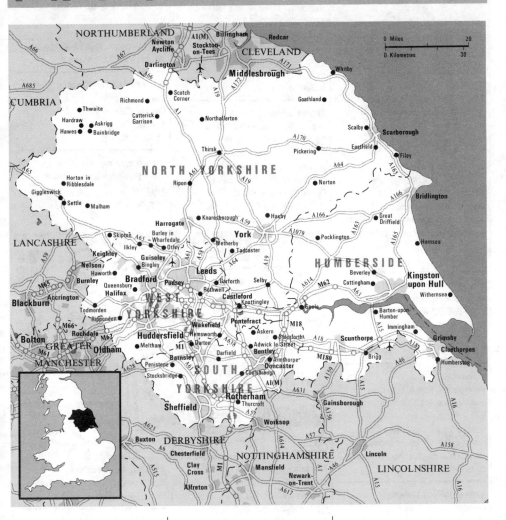

**Cusworth Hall Museum
of South Yorkshire Life**
Cusworth Lane, Doncaster, S. Yorkshire
DN5 7TU ☎ (0302) 782342
Georgian mansion in landscaped park,
containing Museum of South Yorkshire
Life.
Admission free.

Fountains Abbey
Ripon, N. Yorkshire HG4 3DZ
☎ (076 586) 333
Largest monastic ruin in Britain, founded
by Cistercian monks in 1132. Landscaped garden laid out in 1720 – 40,
with lake, formal water-garden and
temples. Deer park.
Admission charge.

Harewood House
Harewood, W. Yorkshire LS17 9LQ
☎ (0532) 886225
18th C Carr/Adam house, with gardens
landscaped by 'Capability' Brown. Fine
Sevres and Chinese porcelain, English and
Italian paintings, Chippendale furniture.
Exotic bird garden.
Admission charge.

►

JORVIK VIKING CENTRE

Jorvik Viking Centre
Coppergate, York, N. Yorkshire
YO1 1NT ☎ (0904) 643211
Visitors travel in electric cars down a
time-tunnel to a recreation of Viking
York. Excavated remains of Viking
houses and display of objects found.
Admission charge.

Museum of Army Transport
Flemingate, Beverley, Humberside
HU17 0NG ☎ (0482) 860445
Four locomotives, 2 aircraft and over 50
vehicles.
Admission charge.

**National Museum of
Photography, Film & Television**
Prince's View, Bradford, W. Yorkshire
BD5 0TR ☎ (0274) 727488
National museum with largest cinema
screen in Britain. Several shows daily.
*Admission to museum free, but charge
for cinema.*

National Railway Museum
Leeman Road, York, N. Yorkshire
YO2 4XJ ☎ (0904) 621261
Collection of locomotives and carriages
with displays depicting the technical,
social and economic development of
Britain's railway heritage.

Normanby Hall
Normanby, Nr. Scunthorpe, Humberside
DN15 9HU ☎ (0724) 720215
Regency mansion by Sir Robert Smirke,
architect of British Museum. Furnished
and decorated in period, with displays
of costume.
Admission charge.

Piece Hall
Halifax, W. Yorkshire HX1 1RE
☎ (0422) 58087
Rectangular, colonnaded Cloth Hall,
surrounding open-air courtyard and
comprising open-air market, art gallery,
museum.
Admission free.

Skipton Castle
Skipton, N. Yorkshire BD23 1AQ
☎ (0756) 2442
One of the most complete and well-
preserved medieval castles in England.
Fully roofed and floored. Beautiful
Conduit Court featured on TV in
'Treasure Hunt'.
Admission charge.

SKIPTON CASTLE

Mark Carolan

Thrybergh Country Park
Doncaster Road, Rotherham,
S. Yorkshire S65 4NU
☎ (0709) 850353
Country park (63 acres) including lake.
Fly fishing, sailing, wind-surfing,
canoeing. Craft for hire. Picnic areas.
*Admission free, but charge for use of
water-sports facilities.*

Transport and Archaeology Museum
36 High Street, Hull, Humberside
☎ (0482) 222737
Horse-drawn vehicles, motor vehicles
1890 – 1910, Humberside archaeology,
Iron Age chariot burial, Romano-British
mosaics.
Admission free.

MAKE A DATE FOR...

Jorvik Viking Festival
Various venues, York, North Yorkshire
28 January – 25 February

**World Professional Snooker
Championships**
Crucible Theatre, Norfolk Street,
Sheffield, South Yorkshire
15 April – 1 May

Harrogate Spring Flower Show
Valley Gardens, Harrogate, North
Yorkshire
27 – 29 April

Wharfdale Music Festival
Various venues, Ilkley, West Yorkshire
13 – 20 May

Great Yorkshire Show
Great Yorkshire Showground, Wetherby
Road, Harrogate, North Yorkshire
11 – 13 July

York Early Music Festival
Various venues including York Minster,
York, North Yorkshire
14 – 23 July

Great Autumn Flower Show
Exhibition Centre, Ripon Road,
Harrogate, North Yorkshire
15 – 16 July

Tourist Information

Tourist and leisure information can be obtained from Tourist Information Centres throughout England. Details of centres in the Yorkshire & Humberside region are listed below. The symbol 🛏 means that an accommodation booking service is provided. Centres marked with a * are open during the summer months only. In the following pages, towns which have a Tourist Information Centre are indicated with the symbol *i* .

Barnsley
S. Yorkshire 🛏
56 Eldon Street
☎ (0226) 206757

Bedale
N. Yorkshire 🛏
Bedale Hall, North End
☎ (0677) 24604

Bentham
N. Yorkshire *
Station Road, via Lancaster
☎ (0468) 62252/61524

Beverley
Humberside
The Guildhall, Register Square 🛏
☎ Hull (0482) 867430
Museum of Army Transport, Flemingate 🛏
☎ Hull (0482) 867813

Boroughbridge
N. Yorkshire 🛏 *
Fishergate
☎ Harrogate (0423) 323373

Bradford
W. Yorkshire 🛏
City Hall
☎ (0274) 753678

Bridlington
Humberside 🛏
Prince Street
☎ (0262) 673474/679626

Brigg
Humberside
7 Market Place
☎ (0652) 57637

Cleethorpes
Humberside 🛏
43 Alexandra Road
☎ (0472) 200220

Danby
N. Yorkshire 🛏 *
The Moors Centre, Lodge Lane, Danby, Whitby
☎ Castleton (0287) 60654

Doncaster
S. Yorkshire 🛏
Central Library, Waterdale
☎ (0302) 734309

Easingwold
N. Yorkshire 🛏 *
Chapel Lane
☎ (0347) 21530

Filey
N. Yorkshire 🛏 *
John Street
☎ Scarborough (0723) 512204

Goole
Humberside 🛏
Central Library, Carlisle Street
☎ (0405) 2187

Grassington
N. Yorkshire 🛏 *
National Park Centre, Hebden Road
☎ (0756) 752748

Great Ayton
N. Yorkshire 🛏
High Green
☎ Stokesley (0642) 722835

Grimsby
Humberside
Central Library, Town Hall Square
☎ (0472) 240410

Halifax
W. Yorkshire 🛏
Piece Hall
☎ (0422) 68725

Harrogate
N. Yorkshire
Royal Baths Assembly Rooms, Crescent Road
☎ (0423) 525666/7/8

ROYAL BATHS, HARROGATE

Jean M Brett

Hartshead Moor
W. Yorkshire 🛏
Hartshead Moor Service Area, M62 Motorway
☎ Bradford (0274) 869167

Hawes
N. Yorkshire 🚂 ✻
Station Yard
☎ (096 97) 450

Haworth
W. Yorkshire 🚂
2 – 4 West Lane
☎ (0535) 42329

Hebden Bridge
W. Yorkshire 🚂
1 Bridge Gate
☎ (0422) 843831

Helmsley
N. Yorkshire 🚂 ✻
Town Hall
☎ (0439) 70173

Holmfirth
W. Yorkshire 🚂
49 – 51 Huddersfield Road
☎ (0484) 684992/687063

Hornsea
Humberside 🚂 ✻
Floral Hall, Esplanade
☎ (0964) 532919

Horton-in-Ribblesdale
N. Yorkshire 🚂
Pen-y-ghent Café
☎ (072 96) 333

Huddersfield
W. Yorkshire 🚂
3 – 5 Albion Street
☎ (0484) 22133 ext. 313
(23877 Saturdays)

Hull
Humberside
See Kingston upon Hull

Humber Bridge
Humberside 🚂
North Bank Viewing Area,
Ferriby Road, Hessle
☎ Hull (0482) 640852

Hutton-le-Hole
N. Yorkshire 🚂 ✻
Ryedale Folk Museum
☎ Lastingham (075 15) 367

Ilkley
W. Yorkshire 🚂
Station Road
☎ (0943) 602319

Ingleton
N. Yorkshire 🚂 ✻
Community Centre Car Park
☎ (0468) 41049

Kingston upon Hull
Humberside
Central Library, Albion Street 🚂
☎ (0482) 223344

75 – 76 Carr Lane 🚂
☎ (0482) 223559

King George Dock, Hedon Road 🚂
☎ (0482) 702118

Knaresborough
N. Yorkshire 🚂 ✻
Information Kiosk, Market Place
☎ Harrogate (0423) 866886

Leeds
W. Yorkshire 🚂
19 Wellington Street
☎ (0532) 462454/5

Leyburn
N. Yorkshire 🚂 ✻
Thornborough Hall
☎ Wensleydale (0969) 23069/
22773

Malton
N. Yorkshire 🚂 ✻
Old Town Hall, Market Square
☎ (0653) 600048

Northallerton
N. Yorkshire 🚂 ✻
Applegarth Car Park
☎ (0609) 6864

KINGSTON UPON HULL

Britain on View

Otley
W. Yorkshire 🚶
Council Offices, 8 Boroughgate
☎ (0943) 465151

Pateley Bridge
N. Yorkshire 🚶 *
Southlands Car Park, High
Street
☎ Harrogate (0423) 711147

Pickering
N. Yorkshire 🚶 *
7 Eastgate Square
☎ (0751) 73791

Reeth
N. Yorkshire 🚶 *
Swaledale Folk Museum
☎ Richmond (0748) 84517

Richmond
N. Yorkshire 🚶
Friary Gardens, Victoria Road
☎ (0748) 850252

Ripon
N. Yorkshire 🚶 *
Minster Road
☎ (0765) 4625

Rotherham
S. Yorkshire 🚶
Brian O'Malley Central Library
and Arts Centre, Walker Place
☎ (0709) 382121 ext. 3611/2
& (0709) 365674 (evenings &
Saturdays)

Scarborough
N. Yorkshire 🚶
St. Nicholas Cliff
☎ (0723) 373333

Scotch Corner
N. Yorkshire 🚶 *
Scotch Corner Hotel (A1/A66)
☎ Richmond (0748) 4864

Scunthorpe
Humberside 🚶
Central Library, Carlton Street
☎ (0724) 860161

Selby
N. Yorkshire 🚶
Bus Station, Park Street
☎ (0757) 703263

Settle
N. Yorkshire 🚶 *
Town Hall, Cheapside
☎ (072 92) 3617

Sheffield
S. Yorkshire 🚶
Town Hall Extension, Union
Street
☎ (0742) 734671/2

Skipton
N. Yorkshire 🚶
8 Victoria Square
☎ (0756) 2809

Sowerby Bridge
W. Yorkshire 🚶
40 Town Hall Street
☎ (0422) 835326

Staithes
N. Yorkshire 🚶 *
The Old School, Staithes Lane
☎ Whitby (0947) 841251

Sutton Bank
N. Yorkshire 🚶 *
National Park Centre
☎ Thirsk (0845) 597426

Thirsk
N. Yorkshire 🚶 *
Thirsk Museum, 16 Kirkgate
☎ (0845) 22755

Todmorden
W. Yorkshire 🚶
15 Burnley Road
☎ (0706) 818181

Wakefield
W. Yorkshire 🚶
Town Hall, Wood Street
☎ (0924) 370211 ext.
7021/7022 & (0924) 370700
(Saturdays only)

Wetherby
W. Yorkshire 🚶
Council Offices, 24 Westgate
☎ (0937) 62706/7

Whitby
N. Yorkshire 🚶
New Quay Road
☎ (0947) 602674

Woodall
S. Yorkshire 🚶
Woodall Service Area,
Northbound Carriageway M1,
Harthill, Nr. Sheffield
☎ Sheffield (0742) 484055

York
N. Yorkshire
De Grey Rooms, Exhibition
Square 🚶
☎ (0904) 21756/7

Railway Station, Outer
Concourse, Station Road 🚶
☎ (0904) 643700

Entries in this regional section are listed in alphabetical order of place name, and then in alphabetical order of establishment. County names are not normally repeated in each establishment entry, but please use the full postal address when writing.

The map references refer to the colour maps towards the end of this guide. The first number is the number of the map, and it is followed by the grid reference.

The Crown Classifications are explained on pages 8 and 9, and the key to symbols is on the flap inside the back cover — keep it open for easy reference.

ACASTER MALBIS

N. Yorkshire
Map ref 4C1

5m S. York

Ship Inn M
Listed
Acaster Malbis, York,
YO2 1UH
☎ York (0904) 703888
Old English inn on the banks of the River Ouse at Acaster Malbis 5 miles from York city centre.
Bedrooms: 2 double & 3 twin.
Bathrooms: 1 public.
Bed & breakfast: £15-£25 single, £29-£49 double.
Half board: £22.50-£32.50 daily, £135-£195 weekly.
Lunch available.
Evening meal 6.30pm (l.o. 9.30pm).
Parking for 90.
Credit: Access, Visa, Amex.
⌂ ⚑ ♥ ✿ 🛈 V 🞑 ▣ ( ) ♩ ► ❦ SP 🈁

ADDINGHAM

W. Yorkshire
Map ref 4B1

3m NW. Ilkley

176 Main Street
Addingham, Ilkley,
LS29 0LU
☎ (0943) 830038
Yorkshire stone, terraced house on the A65, on the outskirts of Addingham village. 3 miles from Ilkley and 6 miles from Skipton.
Bedrooms: 1 single, 1 double & 1 twin.
Bathrooms: 1 public.
Bed & breakfast: max. £9 single, max. £18 double.
Half board: max. £13 daily, max. £75 weekly.
Evening meal 7pm (l.o. 8pm).
Open March-October.
⌂ ✖ UL 🛈 V 🞑 TV ✖ 🈁

ALLERSTON

N. Yorkshire
Map ref 5D3

5m NE. Pickering

Rains Farm
Allerston, Pickering,
YO18 7PQ
☎ Scarborough (0723) 85343
120-acre arable/sheep farm. Renovated farmhouse between Allerston and Yedingham in the peaceful Vale of Pickering.
Bedrooms: 2 double & 1 twin, 2 family rooms.
Bathrooms: 1 private, 1 public.
Bed & breakfast: £18-£22 double.
Half board: £100-£112.50 weekly.
Evening meal 6pm (l.o. 7pm).
Parking for 6.
Open March-October.
⌂ ✖ 4 🛏 UL V ✖ 🞑 TV 🞕 ▣ ✿ 🈁

AMPLEFORTH

N. Yorkshire
Map ref 4C1

10m E. Thirsk
Stone-built village in Hambleton Hills famous for its abbey and college, a Benedictine public school founded in 1802, of which Cardinal Hume was once Abbot.

White Swan M
Listed
Ampleforth, York, YO6 4DA
☎ (043 93) 239
17th C. inn retaining its original low-beamed bar. In a picturesque village in the North York Moors National Park, an ideal tourist centre. Weekly rates available.
Bedrooms: 1 single, 1 double & 1 twin.
Bathrooms: 1 public.

Bed & breakfast: £12-£14 single, £24-£28 double.
Lunch available.
Evening meal 7pm (l.o. 10pm).
Parking for 70.
Credit: Access, Visa, Diners, Amex.
⌂ ⚑ ♥ 🛈 V 🞑 ▣ ▪ ✖ 🈁 🄰 ❦ SP 🈁 T

APPERSETT

N. Yorkshire
Map ref 5B3

1m NW. Hawes

Rigg House West
Appersett, Hawes, DL8 3LR
☎ Hawes (096 97) 712
Fine house 4 miles west of Hawes on the A684 in Wensleydale's Herriot country. Rivers, waterfalls, fells, the Pennine Way and the historic Settle/Carlisle railway on the doorstep.
Bedrooms: 2 double & 1 twin.
Bathrooms: 1 public.
Bed & breakfast: £10-£12 single, £20-£22 double.
Half board: £16.50-£18 daily, £108.50-£126 weekly.
Evening meal 7pm (l.o. 5.50pm).
Parking for 5.
⌂ ✖ 5 🛏 🛈 V 🞑 🞕 TV 🞑 ▪ ♀ ✿ ✖ ❦ SP 🈁

APPLETON-LE-MOORS

N. Yorkshire
Map ref 5C3

5m NW. Pickering
Small village situated on the edge of North York Moors with spired Victorian church.

Appleton Farmhouse
Appleton-le-Moors, York, YO6 6TE
☎ Lastingham (075 15) 275
Large comfortable, stone-built house in the North York Moors National Park. Excellent base for walking, cycling, touring and motoring to the coast.
Bedrooms: 2 double & 1 twin, 1 family room.
Bathrooms: 2 private, 1 public.
Bed & breakfast: £10-£13 single, £20-£23 double.
Half board: £31-£34 daily, £102.50-£123.50 weekly.
Parking for 4.
Open March-November.
⌂ ✖ ♥ UL 🛈 V 🞑 TV 🞕 ▪ 🈁 🄰 SP

APPLETREEWICK

N. Yorkshire
Map ref 4B1

2m SE. Burnsall
A Wharfedale village below the craggy summit of 'Simon's Seat'. Half way through the village is Monks Hall, originally known as 'Mock Beggars Hall', and at the top stands High Hall, former home of the Craven family.

Haughside M
Listed
Appletreewick, Skipton, BD23 6DQ
☎ Burnsall (075 672) 225
Informal comfort in a detached stone bungalow in a secluded, scenic position in Wharfedale. 400 yards from the Dalesway, 8 miles from Skipton and 6 miles from Grassington. Excellent walking area.
Bedrooms: 1 single, 1 double.
Bathrooms: 1 public.
Bed & breakfast: £9.50-£12.50 single, £18-£24 double.
Half board: £13-£16.50 daily, £85-£110 weekly.
Evening meal 7pm (l.o. 8pm).
Parking for 6.
Open March-November.
⌂ ✖ ♿ UL ⓒ UL 🛈 V TV 🞕 ✿ ✖ 🈁

ASKRIGG

N. Yorkshire
Map ref 5B3

4m NW. Aysgarth
The name of this Dales village means 'ash tree ridge'. It is centred on a steep main street of high, narrow three-storey houses and thrived on cotton and later wool in 18th C. TV location for James Herriot series. Once famous for its clock making.

Mrs. B. Percival
Listed
Milton House, Askrigg, Leyburn, DL8 3HJ
☎ Wensleydale (0969) 50217
Large comfortable, family house in a beautiful dales' village, central for touring or walking. Colour TV lounge and wholesome Yorkshire cooking.
Bedrooms: 1 double & 1 twin, 1 family room.
Bathrooms: 2 private, 1 public.
Bed & breakfast: from £15 single, £20-£24 double.

Half board: £15.50-£16.50 daily.
Evening meal 7pm (l.o. 7pm).
Parking for 3.
♿ ⚬ Ⓤ ⓛ 🍴 📺 ▥ ﷽ ⚹

Thornsgill Guest House

Moor Rd., Askrigg, Leyburn,
DL8 3HH
☎ Wensleydale (0969) 50617
*Stone-built early 20th C.
building 50 yards from the
main street, on the Muker
road.*
Bedrooms: 1 single, 1 double,
1 family room.
Bathrooms: 2 private,
1 public.
Bed & breakfast: from £29 double.
Half board: from £21.50 daily.
Evening meal 7pm (l.o. 8pm).
Parking for 4.
♿ ⚬ Ⓤ ⓛ Ⓥ 🍴 📺 ▥ ⌂
▥ ⒹⒶⓅ SP

BAINBRIDGE

N. Yorkshire
Map ref 5B3

This Wensleydale grey-
stone village with fine
views of the River Bain,
reputedly England's
shortest river, was once a
Roman settlement, some
of it still visible. Boating
and water-skiing on
nearby Semerwater.
Ancient foresters' custom
of hornblowing still
continues.

Mrs. M. Iveson ⚠
Listed

High Force Farm,
Bainbridge, Leyburn,
DL8 3DL
☎ Wensleydale (0969) 50379
*470-acre hill/sheep/dairy farm.
Used in the James Herriot TV
series. Close to Lake
Semerwater.*
Bedrooms: 2 family rooms.
Bathrooms: 1 public.
Bed & breakfast: from £10
single, £16-£18 double.
Half board: from £15 daily.
Evening meal 7.30pm.
Parking for 3.
♿ ⚞ ⚬ Ⓤ Ⓥ 📺 ▥ ❁ ▥
▥

BARMBY MOOR

Humberside
Map ref 4C1

2m W. Pocklington

Alder Carr House

York Rd., Barmby Moor,
York, N. Yorkshire
YO4 5HU
☎ Wilberfoss (075 95) 566
*Georgian farmhouse offering
tastefully furnished,
comfortable and quiet
accommodation, overlooking
the Yorkshire Wolds. Excellent
base for touring historic
centres, countryside and coast.*
Bedrooms: 2 double & 1 twin.
Bathrooms: 1 private,
2 public.
Bed & breakfast: £18-£22 double.
Parking for 6.
♿ ⚞ ⚬ 🍴 📺 ▥ ⌂ ∪ ❁
▥ ▥ ⒹⒶⓅ SP

Mohair Farm (Newlands Farm)
Listed

York Rd., Barmby Moor,
York, N. Yorkshire
YO4 5HU
☎ Wilberfoss (075 95) 308
Fax: 07595 8119
*24-acre mixed farm. A quiet
farmhouse set well back from
the road, between York and the
Humber Bridge.*
Bedrooms: 1 twin, 1 family
room.
Bathrooms: 1 public.
Bed & breakfast: £9-£9.50
single, £18-£19 double.
Parking for 10.
♿ ⚬ Ⓔ ⛰ ⚬ Ⓤ Ⓥ ▥ ⌂
⚞ ∪ ∕ ❁ ▥ ⒹⒶⓅ SP

BARTON-UPON-HUMBER

Humberside
Map ref 4C1

Eminent river port on the
Humber before Hull
became important, now a
rambling riverside town
with some attractive
buildings and narrow
winding streets.
Magnificent views of
Humber Bridge.

Southgarth
⛺

2 Caistor Rd., Barton-upon-
Humber, S. Humberside
DN18 5AH
☎ (0652) 32833

---

*Original gatekeeper's lodge at
the entrance to Baysgarth
Park and Museum. Tennis,
swimming, bowls and a putting
green are available in the park.
2 minutes' walk from the town
centre and Humber Bridge.
Close to the motorway.*
Bedrooms: 3 twin.
Bathrooms: 2 public;
2 private showers.
Bed & breakfast: £12-£14
single, £22-£24 double.
Half board: £17-£19 daily,
£100-£120 weekly.
Evening meal 7.30pm (l.o.
6.30pm).
Parking for 7.
♿ ⚞5 Ⓔ ▯ ⚬ Ⓤ ⓛ Ⓥ 🍴 📺
▥ ⌂ ✕ ▥ ⒹⒶⓅ

Willow Tree Lodge

Pasture Road North, Barton-
upon-Humber,
S. Humberside DN18 5RB
☎ (0652) 34416
*Artists' bungalow home in 4
acre grounds with private
fishing, adjoining a nature
reserve and site of special
scientific interest. Children 10
years and over are welcome.*
Bedrooms: 1 double & 1 twin.
Bathrooms: 1 public.
Bed & breakfast: £10-£12.50
single, £20-£24 double.
Half board: £13-£16 daily,
£90-£110 weekly.
Evening meal 7pm (l.o.
5.30pm).
Parking for 7.
♿ ⚞ Ⓤ ⓛ Ⓥ 🍴 📺 ▥ ⌂
∕ ❁ ✕ ▥

BEDALE

N. Yorkshire
Map ref 5C3

Ancient church of St.
Gregory and Georgian
Bedale Hall occupy
commanding positions
over this market town
situated in good hunting
country. The Hall, which
contains interesting
architectural features
including great ballroom
and flying-type staircase,
now houses a library and
museum. Ⓘ

Hyperion House
⛺⛺

88 South End, Bedale,
DL8 2DS
☎ (0677) 22334
*Detached, comfortable large-
roomed house, ideal for touring
the Yorkshire Dales and moors
and the Cleveland and
Hambleton hills. Non-smoking
establishment.*
Bedrooms: 2 double & 1 twin.
Bathrooms: 1 public.

Continued ▶

AYSGARTH

N. Yorkshire
Map ref 5B3

Famous for its beautiful
Falls - a series of 3
cascades extending for
half mile on the River Ure
in Wensleydale. There is
a coach and carriage
museum with a crafts
centre at old Yore Mill
and National Park Centre.

Marlbeck
Listed

Aysgarth, Leyburn,
DL8 3AH
☎ (096 93) 610
*Former 19th C. dales'
smallholding converted to a
picture studio. Located in
Wensleydale in the beautiful
Yorkshire Dales National
Park, a short walk from
Aysgarth's limestone falls.*
Bedrooms: 1 single, 1 twin,
1 family room.
Bathrooms: 1 public.
Bed & breakfast: £9 single,
£18 double.
Open April-October.
♿ ⚞ Ⓤ ⓛ Ⓥ 🍴 📺 ▥ ▥

BARDEN

N. Yorkshire
Map ref 4B1

5m NE. Skipton
Situated in Wharfedale.
17th C Barden Tower
which was restored in
1658 by Lady Anne
Clifford.

Howgill Lodge Barn

Howgill Lodge, Barden,
Skipton, BD23 6DJ
☎ Burnsall (075 672) 655
*17th C. barn, tastefully
converted in 1986 using
original materials where
possible. Ideal base for the
country lover, with fine views of
Wharfedale.*
Bedrooms: 2 double & 2 twin.
Bathrooms: 4 private.
Bed & breakfast: £29-£34
double.
Parking for 4.
♿ ⚬ ⚬ ▯ ▥ ⛰ ⚞ ✕ ▥ ⒹⒶⓅ
SP ▥

THERE IS A SPECIAL
SECTION IN THIS
GUIDE LISTING
ACCOMMODATION
ESPECIALLY
SUITABLE FOR
GROUPS AND
YOUNG PEOPLE.

MAP REFERENCES APPLY TO THE COLOUR
MAPS TOWARDS THE END OF THIS GUIDE.

BEDALE

Continued

Bed & breakfast: £10-£12 single, £20-£24 double.
Parking for 5.

BELLERBY

N. Yorkshire
Map ref 5B3

Small village, the focal point of which is the village green featuring 'The Cross Tree' - a fine sycamore planted in 1818. Bellerby Manor dates back to the 13th C.

Mrs. J. Munro

Hill Top House, Bellerby, Leyburn, DL8 5QN
☎ Wensleydale (0969) 22596
18th C. stone-built farmhouse with log fires, personal attention at all times and home cooking. Emphasis on comfort.
Bedrooms: 1 double & 1 twin.
Bathrooms: 1 public.
Bed & breakfast: £8-£10 single, £16-£20 double.
Half board: £13-£15 daily, £90-£100 weekly.
Lunch available.
Evening meal 6pm (l.o. 10pm).
Parking for 2.

BENTHAM

N. Yorkshire
Map ref 5B3

Bentham is said to mean 'Home on the Common'. A weekly market has been held here since the 14th C. Good walking country.

Lane House Farm

Bentham, Lancaster, Lancashire LA2 7DJ
☎ (0468) 61479
100-acre mixed farm. Family-run near open moorland, overlooking the Yorkshire Dales and within easy reach of the Lakes and coast.
Bedrooms: 2 double, 1 family room.
Bathrooms: 1 public.
Bed & breakfast: £8-£9.50 single, £16-£19 double.
Half board: from £14 daily, from £95 weekly.
Evening meal 6pm.
Parking for 4.

BEVERLEY

Humberside
Map ref 4C1

Beverley's most famous landmark is its beautiful medieval Minster with Percy family tombs. Many attractive squares and streets, notably Wednesday and Saturday Market, North Bar Gateway and The Museum of Army Transport, Flemingate. Famous race course.

Eastgate Guest House

7 Eastgate, Beverley, N. Humberside HU17 0DR
☎ Hull (0482) 868464
Family-run, Victorian guesthouse, established and run by the same proprietor for 20 years. Close to the town centre, Minster, Army Transport Museum and railway station.
Bedrooms: 4 single, 3 double & 4 twin, 4 family rooms.
Bathrooms: 3 public.
Bed & breakfast: £12.50-£13.50 single, £19-£21 double.

BILSDALE WEST

N. Yorkshire
Map ref 5C3

7m NW. Helmsley

Lockton House Farm

Bilsdale West, Helmsley, York, YO6 5NE
☎ Bilsdale (043 96) 303
400-acre mixed farm. Part of the house is a 16th C. cruck house with oak beams and log fires. 7 miles out of Helmsley on the B1257 Teesside road.
Bedrooms: 1 single, 2 double, 1 family room.
Bathrooms: 1 public.
Bed & breakfast: £8.50 single, £17 double.
Half board: £12.50 daily, £87.50 weekly.
Evening meal 6pm (l.o. 6pm).
Parking for 6.

MAP REFERENCES APPLY TO COLOUR MAPS NEAR THE BACK OF THE GUIDE.

BISHOP THORNTON

N. Yorkshire
Map ref 4B1

5m SW. Ripon
Small village near Brimham Rocks.

Hatton House Farm

Bishop Thornton, Harrogate, HG3 3JA
☎ Harrogate (0423) 770315
150-acre dairy/sheep farm. Farmhouse accommodation with special emphasis on well-presented, home-cooked food.
Bedrooms: 1 single, 2 double & 1 twin.
Bathrooms: 1 public.
Bed & breakfast: max. £12 single, max. £24 double.
Half board: max. £16 daily, max. £100 weekly.
Evening meal 6.30pm.
Parking for 10.
Open March-October.

Raventofts Head House

Bishop Thornton, Harrogate, HG3 3JZ
☎ Sawley (076 586) 279
17-acre beef farm. Fully-modernised, stone-built farmhouse providing comfortable and inviting accommodation with a warm welcome. Picturesque countryside near places of historic interest. Evening meal by request only. Tea/coffee available at any time free of charge. Babies welcome.
Bedrooms: 1 single, 1 double & 1 twin.
Bathrooms: 1 private, 1 public.
Bed & breakfast: £10 single, £19-£20 double.
Half board: £14-£14.50 daily, £88.50 weekly.
Parking for 7.
8

PLEASE CHECK PRICES AND OTHER DETAILS AT THE TIME OF BOOKING.

BRADFORD

W. Yorkshire
Map ref 4B1

Once a Victorian city founded on wool, now largely rebuilt and modernised. Attractions include the Cathedral, City Hall, Cartwright Hall, Lister Park, Moorside Mills Industrial Museum and National Museum of Photography and Television.

Carlton House

Listed
1164 Thornton Rd., Thornton, Bradford, BD13 3QE
☎ (0274) 833397
Detached, Victorian house in open countryside between the Bronte villages of Thornton and Haworth.
Bedrooms: 1 double & 1 twin, 1 family room.
Bathrooms: 1 private, 1 public; 1 private shower.
Bed & breakfast: £10-£11 single, £20-£22 double.
Parking for 4.

Marriners

Listed
241 Keighley Rd., Heaton, Bradford, BD9 4JU
Small Victorian guesthouse with a garden and parking facilities. On the major road to the dales and lakes, 1.5 miles from the city centre.
Bedrooms: 1 single, 1 double & 1 twin, 1 family room.
Bathrooms: 1 public; 1 private shower.
Bed & breakfast: £12-£15 single, £24-£26 double.
Half board: £84-£90 weekly.
Parking for 5.

BUCKDEN

N. Yorkshire
Map ref 5B3

Upper Wharfedale village at the foot of Buckden Pike, 2300 ft.

The Buck Inn

Buckden, Skipton, BD23 5JA
☎ Kettlewell (075 676) 227
An attractive stone-built hotel, facing south and overlooking beautiful countryside in the heart of the Yorkshire Dales. Reductions for more than one night's stay.

Bedrooms: 2 single, 5 double & 1 twin, 2 family rooms.
Bathrooms: 3 private, 2 public; 5 private showers.
Bed & breakfast: £17.50-£27 single, £30-£54 double.
Half board: £24.50-£34 daily, £170-£230 weekly.
Lunch available.
Evening meal 6.30pm (l.o. 9pm).
Parking for 30.
Credit: Access, Visa.

CARLTON
N. Yorkshire
Map ref 5B3

4m SW. Wensley

Town Foot Farm
Carlton, Leyburn, DL8 4BA
☎ Wensleydale (0969) 40651
100-acre mixed farm. Farmhouse with an oak-beamed dining room and guests' kitchen, on the outskirts of the village. Free range eggs available. It is planned that all rooms will have private facilities by 1989.
Bedrooms: 2 double & 1 twin.
Bathrooms: 1 private, 1 public.
Bed & breakfast: £24-£28 double.
Half board: £17-£19 daily, £119-£153 weekly.
Evening meal 6.30pm (l.o. 3pm).
Parking for 4.
Open April-October.

CLOUGHTON
N. Yorkshire
Map ref 5D3

4m N. Scarborough
Village close to the east coast and North York Moors.

Red Lion Hotel
High St., Cloughton, Scarborough, YO13 0AE
☎ Scarborough (0723) 870702
Family-run inn with clean, comfortable accommodation and a friendly atmosphere. In a beautiful country village adjacent to the National Park.
Bedrooms: 1 single, 1 twin, 1 family room.
Bathrooms: 2 public.
Bed & breakfast: £12-£15 single, £24-£30 double.
Evening meal 7pm (l.o. 9.30pm).
Parking for 20.

COXWOLD
N. Yorkshire
Map ref 4C1

This well-known beauty spot in Hambleton and Howardian Hills is famous as home of Laurence Sterne, the 18th C country parson and author of 'Tristram Shandy' books who, in 1760, lived at Shandy Hall now open to the public.

Mrs. M. J. Banks
Wakendale House, Oldstead Grange, Coxwold, York, YO6 4BJ
☎ (034 76) 351
160-acre mixed farm. Comfortable accommodation with a friendly family in an attractive farmhouse in lovely countryside. No smoking in the house.
Bedrooms: 1 double & 1 twin, 1 family room.
Bathrooms: 1 public.
Bed & breakfast: £9-£12 single, £18-£20 double.
Parking for 5.
Open February-November.

School House
Coxwold, York, YO6 4AD
☎ (034 76) 356
17th C. cottage, a former coaching house, under the supervision of the owners and offering well-appointed accommodation and home cooking.
Bedrooms: 1 double & 1 twin, 1 family room.
Bathrooms: 2 public.
Bed & breakfast: £11-£12 single, £22-£24 double.
Half board: £16.50-£17 daily, £96-£105 weekly.
Evening meal 7pm (l.o. 7pm).
Parking for 6.
Open April-October.

Yeoman's Course Farm
Listed
Yeoman's Course, Oulston, York, YO6 3PY
☎ (034 76) 437
300-acre mixed farm. 300-year-old farmhouse with views over the Vale of York, 1 mile out of Oulston and 2 miles from Coxwold.
Bedrooms: 2 double.
Bathrooms: 1 public.
Bed & breakfast: £9 single, from £18 double.

Half board: from £15 daily, from £105 weekly.
Evening meal 6pm.

CRAGG VALE
W. Yorkshire
Map ref 4B1

Springfield
Cragg Rd., Cragg Vale, Hebden Bridge, HX7 5SR
☎ Hebden Bridge (0422) 882029
Comfortable, clean, modern house in a beautiful rural setting, providing a real Yorkshire welcome to the Pennines. English breakfast a speciality.
Bedrooms: 2 single, 1 double & 1 twin.
Bathrooms: 2 public.
Bed & breakfast: £10 single, £20 double.
Parking for 3.

CRAKEHALL
N. Yorkshire
Map ref 5C3

2m NW. Bedale

Waterside
Glenaire, Crakehall, Bedale, DL8 1HS
☎ Bedale (0677) 22908
Spacious, modern house with 1 acre of mature gardens and a trout stream, on a smallholding with poultry and a nursery. Central for the Yorkshire Dales and Moors, the gateway to Herriot country.
Bedrooms: 1 double & 1 twin, 1 family room.
Bathrooms: 2 private, 1 public.
Bed & breakfast: £11-£13 single, £22-£26 double.
Parking for 5.

CRAYKE
N. Yorkshire
Map ref 4C1

Pretty hillside village once belonging to the Bishopric of Durham, hence the name of the village inn, the Durham Ox.

The Hermitage
Mill La., Crayke, York, YO6 4TB
☎ Easingwold (0347) 21635
300-acre dairy farm. Stone-built house overlooking our own dairy farm and the Howardian Hills. Offering a warm and friendly welcome.
Bedrooms: 2 twin, 1 family room.
Bathrooms: 1 public.
Bed & breakfast: £10 single, £20 double.
Parking for 4.
Open January-November.

CROW. EDGE
S. Yorkshire
Map ref 4B1

4m W. Penistone

Pennine Inn ♨
Listed
Whams Rd., Crow Edge, Sheffield, S30 5HF
☎ Barnsley (0226) 762286
Telex 51458 Com Hud G Privel
Country inn on the A616, 4 miles from Holmfirth (Summer Wine country) and close to the Peak District.
Bedrooms: 2 single, 3 double.
Bathrooms: 5 private.
Bed & breakfast: from £18.50 single, from £30 double.
Half board: from £26 daily, from £175 weekly.
Lunch available.
Evening meal 7pm (l.o. 9.30pm).
Parking for 100.
Credit: Access, Visa.

THERE IS A SPECIAL SECTION IN THIS GUIDE LISTING ACCOMMODATION ESPECIALLY SUITABLE FOR GROUPS AND YOUNG PEOPLE.

GROUPS, CONSORTIA AND AGENCIES SPECIALISING IN FARM AND COUNTRY HOLIDAYS ARE LISTED IN A SPECIAL SECTION OF THIS GUIDE.

DALTON

N. Yorkshire
Map ref 5C3

Small village in the Vale of York.

Manor Farm
Dalton, Thirsk, YO7 3HS
☎ Thirsk (0845) 577239
20-acre stock farm. Comfortable farmhouse between the A1 and A19 in Herriot country. Central for the Dales, Moors, York and Harrogate. Near many abbeys and country houses.
Bedrooms: 1 single, 1 double & 1 twin, 1 family room.
Bathrooms: 2 public.
Bed & breakfast: £9-£9.50 single, £18-£19 double.
Parking for 4.
Open March-October.
⌖ ⚶ ᵤₗ Ⅴ ⌿ ⛟ ☎ ❋ ⅄
⊠ ₅ₚ

Ye Jolly Farmers of Olden Times
Dalton, Thirsk, YO7 3HY
☎ Thirsk (0845) 577359
Cosy, friendly, picturesque village inn with original beams, set in Herriot country. Real ales and emphasis on food.
Bedrooms: 1 double, 1 family room.
Bathrooms: 1 public.
Bed & breakfast: from £11.50 single, from £23 double.
Lunch available.
Evening meal 7.30pm (l.o. 9.30pm).
Parking for 40.
⌖ ⚶ ⊟ ❍ ☿ ⅃ Ⅴ ⚒ ▨ ◓
⏣ ♨ ⌖ ❋ ⅄

DALTON

N. Yorkshire
Map ref 5C3

6m NW. Richmond

Mrs. L. Brooks
Holmedale, Dalton, Richmond, DL11 7HX
☎ Teesdale (0833) 21236
Georgian house in a quiet village, midway between Richmond and Barnard Castle. Ideal for the Dales and Lakes.
Bedrooms: 1 double, 1 family room.
Bathrooms: 1 public.
Bed & breakfast: from £10 single, from £17 double.
Half board: from £14 daily.
Evening meal 6pm (l.o. 6pm).
Parking for 2.
⌖ ☿ ᵤₗ ⅃ ⚒ ⌿ ⛟ ▨ ▢ ⅄
ᴅᴀᴘ ₅ₚ

DONCASTER

S. Yorkshire

See Skellow.

DUNNINGTON

N. Yorkshire
Map ref 4C1

4m E. York
Near York, this village has an attractive old street, an interesting church and ancient village cross. Known for centuries for its making of farm implements.

Copyhold Cottage Guest House
28 York St., Dunnington, York, YO1 5QT
☎ York (0904) 489098
Tastefully restored 17th C. cottage with open fires and oak beams. In the village of Dunnington, 4 miles from York city centre, on the main Hull road. Tea and coffee free on request.
Bedrooms: 2 double.
Bathrooms: 1 public.
Bed & breakfast: £12-£15 single, £24-£30 double.
Parking for 4.
⌖ ᵤₗ ⅃ Ⅴ ⅄ ⌿ ⛟ ▨ ☎
⊿ ⅄

Horseshoe House ♨
York Rd., Dunnington, York, YO1 5QJ
☎ York (0904) 489369
Well-appointed accommodation in a country setting, half a mile from the A1079 and 4 miles from York city centre. Easy access to the racecourse and golf course. Restaurants close by.
Bedrooms: 1 double & 2 twin.
Bathrooms: 2 private, 1 public.
Bed & breakfast: £18-£21 double.
Parking for 3.
⌖ ⚶ ☿ ᵤₗ ⌿ ⛟ ▨ ⅄ ₅ₚ

EASINGWOLD

N. Yorkshire
Map ref 4C1

Market town of charm and character with a cobbled square and many fine Georgian buildings.
ℹ

Station Hotel ♨
⊟☎☎⊟
Knott La., Easingwold, York, YO6 3NT
☎ (0347) 22635
Small family-run hotel, recently refurbished to reflect the Victorian age.
Bedrooms: 3 double & 2 twin, 2 family rooms.
Bathrooms: 7 private.
Bed & breakfast: £14-£18 single, £24-£32 double.
Lunch available.
Evening meal 7.30pm (l.o. 9.30pm).
Parking for 10.
Credit: Visa.
⌖ ⊟ ☿ ⅃ Ⅴ ⌿ ▨ ♀ ♨
▶ ⅄ ᴅᴀᴘ ₅ₚ ⏣

EAST AYTON

N. Yorkshire
Map ref 5D3

4m SW. Scarborough
Nestling at the southern end of the beautiful Forge Valley on the River Derwent.

Church Farmhouse ♨
Listed
3 Main St., East Ayton, Scarborough, YO13 9HL
☎ Scarborough (0723) 862102
18th C. Yorkshire farmhouse at the entrance to Forge Valley, near the North Yorkshire Moors. Specialising in comfort, food and a warm welcome. A self-catering cottage is also available.
Bedrooms: 1 single, 1 double & 1 twin, 1 family room.
Bathrooms: 1 public.
Bed & breakfast: £14 single, £28 double.
Half board: £24 daily.
Lunch available.
Evening meal 7pm.
Parking for 4.
⌖ ⚶ ⊟ ☿ ⅃ Ⅴ ⌿ ⛟ ▨
⊿ ⚶ ♀ ♙ ⅄ ᴅᴀᴘ ⅄ ₅ₚ ⏣

EAST HESLERTON

N. Yorkshire
Map ref 5D3

9m E. Malton

The Old Vicarage
East Heslerton, Malton, YO17 8RN
☎ West Heslerton (094 45) 200
Beautiful old vicarage with pine woodwork and beams. Set in its own grounds, just off the A64 Malton to Scarborough road. Evening meal by arrangement.
Bedrooms: 2 double & 1 twin.
Bathrooms: 1 private, 1 public.
Bed & breakfast: max. £12 single, £24-£28 double.
Half board: max. £17 daily, max. £112 weekly.
Parking for 3.
Open April-December.
⌖ ☿ ᵤₗ ⅃ Ⅴ ⛟ ▨ ❋ ⅄
⊠ ₅ₚ ⏣

ELLERBY

N. Yorkshire
Map ref 5C3

3m S. Staithes

Ellerby Hotel ♨
⊟
Ellerby, Saltburn-by-the-Sea, Cleveland TS13 5LP
☎ Whitby (0947) 840342
Residential country inn within the North Yorkshire Moors National Park, 9 miles north of Whitby, 1 mile inland from Runswick Bay.
Bedrooms: 2 double, 1 family room.
Bathrooms: 3 private.
Bed & breakfast: £20 single, £30 double.
Lunch available.
Evening meal 7pm (l.o. 10pm).
Parking for 60.
Credit: Access, Visa.
⌖ ⚶ ⊟ ☿ ⅃ Ⅴ ▨ ⊿
⚶ ❋ ⅄ ⏣

ESHTON

N. Yorkshire
Map ref 4B1

Eshton Grange
Eshton, Skipton, BD23 3QE
☎ Skipton (0756) 749383
20-acre stock and stud farm. 18th C. listed farmhouse and Shetland Pony stud, 1 mile from the Pennine Way, close to many beauty spots and James Herriot country. Evening meal by arrangement.

INDIVIDUAL PROPRIETORS HAVE SUPPLIED ALL DETAILS OF ACCOMMODATION. ALTHOUGH WE DO CHECK FOR ACCURACY, WE ADVISE YOU TO CONFIRM PRICES AND OTHER INFORMATION AT THE TIME OF BOOKING.

Bedrooms: 1 double & 3 twin, 1 family room.
Bathrooms: 1 private, 1 public.
Bed & breakfast: £15 single, £26 double.
Half board: £21 daily, £147 weekly.
Parking for 12.

FARNDALE
N. Yorkshire
Map ref 5C3

2m N. Kirkbymoorside
Long, wide valley below Farndale Moor on the west of Blakey Ridge. Famous for its magnificent wild daffodils.

Eller House
Farndale, Kirkbymoorside, York, YO6 6LA
☎ Kirkbymoorside (0751) 23323
155-acre mixed farm. 9 miles north of Kirkbymoorside. Well situated for walking, sightseeing, the moors, coast and York.
Bedrooms: 1 double & 1 twin, 1 family room.
Bathrooms: 1 public.
Bed & breakfast: £7.50-£8 single, £15-£16 double.
Half board: £11-£12 daily, £75-£80 weekly.
Evening meal 6.30pm.
Parking for 3.
Open April-October.

FEIZOR
N. Yorkshire
Map ref 5B3

3m NW. Settle

Scar Close Farm M
Scar Close, Feizor, Austwick, Lancaster, Lancashire LA2 8DF
☎ Settle (072 92) 3496
185-acre dairy and sheep farm. In a picturesque hamlet near Settle, a tourist centre for the lakes, dales and seaside. All rooms have private bathroom.
Bedrooms: 1 double & 1 twin, 1 family room.
Bathrooms: 3 private.
Bed & breakfast: £20-£21 double.
Half board: £16-£16.50 daily, £107-£112 weekly.
Evening meal 5pm (l.o. 6.30pm).
Parking for 5.

FIRBECK
S. Yorkshire
Map ref 4C2

3m SE. Maltby
Near to the romantic setting of the 12th C. ruins of Roche Abbey, the grounds of which were laid out in the 18th C. by Capability Brown.

Yews Farm
Firbeck, Worksop, Nottinghamshire S81 8JW
☎ Worksop (0909) 731458
Charming, grade II listed, Yorkshire stone country house with elegant rooms, in 2.5 acre garden in an idyllic setting.
Bedrooms: 1 single, 2 twin.
Bathrooms: 2 private, 1 public.
Bed & breakfast: from £25 single, £36-£40 double.
Half board: £30-£37 daily.
Evening meal 7pm (l.o. 9pm).
Parking for 5.
Open March-October.

FLAMBOROUGH
Humberside
Map ref 5D3

Village with strong seafaring tradition, high on chalk headland dominated by cliffs of Flamborough Head; a fortress for over 2000 years. St. Oswald's Church is in the oldest part of Flamborough.

Aaheather Cottage Guest House M
Listed
12 Chapel St., Flamborough, Bridlington, N. Humberside YO15 1LQ
☎ Bridlington (0262) 851036
Traditional fisherman's cottage providing comfortable accommodation, with emphasis on food. In the heart of Flamborough village on the Heritage Coast.
Bedrooms: 1 double & 1 twin.
Bathrooms: 1 public.
Bed & breakfast: £18-£22 double.

FORCETT
N. Yorkshire
Map ref 5C3

2m W. Aldbrough
A place of some antiquity with Saxon and Norman connections, as well as being within the ancient area known as the Scots Dike.

Millbank
Forcett, Richmond, DL11 7RZ
☎ Darlington (0325) 718621
Bungalow in a rural area with open views. 3 miles west from Scotch Corner, then 3 miles north on the B6274, midway between Forcett and Eppleby.
Bedrooms: 1 double & 1 twin.
Bathrooms: 1 public.
Bed & breakfast: £9 single, £18 double.
Parking for 2.

GILLAMOOR
N. Yorkshire
Map ref 5C3

2m N. Kirkbymoorside
Village much admired by photographers for its views of Farndale, including 'Surprise View' from the churchyard.

Royal Oak Inn M
Gillamoor, York, YO6 6HX
☎ Kirkbymoorside (0751) 31414
Old country inn with 2 black leaded open fireplaces, on the edge of the North Yorkshire Moors.
Bedrooms: 1 double & 1 twin.
Bathrooms: 2 private.
Bed & breakfast: £14-£16 single, £28-£32 double.
Evening meal 7pm (l.o. 9.30pm).
Parking for 10.

GOATHLAND
N. Yorkshire
Map ref 5D3

Spacious village with several large greens grazed by sheep and an ideal centre for walking North York Moors. Nearby are several waterfalls, among them Mallyan Spout. Plough Monday celebrations held in January.

Dale End Farm
Green End, Goathland, Whitby, YO22 5LJ
☎ Whitby (0947) 85371
140-acre mixed farm. Moorland farmhouse built in 1720 and retaining much of its character, including oak beams and log fires. Home cooking. We have many repeat bookings.
Bedrooms: 1 double, 2 family rooms.
Bathrooms: 1 public.
Bed & breakfast: £9-£9.50 single, £18-£19 double.
Half board: £13.50-£14 daily, £94.50-£98 weekly.
Evening meal 5.45pm.
Parking for 4.

GRASSINGTON
N. Yorkshire
Map ref 5B3

Tourists visit this former lead-mining village to see its 'smiddy', antique and craft shops and Upper Wharfedale Museum of country trades. Popular with fishermen and walkers. Numerous prehistoric sites. Grassington Feast in October. National Park Centre.

Black Horse Hotel M
Garrs La., Grassington, Skipton, BD23 5AT
☎ (0756) 752770
Old coaching inn serving Tetley's and Theakston's real ales. Open coal fires, a warm and friendly atmosphere and all bedrooms with colour TV.
Bedrooms: 7 double & 3 twin, 1 family room.
Bathrooms: 11 private.
Bed & breakfast: £20-£27.50 single, £35-£40 double.
Half board: £29-£36.50 daily, £183-£230.50 weekly.
Lunch available.
Continued ▶

THERE IS A SPECIAL SECTION IN THIS GUIDE LISTING ACCOMMODATION ESPECIALLY SUITABLE FOR GROUPS AND YOUNG PEOPLE.

GRASSINGTON

Continued

Evening meal 6.30pm (l.o. 8.30pm).
Credit: Visa.
⌖ 🏠 📞 ♿ 🛏 Ⅴ 🗄 🖥 📶
🍴 SP 🏤

GREEN HAMMERTON

N. Yorkshire
Map ref 4C1

Skipbridge Farm
Green Hammerton, York,
YO5 8EZ
☎ Boroughbridge
(0423) 331015
12.5-acre sheep/poultry/goat farm. Spacious Regency farmhouse of character, with traditional range in dining room, and old pine furniture and log fires in the public rooms. Old world farm atmosphere in miniature with plenty of animals and space for children to play.
Bedrooms: 2 double, 3 family rooms.
Bathrooms: 3 private, 1 public.
Bed & breakfast: £10 single, £20-£25 double.
Half board: £16-£19 daily.
Evening meal 6pm (l.o. 7pm).
Parking for 12.
⌖ 🛁 🛏 📞 ♿ 🛏 🖥 📶
🍴 DAP 🍴 SP

GRIMSBY

Humberside
Map ref 4D1

Founded by a Danish fisherman named Grim 1000 years ago, Grimsby is today a major fishing port and docks. It has modern shopping precincts and Welholme Galleries Fishing and Maritime Museum. ℹ

County Hotel
Brighowgate, Grimsby,
S. Humberside DN32 0QU
☎ (0472) 44449 & 54422 & 54070 & 241560
Completely modernised hotel with a large lounge bar and friendly atmosphere, next to the coach and railway stations.
Bedrooms: 3 single, 3 double & 3 twin.
Bathrooms: 9 private.
Bed & breakfast: £25-£35 single, £35-£50 double.
Half board: £30-£45 daily.
Lunch available.

Evening meal 5.30pm (l.o. 10pm).
Parking for 12.
Credit: Access, Visa, Amex.
⌖ 📞 ♿ 🛏 Ⅴ 🗄 🖥 ●
📶 🚗 DAP SP

GRINTON

N. Yorkshire
Map ref 5C3

7m SW. Richmond
Village overlooking Richmond whose parish church was originally a mission church run by Augustinians.

Bridge Hotel
Grinton (Swaledale),
Richmond, DL11 6HH
☎ Richmond (0748) 84224
Country inn beside the River Swale with 1.5 miles of private fishing.
Bedrooms: 2 single, 2 double & 3 twin, 2 family rooms.
Bathrooms: 3 private, 2 public.
Bed & breakfast: £12-£15 single, £24-£30 double.
Half board: £18-£20 daily, £115-£135 weekly.
Lunch available.
Evening meal 7pm.
Parking for 25.
Open April-October.
⌖ 🛏 🗄 🖥 📶 🚗 🍴 ✳ 🏤

GROSMONT

N. Yorkshire
Map ref 5D3

6m SW. Whitby
Grosmont is the terminus of North Yorkshire Moors Railway. Planned by George Stephenson in 1833, the railway was closed under Beeching Plan and later reopened by a railway preservation society.

Eskdale
Listed
Grosmont, Whitby,
YO22 5PT
☎ Whitby (0947) 85385
Georgian house, outside the village of Grosmont. All main rooms have extensive views along the Esk Valley.
Bedrooms: 2 single, 2 double.
Bathrooms: 1 public.
Bed & breakfast: £8.50 single, £17-£18 double.
Parking for 4.
Open March-October.
⌖ 🛁 🛏 📶 🏤

Grosmont House ♨
♨♨
Grosmont, Whitby,
YO22 5PE
☎ Whitby (0947) 85539
Spacious Victorian house in its own grounds near the station. An ideal centre for combining rail trips with country walks. Brochure on request.
Bedrooms: 2 double & 1 twin.
Bathrooms: 1 private, 1 public.
Bed & breakfast: £12-£14 single, £18-£22 double.
Evening meal 7pm (l.o. 9.30am).
Parking for 3.
⌖ 8 ♿ 🛏 Ⅴ 🗄 🖥 📶 🚗 ✿ 🏤

HACKFORTH

N. Yorkshire
Map ref 5C3

3m S. Catterick
Village near Bedale, approximately half way between the Dales and Moors.

Mrs. V. K. Anderson
♨♨
Ainderby Myers Farm,
Hackforth, Bedale, DL8 1PF
☎ Northallerton
(0609) 748668
423-acre mixed farm. An historic farmhouse set amidst rolling countryside. An ideal base for touring Herriot country, the moors, Dales, castles, abbeys and towns. Facilities for making drinks, snacks and picnics are available.
Bedrooms: 2 double & 1 twin, 1 family room.
Bathrooms: 2 public.
Bed & breakfast: £12-£12.50 single, £20-£21 double.
Half board: £17.50-£18 daily, £122.50-£126 weekly.
Evening meal 7pm.
Parking for 4.
⌖ ♿ 🛏 🛏 Ⅴ 🍴 🗄 🖥 📶
🚗 ☾ ✿ 🍴 🏤 SP 🏤

HALIFAX

W. Yorkshire
Map ref 4B1

Founded on the cloth trade, and famous for its building society, textiles, carpets and toffee. Most notable landmark is Piece Hall where wool merchants traded, now restored to house shops, museums and art gallery. National Museum of the Working Horse. ℹ

Arundell Guest House ♨
32 Calder Terrace, Copley,
Halifax, HX3 0UQ
☎ Halifax (0422) 42775
Mews cottage offering homely accommodation. In a conservation area, off Huddersfield Road, 2.5 miles from the city centre. Adjacent to woodland countryside, with fishing and canoeing available locally. Convenient for all amenities.
Bedrooms: 1 family room.
Bathrooms: 1 public.
Bed & breakfast: from £9 single, from £16 double.
Half board: from £11 daily, from £75 weekly.
Evening meal 6pm (l.o. 4pm).
Parking for 2.
⌖ 🛡 📞 🛏 ♿ 🛏 Ⅴ 🗄
🖥 🚗 🍴 🏤 SP 🏤

The Elms
Keighley Rd., Illingworth,
Halifax, HX2 8HT
☎ (0422) 244430
Victorian residence with gardens and original ornate ceilings, within 3 miles of Halifax. Some facilities for disabled guests are available including wheelchair, lift and external ramping. For further information contact the proprietor.
Bedrooms: 3 single, 1 double, 1 family room.
Bathrooms: 1 private, 3 public.
Bed & breakfast: £11.50-£13 single, £23-£25 double.
Half board: £16-£18 daily, £100-£110 weekly.
Evening meal 6pm (l.o. 8pm).
Parking for 16.
⌖ 🛏 🛏 Ⅴ 🗄 🖥 📶 🚗 🍴
✿ 🏤

INDIVIDUAL PROPRIETORS HAVE SUPPLIED ALL DETAILS OF ACCOMMODATION. ALTHOUGH WE DO CHECK FOR ACCURACY, WE ADVISE YOU TO CONFIRM PRICES AND OTHER INFORMATION AT THE TIME OF BOOKING.

Stump Cross Inn

Stump Cross, Halifax,
HX3 7AD
☎ (0422) 66004
*Traditional old world roadside
inn with emphasis on friendly
and efficient, personal service.
Grill room open lunchtimes 12
to 2 pm and evenings 7 to 10
pm.*
Bedrooms: 1 single, 5 double
& 5 twin, 1 family room.
Bathrooms: 6 private,
1 public.
Bed & breakfast: £17-£27
single.
Lunch available.
Evening meal 7pm (l.o.
10pm).
Parking for 45.
♒7 🌢 🛢 📺 ▥ ♨ 🎄

HARROGATE

N. Yorkshire
Map ref 4B1

Once popular as a spa,
now a major conference
and exhibition centre.
Beautiful Victorian
architecture offset by
spacious parks and
gardens. Famous for
toffee, fine shops and rich
teas, also its Royal Pump
Rooms and Baths.
Nearby is Ripley Castle. ⓘ

Abbey Lodge
🛏🛏🛏
31 Ripon Rd., Harrogate,
HG1 2JL
☎ (0423) 69712
*Beautifully restored and
ideally situated, offering a
combination of well-appointed
accommodation and a relaxed
atmosphere. Emphasis on food.*
Bedrooms: 1 single, 6 double
& 3 twin, 3 family rooms.
Bathrooms: 8 private,
3 public.
Bed & breakfast: £15-£18
single, £30-£34 double.
Half board: £23-£25 daily,
£150.50-£163 weekly.
Evening meal 7pm (l.o.
8.30pm).
Parking for 12.
Credit: Access, Visa.
♒🌢🛢 ⊡🍴♨ 🛢 Ⓥ ♨ ▥
🌢 🏃 🎄 ᴅᴀᴘ ꜱᴘ ⊤

**MAP REFERENCES
APPLY TO THE
COLOUR MAPS
TOWARDS THE END
OF THIS GUIDE.**

Alexa House Hotel and Stable Cottages ♨
🛏🛏🛏
26 Ripon Rd., Harrogate,
HG2 2JJ
☎ (0423) 501988
*Small hotel, built for Baron de
Ferrier in 1830. Maintaining
the old and gracious traditions
of personal service and true
Yorkshire hospitality.*
Bedrooms: 2 single, 2 double
& 6 twin, 2 family rooms.
Bathrooms: 11 private,
1 public.
Bed & breakfast: from £18
single, max. £36 double.
Parking for 14.
Credit: Access, Visa.
♒1 🌢⊞⊡♨ 🛢 Ⓥ ♨ 📺
▥ 🌢♿🏃🎄🛢 ᴅᴀᴘ ꜱᴘ 🎋
⊤

Brandsby Guest House
🛏
10 Studley Rd., Harrogate,
HG1 5JU
☎ (0423) 501592
*Victorian terraced house with
modern facilities, close to the
town centre. Personal service
from the owners.*
Bedrooms: 2 twin.
Bathrooms: 2 public.
Bed & breakfast: £24 double.
♒⊞⊡♨ ▥ Ⓥ ♨ 📺 ▥
🛢 🎄 🎋

Crescent Lodge ♨
🛏🛏
20 Swan Rd., Harrogate,
HG1 2SA
☎ (0423) 503688
*Elegant and well-appointed
period town house, welcoming a
maximum of 6 guests. Quiet,
yet close to all amenities.*
Bedrooms: 2 single, 2 twin.
Bathrooms: 2 private,
1 public.
Bed & breakfast: £12-£14
single, £24-£28 double.
Parking for 3.
♨ ▥ Ⓥ ♨ 📺 ▥ 🛢 🏃 🎄
🎋

Knox Mill House
🛏🛏
Knox Mill La., Harrogate,
HG3 2AE
☎ (0423) 60650
*Delightfully renovated 200-
year-old millhouse in a quiet
rural setting. Just off the A61
and less than 2 miles from
Harrogate town centre.*
Bedrooms: 1 double & 2 twin.
Bathrooms: 2 public.
Bed & breakfast: from £15
single, £25-£30 double.
Parking for 4.
♒♨ ▥ 🛢 📺 ▥ 🛢 🏃 🎄

HAWES

N. Yorkshire
Map ref 5B3

Fell-climbing is popular
round Hawes and
Wensleydale cheese is
made here. Upper Dales
Folk Museum has
collection of books about
Yorkshire. Nearby is
spectacular Hardraw
Force Waterfall. ⓘ

Dale View

Burtersett Rd., Hawes,
DL8 3NP
☎ (096 97) 752
*Spacious family house on the
A684 between Hawes and
Leyburn. Close to the National
Park Centre and other
amenities.*
Bedrooms: 1 single, 2 double.
Bathrooms: 1 public.
Bed & breakfast: from £11
single, from £22 double.
⊡♨ ▥ ▥ 🎄

White Hart Inn ♨
🛏🛏
Main St., Hawes, DL8 3QL
☎ (096 97) 259
*Small country inn with a
friendly welcome, offering
home-cooked meals using local
produce. An ideal centre for
exploring the Yorkshire Dales.*
Bedrooms: 1 single, 4 double
& 2 twin.
Bathrooms: 2 public.
Bed & breakfast: £12 single,
£24 double.
Lunch available.
Evening meal 7pm (l.o.
8.30pm).
Parking for 7.
♒♨ 🛢 ♨ 📺 🍴 ꜱᴘ 🎋

HAWNBY

N. Yorkshire
Map ref 5C3

6m NW. Helmsley

Cringle Carr Farm
🛏
Hawnby, York, YO6 5LT
☎ Bilsdale (043 96) 264
*75-acre dairy farm. Edwardian
stone-built farmhouse in an
agricultural area close to the
North Yorkshire Moors. The
River Rye runs through the
farmland.*
Bedrooms: 1 twin, 1 family
room.
Bathrooms: 1 public.
Bed & breakfast: £18-£20
double.
Half board: £15-£16.50 daily,
£105-£112 weekly.

Evening meal 6.30pm (l.o.
7.30pm).
Parking for 2.
Open April-October.
♒♨ ▥ 📺 ▥ 🍴 ♨ ✲ 🎄
🎋

Laskill Farm
🛏🛏
Hawnby, York, YO6 5NB
☎ Bilsdale (043 96) 268
*600-acre mixed farm.
Surrounded by beautiful
scenery in a peaceful setting
within the National Park.
Ideal location for bird watching
and walking; pony trekking
available locally. Evening meal
by arrangement only.*
Bedrooms: 1 double & 1 twin,
1 family room.
Bathrooms: 1 public.
Bed & breakfast: £11-£12
single, from £22 double.
Half board: max. £19 daily.
Parking for 6.
Open April-October.
♒⊞ ▥ 🛢 Ⓥ ✂ ♨ 📺 ▥
🛢 ♨ 🍴 🏃 ✐ 🎄 🎋

HAWORTH

W. Yorkshire
Map ref 4B1

This small Pennine town
is famous as home of the
Bronte family. The
parsonage is now a
Bronte Museum where
furniture and possessions
of the family are
displayed. Moors and
Bronte waterfalls nearby
and the Keighley and
Worth Valley Steam
Railway passes through
town. ⓘ

Mrs. M. Adam
(Listed)
42 Ivy Bank La., Haworth,
Keighley, BD22 8PD
☎ (0535) 45768
*Comfortable Victorian family
home with views of moorland
countryside. Lovely walks,
Bronte Museum and a steam
railway all nearby. Home
cooking. No smoking
preferred.*
Bedrooms: 1 double & 1 twin.
Bathrooms: 1 public.
Bed & breakfast: £10 single,
£20 double.
Parking for 2.
♒🛎⊞ ▥ 🛢 Ⓥ ✂ ♨ 📺
▥ 🛢 🏃 🎄

Ebor House
Lees La., Haworth, Keighley
BD22 8RA
☎ (0535) 45869
Continued ▶

HAWORTH

Continued

Yorkshire stone-built house of character, conveniently placed for the main tourist attractions of Haworth, including the Worth Valley Railway and Bronte Parsonage and Museum.
Bedrooms: 2 twin.
Bathrooms: 1 public.
Bed & breakfast: max. £10 single, max. £20 double.
Parking for 2.

Eden Lodge
Spring Head, Lord La.,
Haworth, Keighley,
BD22 7RX
☎ (0535) 44470
Delightful 17th C. open-beamed millworkers' cottage, with private trout fishing on the River Worth which runs through the garden.
Bedrooms: 1 single, 1 double & 1 twin, 1 family room.
Bathrooms: 2 public.
Bed & breakfast: £9 single, £18 double.
Parking for 3.

Howarth's End
Listed
1 Queen St., Haworth,
Keighley, BD22 8QB
☎ (0535) 45079
Small end-of-terrace cottage where a warm, friendly service is offered. Evening meal available by arrangement.
Bedrooms: 1 single, 1 double.
Bathrooms: 1 public.
Bed & breakfast: from £20 double.
Parking for 1.

Old White Lion Hotel ⋒
Haworth, Keighley,
BD22 8DU
☎ (0535) 42313
Family-run hotel with a candlelit restaurant. Close to the museum, parsonage and steam railway. Special weekend breaks available.
Bedrooms: 2 single, 7 double & 2 twin, 1 family room.
Bathrooms: 12 private.
Bed & breakfast: £24 single, £34.50 double.
Half board: £24.75-£33.50 daily.
Lunch available.
Evening meal 7pm (l.o. 10pm).

Parking for 10.
Credit: Access, Visa, Diners, Amex.

Mrs. V. Woodhouse
The Croft, West La.,
Haworth, Keighley,
BD22 8EL
☎ (0535) 43389
A country house with open views, minutes from the Bronte Museum, moors and shops. All bedrooms have their own WC. Tea or coffee served in the evening on request.
Bedrooms: 2 double & 1 twin.
Bathrooms: 2 public.
Bed & breakfast: from £9 single, £18 double.
Parking for 4.

Ye Sleeping House
8 Main St., Haworth, Nr. Keighley, BD22 8DA
☎ (0535) 45992 & 44102
Small and homely Victorian terraced house with well-furnished, spacious rooms, on the main street of the town made famous by the Brontes. Evening meal by arrangement. All rooms suitable for double, twin or family use.
Bedrooms: 1 single, 1 double, 1 family room.
Bathrooms: 1 public.
Bed & breakfast: £9.50-£12.50 single, £19-£25 double.
Half board: £14-£17 daily, £90-£119 weekly.
Parking for 2.
Credit: Access, Visa, Diners, Amex.

HEALEY

N. Yorkshire
Map ref 5C3

3m W. of Masham
Village to the west of the attractive market town of Masham, on the eastern edge of the Yorkshire Dales.

Pasture House ⋒
Healey, Ripon, HG4 4LJ
☎ Ripon (0765) 89149
100-year-old detached house in 3.5 acres at the foot of Colsterdale; a beautiful, small and quiet dale leading to grouse moors. Fishing and golf available by arrangement.
Bedrooms: 1 double & 1 twin, 1 family room.
Bathrooms: 1 public.
Bed & breakfast: from £9 single, from £18 double.

Half board: from £15 daily, from £100 weekly.
Lunch available.
Evening meal 7pm.
Parking for 6.

HEBDEN BRIDGE

W. Yorkshire
Map ref 4B1

Originally small town on packhorse route, Hebden Bridge grew into booming mill town in 18th C with rows of 'up-and-down' houses of several storeys built against hillsides. Ancient 'pace-egg play' custom held on Good Friday. *i*

Leicester House
Market St., Hebden Bridge, HX7 7DD
☎ (0422) 843053
Large rooms and a homely and informal atmosphere, in a central location in the town. An excellent touring area.
Bedrooms: 1 single, 1 double, 1 family room.
Bathrooms: 1 public.
Bed & breakfast: max. £10 single, max. £20 double.
Parking for 2.

Stray Leaves
Listed
Wadsworth, Hebden Bridge, HX7 7TN
☎ Halifax (0422) 842353
Private bungalow in pleasant rural surroundings overlooking Hebden Bridge. 1 mile from the centre. Evening meals available by arrangement.
Bedrooms: 1 single, 1 family room.
Bathrooms: 1 private, 1 public.
Bed & breakfast: £8-£9 single, £16-£18 double.
Half board: £12-£13 daily.
Parking for 4.

HELMSLEY

N. Yorkshire
Map ref 4C1

Pretty North Riding town on the River Rye at the entrance to Ryedale and the North York Moors with large cobbled square and remains of 12th C castle, several inns, notably the 16th C Black Swan, and All Saints' Church. *i*

Beaconsfield Guest House
Bondgate, Helmsley, York, YO6 5BW
☎ (0439) 71346
Large country house with comfortable rooms. Ideal for York, the moors and the East Coast. Double rooms can be let as singles.
Bedrooms: 4 double & 2 twin.
Bathrooms: 2 public.
Bed & breakfast: £17.50-£19 single, £29-£32 double.
Parking for 8.

HEPTONSTALL

W. Yorkshire
Map ref 4B1

1m NW. Hebden Bridge
Quaint village above Hebden Bridge with an assortment of narrow streets, weavers' cottages, weather worn houses and the ruins of a 12th C church. The 17th C Grammar School, now a museum, is situated in a churchyard.

29 Slack Top
Heptonstall, Hebden Bridge, HX7 7HA
☎ Hebden Bridge (0422) 843636
Glorious views overlooking national parkland near the Pennine/Calderdale Ways. Easily accessible by bus, rail or car. Under 1 hour's drive to Leeds/Manchester.
Bedrooms: 1 single, 1 double & 1 twin.
Bathrooms: 1 public.
Bed & breakfast: £10-£12 single, £20-£24 double.
Parking for 4.

THERE IS A SPECIAL SECTION IN THIS GUIDE LISTING ACCOMMODATION ESPECIALLY SUITABLE FOR GROUPS AND YOUNG PEOPLE.

HIBALDSTOW

Humberside
Map ref 4C1

3m SW. Brigg
Village close to the M180, south of the River Humber, once a Roman settlement.

Brookside
😊😊

Beckside, Hibaldstow, Nr. Brigg, S. Humberside DN20 9EQ
☎ Brigg (0652) 54347
Delightful cottage in a beautiful setting on the A15, close to country parks and windmills. Lincoln 23 miles and the Humber Bridge 12 miles away.
Bedrooms: 1 single, 1 double & 1 twin.
Bathrooms: 1 public.
Bed & breakfast: £13-£15 single, £22-£26 double.
Half board: £16-£19 daily, £125-£130 weekly.
Evening meal 6pm (l.o. 6pm).
Parking for 10.
🛇 🗂 💷 🛄 🛈 Ⓥ ✗ 🏮 📺
🏕 🛆 ❀ 🏠 🛗 🏮

HOLTBY

N. Yorkshire
Map ref 4C1

5m E. York
Unspoilt village close to Stamford Bridge. A farming community overlooking the Vale of York with the Wolds in the background.

Holtby Grange M
😊😊

Holtby, York, YO3 9XQ
☎ York (0904) 489933
90-acre arable farm. Peaceful farmhouse in open countryside, offering clean accommodation and emphasis on food. Please send stamp only for brochure. Minimum stay 2 nights.
Bedrooms: 1 double & 1 twin, 1 family room.
Bathrooms: 1 public.
Bed & breakfast: £18 double.
Half board: £13.75 daily, £86.65 weekly.
Evening meal 7pm (l.o. 3pm).
Parking for 3.
Open April-October.
🛇 ❀ 💷 🛄 Ⓥ 🏮 📺 🛗 ✗ 🏮

HORTON-IN-RIBBLESDALE

N. Yorkshire
Map ref 5B3

5m N. Settle
On the River Ribble and an ideal centre for pot-holing. The Pennine Way runs eastward over Pen-y-ghent, one of the famous 'Three Peaks'. 🔢

Wagis Guest House M
Townend, Horton-in-Ribblesdale, Settle, BD24 0EX
☎ (072 96) 320
Farm and barn (dated 1735) conversion in a beautiful limestone area close to the Three Peaks, Pennine Way, Settle/Carlisle Railway and Yorkshire Dales National Park.
Bedrooms: 1 double & 2 twin, 1 family room.
Bathrooms: 3 public.
Bed & breakfast: £10-£10.50 single, £20-£21 double.
Half board: £16.50-£17 daily, max. £110 weekly.
Evening meal 6.30pm (l.o. 6.30pm).
Parking for 10.
🛇 ☕ 🛈 Ⓥ 🏮 💷 ❀ 🐾
💷 🏮

HUBBERHOLME

N. Yorkshire
Map ref 4B1

1m NW. Buckden
Ancient Upper Wharfedale village with a charming and interesting church noted for its rood loft dated 1558, a rare survival in England.

The George Inn
Listed

Kirk Gill, Hubberholme, Skipton, BD23 5JE
☎ Kettlewell (075 676) 223
An ancient inn in the heart of the Yorkshire Dales.
Bedrooms: 3 double & 2 twin.
Bathrooms: 1 public.
Bed & breakfast: £28 double.
Lunch available.
Evening meal 7.30pm (l.o. 9pm).
Parking for 20.
🛇8 ❀ 🛈 💷 ◡ ↲ 🏮 🏮

HUDDERSFIELD

W. Yorkshire
Map ref 4B1

Founded on wool and cloth, has a famous choral society. Town centre redeveloped, but several good Victorian buildings remain, including railway station, St. Peter's Church, Tolson Memorial Museum, art gallery and nearby Colne Valley Museum. Castle Hill overlooks the town. 🔢

Hollies Guest House M
Listed

286 Halifax Old Rd., Grimscar, Huddersfield, HD2 2SP
☎ (0484) 27097
In woodland on the valley side with wildlife, birdwatching and angling. A beautiful area, renowned for its industrial/historic heritage and music. Some rooms with washbasins and colour TV.
Bedrooms: 2 single, 1 double & 1 twin.
Bathrooms: 2 public.
Bed & breakfast: £10-£15 single, £20-£30 double.
Half board: £15-£21 daily, £100-£140 weekly.
Lunch available.
Evening meal 6pm (l.o. 9am).
Parking for 4.
🛇3 🕭 ❀ 🛄 🛈 🏮 📺 💷 🛆
❀ ✗ 🏮 🏮 📺 🗊

Holmcliffe M
😊😊

16 Mountjoy Rd., Edgerton, Huddersfield, HD1 5PZ
☎ (0484) 29598
Large Victorian double-fronted, detached stone house in a quiet residential area. Close to the town centre.
Bedrooms: 1 single, 1 double & 3 twin.
Bathrooms: 1 public.
Bed & breakfast: £11 single, £20 double.
Half board: £13.50-£14.50 daily, £94.50-£100 weekly.
Evening meal 6.30pm (l.o. 5pm).
Parking for 6.
🛇 🗂 ☕ 💷 🛄 🛈 Ⓥ 🏮 📺 💷
🛆 ✗ 🏮 🗊 🗊

HULL

See Kingston-upon-Hull.

HUSTHWAITE

N. Yorkshire
Map ref 4C1

4m N. Easingwold
Attractive village beneath Hambleton Hills of weathered brickwork houses and a green dominated by medieval church of St. Nicholas with some Norman features.

Hunters Lodge
😊😊

Husthwaite, York, YO6 3SY
☎ Coxwold (034 76) 539
Detached residence with a large, scenic garden in a tranquil village in the Howardian Hills. Indoor swimming pool (heated May to September), sauna, solarium and games room.
Bedrooms: 1 double & 1 twin, 1 family room.
Bathrooms: 1 private, 1 public.
Bed & breakfast: £10-£12 single, £20-£22 double.
Parking for 6.
🛇 🛄 📺 💷 🏮 ▲ 🏮 ❀ 🏮

HUTTON CONYERS

N. Yorkshire
Map ref 5C3

2m NE. Ripon

Hutton Grange M
Hutton Moor, Hutton Conyers, Ripon, HG4 5LX
☎ Melmerby (076 584) 520
12-acre smallholding. Large stone-built farmhouse with TV lounge and dining room exclusively for guests' use.
Bedrooms: 2 double & 1 twin.
Bathrooms: 1 public.
Bed & breakfast: £10-£15 single, £20-£23 double.
Half board: £16-£17.50 daily, £120-£122.50 weekly.
Evening meal 7pm (l.o. 8pm).
Parking for 8.
🛇 🏮 🛄 🛈 Ⓥ 🏮 📺 💷 🛆
▲ 🏮 ◔ ❀ 🏮 🗊

GROUPS, CONSORTIA AND AGENCIES SPECIALISING IN FARM AND COUNTRY HOLIDAYS ARE LISTED IN A SPECIAL SECTION OF THIS GUIDE.

INDIVIDUAL PROPRIETORS HAVE SUPPLIED ALL DETAILS OF ACCOMMODATION. ALTHOUGH WE DO CHECK FOR ACCURACY, WE ADVISE YOU TO CONFIRM PRICES AND OTHER INFORMATION AT THE TIME OF BOOKING.

ILKLEY

W. Yorkshire
Map ref 4B1

This moorland spa town, famous for its ballad, is a lively tourist centre with many hotels and shops. 16th C Manor House, now a museum, displays local prehistoric and Roman relics. Popular walk leads up Heber's Ghyll to mysterious Swastika Stone, White Wells, 18th C plunge baths on Ilkley Moor. *i*

Beech House
Listed
5 St. James Rd., Ilkley, LS29 9PY
☎ (0943) 601995
Spacious, Victorian house, close to the town centre and public transport. Quiet location within easy walking distance of riverside and moor.
Bedrooms: 1 double & 1 twin.
Bathrooms: 1 public.
Bed & breakfast: £8.50 single, £17 double.
Parking for 2.
⛵ 🗻 UL �ͅ ⌿ 🛏 TV ▥ ◚ 🐾 🏳

Briarwood
😊
Queens Drive, Ilkley, LS29 9QW
☎ (0943) 600870
Victorian ladies' residence with spacious rooms and excellent views. Visitors are entertained as house guests. 5 minutes' walk from Ilkley Moor and Ilkley College.
Bedrooms: 1 double & 1 twin.
Bathrooms: 1 public.
Bed & breakfast: £8 single, £16 double.
Half board: £12 daily, £80 weekly.
Evening meal 6pm (l.o. 7pm).
Parking for 5.
⛵ UL 🛏 ▥ TV ▥ 🐾 🏳

Lanshaw
19 River View, Leeds Rd., Ilkley, LS29 8LP
☎ (0943) 601261
Small, comfortable house with parking, near bus routes and convenient for touring the Dales. Reduction for week-long bookings.
Bedrooms: 1 double & 1 twin.
Bathrooms: 1 public.
Bed & breakfast: £17-£18 double.
Parking for 3.
Open April-October.
🗻 ♥ ⌿ 🛏 TV ▥ ◚ 🐾 🏳

Star Inn M
😊😊
1 Leeds Rd., Ilkley, LS29 8DH
☎ (0943) 607227
In the town centre, 100 yards from the park which has facilities for rugby, tennis, cricket, boating, putting, swimming and golf.
Bedrooms: 2 twin, 4 family rooms.
Bathrooms: 2 public; 1 private shower.
Bed & breakfast: £13-£14 single, £22-£25 double.
Lunch available.
Parking for 5.
⛵ ♥ 🛏 TV ▥ ◚ 🝙 🐾 🏳

West Hall
Listed
Nesfield, Ilkley, LS29 0BX
☎ Addingham (0943) 830573
Renovated longhouse (originally a timber-framed farmhouse) in a rural location by the River Wharfe, 3 miles from Ilkley and 6 miles from Skipton. Home produce and free range eggs.
Bedrooms: 1 single, 1 double, 1 family room.
Bathrooms: 2 public.
Bed & breakfast: £8.50-£9.50 single, £16-£19 double.
Half board: £13-£14 daily, £70-£90 weekly.
Evening meal 6pm (l.o. 7.30pm).
Parking for 3.
⛵ UL 🛏 V TV ▥ 🐾 DAP

INGLEBY GREENHOW

N. Yorkshire
Map ref 5C3

4m E. Stokesley
Perched on the edge of Cleveland Hills, the village boasts the Norman church of St. Andrew's with well preserved carving and effigies of a priest and a knight. Ingleby Moor rises 1300 ft above village.

Howe Hill Farm
Listed
Ingleby Greenhow, Great Ayton, Cleveland TS9 6RD
☎ Stokesley (0642) 778288
62-acre sheep farm. Spacious, modern, stone farmhouse in one acre of garden, on the western edge of the North Yorkshire Moors.
Bedrooms: 1 single, 1 double & 1 twin.
Bathrooms: 1 public.

Bed & breakfast: £9.50-£12.50 single, £19-£22 double.
Parking for 5.
Open April-October.
⛵ 🗻 UL 🛏 TV ▥ 🐾 🏳

Manor House Farm M
Listed
Ingleby Greenhow, Middlesbrough, Cleveland TS9 6RB
☎ Great Ayton (0642) 722384
164-acre mixed farm. In a picture book setting surrounded by hills and forests, in the National Park. Ideal for nature lovers, walking, touring, riding and relaxing.
Bedrooms: 1 double & 2 twin.
Bathrooms: 2 public.
Bed & breakfast: £13.50-£14.50 single, £27-£29 double.
Half board: £22-£24 daily, £147-£160 weekly.
Evening meal 7pm (l.o. 7pm).
Parking for 36.
⛵6 🗻 ⊡ ♥ 🛏 V 🛏 TV ▥ ◚ 🝙 🕤 ⌂ ▸ ✿ 🐾 🏳

INGLETON

N. Yorkshire
Map ref 5B3

Ingleton is a thriving tourist centre for fell-walkers, climbers and pot-holers. Popular walks up beautiful Twiss Valley to Ingleborough Summit, Whernside and White Scar Caves. *i*

Ingleborough View M
😊😊
Main St., Ingleton, Carnforth, Lancashire LA6 3HH
☎ (052 42) 41523
Family-run guesthouse with a friendly atmosphere and panoramic views. Ideally situated for walking and for touring the Dales and Lake District.
Bedrooms: 2 double & 1 twin.
Bathrooms: 2 public.
Bed & breakfast: £9-£10 single, £18-£20 double.
Parking for 4.
⛵ ♥ 🛏 V 🛏 TV ▥ ◚ 🐾 🏳 SP

Langber Country Guest House
Ingleton, Carnforth, Lancashire LA6 3DT
☎ (0468) 41587
Detached country house with large gardens and panoramic views. Ideal for family holidays. Good touring centre for the Lake District, Yorkshire Dales and coast.

Bedrooms: 1 single, 1 double & 1 twin, 3 family rooms.
Bathrooms: 2 public.
Bed & breakfast: £9.25-£10.50 single, £18.50-£21 double.
Half board: £12.75-£14 daily, £85-£95 weekly.
Evening meal 6.30pm (l.o. 5.30pm).
Parking for 6.
⛵ UL 🛏 V 🛏 TV ▥ ◚ 🝙 ✿ DAP SP

Stacksteads Farm M
😊
Ingleton, Carnforth, Lancashire LA6 3HS
☎ (0468) 41386
Friendly atmosphere and panoramic views on a smallholding in a pleasant, quiet location one mile from the village. Access to the dales, lakes and Lancashire coast. Half a mile from the Masons Arms off the A65.
Bedrooms: 1 double & 1 twin, 1 family room.
Bathrooms: 1 private, 1 public.
Bed & breakfast: £9 single, £18-£20 double.
Evening meal 6.30pm (l.o. 8pm).
Parking for 6.
⛵ UL 🛏 V 🛏 TV ▥ ◚ ⌣ ✿ 🏳

KEIGHLEY

W. Yorkshire
Map ref 4B1

Pleasant Victorian town where Charlotte Bronte used to shop. Cliffe Castle is an art gallery and museum with large collection of Victorian bygones. 17th C East Riddlesden Hall (National Trust) has fine medieval tithe barn. Trips on Keighley and Worth Valley Railway.

Currer Laithe Farm M
Moss Carr Rd., Long Lee, Keighley, BD21 4SL
☎ (0535) 604387
170-acre beef rearing farm. 16th C. farmhouse overlooking 170 acres of pasture in Bronteland. Panoramic views, a warm welcome and a variety of animals. Popular with disabled persons.
Bedrooms: 1 single, 2 double & 3 twin, 1 family room.
Bathrooms: 2 public.
Bed & breakfast: £7.50 single, £15 double.

Half board: £10 daily, £70 weekly.
Evening meal 7pm.
Parking for 10.
ॐ ♿ Ⓤ 🔋 🍴 📺 🏛 ♿ 🏹 ♨

KETTLEWELL
N. Yorkshire
Map ref 5B3

See also Starbotton.
Set in the spectacular scenery of the Yorkshire Dales National Park between Wharfedale and Wensleydale, this former market town is a convenient stopping place for climbers and walkers. Dramatic rock formation of Kilnsey Crag is 3 miles south.

Fold Farm ♨
😁😁
Kettlewell, Skipton,
BD23 5RJ
☎ (075 676) 886
350-acre mixed/hill/sheep farm. 15th C. stone-built farmhouse in the village.
Bedrooms: 2 double & 1 twin.
Bathrooms: 1 public.
Bed & breakfast: max. £12.50 single, £20-£22 double.
Half board: max. £36 daily.
Evening meal 6.30pm (l.o. 11am).
Parking for 8.
Open April-October.
ॐ Ⓤ 🔋 🍴 📺 🏛 ☕ ∪ ↑ ✓ 🏹 ♨

KILBURN
N. Yorkshire
Map ref 4C1

Attractive village of stone cottages with tiled roofs in the Hambleton Hills, famous for its White Horse cut by local schoolmaster, Thomas Hodgson, in 1857 and for the mouse carved in oak which is the famous trade mark of Robert Thompson, whose craft workshop still produces hand made oak furniture.

Church Farm
(Listed)
Kilburn, York, YO6 4AH
☎ Coxwold (034 76) 318
400-acre mixed farm. Large farmhouse in a picturesque village. Ideal area for gliding, walking and touring. Ample parking space. Everyone made welcome. Evening meal optional.

Bedrooms: 1 twin, 1 family room.
Bathrooms: 1 public.
Bed & breakfast: max. £8.50 single, max. £17 double.
Half board: max. £14 daily, max. £90 weekly.
Parking for 4.
Open March-November.
ॐ 🔥 Ⓤ 🍴 📺 🏛 ☕ 🏹

KINGSTON-UPON-HULL
Humberside
Map ref 4C1

Busy seaport with a modern city centre and deep-sea fishing base at junction of the Rivers Hull and Humber, founded by Cistercian monks in 12th C. Maritime traditions in the town, docks and the museum, and the home of William Wilberforce, the slavery abolitionist, whose house is now a museum. The world's longest single span suspension bridge crosses the Humber 5 miles west. 🛈

Earlsmere Hotel
😁😁
76-78 Sunnybank, Off Spring Bank West, Kingston-upon-Hull, N. Humberside
HU3 1LQ
☎ (0482) 41977 Telex 592729 FASTA G FAX: 445691
Small family-run hotel in a quiet area overlooking Hymers College sports fields. Some private suites are available.
Bedrooms: 11 single, 4 family rooms.
Bathrooms: 7 private, 2 public.
Bed & breakfast: £17.25-£26.45 single, £34.50-£40.25 double.
Half board: £27-£36 daily, £185-£250 weekly.
Evening meal 6pm (l.o. 5pm).
ॐ ♿ 🖵 ✿ 🔋 Ⓥ 🍴 📺 🏛 ☕ SP

THERE IS A SPECIAL SECTION IN THIS GUIDE LISTING ACCOMMODATION ESPECIALLY SUITABLE FOR GROUPS AND YOUNG PEOPLE.

KIRBY HILL
N. Yorkshire
Map ref 5B3

4m NW. Richmond
Hamlet in hilly country near Richmond consisting of 17th and 18th C houses grouped round grassy and cobbled square, with almshouses and grammar school founded by John Dakyn in 16th C.

Shoulder of Mutton Inn ♨
😁😁
Kirby Hill, Richmond,
DL11 7JH
☎ Richmond (0748) 2772
Small, family-run country inn with emphasis on service. In beautiful Yorkshire countryside, within 10 minutes of Scotch Corner and central for Ripon, Newcastle, the Lake District and East Coast.
Bedrooms: 3 double & 1 twin, 1 family room.
Bathrooms: 3 private, 1 public.
Bed & breakfast: £25.80-£31 double.
Half board: £21.50-£23.50 daily, £136.50-£150.50 weekly.
Evening meal 7.30pm (l.o. 9pm).
Parking for 30.
ॐ 🖵 🔋 Ⓥ 🍴 ∪ 🏹 ⬎ SP

KIRKBYMOORSIDE
N. Yorkshire
Map ref 5C3

Attractive market town with remains of Norman castle. Good centre for exploring moors and nearby are wild daffodils of Farndale.

Lion Inn
Blakey Ridge, Kirkbymoorside, York,
YO6 6LQ
☎ Lastingham (075 15) 320
13th C. freehouse in the centre of the North York moors, with breathtaking views.
Bedrooms: 3 double & 1 twin, 1 family room.
Bathrooms: 1 public; 1 private shower.
Bed & breakfast: £15 single, £30 double.
Half board: £18.50-£25 daily.
Lunch available.
Evening meal 5.30pm (l.o. 10.30pm).
Parking for 100.
ॐ 🖵 ☕ 🔋 Ⓥ 🍴 ☕ ✿ 🏹 ♨

KIRKHAM
N. Yorkshire
Map ref 4C1

5m SW. Malton

Old Station House
(Listed)
Kirkham Abbey, York,
YO6 7JS
☎ Whitwell-on-the-Hill (065 381) 658
Family-run guesthouse with views across the River Derwent to the Old Priory. Near York, Castle Howard, the moors and Ryedale.
Bedrooms: 1 double & 1 twin.
Bathrooms: 1 private, 1 public.
Bed & breakfast: £20-£24 double.
Lunch available.
Evening meal 4pm (l.o. 5.45pm).
Parking for 20.
Open March-October.
Credit: Access, Visa.
ॐ 🔥 🖵 ✿ 🔋 Ⓥ 🍴 ⬎ 🏹 ♨

KIRTON IN LINDSEY
Humberside
Map ref 4C1

Small town within easy reach of Scunthorpe, Brigg and Gainsborough, and not far from the Lincolnshire Wolds.

Mount Pleasant Mill
North Cliff Rd., Kirton in Lindsey, Gainsborough, Lincolnshire DN21 4NH
☎ Kirton Lindsey (0652) 648251
Grade II listed windmill and millhouse with fine views, set in 1.5 acres, on the B1398 half a mile north of Kirton in Lindsey. All bedrooms can be let as single occupancy.
Bedrooms: 3 double & 1 twin, 1 family room.
Bathrooms: 2 private, 1 public.
Bed & breakfast: £12.50-£22.50 single, £25-£32 double.
Half board: £17.50-£27.50 daily, £122.50-£192.50 weekly.
Lunch available.
Evening meal 5pm.
Parking for 20.
Credit: Access, Visa.
ॐ ☕ Ⓤ 🔋 Ⓥ 🍴 📺 🏛 ☕ ❄ 🏹 ♨

WE ADVISE YOU TO CONFIRM YOUR BOOKING IN WRITING.

KNARESBOROUGH

N. Yorkshire
Map ref 4B1

Picturesque market town on the River Nidd, famous for its 11th C castle ruins overlooking town and river gorge. Attractions include oldest chemist's shop in country, prophetess Mother Shipton's cave near Dropping Well and Court House Museum. Boating on river. ℹ️

Ebor Mount 𝖒
♨️♨️

18 York Place,
Knaresborough, HG5 0AA
☎ Harrogate (0423) 863315
250-year-old coaching house with large, comfortable rooms. Ideal touring centre.
Bedrooms: 2 double & 2 twin,
3 family rooms.
Bathrooms: 2 public;
6 private showers.
Bed & breakfast: £12-£20 single, £25-£30 double.
Half board: £18-£26 daily,
£120-£140 weekly.
Evening meal 6.30pm (l.o. midday).
Parking for 10.
Credit: Visa.
♿ ▯ ▯ ♻ ▮ ﹣ ▥ ▬ ▯ ▯
▯ ▯

Yorkshire Lass 𝖒
♨️♨️♨️

High Bridge, Harrogate Rd.,
Knaresborough, HG5 8DA
☎ Harrogate (0423) 862962
Detached inn on main Harrogate/York road, with three cottage-style bedrooms overlooking River Nidd. Real ales, wines, large selection of spirits. Specialising in traditional Yorkshire dishes.
Bedrooms: 1 double & 2 twin.
Bathrooms: 3 private.
Bed & breakfast: £25-£30 single, £40 double.
Lunch available.
Evening meal 5.30pm (l.o. 10.30pm).
Parking for 20.
Credit: Visa, Amex.
▯ ▯ ♻ ▮ ▯ ▥ ﹣ ▮ ✗
▯

LINTON-ON-OUSE

N. Yorkshire
Map ref 5C3

The Manor House
Linton-on-Ouse, York,
YO6 2AY
☎ (034 74) 391
60-acre poultry/horse farm. Large manor house with oak beams, in its own grounds and garden, with a 4 acre paddock at the rear for horses and animals.
Bedrooms: 1 twin, 2 family rooms.
Bathrooms: 2 private,
1 public.
Bed & breakfast: £10-£12 single, £20-£24 double.
Parking for 33.
♿ ♨ ▯ ▯ ▯ ▮ ﹣ ▯ ▥
▯ ✗ ▯ ▯ ▯

LONG PRESTON

N. Yorkshire
Map ref 4B1

Village surrounded by limestone country and overlooking Ribblesdale.

Maypole Inn 𝖒
♨️♨️

Maypole Green, Main St.,
Long Preston, Skipton,
BD23 4PH
☎ (072 94) 219
17th C. inn on the village green, with easy access to many attractive walks in the surrounding Dales. Tea and coffee making facilities in residents' lounge.
Bedrooms: 2 double & 1 twin,
1 family room.
Bathrooms: 1 public.
Bed & breakfast: £13.50 single, £21.50 double.
Half board: £15-£20 daily,
£115-£150 weekly.
Lunch available.
Evening meal 6pm (l.o. 9pm).
Parking for 25.
♿ ▮ ▯ ▥ ﹣ ▯ ▥ ﹣ ▮ ✗ ▯
▯ ▯ ▯ ▯

LOW BRADLEY

N. Yorkshire
Map ref 4B1

2m SE. Skipton

14 Aire Valley Drive
Low Bradley, Keighley,
W. Yorkshire BD20 9EY
☎ Cross Hills (0535) 33432
Detached bungalow with a spacious lounge/diner, offering a warm welcome and hospitality. Pleasant surroundings, in a village 2 miles from Skipton.
Bedrooms: 1 twin.
Bathrooms: 1 public.
Bed & breakfast: £9-£10 single, £18-£20 double.
Evening meal 6.50pm.
Parking for 1.
Open April-October.
♨ ♻ ▯ ▮ ﹣ ▥ ▬ ﹣ ▯

LUDDENDEN FOOT

W. Yorkshire
Map ref 4B1

In the Calder Valley. Branwell Bronte was put in charge of the station here in 1840.

Crib Farm
♨️♨️♨️

Luddenden Foot, Halifax,
HX2 6JJ
☎ Halifax (0422) 883285
200-acre dairy farm. Family-run farm where a warm welcome is assured. On the Pennine slopes with bracing hill air and open moorland adjacent. Good approach, not isolated.
Bedrooms: 1 single, 1 double,
1 family room.
Bathrooms: 2 private,
1 public.
Bed & breakfast: £10 single, £20-£24 double.
Half board: £16-£18 daily,
£98-£112 weekly.
Evening meal 6.30pm (l.o. 7.30pm).
Parking for 11.
Open January-November.
♿ ▮ ▮ ✗ ﹣ ▥ ▬ ﹣ ▮ ✗
▯ ▯ ✿ ✗ ▯ ▯

MALHAM

N. Yorkshire
Map ref 4B1

11m NNW. Skipton
Hamlet of stone cottages amid rugged limestone scenery in the Yorkshire Dales National Park. Malham Cove is a curving sheer white cliff 240 ft high. Malham Tarn, one of Yorkshire's few natural lakes, belongs to the National Trust. National Park Centre.

Beck Hall Guest House
Malham, Skipton, BD23 4DJ
☎ Airton (072 93) 332
Family-run guesthouse set in a spacious riverside garden. Homely atmosphere, four-poster beds, log fires and home cooking.
Bedrooms: 1 single, 4 double & 4 twin, 3 family rooms.
Bathrooms: 2 private,
3 public.
Bed & breakfast: from £15.50 single, from £21 double.
Half board: from £14.50 daily, from £98 weekly.
Lunch available.
Evening meal 7pm (l.o. 8pm).
Parking for 30.
Open January-November.
♿ ♨ ▯ ▮ ▥ ﹣ ▥ ▬ ▮ ✿
▯

MALTON

N. Yorkshire
Map ref 5D3

A thriving farming town on the River Derwent with large livestock market and famous for race horse training. The local museum has many World War II relics from the 'Eden' Prisoner of war camp on site in the town. Castle Howard within easy reach. ℹ️

Gate Inn
Yorkersgate, Malton,
YO17 0AB
☎ (0653) 692033
Bedrooms: 1 single, 1 double & 1 twin, 2 family rooms.
Bathrooms: 1 public.
Bed & breakfast: £10-£12 single, £20-£24 double.
Parking for 1.
♿ ♨ ▮ ﹣ ▥ ▬ ✗ ▯

Low Easthorpe Farmhouse
Easthorpe, Malton,
YO17 0QX
☎ (0653) 695006

INDIVIDUAL PROPRIETORS HAVE SUPPLIED ALL DETAILS OF ACCOMMODATION. ALTHOUGH WE DO CHECK FOR ACCURACY, WE ADVISE YOU TO CONFIRM PRICES AND OTHER INFORMATION AT THE TIME OF BOOKING.

MAP REFERENCES APPLY TO THE COLOUR MAPS TOWARDS THE END OF THIS GUIDE.

25-acre mixed farm. Farmhouse in beautiful countryside 3 miles west of Malton, with views towards Castle Howard. Ideal location for rambling and pony trekking. Four-poster beds.
Bedrooms: 2 double, 1 family room.
Bathrooms: 1 public.
Bed & breakfast: £9-£10 single, £18-£20 double.
Parking for 6.

Squirrel Cottage

`Listed`

81 Middlecave Rd., Malton, YO17 0NQ
☎ (0653) 692176
Interesting period cottage on the outskirts of town. An ideal centre for touring the Dales and wolds.
Bedrooms: 2 double, 1 family room.
Bathrooms: 1 public.
Bed & breakfast: £9.50-£11 single, £19-£21 double.
Half board: £14-£16 daily, £84-£90 weekly.
Evening meal 6.30pm (l.o. 6.30pm).
Parking for 3.

Small town on the western side of the Yorkshire Wolds. A tablet in the parish church records the death of William Bradley in 1820 at which time he was 7 ft 9 in tall and weighed 27 stone!

Arras Farmhouse ⋒

`Listed`

Arras Farm, Market Weighton, York,
N. Yorkshire YO4 3RN
☎ (0430) 872404
700-acre arable farm. Traditional family farmhouse on the Wolds Way, secluded, but close to the main road.
Bedrooms: 2 double & 1 twin.
Bathrooms: 1 private, 1 public.
Bed & breakfast: £10 single, £20 double.
Half board: £15 daily, £105 weekly.
Evening meal 7.30pm (l.o. 9pm).
Parking for 5.

3m SE. Boroughbridge Village close to the A1 in the Vale of York.

Prospect Farm ⋒

Marton-cum-Grafton, York, YO5 9QT
☎ Boroughbridge (0423) 322045
250-acre mixed farm. 18th C. farmhouse offering modern facilities and a private carp lake. Easy access to York, Harrogate, the Yorkshire Dales, the moors and the A1.
Bedrooms: 1 single, 1 double & 1 twin, 1 family room.
Bathrooms: 2 private, 2 public.
Bed & breakfast: £10-£15 single, £20-£25 double.
Parking for 3.

Famous market town on the River Ure, with a large market square. St. Mary's Church has Norman tower and 13th C spire. Theakston's 'Old Peculier' ale is brewed here.

Bank Villa ⋒

Masham, Ripon, HG4 4DB
☎ Ripon (0765) 89605
Personal service in a charming Georgian house. An excellent touring centre. British Tourist Authority commended.
Bedrooms: 4 double & 3 twin.
Bathrooms: 1 public; 4 private showers.
Bed & breakfast: from £15 single, from £25 double.
Half board: from £22.50 daily, from £140 weekly.
Evening meal 7.30pm (l.o. midday).
Parking for 7.
Open March-October.

2m N. Bingley Small hamlet close to Rombald's Moor and the Leeds Liverpool Canal.

Holroyd House

Beck Rd., Micklethwaite, Nr. Bingley, BD16 3JN
☎ Bradford (0274) 562464
Former mill owner's house overlooking the mill pond, set in the small conservation village of Micklethwaite on the edge of the Yorkshire Dales.
Bedrooms: 2 single, 1 double & 2 twin.
Bathrooms: 2 public.
Bed & breakfast: from £9 single, from £18 double.
Half board: from £15 daily, from £90 weekly.
Evening meal 6pm (l.o. 7pm).
Parking for 12.

7m NE. Market Weighton Held on the third Thursday in March, the Kiplingcote Derby is England's oldest horse race, dating from 1519. It starts at 11 am in the neighbouring village of South Dalton and goes through several parishes terminating at the winning post in Middleton-on-the-Wolds. One unique aspect of this race is that the winner receives less than the horse coming second past the post!

Middleton Wold Cottages ⋒

`Listed`

Middleton-on-the-Wolds, Driffield, N. Humberside YO25 9DD
☎ (037 781) 635
Comfortable old stone cottages in 1.75 acres, offering non-smoking accommodation. Overlooking the wolds, a convenient base for touring and York.
Bedrooms: 1 single, 1 double, 1 family room.
Bathrooms: 2 public.
Bed & breakfast: from £11 single, from £22 double.

Half board: from £16.50 daily, from £115.50 weekly.
Evening meal 7pm.
Parking for 5.

7m NW. York Village on the last stretch of the River Nidd before its confluence with the Ouse. Here is a charming little church with memorials to the Slingsby family, whose former home 'Red House' is now a public school.

Station Guest House ⋒

`Listed`

Marston La., Moor Monkton, York, YO5 8JL
☎ Rufforth (090 483) 639
Family-run guesthouse in a rural setting 5 miles from York on the A59. Close to all local amenities.
Bedrooms: 1 double, 2 family rooms.
Bathrooms: 1 public.
Bed & breakfast: from £11 single, from £18 double.
Parking for 4.
Open February-October.

THERE IS A SPECIAL SECTION IN THIS GUIDE LISTING ACCOMMODATION ESPECIALLY SUITABLE FOR GROUPS AND YOUNG PEOPLE.

GROUPS, CONSORTIA AND AGENCIES SPECIALISING IN FARM AND COUNTRY HOLIDAYS ARE LISTED IN SPECIAL SECTION OF THIS GUIDE.

THE SYMBOLS ARE EXPLAINED ON THE FLAP INSIDE THE BACK COVER.

MYTON-ON-SWALE

N. Yorkshire
Map ref 4C1

*3m SE. Boroughbridge
Small village on the
mighty River Swale.*

Plump House Farm
Listed
Myton-on-Swale, York,
YO6 2RA
☎ Boroughbridge
(0423) 360650
*160-acre mixed farm. A warm
welcome with comfortable
accommodation on a family-
run farm. Easy access to York
and Harrogate and an ideal
centre for the coast, Dales and
moor. Reductions for children.*
Bedrooms: 1 double, 1 family
room.
Bathrooms: 1 public.
Bed & breakfast: from £8.50
single, from £17 double.
Half board: from £13 daily.
Evening meal 6pm (l.o. 8pm).
Parking for 4.
⌂ ▯ Ⓤ ▮ ◁ ⊙ ▥ ❧ ⌖
✿ ⊁ ▦

NEWBIGGIN

N. Yorkshire
Map ref 5B3

*2m S. Aysgarth
Village in Bishopdale with
footpaths to the summit
of Noughtberry Hill and
Buckden Pike.*

Brookside
Newbiggin, Leyburn,
DL8 3TD
☎ Aysgarth (096 93) 433
*Non-working, comfortable
farmhouse in a quiet location
off the main road. In the heart
of Bishopdale, central for
walking and touring. Home
baking.*
Bedrooms: 1 double & 1 twin,
1 family room.
Bathrooms: 1 public.
Bed & breakfast: £12.50-£13
single, £16-£19 double.
Half board: £14.50-£16 daily.
Evening meal 6.30pm.
Parking for 3.
Open March-September.
⌂3 ⊠ ⌁ ⌖ Ⓤ ▮ Ⓥ ▥ ⊁
▦ ᴅᴀᴘ ▦

PLEASE CHECK
PRICES AND OTHER
DETAILS AT THE
TIME OF BOOKING.

NEWBY WISKE

N. Yorkshire
Map ref 5C3

*4m S. Northallerton
Village on the River Wiske
in the Vale of Mowbray.*

Well House
Listed
Newby Wiske,
Northallerton, DL7 9EX
☎ Northallerton (0609) 2253
*Detached house set in a large
garden in a quiet village.*
Bedrooms: 1 double, 1 family
room.
Bathrooms: 1 public.
Bed & breakfast: £11 single,
£19 double.
Parking for 3.
Open April-October.
⌂ ⊠ Ⓤ ⊙ ▥ ✿ ⊁ ▦

NORWOOD

N. Yorkshire
Map ref 4B1

Paddock Hill
Listed
Norwood, Otley,
W. Yorkshire LS21 2QU
☎ Otley (0943) 465977
*Converted ex-farmhouse and
barn. Entirely rural, but within
easy reach of Harrogate, Otley
and the Yorkshire Dales.*
Bedrooms: 1 double & 2 twin.
Bathrooms: 1 public.
Bed & breakfast: from £9
single, from £18 double.
Parking for 3.
⌂ Ⓤ ▮ Ⓥ ▥ ⊙ ▥ ✿ ⊁
▦ ▦

OSGODBY

N. Yorkshire
Map ref 5D3

*Hamlet between
Scarborough and Filey
with panoramic views of
Cayton Bay.*

The Barn
Osgodby La., Osgodby,
Scarborough, YO11 3QH
☎ Scarborough
(0723) 584372
*Converted old manor house
and barn with an old world
restaurant, inglenook fireplace
and an extensive menu. Live
entertainment and disco every
week.*
Bedrooms: 1 single, 3 double
& 2 twin, 1 family room.
Bathrooms: 2 public.
Bed & breakfast: £17-£21
single, £32-£40 double.
Half board: £24-£28 daily.
Lunch available.

Evening meal 7pm (l.o.
9.30pm).
Parking for 100.
Credit: Access, Visa.
⌂ ⌖ Ⓥ ▮ ◁ ⊙ ▥ ❢ ⌖ ▦
⌕ sᴘ ▦

OSMOTHERLEY

N. Yorkshire
Map ref 5C3

*6m NE. Northallerton
The famous 'Lyke Wake
Walk' across the
Cleveland Hills to
Ravenscar 40 miles away
starts here in this ancient
village. Attached to the
village cross is a large
stone table used as a
'pulpit' by John Wesley.*

Vane House
11A North End,
Osmotherley, Northallerton,
DL6 3BA
☎ (060 983) 448
*Small homely guesthouse
offering plain Yorkshire
cooking. In a pretty village on
the edge of the North York
Moors; an ideal walking area.*
Bedrooms: 3 twin, 1 family
room.
Bathrooms: 2 public.
Bed & breakfast: from £9
single, from £18 double.
Parking for 4.
Ⓤ ▮ Ⓥ ▥ ⊙ ▥ ⊁ ▦

OTLEY

W. Yorkshire
Map ref 4B1

Market and
manufacturing town in
Lower Wharfedale, the
birthplace of Thomas
Chippendale. Has a
Maypole, several old inns,
rebuilt medieval bridge
and a local history
museum. All Saints
Church dates from
Norman times. ⓘ

Wood Nook ⋒
⊜
East Chevin Rd., Otley,
LS21 3DE
☎ (0943) 463040
*Convenient for the dales and
Leeds-Bradford airport.
Between Harrogate, Ilkley,
Bradford and Leeds. Next to
Chevin Forest Park with
extensive views.*
Bedrooms: 1 double & 1 twin.
Bathrooms: 1 private,
2 public.
Bed & breakfast: £14-£15
single, from £25 double.
Parking for 4.
⌂ ⌖ Ⓤ ⊙ ▥ ⊿ ✿ ▦

OXENHOPE

W. Yorkshire
Map ref 4B1

This village is the
terminus of the Worth
Valley Railway housing
some fine locomotives.
Location for the film 'The
Railway Children'.

Drop Farm ⋒
Listed
Upper Westfield, Moorside
La., Oxenhope, Keighley,
BD22 9RE
☎ Haworth (0535) 45297
*60-acre dairy farm. Renovated
farmhouse retaining its original
character. Adjoining Haworth
Moor, amidst quiet and
peaceful surroundings and
panoramic views.*
Bedrooms: 1 single, 1 double,
1 family room.
Bathrooms: 2 public.
Bed & breakfast: £8-£10
single, £16-£20 double.
Half board: £12-£14 daily,
£78-£92 weekly.
Evening meal 6pm (l.o.
midday).
Parking for 10.
⌂ ⊠ Ⓤ ▮ Ⓥ ◁ ⊙ ▥
✿ ⊁ ▦

Lily Hall Farm
Upper Marsh La., Oxenhope,
Keighley, BD22 9RH
☎ Haworth (0535) 43999
*3-acre mixed farm. 17th C.
farmhouse beside Penistone
Hill Country Park with
panoramic views of magnificent
countryside from all rooms.
Evening meal available on
request.*
Bedrooms: 1 double & 1 twin,
1 family room.
Bathrooms: 1 public.
Bed & breakfast: £21 double.
Half board: £16-£17.50 daily,
£100-£110 weekly.
Evening meal 6.15pm (l.o.
4pm).
Parking for 6.
⌂ Ⓤ ▮ Ⓥ ⌿ ⊙ ▥ ⊿ ✿
⊁ ▦ ᴅᴀᴘ ▦

Springfield Guest
House ⋒
Listed
Springfield, Shaw La.,
Oxenhope, Keighley,
BD22 9QL
☎ Haworth (0535) 43951
*Elegant Victorian house in
beautiful Bronte country, 1
mile's pleasant walk from
Haworth.*
Bedrooms: 2 double, 1 family
room.
Bathrooms: 1 public.
Bed & breakfast: £10 single,
£19 double.

Half board: £14.50 daily, £90 weekly.
Evening meal 6pm (l.o. 5pm).
Parking for 9.

PATELEY BRIDGE

N. Yorkshire
Map ref 5C3

Small market town at centre of Upper Nidderdale. Flax and linen industries once flourished in this remote and beautiful setting.

Bishop Keld Farm

Blazefield, Pateley Bridge, Harrogate HG3 5DR
Harrogate (0423) 711636
105-acre mixed farm. Farmhouse built in 1865, overlooking the Nidd Valley. From Harrogate take the B6265 to Glasshouses then turn right up the hill directly opposite. Fishing is available free of charge.
Bedrooms: 1 double & 1 twin, 1 family room.
Bathrooms: 1 public.
Bed & breakfast: from £10.50 single, from £21 double.
Half board: from £17.50 daily, from £119 weekly.
Lunch available.
Evening meal 6pm.
Parking for 12.
Open April-December.

PICKERING

N. Yorkshire
Map ref 5D3

Market town and tourist centre on edge of North York Moors. Parish church has complete set of 15th C wall paintings depicting lives of saints. Part of 12th C castle still stands. Beck Isle Museum. The North Yorkshire Moors Railway begins here.

Bramwood Guest House

19 Hallgarth, Pickering, YO18 7AW
(0751) 74066
Homely 18th C. house with an attractive walled garden. Proprietors provide a personal service and offer old English cooking. Non-smoking. Special breaks in Spring and Autumn.
Bedrooms: 3 double & 1 twin, 2 family rooms.
Bathrooms: 2 public;
1 private shower.
Bed & breakfast: £20-£28 double.
Half board: £16-£20 daily, £102-£126 weekly.
Evening meal 6.30pm (l.o. 4.30pm).
Parking for 6.
Credit: Access, Visa, Diners, Amex.

Brickyard Farm

Marton La., Pickering, YO18 8LW
(0751) 72880
70-acre arable farm. At the side of a country lane, 1 mile from the market town of Pickering. Comfortable house with home cooking provided.
Bedrooms: 1 single, 2 double & 1 twin.
Bathrooms: 1 public.
Bed & breakfast: £9 single, £18 double.
Half board: £15 daily, £105 weekly.
Evening meal 6pm (l.o. 6pm).
Parking for 6.
Open April-October.

27 Burgate

Pickering, YO18 7AU
(0751) 73224
Charming, terraced house next to Pickering Castle, with views overlooking the moor's steam railway.
Bedrooms: 1 double & 2 twin.
Bathrooms: 2 public.
Bed & breakfast: £10 single.
Parking for 3.

Kirkham Garth

Whitby Rd., Pickering, YO18 7AT
(0751) 74931
In a quiet location on Whitby Road, 200 yards from the roundabout. Convenient for the town centre. Homely atmosphere, ample parking facilities and a colour TV lounge.
Bedrooms: 1 double & 1 twin, 1 family room.
Bathrooms: 1 public.
Bed & breakfast: £9-£10 single, £18-£20 double.
Parking for 5.

POCKLINGTON

Humberside
Map ref 4C1

Homely market town at the foot of the Yorkshire Wolds. Burnby Hall on outskirts has gardens with finest collection of water lilies in Europe. Penny Arcadia with fine exhibition of amusement machines located in former Ritz cinema.

Feathers Hotel

56 Market Place, Pocklington, York, N. Yorkshire YO4 2UN
(0759) 303155
Comfortable market town hotel, 13 miles from York, 28 miles from Hull and convenient for the East Coast resorts. 1 mile off the main A1079 York - Hull road.
Bedrooms: 4 double & 7 twin, 1 family room.
Bathrooms: 12 private.
Bed & breakfast: £27-£30 single, £40-£50 double.
Half board: £34-£37 daily.
Lunch available.
Evening meal 7pm (l.o. 9.30pm).
Parking for 56.
Credit: Access, Visa, Diners, Amex.

POOL

W. Yorkshire
Map ref 4B1

3m E. Otley

Rawson Garth

Pool Bank Farm, Pool (Wharfedale), Otley, LS21 1EU
Leeds (0532) 843221
6-acre pigs/sheep farm. Attractively-converted coach house with modern facilities and open country views in Emmerdale Farm area. 5 minutes from the airport and well placed for Leeds, Otley, Bradford and Harrogate. Non-smoking establishment.
Bedrooms: 1 double & 1 twin.
Bathrooms: 1 public.
Bed & breakfast: from £20 double.
Parking for 10.

GROUPS, CONSORTIA AND AGENCIES SPECIALISING IN FARM AND COUNTRY HOLIDAYS ARE LISTED IN A SPECIAL SECTION OF THIS GUIDE.

RAVENSCAR

N. Yorkshire
Map ref 5D3

Splendidly positioned small coastal resort with magnificent views over Robin Hood's Bay. Its Old Peak is the end of the famous Lyke Wake Walk or 'corpse way'.

Crag Hill

Ravenhall Rd., Ravenscar, Scarborough, YO13 ONA
Scarborough (0723) 870925
Magnificent coastal views. Bicycles are available at the hotel, and golf and pony trekking are accessible locally. Please send for brochure.
Bedrooms: 3 double & 2 twin.
Bathrooms: 3 private, 1 public.
Bed & breakfast: £22-£26 double.
Half board: £17-£19 daily.
Evening meal 6.30pm.
Parking for 9.

RICHMOND

N. Yorkshire
Map ref 5C3

Pleasant market town on edge of Swaledale with 11th C castle and Georgian and Victorian buildings surrounding large cobbled market place. Green Howards' Museum is in the former Holy Trinity Church. Attractions include the Georgian Theatre, Richmondshire Museum and Easby Abbey.

Pottergate Guest House

4 Pottergate, Richmond, DL10 4AB
(0748) 3826
Small, family-run guesthouse two minutes' stroll from the town centre. Emphasis on comfort and value for money.
Bedrooms: 2 double & 2 twin, 1 family room.
Bathrooms: 2 public.
Bed & breakfast: £14-£18 single, £22-£24 double.
Half board: £28-£30 daily, £130-£140 weekly.
Lunch available.
Evening meal 6pm (l.o. 8pm).
Parking for 5.

RICHMOND
Continued

West End Guest House M
😊😊
45 Reeth Rd., Richmond,
DL10 4EX
☎ (0748) 4783
*19th C. house with a large
garden and ample parking,
close to the town and river.
Home cooking a speciality.
Children and dogs welcome.*
Bedrooms: 2 double & 1 twin,
1 family room.
Bathrooms: 1 private,
2 public.
Bed & breakfast: £11-£17.50
single, £22-£27 double.
Half board: £17.50-£24 daily,
£110.25-£151.20 weekly.
Evening meal 7.30pm (l.o.
5pm).
Parking for 9.
🛇 🖐 📮 ❖ 🛊 Ⅴ ⌘ 🛏 📖
📠 ❖ 🛡 Ⓣ

York Grove
35-39 The Green, Richmond,
DL10 4RG
☎ (0748) 5138
*The house affords panoramic
views of the castle and town,
and offers tasteful, spacious
accommodation. Special
emphasis on food.*
Bedrooms: 2 single, 1 double
& 2 twin.
Bathrooms: 1 private,
1 public.
Bed & breakfast: £12-£12.50
single, £21-£22 double.
Half board: £17-£17.50 daily,
£100-£110 weekly.
Evening meal 6.30pm.
🛇 🕷 ❖ ⓤ 🛊 Ⅴ ⌘ 🛏 📖
📠 🗶 🛡 ⒹⒶ⒫ 🗞 🆂🅿 🕭

RIPON
N. Yorkshire
Map ref 5C3

Small ancient city with
impressive cathedral
containing Saxon crypt
which houses church
treasures from all over
Yorkshire. 'Setting the
Watch' tradition kept
nightly by horn-blower in
Market Square. 🗗

Borrage Croft
(Listed)
39 Borrage La., Ripon,
HG4 2PZ
☎ (0765) 2465
*Detached house, well placed
for town and country.
Delightful, peaceful setting in
extensive gardens bordering the
River Skell.*
Bedrooms: 1 double & 1 twin.

Bathrooms: 1 public.
Bed & breakfast: £22-£24
double.
Parking for 4.
Open April-October.
🛇7 ⒸⒹ ⓤ ⌘ 🛏 📺 📖 📠 🖊 🛡

The Coopers M
😊😊
36 College Rd., Ripon,
HG4 2HA
☎ (0765) 3708
*Spacious rooms in a
comfortable, Victorian house
overlooking countryside in a
quiet area of Ripon, close to
the market place. Special rates
for children under 14.*
Bedrooms: 1 twin, 1 family
room.
Bathrooms: 1 public.
Bed & breakfast: £9-£10
single, £18 double.
🛇5 📮 ❖ ⓤ 🛊 📺 📖 📠 🛡

Crescent Lodge M
😊😊
42-42a North St., Ripon,
HG4 1EN
☎ (0765) 2331
*Reputedly the former
Archbishop of York's town
residence. Early Georgian
house within easy walking
distance of the city centre.
Ample street parking. Special
rates for children.*
Bedrooms: 2 single, 4 double
& 2 twin, 4 family rooms.
Bathrooms: 3 public.
Bed & breakfast: £9.50-£12
single, £10-£12 double.
🛇 🖐 📮 ❖ 🛊 Ⅴ ⌘ 🛏 📺 📖 📠
🗶 🛡 🆂🅿 🕭

Marrick House M
😊😊
21 Iddesleigh Terrace,
Bondgate Green, Ripon,
HG4 1QW
☎ (0765) 2707
*Comfortable, Victorian
terraced house facing the canal
basin, on the B6265,
approximately 300 yards from
Ripon Cathedral and six
minutes' walk from the market
square. Evening meal by
arrangement.*
Bedrooms: 1 single, 1 twin,
1 family room.
Bathrooms: 1 public.
Bed & breakfast: £10-£12
single, £20-£24 double.
Half board: £15.50-£18 daily,
£100-£115 weekly.
🛇5 📮 ❖ ⓤ Ⅴ ⌘ 📺 📖 📠
🛡

Riga
22 Primrose Drive, Ripon,
HG4 1EY
☎ (0765) 2611

*Detached, modern house with
spacious bedrooms and colour
TV, in a quiet cul-de-sac. Non-
smokers only.*
Bedrooms: 1 single, 2 twin.
Bathrooms: 1 public.
Bed & breakfast: £10.50-
£12.50 single, £21-£25 double.
Parking for 3.
Open February-November.
🛇5 ❖ ⓤ 🛊 Ⅴ ⌫ 🛏 📺 📖
📠 🛡

ROBIN HOOD'S BAY
N. Yorkshire
Map ref 5D3

Picturesque village of
red-roofed cottages with
main street running from
cliff top, down ravine, to
seashore. Scene of much
smuggling and
shipwrecks in 18th C.
Robin Hood reputed to
have escaped to
continent by boat from
here.

Falconhurst Wholefood
😊😊
Mount Pleasant South, Robin
Hood's Bay, Whitby,
YO22 4RQ
☎ Whitby (0947) 880582
*Comfortable Edwardian
residence. Home-made
wholemeal breads, preserves,
ice-creams and home cooking
using local organically-grown
produce. Vegetarian/traditional
menu. Non-smoking.*
Bedrooms: 1 double & 1 twin,
1 family room.
Bathrooms: 1 public.
Bed & breakfast: £10 single,
£20 double.
Half board: £16 daily, £110
weekly.
Evening meal 7pm (l.o. 3pm).
🛇 ❖ ⓤ Ⅴ ⌫ 🛏 📺 📖 📠
Ữ 🛡

Meadowfield Bed &
Breakfast
Mount Pleasant North,
Robin Hood's Bay, Whitby,
YO22 4RE
☎ Whitby (0947) 880564
*Comfortable, family-run
Victorian house in a quiet
seaside village. Well-presented
accommodation and meals.*
Bedrooms: 1 single, 1 twin,
1 family room.
Bathrooms: 1 public.
Bed & breakfast: £9-£10
single, £18-£19 double.
Half board: £14-£15 daily,
£98 weekly.
Evening meal 5.30pm (l.o.
4pm).
🛇 ⓤ 🛊 Ⅴ ⌫ 🛏 📺 📖 🗶
🛡 ⒹⒶ⒫

Old School House
😊
Fisherhead, Robin Hood's
Bay, Whitby, YO22 4ST
☎ Whitby (0947) 880723
*The old school of Robin Hood's
Bay has now been converted to
cater for bed and breakfast
guests. Educational and
recreational groups are
welcome. Full board is
available by arrangement.*
Bedrooms: 4 double & 2 twin,
3 family rooms.
Bathrooms: 4 public.
Bed & breakfast: £15-£18
single, £16-£19 double.
Parking for 9.
Open February-October.
🛇1 🖐 ⓤ Ⅴ ⌘ 🛏 📺 📖 ♈ ❖

ROSEDALE ABBEY
N. Yorkshire
Map ref 5C3

Sturdy hamlet built
around Cistercian
Nunnery in the reign of
Henry II in the middle of
Rosedale, largest of the
moorland valleys.

Sevenford House M
(Listed)
Thorgill, Rosedale Abbey,
Pickering, YO18 8SE
☎ Lastingham (075 15) 283
*Large country house nestling in
4 acres of beautiful gardens, in
a tranquil moorland setting.
Panoramic views from all
rooms and a relaxed
atmosphere. Children under 12
half price.*
Bedrooms: 1 double, 3 family
rooms.
Bathrooms: 1 public.
Bed & breakfast: from £12.50
single, £19-£21 double.
Parking for 6.
🛇 ⓤ 🛊 Ⅴ ⌘ 🛏 📺 📖 🏃 ❖
🛡 🆂🅿 🕭

Sycamores Farm
(Listed)
Rosedale Abbey, Pickering,
YO18 8RA
☎ Lastingham (075 15) 448
*150-acre dairy farm. Modern
farmhouse with a friendly
atmosphere, in the heart of the
North Yorkshire Moors
National Park. Central for the
coast and an ideal base for
walking.*
Bedrooms: 2 double & 1 twin.
Bathrooms: 1 public.
Bed & breakfast: max. £16
double.
Half board: max. £12 daily.
Evening meal 6pm.
Parking for 4.
🛇 🕷 ⓤ 🛊 Ⅴ ⌘ 📺 📖 📠
Ữ 🖊 🏃 ❖ 🛡 ⒹⒶ⒫

ROTHERHAM

S. Yorkshire
Map ref 4B2

In the Don Valley, Rotherham became an important industrial town in 19th C with discovery of coal and development of iron and steel industry by Joshua Walker who built Clifton House, now the town's museum. Magnificent 15th C All Saints church is town's showpiece. ℹ

Limes Hotel
Broom La., Rotherham, S60 3EL
☎ (0709) 363431 & 382446
Small hotel with a friendly atmosphere, in a pleasant residential area, 1 mile from the city centre and close to the M1. All bedrooms have a trouser press and hair dryer.
Bedrooms: 11 single, 3 double & 2 twin, 1 family room.
Bathrooms: 17 private.
Bed & breakfast: £21-£32 single, £30-£40 double.
Half board: £28-£39 daily.
Lunch available.
Evening meal 6.30pm (l.o. 9.30pm).
Parking for 30.
Credit: Access, Visa.

RUFFORTH

N. Yorkshire
Map ref 4C1

Village west of York. Rufforth Park is noted as a show jumping venue. There is also a small airfield.

Wellgarth House
Wetherby Rd., Rufforth, York, YO2 3QB
☎ (090 483) 592 & 595
Individual and attractive detached house in the delightful village of Rufforth. Ideal touring base for York and the Yorkshire Dales.
Bedrooms: 1 single, 3 double & 2 twin, 1 family room.
Bathrooms: 2 private, 2 public.
Bed & breakfast: £12-£15 single, £20-£28 double.
Half board: from £15.50 daily.
Parking for 6.
Open February-December.

SCAGGLETHORPE

N. Yorkshire
Map ref 5D3

Small village lying at the foot of the Wolds under the Wold Brow, with outlying farms and low meadows. Old houses and cottages can be seen here.

Mrs. H. H. Stonehouse
Paddock House, Scagglethorpe, Malton, YO17 8EA
☎ Rillington (094 42) 209 & 614
12-acre fruit/vegetable farm. Open views over the Vale of Pickering. Convenient for touring the wolds, coast and York. 2 bedrooms have hot and cold water.
Bedrooms: 1 single, 1 twin, 1 family room.
Bathrooms: 1 public.
Bed & breakfast: £8.25-£8.75 single, £16.50-£17.50 double.
Parking for 3.
Open March-October.

SCARBOROUGH

N. Yorkshire
Map ref 5D3

Large popular east coast seaside resort, formerly a spa town. Beautiful gardens and splendid sandy beaches in North and South Bays. Castle ruins date from 1100, fine Georgian and Victorian houses in old town. September angling, Theatres, cricket festivals and seasonal entertainment. ℹ

Cornelian
43 Cornelian Drive, Scarborough, YO11 3AL
☎ (0723) 354185
Friendly, family-run guesthouse with a large garden, in tranquil surroundings overlooking the sea, castle and South Cliff Golf Course.
Bedrooms: 1 double & 1 twin, 1 family room.
Bathrooms: 1 public.
Bed & breakfast: £10-£11 single, £19-£20 double.
Parking for 2.
Open April-October.

Miricia ⚜
5 Rutland Terrace, Scarborough, YO12 7HR
☎ (0723) 373868
Family-run hotel overlooking the sea and beach, offering a warm welcome to all the family. Home cooking and late snacks provided in the games room.
Bedrooms: 1 single, 3 double & 1 twin, 3 family rooms.
Bathrooms: 3 public.
Bed & breakfast: £12-£14 single, £18-£22 double.
Half board: £15-£17 daily, £77-£84 weekly.
Evening meal 5pm (l.o. 5.30pm).

Premier Hotel ⚜
66 Esplanade, Scarborough, YO11 2UZ
☎ (0723) 361484 & 373926
On the South Cliff offering unsurpassed sea views, among beautiful gardens and pleasant walks.
Bedrooms: 3 single, 7 double & 7 twin, 3 family rooms.
Bathrooms: 20 private.
Bed & breakfast: £23-£25 single, £40-£44 double.
Half board: £28-£30 daily, £161-£182 weekly.
Evening meal 6pm (l.o. 6pm).
Parking for 7.

Riga Hotel ⚜
10 Crown Crescent, Scarborough, YO11 2BJ
☎ (0723) 363994
Family-run, licensed hotel on the South Cliff, overlooking the Crown Gardens and close to the Esplanade.
Bedrooms: 4 single, 2 double & 2 twin, 4 family rooms.
Bathrooms: 3 public.
Bed & breakfast: £9.50-£10.50 single, £19-£21 double.
Half board: £12.75-£13.75 daily, £89.25 weekly.
Evening meal 6pm (l.o. 6.30pm).
Credit: Access, Visa.

Seahaven
52 Scalby Mills Rd., Scarborough, YO12 6RW
☎ (0723) 372465
Small friendly guesthouse overlooking the North Bay and golf course.
Bedrooms: 1 double & 3 twin, 1 family room.
Bathrooms: 1 public.
Bed & breakfast: £9-£9.50 single, £18-£19 double.
Parking for 6.
Open April-October.

Wheatcroft Mini Motel ⚜
156-158 Filey Rd., Scarborough, YO11 3AA
☎ (0723) 374613
Small motel offering comfortable accommodation at reasonable prices. On the South Cliff, away from the busy town centre.
Bedrooms: 1 single, 3 double & 1 twin, 2 family rooms.
Bathrooms: 7 private.
Bed & breakfast: £17-£27 double.
Parking for 7.

SCRUTON

N. Yorkshire
Map ref 5C3

4m NE. Bedale
Little village east of A1 and west of the River Swale. The church is one of only 5 in the country dedicated to St. Radegund.

Teasels
Listed
6 Meadow Court, Scruton, Northallerton, DL7 0QU
☎ Northallerton (0609) 748461
Modern house on the outskirts of the village in sight of dales and moors. 2 miles east of the A1 and 1 mile north of the A684 to Northallerton. Non-smokers only.
Bedrooms: 1 double & 1 twin.
Bathrooms: 1 public.
Bed & breakfast: £18 double.
Parking for 2.
Open February-November.

WE ADVISE YOU TO CONFIRM YOUR BOOKING IN WRITING.

THERE IS A SPECIAL SECTION IN THIS GUIDE LISTING ACCOMMODATION ESPECIALLY SUITABLE FOR GROUPS AND YOUNG PEOPLE.

SELBY

N. Yorkshire
Map ref 4C1

Small market town on the River Ouse, believed to have been birthplace of Henry I, with a magnificent abbey containing much fine Norman and Early English architecture. ℹ

Hazeldene Guest House
👄👄

34 Brook St., Doncaster Rd., Selby, YO8 0AR
☎ (0757) 704809
Attractive, double-fronted Victorian town house, close to the town centre.
Bedrooms: 3 single, 2 twin, 2 family rooms.
Bathrooms: 2 public.
Bed & breakfast: £11-£12 single, £22-£24 double.
Parking for 6.
🛇 ⓤ Ⓥ ⌦ ⓣⓥ ✕ 🗮

SETTLE

N. Yorkshire
Map ref 5B3

Town of narrow streets and Georgian houses in an area of great limestone hills and crags. Panoramic view from Castleberg Crag which stands 300 ft above town. ℹ

Mrs. P. Houlton

Whitebeam Croft, Duke Street, Settle, BD24 9AN
☎ (072 92) 2824
Quiet, modern chalet bungalow with superb views, in its own grounds off the main road. Excellent touring centre, convenient for the railway station. Specialising in home cooking. Evening meal by arrangement.
Bedrooms: 1 double & 1 twin, 1 family room.
Bathrooms: 2 public.
Bed & breakfast: £21-£22 double.
Parking for 3.
Open January-November.
🛇 👄 ⓥ ⓤ 🗮 Ⓥ ⌦ ⓣⓥ ▦
🗮 🗮

SHEFFIELD

S. Yorkshire
Map ref 4B2

Local iron ore and coal gave Sheffield its prosperous steel and cutlery industries. The modern city centre retains many interesting buildings - cathedral, Cutlers' Hall, Crucible Theatre, Graves and Mappin Art Galleries - and has an excellent shopping centre. ℹ

Falcon Hotel 🗮

9-11 Kenwood Park Rd., Nether Edge, Sheffield, S7 1NE
☎ (0742) 552280
Friendly family business with emphasis on service, cleanliness and comfort. Most bedrooms have telephone.
Bedrooms: 10 single, 4 double & 9 twin, 4 family rooms.
Bathrooms: 3 private, 7 public; 22 private showers.
Bed & breakfast: £26-£31 single, £34-£42 double.
Half board: £32-£37 daily.
Lunch available.
Evening meal 7pm (l.o. 9pm).
Parking for 16.
Credit: Access, Visa, Diners, Amex.
🛇 👄 🗮 ⌨ ⓥ 🗮 Ⓥ ⌦ ⓣⓥ
◑ ▦ ▱ 🍴 ⬚ SP

Greensleeves Cottage

183 Foxhill Rd., Birley Carr, Sheffield, S6 1HF
☎ (0742) 321107
Detached stone cottage 4.5 miles north west of the city centre. Take the A61 Penistone road north to Wadsley Bridge, turn left at the traffic lights and follow the signs for Foxhill.
Bedrooms: 1 single, 1 double.
Bathrooms: 1 public.
Bed & breakfast: max. £10 single, max. £18 double.
Parking for 2.
Open January-April, July-December.
🛇 Ⓑ ⓥ ⓤ ⓣⓥ ▦ 🗮

SHIPTON-BY-BENINGBROUGH

N. Yorkshire
Map ref 4C1

5m NW. York
Village on the A19 north of York. Beningbrough Hall (NT) nearby.

Brentwood Cottage
👄👄

Main St., Shipton-by-Beningbrough, York, YO6 1AB
☎ York (0904) 470111
Small, select 18th C. cottage with modern facilities, 5 miles north of York on the A19. Convenient for the city, the coast and the North Yorkshire Moors. Evening meal available by request.
Bedrooms: 1 double & 1 twin, 2 family rooms.
Bathrooms: 1 public; 3 private showers.
Bed & breakfast: £20-£21 double.
Parking for 7.
🛇 ⓤ Ⓥ ⌦ ⓣⓥ ▦ ▱ ✕ 🗮
🃏

SKEEBY

N. Yorkshire
Map ref 5C3

Village between the A1 and Richmond on the edge of the Dales.

Mrs. J.M.B. Brenkley
Listed

Merrifield Farm, Scurragh La., Skeeby, Richmond, DL10 5EF
☎ Richmond (0748) 2391
5-acre mixed farm. Modern, stone-built home offering peaceful, relaxing accommodation. Comfortable lounge, colour TV, hot water at all times. Near the A1, 1 mile from Scotch Corner roundabout, providing easy access north and south and a good base for touring the dales with circular runs from Richmond.
Bedrooms: 1 double & 1 twin, 1 family room.
Bathrooms: 2 public.
Bed & breakfast: from £21 double.
Evening meal 6pm (l.o. 8pm).
Parking for 6.
🛇 🞐 ⓤ ⌦ ⓣⓥ ▦ ▱ ❄ ✕
🗮

SKELLOW

S. Yorkshire
Map ref 4C1

5m NW. Doncaster
Small village just off the A1 north of Doncaster.

Canda 🗮

Hampole Balk La., 5 Lane Ends, Skellow, Doncaster, DN6 8LF
☎ Doncaster (0302) 724028
Family home on the A1, which guests are invited to share. 2 ground floor bedrooms with own access.
Bedrooms: 2 single, 2 double & 1 twin.
Bathrooms: 2 public.
Bed & breakfast: £12.50-£15 single, £25 double.
Parking for 6.
🛇9 👄 ⓥ ⓤ Ⓥ ⓣⓥ ▦ ▱ ⬚
✕ 🗮

SKIPTON

N. Yorkshire
Map ref 4B1

Pleasant market town with farming community atmosphere at gateway to Dales with a Palladian Town Hall, Parish Church and fully roofed Castle at the top of High Street. ℹ

Black Horse Hotel

High St., Skipton, BD23 1JZ
☎ (0756) 2145
17th C. hotel in a pleasant market town. Restaurant, comfortable accommodation and a friendly atmosphere.
Bedrooms: 2 single, 1 double & 2 twin.
Bathrooms: 5 private.
Bed & breakfast: £28-£32 single, £37-£40 double.
Half board: £35-£39 daily.
Lunch available.
Evening meal 7pm (l.o. 10pm).
Credit: Access, Visa, Diners, Amex.
🛇 📞 ⌨ ⓥ 🗮 Ⓥ ▦ 🍴 🗮
⬚ SP 🃏

INDIVIDUAL PROPRIETORS HAVE SUPPLIED ALL DETAILS OF ACCOMMODATION. ALTHOUGH WE DO CHECK FOR ACCURACY, WE ADVISE YOU TO CONFIRM PRICES AND OTHER INFORMATION AT THE TIME OF BOOKING.

MAP REFERENCES APPLY TO THE COLOUR MAPS TOWARDS THE END OF THIS GUIDE.

SLEDMERE

Humberside
Map ref 5D3

7m NW. Driffield

Triton Inn M

Sledmere, Driffield,
N. Humberside YO25 OXQ
☎ Driffield (0377) 86644
*Comfortable country inn
(freehouse) with home-cooked
food, traditional ales and a
warm welcome. Within easy
reach of the coast and Moors
and adjacent to Sledmere
House.*
Bedrooms: 2 single, 3 double
& 2 twin, 1 family room.
Bathrooms: 3 private,
3 public.
Bed & breakfast: £12-£17.50
single, £24-£34 double.
Half board: £17-£22 daily,
£112-£147 weekly.
Lunch available.
Evening meal 7pm (l.o.
10pm).
Parking for 30.
Credit: Access, Visa, Diners.
🛏 🖵 🕯 🛉 🖪 🖤 🕮 🍴
🈁 �🅙 🆎 🇹

SLEIGHTS

N. Yorkshire
Map ref 5D3

4m SW. Whitby
Village close to Whitby at
the bottom of Blue Bank
and on the broad, deep
point of the River Esk.

Mrs. P. Beale M

Ryedale House, 154-
158 Coach Rd., Sleights,
Whitby, YO22 5EQ
☎ Whitby (0947) 810534
*Friendly cottage style house
with a large garden and
beautiful views, at the foot of
the moors and 4 miles from the
coast. Traditional and
vegetarian cooking with plenty
of choice. Established 12 years.
No pets.*
Bedrooms: 1 double & 1 twin,
1 family room.
Bathrooms: 1 public.
Bed & breakfast: max. £9.50
single, max. £19 double.
Half board: max. £15 daily,
max. £95 weekly.
Evening meal 6.30pm (l.o.
7.30pm).
Parking for 3.
Open March-November.
🛏 3 🕮 🛉 🖪 🖤 🕮 🍴 🆎 🛧
🈁 �🅙 🆎

Willow Dale

☀☀☀

17 Carr Hill La., Briggswath,
Sleights, Whitby, YO21 1RS
☎ Whitby (0947) 810525
*Quiet, spacious Edwardian
house in the Esk Valley. 3
miles from Whitby, 100 yards
off the main road. Emphasis on
fresh food. Non smokers only
please.*
Bedrooms: 2 double & 1 twin.
Bathrooms: 2 private,
1 public.
Bed & breakfast: £11-£17
single, £22-£26 double.
Half board: £19-£21 daily,
£125.30-£138.90 weekly.
Evening meal 7pm.
Parking for 4.
Open April-October.
🛏 🖨 🖸 🖵 🕯 🕮 🛉 🖪 🍴
🈁 🎞 ♨ 🛧 🆎 🈁 🆘

SNAINTON

N. Yorkshire
Map ref 5D3

Village on the A170
Thirsk to Scarborough
road with a riding centre.

Hazel Hall Farm

☀☀

Snainton, Scarborough,
YO13 9PN
☎ Scarborough (0723) 85413
*150-acre mixed farm. 18th C.
stone-built farmhouse providing
modern comforts, with
panoramic views. Helpful
information for sightseeing
available. Putting green,
practice golf bunker and public
all-weather golf driving range
on premises.*
Bedrooms: 1 twin, 3 family
rooms.
Bathrooms: 4 private,
1 public.
Bed & breakfast: from £15
single, from £24 double.
Half board: from £18 daily,
from £95 weekly.
Evening meal 6pm (l.o. 7pm).
Parking for 6.
Open March-October.
🛏 🕮 🆎 🖤 ⚡ ✓ ♨ 🛧

**GROUPS, CONSORTIA
AND AGENCIES
SPECIALISING
IN FARM AND
COUNTRY HOLIDAYS
ARE LISTED IN A
SPECIAL SECTION
OF THIS GUIDE.**

Troutsdale Lodge M

☀☀☀

Troutsdale, Snainton,
Scarborough, YO13 OBS
☎ Scarborough (0723) 82209
*An idyllic setting overlooking
the Dale and Wykeham
Forest. Reminiscent of an
Indian hill station with a wide,
shady, south-facing verandah.
From A64 York to
Scarborough road, take A170
to Snainton, left at Peacock
public house, about 4 miles
along dale, signposted after
Rockhouse Farm.*
Bedrooms: 2 single, 2 double
& 2 twin.
Bathrooms: 2 public.
Bed & breakfast: £12.50-
£14.50 single, £25-£29 double.
Half board: from £20.25-£22.25
daily, £145 weekly.
Lunch available.
Evening meal 6pm (l.o.
5.30pm).
Parking for 10.
🛏 🕯 🕮 🛉 🖪 🆎 🖤 🕮 🍴
🔥 ♨ 🛧 🆎 🈁 🆘 🆎 🇹

SOUTH CAVE

Humberside
Map ref 4C1

Lying on the famous
Ermine Street, the Roman
road stretching from
Lincoln to York. Located
only 3 miles from the
River Humber, it is an
ideal centre from which to
tour the County of
Humberside.

Rudstone Walk Farm

Listed

South Cave, Brough,
N. Humberside HU15 2AH
☎ North Cave (043 02) 2230
*303-acre arable farm.
Beautiful 400-year-old wolds'
farmhouse with superb views.
Well-appointed and tastefully
furnished in the traditional
style. Emphasis on Yorkshire
cooking using fresh produce.
Near Beverley, ideal for York
and 2.5 miles from the M62.*
Bedrooms: 1 single, 1 double
& 1 twin, 1 family room.
Bathrooms: 1 private,
2 public.
Bed & breakfast: £12.50-
£14.40 single, £30-£35.65
double.
Half board: from £20 daily,
from £140 weekly.
Evening meal 7pm (l.o. 6pm).
Parking for 10.
Open January-November.
🛏 📻 🖸 🖵 🕮 🛉 🖪 🖤 🆎
🖤 🕮 🍴 🛉 ⚡ ♨ ✓ ♨ 🛧
🈁 🆎

SOUTH MILFORD

N. Yorkshire
Map ref 4C1

Small village, close to the
A1 and just north of Monk
Fryston.

Mill Farm

Listed

Gorse La., South Milford,
Leeds, W. Yorkshire
LS25 6JS
☎ (0977) 682979 & 682810
FAX 0977 685457
*Modernised farmhouse behind
the village post office, in 2.5
acres of mainly horticultural
glasshouses bordered by a beck
and The Willows (Yorkshire
Trust Nature Reserve).*
Bedrooms: 1 single, 1 double
& 1 twin.
Bathrooms: 2 private,
2 public.
Bed & breakfast: £10-£12
single, £20-£24 double.
Half board: £15-£17 daily,
max. £90 weekly.
Evening meal 6pm (l.o. 8pm).
Parking for 3.
🛏 🖸 🕮 🆎 🖤 🕮 🆎

SOUTH OTTERINGTON

N. Yorkshire
Map ref 5C3

Otterington Shorthorn Inn

☀☀

South Otterington,
Northallerton, DL7 9HP
☎ Northallerton (0609) 3816
*Early 19th C. inn with an open
fire and oak beams, serving
traditional ales and offering a
warm welcome. Pool table,
juke box and darts.*
Bedrooms: 1 single, 3 double
& 1 twin.
Bathrooms: 1 public.
Bed & breakfast: £13-£15
single, £22-£24 double.
Half board: £16-£18 daily,
£78-£90 weekly.
Lunch available.
Evening meal 5pm (l.o. 7pm).
Parking for 12.
🛏 📻 🖵 🛉 🕮 🍴 ♨ U 🛧 🆎
🆎

SOWERBY

N. Yorkshire
Map ref 5C3

Doxford House M

☀☀☀

Front St., Sowerby, Thirsk,
YO7 1JP
☎ Thirsk (0845) 23238
Continued ▶

SOWERBY

Continued

Handsome, Georgian house with attractive gardens and paddock with animals, overlooking the greens of Sowerby.
Bedrooms: 1 double & 1 twin, 2 family rooms.
Bathrooms: 4 private.
Bed & breakfast: £11-£15 single, £22 double.
Half board: £17 daily, £112 weekly.
Evening meal 6.30pm.
Parking for 4.
🛇 🖢 ⓤ 🛏 ⓣⓥ 🎞 🛋 🕭 🍷 ❀ 🛏 🏠

Ryecroft
54 Front St., Sowerby, Thirsk, YO7 1JF
☎ Thirsk (0845) 23369
Elegant Regency house with a friendly atmosphere, 5 minutes' walk from James Herriot's town of Thirsk.
Bedrooms: 2 double & 1 twin.
Bathrooms: 3 private.
Bed & breakfast: £20-£24 double.
Parking for 3.
Open April-October.
🛇5 🖢 🕯 ⓤ 🛏 ⓣⓥ 🎞 🍴 🛏

SOWERBY BRIDGE

W. Yorkshire
Map ref 4B1

Busy little town in the Calder Valley near the Calder Hebble Canal.

The Hobbit 🅜
😋😋😋😋
Hob La., Sowerby Bridge, HX6 3QL
☎ Halifax (0422) 832202
Country inn nestling on the hillside above Sowerby Bridge, with panoramic views over the Calder Valley.
Bedrooms: 1 single, 5 double & 10 twin.
Bathrooms: 16 private.
Bed & breakfast: £20-£32 single, £30-£46 double.
Half board: £26-£47 daily.
Lunch available.
Evening meal 5pm (l.o. 11pm).
Parking for 100.
Credit: Access, Visa, Amex.
🛇 🖢 🕻 ⓔ ⓓ 🖢 🕯 ⓥ 🍴
🎞 🛋 ⓨ ⓤ 🏃 ❀ 🍴 🐾 🆂🅿
ⓣ

SPENNITHORNE

N. Yorkshire
Map ref 5C3

2m SE. Leyburn
Quiet rural village with small fragments remaining of a castle and an interesting church.

Old Horn Inn 🅜
😋😋
Spennithorne, Leyburn, DL8 5PR
☎ Wensleydale (0969) 22370
17th C. country inn in beautiful Lower Wensleydale, with a warm, friendly welcome and emphasis on food. Children 10 years and over welcome.
Bedrooms: 2 double.
Bathrooms: 2 private.
Bed & breakfast: £25 double.
Lunch available.
Evening meal 7pm (l.o. 9.30pm).
Parking for 6.
ⓞ 🖢 🕯 🕻 ⓥ 🎞 🛋 🍴 🍴
🆂🅿

SPROXTON

N. Yorkshire
Map ref 5C3

2m S. Helmsley
Pretty village with a 19th C church built for Lord Feversham and close to Duncombe Park, home of the Lords Feversham (1718).

Sproxton Hall
😋😋
Sproxton, York, YO6 5EQ
☎ Helmsley (0439) 70225
300-acre mixed farm. 17th C. grade II listed stone farmhouse, beamed, traditionally decorated and comfortably furnished. In a peaceful setting with panoramic views, 1.5 miles from Helmsley. Excellent base for the North York Moors, York, the coast and Dales. Non-smoking establishment.
Bedrooms: 1 double & 1 twin.
Bathrooms: 2 public.
Bed & breakfast: £25-£30 double.
Parking for 10.
🛇8 🕯 ⓤ ⓨ 🛏 ⓣⓥ 🎞 🛋 ❀
🍴 🛏 🏠

STAITHES

N. Yorkshire
Map ref 5C3

9m NW. Whitby
Busy fishing village until growth of Whitby, Staithes is a maze of steep, cobbled streets packed with tall houses of red brick and bright paintwork. Smuggling was rife in 18th C. Cotton bonnets worn by fisherwomen can still be seen. Strong associations with Captain Cook. ☑

Old Mill 🅜
😋😋
Dalehouse, Staithes, Saltburn-by-the-Sea, Cleveland TS13 5DT
☎ Whitby (0947) 840683
Specifically for vegetarian/vegan guests. Breakfast a speciality and evening meal by arrangement. Beamed rooms in an 18th C. mill house. In a tranquil setting with the ruins of the mill and wooden aquaduct/race nearby.
Bedrooms: 2 double & 1 twin.
Bathrooms: 3 private.
Bed & breakfast: £22-£26 double.
Evening meal 6pm (l.o. 7pm).
Parking for 5.
🛇 ⓞ 🕯 🛏 ⓥ 🛏 ⓣⓥ 🎞
🛋 ❀ 🛏 ⓞⓐⓟ 🆂🅿 🏠

STARBOTTON

N. Yorkshire
Map ref 5B3

2m N. Kettlewell
Quiet, picturesque village midway between Kettlewell and Buckden in Wharfedale. Many buildings belong to the 17th C and several have dated lintels.

Hilltop Country Guest House 🅜
😋😋😋
Starbotton, Skipton, BD23 5HY
☎ Kettlewell (075 676) 321
17th C. house with beckside gardens overlooking an unspoilt dales' village. Spacious and comfortable bedrooms with splendid views. Local and international dishes with sensibly priced wines. Log fires and a welcoming bar.
Bedrooms: 4 double & 2 twin, 1 family room.
Bathrooms: 7 private, 1 public.
Bed & breakfast: from £38 double.

Half board: from £182 weekly.
Evening meal 7.30pm (l.o. 8pm).
Parking for 7.
🛇 🖢 🛏 🕯 🕻 ⓥ 🛏 ⓣⓥ 🎞
🛋 🏃 ❀ 🍴 🐾 🆂🅿 🏠

STITTENHAM

N. Yorkshire
Map ref 5C3

1m NE. Sheriff Hutton

Carr Farm
High Stittenham, Stittenham, York, YO6 7TW
☎ Sheriff Hutton (034 77) 339
30-acre mixed farm. Adjacent to Castle Howard, location of "Brideshead Revisited", and well situated for the East Coast, North York Dales and moors.
Bedrooms: 1 double & 1 twin, 1 family room.
Bathrooms: 1 public.
Bed & breakfast: max. £9 single, max. £18 double.
Parking for 20.
Open April-October.
🛇4 ⚘ ⓤ ⓣⓥ 🛋 🍴 🛏

SUMMER BRIDGE

N. Yorkshire
Map ref 4B1

In Nidderdale. Through the timbered sloping footpath of Braisty Wood lies Brimham Rocks. New York Mill is associated with the manufacture of carpet yarns.

North Pasture Farm 🅜
Listed
Brimham Rocks, Summer Bridge, Harrogate, HG3 4DW
☎ Harrogate (0423) 711470
135-acre dairy farm. The house dates back to 1400 and 1657. John Wesley preached in what is now the lounge.
Bedrooms: 2 double & 1 twin.
Bathrooms: 2 public.
Bed & breakfast: max. £10 single, max. £20 double.
Half board: max. £15 daily, max. £105 weekly.
Evening meal 6.30pm (l.o. 5pm).
Parking for 4.
Open March-October.
🛇 ⓤ 🛏 ⓣⓥ 🎞 🛋 ✓ 🍴 🛏
🏠

THERE IS A SPECIAL SECTION IN THIS GUIDE LISTING ACCOMMODATION ESPECIALLY SUITABLE FOR GROUPS AND YOUNG PEOPLE.

PLEASE MENTION THIS GUIDE WHEN MAKING A BOOKING.

SUTTON BANK

N. Yorkshire
Map ref 5C3

Mrs. K. M. Hope ♨
⊞⊞
High House Farm, Sutton
Bank, Thirsk, YO7 2HA
☎ Thirsk (0845) 597557
113-acre mixed farm. 300-
year-old listed, stone-built
farmhouse with a courtyard
and magnificent views.
Splendid walking country, half
a mile from Sutton Bank
Information Centre. Home-
produced food and emphasis on
comfort and warm hospitality.
Bedrooms: 1 double & 1 twin,
1 family room.
Bathrooms: 1 public.
Bed & breakfast: £9-£9.50
single, £18-£19 double.
Half board: £14-£15 daily.
Parking for 10.
Open March-November.

THIRSK

N. Yorkshire
Map ref 5C3

Thriving market town with
cobbled square
surrounded by old shops
and inns. St. Mary's
church is probably the
best example of
perpendicular work in
Yorkshire. ℓ

Cod Beck Farm
Gristhwaite, Thirsk,
YO7 3HL
☎ (0845) 577536
160-acre mixed farm. Large,
traditional farmhouse in open
countryside, well off the road,
two miles south of Herriot's
Thirsk. Peaceful and
comfortable. Reductions for
children.
Bedrooms: 1 single, 1 double
& 1 twin, 1 family room.
Bathrooms: 2 private,
1 public.
Bed & breakfast: £9-£11
single, £18-£22 double.
Half board: £12.50-£18 daily,
£87.50-£119 weekly.
Evening meal 5pm (l.o. 8pm).
Parking for 12.

Mrs. E. E. Hall
Listed
37 Danum Avenue, Topcliffe
Rd., Thirsk, YO7 1RU
☎ (0845) 22629

Quiet, detached house with a
pleasant garden, offering a
warm welcome. In James
Herriot country, well placed for
touring the dales and coast.
Bedrooms: 1 single, 1 twin.
Bathrooms: 1 public.
Bed & breakfast: £9.50
single, £19 double.
Parking for 2.
Open April-October.

St. James House
35-37 St. James Grove,
Thirsk, YO7 1AQ
☎ (0845) 22676 & 24120
Listed, 18th C., Georgian
house, imposing and tastefully
furnished, on the village green,
two minutes' walk from the
market place. TV in most
rooms. Children 10 years and
over accepted. Non-smokers
only please.
Bedrooms: 2 double, 2 family
rooms.
Bathrooms: 2 private,
3 public.
Bed & breakfast: £26-£34
double.
Parking for 6.
Open March-November.

Station House
Listed
Station Rd., Thirsk,
YO7 4LS
☎ (0845) 22063
Large, detached red brick
building with a unique roof
design of character, originally
a station master's house.
Private garden with an orchard
to the front.
Bedrooms: 1 single, 1 double
& 1 twin.
Bathrooms: 1 public.
Bed & breakfast: £9 single,
£18 double.
Parking for 3.
Open April-October.

THIXENDALE

N. Yorkshire
Map ref 4C1

10m SE. Malton
Tiny remote village in the
Yorkshire Wolds where
many dales meet. Good
walking country.

Round The Bend
Thixendale, Malton,
YO17 9TG
☎ Driffield (0377) 88237
Attractive cottage in an
isolated village in beautiful
countryside. Log fires, home
cooking and a warm welcome.
Brochure on request.

Bedrooms: 1 single, 1 double,
1 family room.
Bathrooms: 1 public.
Bed & breakfast: £11 single,
£22 double.
Half board: £18.25 daily,
£123-£127.75 weekly.
Evening meal 6.30pm (l.o.
midday).
Parking for 3.
Open April-October.

THORALBY

N. Yorkshire
Map ref 5B3

1m S. Aysgarth
Small village south of
Aysgarth in Wensleydale.

Low Green House
⊞⊞⊞
Thoralby, Leyburn, DL8 3SZ
☎ Aysgarth (096 93) 623
Country home providing every
comfort with special emphasis
on cooking, in an unspoilt
dales' village.
Bedrooms: 1 double, 1 family
room.
Bathrooms: 2 private,
1 public.
Bed & breakfast: from £12
single, from £24 double.
Half board: from £19 daily,
from £124.60 weekly.
Evening meal 6.45pm.
Parking for 3.

Pen View ♨
⊞⊞
Thoralby, Leyburn, DL8 3SU
☎ Aysgarth (096 93) 319
South facing, family-run
guesthouse with excellent
views. Located in Bishopdale, 8
miles from Leyburn and
Hawes. Emphasis on home
cooking.
Bedrooms: 1 double, 1 family
room.
Bathrooms: 1 public.
Bed & breakfast: £10.50-£11
single, £19-£20 double.
Half board: £16.50-£17 daily,
£112-£115.50 weekly.
Parking for 3.

THORNTON WATLASS

N. Yorkshire
Map ref 5C3

3m SW. Bedale

The Buck Inn
Thornton Watlass, Ripon,
HG4 4AH
☎ Bedale (0677) 22461
Friendly village inn
overlooking the delightful
cricket green in a small village,
3 miles from Bedale on the
Masham Road, and close to
the A1. In James Herriot
Country. Ideal for walking.
Bedrooms: 2 single, 3 twin,
1 family room.
Bathrooms: 1 public.
Bed & breakfast: from £15
single, from £26 double.
Lunch available.
Evening meal 7pm (l.o.
9.30pm).
Parking for 42.

THRESHFIELD

N. Yorkshire
Map ref 5B3

1m W. Grassington
Wharfedale village, once
an Anglian settlement
which, according to
moormen, probably gave
it its name, being derived
from 'open land where
threshing is done'. In the
Yorkshire Dales National
Park.

Woodland View
1 Woodland View,
Threshfield, Skipton,
BD23 5EX
☎ Grassington (0756) 753166
Comfortable family house with
glorious views of Wharfedale, 1
mile outside charming
Grassington village on the
B6265. Ideal walking and
touring centre.
Bedrooms: 1 single, 1 double
& 1 twin.
Bathrooms: 2 private,
1 public.
Bed & breakfast: max. £10
single, max. £20 double.
Half board: max. £16 daily.
Parking for 4.

INDIVIDUAL PROPRIETORS HAVE SUPPLIED
ALL DETAILS OF ACCOMMODATION.
ALTHOUGH WE DO CHECK FOR ACCURACY, WE
ADVISE YOU TO CONFIRM PRICES AND OTHER
INFORMATION AT THE TIME OF BOOKING.

THURLSTONE

S. Yorkshire
Map ref 4B1

1m W. Penistone
On the River Don and close to the Peak District National Park with 19th C weavers' cottages with long upper windows.

Weaver's Cottages
😀😀

3-5 Tenter Hill, Thurlstone, Sheffield, S30 6RG
☎ Barnsley (0226) 763350
18th C. weavers' cottages with authentic furnishings. 2 private suites, 1 double and 1 twin. Self-catering by arrangement. In a conservation area close to the Peak National Park.
Bedrooms: 1 single, 1 double & 1 twin.
Bathrooms: 2 private, 1 public.
Bed & breakfast: £16-£19 single, £32-£38 double.
Parking for 2.
🛇 🔟 Ⓥ ✕ 🖛 �📺 🏛 🛆 ❄
✕ 🏠 🏘

TODMORDEN

W. Yorkshire
Map ref 4B1

8m NE. Rochdale
In beautiful scenery on the edge of the Pennines at junction of 3 sweeping valleys. Until 1888 the county boundary between Yorkshire and Lancashire cut this old cotton town in half, running through the middle of the Town Hall. ⓘ

Stansfield Cottage Guest House ♨
😀😀😀

Holebottom Rd., Todmorden, Lancashire OL14 8DD
☎ (0706) 812979
Early 19th C. stone-built, south facing house with fine views of the Pennines, in an elevated situation overlooking Todmorden. Within 1 mile of the town centre, bus and railway station.
Bedrooms: 1 single, 1 double & 2 twin.
Bathrooms: 3 private, 2 public.
Bed & breakfast: £18.50-£20 single, £28-£31 double.
Half board: £27-£28.50 daily.
Evening meal 7pm (l.o. 8.30pm).
Parking for 5.
🛇 📞 🖵 ❂ 🔐 🛆 🖛 �📺 🖩
🛆 ✕ 🏘

Todmorden Edge South Guest House
😀😀

Parkin La., Sourhall, Todmorden, Lancashire OL14 7JF
☎ (0706) 813459
Converted 17th C. farmhouse, in a beautiful, open, elevated position in quiet countryside, 1 mile from the town centre. Evening meal by prior arrangement only.
Bedrooms: 2 twin, 1 family room.
Bathrooms: 1 public.
Half board: £19.50-£23 daily, £126-£150 weekly.
Parking for 10.
Open March-December.
🛇 🔟 🖵 ❂ 🖛 �📺 🖩 🛆 ⋃
🏹 ❄ ✕ 🏠 🏘

TOLLERTON

N. Yorkshire
Map ref 5C3

Bungalow Farm
😀😀

Warehills La., Tollerton, York, YO6 2HG
☎ (034 73) 732
7.5-acre smallholding. In a rural setting three quarters of a mile from the A19, on the outskirts of the village. Tea and coffee provided free on request.
Bedrooms: 2 family rooms.
Bathrooms: 1 public; 1 private shower.
Bed & breakfast: £10-£12 double.
Evening meal 6pm (l.o. 9pm).
Parking for 4.
🛇 5 🖵 🖼 🔐 Ⓥ �📺 🖩 🛆 ▶
✕ 🏘

TRIANGLE

W. Yorkshire
Map ref 4B1

2m SW. Sowerby Bridge
Named after the 'Triangle Inn' because of its situation on a triangular piece of ground.

Saw Hill Farm ♨

Dean La., Triangle, Sowerby Bridge, HX6 3DP
☎ Halifax (0422) 822016
Friendly family-run business in a farmhouse with interesting architecture and history, in dramatic countryside. Feature window in the guestroom and a Z-bed for children.

Bedrooms: 1 single, 1 double & 1 twin, 1 family room.
Bathrooms: 2 public.
Bed & breakfast: £12.50 single, £25 double.
Half board: £18.50 daily, £112-£144 weekly.
Parking for 3.
🛇 🔟 🖵 ❂ 🔟 Ⓥ ✕ �📺 🖩
🛆 ❄ 🏠 🏘

WATH

N. Yorkshire
Map ref 5C3

4m N. Ripon

The George Inn ♨
Main St., Wath, Ripon, HG4 5EN
☎ Ripon (0765) 84202
Traditional country inn with a restaurant; in a farmyard setting, just off the A61 Ripon to Thirsk road.
Bedrooms: 1 double & 4 twin.
Bathrooms: 2 public; 2 private showers.
Bed & breakfast: from £18 single, from £32 double.
Half board: from £23 daily, from £150 weekly.
Lunch available.
Evening meal 7pm (l.o. 10pm).
Parking for 50.
Credit: Access, Visa.
🛇 🔟 🖵 ❂ 🔐 Ⓥ ✕ 🖩 🛆
✕ 🏠 🏘 [DAP] 🔟 [SP]

WATH-UPON-DEARNE

S. Yorkshire
Map ref 4B1

5m N. Rotherham
The name means 'ford on the River Dearne'. Wentworth Woodhouse, the stately home with the longest facade in England, is nearby.

Sandygate Hotel
Sandygate, Wath-upon-Dearne, Rotherham, S63 7LR
☎ Rotherham (0709) 877827
Recently refurbished William Younger inn providing well-appointed bedrooms, 3 bar areas, a dining area with extensive menus and a large patio. Parties catered for.
Bedrooms: 4 single, 2 double & 5 twin, 1 family room.
Bathrooms: 12 private.
Bed & breakfast: £25-£28 single, £37-£43 double.
Half board: £32-£35 daily.
Lunch available.

Evening meal 7pm (l.o. 10pm).
Parking for 100.
Credit: Access, Visa.
🛇 📞 🖵 ❂ 🔐 🖼 Ⓥ 🖛 �📺
🖩 🛆 🛐 ✕ 🏠 🏘

WEAVERTHORPE

N. Yorkshire
Map ref 5D3

Star Inn ♨
Listed

Main St., Weaverthorpe, Malton, YO17 8EY
☎ West Lutton (094 43) 273
Country inn, four miles from the A64, among the beautiful rolling wolds. Easy access to York, the coast and the Wolds Way.
Bedrooms: 1 single, 2 family rooms.
Bathrooms: 3 public.
Bed & breakfast: £12.50 single, £25 double.
Half board: £16.50 daily, from £99 weekly.
Lunch available.
Evening meal 7.30pm (l.o. 9.45pm).
Parking for 30.
🛇 🛼 🖼 Ⓥ ✕ 🛆 🔟 ❀ ▶
🏹 🏠 🏘

WENTWORTH

S. Yorkshire
Map ref 4B1

Rockingham Arms
1-5 Main St., Wentworth, Rotherham, S62 7TL
☎ Barnsley (0226) 742198
17th C. period cottages in pleasant gardens opposite the Rockingham Arms, a picturesque, old world country inn, in a delightful village.
Bedrooms: 3 single, 4 double & 5 twin.
Bathrooms: 4 private, 2 public.
Bed & breakfast: £20-£25 single, £28.50-£34 double.
Half board: £27-£32 daily.
Lunch available.
Evening meal 6.30pm (l.o. 9.30pm).
Parking for 40.
Credit: Access, Visa.
🛇 🛼 🖵 ❂ 🔐 🖼 Ⓥ 🖩 🛐 ❄
🗞 [SP] 🏘

MAP REFERENCES
APPLY TO THE
COLOUR MAPS
TOWARDS THE END
OF THIS GUIDE.

WEST BURTON

N. Yorkshire
Map ref 5B3

7m W. Leyburn

Fox & Hounds Inn
West Burton, Leyburn,
DL8 4JY
☎ Aysgarth (096 93) 279
Inn on the green of an unspoilt village in Herriot country, an excellent walking area.
Bedrooms: 2 double & 2 twin, 1 family room.
Bathrooms: 5 private.
Bed & breakfast: from £16 single, £32-£34 double.
Lunch available.
Evening meal 7.30pm (l.o. 9pm).
Parking for 5.
❄8 ♨ ⌂ ♥ ⚓ ⓥ ⊬ ⠿ ⌂
✕ ♨ SP ⊞

WETHERBY

W. Yorkshire
Map ref 4B1

Prosperous market town on the River Wharfe noted for horse racing. *i*

Craiglands
Listed
4 Spofforth Hill, Wetherby,
LS22 4SE
☎ (0937) 65061
Attractive family house in a delightful market town, convenient for Harrogate, York, the Dales and Yorkshire moors.
Bedrooms: 1 double & 1 twin.
Bathrooms: 1 public.
Bed & breakfast: £10-£12 single, £18-£20 double.
Parking for 6.
❄ ♨ ♥ ⓤ ⓥ ⊬ ⓣⓥ ⠿ ♨ ᴅᴀᴘ

Number Fifty ⋈
Listed
50 Westgate, Wetherby,
LS22 4NJ
☎ (0937) 63106
Elegant early Victorian town house with a large garden, close to the market square. Restaurants, Wetherby Racecourse and the A1 are easily accessible.
Bedrooms: 1 double & 1 twin, 1 family room.
Bathrooms: 1 public.
Bed & breakfast: from £15 single, from £25 double.
Parking for 3.
❄ ♨ ⑧ ♥ ⓤ ⓥ ⊬ ⓣⓥ ⠿ ♨
✕ ᴅᴀᴘ

WHITBY

N. Yorkshire
Map ref 5D3

Quaint holiday town with narrow streets and steep alleys at the mouth of the River Esk. Captain James Cook, the famous navigator, lived in Grape Lane. 199 steps lead to St. Mary's church and St. Hilda's Abbey overlooking harbour. Reputed to be where Dracula landed and relived at the "Dracula Experience". Sandy beach. *i*

Argyle House
18 Hudson St., Whitby,
YO21 3EP
☎ (0947) 602733
On the West Cliff with sea views from the front windows. 3 minutes' walk from the beach and close to all amenities. Traditional home cooking; evening meals available on request. Licensed bar.
Bedrooms: 2 single, 2 double, 2 family rooms.
Bathrooms: 3 private, 1 public; 2 private showers.
Bed & breakfast: £12-£15 single, £16-£20 double.
Half board: £12-£14 daily, £84-£91 weekly.
❄2 ♥ ⓥ ⊬ ⓣⓥ ⠿ ♨ ♠ ✕
♨ ᴅᴀᴘ SP

Esklet Guest House
⚌⚌
22 Crescent Avenue, West Cliff, Whitby, YO21 3ED
☎ (0947) 605663
Edwardian guesthouse with a comfortable lounge and colour TV. Home-cooked food served in a pleasant dining room.
Bedrooms: 2 double & 1 twin, 2 family rooms.
Bathrooms: 2 public.
Bed & breakfast: £9-£10 single, £18-£20 double.
Evening meal 6.30pm (l.o. 6pm).
Parking for 1.
Open February-October.
❄ ♥ ⓤ ⚓ ⊬ ⊬ ⓣⓥ ⠿ ⚑
✕ ♨

YORK

N. Yorkshire
Map ref 4C1

Roman walled city nearly 2000 years old containing many well preserved medieval buildings (The Shambles, Stonegate). Its Minster has over 100 stained glass windows spanning 800 years. Castle Museum contains city's history and there is a National Railway Museum. Many attractions including a new Wax Museum, Viking Centre and York Dungeon. *i*

Acer Guest House ⋈
Listed
52 Scarcroft Hill, The Mount, York, YO2 1DE
☎ (0904) 653839
Victorian guesthouse in a quiet residential area adjoining the Knavesmire and racecourse. Half a mile from the city centre.
Bedrooms: 2 double & 2 twin, 2 family rooms.
Bathrooms: 1 public.
Bed & breakfast: £12-£15 single, £20-£24 double.
Half board: £18-£21 daily, £115-£120 weekly.
Lunch available.
Evening meal 6pm (l.o. 8pm).
Parking for 4.
❄ ♨ ⌂ ♥ ⓤ ⚓ ⓥ ⊬ ⓣⓥ
⠿ ♨ ♠ ᴅᴀᴘ ♨ SP ⊞

Ambleside Guest House
62 Bootham Crescent, Bootham, York, YO3 7AH
☎ (0904) 37165 & 637165
Warm, friendly service, with access to rooms at all times. Only minutes from the city centre.
Bedrooms: 5 double & 2 twin, 1 family room.
Bathrooms: 4 private, 2 public.
Bed & breakfast: £20-£32 double.
❄ ♨ ⌂ ♥ ⓤ ⓥ ⊬ ⓣⓥ ⠿ ✕
ᴅᴀᴘ

Anker Guest House ⋈
Listed
53 Bishopthorpe Rd., York,
YO2 1NX
☎ (0904) 625800
Family-run guesthouse with a friendly atmosphere, five minutes' walk from the Castle Museum and half a mile from the railway station.
Bedrooms: 2 double & 3 twin, 1 family room.
Bathrooms: 2 public.

Bed & breakfast: £20-£24 double.
Half board: from £15.50 daily, from £100 weekly.
Evening meal 6pm (l.o. 7pm).
❄5 ♥ ⓤ ⓥ ⊬ ⓣⓥ ⠿ ♨
✕ ♨ ♨ SP

Arndale Hotel ⋈
⚌⚌⚌
290 Tadcaster Rd., York,
YO2 2ET
☎ (0904) 702424
Victorian family-run hotel, formerly a gentlemen's residence on a grand scale overlooking York racecourse. Warm, friendly atmosphere and Yorkshire hospitality.
Bedrooms: 1 single, 5 double & 3 twin, 1 family room.
Bathrooms: 10 private.
Bed & breakfast: £30-£38 double.
Half board: £20-£29 daily, £138.25-£199.50 weekly.
Evening meal 6.30pm (l.o. 6.30pm).
Parking for 15.
❄8 ♨ ⌂ ♥ ⚓ ⌂ ♥ ⊬ ♠
❀ ♨ SP ♨ ⊤

Arnot House ⋈
⚌⚌
17 Grosvenor Terrace, Bootham, York, YO3 7AG
☎ (0904) 641966
A beautifully preserved, Victorian town house with original cornices, fireplaces and staircase. Large rooms, tastefully decorated and well appointed. Five minutes' walk from York Minster. Brochure available.
Bedrooms: 1 single, 2 double & 1 twin, 2 family rooms.
Bathrooms: 2 public.
Bed & breakfast: £9.75-£12.50 single, £19.50-£25 double.
Half board: £17.70-£20.45 daily, £123.90-£143.15 weekly.
Evening meal 6pm (l.o. 7.30pm).
Parking for 2.
❄5 ♨ ⌂ ♥ ⓥ ⊬ ⠿ ♨
✕ ᴅᴀᴘ SP

Bay Horse Hotel
Monkgate, York, YO3 7PE
☎ (0904) 624803 & 610928
Listed Georgian building with an 18th C. external icehouse. 2 minutes' walk form the Minster and close to the city centre. 2 rooms have colour TV.
Bedrooms: 2 single, 4 double.
Bathrooms: 1 public.
Bed & breakfast: £13-£14 single, £26-£28 double.
Lunch available.
Parking for 14.
Open January-November.
⊬ ⓣⓥ ⠿ ♨ ✕ ♨ ♨

THERE IS A SPECIAL SECTION IN THIS GUIDE LISTING ACCOMMODATION ESPECIALLY SUITABLE FOR GROUPS AND YOUNG PEOPLE.

YORK
Continued

Blue Bridge Hotel M
⌂⌂⌂
Fishergate, York, YO1 4AP
☎ (0904) 621193
A friendly private hotel with a warm welcome and a relaxed atmosphere. Emphasis on home-cooked English food with a table d'hote and an a la carte menu. Easy riverside walk to the city.
Bedrooms: 2 single, 6 double & 3 twin, 5 family rooms.
Bathrooms: 14 private, 1 public.
Bed & breakfast: £29-£38 single, £40-£48 double.
Half board: £40-£49 daily, £280-£343 weekly.
Lunch available.
Evening meal 6.30pm (l.o. 9.30pm).
Parking for 20.
Credit: Access, Visa.

Briar Lea Guest House M
Listed
8 Longfield Terrace, Bootham, York, YO3 6HD
☎ (0904) 35061 & 635061
Victorian house, 5 minutes' walk from the city centre and railway station.
Bedrooms: 1 single, 2 double & 1 twin, 2 family rooms.
Bathrooms: 2 public.
Bed & breakfast: £10-£14 single, £17-£24 double.
Parking for 1.

Cottage Guest House
21 Main St., Fulford, York, YO1 4PJ
☎ (0904) 621328
Bedrooms: 4 double & 1 twin, 2 family rooms.
Bathrooms: 2 public.
Bed & breakfast: £12-£20 single, £20-£22 double.
Parking for 8.

Dairy Wholefood Guest House
Listed
3 Scarcroft Rd., York, YO2 1ND
☎ (0904) 639367
Decorated in the style of Habitat, Sanderson and Laura Ashley. The breakfast choice ranges from traditional British to wholefood/vegetarian.
Bedrooms: 2 double & 1 twin, 2 family rooms.

Bathrooms: 2 private, 1 public.
Bed & breakfast: from £22 double.
Open February-November.

Dalescroft Guest House
10 Southlands Rd., Bishopthorpe Rd., York, YO2 1NP
☎ (0904) 626801
Comfortable, family-run guesthouse close to the city centre and racecourse. Full English breakfast.
Bedrooms: 1 double & 1 twin, 1 family room.
Bathrooms: 1 public.
Bed & breakfast: £10-£12 single, £16-£22 double.
Half board: £15-£17 daily, £98-£112 weekly.
Lunch available.
Evening meal 6pm (l.o. 1pm).

Fairfax House, University of York
99 Heslington Rd., York, YO1 5BJ
☎ (0904) 656593
Student residence in quiet, spacious grounds within walking distance of the city centre. Colour TV and car park. Reduced rates for children under 12.
Bedrooms: 85 single.
Bathrooms: 14 public.
Bed & breakfast: £9-£13.50 single.
Parking for 40.
Open July-September.

Hotel Fairmount M
⌂⌂⌂
230 Tadcaster Rd., Mount Vale, York, YO2 2ES
☎ (0904) 38298 & 638298
Large, tastefully-furnished, Victorian villa dated 1881, with open views over the racecourse and within walking distance of medieval York. All rooms have a colour TV, mini bar, tea making facilities and hair dryer. Reduced weekly rates available.
Bedrooms: 2 single, 3 double & 1 twin, 4 family rooms.
Bathrooms: 10 private.
Bed & breakfast: £25-£30 single, £34-£39 double.
Half board: £27-£29.50 daily.
Lunch available.
Evening meal 7pm (l.o. 8pm).
Parking for 10.
Credit: Access, Visa.

Farthings Hotel M
⌂⌂
5 Nunthorpe Ave., York, YO2 1PF
☎ (0904) 53545
Lovingly renovated Victorian residence with a friendly, informal atmosphere. In a quiet cul-de-sac approximately 10 minutes' walk from the city centre.
Bedrooms: 4 double & 1 twin, 2 family rooms.
Bathrooms: 1 private, 2 public.
Bed & breakfast: £20-£26 double.
Half board: £140-£182 weekly.

Foss Bank Guest House M
⌂⌂⌂
16 Huntington Rd., York, YO3 7RB
☎ (0904) 35548 & 635548
Small Victorian family-run guesthouse opposite the River Foss on the north east side of the city. 5 minutes' walk from the city wall.
Bedrooms: 2 single, 2 double & 1 twin.
Bathrooms: 1 public; 1 private shower.
Bed & breakfast: £10-£12 single, £20-£24 double.
Parking for 4.

Fourposter Lodge M
⌂⌂⌂
68-70 Heslington Rd., York, YO1 5AU
☎ (0904) 651170
Victorian town house, sympathetically furnished with Victorian-style, four-poster beds. A warm, friendly welcome is extended to all guests by the proprietors.
Bedrooms: 1 single, 6 double & 1 twin, 2 family rooms.
Bathrooms: 7 private, 1 public; 1 private shower.
Bed & breakfast: £17-£20 single, £27-£36 double.
Half board: £20-£25 daily, £140-£175 weekly.
Evening meal 6.30pm (l.o. 11pm).
Parking for 7.

Heworth Guest House M
⌂
126 East Parade, Heworth, York, YO3 7YG
☎ (0904) 426384

We welcome you to our family-run hotel in a quiet conservation area, with easy parking, 15 minutes' walk from the city centre. Excitingly different menus are our speciality, vegetarian and vegan dishes are always available.
Bedrooms: 3 single, 1 double & 2 twin, 1 family room.
Bathrooms: 2 public.
Bed & breakfast: £10.50-£12.75 single, £21-£25.50 double.
Half board: £17-£19.75 daily, £110-£128 weekly.
Evening meal 6pm (l.o. 3pm).
Parking for 2.
Credit: Access, Visa.

Hobbits Hotel M
9 St. Peter's Grove, York, YO3 6AQ
☎ (0904) 624538 Telex 57476
Edwardian style small hotel in a quiet cul-de-sac, within easy walking distance of the city centre.
Bedrooms: 1 single, 3 twin, 1 family room.
Bathrooms: 5 private.
Bed & breakfast: £16-£20 single, £28-£32 double.
Parking for 5.

Keys House M
Listed
137 Fulford Rd., York, YO1 4HG
☎ (0904) 658488
Comfortable Edwardian house providing spacious bedrooms with showers and WCs. Own key provided.
Bedrooms: 2 double & 2 twin, 1 family room.
Bathrooms: 5 private.
Bed & breakfast: £22-£28 double.
Parking for 6.

Lodge Guest House M
Listed
92 Eldon St., (off Haxby Rd.,) York, YO3 7NE
☎ (0904) 36281 & 636281
Guesthouse in a quiet location with easy car parking, only 10 minutes' walk from the city centre.
Bedrooms: 2 double & 1 twin, 2 family rooms.
Bathrooms: 1 public.
Bed & breakfast: £12-£15 single, £24-£30 double.

Half board: £20-£25 daily, £140-£210 weekly.
Evening meal 6pm (l.o. 9am).

Moorgarth Guest House M

158 Fulford Rd., York, YO1 4DA
☎ (0904) 36768 Telex 57842
Victorian town house with a warm, friendly atmosphere. Close to all tourist attractions and 10 minutes' walk from the city centre.
Bedrooms: 3 single, 2 double, 3 family rooms.
Bathrooms: 4 private, 1 public.
Bed & breakfast: £13-£16 single, £24-£32 double.
Parking for 5.

Mulberry Guest House M

124 East Parade, Heworth, York, YO3 7YG
☎ (0904) 423468
Well-appointed and spacious Victorian townhouse offering a warm welcome. In a conservation area, a short walk from the city centre.
Bedrooms: 1 double & 1 twin.
Bathrooms: 2 private showers.
Bed & breakfast: £12-£14 single, £24-£28 double.
Parking for 2.

Stanley Guest House M

Stanley St., Haxby Rd., York, YO3 7NW
☎ (0904) 37111 & 637111
Large end-of-terrace, Victorian house, 10 minutes' walk from York Minster and the city centre.
Bedrooms: 2 single, 1 double & 1 twin, 2 family rooms.
Bathrooms: 2 public; 2 private showers.
Bed & breakfast: £10-£12.50 single, £20-£24 double.
Parking for 3.

Turnberry House

143 Fulford Rd., York, YO1 4HG
☎ (0904) 658435
Recently restored and refurbished Edwardian house within walking distance of the city and close to Fulford Golf Club.
Bedrooms: 2 double & 1 twin.
Bathrooms: 1 public; 2 private showers.
Bed & breakfast: £24-£32 double.
Parking for 4.

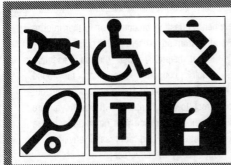

KEY TO SYMBOLS

Open out the flap inside the back cover of this guide and the key to symbols will be easy to use.

When enquiring about accommodation you may find it helpful to use the booking enquiry coupons which can be found towards the end of the guide. These should be cut out and mailed direct to the establishments in which you are interested. Remember to include your name and address and please enclose a stamped addressed envelope (or an international reply coupon if writing from outside Britain).

The BLACK HORSE Hotel

Garrs Lane, Grassington, Skipton, North Yorkshire. BD23 5AT ☎ (0756) 752770

A charming 17th century former coaching inn offering good beer, good food and good company.

This highly recommended freehouse has 11 delightful bedrooms, all of which are en-suite, two with four poster beds and all with colour television, tea & coffee making facilities and full central heating.

Bar meals served every lunch & evening, dinner served every evening.

Spring and Autumn breaks available.

Phone or write for brochure (quote W.T.S.E.)

John and Roberta Black (Resident Proprietors)

AA★

RAC INN

SCARBOROUGH *Heritage Coast*
WHITBY FILEY *and Countryside!*

Enjoy a real holiday or short break on the magnificent Yorkshire Coast.

SCARBOROUGH Golden sands, scenic views, Norman castle and colourful harbour. Fine town with royal history, elegant hotels and attractive guest houses. Theme parks and water sports. Scarborough Spa Orchestra. Alan Ayckbourn plays. Theatre in the Round.
WHITBY Historic town with famous Abbey ruins. Ancient harbour from Captain Cook's day. Sandy bay, sea and river angling.
FILEY Gentle atmosphere of sandy bay in dramatic setting. Charming small resort town with local fishing and glorious coastal scenery.
COUNTRYSIDE Beautiful North Yorkshire National Park. Moors and Wolds, Vale and Forest of Pickering. Villages, country inns, steam railway, walks. **FREE! GUIDE:**
DEPT 99 INFORMATION CENTRE, SCARBOROUGH. Tel: 0723 373333.

When requesting brochures or further information from advertisers in this guide, you may find it helpful to use the advertisement enquiry coupons which can be found towards the end of the guide. These should be cut out and mailed direct to the companies in which you are interested. Remember to include your name and address and enclose a stamped and addressed envelope or stamps if requested by the advertiser.

P L E A S E   N O T E

Individual establishments who have a display advertisement have a line listing under the appropriate town heading

CROWN CLASSIFICATIONS

All the establishments displaying a national classification in this guide are inspected regularly. All can be chosen with confidence.

There are six classifications — from Listed to 5 Crowns; each indicates the level of facilities and services provided.

All classified establishments are required to provide a high standard of cleanliness, courtesy and service and to be well maintained. A lower classification does not imply lower standards; although the range of facilities and services may be smaller, they may be provided to a high standard.

You will find a full explanation of the national Crown Classification Scheme towards the end of this guide.

FOLLOW THE SIGN

It leads to over 550 Tourist Information Centres throughout England offering friendly help with accommodation and holiday ideas as well as suggestions of places to visit and things to do.

In your home town there may be a centre which can help you before you set out. If not, why not send for the Directory of Tourist Information Centres in Great Britain? It is available free from English Tourist Board, Department D, Bromells Road, Clapham, London SW4 0BJ.

INFORMATION

Six counties make up the big Heart of England tourist region: Gloucestershire, Hereford & Worcester, Warwickshire, Shropshire, Staffordshire and the West Midlands.

Old England can still be seen to perfection here — in the wild Marches with their 26 castles, Shropshire's quiet hills, the open moorlands and peaks of Staffordshire, Hereford's Golden Valley and the isolated and peaceful Forest of Dean.

And then there are the pretty limestone villages of the Cotswolds: Broadway, Bibury, Stow-on-the-Wold, Bourton-on-the-Water, Moreton-in-Marsh, Chipping Campden and many more.

The fruitful Vale of Evesham leads to Shakespeare Country, centred on Stratford-upon-Avon and extending to Kenilworth and Warwick. Over on the Welsh border is Ross-on-Wye, centre of the beautiful Wye Valley.

Capital of the Heart of England region is the City of Birmingham with its shops, entertainment and museums. But don't forget the cathedral cities of Coventry, Gloucester, Worcester, Hereford and Lichfield, the elegant spa towns of Cheltenham, Malvern, Droitwich and Leamington Spa and the medieval jewels of Shrewsbury, Ludlow, Ledbury and Tewkesbury.

Whether you are seeking peace, quiet and relaxation or entertainment and excitement, this is the region to explore.

FIND OUT MORE

Further information about holidays and attractions in the Heart of England tourist region is available from: **Heart of England Tourist Board,** Trinity Street, Worcester WR1 2PW. ☎ (0905) 613132.

These publications are available free from the Heart of England Tourist Board:
Bed & Breakfast map
Shakespeare's Country, Cotswolds and Heart of England
Short breaks brochure
Discover the Marches
Area accommodation guides (English Marches, Hereford & Worcester, Staffordshire & The Black Country, Gloucestershire & The Cotswolds, Birmingham, Warwickshire)

Also available are:
Places to Visit in the Heart of England *(£1.50)*
Great Days Out in the Heart of England *(£2.95)*

WHERE TO GO, WHAT TO SEE

Alton Towers Leisure Park
Alton, Staffordshire ST10 4DB
☎ (0538) 702200
Europe's premier leisure park with more than 100 attractions, set in the magnificent former estate of the Earls of Shrewsbury.
Admission charge.

Birmingham Botanical Gardens
Westbourne Road, Edgbaston, Birmingham, West Midlands B15 3TR
☎ 021-454 1860
17 acres of ornamental gardens and ▶

▶ glasshouses. Tropical plants of botanical interest, aviaries with exotic birds. Children's play area.
Admission charge.

The Patrick Collection

180 Lifford Lane, Birmingham, West Midlands B30 3NT ☎ 021-459 9111
Three exhibition halls covering cars from 1913 to 1988 in period settings. Terraced garden with water features.
Admission charge.

Charlecote Park

Charlecote, Wellesbourne, Warwickshire CV35 9ER ☎ (0789) 840277
Home of Lucy family since 1247, present house built 1550. Park landscaped by 'Capability' Brown, supports herd of red and fallow deer. Tudor gatehouse.
Admission charge.

Paul Jones

FALLOW DEER AT CHARLECOTE PARK

Dean Heritage Centre

Camp Mill, Soudley, Cinderford, Gloucestershire GL14 7UG ☎ (0594) 22170
Museum displays housed in old flour mill. Water wheel, beam engine, Forest of Dean history, smallholding. 'The Living Forest' exhibition. Nature trails.
Admission charge.

Black Country Museum

Tipton Road, Dudley, West Midlands DY1 4SQ ☎ 021-557 9643
Open-air museum on 26-acre site, with many rescued buildings including shops, chapel and chainmaker's house. Canal, coalmine and electric tramway.
Admission charge.

Stuart Crystal

Redhouse Glassworks, Wordsley, Stourbridge, West Midlands DY8 4AA ☎ (0384) 71161
Factory tours showing all aspects of the production of world-famous Stuart Crystal from glassblowing and annealing to the final process of cutting and decorating. Redhouse Cone and museum, factory shop.
Admission free.

Nature in Art

Wallsworth Hall, Sandhurst, Gloucestershire GL2 9PA ☎ (0452) 731422
Nature brought to life in masterpieces of wildlife art, in all media and from any period. Nature garden and pond, gallery shop, coffee shop, play area and Kids' Corner.

Britain on View

IRONBRIDGE GORGE MUSEUM TRUST

Ironbridge Gorge Museum Trust

Ironbridge, Nr. Telford, Shropshire TF8 7AW ☎ (095 245) 3522
World's first cast-iron bridge, Severn Warehouse Visitor Centre, Coalport China, Jack Geld Tile Museum, Coalbrookdale Museum, Blists Hill Open-Air Museum, Rosehill House.
Admission charge.

Lichfield Cathedral

Lichfield, Staffordshire WS13 7LD ☎ (054 32) 256120
The only English cathedral with 3 spires. The exterior is a fine example of Early English and Decorated styles.

Especially noteworthy are the Flemish glass windows.
Admission free.

Packwood House

Packwood, Nr. Hockley Heath, West Midlands B94 6AT ☎ (056 43) 2024
Mainly built about 1560, timber-framed house with a wealth of tapestries and furniture. Gardens include Carolean formal garden and notable yew garden.
Admission charge.

Shropshire Country World

Yockleton, Shrewsbury, Shropshire SY5 9PU ☎ (074 384) 217
A day in the country with farm rides, tropical butterfly house, adventure play area. Gift shop and pottery.
Admission charge.

Batsford Arboretum

Batsford, Moreton-in-Marsh, Gloucestershire GL56 9QF ☎ (0608) 50722
500-acre arboretum containing the largest private collection of rare trees in the country, most spectacular in spring and autumn. Garden centre and nursery.
Admission charge.

Aerospace Museum

RAF Cosford, Wolverhampton, West Midlands WV7 3EX ☎ (090 722) 4872
One of the largest collections of aircraft, rockets, missiles and aero engines in Europe. Display includes British,

American, Japanese and German warplanes.
Admission charge.

National Waterways Museum
Llanthony Warehouse, Gloucester Docks, Gloucestershire GL1 2EH
☎ (0452) 25524
Three floors of dockside warehouse with lively displays telling the story of Britain's canals. Outside craft area with demonstration. Shop.
Admission charge.

West Midlands Safari and Leisure Park
Spring Grove, Bewdley, Worcestershire
☎ (0299) 402114
Set in 195 acres of countryside, animal reserves, pets corner. Leisure area with pirate ship, amusement rides, train, canoes, pedal boats. Sealion show.
Admission charge.

Worcester Royal Porcelain
Severn Street, Worcester, Worcester-shire ☎ (0905) 23221
The largest and most comprehensive collection of Worcester Porcelain in the world, covering the period from start of manufacture in 1751 to present day.
Admission free to site, charge for tours.

Warwick Castle
Warwick, Warwickshire CV34 4QU
☎ (0926) 495421
State rooms, armoury, dungeon, torture chamber, clock tower and barbican, towers, in 60 acres of grounds.
Admission charge.

Jinney Ring Craft Centre
Hanbury, Bromsgrove, Worcestershire B60 4BU ☎ (052 784) 272
Old farm buildings converted to craft centre. Craftsmen can be seen working on woodcarving, pottery, jewellery, stained glass, leather, fashion design, crystal glass. Wildlife artist. Shop and gallery.
Admission free.

Royal Shakespeare Company
Stratford-upon-Avon, Warwickshire
☎ (0789) 296655

The RSC has 3 theatres in Stratford-upon-Avon: the Royal Shakespeare Theatre, Swan Theatre and the Other Place. *Admission charge.*

MAKE A DATE FOR...

Horse racing:
Cheltenham Gold Cup meeting
Cheltenham Racecourse, Prestbury, Cheltenham, Gloucestershire
14 – 16 March

Three Counties Agricultural Show
Three Counties Showground, Malvern, Worcestershire *13 – 15 June*

Royal International Horse Show
National Exhibition Centre, Birmingham, West Midlands *15 – 18 June*

Royal International Agricultural Show
National Agricultural Centre, Stoneleigh, Kenilworth, Warwickshire *3 – 6 July*

Shrewsbury International Music Festival
Various venues, Shrewsbury, Shropshire
5 – 12 July

International Air Tattoo
Royal Air Force Fairford, Nr. Cirencester, Gloucestershire *22 – 23 July*

Shrewsbury Flower Show
Quarry Park, Shrewsbury, Shropshire
11 – 12 August

Three Choirs Festival
Gloucester Cathedral, Gloucester, Gloucestershire *18 – 26 August*

Birmingham Super Prix
City Centre Circuit, Birmingham, West Midlands *27 – 28 August*

Cheltenham Festival of Literature
Various venues, Cheltenham, Gloucestershire
30 September – 15 October

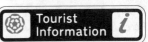

Tourist and leisure information can be obtained from Tourist Information Centres throughout England. Details of centres in the Heart of England region are listed below. The symbol 🛏 means that an accommodation booking service is provided. Centres marked with a ✱ are open during the summer months only. In the following pages, towns which have a Tourist Information Centre are indicated with the symbol *i* .

Bewdley
Worcestershire 🛏
Load Street
☎ (0299) 404740

Birmingham
W. Midlands
2 City Arcade 🛏
☎ 021-643 2514
National Exhibition Centre 🛏
☎ 021-780 4141 & 4321
International Airport
☎ 021-767 5511

Bridgnorth
Shropshire 🛏
The Library, Listley Street
☎ (074 62) 3358

Broadway
Worcestershire 🛏 ✱
1 Cotswold Court, The Green
☎ (0386) 852937

Bromsgrove
Worcestershire 🛏
47 – 49 Worcester Road
☎ (0527) 31809

▶

Bromyard
Herefordshire 🛏
Council Offices,
1 Rowberry Street
☎ (0885) 82341

Burton upon Trent
Staffordshire 🛏
Town Hall
☎ (0283) 45454

Cheltenham
Gloucestershire 🛏
The Promenade
☎ (0242) 522878

Chipping Campden
Gloucestershire 🛏 *
Woolstaplers Hall Museum,
High Street
☎ Evesham (0386) 840289

Church Stretton
Shropshire 🛏 *
County Branch Library,
Church Street
☎ (0694) 723133

Cinderford
Gloucestershire 🛏
Bellevue Road
☎ Dean (0594) 23184

Cirencester
Gloucestershire 🛏
Corn Hall, Market Place
☎ (0285) 654180

Coleford
Gloucestershire 🛏
Forest of Dean
☎ Dean (0594) 36307

Coventry
W. Midlands 🛏
Smithford Way
☎ (0203) 51717/832311

Droitwich
Worcestershire 🛏
Heritage Centre, Heritage Way
☎ (0905) 774312

Dudley
W. Midlands 🛏
39 Churchill Precinct
☎ (0384) 50333

Evesham
Worcestershire 🛏
The Almonry Museum,
Merstow Green
☎ (0386) 6944

Gloucester
Gloucestershire 🛏
St. Michael's Tower, The Cross
☎ (0452) 421188

Hereford
Herefordshire 🛏
Town Hall, St. Owen Street
☎ (0432) 268430

Ironbridge
Shropshire 🛏 *
Ironbridge Toll House
☎ (0952) 882753

Kenilworth
Warwickshire 🛏
11 Smalley Place
☎ (0926) 52595

Kington
Herefordshire
Council Offices, 2 Mill Street
☎ (0544) 230202

Leamington Spa
Warwickshire 🛏
Jephson Lodge, The Parade
☎ (0926) 311470

Ledbury
Herefordshire 🛏
St. Katherine's High Street
☎ (0531) 2461

Leek
Staffordshire 🛏
1 Market Place
☎ (0538) 381000

Leominster
Herefordshire 🛏
School Lane
☎ (0568) 6460

Lichfield
Staffordshire 🛏
Donegal House, Bore Street
☎ (0543) 252109

Ludlow
Shropshire 🛏 *
Castle Street
☎ (0584) 3857

Malvern
Worcestershire 🛏
Winter Gardens, Grange Road
☎ (0684) 892289

Much Wenlock
Shropshire 🛏 *
Guildhall
☎ (0952) 727679

Newcastle-under-Lyme
Staffordshire 🛏
Area Reference Library,
Ironmarket
☎ (0782) 618125

Newport
Shropshire 📠
9 St. Mary Street
☎ (0952) 814109

Northleach
Gloucestershire 📠 *
Cotswold Countryside Collection
☎ (0451) 60715

Nuneaton
Warwickshire 📠
The Library, Church Street
☎ (0203) 384027

Oswestry
Shropshire
Mile End Service Area,
Mile End 📠
☎ (0691) 662488
The Library, Arthur Street 📠
☎ (0691) 662753

Painswick
Gloucestershire 📠
The Library
☎ (0452) 812569

Pershore
Worcestershire 📠
37 High Street
☎ (0386) 554711

Redditch
Worcestershire 📠
9 – 11 Royal Square
☎ (0527) 60806

Ross-on-Wye
Herefordshire 📠
20 Broad Street
☎ (0989) 62768

Rugby
Warwickshire 📠
The Library, St. Matthew Street
☎ (0788) 71813/535348

Shrewsbury
Shropshire 📠
The Square
☎ (0743) 50761/52019

Solihull
W. Midlands
Central Library, Homer Road
☎ 021-705 6789 ext. 504/5

Stoke-on-Trent
Staffordshire 📠
1 Glebe Street
☎ (0782) 411222

Stow-on-the-Wold
Gloucestershire 📠
Talbot Court
☎ (0451) 31082

Stratford-upon-Avon
Warwickshire 📠
Judith Shakespeare's House,
1 High Street
☎ (0789) 293127

Stroud
Gloucestershire 📠
Subscription Rooms
☎ (045 36) 5768

Tamworth
Staffordshire 📠
Municipal Offices,
Marmion House, Lichfield Street
☎ (0827) 64222 ext. 387

Telford
Shropshire 📠
Shopping Arcade
☎ (0952) 505370

Tetbury
Gloucestershire 📠 *
Old Court House, 63 Long Street
☎ (0666) 53552

Tewkesbury
Gloucestershire 📠 *
Tewkesbury Museum,
64 Barton Street
☎ (0684) 295027

Upton-upon-Severn
Worcestershire 📠 *
Heritage Centre, The Pepperpot,
Church Street
☎ (068 46) 4200

Warwick
Warwickshire
Court House, Jury Street
☎ (0926) 492212

Wellington
Shropshire 📠
9 Walker Street
☎ Telford (0952) 48295

Whitchurch
Shropshire 📠
Civic Centre, High Street
☎ (0948) 4577

Winchcombe
Gloucestershire 📠 *
Town Hall, High Street
☎ (0242) 602925

Wolverhampton
W. Midlands 📠
16 Queen Square
☎ (0902) 312951

Worcester
Worcestershire 📠
Guildhall, High Street
☎ (0905) 723471

Entries in this regional section are listed in alphabetical order of place name, and then in alphabetical order of establishment. County names are not normally repeated in each establishment entry, but please use the full postal address when writing.

The map references refer to the colour maps towards the end of this guide. The first number is the number of the map, and it is followed by the grid reference.

The Crown Classifications are explained on pages 8 and 9, and the key to symbols is on the flap inside the back cover — keep it open for easy reference.

ABBOTS BROMLEY

Staffordshire
Map ref 4B3

6m W. Uttoxeter
Attractive village with a Butter Cross, a green, some black and white cottages and 18th C almshouses. It is well-known for the ancient Horn Dance which takes place each year in September when dancers in Tudor dress bear reindeer antlers.

Crown Inn
Market Pl., Abbots Bromley, Rugeley, WS15 3BS
☎ Burton upon Trent (0283) 840227
English country inn in centre of attractive village, famous for the Horn Dance held each year in September.
Bedrooms: 2 single, 2 double & 1 twin, 2 family rooms.
Bathrooms: 2 public.
Bed & breakfast: from £15 single, from £23 double.
Lunch available.
Evening meal 6.30pm (l.o. 10pm).
Parking for 62.
Credit: Access, Visa.
🛏 🖵 🏵 🛎 🍴 Ⓥ ⅙ 🗲 ⊞ 🖺
🖺 🍴 🐾 🏠

ACTON BURNELL

Shropshire
Map ref 4A3

7m S. Shrewsbury
Pleasant little village of black and white cottages and Georgian houses, noted for the ruins of Acton Burnell Castle and the remains of the castle barn where it is thought England's first properly constituted parliament was held in 1283. Acton Burnell Hall, an elegant Georgian building, is now a college.

Parsons Pleasure M
⊞⊞
Acton Pigot, Acton Burnell, Shrewsbury, SY5 7HQ
☎ (069 44) 261
A warm, friendly part-timbered house dating from Tudor times, in beautiful rural Shropshire. Within easy reach of Ironbridge, Ludlow and Shrewsbury and a small unusual plant nursery.
Bedrooms: 2 double & 1 twin.
Bathrooms: 3 private.
Bed & breakfast: £12 single, £24 double.
Parking for 3.
Open April-October.
🏠 🏵 Ⓥ ⅙ 🗲 ⊞ 🖺 🛋
🔎 🐾 🗡 🖺 🏠

THERE IS A SPECIAL SECTION IN THIS GUIDE LISTING ACCOMMODATION ESPECIALLY SUITABLE FOR GROUPS AND YOUNG PEOPLE.

GROUPS, CONSORTIA AND AGENCIES SPECIALISING IN FARM AND COUNTRY HOLIDAYS ARE LISTED IN A SPECIAL SECTION OF THIS GUIDE.

ADFORTON

Hereford & Worcester
Map ref 4A3

7m E. Knighton
Small village close to Wigmore with its Norman church and ruined castle. Croft Castle (National Trust) is nearby.

Lower House M
⊞⊞
Adforton, Leintwardine, Craven Arms, Shropshire SY7 0NF
☎ Wigmore (056 886) 223
Well-furnished 16th C. farmhouse with exposed beams. Open fires and feature inglenook in dining room.
Bedrooms: 1 double & 2 twin.
Bathrooms: 1 public.
Bed & breakfast: £14-£16 single, £28-£32 double.
Half board: £21-£23 daily, £135 weekly.
Evening meal 7pm (l.o. 7.30pm).
Parking for 10.
Open April-October.
🛏 🏵 Ⓤ 🛎 Ⓥ 🗲 ⊞ 🖺 🛋
🖺 ⏛ 🐾 🗡 🖺

ALCESTER

Warwickshire
Map ref 2B1

See also Bidford on Avon, Wootton Wawen.
Town has Roman origins and many old buildings around the High Street. It is close to Ragley Hall, the 18th C Palladian mansion with its magnificent baroque Great Hall.

Glebe Farm M
(Listed)
Exhall, Alcester, B49 6EA
☎ Stratford-upon-Avon (0789) 772202
100-acre mixed farm. Quaint old farmhouse in a very rural setting, 10 minutes' drive from Stratford. Home-cooked meals available.
Bedrooms: 1 single, 1 double & 1 twin.
Bathrooms: 2 public.
Bed & breakfast: £10-£12.50 single, £20-£25 double.
Half board: £16-£19.50 daily, £112-£136.50 weekly.
Evening meal 7pm.
Parking for 6.
🛏 🝔 Ⓤ 🗲 🗲 ⊞ 🛋 🐾 🌣
🖺 🏠

Sambourne Hall Farm M
⊞⊞
Wike La., Sambourne, Redditch, Worcestershire B96 6NZ
☎ Studley (052 785) 2151
315-acre arable & beef farm. Mid 17th C. farmhouse in a peaceful village, close to local pub. Just off the A435 between Alcester and Studley and 9 miles from Stratford.
Bedrooms: 1 single, 2 double.
Bathrooms: 1 private, 1 public.
Bed & breakfast: £15 single, £25 double.
Parking for 7.
🛏 🖵 Ⓤ Ⓥ ⅙ 🗲 ⊞ 🖺 🛋 🌣
🗡 🖺 🏠

The Stag's Head Hotel M
Redhill, Alcester Road, Stratford-upon-Avon, B49 6NQ
☎ (0789) 762440/764634
16th C. inn 4 miles from Stratford-upon-Avon, with all amenities. A la carte restaurant plus bar meals. Open views.
Bedrooms: 4 single, 6 double & 5 twin.
Bathrooms: 14 private, 2 public.
Bed & breakfast: from £32.50 single, £42.50-£55 double.
Lunch available.
Evening meal 7pm (l.o. 9.30pm).
Parking for 200.
Credit: Access, Visa, Diners, Amex.
🛏 10 🖺 🝔 📞 ▣ 🖵 🛎 🎱
Ⓥ 🗲 ⊞ 🖺 🛋 🍴 � 🐾 🌣
🗡 SP

ALDSWORTH

Gloucestershire
Map ref 2B1

10m NE. Cirencester
Village near many interesting places such as Northleach with its beautiful church, Burford, one of the finest Cotswold towns, Chedworth Roman villa and Bibury with its trout farm and famous row of cottages.

The Old Bakery
Aldsworth, Cheltenham, GL54 3QZ
☎ Windrush (045 14) 514
Converted bakehouse attached to a Georgian house, in a lovely village setting.
Bedrooms: 1 double, 1 family room.

Bathrooms: 1 public.
Bed & breakfast: £24 double.
Parking for 4.

Staffordshire
Map ref 4B3

5m NE. Lichfield
Delightful village of black
and white cottages, past
which the willow fringed
Trent runs. The Trent and
Mersey canal enhances
the scene and Fradley
Junction, a mile away, is
one of the most charming
inland waterway locations
in the country.

Main View
[Listed]
18 Burton Rd., Alrewas,
Burton upon Trent,
DE13 7BB
☎ (0283) 790725
*Detached house on the main
A38 northbound. Country
village convenient for
Birmingham and the North
Country. Pleasant views.*
Bedrooms: 1 single, 1 double
& 1 twin.
Bathrooms: 1 public.
Bed & breakfast: £10-£12
single, £19-£20 double.
Half board: £13.50-£14.50
daily, £90 weekly.
Evening meal 5pm (l.o. 6pm).
Parking for 6.

Staffordshire
Map ref 4B2

*See also Cheadle,
Kingsley, Oakamoor.*
Alton Castle, an
impressive 19th C
building now a school,
dominates the village
which is set in
spectacular scenery.
Nearby is Alton Towers, a
romantic 19th C ruin with
innumerable tourist
attractions in its 800
acres of magnificent
gardens.

Rakesdale Cottage
[Listed]
Alton, Stoke-on-Trent,
ST10 4BT
☎ Oakamoor (0538) 702097
*Very large stone-built house
dating from 1850, set in
beautiful grounds featuring
several ponds, walks and
magnificent views.*

Bedrooms: 1 double, 1 family
room.
Bathrooms: 1 public.
Bed & breakfast: max. £15
single, max. £25 double.
Parking for 10.

Tythe Barn House ⋀
Denstone Lane, Alton, Stoke-
on-Trent, ST10 4AX
☎ Oakamoor (0538) 702852
*Comfortable, homely
accommodation in attractive
17th C. farmhouse, with
exposed beams and a quarter
of an acre garden. Reduced
rates for children. 1 mile from
Alton Towers.*
Bedrooms: 1 single, 1 double,
1 family room.
Bathrooms: 1 public.
Bed & breakfast: £8.50-£9.50
single, £17-£19 double.
Parking for 4.

Wild Duck Inn
[Listed]
New Rd., Alton, Stoke-on-
Trent, ST10 4AF
☎ Oakamoor (0538) 702218
*A large country inn, within
view of Alton Towers Leisure
Park. Comfortable bedrooms
and a pleasant restaurant and
bar.*
Bedrooms: 5 family rooms.
Bathrooms: 1 private,
1 public.
Bed & breakfast: £21-£36
double.
Evening meal 7pm (l.o. 9pm).
Parking for 50.
Open March-November.
Credit: Visa.

Shropshire
Map ref 4A3

6m SE. Bridgnorth
Off the Kidderminster to
Bridgnorth road looking
west to the River Severn,
a village of sturdy stone
cottages and a mainly
Norman church with 18th
C battlements.

The Low Farm
⊞⊞
Alveley, Bridgnorth,
WV15 6HX
☎ Arley (Worcs) (029 97) 206
*200-acre mixed farm.
Victorian farmhouse on
working farm in the Severn
Valley near Bewdley,
Kidderminster and Bridgnorth.*
Bedrooms: 1 twin, 1 family
room.

Bathrooms: 1 public.
Bed & breakfast: £8-£9
single, £16-£18 double.
Half board: £13.50-£14.50
daily.
Evening meal 5pm.
Parking for 4.

Gloucestershire
Map ref 2B1

6m SE. Cheltenham
Village not far from
Chedworth Roman Villa
which is owned by the
National Trust. There are
extensive views over the
Cotswolds from Kilkenny
Viewpoint, 1 mile to the
west of the village.

Andoversford Nurseries
⊞
Upper Hannington, Stow
Rd., Andoversford,
Cheltenham, GL54 5SH
☎ Cheltenham (0242) 820270
*10-acre glasshouse and pasture
farm. Modern farmhouse a few
miles from Cheltenham. Good
centre for touring Cotswolds.*
Bedrooms: 2 double & 1 twin.
Bathrooms: 1 private,
1 public.
Bed & breakfast: £8-£15
single, £16-£30 double.
Half board: £14-£20 daily.
Evening meal 6.45pm (l.o.
7.15pm).
Parking for 12.

Staffordshire
Map ref 4B2

The Domvilles Farm ⋀
⊞⊞
Barthomley Rd., Audley,
Stoke-on-Trent, ST7 8HT
☎ Stoke-on-Trent
(0782) 720378
*120-acre mixed farm. Georgian
farmhouse, with oak beams
and staircase, overlooking the
Cheshire Plain, half a mile
from picturesque Barthomley.
Ideal for Alton Towers, the
Potteries and Bridgmere
Garden World. 3 minutes from
junction 16 M6.*
Bedrooms: 2 double, 2 family
rooms.
Bathrooms: 2 private,
1 public.
Bed & breakfast: from £12
single, from £20 double.
Half board: from £18 daily.

Evening meal 6pm (l.o.
7.30pm).
Parking for 12.

Warwickshire
Map ref 2C1

7m NW Banbury
Village on the slopes of
the Dasset Hills, with
good views. The church,
with its impressive tower
and spire, dates from
1868 though it
incorporates a 14th C.
window with 15th C.
glass.

Crandon House ⋀
⊞⊞⊞
Avon Dassett, Leamington
Spa, CV33 0AA
☎ Fenny Compton
(029 577) 652
*20-acre mixed farm.
Comfortable farmhouse in
beautiful countryside, serving
home produce.*
Bedrooms: 1 double & 2 twin.
Bathrooms: 1 private,
1 public.
Bed & breakfast: £15-£20
single, £25-£30 double.
Half board: £18-£24 daily,
£126-£150 weekly.
Evening meal 7pm (l.o. 6pm).
Parking for 22.

West Midlands
Map ref 4B3

6m NW. Kenilworth
Close to Kenilworth and
within easy reach of
Coventry.

Meadow Farm
Guesthouse
⊞⊞
Windmill La., Balsall
Common, CV7 7FG
☎ Berkswell (0676) 32211
*120-acre dairy farm.
Beautifully restored farmhouse
in a secluded position.
Convenient for Warwick and
Stratford. 10 minutes from the
National Exhibition Centre
and the Royal Showground in
Stoneleigh.*
Bedrooms: 2 single, 1 double
& 2 twin.
Bathrooms: 1 private,
1 public.

Continued ▶

123

BALSALL COMMON

Continued

Bed & breakfast: £12 single, £15 double.
Parking for 10.

⬤ 🔲 ⓥ 🛁 📺 🎮 ♨ ❄ ✕ 🏠

BALTERLEY

Staffordshire
Map ref 4A2

2m W. Audley
Hamlet on the Staffordshire/Cheshire border with an interesting modern church and a black and white Tudor hall.

Balterley Hall Farm ⋔
Listed

Balterley, Crewe, Cheshire CW2 5QG
☎ Crewe (0270) 820206
240-acre arable farm. A 17th C. farmhouse offering a warm and friendly welcome. Set in peaceful surroundings near the Potteries. 3.5 miles from the M6.
Bedrooms: 1 single, 1 double, 1 family room.
Bathrooms: 1 private, 1 public.
Bed & breakfast: £10-£15 single, £19-£24 double.
Half board: £15-£29 daily, £91-£105 weekly.
Evening meal 6pm (l.o. 7.30pm).
Parking for 10.

⬤ ⚒ 🔧 🛗 ♨ 🔲 ⓥ 🛁 📺 🎮 ♨ ❄ 🏠 🏡

Pear Tree Lake Farm
Listed

Balterley, Crewe, Cheshire CW2 5QE
☎ Crewe (0270) 820307
115-acre pig and bullock farm. Beams and log fires enhance this lovely old farmhouse. Quiet patio and large gardens. Convenient for Alton Towers.
Bedrooms: 4 double & 1 twin, 2 family rooms.
Bathrooms: 1 private, 2 public.
Bed & breakfast: £12.50-£17.50 single, £20-£25 double.
Half board: £17-£20 daily, £70-£90 weekly.
Lunch available.
Evening meal 8pm (l.o. 8pm).
Parking for 13.

⬤ ⚒ 🛗 🛌 🔲 ♨ 🔲 ⓥ 🛁 📺 ♨ 📡 ❄ 🏠 🏡 📶 SP

BASCHURCH

Shropshire
Map ref 4A3

8m NW. Shrewsbury
The older part of this village forms a compact group around the church and inn, with some black and white buildings. Thomas Telford, the great engineer, was responsible for major work on the church in 1790.

Frankbrook
Listed

Yeaton La., Baschurch, Shrewsbury, SY4 2HZ
☎ (0939) 260778
Attractive, comfortable family home in quiet countryside. 1 mile from Baschurch and a good base for touring Wales, Shrewsbury, Chester and Ironbridge. Sketch map sent on request.
Bedrooms: 2 double & 2 twin.
Bathrooms: 2 public.
Bed & breakfast: £9-£10 single, £18-£20 double.
Half board: £13-£15 daily, £90-£100 weekly.
Evening meal 6.30pm (l.o. 7.30pm).
Parking for 5.

⬤ ⚒ 🔲 🛁 📺 🎮 ♨ U ❄ ✕ 🏠 🏡

BETLEY

Staffordshire
Map ref 4A2

6m W. Newcastle-under-Lyme
Once a market town, now a village with many whitewashed and timber-framed houses. Much of the 17th C. church was paid for by the Egerton Family, whose monuments may be seen inside. Noteworthy is the unusual use of wood in the interior of the church.

Adderley Green Farm ⋔
😊😊

Heighley Castle Lane, Betley, Crewe, Cheshire CW3 9BA
☎ Crewe (0270) 820203
250-acre dairy and mixed farm. Large, attractive farmhouse near picturesque Betley and within easy reach of the Potteries, Stapeley Water Gardens and Alton Towers.
Bedrooms: 1 double & 1 twin, 1 family room.
Bathrooms: 1 private, 2 public.

Bed & breakfast: £10-£15 single, £20-£24 double.
Half board: £16-£21 daily, £100-£142 weekly.
Lunch available.
Evening meal 7pm (l.o. 1pm).
Parking for 9.

⬤ 🔲 🛗 🔲 ♨ 🔲 ⓥ ✂ 🛁 📺 🎮 ♨ ❄ ♀ U ♨ ➤ ✕ ❄ 🏠 🏡

BEWDLEY

Hereford & Worcester
Map ref 4A3

Attractive hillside town situated above the River Severn and approached by a bridge designed by Telford. It has many elegant buildings and an interesting museum. It is the southern terminus of the Severn Valley Steam Railway.

Baytree Farm
Listed

Baveney Wood, Neen Savage, Cleobury Mortimer, Kidderminster, Worcestershire DY14 8JB
☎ Kinlet (029 924) 403 & 382
8-acre non-working farm. Delightful elevated farmhouse on the Worcestershire/Shropshire border with uninterrupted rural views. 5 miles from Bewdley, and close to Bridgnorth, Ludlow, and the Wyre Forest.
Bedrooms: 1 single, 1 double & 1 twin.
Bathrooms: 1 public.
Bed & breakfast: £11.50-£12.50 single, £20-£23 double.
Evening meal 6.50pm (l.o. 7.50pm).
Parking for 10.

⬤ ⚒ 🔲 ♨ 🔲 ⓥ 🛁 📺 🎮 ♨ U ❄ ✕ 🏠

Church Farm ⋔
😊

Suffolks La., Abberley, Worcester, Worcestershire WR6 6BB
☎ Great Witley (0299) 896316
300-acre arable and beef farm. Working farm set in its own orchard, overlooking nature pond and small trout pool. 5 miles from Bewdley and 12 miles from Worcester. Log fires, pretty bedrooms.
Bedrooms: 1 single, 1 double & 1 twin.
Bathrooms: 1 private, 1 public.
Bed & breakfast: £10 single, £20-£24 double.

Half board: £15-£16 daily, from £105 weekly.
Evening meal 6pm (l.o. 6pm).
Parking for 5.
Open April-October.

⬤ ♨ 🔲 🛁 🎮 📺 ✕ 🏠

Rosemary Cottage

Trimpley La., Shatterford, Bewdley, Worcestershire DY12 1RQ
☎ Arley (Worcs) (029 97) 492
300-year-old timbered cottage in 2 acres of garden, with an elevated summer house. Lovely villages, walks and wonderful scenery. Between Kidderminster and Bridgnorth on the A442.
Bedrooms: 1 single, 2 twin.
Bathrooms: 1 public.
Bed & breakfast: £10 single, £20 double.
Parking for 6.

⬤ ⚒ 🔲 🛁 📺 🎮 ❄ ✕ 🏠 DAP

BIDFORD-ON-AVON

Warwickshire
Map ref 2B1

Attractive village with an ancient 8-arched bridge and a main street with some interesting 15th C houses.

Orchard, Horseshoe Cottage
Listed

Honeybourne Rd., Bickmarsh, Bidford-on-Avon B50 4PB
☎ (0789) 778410
White rendered cottage in a quietly located position with beautiful garden and orchard. 1 mile outside Bidford on Honeybourne Road.
Bedrooms: 1 single, 1 double.
Bathrooms: 1 public.
Bed & breakfast: £12.50 single, £25 double.
Half board: £17.50 daily, £122.50 weekly.
Lunch available.
Evening meal 5pm (l.o. 6.30pm).
Parking for 4.

⬤ ⚒ 🔲 ♨ 🔲 🛁 🎮 ♨ ✕ 🏠

> **MAP REFERENCES APPLY TO THE COLOUR MAPS TOWARDS THE END OF THIS GUIDE.**

BIRDLIP

Gloucestershire
Map ref 2B1

7m SE. Gloucester
Hamlet at the top of a
very steep descent down
to the Gloucester Vale
and close to the Crickley
Hill Country Park.

Beechmount
😊😊

Birdlip, Gloucester, GL4 8JH
☎ Gloucester (0452) 862262
*A small family-run guesthouse
with personal attention. Ideal
centre for the Cotswolds.*
Bedrooms: 1 single, 2 double
& 2 twin, 2 family rooms.
Bathrooms: 2 private,
1 public.
Bed & breakfast: £11-£15
single, £18.75-£36 double.
Half board: £17-£25 daily.
Evening meal (l.o. 7pm).
Parking for 6.
⏰ 🛏 ℹ️ ✓ ⬛ 📺 🎮 ▥ 🅰 🎄

Knapp House M
Birdlip Hill, Witcombe,
Gloucester, GL3 4SL
☎ Gloucester (0452) 862213
*A beautiful country house with
outstanding views. Overlooking
the Severn Vale and adjoining
the famous Cotswold Way on
scenic Birdlip Hill.*
Bedrooms: 1 double & 2 twin.
Bathrooms: 1 public.
Bed & breakfast: £12.50-£15
single, £22-£28 double.
Half board: £18.50-£22 daily.
Evening meal 6.30pm (l.o.
7pm).
⏰ 🛏 ℹ️ ⬛ 🎮 📺 ▥ 🅰 ❄ 🎄

BISHAMPTON

Hereford & Worcester
Map ref 2B1

7m NE. Pershore
Mentioned in the
Domesday Book. The
church was restored in
1870 but its Norman
doorways remain.

Nightingale Farm M
😊😊😊

Bishampton, Pershore,
Worcestershire WR10 2NN
☎ (038 682) 384
*200-acre beef and arable farm.
Working farm with many
footpaths and unspoilt views of
the Malverns. Farming a
pedigree herd of Aberdeen
Angus and Belgian Blue cattle.*
Bedrooms: 1 double & 1 twin,
1 family room.
Bathrooms: 3 private.
Bed & breakfast: £20 single,
£32 double.

Half board: £28 daily, £185
weekly.
Lunch available.
Evening meal 7.30pm (l.o.
9.30pm).
Parking for 4.
Credit: Access, Visa.
⏰6 ⬛ 🛏 ℹ️ ⬛ 📺 ◐
▥ 🅰 🕐 ✓ ❄ 🎄 SP 🎄

BISHOPS CASTLE

Shropshire
Map ref 4A3

See also Wentnor.
Small hill-top town on the
Welsh Border close to the
Clun Forest, with some
Tudor houses and a 17th
C public house where the
landlord brews his own
beer. An excellent centre
for exploring Offa's Dyke
and the Shropshire
countryside.

Castle Hotel M
Bishops Castle, SY9 5DG
☎ (0588) 638403
*Coaching hotel of character
built in 1719 on site of castle
keep. Panelled coffee room,
restaurant and bars with log
fires.*
Bedrooms: 3 double & 3 twin,
2 family rooms.
Bathrooms: 1 private,
1 public.
Bed & breakfast: £17-£19
single, £29.50-£34 double.
Lunch available.
Evening meal 7.30pm (l.o.
9.30pm).
Parking for 40.
Credit: Access, Visa, Diners.
⏰ 🕐 ⬛ 📺 ▥ 🍴 SP
🎄 🅣

Old Time
29 High St., Bishops Castle,
SY9 5BE
☎ (0588) 638467
*An old beamed house and shop
at the centre of a small,
unspoilt market town, set in the
south Shropshire Hills.*
Bedrooms: 2 double & 2 twin.
Bathrooms: 2 private,
1 public.
Bed & breakfast: £9-£12
single, £18-£24 double.
⏰ ❄ 🅰 ❄ ℹ️ ⬛ 🅰 🎄
🎄

Waverley Guest
House M
Listed
Montgomery Rd., Bishops
Castle, SY9 5EZ
☎ (0588) 638554
*Large spacious bungalow in
rural setting, 2 minutes' walk
from the centre of this market
town. A la carte evening meals.*

Bedrooms: 2 single, 1 twin,
1 family room.
Bathrooms: 2 public.
Bed & breakfast: £9.50-
£10.50 single, £19-£21 double.
Half board: £15-£16.50 daily,
£105-£115.50 weekly.
Evening meal 7pm (l.o.
8.30pm).
Parking for 8.
⏰ ❄ 🅰 🛏 ℹ️ ⬛ 🎮 ▥
🅰 🕐 ❄ 🎄 🎄 SP

BLEDINGTON

Gloucestershire
Map ref 2C1

4m SE. Stow-on-the-Wold
Village close to the
Oxfordshire border with a
pleasant green and a
beautiful church.

Kings Head Inn &
Restaurant M
😊😊😊

The Green, Bledington,
Kingham, Oxford,
Oxfordshire OX7 6HD
☎ Kingham (060 871) 365
*15th C. inn located in the heart
of the Cotswolds, facing the
village green. Main building
has 2 bars, one with inglenook
fireplace.*
Bedrooms: 1 single, 3 double
& 1 twin, 1 family room.
Bathrooms: 3 private,
3 public.
Bed & breakfast: £24-£29
single, max. £39 double.
Lunch available.
Evening meal 7pm (l.o.
10.15pm).
Parking for 20.
⏰ 🕐 🛏 ℹ️ ⬛ ✓ ▥ 📺 ▥
🅰 🍴 ❄ ❄ 🎄 🎄 OAP SP 🅣

BLITHBURY

Staffordshire
Map ref 4B3

2m NE. Rugeley
Hamlet in the parish of
Mavesyn Ridware, a
charming and historic
village on the banks of
the River Trent.

Lower Newlands
Farm M
Listed
Newlands La., Blithbury,
Rugeley, WS15 3JD
☎ Burton upon Trent
(0283) 840370
*195-acre mixed farm. Listed
16th C. farmhouse with
exposed oak beams. Exclusive
accommodation for up to 6
persons. Home-cooked food,
private dining room and lounge
with open fires.*
Bedrooms: 2 family rooms.

Bathrooms: 1 public.
Bed & breakfast: £10 single,
£20 double.
Half board: £14 daily, £84
weekly.
Evening meal 6pm (l.o. 7pm).
Parking for 10.
Open April-October.
⏰ ❄ ▥ ✗ 📺 🅰 ❄ 🎄 🎄
🎄

BLOCKLEY

Gloucestershire
Map ref 2B1

*3m NW. Moreton-in-
Marsh*
Village's prosperity was
founded in silk mills and
other factories but now it
is a quiet unspoilt place.
An excellent centre for
exploring pretty Cotswold
villages, especially
Chipping Campden and
Broadway.

Park Farm Guest
House M
Listed
Blockley, Moreton-in-Marsh,
GL56 9TA
☎ (0386) 700266
*200-acre mixed farm. A lovely
old farmhouse, carefully
modernised but retaining
original beams and features.
Warm, friendly atmosphere
and wonderful walks.*
Bedrooms: 2 single, 1 twin,
1 family room.
Bathrooms: 1 public.
Bed & breakfast: £10-£12
single, £20 double.
⏰ ❄ 🕐 ▥ ℹ️ ⬛ ▥ 📺 🅰
🅿 ❄ 🎄 🎄

21 Station Rd. M
😊😊

Blockley, Moreton-in-Marsh,
GL56 9ED
☎ (0386) 700402
*Semi-detached Cotswold stone
house on the edge of a
peaceful, attractive village.*
Bedrooms: 2 double & 1 twin.
Bathrooms: 2 public.
Bed & breakfast: £25 double.
Half board: £15 daily.
Parking for 9.
⏰5 ⬛ 🕐 ▥ 📺 ✗ ▥ 📺
▥ 🅰 ❄ 🎄 🎄

┌─────────────────────┐
│ **PLEASE CHECK** │
│ **PRICES AND OTHER** │
│ **DETAILS AT THE** │
│ **TIME OF BOOKING.** │
└─────────────────────┘

BLYTHE BRIDGE

Staffordshire
Map ref 4B2

5m SE. Stoke-on-Trent
Riverside village on the
main Stoke-on-Trent to
Uttoxeter road.

Clovelly Guest House M
Listed
92 Uttoxeter Road, Blythe
Bridge, Stoke-on-Trent,
ST11 9JG
☎ (0782) 398958
*A large Victorian house out of
the town, with a quarter of an
acre garden. Within easy reach
of the countryside, Alton
Towers and the Potteries.*
Bedrooms: 2 single, 2 double
& 1 twin, 1 family room.
Bathrooms: 3 public.
Bed & breakfast: £12-£14
single, £24-£26 double.
Parking for 7.
🛇 🌣 ⓤ Ⓥ 🖴 ⓣ ▥ 🗡 🏠
ᴅᴀᴘ SP

The Limes
Listed
Cheadle Rd., Blythe Bridge,
Stoke-on-Trent, ST11 9PW
☎ (0782) 393278
*Victorian residence of
character in large, landscaped
gardens, near to Alton Towers,
Wedgwood, the Potteries and
Staffordshire Moorlands.*
Bedrooms: 1 single, 1 double,
1 family room.
Bathrooms: 1 public;
2 private showers.
Bed & breakfast: from £13
single, from £24 double.
Half board: from £18 daily.
Evening meal 6pm (l.o. 7pm).
Parking for 10.
🛇 4 ⓤ 🖴 ⓣ ▥ 🌣 🗡 🏠 🏡

BODENHAM

Hereford & Worcester
Map ref 2A1

6m SE. Leominster
An attractive village with
old timbered cottages and
stone houses and an
interesting church. Here
the River Lugg makes a
loop and flows under an
ancient bridge at the end
of the village.

Maund Court
😑😑😑
Bodenham, Hereford,
Herefordshire HR1 3JA
☎ (056 884) 282

*150-acre mixed farm.
Attractive 15th C farmhouse
with a large garden, swimming
pool and croquet. Riding, golf
and pleasant walks nearby.
Ideal centre for touring.*
Bedrooms: 1 double & 2 twin.
Bathrooms: 1 private,
2 public.
Bed & breakfast: £11.50-
£14.50 single, £22-£28 double.
Parking for 8.
Open February-November.
🛇 🌣 ① ♦ ⓤ ▥ 🖴 ₹
ᵾ ⌨ 🌣 🗡 🏠 🏡

BOURTON-ON-THE-WATER

Gloucestershire
Map ref 2B1

Famous Cotswold village
on the River Windrush
which flows through the
village. It has a village
green and cottages and
houses of Cotswold
stone. Its many
attractions include a
model village, Birdland
and a Motor Museum.

The Bell House
😑
Croft Cottage, Riverside,
Bourton-on-the-Water,
Cheltenham, GL54 2HF
☎ Cotswold (0451) 21132
*Situated in the centre of
Bourton-on-the-Water. Four
rooms have a river view.*
Bedrooms: 4 double, 1 family
room.
Bathrooms: 5 private.
Bed & breakfast: £25-£27.50
double.
🛇 🚲 ♦ ⓤ Ⓒⓑ ▥ 🗡
🏠 ᴅᴀᴘ SP 🏡

Duke of Wellington Inn M
Sherborne St., Bourton-on-
the-Water, Cheltenham,
GL54 2BY
☎ Cotswold (0451) 20539
*16th C. Cotswolds inn in the
centre of the village, bordered
by the River Windrush. Real
ales and a beer garden.*
Bedrooms: 3 double.
Bathrooms: 2 public.
Bed & breakfast: £30-£32
double.
Lunch available.
Evening meal 6pm (l.o.
10pm).
Parking for 16.
🛇 ♦ ◻ ♦ 🏠 Ⓥ 🖴 ▥ 🔥
🍴 🗡 🏠 SP 🏡

Hill Farm M
😑😑
Little Rissington, Bourton-
on-the-Water, Cheltenham,
GL54 2ND
☎ Cotswold (0451) 20330
*10-acre market garden. Large
farmhouse in a quiet position in
the heart of the Cotswolds.
Centrally situated for Oxford,
Stratford and Gloucester.
Home-made bread.*
Bedrooms: 2 twin, 1 family
room.
Bathrooms: 1 private,
2 public.
Bed & breakfast: £9-£14
single, £18-£28 double.
Parking for 6.
🛇 🌣 ⓤ Ⓥ 🍴 🖴 ⓣ ▥ 🏠
🌣 🏡

Lansdowne House
Listed
Lansdowne, Bourton-on-the-
Water, Cheltenham,
GL54 2AT
☎ Cotswold (0451) 20812
*Large, period stone, family
house, two minutes' level walk
from the centre of this much
visited and delightful Cotswold
village.*
Bedrooms: 1 double, 2 family
rooms.
Bathrooms: 1 private,
1 public.
Bed & breakfast: £10-£15
double.
Parking for 3.
🛇 🌣 ① ♦ ⓤ Ⓥ 🖴 ⓣ 🏠
🌣 🗡 🏡

Little Rissington Manor M
😑😑
Nr. Bourton-on-the-Water,
Cheltenham, GL54 2NB
☎ Cotswold (0451) 21078
*19th C. Victorian manor house,
set in 11 acres, with fine views
over the Windrush Valley.
Spacious rooms with quality
furnishings. Quiet
surroundings.*
Bedrooms: 1 single, 2 double
& 1 twin, 1 family room.
Bathrooms: 2 private,
1 public.
Bed & breakfast: £16 single,
£32 double.
Open March-September.
🛇 🌣 ⓤ ⓣ ▥ ₹ 🔎 🌣 🗡
🏡

Old New Inn M
😑😑😑
Bourton-on-the-Water,
Cheltenham, GL54 2AF
☎ Cotswold (0451) 20467
*Run by the same family for
over 50 years. Traditional
cooking and service.*

Bedrooms: 9 single, 8 double
& 6 twin, 1 family room.
Bathrooms: 8 private,
3 public; 1 private shower.
Bed & breakfast: £20-£25
single, £40-£50 double.
Half board: £32-£37 daily,
£160-£200 weekly.
Lunch available.
Evening meal 7.30pm (l.o.
8.30pm).
Parking for 32.
Credit: Access, Visa.
🛇 🚲 🏠 🏡 Ⓥ 🖴 ⓣ ▥ 🏠 🌣
🏡 SP 🏡

The Ridge M
😑😑
Whiteshoots, Bourton-on-the-
Water, Cheltenham,
GL54 2LE
☎ Cotswold (0451) 20660
*Large country house
surrounded by beautiful
grounds. Central for visiting
many places of interest and
close to all amenities. Evening
meal by arrangement in off
peak season.*
Bedrooms: 3 double & 1 twin,
1 family room.
Bathrooms: 2 public.
Bed & breakfast: £12-£15
single, £20-£25 double.
Evening meal 6pm.
Parking for 6.
🛇 6 ⓤ 🍴 ⓣ ▥ 🏠 🌣 🗡 🏠
SP

Rooftrees Guesthouse M
😑😑😑
Rissington Road, Bourton-
on-the-Water, Cheltenham,
GL54 2EB
☎ Cotswold (0451) 21943
*A relaxed atmosphere is found
in this homely, detached,
Cotswold stone guest house on
the edge of Bourton-on-the-
Water.*
Bedrooms: 1 twin, 2 family
rooms.
Bathrooms: 1 private,
1 public.
Bed & breakfast: £15-£18
single, £22-£29 double.
Half board: £18-£21.50 daily,
£122.50-£147 weekly.
Evening meal 6.30pm (l.o.
7pm).
Parking for 8.
🛇 2 🚲 ⓤ 🏠 Ⓥ ⓣ ▥ 🏠 ⓖ
🗡 🏡

Stepping Stone
Rectory Lane, Great
Rissington, Cheltenham
☎ Cotswold (0451) 21385
*Large detached house in
country village lane with
private grounds and views
across the Windrush Valley.*

**WE ADVISE YOU TO CONFIRM YOUR BOOKING
IN WRITING.**

Bedrooms: 2 double.
Bathrooms: 2 private.
Bed & breakfast: £15-£20 single, £20-£24 double.
⌷ ⌂ ⒰ Ⓥ ▥ ✽ ⋇ ⌺

Strathspey
Lansdown, Bourton-on-the-Water, Cheltenham,
GL54 2AR
☎ Cotswold (0451) 20694
Character, Cotswold-stone house 400 yards' walk from village centre. Quiet location with pretty riverside walk.
Bedrooms: 1 twin, 1 family room.
Bathrooms: 1 public.
Bed & breakfast: £20-£22 double.
Parking for 2.
Open April-October.
⅃ ⅄ ⌂ ⒰ Ⓥ ▥ ⌂ ⌺

Trevone ⋀
Listed
Moore Rd., Bourton-on-the-Water, Cheltenham,
GL54 2AZ
☎ Cotswold (0451) 21476
Cotswold stone gabled cottage in a quiet location 2 minutes' walk from village centre.
Bedrooms: 1 double, 1 family room.
Bathrooms: 2 public.
Bed & breakfast: £11-£12.50 double.
Parking for 2.
⅃ ⅄ ⒟ ⌂ ⌂ ⒰ ⎵ Ⓥ ⅊
▥ ⌂ ⌺ ⎌

Upper Farm ⋀
☎☎
Clapton on the Hill, Bourton-on-the-Water, Cheltenham,
GL54 1LG
☎ Cotswold (0451) 20453
130-acre mixed farm. 17th C. Cotswold farmhouse, in a quiet, unspoilt village 2.5 miles from Bourton-on-the-Water. Magnificent views. Fresh farm produce.
Bedrooms: 1 double & 1 twin, 1 family room.
Bathrooms: 2 public.
Bed & breakfast: £10-£14 single, £20-£22 double.
Parking for 12.
Open April-October.
⅃ ⒰ ⅊ Ⓣ ▥ ⎍ ✽ ⋇ ⌺
⎗

**MAP REFERENCES
APPLY TO THE
COLOUR MAPS
TOWARDS THE END
OF THIS GUIDE.**

5m NE. Tewkesbury
Hamlet at the foot of Bredon Hill with a substantial Victorian mansion in Tudor style.

Home Farm ⋀
Listed
Bredon's Norton,
Tewkesbury, Gloucestershire
GL20 7HA
☎ Bredon (0684) 72322
*150-acre mixed farm.
Comfortably furnished family farmhouse in a quiet, picturesque village. Tastefully decorated bedrooms.
Woodburning stoves in lounge and dining room. Self-catering accommodation also available.*
Bedrooms: 2 twin, 1 family room.
Bathrooms: 1 public.
Bed & breakfast: £10 single, £20 double.
Half board: £17 daily, £112-£119 weekly.
Evening meal 7pm (l.o. 8pm).
Parking for 7.
Open February-November.
⅃ ⅄ ⒰ ⅊ ⎵ Ⓥ ⅊ Ⓣ ▥
⎵ ⎙ ⌺ SP

Interesting red sandstone town in 2 parts - High and Low linked by a cliff railway. It has much of interest including a ruined Norman keep, half-timbered 16th C houses, Midland Motor Museum and Severn Valley Railway. Ⓘ

Charlcotte Farm
☎☎
Cleobury North, Bridgnorth,
WV16 6RR
☎ Burwarton (074 633) 238
*300-acre mixed farm.
Spacious, Georgian farmhouse set in pleasant grounds on a mixed farm at the foot of the Clee Hills.*
Bedrooms: 1 double & 1 twin,
1 family room.
Bathrooms: 1 private,
1 public.
Bed & breakfast: £12 single, £20-£24 double.
Half board: £18.50 daily.
Lunch available.
Evening meal 6.30pm.
Parking for 6.
⅃ ⒰ ⌂ ⎵ ⅊ Ⓣ ⎵ ✽ ⋇
⌺

Church House ⋀
☎☎
Aston Eyre, Bridgnorth,
WV16 6XD
☎ Morville (074 631) 248
Converted wheelwright's cottage, next to Norman Church, on 6 acre smallholding 4 miles west of Bridgnorth, on B4368. Special weekly terms. Ideal base for touring south Shropshire and Ironbridge.
Bedrooms: 1 twin, 1 family room.
Bathrooms: 2 private.
Bed & breakfast: max. £24 double.
Half board: max. £19 daily.
Evening meal 6pm (l.o. 8pm).
Parking for 4.
Open April-November.
⅃ ⅄ ⒰ ⅊ ⎵ Ⓥ ⅊ ⅊ Ⓣ
▥ ⎵ ✽ ⋇ ⌺

Hillside House
St. Mary's Steps, Bridgnorth,
WV16 4AQ
☎ (074 62) 2205
Family house, built in 1762, overlooking the River Severn with beautiful views from all windows.
Bedrooms: 3 double.
Bathrooms: 1 private,
2 public.
Bed & breakfast: from £12.50 single, from £23 double.
⅃ ⅄ ⒰ Ⓥ ⅊ ▥ ⋇ ⌺ ⌺

Now a district of Dudley and part of Birmingham conurbation, retaining its links with the glassmaking industry.

Saltwells Inn ⋀
☎☎
Saltwells, Brierley Hill,
DY5 1AX
☎ Cradley Heath
(0384) 69224
The Saltwells Inn is set within a 100 acre Nature Reserve and has a large children's play area with swings and slide.
Bedrooms: 2 single, 1 double
& 2 twin.
Bathrooms: 5 private.
Bed & breakfast: £14-£17.25 single, £28.75-£32.20 double.
Lunch available.
Evening meal 8pm (l.o.
10pm).
Credit: Access, Visa.
⅃ ⌷ ⒰ ▥ ⅀ ⌺ ⎗

5m S. Ludlow
Village of thatched and timbered houses near the River Teme, close to Ludlow and looking out towards the Clee Hills of Shropshire.

Bank House
Wyson La., Brimfield,
Ludlow, Herefordshire
SY8 4NW
☎ (058 472) 343
Period family house for non-smokers. Take Wyson Lane by the Forge House Gallery; left at T junction; and Bank House is on the right towards the Grange. Private bathroom for guests' sole use.
Bedrooms: 1 double & 1 twin.
Bed & breakfast: £10.50 single, £19 double.
Parking for 3.
Open April-October.
⅃ 5 ⌂ ⒰ ⅊ ▥ ✽ ⌺

Woodstock House ⋀
☎☎
Brimfield, Ludlow,
Shropshire, SY8 4NY
☎ (058 472) 445
*Building in 2 acres of own grounds. Home grown food and family atmosphere.
Evening meals provided for residents if required. On A49 5 miles south of Ludlow.*
Bedrooms: 1 single, 1 double
& 2 twin, 1 family room.
Bathrooms: 2 public.
Bed & breakfast: £10-£12 single, £18-£20 double.
Half board: £16-£18 daily, £90-£112 weekly.
Lunch available.
Evening meal 7pm (l.o. 9am).
Parking for 10.
⅃ ⒰ ⅊ ⅊ Ⓣ ▥ ⎵ ✽ ⋇
⌺ ⎗

**INDIVIDUAL
PROPRIETORS HAVE
SUPPLIED ALL
DETAILS OF
ACCOMMODATION.
ALTHOUGH WE DO
CHECK FOR
ACCURACY, WE
ADVISE YOU TO
CONFIRM PRICES
AND OTHER
INFORMATION AT
THE TIME OF
BOOKING.**

BROADWAY

Hereford & Worcester
Map ref 2B1

Beautiful Cotswold village
called the 'Show village of
England' with 16th C
stone houses and
cottages. Near the village
is Broadway Tower with
magnificent views over 12
counties and a country
park with nature trails and
adventure playground.

Cotswold Experience M
😊😊

Copgrove, West End,
Broadway, Worcestershire
WR12 7JP
☎ (0386) 852866
*17th C. listed manor house set
in 3 acres of park-like grounds.*
Bedrooms: 1 double & 2 twin.
Bathrooms: 3 private.
Bed & breakfast: £18-£20
single, £35-£40 double.
Parking for 8.
⬛ ↻ ⓤ ⓥ ▦ ↻ ✿ ✗ 🐾
⚓ 🏠

Crown and Trumpet M
😊😊

Church St., Broadway,
Worcestershire WR12 7AE
☎ (0386) 853202
*Traditional English inn with
log fires and oak beams,
quietly located just off the
village green. Home-cooked
English food.*
Bedrooms: 2 double, 1 family
room.
Bathrooms: 1 public.
Bed & breakfast: £27-£28
double.
Half board: £16.50-£17 daily.
Lunch available.
Evening meal 6pm (l.o.
9.30pm).
Parking for 6.
🔾 ⬛ ↻ ⓘ ⓥ ▦ ⚓ ♨ ↻
✿ 🐾 ⓓⒶⓅ ⚓ ⚓ 🏠

Eastbank M
Station Drive, Broadway,
Worcestershire WR12 7DF
☎ (0386) 852659
*Home cooking and friendly
atmosphere. Very quiet
location about half a mile from
the village. Free brochure
available.*
Bedrooms: 1 single, 1 double
& 2 twin, 2 family rooms.
Bathrooms: 5 private,
1 public.
Bed & breakfast: £16.50-
£18.50 single, £24-£28 double.
Half board: £19-£24 daily,
£128-£160 weekly.
Evening meal 7pm (l.o. 10pm).
Parking for 6.
🔾 ⚓ ↻ ⓤ ⓘ ⓥ ↻ ▦
⚓ ✿ 🐾 ⓓⒶⓅ ⓈⓅ

Leasow House M
😊😊😊

Laverton Meadow,
Broadway, Worcestershire
WR12 7NA
☎ Stanton (038 673) 526
*17th C. Cotswold stone
farmhouse tranquilly set in
open countryside close to
Broadway village.*
Bedrooms: 2 double & 2 twin,
3 family rooms.
Bathrooms: 7 private.
Bed & breakfast: £32-£44
double.
Parking for 14.
Credit: Access, Visa.
🔾 ♨ ↻ ⬛ ⓤ ⓘ ⓥ
↻ ⓣⓥ ▦ ⚓ ♨ ↻ ✿ 🐾 ⓈⓅ
🏠

Manor Farm M
😊😊😊

Wormington, Broadway,
Worcestershire WR12 7NL
☎ Stanton (038 673) 302
*200-acre arable, beef farm.
Attractive Tudor farmhouse in
quiet village, 4 miles from
Broadway. Access to mixed
farm with animals and river
fishing.*
Bedrooms: 2 double & 1 twin.
Bathrooms: 1 public;
2 private showers.
Bed & breakfast: £11-£15
single, £22-£28 double.
Parking for 6.
🔾 ⓤ ↻ ⓣⓥ ▦ ⚓ ♨ ✓ 🐾
ⓓⒶⓅ ⓈⓅ 🏠

Mount Pleasant Farm M
😊😊😊

Childswickham, Broadway,
Worcestershire
☎ Broadway (0386) 853424
*250-acre mixed farm. Large
Victorian farmhouse with
excellent views. Very quiet
accommodation with all
modern amenities.
Approximately 3 miles from
Broadway.*
Bedrooms: 3 double.
Bathrooms: 3 private.
Bed & breakfast: £24-£27
double.
Parking for 8.
🔾 ⚓ ↻ ⓤ ↻ ⓣⓥ ▦ ⚓ ↻
♨ ✿ 🐾

The Old Rectory M
😊😊😊😊

Church St., Willersey,
Broadway, Worcestershire
WR12 7PN
☎ (0386) 853729
*A combination of the standards
of a good hotel with the
warmth of a private home.*
Bedrooms: 4 double & 2 twin.
Bathrooms: 6 private.
Bed & breakfast: £39-£59
single, £49-£69 double.

Parking for 10.
Credit: Access, Visa.
↻ ⬛ 🔾 ⚓ ⓤ ⓥ ↻ ⚓ ⓣⓥ
● ▦ ⚓ ↻ ⓟ ✿ 🐾 ⚓ ⚓
ⓈⓅ 🏠

The Old Rectory M
😊😊

Aston Somerville, Broadway,
Worcestershire WR12 7JF
☎ Broadway (0386) 852466
*Cotswold stone rectory in small
village 4 miles from Broadway,
with a one and a quarter acre
garden and a view to
Broadway Tower. Near
Stratford-upon-Avon. Very
near restaurants.*
Bedrooms: 2 twin.
Bathrooms: 2 private.
Bed & breakfast: max. £15
single, max. £25 double.
Parking for 20.
🔾5 ↻ ⓤ ⓘ ⓣⓥ ▦ ⚓ ♀
🔾 ⓟ ✿ 🐾 🐾 ⓈⓅ

The Orchard Bed and Breakfast
The Orchard, Leamington
Rd., Broadway,
Worcestershire WR12 7EB
☎ (0386) 852534
*A modern house in the
Cotswold style, in a large
garden with magnificent views.
On the main Stratford road
between Broadway and
Willersey.*
Bedrooms: 1 single, 1 double
& 1 twin.
Bathrooms: 1 public.
Bed & breakfast: £10 single,
£22-£25 double.
Parking for 4.
🔾7 ⚓ ↻ ⓤ ⓥ ↻ ⓣⓥ ▦ ✿
🐾

Southwold House M
Station Rd., Broadway,
Worcestershire WR12 7DE
☎ (0386) 853681
*Edwardian house with large
garden, only 4 minutes from
the village centre. Traditional
home cooking. Central for
touring.*
Bedrooms: 1 single, 4 double
& 3 twin.
Bathrooms: 3 private,
2 public; 1 private shower.
Bed & breakfast: from £14
single, £28-£32 double.
Half board: £22.50-£24.50
daily, £147-£161 weekly.
Evening meal 7pm (l.o. 4pm).
Parking for 8.
Credit: Access, Visa.
🔾3 ⚓ ↻ ⓤ ⓘ ⓥ ↻ ⓣⓥ ▦
⚓ ♨ 🐾 ⓓⒶⓅ ⓈⓅ

Tuck Mill M
Childswickham Rd.,
Broadway, Worcestershire
☎ Evesham (0386) 852201
*17th C. tucking mill, three
quarters of a mile from
Broadway, in extensive
grounds with pond, stream and
orchards. Building of
interesting Cotswold character.*
Bedrooms: 3 twin, 1 family
room.
Bathrooms: 1 private,
2 public.
Bed & breakfast: £15-£20
single, £26-£30 double.
Parking for 5.
🔾 ⚓ ♨ ↻ ⓤ ⓥ ↻ ⓣⓥ ▦
✿ 🐾 🐾 ⓓⒶⓅ 🏠

BROMSGROVE

Hereford & Worcester
Map ref 4B3

Market town in the Lickey
Hills with an interesting
14th C church with fine
tombs and a Carillon
tower. The Avoncroft
Museum of Buildings is
nearby where many old
buildings have been re-
assembled, having been
saved from destruction.
🄸

Forest Inn M
290 Birmingham Rd.,
Bromsgrove, Worcestershire
B61 0ER
☎ (0527) 72063
*A 19th C. coaching inn on the
main A38, at junction 1 of the
M42.*
Bedrooms: 2 single, 3 double
& 3 twin.
Bathrooms: 2 public.
Bed & breakfast: £18-£24
single, £27-£35 double.
Lunch available.
Evening meal 6.30pm (l.o.
10pm).
Parking for 70.
Credit: Access, Visa, Amex.
🔾 ⚓ ↻ ⓘ ⓥ ⓣⓥ ▦ ⚓ 🍴
ⓓⒶⓅ 🏠

Home Farm
Mill La., Wildmoor,
Bromsgrove, Worcestershire
B61 0BX
☎ (0527) 74964
*35-acre arable farm. Self-
contained unit of Home Farm,
established 1900, with open
views in quiet countryside. 1
mile from the M5 junction 4.*
Bedrooms: 2 double & 1 twin.
Bathrooms: 3 private.
Bed & breakfast: from £12.50
single, from £25 double.
Parking for 6.
🔾1 ♨ ⓤ ↻ ⓣⓥ ▦ ⚓ 🐾 🐾

┌─────────────────────┐
│ **PLEASE MENTION** │
│ **THIS GUIDE WHEN** │
│ **MAKING A BOOKING.** │
└─────────────────────┘

Mrs. B. Graham
Listed

95 Old Station Rd.,
Bromsgrove, Worcestershire
B60 2AF
☎ (0527) 74463
*Modern house in quiet pleasant
location close to the A38, 3
miles from the M5 and 1.5
miles from the M42. Within
easy reach of National
Exhibition Centre, Worcester
and Stratford.*
Bedrooms: 2 single, 1 twin.
Bathrooms: 1 public.
Bed & breakfast: from £9.50
single, from £19 double.
Half board: from £13.50
daily, from £75 weekly.
Evening meal 6pm (l.o. 9am).
Parking for 2.
🛏 2 🗲 ⓊⓁ Ⓥ 📺 ▥ ▬ ⍻ 🐾

BROMYARD
Hereford & Worcester
Map ref 2B1

See also Stoke Lacy.
Market town on the River
Frome surrounded by
orchards with black and
white houses and a
Norman church. Nearby
at Lower Brockhampton
is a 14th C half-timbered
moated manor house
owned by the National
Trust. ⓘ

Coach House
Listed

The Tower House, 1 Tower
Hill, Bromyard,
Herefordshire HR7 4DF
☎ (0885) 83461
*Coach house to Grade II listed
Stuart house of great historic
interest. King Charles I stayed
in the house in 1645 during
Civil War.*
Bedrooms: 3 twin.
Bathrooms: 1 private,
1 public.
Bed & breakfast: £20-£24
double.
Parking for 3.
Open March-November.
🗲 ⓊⓁ 📺 ▥ ▬ ❀ 🐾 🐾

Crown And Sceptre ⋀
Listed

7 Sherford St, Bromyard,
Herefordshire HR7 4DL
☎ (0885) 82441
*A family-run pub specialising
in a wide range of traditional
beers and home-cooked food.*
Bedrooms: 2 single, 2 double
& 1 twin.
Bathrooms: 3 private,
1 public.
Bed & breakfast: £12-£18
single, £24-£36 double.

Lunch available.
Evening meal 6.30pm (l.o.
10pm).
Parking for 14.
🛏 🗲 ⊟ ⌘ 🏆 Ⓥ ▥ ▬ ⍻
🐾 ⓈⓅ

The Granary
Restaurant ⋀

Church House Farm,
Collington, Bromyard,
Herefordshire HR7 4NA
☎ Kyre (088 54) 345
*210-acre mixed farm. In the
beautiful Kyre Valley. Well-
appointed farm accommodation
and restaurant, 7 miles from
Tenbury and 3 miles from
Bromyard.*
Bedrooms: 5 twin.
Bathrooms: 5 private.
Bed & breakfast: from £17.50
single, from £30 double.
Evening meal 6.30pm (l.o.
10pm).
Parking for 30.
▬ ⊙ ⊟ ♥ Ⓥ ▥ 🏆 🐾 🐾

Park House ⋀
☺☺

28 Sherford St., Bromyard,
Herefordshire HR7 4DL
☎ (0885) 82294
*Close to town centre and a
desirable location for touring.*
Bedrooms: 1 single, 1 double
& 1 twin, 2 family rooms.
Bathrooms: 3 private,
1 public.
Bed & breakfast: £10-£12
single, £20-£22 double.
Parking for 6.
🛏 ▬ ⓊⓁ ⊟ 🏆 📺 ▥ 🐾
🐾

Peppercorn
Listed

19 Cruxwell St., Bromyard,
Herefordshire HR7 4EB
☎ (0885) 82277
*Late 17th C. town house with
many exposed beams, in the
centre of an interesting old
town. 3 public car parks close
by. Wide range of home-made
marmalades and jams.*
Bedrooms: 1 twin.
Bathrooms: 1 public.
Bed & breakfast: from £9.50
single, from £18.50 double.
ⓊⓁ ⊟ Ⓥ 🏆 📺 ▥ 🐾 🐾 🐾

GROUPS, CONSORTIA
AND AGENCIES
SPECIALISING
IN FARM AND
COUNTRY HOLIDAYS
ARE LISTED IN A
SPECIAL SECTION
OF THIS GUIDE.

BUCKNELL
Shropshire
Map ref 4A3

4m E. Knighton
Village by the River
Redlake with thatched
black and white cottages,
a Norman church and the
remains of an Iron Age
fort on a nearby hill. It is
near attractive
countryside.

Bucknell House
☺☺

Bucknell, SY7 0AD
☎ (054 74) 248
*70-acre grazing farm. Mellow
Georgian house in large
secluded grounds on fringe of
South Shropshire village.
Scenic countryside amid rolling
wooded hillsides of upper Teme
Valley on Welsh borderland.*
Bedrooms: 2 double & 1 twin.
Bathrooms: 2 public.
Bed & breakfast: £11-£12.50
single, £22-£25 double.
Parking for 3.
Open March-November.
🛏 12 ⊙ ♥ ⓊⓁ Ⓥ ▬ 📺 ▥
▬ 🏇 ♪ ✓ ❀ 🐾 🐾

The Hall ⋀
Listed

Bucknell, SY7 0AA
☎ (054 74) 249
*225-acre mixed farm. Georgian
farmhouse in the picturesque
village of Bucknell, with a
peaceful and relaxed
atmosphere.*
Bedrooms: 1 double & 1 twin,
1 family room.
Bathrooms: 1 public.
Bed & breakfast: from £11
single, from £22 double.
Half board: from £16.50
daily, from £110 weekly.
Evening meal 6pm (l.o.
midday).
Parking for 4.
Open March-November.
🛏 7 🗲 ⓊⓁ ▬ 📺 ⍻ 🐾

BUILDWAS
Shropshire
Map ref 4A3

3m NE. Much Wenlock
Village on the River
Severn with the
substantial remains of a
Norman abbey, now in
the care of the
Department of the
Environment.

Grove Farm House ⋀
Listed

Leighton Rd., Buildwas.
Telford, TF8 7DF
☎ Ironbridge (095 245) 3572

*An attractive 18th C.
farmhouse, recently restored,
with beamed ceilings and log
fires. Overlooking river
meadows and close to
Ironbridge.*
Bedrooms: 1 single, 1 double
& 1 twin.
Bathrooms: 1 public.
Bed & breakfast: £12 single,
£22 double.
Parking for 5.
🗲 ⓊⓁ Ⓥ ▬ ▬ 🐾 ⍻ 🐾

BURTON DASSETT
Warwickshire
Map ref 2C1

9m SE. Leamington Spa
The church tower looks
out over the site of the
Battle of Edgehill and it is
said that Cromwell
himself climbed the tower
to watch the fighting.
Nearby is a 16th C.
beacon tower from which
news of the battle was
sent.

Grove Farm ⋀
☺☺

Burton Dassett, Leamington
Spa, CV33 0AB
☎ Fenny Compton
(029 577) 204
*13-acre grazing, young beef
stock farm. Stone farmhouse
with panoramic views, in a
quiet hamlet on Burton Dassett
Hills. A41 (north) from
Banbury for 9 miles, then take
right turn to Burton Dassett
Country Park.*
Bedrooms: 1 single, 1 twin,
1 family room.
Bathrooms: 1 public.
Bed & breakfast: £11-£15
single, £22-£30 double.
Parking for 5.
🛏 ⊙ ⓊⓁ ♥ ▬ ⌘ Ⓥ ▬ 📺
▥ ▬ ❀ 🐾

INDIVIDUAL
PROPRIETORS HAVE
SUPPLIED ALL
DETAILS OF
ACCOMMODATION.
ALTHOUGH WE DO
CHECK FOR
ACCURACY, WE
ADVISE YOU TO
CONFIRM PRICES
AND OTHER
INFORMATION AT
THE TIME OF
BOOKING.

BURTON UPON TRENT

Staffordshire
Map ref 4B3

An important brewing town with the Bass Museum of Brewing, where the Bass Shire horses are also stabled. There are 3 bridges with views over the river and some interesting public buildings including the 18th C St. Modwen's Church. ℹ

New Inn Farm
Listed

Needwood, Burton upon Trent DE13 9PB
☎ (0283) 435
122-acre mixed dairy farm. In the heart of Needwood Forest on the main B5234 Newborough to Burton upon Trent road. Central for Uttoxeter, Lichfield, Derby, Burton upon Trent, easy access to A38.
Bedrooms: 1 single, 2 double.
Bathrooms: 1 public.
Bed & breakfast: from £8.50 single, from £17 double.
Parking for 6.
⛹ 🏃 🔌 Ⓤ 🍴 ✆ TV 🛋 ❄ ✗ 🏠

CANON FROME

Hereford & Worcester
Map ref 2B1

6m NW. Ledbury
Village in the Frome Valley with a modest Victorian church within the shadow of the 18th C Frome Court.

Mill Cottage
🏠

Canon Frome, Ledbury, Herefordshire HR8 2TD
☎ Trumpet (053 183) 506
Ideal for naturalists, artists, fishermen. Picturesque period cottage in magnificent setting, with river, weir, and woodland walks. Warm, friendly service.
Bedrooms: 1 twin.
Bathrooms: 1 private.
Bed & breakfast: £10-£15 single, £20-£30 double.
Parking for 6.
⛹ 🏃 🔌 Ⓤ Ⓥ ✗ 🍴 TV 🖩
🛋 🐾 🎣 ❄ ✗ 🏠 🏡

MAP REFERENCES APPLY TO COLOUR MAPS NEAR THE BACK OF THE GUIDE.

CHEADLE

Staffordshire
Map ref 4B2

Market town dominated by the 19th C Roman Catholic Church with its 200 ft spire. To the east of the town lie 300 acres of Hawksmoor Nature Reserve with many different birds and trees. Alton Towers is nearby.

Bradley Elms Farm ⚲
🏠🏠

Threapwood, Nr. Cheadle, Stoke-on-Trent, ST10 4RA
☎ (0538) 753135
Modernised farmhouse surrounded by open fields, offering homely and comfortable accommodation. Close to the Potteries and Peak District, 3 miles from Alton Towers.
Bedrooms: 2 double & 2 twin, 2 family rooms.
Bathrooms: 5 private, 1 public.
Bed & breakfast: £13.50-£17.50 single, £20-£28 double.
Half board: £18.50-£23 daily, £98-£135 weekly.
Evening meal 7.30pm (l.o. 9pm).
Parking for 11.
⛹5 🔌 Ⓤ 🍴 Ⓥ ✗ TV 🖩 🛋
◡ ❄ 🏠 DAP SP 🇹

The Coach House ⚲
Listed

Boundary, Cheadle ST10 2NX
☎ (0538) 753462
Private country house on a521, near to Alton Towers, Churnet Valley and the Peak District. Evening meal by arrangement. Licensed boarding kennels adjacent.
Bedrooms: 1 double & 1 twin.
Bathrooms: 1 public.
Bed & breakfast: £9-£11.50 single, £18-£23 double.
Parking for 2.
⛹ 🏃 🔌 🍴 Ⓤ 🍴 TV 🖩 ❄
✗ 🏠

CHELMARSH

Shropshire
Map ref 4A3

4m SE. Bridgnorth
An unspoilt village near the River Severn, with old timbered cottages and an imposing 14th C church.

Bulls Head Inn ⚲
🏠🏠🏠

Chelmarsh, Bridgnorth, WV16 6BA
☎ Highley (0746) 861469

Rural 17th C. inn with traditional atmosphere and modern comforts and service. Home-cooked food served in bars and restaurant. Real ales.
Bedrooms: 1 single, 3 double & 2 twin, 1 family room.
Bathrooms: 6 private, 2 public.
Bed & breakfast: from £15 single, from £28 double.
Half board: £18-£22 daily, from £95 weekly.
Lunch available.
Evening meal 7pm (l.o. 9.30pm).
Parking for 50.
⛹ 🔌 🍴 Ⓥ ✗ ◉ 🖩 🛋 🏠

CHELTENHAM

Gloucestershire
Map ref 2B1

See also Andoversford, Colesbourne, Elkstone.
Cheltenham was developed as a spa town in the 18th C and has some beautiful Regency architecture, in particular the Pittville Pump Room. It holds international music and literature festivals and is also famous for its race meetings and cricket. ℹ

Allards ⚲
🏠🏠🏠

Shurdington Rd., Cheltenham, GL51 5XA
☎ (0242) 862498
On the A46, surrounded by hills and fields. All rooms have modern facilities, providing comfort and convenience.
Bedrooms: 1 single, 5 double & 3 twin, 2 family rooms.
Bathrooms: 11 private, 1 public.
Bed & breakfast: £16-£17 single, £32-£34 double.
Parking for 17.
Credit: Access, Visa.
⛹ 🔌 🍴 ☎ 🔌 Ⓤ ✗ 🛋
❄ ✗ 🏠

Cleyne Hage ⚲
🏠

Southam Lane, Southam, Cheltenham, GL52 3NY
☎ (0242) 518569
Cotswolds-style house on the Cotswold Way, off the A46 at the foot of Cleeve Hill. Open views to Cheltenham Racecourse and the Malvern Hills. Dogs welcome. Non smoking establishment.
Bedrooms: 1 double & 1 twin, 1 family room.
Bathrooms: 1 private, 1 public.
Bed & breakfast: £12-£15 single, £24-£30 double.

Half board: £17-£20 daily, £109-£120 weekly.
Lunch available.
Evening meal 6pm (l.o. 7pm).
Parking for 10.
Open January-October.
⛹ 🔌 Ⓤ 🍴 🍴 Ⓥ ✗ 🍴 TV ◉
🖩 🛋 ◡ 🍴 ❄ 🏠 SP

Columbia House ⚲
🏠

59 Leckhampton Rd., Cheltenham, GL53 0BS
☎ (0242) 525388
Regency house with large bedrooms. A family-run business 1 mile from the town centre.
Bedrooms: 2 twin, 2 family rooms.
Bathrooms: 1 public.
Bed & breakfast: £10 single, £20 double.
Parking for 4.
⛹ 🏃 🔌 Ⓤ Ⓥ 🖩 🏠 🏡
🇹

Glendronach
Listed

24 Christchurch Rd., Cheltenham, GL50 2PL
☎ (0242) 518272
Victorian stone-built house dating from 1885, with large rooms and pleasant aspect. In a quiet, tree-lined road, 5 minutes from the railway station and 10 minutes from the town centre. Dinner on request.
Bedrooms: 1 twin, 1 family room.
Bathrooms: 1 public.
Bed & breakfast: £11-£12.50 single, £21-£24 double.
Parking for 2.
⛹5 🔌 Ⓤ 🍴 Ⓥ 🖩 🐾 🏠 🏠

Hannaford's ⚲
🏠🏠🏠

20 Evesham Rd., Cheltenham, GL52 2AB
☎ (0242) 515181
Comfortable, relaxed and friendly. En-suite bedrooms, each with colour TV and hospitality trays. Well situated, just a short walk from promenade and town centre.
Bedrooms: 3 single, 2 double & 4 twin, 1 family room.
Bathrooms: 9 private, 2 public.
Bed & breakfast: £18.50-£25 single, £36-£40 double.
Evening meal 7pm (l.o. 5pm).
Credit: Access, Visa.
⛹7 🔌 ☎ 🔌 🍴 🍴 Ⓥ ✗
✗ TV 🖩 🛋 🍴 ❄ 🏠 SP 🏡

Hollington House ⚲
🏠🏠

115 Hales Road, Cheltenham, GL52 6ST
☎ (0242) 519718

Detached house in pleasant grounds a few minutes' walk from the town centre. Lounge with colour TV, ample parking space.
Bedrooms: 1 single, 3 double & 1 twin, 2 family rooms.
Bathrooms: 5 private, 1 public.
Bed & breakfast: £17-£24 single, £27-£35 double.
Half board: £25.25-£33 daily, £169-£218 weekly.
Evening meal 6.30pm (l.o. 6.30pm).
Parking for 12.

Hunting Butts M

Swindon La., Cheltenham, GL50 4NZ
☎ (0242) 524982
200-acre beef and arable farm. Farmhouse overlooking Cheltenham with views to the Malverns and Cleeve Hill, within walking distance of Cheltenham and all facilities. Also converted stable annexe, which includes 2 ground floor rooms adapted for disabled visitors.
Bedrooms: 3 double & 3 twin, 2 family rooms.
Bathrooms: 6 private, 1 public.
Bed & breakfast: £10-£12.50 single, £20-£25 double.
Evening meal 6.30pm (l.o. 7pm).
Parking for 20.

Ivy Dene Guest House

145 Hewlett Rd., Cheltenham, GL52 6JS
☎ (0242) 521726
Ideal base for exploring Cotswolds. A charming corner house in its own grounds, situated in a residential area. Within walking distance of the town.
Bedrooms: 3 single, 2 double & 2 twin, 3 family rooms.
Bathrooms: 3 public.
Bed & breakfast: £9.50-£10 single, £19-£20 double.
Parking for 8.

Kielder M

222 London Rd., Charlton Kings, Cheltenham, GL52 6HW
☎ (0242) 37138
Semi-detached, late Victorian, brick-built house with 3 storeys situated on A40.

Bedrooms: 2 twin, 1 family room.
Bathrooms: 1 private, 1 public.
Bed & breakfast: £12-£13 single, £23-£25 double.
Half board: £17.50-£18.50 daily, £112-£119 weekly.
Evening meal 7pm (l.o. 7.30pm).
Parking for 5.
Open March-October.

Lonsdale House M

Montpellier Drive, Cheltenham, GL50 1TX
☎ (0242) 32379
Regency house situated 5 minutes' walk from the Town Hall, Promenade, shopping centre, parks and theatre. Easy access to all main routes.
Bedrooms: 5 single, 2 twin.
Bathrooms: 4 public.
Bed & breakfast: £12.50-£14 single, £25-£28 double.
Parking for 6.

North Hall Hotel M

Pittville Circus Rd., Cheltenham, GL52 2PZ
☎ (0242) 520589
Early Victorian town house situated in a wide tree-lined road near Pittville Park.
Bedrooms: 7 single, 6 double & 5 twin, 2 family rooms.
Bathrooms: 12 private, 7 public.
Bed & breakfast: from £14.95 single, from £25.88 double.
Half board: from £22.18 daily, from £133.08 weekly.
Evening meal 6pm (l.o. 5pm).
Parking for 20.
Credit: Access, Visa.

Old Rectory M

Woolstone, Cheltenham, GL52 4RG
☎ Bishops Cleeve (024 267) 3766
In a peaceful hamlet 4 miles from the Regency town of Cheltenham.
Bedrooms: 2 single, 2 twin.
Bathrooms: 2 private, 2 public.
Bed & breakfast: £12 single, £24 double.
Parking for 6.
Open March-October.

Old Stables M
Listed

239A London Rd., Charlton Kings, Cheltenham, GL52 6YE
☎ (0242) 583660
Former coach house in pleasant surroundings, 2 miles east of Cheltenham town centre on the A40. Easy car access and parking.
Bedrooms: 1 double & 1 twin.
Bathrooms: 1 private, 1 public.
Bed & breakfast: £10 single, £20 double.
Parking for 3.

Old Vineyards

Timbercombe Lane, Off Cirencester Road, Cheltenham, GL53 8EE
☎ (0242) 582893
240-acre mixed farm. Built in 1754. Located off the A435, 4 miles from Cheltenham town centre: car an advantage. Dinner by prior arrangement.
Bedrooms: 1 single, 2 double & 2 twin.
Bathrooms: 2 public.
Bed & breakfast: £14 single, £28 double.
Lunch available.
Evening meal 6.30pm (l.o. 6.30pm).

CHIPPING CAMPDEN
Gloucestershire
Map ref 2B1

Outstanding Cotswold wool town with many old stone gabled houses, a splendid church and 17th C almshouses. There is a collection of historic sports cars and nearby are Kiftsgate Court Gardens and Hidcote Manor Gardens (National Trust). *i*

Trinder House

High St., Chipping Campden, GL55 6AG
☎ Evesham (0386) 840869
Near the centre of the town in a famous high street. The house is reputedly of Tudor origin.
Bedrooms: 1 double, 1 family room.
Bathrooms: 2 public.
Bed & breakfast: £20-£24 double.
Parking for 3.

Weston Park Farm M

Dovers Hill, Chipping Campden, GL55 6WW
☎ (0386) 840835
Self-contained wing in secluded farmhouse, 1 mile from Chipping Campden, adjacent to National Trust land.
Bedrooms: 1 family room.
Bathrooms: 1 private.
Bed & breakfast: max. £12 single, max. £25 double.
Parking for 10.

CHURCH STRETTON
Shropshire
Map ref 4A3

See also Munslow.
Church Stretton lies under the eastern slope of the Longmynd surrounded by hills. It is ideal for walkers, with marvellous views, golf and gliding. The town has a small puppet theatre and Wenlock Edge is not far away. *i*

Acton Scott Farm M
Listed

Church Stretton, SY6 6QN
☎ Marshbrook (069 46) 260
320-acre mixed farm. Traditional farmhouse accommodation on mixed farm in area of outstanding natural beauty near Church Stretton and next to farm museum.
Bedrooms: 1 double, 1 family room.
Bathrooms: 1 public.
Bed & breakfast: £16-£20 double.
Parking for 10.

The Elms

Little Stretton, Church Stretton, SY6 6RD
☎ (0694) 723084
Victorian country house in spacious grounds, decorated and furnished in Victorian style.
Bedrooms: 1 double & 1 twin, 1 family room.
Bathrooms: 2 public.
Bed & breakfast: from £12 single, from £21 double.
Parking for 3.

WE ADVISE YOU TO CONFIRM YOUR BOOKING IN WRITING.

CHURCH STRETTON

Continued

Hope Bowdler Hall M
⚌⚌

Hope Bowdler, Church
Stretton, SY6 7DD
☎ (0694) 722041
*Peaceful, 17th century manor
house on edge of the tiny
village of Hope Bowdler,
surrounded by beautiful hills.
From B4371 approach by
unpaved road leading past
church.*
Bedrooms: 1 single, 2 twin.
Bathrooms: 2 public.
Bed & breakfast: £10-£12
single, £20-£24 double.
Parking for 4.
Open March-October.
🛏10 ⬚ ⚲ ▥ ▦ ▦ ✿ ✕ �🏠 ▦

Littlebrook
38 Ludlow Rd., Church
Stretton, SY6 6AB
☎ (0694) 722307
*A dormer bungalow in one and
a quarter acres adjacent to the
Longmynd. Half a mile from
town centre. 5 course
breakfast. Comfortable rooms.*
Bedrooms: 1 double, 2 family
rooms.
Bathrooms: 1 public.
Bed & breakfast: £12.50-£15
single, £20-£24 double.
Half board: £15-£18 daily,
£98-£117.60 weekly.
Lunch available.
Evening meal 7pm (l.o.
5.30pm).
Parking for 6.
Open February-November.
🛏 ⬚ ⚲ ▯ Ⓥ ⚲ ▥ ▦
▦ ✿ ✕ ▦ SP

Malt House Farm M
Listed

Lower Wood, Church
Stretton, SY6 6LF
☎ Leebotwood (069 45) 379
*80-acre mixed farm. Old
pretty, beamed farmhouse on
the edge of a large area of
unspoilt National Trust land.*
Bedrooms: 2 double & 1 twin.
Bathrooms: 1 public.
Bed & breakfast: £8.50-£9.50
single, £17-£19 double.
Half board: £14.50-£15.50
daily, £101.50-£108.50
weekly.
Evening meal 6pm (l.o. 7pm).
Parking for 4.
Open March-October.
🛏 ▦ ▥ 🖊 ▯ ▥ ▦ ▦ ⊍ ▶
✿ ✕ ▦ ▦

CHURCHAM

Gloucestershire
Map ref 2B1

4m W. Gloucester
Village a few miles west
of Gloucester off the A40,
displaying a delightful
picture of church, court
and willow fringed pond.

Wood Cottage
⚌

Kitesnest La., Churcham,
Gloucester, GL2 8BL
☎ Tibberton (045 279) 457
*Half-timbered interior with
large inglenook fireplace. On
the A40 Gloucester to Ross
Road, right at Bulley Lane,
first right again leading into
500 acres Woodland. Very
quiet and ideal for walking and
birdwatching.*
Bedrooms: 1 double.
Bathrooms: 1 public.
Bed & breakfast: from £9.50
single, max. £19 double.
Parking for 3.
▥ ▥ ▯ ▦ ▦ ▲ ✿ ✕ ▦ ▦

CIRENCESTER

Gloucestershire
Map ref 2B1

See also Fairford.
'Capital of the
Cotswolds', Cirencester
was Britain's second
most important Roman
town with many finds
housed in the Corinium
Museum. It has a very
fine perpendicular church
and old houses around
the Market Place.
Cirencester Park is open
to the public with polo in
summer. 🛈

Abacus House M
⚌⚌

6 Trenchard Gardens, South
Cerney, Cirencester,
GL7 6JA
☎ Cirencester (0285) 860999
*8-bedroomed country house, in
an acre of gardens, 1.5 miles
from Cirencester. 1 mile from
water park with all water
sports.*
Bedrooms: 2 single, 1 double
& 1 twin, 1 family room.
Bathrooms: 2 public.
Bed & breakfast: £10-£12
single, £20-£26 double.
Parking for 8.
🛏 ⚲ ▥ 🖊 ▯ ▥ ▦ ▲ ⊍
✿ ✕ ▦

Abbeymead
⚌⚌

39a Victoria Road,
Cirencester, GL7 1ES
☎ (0285) 3740 due to change
to (0285) 653740
Bedrooms: 1 double & 1 twin,
2 family rooms.
Bathrooms: 3 public.
Bed & breakfast: from £20
double.
Parking for 4.
🛏2 ⚲ ▥ ⚲ ▦ ▯ ▥
DAP SP

Mrs. J. Woodford. M
Listed

115 Cheltenham Rd.,
Cirencester, GL7 2JE
☎ (0285) 61638
*Fifty-year-old house on the
A435 Cheltenham to
Cirencester road. On the edge
of Cirencester with views over
farmland, within easy reach of
the town.*
Bedrooms: 1 double & 3 twin.
Bathrooms: 2 public.
Bed & breakfast: from £10
single, from £20 double.
Parking for 4.
🛏 ⚲ ✕ ⚲ ▥ ▥ ▯ ▦ ▲
▦

The Leauses
⚌⚌

101 Victoria Rd.,
Cirencester, GL7 1EU
☎ (0285) 1416
*Guesthouse with spacious
rooms, near the town centre.
Non-smoking house.*
Bedrooms: 1 double & 2 twin,
3 family rooms.
Bathrooms: 3 private,
2 public.
Bed & breakfast: from £19
double.
Parking for 6.
🛏 ▦ ▥ Ⓥ ▥ ▯ ▦ ▲ ▦
▦ SP

Wimborne House M
⚌⚌⚌

91 Victoria Rd., Cirencester,
GL7 1ES
☎ (0285) 3890
*Cotswold stone house, built in
1886, with a warm and friendly
atmosphere and spacious
rooms.*
Bedrooms: 4 double & 1 twin.
Bathrooms: 5 private.
Bed & breakfast: £15-£25
single, £25-£28 double.
Half board: from £19.50
daily, from £133 weekly.
Evening meal 6.30pm (l.o.
5.30pm).
Parking for 6.
🛏5 ▦ ▯ ▯ ▥ ▥ 🖊 ▲
▯ ▦ ▲ ✿ ✕ ▦ DAP SP

CLEARWELL

Gloucestershire
Map ref 2A1

2m SW. Coleford
Attractive village in the
Forest of Dean, noted for
its castle, built in 1735
and one of the oldest
Georgian Gothic houses
in England. The old mines
in Clearwell Caves are
open to the public.

Mrs. S.W. Reid M
⚌⚌

Tudor Farm, Clearwell,
Coleford, GL16 8JS
☎ Dean (0594) 33046
*Charming 13th C. listed house
with original oak panelling and
unique spiral staircase. Well-
appointed bedrooms and
restaurant.*
Bedrooms: 4 double & 2 twin,
2 family rooms.
Bathrooms: 8 private.
Bed & breakfast: £25-£32.50
single, £33-£42 double.
Evening meal 7pm (l.o. 5pm).
Parking for 17.
Open February-December.
🛏 ▦ ▯ ▯ ⚲ Ⓥ ▥ ▦ ▲
▶ ✿ ▦ ▥ SP ▦ Ⓣ

CLUN

Shropshire
Map ref 4A3

*See also Bucknell,
Clunton.*
Small ancient town on the
Welsh border with flint
and stone tools in its
museum and Iron Age
forts nearby. The
impressive ruins of a
Norman castle lie beside
the River Clun and there
are some interesting 17th
C houses.

Llanhedric Farm M
Clun, Craven Arms,
SY7 8NG
☎ (058 84) 203
*380-acre mixed farm. Old
farmhouse of character just off
A488 road, 3 miles out of
Clun. Few miles from Welsh
border and Offa's Dyke.*
Bedrooms: 1 double, 1 family
room.
Bathrooms: 1 public.
Bed & breakfast: £9-£10
single, £18-£20 double.
Half board: £14.50-£16 daily,
£98-£101.50 weekly.
Parking for 4.
Open April-November.
🛏 ⚲ ▥ ▯ Ⓥ ▥ ▦ ▲ ⚲
🖊 ✿ ✕ ▦

**PLEASE CHECK PRICES AND OTHER DETAILS
AT THE TIME OF BOOKING.**

Woodside Farmhouse
⊜⊜

Woodside, Clun, Craven
Arms, SY7 0JB
☎ (058 84) 695
*250-year-old farmhouse, 1 mile
and 300 feet above Clun,
overlooking the picturesque
Clun Valley. Ordnance Survey
ref. S0310802.*
Bedrooms: 1 double, 1 family
room.
Bathrooms: 1 public.
Bed & breakfast: £10-£12
single, £20-£24 double.
Half board: £15-£18 daily,
£100-£115 weekly.
Lunch available.
Evening meal 7pm (l.o.
11am).
Parking for 4.
Open March-October.
🕭 🕯 ⛤ 🛉 Ⓥ ⊣ ⑲ Ⅲ 🔔
❋ 🏠

CLUNBURY

Shropshire
Map ref 4A3

Village near the River
Clun and close to Hopton
Castle with its ruins of a
Norman moat and bailey.

Hillside ₥
⊜⊜

Twitchen, Clunbury, Craven
Arms, SY7 0HN
☎ Little Brampton
(058 87) 485
*18th C. stone cottage in its own
grounds, in a quiet hamlet in
Clun Valley, 7 miles from
Craven Arms.*
Bedrooms: 1 double & 2 twin.
Bathrooms: 1 public.
Bed & breakfast: £9.50-£10
single, £19-£20 double.
Half board: £14-£15 daily,
from £98 weekly.
Evening meal 6.30pm (l.o.
7.30pm).
Parking for 5.
Open March-November.
🕯 ⛤ 🛉 Ⓥ ⊣ ⑲ 🔔 ❋
🐾

CLUNTON

Shropshire
Map ref 4A3

2m E. Clun
Village near the Welsh
border and Offa's Dyke.

Clun Forest Walks ₥
28/29 Clunton, Craven Arms,
Clunton, SY7 0HU
☎ Little Brampton
(058 87) 652

---

*18th C. pair of stone-built
cottages in an area of
outstanding natural beauty.
Small village, 7 miles due west
of Craven Arms in Clun
Valley.*
Bedrooms: 1 double & 2 twin.
Bathrooms: 1 public.
Bed & breakfast: £10 single,
£20 double.
Half board: £15-£17 daily,
£105-£119 weekly.
Evening meal 6.30pm (l.o.
8pm).
Parking for 4.
Open March-November.
🕭 ⛤ 🛉 Ⓥ ⑲ Ⅲ 🔔 ❋ ⤬
🏠 SP 🏠

Hurst Mill Farm
⊜⊜

Clunton, SY7 0JA
☎ Clun (058 84) 224
*100-acre mixed farm.
Attractive stone farmhouse and
garden, next to disused old mill
by the River Clun. Trails
through local woodland are
ideal for walking enthusiasts.*
Bedrooms: 1 single, 2 double
& 1 twin.
Bathrooms: 2 public.
Bed & breakfast: from £10
single, from £20 double.
Half board: from £15 daily.
Evening meal 6pm (l.o. 8pm).
Parking for 8.
🕭 🕯 ⛤ 🛉 Ⓥ ⊣ ⑲ Ⅲ 🔔
Ự 🏠 🏠

CODSALL

Staffordshire
Map ref 4B3

Expanding residential
village a few miles from
Wolverhampton.

Moors Farm and
Country Restaurant ₥
⊜⊜

Chillington La., Codsall,
Wolverhampton, WV8 1QF
☎ (090 74) 2330
*100-acre mixed farm. 200-
year-old farmhouse, 1 mile
from pretty village. All home
produce used. Many local
walks and places of interest.*
Bedrooms: 1 double & 2 twin,
3 family rooms.
Bathrooms: 1 private,
2 public.
Bed & breakfast: £18-£25
single, £30-£40 double.
Half board: max £32 daily,
£140-£215 weekly.
Lunch available.
Evening meal 6.30pm (l.o.
9pm).
Parking for 20.
🕭 4 ⛤ 🛉 Ⓥ ⊣ ⑲ Ⅲ 🔔 ⓣ
✦ ❋ ⤬ 🏠 🏠 SP 🏠 ⓣ

COLESBOURNE

Gloucestershire
Map ref 2B1

6m SE. Cheltenham
Situated beside the River
Churn, which later flows
into the upper reaches of
the Thames. Parts of the
church are over 800
years old. Nearby
Colesbourne Park
possesses many unusual
trees, like the American
Sequoia, introduced by
Henry Elwes.

Colesbourne Inn ₥
Colesbourne, Cheltenham,
GL53 9NP
☎ Coberley
(024 287) 376/396/397
*Typical Cotswold inn on the
A435 between Cirencester and
Cheltenham.*
Bedrooms: 2 single, 6 double
& 2 twin.
Bathrooms: 10 private.
Bed & breakfast: £28 single,
£40 double.
Half board: £30 daily, £190
weekly.
Lunch available.
Evening meal 6pm (l.o.
10pm).
Parking for 70.
Credit: Access, Visa, Diners,
Amex.
🕭 🕯 🍴 🕻 🕬 🗋 🕯 🛉 Ⓥ ⓣ
❋ 🏠 🕱 SP 🏠

COLESHILL

Warwickshire
Map ref 4B3

9m E. Birmingham
Close to Birmingham's
many attractions
including the 17th C
Aston Hall with its
plasterwork and
furnishings, the Railway
Museum and Sarehole
Mill, an 18th C water-
powered mill restored to
working order.

Maxstoke Priory ₥
⊜⊜⊜

Maxstoke, Coleshill,
Birmingham, West Midlands
B46 2SU
☎ (0675) 62117
*500-acre mixed farm. Historic
farmhouse with unique dining
room, in peaceful surroundings.
Easy access to National
Exhibition Centre, airport and
motorways.*
Bedrooms: 1 double & 1 twin.
Bathrooms: 2 private,
2 public.

Bed & breakfast: £14-£16
single, £28-£32 double.
Parking for 30.
🗋 🕯 ⛤ 🛉 Ⓥ ⊣ ⑲ Ⅲ 🔔
🕯 🍴 🐾 🏠 🏠

CORSE

Gloucestershire
Map ref 2B1

6m N. Gloucester
Near here at Snigs End,
Feargus O'Connor the
Chartist established in
1847 a settlement on the
land for industrial workers
and many of the
characteristic cottages
still remain. There is an
ancient Court with cruck
beams.

Kilmorie
Listed

Gloucester Rd., Corse,
Staunton, Gloucester,
GL19 3RQ
☎ Staunton Court
(045 284) 224
*7-acre livestock & fruit farm.
Grade II listed smallholding
built in 1848 in conservation
area. Own produce when
available. Ideally situated for
touring Cotswolds, Forest of
Dean and Malvern Hills.*
Bedrooms: 4 double & 1 twin.
Bathrooms: 1 public.
Bed & breakfast: from £7
single, from £14 double.
Half board: from £11 daily,
from £77 weekly.
Lunch available.
Evening meal 6pm (l.o.
7.30pm).
Parking for 6.
🕭6 🕮 🕯 ⛤ 🛉 Ⓥ ⊣ ⑲ Ⅲ
🔔 ❋ 🏠 🏠

CORSE LAWN

Hereford & Worcester
Map ref 2B1

6m NW. Gloucester
Attractive rural settlement
on a quiet road near
Tewkesbury and Ledbury.

Corse Hill Farm
Listed

Main Rd., Corse Lawn,
Gloucester, Gloucestershire
GL19 4NT
☎ Staunton Court
(045 284) 503
*100-acre mixed farm. 200-
year-old stone-built farmhouse
with Victorian addition. Lovely
views towards Malvern Hills.
Within easy reach of
Tewkesbury, Cheltenham,
Gloucester and M50.*
Bedrooms: 1 single, 1 family
room.

Continued ▶

CORSE LAWN

Continued

Bathrooms: 1 public.
Bed & breakfast: £11-£12
single, £25-£26 double.
Parking for 5.
Open April-October.

COTSWOLDS

*See Blockley, Bourton-
on-the-Water, Broadway,
Cheltenham, Chipping
Campden, Cirencester,
Frocester, Gloucester,
Guiting Power, Moreton-
in-Marsh, Nailsworth,
Northleach, North Nibley,
Stonehouse, Stow-on-
the-Wold, Stroud,
Tewkesbury,
Winchcombe.*

COVENTRY

West Midlands
Map ref 4B3

*See also Balsall
Common, Meriden.*
Modern city with a long
history. It has many
places of interest
including the post-war
and ruined medieval
cathedrals, art gallery and
museums, some 16th C
almshouses, St. Mary's
Guildhall, Lunt Roman
fort and the Belgrade
Theatre. ℹ

Woodlands
😊😊

Oak Lane, Allesley, Coventry
W. Midlands CV5 9BX
☎ Meriden (0676) 22688
*Comfortable, detached and
privately situated in a beautiful
countryside lane only 150
yards from the A45. Seven
minutes from National
Exhibition Centre and airport,
ideal for Coventry, Stratford-
upon-Avon and Warwick.*
Bedrooms: 3 twin.
Bathrooms: 1 public.
Bed & breakfast: £11-£12
single, £20-£22 double.
Parking for 6.

**THE SYMBOLS ARE
EXPLAINED ON THE
FLAP INSIDE THE
BACK COVER.**

CRAVEN ARMS

Shropshire
Map ref 4A3

See also Clunbury.
Village close to Wenlock
Edge and the Longmynd
and an ideal centre for
walking with many fine
views. It is close to
Stokesay Castle, a 13th
C. fortified manor house,
the ruins of Hopton
Castle and Ludlow.

Ridgway Wood
Edgton, Craven Arms,
SY7 8HW
☎ Lydbury North
(058 88) 278
*Bungalow with 22 acres of
woodland and gardens in a
area of outstanding natural
beauty. Three quarters of a
mile towards Edgton from
A489.*
Bedrooms: 2 single, 1 twin.
Bathrooms: 2 public.
Bed & breakfast: £9 single,
£18 double.
Parking for 5.

Strefford Hall M
Listed

Strefford, Craven Arms,
SY7 8DE
☎ (0588) 672383
*350-acre mixed farm. A
Victorian farmhouse on a
working farm nestling at the
foot of Wenlock Edge. 2 miles
north of the market town of
Craven Arms. Non-smoking
household.*
Bedrooms: 1 double & 1 twin,
1 family room.
Bathrooms: 1 public.
Bed & breakfast: £9-£11
single, £18-£22 double.
Half board: £14-£16 daily,
max. £100 weekly.
Evening meal 7pm.
Parking for 3.
Open April-October.

Woodville M
😊😊

Clun Rd., Craven Arms,
SY7 9AA
☎ (058 82) 2476
*Woodville is a large family
house set in three quarters of
an acre in the heart of some of
the most unspoilt countryside in
Shropshire.*
Bedrooms: 1 double & 1 twin,
1 family room.
Bathrooms: 3 private.
Bed & breakfast: £20-£26
double.

Half board: £15-£16.50 daily,
£95-£120 weekly.
Evening meal 6.30pm (l.o.
8pm).
Parking for 6.

CUSOP

Hereford & Worcester
Map ref 2A1

1m SE. Hay-on-Wye
Village on the Welsh
border, on the outskirts of
Hay-on-Wye which is
world renowned for its
second hand bookshops.

York House
😊😊

Hardwick Road Cusop, Hay-
on-Wye, Hereford,
Herefordshire HR3 5QX
☎ Hay-on-Wye
(0497) 820705
*Quiet Victorian house with
view to mountains over
attractive southerly gardens.
Historic riverside Hay-on-Wye,
"town of books", 5 minutes'
walk away. No smoking
allowed in bedrooms or dining
room.*
Bedrooms: 1 single, 2 double
& 2 twin, 1 family room.
Bathrooms: 2 public.
Bed & breakfast: £11-£13
single, £22 double.
Half board: £18-£20 daily,
£113.40-£126 weekly.
Evening meal 7.30pm (l.o.
5pm).
Parking for 8.

DENSTONE

Staffordshire
Map ref 4B2

Denstone has won
several awards for best
kept village in
Staffordshire. The public
school, Denstone
College, is a handsome
building overlooking the
Churnet Valley.

Ford Croft House Stud
Oak Rd., Denstone,
Uttoxeter, ST14 5HT
☎ Rocester (0889) 590822
*A large detached house on
outskirts of Denstone village;
also a stud farm for
thoroughbred horses. 2 miles
from Alton Towers, Dovedale
and the Peak National Park.*
Bedrooms: 1 double & 1 twin,
1 family room.

Bathrooms: 1 public.
Bed & breakfast: £10-£15
single, £20-£25 double.
Parking for 4.

Hillside Farm
Denstone, Uttoxeter,
ST14 5HE
☎ Rocester (0889) 590760
*Victorian farmhouse with
extensive views to the Weaver
Hills and Churnet Valley.
Situated 2 miles south of Alton
Towers on the B5032.*
Bedrooms: 2 family rooms.
Bathrooms: 1 public.
Bed & breakfast: £10 single,
£18-£20 double.
Parking for 7.
Open April-October.

Manor House Farm M
😊😊

Prestwood, Denstone,
Uttoxeter, ST14 5DD
☎ Rocester (0889) 590415
*178-acre dairy farm. Stone-
built farmhouse with mullion
windows and antique furniture
throughout. 2 miles from Alton
Towers, 6 miles from
Ashbourne. Victorian
summerhouse in traditional
terraced garden, overlooking
the scenic Churnet Valley.*
Bedrooms: 1 double & 1 twin,
1 family room.
Bathrooms: 2 public.
Bed & breakfast: £12-£16
single, £20-£28 double.
Parking for 8.

DIDMARTON

Gloucestershire
Map ref 2B2

6m SW. Tetbury
Attractive village with
stone houses and
interesting architectural
features. It has 2
churches, one of which
has Georgian furnishings.
Didmarton is close to
Badminton House.

Kings Arms
😊

Didmarton, Badminton,
Avon GL9 1DT
☎ (045 423) 245
*Old coaching inn on the
Badminton estate, in the village
of Didmarton; near Westonbirt
Arboretum.*
Bedrooms: 1 double, 1 family
room.
Bathrooms: 1 public.
Bed & breakfast: from £14
single, £28-£30 double.

Half board: £20-£35 daily, £120-£250 weekly.
Lunch available.
Evening meal 7pm (l.o. 9pm).
Parking for 40.
Open January-November.

⛏5 🏤 🖵 ↻ ⊁ 🖾 🛗

Orchard Grove
😊😊

The Street, Didmarton, Badminton, GL9 1DN
☎ (0454) 23731
Picturesque village setting with nature walks, equestrian centre and local inn. Ideal location for exploring the cultural centres of the Cotswolds and the South West. Bath is 4 miles to the south.
Bedrooms: 1 double & 1 twin.
Bathrooms: 2 private, 1 public.
Bed & breakfast: max. £10 single, £16-£24 double.
Parking for 4.

⛏ 🅄 🛢 🖻 🖾 🖻 🎥 ◉ 🕮 ▯
↻ ⊁ 🖾 🖾 🖾 ⊠ 🆂🅿

DILWYN
Hereford & Worcester
Map ref 2A1

6m SW. Leominster
Pretty black and white houses, a village green and a big medieval church form the focal point of this peaceful village which has now been by-passed by the Leominster-Brecon road.

Bedford House
Listed

Dilwyn, Hereford, Herefordshire HR4 8JJ
☎ Pembridge (054 47) 260
20-acre mixed farm. Near an attractive village by-passed by the Leominster - Brecon road.
Bedrooms: 1 twin, 2 family rooms.
Bathrooms: 1 public.
Bed & breakfast: from £9.50 single, from £19 double.
Half board: from £15.50 daily, from £100 weekly.
Evening meal 6.30pm.
Parking for 3.
Open March-October.

⛏ ↻ 🅄 🛢 🖻 🎥 🕮 ↻ ⌡
▶ ✓ ❄ 🖾

**MAP REFERENCES
APPLY TO THE
COLOUR MAPS
TOWARDS THE END
OF THIS GUIDE.**

DOCKLOW
Hereford & Worcester
Map ref 2A1

4m SE. Leominster
Little village on the Leominster to Bromyard road with splendid views stretching away to the Welsh mountains.

Mrs E.T. Brooke
Listed

Nicholson Farm, Docklow, Leominster, Herefordshire HR6 0SL
☎ Steens Bridge (056 882) 269
200-acre dairy farm. 360-year-old farmhouse in delightful scenic valley, with trout and carp in farm lake. Wonderful walking on farm and superb touring in Herefordshire and the Welsh border.
Bedrooms: 1 single, 1 double, 1 family room.
Bathrooms: 3 public.
Bed & breakfast: £8.50-£9.50 single, £17-£19 double.
Evening meal 6pm (l.o. 7.50pm).
Parking for 12.

⛏ 🖾 ↻ 🅄 🛢 🖻 🎥 🕮 ▯
🍽 🏮 ↻ ⌡ ▶ ❄ 🖾 🛗

DORRINGTON
Shropshire
Map ref 4A3

7m S. Shrewsbury
Village on the main Shrewsbury-Ludlow road, mainly of brick houses and cottages and an early Victorian church.

Ashton Lees
😊😊

Dorrington, Shrewsbury, SY5 7JW
☎ (074 373) 378
6 miles south of Shrewsbury on the A49. Well placed for exploring the south Shropshire area.
Bedrooms: 1 single, 1 double & 1 twin.
Bathrooms: 1 public.
Bed & breakfast: from £10 single.
Parking for 6.

⛏ 🖵 ↻ 🅄 🛢 🖻 🎥 ❄ ⊁
🖾 🖾

The Old House ⋈
Listed

Ryton, Dorrington, SY5 7LY
☎ (074 373) 585
Small 17th C. manor house with gardens of 1.5 acres and large lily pond. Isolated setting, 400 yards from village pub. Fine views; very peaceful.
Bedrooms: 2 twin.
Bathrooms: 1 public.
Bed & breakfast: £25-£27.50 double.
Parking for 10.

⛏10 🖾 ◉ ↻ 🅄 🛢 🎥 🕮
🏮 ↻ ⊁ 🖾 🛗

DROITWICH
Hereford & Worcester
Map ref 2B1

See also Hanbury, Himbleton, Ombersley.
Old town with natural brine springs which was developed as a spa town at the beginning of the 19th C. It has some interesting churches, in particular the Church of the Sacred Heart with splendid mosaics. There are several fine parks and a Heritage Centre. ℹ

Wessex House Farm
Trench Lane, Oddingley, Droitwich, Worcestershire WR9 7NB
☎ (0905) 772826
50-acre mixed farm. Modern farmhouse in pleasant surroundings 4 miles from the M5 motorway, 3 miles from Droitwich and within easy reach of Cotswolds. Farmhouse food. Also food available locally.
Bedrooms: 1 double, 1 family room.
Bathrooms: 1 public.
Bed & breakfast: £9-£10 single.
Half board: £12-£14 daily.
Evening meal 6pm (l.o. 8pm).
Parking for 3.
Open March-October.

⛏ ↻ 🅄 🛢 🖻 🎥 🕮 🖾 ⊁
🖾 🖾 🆂🅿

DURSLEY
Gloucestershire

See Uley.

ECCLESHALL
Staffordshire
Map ref 4B3

Small market town with long associations with the Bishops of Lichfield, 6 of whom are buried in the large 12th C parish church. The ruined castle was formerly the residence of these bishops.

Glenwood ⋈
😊😊

Croxton, Eccleshall, Stafford, ST21 6PF
☎ Wetwood (063 082) 238
16th C. timber-framed cottage in an ideal position for visiting the many attractions of Staffordshire and Shropshire.
Bedrooms: 1 double & 2 twin.
Bathrooms: 1 public.
Bed & breakfast: £10-£12 single, £20-£24 double.
Half board: £16-£18 daily.
Evening meal 6pm (l.o. 6.30pm).
Parking for 6.

⛏ 🍴 ◉ ↻ 🅄 🛢 🖾 ✕ 🖻
🎥 🕮 🖾 ❄ 🖾 🖾 🖾 🛗 🆃

King's Arms Hotel
Stafford St., Eccleshall, Stafford, ST21 6BL
☎ Stafford (0785) 850294
16th C. coaching inn.
Bedrooms: 1 single, 2 double, 1 family room.
Bathrooms: 2 public.
Bed & breakfast: £15.50-£18 single, £29.50-£31 double.
Lunch available.
Evening meal 7pm (l.o. 10.30pm).
Parking for 50.
Credit: Access.

⛏ 🖵 ↻ 🛢 ▯ 🖻 🎥 🕮 🖾
🍽 🖾 🛗

EDGE
Gloucestershire
Map ref 2B1

3m N. Stroud
Near the picturesque wool town of Painswick, the village church is of rock-faced stone with freestone dressings.

Upper Doreys Mill
😊

Edge, Stroud, GL6 6NF
☎ Painswick (0452) 812459
18th C. cloth mill with log fires and old beams. By a stream and in a rural setting. Half a mile from Painswick, down Edge Lane.
Bedrooms: 1 double & 1 twin.

Continued ▶

**INDIVIDUAL PROPRIETORS HAVE SUPPLIED
ALL DETAILS OF ACCOMMODATION.
ALTHOUGH WE DO CHECK FOR ACCURACY, WE
ADVISE YOU TO CONFIRM PRICES AND OTHER
INFORMATION AT THE TIME OF BOOKING.**

EDGE

Continued

Bathrooms: 1 public;
1 private shower.
Bed & breakfast: from £12.50
single, from £25 double.
Parking for 6.

ELKSTONE

Gloucestershire
Map ref 2B1

6m S. Cheltenham
Village with remarkable
Norman and later church
with a carved south
doorway, a fine chancel
and gargoyles on the
tower.

Manor Farm Cottage
26 Elkstone, Cheltenham,
GL53 9PB
☎ Coberley (024 287) 418
*Traditional Cotswold country
house adjoining farmland and
historic church. Excellent
walking. Non-smoking
household.*
Bedrooms: 1 single, 1 double
& 1 twin, 1 family room.
Bathrooms: 1 public.
Bed & breakfast: from £12.50
single, from £20 double.
Evening meal 6.30pm.
Parking for 4.

EVESHAM

Hereford & Worcester
Map ref 2B1

Evesham is a market
town in the centre of a
fruit growing area. There
are pleasant walks along
the River Avon and many
old houses and inns. A
fine 16th C Bell Tower
stands between 2
churches.

The Croft.
54 Greenhill, Evesham,
Worcestershire WR11 4NF
☎ (0386) 6035
*A splendid Georgian home
offering comfortable overnight
and holiday accommodation.
Sauna and sunbed facilities,
gardens and private parking.*
Bedrooms: 1 single, 1 twin,
1 family room.
Bathrooms: 1 private,
1 public.

Bed & breakfast: £12.50-£15
single, £25-£30 double.
Parking for 6.
Open February-November.

Far Horizon
Listed
Long Hyde Rd., South
Littleton, Evesham,
Worcestershire WR11 5TH
☎ (0386) 831691
*Elegant family home of
character with fine views of
surrounding Cotswolds and
Malvern Hills. Rural location
4 miles from Evesham.*
Bedrooms: 1 single, 1 double
& 1 twin.
Bathrooms: 1 private,
1 public.
Bed & breakfast: £10-£11
single, £20-£24 double.
Half board: £17.50-£19.50
daily.
Evening meal 6.30pm (l.o.
8.30pm).
Parking for 3.

Park View Hotel
Waterside, Evesham,
Worcestershire WR11 6BS
☎ (0386) 442639
*Riverside hotel offering
personal attention. Traditional
English breakfast included,
evening meal available. Base
for touring Cotswolds and
Shakespeare country.*
Bedrooms: 13 single, 3 double
& 11 twin, 2 family rooms.
Bathrooms: 6 public.
Bed & breakfast: £13.50-£15
single, £27-£30 double.
Half board: £20.50-£22 daily.
Lunch available.
Evening meal 6pm (l.o. 7pm).
Parking for 50.
Credit: Access, Visa.

FAIRFORD

Gloucestershire
Map ref 2B1

Small town with a 15th C
wool church famous for
its complete 15th C
stained glass windows,
interesting carvings and
original wall paintings. It
is an excellent touring
centre and the Cotswolds
Wild Life Park is nearby.

Moor Farm
Fairford, GL7 4AP
☎ Cirencester (0285) 712763

*70-acre arable farm. 17th C.
farmhouse in quiet cul-de-sac
10 minutes' walk from centre
of town. Take A417 east, half
a mile turn right at Eight Bells,
end of lane.*
Bedrooms: 1 single, 2 twin,
1 family room.
Bathrooms: 1 private,
1 public.
Bed & breakfast: from £12
single, from £22 double.
Parking for 6.

FECKENHAM

Hereford & Worcester
Map ref 2B1

5m SW. Redditch
Large and lovely village
containing a number of
elegant Georgian houses
and an interesting church
with a Norman arcade
and a chancel rebuilt by
William Butterfield in
1853.

Manor Farm
Listed
Moors Lane, Feckenham,
Redditch, Worcestershire
B96 6JH
☎ Astwood Bank
(052 789) 3285
*35-acre mixed farm. 15th C.
farmhouse with large gardens
and beautiful views. Large
lounge and dining room with
log fire in season. Farmhouse
breakfast with farm produce.*
Bedrooms: 1 double & 1 twin,
1 family room.
Bathrooms: 1 public.
Bed & breakfast: £8-£9
single, £16-£18 double.
Half board: £12-£14 daily,
£84-£98 weekly.
Parking for 6.

FEN END

West Midlands
Map ref 4B3

5m NW. Kenilworth

Oldwych House Farm
Oldwych Lane, Fen End,
Kenilworth, Warwickshire
CV8 1NR
☎ Berkswell (0676) 33552
*14th C. Warwickshire redbrick
farmhouse on traditional
hedged farmland. 2 pools,
abundant wildlife and farm
animals. 8 miles north of
Warwick on the A41.*
Bedrooms: 2 double.
Bathrooms: 2 private.

Bed & breakfast: £25-£30
double.
Parking for 6.
Open January-November.

FLADBURY

Hereford & Worcester
Map ref 2B1

Attractive riverside village
on the Avon, with half-
timbered and Georgian
buildings, and a former
mill now converted to an
imposing residence.

Chequers Inn
Fladbury, Pershore,
Worcestershire WR10 2PZ
☎ Evesham (0386) 860276 &
860527
*16th C. inn between Evesham
and Pershore, on the edge of
the Cotswolds. Off B4084 and
A44, in a quiet village location,
17 miles from Stratford-upon-
Avon.*
Bedrooms: 3 double & 4 twin,
1 family room.
Bathrooms: 8 private.
Bed & breakfast: £22.50-
£32.50 single, £35-£45 double.
Half board: £32.50-£47.50
daily, £227.50-£332.50
weekly.
Lunch available.
Evening meal 6.30pm (l.o.
10.30pm).
Parking for 30.
Credit: Access, Visa.

FLASH

Staffordshire
Map ref 4B2

4m NW. Longnor
Small and remote,
claiming to be England's
highest village. Flash
came to mean counterfeit
money because nearby
Panniers Pool Bridge was
once the meeting place of
forgers and other
lawbreakers. 2m SW is
Lud's Church, a hidden
but spectacular chasm,
reached by footpath from
Gradbach Mill Youth
Hostel.

New Inn
Flash, Quarnford, Buxton,
Derbyshire SK17 0SW
☎ Buxton (0298) 2941
Village inn over 300 years old.
Bedrooms: 1 double & 2 twin.

**THE SYMBOLS ARE EXPLAINED ON THE FLAP
INSIDE THE BACK COVER.**

Bathrooms: 1 public.
Bed & breakfast: £15 single,
£25 double.
Lunch available.
Evening meal 7pm (l.o.
10pm).
Parking for 12.

🛉 Ⅴ 🛏 📺 🛍 🔾 ✕ 🎠 🏳

FROCESTER

Gloucestershire
Map ref 2B1

*10m SW. Gloucester
Village at the foot of
Frocester Hill with one of
the oldest and best
preserved of the
country's tithe barns.*

Elmtree Farm 🅼
🏮

Frocester, Stonehouse,
GL10 3TG
☎ Stonehouse (045 382) 3274
*201-acre dairy farm. 200-year-
old farmhouse with inglenooks
and beams. Ideal for visiting
Slimbridge Wildfowl Trust,
Berkeley Castle and for
touring the Cotswolds.*
Bedrooms: 2 twin, 1 family
room.
Bathrooms: 1 public.
Bed & breakfast: £12-£14
single, £20-£24 double.
Half board: £60-£65 weekly.
Parking for 5.
Open April-October.

🛏 🖃 🛍 🛡 📺 🛍 🌣 ✕ 🎠

GARWAY

Hereford & Worcester
Map ref 2A1

*5m SE. Pontrilas
A small village in
delightful countryside of
the Monnow Valley. There
is fine Norman work in
the church, which has a
detached tower, and a
nearby circular 14th C
dovecote once belonging
to the Knights Templar.*

Garway Moon

Garway, Hereford,
Herefordshire HR2 8RQ
☎ Skenfrith (060 084) 270
*16th C. inn on the borders of
Wales and the Golden Valley
with Hereford, Monmouth,
Abergavenny and Ross-on-Wye
all within 20 minutes' drive.*
Bedrooms: 1 single, 2 double.
Bathrooms: 1 public.
Bed & breakfast: max. £10
single, max. £20 double.
Half board: £12.50-£20 daily,
£87.50-£140 weekly.
Lunch available.

Evening meal 7pm (l.o.
10pm).
Parking for 40.

🛏5 🛡 🛍 Ⅴ 📖 🛍 🛡 🎠 🔾 🌣 ✕ 🎠 ⅏ 🏳

GLOUCESTER

Gloucestershire
Map ref 2B1

*See also Birdlip, Corse,
Corse Lawn, Churcham,
Hartpury, Newnham.
A Roman city and inland
port on the Severn, its
cathedral is one of the
most beautiful in Britain.
Gloucester's many
attractions include
museums, old buildings
and inns and the house of
Beatrix Potter's 'Tailor of
Gloucester'.* ℹ

Brydone 🅼
Listed

Coopers Hill, Brockworth,
Gloucester, GL3 4RT
☎ Gloucester (0452) 863585
*Typical Cotswold cottage, 5
miles from Cheltenham and 4
miles from Painswick, on the
A46. An area of outstanding
natural beauty.*
Bedrooms: 1 double & 1 twin.
Bathrooms: 1 public.
Bed & breakfast: £10-£11
single, £18-£19 double.
Parking for 2.

🛏1 🛍 🖳 🛡 Ⅴ 🛏 🌣 ✕ 🎠 🏳

Gilbert's
🏮🏮🏮

Brookthorpe, Gloucester,
GL4 0UH
☎ Painswick (0452) 812364
*5-acre organic smallholding. A
grade II listed Jacobean house
near the Cotswolds, Bath,
Oxford and Stratford. A
family home, combining
antiques with modern
amenities.*
Bedrooms: 1 single, 2 double
& 1 twin.
Bathrooms: 2 private,
1 public.
Bed & breakfast: from £15
single, from £30 double.
Parking for 6.

🛏 🔾 🛒 🖳 🛡 Ⅴ 🛏 📖 🛍 🌣 🎠 🏳

Hill Farm
🏮🏮🏮

Bishops Norton, Gloucester,
GL2 9LN
☎ (0452) 730351
*15-acre mixed farm. 14th C.
thatched farmhouse in rural
setting, close to River Severn,
offering facilities for "get away
from it all" breaks.*
Bedrooms: 3 double & 1 twin.
Bathrooms: 2 private,
2 public.
Bed & breakfast: £10-£16.50
single, £20-£33 double.
Half board: £16.50-£23 daily,
£115-£161 weekly.
Evening meal 6.45pm (l.o.
6.45pm).
Parking for 12.

🛏 🖃 🛒 🔾 🛡 Ⅴ 📺 🛍 🛡 🌣 🎠 🏳

The Limes
🏮🏮

Stroud Rd., Brookthorpe,
Gloucester, GL4 0UQ
☎ Painswick (0452) 812645
*A charming Georgian 3-storey
house on the A4173 between
Gloucester and Stroud, set in
the Cotswold Escarpment.*
Bedrooms: 1 single, 1 double
& 2 twin, 1 family room.
Bathrooms: 1 private,
2 public.
Bed & breakfast: max. £15
single, max. £28 double.
Evening meal 6pm (l.o. 8pm).
Parking for 2.
Credit: Access, Visa.

🛏 🛒 🔾 🛡 Ⅴ 🛏 📺 📖 ✕ 🎠 🅳 🛡

Lulworth
🏮🏮

12 Midlands Rd., Gloucester,
GL1 4UF
☎ (0452) 21881
Bedrooms: 2 single, 2 double
& 2 twin, 2 family rooms.
Bathrooms: 2 private,
3 public.
Bed & breakfast: £11-£13
single, £22-£28 double.
Parking for 8.

🛏 🛒 🛒 🔾 🖳 Ⅴ 🛏 📺 📖 🛡 🎠

The Retreat 🅼
🏮🏮🏮

116 Bristol Rd., Quedgeley,
Gloucester, GL2 6NA
☎ (0452) 728296
*Large double-fronted detached
house.*
Bedrooms: 1 single, 4 twin,
3 family rooms.
Bathrooms: 1 private,
5 public; 1 private shower.
Bed & breakfast: £13-£15
single, £25-£30 double.
Parking for 10.

🛏 🖃 🛒 🔾 🛒 🛡 Ⅴ 🖌 🛏 📺 📖 🛡 🗙 ✕

GOODRICH

Hereford & Worcester
Map ref 2A1

*Village standing above
the River Wye with the
magnificent ruins of the
red sandstone castle high
above it, now in the care
of the Department of the
Environment.*

Marstow Court Farm 🅼
Listed

Marstow, Goodrich, Ross-on-
Wye, Herefordshire
HR9 6HD
☎ Symonds Yat
(0600) 890487
*170-acre mixed farm. Early
17th C. farmhouse in the heart
of the Wye Valley. A beautiful
area to explore. Half a mile off
the A40 on the Hereford
A4137 road.*
Bedrooms: 1 single, 1 double
& 1 twin.
Bathrooms: 1 public.
Bed & breakfast: £10 single,
£20 double.
Parking for 4.
Open March-October.

🛏10 🛥 🔾 🖳 Ⅴ 🛏 📺 📖 ✕ 🎠 🏳

Ye Hostelrie Hotel 🅼
🏮🏮

Goodrich, Ross-on-Wye,
Herefordshire HR9 6HX
☎ Symonds Yat
(0600) 890241
*Listed building of pseudo-
Gothic architecture, in a
peaceful village near the
renowned Goodrich Castle,
overlooking the River Wye.
The original building dates
from the 17th C.*
Bedrooms: 1 single, 3 double
& 3 twin, 1 family room.
Bathrooms: 4 private,
2 public.
Bed & breakfast: £18-£20
single, £28-£32 double.
Evening meal 7.30pm (l.o.
9pm).
Parking for 31.

🛏 🔾 🛡 Ⅴ 🛏 📺 📖 🛡 🛡
🗙 🌣 🎠 🛍 🆂🅿 🛡

**MAP REFERENCES
APPLY TO THE
COLOUR MAPS
TOWARDS THE END
OF THIS GUIDE.**

**THERE IS A SPECIAL
SECTION IN THIS
GUIDE LISTING
ACCOMMODATION
ESPECIALLY
SUITABLE FOR
GROUPS AND
YOUNG PEOPLE.**

GUITING POWER

Gloucestershire
Map ref 2B1

5m SE. Winchcombe
Unspoilt village with stone
cottages and a green.
The Cotswold Farm Park
with a collection of rare
breeds is nearby with an
adventure playground
and farm trail.

The Guest House ⋈
😎🏖

Guiting Power, Cheltenham,
GL54 5TZ
☎ (045 15) 470
*Built of Cotswold stone, with
inglenooks and beams. In the
centre of a delightful village
and within easy motoring
distance of Blenheim Palace,
Cheltenham and Stratford.*
Bedrooms: 2 double & 1 twin,
1 family room.
Bathrooms: 2 public.
Bed & breakfast: £11-£12
single, £22 double.
Half board: £18.50 daily,
£120 weekly.
Evening meal 6.45pm.
Parking for 4.
🏃🛇📺🔧🆄🍴 👁 Ⅴℳ🛏📺🎞
🗪🖤🚗🏡

HALFWAY HOUSE

Shropshire
Map ref 4A3

10m W. Shrewsbury
Settlement which gets its
name from its midway
position on the coach
road between
Shrewsbury and
Welshpool, dominated by
the rounded tops of the
Breidden Hills.

Bulthy Farm

Middleton, Welshpool,
Powys SY21 8ER
☎ (0743) 884247
*100-acre mixed farm. Listed
Georgian farmhouse in a
peaceful environment, offering
a warm welcome. Central for
exploring the Welsh and
Shropshire countryside.*
Bedrooms: 1 twin, 2 family
rooms.
Bathrooms: 2 private;
1 private shower.
Bed & breakfast: £12-£14
single, £20-£22 double.
Half board: £18-£20 daily,
£100-£105 weekly.
Evening meal 7pm (l.o. 9pm).
Parking for 40.
Open April-October.
🏃🛇📺🔧🆄 👁 Ⅴℳ🛏🎞 🗪
🎣🎵▶✓🖤 🚗📑🏡

HANBURY

Hereford & Worcester
Map ref 4B3

4m E. Droitwich
Village best known for
Hanbury Hall, built in
1701 in Wren style and
little altered. The
staircase murals and
ceilings were painted by
Thornhill. There is also a
craft centre in Hanbury.

The Cottage ⋈
Listed

Woolmere Green, Droitwich
Road, Hanbury, Nr.
Bromsgrove, Worcestershire
B60 4DD
☎ (052 784) 476 & 021-643
8424
*Friendly family cottage, circa
1820, extensively modernised
and central for touring the
Heart of England.*
Bedrooms: 2 double.
Bathrooms: 2 public.
Bed & breakfast: £10-£15
single, £20-£25 double.
Parking for 6.
Open April-October.
Credit: Access, Visa, Diners,
Amex.
🏃🐎📺🖤🆄 Ⅴℳ🎞 🗪
🖤🖤 🚗📑

Valley Farm ⋈
😎😎

Hanbury Rd., Hanbury,
Bromsgrove, Worcestershire
B61 9HY
☎ (052 784) 678
*17-acre mixed farm. 16th C.
farmhouse recently modernised
but retaining its traditional
charm. Dining room with
inglenook fireplace and wealth
of beams.*
Bedrooms: 2 double & 1 twin.
Bathrooms: 1 private,
1 public.
Bed & breakfast: £12-£15
single, £18-£25 double.
Half board: £18-£23 daily,
£80-£125 weekly.
Evening meal 6.30pm (l.o.
9pm).
Parking for 10.
🏃📑🖤🆄 👁 🛏🖤 🆂🅿🏡

**THERE IS A SPECIAL
SECTION IN THIS
GUIDE LISTING
ACCOMMODATION
ESPECIALLY
SUITABLE FOR
GROUPS AND
YOUNG PEOPLE.**

HARDWICK

Hereford & Worcester
Map ref 2A1

3m E. Hay-on-Wye
Small, scattered village
near the Herefordshire-
Wales border, close to
Clifford with its ruined
castle and the second-
hand bookshops of Hay-
on-Wye.

Royal Oak ⋈
Listed

Hardwick, Hay-on-Wye,
Hereford, Herefordshire
HR3 5TA
☎ Clifford (049 73) 248
*16th C. country inn with
beautiful views of "Golden
Valley", oak beams, log fires,
interesting meals in the bar or
small restaurant.*
Bedrooms: 1 double & 2 twin.
Bathrooms: 1 public.
Bed & breakfast: £12-£13
single, £24-£26 double.
Lunch available.
Evening meal 6pm (l.o.
9.45pm).
Parking for 40.
Credit: Access, Visa.
🏃🛇 👁 Ⅴℳ🛏🎞 🖤 🗪🅳🅰🅿
🆂🅿🏡

HARTPURY

Gloucestershire
Map ref 2B1

Ridgeway ⋈
😎

Broad St., Hartpury,
Gloucester, GL19 3BN
☎ (045 270) 355
*A friendly family home in a
country village on the A417
Gloucester to Ledbury road.
Central for Cotswolds,
Malverns, Wye Valley, Forest
of Dean, Cheltenham,
Gloucester and Tewkesbury.
Small pottery in pleasant
garden.*
Bedrooms: 1 single, 1 twin.
Bathrooms: 1 public.
Bed & breakfast: £9-£9.50
single, £18-£19 double.
Parking for 4.
Open January-November.
🏃8📑🖤🆄 Ⅴℳ📺🎞 🗪✖
🖤 🅳🅰🅿 🆂🅿

HAY-ON-WYE

Powys

*See Cusop, Hardwick,
Michaelchurch Escley,
Whitney-on-Wye.*

HENLEY-IN-ARDEN

Warwickshire
Map ref 4B3

Old market town which in
Tudor times stood in the
Forest of Arden. It has
many ancient inns and a
15th C Guildhall and
parish church. Coughton
Court with its Gunpowder
Plot connections is
nearby.

Impsley Farm ⋈

Henley-in-Arden, Solihull,
W. Midlands B95 5QH
☎ (056 42) 2300
*13-acre smallholding. Heavily
timbered ancient farmhouse on
A34. Totally peaceful with rare
farm animals and large
interesting garden. Handy for
the National Exhibition Centre,
Shakespeare country and the
Cotswolds.*
Bedrooms: 1 single, 2 double
& 3 twin.
Bathrooms: 5 private,
1 public.
Bed & breakfast: £15 single,
£30 double.
Parking for 6.
🏃♨📑🆄🛏📺🎞 🗪🖤
✖🖤🏡

Irelands Farm ⋈
😎😎

Henley-in-Arden, B95 5SA
☎ (056 42) 2476
*220-acre arable and beef farm.
Secluded farmhouse in peaceful
countryside. En suite facilites.
Close to Stratford, Warwick
and the Cotswolds. 1 mile off
A34 between Henley and M42.*
Bedrooms: 2 twin, 1 family
room.
Bathrooms: 2 private,
1 public.
Bed & breakfast: £12-£20
single, from £24 double.
Parking for 3.
🏃📺📑🖤🆄🛏📺🎞 🗪
✓🖤🖤🏡

**GROUPS, CONSORTIA
AND AGENCIES
SPECIALISING
IN FARM AND
COUNTRY HOLIDAYS
ARE LISTED IN A
SPECIAL SECTION
OF THIS GUIDE.**

HEREFORD

*See also Canon Frome,
Kingstone, Little
Dewchurch, Marden,
Much Birch, Sutton St.
Nicholas, Weobley,
Woolhope.*
Agricultural county town,
its cathedral containing
much Norman work and a
large chained library. The
city's varied attractions
include the Bulmer
Railway Centre and
several museums
including a cider museum.
🛈

Amberley
Listed
137 Hampton Dene Rd.,
Hereford, Herefordshire
HR1 1UJ
☎ (0432) 273448
*Modern, detached 4-
bedroomed house in a
residential area, one mile from
the city centre.*
Bedrooms: 1 single, 1 double
& 1 twin.
Bathrooms: 1 public.
Bed & breakfast: £10.50-
£12.50 single, £19-£21 double.
Parking for 3.
🛍10 ⚒ Ⓖ ▭ ♥ Ⓤ ⧄ ⒯
▥ 🏴 🐾

7 Cantilupe St.
Castle Green, Hereford,
Herefordshire HR1 2NU
☎ (0432) 278161
*An elegant Victorian house in a
sunny, quiet position,
overlooking duck pond and
gardens. 400 metres from the
city centre.*
Bedrooms: 1 double & 1 twin.
Bathrooms: 1 public.
Bed & breakfast: £10-£12
single, £20-£24 double.
Parking for 2.
🛍 ▭ ♥ Ⓤ Ⓥ ⧄ 🐾 🏴
SP ⊞

The Hermitage Manor M
😄😄😄
Canon Pyon, Hereford,
Herefordshire HR4 8NR
☎ (0432) 760317
*A combination of country house
elegance and a homely
atmosphere, conducive to
relaxation. Set in 11 acres and
overlooking 600 square miles of
rural Herefordshire. The
Hermitage is only 10 minutes
by car from the cathedral city
of Hereford.*
Bedrooms: 2 double & 1 twin.
Bathrooms: 3 private.

Bed & breakfast: £19.50-£21
single, £30-£35 double.
Parking for 8.
Open March-December.
🛍12 ♥ Ⓤ ⧄ ⒯ ▥ 🐾
🏴 🏴

Hopbine Guest House M
😄😄
The Hopbine, Roman Rd.,
Hereford, Herefordshire
HR1 1LE
☎ (0432) 268722
*Attractive Victorian guesthouse
in own 2 acre grounds on
boundary of city. Half a mile
from leisure centre and golf
course.*
Bedrooms: 1 single, 3 double
& 2 twin, 1 family room.
Bathrooms: 2 private,
2 public.
Bed & breakfast: £9.50-£14
single, £19-£26 double.
Half board: £24.50-£25 daily,
£102-£116 weekly.
Evening meal 6pm (l.o. 5pm).
Parking for 16.
🛍3 ⧄ ▭ ♥ Ⓤ 🛈 Ⓥ ⧄ ⒯
▥ 🐾 🐾 🏴 DAP

Lower Bartestree Farm
😄
Bartestree, Hereford,
Herefordshire HR1 4DT
☎ (0432) 851005
*Comfortable accommodation in
a peaceful setting with splendid
views. Home made bread,
preserves and free-range eggs.*
Bedrooms: 1 double & 1 twin.
Bathrooms: 1 public.
Bed & breakfast: max. £20
double.
Parking for 5.
🛍 ♥ Ⓤ Ⓥ ⧄ ⒯ ▥ 🐾 🐾
🏴

Prospect Cottage M
Listed
Bartestree, Hereford,
Herefordshire HR1 4BY
☎ (0432) 851164
*Part 16th C. black and white
country house on 2-acre
market garden. Beautiful
countryside. 3 miles from the
city centre. Evening meal by
arrangement.*
Bedrooms: 1 double & 1 twin.
Bathrooms: 1 public.
Bed & breakfast: £20 double.
Evening meal 6pm.
Parking for 6.
🛍 ⚒ ♥ ⧄ Ⓤ 🛈 Ⓥ ⧄ ⒯
▥ 🐾 🏴 🏴 ⊞

Westfield House
😄😄
235 Whitecross Rd.,
Hereford, Herefordshire
HR4 0LT
☎ (0432) 267712

*Spacious Victorian house with
large, attractive rooms and
pleasant leisure garden. Less
than a mile from the city.*
Bedrooms: 2 double & 1 twin,
1 family room.
Bathrooms: 3 public;
1 private shower.
Bed & breakfast: £10-£12
single, £20-£24 double.
Parking for 3.
🛍 ♥ Ⓤ Ⓥ ⧽ ⧄ ⒯ ▥ 🐾
🏴

HEWELSFIELD

6m S. Coleford
From the village of
Hewelsfield, Tintern
Abbey, St. Briavels Castle
and Chepstow Castle can
be easily reached.

Hopewell House
😄😄
Hewelsfield, Lydney,
GL15 6XE
☎ Tintern (029 18) 400
*Comfortable 18th C.
farmhouse in secluded rural
area. Private "barn" room en
suite providing fairly limited
self-catering. 1 mile to
Brockweir Bridge.*
Bedrooms: 1 double & 2 twin.
Bathrooms: 1 private,
1 public.
Bed & breakfast: £10-£12.50
single, £20-£25 double.
Parking for 6.
Open February-October.
🛍 Ⓜ ⧄ ♥ Ⓤ Ⓥ ⧄ ⒯ ▥
🐾 ⅏ 🐾 🐾 🏴 SP ⊞

HIMBLETON

4m SE. Droitwich
Pleasant village of half
timbered houses and
church with weather-
boarded bell turret. The
brook here is crossed by
an early packhorse
bridge.

Phepson Farm M
😄😄
Himbleton, Droitwich,
Worcestershire WR9 7JZ
☎ (090 569) 205
*170-acre mixed farm.
Traditional oak-beamed
farmhouse on family stock
farm on Wychavon Way.
Peaceful countryside 5 miles
from the M5.*
Bedrooms: 1 double & 1 twin,
1 family room.
Bathrooms: 2 public.

Bed & breakfast: £10-£12.50
single, £20-£25 double.
Half board: £16-£18.50 daily,
£110-£125 weekly.
Evening meal 6.30pm (l.o.
midday).
Parking for 6.
🛍 ♥ Ⓤ ⧄ ⒯ 🐾 🏴 DAP SP

HUNNINGHAM

5m NE. Leamington Spa
Village close to
Stoneleigh Abbey, the site
of the Royal Agricultural
Show with a farm and
country centre, and to
Kenilworth Castle.

Mr. R.C. Hancock M
😄😄
Snowford Hall, Hunningham,
Leamington Spa, CV33 9ES
☎ Marton (0926) 632297
*250-acre arable/mixed farm.
18th C. farmhouse off the
Fosse Way, on the edge of
Hunningham village. On
elevated ground overlooking
quiet surrounding countryside.*
Bedrooms: 1 double & 1 twin,
1 family room.
Bathrooms: 1 public;
2 private showers.
Bed & breakfast: £15-£20
single, £24-£26 double.
Half board: from £20 daily.
Evening meal 6pm (l.o. 8pm).
Parking for 4.
🛍 ♥ Ⓤ 🛈 ⧽ ⧄ ⒯ ▥ 🐾
⚓ 🐾 🐾 🏴

IRONBRIDGE

Small town on the Severn
where the Industrial
Revolution began. It has
the world's first iron
bridge built in 1774. The
Ironbridge Gorge
Museum contains several
industrial sites and
museums spread over 2
miles and is exceptionally
interesting. 🛈

Paradise House M
😄😄
Coalbrookdale, Telford,
TF8 7NR
☎ (095 245) 3379
*Georgian family home with
large airy rooms, overlooking
the valley. Central for
museums and adjacent to the
Shropshire Way footpath.*
Bedrooms: 1 single, 1 double
& 1 twin, 1 family room.
Bathrooms: 1 private,
3 public.

Continued ▶

IRONBRIDGE

Continued

Bed & breakfast: £12-£15 single, £22-£28 double.
Parking for 2.
Open February-November.

KENILWORTH

Warwickshire
Map ref 4B3

The main feature of the town is the ruined 12th C castle. It has many royal associations but was damaged by Cromwell.

Banner Hill Farmhouse

Rouncil Lane, Kenilworth, CV8 1NN
☎ (0926) 52850
*250-acre mixed farm.
Farmhouse set in Warwickshire countryside with local walks, and bicycles available. Also a 30 foot residential van with 2 bedrooms, bathroom and kitchen.*
Bedrooms: 1 double & 2 twin.
Bathrooms: 1 private,
1 public.
Bed & breakfast: £10-£15 single, £20-£25 double.
Half board: £12.50-£20 daily, £60-£75 weekly.
Lunch available.
Evening meal 6pm (l.o. 9pm).
Parking for 8.

Enderley Guest House

20 Queens Rd., Kenilworth, CV8 1JQ
☎ (0926) 55388
Family-run guesthouse, quietly situated near town centre and convenient for Warwick, Stratford-upon-Avon, Stoneleigh and Warwick University.
Bedrooms: 2 single, 3 twin.
Bathrooms: 2 public.
Bed & breakfast: £13-£16.50 single, £24-£27 double.
Parking for 2.

Honiley Boot Inn

Honiley, Kenilworth, CV8 1NP
☎ Haseley Knob
(092 687) 234

Set in its own grounds and tastefully furnished, with a fully-equipped children's play area and a la carte restaurant.
Bedrooms: 3 single, 2 double & 6 twin.
Bathrooms: 4 public.
Bed & breakfast: £15-£17.50 single, £30-£32 double.
Half board: from £25 daily.
Lunch available.
Evening meal 7pm (l.o. 11pm).
Parking for 150.
Credit: Access, Visa, Amex.

Malt House Farm ⋒

Meer End Rd., Meer End, Kenilworth, CV8 1PW
☎ Berkswell (0676) 33490
12-acre farm. 17th C. oak-beamed farmhouse with log fires, convenient for Stratford, Warwick, Coventry, Leamington and Birmingham Airport. National Exhibition Centre and National Agricultural Centre easily reached.
Bedrooms: 1 single, 1 double & 2 twin.
Bathrooms: 1 public.
Bed & breakfast: £10 single, £20 double.
Half board: £14.50 daily, £101.50 weekly.
Evening meal 7pm (l.o. 4pm).
Parking for 6.

KIDDERMINSTER

Hereford & Worcester
Map ref 4B3

The town is the centre for carpet manufacturing. It has a medieval church with good monuments and a statue of Sir Rowland Hill, a native of the town and founder of the penny post. West Midlands Safari Park is nearby.

Harvington Hall Farm

Harvington, Kidderminster, Worcestershire DY10 4LR
☎ (056 283) 216
250-acre arable farm. 16th C. farmhouse in small hamlet opposite the historic manor house, Harvington Hall. Within easy reach of motorways.
Bedrooms: 1 single, 1 double & 1 twin.
Bathrooms: 1 private,
1 public.

Bed & breakfast: £12.50-£17.50 single, £21-£30 double.
Parking for 10.

KINETON

Warwickshire
Map ref 2C1

See also Avon Dassett, Warmington.
Attractive old village in rolling countryside. 1 mile from site of famous battle of Edgehill. Medieval church of St. Peter.

Caroline and John Howard ⋒

Willowbrook House, Lighthorne Rd., Kineton, Warwick, CV35 0JL
☎ (0926) 640475
Peaceful country house in 4 acres of garden and paddocks, half a mile from Kineton village. Charming views. Sheep, hens and goats kept.
Bedrooms: 1 double & 2 twin.
Bathrooms: 2 public.
Bed & breakfast: from £9.50 single, from £19 double.
Half board: from £15 daily, from £105 weekly.
Evening meal 6.30pm (l.o. 9am).
Parking for 6.

KINGSLAND

Hereford & Worcester
Map ref 2A1

4m NW. Leominster
A monument erected in 1799 commemorates the battle of Mortimers Cross, fought near here in 1461 when Edward of York decisively defeated the Lancastrians and then marched unopposed to London to be crowned as Edward IV.

Wayside

Shirlheath, Kingsland, Leominster, Herefordshire HR6 9RJ
☎ (056 881) 547
In the countryside near Kingsland, 4 miles from Leominster and 12 from Hereford. Central for touring. Home cooking.
Bedrooms: 1 twin, 1 family room.
Bathrooms: 1 private,
1 public.
Bed & breakfast: £11-£12 single, £21-£23 double.

Half board: £17.50-£18.50 daily, £118-£125 weekly.
Evening meal 7pm (l.o. 8pm).
Parking for 2.
Open April-October.

KINGSLEY

Staffordshire
Map ref 4B2

2m N. Cheadle
A village on a hill above the Churnet Valley. The church was remodelled around 1820, but retains its 13th C. tower.

The Church Farm ⋒
Listed

Holt Lane, Kingsley, Stoke-on-Trent, ST10 2BA
☎ Cheadle (0538) 754759
165-acre dairy/beef farm. 18th C., stone farmhouse with oak beams, spiral staircase and old world charm. Five miles from Alton Towers and within easy reach of potteries, Peak District and the Churnet Valley.
Bedrooms: 2 double & 1 twin.
Bathrooms: 1 public.
Bed & breakfast: £9.50-£10 single, £17-£18 double.
Parking for 5.

KINGSTONE

Hereford & Worcester
Map ref 2A1

6m SW. Hereford
Village near the Golden Valley, Abbey Dore Church and Kilpeck Church.

Webton Court Farmhouse ⋒

Kingstone, Hereford, Herefordshire HR2 9NF
☎ Golden Valley
(0981) 250220
280-acre mixed farm. Large black and white Georgian farmhouse in a quiet and peaceful part of Herefordshire. Lunch provided upon request.
Bedrooms: 1 single, 2 double & 2 twin, 2 family rooms.
Bathrooms: 3 public.
Bed & breakfast: £8.50-£10 single, £17-£20 double.
Half board: £29-£31 daily, £196 weekly.
Lunch available.
Evening meal 7pm (l.o. 8pm).
Parking for 10.

KINGTON

Hereford & Worcester

See Lyonshall.

KNOWLE

West Midlands
Map ref 4B3

Knowle lies on the outskirts of Solihull and although there is much modern building, the centre still has some old buildings, including the medieval Chester House, which is now a library. Kenilworth Castle and Packwood House (National Trust) are nearby.

Ivy House

Warwick Rd., Heronfield, Knowle, Solihull, W. Midlands B93 0EB
☎ (056 45) 770247
Set in 6 acres of its own land overlooking fields. Approximately 5 miles from the National Exhibition Centre and airport.
Bedrooms: 1 single, 1 double & 3 twin.
Bathrooms: 5 private.
Bed & breakfast: £13-£18 single, £25-£30 double.
Parking for 20.

LAPWORTH

Warwickshire
Map ref 4B3

The village church is over 800 years old, though its Norman nave has been added to three times in different styles. Among the furnishings are an Elizabethan altar table and chair stalls made from the old rood screen.

Lapworth Lodge

Bushwood Lane, Lapworth, B94 5PJ
☎ (056 43) 3038
Large comfortable 18th C. house with spacious rooms, all with extensive views over peaceful countryside. Convenient for National Exhibition Centre, Stratford, Warwick and the Cotswolds. Vegetarians catered for.
Bedrooms: 2 double & 1 twin, 2 family rooms.
Bathrooms: 5 private.

Bed & breakfast: £23-£28 single, £28-£46 double.
Parking for 20.
Credit: Access, Visa.

Mountford Farm

Church La., Lapworth, Solihull, W. Midlands B94 5NU
☎ (056 43) 3283
28-acre poultry (wild waterfowl etc) farm. Set in rural Warwickshire, a picturesque Tudor farmhouse beside a beautiful duck pond. Comfortable and fully modernised, with heated outdoor swimming pool. Easy access to Stratford and National Exhibition Centre.
Bedrooms: 2 single, 1 double & 1 twin.
Bathrooms: 1 public; 1 private shower.
Bed & breakfast: £14-£16 single, £32-£36 double.
Parking for 4.

LEAMINGTON SPA

Warwickshire
Map ref 2C1

See also Burton Dassett, Princethorpe.
18th C spa town where tea can be taken in the 19th C Pump Room and with many fine Georgian and Regency houses. The attractive Jephson Gardens are laid out alongside the river and there is a museum and art gallery.

Agape

26 St. Mary's Rd., Leamington Spa, CV31 1JW
☎ (0926) 882896
A private house to refresh the visitor to Regency Royal Leamington Spa. Close to historic Warwick and Stratford-upon-Avon.
Bedrooms: 1 single, 1 double & 1 twin.
Bathrooms: 1 public.
Bed & breakfast: £9.50-£10.50 single, £18-£20 double.
Parking for 2.

Mrs. B. Charters

11 Eastnor Grove, Leamington Spa, CV31 1LD
☎ (0926) 25820

Spacious Victorian family house with large garden, in a quiet residential cul-de-sac near the town centre. Supper by arrangement.
Bedrooms: 1 single, 1 double.
Bathrooms: 1 private, 1 public.
Bed & breakfast: £12.50-£15 single, £25-£30 double.
Half board: £17.25-£20 daily, £115-£140 weekly.
Evening meal 6.30pm (l.o. 8.30am).
Parking for 2.

Hawthorne Lodge Guest House

Listed

20 Clarendon Avenue, Leamington Spa, CV32 4RY
☎ (0926) 28175
Victorian town house close to Leamington Royal Priors, Jephson Gardens, Royal Show grounds and National Exhibition Centre.
Bedrooms: 1 single, 1 twin, 1 family room.
Bathrooms: 2 public.
Bed & breakfast: £11-£12 single, £22-£24 double.

Hill Farm

Lewis Rd., Radford Semele, Leamington Spa, CV31 1UX
☎ (0926) 37571
350-acre mixed farm. Farmhouse set in large attractive garden, 2 miles from Leamington town centre and close to Warwick Castle and Stratford.
Bedrooms: 4 double & 2 twin.
Bathrooms: 3 private, 2 public.
Bed & breakfast: £12-£14 single, £20-£24 double.
Half board: £18-£20 daily, £126-£140 weekly.
Evening meal 6.30pm (l.o. 4pm).
Parking for 4.

Westbury House Private Hotel

47 Leam Terrace, Leamington Spa, CV31 1BQ
☎ (0926) 883756
Victorian town house completely redecorated throughout, with new carpets, furniture and double-glazing. TV and central heating in all rooms.
Bedrooms: 5 single, 4 double.
Bathrooms: 4 private, 2 public.

Bed & breakfast: £15-£18 single, £30-£35 double.
Parking for 9.

Westfield House

Weston-under-Wetherley, Leamington Spa, CV33 9BW
☎ Marton (0926) 632368
Large detached house in an acre of garden set back from the road. Each room has modern amenities and extensive views over the surrounding countryside.
Bedrooms: 2 single, 1 twin.
Bathrooms: 1 public.
Bed & breakfast: £12-£16 single, £24-£32 double.
Half board: £18-£22 daily.
Parking for 4.

LECHLADE

Gloucestershire
Map ref 2B1

Attractive village on the River Thames and a popular spot for boating. It has a number of fine Georgian houses and a 15th C church. Nearby is Kelmscott Manor with its William Morris furnishings and 18th C Buscot House (National Trust).

The Apple Tree Inn

Buscot, Faringdon, Oxfordshire SN7 8DA
☎ (0367) 52592
17th C freehouse in National Trust Village near Lechlade: beamed lounge bar, very large garden, central heating. Waitress service.
Bedrooms: 2 double & 1 twin.
Bathrooms: 1 public.
Bed & breakfast: from £25 double.
Lunch available.
Evening meal 7pm (l.o. 9pm).
Parking for 20.

THERE IS A SPECIAL SECTION IN THIS GUIDE LISTING ACCOMMODATION ESPECIALLY SUITABLE FOR GROUPS AND YOUNG PEOPLE.

LEDBURY

Hereford & Worcester
Map ref 2B1

The town has cobbled streets and many black and white timbered houses, including the 17th C Market House and old inns. Nearby is Eastnor Castle with an interesting collection of tapestries and armour. *i*

Hill Farm
Listed

Eastnor, Ledbury,
Herefordshire HR8 1JF
☎ (0531) 2827
200-acre sheep and corn farm. 400-year-old family farmhouse. Comfortable lounge with wood burner and storage heaters in all bedrooms. Woodland walks nearby and close to the Malvern Hills.
Bedrooms: 2 double & 1 twin.
Bathrooms: 1 public.
Bed & breakfast: £9.50-£10 single, £19-£20 double.
Half board: £15.50-£16 daily, £105 weekly.
Evening meal 7pm (l.o. 4pm).
Parking for 6.
⛵ 2 ※ ⌨ UL 🅿 V 🍴 TV ᴀ ♪
U ✓ ❋ 🐾 SP

White House
😊😊

Aylton, Ledbury,
Herefordshire HR8 2RQ
☎ Trumpet (053 183) 349
Beautiful 16th C. half-timbered house, all rooms beamed, set among 2 acres of well-established gardens. Opposite village church.
Bedrooms: 1 single, 1 double, 1 family room.
Bathrooms: 1 public.
Bed & breakfast: £10-£11 single, £22-£24 double.
Parking for 9.
Open April-October.
⛵ ❣ UL 🅿 🍴 TV 🎞 ᴀ ❋
🐾 🐾 🐾

Ye Olde Talbot Hotel ₼
😊😊

New Street, Ledbury,
Herefordshire HR8 2DX
☎ (0531) 2963
Formerly an old coaching house, a grade II listed, timber-framed inn built circa 1596.
Bedrooms: 1 single, 2 double & 1 twin, 3 family rooms.
Bathrooms: 3 private, 2 public.
Bed & breakfast: £16-£22 single, £26-£34 double.
Half board: £24-£30 daily.

Evening meal 7pm (l.o. 9.30pm).
Parking for 5.
Credit: Access, Visa.
⛵ ⌨ ⌨ ❣ 🅿 V 🍴 TV ᴀ
♦ 🅿 ❣ SP 🐾

LEEK

Staffordshire
Map ref 4B2

See also Flash, Onecote, Rudyard, Rushton Spencer, Warslow, Waterhouses.
Old silk and textile town, with some interesting buildings and a number of inns dating from the 17th C. Its art gallery has displays of embroidery. Brindley Mill, designed by James Brindley, has been restored as a museum. *i*

Longview House
26 Westfields Leek,
ST13 5LP
☎ (0538) 387047
Detached house, off Southbank Street, in a quiet cul-de-sac. Well appointed and comfortable. Single bed can be added to either room to make up a family room.
Bedrooms: 1 double & 1 twin.
Bathrooms: 1 public.
Bed & breakfast: £22 double.
Parking for 3.
⛵ 8 ❣ ❋ UL 🎞 🐾 🐾 🐾

The Park
Park Rd., Leek, ST13 8JS
☎ (0538) 384454
Large Victorian 3-storey house with beautiful garden adjoining the park where there is bowls, tennis, squash and swimming.
Bedrooms: 1 single, 1 double & 1 twin, 1 family room.
Bathrooms: 1 private, 2 public.
Bed & breakfast: £10 single, £20 double.
Half board: £15-£18.50 daily, £105-£130 weekly.
Lunch available.
Evening meal 7pm (l.o. midday).
Parking for 3.
❣ ⌨ UL 🅿 V ✗ TV 🎞 ᴀ
🅿 🐾 🐾 🐾

Three Horseshoes Inn ₼
😊😊

Blackshaw Moor, Leek,
ST13 8TW
☎ Blackshaw (053 834) 296
Beneath the Roaches in the Staffordshire moorlands. An ideal centre for pleasure or business and for visiting Alton Towers.
Bedrooms: 2 single, 3 double & 1 twin, 1 family room.

Bathrooms: 2 public; 6 private showers.
Bed & breakfast: £23-£25 single, £28-£30 double.
Lunch available.
Evening meal 7pm (l.o. 9.30pm).
Parking for 100.
Credit: Access, Visa, Diners, Amex.
⛵ ⌨ ⌨ ❣ 🅿 V 🍴 TV
🎞 ᴀ ❣ U 🅿 ❋ SP

LEOMINSTER

Hereford & Worcester
Map ref 2A1

See also Bodenham, Dilwyn, Docklow, Hardwick, Kingsland.
The town owed its prosperity to wool and has many interesting buildings, notably the timber-framed Grange Court, a former Town Hall. The impressive Norman priory church has 3 naves and a ducking stool. Berrington Hall (National Trust) is nearby. *i*

Copper Hall ₼
😊😊

South St., Leominster,
Herefordshire HR6 8JN
☎ (0568) 611622
Comfortable 17th C. house with spacious garden, beamed guest lounge and home cooking. Good touring centre for Wales, Wye Valley and the Malverns.
Bedrooms: 1 double & 1 twin, 1 family room.
Bathrooms: 1 public.
Bed & breakfast: £13.50-£14.50 single, £25-£30 double.
Half board: £21-£23 daily, £127-£140 weekly.
Evening meal 6pm (l.o. 6pm).
Parking for 6.
⛵ ❣ ⌨ 🅿 UL 🅿 V 🍴
ᴀ ❋ 🅿 SP

Highgate House
29 Hereford Rd., Leominster,
Herefordshire HR6 8JS
☎ (0568) 4562
Large Victorian detached house on the edge of a small market town of historic interest.
Bedrooms: 1 single, 2 double, 1 family room.
Bathrooms: 1 public.
Bed & breakfast: £8 single, £16 double.
Parking for 4.
⛵ ❣ UL 🅿 V 🍴 TV 🎞 ᴀ
✗ 🅿 ᴄᴀᴘ SP 🐾

Kimbolton Court ₼
Listed

Leominster, Herefordshire
HR6 0HH
☎ Leysters (056 887) 259
32-acre sheep/cattle farm. Stone built, 100 years old. Dining in garden room overlooking patio and lawn. Sample our own hand-made chocolates. Take A4112 (off A49) through village for one mile, turn left by school; we are a quarter mile down lane by farm buildings on right.
Bedrooms: 1 twin, 1 family room.
Bathrooms: 2 private, 1 public.
Half board: £10-£12 daily.
Evening meal 6pm (l.o. 7.30pm).
Parking for 32.
⛵ ❣ ❋ UL 🅿 V 🍴 TV 🎞
U ❋ ✗ 🅿 🐾

Park Lodge Farm
Eye, Leominster,
Herefordshire HR6 0DP
☎ (0568) 5711
200-acre mixed farm. Homely farmhouse accommodation near Leominster and Ludlow, in a delightful touring area, with many places of historic interest nearby.
Bedrooms: 1 double, 1 family room.
Bathrooms: 2 public.
Bed & breakfast: £10-£12 single, £19-£20 double.
Half board: £13.50-£14.50 daily, £95-£100 weekly.
Evening meal 6.30pm.
Parking for 8.
⛵ ❣ UL 🅿 V 🍴 TV 🎞 ✓ ❋
✗ 🅿 🐾

LEYSTERS

Hereford & Worcester
Map ref 2A1

Tiny village hidden in a remote corner of Herefordshire with ancient farms scattered in the hills about. A field path leads to Wordsworth's Stone, marking the spot which the poet used to visit when staying nearby.

The Hills Farm
Listed

Leysters, Leominster,
Herefordshire HR6 9HP
☎ (056 887) 205
120-acre arable farm. A family-run farm on high ground. A welcoming farmhouse with beamed rooms and pretty gardens.
Bedrooms: 1 double & 1 twin.

Bathrooms: 1 public.
Bed & breakfast: from £9.50
single, from £19 double.
Half board: from £16.50
daily.
Evening meal 6.30pm (l.o.
6pm).
Parking for 4.

ㅎ ☒ ♥ ⑭ Ⅴ ㅔ ⑳ ✿ ⍾

LICHFIELD

Staffordshire

See Blithbury.

LITTLE DEWCHURCH

Hereford & Worcester
Map ref 2A1

*6m SE. Hereford
Village in gently
undulating wooded
countryside to the south
of Hereford. Astonishing
gargoyles look out from
the church's 14th C
tower.*

Cwm Craig Farm ⚘⚘

Little Dewchurch, Hereford,
Herefordshire HR2 6PS
☎ Carey (043 270) 250
*180-acre arable/beef farm.
Spacious Georgian farmhouse
on edge of Wye Valley,
surrounded by superb, unspoilt
countryside. Easy access from
M50.*
Bedrooms: 1 double & 1 twin,
1 family room.
Bathrooms: 2 public.
Bed & breakfast: £10-£12
single, £18-£20 double.
Parking for 4.

ㅎ ♥ ⑭ ㅔ ⑳ Ⅲ ▫ ♣ ✿
✕ ⍾

LONG ITCHINGTON

Warwickshire
Map ref 4B3

*2m N. Southam
Attractive village, with
cottages built round a
village green, the
birthplace of St. Wulfstan,
Saxon Bishop of
Worcester at the time of
the Norman Conquest.*

The Jolly Fisherman ⍾
Banbury Rd., Long
Itchington, Rugby,
CV23 8QJ
☎ Southam (0926) 2296 & In
1989 (0926) 442296

> ### PLEASE MENTION
> ### THIS GUIDE WHEN
> ### MAKING A BOOKING.

---

*Overlooking the village pond.
On the main A432, well placed
for visiting Stratford, Warwick,
Stoneleigh, Leamington and
Rugby. Homely atmosphere.*
Bedrooms: 3 double & 2 twin,
3 family rooms.
Bathrooms: 1 public.
Bed & breakfast: from £11.50
single, from £23 double.
Lunch available.
Evening meal 7.30pm (l.o.
10pm).
Parking for 35.

ㅎ ▮ ⑭ ⑳ ▫ ▾ ♣ ⍾ Ⓓᴬᴾ

LONGDON

Hereford & Worcester
Map ref 2B1

*3m SW. Upton-upon-
Severn*

The Moat House Stud ⍾
⚘⚘
Longdon, Tewkesbury,
Gloucestershire GL20 6AT
☎ Birtsmorton (068 481) 313
Telex 337300
*8-acre stud farm. 16th C. moat
house and thoroughbred stud
farm set in own beautiful
grounds, offering comfortable
accommodation. Emphasis on
cooking. Close to the M5 and
M50.*
Bedrooms: 2 double, 1 family
room.
Bathrooms: 2 private,
1 public.
Bed & breakfast: £26-£32
double.
Half board: £22.50-£26.50
daily, £150-£185 weekly.
Evening meal 8pm (l.o. 5pm).
Parking for 8.

ㅎ ♥ ⑭ ▮ Ⅴ ⅙ ㅔ ⑳ Ⅲ
▫ ⏻ ✿ ⍾ Ⓓᴬᴾ ⓢᴾ ▥ Ⓣ

LOWER SWELL

Gloucestershire
Map ref 2B1

*1m W. Stow-on-the-Wold
Attractive village in the
Cotswolds on the River
Dikler with stone houses,
some dating from the
17th C. There is a large
house and gardens
designed by Lutyens.*

Golden Ball Inn ⍾
⚘⚘
Lower Swell, Cheltenham,
GL54 1LF
☎ Cotswold (0451) 30247
*17th C. Cotswold inn providing
accommodation and real ale.
Separate restaurant also open
Thursday, Friday and
Saturday evenings.*
Bedrooms: 1 single, 2 double.

Bathrooms: 2 public.
Bed & breakfast: £12.50-£15
single, £25-£30 double.
Half board: £22.50-£25 daily.
Lunch available.
Evening meal 7pm (l.o. 9pm).
Parking for 20.

ㅎ ♥ ▮ ⑭ Ⅴ Ⅲ ▫ ✕ ⍾

LOXLEY

Warwickshire
Map ref 2B1

*4m SE. Stratford-upon-
Avon
There is an attractive
black and white
farmhouse and some
cottages in this pleasant
village overlooking a
wooded valley, only a few
miles from Stratford-
upon-Avon and close to
Warwick and Leamington
Spa.*

Loxley Farm ⍾
⚘⚘
Loxley, Warwick, CV35 9JN
☎ Stratford-upon-Avon,
(0789) 840265
*6-acre Shetland ponies farm.
Picturesque, half-timbered
thatched farmhouse dating
from the late 13th C., set in 2
acres of garden.*
Bedrooms: 2 double, 1 family
room.
Bathrooms: 2 private,
3 public.
Bed & breakfast: £20-£22
single, £30-£33 double.
Half board: £25-£26.50 daily,
from £155 weekly.
Evening meal 7pm.
Parking for 20.
Open April-October.

ㅎ ♣ ♥ ⑭ ▮ Ⅴ ㅔ ⑳ Ⅲ
▫ ✿ ⍾ ▥

LUDLOW

Shropshire
Map ref 4A3

*See also Adforton,
Brimfield.
Outstandingly interesting
border town with a
magnificent castle high
above the River Teme, 2
half-timbered old inns and
an impressive 15th C
church. The Reader's
House should also be
seen with its three-storey
Jacobean porch. ℹ*

Church Bank ⍾
Listed
Burrington, Ludlow,
SY8 2HT
☎ Wigmore (056 886) 426

---

*Stone cottage guesthouse in
tiny village. Walking in hills
and forests, and historic places
to visit. 4-course dinner.*
Bedrooms: 1 double & 2 twin.
Bathrooms: 2 public.
Bed & breakfast: £10-£11
single, £20-£22 double.
Half board: £16-£17 daily,
£105-£112 weekly.
Evening meal 7pm.
Parking for 4.
Open April-October.

ㅎ ☒ ▮ Ⅴ ⅙ ㅔ ⑳ Ⅲ
▫ ✿ ✕ ⍾

Haynall Villa ⍾
⚘⚘
Haynall Lane, Little
Hereford, Ludlow, SY8 4BG
☎ Brimfield (058 472) 589
*72-acre dairy/mixed farm.
Victorian farmhouse in
peaceful, rural surroundings,
well placed for touring, farm or
fishing holidays. Home
cooking, families welcome.*
Bedrooms: 1 double & 1 twin,
1 family room.
Bathrooms: 2 public.
Bed & breakfast: £10-£12.50
single, £20-£25 double.
Half board: £16-£20 daily,
£105-£130 weekly.
Evening meal 6pm (l.o. 6pm).
Parking for 6.

ㅎ ⑭ ▮ Ⅴ ㅔ ⑳ Ⅲ ▫
♪ ✓ ✿ ⍾

Lower Upton Farm ⍾
⚘⚘
Little Hereford, Ludlow,
SY8 4BB
☎ Brimfield (058 472) 322
*160-acre mixed farm.
Impressive Victorian farmhouse
in peaceful countryside.
Friendly atmosphere.
Extensive range of home-
cooked meals. Ideal touring
centre.*
Bedrooms: 1 double & 1 twin,
1 family room.
Bathrooms: 1 private,
1 public.
Bed & breakfast: £9-£12
single, £18-£24 double.
Half board: £14-£17 daily,
£98-£119 weekly.
Evening meal 6.30pm (l.o.
6.30).
Parking for 4.

ㅎ ⑭ ▮ ⅙ ㅔ ⑳ Ⅲ ▫ ✕
⍾

Redroofs
Tenbury Rd., Little
Hereford, Ludlow, SY8 4AT
☎ Brimfield (058 472) 439
*In quiet rural surroundings on
the A456, near the historic
town of Ludlow. 3 inns nearby
serve home-cooked food.*
Bedrooms: 1 double, 1 family
room.

Continued ▶

LUDLOW

Continued

Bathrooms: 1 public.
Bed & breakfast: £18-£20
double.
Half board: £14-£15 daily.
Parking for 5.

LYDBROOK

Gloucestershire
Map ref 2A1

Lower Lydbrook is on the
banks of the Wye, Upper
Lydbrook is above it, on
the road leading into the
Forest of Dean. There is
much in the area to
interest the industrial
archaeologist.

Viaduct House **M**

Lower Lydbrook, Lydbrook,
GL17 9NT
☎ Dean (0594) 60550
*Georgian family home by the
River Wye in an area of
outstanding natural beauty. 2
local inns for meals and
snacks. Bus services. Central
for Ross-on-Wye, Monmouth,
Symonds Yat and Forest of
Dean. Beside junction of
B4228 and B4234.*
Bedrooms: 1 double, 1 family
room.
Bathrooms: 2 private.
Bed & breakfast: £10-£20
single, £20-£40 double.

LYDNEY

Gloucestershire
Map ref 2B1

Small town in the Forest
of Dean close to the River
Severn where Roman
remains have been found.
It has a steam centre with
engines, coaches and
wagons.

Lower Viney Farm Guesthouse **M**

Viney Hill, Lydney,
GL15 4LT
☎ Dean (0594) 510218
*Detached period farmhouse set
in delightful gardens of
approximately half an acre.
Lovely rural setting with
extensive views of surrounding
countryside.*
Bedrooms: 3 twin.
Bathrooms: 1 private,
1 public.

Bed & breakfast: £9.50-
£12.50 single, £17-£22.50
double.
Half board: £15-£19 daily,
£75-£100 weekly.
Evening meal 7pm (l.o. 9pm).
Parking for 4.
Credit: Access, Visa, Amex.

LYONSHALL

Hereford & Worcester
Map ref 2A1

3m E. Kington
Village close to the Welsh
border. Hergest Croft
Gardens with their
beautiful displays of
rhododendrons and
azaleas in May and June
are nearby.

Church House **M**

Lyonshall, Kington,
Herefordshire HR5 3HR
☎ (054 48) 350
*Georgian country house in 4.5
acres of garden/paddocks at
junction of A44/A480.
Edwardian style teas and craft
products available.*
Bedrooms: 1 double & 1 twin,
1 family room.
Bathrooms: 1 private,
1 public.
Bed & breakfast: £23-£27
double.
Half board: £17.50-£19.50
daily, £108.50-£122.50
weekly.
Evening meal 6pm (l.o.
8.30pm).
Parking for 10.

MALVERN

Hereford & Worcester
Map ref 2B1

*See also Ledbury,
Suckley.*
Spa town in Victorian
times, its water is today
bottled and sold
worldwide. Six resorts,
set on the slopes of the
Hills, form part of Malvern
and Great Malvern Priory
has splendid 15th C
windows. It is an
excellent walking centre
with fine views from the
Worcestershire
Beacon. **i**

Clarendon House

77 Cowleigh Rd., Malvern,
Worcestershire WR14 1QL
☎ (068 45) 69562

*An Edwardian home on the
Malvern Hills, offering good
food and a warm and friendly
welcome. Magnificent views.
Off the B4219.*
Bedrooms: 1 double & 1 twin,
1 family room.
Bathrooms: 1 public.
Bed & breakfast: £12 single,
£20 double.
Half board: £16-£18 daily,
£98-£114 weekly.
Evening meal 6.30pm (l.o.
6.30pm).
Parking for 5.

Clevelands

41 Alexandria Rd., Malvern,
Worcestershire WR14 1HE
☎ (068 45) 2164
*Pleasant Edwardian house in
quiet area with many mature
trees, adjacent to the Elgar
Route.*
Bedrooms: 1 single, 1 twin.
Bathrooms: 1 private,
1 public.
Bed & breakfast: £8-£10
single, £20-£22 double.
Parking for 2.

Cowleigh Park Farm **M**
Listed

Cowleigh Rd., Malvern,
Worcestershire WR13 5HJ
☎ (068 45) 66750
*2.5-acre mixed, horticultural
farm. Beautifully restored,
grade II listed 17th C.
timbered farmhouse, in a
tranquil setting at the foot of
the Malvern Hills.*
Bedrooms: 1 double & 2 twin.
Bathrooms: 1 public.
Bed & breakfast: £17-£18
single, £22-£26 double.
Half board: £18.50-£25.50
daily, £129.50-£178.50
weekly.
Evening meal 6.30pm (l.o.
midday).
Parking for 6.

Deacon's

34 Worcester Rd., Malvern,
Worcestershire WR14 4AA
☎ (068 45) 66990 & 5323
*Attractive Georgian building in
the heart of Great Malvern,
with easy access to shops,
railway station and the
Malvern Hills.*
Bedrooms: 2 single, 3 double
& 2 twin, 2 family rooms.
Bathrooms: 6 private,
1 public.
Bed & breakfast: £20-£25
single, £30-£35 double.
Half board: £28-£32 daily.

Evening meal 7pm (l.o. 9pm).
Parking for 10.
Credit: Access, Visa, Amex.

Elm Bank **M**

52 Worcester Rd., Malvern,
Worcestershire WR14 4AB
☎ (068 45) 66051
*Elegant late-Regency house
with quiet bedrooms, enjoying
breathtaking views. 5 minutes'
walk from town centre.*
Bedrooms: 3 double & 2 twin,
1 family room.
Bathrooms: 4 private,
1 public.
Bed & breakfast: £18-£22
single, £30-£36 double.
Half board: £23-£30 daily.
Evening meal 7pm (l.o. 7pm).
Parking for 6.

Mellbreak

177 Wells Rd., Malvern
Wells, Malvern,
Worcestershire WR14 4HE
☎ (068 45) 61287
*Near the intersection A449
with B4209 and the Three
Counties Showground. Views
over the Severn and Avon
Valleys and Malvern Hills.*
Bedrooms: 1 single, 1 double
& 1 twin, 1 family room.
Bathrooms: 1 public;
3 private showers.
Bed & breakfast: £10-£11
single, £22 double.
Half board: £17.50-£18.50
daily, £109 weekly.
Lunch available.
Evening meal 6pm (l.o. 9pm).
Parking for 4.

Priory Holme **M**

18 Avenue Rd., Malvern,
Worcestershire WR14 3AR
☎ (068 45) 68455
*Elegantly furnished large
Victorian house in a tree-lined
avenue. Well situated for all
local amenities.*
Bedrooms: 1 single, 1 double
& 1 twin, 1 family room.
Bathrooms: 1 private,
2 public.
Bed & breakfast: max. £12
single, max. £24 double.
Half board: max. £19 daily,
max. £133 weekly.
Evening meal 7pm (l.o. 8pm).
Parking for 5.

Rock House ♠
⚅⚅

144 West Malvern Rd.,
Malvern, Worcestershire
WR14 4NJ
☎ Malvern (068 45) 4536
*Late Georgian house on
Malvern Hills with large
garden and varied views.
Ideal for rambling and touring.*
Bedrooms: 5 double & 3 twin,
2 family rooms.
Bathrooms: 1 private,
3 public.
Bed & breakfast: £22.50
double.
Half board: £18.25 daily,
£118 weekly.
Evening meal 6.30pm.
Parking for 10.
Open January-November.
⚅3 🅿 ☒ ⚓ ⊟ 📺 ▥ ⏣ ✷
☒ ⅅ⅍ SP

Sidney House ♠
⚅⚅⚅

40 Worcester Rd., Malvern,
Worcestershire WR14 4AA
☎ (068 45) 4994
*Small, attractive Georgian
hotel with personal and
friendly service. Magnificent
views over the Worcestershire
countryside. Close to town
centre and hills.*
Bedrooms: 1 single, 3 double
& 2 twin, 1 family room.
Bathrooms: 3 private,
1 public.
Bed & breakfast: £13-£19
single, £26-£32 double.
Half board: £21.25-£27.25
daily, £124-£164 weekly.
Evening meal 6.30pm (l.o.
2pm).
Parking for 8.
Credit: Access, Visa, Diners,
Amex.
⚅ 🅿 ⚓ 🎇 ☒ 📺 ▥
▤ ⏣ ☒ ✵ SP ▥ ⒯

Swan Inn
Listed

Worcester Road, Newland,
Malvern, Worcestershire
WR13 5AY
☎ Leigh Sinton (0886) 32224
*A country inn decorated to
maintain a traditional theme.
Located a few minutes outside
Malvern Link on the
Worcester road.*
Bedrooms: 2 twin.
Bathrooms: 1 public.
Bed & breakfast: £14 single,
£28 double.
Half board: £17.50-£24.75
daily, £120-£170 weekly.
Lunch available.
Evening meal 7pm (l.o.
9.30pm).
Parking for 25.
🎇 🅿 ⚓ 🎇 ☒ ▥ ⏣ ✷
▥

Thornbank
Listed

179 Wells Rd., Malvern
Wells, Malvern,
Worcestershire WR14 4HE
☎ (068 45) 68743
*Large 100-year-old house on
the Malvern Hills with
magnificent views of the
Worcestershire countryside.*
Bedrooms: 2 double & 3 twin,
2 family rooms.
Bathrooms: 2 public.
Bed & breakfast: £9 single,
£18 double.
Half board: £13.50 daily,
£94.50 weekly.
Evening meal 6pm (l.o. 7pm).
Parking for 6.
⚅ 🎇 ⚓ ☒ 🅿 ⏣ 📺 ▥ ▤
✵ ▥ ▥

West Villa ♠
⚅⚅

196 West Malvern Rd.,
Malvern, Worcestershire
WR14 4AZ
☎ (068 45) 61192
*Victorian house on western
slopes of Malvern Hills, with
uninterrupted views due west.
Within easy reach of hills for
walking.*
Bedrooms: 1 double & 1 twin,
1 family room.
Bathrooms: 1 public.
Bed & breakfast: max. £12.50
single, max. £25 double.
Half board: max. £17.50
daily, max. £100 weekly.
Evening meal 6pm (l.o. 8pm).
Parking for 5.
⚅ 🅿 ☒ 🅿 ☒ 📺 ▤ ▥
ⅅ⅍ SP

Village on the banks of
the Lugg with a large
spacious church with an
underfloor well,
supposedly marking the
site where King Ethelbert
of East Anglia was laid
after his murder nearby.

Vauld Farm ♠
The Vauld, Marden,
Hereford, Herefordshire
HR1 3HA
☎ Bodenham (056 884) 898
*16th C. black and white
farmhouse, 7.5 miles north east
of Hereford. Self-catering flat
also available.*
Bedrooms: 1 double & 1 twin,
1 family room.
Bathrooms: 3 private.
Bed & breakfast: £15 single,
£30 double.
Half board: £23.50 daily,
£164.50 weekly.

Evening meal 7pm (l.o.
4.30pm).
Parking for 22.
⚅5 🎇 🅿 ☒ ⚓ ☒ 🅿 ☒ 🅿
📺 ▥ ▤ ⚓ ✷ ▥ 🗲 ▥

Old market town with
black and white buildings
and 17th C houses.
Hodnet Hall is in the
vicinity with its beautiful
landscaped gardens
covering 60 acres.

Aston Farm
Listed

Aston, Pipe Gate, Market
Drayton, TF9 4JF
☎ Pipe Gate (063 081) 296
*88-acre dairy farm.
Comfortable farmhouse in a
peaceful country village on the
Shropshire and Staffordshire
borders. Home cooking and a
quiet atmosphere. Dinner
available if booked in advance.*
Bedrooms: 1 double, 1 family
room.
Bathrooms: 1 public.
Bed & breakfast: £8.50-
£10.50 single, £17-£21 double.
Parking for 4.
Open January-November.
⚅ 🎇 🅿 ☒ 🅿 ☒ 🅿 📺 ▥ ▤
🗲 ✷ ▥

Larksfield
Listed

Stoniford Lane, Aston,
Pipegate, Market Drayton,
TF9 4JB
☎ Pipegate (063 081) 7069
*30-acre arable farm. Modern
country farmhouse with
purpose-built, separate
accommodation, in attractive
Shropshire countryside. Own
shooting ground and small
trout pool.*
Bedrooms: 1 single, 1 double
& 1 twin, 2 family rooms.
Bathrooms: 2 private,
1 public.
Bed & breakfast: £12-£15
single, £24-£30 double.
Parking for 8.
Credit: Access, Visa.
⚅ 🎇 🅿 ⚓ ☒ 🅿 ☒ ▤ ▥
⚓ 🗲 🅿 🗲 ✷ ▥ ▥

5m N. Southam
Bright little village on the
road from Banbury to
Coventry, with an ancient
stone bridge across the
River Leam.

Marton Fields Farm ♠
⚅⚅

Marton, Rugby, CV23 9RS
☎ (0926) 632410
*240-acre mixed farm. 1 mile
off the A423 in Marton village.
Lovely scenery, friendly
welcome and home cooking.*
Bedrooms: 2 single, 2 double
& 2 twin.
Bathrooms: 2 public.
Bed & breakfast: £12-£14
single, £24-£26 double.
Half board: £19-£21 daily.
Evening meal 6.30pm (l.o.
8pm).
Parking for 10.
⚓ ⚓ ☒ 🅿 ☒ 📺 ▥
⚓ 🗲 ▸ 🗲 ✷ ▥ 🗲 SP

Village halfway between
Coventry and Birmingham
said to be the centre of
England, marked by a
cross on the green.

Woodlands Guest
House ♠
⚅⚅

Back La., Meriden,
Coventry, W. Midlands
CV7 7LD
☎ (0676) 22317
*12-acre farm. Oak-beamed,
comfortable house in old
Warwickshire countryside.
Ideal for touring Kenilworth,
Warwick and Stratford-upon-
Avon. Central for theatre,
concert and sports facilities.
Accessible to major road
network, airport, rail and the
National Exhibition Centre.*
Bedrooms: 1 double & 2 twin.
Bathrooms: 2 private,
1 public.
Bed & breakfast: £12-£18
single, £24-£28 double.
Half board: £15-£21 daily.
Evening meal 6pm.
Parking for 10.
⚅5 🎇 ▤ ☒ ▥ 🅿 📺 ▥ ▤
✵ 🗲 ▥

```
THERE IS A SPECIAL SECTION IN THIS
GUIDE LISTING ACCOMMODATION ESPECIALLY
SUITABLE FOR GROUPS AND YOUNG PEOPLE.
```

MICHAELCHURCH ESCLEY

Hereford & Worcester
Map ref 2A1

8m SE. Hay-on-Wye
Inside the village church,
entered by a 300 year old
door, is a large wall
painting of " Christ of the
Trades", a rare subject of
ecclesiastical art.

The Gables M

Listed

Michaelchurch Escley,
Hereford, Herefordshire
HR2 OJS
☎ Michaelchurch
(098 123) 287
*Stone-built family home
offering comfortable and
friendly accommodation. From
Hereford, follow directions to
Hay, left in Vowchurch:
Gables 4 miles.*
Bedrooms: 1 double.
Bathrooms: 1 public.
Bed & breakfast: £18 double.
Half board: £14 daily, £80
weekly.
Evening meal 7pm (l.o. 6pm).
Parking for 9.
🛇 🗆 🕏 🗓 🗺 🏢 ✕ 🏠

MIDDLETON PRIORS

Shropshire
Map ref 4A3

6m S. Much Wenlock
Hamlet of farms and a
few cottages remotely
situated in hilly
countryside near
Bridgnorth and the Clee
Hills.

Middleton Lodge

⛔

Middleton Priors,
Bridgnorth, WV16 6UR
☎ Ditton Priors
(074 634) 228 or 675
*30-acre mixed farm. Imposing
stone building in its own
grounds, in a quiet hamlet in
the Shropshire hills.*
Bedrooms: 2 double & 1 twin.
Bathrooms: 3 private.
Bed & breakfast: £12.50-£15
single, £25-£30 double.
Parking for 4.
🛇2 🗇 🕏 🗓 🗺 🗓 🖩 🏠 ✻
✕ 🏠

```
MAP REFERENCES
APPLY TO THE
COLOUR MAPS
TOWARDS THE END
OF THIS GUIDE.
```

MINCHINHAMPTON

Gloucestershire
Map ref 2B1

4m SE. Stroud
A stone-built town, with
many 17th/18th C.
buildings, owing its
existence to the wool and
cloth trades. A 17th C.
pillared market house
may be found in the town
square, near which is the
Norman and 14th C.
church.

Forwood West

⛔

Well Hill, Minchinhampton,
Stroud, GL6 9AB
☎ Brimscombe
(0453) 885478
*Major part of an 18th C.
Cotswold house on outskirts of
Minchinhampton, with fine
views over Gatcombe.
Directions: quarter of a mile
from centre of village towards
Nailsworth.*
Bedrooms: 1 double & 1 twin.
Bathrooms: 1 public.
Bed & breakfast: £12-£14
single, £24-£28 double.
Parking for 6.
🛇 🗓 🗺 🖩 🏠 🅿 🏢 🅳🅰🅿

MINSTERLEY

Shropshire
Map ref 4A3

9m SW. Shrewsbury
Village with a curious little
church of 1692 and a fine
old black and white hall.
The lofty ridge known as
the Stiperstones is 4
miles to the south.

The Old Post Office

⛔

Bent Lawnt, Minsterley,
Shrewsbury, SY5 0ES
☎ Worthen (074 383) 607
*Old stone, beamed country
cottage with beautiful garden
and panoramic views. On the
A488, 11 miles south of
Shrewsbury.*
Bedrooms: 1 twin.
Bathrooms: 1 private.
Bed & breakfast: max. £27
double.
Half board: max. £19.50
daily, max. £120 weekly.
Lunch available.
Evening meal 7pm (l.o. 8pm).
Parking for 1.
Open April-October.
🛇 🗓 🖩 🕏 🗓 🔋 ✕ 🗺 🏠 🗓
🖩 🏠 🔱 ✕ 🏠

The Stiperstones Inn

The Stiperstones, Minsterley,
Shrewsbury, SY5 0LZ
☎ (0743) 791327
*Old world inn situated in
Shropshire's loveliest hill
country.*
Bedrooms: 1 single, 3 double,
1 family room.
Bathrooms: 2 public.
Bed & breakfast: £9 single,
£18 double.
Half board: £13 daily, £78
weekly.
Lunch available.
Evening meal 6pm (l.o.
10pm).
Parking for 31.
🛇 🗇 🗇 🕏 🔋 🗓 ✕ 🗺 🏠
🍴 ✻ 🏠 🏢

MITCHELDEAN

Gloucestershire
Map ref 2B1

Village at the
northernmost tip of the
Forest of Dean. The ruins
of Goodrich Castle can be
easily reached.

Abenhall House M

Abenhall Rd., Mitcheldean,
GL17 0DT
☎ Dean (0594) 544201
*Period house on the edge of the
village and the Forest of Dean.
Central for walking and
touring in the Wye Valley and
Malverns. Ground floor
bedroom available. Evening
meal by arrangement.*
Bedrooms: 2 double & 2 twin,
1 family room.
Bathrooms: 1 public.
Bed & breakfast: from £9.50
single, from £19 double.
Parking for 6.
🛇 🗓 🕏 🗓 🔋 🗓 🏠 🗺 🏠 🅳🅰🅿

MORETON-IN-MARSH

Gloucestershire
Map ref 2B1

Attractive town of
Cotswold stone with 17th
C houses, an ideal base
for touring the Cotswolds.
Some of the local
attractions include
Batsford Park Arboretum,
the Jacobean Chastleton
House and Sezincote
Garden. 🛈

Blue Cedar House

⛔

Stow Rd., Moreton-in-Marsh,
GL56 0DW
☎ (0608) 50299
*Pleasantly situated in its own
grounds adjacent to the main
Fosseway, 300 yards from the
shops and village centre.*

Bedrooms: 2 double & 1 twin,
1 family room.
Bathrooms: 2 public;
2 private showers.
Bed & breakfast: from £14.50
single, £20-£24 double.
Half board: £30-£34 daily,
£210-£238 weekly.
Evening meal 6pm (l.o. 6pm).
Parking for 7.
Open February-November.
🛇 🕏 🗓 🔋 🗓 🗺 🖩 🏠 🅰 🔱
✕ 🏠

The Cottage M

Oxford St., Moreton-in-
Marsh, GL56 0LA
☎ (0608) 50370
*Interesting, fully modernised,
17th C. cottage, just off the
A429 and A44.*
Bedrooms: 1 double & 1 twin.
Bathrooms: 1 public.
Bed & breakfast: £20-£24
double.
Parking for 3.
🛇7 🗓 🕻 🗓 🕏 🗓 🗓 🗺
🗓 🗓 🏠 ✕ 🏠 🗓 🅂🅿

Dorn Priory

Dorn, Moreton-in-Marsh
☎ (0608) 50152
*10-acre horses farm. 17th C.
Cotswold house in peaceful
surroundings. Set in a small
hamlet on edge of Cotswolds,
within easy reach of Stratford
and Oxford.*
Bedrooms: 2 twin, 1 family
room.
Bathrooms: 1 public.
Bed & breakfast: £10 single,
£20 double.
Parking for 10.
Open May-September.
🛇 🗓 🗓 🗓 🖩 🏠 ✻ 🏢 🏠

Farriers Arms

Todenham, Moreton-in-
Marsh, GL56 9PF
☎ (0608) 50901
*Cotswold village inn, 3.5 miles
from Moreton in Marsh, 4
miles from Shipston on Stour,
within easy reach of Oxford,
Stratford and Cheltenham.*
Bedrooms: 2 single, 3 double,
1 family room.
Bathrooms: 2 public.
Bed & breakfast: £10-£13
single, £25-£28 double.
Half board: £16-£19 daily,
£98-£105 weekly.
Evening meal 7pm (l.o.
10pm).
Parking for 30.
🛇 🗓 🗓 🕏 🗓 🗺 🗓 🏠
🏢 🅳🅰🅿 🅂🅿 🏢 🏠

Home Farm

Draycott, Moreton-in-Marsh,
GL56 9LQ
☎ Evesham (0386) 700380

160-acre arable/sheep farm. Attractive old Cotswold farmhouse in quiet village, well placed for touring the Cotswolds and Shakespeare country.
Bedrooms: 1 double & 1 twin.
Bathrooms: 2 public.
Bed & breakfast: £10.50-£11 single, £21-£22 double.
Parking for 10.
Open April-October.

Lines Farm

Chastleton Rd., Little Compton, Moreton-in-Marsh, GL56 OSL
☎ Barton on the Heath (060 874) 343
27-acre stock farm. Detached Cotswold stone house with good facilities and beautiful views. Easily accessible from A44 between Chipping Norton and Moreton-in-Marsh.
Bedrooms: 1 double, 2 family rooms.
Bathrooms: 1 private, 1 public.
Bed & breakfast: from £10 single, £22-£25 double.
Parking for 10.

New Farm ⋔

Dorn, Moreton-in-Marsh, GL56 9NS
☎ (0608) 50782
250-acre dairy farm. Old Cotswold farmhouse in quiet hamlet of Dorn. Full English breakfast with hot, crispy bread. Dining room has large impressive Cotswolds stone fireplace. Ideal for touring Cotswolds.
Bedrooms: 1 double & 1 twin, 1 family room.
Bathrooms: 1 private, 1 public.
Bed & breakfast: £12-£15 single, £20-£22 double.
Parking for 10.
Open April-October.

Treetops ⋔
Listed

London Road, Moreton-in-Marsh, GL56 0HE
☎ (0608) 51036
Family guesthouse on the A44, set in half an acre of secluded gardens. 5 minutes' walk from the village centre.
Bedrooms: 2 double & 1 twin.
Bathrooms: 1 public.
Bed & breakfast: £12 single, £18-£20 double.
Parking for 6.

MUCH BIRCH

Hereford & Worcester
Map ref 2A1

6m S. Hereford Village on the road between Ross-on-Wye and Hereford with splendid views towards the Black Mountains.

Old School House ⋔

Much Birch, Hereford, Herefordshire HR2 8HJ
☎ Golden Valley (0981) 540006
Interesting Victorian school on A49 Hereford-Ross road.
Bedrooms: 1 double & 1 twin, 1 family room.
Bathrooms: 2 public.
Bed & breakfast: £10-£12 single, £18-£20 double.
Half board: £15.50-£17.50 daily, £100-£112 weekly.
Evening meal 6pm (l.o. 8pm).
Parking for 15.

MUCH WENLOCK

Shropshire

See Buildwas, Middleton Priors.

MUNSLOW

Shropshire
Map ref 4A3

7m NE. Craven Arms Village on the B4368 between Craven Arms and Much Wenlock whose main charm lies in the ancient church and attractive lawned rectory.

Chadstone

Aston Munslow, Craven Arms, SY7 9ER
☎ (058 476) 675
Spacious new bungalow, with modern facilities and superb views of the renowned Corve Dale. On the B4368 Bridgnorth to Craven Arms road.
Bedrooms: 1 single, 2 double.
Bathrooms: 1 public.
Bed & breakfast: £18 single, £29 double.
Parking for 6.
Open April-October.

PLEASE MENTION THIS GUIDE WHEN MAKING A BOOKING.

MYDDLE

Shropshire
Map ref 4A3

Oakfields

Myddle, Shrewsbury, SY4 3RX
☎ Bromere Heath (0939) 290823
Large bungalow in pleasant surroundings, with a happy, friendly atmosphere. 8 miles from Shrewsbury and 20 minutes from Hawkstone Park.
Bedrooms: 1 double & 1 twin, 1 family room.
Bathrooms: 2 public.
Bed & breakfast: £9 single, £17 double.
Parking for 10.

NAILSWORTH

Gloucestershire
Map ref 2B1

See also Nympsfield. Ancient wool town with several elegant Jacobean and Georgian houses, surrounded by wooded hillsides with fine views.

Barley Hill ⋔

Watledge, Nailsworth, Stroud, GL6 0AS
☎ (045 383) 2619
Spacious country house in elevated position with superb views. Large garden backing on to National Trust woods and Minchinhampton Common.
Bedrooms: 2 double & 1 twin.
Bathrooms: 2 public.
Bed & breakfast: £12 single, £22 double.
Half board: £17.50-£20 daily, £110-£125 weekly.
Evening meal 7pm (l.o. 9pm).
Parking for 3.

Heatherville ⋔
Listed

9 Bath Rd., Nailsworth, Stroud, GL6 0JB
☎ (045 383) 4590
Family home offering comfortable accommodation close to the centre of Nailsworth, with riding, gliding and golf nearby. Excellent touring base for Cotswolds.
Bedrooms: 1 double & 2 twin.
Bathrooms: 1 public.
Bed & breakfast: from £20 double.

Orchard Close ⋔

Springhill, Nailsworth, Stroud, GL6 0LX
☎ (045 383) 2503
Large house in secluded garden with lovely views and spacious, well-furnished rooms. Interesting south Cotswold village.
Bedrooms: 1 double & 2 twin.
Bathrooms: 3 private.
Bed & breakfast: £13-£15.50 single, £20-£25 double.
Half board: £16-£18.50 daily, £105-£129.50 weekly.
Parking for 3.
Credit: Access.

NAUNTON

Gloucestershire
Map ref 2B1

A high place on the Windrush, renowned for its wild flowers and with an attractive dovecote.

Eastern Hill Farm ⋔

Naunton, Cheltenham, GL54 3AF
☎ Guiting Power (045 15) 716
150-acre mixed farm. Recently constructed, traditional style Cotswolds farmhouse. Within walking distance of Bourton-on-the-Water and the Slaughters.
Bedrooms: 2 double & 1 twin.
Bathrooms: 3 public.
Bed & breakfast: £20-£22 double.
Parking for 6.
Open April-October.

NEWNHAM

Gloucestershire
Map ref 2B1

Small town on the Severn estuary near the Forest of Dean. It has some 18th C houses and fine views of the Severn.

Upper Hall

Elton, Newnham, GL14 1JJ
☎ Westbury-on-Severn (045 276) 243
17th C. stone-built country house set in large garden on the edge of Royal Forest of Dean. From A48 Cirencester to Chepstow Road, take A4151 to Cinderford and first right to Elton Lane.
Bedrooms: 1 double & 2 twin.
Bathrooms: 3 private.

Continued ▶

NEWNHAM

Continued

Bed & breakfast: £17 single, £28 double.
Parking for 10.

NEWPORT

Shropshire
Map ref 4A3

Small market town on the Shropshire Union Canal, it has a wide high street and its church has some interesting monuments. It is close to Aqualate Mere which is the largest lake in Staffordshire.

Bridge Inn
Listed
Chetwynd End, Newport, TF10 7JB
☎ (0952) 811785
Small, family-run establishment, serving a wide range of home-cooked food. Parts of the building date from 1664.
Bedrooms: 2 single, 1 twin, 2 family rooms.
Bathrooms: 1 public; 2 private showers.
Bed & breakfast: £13.50-£15 single, £27-£30 double.
Lunch available.
Evening meal 7pm (l.o. 10pm).
Parking for 40.
Credit: Visa, C.Bl., Amex.

Sambrook Manor
Listed
Sambrook, Newport, TF10 8AL
☎ Sambrook (095 279) 256
260-acre mixed farm. Old manor farmhouse built in 1702. Close to Stoke potteries, Shrewsbury, Ironbridge, Wolverhampton and many places of historic interest.
Bedrooms: 2 double, 1 family room.
Bathrooms: 1 private, 2 public.
Bed & breakfast: £10 single, £20 double.
Half board: £70 weekly.
Parking for 10.

NORBURY

Staffordshire
Map ref 4B3

4m NE. Newport

Oulton House Farm M
Norbury, Stafford, ST20 0PG
☎ Woodseaves (078 574) 264
230-acre mixed farm. Charming Victorian farmhouse, offering comfortable accommodation, with 4 poster-bed and en-suite facilities. Convenient for Ironbridge, Telford and Potteries. Newport 3 miles.
Bedrooms: 1 single, 1 double & 1 twin.
Bathrooms: 1 private, 1 public.
Bed & breakfast: £10.50-£14 single, £21-£28 double.
Half board: £15.50-£19 daily, £100-£128 weekly.
Lunch available.
Evening meal 6pm (l.o. 9pm).
Parking for 6.

NORTH CERNEY

Gloucestershire
Map ref 2B1

Beautiful village on the little River Churn, with a notable church and Queen Anne rectory.

Bathurst Arms
North Cerney, Cirencester, GL7 7BZ
☎ (028 583) 281
17th C. country inn. Riverside gardens with barbecue in summer, 3 bars with open log fires in the winter. Set back from the Cirencester to Cheltenham road.
Bedrooms: 2 single, 2 double & 2 twin.
Bathrooms: 6 private.
Bed & breakfast: £25 single, £30-£40 double.
Half board: £30-£35 daily, £150-£175 weekly.
Evening meal 7pm (l.o. 10pm).
Parking for 60.
Credit: Visa, Amex.

NORTH NIBLEY

Gloucestershire
Map ref 2B1

2m SW. Dursley
Pleasant little village near Dursley dominated by the Tyndale Monument, a tapering stone tower erected in 1966 in memory of the translator of the New Testament.

The Old Vicarage M
North Nibley, Dursley, GL11 6DJ
☎ Dursley (0453) 47743
A large house with extensive views, set in a small village on the Cotswold Way. All bedrooms will take 2 children's beds.
Bedrooms: 3 twin.
Bathrooms: 3 private.
Bed & breakfast: from £12 single, from £20 double.
Parking for 3.
Open April-October.

NORTHLEACH

Gloucestershire
Map ref 2B1

See also Aldsworth, Shipton.
Village famous for its beautiful 15th C wool church with its lovely porch and interesting interior. There are also some fine houses including 16th C almshouses, a 17th C manor house and a collection of agricultural instruments in the former prison.

Cotteswold House M
Listed
Market Pl., Northleach, Cheltenham, GL54 3EG
☎ Cotswold (0451) 60493
A traditional Cotswold stone house with many interesting architectural features.
Bedrooms: 1 double & 2 twin, 1 family room.
Bathrooms: 3 public.
Bed & breakfast: £13-£17 single, £26-£28 double.

Market House
The Square, Northleach, Cheltenham, GL54 3EJ
☎ Cotswold (0451) 60557
16th C. Cotswold house with exposed beams and inglenook fireplace. In the Cotswolds, close to all holiday routes.
Bedrooms: 2 double & 1 twin.
Bathrooms: 1 public.
Bed & breakfast: £14-£16 single, £24-£28 double.
Lunch available.
Parking for 4.

NYMPSFIELD

Gloucestershire
Map ref 2B1

3m W. Nailsworth
Pretty village, high up in the Cotswolds, with a simple mid-Victorian church, and a prehistoric long barrow nearby.

Rose and Crown Inn M
Listed
Nympsfield, Stonehouse, GL10 3TU
☎ Dursley (0453) 860240
300-year-old inn in extremely quiet Cotswold village, close to Cotswold Way and Nympsfield Gliding Club. Easy access to M4/M5.
Bedrooms: 1 twin, 2 family rooms.
Bathrooms: 1 private, 1 public.
Bed & breakfast: £18 single, £24 double.
Half board: £20-£25 daily, £125-£150 weekly.
Lunch available.
Evening meal 6.30pm (l.o. 10pm).
Parking for 30.
Credit: Access, Visa.

PLEASE CHECK PRICES AND OTHER DETAILS AT THE TIME OF BOOKING.

GROUPS, CONSORTIA AND AGENCIES SPECIALISING IN FARM AND COUNTRY HOLIDAYS ARE LISTED IN A SPECIAL SECTION OF THIS GUIDE.

OAKAMOOR

Staffordshire
Map ref 4B2

3m E. Cheadle
Small village below a steep hill amid the glorious scenery of the Churnet Valley. Its industrial links have now gone, as the site of the factory which made 20,000 miles of copper wire for the first Atlantic cable has been transformed into an attractive picnic site on the riverside.

The Admiral Jervis Inn and Restaurant M

Mill Rd., Oakamoor, Stoke-on-Trent, ST10 3AG
☎ (0538) 702187
Old riverside restaurant and inn with chef-proprietor. Peaceful and picturesque setting. 2 miles from Alton Towers and 9 miles from the Potteries.
Bedrooms: 1 double & 1 twin, 4 family rooms.
Bathrooms: 6 private.
Bed & breakfast: £18.50-£20 single, £30-£33 double.
Lunch available.
Evening meal 7.30pm (l.o. 9.30pm).
Parking for 10.
Credit: Access, Visa, Diners, Amex.

ODDINGTON

Gloucestershire
Map ref 2B1

3m E. Stow-on-the-Wold
Cotswolds village with a beautiful church in an attractive setting, some way from the village. It is near Chastleton House, a Jacobean manor.

Banks Farm M
Listed

Upper Oddington, Moreton-in-Marsh, GL56 0XG
☎ Cotswold (0451) 30475
280-acre mixed farm. Cotswold stone farmhouse overlooking fields to 11th C. church, 3 miles from Stow-on-the-Wold. Central for touring the Cotswolds. Evening meal by arrangement only.
Bedrooms: 1 double & 1 twin.
Bathrooms: 1 public.

Bed & breakfast: £21-£24 double.
Parking for 2.
Open March-November.

Bramley House

Upper Oddington, Moreton-in-Marsh, GL56 0XH
☎ Cotswold (0451) 30403
Detached cottage in delightful Cotswold village. Homely atmosphere, personal service, separate dining and sitting rooms.
Bedrooms: 1 single, 1 double, 1 family room.
Bathrooms: 1 private, 1 public.
Bed & breakfast: £11-£12 single, £21-£23 double.
Parking for 3.

Horse and Groom Inn M

Upper Oddington, Moreton-in-Marsh, GL56 0XH
☎ Cotswold (0451) 30584
16th C old world character inn serving lunchtime and evening meals all year round. Families welcome.
Bedrooms: 4 double & 2 twin, 1 family room.
Bathrooms: 7 private.
Bed & breakfast: £22-£24 single, £34-£38 double.
Half board: £160-£180 weekly.
Lunch available.
Evening meal 7pm (l.o. 10pm).
Parking for 40.

Manor House M
Listed

Lower Oddington, Moreton in Marsh, GL56 0XA
☎ Cotswold (0451) 31316
Early 17th C. Cotswold stone manor house in Lower Oddington. Off the A436, 50 yards from the war memorial and opposite the church. No smoking allowed in house.
Bedrooms: 2 double & 1 twin.
Bathrooms: 2 private, 1 public.
Bed & breakfast: £24-£28 double.
Parking for 2.
Open May-October.

THE SYMBOLS ARE EXPLAINED ON THE FLAP INSIDE THE BACK COVER.

OMBERSLEY

Hereford & Worcester
Map ref 2B1

4m W. Droitwich
A particularly fine village full of black and white houses including the 17th C Dower House and some old inns. The church contains the original box pews.

The Crown and Sandys Arms M

Ombersley, Droitwich, Worcestershire WR9 0EW
☎ Worcester (0905) 620252
A free house with comfortable bedrooms, draught beers and open fires. Home-cooked meals available lunch and evenings, 7 days a week.
Bedrooms: 2 single, 4 double, 1 family room.
Bathrooms: 5 private, 1 public.
Bed & breakfast: £18.50-£23 single, £40 double.
Lunch available.
Evening meal 6pm (l.o. 10pm).
Parking for 100.
Credit: Access.

ONECOTE

Staffordshire
Map ref 4B2

5m E. Leek
Pleasant moorland village in the valley of the River Hamps, with splendid countryside all around.

Pethill Bank

Bottomhouse, Leek, ST13 7PF
☎ Onecote (053 88) 555 or 277 FAX 05388 575
200-year-old former farmhouse enjoying a secluded, elevated position on edge of Peak District. 7 miles from Alton Towers and 9 miles west of Ashbourne.
Bedrooms: 2 double & 1 twin.
Bathrooms: 3 private, 1 public.
Bed & breakfast: £22-£32 double.
Half board: £19-£24 daily, £119-£150.50 weekly.
Evening meal 6.30pm (l.o. 7.30pm).
Parking for 7.

ONNELEY

Staffordshire
Map ref 4A2

6m SW. Newcastle-under-Lyme

The Wheatsheaf Inn at Onneley M

Bar Hill Rd., Onneley, CW3 9QF
☎ Stoke-on-Trent (0782) 751581
18th C. country inn with bars, restaurant, conference and function facilities. On the A525, 3 miles from Bridgemere and Keele University, 7 miles from Newcastle (Staffs).
Bedrooms: 5 double.
Bathrooms: 5 private.
Bed & breakfast: £29.50-£39.50 single, £39.50-£49.50 double.
Half board: £42.45-£52.45 daily.
Lunch available.
Evening meal 6pm (l.o. 10pm).
Parking for 150.
Credit: Access.

OSWESTRY

Shropshire
Map ref 4A3

See also Ruyton-XI-Towns, Weston Rhyn.
Town close to the Welsh border, the scene of many battles. To the north are the remains of a large Iron Age hill fort. An excellent centre for exploring Shropshire and Offa's Dyke.

April Spring Cottage M

Nantmawr, Oswestry, SY10 9HL
☎ Llansantffraid (069 181) 8802
150-year-old cottage with 1 acre of grounds, in rural area 5 miles from Oswestry, on the border of Shropshire and Wales. Offa's Dyke nearby.
Bedrooms: 1 double & 1 twin.
Bathrooms: 1 public.
Bed & breakfast: £10 single, £20 double.
Half board: £15 daily, £105 weekly.
Parking for 6.

OXHILL

Warwickshire
Map ref 2C1

6m SE. Stratford-upon-Avon
Village in the Vale of Red Horse not far from the battlefield of Edgehill. Its church retains much that is Norman.

Mr & Mrs R. Hutsby ♠

Nolands Farm, Oxhill, Warwick, CV35 0RJ
☎ Kineton (0926) 640309
300-acre arable farm. In a tranquil valley surrounded by fields. All rooms in converted barn annexe. Peaceful and quiet, overlooking old stable yard. Stocked lake, woods, walks and wildlife. Elegant four poster bedroom.
Bedrooms: 3 double & 1 twin, 2 family rooms.
Bathrooms: 4 private, 2 public.
Bed & breakfast: from £12.50 single, from £18 double.
Evening meal 6.30pm.
Parking for 10.
Credit: Access, Visa.

PAINSWICK

Gloucestershire
Map ref 2B1

See also Edge.
Picturesque wool town with inns and houses dating from the 14th C. Painswick House is a Palladian mansion with Chinese wallpaper. The churchyard is famous for its yew trees.

Damsells Lodge
The Park, Painswick, Stroud, CL6 6SN
☎ (0453) 813777
A quiet country house enjoying spectacular views.
Bedrooms: 1 double & 1 twin, 1 family room.
Bathrooms: 1 private, 1 public.
Bed & breakfast: £15-£25 single, £28-£33 double.
Parking for 6.

PERSHORE

Hereford & Worcester
Map ref 2B1

See also Bishampton, Fladbury.
Attractive Georgian town on the River Avon close to the Vale of Evesham with fine houses and old inns. The remains of the beautiful Pershore Abbey form the parish church. [i]

Oaklands Farm ♠
Evesham Rd. (A44), Pershore, Worcestershire WR10 3JT
☎ Evesham (0386) 860323
5-acre flower nursery. In the beautiful Vale of Evesham, close to Worcester, the Cotswolds, Stratford-upon-Avon and Cheltenham.
Bedrooms: 1 double & 2 twin, 1 family room.
Bathrooms: 1 public.
Bed & breakfast: £12 single, £22 double.
Half board: max. £22 daily, max. £144 weekly.
Evening meal 7.30pm.
Parking for 20.

Star Hotel ♠
Bridge St., Pershore, Worcestershire WR10 1AL
☎ (0386) 552704 & 552198
Alongside the River Avon, with private mooring. Beer garden; lunches and evening meals available to non-residents.
Bedrooms: 2 single, 4 double & 1 twin, 1 family rooms.
Bathrooms: 2 public; 9 private showers.
Bed & breakfast: from £21 single, from £28 double.
Half board: £29-£35 daily.
Evening meal 7pm (l.o. 9.30pm).
Parking for 50.
Credit: Access, Visa.

PONTESBURY

Shropshire
Map ref 4A3

8m SW. Shrewsbury
With views of the Rea Valley from nearby Pontesford Hill, this village is the site of a 7th C. battle between a King of Mercia and a King of the West Saxons. Most of the village church was rebuilt in the last century, except for the 13th C.chancel which retains its original roof of trussed beams.

Nills Farm
Habberley Rd., Pontesbury, Shrewsbury, SY5 0YN
☎ Shrewsbury (0745) 790495
82-acre mixed farm. Working farm at gateway to Shropshire hill country. Ideal for walking and touring the Welsh Borders. A488 to Pontesbury. Three quarters of a mile on Habberley Road.
Bedrooms: 2 twin.
Bathrooms: 1 public.
Bed & breakfast: £7.50-£10 single, £15 double.
Parking for 4.
Open February-November.

PRINCETHORPE

Warwickshire
Map ref 4B3

Three Horse Shoes ♠
Southam Rd., Princethorpe, Rugby, CV23 9PR
☎ Marton (0926) 632345
Old coaching inn dated 1850, built on Fosseway crossroads. Banbury/Oxford road A423. Countryside setting and near to Coventry, Rugby, Leamington Spa.
Bedrooms: 2 single, 2 double.
Bathrooms: 1 public.
Bed & breakfast: £20 single, £30 double.
Lunch available.
Evening meal 7pm (l.o. 10pm).
Parking for 40.

REDDITCH

Hereford & Worcester

See Feckenham.

ROSS-ON-WYE

Hereford & Worcester
Map ref 2A1

See also Garway, Goodrich, Symonds Yat West.
Attractive market town set above the River Wye with a 17th C Market Hall. There are lovely views over the surrounding countryside from the Prospect and the town is close to Goodrich Castle and the Welsh border. [i]

Aberhall Farm ♠
St. Owen's Cross, Ross-on-Wye, Herefordshire HR2 8LL
☎ Harewood End (098 987) 256
132-acre stock/arable farm. In the heart of the Wye Valley amid quiet, unspoilt countryside. Home cooking on this family-run farm.
Bedrooms: 2 double & 1 twin.
Bathrooms: 1 public.
Bed & breakfast: £20-£21 double.
Half board: £15-£16 daily, £105-£108.50 weekly.
Evening meal 6.30pm (l.o. 2pm).
Parking for 5.

Brookfield House ♠
Over Ross, Ross-on-Wye, Herefordshire HR9 7AT
☎ (0989) 62188
Queen Anne/Georgian listed building close to the town centre.
Bedrooms: 2 single, 2 double & 4 twin.
Bathrooms: 3 private, 3 public.
Bed & breakfast: £11-£12.50 single, £24-£26 double.
Parking for 11.
Open February-October.
Credit: Access, Visa.

Merrivale Place ♠
The Avenue, Ross-on-Wye, Herefordshire HR9 5AW
☎ (0989) 64929
Fine Victorian house in peaceful surroundings in a quiet residential area. Large rooms and lovely views. Family run.
Bedrooms: 1 double & 1 twin, 1 family room.

INDIVIDUAL PROPRIETORS HAVE SUPPLIED ALL DETAILS OF ACCOMMODATION. ALTHOUGH WE DO CHECK FOR ACCURACY, WE ADVISE YOU TO CONFIRM PRICES AND OTHER INFORMATION AT THE TIME OF BOOKING.

Bathrooms: 2 public.
Bed & breakfast: £21-£23 double.
Half board: £17.50-£18.50 daily, £120-£127 weekly.
Evening meal 7pm (l.o. 4pm).
Parking for 6.
Open March-October.

The Old Vicarage M

Bridstow, Ross-on-Wye, Herefordshire HR9 6PZ
☎ (0989) 62371
Spacious Georgian house in 8 acres of garden and paddocks overlooking Ross-on-Wye. 5 minutes from town centre.
Bedrooms: 1 single, 1 twin, 1 family room.
Bathrooms: 1 public.
Bed & breakfast: £10 single, £20 double.
Parking for 4.
Open May-October.

Rudhall Farm

Ross-on-Wye, Herefordshire HR9 7TL
☎ Upton Bishop (098 985) 240
250-acre arable, sheep, hens farm. Charming, spacious farmhouse beside millstream, in large, attractive, walled garden. Ideal for exploring the Wye Valley.
Bedrooms: 1 double & 1 twin.
Bathrooms: 1 public.
Bed & breakfast: £10-£12 single, £20-£22 double.
Parking for 10.
Open April-October.

Thatch Close

Llangrove, Ross-on-Wye, Herefordshire HR9 6EL
☎ Llangarron (098 984) 300
13-acre mixed farm. Secluded Georgian country house (OS 51535196), midway between Ross-on-Wye and Monmouth. Home-produced vegetables and meat. Ideal for country lovers of any age. Map sent on request.
Bedrooms: 1 double & 1 twin.
Bathrooms: 1 public.
Bed & breakfast: £9.50-£10.50 single, £19-£20 double.
Half board: £16-£17 daily, £110-£115 weekly.
Lunch available.
Evening meal 6.30pm (l.o. 6pm).
Parking for 7.
Open March-November.

RUCKHALL

Hereford & Worcester
Map ref 2A1

Riverside hamlet high above the River Wye, with an Iron Age camp.

Ancient Camp Inn M

Ruckhall, Eaton Bishop, Hereford, Herefordshire HR2 9QZ
☎ Golden Valley (0981) 250449
This inn is on the site of an Iron Age fort dating from the 4th - 5th C. BC. Spectacular views of the River Wye.
Bedrooms: 2 double & 1 twin.
Bathrooms: 3 private, 1 public.
Bed & breakfast: £20 single, £35 double.
Lunch available.
Evening meal 7pm (l.o. 9.30pm).
Parking for 45.
Credit: Access, Visa.

RUDYARD

Staffordshire
Map ref 4B2

2m NW. Leek
Village close to the attractive Rudyard Reservoir where there are facilities for fishing, boating and pleasant walks. Rudyard gave its name to the famous writer, Kipling, whose parents are said to have often visited it.

Fairboroughs Farm

Rudyard, Leek, ST13 8PR
☎ Rushton Spencer (026 06) 341
150-acre beef/sheep farm. Comfortable oak-beamed stone house, with log fires and splendid views. The Potteries, Peak District, Cheshire and Alton Towers are within easy reach.
Bedrooms: 1 double & 1 twin, 1 family room.
Bathrooms: 1 public.
Bed & breakfast: max. £10 single, max. £18 double.
Evening meal 6.30pm (l.o. 12.30pm).
Parking for 4.

RUGBY

Warwickshire
Map ref 4C3

See also Marton.
Town famous for its public school which gave its name to Rugby Union football and which featured in 'Tom Brown's Schooldays'. ℹ

Avondale Guest House M

16 Elsee Rd., Rugby, CV21 3BA
☎ (0788) 78639
Victorian town residence close to Rugby School, convenient for Warwick Castle, Coventry Cathedral, Leamington Spa, National Exhibition Centre and Birmingham.
Bedrooms: 2 single, 1 double & 3 twin, 1 family room.
Bathrooms: 1 private, 2 public; 1 private shower.
Bed & breakfast: £15-£17.25 single, £28.75-£34.50 double.
Evening meal 6pm (l.o. 3pm).
Parking for 9.

Lawford Hill Farm M

Lawford Heath Lane, Long Lawford, Rugby, CV23 9HG
☎ (0788) 542001
200-acre mixed farm. Georgian farmhouse with small bygones museum, donkey riding, fishing and children's farmyard. 2 miles from Rugby town centre.
Bedrooms: 1 double & 1 twin, 1 family room.
Bathrooms: 1 private, 1 public.
Bed & breakfast: £11-£12 single, £20-£24 double.
Half board: £16-£17 daily, £105-£120 weekly.
Evening meal 6pm (l.o. 4pm).
Parking for 20.

THERE IS A SPECIAL SECTION IN THIS GUIDE LISTING ACCOMMODATION ESPECIALLY SUITABLE FOR GROUPS AND YOUNG PEOPLE.

RUSHTON SPENCER

Staffordshire
Map ref 4B2

Village with an interesting church which was built in the 14th C of wood, some of which still remains. It is close to the pleasant Rudyard Reservoir.

Barnswood Farm

Rushton Spencer, Macclesfield, Cheshire SK11 0RA
☎ (0260) 226261
100-acre dairy farm. In a lovely setting overlooking Rudyard Lake 400 yards down the field; Alton Towers, Peak District and the Potteries all within 15 mile radius.
Bedrooms: 1 single, 2 double, 1 family room.
Bathrooms: 1 public.
Bed & breakfast: from £11 single, from £20 double.
Parking for 5.

RUYTON-XI-TOWNS

Shropshire
Map ref 4A3

Town got its name from the time when, at the beginning of the 14th C, it was one of 11 towns 'joined' into 1 manor. It is situated above the River Perry and has the remains of a castle in the churchyard.

Brownhill House M
Listed

Ruyton-XI-Towns, Shrewsbury, SY4 1LR
☎ Baschurch (0939) 260626
Family house of character with informal atmosphere. Of particular interest to gardeners and local history enthusiasts. Unique garden bordering the River Perry. Fishing, canoeing, walks, local pubs.
Bedrooms: 1 single, 1 double.
Bathrooms: 1 public.
Bed & breakfast: £7-£8 single, £14-£16 double.
Half board: £10.50-£13 daily, £70-£75 weekly.
Lunch available.
Evening meal 6pm (l.o. 5pm).
Parking for 5.

SHAWBURY

Shropshire
Map ref 4A3

Village near the River
Roden now becoming
almost a small town
centred on the RAF
station here. The area
round the late Norman
church retains much of its
village character.

New Farm M
😊😊
Muckleton, Telford, TF6 6RJ
☎ (0939) 250358
*70-acre arable/mixed farm. A
modernised farmhouse within
easy reach of the Welsh border
country, Shrewsbury, Chester,
Bridgnorth, Ironbridge and the
Potteries.*
Bedrooms: 1 single, 1 double
& 1 twin, 1 family room.
Bathrooms: 1 private,
2 public.
Bed & breakfast: £10-£12
single, £20-£25 double.
Half board: £16-£18 daily,
£100-£110 weekly.
Evening meal 6pm.
Parking for 10.
☎3 ♦ ♥ ⓤ ♉ ⓣⓥ ⅲ ⋇ ♙
⬩

SHIPSTON ON STOUR

Warwickshire
Map ref 2B1

Old market town with
many Georgian houses
and inns. Honington Hall,
a small Carolean house,
is nearby and Stratford,
the Cotswolds, Chipping
Campden and Hidcote
Manor Gardens can be
easily reached.

Admington Lane Farm M
😊😊
Admington, Shipston on
Stour, CV36 4JJ
☎ Alderminster
(078 987) 394
*60-acre arable farm. Working
farm, with Victorian farmhouse
and large garden. Between
Mickleton and Ilmington, eight
miles from Stratford-upon-
Avon.*
Bedrooms: 1 double & 1 twin.
Bathrooms: 2 private.
Bed & breakfast: £14.50-£15
single, £24-£25 double.

**WE ADVISE YOU TO
CONFIRM YOUR
BOOKING IN WRITING.**

Half board: £19-£19.50 daily,
£133-£154 weekly.
Evening meal 6pm (l.o. 8pm).
Parking for 13.
Open February-October.
⬧ ⬝ ♦ ♥ ⓤ ✂ ⅲ ❋ ✕ ♙

The Fox and Hounds
Great Wolford, Shipston on
Stour, CV36 5NQ
☎ Barton-on-the-Heath
(060 874) 220
*Beautifully situated and
peaceful 16th C. coaching inn,
just off the A34 Oxford to
Stratford-upon-Avon road and
4 miles south of Shipston on
Stour.*
Bedrooms: 1 double & 1 twin.
Bathrooms: 2 private.
Bed & breakfast: £32-£40
double.
Lunch available.
Evening meal 7pm (l.o.
10pm).
Parking for 18.
Credit: Access.
🔥 ⓥ ⅲ ♦ ⬩ ⋇ ⓢⓟ ♙

Lower Farm Barn M
Great Wolford, Shipston on
Stour, CV36 5NQ
☎ Barton on the Heath
(060 874) 435
*900-acre arable/mixed farm.
18th C. converted barn.
Modern comforts combined
with exposed beams and
ancient stonework. 3 well-
furnished double bedrooms:
use of attractive drawing room.
Quiet village between A34,
A44 and A429.*
Bedrooms: 1 double & 2 twin,
1 family room.
Bathrooms: 1 private,
1 public.
Bed & breakfast: £9-£10
single, £22-£24 double.
Parking for 42.
👪 ♥ ⅲ ⓥ ⅲ ⓣⓥ ⅲ ⬩ ⟋
⟳ ❋ ♙ ♙

SHIPTON

Gloucestershire
Map ref 2B1

Village close to
Chedworth Roman villa
(National Trust) and
Northleach with its
beautiful church.

Frogmill Inn & Hotel M
Shipton Oliffe,
Andoversford, Cheltenham,
GL54 4HT
☎ Cheltenham (0242) 820547
& 820237
*Cotswold stone building with
an a la carte restaurant and 2
bars serving bar food 7 days a
week. At the junction of the
A40 (Oxford) and the A436.*

Bedrooms: 5 double & 3 twin,
2 family rooms.
Bathrooms: 10 private.
Bed & breakfast: from £30
single, from £44 double.
Lunch available.
Evening meal 6pm (l.o.
10pm).
Parking for 206.
Credit: Access, Visa, Diners,
Amex.
👪 ⅲ ⬩ ♥ ♥ 🅿 ⓥ ⅲ ⓣⓥ
ⅲ ⬩ ⟡ ❋ ⒹⒶⒻ ⓢⓟ ♙ ⓣ

SHREWSBURY

Shropshire
Map ref 4A3

*See also Baschurch,
Dorrington, Minsterley,
Pontesbury, Stiperstones.*
Beautiful historic town on
the River Severn retaining
many fine old timber-
framed houses. Its
attractions include
Rowley's Museum with
Roman finds, remains of
a castle, Clive House
Museum, St. Chad's 18th
C round church and
rowing on the river. ℹ

The Day House M
😊😊
Nobold, Shrewsbury,
SY5 8NL
☎ (0743) 860212
*330-acre dairy and arable
farm. Secluded 19th C.
farmhouse set in landscaped
gardens. Three miles from
medieval town of Shrewsbury.*
Bedrooms: 1 twin, 2 family
rooms.
Bathrooms: 2 private,
1 public.
Bed & breakfast: £16-£18
single, £28-£32 double.
Parking for 7.
👪 ♥ ⓤ 🅿 ⅲ ♦ ⓣⓥ ⅲ ⬩
⟡ ⟳ ♉ ⟋ ❋ ✕ ♙ ♙ ⓣ

Fitz Manor M
Listed
Bomere Heath, Shrewsbury,
SY4 3AS
☎ (0743) 850295
*250-acre mixed farm. Family
home in glorious unspoilt
countryside, within easy reach
of castles, gardens and the
Welsh hills.*
Bedrooms: 1 single, 2 twin.
Bathrooms: 1 public.
Bed & breakfast: £10-£12.50
single, £20-£25 double.
Half board: £17.50-£22.50
daily, £120-£155 weekly.
Lunch available.
Evening meal 6pm (l.o. 9pm).
Parking for 20.
👪 ⅕ ⓪ ♥ ⓤ 🅿 ♦ ✂ ⅲ
ⓣⓥ ⅲ ⬩ ⒹⒶⒻ ⬝ ♉ ⟳ ⟋ ♉
⟋ ❋ ♙ ⒹⒶⒻ ⬩ ⓢⓟ ♙ ⓣ

Mytton Farmhouse
Mytton, Montford Bridge,
Shrewsbury, SY4 1EU
☎ (0743) 850994
*Converted farmhouse in quiet
location 5 miles from
Shrewsbury, offering homely
accommodation. Oak-panelled
dining room with separate
visitors' lounge.*
Bedrooms: 1 single, 3 double.
Bathrooms: 1 private,
2 public.
Bed & breakfast: £10-£11
single, £20-£26 double.
Half board: £15-£18 daily,
£105-£126 weekly.
Evening meal 6pm (l.o. 7pm).
Parking for 8.
👪 ⅕ ⓤ ⅲ ♦ ⓥ ⅲ ⬩ ❋ ♙

The Old School House
😊
Hanwood, Shrewsbury,
SY5 8LJ
☎ (0743) 860694
*Old school house, built in 1863,
in pleasant village 5 minutes'
drive from the town centre.
Adjacent to beautiful
Shropshire hills and
countryside.*
Bedrooms: 1 single, 1 double
& 1 twin, 1 family room.
Bathrooms: 1 public.
Bed & breakfast: £11 single,
£22 double.
Parking for 10.
👪 ⬝ ⓪ ♦ ⅲ ⓤ ⅲ ⓥ ⅲ
ⓣⓥ ⅲ ⬩ ⟳ ♉ ⋇ ♙ ♙ ⒹⒶⒻ ⓢⓟ
♙

Vale Cottages
Valeswood, Nesscliff,
Shrewsbury, SY4 2LH
☎ Nesscliff (074 381) 467
*Oak-beamed sandstone cottage
with spectacular views of the
surrounding Shropshire
countryside, amid beautiful
Welsh mountains. Central
location for touring.*
Bedrooms: 1 double, 1 family
room.
Bathrooms: 1 public.
Bed & breakfast: £18-£24
double.
Half board: £15.50-£18.50
daily, £93-£114 weekly.
Lunch available.
Evening meal 5pm (l.o. 4pm).
Parking for 20.
👪3 ⓪ ♦ ⓤ ⅲ ⓥ ⅲ ⓣⓥ ⅲ
⬩ ⟳ ❋ ♙ ♙ ⬧ ⓢⓟ

**MAP REFERENCES
APPLY TO THE
COLOUR MAPS
TOWARDS THE END
OF THIS GUIDE.**

SOLIHULL

West Midlands
Map ref 4B3

See also Knowle.
On the outskirts of
Birmingham, some Tudor
houses and a 13th C
church remain amongst
the new public buildings
and shopping centre. The
16th C Malvern Hall is
now a school and the
15th C Chester House at
Knowle is now a library.
ℹ

Norton House ▲
230 Norton Lane, Earlswood,
Solihull, W. Midlands
B94 5LT
☎ Earlswood (056 46) 2348
*Comfortable country house, 15
minutes from Birmingham and
the National Exhibition
Centre. Home produce. Car
essential. 5 minutes from A34
and M42 motorway.*
Bedrooms: 1 single, 1 double
& 1 twin.
Bathrooms: 1 public;
1 private shower.
Bed & breakfast: £11.50-
£12.50 single, £20-£23 double.
Half board: £15-£16 daily,
£80-£90 weekly.
Evening meal 7pm (l.o. 9am).
Parking for 8.
ᕲ ⅏ Ⓥ ⊨ ⓣⓥ ▥ ▄ 🖾 ᴳᴬᴾ

STAFFORD

Staffordshire
Map ref 4B3

*See also Eccleshall,
Norbury.*
The town has a long
history and some half-
timbered buildings still
remain, notably the 16th
C High House. There are
several museums in the
town and Shugborough
Hall and the famous
angler Izaak Walton's
cottage, now a museum,
are nearby. ℹ

Littywood House ▲
😊😊😊
Bradley, Stafford ST18 9DW
☎ (0785) 780234
*Country house accommodation,
secluded yet easily accessible
from the M6 (junction 13 - 3
miles). Ideal base for Midlands
or for a stopover.*
Bedrooms: 1 double & 2 twin.
Bathrooms: 3 private.
Bed & breakfast: £20-£22
single, £35-£39 double.
Half board: £30-£35 daily.
Lunch available.

Evening meal 7.30pm (l.o.
9.30pm).
Parking for 8.
⅏ ⅏ Ⅰ Ⓥ ⊨ ⓣⓥ ▥ ▄ ⵙ
🏋 ⏲ ✿ 🖾 🖾

Oakleigh ▲
😊😊
Salters Lane, Enson,
Stafford, ST18 9TA
☎ Sandon (088 97) 432
*A converted barn in the
countryside. Fresh food served
in a large conservatory. 4 miles
north of Stafford off A34.*
Bedrooms: 1 double & 1 twin.
Bathrooms: 2 private.
Bed & breakfast: £18 single,
£27 double.
Evening meal 7pm (l.o. 8pm).
Parking for 4.
ᕲ 🖾 ⬜ ⅏ ⅏ Ⓥ ⊁ ▥ ▄
✿ 🏋 🖾

STIPERSTONES

Shropshire
Map ref 4A3

14m SW. Shrewsbury
Below the spectacular
ridge of the same name,
from which superb views
over moorland, forest and
hills may be enjoyed.

Tankerville Lodge ▲
😊😊
Stiperstones, Minsterley,
Shrewsbury, SY5 0NB
☎ Shrewsbury (0743) 791401
*Country house noted for warm
hospitality, set in superb
landscape, with breathtaking
views. Ideal touring base for
Shropshire and Welsh
borderland. Adjacent to
Stiperstones Nature Reserve.*
Bedrooms: 1 double & 3 twin.
Bathrooms: 2 public.
Bed & breakfast: £11-£13
single, £22 double.
Half board: £17.50-£19.50
daily, £110.25-£122.85
weekly.
Evening meal 7pm (l.o. 4pm).
Parking for 4.
ᕲ ⅏ Ⅰ ⊁ ⊨ ⓣⓥ ▥ ▄ 🖾
🖾 ᔆᴾ

**GROUPS, CONSORTIA
AND AGENCIES
SPECIALISING
IN FARM AND
COUNTRY HOLIDAYS
ARE LISTED IN A
SPECIAL SECTION
OF THIS GUIDE.**

STOKE LACY

Hereford & Worcester
Map ref 2A1

4m SW. Bromyard
Village with small nursery
and garden which
specialise in herbs. The
14th C half-timbered
manor house of Lower
Brockhampton (National
Trust) is close.

Nether Court
Ⓛⁱˢᵗᵉᵈ
Stoke Lacy, Herefordshire
HR7 4HJ
☎ Hereford (0432) 820247
*160-acre mixed farm. A
Victorian farmhouse in
peaceful village surroundings.
A small lake for wildlife is
being constructed. Near to
Hereford, Ludlow, Malvern
and Leominster.*
Bedrooms: 1 double, 1 family
room.
Bathrooms: 1 public.
Bed & breakfast: £10-£11
single, £20-£24 double.
ᕲ ⅏ ⅏ ⅏ ⊨ ⓣⓥ ♀ ♪ ▶
✔ ✿ 🏋 🖾 🖾

STOKE-ON-TRENT

Staffordshire
Map ref 4B2

*See also Audley,
Balterley, Betley,
Onneley.*
Famous for its
Wedgwood pottery,
whose factory, along with
several other famous
makers, can be visited.
The City Museum has
one of the finest pottery
and porcelain collections
in the world. ℹ

The Hollies
😊😊
Clay Lake, Endon, Stoke-on-
Trent, ST9 9DD
☎ Stoke-on-Trent
(0782) 503252
*Delightful, Victorian house in a
quiet country setting off
B5051. Convenient for M6, the
Potteries and Alton Towers.*
Bedrooms: 1 double & 1 twin,
1 family room.
Bathrooms: 1 private,
1 public; 1 private shower.
Bed & breakfast: £12-£15
single, £20-£24 double.
Parking for 5.
ᕲ ⅏ ⅏ Ⓥ ⊁ ⊨ ⓣⓥ ▥ ✿
🖾

STONE

Staffordshire
Map ref 4B2

Town on the River Trent
which has the remains of
a 12th C Augustinian
priory. It is surrounded by
pleasant countryside.
Trentham Gardens with
500 acres of parklands
with recreational facilities
is within easy reach.

The Boat House ▲
😊😊
71 Newcastle Rd., Stone,
ST15 8LD
☎ (0785) 815389
*Renovated 18th C. former inn
adjacent to Trent and Mersey
Canal. Convenient for M6,
Wedgwood, the Potteries and
Stafford.*
Bedrooms: 1 single, 1 double
& 1 twin.
Bathrooms: 1 private,
1 public.
Bed & breakfast: £11.50-£15
single, £24-£30 double.
Parking for 4.
⅏ Ⅰ Ⓥ ⊨ ⓣⓥ ▥ ▄ 🏋 🖾

Byways
185 Lichfield Rd., Stone,
ST15 8QB
☎ (0785) 813674
*Detached 3-bedroomed house
with a third of an acre garden.*
Bedrooms: 1 single, 2 double.
Bathrooms: 1 public.
Bed & breakfast: £10-£11
single, £20-£22 double.
Parking for 3.
ᕲ5 ⅏ ⓣⓥ 🏋 🖾

Couldreys ▲
😊😊
8 Airdale Rd., Stone,
ST15 8DW
☎ (0785) 812500 & 813566
*Large house and garden,
quietly situated on the outskirts
of a small market town, and
convenient for visiting the
Wedgwood factory and The
Potteries.*
Bedrooms: 1 twin.
Bathrooms: 1 private.
Bed & breakfast: max. £24
double.
Parking for 2.
Ⓑ ⅏ ⅏ ⊨ ⓣⓥ ▥ ▄ 🏋 🖾

**MAP REFERENCES APPLY TO THE COLOUR
MAPS TOWARDS THE END OF THIS GUIDE.**

STONEHOUSE

Gloucestershire
Map ref 2B1

*See also Frocester.
Village in the Stroud
valley with an Elizabethan
Court, later restored and
altered by Lutyens.*

Welches Farm
Listed

Standish, Stonehouse,
GL10 3BX
☎ (045 382) 2018
*100-acre dairy farm. Large old
house in beautiful
surroundings, 3 miles from
junction 13 of the M5.*
Bedrooms: 1 single, 1 double,
3 family rooms.
Bathrooms: 1 public.
Bed & breakfast: £9 single,
£18 double.
Parking for 12.

 availabilit symbols

STOULTON

Hereford & Worcester
Map ref 2B1

5m SE. Worcester

Froggery House
Listed

Froggery Lane, Stoulton,
Worcester, Worcestershire
WR7 4RQ
☎ Worcester (0905) 841221
*Modern family home in
pleasant rural situation,
opposite a farm and down a
quiet lane off A44.*
Bedrooms: 2 twin.
Bathrooms: 1 public.
Bed & breakfast: max. £9.50
single, max. £19 double.
Parking for 3.
Open March-December.

INDIVIDUAL
PROPRIETORS HAVE
SUPPLIED ALL
DETAILS OF
ACCOMMODATION.
ALTHOUGH WE DO
CHECK FOR
ACCURACY, WE
ADVISE YOU TO
CONFIRM PRICES
AND OTHER
INFORMATION AT
THE TIME OF
BOOKING.

STOURBRIDGE

West Midlands
Map ref 4B3

Town on the River Stour,
famous for its
glassworks. Several of
the factories can be
visited and glassware
purchased at the factory
shops.

St. Elizabeth's
Cottage M

Woodman Lane, Clent,
Stourbridge, W. Midlands
DY9 9PX
☎ Hagley (0562) 883883
*Beautiful country cottage with
lovely gardens and interior
professionally decorated
throughout. 20 minutes from
Birmingham, and close to all
motorway links.*
Bedrooms: 1 twin.
Bathrooms: 1 private.
Bed & breakfast: £40-£50
double.
Parking for 2.

STOURPORT-ON-
SEVERN

Hereford & Worcester
Map ref 4B3

Town standing at the
confluence of the Rivers
Stour and Severn and on
the Staffordshire and
Worcestershire Canal
which was built in the
18th C and is now a
popular place for
pleasure boats. Some
fine Georgian houses
remain. ☑

Worrall's Farm
Listed

Dunley, Stourport-on-Severn,
Worcestershire DY13 0UL
☎ Great Witley
(029 921) 896245
*5-acre equestrian smallholding.
Early 18th C. mill house near
the Severn Valley. A
millstream setting amid rolling
Worcestershire countryside.*
Bedrooms: 1 twin, 1 family
room.
Bathrooms: 1 public;
1 private shower.
Bed & breakfast: £11 single,
£18 double.
Half board: £16 daily, £112
weekly.
Evening meal 6pm (l.o. 9pm).
Parking for 2.

STOW-ON-THE-
WOLD

Gloucestershire
Map ref 2B1

*See also Bledington,
Naunton, Oddington.*
Attractive Cotswold wool
town with a large Market
Place and some fine
houses, especially the old
Grammar School. There
is an interesting church
dating from Norman
times. Stow-on-the-Wold
is surrounded by lovely
countryside and Cotswold
villages. ☑

Auld Stocks Hotel M

The Square, Stow-on-the-
Wold, Cheltenham,
GL54 1AF
☎ Cotswold (0451) 30666
*17th C. hotel refurbished to
combine modern-day comforts
with original charm and
character. Facing quiet village
green on which original stocks
still stand. Exposed stone
walls, oak timbers and roaring
log fires.*
Bedrooms: 1 single, 13 double
& 1 twin, 2 family rooms.
Bathrooms: 17 private.
Bed & breakfast: £20-£26
single, £40-£52 double.
Half board: £24-£33 daily,
£174-£208 weekly.
Lunch available.
Evening meal 7pm (l.o.
9.30pm).
Parking for 16.
Credit: Access, Visa, Diners,
Amex.

Chipping House M

Park St., Stow-on-the-Wold,
GL54 1AG
☎ Cotswold (0451) 31756
*Friendly welcome in
comfortable 18th C. house.
Ideal for touring the
Cotswolds, Shakespeare
Country and Oxford. No
smoking.*
Bedrooms: 2 double & 1 twin.
Bathrooms: 1 public.
Bed & breakfast: £24-£25
double.
Parking for 3.

Corsham Field
Farmhouse M

Bledington Rd., Stow-on-the-
Wold, Cheltenham,
GL54 1JH
☎ Cotswold (0451) 31750

*100-acre mixed farm. Homely
farmhouse with breathtaking
views; home-made suppers.
Heating, TVs, washbasins, tea
and coffee making facilities in
all bedrooms.*
Bedrooms: 1 double & 1 twin,
1 family room.
Bathrooms: 1 private,
2 public.
Bed & breakfast: £19-£27
double.
Evening meal 6pm.
Parking for 10.

Fairview Farmhouse M

Bledington Rd., Stow-on-the-
Wold, Cheltenham,
GL54 1AN
☎ Cotswold (0451) 30279
*3-acre mixed farm. Charming
farmhouse with outstanding
panoramic views. Peaceful
surroundings, 1 mile from
Stow-on-the-Wold. Warm
welcome. Evening meal by
arrangement.*
Bedrooms: 2 double & 1 twin.
Bathrooms: 2 private,
1 public.
Bed & breakfast: £26-£32
double.
Parking for 7.

The Limes M

Tewkesbury Rd., Stow-on-
the-Wold, Cheltenham,
GL54 1EN
☎ Cotswold (0451) 30034
*Large Georgian house
overlooking fields, 4 minutes
from the town centre. TV
lounge, log fires and an
attractive garden. Four poster
bedroom and one en suite at
small additional cost.*
Bedrooms: 1 single, 2 double
& 2 twin, 1 family room.
Bathrooms: 1 private,
2 public; 1 private shower.
Bed & breakfast: £11-£12
single, £22-£24 double.
Parking for 7.

Wyck Hill Lodge M

Burford Road, Stow-on-the-
Wold, Cheltenham,
GL54 1HT
☎ Cotswold (0451) 30141
*Tastefully furnished lodge in
peaceful rural surroundings,
with extensive views over
Bourton Vale. 1 mile from
Stow-on-the-Wold. Dinner by
arrangement; non-smoking
establishment.*
Bedrooms: 1 double & 1 twin.

Bathrooms: 1 public.
Bed & breakfast: £24-£30
double.
Parking for 8.

STRATFORD-UPON-AVON

Warwickshire
Map ref 2B1

*See also Oxhill,
Wellesbourne, Wilmcote.*
Famous as
Shakespeare's home
town, Stratford's many
attractions include his
birthplace, New Place
where he died, the Royal
Shakespeare Theatre and
Gallery, 'The World of
Shakespeare' audio-
visual theatre, Hall's Croft
(his daughter's house)
and Holy Trinity Church
where he was buried.

34 Banbury Rd.
Stratford-upon-Avon,
CV37 7HY
☎ (0789) 69714
*Homely accommodation in a
warm, clean, friendly
environment.*
Bedrooms: 1 single, 1 twin.
Bathrooms: 1 public.
Bed & breakfast: £9-£9.50
single, £18-£19 double.
Parking for 4.

Barbette M
165 Evesham Rd., Stratford-
upon-Avon, CV37 9BP
☎ (0789) 297822
*10 minutes' walk from the town
centre, with access all day and
ample parking. Meals and
light refreshments on request.
Guests have use of the garden.*
Bedrooms: 2 single, 1 double,
2 family rooms.
Bathrooms: 1 public;
2 private showers.
Bed & breakfast: £12-£14
single, £24-£26 double.
Evening meal 6.30pm.
Parking for 5.

Bishopton Hill Nursery M
Listed
Birmingham Rd., Stratford-
upon-Avon, CV37 0RN
☎ (0789) 67829
*Bungalow set in 4 acres, 2
miles north of Stratford-upon-
Avon on the A34. En-suite
centrally heated
accommodation with ample
parking.*
Bedrooms: 1 double & 1 twin.

Bathrooms: 2 private.
Bed & breakfast: £25-£30
double.
Parking for 4.

Bramdean Guest House
60 Evesham Road, Stratford-
upon-Avon, CV37 9BA
☎ (0789) 298640
*70-year-old house with
interesting period interior.
Antiques, Victorian bedstead
and open fire.*
Bedrooms: 1 double, 1 family
room.
Bathrooms: 1 public;
2 private showers.
Bed & breakfast: £20-£24
double.
Parking for 3.

Brook Lodge M
192 Alcester Rd., Stratford-
upon-Avon, CV37 9DR
☎ (0789) 295988
*Brook Lodge specialises in
offering a wide range of
accommodation to suit a
variety of requirements and
purses.*
Bedrooms: 4 double & 1 twin,
2 family rooms.
Bathrooms: 5 private,
1 public; 2 private showers.
Bed & breakfast: £24-£32
double.
Parking for 13.
Credit: Access, Visa.

Carlton Guest House
22 Evesham Pl., Stratford-
upon-Avon, CV37 6HT
☎ (0789) 293548
*Tasteful decor, elegantly
furnished, combining Victorian
origins with modern facilities.
A peaceful home, happily
shared with guests.*
Bedrooms: 2 single, 2 double
& 1 twin, 1 family room.
Bathrooms: 1 private,
2 public.
Bed & breakfast: £13-£15
single, £23-£32 double.

Cherangani M
61 Maidenhead Road,
Stratford-upon-Avon,
CV37 6XU
☎ (0789) 292655

---

*Pleasant detached house in a
quiet, residential area, offering
warm, attractive
accommodation. Within
walking distance of the town
and theatre.*
Bedrooms: 1 single, 2 twin.
Bathrooms: 1 public.
Bed & breakfast: £12-£15
single, £22-£25 double.
Parking for 3.

Church Farm M
Dorsington, Stratford-upon-
Avon, CV37 8AX
☎ (0789) 720471
*127-acre mixed farm. In
beautiful countryside close to
Stratford, Warwick, Cotswolds
and Evesham.*
Bedrooms: 2 double & 1 twin,
1 family room.
Bathrooms: 1 public.
Bed & breakfast: from £20
double.
Half board: from £17 daily.
Evening meal 6.30pm (l.o.
5pm).
Parking for 3.

Church Farm M
Long Marston, Stratford-
upon-Avon, CV37 8RH
☎ (0789) 720275
*2.5-acre horses farm. Old
family farmhouse with spacious
bedrooms and bathroom. Set in
secluded gardens. Close to
Stratford, Warwick Castle and
the Cotswolds.*
Bedrooms: 1 twin, 1 family
room.
Bathrooms: 1 public.
Bed & breakfast: from £15
single, from £24 double.
Half board: from £20 daily.
Evening meal 7pm (l.o. 8pm).
Parking for 4.

Clomendy Guest House
157 Evesham Rd., Stratford-
upon-Avon, CV37 9BP
☎ (0789) 66957
*Small, detached, mock Tudor
family-run guesthouse,
convenient for town centre,
Anne Hathaway's cottage and
theatres.*
Bedrooms: 1 single, 1 double
& 1 twin.
Bathrooms: 1 public.
Bed & breakfast: £10-£12
single, £20-£24 double.
Parking for 4.

Compton House M
22 Shipston Rd., Stratford-
upon-Avon, CV37 7LP
☎ (0789) 205646
*Small family guesthouse, 5
minutes' walk from the theatre
and town centre.*
Bedrooms: 2 single, 1 double,
2 family rooms.
Bathrooms: 1 public.
Bed & breakfast: £13.50-
£14.50 single, £22-£23.50
double.
Parking for 6.

Eastnor House Hotel M
Shipston Rd., Stratford-upon-
Avon, CV37 7LN
☎ (0789) 68115
*Comfortable hotel with oak
panelling, central open
staircase and spacious rooms.
A short stroll from the River
Avon, theatre and town centre.*
Bedrooms: 2 double & 2 twin,
4 family rooms.
Bathrooms: 5 private,
2 public.
Bed & breakfast: £16-£35
single, £32-£46 double.
Parking for 8.
Credit: Access, Visa, Amex.

Field View M
35 Banbury Rd., Stratford-
upon-Avon, CV37 7HW
☎ (0789) 292694
*10 minutes from Stratford
town centre, offering
comfortable, family type
accommodation.*
Bedrooms: 1 double & 1 twin.
Bathrooms: 1 public.
Bed & breakfast: £20-£24
double.
Parking for 4.

Green Gables M
47 Banbury Road, Stratford-
upon-Avon, CV37 7HW
☎ (0789) 205557
*Edwardian house in a
residential area, within 10
minutes' walk of the town
centre and theatre.*
Bedrooms: 3 double.
Bathrooms: 1 public.
Bed & breakfast: £21-£26
double.
Parking for 3.

STRATFORD-UPON-AVON
Continued

Newlands ⋒
😃😃
7 Broad Walk, Stratford-
upon-Avon, CV37 6HS
☎ (0789) 298449
*Resident hosts' home is only 5
minutes' walk from the Royal
Shakespeare Theatre, town
centre and station.*
Bedrooms: 1 single, 1 double
& 1 twin.
Bathrooms: 1 public.
Bed & breakfast: £10-£12
single, £19-£24 double.
Parking for 2.
🖵 ♥ UL ⌀ 🎳 🗙 🖼

Oxstalls Farm
Listed
Warwick Rd., Stratford-
upon-Avon, CV37 0NS
☎ (0789) 205277
*Beautifully situated stud farm,
overlooking the Welcome Hills
and golf course, in 60 acres.
One mile from Stratford-upon-
Avon.*
Bedrooms: 1 single, 8 double
& 2 twin, 3 family rooms.
Bathrooms: 3 private,
4 public; 6 private showers.
Bed & breakfast: £11.50-£15
single, £23-£30 double.
Parking for 20.
🖐5 ♨ 🖵 ♥ ⌀ 🔟 🎳 🖼
🎵 ⌖ ✿ 🗙 🖼 🖻

Parkfield ⋒
😃😃
3 Broad Walk, Stratford-
upon-Avon, CV37 6HS
☎ (0789) 293313
*Victorian house with large,
comfortable bedrooms. All
rooms with colour TV. Quiet
position, five minutes' walk
from the theatre and town.*
Bedrooms: 1 single, 2 double
& 2 twin, 2 family rooms.
Bathrooms: 4 private,
1 public.
Bed & breakfast: £11-£12
single, £22-£30 double.
Parking for 4.
Credit: Access, Visa.
🖐5 🖵 ♥ UL 🔟 ⌀ 🎳 ⊿

Ravenhurst ⋒
😃😃
2 Broad Walk, Stratford-
upon-Avon, CV37 6HS
☎ (0789) 292515
*Quietly situated a few minutes'
walk from the town centre and
places of historic interest.
Comfortable home, with
substantial breakfast provided.*
Bedrooms: 3 double & 2 twin,
2 family rooms.

Bathrooms: 3 private,
2 public.
Bed & breakfast: £15-£28
single, £19-£30 double.
Credit: Access, Visa, Diners,
Amex.
🖐 🖵 ♥ 🔟 🎳 ⊿ 🗙

Sequoia House ⋒
😃😃😃
51-53 Shipston Rd.,
Stratford-upon-Avon,
CV37 7LN
☎ (0789) 68852 & 294940 &
(0789) 204805
FAX 0789 414559
*Private hotel with large car
park and delightful garden
walk to the theatre, riverside
gardens and Shakespeare
properties.*
Bedrooms: 2 single, 7 double
& 6 twin, 6 family rooms.
Bathrooms: 15 private,
5 public; 2 private showers.
Bed & breakfast: £25-£37
single, £29-£43 double.
Lunch available.
Evening meal 6pm (l.o. 4pm).
Parking for 20.
Credit: Access, Visa.
🖐5 ♨ 📞 🖵 ♥ ⌀ 🔟 🎳 🖼
🔟 🎳 ⊿ ⌖ ✿ 🗙 SP 🖻

Tollgate Cottage
Listed
Stratford Rd., Newbold-on-
Stour, Stratford-upon-Avon,
CV37 8TR
☎ Alderminster
(078 987) 377
*Comfortable, modernised
tollhouse with friendly,
personal service. Near to
Stratford-upon-Avon, Warwick
and the Cotswolds. Enclosed
parking. Evening meals by
prior arrangement.*
Bedrooms: 1 single, 1 double
& 1 twin.
Bathrooms: 2 public.
Bed & breakfast: £9.50-
£10.50 single, £19-£21 double.
Half board: £15-£16 daily.
Parking for 4.
🖐 ⌖ 🖵 ♥ ⌀ 🔟 🎳
🖼

Twelfth Night ⋒
😃😃😃
Evesham Place, Stratford-
upon-Avon, CV37 6HT
☎ (0789) 414595
*Gracious, centrally-located
Victorian villa, formerly owned
by The Royal Shakespeare
Theatre for 21 years for
accommodating actors.
Tastefully refurbished for your
comfort. Non-smokers only.*
Bedrooms: 1 single, 2 double
& 3 twin, 1 family room.
Bathrooms: 5 private,
1 public; 1 private shower.

Bed & breakfast: £15-£16
single, £30-£34 double.
Parking for 3.
🖐5 🖵 ♥ 🖼 ⌀ 🔟 🎳 ⌿ 🖼 🎳
⊿ 🗙 ⧄ 🖻 🔟

Two Eleven
😃😃
211 Evesham Rd., Stratford-
upon-Avon, CV37 9AS
☎ (0789) 299659
*Easy walking distance from
town centre and theatre and
Anne Hathaway's cottage.
Ample parking.*
Bedrooms: 1 twin.
Bathrooms: 1 public.
Bed & breakfast: £9.50-£12
single, £19-£24 double.
Parking for 6.
🖵 ♥ UL 🔟 🎳 🔟 🎳 ⊿ 🗙
🖼 🖓

Whitchurch Farm ⋒
Wimpstone, Stratford-upon-
Avon, CV37 8NS
☎ Alderminster
(078 987) 275
*200-acre mixed farm. Listed
Georgian farmhouse set in
park-like surroundings on the
edge of the Cotswolds. Ideal
for a family holiday. Small
village 4 miles south of
Stratford-upon-Avon.*
Bedrooms: 1 double, 2 family
rooms.
Bathrooms: 2 public.
Bed & breakfast: £10-£11
single, £20-£22 double.
Half board: £14-£15 daily.
Evening meal 6.30pm.
Parking for 3.
🖐 UL 🎳 🔟 🎳 🗙 🖼 🖻

White Horse Inn
😃😃
Banbury Rd., Ettington,
Stratford-upon-Avon,
CV37 7SU
☎ (0789) 740641
*A village inn with open fires
and oak beams, set in the heart
of Shakespeare country.*
Bedrooms: 3 double & 1 twin.
Bathrooms: 1 public.
Bed & breakfast: £10-£18
single, max. £35 double.
Half board: £15-£23 daily.
Lunch available.
Evening meal 7pm (l.o.
10.30pm).
Parking for 30.
Credit: Access, Visa.
🖐7 🖵 ♥ 🔟 🎳 🎳 ⊿ ⧄
🗙 🔟

Wood View
😃😃
Pathlow, Stratford-upon-
Avon, CV37 0RQ
☎ (0789) 295778

*Secluded, beautifully situated
house, with fine views over
fields and woods. Ideal for
touring Stratford-upon-Avon
and the Cotswolds.*
Bedrooms: 2 twin.
Bathrooms: 2 private.
Bed & breakfast: £12-£18
single, £24-£36 double.
Parking for 6.
🖐 ♨ 🖵 ♥ UL 🔟 🎳 ⊿ 🕊
🕊 ✿ 🖼

Woodburn House
Private Hotel ⋒
😃😃😃
89 Shipston Rd., Stratford-
upon-Avon, CV37 7LW
☎ (0789) 204453
*Small hotel 8 minutes' walk to
theatre and town centre.
Private car park. Colour TV
and tea/coffee facilities in
rooms.*
Bedrooms: 1 single, 2 double
& 1 twin, 3 family rooms.
Bathrooms: 4 private,
2 public.
Bed & breakfast: £16 single,
£32-£48 double.
Parking for 10.
🖐5 ♨ 🖵 ♥ UL ⌀ 🔟 🎳 ⊿
🗙 🖼 SP

Woodstock Guest
House ⋒
😃😃
30 Grove Rd., Stratford-
upon-Avon, CV37 6PB
☎ (0789) 299881
*Well-preserved Edwardian
house built in 1910 for the
Reverend Ahbuthnot of
Stratford-upon-Avon. Less
than 10 minutes' walk to
theatre, cinema, town centre
and all main attractions.*
Bedrooms: 1 single, 2 double
& 1 twin.
Bathrooms: 1 private,
1 public.
Bed & breakfast: £12-£14
single, £24-£34 double.
Parking for 3.
🖐3 ♨ ♥ UL ⌀ 🎳 🔟 ● 🎳
⊿ 🖼 🖻

**THERE IS A SPECIAL
SECTION IN THIS
GUIDE LISTING
ACCOMMODATION
ESPECIALLY
SUITABLE FOR
GROUPS AND
YOUNG PEOPLE.**

STROUD

Gloucestershire
Map ref 2B1

This old town has been producing broadcloth for centuries and the local museum has an interesting display on the subject. It is surrounded by attractive hilly country. ℹ️

Burleigh Cottage M
Burleigh, Stroud, GL5 2PW
☎ (0453) 884703
Original Cotswold stone building; 400 years old. On Minchinhampton Common with breathtaking views over the Golden Valley.
Bedrooms: 3 double.
Bathrooms: 3 private.
Bed & breakfast: £27-£32 double.
Parking for 3.
�🖵 ❖ ㉅ 🗓 📺 ▥ ⋃
► ❄ 🎢 🎬 SP 🏠

Cairngall Guest House
⬗⬗
65 Bisley Old Rd., Stroud, GL5 1NF
☎ (045 36) 4595
Unique, Bath-stone house in French style with porticoed west front, furnished to complement the architectural design.
Bedrooms: 1 single, 1 double, 1 family room.
Bathrooms: 1 public.
Bed & breakfast: £9-£11 single, £20-£22 double.
Parking for 3.
➤ ❖ 🗓 🛈 📺 ▥ ➡ 🏠

Highcroft
Gunhouse La., Bowbridge, Stroud, GL5 2DB
☎ (045 36) 3387
17th C. cottage within level walking distance of the town centre and railway station. Ground floor accommodation suitable for the partially disabled. Guests' private payphone. Excellent touring centre.
Bedrooms: 1 double, 1 family room.
Bathrooms: 1 public.
Bed & breakfast: £19-£20 double.
Parking for 3.
➤ 🖒 ❖ 🗓 📺 ▥ ♿ 🎢 🏠

New Inn House M
Listed
The Camp, Stroud, GL6 7HL
☎ Miserden (028 582) 336

In a small hamlet amid unspoilt Cotswold countryside, convenient for Severn Wildfowl Trust and Prinknash Abbey. Oak beams and inglenook fireplace.
Bedrooms: 1 single, 1 twin.
Bathrooms: 1 public.
Bed & breakfast: £10-£12 single, £20-£24 double.
Half board: £16.50-£18.50 daily.
Evening meal 7pm (l.o. 2pm).
Parking for 3.
Open May-November.
➤ 10 ❖ 🗓 📺 ▥ ⋃ ❖ 🏠

Woodside M
⬗⬗⬗
Burleigh, Stroud, GL5 2PA
☎ Brimscombe
(0453) 884350 Telex 437349
Beautiful Cotswold home with attractive furnishings. Lovely garden with views of the Golden Valley. 2.5 miles from Stroud and near Minchinhampton Common; an excellent centre for touring.
Bedrooms: 2 double, 1 family room.
Bathrooms: 3 private.
Bed & breakfast: £16.40-£23 single, £29.90-£37.95 double.
Half board: £26.40-£33 daily, £161-£207 weekly.
Parking for 8.
➤ ⬗ 🖵 ❖ 🛈 ▣ ➡ 📺 ▥ ➡ 🍴 ⋃ ► ❄ 🎢 🎬 🏠

SUCKLEY

Hereford & Worcester
Map ref 2B1

8m SW. Worcester
Village set amid the remote and beautiful wooded countryside of the Suckley Hills.

The Barrow
⬗⬗
Suckley, Worcester, Worcestershire WR6 5EJ
☎ (088 64) 208
Stone-built farmhouse in rural setting. Home cooking, friendly atmosphere.
Bedrooms: 1 double & 1 twin, 1 family room.
Bathrooms: 3 private.
Bed & breakfast: £30 double.
Half board: £20 daily, £130 weekly.
Evening meal 7pm (l.o. 9am).
Parking for 10.
➤ 🖵 ❖ 🗓 🛈 ▥ ➡ ❄ 🎢 🎬 SP

SUTTON ST. NICHOLAS

Hereford & Worcester
Map ref 2A1

4m NE. Hereford
The tower and chancel of the church date from the 13th C, the transept being added a century later. Inside, the altar table and pulpit are 17th C. while the oak screen has 15th C. linenfold panels.

Amberley House
Sutton St. Nicholas, Herefordshire HR1 3BX
☎ (043 272) 564
Family home with large garden and swimming pool. Children and pets welcome. Opposite New Inn, between Sutton St. Nicholas and Bodenham.
Bedrooms: 1 double & 1 twin.
Bathrooms: 2 public.
Bed & breakfast: £8-£10.50 single, £15-£20 double.
Half board: £11.50-£14 daily, £65-£85 weekly.
Evening meal 6pm (l.o. 8pm).
Parking for 3.
Open January-November.
➤ ⬗ ▣ 🖵 ❖ 🗓 ▣ ➡ 📺 ▥ ⋃ ❄ 🎢 🏠

SYMONDS YAT WEST

Hereford & Worcester
Map ref 2A1

Jubilee maze and exhibition was created here in 1977 to commemorate Queen Elizabeth II's Jubilee. The area of Symonds Yat is a world renowned beauty spot.

Ye Olde Ferrie Inne M
⬗⬗
Symonds Yat West, Ross-on-Wye, Herefordshire HR9 6BL
☎ Symonds Yat West (0600) 890232
In the heart of the beautiful Wye Valley in Symonds Yat West which is an area of outstanding natural beauty.
Bedrooms: 1 single, 3 double & 3 twin.
Bathrooms: 4 private, 1 public.
Bed & breakfast: £15-£17.50 single, £25-£40 double.
Half board: £24-£26.50 daily, £168-£183.50 weekly.
Lunch available.

Evening meal 7pm (l.o. 9.45pm).
Parking for 60.
Credit: Access, Visa, Diners.
➤ 🖒 🖵 ❖ 🛈 ▣ V ▥ 🍴 🏮
⋃ 🎵 ❄ 🎢 SP 🏠

TAMWORTH

Staffordshire
Map ref 4B3

Town with a Norman castle which has a Tudor banqueting hall and a museum with coins minted at Tamworth in Saxon times when it was an important royal town. The church has a magnificent tower. ℹ️

The Fox Inn M
⬗⬗⬗
Lichfield Rd., Tamworth, B79 7SH
☎ (0827) 64647 & 58548
Inn on outskirts of Tamworth with extensive selection of bar food.
Bedrooms: 2 single, 1 double & 4 twin.
Bathrooms: 2 public; 1 private shower.
Bed & breakfast: £17.25 single, £29.90 double.
Half board: £19-£23.25 daily.
Lunch available.
Evening meal 6pm (l.o. 8.50pm).
Parking for 200.
➤ 🖵 🛈 ➡ 📺 ▥ ➡ ❄ 🎢

TARRINGTON

Hereford & Worcester
Map ref 2A1

7m E. Hereford
Pretty village half-way between Hereford and Ledbury, containing cottages with timbered walls and thatched roofs.

Mrs. J. Phillips
⬗⬗
Wilton Oaks, Tarrington, Hereford, Herefordshire HR1 4ET
☎ (043 279) 212
30-acre mixed farm. Attractive house near village half a mile off the A438 Hereford - Ledbury road. Large peaceful gardens with beautiful views.
Bedrooms: 2 double & 1 twin.
Bathrooms: 1 public.
Bed & breakfast: £11 single, £22 double.
Half board: £17 daily, £110 weekly.
Evening meal 6pm (l.o. 6pm).
Parking for 6.
❖ 🗓 🛈 ➡ 📺 ▥ ➡ ❄ 🎢 🏠

PLEASE CHECK PRICES AND OTHER DETAILS AT THE TIME OF BOOKING.

TEDDINGTON

Gloucestershire
Map ref 2B1

5m E. Tewkesbury
Village a few miles east of
Tewkesbury and north of
Cheltenham, with just a
few farms and houses,
but an interesting church.

Bengrove Farm
😃

Bengrove, Teddington,
Tewkesbury, GL20 8JB
☎ Alderton (024 262) 332
*10-acre mixed farm. Large
interesting 14th C. farmhouse
with attractive rooms, timbered
and beamed. 2 twin rooms,
lounge and guests' bathroom.
Comfortably furnished.*
Bedrooms: 2 twin.
Bathrooms: 1 public.
Bed & breakfast: £9 single,
£18 double.
Parking for 10.
Open March-November.
➘ ♥ ▥ ▮ ⌿ ☎ ▥ ▦ ▱
❀ ⋈ ⊞

Wren's Nest ♨
Stow Rd., Teddington
Hands, Tewkesbury,
GL20 8NF
☎ Overbury (038 689) 382
*Country house in beautiful
surroundings. All rooms have
private entrance. Teashop
serving cream teas and home-
made cakes. Licensed
restaurant and residents' bar
now open. Dinner by
arrangement.*
Bedrooms: 4 double & 1 twin.
Bathrooms: 5 private.
Bed & breakfast: £18-£25
single, £30-£35 double.
Half board: £23-£42 daily,
£161-£294 weekly.
Lunch available.
Evening meal 7.30pm (l.o.
10pm).
Parking for 40.
Credit: Access, Diners,
Amex.
➘ ♥ ✆ ▢ ♥ ▥ ▮ ▣ ▦ ☎
▥ ▱ ♈ ❀ ☂ ⊞ ▦
⊞

┌─────────────────────┐
│ **GROUPS, CONSORTIA** │
│ **AND AGENCIES** │
│ **SPECIALISING** │
│ **IN FARM AND** │
│ **COUNTRY HOLIDAYS** │
│ **ARE LISTED IN A** │
│ **SPECIAL SECTION** │
│ **OF THIS GUIDE.** │
└─────────────────────┘

TELFORD

Shropshire
Map ref 4A3

See also Newport.
New Town named after
Thomas Telford the
famous engineer who
designed many of the
country's canals, bridges
and viaducts. It is close to
Ironbridge with its
monuments and
museums to the Industrial
Revolution, including
restored 18th C buildings.

Calcutts House
🄻🄸🅂🅃🄴🄳

Jackfield, Telford, TF8 7LH
☎ (0952) 882631
*Built in 1755 by the 9th Earl
of Dundonald, who was deeply
involved in the industrial
development of the Ironbridge
Gorge. The house is steeped in
the history of the area.*
Bedrooms: 1 double, 1 family
room.
Bathrooms: 2 private.
Bed & breakfast: £19-£29
double.
Parking for 7.
➘ ▦ ▥ ▮ ▥ ☎ ▥ ▦ ⌣ ▶
❀ ⊞ ⊞

Church Farm ♨
😃

Wrockwardine, Wellington,
Telford, TF6 5DG
☎ (0952) 244917
*140-acre mixed farm. 200-
year-old listed farmhouse
offering comfortable
accommodation only 1 mile
from the M54 and A5.
Centrally situated for touring
the Midland counties.*
Bedrooms: 1 single, 2 double
& 2 twin, 1 family room.
Bathrooms: 2 private,
1 public.
Bed & breakfast: £12-£16
single, £24-£32 double.
Half board: £19-£23 daily,
£126-£154 weekly.
Evening meal 6.30pm.
Parking for 10.
➘ ♥ ▢ ♥ ▥ ▮ ▥ ☎ ▥
▮ ▶ ⌣ ▶ ❀ ⋈ ⊞

The Lodge
Sunniside, Coalbrookdale,
Telford, TF8 7EX
☎ Ironbridge (095 245) 2423
*Private, secluded country house
in 1.5 acres, within 10 minutes
of all Ironbridge Gorge
Museum sites.*
Bedrooms: 1 single, 2 double.
Bathrooms: 1 public.
Bed & breakfast: £12-£14
single, £22-£24 double.
Parking for 6.
➘ ♨ ▥ ▦ ☎ ▥ ⋈ ⊞

Old Rectory
Stirchley Village, Telford,
TF3 1DY
☎ (0952) 596308
*Former rectory set in an acre
of secluded gardens, on the
edge of the park and central
for local attractions.*
Bedrooms: 2 single, 1 twin,
1 family room.
Bathrooms: 2 public.
Bed & breakfast: £12-£15
single, £24 double.
Half board: £16.50-£19.50
daily, £115.50-£136.50
weekly.
Evening meal 6.30pm (l.o.
10.30pm).
Parking for 6.
➘ ♥ ▥ ▮ ▥ ⌿ ▥ ☎ ▥
▮ ▼ ⌣ ▶ ❀ ⋈ ⊞ ⊞

46 Wigmore
Woodside, Telford, TF7 5NB
☎ (0952) 583748
*Privately-owned house with hot
and cold water available at all
times. Garden and garaging at
rear.*
Bedrooms: 1 single, 1 double.
Bathrooms: 1 public.
Bed & breakfast: £8-£10
single, £16-£20 double.
Half board: £11.50-£12.50
daily, £70-£73.50 weekly.
Evening meal 5pm.
Parking for 2.
⋊ ▢ ▥ ▮ ▥ ▦ ⋈ ⊞

Willow House
137 Holyhead Rd.,
Wellington, Telford,
TF1 2DH
☎ (0952) 223817
*Comfortable guesthouse with
personal service.*
Bedrooms: 1 single, 6 twin.
Bathrooms: 2 public.
Bed & breakfast: £12.50-£15
single, £25-£30 double.
Parking for 7.
➘ ♨ ▢ ▥ ▮ ▥ ⋈ ❀ ⋈
⊞

Wrockwardine Farm ♨
😃

Wrockwardine, Telford,
TF6 5DG
☎ (0952) 242278
*250-acre mixed farm. Early
Georgian farmhouse, built in
1722, in the quiet village of
Wrockwardine, 1.5 miles from
the M54 junction 7.*
Bedrooms: 1 double & 1 twin,
1 family room.
Bathrooms: 1 private,
1 public.
Bed & breakfast: £10-£12
single, £18-£20 double.

┌─────────────────────┐
│ **PLEASE MENTION** │
│ **THIS GUIDE WHEN** │
│ **MAKING A BOOKING.** │
└─────────────────────┘

Half board: £16-£18 daily,
£100-£112 weekly.
Evening meal 7pm.
Parking for 6.
➘ ♥ ▥ ▮ ▥ ☎ ▥ ⋈ ♪
❀ ⋈ ⊞

TENBURY WELLS

Hereford & Worcester
Map ref 4A3

See also Leysters.
Small market town on the
Teme possessing many
fine black and white
buildings. In 1839 mineral
springs were found here
and there were hopes of
a spa centre developing.
The waters never became
fashionable and today
only the old Pump Room
remains, a curious iron
structure which has a
wistful attraction. Nearby
Burford House Gardens
contain many unusual
and rare plants and trees.

Hunt House Farm
😃😃😃

Frith Common, Tenbury
Wells, Worcestershire
WR15 8JY
☎ Clows Top (029 922) 277
*180-acre arable/sheep farm.
Beautiful period farmhouse
providing comfort, tranquillity
and a warm welcome.
Surrounded by breathtaking
views.*
Bedrooms: 2 double & 1 twin.
Bathrooms: 3 private.
Bed & breakfast: from £12
single, from £24 double.
Parking for 8.
➘ ♥8 ♥ ▥ ▥ ☎ ▥ ⋈ ⌣ ⌿
❀ ⋈ ⊞ ⊞

TETBURY

Gloucestershire
Map ref 2B2

See also Didmarton.
Small market town with
18th C houses and an
attractive 17th C Town
Hall. It is a good touring
centre with many places
of interest nearby
including Badminton
House and Westonbirt
Arboretum. ℹ

Crown Inn
😃😃

Gumstool Hill, Tetbury,
GL8 8DG
☎ (0666) 52469
*Historic Cotswold inn with a
great deal of character.
Conservatory restaurant/dining
room providing home cooking.
Friendly family atmosphere.*

Bedrooms: 1 single, 2 double, 1 family room.
Bathrooms: 2 public.
Bed & breakfast: £18 single, £28 double.
Lunch available.
Evening meal 7pm (l.o. 9.30pm).
Parking for 8.
Credit: Access, Visa, Diners, Amex.
🐾 🖵 ♿ ⓘ Ⓥ ▦ ♨ ⓘ ♨
SP ⊞

Priory Inn and Restaurant M
🎫🎫

London Rd., Tetbury, GL8 8JJ
☎ (0666) 52251
Attractive Cotswold inn with many interesting features. Large car park with direct access to letting rooms.
Bedrooms: 1 single, 1 double & 1 twin, 1 family room.
Bathrooms: 2 public.
Bed & breakfast: £17.50-£18.50 single, £31.50-£33.50 double.
Half board: £27.50-£30.50 daily, £132-£150 weekly.
Lunch available.
Evening meal 7pm (l.o. 10pm).
Parking for 50.
Credit: Access, Visa.
🐾 🖵 ⓘ Ⓥ ✂ ▦ ♨ ♨ ♨

Gloucestershire
Map ref 2B1

See also Bredon's Norton, Teddington, Twyning.
Tewkesbury's outstanding possession is its magnificent church, built as an abbey with a great Norman tower and beautiful 14th C interior. The town stands at the confluence of the Severn and Avon and has many old houses, inns and several museums. ⓘ

The Abbey Hotel M
67 Church St., Tewkesbury, GL20 5RX
☎ (0684) 294247 & 294097
Family-run hotel offering private and business accommodation. Colour TV in all rooms.
Bedrooms: 2 single, 5 double & 5 twin, 3 family rooms.
Bathrooms: 13 private, 2 public.
Bed & breakfast: £25-£35 single, £30-£45 double.
Half board: £30-£45 daily, £150-£210 weekly.

Evening meal 6pm (l.o. 8.30pm).
Parking for 11.
Credit: Access, Visa, Amex.
🐾 ☎ 🖵 ♨ ⓘ Ⓥ ▦ ♨ ♨
♨ SP ⊤

The Corner House
🎫🎫

Longdon, Tewkesbury, GL20 6AT
☎ Birtsmorton (068 481) 261
16th C. cottage. Homely and comfortable with home cooking. Set in beautiful countryside and ideal for touring and walking. Within easy reach of M5 and M50.
Bedrooms: 1 single, 1 double.
Bathrooms: 1 private, 1 public.
Bed & breakfast: £10-£12 single, £20-£24 double.
Parking for 2.
♨ ⓤⓛ ▦ ♨ ⓣⓥ ▦ ❄ ✗ ♨
♨

Malvern View Guest House M
Listed

1 St. Mary's Rd., Tewkesbury, GL20 5SF
☎ (0684) 292776
Approximately 200 metres from the town centre and in a quiet situation overlooking the River Avon. Ideal for fishing, boating and other interests.
Bedrooms: 1 single, 2 double & 2 twin, 1 family room.
Bathrooms: 2 public.
Bed & breakfast: £12.50-£13.50 single, £25-£27 double.
Evening meal 6.30pm (l.o. 7.30pm).
🐾 ♨ Ⓜ ♨ 🖵 ♨ ⓤⓛ ⓘ Ⓥ
♨ ⓣⓥ ▦ ♨ ♨

Newton Farm M
Listed

Ashchurch, Tewkesbury, GL20 7BE
☎ (0684) 295903
Easy to find accommodation; half a mile off the M5 at junction 9, then on the A438 heading towards Stow.
Bedrooms: 3 family rooms.
Bathrooms: 2 public.
Bed & breakfast: £10.50 single, £20 double.
Half board: £16 daily, £110 weekly.
Parking for 10.
🐾 ♨ ⓘ Ⓥ ▦ ♨ ⓣⓥ ▦ ♨ ∪
♨ ❄ ♨ ♨ ♨ ▦

Stanley Villas M
4 Rope Walk, Tewkesbury, GL20 5DS
☎ (0684) 294173

Attractive Victorian property in a quiet cul-de-sac, 4 minutes from the town centre. 3 double bedrooms, bathroom with shower room, TV lounge and pretty garden.
Bedrooms: 1 double & 1 twin, 1 family room.
Bathrooms: 1 public.
Bed & breakfast: £22-£24 double.
Evening meal 6pm (l.o. 6pm).
Parking for 2.
🐾 ♨ ⓤⓛ Ⓥ ♨ ⓣⓥ ▦ ♨ ♪
✗ ▦ ♨ SP

Town Street Farm M
🎫🎫

Tirley, Gloucester, GL19 4HG
☎ Tirley (045 278) 442
500-acre mixed farm. 18th C. farmhouse set in beautiful surroundings and within half a mile of the River Severn.
Bedrooms: 1 twin, 1 family room.
Bathrooms: 1 public; 1 private shower.
Bed & breakfast: from £15 single, from £24 double.
Parking for 4.
🐾 ♨ ⓤⓛ ⓘ Ⓥ ▦ ♨
♪ ∪ ❄ ▦

Gloucestershire
Map ref 2B1

2m N. Tewkesbury
Attractive and quiet village near Tewkesbury with village green, several timber framed cottages and Norman church with interesting monuments.

Abbots Court Farm M
🎫🎫🎫

Church End, Twyning, Tewkesbury, GL20 6DA
☎ (0684) 292515
450-acre dairy/arable farm. Large comfortable farmhouse with spacious rooms and lovely views. Games room and bowling green. Carp lake.
Bedrooms: 1 single, 1 twin, 5 family rooms.
Bathrooms: 3 private, 1 public; 1 private shower.
Bed & breakfast: £12-£13 single, £22-£24 double.
Half board: £17.50 daily, £104-£110 weekly.
Evening meal 6.30pm (l.o. 6.30pm).
Parking for 20.
🐾 ♨ 🖵 ♨ ⓘ Ⓥ ♨ ⓣⓥ ▦
♨ ♨ ♪ ∪ ♪ ❄ ▦ ♨ SP
▦

Gloucestershire
Map ref 2B1

2m E. Dursley
Former cloth weaving village straggling down a hillside with many houses of great distinction, and a Neolithic long barrow, Hetty Pegler's Tump, on the edge of the escarpment above.

Mrs. C.C. Cobham
🎫🎫

61A The Street, Uley, Dursley, GL11 5SL
☎ Dursley (0453) 860313
Large bungalow with garden, near the Cotswold Way, Slimbridge Wildfowl Trust, Tetbury, Cheltenham, Cirencester, Berkeley Castle and many places of interest. Disabled welcome. Pets under control accepted.
Bedrooms: 1 double & 1 twin.
Bathrooms: 1 public.
Bed & breakfast: £11 single, £22 double.
Evening meal 7pm (l.o. 8.30pm).
Parking for 7.
♨ ♨ ⓤⓛ ⓘ Ⓥ ♨ ⓣⓥ ▦ ♨
♨ ❄ ▦

Gloucestershire
Map ref 2B1

3m SE. Gloucester
Village in a lovely setting below hills, with many old houses and a part Norman church.

Hill Farm
🎫

Upton St. Leonards, Gloucester, GL4 8DA
☎ Gloucester (0452) 614081
Located 2 miles from Gloucester, with panoramic views of the Cotswolds. Close to dry ski slopes and golfing facilities. Ideal for walking. Country pub nearby serving food.
Bedrooms: 1 double & 2 twin.
Bathrooms: 3 private.
Bed & breakfast: £15-£20 single, £25-£30 double.
Parking for 6.
🐾 🖵 ♨ ⓤⓛ Ⓥ ♨ ♨ ❄ ▦

MAP REFERENCES APPLY TO THE COLOUR MAPS TOWARDS THE END OF THIS GUIDE.

UPTON-UPON-SEVERN

Hereford & Worcester
Map ref 2B1

See also Longdon.
Attractive country town on the banks of the Severn which is a good river cruising centre. It has many pleasant old houses and inns.

Kings Head Inn
Riverside, Upton-upon-Severn, Worcestershire
WR8 0HF
☎ (068 46) 2621
Riverside coaching inn.
Bedrooms: 3 double & 2 twin.
Bathrooms: 2 public.
Bed & breakfast: from £16.50 single, from £30 double.
Lunch available.
Evening meal 7pm (l.o. 9pm).
Parking for 12.
⛵ ♿ 🅿 V ⁂ ⏰ ♪ ✕ 🅿 🏠

UTTOXETER

Staffordshire
Map ref 4B2

See also Abbots Bromley, Denstone.
Small market town which is famous for its race course. There are half-timbered buildings round the Market Square.

Spar Flat Farm M
Listed
Beamhurst, Uttoxeter,
ST14 5DZ
☎ Hollington (088 926) 238
Secluded homely farmhouse with fine views, set back from the road, and convenient for Alton Towers, the Potteries and Peak District. Ample car parking. Dinner by arrangement.
Bedrooms: 1 double & 1 twin, 1 family room.
Bathrooms: 1 public.
Bed & breakfast: from £10 single, from £20 double.
Parking for 10.
⛵ ⛹ 🅄 🅿 ⏰ ⁂ ⚓ ✕ 🅿

West Lodge M
Bramshall, Uttoxeter,
ST14 5BG
☎ (0889) 566000
Detached residence in an acre of attractive garden, on the B5027, 2 miles from Uttoxeter. Easy access to the Derbyshire Dales and Alton Towers.
Bedrooms: 2 double & 1 twin.
Bathrooms: 2 public.

Bed & breakfast: £7.50-£10 single, £20 double.
Parking for 8.
⛵ 🖵 ♿ 🅄 V ⏰ ⁂ ⚓ ⁂ ✕ 🅿

WARMINGTON

Warwickshire
Map ref 2C1

Warmington Manor
The Green, Warmington, Nr Banbury, Oxon OX17 1BU
☎ Farnborough
(029 589) 239
Telex 837333 TEAMWK G
Small, listed manor house in traditional South Warwickshire village. Off A41 North of Banbury. Stratford and Warwick 12 miles.
Bedrooms: 2 double.
Bathrooms: 2 public.
Bed & breakfast: £17-£20 single, £30-£35 double.
Parking for 2.
🅿 🅄 ⏰ ⏰ ⁂ ✕ 🅿 🏠

WARSLOW

Staffordshire
Map ref 4B2

7m E. Leek

The Greyhound Inn
Listed
Warslow, Buxton, Derbyshire
SK17 0JN
☎ Hartington (029 884) 249
A stone-built country inn, in the pleasant village of Warslow. Set in the Peak National Park, close to the Maniford Valley.
Bedrooms: 2 single, 2 double.
Bathrooms: 1 public.
Bed & breakfast: £10-£12 single, £20-£24 double.
Lunch available.
Evening meal 6pm (l.o. 10.30pm).
Parking for 20.
⛵⛹ 🅄 🅿 V ⏰ ⚓ ⁂ ⚓ 🅿 🅿
SP

WARWICK

Warwickshire
Map ref 2C1

See also Lapworth.
Warwick is outstanding for its castle rising above the River Avon with its splendid State Rooms. ℹ

Chesterfield M
😊
84 Emscote Rd., Warwick,
CV34 5QJ
☎ Warwick (0926) 492396

Family-run guest house with pleasant decor throughout and colour TV in all rooms.
Bedrooms: 2 single, 4 double & 2 twin.
Bathrooms: 1 public;
5 private showers.
Bed & breakfast: £11.50-£13.50 single, £23-£27 double.
Half board: £17.50-£19.50 daily.
Evening meal 7pm (l.o. 6pm).
Parking for 10.
Credit: Access, Visa.
⛵ ⏰ 🅿 ♿ 🅄 V ⏰ ⚓ DAP
SP

The Croft M
😊😊
Haseley Knob, Warwick,
CV35 7NL
☎ Haseley Knob
(092 687) 447
Friendly family atmosphere in picturesque rural setting. On A4177 between Balsall Common and A41, convenient for the National Exhibition Centre, National Agricultural Centre and Stratford.
Bedrooms: 1 double & 1 twin, 1 family room.
Bathrooms: 1 private, 2 public.
Bed & breakfast: £10-£15 single, £26-£30 double.
Half board: £15-£22 daily, £105-£130 weekly.
Evening meal 6pm (l.o. 10pm).
Parking for 11.
⛵⛹ 🕓 ⏰ 🅿 🅄 ⏰ V ⏰
⚓ ⁂ ✕ 🅿

Mrs. E. Draisey M
😊😊😊
44 High St., Warwick,
CV34 4AX
☎ (0926) 401512
Georgian house in town centre. Ground floor guest suite comprises sitting room, bedroom and bathroom. Entrance through secluded walled garden.
Bedrooms: 1 twin.
Bathrooms: 1 private.
Bed & breakfast: £16-£22 single, £25-£30 double.
Parking for 1.
⛵⛹ 🕓 ⏰ 🅿 🅄 ⏰ ✂ ⚓
⏰ ⏰ ⚓ ✕ 🅿 🏠

Laurel House
Shipston Rd., Tysoe,
CV35 0TR
☎ (029 588) 285
Stone house standing in lawns and gardens, 2 miles off A422 Banbury to Stratford road, below Edgehill.

Bedrooms: 1 double, 1 family room.
Bathrooms: 1 public.
Bed & breakfast: from £18 double.
Parking for 4.
⛵ 🅄 V ⚓ ⏰ ⏰ ⁂ 🅿

Merrywood
Listed
Hampton-on-the-Hill,
Warwick, CV35 8QR
☎ (0926) 492766
Family house in small village 2 miles from Warwick, with open views from 2 of the rooms.
Bedrooms: 2 single, 1 double.
Bathrooms: 2 public.
Bed & breakfast: £9.50-£11 single, £18-£20 double.
Parking for 3.
⛵⛹ ⛱ ⏰ 🅿 🅄 ⚓ ⏰ ✕ 🅿
DAP

Northleigh House M
😊😊😊
Five Ways Rd., Hatton,
Warwick, CV35 7HZ
☎ Haseley Knob
(092 687) 203
Comfortable, peaceful country house where the elegant rooms all have colour TV and are individually designed.
Bedrooms: 1 single, 2 double & 2 twin.
Bathrooms: 5 private.
Bed & breakfast: £20-£28 single, £32-£38 double.
Parking for 6.
⛵⛹ 🅿 ⏰ 🅄 V ⚓ ⏰ ⏰
⚓ ⁂ 🅿

Old Rectory
Stratford Rd., Sherbourne,
Warwick, CV35 8AB
☎ Barford (0926) 624562
A Georgian country house with beams and inglenook fireplaces; furnished with antiques. Well-appointed bedrooms, many with brass beds. Dinner is available from October to Easter.
Bedrooms: 5 double & 1 twin, 2 family rooms.
Bathrooms: 7 private, 1 public.
Bed & breakfast: £15-£23 single, £24-£35 double.
Half board: £20-£28 daily.
Evening meal 7pm (l.o. 4pm).
Parking for 9.
⛵⛹ ⏰ 🅿 V ⚓ ⏰ ⏰ ⚓
♿ ⁂ 🅿 SP 🏠

```
┌─────────────────────────────────┐
│  WE ADVISE YOU TO CONFIRM YOUR   │
│         BOOKING IN WRITING.      │
└─────────────────────────────────┘
```

Redlands Farm House M
●

Banbury Rd., Lighthorne, Warwick, CV35 0AH
☎ Leamington Spa (0926) 651241
Built in local stone, mainly 17th C., tastefully restored and with a wealth of timber beams. Centrally located for Warwick and Stratford.
Bedrooms: 1 single, 1 double, 1 family room.
Bathrooms: 1 private, 2 public.
Bed & breakfast: £10.50-£12 single, £21-£24 double.
Half board: £14 daily, £98-£119 weekly.
Evening meal 6.30pm (l.o. 3pm).
Parking for 6.
➤ ⬟ ⬙ ▮ ⬙ ⇥ ⬙ ▥ ❋ ⚹ ⍾ ⊞

Shrewley House M
Listed

Shrewley, Warwick, CV35 7AT
☎ Claverdon (092 684) 2549
Listed farmhouse in Warwickshire countryside, in 1.5 acres of garden. 3 miles from Warwick and 12 miles from the National Exhibition Centre.
Bedrooms: 2 double.
Bathrooms: 2 private, 1 public.
Bed & breakfast: from £20 single, from £30 double.
Parking for 22.
➤ ⬙ ⬙ ⬟ ⬙ ▮ ⬙ ⌇ ⇥ ⬙
▥ ⬛ ❋ ⍾ ⎚ ⊞

8m SE. Leek
Village in the valley of the River Hamps, once the terminus of the Leek and Manifold Light Railway, 8 miles of which is now a macadamised walkers' path.

Back Lane Farm M
●●

Winkhill, Leek, ST13 7PJ
☎ Waterhouses (053 86) 273
Farmhouse bed and breakfast, set in 20 acres of land on the edge of the Peak Park, close to A523.
Bedrooms: 1 single, 1 double & 1 twin.
Bathrooms: 1 private, 1 public.
Bed & breakfast: £9-£15.50 single, £22-£26 double.

Half board: £15.50-£22 daily, £102.20-£127.40 weekly.
Evening meal 7pm (l.o. 5.50pm).
Parking for 12.
Open March-December.
➤ ⬟ ▮ ⬙ ⇥ ⬙ ▥ ❋ ⍾

Mrs. K. Watson M
●●

Weaver Farm, Waterhouses, Stoke-on-Trent, ST10 3HE
☎ Oakamoor (0538) 702271
270-acre dairy/mixed farm. Stone built farmhouse on the Weaver Hills. Ideal for touring Derbyshire and Staffordshire. 5 miles from Alton Towers.
Bedrooms: 1 single, 2 double & 1 twin, 1 family room.
Bathrooms: 1 public.
Bed & breakfast: from £10 single, £16-£20 double.
Half board: from £14 daily, from £80 weekly.
Evening meal 6pm (l.o. 3pm).
Parking for 6.
➤ ⬙ ⬟ ▮ ⬙ ⇥ ⬙ ▥ ⍾
⊙ ⎘ ❋ ⍾ ⎚ ⊞

Picturesque village with several noteworthy pubs. The River Dene which divides the place in two once separated Wellesbourne Hastings from Wellesbourne Mountford, but now both parts are regarded as one village.

Dunrovin
●●

Friz Hill, Wellesbourne, Warwick, CV35 9HH
☎ Stratford-upon-Avon (0789) 841544
17th C. converted barn in a peaceful rural setting. Within easy reach of the Cotswolds, Stratford-upon-Avon, Warwick and the National Exhibition Centre.
Bedrooms: 1 double & 1 twin.
Bathrooms: 1 public.
Bed & breakfast: £22-£24 double.
Parking for 3.
⬟ ⬙ ⎚ ⍾ ⊞

```
PLEASE CHECK
PRICES AND OTHER
DETAILS AT THE
TIME OF BOOKING.
```

See also Shawbury.
Small town connected with Judge Jeffreys who lived in Lowe Hall. Well-known for its ales.

Castle Hotel M
●●

High St., Wem, Shrewsbury, SY4 5AA
☎ (0939) 32430
The hotel retains old world charm from the original coaching house in the centre of the market town of Wem.
Bedrooms: 2 single, 2 double & 2 twin.
Bathrooms: 1 public.
Bed & breakfast: £12-£15 single, £20-£28 double.
Lunch available.
Evening meal 7pm (l.o. 10pm).
Parking for 20.
➤ ⬙ ▮ ⇥ ⎚ ⎚ ⍾ ⎓ ⊞

Lowe Hall Farm M
●●

Wem, Shrewsbury, SY4 5UE
☎ (0939) 32236
134-acre dairy farm. Historically famous grade II listed farmhouse, once the country residence of Judge Jeffries, 1648-1689. Splendid Jacobean staircase and Charles II fireplace. Excellent touring centre.
Bedrooms: 1 double & 1 twin, 1 family room.
Bathrooms: 1 public.
Bed & breakfast: £10 single, £20 double.
Half board: £70 weekly.
➤ ⬙ ⬟ ⬙ ▮ ⬙ ⇥ ⎚ ⎚
⍾ ⍾ ⎚ ❋ ⚹ ⍾ ⊞

Soulton Hall M
●●●

Wem, Shrewsbury, SY4 5RS
☎ (0939) 32786
560-acre mixed farm. Tudor manor house with moated Domesday site in grounds, offering relaxing holiday. Private riverside and woodland walks.
Bedrooms: 1 double & 2 twin.
Bathrooms: 2 private, 1 public.
Bed & breakfast: £15-£18 single, £30-£36 double.
Half board: £23-£26 daily, £161-£182 weekly.
Evening meal 7pm (l.o. 8.30pm).
Parking for 4.
➤ ⬙ ⬙ ⊞ ⬟ ▮ ⬙ ⇥
⍾ ⍾ ⎓ ⎘ ⟋ ❋ ⍾ ⎚ ⎚
⊞

5m NE. Bishops Castle
Village near the lovely countryside of the Longmynd and close to the Welsh border and Offa's Dyke.

Crown Inn M
Listed

Wentnor, Bishops Castle, SY9 5EE
☎ Linley (058 861) 613
On the western side of the Longmynd hills which offer unrestricted walking in thousands of acres of National Trust Land. Easy access to Midland Gliding Club; private fishing nearby.
Bedrooms: 1 double & 2 twin, 1 family room.
Bathrooms: 2 public.
Bed & breakfast: £10.50-£15 single, £21-£25 double.
Lunch available.
Evening meal 7pm (l.o. 10pm).
Parking for 12.
➤⬤ ⬚ ⬙ ▮ ⬙ ⎚ ⍾ ⎚ ⍾ ⎓
⍾ ⎘ ⟋ ❋ ⍾ ⍾ ⎚ ⊞

One of the most beautiful Herefordshire villages and full of attractive black and white timber-framed houses. It is dominated by the church which has a fine spire.

Mellington House M
Listed

Broad St., Weobley, Hereford, Herefordshire HR4 8SA
☎ (0544) 318537
A half-timbered structure with a Queen Anne style frontage added in 1926. Interesting historical features.
Bedrooms: 1 double & 2 twin.
Bathrooms: 2 private, 1 public.
Bed & breakfast: £11.50-£13.50 single, £23-£27 double.
Half board: £18.50-£19.50 daily, £125.50-£140.50 weekly.
Evening meal 7.30pm (l.o. 8.30pm).
➤ ⬙ ⬚ ⬚ ⬟ ⬙ ⎚ ⍾ ⎚ ⎚
⍾ ❋ ⚹ ⍾ ⎚ ⎚ ⊞

WESTON RHYN

Shropshire
Map ref 4A2

4m N. Oswestry
Agricultural parish close
to the River Ceiriog and
the Chirk Valley. The
Druids Temple is a folly
built by a local landowner
in the last century.

Rhoswiel Lodge ⋔
Listed
Weston Rhyn, Oswestry,
SY10 7TG
☎ Chirk (0691) 777609
*Victorian house with modern
annexe in pleasant
surroundings beside Llangollen
Canal. 300 yards from the A5.*
Bedrooms: 2 single, 1 double
& 2 twin, 1 family room.
Bathrooms: 3 public.
Bed & breakfast: £9-£12
single, £18-£22 double.
Half board: £14-£17 daily,
£95 weekly.
Evening meal 7pm (l.o.
5.30pm).
Parking for 6.
⑤ ⅏ ↝ ♥ 🅸 ▾ 🆅 🆃🆅 ⌨ ✿
🐾

WHITNEY-ON-WYE

Hereford & Worcester
Map ref 2A1

Here the main Hereford-
Brecon road crosses into
Wales and nearby the
Wye is spanned by its
only surviving toll bridge,
the owners of which are
exempt, by the terms of
an Act of George III, from
payments of taxes.

The Rhydspence Inn ⋔
⊕ ⊕ ⊕
Whitney-on-Wye, Hereford,
Herefordshire HR3 6EU
☎ Clifford (049 73) 262
*16th C. black and white
country inn offering food and
hospitality, in the superb Wye
Valley and Black Mountains
countryside.*
Bedrooms: 1 single, 3 double
& 1 twin.
Bathrooms: 5 private.
Bed & breakfast: £22 single,
£44 double.
Lunch available.
Evening meal 7.30pm (l.o.
9.30pm).
Parking for 60.
Credit: Access, Visa, Amex.
⑤ ↝ ▯ ♥ 🅸 ▾ ⌨ ⌨ 🐾 ✿
🐾 🐾 🆂🅿 🏠

WIGMORE

Hereford & Worcester
Map ref 4A3

9m NW. Leominster
Village with a Norman
church and some
attractive half-timbered
houses. There are the
remains of Wigmore
Castle and Wigmore
Abbey and Croft Castle
(National Trust) is nearby.

Queen's House
Wigmore, Leominster,
Herefordshire HR6 9UJ
☎ (056 886) 451
*Spacious 2-storey house,
mainly black and white, with
beams in all rooms. Furnished
with antiques.*
Bedrooms: 1 single, 2 double
& 1 twin, 1 family room.
Bathrooms: 2 public.
Bed & breakfast: £10 single,
£20 double.
Half board: £13-£18 daily,
£77-£112 weekly.
Lunch available.
Evening meal 8pm (l.o. 6pm).
Parking for 8.
⑤ ↝ 🆄🅻 ▾ 🅸 🝤 🆃🆅 ⌨ 🝤
🐾 🝤 🆂🅿 🏠

WILMCOTE

Warwickshire
Map ref 2B1

*3m NW. Stratford-upon-
Avon*
Village where
Shakespeare's mother,
Mary Arden, lived. Her
home has an attractive
cottage garden and now
houses a museum of
rural life.

Swan Cottage
The Green, Wilmcote,
Stratford-upon-Avon,
CV37 9XJ
☎ Stratford-upon-Avon
(0789) 66480
*Old cottage on the village
green, overlooking Mary
Arden's house. Pleasant garden
available to guests. Farmhouse
museum and gardens.*
Bedrooms: 1 double & 1 twin.
Bathrooms: 1 public.
Bed & breakfast: £22-£25
double.
Parking for 4.
⑤ ⅏ 🆄🅻 🆃🆅 ⌨ 🝤 🐾 🐾 🏠

WOLVERHAMPTON

West Midlands

See Codsall.

WINCHCOMBE

Gloucestershire
Map ref 2B1

Ancient town with a folk
museum and railway
museum. To the south
lies Sudeley Castle with
its fine collection of
paintings and toys and an
Elizabethan garden. 🅸

Gower House
16 North St., Winchcombe,
Cheltenham, GL54 5LH
☎ Cheltenham (0242) 602616
*17th C. house in town centre,
close to shops. Large garden
and parking space at rear.*
Bedrooms: 1 double & 2 twin.
Bathrooms: 2 public.
Bed & breakfast: £10-£20
single, £20 double.
Parking for 4.
⑤ ↝ 🆄🅻 🆃🆅 ⌨ 🝤 🐾 🐾 🏠

Great House
Castle St., Winchcombe,
Cheltenham, GL54 5JA
☎ (0242) 602490
*A Jacobean house within half a
mile of Sudeley Castle, on the
route of the Cotswold Way.*
Bedrooms: 1 double, 1 family
room.
Bathrooms: 1 public.
Bed & breakfast: £22-£25
double.
⑤ ↝ 🝤 🆃🆅 ⌨ 🐾 🐾 🏠

Old Station House
⊕ ⊕
Winchcombe, Cheltenham,
GL54 5LD
☎ (0242) 602283
*Cotswold stone former
stationmaster's house in quiet
rural setting. Central for
touring the Cotswolds.
Restaurant facilities nearby.*
Bedrooms: 1 double, 1 family
room.
Bathrooms: 1 public.
Bed & breakfast: £18-£20
double.
Parking for 3.
⑤ 🆄🅻 🝤 🆃🆅 ⌨ 🐾 🐾 🏠

WOOLHOPE

Hereford & Worcester
Map ref 2A1

7m SE. Hereford
Village amid woods and
hills where 5 major roads
meet and whose part-
Norman church contains
a window showing Lady
Godiva, once the owner
of the manor, riding
through Coventry. Haugh
Wood, with nature trail, is
nearby.

Butchers Arms ⋔
Listed
Woolhope, Hereford,
Herefordshire HR1 4RF
☎ Fownhope (043 277) 281
*A 14th C. listed, half-timbered
inn in rural and wooded
countryside. Low oak beams,
log fires, traditional ales,
restaurant and bar food.*
Bedrooms: 2 double & 1 twin.
Bathrooms: 1 public.
Bed & breakfast: from £20.50
single, from £33 double.
Lunch available.
Evening meal 7.30pm (l.o.
9pm).
Parking for 80.
🝤 ↝ 🅸 ▾ ⌨ 🐾 🐾 🐾 🆂🅿 🏠

WOOTTON WAWEN

Warwickshire
Map ref 4B3

*4m NW. Stratford-upon-
Avon*
Attractive village which
has an unspoilt church
with an Anglo-Saxon
tower, the only chained
library in Warwickshire
and some good brasses
and monuments.

Wootton Park Farm
Alcester Rd., Wootton
Wawen. Solihull, W.
Midlands B95 6HJ
☎ Henley-in-Arden
(056 42) 2673
*330-acre dairy/arable farm.
Delightful 16th C. half-
timbered farmhouse with a
wealth of oak beams. 5 miles
north of Stratford-upon-Avon
in quiet countryside.
Conveniently situated for the
National Agricultural Centre
and the National Exhibition
Centre.*
Bedrooms: 1 double & 1 twin,
1 family room.
Bathrooms: 1 private,
1 public.

**GROUPS, CONSORTIA AND AGENCIES
SPECIALISING IN FARM AND COUNTRY
HOLIDAYS ARE LISTED IN A SPECIAL
SECTION OF THIS GUIDE.**

Bed & breakfast: £13-£14 single, £25-£26 double. Parking for 6.

🛇 🛆 ⬜ ⓘ Ⅴ ✂ ⌫ TV ▥ 🛆 ❉ ✕ 🎄 🅐ⓟ SP 🎏

See also Stoulton.
Lovely city which is dominated by its Norman and Early English cathedral, King John's burial place. The city has many old buildings including the 15th C Commandery and the 18th C Guildhall. There are several museums and the Royal Worcester Porcelain factory. *i*

Ailsa ⬱⬱
49 Park Avenue, Barbourne, Worcester, Worcestershire WR3 7AJ
☎ (0905) 23707
A roomy, mid-terrace Victorian house located in a very attractive, quiet, tree-lined road, within easy reach of the city.
Bedrooms: 1 double & 1 twin.
Bathrooms: 1 public; 1 private shower.
Bed & breakfast: £18-£21 double.
Parking for 2.
🛇 🖰 ⬜ TV ▥ 🎄

49 Britannia Sq. ⋒
Listed
Worcester, Worcestershire WR1 3HP
☎ (0905) 22756
An attractive grade II listed Georgian house with comfortable accommodation, in a quiet and pleasant square near the city centre.
Bedrooms: 1 single, 1 double & 1 twin.
Bathrooms: 1 private, 1 public.
Bed & breakfast: £15-£20 single, £28-£33 double.
Parking for 2.
🛇 🛆 ⓑ ▢ 🖰 ⬜ Ⅴ ✂ TV ▥ 🛆 ❉ 🎄 🎏

Burgage House
Listed
4 College Precincts, Worcester, Worcestershire WR1 2LG
☎ (0905) 25396
Comfortable accommodation in a fine grade II listed Georgian house adjacent to Worcester Cathedral, overlooking the cathedral grounds.

Bedrooms: 1 single, 2 double & 1 twin, 1 family room.
Bathrooms: 2 public.
Bed & breakfast: £13-£15 single, £26-£30 double.
Half board: from £18.50 daily, from £125 weekly.
Evening meal 7pm.
🛇 ⚘ ▢ ⬜ 🖰 ⬜ Ⅴ ✂ ⌫ ▥ 🛆 ✕ 🎄 🅐ⓟ SP 🎏 Ⓣ

Diglis Hotel ⋒
Riverside, Worcester, Worcestershire WR1 2NF
☎ (0905) 353518
Old riverside mansion.
Bedrooms: 6 single, 2 double & 4 twin, 3 family rooms.
Bathrooms: 3 private, 2 public; 2 private showers.
Bed & breakfast: £22.50-£27.50 single, £37.50-£45 double.
Half board: £31-£36 daily, £165-£195 weekly.
Evening meal 7pm (l.o. 9.45pm).
Parking for 60.
Credit: Access, Visa.
🛇 ⓑ ⓘ Ⅴ ⌫ TV ▥ ⓣ ♪
SP 🎏

Mrs. J. Popplewell ⬱⬱
Hilltop House, Cotheridge, Worcester, Worcestershire WR6 5LX
☎ Cotheridge (090 566) 288
*A Queen Anne, former farmhouse with extension built earlier this century.
Outstanding views across the Teme Valley. Located on the A44.*
Bedrooms: 2 twin, 1 family room.
Bathrooms: 1 public.
Bed & breakfast: £10-£12 single, £20-£23 double.
Parking for 7.
🛇 ⚘ ⬜ 🖰 Ⅴ ⌫ TV ▥ 🛆 🛆 ❉ 🎄

Leigh Court ⋒ ⬱⬱
Leigh, Worcester, Worcestershire WR6 5LB
☎ Leigh Sinton (0886) 32275
270-acre sheep/arable farm. Period Teme Valley farmhouse beside the river, with Worcester and Malvern within five miles. Friendly, informal atmosphere. Home cooking and river fishing. French spoken.
Bedrooms: 1 double & 1 twin, 1 family room.
Bathrooms: 2 public.
Bed & breakfast: £15-£16 single, £24-£26 double.
Half board: £24-£25 daily, £136 weekly.

Evening meal 7pm.
Parking for 6.
Open March-October.
🛇 ⓑ ⚘ TV ⬜ 🖰 Ⅴ ⌫ TV ▥ 🛆 ⚘ ♪ ✎ ❉ 🎄 🎏

Lightwood Farm Holidays ⬱⬱
Little Lightwood Farm, Cotheridge, Worcester, Worcestershire WR6 5LT
☎ Cotheridge (090 566) 236
56-acre dairy farm. Farmhouse accommodation with shaver points and heating in all bedrooms. Delightful views of the Malvern Hills. Just off the A44 from Worcester to Leominster, 3.5 miles from Worcester.
Bedrooms: 1 double & 1 twin, 1 family room.
Bathrooms: 1 public.
Bed & breakfast: £9-£12 single, £18-£24 double.
Half board: £15-£18 daily, £100-£120 weekly.
Evening meal 6pm.
Parking for 6.
Open March-November.
🛇 1 ⚘ ⬜ ⓘ Ⅴ ⌫ TV ▥ 🛆 ✕ 🎄 🎏

Loch Ryan Hotel ⋒
119 Sidbury, Worcester, Worcestershire WR5 2DH
☎ (0905) 351143
Historic hotel very close to the cathedral, Royal Worcester Porcelain Factory and Commandery. Attractive terraced garden.
Bedrooms: 11 single, 3 double & 3 twin, 2 family rooms.
Bathrooms: 2 private, 3 public.
Bed & breakfast: £18-£22 single, £30-£40 double.
Half board: from £22.50 daily.
Lunch available.
Evening meal 7pm (l.o. 8.30pm).
🛇 🛆 ⬜ ⌫ TV ▥ 🛆 ♪ ✕ 🅐ⓟ SP 🎏 Ⓣ

Osborne House ⬱
17 Chestnut Walk, Worcester, Worcestershire WR1 1PR
☎ (0905) 22296
Comfortable accommodation in restored Victorian house in a quiet position near swimming baths and antique shops.
Bedrooms: 1 double & 1 twin, 1 family room.

Bathrooms: 3 private showers.
Bed & breakfast: £10-£15 single, £23 double.
Parking for 4.
🛇 ⚘ ⬜ Ⅴ ⌫ TV ▥ ✕ 🎄

9m SW. Hereford
Village in the Golden Valley close to the very beautiful churches at Kilpeck and Abbey Dore.

Duffryn Farm ⋒ ⬱⬱
Wormbridge, Hereford, Herefordshire HR2 9EJ
☎ (098 121) 217
251-acre beef, arable & sheep farm. Hospitable farmhouse where guests are welcome to take an interest in the farm. Traditional farmyard with duck pond.
Bedrooms: 1 double, 2 family rooms.
Bathrooms: 1 public.
Bed & breakfast: max. £12 single, max. £24 double.
Evening meal 6.30pm (l.o. 5pm).
Parking for 6.
🛇 ⚘ ⬜ ⓘ Ⅴ ⌫ TV ▥ 🛆 ❉ 🎄 🎏

INDIVIDUAL
PROPRIETORS HAVE
SUPPLIED ALL
DETAILS OF
ACCOMMODATION.
ALTHOUGH WE DO
CHECK FOR
ACCURACY, WE
ADVISE YOU TO
CONFIRM PRICES
AND OTHER
INFORMATION AT
THE TIME OF
BOOKING.

THE SYMBOLS ARE EXPLAINED ON THE FLAP
INSIDE THE BACK COVER.

Leasow House

Laverton Meadows, Broadway, Worcestershire WR12 7NA
☎ *Stanton (0386 73) 526*

*Tranquilly situated approximately one mile off the B4632 (A46) &
some three miles south of Broadway, making it ideally situated as a
centre for touring the Cotswolds & the Vale of Evesham.
We offer spacious accommodation with all the refinements of the 20th
Century. All bedrooms have private shower/bathroom en suite, colour
television, tea & coffee making facilities. Ground floor facilities for
elderly & disabled people.*

*Leasow House is personally run by your hosts:
BARBARA & GORDON MEEKINGS*

Rakesdale House

Rakesdale, Alton, Staffordshire ST10 4BT.
☎ **(0538) 702097 Proprietors: Eva & Terry Pickard.**

Enjoy a truly peaceful holiday in this beautiful country house, lying
in its own 13½ acre dale. Look out of the stone mullioned
windows, over the cascade of waterfalls and trout filled ponds.
Superb walking country. (Alton Towers, 1 mile). All double and
family rooms have antique pine and wash basins. The English
breakfast is served in a galleried dining room.
Terms: B&B £12.50 per person (reductions for children sharing a
family room).

When requesting brochures or further information from advertisers in this guide, you may
find it helpful to use the advertisement
enquiry coupons which can be found
towards the end of the guide. These should be cut out
and mailed direct to the companies in which you are
interested. Remember to include your name and address
and enclose a stamped and addressed envelope or
stamps if requested by the advertiser.

P L E A S E   N O T E
Individual establishments who have a display advertisement have a line listing under the appropriate town heading

CROWN CLASSIFICATIONS

All the establishments displaying a national classification in this guide are inspected regularly. All can be chosen with confidence.

There are six classifications — from Listed to 5 Crowns; each indicates the level of facilities and services provided.

All classified establishments are required to provide a high standard of cleanliness, courtesy and service and to be well maintained. A lower classification does not imply lower standards; although the range of facilities and services may be smaller, they may be provided to a high standard.

You will find a full explanation of the national Crown Classification Scheme towards the end of this guide.

The town or village you wish to visit may not have accommodation entirely suited to your needs, but there could be somewhere ideal quite close by. From the colour maps towards the end of this guide you will be able to identify nearby towns and villages with accommodation listed in the guide. You can then use the index to find the relevant page numbers.

♣ Enjoy the countryside and respect its life and work ♣ Guard against all risk of fire ♣ Fasten all gates ♣ Keep your dogs under close control ♣ Keep to public paths across farmland ♣ Use gates and stiles to cross fences, hedges and walls ♣ Leave livestock, crops and machinery alone ♣ Take your litter home ♣ Help to keep all water clean ♣ Protect wildlife, plants and trees ♣ Take special care on country roads ♣ Make no unnecessary noise

East Midlands

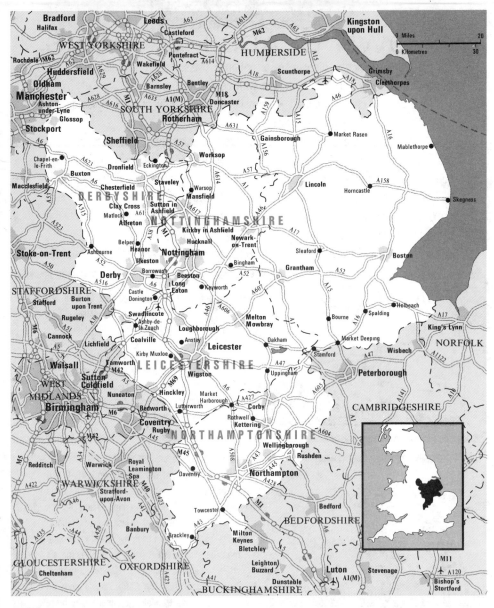

INFORMATION

T he Shires of Middle England — that's the other name for the five counties of Derbyshire, Leicestershire, Lincolnshire, Northamptonshire and Nottinghamshire which together form the East Midlands tourist region.

Each county has its own character and attractions but, together, they offer the peace of the countryside, the pulse of the city and the fun of the seaside.

The beautiful Peaks of Derbyshire, famous Sherwood Forest in Nottinghamshire, the unspoilt coast and rolling wolds of Lincolnshire, the quiet, rural havens of Leicestershire, the rich history and splendid historic houses of Northamptonshire add up to a region full of inviting possibilities.

Paul Anscomb

SHERWOOD FOREST   ROBIN HOOD COUNTRY

From the depths of the countryside to the nightlife of the cities — taking in the dramatic castles, majestic cathedrals, hills, woods, rivers, lakes, canals and coast on the way — the Shires offer something for everyone.

And in 1989, the region will be playing its full part in the Celebration of British Food and Farming. Lincolnshire's rich soil is renowned for its vegetables and bulbs; Stilton, Leicester and Sage Derby cheeses have a world reputation; and there's Bakewell Pudding, Grantham and Ashbourne gingerbread and Buxton Spring Water to delight the palate.

FIND OUT MORE

Further information about holidays and attractions in the East Midlands tourist region is available from:
East Midlands Tourist Board, Exchequergate, Lincoln LN2 1PZ. ☎ (0522) 531521.

These publications are available from the East Midlands Tourist Board (prices include post and packing):
Shires of Middle England (information guide) £1
Shires of Middle England (descriptive brochure) 95p
Shires of Middle England (leisure map) £2.50
Peak District Holidays 80p

Also available is an **Events List** (free, but large stamped and addressed envelope would be appreciated)

WHERE TO GO, WHAT TO SEE

Chatsworth
Bakewell, Derbyshire DE4 1PP
☎ (024 688) 2204
Built between 1687 – 1707. Gardens laid out by 'Capability' Brown. Collection of pictures, books, drawings and furniture.
Admission charge.

▶

Poole's Cavern
Green Lane, Buxton, Derbyshire
SK17 9DH ☎ (0298) 6978
One of the finest natural limestone
caves. Stalactites and stalagmites.
Exhibition area, video show.
Admission charge.

Wirksworth Heritage Centre
Crown Yard, Market Place, Wirksworth,
Derbyshire DE4 4ET
☎ (062 982) 5225
Interpretative displays of town's past,
present and future. Cafe and working
smithy. Crown Yard also holds a
silversmith's workshop and cabinet
maker's workshop.
Admission charge.

Sherwood Forest Visitor Centre and Country Park
Edwinstowe, Nr. Mansfield,
Nottinghamshire NG21 9HN
☎ (0623) 823202
450 acres of ancient Sherwood Forest
containing the Major Oak, with Robin
Hood associations. Visitor Centre
includes Robin Hood exhibition, slide
shows, films, talks, shop.
Admission charge.

Belvoir Castle
Belvoir, Nr. Grantham, Lincolnshire
NG32 1PD ☎ (0476) 870262
Seat of the Dukes of Rutland since
Henry VIII's time, rebuilt by Wyatt in
1816. Notable pictures, state rooms and
museum of 17th/21st Lancers.
Admission charge.

Kedleston Hall
Kedleston, Derby, Derbyshire DE6 4JN
☎ (0332) 842191
The finest Robert Adam house, built
1759 – 65, including unique Marble Hall
and the Saloon. Collection of Old
Masters. Marquis Curzon's Indian
Museum.
Admission charge.

University of Leicester Botanic Gardens
Beaumont Hall, Stoughton Drive South,
Oadby, Leicester, Leicestershire
LE2 2NA ☎ (0533) 717725

WATERWAYS MUSEUM BESIDE THE GRAND UNION CANAL

Britain on View

16 acres containing several individual
gardens of different character.
Admission free.

Hartsholme Country Park
Skellingthorpe Road, Lincoln,
Lincolnshire ☎ (0522) 686264
Lake surrounded by 88 acres of
grassland and woodland. Information
centre with natural history displays.
Nature trail, cafe.
Admission free.

Newark Air Museum
The Airfield, Winthorpe,
Newark-on-Trent, Nottinghamshire
NG24 2NY ☎ (0636) 707170
Collection of over 30 aircraft and
aviation-related items. Large exhibition
hall, book and model shop.
Admission charge.

The Lace Hall
High Pavement, Nottingham,
Nottinghamshire NG1 1HN
☎ (0602) 484221
The Story of Nottingham Lace
exhibition, including audio-visual
presentation, with lace shops and coffee
shop, in fine converted church building.
Admission charge.

Church Farm Museum
Church Road South, Skegness,
Lincolnshire ☎ (0754) 66658
19th C farm buildings house the
Bernard Best collection of local

agricultural machinery and the
farmhouse is furnished as the home of
a tenant farmer of about 1900.
Exhibitions.
Admission charge.

Waterways Museum
Stoke Bruerne, Nr. Towcester,
Northamptonshire ☎ (0604) 862229
Colourful display beside the Grand
Union Canal brings to life the rich
history of over 200 years on the canals
and waterways of the whole country.
Admission charge.

Turner's Musical Merry-Go-Round
Queen Eleanor Vale, Newport Pagnell
Road, Wootton, Northampton,
Northamptonshire NN4 0HU
☎ (0604) 763314
Unique collection of mechanical musical
instruments presented as a spectacular
show. Dancing to one of the largest
Wurlitzer theatre organs in Europe.
Fairground carousel.
Admission charge.

MAKE A DATE FOR...

Spalding Flower Festival and Parade
Spalding, Lincolnshire *6 – 8 May*

Nottingham Festival
Various venues, Nottingham,
Nottinghamshire *30 May – 16 June*

Lincoln Mystery Plays
Lincoln Cathedral, Lincoln, Lincolnshire
12 – 20 July

Buxton International Festival
Various venues, Buxton, Derbyshire
22 July – 13 August

Medieval Jousting Tournament
Belvoir Castle, Belvoir, Leicestershire
27 – 28 August

Nottingham Goose Fair
Forest Recreation Ground, Nottingham,
Nottinghamshire *5 – 7 October*

World Conker Championship
Village Green, Ashton, Nr. Oundle,
Northamptonshire *8 October*

Lincoln Christmas Market
Bailgate and Castle Hill, Lincoln,
Lincolnshire *14 – 17 December* *

* Provisional dates only

ASHBOURNE, DERBYSHIRE

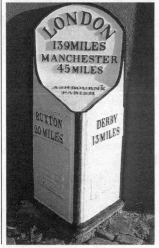

LONDON
139 MILES
MANCHESTER
45 MILES
ASHBOURNE
PARISH

BUXTON
20 MILES

DERBY
13 MILES

Britain on View

Tourist Information *i*

Tourist and leisure information can be obtained from Tourist Information Centres throughout England. Details of centres in the East Midlands region are listed below. The symbol means that an accommodation booking service is provided. Centres marked with a ✱ are open during the summer months only. In the following pages, towns which have a Tourist Information Centre are indicated with the symbol *i*.

Ashbourne
Derbyshire
13 Market Place
☎ (0335) 43666

Ashby-de-la-Zouch
Leicestershire ✱
North Street
☎ (0530) 510034

Bakewell
Derbyshire
Old Market Hall, Bridge Street
☎ (062 981) 3227

Bosworth Battlefield
Leicestershire ✱
Visitor Centre, Sutton Cheney,
Nr. Market Bosworth
☎ (0455) 292239

Buxton
Derbyshire
The Crescent
☎ (0298) 5106, changing during 1989 to (0298) 25106

Chesterfield
Derbyshire
The Peacock, TIC & Heritage Centre, Low Pavement
☎ (0246) 207777

Coalville
Leicestershire
Public Library, High Street
☎ (0530) 35951

Corby
Northamptonshire
Civic Centre, George Street
☎ (0536) 402551

Daventry
Northamptonshire
Moot Hall, Market Square
☎ (0327) 300277

Derby
Derbyshire
Central Library, The Wardwick
☎ (0332) 290664

Glossop
Derbyshire
Railway Station Forecourt, Norfolk Street
☎ (045 74) 5920

Grantham
Lincolnshire
Grantham Museum,
St. Peter's Hill
☎ (0476) 66444

Heckington
Lincolnshire
The Pearoom Craft Heritage Centre, Station Yard, Nr. Sleaford
☎ Sleaford (0529) 60088

▶

Hinckley
Leicestershire 🛏
Public Library, Lancaster Road
☎ (0455) 30852/635106

Kettering
Northamptonshire 🛏
The Coach House, Sheep Street
☎ (0536) 410266/410333

Leicester
Leicestershire
25 – 27 St. Martin's Walk
☎ (0533) 511300
St Margaret's Bus Station 🛏
☎ (0533) 532353

Lincoln
Lincolnshire
9 Castle Hill 🛏
☎ (0522) 29828
Cornhill 🛏
☎ (0522) 512971

Loughborough
Leicestershire 🛏
John Storer House, Wards End
☎ (0509) 230131

Mablethorpe
Lincolnshire 🛏
The Dunes Family Entertainment
Centre, Central Promenade
☎ (0521) 72496

Market Harborough
Leicestershire 🛏
Pen Lloyd Library,
Adam and Eve Street
☎ (0858) 62649/62699

Matlock
Derbyshire 🛏
Matlock Bath Pavilion,
Matlock Bath
☎ (0629) 55082

Melton Mowbray
Leicestershire 🛏
Melton Carnegie Museum,
Thorpe End
☎ (0664) 69946

Newark
Nottinghamshire 🛏
The Ossington,
Beast Market Hall
☎ (0636) 78962

Northampton
Northamptonshire 🛏
21 St. Giles Street
☎ (0604) 22677/34881 Ext.
404

Nottingham (West Bridgford)
Nottinghamshire
County Hall, West Bridgford
☎ (0602) 823823
14 – 16 Wheeler Gate 🛏
☎ (0602) 470661

Oakham
Leicestershire 🛏
Public Library, Catmos Street
☎ (0572) 2918

Ollerton
Nottinghamshire 🛏
Sherwood Heath, Ollerton
Roundabout, Nr. Newark
☎ Mansfield (0623) 824545

Oundle
Northamptonshire 🛏
Market Place
☎ (0832) 74333

Retford
Nottinghamshire 🛏
Town Hall, The Square
☎ (0777) 706741

Sherwood Forest
Nottinghamshire 🛏
Sherwood Forest Visitor Centre,
Edwinstowe
☎ Mansfield (0623) 823202

Skegness
Lincolnshire 🛏 *
Embassy Centre, Grand Parade
☎ (0754) 4821

Sleaford
Lincolnshire 🛏 *
Moneys Yard Car Park,
Carre Street
☎ (0529) 60088

Spalding
Lincolnshire 🛏
Ayscoughfee Hall, Churchgate
☎ (0775) 5468

Spilsby
Lincolnshire
Council Offices, 41B High Street
☎ (0790) 52301

Stamford
Lincolnshire 🛏
Stamford Museum, Broad Street
☎ (0780) 55611

Wellingborough
Northamptonshire 🛏
Wellingborough Library,
Pebble Lane
☎ (0933) 225365

Worksop
Nottinghamshire
Queen's Buildings, Potter Street
☎ (0909) 475531

Entries in this regional section are listed in alphabetical order of place name, and then in alphabetical order of establishment. County names are not normally repeated in each establishment entry, but please use the full postal address when writing.

The map references refer to the colour maps towards the end of this guide. The first number is the number of the map, and it is followed by the grid reference.

The Crown Classifications are explained on pages 8 and 9, and the key to symbols is on the flap inside the back cover — keep it open for easy reference.

ABNEY
Derbyshire
Map ref 4B2

2m SW. Hathersage

Lane End Farm
Listed
Abney, Hathersage, Via
Sheffield S30 1AA
☎ Hope Valley (0433) 50371
*Between Hathersage and
Tideswell. Farm trail and
horse riding available. Holiday
flat also available.*
Bedrooms: 1 double & 1 twin,
1 family room.
Bathrooms: 1 public.
Bed & breakfast: £11-£14
single, £22-£28 double.
Parking for 8.

ABTHORPE
Northamptonshire
Map ref 2C1

3m SW. Towcester

Mr. & Mrs. M.J.C. Brodie, Fawe Park
17 Wappenham Road,
Abthorpe, Towcester,
NN12 8QU
☎ Silverstone (0327) 857544
*A country house built 1957, in
its own large garden with
extensive views over farmland.
Quiet village convenient for the
Cotswolds, Stratford, Oxford
and Silverstone Race Track.*
Bedrooms: 2 twin.
Bathrooms: 1 public.
Bed & breakfast: £13 single,
£24 double.
Evening meal 6pm (l.o. 9pm).
Parking for 5.

ALDWARK
Derbyshire
Map ref 4B2

5m SW. Matlock

Tithe Farm
Grange Mill, Aldwark, Via
Derby, DE4 4HX
☎ Carsington (062 985) 263
*Peacefully situated, within 10
miles of Matlock, Bakewell,
Ashbourne, the Dales and
historic houses. Fresh produce
and home baking are a
speciality.*
Bedrooms: 3 twin.
Bathrooms: 1 public.
Bed & breakfast: £20.50
double.
Half board: £16.75 daily,
£100.50 weekly.
Evening meal 7pm (l.o. 6pm).
Parking for 6.
Open April-October.

ALKMONTON
Derbyshire
Map ref 4B2

4m NE. Sudbury

Dairy House Farm
Alkmonton, Longford,
Derby, DE6 3DG
☎ Great Cubley
(033 523) 359
*82-acre dairy farm. Old, red
brick farmhouse with oak-
beams, an inglenook fireplace
and a comfortable atmosphere.
Guests have their own lounge
and dining room.*
Bedrooms: 2 single, 1 double
& 1 twin, 2 family rooms.
Bathrooms: 2 public.
Bed & breakfast: £10-£12
single, £20-£24 double.
Half board: £16-£18 daily,
£116-£126 weekly.

Evening meal 6.30pm (l.o. 8.30pm).
Parking for 9.

ANCASTER
Lincolnshire
Map ref 3A1

5m W. Sleaford

Woodlands
West Willoughby, Nr.
Ancaster, Grantham,
NG32 3SH
☎ Loveden (0400) 30340
*12-acre mixed farm. A quiet
farmhouse on the A153. 1 mile
west of Ancaster, 4 miles from
Belton House, 9 miles from the
A1 and 20 miles from Lincoln.
We offer farmhouse breakfasts
and home-cooked food with
vegetables from our own
garden where possible.*
Bedrooms: 1 single, 1 twin,
1 family room.
Bathrooms: 1 public.
Bed & breakfast: £9-£9.50
single, £18-£19 double.
Half board: £13-£13.50 daily,
£88 weekly.
Evening meal 5pm (l.o. 9pm).
Parking for 6.
Open April-October.

ASHBOURNE
Derbyshire
Map ref 4B2

Market town on the edge
of the Peak National Park
and an excellent centre
for walking. Its impressive
church with 212 ft spire
stands in an untouched
old street. Ashbourne is
well-known for
gingerbread and its
Shrovetide football
match.

Bentley Brook
Fenny Bentley, Nr.
Ashbourne, DE6 1LF
☎ Thorpe Cloud
(033 529) 278
*A traditional owner-operated
country inn in the Peak
District National Park, close to
Dovedale, Manifold Valley
and Chatsworth. Specialising
in food, wine and real ales.*
Bedrooms: 1 single, 4 double
& 2 twin, 1 family room.
Bathrooms: 3 private,
2 public.
Bed & breakfast: £25-£30
single, £35-£45 double.
Half board: £34.25-£39.25
daily.

Lunch available.
Evening meal 7pm (l.o. 9.30pm).
Parking for 60.
Credit: Access, Visa.

Collycroft Farm
Listed
Clifton, Ashbourne,
DE6 2GN
☎ (0335) 42187
*260-acre mixed farm. Located
south of Ashbourne on the
A515 in lovely countryside.
Within easy reach of Alton
Towers and the Peak District.*
Bedrooms: 1 double & 1 twin,
1 family room.
Bathrooms: 1 public.
Bed & breakfast: £10-£12
single, £20-£24 double.
Parking for 8.

Little Park Farm
Mappleton, Nr. Ashbourne,
DE6 2BR
☎ Thorpe Cloud
(033 529) 341
*123-acre mixed farm. Listed
oak-beamed farmhouse, 300
years old, in the Dove Valley 3
miles from Ashbourne.*
Bedrooms: 1 double & 1 twin,
1 family room.
Bathrooms: 1 public.
Bed & breakfast: £10 single,
£17-£19 double.
Half board: £15 daily.
Evening meal 6.30pm.
Parking for 3.
Open March-October.

The Mount Cottage
North Avenue, Ashbourne,
DE6 1EZ
☎ (0335) 45552 & 46071
*Part of an imposing Victorian
residence with a mature
garden, in an elevated position
overlooking the town. A warm
welcome is assured!*
Bedrooms: 1 double & 2 twin.
Bathrooms: 1 private,
1 public.
Bed & breakfast: £16-£20
single, £24-£32 double.
Half board: £20-£24 daily,
£100-£120 weekly.
Parking for 4.

**WE ADVISE YOU TO
CONFIRM YOUR
BOOKING IN WRITING.**

ASHBOURNE
Continued

Water Keepers Cottage
Mappleton, Ashbourne,
DE6 2AB
☎ Thorpe Cloud
(033 529) 444
*A cosy cottage in a quiet
village midway between
Ashbourne and Thorpe, on the
border of Staffordshire and
Derbyshire.*
Bedrooms: 1 single, 1 double
& 1 twin.
Bathrooms: 1 public.
Bed & breakfast: £9-£10
single, £18-£20 double.
Half board: £14-£15 daily,
£95-£105 weekly.
Evening meal 5pm (l.o. 9pm).
Parking for 3.
🛇 🕭 Ⓤ 🖷 Ⓥ ✂ 🛏
🔌 ⋃ ✿ 🎇 🕸

Mrs. Sylvia Woolliscroft
👄👄
Anacre Hill, Snelston,
Ashbourne, DE6 2DN
☎ Ellastone (033 524) 326
*A guesthouse in a quiet and
lovely part of Derbyshire,
offering home cooking using
fresh local produce. Within
easy reach of Alton Towers.
Non-smokers please.*
Bedrooms: 1 twin, 1 family
room.
Bathrooms: 2 public.
Bed & breakfast: £10-£12
single, £20-£22 double.
Half board: £15-£17 daily,
£95-£105 weekly.
Evening meal 6pm.
Parking for 2.
Open April-October.
🛇10 ⊙ Ⓤ ✂ Ⓣ 🖷 🎇 🕸

**INDIVIDUAL
PROPRIETORS HAVE
SUPPLIED ALL
DETAILS OF
ACCOMMODATION.
ALTHOUGH WE DO
CHECK FOR
ACCURACY, WE
ADVISE YOU TO
CONFIRM PRICES
AND OTHER
INFORMATION AT
THE TIME OF
BOOKING.**

ASHFORD-IN-THE-WATER
Derbyshire
Map ref 4B2

2m NW. Bakewell
Limestone village in
attractive surroundings of
the Peak District
approached by 3 bridges
over the River Wye. There
is an annual well-dressing
ceremony and the village
was well-known in the
18th C for its black
marble quarries.

Gritstone House
👄👄
Greaves Lane, Ashford-in-
the-Water, Bakewell,
DE4 1QH
☎ Bakewell (062 981) 3563
*This charming 18th C.
Georgian house offers friendly
service, and accommodation
designed with comfort and
style in mind. It is an ideal
centre for exploring the Peak
District's scenery and country
houses, and is close to an
extensive range of dining-out
facilities.*
Bedrooms: 2 double & 1 twin.
Bathrooms: 1 public.
Bed & breakfast: £20-£24
double.
Open April-October.
Ⓤ Ⓣ 🖷 ✕ 🎇 🕸

ASHOVER
Derbyshire
Map ref 4B2

7m SW. Chesterfield
Unspoilt village with a
13th C church.

Fairhaven
Stonerows Lane, The Hay,
Ashover, Chesterfield,
S45 0HE
☎ Chesterfield (0246) 590405
*A secluded stone-built, oak-
beamed cottage with log fires
in winter, close to the Peak
District and Matlock, offering
a friendly family atmosphere.
We try to oblige! 5 miles
towards Matlock from the M1
junction 29.*
Bedrooms: 1 single, 1 double,
1 family room.
Bathrooms: 1 public.
Bed & breakfast: £9.50
single, £19 double.
Half board: £14.50 daily, £95-
£100 weekly.
Evening meal 4pm (l.o. 9pm).
Parking for 5.
🛇 🕭 Ⓛ ⊙ Ⓤ 🛍 Ⓥ ✂ 🛏
Ⓣ 🖷 🔌 ⋃ ⋗ ✿ 🆂🅿

AYNHO
Northamptonshire
Map ref 2C1

2m SW. Silverstone

Cartwright Arms Hotel and Restaurant
👄👄
Aynho, Near Banbury, Oxon
OX17 3BE
☎ Croughton
(0869) 810218/810656
*A 16th C. coaching inn behind
the village green, in the
picturesque village of Aynho.
On the A41 between Bicester
and Banbury.*
Bedrooms: 2 single, 4 double
& 3 twin, 1 family room.
Bathrooms: 8 private,
2 public.
Bed & breakfast: £30-£35
single, £45-£50 double.
Half board: £45-£50 daily,
£254-£315 weekly.
Lunch available.
Evening meal 6.30pm (l.o.
10pm).
Parking for 20.
Credit: Access, Visa, Diners,
Amex.
🛇 🕭 🕮 ⊙ 🖵 🛍 🍴 Ⓥ 🌢
Ⓣ 🖷 🔌 🍽 ⋃ 🎇 🕸

BAKEWELL
Derbyshire
Map ref 4B2

Pleasant market town,
famous for its pudding. It
is set in beautiful
countryside on the River
Wye and is an excellent
centre for exploring the
Derbyshire Dales, the
Peak National Park,
Chatsworth and Haddon
Hall. *i*

Bourne House
The Park, Haddon Road,
Bakewell, DE4 1ET
☎ (062 981) 3274
*A friendly home overlooking
the park, offering a hearty
breakfast in a comfortable
atmosphere. Ideal base for
touring the Peak District; only
three miles from Chatsworth
House.*
Bedrooms: 2 double & 1 twin.
Bathrooms: 1 public.
Bed & breakfast: £21-£22
double.
Parking for 5.
🛇6 ⊙ Ⓤ 🛍 Ⓥ 🛏 Ⓣ 🖷 🔌
🎇 🕸

Everton
Haddon Road, Bakewell,
DE4 1AW
☎ (062 981) 3725
*Located near the park. Everton
offers home comforts and
makes an excellent base for
visiting the stately homes and
dales of the Peak District.*
Bedrooms: 2 double & 1 twin.
Bathrooms: 1 public.
Bed & breakfast: max. £20
double.
Parking for 3.
🛇 🖵 Ⓤ 🛍 Ⓥ 🖷 🔌 ⋃
⋗ 🎇 🕸

Holly Cottage
Listed
Rowland, Bakewell,
DE4 1NR
☎ Great Longstone
(062 987) 624
*A 200-year-old cottage which
has been extended to a house,
in a peaceful setting on a no-
through road. The large
comfortable lounge and dining
room are furnished with many
antiques.*
Bedrooms: 2 twin.
Bathrooms: 1 public.
Bed & breakfast: max. £14
single, max. £28 double.
Half board: max. £20 daily.
Evening meal 7pm (l.o. 8pm).
Parking for 2.
🛇5 🕭 ⊙ Ⓤ Ⓥ 🛏 Ⓣ 🖷 🔌
🎇 🅿 🆂🅿

BARKESTONE-LE-VALE
Leicestershire
Map ref 4C2

8m W. Grantham

The Old Vicarage
Listed
Barkestone-le-Vale, Nr.
Belvoir, Nottingham,
Nottinghamshire NG13 0JA
☎ Bottesford (0949) 42258
*600-acre dairy and arable
farm. The Old Vicarage is an
attractively restored house
surrounded by trees and
garden, with an uninterrupted
view of Belvoir Castle. All-
weather tennis court is near
completion.*
Bedrooms: 2 double & 2 twin.
Bathrooms: 1 private,
2 public.
Bed & breakfast: £13-£15
single, £24-£30 double.
Parking for 9.
Open April-October.
🛇6 🕭 ⊙ 🖵 🛍 Ⓥ ✂ 🛏
Ⓣ 🖷 🔌 ⋃ ⋗ ✿ 🎇
🅳🅰🅿 🆂🅿 🕸

BASLOW

Derbyshire
Map ref 4B2

Small village on the River Derwent with a stone built toll-house and a packhorse bridge. Chatsworth, home of the Duke of Devonshire, is close by.

Bubnell Cliff Farm
Bubnell, Baslow, Nr. Bakewell, DE4 1RH
☎ (024 688) 2454
250-acre mixed farm. Ideal for touring the Peak District. The farm has magnificent views of Chatsworth and the surrounding area.
Bedrooms: 1 double, 1 family room.
Bathrooms: 1 public.
Bed & breakfast: max. £21 double.
Parking for 6.
🛏 🐾 ✧ Ⓤ ⓉⓋ ▱ ☂ ✕ 🏠

Wheatsheaf Hotel 🅼
Netherend, Baslow, Bakewell, DE4 1SR
☎ (024 688) 2240
An old Derbyshire stone building with beams, an open fire in winter and home-cooked food.
Bedrooms: 3 double & 1 twin, 2 family rooms.
Bathrooms: 1 private, 1 public.
Bed & breakfast: £20-£30 single, £30-£40 double.
Half board: £27-£37 daily.
Lunch available.
Evening meal 7pm (l.o. 9.30pm).
Parking for 100.
🛏 ▱ ✧ 🛉 Ⓥ ▥ ♨ ❊ ✕ 🏠

BELPER

Derbyshire
Map ref 4B2

Chevin Green Farm 🅼
😊😊😊
Chevin Road, Belper, Derby, DE5 2UN
☎ (0773) 822328
40-acre mixed farm. In pleasant position overlooking the Derwent Valley. The bedrooms have a comfortable atmosphere, and one is en-suite.
Bedrooms: 2 single, 1 twin, 2 family rooms.
Bathrooms: 3 private, 1 public.
Bed & breakfast: £11-£14 single, £21-£26 double.

Half board: £68.50-£85 weekly. ·
Parking for 8.
🛏 ▱ 🛉 Ⓤ ▥ ⓉⓋ ▥ ▱ ☂ ☂ ✕ 🏠

BLAKESLEY

Northamptonshire
Map ref 2C1

4m NW. Towcester

The Old Vicarage
😊😊
Church Street, Blakesley, Towcester, NN12 8RA
☎ (0327) 860200
An old Victorian vicarage of mellow sandstone, in its own spacious grounds. Outdoor pool and hard tennis court.
Bedrooms: 1 twin.
Bathrooms: 1 private.
Bed & breakfast: £15 single, £28-£30 double.
Parking for 3.
🛏 ☎ ▱ ✧ Ⓤ ▥ ⓉⓋ ▥ ✤ ❊ ✕ 🏠 ⒹⒶ⒫ 🏠

BLYTH

Nottinghamshire
Map ref 4C2

Village on the old Great North Road. A busy staging post in Georgian times with many examples of Georgian Gothic architecture. The remains of a Norman Benedictine priory survive as the parish church.

Angel Inn
〔Listed〕
High Street, Blyth, Worksop, S81 8HG
☎ (090 976) 213
An old coaching inn improved over recent years but still retaining its old charm.
Bedrooms: 3 double & 1 twin, 2 family rooms.
Bathrooms: 2 public.
Bed & breakfast: from £14 single, from £26 double.
Half board: from £19 daily, from £133 weekly.
Lunch available.
Evening meal 7pm (l.o. 10pm).
Parking for 50.
🛏 🚶 🛉 ⓉⓋ ▥ ♨ ❊ 🏠 🏠

Priory Farm Guest House 🅼
〔Listed〕
Hodsock Priory Estate, Blyth, Nr. Worksop, S81 0TY
☎ (090 976) 768

1000-acre mixed farm. A farmhouse in peaceful surroundings on a private country estate. Easy access from the A1(M).
Bedrooms: 2 single, 1 double & 1 twin.
Bathrooms: 2 private, 1 public.
Bed & breakfast: £11.50-£12.50 single, £23-£25 double.
Half board: £16-£17 daily, £90-£99 weekly.
Evening meal 6pm (l.o. 8pm).
Parking for 6.
🛏 🐾 ✧ 🛉 Ⓥ ▥ ⓉⓋ ▱ ✕ ⒹⒶ⒫ 🏠

BRACKLEY

Northamptonshire
Map ref 2C1

8m E. Banbury

Robert & Eileen McCulloch, Welbeck House
😊
Pebble Lane, Brackley, NN13 5DA
☎ (0280) 702364
A large house in a quiet, attractive area of Brackley, close to the A43 and many places of interest. We pride ourselves on our full-scale breakfasts: a wide choice, extra helpings galore, and a bottomless tea and coffee pot.
Bedrooms: 1 single, 2 double.
Bathrooms: 1 public.
Bed & breakfast: £10.50 single, £21.50 double.
Parking for 4.
✧ Ⓤ ⓉⓋ ▥ ▱ ☂ ❊ ✕ 🏠

BUXTON

Derbyshire
Map ref 4B2

The highest market town in England and one of the oldest spas, with an elegant Crescent, Micrarium, Poole's Cavern, Opera House and attractive Pavilion Gardens. An excellent centre for exploring the Peak District.ℹ

Coningsby
😊😊😊
6 Macclesfield Road, Buxton, SK17 9AH
☎ (0298) 6735
A comfortable detached Victorian house of character in a pleasant area, close to the Pavilion Gardens and the many other attractions of this splendid spa resort. Non-smokers only please.

Bedrooms: 1 single, 1 double & 1 twin.
Bathrooms: 1 private, 2 public.
Bed & breakfast: £23-£29 double.
Half board: £19-£22 daily, £120-£140 weekly.
Evening meal 7pm (l.o. 4pm).
Parking for 8.
☎ ▱ ✧ Ⓤ 🛉 Ⓥ ✕ ▥ ☂
▥ ▱ ☂ ☂ ✕ ❊ 🏠 ⒹⒶ⒫ SP

Lynstone Guest House
😊😊
3 Grange Road, Buxton, SK17 6NH
☎ (0298) 77043
A spacious, welcoming and homely Victorian house, recently modernised and centrally, yet quietly located. Both family rooms can be used as singles, doubles or twins.
Bedrooms: 2 family rooms.
Bathrooms: 2 public.
Bed & breakfast: £10-£12 single, £19-£21 double.
Half board: £15-£16 daily, £105-£112 weekly.
Evening meal 6.30pm.
Parking for 3.
🛏 ✧ Ⓤ ▥ ⓉⓋ ▥ ☂ ✕
🏠 SP

Pedlicote Farm
😊😊
Peak Forest, Buxton, SK17 8EG
☎ (0298) 2241
An old farmhouse conversion in the Peak District National Park, full of character, with a charming atmosphere and magnificent views.
Bedrooms: 2 twin.
Bathrooms: 1 private, 1 public.
Bed & breakfast: £12 single, £24 double.
Half board: £17.50 daily, £110 weekly.
Evening meal 7pm (l.o. 9pm).
Parking for 7.
🛏 8 ☎ ▱ ✧ 🛉 Ⓥ ✕ ▥
ⓉⓋ ▥ ☂ ❊ 🏠 🏠

Mr. & Mrs. D. Smith
😊😊
Hawthorn Farm Guest House, Fairfield Road, Buxton, SK17 7ED
☎ (0298) 3230
A 400-year-old ex-farmhouse which has been in the family for ten generations. Full English breakfast.
Bedrooms: 3 single, 4 double & 3 twin, 2 family rooms.
Bathrooms: 2 public.
Continued ▶

BUXTON

Continued

Bed & breakfast: £11-£12 single, £22-£24 double.
Parking for 15.
Open March-November.

CALVER

Derbyshire
Map ref 4B2

4m NE. Bakewell
Attractive Peak District village beside the River Derwent.

Knouchley Farm

Calver, S30 1XY
☎ Hope Valley (0433) 30433
220-acre mixed farm. This farmhouse is only 4 miles from Chatsworth and offers a large bedroom which can be let as a single, twin or family room as well as a double.
Bedrooms: 1 double.
Bathrooms: 1 private.
Bed & breakfast: £13-£15 single, £26 double.

CASTLE BYTHAM

Lincolnshire
Map ref 3A1

8m N. Stamford
Attractive village with castle earthworks dating from Saxon times and a parish church, church yard and several houses of interest. It also has a duck pond and stream.

Mrs. S. Dean

15 Castlegate, Castle Bytham, Grantham, NG33 4RU
☎ (078 081) 274
A 16th C. beamed cottage with open log fires, in a beautiful and historic village near the A1, Rutland Water and Stamford.
Bedrooms: 1 double & 1 twin.
Bathrooms: 1 public.
Bed & breakfast: max. £12.50 single, max. £22 double.
Parking for 2.
Open February-December.

CASTLE DONINGTON

Leicestershire
Map ref 4C3

A Norman castle once stood here. The world's largest collection of single-seater racing cars is displayed at Donington Park alongside the racing circuit, and an Aeropark Visitor Centre can be seen at nearby East Midlands Airport.

High Barn Farm M

Listed
Isley Walton, Castle Donington, Derby, DE7 2RL
☎ Derby (0332) 810360
184-acre mixed farm. 2 of the guest bedrooms on this beautifully situated farm are self-contained, in a cottage adjacent to the farmhouse. The third is in the farmhouse itself. Rooms can be adapted to family rooms on request.
Bedrooms: 3 twin.
Bathrooms: 3 public.
Bed & breakfast: £12 single, £24 double.
Parking for 6.

Park Farmhouse M

Melbourne Road, Isley Walton, Castle Donington, Nr. Derby, Derbyshire DE7 2RN
☎ Derby (0332) 862409
40-acre mixed farm. A half-timbered farmhouse dating back to the 1760s, in its own grounds. Old world charm, log fires, spacious rooms and a warm, friendly atmosphere.
Bedrooms: 3 double & 2 twin, 1 family room.
Bathrooms: 2 private, 2 public.
Bed & breakfast: £20-£29 single, £30-£40 double.
Half board: £23.50-£39 daily.
Evening meal 6pm (l.o. 8pm).
Parking for 15.
Credit: Access, Visa, Diners, Amex.

CASTLETON

Derbyshire
Map ref 4B2

5m W. Hathersage
Large village in a spectacular setting with a ruined Norman castle and 4 great show caverns, where the Blue John stone and lead were mined. One cavern offers a mile-long underground boat journey.

Mrs. B. Johnson, Myrtle Cottage

Market Place, Castleton, Sheffield, S. Yorkshire S30 2WZ
☎ Hope Valley (0433) 20787
A centrally situated, 200-year-old cottage with a comfortable atmosphere, friendly service and substantial English breakfasts.
Bedrooms: 3 double & 1 twin, 2 family rooms.
Bathrooms: 1 public.
Bed & breakfast: £19-£20 double.
Parking for 5.

Ye Olde Cheshire Cheese Inn

How Lane, Castleton, Sheffield, S. Yorkshire S30 2WJ
☎ Hope Valley (0433) 20330
A 17th C. inn providing home-cooked food, set in the heart of the Peak District.
Bedrooms: 1 single, 3 double & 2 twin.
Bathrooms: 6 private.
Bed & breakfast: £16.50-£22.50 single, £33-£38 double.
Half board: £26.50-£32.50 daily.
Lunch available.
Evening meal 6pm (l.o. 10.50pm).
Parking for 100.

CHESTERFIELD

Derbyshire
Map ref 4B2

Famous for the twisted spire of its parish church. It has some fine modern buildings and excellent shopping facilities, including a large traditional open air market. Hardwick Hall and Bolsover Castle are nearby.

34 Gladstone Road

Listed
Chesterfield, S40 4TE
☎ Chesterfield (0246) 209060
Private 4-bedroomed, detached house, built in 1982 but in old, quiet part of town and within walking distance of centre of town. Car parking space available.
Bedrooms: 1 single, 1 double.
Bathrooms: 1 public.
Bed & breakfast: £9 single, £18 double.
Parking for 1.

CLAYBROOKE

Leicestershire
Map ref 4C3

4m NW. Lutterworth

Claybrooke Rectory

Claybrooke Parva, Lutterworth, LE17 5AE
☎ Leire (0455) 209277
Telex 311754 CHACOM G
A Queen Anne rectory with High Gothic extension, in spacious grounds next to the church. The A5, M1, M69 and M6 are nearby.
Bedrooms: 1 single, 1 double & 1 twin, 1 family room.
Bathrooms: 1 public.
Bed & breakfast: max. £10 single, max. £20 double.
Parking for 10.

INDIVIDUAL PROPRIETORS HAVE SUPPLIED ALL DETAILS OF ACCOMMODATION. ALTHOUGH WE DO CHECK FOR ACCURACY, WE ADVISE YOU TO CONFIRM PRICES AND OTHER INFORMATION AT THE TIME OF BOOKING.

THERE IS A SPECIAL SECTION IN THIS GUIDE LISTING ACCOMMODATION ESPECIALLY SUITABLE FOR GROUPS AND YOUNG PEOPLE.

GROUPS, CONSORTIA AND AGENCIES SPECIALISING IN FARM AND COUNTRY HOLIDAYS ARE LISTED IN A SPECIAL SECTION OF THIS GUIDE.

CLAYBROOKE PARVA

Leicestershire
Map ref 4C3

4m NW. Lutterworth

Claybrooke House
Claybrooke Parva,
Lutterworth, LE17 5AE
☎ Leire (0455) 209968
*10-acre smallholding. A family
country house in quiet rural
surroundings, supporting 2
Suffolk Punch heavy horses,
dogs, cats, ponies, chickens,
ducks, swans and goats. We
can also stable other horses.*
Bedrooms: 1 double, 1 family
room.
Bathrooms: 1 public.
Bed & breakfast: £8.50
single, £17 double.
Half board: £11.50 daily.
Evening meal 7pm (l.o. 9pm).
Parking for 4.
� ⚡ Ⓤ 🖥 ∤ ⊣ 🖵 🚽
⬛ ∪ ⚲ ✿ 🗙 🏠

CONINGSBY

Lincolnshire
Map ref 4D2

4m SE. Woodhall Spa

White Bull Inn
55 High Street, Coningsby,
LN4 4RB
☎ (0526) 42439
*A warm welcome to our
friendly pub with real ale, a
riverside beer garden and a
large, children's playground.
Traditional, home-made meals
are available every day.*
Bedrooms: 2 single, 2 double
& 1 twin.
Bathrooms: 1 public.
Bed & breakfast: £10–£12
single, £20–£25 double.
Half board: £15–£17 daily,
£90–£110 weekly.
Evening meal 7.30pm (l.o.
10pm).
Parking for 100.
� 🖩 ☐ ⚡ 🖥 Ⓥ 🖵 🖵 ⬛
♩ ⚲ ✿ 🏠

**MAP REFERENCES
APPLY TO THE
COLOUR MAPS
TOWARDS THE END
OF THIS GUIDE.**

COTGRAVE

Nottinghamshire
Map ref 4C2

6m SE. Nottingham

Jerico Farm
Fosse Way, Cotgrave,
NG12 3HG
☎ Kinoulton (0949) 81733
*120-acre mixed farm. On the
Fosse Way between Newark
and Leicester. 8 miles from
Nottingham and Melton
Mowbray. Evening meals must
be pre-booked.*
Bedrooms: 2 twin.
Bathrooms: 1 public.
Bed & breakfast: £10–£11
single, £20 double.
Half board: £17–£18 daily,
£112–£115.50 weekly.
Evening meal 6pm.
Parking for 3.
� ⚡ Ⓤ 🖥 Ⓥ ⊣ 🖵 ✎ ⌁
🗙 🏠

COTTINGHAM

Northamptonshire
Map ref 4C3

3m W. Corby

Hunting Lodge
High Street, Cottingham,
Market Harborough,
Leicestershire LE16 8XN
☎ Kettering (0536) 771370
*An old world 16th C. free
house and motel, offering a la
carte and table d'hote menus
and bar meals.*
Bedrooms: 2 single, 15 double
& 6 twin.
Bathrooms: 15 private;
8 private showers.
Bed & breakfast: £25–£37.50
single, £30–£47.50 double.
Lunch available.
Evening meal 7pm (l.o.
10pm).
Parking for 80.
Credit: Access, Visa, Diners.
☒ ⚡ ☐ ☎ 🖥 Ⓥ 🖵 🖵 ⬛
⬛ ⚲ ✿ 🗙 🏠 SP T

COVENHAM

Lincolnshire
Map ref 4D1

8m NE. Louth

Mrs. Phyl Shaw
Listed
The Grange, Grange Lane,
Covenham-St-Bartholomew,
Nr. Louth, LN11 0PD
☎ Fulstow (050 786) 678

*700-acre mixed farm.
Welcome to our large and
fully-modernised old
farmhouse, in lovely
countryside, with a comfortable
atmosphere and a real
Lincolnshire breakfast.*
Bedrooms: 1 single, 1 double,
1 family room.
Bathrooms: 1 public.
Bed & breakfast: £10–£12
single, £20–£22 double.
Parking for 6.
☒ ⚡ Ⓤ 🖥 ⊣ 🖵 🖵 ✎ ⚲
🏠

CROWLAND

Lincolnshire
Map ref 3A1

Abbey Hotel
⊕⊕
East Street, Crowland,
Peterborough,
Cambridgeshire PE6 0EN
☎ Peterborough
(0733) 210200
*An old country pub with a
lounge, bar, dining room and
children's room.*
Bedrooms: 2 single, 3 twin.
Bathrooms: 1 public.
Bed & breakfast: max. £13
single, max. £24 double.
Evening meal 7pm (l.o.
9.30pm).
Parking for 20.
☒ 🖥 Ⓥ ⊣ 🖵 ☂ 🗙 SP

CULWORTH

Northamptonshire
Map ref 2C1

2m NW. Sulgrave

Paddocks Farm Guest House
Culworth, Banbury,
Oxfordshire OX17 2BE
☎ Sulgrave (029 576) 491
*This licensed guesthouse is a
cosy converted 17th C.
farmhouse offering home
produce where possible, in
unspoilt countryside ideal for
ramblers.*
Bedrooms: 1 single, 1 double
& 3 twin, 2 family rooms.
Bathrooms: 2 public.
Bed & breakfast: £11.50–
£14.50 single, £23 double.
Half board: £17.50–£20.50
daily, £111–£129 weekly.
Evening meal 6.30pm (l.o.
5pm).
Parking for 21.
☒ ✎ 🖥 Ⓥ ⊣ 🖵 🖵 ✎ ⚲
🗙 🏠

DAVENTRY

Northamptonshire
Map ref 2C1

Ancient market town with
an Iron Age camp on
Borough Hill, from which
7 counties can be seen.
The town still retains
some Georgian buildings
and 2 old inns and there
is a country park with a
reservoir nearby. 🄸

Drayton Lodge
Daventry, NN11 4NL
☎ (0327) 702449 or 76365
*12-acre mixed farm. An
attractive, family home with a
warm and friendly atmosphere.
Local inns within a one mile
radius serve food.*
Bedrooms: 1 single, 1 double
& 1 twin, 1 family room.
Bathrooms: 2 public.
Bed & breakfast: £15–£20
single, £30–£40 double.
Half board: £22.50–£25 daily,
from £87.50 weekly.
Lunch available.
Evening meal 6pm (l.o.
9.30pm).
Parking for 30.
☒ ☒ ⊕ ⚡ Ⓤ 🖥 Ⓥ ⊣
🖵 🖵 ⬛ ⓣ ∪ ⚲ ✿ 🗙 🏠

DERBY

Derbyshire
Map ref 4B2

Modern industrial city but
with ancient origins.
There is a wide range of
facilities including several
museums (notably Royal
Crown Derby), a theatre,
a concert hall, the
cathedral with fine
ironwork and Bess of
Hardwick's tomb, and
Elvaston Castle Country
Park. 🄸

Bonehill Farm
Listed
Etwall Road, Mickleover,
Derby, DE3 5DN
☎ (0332) 513553
*120-acre mixed farm. A
traditional farmhouse in a
rural setting, three miles from
Derby. Alton Towers, the Peak
District, historic houses and the
potteries are all within easy
reach.*
Bedrooms: 1 double & 1 twin,
1 family room.
Bathrooms: 1 public.
Bed & breakfast: £9.50–£11
single, £19–£22 double.
Parking for 4.
☒ ☒ ⚡ Ⓤ 🖥 Ⓥ ⊣ 🖵 🖵
♫ ♩ ∤ ✿ 🗙 🏠

**THE SYMBOLS ARE EXPLAINED ON THE FLAP
INSIDE THE BACK COVER.**

DERBY

Continued

Braemar Guest House M

1061 London Road, Alvaston, Derby, DE2 8PZ
☎ (0332) 72522 or 572522
A friendly guesthouse near Derby city. Easy access to the Derbyshire Dales, stately homes, Alton Towers, American Adventure Park, potteries and good fishing rivers.
Bedrooms: 7 single, 2 double & 3 twin, 1 family room.
Bathrooms: 4 public; 5 private showers.
Bed & breakfast: £11-£12 single, max. £20 double.
Half board: £15-£16 daily, £90-£96 weekly.
Evening meal 6pm (l.o. 7pm). Parking for 10.
⏚ ⚒ ⛛ ✿ Ⓤ 🛉 Ⓥ ✂ ♨
📺 ⦀ ⚓ 🏠 ⓓ ⤢

Rangemoor Hotel
⛉

67 Macklin Street, Derby, DE1 1LF
☎ (0332) 47252
A city centre bed and breakfast hotel, close to all amenities, with a large lock-up private car park.
Bedrooms: 12 single, 5 double & 4 twin, 3 family rooms.
Bathrooms: 4 public.
Bed & breakfast: £14-£14.50 single, £24-£24.50 double.
Parking for 28.
⏚ ⚒ ✿ Ⓤ 🛉 ♨ 📺 ⦀ ⚓

DOVERIDGE

Derbyshire
Map ref 4B2

The Beeches Farmhouse M
⛉⛉⛉

The Beeches, Waldley, Doveridge, DE6 5LR
☎ Rocester (0889) 590288
160-acre dairy farm. A 200-year-old beamed farmhouse in beautiful Derbyshire close to Alton Towers and Dovedale.
Bedrooms: 2 double & 2 twin, 2 family rooms.
Bathrooms: 2 private, 2 public.
Bed & breakfast: £14 single, £20-£28 double.
Half board: £16-£24 daily, £112-£168 weekly.
Evening meal 6.30pm (l.o. 8.30pm).
Parking for 15.
Credit: Access, Visa.
⏚ 📺 ✿ 🛉 Ⓥ ⚓ ⦀ ⚓ 🍴
♨ ✿ 🏠 ⓓ ⤢ ⑀

EDWINSTOWE

Nottinghamshire
Map ref 4C2

Village close to Sherwood Forest, famous for the legend of Robin Hood. The Visitor Centre and Country Park includes a Robin Hood exhibition, and there are guided walks and many special events. ℹ

Friars Lodge Guest House M
Listed

3 Mill Lane, Edwinstowe, Mansfield, NG21 9QY
☎ Mansfield (0623) 823405
A small guesthouse of character close to Sherwood Forest in the heart of the Dukeries.
Bedrooms: 2 single, 1 double & 1 twin.
Bathrooms: 1 public.
Bed & breakfast: max. £10.50 single, max. £20 double.
Half board: max. £15 daily, max. £90 weekly.
Evening meal 6.30pm (l.o. 4pm).
Parking for 4.
⏚ ⚒ ⚓ Ⓤ 🛉 ⚓ 📺 ⦀ ⚓ 🏠

FARTHINGSTONE

Northamptonshire
Map ref 2C1

5m SE. Daventry

Barn Court
Farthingstone, Towcester, NN12 8HE
☎ Preston Capes (032 736) 580
This stone village house has beautiful views to the rear and many walks and historic houses within easy reach. A golf and squash club and a pub serving food are close by, although we can serve evening meals by arrangement.
Bedrooms: 2 single, 2 double & 1 twin.
Bathrooms: 2 public.
Bed & breakfast: from £15 single, from £25 double.
Parking for 5.
⏚ ⚒ Ⓤ ⚓ 📺 ⦀ ∪ ▶ ✗
🏠

FOTHERINGHAY

Northamptonshire
Map ref 3A1

4m NE. Oundle

Castle Farm Guest House M
⛉⛉

Castle Farm, Fotheringhay, Peterborough, Cambridgeshire PE8 5HZ
☎ Cotterstock (083 26) 200
An early 19th C. stone farmhouse in beautiful surroundings, with lawns running down to the River Nene and adjoining the Fotheringhay Castle site. Two rooms can be adapted to family rooms.
Bedrooms: 1 single, 4 twin.
Bathrooms: 3 private, 1 public.
Bed & breakfast: £15-£18 single, £25-£30 double.
Half board: £22-£25 daily, £154-£175 weekly.
Evening meal 7.30pm.
Parking for 10.
⏚ Ⓤ ⚓ 📺 ⦀ ⚓ ♪ ∪ ♩
✿ 🏠 🏠

FROGGATT EDGE

Derbyshire
Map ref 4B2

3m N. Baslow

Chequers Inn
Froggatt Edge, Bakewell, Near Sheffield S30 1ZB
☎ Hope Valley (0433) 30231
In the heart of the Peak National Park, 3 miles from Chatsworth House.
Bedrooms: 1 single, 2 double & 1 twin.
Bathrooms: 1 public.
Bed & breakfast: max. £18 single, max. £28 double.
Half board: max. £28 daily.
Lunch available.
Evening meal 7.30pm (l.o. 9.15pm).
Parking for 60.
Credit: Access.
⦀ ✿ 🛉 Ⓥ ⚓ ⦀ ⚓ 🍴 ✿
🏠

GAINSBOROUGH

Lincolnshire
Map ref 4C2

Laundry Cottage
Knaith Hill, Knaith, Gainsborough, DN21 5PF
☎ (0427) 3248
An attractive family cottage with character, converted from an old laundry, 3 miles south of Gainsborough. There are some local inns which serve food.
Bedrooms: 1 single, 1 double & 2 twin.
Bathrooms: 2 public.
Bed & breakfast: from £10.50 single, from £21 double.
Parking for 6.
⏚6 ⚒ ⚓ Ⓤ ⚓ 📺 ⦀ ⚓ ✿
✗ 🏠

GREETHAM

Leicestershire
Map ref 4C3

6m NE. Oakham
Village in the former county of Rutland and close to Rutland Water. Nearby can be found the outstanding church of Exton with its exceptional monuments.

Greetham House
⛉⛉⛉

Greetham, Oakham, LE15 7NJ
☎ Oakham (0572) 813078
A Grade II listed country house in attractive gardens, conveniently placed for Rutland Water, Burghley House and Cottesmore.
Bedrooms: 3 double.
Bathrooms: 3 private.
Bed & breakfast: £18 single, £32 double.
Half board: £28.50 daily, £175 weekly.
Evening meal 7pm (l.o. 9am).
Parking for 10.
⏚8 ⑩ 🖵 ⚒ ⚓ ⦀ ⚓ ⚓ ♪
∪ ✿ 🏠 🏛

```
MAP REFERENCES
APPLY TO THE
COLOUR MAPS
TOWARDS THE END
OF THIS GUIDE.
```

```
INDIVIDUAL PROPRIETORS HAVE SUPPLIED
ALL DETAILS OF ACCOMMODATION.
ALTHOUGH WE DO CHECK FOR ACCURACY, WE
ADVISE YOU TO CONFIRM PRICES AND OTHER
INFORMATION AT THE TIME OF BOOKING.
```

GRIMOLDBY

Lincolnshire
Map ref 4D2

Manby Arms ♨
😊

Middlegate, Grimoldby, Nr.
Louth, LN11 8SU
☎ South Cockerington
(050 782) 351
*A small village pub 4 miles
from the market town of Louth
and the Wolds, 7 miles from
the coastal resort of
Mablethorpe.*
Bedrooms: 1 double & 3 twin.
Bathrooms: 1 public.
Bed & breakfast: £9.50-£12
single.
🛏6 ♿ 📺 ▥ ☎ ♣ ❄ ✗
🕮

HAINTON

Lincolnshire
Map ref 4C2

Old Vicarage
😊😊

School Lane, Hainton,
Lincoln, LN3 6LW
☎ Burgh on Bain
(050 781) 660
*A quiet non-smoking country
household in the Wolds, in 1
acre of secluded gardens. We
offer home baking and
produce, and are convenient for
the Viking Way, the coast and
Lincoln. Evening meals by
arrangement.*
Bedrooms: 1 double & 1 twin.
Bathrooms: 2 public.
Bed & breakfast: from £10
single, from £19 double.
Half board: from £14 daily,
from £93 weekly.
Evening meal 7pm (l.o. 9pm).
Parking for 6.
⑮ ♿ ▥ ⅄ ▥ ▦ ❄ ✗ 🕮
🅿 🕮

HATHERSAGE

Derbyshire
Map ref 4B2

Hillside village in the Peak
District, dominated by the
church which has many
good brasses and
monuments to the Eyre
family which provide a
link with Charlotte Bronte.
Little John, friend of
Robin Hood, is said to be
buried here.

The Old Vicarage
😊😊

Church Bank, Hathersage,
Sheffield, S. Yorkshire
S30 1AB
☎ Hope Valley (0433) 51099

*In 1845 Charlotte Bronte
stayed in this listed building
which is beside Little John's
grave overlooking the Hope
Valley. It is central for
Chatsworth House, the Caves,
fishing and walking. Dinners
served by arrangement only.*
Bedrooms: 2 double & 1 twin.
Bathrooms: 2 public.
Bed & breakfast: £12-£13
single, £20-£24 double.
Half board: £18-£19 daily,
£120-£125 weekly.
Evening meal 6pm (l.o.
8.30pm).
Parking for 3.
🛏 ♿ ♿ ▥ ☎ 📺 ▥ ♨
❄ 🕮 🕮

Mrs. Sheila Payton, Windrush
Listed

6 Park Edge, Hathersage,
Sheffield, S. Yorkshire
S30 1BS
☎ Hope Valley (0433) 50531
*An Edwardian house in superb
scenery, overlooking the village
and grazing sheep. Large
rooms, a comfortable
atmosphere, a warm welcome
and English country cooking.*
Bedrooms: 1 double, 1 family
room.
Bathrooms: 1 public.
Bed & breakfast: £10-£12
single, £20-£24 double.
Half board: £16-£18 daily.
Evening meal 7pm.
Parking for 2.
🛏 ♿ ♿ ▥ ⓘ ▣ ⅄ 📺 ▥
🕮

HINCKLEY

Leicestershire
Map ref 4B3

The town has an
excellent leisure centre
and the site of the Battle
of Bosworth, with its
Visitor Centre and Battle
Trail, is 5 miles away. ⓘ

Hoults of Hollygrange ♨
😊😊

101 Hollycroft, Hinckley,
LE10 0HF
☎ (0455) 30154
*Hollygrange is a family
residence built in 1930, with a
friendly and homely
atmosphere.*
Bedrooms: 1 single, 2 twin,
2 family rooms.
Bathrooms: 1 public.
Bed & breakfast: £10-£13
single, £20-£22 double.

Half board: £13.50-£17 daily,
£94.50-£119 weekly.
Evening meal 6pm (l.o. 3pm).
Parking for 6.
🛏 ♿ ♿ ▥ ⓘ 📺 📺 ▥
▣ 🕮

HOPE

Derbyshire
Map ref 4B2

Village in the Hope Valley
which is an excellent
base for walking in the
Peak District and for
fishing and shooting.
There is a well-dressing
ceremony each June and
its August sheep dog
trials are well-known.
Castleton caves are
nearby.

Cheshire Cheese Inn ♨
Edale Road, Hope, S30 2RF
☎ (0433) 20381
*A delightful 16th C.
freehouse/inn offering hand-
drawn ales and day and
evening menus. Close to the
Pennine Way and well placed
for touring the Peak District.*
Bedrooms: 1 twin, 1 family
room.
Bathrooms: 2 private.
Bed & breakfast: £12.50-£14
single, £25-£28 double.
Lunch available.
Evening meal 5pm (l.o. 9pm).
Parking for 6.
🛏 ♿ ♿ ♿ ▥ 📺 ♣ ∪
✗ 🕮

HORNCASTLE

Lincolnshire
Map ref 4D2

Pleasant market town
near the Lincolnshire
Wolds, which was once a
walled Roman settlement.
It was the scene of a
decisive Civil War battle,
relics of which can be
seen in the church.
Tennyson's bride lived
here.

Nags Head Cottage ♨
Sotby, Lincoln LN3 5LH
☎ Stenigot (050 784) 756
*A comfortable home with a
friendly atmosphere, in the
quiet countryside of the
Lincolnshire Wolds. Non-
smokers preferred, please.*
Bedrooms: 1 single, 2 double.
Bathrooms: 1 private,
1 public.

Bed & breakfast: from £12.50
single, £18-£22 double.
Parking for 3.
Open April-October.
🛏 ♿ ▥ ▣ ⅄ 📺 ▥ ❄ ✗

HOUGH-ON-THE-HILL

Lincolnshire
Map ref 3A1

Brownlow Arms
😊😊😊

Hough-on-the-Hill,
Grantham, NG32 2AZ
☎ Loveden (0400) 50292
*A 17th C. family-run country
inn and restaurant with an a la
carte menu. Bar meals are also
available.*
Bedrooms: 1 single, 2 double
& 1 twin.
Bathrooms: 2 private,
2 public.
Bed & breakfast: £15-£20
single, £28-£35 double.
Evening meal 7pm (l.o.
9.45pm).
Parking for 40.
🛏3 ⑮ ♿ ⓘ ▣ ▣ ▦ ✗ 🕮

HUSBANDS BOSWORTH

Leicestershire
Map ref 4C3

Mrs. J. Armitage
😊

31-33 High Street, Husbands
Bosworth, Lutterworth,
LE17 6LJ
☎ Market Harborough
(0858) 880066
*A Georgian house of character,
set in the centre of this village
on the A427, with wholesome
cooking and a warm welcome.*
Bedrooms: 1 single, 2 twin.
Bathrooms: 1 public.
Bed & breakfast: £10 single,
£20 double.
Parking for 6.
🛏 ▥ ▣ 📺 ▥ ∪ ✗ 🕮 Ⓣ

ISLIP

Northamptonshire
Map ref 3A2

1m W. Thrapston

The 16th C. Woolpack Inn ♨
😊😊

6 Kettering Road, Islip, Nr.
Thrapston, NN14 3JU
☎ (080 12) 2578
*Overlooking the River Nene,
this 16th C. inn is in a quiet
village.*

Continued ▶

**WE ADVISE YOU TO CONFIRM YOUR BOOKING
IN WRITING.**

ISLIP

Continued

Bedrooms: 1 double &
12 twin.
Bathrooms: 13 private.
Bed & breakfast: from £30
single, from £44 double.
Lunch available.
Evening meal 7pm (l.o.
9.30pm).
Parking for 50.

ﾠ⟡🖵🔌💁📞❄️✈️
🎋

KERSALL

Nottinghamshire
Map ref 4C2

5m SE. Ollerton

Hill Farm Guest House
Kersall, Newark, NG22 0BJ
☎ Caunton (063 686) 274
*A 17th C. farm cottage with
splendid views over the
countryside, a beamed dining
room and a comfortable lounge
with an open log fire.
Southwell Minster, Newark
and the Sherwood Forest
Visitor Centre are all nearby.*
Bedrooms: 1 single, 1 twin.
Bathrooms: 1 private,
1 public.
Bed & breakfast: from £15
single, £22-£25 double.
Parking for 6.
Open April-September.
🔌5🖵🔌💁📺▦▤
📞❄️✈️🎋🎋

KETTERING

Northamptonshire
Map ref 3A2

Ancient industrial town
based on shoe-making.
Wicksteed Park to the
south has many
children's amusements.
The splendid 17th C ducal
mansion of Boughton
House is to the north.ℹ️

Pennels Guest House ♨
Listed
175 Beatrice Road,
Kettering, NN16 9QR
☎ (0536) 81940
*A small homely guest house
with a secluded garden for
guests' use. Quiet area of
Kettering near places of
interest.*
Bedrooms: 2 single, 1 double
& 3 twin.
Bathrooms: 3 public.
Bed & breakfast: £12-£12.50
single, £24 double.
Half board: £17-£17.50 daily,
£119-£122.50 weekly.

Lunch available.
Evening meal 6pm (l.o. 5pm).
Parking for 4.

🔌🖵💁▦💁📺🎋▤
📞❄️🎋

KNEESALL

Nottinghamshire
Map ref 4C2

4m SE. Ollerton

The Mill House
Listed
Kneesall, Newark,
NG22 0AZ
☎ Mansfield (0623) 862525
*This beautiful house with a
large, but quiet and pleasant
garden is on the site of an old
windmill on the edge of the
Sherwood Forest area and has
wonderful views from all
windows.*
Bedrooms: 1 double & 1 twin,
1 family room.
Bathrooms: 2 public.
Bed & breakfast: from £15
single, £22-£26 double.
Parking for 6.
Open April-October.
🔌5❄️📞🔌💁▦▤▥
📞❄️✈️🎋

LAXTON

Nottinghamshire
Map ref 4C2

9m NW. Newark
The only village in
England where medieval
open-field strip farming is
still practised, preserved
as an official Ancient
Monument. Three large
fields survive and there
are remains of a splendid
motte and bailey castle.

Mrs. C. Manning
Listed
Kneesall Cottage, Laxton,
Newark, NG22 0NU
☎ Tuxford (0777) 870844
*Guests have a private entrance
and stairway to their room,
which is a modern extension to
our 300-year-old cottage with
its stream and private back
garden.*
Bedrooms: 1 family room.
Bathrooms: 1 public.
Bed & breakfast: from £10
single, from £17 double.
Parking for 1.
🔌❄️🖵💁▦▤▥✈️
🎋🎋

**PLEASE MENTION
THIS GUIDE WHEN
MAKING A BOOKING.**

LEICESTER

Leicestershire
Map ref 4C3

Modern industrial city
with a wide variety of
attractions including
Roman remains, ancient
churches, Georgian
houses and a Victorian
clock tower. There are
pedestrianised shopping
precincts, an excellent
market, several
museums, theatres,
concert hall and sports
and leisure centres. ℹ️

Waltham House
500 Narborough Road,
Leicester, LE3 2FU
☎ (0533) 891129
Victorian detached house.
Bedrooms: 1 single, 1 twin.
Bathrooms: 1 public.
Bed & breakfast: £12-£14
single, £20-£22 double.
Half board: £18-£20 daily,
£119-£133 weekly.
Parking for 3.
🔌❄️▦💁📺▤✈️🎋
▥◀️

LINCOLN

Lincolnshire
Map ref 4C2

Ancient city dominated by
the magnificent 11th C
cathedral with its triple
towers. A Roman
gateway is still used and
there are medieval
houses lining narrow
cobbled streets. Other
attractions include the
Norman castle, several
museums and the Usher
Gallery. ℹ️

Birchside
Listed
7 The Grove, Off Nettleham
Road, Lincoln, LN2 1RG
☎ (0522) 28769
*A Victorian house in a quiet
cul-de-sac. Close to the
cathedral, the historic Bailgate
area and Lindum Sports
Ground.*
Bedrooms: 2 double & 1 twin.
Bathrooms: 1 public.
Bed & breakfast: £9.50-£10
single, £19-£20 double.
Parking for 3.
🔌❄️🔌💁▤▥▦📺▤
🎋

Carline Guest House
♨♨♨
3 Carline Road, Lincoln,
LN1 1HN
☎ (0522) 30422

*A friendly, family-run guest
house, in a quiet location five
minutes from the cathedral.*
Bedrooms: 1 single, 2 double
& 1 twin, 2 family rooms.
Bathrooms: 4 private;
2 private showers.
Bed & breakfast: £11-£17
single, £20-£23 double.
Parking for 7.
🔌❄️🔌🖵💁▦▤▥
📞🎋

D'Isney Place Hotel ♨
Eastgate, Lincoln, LN2 4AA
☎ (0522) 38881 or 538881
*A small family-run hotel near
the cathedral, with individually
styled bedrooms and an
emphasis on comfort and
privacy.*
Bedrooms: 2 single, 10 double
& 4 twin, 2 family rooms.
Bathrooms: 18 private.
Bed & breakfast: £36-£40
single, £51-£57 double.
Parking for 12.
Credit: Access, Visa, Diners,
Amex.
🔌❄️▦⟡🔌🖵💁▦
▤✂️▦▤🎋📞❄️🎋▤
SP 🎋

The Grange
♨♨♨
Torrington Lane, East
Barkwith, Lincoln LN3 5RY
☎ Wragby (0673) 858249
*315-acre mixed farm. Spacious
Georgian Farmhouse in
extensive grounds. Herb
garden, lawn tennis, croquet
and bowls.*
Bedrooms: 1 double & 1 twin.
Bathrooms: 2 private.
Bed & breakfast: £25-£30
double.
Half board: from £18.50
daily, from £100 weekly.
Evening meal 6.30pm (l.o.
7.30pm).
🖵💁▦💁📺▤✂️▤▥
📞🔎🔌🖊️❄️🎋

Mayfield Guest House
♨♨
213 Yarborough Road,
Lincoln, LN1 3NQ
☎ (0522) 533732
*Small homely guesthouse with
views of the Trent Valley, a
short walk from the cathedral.
Private enclosed car park.*
Bedrooms: 1 single, 1 twin,
2 family rooms.
Bathrooms: 3 private,
1 public.
Bed & breakfast: £10-£10.50
single, £19-£22 double.
Parking for 4.
🔌▦🖵💁▦📞💁▤✂️▤
📺▥📞✈️🎋

New Farm

Burton, Nr. Lincoln,
LN1 2RD
☎ (0522) 27326
*360-acre dairy and arable
farm. Twin-bedded room with
a bathroom and use of lounge
with colour TV. 2 miles north
of Lincoln. Packed lunches
provided on request.*
Bedrooms: 1 twin.
Bathrooms: 1 private.
Bed & breakfast: from £12.50
single, from £21 double.
Half board: from £17.50
daily, from £120 weekly.
Parking for 10.
Open March-November.

Newport Guest House ♨

26-28 Newport, Lincoln,
LN1 3DF
☎ (0522) 28590
*Part of a Victorian terrace
within walking distance of the
city centre and main tourist
attractions.*
Bedrooms: 2 single, 2 double
& 3 twin, 2 family rooms.
Bathrooms: 3 public.
Bed & breakfast: £12.50
single, £25 double.
Parking for 6.

Winnowsty House

Winnowsty Lane, Lincoln,
LN2 5RZ
☎ (0522) 28600
*A pretty, Victorian family
house in the shadow of the
cathedral, 2 minutes' walk
from the historic centre of
Lincoln.*
Bedrooms: 1 double.
Bathrooms: 1 public.
Bed & breakfast: from £25
double.
Parking for 2.

THERE IS A SPECIAL
SECTION IN THIS
GUIDE LISTING
ACCOMMODATION
ESPECIALLY
SUITABLE FOR
GROUPS AND
YOUNG PEOPLE.

LONG WHATTON

Leicestershire
Map ref 4C3

5m NW. Loughborough
Village with many
interesting old houses
close to Castle
Donington's Aeropark
Visitor Centre and Racing
Car museum. Melbourne
Hall with its beautiful
gardens, Staunton Harold
Church and Whatton
Gardens are nearby.

Mr. & Mrs. Tolton
Listed

Uplands Farm, West End,
Long Whatton,
Loughborough, LE12 5DN
☎ Loughborough
(0509) 842244
*10-acre mixed farm. A cosy
old 17th C. farmhouse with all
home cooking and personal
service at all times.*
Bedrooms: 3 single, 2 double
& 2 twin, 3 family rooms.
Bathrooms: 2 public.
Bed & breakfast: £11-£12
single, £20-£23 double.
Half board: £17-£18 daily.
Evening meal 6pm (l.o. 7pm).
Parking for 30.

MARKET RASEN

Lincolnshire
Map ref 4D2

Market town on the edge of
the Lincolnshire Wolds.
The race course and the
picnic site and forest
walks at Willingham
Woods are to the east of
the town.

Bleasby House Farm

Bleasby House, Legsby,
Market Rasen, LN8 3QN
☎ (0673) 842383
*1200-acre mixed farm. In
pleasant surroundings only 3
miles from Market Rasen.
Evening meals are available by
prior arrangement.*
Bedrooms: 2 twin.
Bathrooms: 1 private,
1 public.
Bed & breakfast: £10-£15
single, £20-£25 double.
Half board: £15-£17.50 daily,
£100-£120 weekly.
Evening meal 6pm (l.o.
8.30pm).
Parking for 20.

MATLOCK

Derbyshire
Map ref 4B2

The town lies beside the
narrow valley of the River
Derwent surrounded by
steep wooded hills. The
19th C Riber Castle, with
its 60 acre wildlife park,
lies above. Good centre
for exploring Derbyshire's
best scenery.

Boat House ♨

Dale Road, Matlock,
DE4 3PP
☎ (0629) 583776
*In the picturesque Matlock
Dale overlooking the River
Derwent. Near the town centre
and Matlock Bath.*
Bedrooms: 1 single, 1 double
& 1 twin, 1 family room.
Bathrooms: 1 public.
Bed & breakfast: from £13
single, £23-£26 double.
Lunch available.
Evening meal 7pm (l.o. 9pm).
Parking for 25.

Farley Farm

Farley, Matlock, DE4 5LR
☎ (0629) 582533
*225-acre mixed farm. This
natural stone farmhouse, built
in 1610, in open countryside
above Matlock, with all
amenities close by.*
Bedrooms: 1 double & 1 twin,
1 family room.
Bathrooms: 2 public.
Bed & breakfast: £10 single,
£20 double.
Half board: £15 daily, £105
weekly.
Evening meal 5pm (l.o. 7pm).
Parking for 10.

Robertswood

Farley Hill, Matlock
☎ (0629) 55642
*A spacious Victorian residence
on the edge of Matlock, with
panoramic views. Near
Chatsworth.*
Bedrooms: 3 double & 4 twin.
Bathrooms: 7 private.
Bed & breakfast: from £20
single, from £36 double.
Half board: £28-£52 daily.
Evening meal 7pm (l.o.
midday).
Parking for 8.

MEASHAM

Leicestershire
Map ref 4B3

The Laurels Guest House

17 Ashby Road, Measham,
Burton-upon-Trent,
Staffordshire DE15 0LB
☎ (0530) 72567
*A modern guesthouse on the
A453, convenient for the M42.
The back of the guest house
looks out onto a rural location
and the garden is well
maintained.*
Bedrooms: 1 single, 1 double
& 1 twin.
Bathrooms: 2 public.
Bed & breakfast: £12 single,
£24 double.
Half board: £110 weekly.
Parking for 5.

MELTON MOWBRAY

Leicestershire
Map ref 4C3

Close to the attractive
Vale of Belvoir and
famous for its fox-
hunting, pork pies and
Stilton cheese which are
the subjects of special
displays in the museum. It
has a beautiful church
with a tower 100 ft
high.

Manor House ♨

Saxelby, Melton Mowbray,
LE14 3PA
☎ (0664) 812269
*125-acre dairy and sheep farm.
We offer home cooking and a
warm welcome in our oak-
beamed farmhouse. Parts date
back several hundred years
including a unique 400-year-
old staircase.*
Bedrooms: 1 twin, 2 family
rooms.
Bathrooms: 1 public.
Bed & breakfast: from £14.50
single, from £22 double.
Half board: from £17.50
daily, from £113 weekly.
Evening meal 7pm (l.o.
midday).
Parking for 6.
Open April-October.

MAP REFERENCES
APPLY TO COLOUR
MAPS NEAR THE
BACK OF THE GUIDE.

Derbyshire
Map ref 4B2

5m W. Bakewell

Sheldon House
Chapel Street, Monyash,
DE4 1JJ
☎ Bakewell (062 981) 3067
*Comfortable accommodation in
the heart of the Peak District.*
Bedrooms: 2 double & 1 twin.
Bathrooms: 1 public.
Bed & breakfast: £12-£15
single, £20-£24 double.
Parking for 6.

MOUNTSORREL

Leicestershire
Map ref 4C3

The Poplars ♠
Watling Street, Mountsorrel,
Loughborough, LE12 7BD
☎ Leicester (0533) 302102
*A Victorian house with a
wooded secluded garden, on a
hill overlooking the Soar
Valley.*
Bedrooms: 5 single, 1 twin,
1 family room.
Bathrooms: 1 public.
Bed & breakfast: £12.50
single, £23 double.
Parking for 15.

NEWARK

Nottinghamshire
Map ref 4C2

The town has many fine
old houses and ancient
inns near the market
place. The 12th C castle
where King John died is
well preserved and has
many features of interest.
There are several
museums and Sherwood
Forest is nearby. ℹ

Red Roofs
Main Street, Coddington, Nr.
Newark, NG24 2AN
☎ (0636) 702092
*A bungalow in a rural setting,
near the town of Newark.
Handicapped visitors welcome.*
Bedrooms: 1 twin.
Bathrooms: 1 public.
Bed & breakfast: from £12.50
single, from £25 double.
Half board: from £15 daily,
from £100 weekly.
Lunch available.
Parking for 5.

Wilmot House ♠
Church Walk, Dunham-on-
Trent, Newark, NG22 0TX
☎ (077 785) 226
*A listed building with its
original oak beams. Offering
spacious accommodation in a
rural setting.*
Bedrooms: 1 single, 1 double
& 1 twin, 1 family room.
Bathrooms: 2 public.
Bed & breakfast: £11 single,
£22 double.
Half board: £15-£16 daily.
Evening meal 6pm (l.o. 9pm).
Parking for 6.

NORTHAMPTON

Northamptonshire
Map ref 2C1

A bustling town and a
shoe manufacturing
centre, with excellent
shopping facilities, a
theatre, concert hall and
several museums and
parks. There are at least
3 old churches including
one of only four round
churches in Britain. ℹ

Aarandale Regent Hotel & Guest House ♠
😃😃
6-7 Royal Terrace, Barrack
Road, Northampton,
NN1 3RF
☎ (0604) 31096
*Small and cosy, family-run
hotel and guesthouse within
easy walking distance of town
centre, bus and train stations.*
Bedrooms: 2 single, 4 double
& 6 twin, 2 family rooms.
Bathrooms: 3 public.
Bed & breakfast: £16-£18
single, £27-£29 double.
Half board: £22-£24 daily.
Evening meal 6pm (l.o.
7.15pm).
Parking for 14.

Quinton Green Farm
Quinton, Northampton,
NN7 2EG
☎ (0604) 862484
*1200-acre dairy & arable farm.
350-year-old farmhouse 4 miles
south of Northampton and 3
miles from the M1.*
Bedrooms: 1 single, 1 double
& 1 twin.
Bathrooms: 1 public.
Bed & breakfast: £14-£16
single, £28-£32 double.
Parking for 8.

NOTTINGHAM

Nottinghamshire
Map ref 4C2

Modern city with a wide
range of industries
including lace. Its castle is
now a museum and art
gallery with a statue of
Robin Hood outside. The
many attractions include
excellent shopping
facilities, theatres,
museums, Wollaton Hall
and the National Water
Sports Centre. ℹ

Ivy House Farm
Listed
Hawksworth, Nottingham,
NG13 9DD
☎ Whatton (0949) 50361
*200-acre arable farm. Our
18th C. farmhouse is on the
edge of a pleasant conservation
area village. A warm welcome
awaits our guests.*
Bedrooms: 1 double & 1 twin.
Bathrooms: 1 public.
Bed & breakfast: £12-£14
single, £24-£28 double.
Parking for 4.
Open April-October.

OAKHAM

Leicestershire
Map ref 4C3

Pleasant former county
town of Rutland has a
fine 12th C Great Hall,
part of its castle, housing
a historic collection of
horse-shoes. An
octagonal Butter Cross
stands in the Market
Place and Rutland County
Museum, Rutland Farm
Park and Rutland Water
are other attractions. ℹ

Brooke Priory
Brooke, Nr. Oakham,
LE15 8DG
☎ (0572) 2769
*23-acre cattle and horse farm.
Historic house set in its own
grounds, 1.5 miles from
Oakham. Peaceful and quiet.*
Bedrooms: 3 twin.
Bathrooms: 1 public.
Bed & breakfast: £11 single,
£22 double.
Parking for 6.
Open March-October.

RAGNALL

Nottinghamshire
Map ref 4C2

13m N. Newark-on-Trent

Ragnall House
😃😃
Ragnall, Newark,
NG22 0UR
☎ Dunham-on-Trent
(077 785) 575
*A large listed Georgian family
house with a late Victorian
extension, in three quarters of
an acre of grounds. Close to
the River Trent in rolling
countryside. There are good
pubs and restaurants nearby.*
Bedrooms: 2 twin, 1 family
room.
Bathrooms: 1 private;
2 private showers.
Bed & breakfast: £9.50-£10
single, £19-£20 double.
Half board: £13-£13.50 daily.
Evening meal 6pm (l.o.
7.15pm).
Parking for 7.

REDMILE

Leicestershire
Map ref 4C2

8m W. Grantham
Vale of Belvoir village
overlooked by the hilltop
castle.

Marjorie & Peter Need
😃😃
Peacock Farm, Redmile,
Nottingham,
Nottinghamshire NG13 0GQ
☎ Bottesford (0949) 42475
*Peter and Marjorie Need
welcome you to their old
farmhouse in the delightful
Vale of Belvoir, close to the
castle. A small licensed
restaurant is attached, and
there is a sunbed, exercise
room and small covered pool.*
Bedrooms: 1 single, 2 double
& 1 twin, 2 family rooms.
Bathrooms: 4 private,
2 public.
Bed & breakfast: £13.50-£21
single, £23-£28 double.
Half board: from £31 daily.
Lunch available.
Evening meal 6pm (l.o.
9.30pm).
Parking for 20.
Credit: Access.

PLEASE CHECK PRICES AND OTHER DETAILS
AT THE TIME OF BOOKING.

RETFORD

Nottinghamshire
Map ref 4C2

Market town on the River
Idle with a pleasant
market square and
Georgian houses. The
surrounding villages were
the homes and meeting
places of the early Pilgrim
Fathers .🖻

Tirl House

Mattersey Road, Ranskill,
Nr. Retford, DN22 8ND
☎ (0777) 818940
*A small friendly guesthouse
with traditional home-cooked
food. Located a few minutes
from the A1.*
Bedrooms: 1 single, 2 twin.
Bathrooms: 1 public.
Bed & breakfast: £10.50
single, £19 double.
Half board: £13.50 daily, £91
weekly.
Evening meal 5.30pm (l.o.
6.30pm).
Parking for 5.
Ⓤ🖤 ⊢ ⊕ ▥ ▲ ⊀

ROSTON

Derbyshire
Map ref 4B2

4m SW. Ashbourne
Small village featured in
George Eliot's novel
'Adam Bede'. Close to
Dovedale and the Peak
National Park.

Mrs. E. Prince
Listed

Roston Hall Farm, Roston,
Ashbourne, DE6 2EH
☎ Ellastone (033 524) 287
*90-acre beef and arable farm.
A spacious farmhouse in a
quiet village, well placed for
the Derbyshire Dales, Alton
Towers and stately homes.
Ploughman's suppers and
snacks are available in the
evening.*
Bedrooms: 1 twin, 1 family
room.
Bathrooms: 1 public.
Bed & breakfast: £9.50-
£10.50 single, £19-£21 double.
Parking for 4.
Open May-September.
🖤13 ⊼ ✿ Ⓤ ⊕ ✳ ⊀ ⊀

**THE SYMBOLS ARE
EXPLAINED ON THE
FLAP INSIDE THE
BACK COVER.**

SCAMBLESBY

Lincolnshire
Map ref 4D2

6m N. Horncastle

The Old Vicarage

Scamblesby, Near Louth,
LN11 9XL
☎ Stenigot (050 784) 790
*A Victorian vicarage with a
large secluded garden, set in a
quiet village on the
Lincolnshire Wolds.*
Bedrooms: 1 double & 2 twin.
Bathrooms: 3 private.
Bed & breakfast: £12-£15
single, £18-£24 double.
Parking for 6.
🖤 ⊿ ⊡ ✿ Ⓤ CB ✳ ⊀ ⊀
DAP SP

SCAMPTON

Lincolnshire
Map ref 4C2

5m N. Lincoln

The Copse
Listed

Brigg Road, Scampton,
Lincoln, LN1 2SY
☎ Lincoln (0522) 43870
*Located 4 miles north of
Lincoln, opposite the
showground and the Red
Arrows' base. We offer lovely
views and a homely
atmosphere.*
Bedrooms: 1 single, 1 double
& 1 twin.
Bathrooms: 1 public.
Bed & breakfast: £9-£9.50
single, £18-£19 double.
Half board: £13-£13.50 daily,
£85 weekly.
Evening meal 7.30pm.
Parking for 3.
🖤 ⊼ Ⓤ 🖤 ⊕ ▥ ▲ ⊀
DAP

SHEARSBY

Leicestershire
Map ref 4C3

7m NE. Lutterworth

Knaptoft House Farm
☺☺

Bruntingthorpe Road, Nr.
Shearsby, Lutterworth,
LE17 6PR
☎ Leicester (0533) 478388
*145-acre mixed farm. Warm
and comfortable
accommodation overlooking
peaceful and rolling
countryside. Easy access to the
M1 (Exit 20).*
Bedrooms: 1 single, 1 twin,
1 family room.
Bathrooms: 1 public;
1 private shower.

Bed & breakfast: £10-£15
single, £22-£24 double.
Evening meal 6pm (l.o. 2pm).
Parking for 5.
Credit: Access.
🖤 ⊿ ✿ 🖤 Ⓥ ⊕ ⊕ ▥ ▲
⊿ ✓ ✳ ⊀ ⊀

SKILLINGTON

Lincolnshire
Map ref 3A1

Mrs. Whatton
Listed

Sproxton Lodge, Skillington,
Grantham, NG33 5HJ
☎ Grantham (0476) 860307
*213-acre arable farm. A quiet
family farmhouse with large
lawns, providing a good
farmhouse breakfast. Evening
meals may be obtained at the
local inns. Located about 3
miles off the A1 trunk road.*
Bedrooms: 1 single, 1 double
& 2 twin.
Bathrooms: 1 public.
Bed & breakfast: max. £9
single, max. £18 double.
Parking for 4.
🖤 ⊼ ⊡ ✿ Ⓤ 🖤 Ⓥ ⊕ ⊕
▥ ▲ ✳ ⊀ ⊀ ⊓

SNARESTONE

Leicestershire
Map ref 4B3

5m S. Ashby-de-la-Zouch

Snarestone Lodge
Listed

Measham Road, Snarestone,
Burton upon Trent,
Staffordshire DE12 7DA
☎ Measham (0530) 70535
*Snarestone Lodge is a
Georgian country house of
character in 4 acres of
beautiful grounds through
which the Ashby Canal runs.
We are in Ivanhoe country,
close to Twycross Zoo, the
Battlefield of Bosworth, Calke
Abbey and 2 miles from the
M42.*
Bedrooms: 3 single, 1 twin,
1 family room.
Bathrooms: 4 public.
Bed & breakfast: £12-£15
single, £25-£30 double.
Parking for 11.
🖤 ⊼ ⊡ 🖤 Ⓤ ⊕ 🖤 ▥ ▲ 🍸
⊍ ⊿ ⊢ ✳ ⊀ ⊀ ⊓

**MAP REFERENCES
APPLY TO COLOUR
MAPS NEAR THE
BACK OF THE GUIDE.**

SOUTH LUFFENHAM

Leicestershire
Map ref 4C3

Boot & Shoe Inn
☺☺

The Street, South Luffenham,
Oakham, LE15 8NX
☎ Stamford (0780) 720177
*A traditional old world inn
with stone walls, beams and
lots of brassware. Restaurant,
an interesting bar menu and
homely accommodation.*
Bedrooms: 1 single, 1 double
& 2 twin.
Bathrooms: 2 public.
Bed & breakfast: £12.50
single, £25 double.
Lunch available.
Evening meal 7pm (l.o.
10pm).
Parking for 30.
Credit: Visa.
🖤 ⊡ 🖤 Ⓥ ▥ ▲ 🍸 🕏
⊀

SOUTHWELL

Nottinghamshire
Map ref 4C2

Town dominated by the
Norman Minster which
has some beautiful 13th C
stone carvings in the
Chapter House. Charles I
spent his last night of
freedom in one of the
inns. The original Bramley
apple tree can still be
seen.

Old National School
Hotel
☺☺☺

Nottingham Road,
Southwell, NG25 0LG
☎ (0636) 814360
*A former Church of England
National School, circa 1840,
carefully converted by the
resident owners to provide
comfort and style for their
guests. Double rooms can be
adapted for family use by
arrangement.*
Bedrooms: 2 double & 4 twin.
Bathrooms: 6 private.
Bed & breakfast: £16-£18
single, £28-£30 double.
Parking for 6.
Credit: Access, Visa.
🖤 ⊼ ⊡ ✿ Ⓤ ⊁ ▥ ▲
🍸 ⚷ ✳ ⊀ SP

Mrs. S. Woodhull
☺☺☺

Upton Fields House, Upton
Fields, Southwell,
NG25 0QA
☎ (0636) 812303
Continued ▶

SOUTHWELL
Continued

This large country house has spacious rooms with open country views, an inlaid galleried staircase and stained glass windows.
Bedrooms: 3 double & 2 twin.
Bathrooms: 5 private.
Bed & breakfast: £15-£20 single, £30-£34 double.
Parking for 7.
⌂5 ▯ ♨ Ⓤ 🍴 ▦ ⛱ 🅿 🐾 ⊁ 🐕 🏠

STAMFORD
Lincolnshire
Map ref 3A1

Exceptionally beautiful and historic town with many houses of architectural interest, several notable churches and other public buildings all in the local stone. Burghley House, built by William Cecil, is a magnificent Tudor mansion on the edge of the town. ℹ

Birch House
4 Lonsdale Road, Stamford, PE9 2RW
☎ (0780) 54876
A comfortable, family-run detached house only three quarters of a mile from the town centre.
Bedrooms: 2 single, 1 double & 1 twin.
Bathrooms: 1 public.
Bed & breakfast: £11-£12.50 single.
Half board: £15-£17 daily, £75-£95 weekly.
Evening meal 6pm (l.o. 7pm).
Parking for 4.
⌂ ❄ ▯ ▦ ⊁ 🏠

The Lincolnshire Poacher
Broad Street, Stamford, PE9 1PF
☎ (0780) 64239
A former brewery in the centre of Stamford, convenient for Burghley House and Rutland Water. 2 miles from the A1.
Bedrooms: 1 single, 1 twin, 1 family room.
Bathrooms: 1 public.
Bed & breakfast: from £15 single.
Lunch available.
Evening meal 6pm (l.o. 9.30pm).
⌂ ❄ ▯ ♨ 🛏 ▯ 🅅 ▯ 📺 ▦ ⊁ 🏠

STANTON ON THE WOLDS
Nottinghamshire
Map ref 4C2

7m SE. Nottingham

Laurel Farm
Browns Lane, Stanton on the Wolds, Keyworth, Nottingham, NG12 5BL
☎ Plumtree (060 77) 3488
4-acre farm. An old farmhouse adjacent to a church with easy access from the A46. All rooms may be let as singles subject to availability.
Bedrooms: 1 double & 2 twin.
Bathrooms: 1 public.
Bed & breakfast: £10 single, £20 double.
Half board: £17.50 daily, £120 weekly.
Evening meal 7pm (l.o. 7pm).
Parking for 3.
⌂5 ❄ ♨ ▯ ▦ 🛏 ↺ 🐾 🏠

SWINDERBY
Lincolnshire
Map ref 4C2

9m SW. Lincoln

Mrs. Underwood
Halfway Farm Motel & Guest House, (A46), Swinderby, Lincoln, LN6 9HN
☎ (052 286) 749
An old farmstead converted to provide accommodation at reasonable cost, operated by the owners. Licensed restaurant close by.
Bedrooms: 5 single, 2 double & 1 twin, 6 family rooms.
Bathrooms: 7 private, 3 public.
Bed & breakfast: £12-£20 single, £24-£36 double.
Parking for 20.
Credit: Access.
⌂2 🛏 ♨ Ⓤ ▯ 📺 ▦ 🛏 ⊁ 🏠

TETFORD
Lincolnshire
Map ref 4D2

6m NE. Horncastle

Tetford House
Tetford, Horncastle, LN9 6QQ
☎ (065 883) 639
An old country house in an area of outstanding natural beauty in the heart of the Lincolnshire Wolds and Tennyson country. The double room may also be let as a single room or as a family room by prior arrangement.

Bedrooms: 1 double.
Bathrooms: 1 private.
Bed & breakfast: £15 single, £24 double.
Parking for 2.
⌂ ▯ ♨ Ⓤ ▦ ▦ 🛏 🐾 ⊁ 🐕 🏠 🅿

UPPINGHAM
Leicestershire
Map ref 4C3

Quiet market town dominated by its famous public school which was founded in 1584. It has many stone houses and is surrounded by attractive countryside.

Falcon Hotel ▥
😊😊😊😊
Market Place, Uppingham, Oakham, LE15 9PY
☎ (0572) 823535
A 16th C. coaching inn with a cobbled yard and beams, in a central yet secluded situation.
Bedrooms: 10 single, 9 double & 5 twin, 1 family room.
Bathrooms: 25 private.
Bed & breakfast: £47-£52 single, £70-£80 double.
Lunch available.
Evening meal 7pm (l.o. 10pm).
Parking for 23.
Credit: Access, Visa, Diners, Amex.
⌂ 🛏 🛏 📞 ▯ ▯ 🅅 🛏 📺 ● ▦ 🛏 🍴 🐾 ⓈⓅ 🏠 Ⓣ

Old Rectory ▥
😊😊😊
Belton in Rutland, Uppingham, LE15 9LE
☎ Belton (057 286) 279
30-acre pedigree miniature breed farm. A Victorian country house with a retail craft centre, a display of bygones, and a miniature farm of British rare breeds. 3 miles from Uppingham, and is accessible from the A47, following the AA signs.
Bedrooms: 2 double & 1 twin, 5 family rooms.
Bathrooms: 7 private, 2 public.
Bed & breakfast: £13.50-£20 single, £25-£35 double.
Half board: £20-£29.50 daily, £90-£120 weekly.
Lunch available.
Evening meal 5pm (l.o. 8pm).
Parking for 6.
⌂6 🛏 ♨ ▯ ▯ ♨ Ⓤ 🔔 🅅 ⊁ 🛏 📺 ● ▦ 🛏 🍴 ↺ ❄ 🏠

UPTON
Nottinghamshire
Map ref 4C2

4m W. Newark

Honey Cottage
The Green, Upton Newark NG23 5SU
☎ Southwell (0636) 813318
A cottage in the heart of a conservation village, ideal for touring Robin Hood country. Bar and restaurant meals are available in the pubs in the village.
Bedrooms: 1 twin, 1 family room.
Bathrooms: 1 private, 1 public.
Bed & breakfast: £11-£15 single, £20-£25 double.
Parking for 2.
⌂ ♨ ▯ 🛏 📺 ▦ 🛏 ⊁ 🏠

WALTHAM-ON-THE-WOLDS
Leicestershire
Map ref 4C3

5m NE. Melton Mowbray

Royal Horseshoes
Listed
Melton Road, Waltham-on-the-Wolds, Nr. Melton Mowbray, LE14 4AJ
☎ (066 478) 289
A listed thatched country inn, approximately 400 years old. The accommodation is separate from the main building.
Bedrooms: 4 twin.
Bathrooms: 4 private.
Bed & breakfast: £21.50 single, £37.50 double.
Lunch available.
Evening meal 6pm (l.o. 9pm).
Parking for 50.
⌂ ▯ ♨ 🛏 ▦ ⊁ 🏠 ⓈⓅ 🏠

WEEDON
Northamptonshire
Map ref 2C1

Globe Hotel ▥
😊😊😊
High Street, Weedon, Northampton, NN7 4QD
☎ (0327) 40336
A 17th C. countryside inn with a Royal Charter. Old world atmosphere and free house hospitality with English catering.
Bedrooms: 3 single, 5 double & 5 twin, 2 family rooms.
Bathrooms: 15 private.
Bed & breakfast: £29-£34 single, £35-£42 double.
Half board: £34-£40 daily.

Lunch available.
Evening meal 6.30pm (l.o. 9.30pm).
Parking for 45.
Credit: Access, Visa, Diners, Amex.

🛇 🏠 📞 ⊕ 🖵 ❖ ᵢ Ⅴ ⊨
Ⅳ ▥ ▲ 🍴 ♠ ⍓ ✕ SP ⊞

The Narrow Boat Inn
😊😊

Watling Street (A5), Stowe Hill, Weedon, NN7 6RZ
☎ (0327) 40536
An inn with real ales and bar food and a restaurant which serves Cantonese meals. On the A5 by the Grand Union Canal, 5 minutes from the M1.
Bedrooms: 7 twin.
Bathrooms: 7 private.
Bed & breakfast: £29.50-£34.50 single, £34.50-£39.50 double.
Lunch available.
Evening meal 6.30pm (l.o. 10.30pm).
Credit: Access, Visa, Diners, Amex.

🛇 ♿ 📞 ⊕ 🖵 ❖ ᵢ Ⅴ ◉
▥ ▲ 🍴 ♿ ♠ ⍓ ✿ 🗡 ⊞
SP

Derbyshire
Map ref 4B2

6m NW. Derby

Parkview Farm
😊😊

Weston Underwood, Derby, DE6 4PA
☎ Ashbourne (0335) 60352

370-acre arable farm. An attractive farmhouse in a large garden, overlooking our own land and Kedleston Hall and Park.
Bedrooms: 1 double & 2 twin.
Bathrooms: 2 public.
Bed & breakfast: from £13 single, £26-£28 double.
Parking for 10.

🛇 🏠 ❖ ⊔ᴸ ⊨ Ⅳ ▥ ▲ ✿ 🗡

Derbyshire
Map ref 4B2

Old textile town, whose canal warehouses are a reminder of its former importance, at the junction of the Peak Forest Canal and the Cromford and High Peak Railway. Surrounded by hills and with splendid views.

Fernilee Hall
Fernilee, Whaley Bridge, SK12 7HP
☎ (066 33) 2258
A small secluded Victorian hall in large grounds, with spectacular views over the Goyt Valley.
Bedrooms: 1 double & 1 twin, 1 family room.
Bathrooms: 1 public.
Bed & breakfast: £20 double.
Evening meal 7.30pm.
Open June-September.

🛇 ♿ ⊔ᴸ ᵢ Ⅴ ⊨ Ⅳ ▥ ▲
✿ ✕ 🗡

Nottinghamshire
Map ref 4C2

Market town close to the Dukeries, where a number of Ducal families had their estates, some of which, like Clumber Park, may be visited. The upper room of the 14th C. gatehouse of the priory housed the country's first elementary school in 1628. ℹ

The Old Rectory
29 High Street, Whitwell, Worksop, S80 4RE
☎ (0909) 721089
A stone-built house set in an acre of garden. 5 minutes from the M1 junction 30, off the A619 Chesterfield to Worksop road.
Bedrooms: 1 single, 2 twin.
Bathrooms: 1 private, 2 public.
Bed & breakfast: £12.50-£14 single, £24-£28 double.
Half board: £18.50-£22 daily, £75-£138 weekly.
Evening meal 7.30pm (l.o. 9pm).
Parking for 4.

🛇 ♿ ⊔ᴸ ᵢ Ⅴ ⊨ Ⅳ ▥ ▲
🍴 ✿ 🗡 ⊞

Northamptonshire
Map ref 2C1

5m SE. Towcester

Old Wharf Farm
Listed

Yardley Gobion, Nr. Towcester, NN12 7UE
☎ Milton Keynes (0908) 542454
9-acre smallholding. Unique complex of old farm buildings with its own working wharf on to the Grand Union Canal. Now a family home, smallholding and narrow boat maintenance base.
Bedrooms: 1 single, 1 double, 1 family room.
Bathrooms: 2 public.
Bed & breakfast: £12 single, £24 double.
Parking for 5.

🛇 ♿ ⊔ᴸ ⊨ ▥ 🗡 ✿ 🗡 ⊞

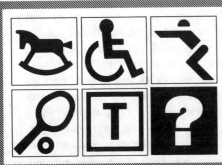

KEY TO SYMBOLS
Open out the flap inside the back cover of this guide and the key to symbols will be easy to use.

The Bentley Brook

TAKE A BREAK WITH US IN THE PEAK DISTRICT NATIONAL PARK

Two miles north of the early Georgian town of Ashbourne the lovely old half timbered Inn is set in over two acres of lawned garden with a further five acres of woods and meadow leading to the Bentley Brook, a tributary of the Dove, one of Englands most famous trout streams. There are two restaurants and a busy lounge bar serving real ales. The main menu lists a fine selection of classical and traditional dishes typical of an English Inn, whilst the Travellers menu provides substantial but less formal meals.

☎ **THORPE CLOUD (033 529) 278**

When requesting brochures or further information from advertisers in this guide, you may find it helpful to use the advertisement enquiry coupons which can be found towards the end of the guide. These should be cut out and mailed direct to the companies in which you are interested. Remember to include your name and address and enclose a stamped and addressed envelope or stamps if requested by the advertiser.

P L E A S E   N O T E

Individual establishments who have a display advertisement have a line listing under the appropriate town heading

🍀 Enjoy the countryside and respect its life and work 🍀 Guard against all risk of fire 🍀 Fasten all gates 🍀 Keep your dogs under close control 🍀 Keep to public paths across farmland 🍀 Use gates and stiles to cross fences, hedges and walls 🍀 Leave livestock, crops and machinery alone 🍀 Take your litter home 🍀 Help to keep all water clean 🍀 Protect wildlife, plants and trees 🍀 Take special care on country roads 🍀 Make no unnecessary noise

FOLLOW THE COUNTRY CODE

CROWN CLASSIFICATIONS

All the establishments displaying a national classification in this guide are inspected regularly. All can be chosen with confidence.

There are six classifications — from Listed to 5 Crowns; each indicates the level of facilities and services provided.

All classified establishments are required to provide a high standard of cleanliness, courtesy and service and to be well maintained. A lower classification does not imply lower standards; although the range of facilities and services may be smaller, they may be provided to a high standard.

You will find a full explanation of the national Crown Classification Scheme towards the end of this guide.

FOLLOW THE SIGN

It leads to over 550 Tourist Information Centres throughout England offering friendly help with accommodation and holiday ideas as well as suggestions of places to visit and things to do.

In your home town there may be a centre which can help you before you set out. If not, why not send for the Directory of Tourist Information Centres in Great Britain? It is available free from English Tourist Board, Department D, Bromells Road, Clapham, London SW4 0BJ.

Thames & Chilterns

Old Father Thames is very much the focal point of the Thames & Chilterns tourist region, which takes in Bedfordshire, Berkshire, Buckinghamshire, Hertfordshire and Oxfordshire.

So why not take a river cruise from Oxford, Abingdon, Reading or Windsor? Or hire your own boat and meander on the river through old towns like Wallingford, Maidenhead and Marlow. If you prefer to stay firmly on dry land, just stroll along the banks of this great river, calling in at pretty local restaurants and pubs on the way. The Thames is there to enjoy.

And there are other rivers, too: the Great Ouse, leading to Bedford; the Evenlode, winding through the old hunting forests of the Wychwoods; the Windrush, weaving through gentle limestone hills; the Cherwell and the Isis, slipping past Oxford's dreaming spires.

If your interest is in historic towns and settlements, the region has riches in store: Royal Windsor and Roman St. Albans; the market towns of Banbury, Wantage and Aylesbury; and the picture postcard towns and villages in the Oxfordshire Cotswolds.

The historical theme continues with great houses and estates — Woburn Abbey, Hatfield House, Blenheim Palace and dozens more. And don't forget the abundance of glorious gardens that will be open for your delight in 1989.

Paul Anscomb

WINDSOR SAFARI PARK

FIND OUT MORE

Further information about holidays and attractions in the Thames & Chilterns tourist region is available from: **Thames & Chilterns Tourist Board,** The Mount House, Church Street, Church Green, Witney, Oxfordshire OX8 6DZ.
☎ (0993) 778800.

These publications are available free from the Thames & Chilterns Tourist Board:
A Cottage in the Country (Self-Catering Holidays)
Historic Houses in the Thames & Chilterns

Also available are: **Where to Go in the Thames & Chilterns** (£1.95)
Churches of the Thames & Chilterns (25p)

WHERE TO GO, WHAT TO SEE

Waddesdon Manor
Aylesbury, Buckinghamshire HP18 0JH
☎ (0296) 651211/651282
House built 1874 – 89 for Baron Ferdinand de Rothschild. Fine collection of French 17th – 18th C works of art; English portraits. Grounds, aviary and play area.
Admission charge.

▶

SHUTTLEWORTH COLLECTION

Britain on View

Shuttleworth Collection
Old Warden Aerodrome, Biggleswade,
Bedfordshire SG18 9ER
☎ (076 727) 288
In a charming rural setting on a classic
grass aerodrome, a unique collection of
flyable historic aeroplanes from 1909
Bleriot to 1941 Spitfire. Cars dating
from an 1898 Panhard Levassor.
Admission charge.

Didcot Railway Centre
Didcot, Oxfordshire OX11 7NJ
☎ (0235) 817200
Steam locomotives and rolling stock
from the Great Western Railway; original
engine shed and depot, train rides.
Admission charge.

Greys Court
Rotherfield Greys, Henley-on-Thames,
Oxfordshire RG9 4PG ☎ (049 17) 529
Jacobean manor house in a garden set
amid remains of 14th C walls and
towers of a fortified house; early Tudor
donkey wheel-house.
Admission charge.

Littlecote House
Hungerford, Berkshire RG17 0SS
☎ (0488) 82170
Elizabethan country house and park.
Cromwellian armour exhibition, medieval
farm, narrow-gauge railway. All-round
family day out.
Admission charge.

Ashmolean Museum
Beaumont Street, Oxford, Oxfordshire
OX1 2PH ☎ (0865) 278000
The University of Oxford's museum and
picture gallery. World renowned
collections of paintings and sculpture.
Oriental art; artefacts from Egypt,
Greece and Rome. Coins and medals of
the world.
Admission charge.

Museum of English Rural Life
The University, Whiteknights, Reading,
Berkshire RG6 2AG
☎ (0734) 875123 Ext. 475
A national collection of material relating
to the history of the English countryside.
Admission charge.

Cathedral and Abbey Church
of St. Alban
Sumpter Yard, St. Albans, Hertfordshire
AL1 1BY ☎ (0727) 60780/64738
Medieval abbey/cathedral.
Admission charge.

Kingstone Lisle Park
Kingstone Lisle, Wantage, Oxfordshire
OX12 9QG ☎ (036 782) 223
House contains a superb flying
staircase, fine furniture and a collection
of glass, needlework and carpets.
Excellent gardens and the unusual
Blowing Stone.
Admission charge.

West Wycombe Caves
West Wycombe, Buckinghamshire
HP14 3AJ ☎ (0494) 33739
The caves are approached through a
large flint forecourt which looks rather
like the interior of a Gothic church.
Great Hall filled with classical statues.
Admission charge.

Windsor Safari Park
Winkfield Road, Windsor, Berkshire
SL4 4AY ☎ (0753) 869841
Attractions include 7 drive-through
reserves including bear reserve, killer
whale, dolphin and sealion shows, birds
of prey show, parrot show, unique
Africa 'Tiki' show plus walk-through
tropical plant and butterfly house.
Admission charge.

Blenheim Palace
Woodstock, Oxfordshire OX7 1PX
☎ (0993) 811325
Park by 'Capability' Brown. Architecture
by Vanbrugh. Churchill's birth room and
exhibition. Fine furniture, paintings,
bronzes, Marlborough victories,
tapestries. Butterfly house.
Admission charge.

Knebworth House and Park
Knebworth, Nr. Stevenage, Hertfordshire
SG3 6PY ☎ (0438) 812661
15th C house refashioned in 19th C;
home of novelist Bulwer Lytton; deer
park and Lutyens Garden. Adventure
playground, railway.
Admission charge.

The Gardens of the Rose
Royal National Rose Society, Chiswell
Green, St. Albans, Hertfordshire
AL2 3NR ☎ (0727) 50461
12 acres of showground and trial
grounds for new varieties. 30,000 roses
of all types, 1,700 different varieties.
Admission charge.

The Oxford Story
6 Broad Street, Oxford, Oxfordshire
☎ (0865) 728822
Original and imaginative presentation of
the history of the City of Oxford, its
University and its people.
Admission charge.

MAKE A DATE FOR...

**Golf: Dunhill British Masters
Golf Tournament**
Woburn Golf & Country Club, Bow
Brickhill, Milton Keynes,
Buckinghamshire *1 — 4 June*

Horse racing: Royal Ascot
Ascot Racecourse, Ascot, Berkshire
20 — 23 June

Henley Royal Regatta
Henley-on-Thames, Oxfordshire
28 June — 2 July

Henley Festival of Music and the Arts
Steward's Enclosure, Remenham,
Henley-on-Thames, Oxfordshire
5 — 8 July

Paul Jones

British Rose Festival
Gardens of the Rose, Chiswell Green
Lane, St. Albans, Hertfordshire
8 — 9 July

St. Albans Organ Festival
St. Albans Abbey, St. Albans,
Hertfordshire *8 — 15 July*

Tourist Information ℹ

Tourist and leisure information can be obtained from Tourist Information Centres throughout England. Details of centres in the Thames & Chilterns region are listed below. The symbol 🛏 means that an accommodation booking service is provided. Centres marked with a ✱ are open during the summer months only. In the following pages, towns which have a Tourist Information Centre are indicated with the symbol *i* .

Abingdon
Oxfordshire 🛏
The Old Gaol, Bridge Street
☎ (0235) 22711

Ampthill
Bedfordshire
12 Dunstable Street
☎ (0525) 402051

Aylesbury
Buckinghamshire
County Hall, Walton Street
☎ (0296) 395000

Banbury
Oxfordshire 🛏
8 Horsefair
☎ (0295) 59855

Bedford
Bedfordshire 🛏
10 St Paul's Square
☎ (0234) 215226

Berkhamsted
Hertfordshire
County Library, Kings Road
☎ (044 27) 4545

Bishop's Stortford
Hertfordshire
Council Offices, The Causeway
☎ (0279) 55261

Borehamwood
Hertfordshire
Civic Office, Elstree Way
☎ 01-207 2277

Bracknell
Berkshire
Central Library, Town Square
☎ (0344) 423149

Burford
Oxfordshire 🛏
The Brewery, Sheep Street
☎ (099 382) 3590

Chipping Norton
Oxfordshire 🛏
New Street Car Park
☎ (0608) 44379

Cropredy
Oxfordshire ✱
Country Crafts, The Green
☎ Cropredy (029 575) 8203

Dunstable
Bedfordshire 🛏
Dunstable Library, Vernon Place
☎ (0582) 608441

Faringdon
Oxfordshire 🛏 ✱
Pump House,
5 The Market Square
☎ (0367) 22191

Hemel Hempstead
Hertfordshire
The Pavilion, Marlowes
☎ (0442) 64451

Henley-on-Thames
Oxfordshire 🛏
Town Hall, Market Place
☎ (0491) 578034

Hertford
Hertfordshire 🛏
The Castle
☎ (0279) 55261

High Wycombe
Buckinghamshire 🛏
Wycombe District Council,
Queen Victoria Road
☎ (0494) 26100

Hitchin
Hertfordshire
County Library, Paynes Park
☎ (0462) 34738

Luton
Bedfordshire
Advice & Information Bureau,
45 – 47a Alma Road
☎ (0582) 401579

Maidenhead
Berkshire
Central Library, St. Ives Road
☎ (0628) 781110

Marlow
Buckinghamshire 🛏 *
Higginson Park, Pound Lane
☎ (062 84) 3597

Milton Keynes
Buckinghamshire 🛏
Saxon Court,
502 Avebury Boulevard
☎ (0908) 691995

Newbury
Berkshire 🛏
Newbury District Museum,
The Wharf
☎ (0635) 30267

Oxford
Oxfordshire
St. Aldates 🛏
☎ (0865) 726871

Erskine Bureaux Ltd., Railway
Station (personal callers only)

Reading
Berkshire
Civic Offices, Civic Centre
☎ (0734) 55911/592388

Rickmansworth
Hertfordshire
Three Rivers District Council,
17 – 23 High Street
☎ (0923) 776611

St. Albans
Hertfordshire 🛏
37 Chequer Street
☎ (0727) 64511/66100 ext.
294

Stevenage
Hertfordshire
Central Library, Southgate
☎ (0438) 369441

Thame
Oxfordshire
Town Hall
☎ (084 421) 2834

Wallingford
Oxfordshire 🛏
Council Offices,
9 St. Martins Street
☎ (0491) 35351 ext. 3810

Welwyn Garden City
Hertfordshire 🛏
The Campus
☎ (0707) 332880

Wendover
Buckinghamshire
The Clock Tower
☎ (0296) 623056

Windsor
Berkshire 🛏
Windsor and Eton Central
Station
☎ (0753) 852010

Witney
Oxfordshire
Town Hall, Market Square
☎ (0993) 704379

Woburn
Bedfordshire *
Heritage Centre, Bedford Street
(personal callers only)

Woodstock
Oxfordshire 🛏 *
Hensington Road
☎ (0993) 811038

Entries in this regional section are listed in alphabetical order of place name, and then in alphabetical order of establishment. County names are not normally repeated in each establishment entry, but please use the full postal address when writing.

The map references refer to the colour maps towards the end of this guide. The first number is the number of the map, and it is followed by the grid reference.

The Crown Classifications are explained on pages 8 and 9, and the key to symbols is on the flap inside the back cover — keep it open for easy reference.

ABINGDON

Oxfordshire
Map ref 2C1

See also Wootton, Didcot, Drayton.
Attractive former county town on River Thames with many interesting buildings, including 17th C County Hall, now a museum, in Market Place and the remains of an abbey. *i*

Conifer House
14 Lower Radley, Abingdon, OX14 3AX
☎ (0235) 31793
Comfortable family home in quiet country lane leading to River Thames. Secluded gardens with swimming pool.
Bedrooms: 1 double & 1 twin.
Bathrooms: 2 private.
Bed & breakfast: £11 single, £22 double.
Half board: £16.50 daily, £105 weekly.
Parking for 4.
☎10 ⌘ ⛳ ⓤ ⓣ ▥ ⚓ ✕ 🐴

The Gables
46 Oxford Road, Abingdon, OX14 2DZ
☎ (0235) 20460
Edwardian house of character within walking distance of town centre. Run by English/French speaking family.
Bedrooms: 1 double & 1 twin.
Bathrooms: 1 public.
Bed & breakfast: £22-£26 double.
☎ ⌘ ⓤ 🛏 ⓥ ⇌ ⓣ ▥ ✕ 🐴 DAP

Mrs. S. Howard
22 East St. Helen Street, Abingdon, OX14 5EB
☎ (0235) 33278
A terraced Georgian house in the town centre. The atmosphere is warm and informal.
Bedrooms: 1 double & 1 twin.

Bathrooms: 2 public.
Bed & breakfast: £10-£12 single, £18-£20 double.
Half board: £63 weekly.
☎ ⌘ ⛳ ⓤ ⓥ ▥ ⚓ ✕ 🐴 DAP 🏠

ADDERBURY

Oxfordshire
Map ref 2C1

3m S. Banbury
Village with fine ironstone houses set around a green. Its perpendicular church has a magnificent spire.

The Grange
Adderbury, Nr. Banbury, OX17 3LS
☎ Banbury (0295) 810739
17th C. manor house on the site of a 13th C. vicarage. A grade II listed building in the heart of the village, close to a mill stream.
Bedrooms: 2 twin.
Bathrooms: 2 private.
Bed & breakfast: £15 single, £25 double.
Parking for 3.
Open May-September.
☎ ⓤ ⇌ ▥ ⚓ ✕ 🐴 🏠

ASCOT

Berkshire
Map ref 2C2

Small country town famous for its racecourse which was founded by Queen Anne. The race meeting each June is attended by the Royal Family.

J. & W. Glynn
56 King Edwards Road, Ascot, SL5 8NY
☎ Winkfield Row (0344) 883229

Chalet bungalow in very quiet area. Convenient for Heathrow Airport, trains to London, Windsor, and Ascot races.
Bedrooms: 1 single, 1 double & 2 twin, 1 family room.
Bathrooms: 2 public.
Bed & breakfast: £15-£17 single, £28-£30 double.
Parking for 6.
☎ ⌘ ⛳ ⓤ ⓥ ✄ ⇌ ⓣ ▥ ⚓ ✿ 🐴

ASTHALL LEIGH

Oxfordshire
Map ref 2C1

See also Witney.

Warwick House
Asthall Leigh, OX8 5PX
☎ (099 387) 336
5-acre mixed farm. Delightful chalet bungalow, in quiet location, overlooking open farmland on edge of Windrush Valley in the Cotswolds, between Witney and Burford.
Bedrooms: 2 double & 2 twin.
Bathrooms: 4 private.
Bed & breakfast: £15-£20 single, £27-£32 double.
Parking for 3.
Open January, March-December.
⛳ ⌘ ⛳ ⓤ ▥ 🔎 ✿ ✕ 🐴 DAP

ASTON CLINTON

Buckinghamshire
Map ref 2C1

See also Aylesbury.
Village far-spread on the escarpment of the Downs, with many Jacobean thatched cottages and an inn which has been receiving travellers since John Hampden's days. 14th C church with its original chancel and fine arch still stands today.

The Haven
Listed
7 Lower Icknield Way, Aston Clinton, HP22 5JS
☎ Aylesbury (0296) 630751
Friendly, comfortable and homely bungalow 300 yards from A41 on the B489 to Dunstable. Ideal for touring adjoining counties and Chilterns.
Bedrooms: 1 single, 1 twin.
Bathrooms: 1 public.
Bed & breakfast: £10-£12 single, £20-£24 double.
Parking for 2.
⛳ ⊙ ⌘ ⓤ 🛏 ⇌ ⓣ ▥ ✕ 🐴 DAP SP

AYLESBURY

Buckinghamshire
Map ref 2C1

See also Aston Clinton, Winslow.
Historic county town in the Vale of Aylesbury. The cobbled Market Square has a Victorian clock tower and the 15th C King's Head Inn (National Trust). Interesting County Museum and 13th C parish church. Twice weekly livestock market. *i*

Grange Leys
Listed
67 North End Road, Quainton, Aylesbury, HP22 4BG
☎ Quainton (029 675) 348
Turn of the century detached country home on the outskirts of picturesque village, 6 miles from Aylesbury.
Bedrooms: 2 double.
Bathrooms: 1 public.
Bed & breakfast: £10 single, £20 double.
Parking for 3.
⇌ ⓤ 🛏 ⓣ ▥ ⚓ ✿ ✕ 🐴

Jasmine House
Listed
Ashendon, Aylesbury, HP18 0HB
☎ (0296) 651200
Comfortable, spacious detached house set high in beautiful countryside overlooking the Chilterns. A quiet haven, 2.5 miles from A41 London to Birmingham road. Car essential.
Bedrooms: 1 double & 1 twin.
Bathrooms: 1 public.
Bed & breakfast: from £9.50 single, from £19 double.
Parking for 2.
Open April-September.
⛳ ⓤ ⓣ ▥ ✕ 🐴 DAP

The Wheatsheaf ⋀
Listed
Weedon, Nr. Aylesbury, HP22 4NS
☎ (0296) 641581
Old Elizabethan coaching inn, furnished with antiques.. Courtyard surrounded by cottage and stable-cots. Home-from-home treatment and atmosphere.
Bedrooms: 2 single, 1 double.
Bathrooms: 2 public.
Bed & breakfast: £22-£25 single, £44-£50 double.
Continued ▶

AYLESBURY
Continued

Lunch available.
Parking for 14.

🚳 🎿 Ⓜ 🚲 🅿 Ⓤ ♿ 🅅 ⚡
🍴 📺 🆚 ⚓ 🍽 ☺ 🐾 🚩 SP
🏘

BAMPTON
Oxfordshire
Map ref 2C1

See also Standlake, Witney.
Small market town well known for its Spring Bank Holiday Monday Fete with Morris Dance Festival.

Romany Inn
Listed

Bridge Street, Bampton, OX8 2HA
☎ Bampton Castle (0993) 850237
A listed building dating from the 17th C. Lounge bar with separate dining room. Log fires in winter.
Bedrooms: 2 double & 1 twin.
Bathrooms: 1 public.
Bed & breakfast: max. £15 single, max. £23 double.
Lunch available.
Evening meal 6.30pm (l.o. 10pm).
Parking for 3.

🚳 ☺ 🍴 🚩 📺 🍽 🚩 🏘

BANBURY
Oxfordshire
Map ref 2C1

See also Deddington.
Famous for its cattle market, cakes and Nursery Rhyme Cross. Founded in Saxon times it has some fine houses and interesting old inns. A good centre for touring Warwickshire and the Cotswolds. *i*

Belmont Guest House
👄👄

34 Crouch Street, Banbury, OX16 9PR
☎ (0295) 62308
Family-run guesthouse approximately 200 yards from Banbury Cross. Away from the main road.
Bedrooms: 3 single, 2 double & 1 twin, 2 family rooms.
Bathrooms: 3 private, 1 public.
Bed & breakfast: £13-£18 single, £22-£28 double.
Parking for 6.
Credit: Access, Visa.

🚳 🚲 🖾 ☺ 🅅 🚩 🍽 ⚓ 🅖
🚩 🏘

The Mill Barn
Lower Tadmarton, Banbury, OX15 5SU
☎ Swalcliffe (029 578) 349
Family home offering ground floor accommodation in a beautifully converted stone barn, set in an acre of grounds. Convenient for Oxford, Stratford and the Cotswolds.
Bedrooms: 1 double, 1 family room.
Bathrooms: 2 private.
Bed & breakfast: max. £15 single, max. £30 double.
Parking for 4.

🚳 🎿 🚲 Ⓤ 🚩 📺 🍽 ⚓ ☺
🚩 🏘

The Mill House 👄
North Newington, Nr. Banbury, OX15 6AA
☎ Wroxton St. Mary (029 573) 212
17th C. miller's house set in beautiful countryside on edge of Cotswolds. Half a mile from Broughton Castle, close to Stratford, Warwick and Oxford.
Bedrooms: 4 double & 2 twin.
Bathrooms: 6 private.
Bed & breakfast: £38-£44 double.
Half board: from £31 daily, £206-£226 weekly.
Evening meal 8pm (l.o. midday).
Parking for 9.
Credit: Access, Visa, Diners.

🚳 🚲 Ⓓ 🖾 ☺ 🅅 🚩 🍽
⚓ 🍴 ☺ 🚩 SP 🏘

The Old Manor
Listed

Cropredy, Banbury, OX17 1PS
☎ Cropredy (029 575) 235
Partially moated manor house alongside Oxford Canal and in centre of village. Rare breed farm animals and private motor museum.
Bedrooms: 2 twin.
Bathrooms: 1 private, 1 private shower.
Bed & breakfast: £25-£30 double.
Parking for 16.

🚳 🎿 ☺ Ⓤ 🅅 🍽 ⚓ 🥄 ☺
🚩 🚩 🏘

Prospect House Guest House 👄
👄👄

70 Oxford Road, Banbury, OX16 9AN
☎ (0295) 68749
Detached house with lovely grounds. Situated in the most convenient area of town.

Bedrooms: 3 double & 2 twin, 1 family room.
Bathrooms: 6 private.
Bed & breakfast: £23-£26 single, £28.75-£35 double.
Parking for 8.

🚳 🚲 🖾 🚩 🍽 🚩 ⚓ ☺
🚩 🚩 SP

Wisteria House 👄
Listed

3 Church Lane, Middleton Cheney, Nr. Banbury, OX17 2NR
☎ Banbury (0295) 711086
Grade II listed building offering comfortable accommodation. Well placed for visiting Stratford, Leamington Spa and the Cotswolds. Ancient town of Banbury 3 miles away. Local public golf course nearby.
Bedrooms: 1 family room.
Bathrooms: 1 private.
Bed & breakfast: max. £14 single, £26-£28 double.
Open January-November.

🚳 🍴 ☎ Ⓓ Ⓤ 🍽 ⚓ ☺ 🚩 🚩
SP 🏘

BEDFORD
Bedfordshire
Map ref 2D1

Busy county town with interesting buildings and churches near the River Ouse which has pleasant riverside walks. Many associations with John Bunyan including Bunyan Meeting House, museum and statue. The Bedford Museum and Cecil Higgins Art Gallery are of interest. *i*

No. 1 The Grange
👄👄👄

Sunderland Hill, Ravensden, MK44 2SH
☎ Bedford (0234) 771771
Spacious family-run accommodation set in elegant rural surroundings.
Bedrooms: 2 double & 2 twin.
Bathrooms: 1 private, 2 public.
Bed & breakfast: from £14 single, max. £28 double.
Half board: max. £24 daily, max. £150 weekly.
Evening meal 6.30pm (l.o. midday).
Parking for 10.

🚳 3 🚩 ☺ Ⓤ 🍴 🅅 🚩 📺 🍽
⚓ ☺ 🚩 🚩 🏘

BENSON
Oxfordshire
Map ref 2C2

See also Berrick Salome, Wallingford.
On a river plain by the Thames, this village is notable for its 13th C church and 17th C coaching inn. Nearby is a large airfield, famous for housing the Queen's Flight.

Mrs. A. H. Belcher
Hale Farm, Benson, OX9 6NE
☎ Wallingford (0491) 36818
350-acre arable and beef farm. Late Georgian farmhouse with large rooms. Self-catering units also available.
Bedrooms: 1 single, 1 double & 1 twin, 1 family room.
Bathrooms: 1 public.
Bed & breakfast: from £9 single, from £18 double.
Parking for 5.
Open April-October.

🚳 🎿 ☺ Ⓤ 🍴 🅅 🚩 📺 🍽
☺ 🚩 🚩

BERRICK SALOME
Oxfordshire
Map ref 2C2

See also Wallingford.

Lower Farm
👄👄

Berrick Salome, Oxford, OX9 6JL
☎ Stadhampton (0865) 891073
24-acre arable farm. Family home with comfortable rooms, on small farm with horses. An old house with architecturally interesting connections with the Civil War.
Bedrooms: 2 family rooms.
Bathrooms: 1 private, 1 public.
Bed & breakfast: £17.50-£22.50 single, £30-£40 double.
Half board: £22.50-£27.50 daily, £120-£140 weekly.
Lunch available.
Evening meal 7pm (l.o. 11pm).
Parking for 4.

🚳 🚩 Ⓓ 🚩 🚩 Ⓤ 🍴 🅅 🚩
📺 🍽 ⚓ ☺ ☺ 🚩 🐾 SP 🏘

GROUPS, CONSORTIA AND AGENCIES SPECIALISING IN FARM AND COUNTRY HOLIDAYS ARE LISTED IN A SPECIAL SECTION OF THIS GUIDE.

BICESTER

Oxfordshire
Map ref 2C1

See also Bletchington.
Market town with large Army depot and well-known hunting centre with hunt established in the late 18th C. The ancient parish church displays work of many periods. Nearby is the Jacobean mansion of Rousham House with gardens landscaped by William Kent.

The Old Rectory ⋈
Listed
Launton, Bicester, OX6 0DP
☎ (0869) 252471
Stylish bed and breakfast accommodation in a Grade II listed house. Bedrooms are well furnished and decorated.
Bedrooms: 2 double & 1 twin.
Bathrooms: 1 private,
1 public.
Bed & breakfast: £15-£18 single, £24-£30 double.
Parking for 4.
⛫ ※ ⌷ ▮ ☎ � ⋈ ▥ ⋒ ✿ ⋈ ⋒

BLETCHINGTON

Oxfordshire
Map ref 2C1

See also Bicester.
Thatched and stone-roofed cottages surround the village green with magnificent views of Otmoor and the hills beyond.

Stonehouse Farm
Listed
Bletchington, OX5 3EA
☎ (0869) 50585
560-acre arable farm. Off the beaten track with lovely summer walks. Only 15 minutes north of Oxford and 20 minutes south of Banbury. Near the A423 and A43, between the villages of Weston-on-the-green and Bletchington.
Bedrooms: 1 double & 2 twin, 1 family room.
Bathrooms: 2 public.
Bed & breakfast: £12-£14 single, £22-£25 double.
Parking for 11.
⛫ ※ ⌷ ▮ ⌷ ▮ ☎ ▮ ✿ ⋈ ⋈ SP ⋒

BOXFORD

Berkshire
Map ref 2C2

See also Hungerford, Newbury.

Honeysuckle Cottage
Boxford, Newbury,
RG16 8DP
☎ Boxford (048 838) 442
Charming 300-year-old thatched and beamed cottage in a picturesque village.
Bedrooms: 2 twin.
Bathrooms: 1 private,
1 public.
Bed & breakfast: from £12 single, from £22 double.
Half board: from £18 daily, from £110 weekly.
Parking for 3.
⛫ ※ ⌷ ▮ ☎ ⋒ ⋈

BRACKNELL

Berkshire
Map ref 2C2

Designated a New Town in 1949, the town has ancient origins. Set in heathlands, it is an excellent centre for golf and walking. South Hill Park, an 18th C mansion, houses an art centre. ℹ

Bear Farm
☺
Binfield, Bracknell,
RG12 5QE
☎ Twyford (0734) 343286
65-acre mixed farm. 17th C. oak-beamed farmhouse surrounded by 2 acres of well kept gardens, with guest bedrooms in an adjoining converted farmbuilding.
Bedrooms: 1 double & 1 twin.
Bathrooms: 1 public.
Bed & breakfast: £18 single, £30 double.
Parking for 6.
⛫ ◢ ⌷ ▮ ☎ ⋒ ✿ ⋈ ⋈ ⋒

BRADFIELD

Berkshire
Map ref 2C2

See also Pangbourne.

Boot Farm
☺☺
Southend Road, Bradfield,
Nr. Reading, RG7 6ES
☎ Reading (0734) 744298

150-acre dairy and mixed farm. Midway between Reading and Newbury. Day trips to London, Windsor and Oxford. Own riding school and livery yard. 7 minutes from the M4 exit 12 and 40 minutes from Heathrow.
Bedrooms: 1 single, 1 double & 1 twin.
Bathrooms: 1 private,
2 public.
Bed & breakfast: £12 single, £24-£25 double.
Lunch available.
Parking for 6.
⛫ ⑩ ⊛ ▮ ▮ ☎ ⓣⓥ ⋒ ⋒ ⋓ ✿ ⋈ ⋈

BRAY

Berkshire
Map ref 2C2

See also Maidenhead.

Old Court Cottage
Upper Bray Road, Bray,
Maidenhead, SL6 2DB
☎ Maidenhead (0628) 32833
Approximately 27 miles from London, 5 miles from Windsor and M4, 20 minutes' drive from Henley and 40 minutes' drive from Oxford. Close to mainline station.
Bedrooms: 2 double.
Bathrooms: 2 private.
Bed & breakfast: £30-£35 single, £35-£40 double.
Parking for 3.
⛫ ® ⌷ ⊛ ⌷ ▮ CB ⅍ ⋒ ▥
▮ ⋈ ▮ ▮ GAP SP ⋒

BRIMPTON

Berkshire
Map ref 2C2

4m NE. Kingsclere

Manor Farm ⋈
Listed
Brimpton, Nr. Reading,
RG7 4SQ
☎ Woolhampton
(0734) 713166
600-acre mixed farm. Working family farm in Brimpton village. Interesting house and chapel, once of the Knights Hospitallers. Close to A4, M4 and M3.
Bedrooms: 1 double & 1 twin.
Bathrooms: 1 public.
Bed & breakfast: £12-£15 single, £24-£30 double.
Parking for 4.
⛫ ※ ® ⌷ ▮ ☎ ⋒ ⋈ ⋈ ⋒

BRIZE NORTON

Oxfordshire
Map ref 2C1

Village closely associated with the American Air Force. The medieval church is the only church in England dedicated to St. Brice, from whom the village takes its name.

Montrose
Manor Road, Brize Norton,
OX8 3LZ
☎ (0993) 842211
Late 17th C. Cotswold stone house, very comfortable, with separate guest sitting room. Close to the Cotswolds and Oxford.
Bedrooms: 1 double & 1 twin.
Bathrooms: 1 public.
Bed & breakfast: £11-£12 single, £22 double.
Parking for 3.
⛫ ※ ⊛ ⌷ ▮ ⓥ ⋒ ▥
⋒ ✿ ⋈ ▮ SP ⋒

BURFORD

Oxfordshire
Map ref 2B1

One of the most beautiful Cotswold wool towns with Georgian and Tudor houses, many antique shops and a picturesque High Street. ℹ

The Dower House
☺☺☺
Westhall Hill, Fulbrook,
Burford, OX8 4BJ
☎ (099 382) 2596
Elegant, newly-restored period accommodation in an imposing Cotswold dower house. Superb and tranquil setting, with commanding views over Burford and beautiful surrounding countryside. South facing bedrooms and picturesque gardens.
Bedrooms: 2 double.
Bathrooms: 1 private,
1 public.
Bed & breakfast: £15-£18 single, £22-£26 double.
Parking for 3.
⌷ ⌷ ▮ ⓥ ⅍ ⋒ ⓣⓥ ▥ ⋒ ✿
⋈ ▮ ⋒

Glenthorne House
☺☺☺
The Hill, Burford, OX8 4QY
☎ (099 382) 2418
The house incorporates many original medieval features, including the circular staircase, fireplaces, panelling and painted beams. Comfortable, modernised accommodation.

Continued ▶

PLEASE MENTION THIS GUIDE WHEN MAKING A BOOKING.

THERE IS A SPECIAL SECTION IN THIS GUIDE LISTING ACCOMMODATION ESPECIALLY SUITABLE FOR GROUPS AND YOUNG PEOPLE.

BURFORD

Continued

Bedrooms: 1 double & 2 twin.
Bathrooms: 1 private,
1 public.
Bed & breakfast: £12.50-£15
single, £25-£30 double.
Parking for 5.
🐕10 ⓤⓛ ⊡ ▥ ❀ ⊁ ☂ SP ⊞

Lower Pound
🍴🍴

Fulbrook, Burford, OX8
☎ (099 382) 3457
*Modern Cotswold stone house
in pleasant gardens. Half a
mile from Burford on the
A361.*
Bedrooms: 1 double & 1 twin.
Bathrooms: 2 private.
Bed & breakfast: £12.50-£13
single, £25-£27 double.
Parking for 6.
⌷ ♥ ⎸ ⓘ Ⓥ ⊿ ⊡ ▥ ⚊
⊁ ☂

Rylands
[Listed]

Cheltenham Road, Burford,
OX8 4PJ
☎ (099 382) 3054
*Comfortable accommodation
with lovely views over adjoining
fields. Conveniently placed for
touring the Cotswolds.*
Bedrooms: 1 single, 1 double
& 2 twin.
Bathrooms: 2 private,
1 public.
Bed & breakfast: £12-£15
single, £24-£27 double.
Parking for 4.
Open January-November.
🐕 ⚗ ♥ ⓤⓛ ⊡ ▥ ⊁ ☂

St. Andrews Bed and
Breakfast

Oxford Road, (A40) Burford,
OX8 4TU
☎ (099 382) 3281
*Cotswold stone house on
outskirts of Burford.
Panoramic views overlooking
Windrush River. Relaxed
family atmosphere.*
Bedrooms: 1 double & 1 twin,
1 family room.
Bathrooms: 2 public.
Bed & breakfast: £20-£25
double.
Parking for 10.
🐕 ♥ ⓤⓛ Ⓥ ⊿ ⊡ ⚊ ♣ ❀
☂

Treetops
[Listed]

10 Windrush Close, Burford,
OX8 4SL
☎ (099 382) 2340

---

*Picturesque Cotswold stone
cottage in the historic town of
Burford. Within easy reach of
Oxford and Stratford, 75 miles
from London.*
Bedrooms: 1 double, 1 family
room.
Bathrooms: 1 private,
1 public.
Bed & breakfast: £20-£22
double.
Parking for 2.
🐕4 ⚗ ⓘ ♥ ⓤⓛ ▥ ⊁ ☂

Westfarthing Cottage

1 Lawrence Lane, Lower
High Street, Burford,
OX8 4RP
☎ (099 382) 3542
*15th C. cottage off Burford
High Street offering
comfortable, friendly bed and
breakfast accommodation.*
Bedrooms: 1 double.
Bathrooms: 1 private.
Bed & breakfast: £24 double.
⌷ ♥ ⚘ ⊁ ☂ ⊞

CASSINGTON

Oxfordshire
Map ref 2C1

*See also Oxford,
Woodstock.*
Pretty village with
thatched cottages around
a green. Close to Oxford
and Blenheim Palace.

Mill Cottage
[Listed]

Cassington Mill, Cassington,
OX8 1DB
☎ Oxford (0865) 881542
*Modernised Victorian cottage
in quiet position. Oxford 6
miles. From A40 follow
Cassington Mill Caravan Park
signs.*
Bedrooms: 1 double & 1 twin.
Bathrooms: 1 public.
Bed & breakfast: £10-£11
single, £20-£22 double.
Parking for 2.
🐕 ⚗ ⓤⓛ ⎸ ⊿ ⊡ ▥ ⚊ ☂

GROUPS, CONSORTIA AND AGENCIES
SPECIALISING IN FARM AND COUNTRY
HOLIDAYS ARE LISTED IN A SPECIAL
SECTION OF THIS GUIDE.

INDIVIDUAL PROPRIETORS HAVE SUPPLIED
ALL DETAILS OF ACCOMMODATION.
ALTHOUGH WE DO CHECK FOR ACCURACY, WE
ADVISE YOU TO CONFIRM PRICES AND OTHER
INFORMATION AT THE TIME OF BOOKING.

CASTLETHORPE

Buckinghamshire
Map ref 2C1

3m N. Stony Stratford

Milford Leys Farm ⋔

Castlethorpe, Milton Keynes,
MK19 7HH
☎ (0908) 510153
*140-acre mixed farm. Pleasant
farmhouse in own grounds,
surrounded by fields.*
Bedrooms: 3 twin.
Bathrooms: 2 public.
Bed & breakfast: from £24
double.
Parking for 4.
🐕 ⚗ ⓤⓛ ⊿ ⊡ ▥ ⚊ ♪ ❀
⊁ ☂

CHINNOR

Oxfordshire
Map ref 2C1

4m SE. Thame

Crowell End ⋔
[Listed]

Spriggs Alley, Crowell Hill,
Nr. Chinnor, OX9 4BT
☎ Kingston Blount
(0844) 52726
*Family house in beautiful
surroundings, half a mile from
the Ridgeway Walk. 2 miles
from Chinnor via Chinnor Hill
to Spriggs Alley. Ideal base for
walking, riding and touring.*
Bedrooms: 1 single, 1 double
& 1 twin.
Bathrooms: 2 private,
1 public.
Bed & breakfast: £10-£12.50
single, £25-£30 double.
Half board: £16.50-£21.60
daily, £90-£120 weekly.
Parking for 6.
Open March-November.
🐕 ⚗ ⚘ ⌷ ♥ ⓤⓛ Ⓥ ▥ ⚊
Ʊ ✓ ❀ ⊁ ☂ ᴰᴬᴾ

CHISLEHAMPTON

Oxfordshire
Map ref 2C1

Village close to Oxford
near the site of the
famous Civil War Battle of
Chalgrove Field. An
obelisk marks the site.

Mrs. S. Bacon
[Listed]

Maxfield, Chislehampton,
Nr. Oxford, OX9 7XE
☎ Stadhampton
(0865) 890544
*Comfortable and homely
bungalow in a peaceful setting,
close to the river in a small
village. Oxford is 6 miles
away. Ideal for touring the
Cotswolds and Chilterns.*
Bedrooms: 2 twin.
Bathrooms: 1 public.
Bed & breakfast: £22 double.
Parking for 3.
🐕 ⚗ ⚘ ♥ ⓤⓛ ⊡ ▥ ⚊ ☂

COOKHAM DEAN

Berkshire
Map ref 2C2

3m N. Maidenhead

Cartlands Cottage

Kings Lane, Cookham Dean,
Maidenhead, SL6 9AY
☎ Marlow (062 84) 2196
*Delightful timbered character
cottage with exposed beams.
Traditional cottage garden
surrounded by National Trust
common land. Family room in
self-contained garden studio.
Very quiet.*
Bedrooms: 1 single, 1 family
room.
Bathrooms: 1 public.
Bed & breakfast: £14-£15
single, £28-£30 double.
Parking for 4.
🐕 ⚗ ⚘ ⓘ ♥ ⓤⓛ ⎸ ⊿ ⊡
▥ ❀ ⊁ ☂ ⊞

DEDDINGTON

Oxfordshire
Map ref 2C1

See also Banbury.
Attractive former market
town with a large market
square and many fine old
buildings.

Earls Farm
🍴

Deddington, Oxford,
OX5 4TH
☎ (0869) 38243
230-acre arable farm. .
Bedrooms: 2 double & 2 twin,
1 family room.
Bathrooms: 2 public.

Bed & breakfast: £11-£13
single, £22-£25 double.
Parking for 4.
Open April-October.
🛇 ♿ ☺ Ⓤ 🛏 �📺 📖 🍽 ↴
🍴 ⌘

DIDCOT

Oxfordshire
Map ref 2C2

See also Abingdon.
Important railway junction
where steam engines can
still be seen at the Didcot
Railway Centre, together
with a re-created station
and a small relics
museum.

North Croft Cottage
😊😊

North Croft, East
Hagbourne, Didcot,
OX11 9LT
☎ (0235) 813326
*17th C. low white cottage with
oak beams inside and out,
inglenook fireplace and leaded
windows.*
Bedrooms: 3 single, 1 double.
Bathrooms: 4 private.
Bed & breakfast: max. £15
single, max. £25 double.
Parking for 3.
Open April-October.
🛇5 ♿ Ⓤ 🛏 📺 📖 🍽 ✤ 🍴
⌘ 🏠

Mrs. J.M. Wilden

Hacca's Cottage, Fieldside,
East Hagbourne, Didcot,
OX11 9LQ
☎ (0235) 814324
*Two cottages combined and
modernised for maximum
comfort. Rural setting in a
delightful village, with views
over fields and downs.*
Bedrooms: 2 single, 1 double.
Bathrooms: 3 private.
Bed & breakfast: from £14
single, from £28 double.
Evening meal 6pm (l.o. 8pm).
Parking for 2.
Ⓤ 🔥 Ⓥ 📺 📖 ↴ ✤ 🍴 ⌘

DRAYTON

Oxfordshire
Map ref 2C1

See also Abingdon.
Mellow and leafy old
village with a wide High
Street and a number of
beautiful cottages.
Approached through a
ribbon development of
small bungalows along
the A34.

Forge Cottage
Listed

55 High Street, Drayton, Nr.
Abingdon, OX14 4JW
☎ (0235) 31232
*Converted early 16th C.
blacksmith's forge, close to
Abingdon. Places of interest
nearby are Blenheim Palace
and Oxford colleges. Good for
touring the Cotswolds.*
Bedrooms: 2 double.
Bathrooms: 1 public.
Bed & breakfast: £9 single,
£18 double.
Parking for 3.
🛇 ♿ Ⓤ Ⓥ 🛏 📺 📖 ↴ ✤
🍴 ⌘ 🏠

DUNSTABLE

Bedfordshire
Map ref 2D1

Modern town with
remains of a 12th C
Augustinian priory in the
parish church. The
Dunstable Downs are
famous for gliding and in
the parkland of
Whipsnade Zoo on the
edge of the Downs many
animals roam freely. ℹ

Priory Guest House ⋔
😊😊

30 Priory Road, Dunstable,
LU5 4HR
☎ (0582) 61900
*Roomy Edwardian house in
quiet tree-lined road, 3
minutes' walk from town
centre. Convenient for
Whipsnade, Woburn and Luton
Hoo.*
Bedrooms: 2 single, 5 twin,
1 family room.
Bathrooms: 2 public.
Bed & breakfast: £15-£19
single, £26 double.
Parking for 9.
🛇 Ⓤ 🛏 📺 📖 ↴ ✤ ⌘

ENSTONE

Oxfordshire
Map ref 2C1

Swan Lodge
😊😊😊

Oxford Road, Enstone,
Oxford, OX7 4NE
☎ (060 872) 8736
Cotswold country house.
Bedrooms: 1 twin, 2 family
rooms.
Bathrooms: 3 private.
Bed & breakfast: £20-£30
single, £35-£45 double.
Evening meal 5pm (l.o. 7pm).
Parking for 10.
Credit: Access, Visa.
🛇 Ⓑ 📺 🔥 Ⓤ 🛏 Ⓥ 🛏 📺
📖 ↴ 🍴 ✤ ⌘ 🏠 DAP SP

FARINGDON

Oxfordshire
Map ref 2C2

See also Uffington.
Ancient stone built market
town in the Vale of the
White Horse. The 17th C
Market Hall stands on
pillars and the 13th C
church has some fine
monuments. The great
monastic tithe barn is
nearby at Great Coxwell.
ℹ

The Apple Tree Inn ⋔
Buscot, Faringdon, SN7 8DA
☎ (0367) 52592
*17th C. freehouse in National
Trust Village near Lechlade.
Beamed lounge bar, central
heating and very large garden.*
Bedrooms: 2 double & 1 twin.
Bathrooms: 1 public.
Bed & breakfast: from £25
double.
Lunch available.
Evening meal 7pm (l.o. 9pm).
Parking for 20.
🛇 ♿ 📖 ↴ 🍴 🌺 ✤ ⌘
🍴 🏠

The Bell Hotel ⋔
Market Place, Faringdon,
SN7 7HP
☎ (0367) 20534
*A 16th C. posting house. The
original character and
structure have been
maintained, although many
improvements have been made.
Ideal for exploring the beauty
of the Vale of White Horse
and the Cotswolds.*
Bedrooms: 3 single, 3 double
& 2 twin, 3 family rooms.
Bathrooms: 9 private,
1 public.
Bed & breakfast: £22-£36
single, £28-£46 double.
Half board: £32-£51 daily.

Evening meal 7.30pm (l.o.
9.30pm).
Parking for 25.
Credit: Access, Visa, Diners,
Amex.
🛇 Ⓑ ♿ Ⓥ 🛏 📺 📖 ↴ 🍴
♿ SP 🏠

Bowling Green Farm ⋔
😊😊😊

Stanford Road, Faringdon,
SN7 8EZ
☎ (0367) 20229
*30-acre mixed farm. 17th C.
farmhouse in 30 acres of
farmland, on the edge of the
Cotswolds and the Ridgeway,
breeding horses and calves.*
Bedrooms: 2 family rooms.
Bathrooms: 2 private.
Bed & breakfast: from £17
single, from £27 double.
Parking for 7.
🛇 ♿ 🛏 🔥 Ⓤ 🛏 📖 ↴ ⌘
DAP SP

Manor Farm ⋔

Kelmscott, Nr. Lechlade,
Gloucestershire GL7 3HJ
☎ (0367) 52620
*311-acre mixed farm. 17th C.
Cotswold stone farmhouse with
attractive gardens and lawns in
quiet country village. Close to
the River Thames. M4 junction
15 minutes away.*
Bedrooms: 2 family rooms.
Bathrooms: 1 public.
Bed & breakfast: max. £16
single, max. £24 double.
Lunch available.
Parking for 6.
🛇 ☺ Ⓤ 🛏 🔥 📺 📖 ↴ ⌘ ∪
🍴 ✤ 🍴 ⌘ DAP SP

FOREST HILL

Oxfordshire
Map ref 2C1

See also Oxford.
This hilltop village affords
excellent views of the
valley to Thorn and
Shotover Hills and the
church's bell rang out for
Milton's wedding.

Manor Farm
Listed

Forest Hill, OX9 1EB
☎ Wheatley (086 77) 2434
*450-acre dairy and arable
farm. Working farm, spacious
and comfortable. 500 yards off
A40, next to church.*
Bedrooms: 1 double, 1 family
room.
Bathrooms: 1 public.
Bed & breakfast: £11-£12
single, £22-£24 double.
Continued ▶

THERE IS A SPECIAL SECTION IN THIS
GUIDE LISTING ACCOMMODATION ESPECIALLY
SUITABLE FOR GROUPS AND YOUNG PEOPLE.

FOREST HILL

Continued

Half board: £16-£17 daily, £105-£112 weekly.
Parking for 20.

Mead Close
Listed

Forest Hill, Oxford,
OX9 1EB
☎ Wheatley (086 77) 2248
*500-acre mixed farm. Warm
and welcoming family
farmhouse, conveniently
situated in village near the A40
London Road, 1 hour from
Heathrow.*
Bedrooms: 1 single, 1 double
& 1 twin.
Bathrooms: 2 public.
Bed & breakfast: £10-£15
single, £20-£28 double.
Half board: £15-£20 daily,
£70-£105 weekly.
Parking for 3.

FYFIELD

Oxfordshire
Map ref 2C1

6m W. Abingdon
Village established by the
Golofre family. The first
John Golofre rebuilt the
church in the 14th C and
erected part of the
splendid Manor House
before his death in 1363.
The main body of the
house was built between
1290 and 1320, making it
one of the country's
oldest.

Manor Farm
Listed

Fyfield, Abingdon,
OX13 5LR
☎ Frilford Heath
(0865) 390485
*750-acre mixed farm. A
working family farm. Queen
Anne type building, over 300
years old, set in the centre of a
small village.*
Bedrooms: 2 family rooms.
Bathrooms: 2 public.
Bed & breakfast: from £10
single, from £19 double.
Parking for 3.

**THE SYMBOLS ARE
EXPLAINED ON THE
FLAP INSIDE THE
BACK COVER.**

GERRARDS CROSS

Buckinghamshire
Map ref 2D2

On the London Road,
Gerrards Cross is
distinguished by its wide
gorse and beech tree
common.

Mr. & Mrs. I. Lee-Duncan
Listed

1 White House Close,
Chalfont St. Peter, Gerrards
Cross, SL9 0DA
☎ Gerrards Cross
(0753) 885401
*Ground floor room. On bus
route to British Rail, London
half an hour. 3 miles from the
M40, 4 miles from the M25.*
Bedrooms: 1 twin.
Bathrooms: 1 private.
Bed & breakfast: £20 single,
£35 double.
Parking for 2.

GORING ON THAMES

Oxfordshire
Map ref 2C2

Riverside town on the
Oxfordshire/Berkshire
border, linked by an
attractive bridge to
Streatley with views to
the Goring Gap.

The John Barleycorn
Listed

Manor Road, Goring on
Thames, RG8 9DP
☎ (0491) 872509
*16th C. inn with exposed
beams. Close to the river,
lovely walks.*
Bedrooms: 2 single, 2 double
& 1 twin, 1 family room.
Bathrooms: 2 public.
Bed & breakfast: £16-£18
single, £28-£30 double.
Lunch available.
Evening meal 7pm (l.o.
10pm).
Parking for 2.

GREAT BRICKHILL

Buckinghamshire
Map ref 2C1

Duncombe Arms
😃😃

32 Lower Way, Great
Brickhill, Nr. Milton Keynes,
MK17 9AG
☎ (052 526) 226

---

*Premises set in 2 acres of
gardens in the centre of village.
Restaurant and two bars,
children's garden. 18-hole
putting green and 16 floodlit
petanque pitches, garden
skittles, pitching American
horseshoes.*
Bedrooms: 3 twin.
Bathrooms: 3 private.
Bed & breakfast: £28-£32
single, £35-£45 double.
Half board: £36-£38 daily.
Lunch available.
Evening meal 7.30pm (l.o.
10.30pm).
Parking for 17.
Credit: Access, Visa.

Partridge House

Great Brickhill, Milton
Keynes, MK17 9BH
☎ Soulbury (052 527) 470
*100-acre fruit and arable farm.
Located by the river, off the
A4146 Leighton Buzzard to
Bletchley Road. Woburn,
Milton Keynes and Silverstone
easily reached.*
Bedrooms: 1 single, 3 double
& 3 twin, 2 family rooms.
Bathrooms: 4 private,
2 public; 2 private showers.
Bed & breakfast: £25-£30
single, £40-£50 double.
Parking for 20.
Credit: Access, Visa, C.Bl.,
Diners, Amex.

GREAT TEW

Oxfordshire
Map ref 2C1

5m E. Chipping Norton
Village of thatched and
gabled roofs, mullioned
windows and rustic
porches, with charming
flowerbeds, green
meadows and fruit
orchards running down to
a small brook.

Falkland Arms
😃😃

Great Tew
☎ (060 883) 653
*Comfortable inn in beautiful
Oxfordshire village, tucked
away in the hollow of the low
hills, with thatched cottages
around the green.*
Bedrooms: 1 single, 2 double,
1 family room.
Bathrooms: 1 public;
2 private showers.

Bed & breakfast: £18-£20
single, £30-£32 double.
Lunch available.
Parking for 20.

Hornbeam House
😃😃😃

Old Road, Great Tew,
OX7 4AN
☎ (060 883) 246
*14th - 17th C. buildings around
a courtyard in a unique and
totally unspoilt 17th C. village.
Built on wooded hillside/valley
in a special conservation area.
Magnificent views.*
Bedrooms: 1 double & 1 twin.
Bathrooms: 2 private.
Bed & breakfast: £28-£34
double.
Half board: £20-£23 daily,
£130-£150 weekly.
Lunch available.
Parking for 8.

HAMPSTEAD NORRIS

Berkshire
Map ref 2C2

6m NE. Newbury

The New Inn

Yattendon Road, Hampstead
Norris, RG16 0TF
☎ Newbury (0635) 201301
*A secluded country inn in a
small Berkshire village 9 miles
from Newbury.*
Bedrooms: 1 single, 1 double
& 1 twin.
Bathrooms: 1 public.
Bed & breakfast: £15 single,
£20 double.
Lunch available.
Evening meal 7pm (l.o.
9.45pm).
Parking for 50.

HANSLOPE

Buckinghamshire
Map ref 2C1

Village famous for the
height of its church spire
which was built in the
15th C. The High Street
has some attractive
cottages and Georgian
houses.

Chantry Farm
Listed

Pindon End, Hanslope, Nr.
Stony Stratford, Milton
Keynes, MK19 7HL
☎ (0908) 510269

500-acre mixed farm. Old farmhouse built of Northamptonshire stone and set deep in the country.
Bedrooms: 1 double, 1 family room.
Bathrooms: 1 public.
Bed & breakfast: £15 single, £30 double.
Half board: £20 daily, £100-£105 weekly.
Evening meal 7pm (l.o. 9pm).
Parking for 7.

HARPENDEN

Hertfordshire
Map ref 2D1

Delightful country town with many scenic walks through surrounding woods and fields.

Schiehallion

235 Luton Road, Harpenden, AL5 3DE
☎ (058 27) 3524
Modern, comfortable rooms in family home, overlooking farmland. Convenient for London, M1, M25, Luton Airport and St. Albans. Phone number will change to (0582) 713524 in July 1989.
Bedrooms: 1 twin, 1 family room.
Bathrooms: 1 public.
Bed & breakfast: £22-£24 double.
Parking for 3.
Open April-October.

HENLEY-ON-THAMES

Oxfordshire
Map ref 2C2

The famous Thames regatta is held in this prosperous and attractive town at the beginning of July each year. The town has many Georgian buildings and old coaching inns and the parish church has some fine monuments. ℹ

New Lodge

😊
Henley Park, Nr. Fawley, Henley-on-Thames, RG9 6HU
☎ (0491) 576340
Victorian lodge in historic park. Area of outstanding natural beauty with plenty of walks and lovely views.
Bedrooms: 1 single, 1 double.

Bathrooms: 1 private, 1 public.
Bed & breakfast: £15-£18 single, £22-£26 double.
Half board: £20-£23 daily.
Lunch available.
Evening meal 6.30pm (l.o. 7.30pm).
Parking for 11.

HENTON

Oxfordshire
Map ref 2C1

4m SE. Thame

The Peacock 🅼

(awards)
Henton, Nr. Chinnor
☎ Kingston Blount (0844) 53519
Charming thatched country inn providing lounge bars, separate dining room and en-suite bedrooms, and serving traditional real ales.
Bedrooms: 6 single, 3 double & 2 twin.
Bathrooms: 11 private.
Bed & breakfast: £30-£45 single, £40-£55 double.
Half board: £42-£57 daily, £294-£399 weekly.
Lunch available.
Evening meal 6pm (l.o. 10.30pm).
Parking for 60.
Credit: Access, Visa, Amex.

HITCHIN

Hertfordshire
Map ref 2D1

Once a flourishing wool town and full of interest with many fine old buildings centred around the Market Square. These include the 17th C. almshouses, old inns and the Victorian Corn Exchange. ℹ

Beechlea

Kings Walden Road, Offley, Hitchin, SG5 3DV
☎ Offley (046 276) 703
Spacious, modern house set in quiet, rural location opposite village church. 6 miles from Luton Airport.
Bedrooms: 1 single, 1 double & 1 twin.
Bathrooms: 1 private, 1 public.
Bed & breakfast: £14-£15 single, £23-£26 double.
Parking for 4.

HUNGERFORD

Berkshire
Map ref 2C2

See also Boxford.
Attractive town on the Avon Canal and the River Kennet, famous for its fishing. It has a wide High Street and many antique shops. Nearby is the Tudor manor of Littlecote with its large Roman mosaic.

Marshgate Cottage 🅼

😊😊
Marsh Lane, Hungerford, RG17 0QX
☎ (0488) 82307
Delightful 350-year-old thatch and tiled cottage overlooking marshland, trout streams and canal. Lovely walks and plenty of birdwatching. Important antiques centre. 1 hour from Heathrow. Foreign languages spoken.
Bedrooms: 1 single, 1 double & 2 twin.
Bathrooms: 1 private, 1 private shower.
Bed & breakfast: £19.50-£32.50 single, £26.50-£37.50 double.
Parking for 8.

HURLEY

Berkshire
Map ref 2C2

4m NW. Maidenhead

Old Farm House

High Street, Hurley, SL6 5NB
☎ Littlewick Green (062 882) 4271
Bedrooms: 1 double & 2 twin.
Bathrooms: 1 public.
Bed & breakfast: £12.50-£15 single, £20-£25 double.
Parking for 4.

KINGHAM

Oxfordshire
Map ref 2B1

Small village set in beautiful scenery near the River Evenlode and the woodlands of Wychwood. Popular with ornithologists due to the variety of the rare birds which can be seen here.

Bould Farmhouse

Bould Farm, Bould, Kingham, OX7 6RT
☎ (060 871) 8850
300-acre mixed farm. Farmhouse with beamed attics, 10 minutes' drive from Stow-on-the-Wold, Bourton-on-the-Water and Burford. Nature trails adjoining wood. Learn to spin.
Bedrooms: 1 twin, 1 family room.
Bathrooms: 1 public.
Bed & breakfast: £10-£12.50 single, £20-£25 double.
Parking for 6.

Kings Head Inn & Restaurant

The Green, Bledington, Nr. Kingham, OX7 6HD
☎ Kingham (060 871) 365
Home comfort, set in village green in the heart of the Cotswolds. 15th C. inn with real ale.
Bedrooms: 4 double & 1 twin, 2 family rooms.
Bathrooms: 7 private.
Bed & breakfast: £24 single, £39 double.
Lunch available.
Evening meal 6pm (l.o. 10pm).
Parking for 20.

KNOWL HILL

Berkshire
Map ref 2C2

3m NE. Twyford

Laurel Cottage

Bath Road, Knowl Hill, Nr. Reading, RG10 9UP
☎ Littlewick Green (062 882) 5046
Attractive oak-beamed cottage on the A4. Convenient for Bath, London, Henley, Ascot and Heathrow. Evening meal by arrangement only.
Bedrooms: 1 single, 1 double, 1 family room.

Continued ▶

THERE IS A SPECIAL SECTION IN THIS GUIDE LISTING ACCOMMODATION ESPECIALLY SUITABLE FOR GROUPS AND YOUNG PEOPLE.

197

KNOWL HILL

Continued

Bathrooms: 1 public.
Bed & breakfast: £12-£14
single, £24-£28 double.
Half board: £15-£17 daily.
Parking for 3.

LEWKNOR

Oxfordshire
Map ref 2C1

Village with much open
space, some attractive
cottages and an 18th C
moated farmhouse.

The Manor House
Listed

Weston Road, Lewknor,
OX9 5RU
☎ Kingston Blount
(0844) 51680
*Parts of house are 400 years
old. Dark-oak-panelled
bedroom and hall. All rooms
are spacious bed-sitters.*
Bedrooms: 1 double & 1 twin,
1 family room.
Bathrooms: 1 public.
Bed & breakfast: £13.50-£18
single, £26-£35 double.
Half board: £21.50-£26 daily,
£143-£174 weekly.
Lunch available.
Evening meal 7pm (l.o.
8.30pm).
Parking for 6.

LONG HANBOROUGH

Oxfordshire
Map ref 2C1

Mrs. A.M. Apperly, Longlands

48 Millwood End, Long
Hanborough, OX7 2BY
☎ Freeland (0993) 881475
*In a pleasant situation
overlooking Blenheim Estate.*
Bedrooms: 1 single, 1 double
& 1 twin.
Bathrooms: 1 public.
Bed & breakfast: max. £12.50
single, max. £23 double.
Parking for 1.

LUTON

Bedfordshire
Map ref 2D1

Bedfordshire's largest
town with its own airport,
several industries and an
excellent shopping
centre. The town's history
is depicted in the
museum and art gallery in
Wardown Park. Luton
Hoo has a magnificent
collection of treasures. *i*

Applemoore

54 St. Ethelbert Avenue,
Luton, LU3 1QJ
☎ (0582) 33359
*Family-run guesthouse,
convenient for Luton Airport.
Free parking on premises
whilst away.*
Bedrooms: 1 twin, 1 family
room.
Bathrooms: 1 public.
Bed & breakfast: from £15
single, from £24 double.
Half board: from £18 daily,
from £126 weekly.
Evening meal 6pm (l.o. 9pm).
Parking for 4.

LYFORD

Oxfordshire
Map ref 2C2

4m N. Wantage

Manor Farm ⋔

Lyford, Wantage, OX12 0EG
☎ West Hanney
(023 587) 204
*600-acre mixed farm. Our
farmhouse is in a peaceful,
unspoilt hamlet but close
enough to visit the many
attractions of the Cotswolds.*
Bedrooms: 1 twin, 1 family
room.
Bathrooms: 1 public.
Bed & breakfast: £13.50
single, £24 double.
Parking for 8.

MAIDENHEAD

Berkshire
Map ref 2C2

See also Bray.
Attractive town on the
River Thames which is
crossed by an elegant
18th C. bridge and by
Brunel's well-known
railway bridge. It is a
popular place for boating
with delightful riverside
walks. The Courage Shire
Horse Centre is nearby.
i

Ray Corner
Listed

141 Bridge Road,
Maidenhead, SL6 8NQ
☎ (0628) 32784
*Detached guesthouse close to
the River Thames.*
Bedrooms: 1 single, 2 twin.
Bathrooms: 1 public.
Bed & breakfast: £13-£15
single, £26-£30 double.
Parking for 5.

Thamesbrook Guest House
⊟

18 Ray Park Avenue,
Maidenhead, SL6 8DS
☎ (0628) 783855
*Spacious, well-decorated
Victorian residence close to the
river, Boulters Lock,
Maidenhead Bridge and town
centre. Pubs and restaurants
nearby.*
Bedrooms: 1 single, 1 double
& 2 twin, 1 family room.
Bathrooms: 1 private,
2 public.
Bed & breakfast: £18-£22
single, £28-£32 double.
Parking for 6.

Woolley Cottage

(Off Cherry Garden Lane),
The Thicket, Maidenhead,
SL6 3QE
☎ Littlewick Green
(062 882) 2605
*Spacious, secluded country
house bounded by woodland
and farmland. Half a mile
from the motorway and
convenient for London Airport
and Windsor.*
Bedrooms: 1 single, 1 family
room.
Bathrooms: 1 public.
Bed & breakfast: £15 single,
£25 double.
Parking for 4.

MARLOW

Buckinghamshire
Map ref 2C2

Attractive Georgian town
on the River Thames
famous for its 19th C
suspension bridge. The
High Street contains
many old houses and its
connections with writers
include Shelley and the
poet T.S. Eliot. *i*

Mrs. S. Bendall

5 Pound Lane, Marlow,
SL7 2AE
☎ (062 84) 2649
*Older style house, just off town
centre, 2 minutes from River
Thames. Double room has own
balcony with delightful view.*
Bedrooms: 1 double & 1 twin,
1 family room.
Bathrooms: 1 public;
1 private shower.
Bed & breakfast: £15-£17.50
single, £25-£27.50 double.
Parking for 2.
Open January-November.

Mrs J M Kimber

Monkton Farm, Little
Marlow, SL7 3RF
☎ High Wycombe
(0494) 21082
*150-acre dairy farm. 14th C.
cruckhouse set in beautiful
countryside, easily reached by
motorway, and close to all
shopping and sporting facilities.*
Bedrooms: 1 single, 1 twin,
1 family room.
Bathrooms: 1 public.
Bed & breakfast: from £15
single, from £30 double.
Parking for 6.

MILTON COMMON

Oxfordshire
Map ref 2C1

See also Oxford.

The Three Pigeons Inn
⊟

Milton Common, OX9 2NS
☎ Great Milton (084 46) 247
& 251
*16th C. coaching inn with rural
surroundings, right on junction
7 of the M40.*
Bedrooms: 2 double & 1 twin.
Bathrooms: 3 private.
Bed & breakfast: from £25
single, from £40 double.
Half board: from £33 daily,
from £150 weekly.
Lunch available.

**INDIVIDUAL PROPRIETORS HAVE SUPPLIED
ALL DETAILS OF ACCOMMODATION.
ALTHOUGH WE DO CHECK FOR ACCURACY, WE
ADVISE YOU TO CONFIRM PRICES AND OTHER
INFORMATION AT THE TIME OF BOOKING.**

Evening meal 6pm (l.o. 8pm).
Parking for 100.
Credit: Access, Visa, Diners.
💿 🖭 □ ❖ 🛉 Ⓥ 📺 🕮 ⚡
🏧 ♨ ❄ 🏠 🎍

MILTON KEYNES

Buckinghamshire
Map ref 2C1

See also Winslow.
Designated a New Town
in 1967, Milton Keynes
offers a wide range of
housing and is
abundantly planted with
trees. It has excellent
shopping facilities and 3
centres for leisure and
sporting activities. The
Open University is based
here. ℹ

The Grange Stables
Winslow Road, Great
Horwood, Milton Keynes,
MK17 0QN
☎ Winslow (029 671) 2051
*A recently converted stable
block offering comfortable and
spacious accommodation.
Conveniently situated opposite
the Swan pub.*
Bedrooms: 3 twin.
Bathrooms: 1 public.
Bed & breakfast: from £24
single, from £35 double.
Parking for 5.
Credit: Access, Visa.
🏖 ♨ 📞 □ 🕮 🕮 🗡 🏠 🎍

Michelville House
Newton Road, Bletchley,
Milton Keynes, MK3 5BN
☎ (0908) 71578
*Clean compact establishment
within easy reach of railway
station, M1, shopping and
sporting facilities. 10 minutes
from Milton Keynes shopping
centre.*
Bedrooms: 10 single, 6 twin.
Bathrooms: 4 public.
Bed & breakfast: £14.95-
£16.10 single, £27.60-£29.90
double.
Parking for 16.
💿6 ♨ □ ❖ 🕮 🗡 🕮 🗡

Miss F. Thornton
12 Yarrow Place,
Conniburrow, Milton
Keynes, MK14 7AX
☎ (0908) 607613
*3-storey town house in
residential area. Close to city
centre.*
Bedrooms: 1 single, 2 double.
Bathrooms: 1 public.
Bed & breakfast: £11-£12
single, £20-£22 double.

Half board: £13 daily.
Evening meal 6pm (l.o. 8pm).
Parking for 3.
💿 🏖 □ ❖ 🛉 🕮 Ⓥ 🕮 🎍
🏠 🅳🅰🅿

Vignoble ♨
Listed
2 Medland, Woughton Park,
Milton Keynes, MK6 3BH
☎ (0908) 666804
*House situated in quiet cul-de-
sac. Within walking distance of
the Open University. 2.5 miles
from the city centre.*
Bedrooms: 1 single, 1 double
& 1 twin.
Bathrooms: 1 public.
Bed & breakfast: £13.50-£15
single, £25-£30 double.
Parking for 2.
💿5 🏖 ♨ □ ❖ 🕮 🗡 📺 🕮
🗡 🏠

MINSTER LOVELL

Oxfordshire
Map ref 2C1

See also Witney.
Picturesque village on the
River Windrush with
thatched cottages and
19th C. houses. Minster
Lovell Hall, built in the
15th C. by the Lovell
family, is the subject of
several legends and now
stands in ruins in a
beautiful riverside setting.

Mrs. K. Brown, Hill Grove Farm
🔵
Crawley Road, Minster
Lovell, OX8 5NA
☎ Witney (0993) 3120 or
703120
*250-acre mixed farm. A
Cotswold farmhouse run on a
family basis, in an attractive
setting overlooking the
Windrush Valley.*
Bedrooms: 1 double & 1 twin.
Bathrooms: 1 private,
1 public.
Bed & breakfast: £24-£26
double.
Parking for 4.
💿 ❖ 🕮 📺 🕮 🖭 ❄ 🗡 🏠

MOULSFORD ON THAMES

Oxfordshire
Map ref 2C2

See also Wallingford.

White House
Listed
Reading Road, Moulsford,
Wallingford, OX10 9JD
☎ Cholsey (0491) 651397

*Homely accommodation in
private location with
picturesque surroundings. Close
to the river.*
Bedrooms: 1 double & 1 twin.
Bathrooms: 1 public.
Bed & breakfast: £12-£16
single, £24-£32 double.
Parking for 3.
💿5 🏖 ♨ 🕮 🛉 🕮 🖭 ❄ ♨
🏠

NEWBURY

Berkshire
Map ref 2C2

Ancient town surrounded
by the Downs and on the
Kennet and Avon canal, it
has many buildings of
interest, including the
17th C Cloth Hall, which
is now a museum. The
famous race course is
nearby. ℹ

Cleremede
Fox's Lane, Kingsclere, Nr.
Newbury, RG15 8SL
☎ Kingsclere (0635) 297298
Bedrooms: 1 double.
Bathrooms: 1 private.
Bed & breakfast: £15-£17
single, £25-£30 double.
Parking for 1.
💿10 □ ❖ 🕮 🕮 🖭 ♀ ❄
🏠

"Greenways"
🔵🔵
Garden Close Lane,
Newbury, RG14 6PP
☎ (0635) 40496
*Comfortable country house set
in secluded parkland gardens.
Ideally situated for London
and many other touring
attractions.*
Bedrooms: 1 double & 1 twin.
Bathrooms: 2 public.
Bed & breakfast: from £12.50
single, from £25 double.
Parking for 6.
□ ❖ 🕮 Ⓥ ❄ 📺 🕮 🖭 ♨
▶ ❄ 🏠

Mousefield Farm
Listed
Long Lane, Shaw, Newbury,
RG16 9LG
☎ (0635) 40333
*500-acre dairy/arable/beef/pigs
farm. Farmhouse overlooking
our own farmland, set in an
area of outstanding natural
beauty. Well-kept gardens and
plenty of nature trails.*
Bedrooms: 3 single, 1 double
& 1 twin, 1 family room.
Bathrooms: 3 public.
Bed & breakfast: £12-£15
single, £24-£30 double.

Half board: £18-£21 daily,
£100-£120 weekly.
Evening meal 6pm (l.o. 9pm).
Parking for 7.
💿 🏖 🕮 🛉 Ⓥ ✂ 🖭 📺 🕮
🖭 🖱 ✂ ❄ 🏠 🎍

Starwood
1 Rectory Close, Newbury,
RG14 6DF
☎ (0635) 49125
*Large family house set in own
gardens, with off-street
parking. Within 5 minutes'
walk of town centre.*
Bedrooms: 1 single, 1 double
& 1 twin.
Bathrooms: 1 private,
1 public.
Bed & breakfast: from £12
single, £24-£28 double.
Parking for 3.
Open January-November.
🏖 ❖ 🕮 🖭 🕮 🗡 🏠

The White Hart Inn
Hamstead Marshall,
Newbury, RG15 0HW
☎ Kintbury (0488) 58201
*Traditional English inn with
modern accommodation run by
Anglo-Italians.*
Bedrooms: 2 single, 2 twin,
2 family rooms.
Bathrooms: 6 private.
Bed & breakfast: £35-£40
single, £45-£50 double.
Lunch available.
Evening meal 7pm (l.o.
10pm).
Parking for 35.
Credit: Access, Visa, Diners,
Amex.
💿 📞 □ 🛉 Ⓥ 🖱 🕮 ♨
⚡ ❄ 🗡 🏠

Woodlands Park Farm
🔵🔵
Ashford Hill, Newbury,
RG15 8AY
☎ Headley (063 523) 258
*240-acre beef farm.
Accommodation in this
friendly, busy household is
comfortable and a hearty
breakfast is provided. Public
footpaths are plentiful on the
pretty, wooded farm.*
Bedrooms: 2 single, 2 twin.
Bathrooms: 1 public.
Bed & breakfast: from £17
single, from £30 double.
Parking for 5.
💿 🏖 🕮 ❖ 🕮 🛉 Ⓥ 🖱 📺
🕮 ♨ ❄ 🏠

**MAP REFERENCES
APPLY TO THE
COLOUR MAPS
TOWARDS THE END
OF THIS GUIDE.**

199

NEWPORT PAGNELL

Buckinghamshire
Map ref 2C1

Busy town situated on 2 rivers with some Georgian as well as modern buildings.

Swan Revived Hotel M
😔😔😔
High Street, Newport Pagnell, Milton Keynes MK16 8AR
☎ (0908) 610565
Telex 826801
Famous coaching inn, where guests can enjoy every modern comfort. Perfect stopping place for those travelling north or south, or for exploring.
Bedrooms: 15 single, 5 double & 11 twin.
Bathrooms: 31 private.
Bed & breakfast: £20-£42 single, £32-£46 double.
Half board: £27-£52 daily, £275 weekly.
Lunch available.
Evening meal 7.15pm (l.o. 10pm).
Parking for 18.
Credit: Access, Visa, Diners, Amex.
⛄ 🅿 📞 🔟 🖵 🖤 🌡 Ⓥ 🖾
◑ 🎘 Ⅲ ▲ 🏖 ᐸ ⍟ ₪
Ⓣ

Wood End House
Cranfield Road, Moulsoe, Nr. Newport Pagnell, MK16 0HB
☎ Milton Keynes (0908) 615648
Small country house, 2 miles from the M1 and 3 miles outside Milton Keynes.
Bedrooms: 2 double & 2 twin.
Bathrooms: 4 private.
Bed & breakfast: from £25 single, from £40 double.
Parking for 7.
🖵 🖤 🅿 Ⓥ 🖾 Ⅲ ✿ 🗙 🖾

OLNEY

Buckinghamshire
Map ref 2C1

The Mill House
😔😔😔
Church Street, Olney, MK46 4AD
☎ Bedford (0234) 711381
A Georgian country house in a large garden with a river flowing through. Beside historic church associated with poets Cowper and Newton.
Bedrooms: 1 double & 2 twin.
Bathrooms: 2 private, 1 public.
Bed & breakfast: max. £24 single, max. £48 double.

Half board: £36-£45 daily.
Evening meal 7.30pm (l.o. midday).
Parking for 3.
Ⓥ 🐾 🌡 Ⓥ 🖾 🔟 Ⅲ ▲ ✦
✿ 🗙 🖾 🏘

OXFORD

Oxfordshire
Map ref 2C1

See also Forest Hill.
Beautiful university town with many ancient colleges, some dating from the 13th C, and numerous buildings of historic and architectural interest. The Ashmolean Museum has outstanding collections. There are lovely gardens and meadows with punting on the Cherwell. *i*

Acorn Guest House
😔
260 Iffley Road, Oxford, OX4 1SE
☎ (0865) 247998
Comfortable, friendly, convenient for all local amenities and close to the river.
Bedrooms: 2 single, 1 twin, 3 family rooms.
Bathrooms: 2 public.
Bed & breakfast: £13-£16 single, £24-£30 double.
Parking for 5.
🖤 🖵 🐾 🖤 Ⓥ 🖾 Ⅲ ▲ 🗙

Ascot Guest House
283 Iffley Road, Oxford, OX4 4AQ
☎ (0865) 240259
Small guest house, one mile from city centre, with comfortable lounge.
Bedrooms: 1 single, 1 double & 2 twin, 2 family rooms.
Bathrooms: 1 public; 1 private shower.
Bed & breakfast: £11-£16 single, £22-£30 double.
Parking for 2.
Credit: Access, Visa.
⛄ 🖤 🖵 🖵 🐾 🖤 Ⓥ 🖾
🔟 Ⅲ ▲ 🗙 🖾 ₪ ₪

The Athena Guest House M
Listed
253 Cowley Road, Oxford, OX4 1XQ
☎ (0865) 243124
Victorian 3-storey house on main bus route to station and city centre.
Bedrooms: 1 single, 1 double & 2 twin, 2 family rooms.

Bathrooms: 1 public.
Bed & breakfast: £12-£14 single, £24-£28 double.
Parking for 4.
🐾10 🖤 🖾 🔟 Ⅲ ▲ 🗙

Mrs. G. M. Baleham
😔
21 Lincoln Road, Oxford, OX1 4TB
☎ (O865) 246944
Quiet, cosy semi-detached house with ground floor annexe. Close to city centre.
Bedrooms: 1 twin.
Bathrooms: 1 private.
Bed & breakfast: max. £20 single, max. £25 double.
Parking for 2.
♨ 🅿 🖵 🐾 🌡 ✂ 🔟 Ⅲ
▲ ᐸ 🗙 🖾

Burren Guest House
374 Banbury Road, Summertown, Oxford, OX2 7PP
☎ (0865) 513513
Early Victorian house, centrally located for shops, restaurants and sports facilities. Frequent bus service to city.
Bedrooms: 2 single, 2 double & 1 twin, 2 family rooms.
Bathrooms: 2 private, 2 public.
Bed & breakfast: £13-£16 single, £26-£32 double.
Parking for 4.
🐾5 🅿 🖵 🖤 🌡 🖾 🔟 ▲
🗙

Cedarlea
😔😔
41 Sandford Lane, Kennington, Oxford, OX1 5RW
☎ (0865) 735591
Spacious bungalow with a pleasant garden, in a cul-de-sac leading to Sandford Lock. Picturesque walks along River Thames.
Bedrooms: 1 double.
Bathrooms: 1 public.
Bed & breakfast: £18-£20 double.
Parking for 4.
🐾5 ♨ ♨ 🅿 🖵 🖤 🌡 Ⓥ
✂ 🖾 🔟 Ⅲ ▲ 🗙 🖾 🖾 ₪

Combermere House
Listed
11 Polstead Road, Oxford, OX2 6TW
☎ (0865) 56971
Victorian house in a quiet tree-lined road.
Bedrooms: 4 single, 2 twin, 2 family rooms.
Bathrooms: 4 private, 1 public.

Bed & breakfast: £13-£16 single, £24-£30 double.
Parking for 3.
🐾 ♨ 🅿 🌡 🖤 Ⓥ ✂ Ⅲ
▲ 🖾 Ⓣ

Mrs. L. Gledic
375 Iffley Road, Oxford, OX4 4DP
☎ (0865) 778458
Pleasant semi-detached house on main road, 1 mile from city centre.
Bedrooms: 1 double & 1 twin.
Bathrooms: 1 public.
Bed & breakfast: £10-£12 single, £20-£24 double.
Parking for 3.
🐾 ♨ 🌡 🖾 🔟 Ⅲ ▲ 🖾 🖾
₪ ₪ Ⓣ

Mrs. B. Harris
Listed
31 Faulkner Street, St. Ebbes, Oxford, OX1 1UA
☎ (0865) 251898
Bedrooms: 1 double & 1 twin.
Bathrooms: 1 public.
Bed & breakfast: £10-£12 single, £20-£25 double.
Half board: £14-£16 daily, £70-£85 weekly.
Parking for 1.
🐾 ♨ 🖤 🌡 ✂ Ⅲ 🗙 🖾

Hill Farm
Cuddesdon Road, Horspath, Oxford, OX9 1JA
☎ Wheatley (086 77) 3944
240-acre mixed farm. Stone-built farmhouse with large garden and lovely views over farmland. 5 miles from Oxford city centre.
Bedrooms: 1 single, 2 twin.
Bathrooms: 1 public.
Bed & breakfast: £22 double.
Parking for 4.
🐾 ♨ 🖤 🖤 🌡 🔟 Ⅲ ▲ ✓
✿ 🖾

The Lawns M
😔😔😔
12 Manor Road, South Hinksey, Oxford, OX1 5AS
☎ (0865) 739980
Secluded accommodation with every comfort, within walking distance of the city centre. Just off the A34.
Bedrooms: 2 double.
Bathrooms: 1 private, 1 public.
Bed & breakfast: max. £12.50 single, £25-£28 double.
Parking for 2.
Open March-December.
🐾 ♨ 🖵 🖤 🖤 Ⓥ 🔟 Ⅲ ▲
🍴 🖾

PLEASE MENTION THIS GUIDE WHEN MAKING A BOOKING.

Mulberry Guest House
😃😃

265 London Road,
Headington, Oxford,
OX3 9EH
☎ (0865) 67114
*Mulberry Guest House is on
the London Road close to the
ring road. Bus stops outside for
the city centre and the colleges.*
Bedrooms: 1 single, 1 double
& 2 twin, 1 family room.
Bathrooms: 2 public.
Bed & breakfast: £14-£20
single, £24-£30 double.
Half board: £23-£29 daily,
max. £190 weekly.
Evening meal 6pm (l.o.
10pm).
Parking for 3.

Old Mitre Rooms, Lincoln College
Listed

Turl Street, Oxford,
OX1 3DR
☎ (0865) 279821
*The accommodation forms part
of a medieval inn given to the
college in the 15th C., which is
now student rooms.*
Bedrooms: 35 single, 15 twin.
Bathrooms: 3 private,
11 public.
Bed & breakfast: £12.25-
£12.75 single, £23.50-£26
double.
Open July-August.

Portland House
😃😃

338 Banbury Road, Oxford,
OX2 7PR
☎ (0865) 52076 & 53796
*Light, spacious, Edwardian
character house. Few minutes'
walk to various restaurants,
sports facilities, river and
parks. Close to city centre.*
Bedrooms: 1 single, 2 double
& 1 twin, 1 family room.
Bathrooms: 3 public;
2 private showers.
Bed & breakfast: £14-£16
single, £24-£29 double.
Parking for 5.

The Ridings
😃😃

280 Abingdon Road, Oxford,
OX1 4TA
☎ (0865) 248364
*Friendly, comfortable
guesthouse with tastefully
furnished rooms and homely
atmosphere. Close to city
centre, theatres, shops and
university.*
Bedrooms: 1 single, 2 double.

Bathrooms: 1 public;
2 private showers.
Bed & breakfast: £11-£14
single, £22-£28 double.
Parking for 3.

Two Chimneys
Listed

25 Old Wootton Village,
Boars Hill, Oxford, OX1 5HP
☎ (0865) 739144
*17th C. thatched cottage with
separate guest accommodation.*
Bedrooms: 1 twin.
Bathrooms: 1 private.
Bed & breakfast: £10.50-
£13.50 single, £21-£27 double.
Parking for 1.
Open March-October.

Willow Reaches Private Hotel ♠
😃😃😃

1 Wytham Street, Oxford,
OX1 4SU
☎ (0865) 721545/243767
*A comfortable, small hotel in a
quiet location, 20 minutes' walk
from the city centre.*
Bedrooms: 3 single, 2 double
& 2 twin, 2 family rooms.
Bathrooms: 4 private,
2 public.
Bed & breakfast: £19-£22
single, £36-£39 double.
Half board: £26.50-£31 daily,
£185-£196 weekly.
Evening meal 7pm (l.o.
6.30pm).
Parking for 6.
Credit: Access, Visa, Diners,
Amex.

Windrush
Listed

11 Iffley Road, Oxford,
OX4 1EA
☎ (0865) 247933
*200 yards from Oxford High
Street and close to Magdalen
College and River Cherwell.
Ideal touring centre for the
Chilterns, Cotswolds and
Thames.*
Bedrooms: 1 single, 2 double
& 3 twin, 2 family rooms.
Bathrooms: 2 public.
Bed & breakfast: £10.50-£14
single, £21-£27 double.

Windsor Hotel
Listed

226 Iffley Road, Oxford,
OX4 1SE
☎ (0865) 248649 & 242909
*Friendly family service. 1 mile
from the city centre.*

Bedrooms: 1 single, 1 double
& 1 twin, 3 family rooms.
Bathrooms: 2 public.
Bed & breakfast: £20-£25
single, £35-£40 double.
Half board: £24.50-£27.50
daily.
Evening meal 6.30pm (l.o.
10pm).
Parking for 12.

PANGBOURNE
Berkshire
Map ref 2C2

See also Bradfield.
A pretty stretch of river
where the Pang joins the
Thames with views of the
lock, weir and toll bridge.
Once the home of
Kenneth Grahame, author
of 'Wind in the Willows'.

Tudor House
Listed

Farm Lane, Maidenhatch,
Pangbourne, Reading,
RG8 8HP
☎ Bradfield (0734) 744482
*Secluded, private residence in
sunny position in the Pang
Valley; an area of outstanding
natural beauty.*
Bedrooms: 1 double & 1 twin.
Bathrooms: 1 public.
Bed & breakfast: £16 single,
£32 double.
Parking for 4.

Weir View Guest House
😃😃

9 Shooters Hill, Pangbourne,
RG8 7DZ
☎ (073 57) 2120
*House with superb views
overlooking weir and River
Thames. Main line railway
station immediately at rear of
premises.*
Bedrooms: 1 double & 2 twin.
Bathrooms: 1 private,
1 public.
Bed & breakfast: £17.50-
£22.50 single, £30-£35 double.
Parking for 4.
Credit: Access, Visa.

PULLOXHILL
Bedfordshire
Map ref 2D1

4m SE. Ampthill

Pond Farm
Listed

7 High Street, Pulloxhill,
MK45 5HA
☎ Flitwick (0525) 712316

---

*70-acre cereal and horses farm.
This farmhouse is a listed
building. An ideal base for
touring. Close to Woburn
Abbey, Whipsnade Zoo, the
Shuttleworth Collection of old
aircraft and Luton Airport.*
Bedrooms: 1 double & 1 twin,
1 family room.
Bathrooms: 1 public.
Bed & breakfast: £12-£17
single, from £24 double.
Evening meal 6pm.
Parking for 20.

RADNAGE
Buckinghamshire
Map ref 2C2

2m NE. Stokenchurch

Mrs. P. Rowe
😃😃

The Elms, Radnage, Nr.
High Wycombe, HP14 4DW
☎ (024 026) 2175
*17th C. farmhouse in 2 acres of
garden with panoramic views,
overlooking an 11th C. church.
Area of outstanding natural
beauty, ideal for children.*
Bedrooms: 1 single, 2 double,
1 family room.
Bathrooms: 2 public.
Bed & breakfast: £17-£20
single, £27-£30 double.
Half board: £25-£28 daily.
Evening meal 6pm (l.o. 5pm).
Parking for 7.

Three Horseshoes Inn
😃😃

Bennett End, Radnage, Nr.
High Wycombe
☎ Radnage (024 026) 3273
*18th C. inn set amongst the
rural Chilterns. Lots of country
walks.*
Bedrooms: 2 double & 1 twin.
Bathrooms: 3 private.
Bed & breakfast: £32 single,
£42 double.
Half board: £37-£45 daily,
£240-£300 weekly.
Lunch available.
Evening meal 7pm (l.o.
10pm).
Parking for 35.

**GROUPS, CONSORTIA
AND AGENCIES
SPECIALISING
IN FARM AND
COUNTRY HOLIDAYS
ARE LISTED IN A
SPECIAL SECTION
OF THIS GUIDE.**

RICKMANSWORTH

Hertfordshire
Map ref 2D2

Old town, where 3 rivers meet, now mainly residential. The High Street is full of interesting buildings, including the home of William Penn. Moor Park Mansion, a fine 18th C house, is now a golf club-house.

Mrs. E. Childerhouse
6 Swallow Close, Nightingale Road, Rickmansworth, WD3 2DZ
☎ (0923) 720069
Home baking and home-grown produce a speciality. 30 minutes from London by underground and close to Watford, M25 and Moorpark Golf Course. Non-smokers preferred please.
Bedrooms: 1 single, 1 double, 1 family room.
Bathrooms: 1 private, 1 public.
Bed & breakfast: from £14 single, from £28 double.
Half board: from £19 daily.
Parking for 3.

The Millwards
30 Hazelwood Road, Croxley Green, Rickmansworth, WD3 3EB
☎ Watford (0923) 33751 & 226666
A homely service is offered at this comfortable guesthouse which is pleasantly situated beside the River Gade, Great Union Canal and Common Moor.
Bedrooms: 1 single, 3 double.
Bathrooms: 1 public
Bed & breakfast: £12.50 single, £25 double.
Parking for 3.

Mrs. J. Sharp
Listed
27 Mount View, Rickmansworth, WD3 2BB
☎ (0923) 774408 & 776529
Detached house in quiet road. Central for London and Heathrow. Easy access to M1, M25 and M40.
Bedrooms: 2 single, 1 twin.
Bathrooms: 1 public.
Bed & breakfast: £14-£15 single, £28-£30 double.
Parking for 2.

ROTHERFIELD GREYS

Oxfordshire
Map ref 2C2

2m W. Henley-on-Thames

Shepherds
Shepherds Green, Rotherfield Greys, Henley-on-Thames, RG9 4QL
☎ Rotherfield Greys (049 17) 413
Private house with pretty garden set on secluded village green. Warm welcome to guests. Lovely walks nearby. Easy reach of Heathrow Airport, London, Windsor, Oxford, Thames Valley and Chilterns.
Bedrooms: 1 single, 1 double & 1 twin.
Bathrooms: 2 private, 1 public.
Bed & breakfast: £15-£25 single, from £40 double.
Half board: £27-£37 daily.
Parking for 6.

ST ALBANS

Hertfordshire
Map ref 2D1

As Verulamium this was one of the largest towns in Roman Britain and its remains can be seen in the museum. The Norman cathedral was built from Roman materials to commemorate Alban, the first British Christian martyr. The fortified clock tower is one of only two in Britain.

The Care Inn
29 Alma Road, St. Albans, AL1 3AT
☎ (0727) 67310
Comfortable family atmosphere, ideally located close to station, town and cathedral.
Bedrooms: 1 single, 1 double & 1 twin, 1 family room.
Bathrooms: 1 private, 2 public.
Bed & breakfast: £13-£15 single, £24-£28 double.
Parking for 5.

Mrs. G. Rennick
24 Beaconsfield Road, St. Albans, AL1 3RB
☎ (0727) 55540

Large Edwardian house, 10 minutes' walk from city centre. Recently restored and modernised to high standard without altering its original character. Railway station nearby - London 18 minutes.
Bedrooms: 1 single, 1 double & 1 twin, 1 family room.
Bathrooms: 1 private, 2 public.
Bed & breakfast: max. £15 single, £26-£28 double.
Parking for 2.

SANDY

Bedfordshire
Map ref 2D1

Small town on the River Ivel on the site of a Roman settlement. Sandy is mentioned in Domesday.

Highfield Farm
Sandy, SG19 2AQ
☎ (0767) 82332
300-acre arable farm. Attractive period farmhouse set back in its own grounds. 1 mile north of Sandy roundabout on A1.
Bedrooms: 1 twin, 1 family room.
Bathrooms: 1 private, 1 public.
Bed & breakfast: £15-£16.50 single, £24-£26 double.
Half board: £20-£22 daily, £126-£138.60 weekly.
Evening meal 6.30pm.
Parking for 6.

Orchard Cottage
1 High Street, Wrestlingworth, Sandy, SG19 2EW
☎ Wrestlingworth (076 723) 355
A picturesque period thatched cottage with modern extension, once the village bakery. In country location with open views over large garden.
Bedrooms: 1 family room.
Bathrooms: 1 public.
Bed & breakfast: max. £12.50 single, max. £24 double.
Parking for 2.
Open February-November.

THE SYMBOLS ARE EXPLAINED ON THE FLAP INSIDE THE BACK COVER.

SHABBINGTON

Buckinghamshire
Map ref 2C1

3m NW. Thame

Manor Farm
Listed
Shabbington, Aylesbury, HP18 9HJ
☎ Long Crendon (0844) 201103
188-acre cattle and sheep farm. In rural setting, within 20 minutes of historic Oxford, on the fringes of the scenic Thames Valley, Chilterns and Cotswolds.
Bedrooms: 2 single, 2 double.
Bathrooms: 1 private, 1 public.
Bed & breakfast: £13-£15 single, £26-£30 double.
Parking for 10.

SHIPLAKE

Oxfordshire
Map ref 2C2

3m W. Henley

Crowsley House
Crowsley Road, Shiplake, Nr. Henley-on-Thames, RG9 3JT
☎ Wargrave (073 522) 3197
Family home in a quiet village location, close to Henley-on-Thames, and convenient for Oxford and London.
Bedrooms: 2 twin.
Bathrooms: 1 public.
Bed & breakfast: from £12 single, from £24 double.
Parking for 2.

SKIRMETT

Oxfordshire
Map ref 2C2

5m SW. High Wycombe

Kings Arms Hotel
Listed
Skirmett, Henley-on-Thames, RG9 6TG
☎ Turville Heath (049 163) 247
In the beautiful Hambleden Valley overlooking pleasant countryside near Henley-on-Thames. Close to many places of beauty and historic interest.
Bedrooms: 1 double & 3 twin.
Bathrooms: 2 private, 1 public.
Bed & breakfast: £33 single, £44 double.
Half board: £43 daily, £300 weekly.

Evening meal 7pm (l.o. 9.30pm).
Parking for 15.
Credit: Access, Visa.

⌷ ⑳ ❖ ⚊ ▮ Ⓥ ▥ ♨ ☽ ✳
✗ ☷ ➘ SP ⌗

The Old Bakery
Skirmett, Nr. Henley-on-Thames, RG9 6TD
☎ Turville Heath (049 163) 309
On the site of an old bakery, in a country village with excellent walks and local pubs. Beamed drawing room; attractive garden with outstanding rural views.
Bedrooms: 4 single, 2 double, 1 family room.
Bathrooms: 2 public.
Bed & breakfast: £12.50-£15 single, £25-£30 double.
Half board: £17.50-£20 daily, £100-£120 weekly.
Evening meal 7pm (l.o. 9pm).
Parking for 7.

⌷ ⌾ ⇘ ⓐ ⌶ ❖ ⓤ ⚊ ▮ Ⓥ
✄ ✑ ⓣ ▥ ⌷ ⚑ ⟟ ☽ ✳ ☷
SP

SLOUGH
Berkshire
Map ref 2D2

A busy town with a large trading estate, Slough is an excellent centre for recreation with many open spaces. The ancient village of Upton, now part of Slough, has an interesting Norman church and Cliveden House is nearby.

Highways Guest House ⚠
☎ — *£23022*
95 London Road, Langley, Slough, SL3 7RS
☎ (0753) 24715 & 23022
Comfortable accommodation set in half an acre of pleasant garden. Located on A4, convenient for London, Heathrow Airport and Windsor.
Bedrooms: 2 single, 2 double & 4 twin, 2 family rooms.
Bathrooms: 2 public.
Bed & breakfast: £18.50-£21.50 single, £32-£37.50 double.
Parking for 15.

⌷ ⇘ ⚏ ⌷ ❖ ⓤ Ⓥ ✄ ⓣ ▥
⚑ ✳ ✗ ☷ DAP SP ⌗

SOUTH MIMMS
Hertfordshire
Map ref 2D1

Best known today for its location at the junction of M25 and A1M and the only service station on the M25.

The Black Swan
62-64 Blanche Lane, South Mimms, Potters Bar, EN6 3PD
☎ Potters Bar (0707) 44180
Self-contained flat, breakfast provided.
Bedrooms: 1 family room.
Bathrooms: 1 private.
Bed & breakfast: from £20 single, from £35 double.
Parking for 2.

⌷ ⇘ ⓐ ⑳ ❖ ⓤ Ⓥ ▥ ⚑ ☷
⌗ ⓣ

STANDLAKE
Oxfordshire
Map ref 2C1

13th C. church with an octagonal tower and spire standing beside the Windrush. The interior of the church is rich in woodwork.

The Old Rectory ⚠
⚉⚉⚉
Church End, Standlake, Nr. Witney, OX8 7SG
☎ (086 731) 559
Delightful house of historic interest standing in grounds of 5 acres, on the banks of the River Windrush.
Bedrooms: 2 double & 2 twin.
Bathrooms: 4 private.
Bed & breakfast: £18-£30 single, £28-£50 double.
Half board: £30-£37 daily, £190-£210 weekly.
Evening meal 7.30pm.
Parking for 30.

⌷ ⇘5 ⌗ ⑳ ⌷ ❖ ⓤ ⚊ ▮ Ⓥ ✄
▥ ⚑ ♨ ☽ ✳ ✗ ☷ ➘
SP ⌗

STANTON HARCOURT
Oxfordshire
Map ref 2C1

3m SW. Eynsham

Staddle Stones
Listed
Linch Hill, Stanton Harcourt, Nr. Eynsham, OX8 1BB
☎ Oxford (0865) 882256

Large house in 5 acres of picturesque surroundings. Paddock with donkey and horse, and large ornamental pool.
Bedrooms: 1 single, 1 double & 1 twin.
Bathrooms: 2 public.
Bed & breakfast: £12 single, £24 double.
Half board: £18 daily, £125 weekly.
Evening meal 7.30pm (l.o. 6.30pm).
Parking for 20.

⌷ ⇘ ⚏ ⓤ ⚊ ▮ Ⓥ ✄ ⓣ ▥
⚑ ⇘ ✳ ☷

STEVENTON
Oxfordshire
Map ref 2C1

Below the Causeway the village has several framed timber houses which still have 19th C. lead and copper fire insurance badges nailed to their walls.

Willowbrook Farmhouse
⚉⚉
Willowbrook Farm, Hanney Road, Steventon, Nr. Abingdon, OX13 6BE
☎ West Hanney (023 587) 8188
338-acre arable, beef and sheep farm. Very spacious and comfortable stone house built in 1986. Surrounded by open farmland, adjacent to bridle path and old canal walk.
Bedrooms: 1 double.
Bathrooms: 1 private.
Bed & breakfast: £20-£24 double.
Parking for 2.
Open May-September.

⌷ ❖ ⓤ ▥ ⚑ ✳ ✗ ☷

UFFINGTON
Oxfordshire
Map ref 2C2

See also Faringdon.
Village famous for the great White Horse cut in the chalk, possibly dating from the Iron Age. Above it is Uffington Castle, a prehistoric hill fort.

The Craven
Listed
Fernham Road, Uffington, SN7 7RD
☎ (036 782) 449
1.5-acre mixed farm. Large 17th C. thatched farmhouse, originally an inn. Surrounded by lovely scenery on outskirts of pretty village, near the Ridgeway Path.

Bedrooms: 1 single, 2 double & 1 twin.
Bathrooms: 1 private, 1 public.
Bed & breakfast: £14-£18 single, £28-£38 double.
Half board: £19-£25 daily.
Lunch available.
Evening meal 6pm (l.o. midday).
Parking for 11.

⌷ ⇘ ⚏ ⓐ ⌷ ⓤ ▮ Ⓥ ✄ ✑
ⓣ ▥ ⚑ ⟟ ☽ ⟟ ⇘ ✳ ✗
☷ SP ⌗

WALLINGFORD
Oxfordshire
Map ref 2C2

See also Benson, Berrick Salome, Moulsford on Thames.
Site of an ancient ford over the River Thames, now crossed by a 900 ft long bridge. The town has many timber-framed and Georgian buildings, Gainsborough portraits in the 17th C. Town Hall and a few remains of a Norman Castle. ⓘ

North Farm
⚉⚉
Shillingford Hill, Wallingford, OX10 8ND
☎ Warborough (086 732) 8406
500-acre mixed farm. Comfortable farmhouse close to River Thames; approached through Shillingford Bridge Hotel car park. In quiet position with lovely views.
Bedrooms: 1 double & 1 twin.
Bathrooms: 2 private.
Bed & breakfast: from £18 single, £25-£30 double.
Parking for 4.

⌷ ⌷ ❖ ⓤ ▥ ⚑ ⌒ ✓ ⌗
DAP

The Old Post Office
5 Wharf Road, Shillingford, Wallingford, OX9 8EW
☎ Warborough (086 732) 8498
Period cottage situated very close to the River Thames, in a rural setting. Quiet lane off the A423 halfway between Oxford and Henley.
Bedrooms: 1 double & 1 twin.
Bathrooms: 1 private, 2 public.
Bed & breakfast: £10-£12 single, £20-£22 double.
Parking for 4.

⌷ ⑳ ❖ ⓤ ▥ ⓣ ▥ ⚑ ✳
✗ ☷

PLEASE MENTION THIS GUIDE WHEN MAKING A BOOKING.

WARGRAVE

Berkshire
Map ref 2C2

Attractive village with timber-framed and Georgian houses. The Thames meets the River Loddon near by and it is a popular place for boating.

Windy Brow
204 Victoria Road, Wargrave, Reading, RG10 8AJ
☎ Wargrave (073 522) 3336
Windy Brow provides friendly accommodation in a spacious Victorian house with garden overlooking farmland. 3 miles from Henley-on-Thames, 12 miles from Windsor. 1 mile from fast bus route to London and from station to Paddington. Heathrow Airport half an hour away.
Bedrooms: 2 single, 2 twin, 1 family room.
Bathrooms: 2 public.
Bed & breakfast: £15-£16 single, £28-£30 double.
Parking for 7.
Open March-October.
♿ 🛏 💆 ⓤⓛ Ⓥ ⓣⓥ 🖫 ▦ ✿ 🖾 ▥

WATERPERRY

Oxfordshire
Map ref 2C1

7m E. Oxford
Location of the well-known Waterperry Horticultural centre open to visitors for most of the year.

Mrs. S. Fonge
Manor Farm, Waterperry, OX9 1LB
☎ Ickford (084 47) 263
140-acre mixed farm. 17th C. manor farm in peaceful village location. Guests may walk beside or fish in the nearby River Thames.
Bedrooms: 2 double & 1 twin.
Bathrooms: 2 public.
Bed & breakfast: £11.50-£14.50 single, £22-£27 double.
Half board: £19.50-£22.50 daily, £133-£147 weekly.
Evening meal 6.30pm (l.o. 9pm).
Parking for 4.
♿ ⓤⓛ 🍴 Ⓥ ⊣ ⓣⓥ 🖫 ▵ 🗡 ✿ 🖾 SP

WEST ILSLEY

Berkshire
Map ref 2C2

Attractive village near Wantage.

The Harrow
West Ilsley, Nr. Newbury, RG16 0AR
☎ (063 528) 260
A small village pub situated opposite the duck pond and the cricket pitch in West Ilsley, on the edge of the Berkshire Downs. 1 mile from the A34, 10 miles north of Newbury.
Bedrooms: 2 double & 1 twin.
Bathrooms: 1 public.
Bed & breakfast: max. £15 single, max. £30 double.
Half board: £20.50-£25 daily.
Lunch available.
Evening meal 7pm (l.o. 9.30pm).
Parking for 12.
Credit: Access, Visa.
♿ ✿ 🍴 Ⓥ ⓣⓥ 🖫 🖾

WESTON TURVILLE

Buckinghamshire
Map ref 2C1

Village with many thatched cottages, Georgian houses and beautiful orchards. Quarterly meetings of the Quakers from a very wide area were held here from 1678 to 1723.

Chandos Arms
Listed
1 Main Street, Weston Turville, Nr. Aylesbury, HP22 5RR
☎ Stoke Mandeville (029 661) 3532
Public house with large beer garden and children's play area. German cooking a speciality. 2 miles south of Aylesbury and 2 miles north of Wendover.
Bedrooms: 2 twin.
Bathrooms: 1 public.
Bed & breakfast: £20 single, £30 double.
Lunch available.
Evening meal 7pm (l.o. 9pm).
Parking for 20.
⑩ 🖵 🍴 🖫 ▵ ⊍ ▶ ✿ 🗡 🖾 ▦

WESTON-ON-THE-GREEN

Oxfordshire
Map ref 2C1

9m N. Oxford
Pretty village with stocks on the village green and thatched cottages. The church of St. Mary's has an attractive setting and a fine tower dating from the 12th C.

Newby Cottage
Weston-on-the-Green, Nr. Bicester, OX6 8QL
☎ Bletchington (0869) 50662
18th C. brick and stone thatched cottage overlooking farmland. Convenient for Oxford, Woodstock and the Oxfordshire Way.
Bedrooms: 1 single, 2 double.
Bathrooms: 1 public.
Bed & breakfast: £10-£11 single, £20-£22 double.
Half board: £13.50-£14.50 daily.
Parking for 3.
♿ 🖵 ⓤⓛ 🍴 Ⓥ ⅄ 🖫 🗡 🖾 ▦

WINDSOR

Berkshire
Map ref 2D2

Town dominated by the spectacular castle and home of the royal family for over 900 years. Parts are open to the public. There are many attractions including the Great Park, Eton, Windsor Safari Park and trips on the river. 🖊

Alba
Listed
3 St. Marks Road, Windsor, SL4 3BD
☎ (0753) 860869
Victorian town house in Windsor town centre, renovated to give the atmosphere of the Victorian era.
Bedrooms: 3 double.
Bathrooms: 2 public.
Bed & breakfast: from £28 double.
Evening meal 7pm (l.o. 9pm).
Parking for 2.
🍳 🖵 ⓤⓛ ⊣ ⓣⓥ 🖫 ▵ 🗡 🖾 ⅋ SP ▦ Ⓣ

Alma House
Listed
56 Alma Road, Windsor, SL4 3HA
☎ (0753) 862983 & 855620

An elegant Victorian house within 5 minutes' walk of Windsor Castle, town centre, river and parks. Heathrow Airport 11 miles.
Bedrooms: 1 single, 1 double, 1 family room.
Bathrooms: 1 public; 2 private showers.
Bed & breakfast: £15-£16 single, £28-£30 double.
Parking for 4.
♿ 🖵 ⓤⓛ 🖫 🖾

Brookvilla Guest House
99 Eton Wick Road, Eton Wick, Windsor, SL4 6NQ
☎ (0753) 866263
Private guesthouse in Thames Valley, by open commonland and a stream. Convenient for the castle, college, river and airport.
Bedrooms: 2 single, 3 double & 2 twin.
Bathrooms: 1 private, 2 public.
Bed & breakfast: £20-£28 single, £30-£40 double.
Parking for 10.
Open April-October.
♿ 💆 🖵 ✿ ⊣ ▵ 🗡 🖾 ▦ Ⓣ

Fir Trees
Listed
69 Imperial Road, Windsor, SL4 3RU
☎ (0753) 852836
Large welcoming chalet bungalow within walking distance of all the delights of Royal Windsor. 10 minutes' drive from Heathrow Airport.
Bedrooms: 1 single, 1 double & 2 twin.
Bathrooms: 2 public.
Bed & breakfast: £15-£18 single, £26-£28 double.
Parking for 6.
♿ 💆 🖵 ✿ ⓤⓛ ⅄ ⊣ ▵ 🗡 🖾 Ⓣ

Mrs. E. E. Pliszka
64 Bolton Road, Windsor, SL4 3JL
☎ (0753) 860789
Pleasant accommodation with good facilities, very near Windsor town centre.
Bedrooms: 2 family rooms.
Bathrooms: 2 private.
Bed & breakfast: £15-£20 single, £30 double.
Half board: £19-£20 daily, £133-£140 weekly.
Lunch available.
Evening meal 6pm (l.o. 7pm).
Parking for 5.
♿ ⑩ 🖵 ✿ ⓤⓛ 🍴 ⅄ ⊣ ⓣⓥ 🖫 ▵ 🗡 🖾 ⒼⒶ⒫

GROUPS, CONSORTIA AND AGENCIES SPECIALISING IN FARM AND COUNTRY HOLIDAYS ARE LISTED IN A SPECIAL SECTION OF THIS GUIDE.

WINSLOW

Buckinghamshire
Map ref 2C1

Small town with Georgian houses, a little market square and a fine church with 15th C. wall-paintings. Winslow Hall, built to the design of Sir Christopher Wren in 1700, is open to the public.

Foxhole Farm
Winslow, MK18 3JW
☎ (029 671) 4550
70-acre livestock farm. A very fine modern farmhouse set in pasture and woodland, close to the small market town of Winslow.
Bedrooms: 1 single, 2 double.
Bathrooms: 1 public.
Bed & breakfast: from £12 single, from £21 double.
Parking for 6.
🌲 Ⓤ ℡ ▥ ⟋ ⚘ ✕ 🅗

WITNEY

Oxfordshire
Map ref 2C1

See also Minster Lovell.
Town famous for its blanket-making and mentioned in the Domesday Book. The market place contains the Butter Cross, a medieval meeting place, and there is a green with merchants' houses. ℹ

The Red Lion Hotel
Listed
1-3 Corn Street, Witney,
OX8 7DB
☎ (0993) 703149
Situated in the town centre. Rooms have a country cottage feel, which is complemented by pretty fabric and attractive furnishings.
Bedrooms: 1 single, 4 twin, 1 family room.
Bathrooms: 2 private, 1 public.
Bed & breakfast: £16.10-£18.70 single, £29.90-£34.50 double.
Half board: £18.70-£23 daily, £136.85-£161 weekly.
Lunch available.
Evening meal 6pm (l.o. 10pm).
Credit: Access.
🌲 🌲 ➡ ♥ 🛈 Ⓥ ▥ ◣ ◆ ✕ 🅗

WOBURN

Bedfordshire
Map ref 2D1

Attractive village with thatched cottages, Victorian almshouses and an impressive inn. Woburn Abbey, an 18th C. mansion set in 3000 acres of parkland, is a major tourist attraction with a splendid art collection. ℹ

Serendib
15 Market Place, Woburn,
Nr. Milton Keynes,
MK17 9PZ
☎ Woburn (0525) 290464
Georgian building in historic Woburn village, near the abbey, safari park and golf course. Comfortable and friendly atmosphere. 4 miles from M1 junction 12 or 13.
Bedrooms: 2 single, 1 double & 1 twin.
Bathrooms: 1 public.
Bed & breakfast: from £10 single, £21-£23 double.
Parking for 1.
Credit: Access, Visa.
🛏 5 🌲 ♥ Ⓤ ▥ ℡ ◣ ✕ 🅗 🅖

WOLVERTON

Buckinghamshire
Map ref 2C1

6m NW. Bletchley

Roman Room Restaurant
42 Church Street, Wolverton, Milton Keynes, MK12 5JN
☎ (0908) 318020 & 562869 & (0908) 568793 after 6 pm.
Italian and Continental restaurant, also English cooking. Weekly rates available.
Bedrooms: 3 twin, 1 family room.
Bathrooms: 1 public.
Bed & breakfast: £17-£18.50 single, £29-£35 double.
Half board: £23-£25.50 daily.
Lunch available.
Evening meal 7pm (l.o. 10.30pm).
Parking for 10.
Credit: Access, Visa, Diners, Amex.
🛏 🀄 ♥ 🛈 Ⓥ ⟋ ▥ ◣ 🍴 ✕ 🅗 🅖 ⬚

WOODSTOCK

Oxfordshire
Map ref 2C1

See also Cassington.
Small country town clustered around the park gates of Blenheim Palace, the superb 18th C home of the Duke of Marlborough. The town has well-known inns and an interesting museum. Sir Winston Churchill was born and buried nearby. ℹ

The Blenheim
17 Park Street, Woodstock, OX1 1SJ
☎ (0993) 811467
Attractive 18th C. building adjacent to Blenheim Palace. Guest rooms are in family home above traditional tea room.
Bedrooms: 2 double, 1 family room.
Bathrooms: 3 private.
Bed & breakfast: £24 single, £35 double.
🛏 ➡ ♥ 🛈 ▥ 🅗 🏮

Cedar Gable
Listed
46 Green Lane, Woodstock, OX7 1JZ
☎ (0993) 812231
Detached bungalow in a delightful, quiet location near the Glyme Valley at Woodstock. Large garden and patio. Non-smokers only.
Bedrooms: 2 double & 1 twin, 1 family room.
Bathrooms: 1 public.
Bed & breakfast: £26-£28 double.
Half board: £16-£17 daily.
Parking for 2.
Credit: Access.
🛏 5 🀄 Ⓤ ▥ ℡ ▥ ◣ ✕ 🅗

Hamilton House
⊜
43 Hill Rise, Woodstock, OX7 1AB
☎ (0993) 812206
Convenient for touring the Cotswolds, Oxford and Stratford.
Bedrooms: 2 double & 1 twin.
Bathrooms: 1 public.
Bed & breakfast: £13-£15 single, £22-£24 double.
Parking for 1.
♥ Ⓤ ▥ ℡ ▥ ✕ 🅗

Merrydown ⚕
⊜⊜
37 Brook Hill, Woodstock, OX7 1JE
☎ (0993) 811835

Detached house in quiet, secluded position overlooking Glyme Valley in Woodstock. Short walk from town centre and Blenheim Palace.
Bedrooms: 2 double.
Bathrooms: 2 public.
Bed & breakfast: £13 single, £20 double.
Half board: £14.50 daily, £98 weekly.
Evening meal 6pm (l.o. 6.30pm).
Parking for 5.
🛏 1 ⊛ ➡ ♥ ▥ Ⓥ ▥ ℡ ▥
◣ 🅗 ⚞ 🅖

Shepherds Hall Inn
Witney Road, Freeland, Woodstock, OX7 2HQ
☎ Freeland (0993) 881256
Well-appointed inn offering good accommodation. Ideally situated for Oxford, Woodstock and the Cotswolds, on the A4095 Woodstock to Witney road.
Bedrooms: 1 single, 2 double & 2 twin.
Bathrooms: 5 private.
Bed & breakfast: £20 single, £30-£35 double.
Lunch available.
Evening meal 7pm (l.o. 10pm).
Parking for 50.
🛏 ⊛ ➡ ♥ 🛈 ▥ 🍴 🅗

Tiffany's of Woodstock
Listed
36 Oxford Street, Woodstock, OX7 1TT
☎ (0993) 811751
An old building with modernised, comfortable bedrooms. Centre of Woodstock, near Blenheim Palace.
Bedrooms: 1 double & 2 twin, 3 family rooms.
Bathrooms: 1 public.
Bed & breakfast: £25-£26.50 double.
Lunch available.
🛏 🛈 ▥ 🅗 🅖

WOOTTON

Oxfordshire
Map ref 2C1

Manor Farm
Wootton, Woodstock
☎ (0993) 811479
200-acre mixed farm. Facing south, overlooking River Glyme with views towards Blenheim. In the centre of Wootton, close to the church, shop and inn.
Bedrooms: 2 family rooms.
Bathrooms: 2 public.
Continued ▶

THERE IS A SPECIAL SECTION IN THIS GUIDE LISTING ACCOMMODATION ESPECIALLY SUITABLE FOR GROUPS AND YOUNG PEOPLE.

WOOTTON

Continued

Bed & breakfast: from £14 single, from £28 double. Parking for 10.

WRAYSBURY

Berkshire
Map ref 2D2

See also Windsor.

Nan & Clive Bristow

37 Gloucester Drive,
Wraysbury, Staines,
Middlesex TW18 4TY
☎ Staines (0784) 64858
Detached private house, 10 minutes' walk from Staines station and close to Heathrow Airport. Spacious garden with fruit trees and stream.
Bedrooms: 2 double & 1 twin.
Bathrooms: 1 private,
1 public.
Bed & breakfast: £26-£28 double.
Parking for 6.

hen enquiring about accommodation you may find it helpful to use the booking enquiry coupons which can be found towards the end of the guide. These should be cut out and mailed direct to the establishments in which you are interested. Remember to include your name and address and please enclose a stamped addressed envelope (or an international reply coupon if writing from outside Britain).

FOLLOW THE SIGN

It leads to over 550 Tourist Information Centres throughout England offering friendly help with accommodation and holiday ideas as well as suggestions of places to visit and

Tourist information

things to do. In your home town there may be a centre which can help you before you set out. If not, why not send for the Directory of Tourist Information Centres in Great Britain? It is available free from English Tourist Board, Department D, Bromells Road, Clapham, London SW4 0BJ.

CROWN CLASSIFICATIONS

All the establishments displaying a national classification in this guide are inspected regularly. All can be chosen with confidence.

There are six classifications — from Listed to 5 Crowns; each indicates the level of facilities and services provided.

All classified establishments are required to provide a high standard of cleanliness, courtesy and service and to be well maintained. A lower classification does not imply lower standards; although the range of facilities and services may be smaller, they may be provided to a high standard.

You will find a full explanation of the national Crown Classification Scheme towards the end of this guide.

The town or village you wish to visit may not have accommodation entirely suited to your needs, but there could be somewhere ideal quite close by. From the colour maps towards the end of this guide you will be able to identify nearby towns and villages with accommodation listed in the guide. You can then use the index to find the relevant page numbers.

Enjoy the countryside and respect its life and work ♣ Guard against all risk of fire ♣ Fasten all gates ♣ Keep your dogs under close control ♣ Keep to public paths across farmland ♣ Use gates and stiles to cross fences, hedges and walls ♣ Leave livestock, crops and machinery alone ♣ Take your litter home ♣ Help to keep all water clean ♣ Protect wildlife, plants and trees ♣ Take special care on country roads ♣ Make no unnecessary noise

East Anglia

East Anglia — once an ancient kingdom cut off by undrained marshlands and impenetrable forests — is an increasingly popular area for tourist exploration.

Its counties of Norfolk, Suffolk, Cambridgeshire and Essex stretch the region from medieval King's Lynn in the north, through Cambridge and historic Colchester right down to the outskirts of London in the south.

A flavour of its hidden, brooding past can still be sampled in the flat, open fens of Cambridgeshire, the sandy heaths and woodlands of Breckland, the reedy Norfolk Broads and the undisturbed saltings, dunes and marshes around the coast.

But East Anglia is not all beautifully wild

NORFOLK SHIRE HORSE CENTRE

— it's a little woolly, too, as you'll find in the picturesque old wool towns and villages of Suffolk.

No exploration of the region's delights would be complete without a visit to the great cities of Norwich and Cambridge — the former with its Norman castle and cathedral, the latter with its famous colleges, some dating back to the 13th century.

And don't forget the coastal playgrounds: down to earth Southend-on-Sea, popular Great Yarmouth, Lowestoft, Clacton-on-Sea and Felixstowe plus a host of smaller resorts specialising in restful holidays by the sea.

FIND OUT MORE

Further information about holidays and attractions in the East Anglia tourist region is available from: **East Anglia Tourist Board,** Toppesfield Hall, Hadleigh, Suffolk IP7 5DN. ☎ (0473) 822922.

These publications are available free from the East Anglia Tourist Board:
Farm Holidays in East Anglia
Norfolk Coast and Countryside (accommodation guide)
Norwich — Fine City Breaks

Also available are:
East Anglia Guide (£2.35 inc post and packing)
East Anglia Leisure Map (£2.50 inc post and packing)
A Celebration of Gardens (50p)
Accommodation Guide — hotels, self-catering, camping and caravan parks (50p).

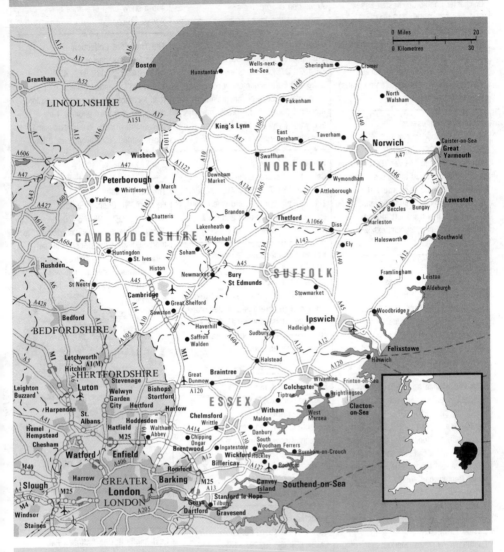

WHERE TO GO, WHAT TO SEE

**Audley End House
and Miniature Railway**
Saffron Walden, Essex
☎ (0799) 22399
Jacobean house in superb grounds, landscaped by 'Capability' Brown, lake and river. Also 10.25 inch gauge miniature railway line.
Admission charge.

**Brandeston Priory
Vineyards and Garden**
The Priory, Brandeston, Nr. Wickham Market, Suffolk IP13 7AU
☎ (072 882) 462
Vineyards, garden, shop, winery, picnic area, children's playground, woodland walk, wine and cider tastings.
Admission charge.

▶

Colchester and Essex Museum
Colchester Castle, Colchester, Essex
CO1 1TJ ☎ (0206) 712481/2
Colchester Castle (archaeology,
particularly Roman), Hollytrees Museum
(domestic items, costumes), Natural
History Museum (dioramas), Social
History Museum (country life and crafts).
Admission charge.

Imperial War Museum
Duxford, Cambridgeshire CB2 4QR
☎ (0223) 833963/835000
A major collection of over 100 military
and civil aircraft and armoured fighting
vehicles, including Concorde 101.
Special attractions include adventure
playground, free transport around
museum and many special exhibitions.
Admission charge.

Ely Cathedral
The College, Ely, Cambridgeshire
CB7 4DL ☎ (0353) 67735
The 'Ship of the Fens', Ely Cathedral is
one of the finest examples of the
Romanesque style with the Octagon as
one of its best features.
Admission charge.

Flag Fen Bronze Age Excavations
Fourth Drove, Fengate, Peterborough,
Cambridgeshire PE1 5UR
☎ (0773) 313414
Excavation of Bronze Age timber 'Lake
Village'. Visitors can see and handle
3,000-year-old timber. Site includes an
intact Roman road. Visitor centre and
gift shop.
Admission charge.

Easton Farm Park
Easton, Nr. Wickham Market,
Woodbridge, Suffolk IP13 0EQ
☎ (0738) 746475
Victorian farm setting for over 40
species of farm animals, including rare
breeds. Modern milking unit, Victorian
dairy, working Suffolk horses. Trail.
Admission charge.

Kilverstone Wildlife Park
Thetford, Norfolk IP24 2RL
☎ (0842) 5369/66606
Latin-American wildlife park and

miniature horse stud.
Admission charge.

Norfolk Shire Horse Centre
West Runton Stables, West Runton,
Cromer, Norfolk NR27 9QH
☎ (026 375) 339
Shire and Suffolk horses working and
on display. Breeds of mountain and
moorland ponies. Horse-drawn machinery
and wagons, video, photographs.
Admission charge.

Norfolk Lavender
Caley Mill, Heacham, King's Lynn,
Norfolk PE31 7JE ☎ (0485) 70384
The only place in England where you
can see lavender grown and distilled.
Admission charge.

National Horseracing Museum
99 High Street, Newmarket, Suffolk
☎ (0638) 667333
Story of Britain's greatest sport told in
fine paintings, bronzes and memorabilia
of personalities connected with the
sport. Five galleries, video of famous
races, coffee and gift shop.
Admission charge.

Never, Never Land
Southend-on-Sea, Essex
☎ (0702) 460618
2.5-acre children's fantasy park
featuring Snow White's Cottage,
Badger's House, model railway, Masters
of the Universe, Merlin and the Dragon,
etc. Illuminated after dusk.
Admission charge.

Stansted Mountfitchet Castle
Bayley Walls, Stansted, Essex
CM24 8SP ☎ (0279) 813237
Reconstruction of a Norman motte-and-
bailey castle, the only one in the world
on its original site. Complete with living
Norman village, Lord's Tower and Grand
Hall.
Admission charge.

**Pleasurewood Hills
American Theme Park**
Corton Road, Lowestoft, Suffolk
NR32 5DZ ☎ (0502) 513626/7
Number one theme park in East Anglia.

Fifty acres, over 40 rides, attractions
and a show on a one-price basis.
Admission charge.

The Thursford Collection
Thursford, Fakenham, Norfolk
NR21 0AS ☎ (032 877) 477
The world's greatest collection of steam
road locomotives, showmen's traction,
ploughing and barn engines. Nine
mechanical organs. Wurlitzer cinema
organ, various steam engines, 2 foot
gauge locomotive train.
Admission charge.

The Otter Trust
Earsham, Nr. Bungay, Suffolk
NR35 2AF ☎ (0986) 3470
A conservation organisation devoted to
the breeding of the British otter, an
endangered species, and the return of
these animals, after the relevant
research work, to a suitable habitat.
*Admission
charge.*

Paul Jones

MAKE A DATE FOR...

Whittlesey Straw Bear Festival
Whittlesey, Cambridgeshire
7 January

East Anglia Spring Antiques Fair
The Athenaeum, Angel Hill, Bury St.
Edmunds, Suffolk *2 — 4 March*

Norfolk Country Music Festival
St. Andrews Hall and Blackfriars Hall,
Norwich, Norfolk *2 — 12 March*

Mildenhall Air Fete
Royal Air Force Mildenhall, Mildenhall,
Suffolk *27 — 28 May*

NEVER, NEVER LAND

Suffolk Show
Suffolk Showground, Ipswich, Suffolk
31 May – 1 June

**Aldeburgh Festival of
Music and the Arts**
Snape Maltings, Snape, Aldeburgh,
Suffolk *9 – 25 June*

Essex County Show
Essex County Showground, Great
Leighs, Chelmsford, Essex
16 – 18 June

Royal Norfolk Show
The Showground, Dereham Road,
Norwich, Norfolk *28 – 29 June*

 ## Tourist Information

Tourist and leisure information can be obtained from Tourist Information Centres throughout England. Details of centres in the East Anglia region are listed below. The symbol 🛏 means that an accommodation booking service is provided. Centres marked with a ✷ are open during the summer months only. In the following pages, towns which have a Tourist Information Centre are indicated with the symbol 𝒊

Aldeburgh
Suffolk 🛏 ✷
The Cinema, High Street
☎ (072 885) 3637

Beccles
Suffolk 🛏 ✷
The Quay, Fen Lane
☎ (0502) 713196

Braintree
Essex ✷
Town Hall Centre, Market Square
☎ (0376) 43140

Bury St. Edmunds
Suffolk 🛏
6 Angel Hill
☎ (0284) 763233

Cambridge
Cambridgeshire 🛏
Wheeler Street
☎ (0223) 322640

Clacton-on-Sea
Essex
23 Pier Avenue
☎ (0225) 423400

Chelmsford
Essex 🛏
County Hall, Duke Street
☎ (0245) 492211

Colchester
Essex 🛏
1 Queen Street
☎ (0206) 712233

Cromer
Norfolk 🛏 ✷
Old Town Hall,
Prince of Wales Road
☎ (0263) 512497

Dedham
Essex 🛏 ✷
Countryside Centre, Duchy Barn
☎ Colchester (0206) 323447

Ely
Cambridgeshire 🛏
The Library, Palace Green
☎ (0353) 2062

Fakenham
Norfolk 🛏 ✷
Red Lion House, 37 Market Place
☎ (0328) 51981

Felixstowe
Suffolk
Felixstowe Leisure Centre,
Sea Front
☎ (0394) 282126

Great Dunmow
Essex 🛏
Council Offices, High Street
☎ (0371) 4533

Great Yarmouth
Norfolk
Publicity Department,
1 South Quay
☎ (0493) 846345

▶

Great Yarmouth continued
Marine Parade 🛏 *
☎ (0493) 842195

Hadleigh
Suffolk 🛏
Toppesfield Hall
☎ (0473) 822922

Harwich
Essex 🛏
Parkeston Quay, Parkeston
☎ (0255) 506139

Hoveton
Norfolk 🛏 *
Station Road
☎ Wroxham (060 53) 2281

Hunstanton
Norfolk 🛏
The Green
☎ (048 53) 2610

Huntingdon
Cambridgeshire 🛏
The Library, Princes Street
☎ (0480) 425831/425801

Ipswich
Suffolk 🛏
Town Hall, Princes Street
☎ (0473) 58070

King's Lynn
Norfolk 🛏
The Old Gaol House,
Saturday Market Place
☎ (0553) 763044

Lavenham
Suffolk 🛏
The Guildhall, Market Place
☎ (0787) 248207

Lowestoft
Suffolk 🛏
The Esplanade
☎ (0502) 565989

Maldon
Essex 🛏
Oakwood Arts Centre,
2 High Street
☎ (0621) 56503

Mundesley
Norfolk *
2a Station Road
☎ (0263) 721070

Norwich
Norfolk 🛏
Guildhall, Gaol Hill
☎ (0603) 666071

Peterborough
Cambridgeshire
Town Hall, Bridge Street 🛏
☎ (0733) 63141/317336
Reference Library, Broadway
☎ (0733) 48343/43146

Ranworth
Norfolk 🛏 *
The Staith
☎ (060 549) 453

Saffron Walden
Essex 🛏
Corn Exchange, Market Square
☎ (0799) 24282

Sheringham
Norfolk 🛏 *
Station Car Park
☎ (0263) 824329

Southend-on-Sea
Essex
Civic Centre, Victoria Avenue 🛏
☎ (0702) 355122
High Street Precinct 🛏
☎ (0702) 355120

Southwold
Suffolk 🛏 *
Town Hall
☎ (0502) 722366

Stowmarket
Suffolk 🛏
Wilkes Way
☎ (0449) 676800

Sudbury
Suffolk
Sudbury Library, Market Hill
☎ (0787) 72092

Thetford
Norfolk
Ancient House Museum,
21 White Hart Street
☎ (0842) 2599

Walsingham
Norfolk *
Shirehall Museum, Common Place
☎ (032 872) 510

Walton-on-the-Naze
Essex 🛏 *
Princess Esplanade
☎ Frinton-on-Sea (025 56) 5542

Wells-next-the-Sea
Norfolk 🛏 *
Wells Centre, Staithe Street
☎ (0328) 710885

Wisbech
Cambridgeshire 🛏
District Library, Ely Place
☎ (0945) 583263/64009

Entries in this regional section are listed in alphabetical order of place name, and then in alphabetical order of establishment. County names are not normally repeated in each establishment entry, but please use the full postal address when writing.

The map references refer to the colour maps towards the end of this guide. The first number is the number of the map, and it is followed by the grid reference.

The Crown Classifications are explained on pages 8 and 9, and the key to symbols is on the flap inside the back cover — keep it open for easy reference.

ABBERTON

Essex
Map ref 3B2

4m S. Colchester

The Maltings
♨

Mersea Rd., Abberton, Colchester. CO5 7NR
☎ Peldon (020 635) 780
Attractive period house with a wealth of beams and an open log fire, in walled garden with swimming pool.
Bedrooms: 1 single, 1 twin, 1 family room.
Bathrooms: 1 public.
Bed & breakfast: £10.50-£12.50 single, £21-£25 double.
Lunch available.
Parking for 8.
🐓 ⛱ 🗑 Ⓤ ℹ Ⓥ ⅋ 🏧 🅃Ⓥ Ⅲ ♨
➹ ✿ ✗ 🐴 🐎

ALDHAM

Essex
Map ref 3B2

1m NE. Hadleigh

Old House
Listed

Aldham, Colchester, CO6 3PH
☎ (0206) 240456
Bed and breakfast in 14th C. family home with friendly atmosphere, oak beams and large garden. Between Harwich and Cambridge, Felixstowe and London. On A604, 5 miles west of Colchester.
Bedrooms: 1 single, 1 double & 1 twin, 1 family room.
Bathrooms: 1 private, 2 public.
Bed & breakfast: £12-£16 single, £22.50-£27.50 double.
Parking for 8.
🐓 ⑩ 🗑 🏧 🅃Ⓥ Ⅲ ➹ ✿
🐴 🐎

ARDLEIGH

Essex
Map ref 3B2

5m NE. Colchester

Bovills Hall ♨
👄👄

Station Rd., Ardleigh, Colchester, CO7 7RT
☎ Colchester (0206) 230217
Small manor house with a wealth of exposed beams, on edge of Dedham Vale.
Bedrooms: 1 double & 1 twin, 1 family room.
Bathrooms: 1 private, 1 public.
Bed & breakfast: £15-£20 single, £25-£30 double.
Parking for 6.
Open February-November.
✗ 🐴 🐎

Dundas Place ♨
Listed

Colchester Rd., Ardleigh, Colchester, CO7 7NP
☎ Colchester (0206) 230625
300-year-old cottage with exposed oak beams throughout, a large open fireplace and a picturesque old world garden. Located in the centre of the village. 4 night bed and breakfast package - £90, including use of Ordnance Survey maps and local information pack.
Bedrooms: 2 twin.
Bathrooms: 1 public.
Bed & breakfast: £15 single, £24 double.
Parking for 2.
🐓 2 🗑 🏧 Ⓤ Ⓥ ⅋ 🅃Ⓥ Ⅲ 🐴
🐎

MAP REFERENCES APPLY TO COLOUR MAPS NEAR THE BACK OF THE GUIDE.

ATTLEBOROUGH

Norfolk
Map ref 3B1

Swangey Farm

Swangey Lane, Attleborough, Norfolk NR17 1XL
☎ (0953) 455093
5-acre mixed farm. 230-year-old farmhouse in 5 acres, bounded by stream; fishing lake adjacent. Beamed bedrooms. 2 miles from A11.
Bedrooms: 1 single & 1 twin.
Bathrooms: 1 public.
Bed & breakfast: £20 double.
Half board: £15 daily, £100 weekly.
Evening meal 6pm (l.o. 9pm).
Parking for 6.
🐓 ⛱ 🗑 Ⓤ ℹ Ⓥ ⅋ 🅃Ⓥ Ⅲ
➹ ✿ ✗ 🐴 🐎

AYLSHAM

Norfolk
Map ref 3B1

See also Reepham.
Small town on the River Bure with an attractive market-place, interesting church and several fine houses. Nearby is Blickling Hall (National Trust).

Manor Farm
👄👄

Colby, Aylsham, NR11 7EE
☎ (0263) 761233
150-acre arable farm. Secluded 18th C. farmhouse. Georgian front with flint courtyard at rear, set in 150 acres of private land. Facilities for walking and fishing.
Bedrooms: 1 double & 1 twin, 1 family room.
Bathrooms: 3 private.
Bed & breakfast: from £25 double.
Open April-October.
🐓 🗑 🏧 🅃Ⓥ Ⅲ ➹ ⓤ
✈ ⚫ ✿ ✗ 🐴

BABRAHAM

Cambridgeshire
Map ref 2D1

7m SE. Cambridge

Worsted Barrows Guest House

Babraham, Cambridge, CB2 4AX
☎ (0223) 833298
Small country house close to Cambridge and Newmarket, 4 miles from the M11.

Bedrooms: 1 single, 2 double & 1 twin, 1 family room.
Bathrooms: 1 private, 2 public.
Bed & breakfast: £11-£13.50 single, £24-£26 double.
Evening meal 6.30pm (l.o. 8.30pm).
Parking for 8.
🐓 ⛱ 🗑 Ⓤ ℹ Ⓥ ⅋ 🅃Ⓥ Ⅲ
➹ ✿ ✗ 🐴

BADLEY

Suffolk
Map ref 3B2

2m SE. Stowmarket

Mill House

Badley, Ipswich, IP6 8RR
☎ Needham Market (0449) 720154
16th C. farmhouse of traditional Suffolk design, midway between Stowmarket and Needham Market on the B1113 in the heart of Gipping Valley.
Bedrooms: 1 single, 2 twin, 1 family room.
Bathrooms: 2 public.
Bed & breakfast: from £12.50 single, from £25 double.
Half board: £17-£19 daily, £110-£124 weekly.
Evening meal 6pm.
Parking for 6.
🐓 5 🗑 🏧 ℹ Ⓥ ⅋ ⅋ ➹
✿ ✗ 🐴 🐎

BARTON

Cambridgeshire
Map ref 2D1

3m SW. Cambridge

King's Tithe
Listed

13a Comberton Rd., Barton, Cambridge, CB3 7BA
☎ (0223) 263610
Private house with 2 bedrooms with adjacent bathroom and toilet. Good bar food at village pub approximately 300 yards from house. Will provide evening meal only when pub is closed.
Bedrooms: 2 twin.
Bathrooms: 1 public.
Bed & breakfast: £12-£15 single, £24-£26 double.
Evening meal 6.30pm (l.o. 3pm).
Parking for 3.
🐓 8 ⑩ 🗑 🏧 Ⓤ ℹ ➹ ✗
🐴

THE SYMBOLS ARE EXPLAINED ON THE FLAP INSIDE THE BACK COVER.

BECCLES

Suffolk
Map ref 3C1

See also Burgh St. Peter.
Fire destroyed the town in
the 16th C and it was
rebuilt in Georgian red
brick. The River Waveney
on which the town stands
is popular with boating
enthusiasts and has an
annual regatta. ⓩ

Corner Farmhouse
Ringsfield Rd., Ilketshall St.
Andrew, Beccles, NR34 8NR
☎ (098 681) 380
*108-acre mixed farm.
Modernised farmhouse in a
quiet village, with beams and
inglenook fireplace. Small
garden, home country cooking.*
Bedrooms: 2 double, 1 family
room.
Bathrooms: 1 private,
1 public.
Bed & breakfast: £9-£10.50
single, £18-£21 double.
Half board: £13-£14 daily,
£73.50-£83.50 weekly.
Lunch available.
Evening meal 6pm (l.o. 8pm).
Parking for 4.
🐾 🐕 🖤 🗒 🛉 Ⓥ 🛏 TV IIII
🖿 ♨ 🕯

The Swan
Loddon Rd., Gillingham,
Beccles, NR34 0LD
☎ (0502) 712055
*Small family-run motel
offering chalet-type
accommodation in 5 acres of
grounds. Close to Norfolk
Broads and historic town.*
Bedrooms: 3 double & 1 twin,
3 family rooms.
Bathrooms: 7 private.
Bed & breakfast: £14-£16
single, £28-£32 double.
Half board: £18-£20 daily.
Lunch available.
Evening meal 7pm (l.o.
9.30pm).
Parking for 50.
Credit: Access, Visa.
🐾5 �& 📞 🖪 🖵 🖤 IIII 💃 🕯
🕯 DAP

BEYTON

Suffolk
Map ref 3B2

Dibolds
Thurston Rd., Beyton, Bury
St. Edmunds, IP30 9AE
☎ (0359) 70467
*17th C. thatched cottage close
to village green. Convenient for
the A45.*
Bedrooms: 2 double.
Bathrooms: 2 private.
Bed & breakfast: £20 double.

Half board: £17 daily.
Evening meal 7.30pm (l.o.
4pm).
Parking for 2.
UL 🛏 TV ☲ IIII 🖿 🕯

BILDESTON

Suffolk
Map ref 3B2

6m NW. Hadleigh

The Crown Hotel ⋒
104 High St., Bildeston,
IP7 7EB
☎ (0449) 740510
*Small 15th C. building,
originally a wool merchant's
house, with a wealth of beams
and fireplaces. Bars,
restaurants, and function hall.*
Bedrooms: 2 double & 5 twin,
2 family rooms.
Bathrooms: 5 private,
2 public.
Bed & breakfast: £20-£30
single, £30-£50 double.
Lunch available.
Evening meal 7pm (l.o.
9.30pm).
Parking for 30.
Credit: Visa, Amex.
🐾 🐕 🖤 🛉 Ⓥ 🛏 TV IIII 💃 🍴
🖑 🅿 ♨ 🕯 🕯 SP 🎠

BLAKENEY

Norfolk
Map ref 3B1

5M NW. Holt
Picturesque village on the
north coast of Norfolk
and a former port and
fishing village. The 15th C
red bricked Guildhall
stands on a brick-vaulted
undercroft. Marshy
creeks which extend
towards Blakeney Point
are a paradise for
naturalists.

Bramble Lodge
3 Morston Rd., Blakeney,
Holt, NR25 7PF
☎ (0263) 740191
*Bramble Lodge has ample
parking and is close to quay
and shops.*
Bedrooms: 2 double & 1 twin.
Bathrooms: 2 private,
1 public.
Bed & breakfast: max. £15
single, £23-£25 double.
Half board: £17.50-£18.50
daily, max. £120 weekly.
Evening meal 7pm.
Parking for 6.
🐾 🖵 🖤 IIII 🖋 🛏 TV IIII 💃
♨ 🕯 🖑 SP

BLAXHALL

Suffolk
Map ref 3C2

4m S. Saxmundham
Unspoilt village
immortalised in the
writings on country lore
of George Ewart Evans.
Sheep used to graze on
the former common lands
beside the River Alde and
smuggling was popular.

The Forge
Church Rd., Blaxhall,
Woodbridge, IP12 2DH
☎ Snape (072 888) 346
*7-acre smallholding. Guests
occupy one end of this house,
set in beautiful countryside
near Snape Maltings. Central
for walking, golf, sailing,
birdwatching and the beach.
Choice of evening meal
available.*
Bedrooms: 1 double & 1 twin.
Bathrooms: 1 public.
Bed & breakfast: £12-£15
single, £22-£26 double.
Half board: £19.50-£22.50
daily, £112-£130 weekly.
Evening meal 7pm (l.o. 8pm).
Parking for 3.
🐾 🐕 🖤 UL 🛉 Ⓥ 🛏 IIII 💃
♨ 🕯 DAP SP

BRAINTREE

Essex
Map ref 3B2

See also Halstead.
On the old Roman road
from St. Albans to
Colchester. Textiles have
brought prosperity to the
town, first in woollen cloth
and then silk-weaving
started by the Courtauld
family. ⓩ

Corkers
Shalford Green, Braintree,
CM7 5AZ
☎ Great Dunmow
(0371) 850376
*Two 16th C., original farm
cottages, tastefully converted.
Lathe and plaster with oak
beams. Half a mile from
Shalford.*
Bedrooms: 2 single, 1 double.
Bathrooms: 1 public.
Bed & breakfast: £12 single,
£24 double.
Parking for 3.
🖤 UL 🛉 Ⓥ TV IIII 💃 ♨ 🕯
🕯

The Old House ⋒

11 Bradford St., Braintree,
CM7 6AS
☎ (0376) 25430
*16th C. timber-framed house
with a wealth of exposed
beams, giving a warm homely
atmosphere. Set in half an acre
of secluded gardens.*
Bedrooms: 2 double.
Bathrooms: 1 public.
Bed & breakfast: £16.50-£19
single, £30-£35 double.
Half board: £24-£26.50 daily,
£142-£158 weekly.
Evening meal 7.30pm (l.o.
8.30pm).
Parking for 8.
Open January-November.
🐾 🖪 🖤 🖵 🛉 UL 🛉 🖋 🛏 TV
IIII 💃 ♨ 🕯 🕯 DAP SP 🎠

BRAMERTON

Norfolk
Map ref 3C1

5m SE. Norwich

Rolling Acre
Wood's End, Bramerton,
Norwich, NR14 7ED
☎ Surlingham (050 88) 529
*Happy family home built in
Victorian times, very quiet with
pretty views. 2 minutes' walk
from picturesque stretch of
River Yare and 5 miles from
Norwich.*
Bedrooms: 1 family room.
Bathrooms: 1 private.
Bed & breakfast: £26 double.
Parking for 2.
🐾5 🚣 🖪 🖵 🖤 UL IIII 💃 ♨
🕯

BRECKLES

Norfolk
Map ref 3B1

5m SE. Watton

Church Cottage ⋒

Breckles, Attleborough,
NR17 1EW
☎ Great Hockham
(095 382) 286
*18th C. home with large
garden in Breckland. Own
produce, home cooking. 40
miles from all coastal resorts
between Hunstanton and
Southwold. Evening meals by
arrangement.*
Bedrooms: 1 single, 2 double
& 1 twin.
Bathrooms: 1 public.
Bed & breakfast: £12.50-£13
single, £25-£26 double.
Half board: £20-£21 daily,
£140-£147 weekly.

**WE ADVISE YOU TO CONFIRM YOUR BOOKING
IN WRITING.**

Evening meal 7pm (l.o. midday).
Parking for 10.

[symbols]

BUCKLESHAM

Suffolk
Map ref 3B2

The White House

Bucklesham, Nr. Ipswich,
IP10 0DR
☎ Nacton (047 388) 325
Private country farmhouse in quiet village. Garden produce, home-made bread. 10 minutes from Orwell Bridge and Felixstowe. Non-smokers only.
Bedrooms: 1 single, 2 twin, 1 family room.
Bathrooms: 1 private, 2 public.
Bed & breakfast: £10.50-£11.50 single, £20-£23 double.
Half board: £17-£18 daily.
Evening meal 6.30pm (l.o. 8pm).
Parking for 8.

[symbols]

BULPHAN

Essex
Map ref 3B3

5m SW. Basildon

Bonny Downs Farm

Listed
Doesgate Lane, Bulphan,
RM14 3TB
☎ Basildon (0268) 42129
60-acre mixed farm. Large comfortable farmhouse conveniently placed for all road links.
Bedrooms: 2 twin, 1 family room.
Bathrooms: 1 private, 1 public.
Bed & breakfast: £12-£15 single, £24 double.
Half board: £17-£20 daily, £119-£140 weekly.
Evening meal 6pm (l.o. 8pm).
Parking for 4.

[symbols]

BUNGAY

Suffolk
Map ref 3C1

14m SE. Wymondham
Market town and yachting centre on the River Waveney with the remains of a great 12th C castle. In the market place stands the Butter Cross erected in 1689 after being largely destroyed by fire.

Abbots Manor

Listed
Old Bungay Rd., Kirby Cane, Bungay, NR35 2HP
☎ Kirby Cane (050 845) 703
Thatched Jacobean farmhouse in secluded rural setting commanding excellent views across the Waveney Valley. Friendly family atmosphere.
Bedrooms: 1 double & 1 twin.
Bathrooms: 2 public.
Bed & breakfast: max. £9.50 single, max. £19 double.
Parking for 4.

[symbols]

BURGH ST. PETER

Norfolk
Map ref 3C1

3m SE. Haddiscoe
Church with unusually narrow thatched nave and 16th C tower overlooking Oulton Broad.

Shrublands Farm

😄😄
Burgh St. Peter, Nr. Beccles,
Suffolk NR34 0BB
☎ Aldeby (050 277) 241
480-acre mixed farm. Working family farm offering home-cooked English breakfast. Coarse fishing facilities free on the River Waveney. Meals available at the nearby River Centre.
Bedrooms: 1 double & 1 twin, 1 family room.
Bathrooms: 2 public.
Bed & breakfast: £10.50-£11.50 single, £21-£23 double.
Parking for 6.

[symbols]

BURY ST. EDMUNDS

Suffolk
Map ref 3B2

23m NW. Ipswich
Ancient market and cathedral town which takes its name from the martyred Saxon King, St. Edmund. Bury has many fine buildings including the Athenaeum and Moyses Hall, claimed to be the oldest Norman house in the county. ⓘ

The Grange Farmhouse

😄😄
Beyton, Bury St. Edmunds,
IP30 9AG
☎ (0359) 70184
6-acre horse farm. Traditional 18th C. Suffolk farmhouse in an attractive mature garden and meadow setting. 4 miles from Bury St. Edmunds.
Bedrooms: 1 double & 2 twin.
Bathrooms: 1 private, 1 public.
Bed & breakfast: £12.50-£15 single, £25-£30 double.
Evening meal 7pm (l.o. 4pm).
Parking for 10.

[symbols]

Hamilton House

4 Nelson Rd., Bury St. Edmunds
☎ (0284) 702201
Refurbished Victorian house, 2 minutes' walk from town centre. On-street parking. Guests' lounge and breakfast room.
Bedrooms: 2 single, 1 twin, 1 family room.
Bathrooms: 2 private, 2 public.
Bed & breakfast: £12-£15 single, £28-£32 double.

[symbols]

> **INDIVIDUAL PROPRIETORS HAVE SUPPLIED ALL DETAILS OF ACCOMMODATION. ALTHOUGH WE DO CHECK FOR ACCURACY, WE ADVISE YOU TO CONFIRM PRICES AND OTHER INFORMATION AT THE TIME OF BOOKING.**

CAMBRIDGE

Cambridgeshire
Map ref 2D1

A most important and beautiful city on the River Cam with 31 colleges forming one of the oldest universities in the world. Numerous museums, good shopping centre, restaurants, theatres, cinema and fine bookshops. ⓘ

Carlton Lodge ⋒

Listed
245 Chesterton Rd.,
Cambridge CB4 1AS
☎ (0223) 67792
Small family-run business within a minute's walking distance from the city centre.
Bedrooms: 1 double & 1 twin, 1 family room.
Bathrooms: 3 private, 1 public.
Bed & breakfast: £14-£20 single, £28-£32 double.
Parking for 6.

[symbols]

Cristinas ⋒

😄😄😄
47 St. Andrews Rd.,
Cambridge, CB4 1DL
☎ (0223) 65855
Small family-run business in quiet location 15 minutes' walking distance from city centre and colleges.
Bedrooms: 1 twin, 2 family rooms.
Bathrooms: 2 private, 1 public.
Bed & breakfast: £14-£20 single, £26-£30 double.
Parking for 3.

[symbols]

Dresden Villa Guest House

😄😄😄
34 Cherry Hinton Rd.,
Cambridge, CB1 4AA
☎ (0223) 247539
Friendly family guesthouse near the railway station, within easy reach of the city centre.
Bedrooms: 2 single, 2 double & 2 twin, 2 family rooms.
Bathrooms: 3 private, 2 public; 1 private shower.
Bed & breakfast: £16 single, £26-£30 double.
Half board: £23 daily, £161 weekly.
Evening meal 7pm (l.o. 8pm).
Parking for 8.

[symbols]

> **GROUPS, CONSORTIA AND AGENCIES SPECIALISING IN FARM AND COUNTRY HOLIDAYS ARE LISTED IN A SPECIAL SECTION OF THIS GUIDE.**

CAMBRIDGE
Continued

Lyndewode Lodge
Listed
2 Lyndewode Rd.,
Cambridge, CB1 2HL
☎ (0223) 356161
Central Cambridge, within walking distance of the principal colleges, city centre and railway station. Close to bus routes, restaurants and shops.
Bedrooms: 2 single, 2 double & 4 twin, 1 family room.
Bathrooms: 4 public.
Bed & breakfast: £15-£16 single, £24-£25 double.
Parking for 5.
≿ 🛁 ♥ ☐ ☪ ▥ ▥ ♨ 爾

Number Eleven M
Listed
11 Glisson Rd., Cambridge,
CB1 2HA
☎ (0223) 311890
Breakfast in charming rooms in a fine, 19th C., university town house, close to the colleges and city centre.
Bedrooms: 1 double & 1 twin, 1 family room.
Bathrooms: 1 private, 1 public.
Bed & breakfast: £20-£22 single, £28-£32 double.
Evening meal 7pm (l.o. 8.30pm).
≿ ® ☐ ♥ ▥ 🛉 Ⓥ ♨ 爾
OAP SP T

The Old Rectory
Swaffham Bulbeck,
Cambridge, CB5 0LX
☎ (0223) 811986
Former Georgian vicarage set in own grounds. Located 6 miles from Cambridge and 4 miles from Newmarket.
Bedrooms: 1 single, 2 double & 1 twin.
Bathrooms: 1 private, 2 public; 2 private showers.
Bed & breakfast: £11.50-£14.50 single, £25-£40 double.
Half board: £18-£21 daily, £110-£130 weekly.
Evening meal 7.30pm (l.o. 9.30pm).
Parking for 20.
≿ ▥ 🛉 Ⓥ ⤬ ♨ ☎ ▥ ♨
🛉 ♠ ⤬ ♪ ❄ ✗ 爾 爾

Mrs. S. Hofford
15 St. Margarets Rd., Girton,
Cambridge, CB3 0LT
☎ Cambridge (0223) 276097
In a quiet residential area adjacent to Girton College, 5 minutes by car from Cambridge city centre.
Bedrooms: 2 single, 1 twin.

Bathrooms: 1 private, 3 public.
Bed & breakfast: £12-£15 single, £24-£30 double.
Parking for 6.
≿ ▥ ▥ 爾

St. Mark's Vicarage
Barton Rd., Cambridge,
CB3 9JZ
☎ (0223) 63339
Victorian vicarage with pleasant garden, a short walk from central Cambridge. Cycles available for guests' use. Near the M11 junction 12.
Bedrooms: 1 single, 1 twin, 1 family room.
Bathrooms: 1 public.
Bed & breakfast: £13-£14 single, £24-£26 double.
Parking for 3.
≿ ☐ ♥ ▥ 🛉 Ⓥ ♨ ▥ ▥
♠ ❄ ✗ 爾

Segovia Lodge
😑😑😑
2 Barton Rd., Newnham,
Cambridge, CB3 9JZ
☎ (0223) 354105
Within walking distance of the city centre and colleges. Next to cricket and tennis fields. Warm welcome and personal service.
Bedrooms: 1 twin, 1 family room.
Bathrooms: 1 private, 1 public; 1 private shower.
Bed & breakfast: £12-£15 single, £24-£30 double.
Parking for 4.
≿ ☐ ♥ ▥ 🛉 ♨ Ⓥ ♨ ●
▥ ♠ ✗ 爾

The Willows
102 High St., Landbeach,
CB4 4DT
☎ (0223) 860332
250-acre arable farm. Georgian house with friendly atmosphere. 2 rooms for up to 6 persons. 3 miles from Cambridge.
Bedrooms: 1 twin, 1 family room.
Bathrooms: 1 public.
Bed & breakfast: £12.50-£14 single, £25-£28 double.
Parking for 4.
≿ ♥ ▥ ⤬ ♨ ▥ ♠ 爾 爾

THERE IS A SPECIAL
SECTION IN THIS
GUIDE LISTING
ACCOMMODATION
ESPECIALLY
SUITABLE FOR
GROUPS AND
YOUNG PEOPLE.

CASTLE HEDINGHAM
Essex
Map ref 3B2

4m NW. Halstead

The Old School House M
😑😑😑
St. James St., Castle
Hedingham, CO9 3EW
☎ Hedingham (0787) 61370
Once the village school, in a lovely walled garden. In the main street with the castle 5 minutes' walk away.
Bedrooms: 1 single, 1 double & 1 twin.
Bathrooms: 2 private, 1 public.
Bed & breakfast: £15-£22.50 single, £30-£37 double.
Parking for 3.
® ♥ ▥ ⤬ ♨ ▥ ♠ ❄ ✗
爾 爾

The Pottery
St. James St., Castle
Hedingham, Nr. Halstead,
C09 3EW
☎ (0787) 60036
Comfortable late-Georgian house in medieval village with Norman castle. No smoking. Working pottery behind house with day courses available.
Bedrooms: 1 double & 1 twin.
Bathrooms: 1 public.
Bed & breakfast: £13.50-£14.50 single, £23-£25 double.
Parking for 5.
♥ ▥ Ⓥ ⤬ ▥ ♠ ✗ 爾

CAVENDISH
Suffolk
Map ref 3B2

4m W. Long Melford
One of the most picturesque villages in East Anglia, with a number of pretty thatched timber-framed and colour-washed cottages grouped around a large green.

George Inn
😑
The Green, Cavendish,
Sudbury, CO10 8BA
☎ Glemsford (0787) 280248
A 15th C. inn in picturesque Suffolk village, adjacent to green.
Bedrooms: 2 double & 1 twin.
Bathrooms: 1 public; 1 private shower.
Bed & breakfast: max. £13 single, max. £26 double.
Half board: £18.95-£21.95 daily.

Lunch available.
Evening meal 7pm (l.o. 9.30pm).
Parking for 8.
≿ 5 ☐ 🛉 ▥ ✗ 爾 SP 爾

CHATTERIS
Cambridgeshire
Map ref 3A2

7m S. March

Guest House De Klomp
😑
39 London Rd., Chatteris,
PE16 6AS
☎ (035 43) 2136
150 - 200-year-old Georgian house with oak beams and inglenook fireplaces. A quarter of a mile from Chatteris town centre.
Bedrooms: 1 double & 2 twin, 1 family room.
Bathrooms: 2 public.
Bed & breakfast: max. £24 double.
Half board: max. £15 daily, max. £87.50 weekly.
Evening meal 6pm.
Parking for 4.
≿ ® ♥ ▥ 🛉 Ⓥ ♨ ▥ ▥
♠ ✗ 爾 爾

CHEDISTON
Suffolk
Map ref 3C2

3m W. Halesworth

Saskiavill M
😑😑
Chediston, Halesworth,
IP19 0AR
☎ Halesworth (098 67) 3067
Travelling west from Halesworth on the B1123, turn right after 2 miles at the signpost for Chediston Green. After crossing the hump-backed bridge over the stream, we are the fourth property on the left.
Bedrooms: 2 double & 2 twin, 1 family room.
Bathrooms: 2 private, 2 public.
Bed & breakfast: £9.50-£11.50 single, £19-£23 double.
Half board: £11-£14.50 daily, £75-£90 weekly.
Evening meal 6.30pm.
Parking for 8.
≿ 3 🛁 ♥ ▥ 🛉 ♨ ▥ ♠
♣ ❄ ✗ 爾 OAP SP

MAP REFERENCES
APPLY TO COLOUR
MAPS NEAR THE
BACK OF THE GUIDE.

CHELMSFORD

Essex
Map ref 3B3

The county town of Essex, situated in the heart of heavily cultivated farmland with an important livestock market. Growth of the town's industry can be traced in the excellent Museum in Oaklands Park. ℹ

Beechcroft Private Hotel
😁 😁

211 New London Rd., Chelmsford, CM2 0AJ
☎ (0245) 352462
A central hotel offering clean and comfortable accommodation with friendly service. Under family ownership and management.
Bedrooms: 15 single, 3 double & 3 twin, 2 family rooms.
Bathrooms: 2 private, 5 public.
Bed & breakfast: £20.45 single, £32.75 double.
Parking for 15.

CLARE

Suffolk
Map ref 3B2

7m NW. Sudbury
Attractive village with many of the houses displaying pargetting work and the site of a castle first mentioned in 1090. Clare Country Park occupies the site of the castle bailey and old railway station.

Bachelor's Hall
Listed

Hundon, Clare CO10 8DY
☎ Hundon (044 086) 236
Small family-run country house set in large garden. In quiet rural position half a mile from the nearest village. Padder tennis available.
Bedrooms: 1 single, 1 double & 1 twin.
Bathrooms: 1 public.
Bed & breakfast: £12-£15 single, £24-£30 double.
Parking for 10.

Mr. T. Bell
Listed

37 Bridewell St., Clare, Sudbury, CO10 8QD
☎ (0787) 277538

Charming, early Georgian grade II listed village house with antique furniture. Comfortable family atmosphere, home cooking.
Bedrooms: 1 double & 1 twin.
Bathrooms: 1 public.
Bed & breakfast: £10-£15 single, £20 double.
Half board: £16.50 daily, £112.50 weekly.
Evening meal 7pm (l.o. 6pm).

COCKFIELD

Suffolk
Map ref 3B2

Crauford House

Howe Lane, Cockfield, IP30 0HA
☎ Bury St Edmunds (0284) 828216
Self-contained ground floor unit overlooking pleasant countryside. Lavenham 4 miles, Bury St. Edmunds 7 miles.
Bedrooms: 1 single, 1 double & 1 twin.
Bathrooms: 1 private, 1 public.
Bed & breakfast: £11 single, £20 double.
Parking for 5.

COLCHESTER

Essex
Map ref 3B2

Britain's oldest recorded town standing on the River Colne and famous for its oysters. Numerous historic buildings, ancient remains and museums. Plenty of parks and gardens, extensive shopping centre, theatre and zoo. ℹ

Mrs. C. Claydon
😁

66 Abbots Rd., Colchester, CO2 8BG
☎ (0206) 579822
Modern, detached family home with a large garden. Near coast and nature reserves, 3 miles from town centre.
Bedrooms: 1 twin, 1 family room.
Bathrooms: 1 public.
Bed & breakfast: £12-£15 single, £22-£28 double.
Parking for 5.

The Old Manse ♨
😁 😁

15 Roman Rd., Colchester, CO1 1UR
☎ (0206) 45154
Victorian family house in a quiet square beside the castle park. 3 minutes' walk from town centre. Roman wall in the garden. No smoking.
Bedrooms: 1 single, 2 twin, 1 family room.
Bathrooms: 2 public.
Bed & breakfast: £12-£18 single, £20-£25 double.
Parking for 2.

Scheregate Hotel ♨
😁

36 Osborne St., Colchester, CO2 7DP
☎ (0206) 573034
Interesting 15th C. building, centrally situated, providing accommodation at moderate prices.
Bedrooms: 14 single, 10 twin, 1 family room.
Bathrooms: 4 public.
Bed & breakfast: £10-£13 single, £20-£24 double.
Parking for 30.

CROMER

Norfolk
Map ref 3C1

Once a small fishing village and now a delightful resort with sandy beaches and excellent bathing, fringed by cliffs. The narrow streets of old Cromer encircle the church of SS. Peter and Paul which has a splendid tower. ℹ

The Grove Guest House ♨
😁 😁

95 Overstrand Rd., Cromer, NR27 0DJ
☎ (0263) 512412
Georgian holiday home in 3 acres, with beautiful walks through fields and woods to the cliffs and beach.
Bedrooms: 2 single, 4 double & 2 twin, 3 family rooms.
Bathrooms: 1 private, 3 public; 4 private showers.
Bed & breakfast: £11.50-£14.50 single, £23-£29 double.
Half board: £17-£20 daily, £110-£130 weekly.

Evening meal 6.30pm (l.o. 6.30pm).
Parking for 15.
Open March-October.

DARSHAM

Suffolk
Map ref 3C2

2m NE. Oxford

Priory Farm
Listed

Darsham, Saxmundham, IP17 3QD
☎ Yoxford (072 877) 459
200-acre mixed farm. Comfortable, 17th C. farmhouse on working family farm with farm trail. Own produce. Three miles from heritage coast.
Bedrooms: 1 double & 1 twin.
Bathrooms: 1 public.
Bed & breakfast: £10-£15 single, £20-£25 double.
Half board: £14.95-£17.45 daily, £100-£122.15 weekly.
Parking for 10.
Open April-October.

DEPDEN

Suffolk
Map ref 3B2

6m SW. Bury

Elms Farm
😁 😁

Depden, Bury St. Edmunds, IP29 4BS
☎ Chevington (0284) 850289
350-acre mixed farm. 17th C. farmhouse, located at the highest point in Suffolk.
Bedrooms: 1 single, 1 double, 1 family room.
Bathrooms: 1 public.
Bed & breakfast: £12-£14 single, £25-£28 double.
Parking for 10.

GROUPS, CONSORTIA AND AGENCIES SPECIALISING IN FARM AND COUNTRY HOLIDAYS ARE LISTED IN A SPECIAL SECTION OF THIS GUIDE.

DEREHAM

Norfolk
Map ref 3B1

16m W. Norwich
East Dereham is famous for its associations with the poet William Cowper and also Bishop Bonner, chaplain to Cardinal Wolsey. His home is now an archaeological museum. Round the charming market place are many notable buildings.

Clinton House
Well Hill, Clint Green, Yaxham, Dereham, NR19 1RX
☎ (0362) 692079
Very pretty white house in one acre of grounds. It is approximately 200 years old, with an open brick fireplace and oak beams.
Bedrooms: 1 single, 2 double & 1 twin, 1 family room.
Bathrooms: 2 public.
Bed & breakfast: £10.50-£12.50 single, £19-£24 double.
Parking for 6.
🌄 🗙 ❄ 🖽 🛉 Ⓥ 🖾 ⊙ 🎺 💷
🛳 ❄ 🗓 🔖 💷

DISS

Norfolk
Map ref 3B2

See also Garboldisham, Gissing, South Lopham.
An old market town which has been modernised. However, interesting Tudor, Georgian and Victorian buildings around the Market Place remain. St Mary's Church has a fine knapped flint chancel.

Strenneth Farmhouse ₼
😄😄😄
Old Airfield Rd., Fersfield, Nr. Diss, IP22 2BP
☎ Bressingham
(037 988) 8182
Fully-renovated period farmhouse with oak beams and log fires, in quiet countryside with many local places of interest to visit. Chauffeured Anglian discovery tours available.
Bedrooms: 1 single, 1 double & 1 twin, 2 family rooms.
Bathrooms: 2 private, 1 public.
Bed & breakfast: £11-£15 single, £22-£30 double.
Half board: £18-£22 daily, £119-£147 weekly.

Evening meal 6.30pm (l.o. 9pm).
Parking for 6.
🌄 🖾 ❄ 🖽 🛉 Ⓥ ⅄ 🔫 ⊙ 💷
🛳 ❄ 🗓 🔖 💷 🎺

The Sun Inn ₼
😄
43 Mere St., Diss, IP22 3AG
☎ (0379) 651076
One of the oldest pubs in Diss, which is an old market town, overlooking the Mere.
Bedrooms: 2 single, 3 double & 1 twin.
Bathrooms: 6 private.
Bed & breakfast: £20-£28 single, £29.50-£37.50 double.
Half board: £25-£29.50 daily, £140-£170 weekly.
Lunch available.
Evening meal 6.30pm (l.o. 10.30pm).
Parking for 6.
Credit: Access, Visa, Diners, Amex.
🌄 📞 🖼 🖵 ❄ 🛉 Ⓥ 💷 🛳
🗲 🗙 🗓 🔖 💷 🎺

DOCKING

Norfolk
Map ref 3B1

11m NW. Fakenham
Conservation village still retaining village stocks, lock-up, blacksmith's forge and ponds. Well situated for the north Norfolk coast 5 miles away.

Holland House
😄😄
Chequers St., Docking, King's Lynn, PE31 8LH
☎ (048 58) 295
Charming, Georgian house with spacious rooms and a delightful garden.
Bedrooms: 2 single, 1 double & 2 twin.
Bathrooms: 3 public.
Bed & breakfast: £11-£13 single, £22-£26 double.
Parking for 8.
🌄 🗓 ❄ 🖽 🔫 ⊙ 💷 🎺 🎺

North Farmhouse
Station Rd., Docking, King's Lynn, PE31 8LS
☎ (048 58) 493
Attractive flint and brick farmhouse in conservation area, within easy reach of Sandringham. 5 miles from bird reserves, Burnham Market and sandy beaches.
Bedrooms: 4 double.
Bathrooms: 3 private, 2 public.
Bed & breakfast: £12-£15 single, £20-£25 double.
Half board: £17.50-£20 daily, £100-£120 weekly.

Evening meal 7.30pm (l.o. 10am).
Parking for 10.
🌄 🖾 ❄ 🖽 Ⓥ 🖾 💷 🛳 🗲 ❄
🗓 ⒹⒶⓅ

DOWNHAM MARKET

Norfolk
Map ref 3B1

10m S. King's Lynn
Market town above the surrounding Fens on the River Ouse and 12 miles from King's Lynn.

Greybridge House
Nordelph, Downham Market, PE38 0BL
☎ (036 68) 263
Comfortable bedrooms in riverside home. Full facilities, fishing, boating, birdwatching. Convenient for coast, Sandringham, 4 miles from Downham Market.
Bedrooms: 1 double & 1 twin.
Bathrooms: 2 private.
Bed & breakfast: £11-£12.50 single, £22-£25 double.
Half board: £16-£17.50 daily, £101.80-£110.25 weekly.
Evening meal 6pm (l.o. 7.30pm).
Parking for 4.
🌄 🗲 ❄ 🖽 🛉 Ⓥ ⅄ ⊙ 💷
🛳 🗲 🗓 ⒹⒶⓅ 🔖

Park House
74 London Rd., Downham Market, PE38 9AT
☎ (0366) 387035
Old farmhouse, 5 minutes' walk from the centre of town. On the B1507, which was the A10, near the police station.
Bedrooms: 1 double, 2 family rooms.
Bathrooms: 1 public.
Bed & breakfast: from £10 single, from £20 double.
Half board: from £15 daily, from £105 weekly.
Evening meal 6pm (l.o. 6.30pm).
Parking for 6.
🌄 🖽 🛉 🔫 ⊙ 💷 🛳 🗓

DRINKSTONE GREEN

Suffolk
Map ref 3B2

6m NW. Stowmarket

Grovebury
Rattlesden Rd., Drinkstone Green, Bury St. Edmunds, IP30 9TL
☎ Rattlesden (044 93) 683
A pleasant village location offering home cooking and home-baked bread.
Bedrooms: 1 single, 2 double.

Bathrooms: 2 public.
Bed & breakfast: £10 single, £20 double.
Parking for 3.
🖾 🖽 🛉 🔫 ⊙ 💷 🛳 ❄ 🎇

DRY DRAYTON

Cambridgeshire
Map ref 2D1

5m NW. Cambridge

Arden House
😄
4 Pettitts Close, Dry Drayton, Cambridge, CB3 8DQ
☎ Crafts Hill (0954) 80975
Comfortable, modern detached house in quiet village, 5 miles from historic Cambridge. Easy access from all major roads. Packed lunch on request.
Bedrooms: 1 single, 1 double & 1 twin.
Bathrooms: 1 public; 2 private showers.
Bed & breakfast: £11-£13 single, £22-£26 double.
Half board: £17.50-£19.50 daily, £116-£129 weekly.
Evening meal 7pm.
Parking for 2.
🌄 🖼 🖵 ❄ 🖽 🛉 Ⓥ 🔫
🛳 🗓 ⒹⒶⓅ 🔖

DUDDENHOE END

Essex
Map ref 2D1

5m W. Saffron Walden

Duddenhoe End Farm
🅛🅘🅢🅣🅔🅓
Duddenhoe End, Saffron Walden, CB11 4UU
☎ Royston (0763) 838258
230-acre mixed farm. The farmhouse is 18th C. and has a wealth of beams and inglenook fireplace. Situated in a quiet rural area.
Bedrooms: 2 double.
Bathrooms: 2 private.
Bed & breakfast: max. £24 double.
Parking for 3.
🌄3 🖼 ❄ 🖽 🔫 ⊙ 💷 🗲 ❄
🎇 🗓

Rockells Farm
😄😄
Duddenhoe End, Saffron Walden, CB11 4UY
☎ Royston (0763) 838053
420-acre arable farm. Georgian house in rolling countryside with plenty of opportunities for walking and sightseeing. The 3 acre lake provides excellent fishing.
Bedrooms: 1 single, 1 double & 1 twin, 1 family room.

Bathrooms: 2 private,
2 public.
Bed & breakfast: £11-£13
single, £22-£26 double.
Half board: £17-£19 daily,
£119 weekly.
Lunch available.
Evening meal 6pm (l.o. 4pm).
Parking for 4.

EAST BERGHOLT
Suffolk
Map ref 3B2

7m NE. Colchester
John Constable, the
famous East Anglian
artist, was born here in
1776 and at the church of
St. Mary are reminders of
his family's associations
with the area.

The Haywain
Burnt Oak Corner, East
Bergholt, Colchester, Essex
CO7 6TJ
☎ (0206) 298300
*Licensed restaurant and tea
rooms.*
Bedrooms: 1 twin.
Bathrooms: 1 public.
Bed & breakfast: £15-£16.50
single, £25-£30 double.
Half board: from £105
weekly.
Lunch available.
Open February-December.
Credit: Visa.

Wren Cottage ⋔
The Street, East Bergholt,
Nr. Colchester, CO7 6SE
☎ Colchester (0206) 298327
*Beamed character cottage in
the heart of Constable
Country. In the middle of the
village, an easy walk from
Flatford. 30 minutes' drive
from Harwich. Off street
parking.*
Bedrooms: 2 twin.
Bathrooms: 2 private.
Bed & breakfast: £14 single,
£24-£30 double.
Parking for 2.

EAST WINCH
Norfolk
Map ref 3B1

Dentons Cottage
Common Rd., East Winch,
Kings Lynn, PE32 1JX
☎ (0553) 840429 & 01-741
3751

*300-year-old cottage with
exposed beams. Turn off at
Carpenters Arms, East Winch.*
Bedrooms: 5 double.
Bathrooms: 5 private.
Bed & breakfast: £10-£15
single, £20-£30 double.
Half board: £15-£20 daily,
£95-£120 weekly.
Lunch available.
Evening meal 7pm (l.o.
8.30pm).

ELY
Cambridgeshire
Map ref 3A2

14m NE. Cambridge
Until the 17th C when the
Fens were drained, Ely
was an island. The
cathedral completed in
1189 dominates the
surrounding area. One
particular feature is the
central octagonal tower
with a fan-vaulted timber
roof and wooden lantern.
Also has a local history
museum and stained
glass museum. ℹ

The Black Hostelry
The Cathedral Close, The
College, Firmary Lane, Ely,
CB7 4DL
☎ (0353) 662612
*One of the finest collections of
medieval domestic buildings
still in use in England.
Situated on the south side of
Ely Cathedral.*
Bedrooms: 1 double, 1 family
room.
Bathrooms: 2 private.
Bed & breakfast: £15-£17.50
double.
Parking for 20.

Springfields
Ely Rd., Little Thetford, Ely,
CB6 3HJ
☎ (0353) 3130 & 3637
*Non-smoking establishment on
A10, 2 miles from cathedral
and city centre. Quiet setting
in an acre of landscaped
gardens.*
Bedrooms: 1 double & 2 twin.
Bathrooms: 1 private,
1 public.
Bed & breakfast: max. £20
single, £30-£35 double.
Parking for 8.

EYKE
Suffolk
Map ref 3C2

3m NE. Woodbridge

The Old House ⋔
Eyke, Woodbridge,
IP12 2QW
☎ (0394) 460213
*17th C. house with beams and
open fires. In the centre of the
village with general store, pub
and church. River walks close
by. Views over the Deben
Valley. Dinner can be provided
by arrangement.*
Bedrooms: 1 single, 1 double
& 1 twin, 1 family room.
Bathrooms: 2 public.
Bed & breakfast: £12.50-£16
single, £25-£28 double.
Half board: £19-£24 daily,
£133-£168 weekly.
Evening meal 7pm (l.o.
8.30pm).
Parking for 5.

FAKENHAM
Norfolk
Map ref 3B1

See also West Rudham.
Busy small town in centre
of agricultural area, with
interesting Georgian
coaching inns. ℹ

Creswick House
77 Norwich Rd., Fakenham,
NR21 8HH
☎ (0328) 2739
*Easy access to town centre.
Convenient for coast, north
Norfolk countryside and many
places of interest.*
Bedrooms: 1 double & 1 twin,
1 family room.
Bathrooms: 1 public.
Bed & breakfast: £12.50-£14
single, £25-£28 double.
Parking for 12.

The Flintstones
9 Salmons Way, Fakenham,
NR21 8NG
☎ (0328) 3954
*Modern house, not far from the
roundabout on the Norwich
road.*
Bedrooms: 1 double, 2 family
rooms.
Bathrooms: 1 private,
2 public.
Bed & breakfast: from £12.50
single, from £25 double.
Half board: from £14 daily.
Parking for 2.

Hardlands
Listed
East Raynham, Fakenham,
NR21 7EQ
☎ (0328) 2567
*Friendly welcome and relaxing
atmosphere in modern
detached house, set in peaceful,
rural countryside 4 miles from
Fakenham on the A1065. Well
placed for visiting many north
Norfolk attractions, including
National Trust properties and
Sandringham. Evening meal by
arrangement.*
Bedrooms: 1 single, 1 double
& 2 twin, 1 family room.
Bathrooms: 2 public.
Bed & breakfast: £11-£15
single, £22-£26 double.
Half board: £17.50-£21.50
daily, £115-£135 weekly.
Evening meal 7pm (l.o.
midday).
Parking for 10.

FELIXSTOWE
Suffolk
Map ref 3C2

11m SE. Ipswich
Seaside resort that
developed at the end of
the 19th C. Lying in a
gently curving bay with a
2 mile long beach and
backed by a wide
promenade of lawns and
floral gardens. Ferry links
to the continent. ℹ

Fludyer Arms Hotel ⋔
Undercliff Rd. East,
Felixstowe, IP11 7LU
☎ (0394) 283279
*Small family-run hotel on
beach road, with restaurant
and bar meals. Sea views from
all rooms. The hotel has 2 bars
and specialises in home-cooked
food.*
Bedrooms: 2 single, 2 double
& 3 twin, 2 family rooms.
Bathrooms: 1 private,
2 public.
Bed & breakfast: £16-£19
single, £28-£34 double.
Lunch available.
Evening meal 7pm (l.o.
10pm).
Parking for 14.
Credit: Access, Visa.

Ordnance Hotel ⋔
1 Undercliff Rd. West,
Felixstowe, IP11 8AN
☎ (0394) 273427
Telex 987129

Continued ▶

219

FELIXSTOWE

Continued

Felixstowe's oldest hotel, with garden frontage and ample car parking space, now features the popular YoYo's Bistro and a comfortable lounge bar. 2 minutes' walk from Felixstowe's new seafront leisure centre and 5 minutes' drive from the continental ferry terminal.
Bedrooms: 3 single, 1 double & 6 twin, 1 family room.
Bathrooms: 4 private, 2 public.
Bed & breakfast: £25.95-£36.95 single, £38-£48 double.
Half board: £34.95-£45.95 daily.
Lunch available.
Evening meal 7pm (l.o. 10.30pm).
Parking for 55.
Credit: Access, Visa, Diners, Amex.

Redbanks
Listed
11 Gainsborough Rd., Felixstowe, IP11 7HT
☎ (0394) 278080
Detached Victorian house very close to shops, 3 minutes from station and 5 minutes from sea. Non-smokers only.
Bedrooms: 1 double & 2 twin.
Bathrooms: 1 public.
Bed & breakfast: max. £11 single, max. £22 double.

FRAMLINGHAM
Suffolk
Map ref 3C2

See also Hacheston, Monk Soham.
Pleasant old market town with an interesting church and impressive castle and some attractive houses round Market Hill. The town's history can be traced at the Lanman Museum.

Boundary Farm
Saxmundham Rd., Framlingham, Woodbridge, IP13 9NU
☎ (0728) 723401
17th C. grade II listed farmhouse set in 1.5 acres of garden with large pond, amidst open countryside. Lunch and evening meal available if required.
Bedrooms: 1 double & 1 twin, 1 family room.
Bathrooms: 1 public.

Bed & breakfast: £11-£13 single, £22-£25 double.
Half board: £17.50-£19.50 daily, from £122.50 weekly.
Lunch available.
Parking for 6.

GARBOLDISHAM
Norfolk
Map ref 3B2

7m W. Diss

Ingleneuk Guest House ⚘

Hopton Rd., Garboldisham, Diss, IP22 2RQ
☎ (095 381) 541
Modern bungalow in quiet wooded countryside. South facing patio and riverside walk. Central for touring. On B1111, 1 mile south of village.
Bedrooms: 1 single, 2 double & 2 twin, 1 family room.
Bathrooms: 5 private, 1 public.
Bed & breakfast: £15.50-£21 single, £26-£33 double.
Half board: £22.50-£30.50 daily, £144-£199 weekly.
Evening meal 6.30pm (l.o. 1pm).
Parking for 10.
Credit: Visa.

GISSING
Norfolk
Map ref 3B2

4m NE. Diss

The Old Rectory
Gissing, Diss, IP22 3XB
☎ Tivetshall (037 977) 575
Private Victorian country house in 3 acres, offering peaceful and comfortable accommodation. Traditional home cooking.
Bedrooms: 1 double & 1 twin, 1 family room.
Bathrooms: 1 private, 1 public.
Bed & breakfast: £19-£23 single, £28-£32 double.
Half board: £22-£24 daily, £154-£168 weekly.
Evening meal 7.45pm (l.o. 7.45pm).
Parking for 6.

GREAT YARMOUTH
Norfolk
Map ref 3C1

See also Rollesby.
One of Britain's major seaside resorts with 5 miles of seafront and every possible amenity including a leisure complex. Busy harbour and fishing centre. Interesting area around the quay with a number of museums. Maritime Museum on seafront. ℹ

Burlington Hotel ⚘
North Drive, Great Yarmouth, NR30 1EG
☎ (0493) 844568
Views of the sea and sandy beach. Facilities include a pool, solarium, sauna and car park.
Bedrooms: 5 single, 12 double & 8 twin, 7 family rooms.
Bathrooms: 26 private, 4 public.
Bed & breakfast: £27-£45 single, £32-£54 double.
Half board: from £24 daily, £120-£180 weekly.
Lunch available.
Evening meal 6pm (l.o. 8pm).
Parking for 40.
Open March-December.
Credit: Access, Visa.

MacLeod's
Church Farm, Burgh Castle, Great Yarmouth, NR31 9QG
☎ (0493) 780251
250-acre mixed farm. The farm encompasses the famous fort of Burgh castle. Quiet, peaceful, relaxing location overlooking Breydon water. Within easy reach of Great Yarmouth. Gorleston Golf Club and Great Yarmouth Golf Club nearby.
Bedrooms: 1 single, 1 double & 1 twin, 2 family rooms.
Bathrooms: 3 private, 1 public; 1 private shower.
Bed & breakfast: £9.50-£10 single, £20-£25 double.
Parking for 16.

Georgian House Private Hotel
16-17 North Drive, Great Yarmouth, NR30 4EW
☎ (0493) 842623

Detached building in its own grounds, overlooking the sea at front and recreation grounds at rear.
Bedrooms: 6 single, 14 double & 4 twin, 1 family room.
Bathrooms: 15 private, 3 public.
Bed & breakfast: £20-£30 single, £26-£40 double.
Parking for 24.
Open February-November.

Ocean Dawn Guest House
Listed
27 North Drive, Great Yarmouth, NR30 4EW
☎ (0493) 844746
Located on the seafront with ample car parking and a friendly atmosphere.
Bedrooms: 2 single, 2 double & 1 twin, 1 family room.
Bathrooms: 1 public.
Bed & breakfast: £8.50-£11.50 single, £17-£23 double.
Parking for 9.

Palm Court Hotel ⚘
North Drive, Great Yarmouth, NR30 1EF
☎ (0493) 844568
Sea views, heated indoor pool, sauna, solarium, lift and car park, in a resort with sandy beaches and crammed with history.
Bedrooms: 6 single, 11 double & 23 twin, 8 family rooms.
Bathrooms: 38 private, 5 public.
Bed & breakfast: £27-£45 single, £32-£54 double.
Half board: from £32.50 daily, £120-£180 weekly.
Lunch available.
Evening meal 6pm (l.o. 9pm).
Parking for 40.
Open March-December.
Credit: Access, Visa.

Trotwood Private Hotel
2 North Drive, Great Yarmouth, NR30 1ED
☎ (0493) 843971 & 844758
In a quiet area on the seafront overlooking bowling greens, beach and sea. Within walking distance of all amenities.
Bedrooms: 7 double & 1 twin, 1 family room.
Bathrooms: 7 private, 1 public.
Bed & breakfast: £15-£18 single, £26-£30 double.
Parking for 11.

HACHESTON

Suffolk
Map ref 3C2

3m S. Framlingham

Cherry Tree House
Hacheston, Woodbridge,
IP13 0DR
☎ Wickham Market
(0728) 746371
*Large farmhouse built 1641
with mature garden for guests'
use. Ample parking.
Imaginative English and
continental cooking using fresh
garden produce. Evening meal
by arrangement.*
Bedrooms: 1 single, 1 double.
Bathrooms: 2 public.
Bed & breakfast: £11-£13
single, £22-£26 double.
Half board: £17.50-£19.50
daily, £120-£130 weekly.
Evening meal 6.30pm (l.o.
8pm).
Parking for 3.
⌧ 🅿 🛉 🖭 🗲 📺 🎕 🏊 ✻ 🛪
🏠 🞸

HADLEIGH

Suffolk
Map ref 3B2

See also Hitcham, Offton.
Former wool town, lying
on a tributary of the River
Stour. The church of St.
Mary stands among a
remarkable cluster of
medieval buildings. 🛈

Odds and Ends House ⋒
131,High Street, Hadleigh,
Ipswich, IP7 5EG
☎ Ipswich (0473) 822032
*Until recently the house of the
local miller. Dates from 15th
C. with Georgian remodelling.
Situated at the end of the high
street.*
Bedrooms: 3 single, 4 twin.
Bathrooms: 2 private,
2 public.
Bed & breakfast: £14-£20
single, £26-£32 double.
Half board: £20-£26 daily.
Evening meal 6.30pm (l.o.
midday).
⌧ 12 🛉 🖭 🗲 📺 🎕
🏠 🞸 SP 🞸

Town House Fruit Farm
Hook Lane, Hadleigh,
IP7 5PH
☎ (0473) 823260
*85-acre fruit farm. Converted
barn close to Constable country
and East Anglian wool
villages.*
Bedrooms: 2 double & 1 twin.

Bathrooms: 2 public.
Bed & breakfast: from £11
single, from £20 double.
Parking for 20.
⌧ 6 🛉 🖭 🗲 📺 🎕 🞸 🛪

HALESWORTH

Suffolk
Map ref 3C2

24m NE. Ipswich
Small market town which
grew firstly with
navigation on the Blyth in
the 18th C and then with
the coming of the
railways in the 19th C.
Opposite the church in a
beautiful 14th C building
is the Halesworth Gallery.

The Grange
😊😊
St. James, South Elmham,
Halesworth, IP19 0HN
☎ St Cross (098 682) 246
*12-acre pig farm. Spacious,
comfortable Victorian
farmhouse with a third of an
acre of grounds in a
picturesque and historic area of
Suffolk.*
Bedrooms: 2 double & 1 twin.
Bathrooms: 2 private,
2 public.
Bed & breakfast: £10 single,
£20 double.
Parking for 8.
⌧ 🛉 🖭 🗲 📺 🎕 🞸

HALSTEAD

Essex
Map ref 3B2

*See also Castle
Hedingham.*

White Hart Inn ⋒
😊😊
15 High St., Halstead,
CO9 2AA
☎ (0787) 475657
Bedrooms: 2 double & 2 twin,
1 family room.
Bathrooms: 1 public;
1 private shower.
Bed & breakfast: from £16
single, from £30 double.
Lunch available.
Evening meal 7pm (l.o.
9.30pm).
Parking for 34.
Credit: Access, Visa.
⌧ 5 🖭 🗲 🛉 🎕 🛪 🞸 🛪

HARDINGHAM

Norfolk
Map ref 3B1

2m NE. Hingham

The Smithy
Listed
Low St., Hardingham,
NR9 4EL
☎ Attleborough
(0953) 851065
*In a peaceful hamlet
surrounded by countryside
between Wymondham and
Dereham. Easy access to
Norwich. Also self-contained
annexe.*
Bedrooms: 1 double & 2 twin.
Bathrooms: 2 public.
Bed & breakfast: £9-£10
single, £18-£20 double.
Half board: £13-£16 daily,
£70-£80 weekly.
Evening meal 6pm (l.o. 9pm).
Parking for 7.
⌧ 🞸 🖭 🛉 🗲 📺 🞸 ✻
🛪 🞸 SP

HARLOW

Essex
Map ref 2D1

Although one of the New
Towns it was so planned
that it could develop
alongside the existing old
town. It has a museum of
local history and a Nature
Reserve with nature trails
and study centre.

5 Willow Place
Hastingwood, Harlow,
CM17 9JH
☎ (0279) 28138
*Chalet bungalow in a third of
an acre plot. Countryside
location overlooking fields, 1.5
miles from the M11/M25 exit
7.*
Bedrooms: 1 double & 1 twin.
Bathrooms: 1 public.
Bed & breakfast: max. £12.50
single, max. £25 double.
Half board: max. £17 daily,
max. £110 weekly.
Evening meal 7pm (l.o. 6pm).
Parking for 1.
Open March-October.
⌧ 🞸 🖭 🗲 🛉 🎕 🞸 📺
🎕 🞸 🛪 🞸

HAVERHILL

Suffolk
Map ref 3B2

*See also Steeple
Bumpstead, Withersfield.*

Hanchett House
Cambridge Rd.,
Withersfield, Haverhill,
CB9 7SW
☎ (0440) 702891
*Large bungalow in own
grounds, on the A604
Cambridge road, within 20
minutes' drive of Cambridge
and one and a quarter hours
from Harwich.*
Bedrooms: 1 double, 1 family
room.
Bathrooms: 1 public.
Bed & breakfast: £10 single,
£18 double.
Parking for 6.
⌧ 🞸 🖭 🗲 📺 🎕 ✻ 🛪
🞸

HEACHAM

Norfolk
Map ref 3B1

2m S. Hunstanton
The portrait of a Red
Indian princess who
married John Rolfe of
Heacham Hall in 1614
appears on the village
sign. Caley Mill is the
centre of lavender
growing.

Caley House
Station Rd., Heacham,
King's Lynn, PE31 7HG
☎ (0485) 71178
*Georgian farmhouse in peaceful
wooded grounds in centre of
coastal village. Close to
Sandringham and Hunstanton.*
Bedrooms: 1 double & 1 twin,
1 family room.
Bathrooms: 1 public.
Bed & breakfast: £10-£14
single, £20-£28 double.
Parking for 8.
⌧ 🞸 🞸 🖭 🗲 📺 🎕 ✻
🛪 🞸

HEMPNALL

Norfolk
Map ref 3C1

Mill House
Listed
Field Lane, Hempnall, Nr.
Norwich, NR15 2PB
☎ (050 842) 552

Continued ▶

GROUPS, CONSORTIA AND AGENCIES
SPECIALISING IN FARM AND COUNTRY
HOLIDAYS ARE LISTED IN A SPECIAL
SECTION OF THIS GUIDE.

HEMPNALL

Continued

Family accommodation in comfortable Victorian house. Large garden, chickens, donkey. Within easy reach of seaside, Broads, Norwich. Quiet village.
Bedrooms: 2 twin.
Bathrooms: 1 public.
Bed & breakfast: max. £12 single, max. £20 double.
Parking for 2.

HIGHAM

Suffolk
Map ref 3B2

4m S. Hadleigh

The Bauble
Listed

Higham, Colchester,
CO7 6LA
☎ (020 637) 254
Telex 987478 WSR
Modernised country house in mature gardens adjacent to the Rivers Brett and Stour. Ideal for touring Constable country and wool industry villages. Will accept children over 12 years old.
Bedrooms: 1 single, 2 twin.
Bathrooms: 1 public.
Bed & breakfast: £13-£18 single, £26-£36 double.

HILDERSHAM

Cambridgeshire
Map ref 2D1

4m NE. Gt Chesterford

The Watermill

Hildersham, Cambridge,
CB1 6BS
☎ (0223) 891520
19th C. mill house on River Granta with waterwheel, surrounded by water meadows and interesting bird life. Large, attractively furnished room overlooking mill race.
Bedrooms: 1 family room.
Bathrooms: 1 private.
Bed & breakfast: from £26.50 double.
Half board: £17.75-£22 daily.
Lunch available.
Evening meal 7pm (l.o. 4pm).
Parking for 3.

HINTLESHAM

Suffolk
Map ref 3B2

4m E. Hadleigh

College Farm

Hintlesham, Ipswich,
IP8 3NT
☎ Ipswich (0473) 87253
160-acre arable farm. Tudor farmhouse in quiet position on the west side of Hintlesham on the A1071, five miles west of Ipswich.
Bedrooms: 1 double, 1 family room.
Bathrooms: 1 private, 1 public.
Bed & breakfast: £12-£15 single, £20-£26 double.
Lunch available.
Parking for 10.
Open March-November.

HITCHAM

Suffolk
Map ref 3B2

6m NW. Hadleigh

Wetherden Hall
Listed

Hitcham, Ipswich, IP7 7PZ
☎ Bildeston (0449) 740412
270-acre mixed/arable farm. Attractive 19th C. farmhouse on the edge of a very pretty village. A good centre for visiting medieval Lavenham, Bury St.Edmunds, Ipswich, Cambridge and Constable country.
Bedrooms: 2 double, 1 family room.
Bathrooms: 1 public.
Bed & breakfast: £10.50-£12.50 single, £19-£22 double.
Parking for 10.
Open January-November.

HOLBROOK

Suffolk
Map ref 3B2

The Mill House ♨
Listed

Holbrook, Ipswich, IP9 2QN
☎ (0473) 328249
17th C. mill house offering comfortable accommodation and family atmosphere. All bedrooms have lake views. Fishing available. Large attractive garden.
Bedrooms: 1 twin, 1 family room.

Bathrooms: 1 public.
Bed & breakfast: max. £18 single, max. £28 double.
Parking for 6.

HORSEHEATH

Cambridgeshire
Map ref 3B2

4m W. Haverhill

Grange Farm
Listed

Mill Green, Horseheath,
CB1 6QZ
☎ Ashdon (079 984) 297
16-acre arable farm. Delightful 18th C. farmhouse set in peaceful rural location. Easy access from the M11 to Cambridge and Newmarket. Places of historic interest nearby.
Bedrooms: 2 double & 1 twin.
Bathrooms: 1 private, 1 public; 1 private shower.
Bed & breakfast: £13-£18 single, £20-£28 double.
Parking for 5.
Open April-October.

HORSFORD

Norfolk
Map ref 3B1

5m NW. Norwich

Becklands

105 Holt Rd., Horsford,
Norwich, NR10 3AB
☎ (0603) 898582 & 898020
Quietly located modern house overlooking open countryside. 5 miles north of Norwich. Central for the Broads and coastal areas.
Bedrooms: 7 single, 1 double & 2 twin.
Bathrooms: 4 public.
Bed & breakfast: £12-£14 single, £24-£28 double.
Parking for 20.

HUNSTANTON

Norfolk
Map ref 3B1

14m NE. King's Lynn
Seaside resort which faces the Wash. The shingle and sand beach are backed by striped cliffs and many unusual fossils can be found here. The town, sometimes known as Hunstanton St. Edmund, is predominantly Victorian. ℹ

Glenmaye Guest House

8 Belgrave Avenue,
Hunstanton, PE36 6DQ
☎ (048 53) 2867
Family-run guesthouse offering comfortable accommodation with home cooking. Close to beach, shops and places of interest.
Bedrooms: 1 double & 1 twin, 1 family room.
Bathrooms: 1 public.
Bed & breakfast: £9 single, £18 double.
Half board: £13 daily, £85 weekly.
Evening meal 6pm (l.o. 4.30pm).
Parking for 3.

Ocean View Guest House

66 Northgate, Hunstanton,
PE36 6DS
☎ (048 53) 2364
A family-run guesthouse offering home-cooked food, with a TV lounge available at all times. Close to the shops, beach and places of interest.
Bedrooms: 2 single, 2 double, 1 family room.
Bathrooms: 1 public.
Bed & breakfast: £9.50 single, £19 double.
Evening meal 6pm (l.o. 6pm).
Parking for 4.

THERE IS A SPECIAL SECTION IN THIS GUIDE LISTING ACCOMMODATION ESPECIALLY SUITABLE FOR GROUPS AND YOUNG PEOPLE.

INDIVIDUAL PROPRIETORS HAVE SUPPLIED ALL DETAILS OF ACCOMMODATION. ALTHOUGH WE DO CHECK FOR ACCURACY, WE ADVISE YOU TO CONFIRM PRICES AND OTHER INFORMATION AT THE TIME OF BOOKING.

Cambridgeshire
Map ref 3A2

15m NW. Cambridge
Attractive town with much of interest and which abounds in associations with the Cromwell family. The town is connected to Godmanchester by a beautiful 14th C bridge over the great River Ouse. ℹ

Mrs. S. Rook
Listed
38 High St., Hemingford Grey, Huntingdon, PE18 9BJ
☎ St. Ives (0480) 301203
Private detached house in centre of village, with large garden and quiet surroundings. All home cooking. 1 mile from the A604.
Bedrooms: 2 single, 2 double.
Bathrooms: 1 public.
Bed & breakfast: max. £12 single, max. £24 double.
Half board: max. £18 daily.
Evening meal 7.30pm (l.o. 4pm).
Parking for 4.
Open January-November.

Suffolk
Map ref 3B2

Interesting county town and major port on the River Orwell. Birthplace of Cardinal Wolsey. Christchurch Mansion set in a fine park contains a good collection of furniture and pictures with works by Gainsborough, Constable and Munnings. ℹ

Mulberry Hall
Burstall, Ipswich, IP8 3DP
☎ Hintlesham (047 387) 348
16th C. beamed farmhouse once owned by Cardinal Wolsey (1523). In small village 5 miles west of Ipswich. Log fires and home cooking.
Bedrooms: 1 single, 1 double & 1 twin.
Bathrooms: 2 public.
Bed & breakfast: from £15 single, £25-£30 double.
Evening meal (l.o. 11am).
Parking for 6.

Priory Farmhouse
Orwell Meadows, Nacton, Ipswich, IP10 0JS
☎ (0473) 726666
Large modern country house within 30-acre caravan and stable complex. Ideally located off the A45 for Ipswich, Felixstowe and Woodbridge.
Bedrooms: 1 single, 1 double, 1 family room.
Bathrooms: 2 public.
Bed & breakfast: £12-£14 single, £24-£28 double.
Parking for 4.

The Vale Farm
Harkstead, Nr. Ipswich, IP9 1BH
☎ Shotley (047 334) 589
7-acre horse farm. Tudor farmhouse with many facilities, tucked away in a secluded valley. Ideal for country lovers and sporting people.
Bedrooms: 3 double & 1 twin, 1 family room.
Bathrooms: 2 private, 1 public.
Bed & breakfast: £15-£19 single, £28-£30 double.
Half board: £23-£29 daily, £145-£183 weekly.
Evening meal 7pm (l.o. 9pm).
Parking for 12.

Norfolk
Map ref 3B1

The White House
Listed
West Church St., Kenninghall, Norwich, NR16 2EN
☎ Quidenham (095 387) 472
18th century house with secluded garden.
Bedrooms: 2 single, 1 double.
Bathrooms: 1 public.
Bed & breakfast: £10 single, £20 double.
Half board: £15 daily, £95 weekly.
Lunch available.
Evening meal 6.30pm (l.o. 9.30pm).
Parking for 3.
Open April-September.

THE SYMBOLS ARE EXPLAINED ON THE FLAP INSIDE THE BACK COVER.

Suffolk
Map ref 3C2

2m SW. Framlingham

Rookery Farm
Framlingham Rd., Kettleburgh, Woodbridge, IP13 7LL
☎ Framlingham (0728) 723248
Lovely Georgian farmhouse in 3.5 acres of wooded garden and surrounded by open farmland.
Bedrooms: 2 twin, 1 family room.
Bathrooms: 1 public.
Bed & breakfast: £10-£10.50 single, £20-£21 double.
Half board: £16-£16.50 daily, £112 weekly.
Evening meal 7pm (l.o. 6pm).
Parking for 3.
Open March-November.

Norfolk
Map ref 3B1

See also Terrington St. Clement.
Combines the attractions of a busy town, port and agricultural centre. Many outstanding buildings. The Guildhall and Town Hall are both built of flint in a striking chequer design. The Customs House was built in 1683. ℹ

Havana Guest House
⌂⌂
117 Gaywood Rd., King's Lynn, PE30 2PU
☎ (0553) 772331
Charming Victorian family-run guesthouse within easy walking distance of town centre and convenient for main access routes.
Bedrooms: 2 single, 2 double & 1 twin, 2 family rooms.
Bathrooms: 1 private, 1 public.
Bed & breakfast: £12 single, £20 double.
Half board: £16.50-£18.50 daily, £115.50-£133 weekly.
Evening meal 6pm (l.o. 1pm).
Parking for 8.

Maranatha Guest House ⋒
Listed
115 Gaywood Rd., Gaywood, King's Lynn, PE30 2PU
☎ (0553) 774596
Large carrstone and brick residence with gardens front and rear. 10 minutes' walk from the town centre. Direct road to Sandringham and the coast.
Bedrooms: 1 single, 1 double & 2 twin, 2 family rooms.
Bathrooms: 1 private, 2 public.
Bed & breakfast: £10 single, £18 double.
Half board: £13.50 daily.
Evening meal 6pm (l.o. 8pm).
Parking for 6.

Orchard Farmhouse
Gayton, King's Lynn, PE32 1PA
☎ Gayton (055 386) 623
Orchard Farmhouse offers bed and breakfast accommodation in the Norfolk countryside. Cycling weekends a speciality - cycles for hire. Evening meal available by arrangement.
Bedrooms: 1 double & 1 twin.
Bathrooms: 1 private, 1 public.
Bed & breakfast: from £12 single, from £22 double.
Half board: from £100 weekly.
Evening meal 6pm (l.o. 7.30pm).
Parking for 3.

Cambridgeshire
Map ref 3B2

5m SE. Newmarket

Queen's Head ⋒
⌂⌂
Kirtling, Nr. Newmarket, Cambs CB8 9PA
☎ Newmarket (0638) 730253
Built as an inn in the first year of Elizabeth I's reign. A wide range of home-cooked food and real ales.
Bedrooms: 2 single, 1 double & 1 twin.
Bathrooms: 1 public.
Bed & breakfast: £14-£16 single, max. £30 double.
Lunch available.
Evening meal 7.30pm (l.o. 10.30pm).
Parking for 35.

KNEESWORTH

Cambridgeshire
Map ref 2D1

2m N. Royston

The Grange
Old North Rd., Kneesworth,
Nr. Royston, Hertfordshire
SG8 5DS
☎ (0763) 48674
*18th C. farmhouse with
inglenook fireplace, panelled
dining room and Victorian
conservatory. Adjacent to A14
on edge of village, 15 minutes
from Cambridge and A1(M).*
Bedrooms: 2 double & 3 twin,
1 family room.
Bathrooms: 3 private,
2 public.
Bed & breakfast: £14-£36
single, £28-£72 double.
Half board: £24-£46 daily,
£154-£300 weekly.
Evening meal 6pm (l.o. 8pm).
Parking for 12.

LAVENHAM

Suffolk
Map ref 3B2

6m NE. Sudbury
A former prosperous
wool town of timber-
framed buildings with the
cathedral-like church and
its tall tower. The market
place is 13th C. and the
Guildhall now houses a
museum.

Weaners Farm
Listed

Bears Lane, Lavenham,
Sudbury, CO10 9RX
☎ (0787) 247310
*20-acre mixed farm. Modern
farmhouse in peaceful location
with farmland views. 10
minutes' walk from historic
village where eating places are
available.*
Bedrooms: 1 double & 1 twin.
Bathrooms: 1 public.
Bed & breakfast: from £12
single, from £23 double.
Parking for 3.

**PLEASE CHECK
PRICES AND OTHER
DETAILS AT THE
TIME OF BOOKING.**

LAWSHALL

Suffolk
Map ref 3B2

5m N. Long Melford

Truin Farms, Brighthouse Farm

Melford Rd., Lawshall, Bury
St. Edmunds, IP29 4PX
☎ (0284) 830385
*300-acre arable and stock
farm. 200-year-old farmhouse
set in 3 acres of gardens. Close
to many places of historic
interest.*
Bedrooms: 1 single, 2 double,
1 family room.
Bathrooms: 2 public;
1 private shower.
Bed & breakfast: £12-£14
single, £24-£28 double.
Parking for 10.

LEISTON

Suffolk
Map ref 3C2

4m E. Saxmundham
Busy industrial town near
the coast. The abbey
sited here in 1363 was for
hundreds of years used
as a farm until it was
restored in 1918.

The Beeches
117 High St., Leiston,
IP16 4BX
☎ (0728) 832541
*Large, modern detached house.
Easy access to all town
facilities and Aldeburgh
Festival activities. 2 miles from
beach.*
Bedrooms: 1 single, 3 twin,
1 family room.
Bathrooms: 1 public.
Bed & breakfast: £19-£28
double.
Evening meal 6pm (l.o. 9am).
Parking for 4.

LETHERINGSETT

Norfolk
Map ref 3B1

1m W. Holt

Glavenside M
Listed

Letheringsett, Holt,
NR25 7AR
☎ Holt (0263) 713181

*River Glaven flows through the
grounds to the sea at Blakeney,
5 miles away. Rock and water
gardens. Boating. Good base
for many places of interest.*
Bedrooms: 2 single, 3 double
& 1 twin, 2 family rooms.
Bathrooms: 3 public.
Bed & breakfast: £10-£16
single, £20-£32 double.
Parking for 8.

LEVINGTON

Suffolk
Map ref 3C2

6m SE. Ipswich
Attractive farming village
with views of the River
Orwell.

Redhouse
Bridge Rd., Levington,
Ipswich, IP10 0LZ
☎ Nacton (047 388) 670
*Farmhouse in quiet village
overlooking River Orwell, in an
area of outstanding natural
beauty. Fresh produce, home
cooking, catering for special
diets, free range eggs.
Felixstowe 6 miles.*
Bedrooms: 1 twin, 1 family
room.
Bathrooms: 1 public.
Bed & breakfast: from £11
single, from £22 double.
Half board: from £17 daily,
from £180 weekly.
Evening meal 6.30pm.
Parking for 20.
Open March-October.

LITTLE BARNEY

Norfolk
Map ref 3B1

The Old Brick Kilns
Little Barney, Fakenham,
NR12 0NL
☎ Thursford (032 877) 305
*Converted cottages in rural
setting. Turn right off A48
Fakenham Holt road. 200
yards on right to Barney, left
into Little Barney, house at
end of lane.*
Bedrooms: 1 single, 1 double
& 1 twin.
Bathrooms: 3 private.
Bed & breakfast: £11.75-
£12.75 single, £23.50-£25.50
double.
Half board: £18.75-£19.75
daily, £123-£129 weekly.

Evening meal 6pm (l.o.
10am).
Parking for 8.

LITTLE EVERSDEN

Cambridgeshire
Map ref 2D1

6m SW. Cambridge

Church Farm
Church Lane, Little
Eversden, Cambridge,
CB3 7HQ
☎ (0223) 262228
*500-acre arable farm. 17th C.
listed house in lovely gardens.
The house has retained much
of the original character.
Farmhouse cooking. Located 7
miles south west of Cambridge.*
Bedrooms: 3 twin.
Bathrooms: 2 private,
2 public.
Bed & breakfast: £20 single,
£30-£35 double.
Half board: £24.50-£26 daily,
£171.50 weekly.
Evening meal 6pm (l.o. 5pm).
Parking for 8.
Credit: Visa.

LITTLE SHELFORD

Cambridgeshire
Map ref 2D1

5m S. Cambridge
Little Shelford was
developed by academics
from nearby Cambridge
during Victorian times and
there are several old
timber-framed buildings.

Mrs. D. Franklin

31 Newton Rd., Little
Shelford, Cambridge,
CB2 5HL
☎ (0223) 842276
*A modern family house in a
large garden, 4 miles south of
Cambridge with easy access
from the M11.*
Bedrooms: 1 twin.
Bathrooms: 1 private.
Bed & breakfast: £22-£27
single, £27-£32 double.
Parking for 2.

St. Andrews M

16 Church St., Little
Shelford, Cambridge,
CB2 5HG
☎ (0223) 842254

**MAP REFERENCES APPLY TO THE COLOUR
MAPS TOWARDS THE END OF THIS GUIDE.**

Quiet select village. Bedrooms overlook flower garden and grazing paddock.
Bedrooms: 1 double & 1 twin.
Bathrooms: 1 public.
Bed & breakfast: £24-£26 double.
Parking for 3.
Open April-October.

LONG MELFORD

Suffolk
Map ref 3B2

3m N. Sudbury
One of Suffolk's loveliest villages, remarkable for the length of its main street. Holy Trinity Church is considered to be the finest village church in England. The National Trust own the Elizabethan Melford Hall and nearby Kentwell Hall is also open to the public.

Crown Inn Hotel M

Hall Street, Long Melford, Sudbury, CO10 9JL
☎ Sudbury (0787) 77666
Family-run hotel in an historic village. Traditional English food, a range of bar snacks and 5 real ales available. Log fires in the winter.
Bedrooms: 2 single, 6 double & 3 twin, 1 family room.
Bathrooms: 7 private, 2 public.
Bed & breakfast: £22.50-£31.50 single, £32.50-£45 double.
Lunch available.
Evening meal 7pm (l.o. 9.30pm).
Parking for 6.
Credit: Access, Visa, Diners, Amex.

The George & Dragon M

Long Melford, Sudbury, CO10 9JB
☎ Sudbury (0787) 71285
An English country inn offering traditional service and hospitality.
Bedrooms: 1 single, 1 double & 2 twin.
Bathrooms: 2 public.
Bed & breakfast: £15 single, £30 double.
Lunch available.
Evening meal 6pm (l.o. 10pm).
Parking for 5.

Holly Cottage

3 Borley Rd., Rodbridge, Long Melford, CO10 9HH
☎ Sudbury (0787) 79848
200 yards from River Stour and the "Valley walk". Free-range eggs available. Garden/orchard for guests' use. Cottage just off the main road.
Bedrooms: 1 double & 2 twin.
Bathrooms: 1 private, 2 public.
Bed & breakfast: £11-£15 single, £19.50-£25 double.
Parking for 3.

LOUND

Suffolk
Map ref 3C1

5m NW. Lowestoft
Lound Manor Bird Farm with its tropical birds, pheasants and waterfowl is open all year round.

Hall Farm, Jay Lane

Church Lane, Lound, Lowestoft, NR32 5LJ
☎ (0502) 730415
101-acre arable farm. Traditional 16th C. Suffolk farmhouse. Take A12 north from Lowestoft, 4 miles turn left into Jay Lane, down private lane on the left, farm is on the right. Within 2 miles of the sea.
Bedrooms: 1 single, 1 double & 1 twin, 1 family room.
Bathrooms: 1 public.
Bed & breakfast: £11-£12 single, £22-£25 double.
Parking for 4.
Open February-November.

LOWESTOFT

Suffolk
Map ref 3C1

Seaside town with wide sandy beaches. Important fishing port with picturesque fishing quarter and also the site of the first recorded lighthouse in England. Home of the famous Lowestoft porcelain and birthplace of Benjamin Britten. Several museums with a maritime flavour. *i*

Ms. J. Beech

Listed
18 Kirkley Cliff, Lowestoft, NR33 0BY
☎ (0503) 515839

Comfortable and friendly guesthouse with some rooms overlooking the sea.
Bedrooms: 4 single, 1 twin, 5 family rooms.
Bathrooms: 2 public.
Bed & breakfast: £10-£11 single, £18-£20 double.
Evening meal 5pm (l.o. 5pm).
Parking for 4.

MARCH

Cambridgeshire
Map ref 3A1

14m E. Peterborough
This is the heart of a railway system linking the Fens to surrounding counties. St. Wendreda's church makes the town famous for the roof is of double hammer-beam construction with a host of carved angels spreading their wings.

The Old Brew House

Listed
52 West End, March, PE15 8DL
☎ (0354) 53793
Period 17th C. cottage with an oak-beamed lounge/dining room and a river garden. A good base for touring or for a quiet break. Listed building. Swimming pool nearby.
Bedrooms: 1 single, 1 double & 1 twin.
Bathrooms: 2 public.
Bed & breakfast: £12-£15 single, £24-£30 double.
Half board: £17-£20 daily.
Evening meal 6pm (l.o. 10pm).
Parking for 2.

MARGARET RODING

Essex
Map ref 3B2

1m S. Leaden Roding

Greys

Listed
Ongar Rd., Margaret Roding, Nr. Great Dunmow, CM6 1QR
☎ Good Easter (024 531) 509
340-acre arable/sheep farm. Small, quiet guest house on family farm. Just off A1060, easy distance London, Cambridge, coast. Tea and coffee available. Children over 10 years welcome.
Bedrooms: 2 double & 1 twin.
Bathrooms: 1 public.

Bed & breakfast: £12.50-£15 single, £20 double.
Parking for 6.
Open April-October.

MENDHAM

Suffolk
Map ref 3C2

2m E. Harleston

Weston House Farm

Mendham, Harleston, Norfolk IP20 0PB
☎ St. Cross (098 682) 206
300-acre mixed farm. 17th C. Grade II listed farmhouse set in an acre of garden, overlooking pasture land.
Bedrooms: 1 double & 1 twin, 1 family room.
Bathrooms: 1 public.
Bed & breakfast: £18-£20 double.
Parking for 6.
Open April-October.

MENDLESHAM GREEN

Suffolk
Map ref 3B2

4m NE. Stowmarket

Cherry Tree Farm

Mendlesham Green, Stowmarket, IP14 5RQ
☎ Stowmarket (0449) 766376
Farmhouse offering home cooking, with our own bread and fresh vegetables. Well placed for touring Suffolk.
Bedrooms: 1 double & 1 twin.
Bathrooms: 1 public.
Bed & breakfast: £24-£26 double.
Half board: £20-£22 daily.
Evening meal 7pm (l.o. 2pm).
Parking for 3.

GROUPS, CONSORTIA AND AGENCIES SPECIALISING IN FARM AND COUNTRY HOLIDAYS ARE LISTED IN A SPECIAL SECTION OF THIS GUIDE.

MILDENHALL

Suffolk
Map ref 3B2

8m NE. Newmarket
Town that has grown considerably in size in the last 20 years but still manages to retain a pleasant small country-town centre. The church is one of the finest in the area.

Bell Hotel
(crowns symbol)

High St., Mildenhall,
IP28 7EA
☎ (0638) 717272
Telex 94011647
A former coaching inn in a busy market town. Inglenook fireplaces, low ceilings and beamed rooms.
Bedrooms: 5 single, 3 double & 6 twin, 3 family rooms.
Bathrooms: 16 private, 2 public.
Bed & breakfast: £27.50-£33 single, £41-£45 double.
Lunch available.
Evening meal 7pm (l.o. 9pm).
Parking for 25.
Credit: Access, Visa, Diners, Amex.
(symbols)

Smoke House Inn ⋒
(crowns symbol)

Beck Row, Mildenhall,
IP28 8DH
☎ (0638) 713223
Telex 817430 SMOKE G
Recently constructed hotel/motel complex adjoining listed buildings. Lounge bar, cocktail bar, fully-licensed restaurant. Open 24 hours a day.
Bedrooms: 80 twin.
Bathrooms: 80 private.
Bed & breakfast: £40-£45 single, £50-£60 double.
Half board: £50-£60 daily, £265-£300 weekly.
Lunch available.
Evening meal 6pm (l.o. 10pm).
Parking for 200.
Credit: Access, Visa, Amex.
(symbols)

MAP REFERENCES APPLY TO COLOUR MAPS NEAR THE BACK OF THE GUIDE.

MOLESWORTH

Cambridgeshire
Map ref 3A2

5m E. Thrapston

The Cross Keys ⋒
(symbol)

Molesworth, Huntingdon,
PE18 0QF
☎ Bythorn (080 14) 283
Friendly country inn in quiet village offering modern accommodation, a warm welcome and home-cooked food.
Bedrooms: 1 single, 2 double & 5 twin, 2 family rooms.
Bathrooms: 7 private, 1 public; 1 private shower.
Bed & breakfast: £17.25-£18.50 single, £28.50-£30 double.
Lunch available.
Evening meal 6pm (l.o. 10pm).
Parking for 30.
(symbols)

MONK SOHAM

Suffolk
Map ref 3C2

4m NW. Framlingham

Abbey House

Monk Soham, Woodbridge,
IP13 7EN
☎ Earl Soham (072 882) 225
10-acre mixed farm. Peaceful Victorian rectory with friendly animals and country cooking.
Bedrooms: 1 twin, 2 family rooms.
Bathrooms: 3 private.
Bed & breakfast: £14-£17 single, £28-£34 double.
Half board: £22.50-£25.50 daily, £143.50-£164.50 weekly.
Evening meal 6pm (l.o. midday).
Parking for 6.
(symbols)

MORLEY ST. BOTOLPH

Norfolk
Map ref 3B1

3m W. Wymondham

Fir Grove

Morley St. Botolph,
Wymondham, NR18 9AA
☎ (0953) 602127
16th C. thatched house, with oak beams and steep spiral staircase, in woodland grounds. Twin bed/sitting room with TV.

Bedrooms: 1 single, 1 twin.
Bathrooms: 1 public.
Bed & breakfast: £10-£12 single, £20-£24 double.
Parking for 4.
(symbols)

MUNDESLEY-ON-SEA

Norfolk
Map ref 3C1

4m NE. Walsham
Small seaside resort with a superb sandy beach and excellent bathing. Nearby is a smock-mill still with cap and sails. (i)

The Grange

High St., Mundesley-on-Sea,
Norwich, NR11 8JL
☎ (0263) 721556
Beautiful, well-furnished house in attractive half-acre garden. Home cooking a speciality. Ideal for the Broads and Norwich, birdwatching, fishing and the beach.
Bedrooms: 2 double & 1 twin, 1 family room.
Bathrooms: 2 public.
Bed & breakfast: £11-£12 single, £22-£44 double.
Half board: £19-£20 daily.
Evening meal 6pm (l.o. 5pm).
Parking for 10.
(symbols)

NAYLAND

Suffolk
Map ref 3B2

6m N. Colchester
Charmingly located village on the River Stour which owed its former prosperity to the cloth trade. The hub of the village is the 15th C Alston Court. The altar-piece of St. James Church was painted by John Constable.

Gladwins Farm

Harpers Hill, Nayland,
Colchester, CO6 4NU
☎ (0206) 262261
22-acre smallholding. Peaceful wooded surroundings overlooking Stour valley. Entrance on main A134 road. Ideal for touring and bird watching. Golf 2 miles away.
Bedrooms: 1 single, 2 double & 1 twin, 1 family room.
Bathrooms: 2 private, 1 public.

Bed & breakfast: £11-£14 single, £22-£38 double.
Parking for 7.
(symbols)

NEATISHEAD

Norfolk
Map ref 3C1

4m NE. Wroxham

Regency Guest House
(symbol)

Neatishead Village Post Office Stores, Neatishead,
NR12 8AD
☎ Horning (0692) 630233
Ideal location for Broads boating and fishing activities. Accent on personal service. 10 minutes from Norwich off the A1151, 6 miles from the coast. Radio or TV in all bedrooms.
Bedrooms: 2 double & 3 twin, 2 family rooms.
Bathrooms: 2 public.
Bed & breakfast: from £16 single, from £24 double.
Parking for 8.
(symbols)

NORTH WALSHAM

Norfolk
Map ref 3C1

14m N. Norwich
Weekly market has been held here for 700 years. One mile south of town is a cross commemorating the Peasants' Revolt of 1381.

Ockley House

Meeting Hill, Nr. North Walsham, NR28 9LS
☎ (0692) 402946
Comfortable accommodation with a friendly atmosphere, in a quiet rural setting 2 miles south east of North Walsham. Ideal for coast, Broads and Norwich.
Bedrooms: 2 double & 1 twin.
Bathrooms: 1 public.
Bed & breakfast: £9-£10 single, £18-£20 double.
Evening meal 6pm (l.o. 7.30pm).
Parking for 3.
(symbols)

THE SYMBOLS ARE EXPLAINED ON THE FLAP INSIDE THE BACK COVER.

Norfolk
Map ref 3C1

See also South Walsham.
Beautiful cathedral city and county town on the River Wensum with many fine museums and medieval churches. Norman castle, Guildhall and interesting medieval streets. Good shopping centre and market.

Aberdale Lodge
211 Earlham Rd., Norwich, NR2 3RQ
☎ (0603) 502100
Family-run Victorian guest house in historic city of Norwich. Easy reach of Norfolk Broads, heritage coastline and countryside.
Bedrooms: 3 single, 1 double & 1 twin, 1 family room.
Bathrooms: 1 public.
Bed & breakfast: £10.50-£11 single, £21-£22 double.

Albion House
Listed
185 Dereham Rd., Norwich, NR2 3TE
☎ (0603) 617555
Close to city centre. On A47 from the North and Midlands. Easy access from ring road. Parking on premises.
Bedrooms: 1 single, 1 twin, 1 family room.
Bathrooms: 1 public.
Bed & breakfast: max. £10 single, max. £20 double.
Parking for 8.

Androse House
272 Unthank Rd., Norwich, NR2 2AJ
☎ (0603) 54276
Attractive Edwardian family house in fine area near city, university and bus routes. Pleasant bedrooms and a warm welcome.
Bedrooms: 1 double & 1 twin.
Bathrooms: 1 public.
Bed & breakfast: £12-£13 single, £22-£23 double.
Parking for 3.

Arodet House
132 Earlham Rd., Norwich, NR2 3HF
☎ (0603) 503522
Modernised Victorian guesthouse offering personal attention. Convenient for city centre and university.

Bedrooms: 2 single, 2 double.
Bathrooms: 1 public.
Bed & breakfast: £11.50-£12.50 single, £23-£25 double.

Arrow Hotel
2 Britannia Rd., Norwich, NR1 4HP
☎ (0603) 628051
Family-run hotel in peaceful surroundings on the edge of conservation area, overlooking the city. Home cooking a speciality.
Bedrooms: 5 single, 2 double & 3 twin, 2 family rooms.
Bathrooms: 4 public; 3 private showers.
Bed & breakfast: £14-£18 single, £26-£30 double.
Half board: £20-£24 daily, £126-£147 weekly.
Evening meal 6.30pm (l.o. 7pm).
Parking for 10.

Mrs. F. Warns
64 Bishopgate, Norwich, NR1 4AA
☎ (0603) 627307
Victorian house situated between the cathedral and historic Bishopbridge. All bedrooms overlook the spacious garden.
Bedrooms: 1 double & 1 twin.
Bathrooms: 1 public.
Bed & breakfast: £22-£24 double.
Parking for 1.

Blue Cedar Lodge
Listed
391 Earlham Rd., Norwich, NR2 3RQ
☎ (0603) 58331
Quiet modern house run by friendly family, set in wooded grounds. Convenient for city centre and University of East Anglia.
Bedrooms: 1 single, 1 double & 1 twin, 1 family room.
Bathrooms: 1 public.
Bed & breakfast: £10.50-£11 single, £21-£22 double.
Parking for 8.

Church Farmhouse
Howe, Norwich, NR15 1HD
☎ Brooke (0508) 50565
Grade II listed farmhouse with original beams and studwork, in a peaceful rural village 7 miles south of Norwich. Abundance of wild life.
Bedrooms: 1 double & 1 twin.
Bathrooms: 1 public.
Bed & breakfast: £12-£14 single, £24-£48 double.
Parking for 8.

Gables Farm
Hemblington, Norwich, NR13 4PT
☎ South Walsham (060 549) 548
400-acre arable farm. Comfortable period thatched farmhouse near Broads. Facilities for bird watching, walking and private coarse fishing. Non-smokers only please. 6 miles east of Norwich.
Bedrooms: 1 twin, 1 family room.
Bathrooms: 1 public.
Bed & breakfast: £14 single, £25 double.
Parking for 3.

The Limes
188 Unthank Rd., Norwich, NR2 2AH
☎ (0603) 54282
Large airy, comfortable rooms, close to the city centre and university. Run by a young, friendly family.
Bedrooms: 1 single, 1 double, 1 family room.
Bathrooms: 2 public.
Bed & breakfast: £12-£14 single, £24-£26 double.

Witton Hall
Norwich, NR13 5DN
☎ (0603) 714580
Elegant Georgian farmhouse in the heart of Norfolk. Peaceful, mature grounds. Swimming pool in walled garden.
Bedrooms: 1 double & 1 twin, 1 family room.
Bathrooms: 3 private.
Bed & breakfast: £24 double.
Parking for 7.
Open April-October.

Suffolk
Map ref 3B2

5m NE. Hadleigh

Mount Pleasant Farm, Coward-Redman Farms Ltd.
Offton, Ipswich, IP8 4RP
☎ (047 333) 8896
8-acre smallholding. Genuinely secluded, typical Suffolk farmhouse. 30 minutes from the sea, water park five minutes away. Many local beauty spots. Evening meals a speciality.
Bedrooms: 3 double & 1 twin.
Bathrooms: 2 public.
Bed & breakfast: £10.50-£11.50 single, £20-£20.50 double.
Half board: £16.50-£17.50 daily, £105-£110 weekly.
Lunch available.
Evening meal 7pm (l.o. 8pm).
Parking for 10.

Norfolk
Map ref 3C1

5m NE. Norwich

Manor Barn House
Back Lane, Rackheath, Norwich, NR13 6NN
☎ (060 53) 3543
6 miles north of Norwich, just off the B1150, 2 miles from Wroxham (Broads area). Beautiful quiet setting, pleasant gardens, family atmosphere.
Bedrooms: 1 single, 2 double.
Bathrooms: 1 private, 2 public.
Bed & breakfast: £12.50 single, £25 double.
Parking for 2.

Essex
Map ref 2D1

4m E. Saffron Walden

Newhouse Farm
Radwinter, Saffron Walden, CB10 2SP
☎ (079 987) 211

Continued ▶

WE ADVISE YOU TO CONFIRM YOUR BOOKING IN WRITING.

RADWINTER

Continued

300-acre mixed farm. Georgian and Tudor farmhouse set in 3 acres of gardens with lake and moat. Cambridge, Saffron Walden, Ardley End Mansion and the Imperial War Museum are nearby.
Bedrooms: 2 twin.
Bathrooms: 1 private, 1 public.
Bed & breakfast: £12 single, £24 double.
Half board: £17 daily.
Evening meal 7pm (l.o. 9pm).
Parking for 4.

RAMSEY

Cambridgeshire
Map ref 3A2

10m SE. Peterborough

The Leys
Listed
25 Bury Rd., Ramsey, Huntingdon, PE17 1NE
☎ (0487) 813221
Large family house with a friendly atmosphere. On the B1040 on the southern outskirts of Ramsay, between Huntingdon and Peterborough.
Bedrooms: 1 single, 1 twin, 2 family rooms.
Bathrooms: 2 public.
Bed & breakfast: £10-£11.50 single, £20-£23 double.
Half board: £15-£16.50 daily, from £105 weekly.
Evening meal 8.30pm.
Parking for 6.

REEPHAM

Norfolk
Map ref 3B1

6m SW. Aylsham
An important market town in the 18th C and an air of prosperity lingers on. Bordering the attractive market place are Dial House, a large town house, and St. Michael's Church. Nearby is the Norfolk Wildlife Park.

Rookery Farm
Church St., Reepham, NR10 4JW
☎ Norwich (0603) 871847
Very attractive listed farmhouse in centre of small market town in conservation area. Within easy reach of Norwich, coast and Broads.

Bedrooms: 1 double & 1 twin, 1 family room.
Bathrooms: 3 private.
Bed & breakfast: £15-£17 single, £26-£30 double.
Parking for 3.

RENDHAM

Suffolk
Map ref 3C2

3m NW. Saxmundham

Yew Tree Cottage
Rendham, Saxmundham, IP17 2AF
☎ (072 878) 746
Picturesque country cottage in small quiet village. Annexed to owner's home. Rendham village 2.5 miles west A12. Use of garden.
Bedrooms: 1 double & 2 twin.
Bathrooms: 1 public.
Bed & breakfast: £8.50-£9 single, £17-£18 double.
Open April-October.

ROLLESBY

Norfolk
Map ref 3C1

7m NW. Great Yarmouth
Rollesby Broad forms part of the Ormesby Broad complex and fine views can be seen from the road which runs through the middle.

The Old Court House ♠
Listed
Court Rd., Rollesby, Great Yarmouth, NR29 5HG
☎ Fleggburgh (049 377) 665
Specialising in family holidays with a friendly atmosphere and home cooking. Bicycles for hire. Free tennis nearby. Fishing in local broad. Row boats for hire locally.
Bedrooms: 1 single, 1 double & 1 twin, 4 family rooms.
Bathrooms: 3 private, 2 public.
Bed & breakfast: £22-£26 single, £26-£30 double.
Evening meal 6.30pm (l.o. 6.30pm).
Parking for 20.
Open February-November.

SHERINGHAM

Norfolk
Map ref 3B1

22m N. Norwich
Holiday resort with Victorian and Edwardian hotels and a sand and shingle beach where the fishing boats are hauled up. The North Norfolk Railway operates from Sheringham Station during the summer. *i*

Sandy Lodge, No. 12
The Boulevard, Sheringham, NR26 8LJ
☎ (0263) 825779
Family home 2 minutes' walk from sea or town centre. Large rooms with all modern facilities.
Bedrooms: 1 double & 1 twin, 1 family room.
Bathrooms: 1 public; 2 private showers.
Bed & breakfast: £9.50 single, £19 double.
Open April-October.

SIBLE HEDINGHAM

Essex
Map ref 3B2

Comfrey Cottage
29/31 Queen St., Sible Hedingham, CO9 3RH
☎ (0787) 60271
Two Victorian cottages converted into one, keeping its charm, with modern facilities. Home produce and fresh food.
Bedrooms: 2 single, 1 twin, 1 family room.
Bathrooms: 1 private, 1 public.
Bed & breakfast: £10-£12 single, £20-£30 double.
Parking for 7.

SOUTH LOPHAM

Norfolk
Map ref 3B2

4m NW. Diss

Maltings Farm
Blo Norton Rd., South Lopham, Diss, IP22 2HT
☎ Bressingham (037 988) 201
70-acre dairy farm. Recently renovated, timber-framed farmhouse with inglenook fireplaces.
Bedrooms: 1 twin, 2 family rooms.
Bathrooms: 2 public.

Bed & breakfast: from £24 double.
Half board: from £19 daily, from £126 weekly.
Evening meal 6pm (l.o. 6.30pm).
Parking for 10.

SOUTH WALSHAM

Norfolk
Map ref 3C1

3m NW. Acle
Village famous for having 2 churches in adjoining churchyards. South Walsham Broad consists of an inner and outer section, the former being private. Alongside, the Fairhaven Garden Trust has woodland and water-gardens open to the public.

Holly Farm ♠
South Walsham, Norwich, NR13 6EQ
☎ (060 549) 220
100-acre arable farm. Adjacent to Upton Fen - 160-acre wood owned by Norfolk Naturalists Trust. Peaceful but not isolated.
Bedrooms: 1 single, 1 double, 1 family room.
Bathrooms: 2 public.
Bed & breakfast: max. £12 single, max. £24 double.
Parking for 6.
Open March-October.

Mrs. V.M. Dewing ♠
Old Hall Farm, South Walsham, Norwich, NR13 6DS
☎ (060 549) 271
80-acre mixed farm. Thatched farmhouse dating from 17th C., on the edge of Broadland village. A47 from Norwich towards Great Yarmouth; left towards South Walsham. 2 miles on the right.
Bedrooms: 2 double & 1 twin.
Bathrooms: 1 private, 2 public.
Bed & breakfast: £12-£13.50 single, £20-£25 double.
Parking for 4.

PLEASE MENTION THIS GUIDE WHEN MAKING A BOOKING.

WE ADVISE YOU TO CONFIRM YOUR BOOKING IN WRITING.

SOUTHEND-ON-SEA

Essex
Map ref 3B3

On the Thames estuary and the nearest seaside resort to London. Amusements abound along the seafront, culminating in the Kursaal Amusement Park. There are 3 museums, including Prittlewell Priory set in lovely parkland. ℹ

Ilfracombe House Hotel ⚋

😊😊😊😊

11-13 Wilson Rd., Southend-on-Sea, SS1 1HQ
☎ (0702) 351000
Victorian house in a conservation area adjacent to cliff gardens, the sea and the town centre.
Bedrooms: 5 single, 4 double & 3 twin, 1 family room.
Bathrooms: 13 private.
Bed & breakfast: £28-£33 single, £42 double.
Half board: £37-£42 daily, £196-£231 weekly.
Lunch available.
Evening meal 6.30pm (l.o. 7.30pm).
Credit: Access, Visa, Diners, Amex.
🛁 👌 🖐 📞 ☕ 🍴 🛏 📺 🌐 ⚓ ✗ 🔯 SP Ⓣ

SOUTHWOLD

Suffolk
Map ref 3C2

8m E. Halesworth
Pleasant and attractive seaside town with a triangular market square and spacious greens around which stand flint, brick and colour wash cottages. The parish church of St. Edmund is one of the greatest churches in Suffolk. ℹ

Dunburgh Guest House

28 North Parade, Southwold, IP18 6LT
☎ (0502) 723253
House overlooking the sea. All bedrooms have seaviews. Comfortable and relaxed atmosphere. Home cooking.
Bedrooms: 2 double & 1 twin.
Bathrooms: 2 public.
Bed & breakfast: £15-£16 single, £30-£32 double.
Half board: £22-£24 daily.
Evening meal 7pm (l.o. 7pm).
🛁 📞 🌐 🛏 📺 🌐 ⚓ 🔯

Mrs. R.D. Hemsley

28 Field Stile Rd., Southwold, IP18 6LD
☎ (0502) 723588
A small private house near beach and town centre. Pets welcome.
Bedrooms: 1 single, 1 double & 1 twin.
Bathrooms: 1 public.
Bed & breakfast: £20 single.
Half board: £30 daily.
Lunch available.
Evening meal 6.30pm (l.o. 9.30pm).
🛁 👌 🖐 📞 ☕ 🍴 🛏 📺 🌐 ⚓ 🔯

Long Shore House

22 North Parade, Southwold, IP18 6LT
☎ (0502) 722768
Seafront, comfortable, friendly Victorian family house. Fresh fish for sale to order.
Bedrooms: 1 single, 2 double & 2 twin, 1 family room.
Bathrooms: 2 public.
Bed & breakfast: £13 single, £26 double.
Half board: £20 daily, £133 weekly.
Evening meal 7pm (l.o. 7.30pm).
🛁 📞 ☕ 🌐 Ⓥ 🔯 📺 🌐 ⚓

Red Lion

🅔

2 South Green, Southwold, IP18 6ET
☎ (0502) 722385
17th C. inn with accommodation. Comfortable public lounge, dining room, private breakfast room. Lunches and evening meals served.
Bedrooms: 2 double & 1 twin.
Bathrooms: 1 private, 1 public.
Bed & breakfast: £27.50-£37.50 double.
Parking for 3.
☕ Ⓥ 🌐 ⚓ ✗ 🔯 OAP SP

STEEPLE BUMPSTEAD

Essex
Map ref 3B2

3m S. Haverhill
An interesting building in the village is the Moot Hall, which in the 17th C served as a village school and was restored as part of the 1977 Jubilee celebrations.

Yew Tree House

Listed

15 Chapel St., Steeple Bumpstead, Haverhill, Suffolk CB9 7DQ
☎ (044 084) 364
Charming Victorian house in centre of Steeple Bumpstead, next to village shop.
Bedrooms: 1 double & 1 twin.
Bathrooms: 1 public.
Bed & breakfast: £8.50-£9.50 single, £19-£21 double.
Half board: £15.50-£17 daily, £105-£112 weekly.
Evening meal 6pm (l.o. 8pm).
Parking for 2.
🛁2 ✗ ☕ 🌐 Ⓥ 📺 🌐 ✗ 🔯

STRADBROKE

Suffolk
Map ref 3B2

7m NW. Framlington
Thought to be the birthplace of Robert Grosseteste, once Bishop of Lincoln and writer.

The Ivy House Public House

Listed

Wilby Rd., Stradbroke, Eye, IP21 5JN
☎ (037 984) 634
A small thatched public house in a village with shops, hairdressers and bank twice a week. Food provided during opening hours.
Bedrooms: 1 double & 1 twin.
Bathrooms: 1 public.
Bed & breakfast: from £10 single, from £20 double.
Parking for 20.
Open April-September.
📞 ☕ ✗ 🔯

STRATFORD ST. MARY

Suffolk
Map ref 3B2

6m NE. Colchester
Set in countryside known as Constable country.

Rosebank

Lower St., Stratford St. Mary, CO7 6JS
☎ Colchester (0206) 322259
Attractive 600-year-old listed manor house, part Tudor, in Constable country. Gardens with river frontage. Boating and fishing available. Just off the A12.
Bedrooms: 3 twin, 1 family room.
Bathrooms: 1 private, 1 public.
Bed & breakfast: £13.50-£15 single, £25-£28 double.
Parking for 6.
🛁 👌 🖐 📞 ☕ 🌐 Ⓥ 🛏 🌐 ⚓ ♿ 🚶 🔯 🏕

SUDBOURNE

Suffolk
Map ref 3C2

2m N. Orford

Gemini Cottage

Listed

7 Long Row, Snape Rd., Sudbourne, Woodbridge, IP12 2AT
☎ Orford (0394) 450207
Modernised period cottage, ideal for walkers, cyclists and motorists, offering an optional 3-course dinner with fresh garden produce.
Bedrooms: 1 single, 1 double & 1 twin.
Bathrooms: 1 public.
Bed & breakfast: £8.50 single, £17 double.
Half board: £13.50 daily, £78 weekly.
Evening meal 7pm (l.o. 5pm).
Parking for 3.
Open April-October.
🛁8 ☕ 🌐 🖐 Ⓥ 🔯 📺 🌐 🔯

Long Meadows

Listed

Gorse Lane, Sudbourne, Woodbridge, IP12 2BD
☎ (0394) 450269
Rural situation among meadows. Plantsman's garden! Modern bungalow, modified to cottage style.
Bedrooms: 1 single, 2 twin.
Bathrooms: 1 private, 2 public.

Continued ▶

INDIVIDUAL PROPRIETORS HAVE SUPPLIED ALL DETAILS OF ACCOMMODATION. ALTHOUGH WE DO CHECK FOR ACCURACY, WE ADVISE YOU TO CONFIRM PRICES AND OTHER INFORMATION AT THE TIME OF BOOKING.

SUDBOURNE

Continued

Bed & breakfast: £9-£10.50 single, £18-£21 double. Parking for 4.
🛇14 🖧 ⏻ Ⓤ 🛏 📺 🎞 ⌂ ❀ 🍴

SUTON

Norfolk
Map ref 3B1

1.5m SW. Wymondham

Rose Farm
Listed

Suton, Wymondham, NR18 9JN
☎ Wymondham (0953) 603512
2-acre poultry farm. Homely farmhouse accommodation within easy reach of Norwich, Broads and Breckland. Bus and train services close by.
Bedrooms: 2 single, 1 double, 1 family room.
Bathrooms: 2 public.
Bed & breakfast: £11 single, £22 double.
Half board: £16 daily, £105 weekly.
Evening meal 7pm.
Parking for 4.
🛇 🦮 🖵 🕾 🛏 📺 🎞 ⌂ ♪ ❀ 🍴

SWAFFHAM

Norfolk
Map ref 3B1

14m SE. King's Lynn
Busy market town with a triangular market-place, a domed rotunda built in 1783 and a number of Georgian houses. The church possesses a large library of ancient books.

Home Farm
Listed

South Pickenham, Swaffham, PE37 8DZ
☎ Great Cressingham (076 06) 259/221
Old beamed farmhouse, gardens and patio within easy reach of Sandringham and the coast. 4-course evening meal, friendly atmosphere.
Bedrooms: 1 single, 1 double & 1 twin, 1 family room.
Bathrooms: 2 public; 1 private shower.
Bed & breakfast: from £12.50 single, from £25 double.
Half board: from £21.50 daily, £150-£175 weekly.

Evening meal 4.50pm (l.o. 10pm).
Parking for 50.
🛇 🦮 Ⓤ 🛏 ⏻ Ⓥ 🛏 📺 🎞 ⌂ ❀ 🍴 🐾 Ⓣ

TERRINGTON ST. CLEMENT

Norfolk
Map ref 3B1

4m W. King's Lynn

Homelands
😀😀

79 Sutton Rd., Terrington St. Clement, King's Lynn, PE34 4PJ
☎ King's Lynn (0553) 828401
A detached house in 1 acre of gardens, 5 miles from King's Lynn and 10 miles from Sandringham. Home cooking. Evening meals by arrangement.
Bedrooms: 1 double & 1 twin.
Bathrooms: 2 public.
Bed & breakfast: £14.50 single, £22 double.
Half board: from £18 daily, £122.50 weekly.
Parking for 4.
Open April-October.
🛇 Ⓤ 🕊 🛏 📺 🎞 ❀ 🍴

THEBERTON

Suffolk
Map ref 3C2

Theberton Grange ♨
😀😀😀

Theberton, IP16 4RR
☎ Leiston (0728) 830625
An elegant country house retaining the warmth and informality of a family home. An ideal base for Aldeburgh Festival, Minsmere and heritage coast.
Bedrooms: 1 single, 2 double & 3 twin.
Bathrooms: 4 private, 1 public.
Bed & breakfast: £17-£40 single, £38-£55 double.
Half board: £29.50-£52.50 daily.
Evening meal 7pm (l.o. 9pm).
Parking for 15.
Open February-December.
Credit: Access, Visa.
🛇5 🕾 🖵 🕊 🛏 🎞 ⌂ ▶ ❀ 🍴 🐾 🐾 SP 🎏

PLEASE CHECK PRICES AND OTHER DETAILS AT THE TIME OF BOOKING.

THOMPSON

Norfolk
Map ref 3B1

3m S. Watton

College Farm ♨
Listed

Thompson, Thetford, IP24 1QG
☎ Caston (095 383) 318
15-acre non working farm. 14th C. farmhouse, formerly a college for priests. In quiet village away from main road. Meals provided by nearby inns.
Bedrooms: 1 single, 1 double & 2 twin.
Bathrooms: 2 public.
Bed & breakfast: £12-£14 single, £24-£28 double.
Parking for 10.
🛇7 🦮 🖵 Ⓤ 🎞 ⌂ ❀ 🍴 🎏

Thatched House

Pockthorpe Corner, Thompson, Thetford, IP24 1PJ
☎ Caston (095 383) 577
Thatched country house situated on the edge of quiet Breckland village of Thompson.
Bedrooms: 1 single, 1 double & 2 twin, 1 family room.
Bathrooms: 2 public.
Bed & breakfast: from £12 single, from £24 double.
Half board: from £17 daily, from £100 weekly.
Evening meal 6pm (l.o. 10pm).
Parking for 6.
🛇 🦮 🦮 🖩 🖵 ⏻ Ⓤ ⚫ Ⓥ 🛏 📺 🎞 🍴 🎏

TUNSTEAD

Norfolk
Map ref 3C1

4m N. Wroxham

Carinya
Listed

Anchor St., Tunstead, Norwich, NR12 8HW
☎ Smallburgh (069 260) 545
Large family home in peaceful rural setting, 4 miles from Wroxham. 14 miles north east of Norwich on B1151, turn off for 1.5 miles on minor road. Full directions are given by phone and map sent at time of booking. Own car is essential.
Bedrooms: 3 double.
Bathrooms: 1 public.
Bed & breakfast: from £12 single.
Evening meal 5pm (l.o. 9pm).
Parking for 3.
🛇 🦮 🖩 ⏻ Ⓤ ⚫ Ⓥ 🛏 📺 🎞 ⌂ 🔨 🍴 🎏

WALTON-ON-THE-NAZE

Essex
Map ref 3C2

7m NE. Clacton-on-Sea
Seaside resort on the Ness peninsula with lovely sands and good sea-bathing. The cliffs contain many interesting fossils. There is a pier, the Naze Tower and a Martello Tower. 🛈

West Lodge Guest House

Saville St., Walton-on-the-Naze, CO14 8P
☎ Frinton-on-Sea (0225) 677172
Large detached Victorian house, minutes by foot from sandy beaches, shops and public transport.
Bedrooms: 1 single, 3 double & 1 twin, 2 family rooms.
Bathrooms: 2 public.
Bed & breakfast: £8-£10 single, £16-£20 double.
Parking for 3.
🛇 🦮 ⏻ Ⓥ 🛏 📺 🎞 🎏 DAP

WELLS-NEXT-THE-SEA

Norfolk
Map ref 3B1

9m N. Fakenham
Seaside resort and small port on the North Coast. The Buttlands is a large tree-lined green surrounded by Georgian houses and from here narrow streets lead to the quay. 🛈

Ilex House

Bases Lane, Wells-next-the-Sea, NR23 1DH
☎ Fakenham (0328) 710556
Small Georgian home. Grade II listed building set in approximately 1 acre of secluded, walled garden. Near Wells-next-the-Sea and amenities.
Bedrooms: 1 double & 1 twin, 2 family rooms.
Bathrooms: 1 public; 3 private showers.
Bed & breakfast: from £16 single, from £27 double.
Half board: from £24 daily, from £168 weekly.
Evening meal 7.30pm (l.o. 10am).
Parking for 8.
🛇 🦮 ⏻ ⏻ Ⓥ 🛏 📺 🎞 ⌂ ❀ 🍴 🎏

Ingledene
Listed
47 Freeman St., Wells-next-the-Sea, NR23 1BQ
☎ Fakenham (0328) 710404
Large friendly old house of historic interest in conservation area, a few yards from the seafront. Garage and parking space.
Bedrooms: 1 double, 2 family rooms.
Bathrooms: 1 private, 1 public.
Bed & breakfast: £9-£12 single, £18-£24 double.
Parking for 4.
Open February-October.
⚏ 🛱 Ⓤ Ⓥ 🚪 Ⓣ 🏊 ➡ ► 🅿
🏠

Mill House Guest House
Northfield Lane, Wells-next-the-Sea, NR23 1JZ
☎ Fakenham (0328) 710739
Former mill owner's house in secluded garden with croquet lawn and badminton. Close to town centre and 2 minutes' walk from quay.
Bedrooms: 2 single, 4 double & 1 twin, 1 family room.
Bathrooms: 3 public.
Bed & breakfast: £12.50-£15 single, £23-£28 double.
Half board: £20-£21.50 daily, £136.50-£147 weekly.
Evening meal 6.30pm (l.o. midday).
Parking for 10.
⚏ 🍴 🥄 Ⓥ 🚪 Ⓣ 🏊 ➡ 🍴
✿ 🏠 SP 🏠

West End House
26 Dogger Lane, Wells-next-the-Sea, NR23 1BE
☎ Fakenham (0328) 711190
Small, friendly guest house run by owners. No restrictions, easy going atmosphere. All welcome.
Bedrooms: 2 double & 1 twin, 1 family room.
Bathrooms: 2 public; 1 private shower.
Bed & breakfast: £20-£24 double.
Parking for 3.
⚏ Ⓤ Ⓥ 🚪 Ⓣ 🏊 🏠

West End of Mersea Island
Weatherboarded and Georgian brick cottages still remain as evidence of the old fishing, oyster and sailing centre and the small museum includes fishing exhibits.

Hazel Oak
28 Seaview Avenue, West Mersea, CO5 8HE
☎ (0206) 3030
Hazel Oak is a quiet family residence 5 minutes' walk to the beach and 15 minutes to the yachting centre. Non-smokers only.
Bedrooms: 1 twin, 1 family room.
Bathrooms: 1 private, 1 public.
Bed & breakfast: £12-£15 single, £25-£30 double.
Parking for 2.
⚏ 🍴 🥄 Ⓤ ✂ Ⓣ 🏊 ► 🍴
🏠

7m W. Fakenham

White House Farm
🏠🏠
Lynn Rd., West Rudham, King's Lynn, PE31 8RW
☎ (048 522) 327
17th C. farmhouse near Sandringham, Walsingham and Houghton Hall. Off-season two day breaks available.
Bedrooms: 1 double & 2 twin, 2 family rooms.
Bathrooms: 3 private, 2 public.
Bed & breakfast: £28-£40 double.
Half board: £20-£28 daily, £120-£168 weekly.
Lunch available.
Evening meal 7.30pm (l.o. 5pm).
Parking for 10.
⚏ 🥄 🍴 Ⓥ 🚪 Ⓣ 🏊 ➡
✿ 🏠 SP 🏠

3m NW. Stowmarket

The Old Rectory
Listed
Wetherden, Stowmarket
☎ Elmswell (0359) 40144
Comfortable well-furnished Georgian house in 12 acres overlooking village. Situated off the A45 between Stowmarket and Bury St. Edmunds.
Bedrooms: 1 single, 1 double & 1 twin.
Bathrooms: 1 private, 2 public.
Bed & breakfast: £15 single, £30 double.
Parking for 10.
⚏ 🏊 Ⓤ 🍴 Ⓣ 🏊 ➡ 🍴 ✿
🍴 🏠 🏠

Haygreen Farm
Whepstead, Bury St. Edmunds, IP29 0UD
☎ Chevington (0284) 850567
6-acre mixed farm. Listed 18th C. Suffolk farmhouse on smallholding with horses, sheep, goats and other livestock. Within easy reach of Cambridge, Newmarket, Long Melford and Lavenham.
Bedrooms: 1 single, 1 double, 1 family room.
Bathrooms: 1 public.
Bed & breakfast: £10.50 single, £20 double.
Parking for 6.
⚏ 🛱 🖵 🥄 Ⓤ 🏊 ∪ 🍴 🏠
🏠

4m S. Fakenham

The Old Bakery
High St., Whissonsett, Dereham, NR20 5AP
☎ Fakenham (0328) 700464
Modernised early 19th C. house in a village 4 miles south of Fakenham, 2 miles east of the A1065. Touring centre for north Norfolk.
Bedrooms: 1 single, 1 double & 1 twin.
Bathrooms: 1 public.
Bed & breakfast: from £9.50 single, from £19 double.

Half board: from £15.50 daily, from £106 weekly.
Evening meal 6.30pm.
Parking for 2.
⚏ 🛱 Ⓤ 🍴 🚪 Ⓣ 🏊 ➡ 🍴
🏠

7m S. Cambridge

Red Lion Hotel 🅼
😊😊😊
Station Rd., Whittlesford, Cambridge, CB2 4NL
☎ Cambridge (0223) 832047 & 832115
Traditional English inn with modern facilities. Well situated for Cambridge with excellent road and rail connections. 1 mile from Duxford Imperial War Museum. Entertainment in night spot at weekends or by special arrangement. Weekly rates available.
Bedrooms: 7 single, 6 double & 1 twin, 4 family rooms.
Bathrooms: 18 private.
Bed & breakfast: from £32.50 single, from £42.50 double.
Half board: £35.50-£47.50 daily.
Lunch available.
Evening meal 7pm (l.o. 10pm).
Parking for 200.
Credit: Visa, Diners, Amex.
⚏ 🛱 📞 🖵 🥄 🍴 Ⓥ 🏊
➡ 🍴 ✿ ✿ 🍴 DAP SP 🏠

Clare Farm House
Listed
86-88 Main St., Witchford, Nr. Ely, CB6 2HQ
☎ Ely (0353) 664135
450-acre arable farm. Large modern farmhouse in village 2 miles from Ely and 16 miles from Newmarket.
Bedrooms: 1 single, 1 twin, 1 family room.
Bathrooms: 1 private, 2 public.
Bed & breakfast: £10-£15 single, £20-£30 double.
Parking for 10.
⚏ 🍴 🏊 🖵 🥄 Ⓤ 🏊 ✿ 🍴
🏠

INDIVIDUAL PROPRIETORS HAVE SUPPLIED ALL DETAILS OF ACCOMMODATION. ALTHOUGH WE DO CHECK FOR ACCURACY, WE ADVISE YOU TO CONFIRM PRICES AND OTHER INFORMATION AT THE TIME OF BOOKING.

MAP REFERENCES APPLY TO THE COLOUR MAPS TOWARDS THE END OF THIS GUIDE.

WITHERSFIELD

Suffolk
Map ref 3B2

2m NW. Haverhill

Leighswood

Rose Hill, Withersfield, Near
Haverhill, CB9 7SE
☎ (0440) 62783
*In the quiet village of
Withersfield, in gently rolling
Suffolk countryside, within
easy touring distance of
Saffron Walden, Lavenham,
Ely, Bury St. Edmunds,
Newmarket and Cambridge.
Close to many stately homes
and unspoilt villages. 1 hour
from London by M11.*
Bedrooms: 1 double & 2 twin.
Bathrooms: 1 private,
1 public.
Bed & breakfast: £12.50-£15
single, £20-£25 double.
Parking for 10.
‰Ⓡ🖵🖐️Ⓤ🗡️🔟☀️🗡️📶

WIX

Essex
Map ref 3B2

5m SE. Manningtree

New Farm House 🅼
😀😀😀

Spinnell's Lane, Wix,
Manningtree, CO11 2UJ
☎ (0255) 870365
*52-acre arable farm. Modern
comfortable farmhouse in large
garden, convenient for Harwich
port and Constable Country.
From Wix village crossroads,
take Bradfield Road, turn right
at top of hill; first house on the
left.*
Bedrooms: 2 single, 2 double
& 2 twin, 5 family rooms.
Bathrooms: 6 private,
2 public.
Bed & breakfast: £12.50-£16
single, £25-£32 double.
Half board: £19-£22.50 daily,
£126.50-£151 weekly.
Evening meal 6.30pm (l.o.
6pm).
Parking for 11.
Credit: Visa.
‰👜Ⓡ🖵🖐️🍴Ⓥ🗡️🗡️
📺🔟🔌👤☀️🚲

**THERE IS A SPECIAL
SECTION IN THIS
GUIDE LISTING
ACCOMMODATION
ESPECIALLY
SUITABLE FOR
GROUPS AND
YOUNG PEOPLE.**

WOODBRIDGE

Suffolk
Map ref 3C2

*See also Eyke,
Framlingham.*
Once a busy seaport, the
town is now a sailing
centre on the River
Deben. There are many
buildings of architectural
merit including The Bell
and Angel Inns. The 18th
C Tide Mill is now
restored and open to the
public.

Bantry 🅼
😀😀😀

Chapel Rd., Saxtead,
Woodbridge, IP13 9RB
☎ Earl Soham (072 882) 578
*Self-contained suite, ideal for
family holidays, in picturesque
village near historic
Framlingham. Central for
touring East Anglia.*
Bedrooms: 1 family room.
Bathrooms: 1 private,
1 public.
Bed & breakfast: £13-£14
single, £26-£28 double.
Half board: £18.50-£19.50
daily, £129.50 weekly.
Evening meal 6.30pm (l.o.
7.30pm).
Parking for 3.
‰👜Ⓡ🖵🖐️Ⓤ🍴🗡️🔟
🔌🕛👤☀️🗡️📶🆖

Meadow View

School Lane, Bromeswell,
Woodbridge, IP12 2PY
☎ Eyke (0394) 460635
*Beams throughout. Opposite a
golf course. 3 miles from
Woodbridge.*
Bedrooms: 1 twin, 1 family
room.
Bathrooms: 2 public.
Bed & breakfast: from £10
single, from £20 double.
‰👜🖵🖐️Ⓤ Ⓥ🗡️📺🔟
🔌🕛☀️🗡️📶🆖🏠

Moat Barn

Bredfield, Woodbridge,
IP13 6BD
☎ Charsfield (047 337) 520
*Renovated Suffolk barn with
exposed beams and original
features in over one acre of
grounds. The village has a pub,
general stores and church, and
is just three miles from the
market town of Woodbridge.*
Bedrooms: 1 single, 2 double
& 1 twin.
Bathrooms: 1 public.
Bed & breakfast: £15 single,
£25 double.
Parking for 10.
‰👜🖵🖐️Ⓤ🔟🔌▶️🗡️
🏠

Spion Kop
😀😀

Spring Lane, Ufford,
Woodbridge, IP13 6EF
☎ Eyke (0394) 460277
*Thatched house, built around
the turn of the century set in
environmentally sensitive rural
surroundings, with pleasant
walks to River Deben.*
Bedrooms: 1 double & 1 twin.
Bathrooms: 1 private,
2 public.
Bed & breakfast: £12-£14
single, £24-£28 double.
Half board: £20-£22 daily.
Evening meal 6pm.
Parking for 3.
‰🗡️🖵🖐️Ⓤ🔟🔌🕛☀️
🆖

WOOLPIT

Suffolk
Map ref 3B2

5m NW. Stowmarket
Village with some
attractive timber-framed
Tudor and Georgian
houses. St. Mary's
Church is one of the most
beautiful churches in
Suffolk and has a fine
porch. The brass eagle-
lectern is said to have
been donated by
Elizabeth I.

Bull Inn

The Street, Woolpit, Bury St.
Edmunds, IP30 9SA
☎ Elmswell (0359) 40393
*Public house and restaurant in
1 acre of land with ample
parking.*
Bedrooms: 1 double & 1 twin.
Bathrooms: 2 public.
Bed & breakfast: £10-£12.50
single, £20-£25 double.
Lunch available.
Evening meal 6pm (l.o.
10pm).
Parking for 50.
🖵🖐️ Ⓥ🔟🔌🍴🗡️🗡️🆖

Grange Farm

The Grange, Woolpit, Bury
St. Edmunds, IP30 9RG
☎ Elmswell (0359) 41143
*120-acre arable farm. Fine
Victorian farmhouse, three
quarters of a mile from
Woolpit village centre on the
Rattlesden road. Set in
pleasant grounds with
surrounding ponds.*
Bedrooms: 2 single, 3 twin.
Bathrooms: 2 public.
Bed & breakfast: £10-£12
single, £20-£24 double.
Parking for 10.
‰🗡️Ⓤ🔟🔌📺🔌🗡️🏠

The Swan Inn 🅼
Listed

Woolpit, Bury St. Edmunds,
IP30 9QN
☎ Elmswell (0359) 40482
*Village inn with modernised
bedroom annexe. Ideal centre
for touring Suffolk. Several
good golf courses within easy
reach. Evening meal sometimes
available.*
Bedrooms: 1 single, 1 double
& 1 twin, 1 family room.
Bathrooms: 1 private,
1 public.
Bed & breakfast: £13-£14
single, £24-£29 double.
Parking for 12.
‰🗡️🖵🖐️🔌🗡️🗡️🏠

WROXHAM

Norfolk
Map ref 3C1

7m NE. Norwich
Yachting centre on the
River Bure which houses
the headquarters of the
Norfolk Broads Yacht
Club. The church of St.
Mary has a famous
doorway and the manor
house nearby dates back
to 1623.

Staitheway House
Listed

Staitheway Rd., Wroxham,
NR12 8TH
☎ (060 53) 3347
*Fine Victorian house in quiet
location, within easy walking
distance of village and river.*
Bedrooms: 1 double & 1 twin,
1 family room.
Bathrooms: 1 public.
Bed & breakfast: £14-£16
single, £26-£28 double.
Parking for 4.
‰🖐️Ⓤ Ⓥ🔌🔟🔌🗡️
🆖

Wroxham Park Lodge
😀😀

142 Norwich Rd., Wroxham,
Norwich, NR12 8SA
☎ (060 53) 2991
*Comfortable Victorian house in
lovely gardens, 1.5 miles from
Wroxham Broads and town
centre. Central for all Broads
amenities. Open all year round.*
Bedrooms: 2 double & 2 twin,
1 family room.
Bathrooms: 1 private,
1 public.
Bed & breakfast: from £16
single, £24-£28 double.
Parking for 6.
‰👜🚲🖵🖐️Ⓤ🍴🔟☀️
🗡️🆖🗡️🆖

King's Head Hotel

Gt. Bircham, King's Lynn, Norfolk PE31 6RJ
Tel: Syderstone (048 523) 265
(On B1153)

Family run hotel and restaurant, situated close to Sandringham, King's Lynn and the coast.

Five en suite bedrooms, tea/coffee making facilities and colour TV.

Wine and Dine in the lodge restaurant, food especially prepared by the proprietor. English and Continental cuisine. Fresh Norfolk seafood and produce, a la carte available lunchtime and evening, traditional Sunday lunch.

When requesting brochures or further information from advertisers in this guide, you may find it helpful to use the advertisement enquiry coupons which can be found towards the end of the guide. These should be cut out and mailed direct to the companies in which you are interested. Remember to include your name and address and enclose a stamped and addressed envelope or stamps if requested by the advertiser.

P L E A S E   N O T E

Individual establishments who have a display advertisement have a line listing under the appropriate town heading

FOLLOW THE SIGN

It leads to over 550 Tourist Information Centres throughout England offering friendly help with accommodation and holiday ideas as well as suggestions of places to visit and

things to do. In your home town there may be a centre which can help you before you set out. If not, why not send for the Directory of Tourist Information Centres in Great Britain? It is available free from English Tourist Board, Department D, Bromells Road, Clapham, London SW4 0BJ.

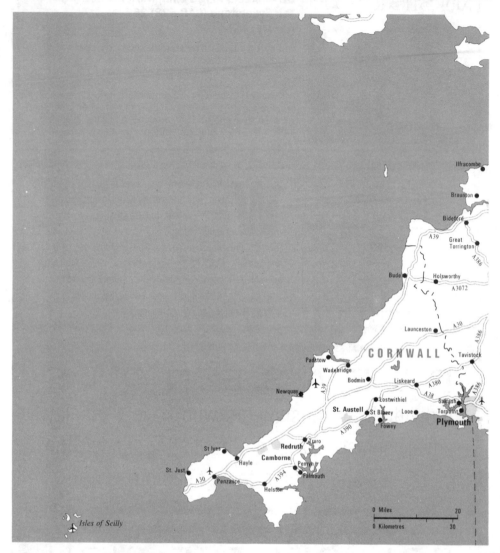

Perhaps England's most **West Country**
area, the West Country brings together the six counties of Avon, Cornwall (with
the Isles of Scilly), Devon, western Dorset, Somerset and Wiltshire into a tourist region
renowned for its fabulous coast and beautiful countryside.

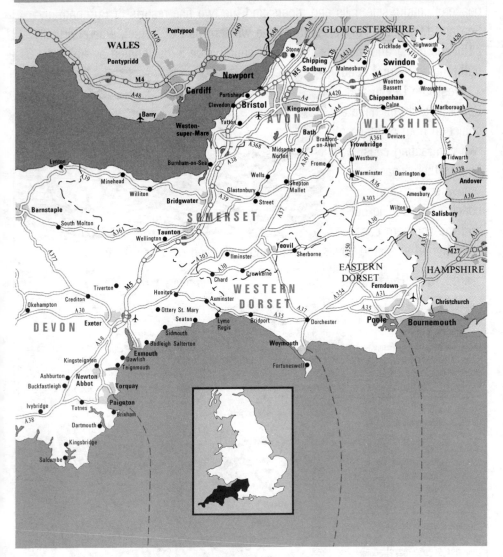

Let's start with Wiltshire — an inland county which typifies rural England at its best. Early man found this area most amenable and the evidence of his long occupation makes Wiltshire the premier county for exploring prehistoric remains.

Go west to Avon and you'll find the major city of Bristol, built on the shipping trade; the city of Bath, Britain's oldest and most famous spa; and the popular resort of Weston-super-Mare.

▶

Move south-west and you're into Somerset — a county well-endowed with peaceful countryside, hills and moors and the two fine resorts of Burnham-on-Sea and Minehead. Further south is the western part of Dorset, where virtually all of the coast and much of the inland countryside is designated an area of outstanding natural beauty.

West into Devon and Cornwall and you have a choice in both counties of two contrasting coastlines. The northern coast, renowned for sandy beaches and rolling surf, and the southern coast, with myriad sheltered coves, little fishing ports and popular resorts.

Paul Anscomb

WHERE TO GO, WHAT TO SEE

Bath Industrial Heritage Centre
Camden Works, Julian Road, Bath, Avon BA1 2RH ☎ (0225) 318348
Recreation of a Victorian engineering brass foundry and mineral water business. Bath Stone display.
Admission charge.

The Exploratory
Hands-on Science Centre
The Victoria Rooms, Queen's Road, Bristol, Avon ☎ (0272) 634321
Exhibition covering lights, lenses, lasers, bubbles, bridges, illusions, gyroscopes and much more.
Admission charge.

Maritime Heritage Centre
Wapping Wharf, Gas Ferry Road, Bristol, Avon BS1 6TY ☎ (0272) 20680
Museum introduces the theme of 200 years of Bristol shipbuilding, with particular reference to Charles Hill & Sons and their predecessor, James Hilhouse.
Admission free.

Roman Baths Museum
Pump Room, Abbey Church Yard, Bath, Avon ☎ (0225) 461111 Ext. 2785
Roman Baths and Temple Precinct; hot springs and Roman monuments.

FIND OUT MORE

Further information about holidays and attractions in the West Country tourist region is available from:
West Country Tourist Board, Trinity Court, Southernhay East, Exeter, Devon EX1 1QS. ☎ (0392) 76351.

These publications are available free from the West Country Tourist Board:
West Country Holidays '89
Bed and Breakfast Touring Map
Graded Camping and Caravan Parks
Also available are:
Places to Visit (published March 1989) *£1.95*
Where to Stay in the West Country 1989 *£1.95*

THE EXPLORATORY HANDS-ON SCIENCE CENTRE, BRISTOL

Paul Anscomb

Jewellery, coins.
Admission charge.

Tropicana Pleasure Beach
Marine Parade, Weston-super-Mare, Avon BS23 1BE ☎ (0934) 26581
Heated surf pool with water chutes.

Play equipment for children of all ages. Toddlers' pool, fountains, ice-skating, amusements, solarium.
Admission charge.

Dairyland Farm Park and Country Life Museum

Tresillian Barton, Summercourt, Newquay, Cornwall TR8 5AA
☎ (0872) 510246
Farm park with animals, pets, wildfowl, game-birds, pheasants. Country life museum. Adventure playground, farm nature trail. *Admission charge.*

Flambards Triple Theme Park

Culdrose Manor, Helston, Cornwall TR13 0GA ☎ (0326) 574549
Recently extended award-winning authentic life-size Victorian village with fully-stocked shops, carriages and fashions. 'Britain in the Blitz' recreation of a life-size wartime street. Gardens. *Admission charge.*

Goonhilly Satellite Earth Station

Goonhilly Downs, Helston, Cornwall TR12 6LQ ☎ (0872) 78551
Satellite tracking station with 10 steerable dish aerials. Automatic audio-visual show. Viewing gallery. Model of station. Bus tour of site. *Admission charge.*

Land's End

Sennen, Cornwall TR19 7AA
☎ (0736) 871501
Spectacular cliffs with breathtaking vistas. Superb multi-sensory Last Labyrinth show, and many other attractions and exhibitions. *Admission charge.*

Lanhydrock

Nr. Bodmin, Cornwall PL30 4AD
☎ (0208) 3320
17th C house largely rebuilt after fire in 1881. 116 foot gallery with magnificent plaster ceiling illustrating scenes from the Old Testament. Park, gardens, walks. *Admission charge.*

Tamar Otter Park and Wild Wood

North Petherwin, Nr. Launceston, Cornwall PL15 8LW ☎ (056 685) 646
Wooded valley with collection of otters in large open natural enclosures. Waterfowl lakes, aviaries, woodland trail with deer, peacocks, pheasants.

Breeding owls.
Admission charge.

Trebah Gardens

Mawnan Smith, Nr. Falmouth, Cornwall TR11 5JZ ☎ (0326) 250448
Unique 25-acre ravine garden leading to private beach on River Helford. Extensive collection of rare and sub-tropical plants and trees. Water garden with Koi carp, children's play area. *Admission charge.*

Wheal Martyn Museum

Carthew, St. Austell, Cornwall PL26 8XG
☎ (0726) 850362
Restored 19th C clay works with working water wheels and static steam locomotive. Fully restored 1916 Peerless lorry. Nature trail, children's adventure trail.
Admission charge.

The Big Sheep

Abbotsham Barton, Bideford, Devon EX39 5AP ☎ (023 72) 72366
Sheep milking parlour with gallery, dairy and production rooms, part of a commercial sheep farm with 500 ewes. Exhibition, video slide show and play area. Extensive nature trail. *Admission charge.*

Buckfast Butterfly Farm

Buckfastleigh, Devon ☎ (0364) 42916
Tropical landscaped garden with waterfalls and large pond under cover where exotic butterflies and moths from all over the world are free-flying. Picnic areas, gift shop.
Admission charge.

Buckland Abbey

Nr. Yelverton, Devon PL20 6EY
☎ (0822) 853607
Originally Cistercian monastery, then home of Sir Francis Drake.
Admission charge.

City Museum and Art Gallery

Drake Circus, Plymouth, Devon PL4 8AJ
☎ (0752) 668000 Ext. 4878
Collections of fine and decorative arts, including Plymouth porcelain and silver, archaeology and local history, natural history.
Admission free.

English Riviera Centre

Chestnut Avenue, Torquay, Devon TQ2 5LZ ☎ (0803) 299992
Leisure area and health spa. Squash courts, video game machines, restaurant and bar.
Admission free, but charge for use of facilities.

Gorse Blossom Miniature Railway

Liverton, Newton Abbot, Devon TQ12 6JD ☎ (062 682) 361, changing to (0626) 821361 during 1989
Passenger-carrying miniature steam railway running through 10 acres of gardens, woodland and picnic areas. *Admission charge.*

Quaywest Beach Resort

Goodrington Sands, Paignton, Devon TQ4 6LN ☎ (0803) 555550
Wide variety of entertainment, sports and catering facilities.
Admission charge.

Rougemont House Museum of Costume and Lace

Castle Street, Exeter, Devon
☎ (0392) 265858
Elegant Regency house in parkland setting. Costumes displayed in period rooms, lace exhibitions and demonstrations.
Admission charge.

The Dinosaur Museum

Icen Way, Dorchester, Dorset DT1 1EW
☎ (0305) 69880
Fossils, full-size models, computerised, mechanical and electronic displays. Video gallery.
Admission charge.

Diving Museum and Shipwreck Centre

9 Custom House Quay, Weymouth, Dorset DT4 8BG ☎ (0305) 760690 ▶

▶ The story of diving with full-size models of early diving apparatus, diving bells and equipment as used in North Sea.
Admission charge.

Dorset County Museum
High West Street, Dorchester, Dorset DT1 1XA ☎ (0305) 62735
Archaeology, natural history and geology of Dorset. Local history displays.
Admission charge.

Britain on View

Parnham
Beaminster, Dorset DT8 3NA
☎ (0308) 862204
Tudor manor house with additions and embellishments by John Nash in 1810. Home of John Makepeace and his famous furniture-making workshops. 14 acres of gardens.
Admission charge.

Sherborne Castle
Sherborne, Dorset ☎ (0935) 813182
Built by Sir Walter Raleigh in 1594. Elizabethan Hall and Jacobean Oak Room.
Admission charge.

Worldwide Butterflies and Lullingstone Silk Farm
Compton House, Nr. Sherborne, Dorset DT9 4QN ☎ (0935) 74608
Tropical jungle with butterflies hatching

and flying. Silk farm.
Admission charge.

Cleeve Abbey
Washford, Nr. Watchet, Somerset TA22 0TS ☎ (0272) 734472
Cistercian Abbey founded in 12th C. Great 13th C dormitory and 15th C refectory with superb timber roof.
Admission charge.

Combe Sydenham
Monksilver, Nr. Taunton, Somerset TA4 4JG ☎ (0984) 56284
Elizabethan hall, gardens, deer park, waymarked woodland walks, trout ponds. Tearoom and shop.
Admission charge.

Cricket St. Thomas Wildlife Park
Cricket St. Thomas, Chard, Somerset TA20 4DD ☎ (046 030) 755
Wildlife park, heavy horse centre, countryside museum, playground, woodland railway. Restaurant.
Admission charge.

Dunster Castle
Dunster, Nr. Minehead, Somerset TA24 6SL ☎ (0643) 821314
Fortified home of the Luttrells for 600 years, remodelled 100 years ago. Fine 17th C staircase and plaster ceilings. Terrace garden of rare shrubs.
Admission charge.

The East Somerset Railway
The Station, Cranmore, Shepton Mallet, Somerset BA4 4DP ☎ (074 988) 417
Museum, art gallery, replica of Victorian engine shed, steam engines, collection of historic coaches and wagons.
Admission charge.

Fleet Air Arm Museum
Royal Naval Air Station, Yeovilton, Somerset BA22 8HT
☎ (0935) 840565
Over 50 historic aircraft, plus displays and equipment, including Concorde 002 prototype, Falklands Campaign Exhibition and Kamikaze exhibition.
Admission charge.

The Peat Moors Visitor Centre
Shapwick Road, Westhay, Glastonbury, Somerset BA6 9TT ☎ (045 86) 257
Archaeology, peat and wildlife exhibition. Traditional peat cutting display, demonstration hall, play area, garden centre.
Admission charge.

Wells Cathedral
Wells, Somerset BA5 2PA
☎ (0749) 74483
Dating from 12th C and built in the Early English Gothic style. Magnificent west front with 296 medieval groups of sculpture.
Admission free but donations welcomed.

Bowood House and Gardens
Calne, Wiltshire SN11 0LZ
☎ (0249) 812102
18th C house by Robert Adam. Paintings, watercolours, Victoriana, Indiana and porcelain. Landscaped park with lake, terraces, waterfall, grottos. Adventure playground, gift shop, garden centre.
Admission charge.

Fox Talbot Museum of Photography
Lacock, Nr. Chippenham, Wiltshire SN15 2LG ☎ (024 973) 459
Displays of apparatus, photographs related to Fox Talbot. Gallery with 3 changing exhibitions.
Admission charge.

Lackham Agricultural Museum and Gardens
Lacock, Nr. Chippenham, Wiltshire SN15 2NY ☎ (0249) 443111
Rare breeds centre. Agricultural tools and early farm machinery and buildings. Displays on trapping, woodland craft.
Admission charge.

Oasis Leisure Centre
North Star Avenue, Swindon, Wiltshire SN2 1EP ☎ (0793) 33404
Large lagoon pool, 3 flumes, large sports hall, squash courts, health suite.
Admission charge.

Salisbury and South Wiltshire Museum
The King's House, 65 The Close, Salisbury, Wiltshire SP1 2EN

☎ (0722) 332151
Archaeology, Pitt-Rivers Wessex collections, ceramics, local history, prints and drawings. New costume gallery.
Admission charge.

Sheldon Manor
Nr. Chippenham, Wiltshire SN14 0RG
☎ (0249) 653120
Ancient manor house with fine example of 13th C porch. Early English oak furniture and Nailsea glass. Gardens.
Admission charge.

MAKE A DATE FOR...

Badminton Horse Trials
Badminton House, Badminton, Avon
4 – 7 May

Helston Furry Dance
Through the streets of Helston, Cornwall
6 May

Devon County Show
The Showground, Whipton, Exeter, Devon *18 – 20 May*

Bath Festival
Various venues, Bath, Avon
26 May – 11 June

Weymouth Trawler Race
The Harbour, Weymouth, Dorset *29 May*

Royal Bath and West Show
The Showground, Shepton Mallet, Somerset *31 May – 3 June*

Royal Cornwall Show
The Showground, Wadebridge, Cornwall
8 – 10 June

International Air Day
Royal Naval Station, Yeovilton, Somerset
29 July

Sidmouth Festival
Various venues, Sidmouth, Devon
4 – 11 August

Melplash Show
West Bay Road, Bridport, Dorset
31 August

Tourist and leisure information can be obtained from Tourist Information Centres throughout England. Details of centres in the West Country region are listed below. The symbol 🛏 means that an accommodation booking service is provided. Centres marked with a ✳ are open during the summer months only. In the following pages, towns which have a Tourist Information Centre are indicated with the symbol *i*.

Amesbury
Wiltshire 🛏
Redworth House, Flower Lane
☎ (0980) 23255

Avebury
Wiltshire 🛏 ✳
The Great Barn
☎ (067 23) 425

Axminster
Devon 🛏 ✳
Old Courthouse, Church Street
☎ (0297) 34386

Barnstaple
Devon 🛏
North Devon Library, Tuly Street
☎ (0271) 47177

Bath
Avon 🛏
Abbey Churchyard
☎ (0225) 462831

Bideford
Devon 🛏 ✳
The Quay
☎ (023 72) 77676

Bodmin
Cornwall 🛏
Shire House, Mount Folly Square
☎ (0208) 6616

Bovey Tracey
Devon 🛏 ✳
Lower Car Park, Station Road
☎ (0626) 832047

Bradford-on-Avon
Wiltshire 🛏
34 Silver Street
☎ (022 16) 5797

Braunton
Devon 🛏 ✳
The Car Park
☎ (0271) 816400

Bridgwater
Somerset 🛏 ✳
Town Hall, High Street
☎ (0278) 427652

Bridport
Dorset 🛏 ✳
32 South Street
☎ (0308) 24901

Bristol
Avon 🛏
Colston House, Colston Street
☎ (0272) 293891/260767

Bristol Airport
Avon 🛏
☎ (027 587) 4441

Brixham
Devon 🛏
The Old Market House, The Quay
☎ (080 45) 2861

▶

Bude
Cornwall
The Crescent Car Park ᐳᐊ ✱
☎ (0288) 4240/3576
Stamford Hill (A39), Stratton ᐳᐊ ✱
☎ (0288) 3781

Budleigh Salterton
Devon ᐳᐊ ✱
Fore Street
☎ (039 54) 5275

Burnham-on-Sea
Somerset ᐳᐊ
Berrow Road
☎ (0278) 787852/782377
ext. 31

Camelford
Cornwall ᐳᐊ ✱
North Cornwall Museum,
The Clease
☎ (0840) 212954

Chard
Somerset ᐳᐊ ✱
The Guildhall, Fore Street
☎ (0460) 67463

Cheddar
Somerset ᐳᐊ ✱
The Gorge
☎ (0934) 744071

Chippenham
Wiltshire ᐳᐊ
The Neeld Hall, High Street
☎ (0249) 657733

Combe Martin
Devon ᐳᐊ ✱
Sea Cottage, Cross Street
☎ (027 188) 3319/2692

Corsham
Wiltshire ᐳᐊ ✱
Arnold House, 31 High Street
☎ (0249) 714660

Dartmouth
Devon ᐳᐊ ✱
Royal Avenue Gardens
☎ (080 43) 4224

Dawlish
Devon ᐳᐊ
The Lawn
☎ (0626) 863589

Devizes
Wiltshire ᐳᐊ ✱
The Canal Centre, The Wharf,
Couch Lane
☎ (0380) 71069

**THE DINOSAUR MUSEUM,
DORCHESTER**

Dorchester
Dorset ᐳᐊ
7 Acland Road
☎ (0305) 67992

Exeter
Devon ᐳᐊ
Civic Centre, Paris Street
☎ (0392) 265297

Exeter Services
Devon ᐳᐊ
Exeter Services Area,
Sandygate (M5), Nr. Exeter
☎ (0392) 37581/79088

Exmouth
Devon ᐳᐊ ✱
Alexandra Terrace
☎ (0395) 263744

Falmouth
Cornwall ᐳᐊ
Town Hall, The Moor
☎ (0326) 312300

Fowey
Cornwall ᐳᐊ
The Post Office,
4 Custom House Hill
☎ (072 683) 3616

Frome
Somerset ᐳᐊ ✱
Cattle Market Car Park
☎ (0373) 67271

Glastonbury
Somerset ᐳᐊ ✱
1 Marchants Buildings,
Northload Street
☎ (0458) 32954

Gordano
Avon 🛏 ✱
Gordano Service Area (M5),
Portbury, Nr. Bristol
☎ Pill (027 581) 3382

Hayle
Cornwall 🛏 ✱
A30 Southern Cross Self-Serve,
Loggans Moor
☎ (0736) 755485

Honiton
Devon 🛏 ✱
Angel Hotel Car Park, High Street
☎ (0404) 3716

Ilfracombe
Devon 🛏
The Promenade
☎ (0271) 63001

Ilminster
Somerset 🛏 ✱
Shrubbery Hotel Car Park,
Station Road
☎ (0460) 57294

Ivybridge
Devon 🛏
Leonards Road
☎ (0752) 897035

Kingsbridge
Devon 🛏
The Quay
☎ (0548) 3195

Laity
Cornwall 🛏 ✱
Lizard & Helston TIC, Laity,
Nr. Wendron
☎ (0326) 40899

Launceston
Cornwall 🛏
Market House Arcade,
Market Street
☎ (0566) 2321

Looe
Cornwall 🛏 ✱
The Guildhall, Fore Street
☎ (050 36) 2072

Lostwithiel
Cornwall 🛏
Lostwithiel Community Centre,
Liddicoat Road
☎ Bodmin (0208) 872207

Lyme Regis
Dorset 🛏
The Guildhall, Bridge Street
☎ (029 74) 2138

Lynton
Devon 🛏
Town Hall, Lee Road
☎ (0598) 52225

Malmesbury
Wiltshire 🛏
Town Hall, Cross Hayes
☎ (0666) 822143/823748

Marlborough
Wiltshire 🛏 ✱
St. Peter's Church, High Street
☎ (0672) 53989

Melksham
Wiltshire 🛏
The Roundhouse, Church Street
☎ (0225) 707424

Mere
Wiltshire 🛏
The Square, Church Street
☎ (0747) 860341

Minehead
Somerset 🛏
Market House, The Parade
☎ (0643) 2624

Modbury
Devon 🛏 ✱
31 Church Street
☎ (0548) 830159

Newquay
Cornwall 🛏
Cliff Road
☎ (0637) 871345

Newton Abbot
Devon 🛏
8 Sherborne Road
☎ (0626) 67494

Okehampton
Devon 🛏 ✱
3 West Street
☎ (0837) 3020

Ottery St. Mary
Devon 🛏 ✱
The Old Town Hall, The Flexton
☎ (040 481) 3964

Paignton
Devon 🛏
The Esplanade
☎ (0803) 558383

Penzance
Cornwall 🛏
Station Road
☎ (0736) 62207

Plymouth
Devon
Civic Centre, Royal Parade 🛏
☎ (0752) 264849/264851
12 The Barbican 🛏 ✱
☎ (0752) 223806

▶

Portland
Dorset 🛏
St. George's Centre, Reforne
☎ (0305) 823406

St. Ives
Cornwall 🛏
The Guildhall, Street-an-Pol
☎ Penzance (0736) 796297

Salcombe
Devon 🛏 *
Russell Court Studios,
Russell Court, Fore Street
☎ (054 884) 2736

Salisbury
Wiltshire 🛏
Fish Row
☎ (0722) 334956

Isles of Scilly 🛏
Porthcressa Bank, St. Mary's
☎ Scillonia (0720) 22536

Seaton
Devon 🛏 *
18 The Esplanade
☎ (0297) 21660

Sedgemoor Services
Somerset 🛏 *
Sedgemoor Services, M5 South,
Axbridge
☎ Edingworth (093 472) 833

Shepton Mallet
Somerset 🛏 *
2 Petticoat Lane
☎ (0749) 5258

Sherborne
Dorset 🛏 *
Hound Street
☎ (0935) 815341

Sidmouth
Devon 🛏 *
The Esplanade
☎ (039 55) 6441

South Molton
Devon 🛏 *
1 East Street
☎ (076 95) 4122/2378

Swindon
Wiltshire 🛏
32 The Arcade, Brunel Centre
☎ (0793) 30328/26161

Taunton
Somerset 🛏
The Library, Corporation Street
☎ (0823) 274785/270479

Tavistock
Devon 🛏 *
Town Hall, Bedford Square
☎ (0822) 2938

Teignmouth
Devon 🛏
The Den, Sea Front
☎ (062 67) 79769

Tideford
Cornwall 🛏 *
Heskyn Hill (A38), Nr. Saltash
☎ Landrake (075 538) 397

Tiverton
Devon 🛏
Phoenix Lane
☎ (0884) 255827

Tiverton Services
Devon 🛏 *
Tiverton Services, Junction 27
(M5), Nr. Sampford Peverell
☎ (0884) 821242

Torquay
Devon 🛏
Vaughan Parade
☎ (0803) 27428

Torrington
Devon 🛏 *
Town Hall, High Street
☎ (0805) 24324

Totnes
Devon 🛏 *
The Plains
☎ (0803) 863168

Trowbridge
Wiltshire 🛏 *
St. Stephens Place,
Adjacent Multi-storey Car Park
☎ (0225) 777054

Truro
Cornwall 🛏
Municipal Buildings,
Boscawen Street
☎ (0872) 74555

Victoria
Cornwall 🛏 *
A30 Victoria, Nr. Roche
☎ (0726) 890481

Wadebridge
Cornwall 🛏 *
Town Hall
☎ (020 881) 3725

Warminster
Wiltshire 🛏 *
The Library,
Three Horseshoes Mall
☎ (0985) 218548

Wellington
Somerset 🛏 *
The Museum, Fore Street
☎ (082 347) 4747

Wells
Somerset 🛏
Town Hall, Market Place
☎ (0749) 72552/75987

Westbury
Wiltshire 🛏 *
Library Car Park, Edward Street
☎ (0373) 827158

Weston-super-Mare
Avon 🛏
Beach Lawns
☎ (0934) 626838

Weymouth
Dorset
Pavilion Theatre Complex,
The Esplanade 🛏
☎ (0305) 785747
The Esplanade 🛏 *
☎ (0305) 785747

Wincanton
Somerset 🛏
The Library, 7 Carrington Way
☎ (0963) 32173

Woolacombe
Devon 🛏 *
Hall '70, Beach Road
☎ (0271) 870553

Yeovil
Somerset 🛏
Petter's House, Petter's Way
☎ (0935) 71279

Yeovilton
Somerset 🛏 *
Fleet Air Arm Museum, R.N.A.S.
Yeovilton
☎ Yeovil (0935) 841083

CROWN CLASSIFICATIONS

All the establishments displaying a national classification in this guide are inspected regularly. All can be chosen with confidence.

There are six classifications — from Listed to 5 Crowns; each indicates the level of facilities and services provided.

All classified establishments are required to provide a high standard of cleanliness, courtesy and service and to be well maintained. A lower classification does not imply lower standards; although the range of facilities and services may be smaller, they may be provided to a high standard.

You will find a full explanation of the national Crown Classification Scheme towards the end of this guide.

Entries in this regional section are listed in alphabetical order of place name, and then in alphabetical order of establishment. County names are not normally repeated in each establishment entry, but please use the full postal address when writing.

The map references refer to the colour maps towards the end of this guide. The first number is the number of the map, and it is followed by the grid reference.

The Crown Classifications are explained on pages 8 and 9, and the key to symbols is on the flap inside the back cover — keep it open for easy reference.

ABBOTS BICKINGTON

Devon
Map ref 1C2

7m NE. Holsworthy

Court Barton Farm

Abbots Bickington, Milton Damerel, Holsworthy, EX22 7LQ
☎ (040 926) 214
Situated in beautiful countryside on the River Torridge. Centrally placed for touring in north Devon and Cornwall. Home cooking.
Bedrooms: 2 single, 1 double, 1 family room.
Bathrooms: 1 public.
Bed & breakfast: £8-£9 single, £16-£18 double.
Half board: £13-£14 daily, £85-£90 weekly.
Evening meal 6.30pm (l.o. 5pm).
Parking for 10.
Open May-October.
১3☼⽥曲戸◉🅰🅄🥂♪▶
✓☼🅇📮

INDIVIDUAL PROPRIETORS HAVE SUPPLIED ALL DETAILS OF ACCOMMODATION. ALTHOUGH WE DO CHECK FOR ACCURACY, WE ADVISE YOU TO CONFIRM PRICES AND OTHER INFORMATION AT THE TIME OF BOOKING.

ABBOTSBURY

Dorset
Map ref 2A3

8m NW. Weymouth
Beautiful village near Chesil Beach, with a long main street of mellow stone and thatched cottages and the ruins of a Benedictine monastery. High above the village on a hill is a prominent 15th C chapel. Abbotsbury's famous swannery and sub-tropical gardens lie just outside the village.

Abbey House

Church St., Abbotsbury, Weymouth, DT3 4JJ
☎ (0305) 871330
Surrounded by its own grounds, the house is of 12th/13th C. origin with 17th/18th C. additions and also incorporates a small vineyard.
Bedrooms: 1 single, 2 double & 1 twin, 1 family room.
Bathrooms: 1 public.
Bed & breakfast: £11-£15 single, £22-£30 double.
Evening meal 7pm (l.o. 4pm).
Parking for 6.
১☼🅇⽥ 🅸 🆅 戸◉🏠
📮🅄☼🅇📮🏠

ALDERBURY

Wiltshire
Map ref 2B3

3m SE. Salisbury

St. Marie's Grange ♠
🖤🖤

Alderbury, Salisbury, SP5 3DJ
☎ Salisbury (0722) 710351
Pugins house set in beautiful grounds beside the Avon. Views across water meadows. Firm beds and English hospitality. Price reductions for 2 or more nights.

Bedrooms: 2 double & 1 twin.
Bathrooms: 1 public.
Bed & breakfast: £15-£22.50 single, £30-£45 double.
Half board: £27.50-£37.50 daily, £162.50-£232.50 weekly.
Evening meal 7pm (l.o. 6pm).
Parking for 4.
১☼⽥⽺◉🏠🍷🅄♪
☼🅇📮🆂🅿🏠

ALLERFORD

Somerset
Map ref 1D1

4m W. Minehead
Village of picturesque stone and thatch cottages with a packhorse bridge, set in the beautiful Vale of Porlock.

Fern Cottage
🖤🖤

Allerford, Nr. Porlock, West Somerset, TA24 8HN
☎ Porlock (0643) 862215
16th C. traditional Exmoor cottage in National Trust wooded vale. Dramatic scenery and wildlife. All the expected comforts of a country home.
Bedrooms: 3 double & 1 twin, 1 family room.
Bathrooms: 1 public.
Bed & breakfast: £11.50 single, £23 double.
Half board: £18.50 daily, £118 weekly.
Evening meal 7pm (l.o. 8pm).
Parking for 7.
১☼🅇 🆅 ⽺戸◉🏠🅄
▶🅇⬛

Lynch Country House Hotel

Allerford, Minehead, TA24 8HJ
☎ Porlock (0643) 862800
Delightful country house in elevated woodland setting, overlooking sea and moors. River Aller flows through the landscaped gardens. Near lake. Comfortably furnished rooms.

THERE IS A SPECIAL SECTION IN THIS GUIDE LISTING ACCOMMODATION ESPECIALLY SUITABLE FOR GROUPS AND YOUNG PEOPLE.

Bedrooms: 1 double & 1 twin.
Bathrooms: 1 public.
Bed & breakfast: £15 single, £27 double.
Parking for 12.
১☼✿⽥戸◉🅄🖾🏠🅀
♪🅄☼☼🅇⬛

ASH MILL

Devon
Map ref 1C1

5m SE. South Molton

Nutcombe Cottage
🖤🖤

Little Ashmoor, Ash Mill, South Molton, EX36 4QT
☎ Bishops Nympton (076 97) 486
In heart of country on B3221. Ideal for touring and walking. Open fires, beams and country food. Owned by Devonshire family.
Bedrooms: 1 double, 1 family room.
Bathrooms: 2 public.
Bed & breakfast: £16-£19 double.
Half board: £11-£12.50 daily, £75-£84 weekly.
Evening meal 6pm (l.o. 9pm).
Parking for 13.
১☼🅇⽥◉🖾🏠☼🅇
⬛

ASHBRITTLE

Somerset
Map ref 1D1

6m W. Wellington

Higher Westcott Farm
🖤🖤

Ashbrittle, Wellington, TA21 0HZ
☎ Clayhanger (039 86) 258
230-acre mixed farm. Lovely views from the farmhouse. Home-produced meat, eggs and vegetables. Quantock Hills, Exmoor and National Trust properties nearby. Children's paradise with the animals.
Bedrooms: 2 family rooms.
Bathrooms: 1 public.
Bed & breakfast: £8.50-£9.50 single, £17-£19 double.
Half board: £12.50-£13.50 daily, £85-£95 weekly.
Evening meal 6.30pm (l.o. 5.30pm).
Parking for 4.
১🅄🅇⽥◉🖾🏠✓☼🅇
⬛

Lower Westcott Farm
🖤🖤

Ashbrittle, Wellington, TA21 0HZ
☎ Clayhanger (039 86) 296

214-acre mixed farm. Devon/Somerset borders family farm. Ideal for touring Exmoor and the coast. Beautiful countryside, comfort and homeliness. Children welcome.
Bedrooms: 1 double & 1 twin, 1 family room.
Bathrooms: 1 public.
Bed & breakfast: £9-£9.50 single, £18-£19 double.
Half board: £13-£14 daily, £90-£95 weekly.
Evening meal 6pm (l.o. 5.30pm).
Parking for 6.

ASHBURTON

Devon
Map ref 1C2

Formerly a thriving wool centre and important as one of Dartmoor's 4 stannary towns. Today's busy market town retains many period buildings and an atmosphere of medieval times. Ancient tradition is maintained in the annual ale-tasting and bread-weighing ceremony. Good centre for exploring Dartmoor or the south Devon coast.

Bremridge Farm Guest House

Woodland, Ashburton, TQ13 7JX
☎ (0364) 52426
7-acre mixed farm. Small working farm set amid beautiful countryside, centrally placed for moors, sea, Exeter and Plymouth.
Bedrooms: 1 single, 2 double, 2 family rooms.
Bathrooms: 1 private, 2 public.
Bed & breakfast: £10-£12 single, £20-£24 double.
Half board: £12.50-£17.50 daily, £80-£100 weekly.
Evening meal 6.30pm (l.o. 5.30pm).
Parking for 6.

Wellpritton Farm

Holne, Ashburton, TQ13 7RX
☎ Poundsgate (036 43) 273
15-acre livestock farm. Plenty of mouthwatering farm-produced food in a tastefully modernised farmhouse on the edge of Dartmoor. Special diets catered for by arrangement and packed lunches available. A warm welcome guaranteed.
Bedrooms: 2 double & 2 twin, 1 family room.
Bathrooms: 4 private, 1 public.
Bed & breakfast: £10-£12 single, £20-£24 double.
Half board: £17-£18 daily, £98-£105 weekly.
Evening meal 6pm (l.o. 9pm).
Parking for 5.

ASHTON KEYNES

Wiltshire
Map ref 2B2

Thameside village, with houses standing along the edge of the stream reached by bridges from the road on the opposite bank. Nearby stands the manor, Ashton House.

Old Manor Farmhouse

Ashton Keynes, Swindon, SN6 6QR
☎ Cirencester (0285) 861770
15th C. Cotswold farmhouse set in 1.5 acres. Close to Cotswold Water Park, with sailing, windsurfing, fishing. Good touring area.
Bedrooms: 1 single, 2 double & 1 twin, 1 family room.
Bathrooms: 1 private, 2 public.
Bed & breakfast: £14-£16 single, £22-£24 double.
Half board: £20.50-£25 daily, £128.50-£158 weekly.
Evening meal 7pm (l.o. 8.30pm).
Parking for 13.

AVEBURY

Wiltshire
Map ref 2B2

6m W. Marlborough
Set in a landscape of earthworks and megalithic standing stones, Avebury has a fine church and an Elizabethan manor with topiary and dove-cote. Fragments from Neolithic stone avenues and circles were used in the buildings; other remains from excavations are seen in the museum. The area abounds in important prehistoric sites, among them Silbury Hill, while Stonehenge stands about 20 miles due south. ℹ

Windmill House

Winterbourne Monkton, Swindon, SN4 9NN
☎ (067 23) 446
Secluded former 18th C. mill house surrounded by open farmland, with magnificent views of Avebury and Marlborough Downs. Home cooking.
Bedrooms: 1 single, 1 double, 1 family room.
Bathrooms: 2 public.
Bed & breakfast: £11-£12.50 single, £22-£25 double.
Half board: £16.50-£18 daily, £108.50-£120 weekly.
Lunch available.
Evening meal 6.15pm (l.o. 4pm).
Parking for 8.

AVETON GIFFORD

Devon
Map ref 1C3

3m NW. Kingsbridge
Village beside a tidal lagoon, at the head of Devonshire's River Avon. Good trout fishing upstream.

Marsh Mills Guest House

Aveton Gifford, Kingsbridge, TQ7 4JW
☎ Kingsbridge (0548) 550549
Mill house, now a smallholding, with leat and pond, gardens and orchard. Peacefully secluded, just off the A379.
Bedrooms: 1 single, 1 double & 2 twin.
Bathrooms: 1 public.
Bed & breakfast: £8-£9 single, £16-£18 double.

Half board: £12-£13 daily, £80-£85 weekly.
Evening meal 7pm (l.o. 10am).
Parking for 6.
Open January-November.

AWLISCOMBE

Devon
Map ref 1D2

Lelamarie ♏

Awliscombe, Honiton, EX14 0PP
☎ Honiton (0404) 44646
Detached bungalow in a third of an acre of patio. On the A373, 2.5 miles from Honiton and 7 miles from Cullompton, M5 junction 28.
Bedrooms: 1 double & 1 twin.
Bathrooms: 1 private, 1 public.
Bed & breakfast: £16-£20 double.
Parking for 4.

BAMPTON

Devon
Map ref 1D1

6m N. Tiverton
Riverside market town, famous for its fair each October.

Blights Farm

Morebath, Bampton, EX16 9DD
☎ (0398) 31423
300-year-old farmhouse situated on the edge of Exmoor in a quiet location, within easy reach of north and south Devon coasts.
Bedrooms: 1 single, 1 twin, 1 family room.
Bathrooms: 1 public.
Bed & breakfast: from £10 single, from £18 double.
Evening meal 7pm (l.o. 8.30pm).
Parking for 5.
Open April-October.

Cider Barn

Lower Bowdens Farm, Shillingford, Bampton, EX16 9EL
☎ (0398) 31573
Converted 18th C. cider barn overlooking its own small lake. Easy access from Taunton, just off the A361.
Bedrooms: 2 double & 1 twin.
Continued ▶

THE SYMBOLS ARE EXPLAINED ON THE FLAP INSIDE THE BACK COVER.

GROUPS, CONSORTIA AND AGENCIES SPECIALISING IN FARM AND COUNTRY HOLIDAYS ARE LISTED IN A SPECIAL SECTION OF THIS GUIDE.

BAMPTON

Continued

Bathrooms: 2 private,
1 public.
Bed & breakfast: £21-£29
double.
Parking for 7.
Open April-October.

⌂ ♥ ⓤ ⇥ ◈ ⓣⓥ ▱ ♠ ♦ ⚘
✕ ▨

Jasmine

2-4 Brook St., Bampton,
EX16 9LY
☎ (0398) 31310
*Comfortable accommodation in
part of 17th C. old world tea
rooms.*
Bedrooms: 2 double & 1 twin.
Bathrooms: 1 private,
1 public.
Bed & breakfast: £12-£14
single, £20-£24 double.
Half board: £16.50-£18.50
daily, £94.50-£108.50 weekly.
Lunch available.
Evening meal 6.30pm (l.o.
9.30pm).
Credit: Access.

⌂ ✕ ⓓ ⓤ ⓘ ⓥ ⇥ ⓣⓥ ▱
▨ SP

BANTHAM

Devon
Map ref 1C3

4m W. Kingsbridge
Village at the mouth of
the River Avon, with a
fine sandy beach.

Sloop Inn ⋔

⚶⚶

Bantham, Nr Kingsbridge,
TQ7 3AJ
☎ Kingsbridge (0548) 560489
& 560215
*Part 16th C. inn in old world
fishing village, with log stove in
bar. Sea and river estuary
overlooked by some rooms.*
Bedrooms: 3 double, 2 family
rooms.
Bathrooms: 4 private,
1 public.
Bed & breakfast: £16-£17.50
single, £32-£35 double.
Half board: £157-£183
weekly.
Lunch available.
Evening meal 7pm (l.o.
10pm).
Parking for 35.

⌂ ▱ ♥ ⓘ ▥ ▱ ► ▨ ☐
SP

BARFORD ST. MARTIN

Wiltshire
Map ref 2B3

Glebe Cottage

⚶⚶

Mount La., Barford St.
Martin, Salisbury, SP3 4AG
☎ (0722) 743293
*Comfortable cottage, built
circa 1780, which has recently
been renovated. 2 bedrooms
with full en-suite facilities.
Excellent views of the
surrounding area.*
Bedrooms: 1 double & 1 twin.
Bathrooms: 2 private.
Bed & breakfast: max. £25
double.
Parking for 4.
Open April-October.

Ⓑ ♥ ⓤ ⇥ ▥ ✕ ▨ ▦

BARNSTAPLE

Devon
Map ref 1C1

*See also Bratton Fleming,
Shirwell, West Buckland.*
At the head of the Taw
estuary, former ship-
building and textile town
and one of England's
oldest boroughs. Now an
important agricultural
centre with attractive
areas of period building, a
modern Civic Centre and
riverside Leisure Centre.
In Queen Anne's Walk, a
charming colonnaded
arcade, merchants and
shipowners traded.
Pannier Market and
Cattle Market open on
Friday. The Athenaeum
by 15th C arched bridge
houses a library. ⓘ

East Bodley

Parracombe, Barnstaple
EX31 4PR
☎ (059 83) 295
*7-acre smallholding. Historic
Exmoor farmhouse on the edge
of the village of Parracombe.
Private lounge. Excellent
centre for walking or touring.*
Bedrooms: 2 double.
Bathrooms: 2 public.
Bed & breakfast: £9 single,
£22 double.
Half board: £14.50-£16.50
daily, £94.50-£108.50 weekly.
Evening meal 7.30pm (l.o.
9pm).
Parking for 2.

⌂ ✕ ▱ ♥ ⓤ ▥ ⓥ ⇥ ▥ ▱
⊍ ▨ ▦

BATH

Avon
Map ref 2B2

*See also Batheaston,
Box, Hinton
Charterhouse, Monkton
Combe.*
Georgian spa city
encircled by hills beside
the River Avon. Important
Roman site with
impressive reconstructed
Baths, uncovered in 19th
C. Bath Abbey built over
Norman abbey on site of
monastery where first
king of England was
crowned (AD 973). Fine
architecture in mellow
local stone. Pump Room,
Art Gallery and other
museums. ⓘ

Astor House

⚶⚶

14 Oldfield Rd., Bath,
BA2 3ND
☎ (0225) 429134
*Lovely Victorian house with
comfortable, spacious rooms
and large secluded garden.
Peaceful, elegant atmosphere.*
Bedrooms: 3 double & 4 twin.
Bathrooms: 2 public.
Bed & breakfast: £25 double.
Parking for 4.
Open April-October.

⌂ 7 ♥ ⓤ ⓥ ⇥ ⓣⓥ ▥ ▱
⚘ ✕ ▨ ▦

Audley House

⚶⚶⚶

Park Gdns., Bath, BA1 2XP
☎ (0225) 333110
*Fine listed residence in a
secluded acre of lawns and
mature trees, close to the city
centre. Non-smokers only.*
Bedrooms: 1 double & 2 twin.
Bathrooms: 3 private.
Bed & breakfast: £45 double.
Parking for 7.
Open February-December.
Credit: Visa.

☎ ▦ ▱ ♥ ⓤ ⓘ ⇥ ⇥ ⇥
▱ ⚘ ✕ ▨ ▦

Bathurst Guest House ⋔

⚶⚶

11 Walcot Pde., London Rd.,
Bath, BA1 5NF
☎ (0225) 421884
*Spacious family home on listed
Georgian parade. Owners give
personal attention. Exclusively
for non-smokers. 10 minutes'
level walk from abbey.*
Bedrooms: 1 single, 2 double
& 2 twin, 1 family room.
Bathrooms: 2 public.

Bed & breakfast: £11-£13.50
single, £20-£26 double.
Parking for 3.

⌂ ♥ ▱ ⇥ ⓤ ▥ ⇥ ⇥ ▥
⚘ ✕ ▨ ▦ ▦

Claremont Guest House

⚶⚶

9 Grosvenor Villas,
Claremont Rd., Bath,
BA1 6QL
☎ (0225) 428859
*Early Victorian semi-detached
house, away from the main
road on the outskirts of Bath.
Pleasant views from bedrooms,
off-street parking.*
Bedrooms: 2 double & 3 twin,
1 family room.
Bathrooms: 3 private,
1 public.
Bed & breakfast: £25-£35
double.
Parking for 4.

⌂ ▦ ▱ ♥ ⓤ ▥ ⇥ ⇥ ⓣⓥ
▥ ▱ ⚘ ✕ ▨ SP

Forres Guest House

⚶⚶

172 Newbridge Rd., Lower
Weston, Bath, BA1 3LE
☎ (0225) 427698
*Edwardian family guesthouse
with friendly, informative hosts,
who are ex-teachers and love
Bath. River Avon and
Cotswold Way close by.
Traditional and vegetarian
breakfasts. Colour TV in all
rooms.*
Bedrooms: 2 double & 2 twin,
1 family room.
Bathrooms: 3 private,
2 public.
Bed & breakfast: £21-£26
double.
Parking for 5.
Open April-October.

⌂ ▦ ▱ ♥ ⓤ ▥ ⇥ ▥ ⚘
✕ ▨ ▦ SP

Gainsborough Hotel ⋔

⚶⚶⚶

Weston La., Bath, BA1 4AB
☎ (0225) 311380
*Small country house hotel in
quiet, secluded garden near
Victoria Park. The Abbey and
Roman baths are 1.25 miles
away.*
Bedrooms: 2 single, 8 double
& 4 twin, 2 family rooms.
Bathrooms: 16 private.
Bed & breakfast: £22-£27.50
single, £40-£52 double.
Half board: £30.50-£35.50
daily, £210-£245 weekly.
Lunch available.
Evening meal 7pm (l.o.
8.30pm).
Parking for 18.
Credit: Access, Visa, Amex.

⌂ ▦ ▱ ⓛ ⓓ ▱ ⇥ ▥
⚘ ✕ ▨ SP ⊤

**PLEASE CHECK PRICES AND OTHER DETAILS
AT THE TIME OF BOOKING.**

Haute Combe
☺☺☺

176 Newbridge Rd., Bath,
BA1 3LE
☎ (0225) 420061
*Elegant family-run Edwardian
guesthouse, with off-the-road
parking, just 2 miles from Bath
city centre. On A4 Bristol side
of Bath.*
Bedrooms: 1 single, 3 double
& 1 twin, 2 family rooms.
Bathrooms: 3 private,
2 public; 1 private shower.
Bed & breakfast: £14-£20
single, £22-£36 double.
Half board: £18.50-£27.50
daily, £140-£178 weekly.
Evening meal 8pm (l.o. 4pm).
Parking for 8.
Credit: Access.
🛇🕭☐♥ 🛉 Ⅴ ⊸ ⊺ꝟ ▥
▣ 🛪 🛱 ᴰᴬᴾ ꜱᴾ

Leighton House
☺☺☺

139 Wells Rd, Bath,
BA2 4QE
☎ (0225) 314769
*An elegant and spacious
Victorian guesthouse set in
gardens of one third of an acre.
10 minutes' walk from city
centre.*
Bedrooms: 3 double & 2 twin,
2 family rooms.
Bathrooms: 4 private,
1 public; 2 private showers.
Bed & breakfast: £22-£33
single, £32-£42 double.
Parking for 8.
Credit: Access, Visa.
🛇🕭☐♥ ᵁᴸ 🛉 Ⅴ ⊸ ▥
▣ 🛪 🛱 ꜱᴾ

Membland
Listed

7 Pulteney Ter., Pulteney
Rd., Bath, BA2 4HJ
☎ 0225 (336 712)
*Spacious, comfortable guest
house in the heart of historic
Bath, two minutes' walk from
canal and countryside.*
Bedrooms: 2 twin, 1 family
room.
Bathrooms: 1 public;
2 private showers.
Bed & breakfast: £16.50-£19
single, £33-£38 double.
Half board: £20-£27.50 daily,
£140-£192 weekly.
Evening meal 7.15pm (l.o.
8pm).
Parking for 3.
🛇☐♥ ᵁᴸ 🛉 Ⅴ ▥ ▣ 🛪
ᴰᴬᴾ ꜱᴾ

Monmouth Lodge
Norton St. Philip, Bath,
BA3 6LH
☎ Faulkland (037 387) 367
*Secluded county home set in an
acre of garden with views.
Situated in a heritage village.
Friendly welcome. German
spoken.*
Bedrooms: 1 double & 1 twin,
1 family room.
Bathrooms: 3 private.
Bed & breakfast: £32-£34
double.
Parking for 5.
Open April-October.
🛇5🕭☐♥ ᵁᴸ Ⅴ ⊸ ▱ ꝟ
▥ ▣ ✿ 🛪 🛱 ᴰᴬᴾ ꜱᴾ

Oakleigh Guest
House ♨
☺☺☺

19 Upper Oldfield Pk., Bath,
BA2 3JX
☎ (0225) 315698
*Your comfort is assured at this
tastefully modernised Victorian
home, quietly situated only 10
minutes from the city centre.*
Bedrooms: 3 double & 1 twin.
Bathrooms: 4 private.
Bed & breakfast: £25-£35
single, £30-£40 double.
Parking for 4.
Credit: Access, Visa.
▣☐♥ ᵁᴸ Ⅴ ⊸ ▥ ▣
🛪 🛱 ᴰᴬᴾ ꜱᴾ

Poplar Farm
Listed

Stanton Prior, Bath,
BA2 9HX
☎ Timsbury (0761) 70382
*320-acre mixed farm. In
village of Stanton Prior
beneath Iron Age fort on
Stantonbury Hill. 5 miles west
of Bath.*
Bedrooms: 2 double, 1 family
room.
Bathrooms: 1 private,
1 public.
Bed & breakfast: £24-£30
double.
Parking for 11.
🛇☒ ᵁᴸ ꝟ ▥ ▣ ♠ ∪ ✿
🛪 🛱

Press Barrow Farm
Listed

Priston, Bath, BA2 9EH
☎ Timsbury (0761) 70354
*200-acre dairy farm.
Comfortable, tastefully
furnished 300-year-old
farmhouse in peaceful village 5
miles from Bath. Lovely views,
farmhouse cooking.*
Bedrooms: 1 double & 2 twin.
Bathrooms: 1 public.
Bed & breakfast: £12 single,
£20 double.
Open April-November.
🛇☒ ᵁᴸ ᴄᴮ 🛪 🛱

Sherford House
Lansdown Rd., Bath,
BA1 5SU
☎ (0225) 316445
*Spacious Victorian gable-
fronted house close to
Lansdown Crescent and within
walking distance of main
tourist attractions. Regular bus
service nearby.*
Bedrooms: 1 single, 1 double.
Bathrooms: 1 public.
Bed & breakfast: £12.50-£15
single, £25-£30 double.
🛇3☒♥ ᵁᴸ ▥ 🛪 🛱

Sheridan
Listed

95 Wellsway, Bearflat, Bath,
BA2 4RU
☎ (0225) 429562
*Quiet, comfortable family
guesthouse. A few minutes'
drive from city centre and on
main bus route to city and
railway station. A non-smoking
house.*
Bedrooms: 1 double, 1 family
room.
Bathrooms: 1 public.
Bed & breakfast: £10-£12
single, £22-£24 double.
🛇3♥ ᵁᴸ Ⅴ ⊸ ▱ ꝟ ▥ 🛪
🛱

Stonehouse Bed &
Breakfast
☺

120 Lower Oldfield Pk.,
Bath, BA2 3HS
☎ (0225) 422743
*Victorian house, a family home
10 minutes' walk to city centre.
Excellent view of Bath from all
bedrooms which have tea and
coffee making facilities and
colour TV.*
Bedrooms: 1 twin, 1 family
room.
Bathrooms: 1 public.
Bed & breakfast: from £20
double.
Parking for 2.
🛇☐♥ ᵁᴸ Ⅴ ▥ ▣ ♠ 🛪
🛱

Tacoma Guest House ♨
☺☺

159 Newbridge Hill, Bath,
BA1 3PX
☎ (0225) 310197
*Old Victorian house in quiet
location with pleasant views.
Good bus service. 1.5 miles
from city centre.*
Bedrooms: 2 single, 2 double
& 2 twin, 2 family rooms.
Bathrooms: 2 public;
2 private showers.
Bed & breakfast: £11-£12
single, £20-£24 double.
Parking for 5.
🛇♥ ᵁᴸ ▱ ꝟ ▥ ▣ 🛪
🛱 ꜱᴾ

Tor View
☺☺☺

Rock Hall La., Combe
Down, Bath, BA2 5JF
☎ (0225) 833326
*Victorian house within easy
reach of city centre, with
comfortable bedrooms and
panoramic views.*
Bedrooms: 3 double.
Bathrooms: 3 private.
Bed & breakfast: £30-£40
double.
Parking for 4.
Open March-October.
▣☐♥ ▱ ▥ ▥ ▣ ✿ 🛪
🛱

Wansdyke Cottage
Marksbury Gate, Bath,
BA2 9HE
☎ Saltford (0225) 873674
*Private family house
specialising in traditional
cottage-style accommodation
including self-contained suite of
bedroom, bathroom, kitchen
and lounge.*
Bedrooms: 1 single, 1 double
& 1 twin.
Bathrooms: 1 private,
1 public.
Bed & breakfast: £10-£12
single, £20-£24 double.
Half board: £15-£17 daily,
£105-£119 weekly.
Lunch available.
Evening meal 7pm (l.o. 7pm).
Parking for 4.
🛇🕭🕭☐♥ 🛉 Ⅴ ⊸
ꝟ ▥ ▣ ✿ 🛪 🛱

Wellsway Guest House
51 Wellsway, Bath, BA2 4RS
☎ (0225) 423434
*Comfortable, clean, warm
small guesthouse on bus route.
Close to local shops, only a few
minutes' walk from city centre.*
Bedrooms: 1 double & 2 twin,
1 family room.
Bathrooms: 1 public.
Bed & breakfast: £18-£26
double.
Parking for 3.
🛇🕭☐♥ ᵁᴸ Ⅴ ⊸ ▥ ▣
► 🛱 ᴰᴬᴾ ⊤

THERE IS A SPECIAL
SECTION IN THIS
GUIDE LISTING
ACCOMMODATION
ESPECIALLY
SUITABLE FOR
GROUPS AND
YOUNG PEOPLE.

MAP REFERENCES
APPLY TO COLOUR
MAPS NEAR THE
BACK OF THE GUIDE.

BATHEASTON

Avon
Map ref 2B2

Suburb north east of Bath, within easy reach of city and Bristol. Nearby Little Solsbury Hill has an Iron Age fort (National Trust).

Old Mill Hotel & Restaurant M

Tollbridge Rd., Batheaston, Bath, BA1 7DE
☎ Bath (0225) 858476
Pleasantly located former mill on banks of River Avon, 2 miles from Georgian Bath. Offering a warm welcome from resident proprietors.
Bedrooms: 2 single, 5 double & 6 twin, 2 family rooms.
Bathrooms: 14 private, 2 public; 1 private shower.
Bed & breakfast: from £35 single, from £48 double.
Lunch available.
Evening meal 7.30pm (l.o. 9.30pm).
Parking for 30.
Credit: Access, Visa, Diners, Amex.

BEAMINSTER

Dorset
Map ref 2A3

Old country town of mellow local stone set amid hills and rural vales. Mainly Georgian buildings; attractive almshouses date from 1603. The 17th C church with its ornate, pinnacled tower, was extensively restored inside by the Victorians.

Manor House

Beaminster
☎ (0308) 862311
Georgian manor house in beautiful surroundings, with lake and waterfalls. Comfortable, spacious rooms, special diets and home-grown produce.
Bedrooms: 1 double & 2 twin.
Bathrooms: 1 private, 2 public.
Bed & breakfast: £14-£20 single, £28-£36 double.
Half board: £21-£25 daily.
Evening meal 7pm.

BEAWORTHY

Devon
Map ref 1C2

Maplehill Farm

East Chilla, Beaworthy, EX21 5XF
☎ (040 922) 217
30-acre beef farm. Comfortable period farmhouse. Guests have a private bathroom. Quiet and relaxing atmosphere, superb views. Local produce used for English breakfast.
Bedrooms: 1 double & 1 twin.
Bathrooms: 1 private, 1 public.
Bed & breakfast: from £12 single, from £24 double.
Parking for 5.

Middle Beamsworthy

Beaworthy, EX21 5AN
☎ (040 922) 414
Cottage with beautiful views offering organically-grown home produce.
Bedrooms: 1 single, 1 double.
Bathrooms: 1 public.
Bed & breakfast: £7.50 single, £15 double.
Half board: £12.50 daily, £75 weekly.
Evening meal 7pm (l.o. 7pm).
Parking for 2.

BIDEFORD

Devon
Map ref 1C1

See also Buckland Brewer, Hartland.
Once the home port of Sir Richard Grenville, this handsome town with its 17th C merchants' houses flourished as a shipbuilding and cloth town, later dealing in Newfoundland cod and American tobacco. The mile long quay is still busy with light shipping as well as pleasure craft. The bridge of 24 arches, recently strengthened, was built about 1460. Charles Kingsley stayed here while writing Westward Ho!

Chope Barton
⊟⊟

Chope Rd., Northam, Bideford, EX39 3QE
☎ (023 72) 77833

Large detached house in peaceful setting with open views, 5 minutes' walk to village and all amenities. Only 1.5 miles from the sea.
Bedrooms: 1 double & 1 twin, 1 family room.
Bathrooms: 1 public.
Bed & breakfast: £10-£11 single, £20-£22 double.
Half board: £15-£16 daily, £100-£107 weekly.
Evening meal 6.30pm (l.o. 5pm).
Parking for 6.

BISHOP'S LYDEARD

Somerset
Map ref 1D1

4m NW. Taunton

Slimbridge Station Farm
⊟⊟⊟

Bishop's Lydeard, Taunton, TA4 3BX
☎ (0823) 432223
120-acre farm. Victorian house next to the privately-owned West Somerset Steam Railway with a limited number of trains running in the summer.
Bedrooms: 1 single, 1 double & 1 twin.
Bathrooms: 1 public.
Bed & breakfast: £10-£12 single, £20-£24 double.
Parking for 4.

BISHOP'S NYMPTON

Devon
Map ref 1C1

3m SE. South Molton

North Hayne

Bishops Nympton, South Molton, EX36 3QR
☎ (076 97) 323
Well restored 13th C. farmhouse in its own smallholding of 10 acres. Very secluded with views over Exmoor.
Bedrooms: 1 single, 1 double, 2 family rooms.
Bathrooms: 2 private, 1 public.
Bed & breakfast: £12-£13 single, £22-£26 double.
Half board: £17-£18 daily, £84-£91 weekly.
Evening meal 8pm (l.o. 9am).
Parking for 20.

BISHOPSWOOD

Somerset
Map ref 1D2

5m NW. Chard

Hawthorne House

Bishopswood, Chard, TA20 3RS
☎ Buckland St. Mary (046 034) 482
19th C. detached house in small village on Blackdown Hills. Home cooking.
Bedrooms: 1 double & 1 twin.
Bathrooms: 1 public.
Bed & breakfast: £10.50 single, £17-£20 double.
Half board: £13.50-£15 daily, £90-£100 weekly.
Evening meal 6pm (l.o. 8pm).
Parking for 2.

BLACKAWTON

Devon
Map ref 1D3

5m W. Dartmouth
Deep in rural Devon, this village with its spacious church makes a peaceful base for journeys to Dartmoor or the coast. Among other interesting items in the church, which dates from the 12th C, is a richly-carved sandstone font of about the same age.

Normandy Arms
Listed

Chapel St., Blackawton, Totnes, TQ9 7BN
☎ (080 421) 316
Traditional, friendly inn with restaurant and family room.
Bedrooms: 3 double & 2 twin.
Bathrooms: 2 private, 1 public.
Bed & breakfast: £14.50-£17.50 single, £29-£35 double.
Half board: £24.50-£27.50 daily, £171.50-£194.50 weekly.
Lunch available.
Evening meal 7pm (l.o. 10pm).
Parking for 10.

THE SYMBOLS ARE EXPLAINED ON THE FLAP INSIDE THE BACK COVER.

BLACKFORD

Somerset
Map ref 1D1

2m W. Wedmore

Overbrook Farm

Pool Bridge Rd., Blackford, Wedmore, BS28 4PA
☎ Wedmore (0934) 712081
6-acre smallholding. Comfortable, homely farmhouse set in walled gardens. Peaceful surroundings close to cathedral cities, Somerset Levels, Wookey and Cheddar Caves.
Bedrooms: 2 double & 1 twin.
Bathrooms: 3 private.
Bed & breakfast: £24 double.
Parking for 6.
Open February-October.

BOSCASTLE

Cornwall
Map ref 1B2

Small unspoilt village in Valency Valley, steeply built at meeting of 2 rivers. Active as a port until onset of railway era and tourism, its dramatic natural harbour affords rare shelter on this wild coast. Attractions include spectacular blow-hold, Celtic field strips, part-Norman church. 2 miles east, St. Juliot church was restored by Thomas Hardy (1872).

Forrabury House

Forrabury Common, Boscastle, PL35 0DJ
☎ Boscastle (084 05) 469
The former rectory to Forabury Church. Offers bed and breakfast, full board or half board accommodation. Various diets catered for on request.
Bedrooms: 2 double & 1 twin, 1 family room.
Bathrooms: 1 public; 4 private showers.
Bed & breakfast: £9.50-£11.50 single, £19-£21 double.
Half board: £15-£16 daily, £98-£105 weekly.
Lunch available.
Evening meal 6.30pm (l.o. 10am).
Parking for 5.

The Old Post House

Fore St., Boscastle, PL35 0AX
☎ (084 05) 342
16th C. listed historic house, comfortably modernised, in 2 acres of wooded garden in conservation area near Elizabethan harbour, beaches and moors.
Bedrooms: 1 double & 2 twin.
Bathrooms: 2 public.
Bed & breakfast: £11.50-£12.50 single, £23-£25 double.
Parking for 3.

Wellington Hotel

The Harbour, Boscastle, PL35 0AQ
☎ (084 05) 202
Historic listed 16th C. coaching inn by Elizabethan harbour and National Trust walks. Georgian restaurant with Anglo-French cuisine. Free house, real ales and buffet. Open fire and beams.
Bedrooms: 5 single, 8 double & 6 twin, 2 family rooms.
Bathrooms: 12 private, 2 public.
Bed & breakfast: £14-£19.50 single, £27-£38 double.
Half board: £22-£27.50 daily, £142-£173 weekly.
Lunch available.
Evening meal 7pm (l.o. 9.30pm).
Parking for 20.
Open February-November.
Credit: Access, Visa, Diners, Amex.
2

BOVEY TRACEY

Devon
Map ref 1D2

See also Manaton.
Standing by its river just east of Dartmoor National Park, this old town has good moorland views. Its church, with a 14th C tower, holds one of Devon's finest medieval rood screens.

Corbyns Brimley

Higher Brimley, Bovey Tracey, TQ13 9JT
☎ (0626) 833332
16th C. thatched cottage in foothills of Haytor, within Dartmoor National Park. Comfortable and friendly atmosphere, secluded garden, panoramic views of surrounding countryside. Overseas visitors welcome. Leave Bovey Tracey on Haytor Road, straight on at island. Take left at fork, forward to cross roads. Turn left, forward to T junction, turn right. Corbyns is first thatched cottage 2/3 mile on right.
Bedrooms: 2 twin.
Bathrooms: 1 private, 1 public.
Bed & breakfast: £24 double.
Parking for 2.

Lower Warmhill Farm

Hennock, Newton Abbot, TQ13 9QH
☎ (0626) 833129
30-acre horse farm. Old converted barn with unrivalled views over the Teign Valley, 3 miles from A38. Located in Dartmoor National Park.
Bedrooms: 1 single, 2 double & 1 twin, 1 family room.
Bathrooms: 2 public.
Bed & breakfast: £12-£14 single, £24-£28 double.
Parking for 10.

BOX

Wiltshire
Map ref 2B2

Fogleigh Lodge

Box Hill, Box, Corsham, SN14 9ES
☎ (0225) 742434
A small intimate family home, friendly and well furnished, with panoramic country views.
Bedrooms: 2 double & 1 twin.
Bathrooms: 1 public.
Bed & breakfast: £12-£15 single, £19-£22 double.
Parking for 7.
Open March-December.
5

GROUPS, CONSORTIA AND AGENCIES SPECIALISING IN FARM AND COUNTRY HOLIDAYS ARE LISTED IN A SPECIAL SECTION OF THIS GUIDE.

BRADFORD-ON-AVON

Wiltshire
Map ref 2B2

Huddled steeply beside the river the old stone buildings of this former cloth-weaving town reflect continuing prosperity from the Middle Ages. Earlier still is a tiny Anglo-Saxon church, among the most complete in England, part of a monastery sacked by Danes. The part-14th C bridge carries a medieval chapel, later used as a lock-up. Interesting places nearby include one of England's largest tithe barns at Barton Farm, Great Chalfield Manor and Westwood Manor.

Priory Steps

Newtown, Bradford-on-Avon, BA15 1NQ
☎ (022 16) 2230
17th C. house in delightful location, with fine views over the Avon Valley. Comfortable and well-appointed accommodation.
Bedrooms: 3 double & 2 twin.
Bathrooms: 5 private.
Bed & breakfast: £28-£30 single, £38-£44 double.
Half board: £31-£34 daily, £200-£250 weekly.
Evening meal 7.30pm.
Parking for 7.
Credit: Access, Visa.

The Roundhouse

4 Masons La., Bradford-on-Avon, BA15 1QN
☎ (022 16) 6842
Converted stone tower windmill in quiet, secluded woodland setting, enjoying extensive views over Bradford. Short walk from town centre.
Bedrooms: 2 single, 1 double, 1 family room.
Bathrooms: 1 public.
Bed & breakfast: £12.50-£16 single, £24-£39 double.
Half board: £22-£29.50 daily, £143.50-£196 weekly.
Evening meal 8pm (l.o. 10am).
Parking for 3.
Open January-October.
5

PLEASE CHECK PRICES AND OTHER DETAILS AT THE TIME OF BOOKING.

BRADFORD-ON-AVON

Continued

Weavers Mill

Avoncliff, Bradford-on-Avon,
BA15 2HB
☎ (022 16) 5128
*Picturesque location on the
banks of the River Avon. 1.5
miles downstream from
Bradford on Avon, with private
fishing rights.*
Bedrooms: 2 single, 1 double,
1 family room.
Bathrooms: 2 public.
Bed & breakfast: £12.50-£15
single, £25-£30 double.
Parking for 6.

BRADWORTHY

Devon
Map ref 1C2

7m N. Holsworthy
Rural village surrounded
by many scenic
attractions and the
superb North Devon
coast.

Bradworthy Inn

Bradworthy, Holsworthy,
EX22 7SS
☎ (040 924) 208
*12th C. comfortable, friendly
inn with personal supervision.
Tamar Lake, a popular fishing
resort, is 3 miles away.*
Bedrooms: 2 single, 2 double
& 1 twin, 1 family room.
Bathrooms: 1 public.
Bed & breakfast: £11 single,
£22 double.
Half board: £14 daily, £75
weekly.
Evening meal 7pm (l.o. 6pm).
Parking for 6.

BRANSCOMBE

Devon
Map ref 1D2

5m E. Sidmouth
Scattered village of
unusual character.
Houses of cob and thatch
are sited irregularly on
the steep wooded slopes
of a combe, which widens
towards the sea. Much of
Branscombe Estate is
National Trust property.

Portselda

Listed
Branscombe, Seaton,
EX12 3DJ
☎ (029 780) 213

*Small guesthouse in village of
outstanding beauty, specialising
in fresh seafood, with a homely
atmosphere.*
Bedrooms: 1 double & 1 twin.
Bathrooms: 1 public.
Bed & breakfast: £10.50-
£12.50 single, £21-£25 double.
Half board: £21-£25 daily,
£97.50 weekly.
Evening meal 7pm (l.o. 8pm).
Parking for 1.

Three Horseshoes ⚏

Branscombe, Seaton,
EX12 3BR
☎ (029 780) 251
*Family run inn with beams,
brasses, log fires. Short
distance from several seaside
resorts. Beautiful countryside
with excellent walks.*
Bedrooms: 2 single, 7 double
& 2 twin, 1 family room.
Bathrooms: 5 private,
2 public.
Bed & breakfast: £11.50-
£18.50 single, £21-£34 double.
Evening meal 6pm (l.o.
10pm).
Parking for 100.
Credit: Access, Visa, Diners,
Amex.

BRATTON CLOVELLY

Devon
Map ref 1C2

8m W. Okehampton

Four Chimneys

Listed
Bratton Clovelly,
Okehampton, EX20 4JS
☎ (083 787) 409
*Charming house in large,
secluded garden just outside
village. Okehampton 9 miles,
Tavistock 13.5, Launceston
12; easy access to Cornwall.
Evening meal or packed lunch
by arrangement.*
Bedrooms: 2 twin.
Bathrooms: 1 public.
Bed & breakfast: £9-£10
single, £18-£20 double.
Half board: £14-£15 daily,
£94-£101 weekly.
Evening meal 7pm (l.o.
10am).
Parking for 3.
Open March-October.

BRATTON FLEMING

Devon
Map ref 1C1

6m NE. Barnstaple
On western fringe of
Exmoor with easy access
to the magnificent
beaches and coastline of
North Devon.

Holywell

⚏⚏
Bratton Fleming, Barnstaple,
EX31 4SD
☎ (0598) 710213
*House in valley designated as
'an area of great landscape
value'. Peaceful, warm and
comfortable accommodation.
English breakfast.*
Bedrooms: 1 double & 1 twin.
Bathrooms: 2 private.
Bed & breakfast: £12 single,
£24 double.
Parking for 2.
Open April-October.

BRAUNTON

Devon
Map ref 1C1

Large village just north of
the Taw estuary and
close to botanically-
important dunelands,
National Nature Reserve,
at Braunton Burrows on
Devon's north coast.
Braunton Great Field
shows rare example of
ancient field-strip
cultivation. The church
has a prominent Norman
tower and lead-shingled
spire. ℹ

Park Farm

Lower Park Rd., Braunton,
Devon. EX33 2LQ
☎ (0271) 812079
*400-acre mixed farm. The
famous beaches of Saunton,
Croyde and Putsborough are
within easy reach. Meals are
prepared with care using fresh
produce daily from farm.
Guests can be sure of a
cheerful welcome and
hospitality.*
Bedrooms: 2 double, 2 family
rooms.
Bathrooms: 1 public.
Bed & breakfast: £10-£12
single, £18-£20 double.
Parking for 6.
Open April-October.

BRIDESTOWE

Devon
Map ref 1C2

6m SW. Okehampton
Small Dartmoor village
with a much restored 15th
C church, and Great
Links Tor rising to the
south east.

The Knole Farm

⚏⚏
Bridestowe, Okehampton,
EX20 4HA
☎ (083 786) 241
*83-acre mixed farm. Late 19th
C. residence, formerly a
gentleman's residence, with
beautiful views of Dartmoor.*
Bedrooms: 2 double & 1 twin,
1 family room.
Bathrooms: 1 public.
Bed & breakfast: £9.50-£10
single, £19-£20 double.
Half board: £14-£15 daily,
£98-£105 weekly.
Evening meal 6pm (l.o. 4pm).
Parking for 4.

Week Farm

⚏⚏⚏
Bridestowe, Okehampton,
EX20 4HZ
☎ (083 786) 221
*200-acre dairy farm. A warm
welcome awaits you at this
homely 17th C. farmhouse, set
in peaceful countryside three
quarters of a mile from the
A30. Home cooking and every
comfort.*
Bedrooms: 1 single, 2 double
& 2 twin, 3 family rooms.
Bathrooms: 1 private,
1 public; 1 private shower.
Bed & breakfast: £20-£22
double.
Half board: £15-£15.50 daily,
£96-£100 weekly.
Evening meal 7pm (l.o. 5pm).
Parking for 10.

THERE IS A SPECIAL
SECTION IN THIS
GUIDE LISTING
ACCOMMODATION
ESPECIALLY
SUITABLE FOR
GROUPS AND
YOUNG PEOPLE.

MAP REFERENCES APPLY TO COLOUR MAPS
NEAR THE BACK OF THE GUIDE.

BRIDGERULE

Cornwall
Map ref 1C2

4m W. Holsworthy

Elm Park Farm
Listed

Bridgerule, Holsworthy,
Devon EX22 7EL
☎ (028 881) 231
*208-acre mixed farm. Modern
farmhouse overlooking
countryside, with a friendly
atmosphere, home cooking and
a pony for children. Surfing
beaches within five miles. Close
to village.*
Bedrooms: 1 twin, 3 family
rooms.
Bathrooms: 1 public.
Bed & breakfast: max. £9
single, max. £18 double.
Half board: £12-£13 daily,
£75-£80 weekly.
Evening meal 6.30pm (l.o.
6.30pm).
Parking for 4.
Open March-November.
🖙 🗄 📺 ⚫ ♨ U ✔ ❀ 🐾

BRIDGWATER

Somerset
Map ref 1D1

See also Kilve.
Originally major medieval
port on the River Parrett,
now small industrial town
with mostly 19th C or
modern architecture.
Georgian Castle Street
leads to West Quay and
site of 13th C castle.
Birthplace of Cromwellian
admiral Robert Blake is
now a museum. Arts
centre and theatre, lido.
i

Waterpitts Farm
Broomfield, Bridgwater,
TA5 1AT
☎ Kingston St. Mary
(082 345) 679
*5-acre mixed farm. In quiet
secluded part of the Quantock
Hills. Convenient for riding,
walking, fishing, golf and pub.
Midway between Taunton and
Bridgwater.*
Bedrooms: 1 double, 1 family
room.
Bathrooms: 1 public.
Bed & breakfast: £9-£10
single, £18-£20 double.
Half board: £14-£16 daily,
£95-£110 weekly.
Evening meal 6pm (l.o. 6pm).
Parking for 20.
🖙 ❀ 🗄 🔌 📺 📟 🔉 U ►
❀ 🐾

BRIDPORT

Dorset
Map ref 2A3

See also Powerstock.
Market town and chief
producer of nets and
ropes just inland of
dramatic Dorset coast.
Earlier ropes made for
hangman's noose as well
as for shipping and
fishing boats. Old, broad
streets built for drying
and twisting, long back
gardens for rope-walks.
Grand arcaded Town Hall
and Georgian buildings,
traditional inns. Local
history museum has
Roman relics. Charles II
stopped here on his flight
to France. *i*

The Marquis of Lorne ♨
😕

Nettlecombe, Bridport,
DT6 3SY
☎ (030 885) 236
*Picturesque village inn only 4
miles from coast and Bridport.*
Bedrooms: 1 single, 2 double
& 3 twin, 2 family rooms.
Bathrooms: 4 private,
1 public.
Bed & breakfast: £14-£17
single, £28-£34 double.
Half board: £19-£28 daily,
£143.50-£175 weekly.
Lunch available.
Evening meal 7pm (l.o.
9.30pm).
Parking for 80.
Credit: Access.
🖙 ❀ 🔌 Ⓥ 🗄 📺 ❀ 🐾 SP
📟 🔉

BRISTOL

Avon
Map ref 2A2

Important since Saxon
times, today a university
town and major port. City
grew round medieval river
docks, now the Floating
Harbour, then busy with
fish, trade, sea warfare
and exploration (Cabots
sailed for Newfoundland
1499). Merchant
Venturers founded here
1552. Fine old churches
and cathedral; Georgian
theatre and Exchange;
wide views of Avon
Gorge from Brunel's
Clifton Bridge. *i*

Portbury Priors
Station Rd., Portbury,
Bristol, BS20 9TN
☎ Pill (027 581) 3165
*16th C. farmhouse, three
quarters of a mile from
Junction 19 of the M5, 8 miles
from Bristol centre. Log fires
in winter. Situated close to the
vilage pub.*
Bedrooms: 1 double & 2 twin.
Bathrooms: 1 public.
Bed & breakfast: from £15
single, from £22 double.
Parking for 3.
🖙 ❀ 🗄 🔌 Ⓥ 📺 🔉
🐾 🐾 📟

BRIXHAM

Devon
Map ref 1D2

Famous for its trawling
fleet in the 19th C, a
steeply-built fishing port
overlooking the harbour
and fish market. A statue
of William of Orange
recalls his landing here
before deposing James II.
There is an aquarium and
museum. Good cliff views
and walks. *i*

Richmond House Hotel
😕

Higher Manor Rd., Brixham,
TQ5 8HA
☎ (0803) 882391
*Detached Victorian home
decorated in Laura Ashley
style. Central for the shops and
harbour, yet quiet. First left
after the Golden Lion. Access
at all times.*
Bedrooms: 2 single, 2 double
& 1 twin, 3 family rooms.
Bathrooms: 3 public.
Bed & breakfast: from £11.25
single, from £20.50 double.
Parking for 5.
Open March-October.
Credit: Visa.
🖙 ❀ 📺 🔌 Ⓥ ✂ 🗄 📺
📟 📟 🐾 SP 📟 🔉

BROAD CHALKE

Wiltshire
Map ref 2B3

5m SW. Wilton
Delightful River Ebble
valley village with a 13th
C church displaying a
notable porch and central
tower.

The Queens Head Inn
😕

Broad Chalke, Salisbury,
SP5 5EN
☎ (0722) 780344
*15th C. building with stone
walls and old beams. Set in the
beautiful Chalke Valley, 8
miles from Salisbury.*
Bedrooms: 3 double & 1 twin.
Bathrooms: 4 private.
Bed & breakfast: £25-£30
single, £36-£40 double.
Evening meal 7pm (l.o.
9.30pm).
Parking for 40.
Credit: Visa.
🖙 5 ❀ 🔌 🗄 🔌 Ⓥ 📺
📟 🔉 🐾

GROUPS, CONSORTIA AND AGENCIES
SPECIALISING IN FARM AND COUNTRY
HOLIDAYS ARE LISTED IN A SPECIAL
SECTION OF THIS GUIDE.

PLEASE CHECK PRICES AND OTHER DETAILS
AT THE TIME OF BOOKING.

INDIVIDUAL PROPRIETORS HAVE SUPPLIED
ALL DETAILS OF ACCOMMODATION.
ALTHOUGH WE DO CHECK FOR ACCURACY, WE
ADVISE YOU TO CONFIRM PRICES AND OTHER
INFORMATION AT THE TIME OF BOOKING.

BROADWINDSOR

Dorset
Map ref 1D2

3m W. Beaminster
Steeply-built village of
period terraces
overlooked by its
brownstone church. King
Charles II stayed at a
terraced cottage near the
centre on his flight to
France after defeat at the
Battle of Worcester. A
few miles westward,
Pilsdon Pen has
extensive views over
Marshwood Vale. Just
west of the hill William
and Dorothy Wordsworth
lived for a while at
Racedown House.

Burstock Grange Farm
Broadwindsor, Beaminster,
DT8 3LL
☎ (0308) 68527
290-acre mixed farm.
Thatched 13th C. farmhouse
on family-run farm. Warm and
friendly, personal attention.
Games room and TV lounge.
Children welcome.
Bedrooms: 1 double & 1 twin.
Bathrooms: 1 private,
1 public.
Bed & breakfast: from £12.50
single, from £25 double.
Parking for 6.
Open April-October.

BROMHAM

Wiltshire
Map ref 2B2

Durlett Farm House
Durlett Rd., Bromham,
Chippenham, SN15 2HY
☎ (0380) 850524
100-year-old farmhouse with
spacious rooms and children's
facilities.
Bedrooms: 1 double & 2 twin.
Bathrooms: 1 public.
Bed & breakfast: £20-£25
double.
Half board: £15-£17.50 daily,
£100-£110 weekly.
Evening meal 7pm (l.o. 8pm).
Parking for 3.

BUCKFASTLEIGH

Devon
Map ref 1C2

Small market and
manufacturing town just
south of Buckfast Abbey
on the fringe of Dartmoor.
Trips can be taken by
steam train on a
reopened line along the
beautiful Dart Valley to
the head of the estuary,
Totnes.

The George Inn ▲
Plymouth Rd., Buckfastleigh,
TQ11 0DH
☎ (0364) 42708
Pretty 18th C. inn just off the
A38. Ideal centre for touring,
walking, fishing, bird watching.
Home-made food.
Bedrooms: 3 double, 4 family
rooms.
Bathrooms: 7 private.
Bed & breakfast: £20-£25
single, £30-£40 double.
Lunch available.
Evening meal 7pm (l.o.
10pm).
Parking for 25.
Credit: Access, Visa.

Royal Oak House ▲
59 Jordan St., Buckfastleigh,
TQ11 0AX
☎ (0364) 43611
Small family-run guesthouse on
the edge of Dartmoor, with
spacious rooms and home
cooking.
Bedrooms: 1 double & 1 twin,
3 family rooms.
Bathrooms: 2 private,
2 public.
Bed & breakfast: £10-£14
single, £20-£26 double.
Half board: £16-£20 daily,
£120-£144 weekly.
Evening meal 6.30pm (l.o.
4.30pm).
Open April-November.

BUCKLAND BREWER

Devon
Map ref 1C1

4m SW. Bideford

Meadow View
Buckland Brewer, Bideford,
EX39 5LU
☎ Horns Cross (023 75) 511
45-acre stock farm. Situated
on outskirts of pleasant village.
Near the sea, ideal touring
area. Bideford and Torrington
are equidistant. Off A386 at
Landcross.
Bedrooms: 3 double & 2 twin,
1 family room.
Bathrooms: 1 public.
Bed & breakfast: £10-£12
single, £18-£20.50 double.
Half board: £13-£15 daily,
£82-£87 weekly.
Evening meal 6pm (l.o.
10am).
Parking for 4.
Open March-November.

BUDE

Cornwall
Map ref 1C2

See also Crackington
Haven, Morwenstow.
Sandy resort on dramatic
Atlantic coast. High cliffs
give spectacular sea and
inland views. Georgian
cottages beside canal
basin, otherwise 19th and
20th C development. Golf
course, cricket pitch, folly,
surfing, coarse-fishing
and boating. Mother-town
Stratton was base of
Royalist Sir Bevil
Grenville and birthplace
of his famous retainer,
the 'Cornish Giant',
Anthony Payne. ℹ

Cliff Hotel ▲
Maer Down, Bude,
EX23 8NG
☎ (0288) 3110
Indoor pool and spa, putting
green and tennis court. In 5
acres of land, near National
Trust cliffs and 200 yards from
the beach. Chef-proprietor.
Bedrooms: 1 single, 3 double
& 1 twin, 10 family rooms.
Bathrooms: 15 private.
Bed & breakfast: £15-£18
single, £30-£36 double.
Half board: £21-£24 daily,
£125-£150 weekly.
Lunch available.
Evening meal 6.30pm (l.o.
6.30pm).

Parking for 15.
Open April-October.

Lower Northcott Farm
Poughill, Bude, EX23 9EL
☎ (0288) 2350
400-acre mixed farm. Georgian
farmhouse in secluded grounds
with children's safe play area.
Visitors welcome to wander
around and meet the animals.
Bedrooms: 1 single, 1 double
& 1 twin, 2 family rooms.
Bathrooms: 2 public.
Bed & breakfast: from £8.50
single, from £17 double.
Half board: from £14 daily,
from £89 weekly.
Evening meal 6.30pm (l.o.
6.30pm).
Parking for 4.
Open January-November.

BULKWORTHY

Devon
Map ref 1C2

7m SW. Torrington

Blakes
Bulkworthy, Holsworthy,
EX22 7UP
☎ Milton Damerel
(040 926) 249
4-acre mixed farm. A really
handsome farmhouse with well-
appointed accommodation and
modern facilities. Well placed
for touring this facinating part
of Devonshire.
Bedrooms: 1 double, 1 family
room.
Bathrooms: 1 public.
Bed & breakfast: £19-£20
double.
Parking for 6.
Open May-September.

GROUPS, CONSORTIA AND AGENCIES
SPECIALISING IN FARM AND COUNTRY
HOLIDAYS ARE LISTED IN A SPECIAL
SECTION OF THIS GUIDE.

THERE IS A SPECIAL
SECTION IN THIS
GUIDE LISTING
ACCOMMODATION
ESPECIALLY
SUITABLE FOR
GROUPS AND
YOUNG PEOPLE.

BURBAGE

Wiltshire
Map ref 2B2

4m E. Pewsey
Village close to
Savernake Forest,
famous as a habitat for
deer. Close by are the
remains of former Wolf
Hall mansion, where a
great banquet in honour
of Jane Seymour took
place in 1536.

The Old Vicarage ♨

Burbage, Marlborough,
SN8 3AG
☎ (0672) 810495
*Victorian country house in 2-
acre garden, close to
Savernake Forest, Kennet and
Avon Canal.*
Bedrooms: 1 single, 2 twin.
Bathrooms: 3 private.
Bed & breakfast: from £25
single, from £40 double.
Lunch available.
Evening meal 7pm (l.o. 8pm).
Parking for 10.
☎ ⊚ ⊡ ♥ ⓤ ▮ ⱽ ⅄ ⊨
⊺ ▥ ▲ ♡ ➤ ❀ ⋈ ❦ ⊤

BURTON BRADSTOCK

Dorset
Map ref 2A3

3m SE. Bridport
Lying amid fields beside
the River Bride, a village
of old stone houses, a
14th C church, a
Wesleyan chapel (now
the library) and a village
green. The beautiful coast
road from Abbotsbury to
Bridport passes by and
Iron Age forts top the
surrounding hills. Beyond
the cliffs, the sheltered
river valley makes a
staging post for migrating
birds.

Common Knapp House ♨
⊕⊕
Coast Rd., Burton Bradstock,
Bridport, DT6 4RJ
☎ (0308) 897428
*Quiet guesthouse with
extensive sea and country
views. Access to beach.
Optional evening meal using
produce from own garden.*
Bedrooms: 2 single, 5 double
& 5 twin, 1 family room.
Bathrooms: 10 private,
1 public.
Bed & breakfast: £15-£17
single, £32-£36 double.
Half board: £23-£25 daily,
£158-£205 weekly.

Evening meal 6.30pm (l.o.
4pm).
Parking for 21.
Open February-November.
⅃ ⚲ ⊞ ♡ ▮ ⊨ ⊺ ▥ ❀
⋈ ❦ SP

BUTLEIGH

Somerset
Map ref 2A2

3m SE. Street

Butleigh Court Tower
Butleigh, Glastonbury,
BA6 8SA
☎ (0458) 50824
*Neo-Gothic stately home 3
miles south of Glastonbury,
with unsurpassed view of the
Tor and countryside.*
Bedrooms: 1 double & 1 twin.
Bathrooms: 2 private.
Bed & breakfast: £16 single,
£32 double.
Parking for 3.
☎▮♡ ⓤ ⱽ ⅄ ⊨ ⊺ ▲
⋈ ❦ ⊞

CALLINGTON

Cornwall
Map ref 1C2

8m NW. Saltash
A quiet market town
standing on high ground
above the River Lynher.
The 15th C church of St.
Mary's has an alabaster
monument to Lord
Willoughby de Broke,
Henry VII's marshal. A
15th C chapel 1 mile east
houses Dupath Well, one
of the Cornish Holy Wells.

Higher Manaton Farm
Callington, PL17 8PX
☎ Stoke Climsland
(0579) 70460
*160-acre mixed farm. Early
19th C. farmhouse in pleasant
rural surroundings, with views
of Bodmin Moor. 2.5 miles
north west of Callington on the
B3257.*
Bedrooms: 1 twin, 1 family
room.
Bathrooms: 1 public.
Bed & breakfast: £7.50-£8.50
single, £15-£17 double.
Half board: £10.50-£11.50
daily, £73-£77 weekly.
Evening meal 6pm (l.o.
7.30pm).
Parking for 4.
Open January-November.
⅃ ⚲ ⓤ ⅄ ⊺ ▲ ⋈ ❦

CALNE

Wiltshire
Map ref 2B2

Prosperity from wool in
the 15th C endowed this
ancient market town with
a fine church in the
perpendicular style. To
the east are chalk
downlands and at
Oldbury Castle, an Iron
Age fort, a 17th C white
horse is carved into the
hillside.

Highway Farmhouse
⊕
Highway, Hilmarton, Calne,
SN11 8SR
☎ (024 976) 283
*800-acre mixed farm. A south
facing family house with lovely
views towards woodland. Easy
access to M4, Bath, Salisbury,
Devizes and Marlborough.
Comfortable bedrooms and
spacious gardens. 5 miles north
of Calne off Calne-Lyneham
road.*
Bedrooms: 1 single, 2 twin,
1 family room.
Bathrooms: 1 public.
Bed & breakfast: £12.50-£15
single, £22-£30 double.
Half board: from £15 daily,
£80-£90 weekly.
Evening meal 6pm (l.o. 9pm).
Parking for 6.
Open January-November.
⅃ ⚲ ⊞ ♡ ⓤ ⊺ ▥ ▲ ⅄ ♩
❀ ⋈ ❦ SP

South Farm
Listed
Calstone Wellington, Calne,
SN11 8PZ
☎ (0249) 815843
*500-acre mixed farm.
Comfortable, spacious house in
tranquil downland setting.
Ideal for walkers. Sports
facilities, riding and historic
sites close by. Friendly helpful
atmosphere. French spoken.*
Bedrooms: 1 single, 1 twin,
1 family room.
Bathrooms: 1 private,
1 public.
Bed & breakfast: £10-£12
single, £24-£26 double.
Half board: £18-£20 daily.
Evening meal 7pm (l.o. 5pm).
Parking for 8.
Open June-September.
⅃7 ⚲ ♡ ⓤ ▮ ⊺ ▥ ▲ ♩
❀ ⋈ ❦

CAMELFORD

Cornwall
Map ref 1B2

See also St. Teath.
Old market town set
between the coast and
the moorlands on the
north-west edge of
Bodmin Moor. Tennyson
thought of it as Arthur's
Camelot. At the northern
end of the town a hilly
track leads to Cornwall's
second-highest hill,
Roughtor. Local history
museum, ornamental
gardens. ℹ

Wilsey Down Inn
⊕⊕
Hallworthy, Camelford,
PL32 9SH
☎ Otterham Station
(084 06) 205
*Fine country inn offering
homely hospitality. Panoramic
views of the countryside.
Within easy reach of the coast.*
Bedrooms: 2 single, 1 double
& 2 twin, 1 family room.
Bathrooms: 2 public;
1 private shower.
Bed & breakfast: £12.65-
£13.80 single, £25.30-£27.60
double.
Half board: from £18.65
daily.
Lunch available.
Evening meal 6pm (l.o. 9pm).
Parking for 20.
⅃12 ♡ ▮ ⱽ ⊨ ⊺ ▥ ▲
♩ ♠ ❀ ⋈ ❦

CARBIS BAY

Cornwall
Map ref 1B3

Overlooking St. Ives Bay
and with fine beaches.

Bella Vista Guest House
Listed
St. Ives Rd., Carbis Bay,
TR26 2SF
☎ Penzance (0736) 796063
*Located 1 mile from town with
good access to rail and bus.
700 yards from beach where
local activities include surfing
and sailing. Pony trekking and
fishing.*
Bedrooms: 3 single, 2 double,
2 family rooms.
Bathrooms: 1 public.
Bed & breakfast: from £9
single, from £18 double.
Half board: from £14 daily,
from £89 weekly.
Evening meal 6pm (l.o. 3pm).
Parking for 7.
⅃ ⚲ ⊚ ⓤ ▮ ⱽ ⊨ ⊺ ▥
▲ ⋈ ❦ ⤬ SP

PLEASE MENTION THIS GUIDE WHEN MAKING A BOOKING.

CARHAMPTON

Somerset
Map ref 1D1

Village at the eastern end of Exmoor National Park, and close to Dunster Castle (National Trust).

Winnibrook House M
⛺⛺⛺

Park La., Carhampton, Minehead, TA24 6NN
☎ Dunster (0643) 821232
Country guesthouse in 1.5 acres on quiet by-road. Magnificent country and coastal views from all rooms.
Bedrooms: 1 double & 1 twin, 1 family room.
Bathrooms: 2 public.
Bed & breakfast: £10-£11 single, £19-£21 double.
Parking for 8.
🛏 ♨ ❖ UL 🅿 🍴 📺 ▥ ⚓ ❄ 🐾 🏠

CHARLTON

Wiltshire
Map ref 2B2

2m NE. Malmesbury

Bullocks Horn Farm
Listed

Charlton, Malmesbury, SN16 9OZ
☎ Crudwell (066 67) 458
12-acre livestock farm. Modern farmhouse in beautiful, peaceful surroundings with large well-tended gardens. Easy access M4. Travelling east through Chalton, 2nd road left after 'Horse and Groom'.
Bedrooms: 2 single, 1 double & 1 twin.
Bathrooms: 2 public.
Bed & breakfast: £11-£11.50 single, £20-£21 double.
Parking for 6.
🛏8 ✗ UL 📺 ▥ ∪ ❖ 🏠

CHARLTON MUSGROVE

Somerset
Map ref 2B3

1m NE. Wincanton

Lower Church Farm
⛺⛺

Rectory Lane, Charlton Musgrove, Wincanton, BA9 8ES
☎ (0963) 32307
60-acre dairy farm. 18th C. brick farmhouse with beams and inglenooks, in a quiet area surrounded by lovely countryside. Ideal for touring.

Bedrooms: 1 double & 1 twin, 1 family room.
Bathrooms: 1 public.
Bed & breakfast: max. £9.50 single, max. £19 double.
Half board: max. £15 daily, max. £90 weekly.
Evening meal 6.30pm (l.o. 10am).
Parking for 5.
Open April-October.
🛏 ❖ UL 🅿 V 🍴 📺 ▥ ⚓ ❄ 🏠 🏠

CHARMOUTH

Dorset
Map ref 1D2

Set back from the fossil-rich cliffs, a small coastal town where Jane Austen stayed. Charles II came to the Queen's Armes when seeking escape to France. Just south at low tide, the sandy beach rewards fossil-hunters; at Black Ven in 1811 a fossilised ichthyosaurus (now in London's Natural History Museum) was found.

Beech House
⛺⛺

The Street, Charmouth, Dorset. DT6 6PN
☎ (0297) 60316
Charming Georgian town house with walled garden in historic coastal village. Only short distance from cliff paths and the sea.
Bedrooms: 1 twin, 2 family rooms.
Bathrooms: 1 public.
Bed & breakfast: £10.50-£11.50 single, £21-£23 double.
Open March-November.
🛏 ❖ UL 🅿 V 🍴 ⚓ 🏠 OAP SP 🏠

Springfield House

Axminster Rd., Charmouth, DT6 6PB
☎ (0297) 60509
17th C. cottage guesthouse. Residents' lounge with inglenook fireplace. Full English breakfast. TV lounge.
Bedrooms: 2 single, 2 double, 1 family room.
Bathrooms: 1 public.
Bed & breakfast: £10.50-£11.50 single, £21-£23 double.
Parking for 6.
🛏 UL V 🍴 📺 ⚓ 🏠 SP 🏠

West Poplars
⛺

Higher Sea La., Charmouth, Bridport, DT6 6BD
☎ (0297) 60904

Attractive house with pretty garden in quiet position, 3 minutes' walk along footpath to beach.
Bedrooms: 1 double, 1 family room.
Bathrooms: 1 public.
Bed & breakfast: £20-£24 double.
Parking for 2.
🛏3 ❖ UL V 🍴 📺 ▥ ⚓ 🍴 🏠

CHEDDAR

Somerset
Map ref 2A2

Large village at foot of Mendips just south of the spectacular Cheddar Gorge. Close by are Roman and Saxon sites. Traditional Cheddar cheese is still made here. ℹ

The Forge

Cliff St., Cheddar, BS27 3PL
☎ (0934) 742345
Traditional working forge. Comfortable old house built of local stone, with large garden. Easy 10 minute walk to gorge.
Bedrooms: 1 double & 1 twin, 1 family room.
Bathrooms: 1 public.
Bed & breakfast: from £9 single, from £18 double.
Parking for 4.
🛏 ✗ UL 🅿 ✂ 📺 ⚓ 🏠 🏠

Westfield
⛺⛺

The Barrows, Cheddar, BS27 3BG
☎ (0934) 743066
Detached house, built in 1840 of Cheddar stone, with walled garden. Full traditional breakfast.
Bedrooms: 2 double & 1 twin.
Bathrooms: 1 private, 1 public.
Bed & breakfast: £20-£27 double.
Parking for 3.
♨ ❖ UL 📺 ▥ 🏠 🏠 🏠

> **THERE IS A SPECIAL SECTION IN THIS GUIDE LISTING ACCOMMODATION ESPECIALLY SUITABLE FOR GROUPS AND YOUNG PEOPLE.**

CHEW MAGNA

Avon
Map ref 2A2

Prosperous redstone village in the Mendip Hills with fine houses, cottages and inns of varying periods. High Street rises between railed, raised pavements from a part-Norman church with lofty 15th C tower.

Woodbarn Farm
Listed

Denny La., Chew Magna, Bristol, BS18 8S2
☎ Bristol (0272) 332599
75-acre mixed farm. Central for touring Bath, Bristol, Wells and Cheddar. 3 minutes' drive from Chew Valley Lake, trout fishing and birdwatching. Friendly, flexible atmosphere.
Bedrooms: 2 family rooms.
Bathrooms: 1 public.
Bed & breakfast: £10-£11 single, £18-£20 double.
Parking for 6.
Open March-October.
🛏 ❖ UL 🅿 🍴 📺 ❖ 🏠 🏠

CHIDEOCK

Dorset
Map ref 1D2

Village of creamy sandstone thatched cottages sheltering in valley near the dramatic Dorset coast. The church holds an interesting processional cross in mother-of-pearl and the manor house close by is associated with the richly-decorated Victorian Roman Catholic church. Seatown's pebble beach is flanked by limestone cliffs.

Chideock House Hotel M
⛺⛺⛺

Chideock, Bridport, DT6 6JN
☎ (0297) 89242
15th C. thatched house in Chideock village. Situated on the A35, 3 miles west of Bridport and less than 1 mile from the sea.
Bedrooms: 3 double & 3 twin, 3 family rooms.
Bathrooms: 7 private, 1 public; 1 private shower.
Bed & breakfast: £36-£40 double.

Evening meal 7pm (l.o. 9.30pm).
Credit: Access, Visa.
🐕 🖵 ⚡ Ⓥ 🗲 🞉 ⌂ ∪ ✿ 🞉 ᴰᴬᴾ ˢᴾ 🞉

Hell Farmhouse
😟

Hell La., North Chideock, Bridport, DT6 6LA
☎ (0297) 89589
Secluded, 18th C. thatched farmhouse in picturesque countryside, two miles from sea. Lounge with inglenook, large garden and parking.
Bedrooms: 1 double & 1 twin, 1 family room.
Bathrooms: 1 public.
Bed & breakfast: £9.50-£10.50 single, £19-£21 double.
Half board: £18-£20 daily, £119-£133 weekly.
Evening meal 7pm (l.o. 10am).
Parking for 5.
Open March-December.
🐕 ✿ ⓤ 🗲 📺 🞉 🞉 ✿ 🞉 ᴰᴬᴾ 🞉

4m E. Kingsbridge

Chillington Inn
😟😟

Chillington, Kingsbridge, TQ7 2JS
☎ Kingsbridge (0548) 580244
17th C. inn in the heart of the South Hams 2 miles from beaches and some of England's most beautiful coastline. Bar snacks available.
Bedrooms: 3 single, 3 double, 1 family room.
Bathrooms: 7 private.
Bed & breakfast: £13.50-£17.50 single, £27-£35 double.
Half board: £23.50-£30 daily, £150-£200 weekly.
Evening meal 7pm (l.o. 9.30pm).
Credit: Visa, Amex.
🐕 🖵 ✿ CB 🞉 🞉 🞉 ✿ 🞉 ᴰᴬᴾ 🞉 ˢᴾ 🞉

Plume of Feathers ⋔
Burton, Chippenham, SN14 7LP
☎ Badminton (045 421) 251
15th C. Cotswold stone inn.
Bedrooms: 1 double & 1 twin.
Bathrooms: 2 private.
Bed & breakfast: £25 single, £28 double.
Half board: £32 daily, £200 weekly.
Lunch available.
Evening meal 7pm (l.o. 9.45pm).
Parking for 80.
🐕 ✿ 🞉 Ⓥ ⦿ 🍽 🞉 🞉

75 Rowden Hill
😟
Chippenham, SN15 2AL
☎ (0249) 652981

See also Christian Malford, Kington Langley, Lacock.
Ancient market town with modern industry, retaining a large cattle market and some half-timbered houses. Notable early buildings include the medieval Town Hall and the gabled 15th C Yelde Hall, now a local history museum, which has a wooden turret. On the outskirts Hardenhuish has a charming hilltop church by the Georgian architect John Wood of Bath. 🛈

Fosse Farmhouse ⋔
😟😟

Nettleton Shrub, Nettleton, Chippenham, SN14 7NJ
☎ (0249) 782286
Nestling beside the Roman Fosseway in an area of outstanding natural beauty. Take the A420 from Chippenham to Bristol, turn right at the 'Shoe' pub, 1.5 miles along the Fosseway on the left hand side.
Bedrooms: 1 single, 2 double & 1 twin.
Bathrooms: 2 private, 1 public; 1 private shower.
Bed & breakfast: £18-£26 single, £32-£48 double.
Half board: £30-£38 daily, £200-£250 weekly.
Lunch available.
Evening meal 6pm (l.o. 9pm).
Parking for 6.
Open April-October.
Credit: Visa, Amex.
🐕 🖵 ✿ 🞉 Ⓥ 📺 🞉 ⌂ 🍽 ∪ ▶ ✿ 🞉 🞉 ᴰᴬᴾ ˢᴾ Ⓣ

Near National Trust village of Lacock and attractive Castle Combe. Cotsham Court also nearby. Friendly welcome assured.
Bedrooms: 1 double & 1 twin.
Bathrooms: 1 public.
Bed & breakfast: £10 single, £18 double.
Parking for 5.
🐕 5 ⓤ 🗲 📺 🞉 🞉

6m W. Yeovil

Manor Farm ⋔
😟😟

Chiselborough, Stoke-sub-Hamdon, TA14 6TQ
☎ (093 588) 203
450-acre mixed farm. Mellow ham stone farmhouse specialising in imaginative menus using local and own produce. Excellent touring base and 18 miles from sea.
Bedrooms: 2 double & 1 twin, 1 family room.
Bathrooms: 2 public.
Bed & breakfast: £12-£13 single, £24-£26 double.
Half board: £20-£22 daily, £126-£133 weekly.
Evening meal 7.30pm (l.o. 5pm).
Parking for 4.
Open April-October.
🐕 ✿ ⓤ 🗲 📺 🞉 ⌂ 🞉 ♪ ✓ ✿ 🍽 🞉 🞉

15m SW. Swindon

Malford House
😟😟

Christian Malford, Chippenham, SN15 4DG
☎ Bradenstoke (0249) 890578
Charming, black and white, 16th C. Tudor country house with oak beams and inglenooks, in 1.5 acres of grounds. Convenient for M4.
Bedrooms: 1 single, 1 double & 1 twin.
Bathrooms: 2 public.
Bed & breakfast: £12-£15 single, £27-£30 double.
Parking for 20.
🐕 🞉 ⓒ 🖵 ✿ ⓤ Ⓥ 🗲 📺 🞉 ⌂ ✿ 🞉 ᴰᴬᴾ ˢᴾ 🞉

The Mermaid Inn
Christian Malford, Chippenham, SN15 4BE
☎ Seagry (0249) 720313
Near the River Avon in a very pretty village, within easy reach of places of interest in Wiltshire.
Bedrooms: 1 single, 1 twin, 1 family room.
Bathrooms: 1 public.
Bed & breakfast: £13 single, £26 double.
Half board: £17 daily.
Evening meal 7.30pm (l.o. 10pm).
Parking for 60.
🐕 🞉 🞉 🞉 🗲 📺 🞉 ⌂ 🍽 🞉

Swallett Lodge
Main Road, Christian Malford, Chippenham, SN15 4DD
☎ Bradenstoke (0249) 890253
Comfortable country house and recently converted stable block. Beamed rooms, log fires.
Bedrooms: 1 single, 2 double.
Bathrooms: 2 private, 1 public.
Bed & breakfast: £12-£13.50 single, £24-£27 double.
Parking for 6.
🐕 10 🞉 🖵 ✿ ⓤ Ⓥ ✂ 🗲 📺 🞉 ⌂ ∪ ▶ ✿ 🞉 🞉 🞉 🞉

Small market town close to main Exeter to Plymouth road. To the south is Chudleigh Rock, a dramatic limestone outcrop containing prehistoric caves.

Rose Cottage
Luton, Chudleigh, Newton Abbot, TQ13 0BL
☎ Teignmouth (0626) 772194
Large country house in unspoilt village near seaside towns of Teignmouth, Dawlish and Torquay. Local 16th C. inn provides lunch and evening meals.
Bedrooms: 3 double.
Bathrooms: 3 public.
Bed & breakfast: £8.50-£9.50 single, £17-£19 double.
Parking for 10.
🐕 ⛟ ⓤ 🗲 📺 🞉 ⌂ ⤳ ✿ 🞉 ˢᴾ

GROUPS, CONSORTIA
AND AGENCIES
SPECIALISING
IN FARM AND
COUNTRY HOLIDAYS
ARE LISTED IN A
SPECIAL SECTION
OF THIS GUIDE.

MAP REFERENCES
APPLY TO COLOUR
MAPS NEAR THE
BACK OF THE GUIDE.

CLEVEDON

Avon
Map ref 1D1

Handsome Victorian resort on shingly shores of Severn estuary. Seafront entertainments and pier, golf links with ruined folly, part-Norman clifftop church. Tennyson and Thackeray stayed at the splendid Clevedon Court just to the east. Basically medieval with later additions, the manor and its fine chapel window overlook terraces with rare plants. Walk-round pottery nearby.

Brighton House
2 Copse Rd., Clevedon, BS21 7QL
☎ (0272) 343566
Family-run grade II listed building just off the seafront. Comfortable accommodation, convenient for the M4 and M5.
Bedrooms: 1 single, 2 double & 1 twin, 1 family room.
Bathrooms: 2 public.
Bed & breakfast: £11 single, £20 double.
Parking for 4.
ॐ ♥ ⓤ ☵ ⓣⓥ ⅲ ⍤ ⍥

CLOVELLY

Devon
Map ref 1C1

Clinging to wild wooded cliffs, fishing village with steep cobbled street zigzagging, or cut in steps, to harbour. Carrying sleds stand beside whitewashed flower-decked cottages. Charles Kingsley's father was rector of the church with its Norman porch, set high up near the Hamlyn family's Clovelly Court.

Burscott Farm
Higher Clovelly, Bideford, EX39 5RR
☎ (023 73) 252
170-acre dairy farm. Farmhouse accommodation with beautiful sea views.
Bedrooms: 1 twin, 1 family room.
Bathrooms: 1 public.
Bed & breakfast: £9-£10 single, £15-£19 double.
Half board: £14-£15 daily, £95-£100 weekly.

Evening meal 6.30pm (l.o. 5.30pm).
Parking for 3.
Open February-November.
ॐ ⓑ ♥ ⓤ ⅃ ☵ ⓣⓥ ⅲ ⍤ ⍥

Jonquil
Burscott Rd., Clovelly, Bideford, EX39 5RR
☎ (023 73) 346
Just off the road into Clovelly on the beautiful North Devon coast, with panoramic views over adjoining farmland.
Bedrooms: 1 double & 1 twin.
Bathrooms: 1 public.
Bed & breakfast: £15-£17 double.
Parking for 3.
ॐ ⓤ ☵ ⓣⓥ ⅲ ⍤ ⍥

CLYST HYDON

Devon
Map ref 1D2

4m S. Cullompton

The Old Manor
☺☺
Clyst Hydon, Cullompton, EX15 2ND
☎ Plymtree (088 47) 338
Large period family house, central in a small village. Well placed for touring Exmoor, Dartmoor, Exeter and the coast.
Bedrooms: 1 single, 1 double, 1 family room.
Bathrooms: 2 public.
Bed & breakfast: £9 single, £18 double.
Parking for 3.
ॐ ⓤ ☵ ⓣⓥ ⅲ ⍤ ⍥ ⍤ ⍥ ⍤

COLYTON

Devon
Map ref 1D2

Surrounded by fertile farmland, this small riverside town was an early Saxon settlement. Medieval prosperity from the wool trade built the grand church tower with its octagonal lantern and the church's fine west window.

Road Green House
Colyton, EX13 6DT
☎ (0297) 52828
Interesting old house with views over hills and walks beside the River Coly.
Bedrooms: 3 twin.
Bathrooms: 2 public.
Bed & breakfast: max. £10 single, max. £20 double.
Parking for 2.
ॐ ⍤ ⓤ ☵ ⓣⓥ ⅲ ⍤ ⍥

Smallicombe Farm
Northleigh, Colyton, Axminster, EX13 6BU
☎ Wilmington (040 483) 310
7-acre mixed farm. On A30 to Honiton, follow the signs for Colyton and Widworthy. Small mixed farm with pigs and numerous poultry. Fresh farm produce. Children's play area.
Bedrooms: 1 double & 1 twin, 1 family room.
Bathrooms: 3 private.
Bed & breakfast: £9-£11 single, £18-£22 double.
Half board: £14-£16 daily, £94-£105 weekly.
Evening meal (l.o. 4pm).
Open April-October.
ॐ ⍤ ☐ ♥ ⍤ ⍥ ⍥ SP

COMBE MARTIN

Devon
Map ref 1C1

Seaside village spreading along its valley to a rocky beach. Silver was mined here in the Middle Ages, market gardening yields today's produce. An unusual sight is the Pack of Cards pub, while the church with its gargoyles is noted for panel paintings on the 15th C rood screen. ℹ

Challacombe House
☺☺
West Challacombe Lane, Combe Martin, EX34 0DR
☎ (027 188) 3331
Modern character house 5 minutes from the sea and shops. Close to Hangman Hills and Wild Pear Beach.
Bedrooms: 1 single, 2 double.
Bathrooms: 1 private, 1 public.
Bed & breakfast: £9 single, £18-£22 double.
Half board: £15 daily, £100-£110 weekly.
Parking for 4.
ॐ ⓤ ⓥ ☵ ⓣⓥ ⅲ ⍤ ⍥ ⍤ ⍥ ⍤

The London Inn
Leigh Rd., Combe Martin, EX34 0NA
☎ (027 188) 3409
An immaculate family-run coastal village inn/hotel on fringe of Combe Martin, adjacent to Exmoor. Fishing, riding, golf and cliff walks.
Bedrooms: 2 single, 3 double & 1 twin, 2 family rooms.
Bathrooms: 3 public.
Bed & breakfast: £13-£15 single, £24-£28 double.

Half board: £18-£20 daily, £117-£131 weekly.
Lunch available.
Evening meal 7pm (l.o. 8pm).
Parking for 50.
Credit: Access.
ॐ ♥ ⍤ ⓥ ☵ ⓣⓥ ⍤ ⍥ ⍥ ⍥

CONNOR DOWNS

Cornwall
Map ref 1B3

Traleste
Angarrack La., Connor Downs, TR27 5JF
☎ Hayle (0736) 754928
Pleasant detached house in quiet country lane. Ideal situation for touring. Hairdryers provided in bedrooms.
Bedrooms: 1 double & 1 twin.
Bathrooms: 2 private.
Bed & breakfast: £10 single, £20 double.
Parking for 2.
ॐ10 ⓑ ☐ ⓤ ⓥ ☵ ⓣⓥ ⅲ ⍤ ⍥ ⍥

CORTON DENHAM

Somerset
Map ref 2B3

Corton Ash
Corton Denham, Sherborne, Dorset DT9 4LS
☎ (096 322) 450
Modern house with garden in peaceful rural countryside, offering hospitality. Ideal for Dorset and Somerset visits, with lovely views and walks. Near Cadbury on the A303/A30.
Bedrooms: 1 double & 1 twin.
Bathrooms: 2 private.
Bed & breakfast: £9-£12 single, £18-£24 double.
Half board: £15-£18 daily.
Lunch available.
Evening meal 7.30pm (l.o. 8.30pm).
Parking for 6.
ॐ4 ⓑ ♥ ⓤ ⅃ ☵ ⓣⓥ ⅲ ⍤ ⍥ ⍥ ⍥

THERE IS A SPECIAL SECTION IN THIS GUIDE LISTING ACCOMMODATION ESPECIALLY SUITABLE FOR GROUPS AND YOUNG PEOPLE.

COUNTISBURY

Devon
Map ref 1C1

2m E. Lynton
Small village in Exmoor National Park and close to the sea. One mile south is Watersmeet (National Trust).

Coombe Farm M
😊😊
Countisbury, Lynton,
EX35 6NF
☎ Brendon (059 87) 236
365-acre hill stock farm. Situated half a mile off the A39 and 3 miles from Lynmouth.
Bedrooms: 2 double & 1 twin, 2 family rooms.
Bathrooms: 2 private, 2 public.
Bed & breakfast: £20.50-£26.50 double.
Half board: £18.50-£20.75 daily, £115-£132 weekly.
Evening meal 7pm (l.o. 5pm).
Parking for 6.
Open April-October.

The Exmoor Sandpiper
😊😊😊
Countisbury, Lynton,
EX35 6NE
☎ (059 87) 263
Beamed character inn/hotel, part 13th C., amidst thousands of acres of rolling Exmoor hills. A few hundred yards from Cantisbury sea cliffs.
Bedrooms: 7 double & 2 twin, 2 family rooms.
Bathrooms: 11 private.
Bed & breakfast: £27.83 single, £55.66 double.
Half board: £41.75 daily, £251.74 weekly.
Lunch available.
Evening meal 7pm (l.o. 9.30pm).
Parking for 50.

COXLEY

Somerset
Map ref 2A2

2m SW. Wells

Coxley House M
😊😊
Upper Coxley, Wells,
BA5 1QS
☎ Wells (0749) 72180
Period country house in large, quiet garden away from main road. Antique furnishings, family-run atmosphere.
Bedrooms: 1 single, 1 double & 1 twin.
Bathrooms: 2 private, 2 public.
Bed & breakfast: £12 single, £30-£40 double.
Parking for 4.

Home Farm
Stoppers La., Coxley, Wells,
BA5 1QS
☎ (0749) 72434
10-acre market garden and pig farm. 1.5 miles from Wells, in a quiet spot just off the A39. Extensive views of the Mendip Hills.
Bedrooms: 1 single, 2 double & 1 twin, 3 family rooms.
Bathrooms: 3 public.
Bed & breakfast: £10-£11 single, £20-£22 double.
Parking for 10.

CRACKINGTON HAVEN

Cornwall
Map ref 1C2

5m NE. Boscastle
Tiny village on the North Cornwall coast, with a small sandy beach and surf bathing. The highest cliffs in Cornwall lie to the south.

Crackington Manor Hotel M
😊😊😊
Crackington Haven, Bude,
EX23 0JG
☎ St. Gennys
(084 03) 397/536
Country house hotel in a quiet Cornish cove, 100 yards from the sea. Swimming pool, sauna, solarium and games room available.
Bedrooms: 2 single, 7 double & 4 twin, 2 family rooms.
Bathrooms: 12 private, 2 public; 1 private shower.
Bed & breakfast: £18-£20 single, £36-£40 double.
Half board: £28-£32 daily, £190-£218 weekly.
Lunch available.
Evening meal 7.30pm (l.o. 9pm).
Parking for 25.
Credit: Access, Visa.

Hallagather
😊😊
Crackington Haven, Bude,
EX23 0LA
☎ St. Gennys (084 03) 276
14th C. farmhouse, 4 miles north Boscastle, on a 184 acre commercial beef/sheep farm. Granite fireplace, oak beams. Individual attention, evening meals by arrangement. Youngsters welcome.
Bedrooms: 1 single, 1 double, 1 family room.
Bathrooms: 2 public.
Bed & breakfast: £8.50-£10 single, £17-£19 double.
Evening meal 6pm (l.o. 7.30pm).
Parking for 6.
Open June-September.

Pendennis
Crackington Haven, Bude,
EX23 0JJ
☎ St. Gennys (084 03) 567
Rurally situated, 1 mile from the beach. Leave the A39 at Wainhouse Corner, follow signs marked Crackington Haven. Turn right on reaching beach, continue up the hill for 1 mile to Higher Crackington.
Bedrooms: 1 single, 1 double & 1 twin, 2 family rooms.
Bathrooms: 1 public.
Bed & breakfast: £8.50-£9 single, £17-£18 double.
Half board: £12-£15 daily, £84-£105 weekly.
Evening meal 6.30pm (l.o. 6pm).
Parking for 6.

Trenance Farm Guest House
😊😊😊
Crackington Haven, Bude,
EX23 0JQ
☎ St. Gennys (084 03) 273
4.8-acre smallholding. Large country house close to sandy surfing beach. Superb views over the haven, sea and cliffs. Coastal and country footpaths. Completely unspoilt. Homely atmosphere.
Bedrooms: 1 single, 2 double & 2 twin, 2 family rooms.
Bathrooms: 2 private, 2 public.
Bed & breakfast: £10.50-£14 single, £18-£28 double.
Half board: £15-£20 daily, £110-£147 weekly.
Evening meal 6.30pm (l.o. 4pm).
Parking for 22.

CREDITON

Devon
Map ref 1D2

Ancient town in fertile valley, once prosperous from wool, now active in cider-making. Said to be the birthplace of St. Boniface. The 13th C Chapter House, the church governors' meeting place, holds a collection of armour from the Civil War.

Birchmans Farm M
😊😊
Colebrook, Crediton,
EX17 5AD
☎ Bow (036 33) 393
200-acre mixed farm. In the centre of Devon within easy reach of Exeter and Dartmoor. Home produce includes milk, meat, cream and garden vegetables.
Bedrooms: 2 double & 1 twin.
Bathrooms: 3 private.
Bed & breakfast: £20-£24 double.
Half board: £14-£16 daily, £90-£110 weekly.
Evening meal 6.30pm (l.o. 6.30pm).
Parking for 6.

CREWKERNE

Somerset
Map ref 1D2

Stone-built light-industrial market town with Roman and Saxon origins, set in undulating farmland. The traditional industry of sail making was later added to by webbing production and shirt making. The cathedral-like church with its imposing west front dates from the 15th C. The St. Bartholomew's Fair is held in September.

Broadview
😊😊😊
43 East St., Crewkerne,
TA18 7AG
☎ (0460) 73424
Secluded colonial style bungalow set in three quarters of an acre with lovely views. Comfortable, individually decorated and furnished en-suite rooms. Home cooking.
Bedrooms: 1 double & 2 twin.
Bathrooms: 3 private.
Bed & breakfast: £15-£17.50 single, max. £25 double.
Half board: max. £20 daily, max. £140 weekly.

Continued ▶

257

CREWKERNE
Continued

Evening meal 6.30pm (l.o. 5.30pm).
Parking for 4.

CRICKLADE
Wiltshire
Map ref 2B2

Standing on the upper Thames, an old town and former Anglo-Saxon settlement. The Roman road from Cirencester passes through and canals pass to north and south. The church, its lofty Tudor tower dominating the town, has work of varying periods from the 12th C to 1930.

The White Lion
50 High St., Cricklade, Swindon, SN6 6DA
☎ Swindon, (0793) 750443
Old coaching inn dating back to the late 1600's, in the 9th C. Saxon town of Cricklade.
Bedrooms: 1 double & 2 twin.
Bathrooms: 1 public.
Bed & breakfast: £15 single, £24.50 double.
Lunch available.
Evening meal 7.30pm (l.o. 9.30pm).
Parking for 22.
Credit: Access.

CROWCOMBE
Somerset
Map ref 1D1

6m SE. Watchet
Village at the foot of the Quantock Hills, with an early medieval market cross. The church is adorned with rich 16th C bench ends and the fine Church House is of about the same period. A large Georgian house, Crowcombe Court, stands next to the church.

The Carew Arms M
Listed
Crowcombe, Taunton, TA4 4AD
☎ (098 48) 631
A charming period inn in the centre of the Quantocks. Home cooking. Bar snacks available.
Bedrooms: 3 double & 1 twin.
Bathrooms: 2 public.

Bed & breakfast: £9.50 single, £19 double.
Half board: from £16 daily, from £112 weekly.
Evening meal 8pm (l.o. 9pm).
Parking for 30.
Credit: Access, Visa.

CUCKLINGTON
Somerset
Map ref 2B3

3m E. Wincanton

Hale Farm
Cucklington, Wincanton, BA9 9PN
☎ Wincanton (0963) 33342
55-acre mixed farm. 17th C. farmhouse with beams, offering home cooking. In peaceful situation near A303, central for touring.
Bedrooms: 1 double, 1 family room.
Bathrooms: 1 public.
Bed & breakfast: from £10 single, from £19 double.
Half board: from £15 daily, from £90 weekly.
Evening meal 6pm (l.o. 10am).
Parking for 3.
Open April-September.

CULLOMPTON
Devon
Map ref 1D2

See also Clyst Hydon.
Market town on former coaching routes, with pleasant tree-shaded cobbled pavements and some handsome 17th C houses. Earlier prosperity from the wool industry is reflected in the grandness of the church with its fan-vaulted aisle built by a wool-stapler in 1526.

Hayne Oak Farm
Cullompton, EX15 1PS
☎ (0884) 38189
20-acre sheep farm. 19th C. farmhouse set in peaceful valley with views to the Blackdown Hills. Non smokers only.
Bedrooms: 1 double, 1 family room.
Bathrooms: 2 private showers.
Bed & breakfast: from £22 double.
Half board: from £110 weekly.

Evening meal 6.30pm (l.o. 9am).
Parking for 2.
Open April-December.

CURRY RIVEL
Somerset
Map ref 1D1

Hillards M
High St., Curry Rivel, Langport, TA10 0EY
☎ Langport, (0458) 251737
Full of old world charm, with a wealth of oak and elm panelled walls, beamed ceilings, large open fireplaces and an intimate and homely atmosphere. On the A378, a short drive from the A303 and junction 25 of the M5.
Bedrooms: 1 single, 3 double & 2 twin.
Bathrooms: 3 private, 1 public.
Bed & breakfast: £15 single, £30-£36 double.
Parking for 9.

DARTMOOR

See Bovey Tracey, Bridestowe, Buckfastleigh, Lydford, Manaton, Moretonhampstead, Okehampton, Peter Tavy, Poundsgate, Throwleigh, Widecombe-in-the-Moor.

INDIVIDUAL PROPRIETORS HAVE SUPPLIED ALL DETAILS OF ACCOMMODATION. ALTHOUGH WE DO CHECK FOR ACCURACY, WE ADVISE YOU TO CONFIRM PRICES AND OTHER INFORMATION AT THE TIME OF BOOKING.

DARTMOUTH
Devon
Map ref 1D3

Ancient port, now a resort, on wooded slopes above natural harbour at mouth of Dart. Has fine period buildings, notably town houses near Quay and Butterwalk of 1635. The church is richly furnished and the harbour castle ruin recalls earlier importance when Crusader fleets assembled here. Royal Naval College, grandly built in 1905, dominates from hill. Carnival, June; Regatta, August.

Boringdon House
1 Church Rd., Dartmouth, TQ6 9HQ
☎ (080 43) 2235
Spacious, welcoming Georgian house in large secluded garden overlooking Dartmouth town and harbour. Minute's walk to town centre.
Bedrooms: 1 double & 2 twin.
Bathrooms: 3 private.
Bed & breakfast: £30 double.
Parking for 3.

The Captains House
18 Clarence St., Dartmouth, TQ6 9NW
☎ (080 43) 2133
18th C. listed house. Tasteful decor and personal service. Close to river and shops. Special diets on request.
Bedrooms: 3 double & 2 twin.
Bathrooms: 5 private.
Bed & breakfast: £14-£19 single, £24-£32 double.

Kentor Guest House
15 Smith St., Dartmouth, TQ6 9QR
☎ (080 43) 5333
Small guesthouse with own garden patio.
Bedrooms: 2 double & 2 twin.
Bathrooms: 2 public.
Bed & breakfast: £9.50-£11 single, £23-£25 double.

PLEASE CHECK PRICES AND OTHER DETAILS AT THE TIME OF BOOKING.

Royal Castle Hotel M
⌂⌂⌂

11 The Quay, Dartmouth,
TQ6 9PS
☎ (080 43) 4004
*Historic 17th C. quayside
coaching inn with resident
proprietors, offering traditional
style food and service. Open
fires, comfortable bedrooms.*
Bedrooms: 4 single, 8 double
& 5 twin, 4 family rooms.
Bathrooms: 21 private.
Bed & breakfast: £28-£36
single, £50-£72 double.
Half board: £32.75-£42.75
daily, £210-£260 weekly.
Lunch available.
Evening meal 7pm (l.o.
9.45pm).
Parking for 3.
Credit: Access, Visa.

Shepherds Dartmouth
⌂

3 Vicarage Hill, Dartmouth,
TQ6 9EW
☎ (080 43) 3341
*Comfortable home in pleasant
position in side road
overlooking bowling green.
Near shops and river.*
Bedrooms: 1 single, 1 double
& 1 twin.
Bathrooms: 1 public.
Bed & breakfast: £12-£15
single, £19-£23 double.

DEVIZES
Wiltshire
Map ref 2B2

Standing on the Kennet
and Avon Canal, old
market town near the
Vale of Pewsey. Rebuilt
Norman castle, good 18th
C buildings and old inns.
All 3 churches are of
interest, notably St.
John's with 12th C work
and Norman tower.
Museum of Wiltshire's
archaeology and natural
history reflects wealth of
prehistoric sites on
Salisbury Plain and at
other locations nearby. *i*

The Artichoke Inn
The Nurseries, Bath Rd.,
Devizes, SN10 2AR
☎ (0380) 3400
*Comfortable, friendly, homely
atmosphere. Private garden for
guests' use.*
Bedrooms: 1 single, 1 double
& 1 twin, 1 family room.

Bathrooms: 1 public.
Bed & breakfast: max. £11
single, max. £22 double.

Clifton Cottage
⌂⌂

Bath Road, Devizes,
SN10 2AY
☎ Devizes (0380) 5717
*Half a mile from Devizes, 20
miles from Salisbury, 15 miles
from Bath. On the canal with
the famous 27 locks. Pleasant
walks to the downs and White
Horse.*
Bedrooms: 1 double & 2 twin.
Bathrooms: 3 private,
1 public.
Bed & breakfast: £12 single,
£24 double.
Half board: £14 daily, £90
weekly.
Lunch available.
Evening meal 6pm (l.o. 8pm).
Parking for 2.

Craven House
Station Rd., Devizes,
SN10 1BZ
☎ (0380) 3514
*Victorian town house, one
minute from town centre and
market place. Easy walking
distance for shops and
restaurants.*
Bedrooms: 1 double & 1 twin,
1 family room.
Bathrooms: 2 public.
Bed & breakfast: £12 single,
£20 double.

Easton Farmhouse
⌂⌂

Bishops Cannings, Devizes,
SN10 2LR
☎ Cannings (038 086) 228
*600-acre mixed farm.
Victorian farmhouse quietly
placed, 1 mile from village.
Ideal walking area along the
Kennet and Avon canal.*
Bedrooms: 2 twin.
Bathrooms: 1 public.
Bed & breakfast: £20-£24
double.
Parking for 4.

Rathlin
⌂⌂⌂

Wick Lane, Devizes,
SN10 5DP
☎ (0380) 71999
*Detached 1920's house in quiet
residential area. Elegantly
furnished with numerous
antiques. Family atmosphere.*
Bedrooms: 1 single, 1 double
& 2 twin.
Bathrooms: 4 private,
1 public.
Bed & breakfast: £15 single,
£28 double.
Parking for 5.

DODDISCOMBS-
LEIGH
Devon
Map ref 1D2

Riverside village amid
hilly rural countryside just
east of Dartmoor. Former
manor house built by
Ralph de Doddiscumbe
stands beside granite
church which was richly
endowed by the medieval
wool trading community.
Spared from the
Roundheads by its
remoteness, its chief
interest lies in glowing
15th C windows of the
north aisle, said to
contain Devon's largest
and finest collection of
medieval glass.

Whitemoor Farm
Listed

Doddiscombsleigh, Exeter,
EX6 7PU
☎ Christow (0647) 52423
*284-acre mixed farm. Homely
thatched farmhouse in 2 acres
of established garden, with
easy access to Dartmoor,
Haldon Forestry walks.
Evening meals available at
local pubs. Children's evening
meals catered for.*
Bedrooms: 2 single, 1 double
& 1 twin.
Bathrooms: 1 public.
Bed & breakfast: £9-£9.50
single, £18-£19 double.

DORCHESTER
Dorset
Map ref 2B3

See also Piddletrenthide.
Busy medieval county
town (cloth and ale-
producing centre)
destroyed by fires in 17th
and 18th C. Cromwellian
stronghold and scene of
Judge Jeffrey's Bloody
Assize (his High Street
lodging is now a
restaurant) after
Monmouth Rebellion of
1685. Tolpuddle Martyrs
tried in Shire Hall.
Museum has Roman and
earlier exhibits and Hardy
relics. *i*

Birkin House
⌂⌂⌂

Stinsford, Dorchester,
DT2 8QD
☎ (0305) 64147
*Beautiful Victorian mansion set
in 15 acres of gardens and
parkland. Each room
decorated in its own style.
Quiet location.*
Bedrooms: 1 single, 5 double
& 4 twin, 1 family room.
Bathrooms: 5 private,
3 public.
Bed & breakfast: £15-£25
single, £25-£35 double.
Parking for 15.

30 Mountain Ash Rd.
⌂⌂

Dorchester, DT1 2PB
☎ (0305) 64811
*Comfortably furnished,
typically English home with
owner interested in meeting
people, cooking and the county
of Dorset.*
Bedrooms: 1 single, 1 double
& 1 twin.
Bathrooms: 2 public.
Bed & breakfast: £11 single,
£22 double.
Evening meal 6pm (l.o. 4pm).
Parking for 4.

GROUPS, CONSORTIA AND AGENCIES
SPECIALISING IN FARM AND COUNTRY
HOLIDAYS ARE LISTED IN A SPECIAL
SECTION OF THIS GUIDE.

MAP REFERENCES
APPLY TO COLOUR
MAPS NEAR THE
BACK OF THE GUIDE.

DORCHESTER
Continued

Port Bredy
⌂⌂

107 Bridport Rd., Dorchester,
DT1 2NH
☎ (0305) 65778
*Large semi-detached house,
with private guest annexe, on
the A35. Annexe suitable for
disabled persons.*
Bedrooms: 1 double, 1 family
room.
Bathrooms: 1 private;
1 private shower.
Bed & breakfast: £22-£24
double.
Parking for 3.
Open April-October.
⌖ ⌂ ⌖ 🅤🅛 ⌖ ⌖ 🆃🆅 ▦ ◪
⌖ ⌖ 🅗🅗

Towns End Farm
Pulham, Dorchester
☎ (030 05) 220
*In the heart of Dorset with
beautiful views, close to many
historic towns. Bed and
breakfast in comfortable
farmhouse with a friendly
welcome assured. Car
essential.*
Bedrooms: 1 double, 1 family
room.
Bathrooms: 1 private,
1 public.
Bed & breakfast: from £8
single, from £16 double.
⌖2 🛇 ⊚ 🅤🅛 ⌖ 🆃🆅 ▦ ⌖ ⌖
🅗🅗

DOWNTON .
Wiltshire
Map ref 2B3

6m S. Salisbury
Anglers' haunt with
medieval houses, watered
by the River Avon. The
large church of varying
periods occupies the site
of a Saxon church. The
18th C Moot House and
amphitheatre stand near
the remains of a Roman
villa, excavated in the
1950's.

47 The Borough
Downton, Salisbury,
SP5 3NB
☎ Downton (0725) 20078
*Attractive part 17th C. cottage
in picturesque village. French
and German spoken.*
Bedrooms: 1 twin.
Bathrooms: 1 private,
1 public.
Bed & breakfast: £25-£30
double.
⌖7 ⊚ 🅤🅛 ▦ ◪ 🅗🅗 🅗🅗

The Dragon House
⌂⌂

134 The Borough, Downton,
Salisbury, SP5 3LT
☎ (0725) 20441
*Close to Salisbury and New
Forest, in a charming village.
Dragon House Cottage is self
contained and is the former
brew house to an 18th C. Inn.
It affords privacy in a
delightful large garden with
river frontage.*
Bedrooms: 1 twin.
Bathrooms: 1 private.
Bed & breakfast: from £27
double.
⌂ ⌖ 🅤🅛 🛇 🅥 ⌖ 🆃🆅 ▦ ◪
⌖ 🅗🅗 🅗🅗 🅒🅐🅟 🅢🅟 🅗🅗

DULVERTON
Somerset
Map ref 1D1

Set among woods and
hills of south-west
Exmoor, a busy riverside
town with a 13th C
church. The Rivers Barle
and Exe are rich in
salmon and trout. The
Exmoor National Park
Headquarters at
Dulverton Information
Centre are open
throughout the year.

Town Mills
⌂⌂

High Street, Dulverton,
Somerset. TA22 9HB
☎ (0398) 23124
*Secluded mill house in the
centre of Dulverton. Spacious
bedrooms providing bedsitting
facilities and breakfast served
in rooms. Log fires.*
Bedrooms: 3 double & 2 twin.
Bathrooms: 2 private,
1 public.
Bed & breakfast: £15-£17
single, £22-£30 double.
Parking for 5.
⌖ ⌂ ⌖ 🅤🅛 🅥 ◪ ⌖ 🅗🅗
🅗🅗

**THERE IS A SPECIAL
SECTION IN THIS
GUIDE LISTING
ACCOMMODATION
ESPECIALLY
SUITABLE FOR
GROUPS AND
YOUNG PEOPLE.**

DUNSTER
Somerset
Map ref 1D1

Ancient town with views
of Exmoor and the
Quantocks whose historic
hilltop castle has been
continuously occupied
since it was begun in
1070. Medieval prosperity
from cloth built the
octagonal Yarn Market,
late 16th C and the
church with its broad
wagon roof. A riverside
mill, packhorse bridge
and 18th C hilltop folly
occupy other interesting
corners in the town.

Burnells Farm
Knowle La., Dunster,
TA6 6UU
☎ (0643) 821841
*46-acre mixed farm. Modern,
comfortable farmhouse in
Exmoor National Park. 1.5
miles from Dunster and 2.5
miles from Minehead.*
Bedrooms: 1 double & 1 twin,
1 family room.
Bathrooms: 2 public.
Bed & breakfast: £9 single,
£18 double.
Half board: £13.50 daily, £88
weekly.
Evening meal 7pm.
Parking for 4.
⌖ 🅤🅛 🛇 🅥 ◪ 🆃🆅 ▦ ⌖ 🅗🅗
🅗🅗

EAST ALLINGTON
Devon
Map ref 1D3

3m NE. Kingsbridge

Fortescue Arms ♨
East Allington, Totnes,
TQ9 7RA
☎ (054 852) 215
*Rural inn, ideal for touring,
offering warm friendly service.
1 mile off the A381 main
Totnes to Kingsbridge road.*
Bedrooms: 1 double & 1 twin,
2 family rooms.
Bathrooms: 2 public.
Bed & breakfast: £11.50
single, £23 double.
Lunch available.
Evening meal 7pm (l.o.
10pm).
Parking for 15.
⌖ ⌖ ⌖ 🛇 🅥 ⌖ ⌖ ◪ 🆃 ◪
⌖ 🅗🅗 🅗🅗 🅢🅟

Higher Torr Farm
East Allington, Totnes,
TQ9 7QH
☎ (054 852) 248

*Quiet peaceful spot, but easily
found off the main road, near
moors and beaches. Home
produce served whenever
possible. Homely cooking in a
family atmosphere.*
Bedrooms: 1 single, 1 twin,
1 family room.
Bathrooms: 1 public.
Bed & breakfast: £8.50-£12
single, £17-£24 double.
Half board: £13.50-£17 daily,
£79-£82 weekly.
Evening meal 7pm (l.o. 6pm).
Parking for 3.
Open April-October.
⌖ 🛇 🅤🅛 🅥 ◪ 🆃🆅 ◪ ⌖ 🅗🅗

EAST BRENT
Somerset
Map ref 1D1

Prospect Farm
Strowlands, East Brent,
TA9 4JH
☎ Brent Knoll (0278) 760507
*4-acre smallholding. 17th C.
Somerset farmhouse with
inglenook fire places, bread
ovens, beamed ceilings and a
colourful history. 1 bedroom
available with own toilet
facilities.*
Bedrooms: 2 double & 1 twin,
1 family room.
Bathrooms: 2 public.
Bed & breakfast: £10-£12
single, £20-£24 double.
Parking for 8.
⌖ 🛇 🅤🅛 ◪ 🆃🆅 ▦ ∪ 🅗🅗

ERLESTOKE
Wiltshire
Map ref 2B2

6M E. Westbury

Longwater
⌂⌂

Lower Rd., Erlestoke,
Devizes, SN10 5UE
☎ Bratton (0380) 830095
*166-acre beef, fish and
woodland farm. Quarter of a
mile from farmyard and
overlooking our own parkland
and lakes with coarse and
trout fishing. Near to many National
Trust areas.*
Bedrooms: 1 double & 1 twin,
1 family room.
Bathrooms: 3 private.
Bed & breakfast: £12.50
single, £23 double.
Half board: £18 daily, £120
weekly.
Evening meal 7pm (l.o. 5pm).
Parking for 12.
⌖ ⌖ ⊚ ⌂ ⌖ 🅤🅛 🛇 🅥 ◪
🆃🆅 ▦ ◪ 🅙 ⌖ 🅗🅗

EXETER

Devon
Map ref 1D2

University city rebuilt after 1940s around its venerable cathedral. Suffered Danish raids under Anglo-Saxons but repulsed William I until 1068. Fragments of Roman wall survive; early Norman towers preserved in 13th C cathedral with fine west front. Notable waterfront buildings, Maritime Museum, Guildhall, old inns; Cathedral library, Rougemont House Museum of Costume and Lace, Royal Albert Memorial Museum, Northcott Theatre. 🛈

Clock Tower Guest House ⋔
16 New North Rd., Exeter, EX4 4HF
☎ (0392) 52493
Homely accommodation in the city centre for all tourists, coach and railway stations within ten minutes' walk. All modern facilities.
Bedrooms: 1 single, 5 double & 3 twin, 2 family rooms.
Bathrooms: 3 private, 3 public.
Bed & breakfast: £8.95-£10.95 single, £16.95-£20.95 double.
Half board: £12.95-£14.95 daily, £77.70-£89.70 weekly.
Evening meal 6pm (l.o. 4pm).
Credit: Access, Visa, Diners, Amex.
🛏 📞 🖨 🍴 🛁 🔟 🛈 Ⅴ 🍴
🎬 🛒 💂 OAP SP 🅿 T

Culm Vale Country House
Stoke Canon, Exeter, EX5 4EG
☎ Stoke Canon (039 284) 615
Comfortable accommodation in beautiful old country house 4 miles north east of Exeter. Friendly relaxed atmosphere, lovely gardens, ample free parking. Ideal touring centre.
Bedrooms: 2 double & 1 twin.
Bathrooms: 1 public; 1 private shower.
Bed & breakfast: £10-£12 single, £20-£22 double.
Parking for 6.
Open February-November.
🛏 🖨 🔟 🖨 🔟 🎬 🛒 ✳ ✗ 🛒 🎬

The Grange
Stoke Hill, Exeter, EX4 7JH
☎ (0392) 59723
Country house set in 3 acres of woodlands, 1.5 miles from the city centre. Ideal for holidays and off-season breaks.
Bedrooms: 2 double & twin, 1 family room.
Bathrooms: 2 public.
Bed & breakfast: £10-£12 single, £18-£20 double.
Parking for 11.
🛏 🖨 🔟 🔟 🎬 🛒 🛁 🍴 🔟 ✳
✗ 🎬 OAP SP

Willoughby
1 New North Rd., Exeter, EX4 4HH
☎ (0392) 31724
Comfortable, friendly Victorian guesthouse extending personal service. Centrally situated, convenient for city, country or coast. Railway stations within walking distance.
Bedrooms: 2 single, 1 twin, 1 family room.
Bathrooms: 1 public.
Bed & breakfast: max. £9 single, max. £18 double.
🛏 🔟 🔟 🖨 🔟 🎬 🛒 🛁 🎬 OAP
SP

EXMOOR

See Allerford, Carhampton, Combe Martin, Countisbury, Martinhoe, Porlock, Simonsbath, West Anstey.

EXMOUTH

Devon
Map ref 1D2

Developed as a seaside resort in George III's reign, set against the woods of the Exe estuary and red cliffs of Orcombe Point. Extensive sands, small harbour, chapel and almshouses, A la Ronde, a sixteen sided house and a model railway. 🛈

The Mews
Knappe Cross, Brixington La., Exmouth, EX8 5DL
☎ (0395) 272198
Large part of a delightfully secluded mews building in a country setting.
Bedrooms: 1 single, 2 twin.
Bathrooms: 1 public.
Bed & breakfast: £9.50-£11.50 single, £19-£23 double.
Parking for 10.
🛏 3 🔟 Ⅴ 🖨 🔟 🎬 🛒 🛁 🔄 ✳
✗ 🎬

FALFIELD

Avon
Map ref 2B2

4m NE. Thornbury

Green Farm Guest House
A38, Falfield, Wotton under Edge, Gloucs GL12 8DL
☎ (0454) 260319
16th C. stone farmhouse tastefully converted into a comfortable guesthouse. Convenient for M4 and M5. Surrounded by 100 acres of farmland. Candlelit suppers and log fires.
Bedrooms: 1 single, 3 double & 3 twin, 1 family room.
Bathrooms: 1 private, 2 public.
Bed & breakfast: £13-£20 single, £22-£30 double.
Half board: £18-£21 daily.
Evening meal 6.30pm (l.o. 10pm).
Parking for 12.
🛏 🖨 🖨 🔟 🛈 Ⅴ 🖨 🔟 🎬
🛁 🔄 🔎 ✳ ✳ 🎬 🐾 🎬

FALMOUTH

Cornwall
Map ref 1B3

Busy port and fishing harbour, popular resort on the balmy Cornish riviera. Henry VIII's Pendennis Castle faces St. Mawes Castle across the broad natural harbour and yacht basin Carrick Roads, which receives 7 rivers. 🛈

Grove Hotel
Grove Pl., Falmouth, TR11 4AU
☎ (0326) 319577
Owner-managed, homely harbourside hotel. Level walk to coaches, railway, town and quays. Public car and dinghy parks opposite.
Bedrooms: 2 single, 5 double & 5 twin, 3 family rooms.
Bathrooms: 8 private, 3 public.
Bed & breakfast: £14.25-£15.50 single, £28.50-£31 double.
Half board: £20.25-£21.50 daily, £120.75-£140 weekly.
Evening meal 6.30pm (l.o. 10pm).
Open February-November.
Credit: Access, Visa.
🛏 🖨 🔟 🛈 Ⅴ 🖨 🔟 🎬 🛁
🍴 🐾 SP 🎬 T

Raffles
Fenwick Rd., Falmouth
☎ (0326) 313012
Beautiful Georgian house built 1780, south facing in 1.5 acres of grounds. Peaceful and tranquil yet only 200 yards from beach.
Bedrooms: 3 double & 2 twin.
Bathrooms: 1 public.
Bed & breakfast: £12-£15 single, £24-£30 double.
Parking for 8.
🖨 🔟 🛈 Ⅴ 🖨 🔟 🎬 🛁 ✳
✗ 🎬 🎬

Ropers Walk
99 Dracaena Ave, Falmouth, TR11 2EP
☎ (0326) 312511
Neo Georgian, detached house in beautiful, quarter-acre garden, close to town and beaches. Central for touring western Cornwall.
Bedrooms: 2 double, 1 family room.
Bathrooms: 1 public.
Bed & breakfast: £19-£23 double.
Parking for 10.
Open March-November.
🛏 5 🔟 🛈 🔟 🎬 ✗ 🎬 OAP SP

FENITON

Devon
Map ref 1D2

4m W. Honiton

Higher Curscombe
Feniton, Honiton, EX14 0EU
☎ Honiton (0404) 850265
104-acre dairy/sheep farm. A30 Honiton to Exeter. Turn at Fenny Bridges direction Feniton. First right after Post Office to Curscombe. 1.25 miles further on.
Bedrooms: 1 double & 1 twin, 1 family room.
Bathrooms: 1 public.
Bed & breakfast: £9-£10 single, £18-£20 double.
Half board: £12-£13 daily, £84 weekly.
Evening meal 6.30pm.
Parking for 3.
Open April-October.
🛏 🐾 🔟 🖨 🔟 ✗ 🎬

GROUPS, CONSORTIA
AND AGENCIES
SPECIALISING
IN FARM AND
COUNTRY HOLIDAYS
ARE LISTED IN A
SPECIAL SECTION
OF THIS GUIDE.

FIGHELDEAN

Wiltshire
Map ref 2B3

4m N. Amesbury

Vale House
Figheldean, Salisbury,
SP4 8JJ
☎ Stonehenge (0980) 70713
*Secluded house in centre of
picturesque village. Easy
access to river, village pub
nearby. Figheldean is on the
A345, 4 miles north of
Amesbury, 2 miles from
Stonehenge and 12 miles from
Salisbury.*
Bedrooms: 1 double & 1 twin.
Bathrooms: 1 public.
Bed & breakfast: £9 single,
£18 double.
Parking for 4.
Open April-October.
⊛ ⚲ ⚱ Ⓤ ⊨ ⚱ ⊞ ⌕ ⚘
⚶

FROME

Somerset
Map ref 2B2

*See also Norton St.
Philip.*
Old market town with
modern light industry, its
medieval centre watered
by the River Frome.
Above Cheap Street with
its flagstones and
watercourse is the church
showing work of varying
periods. Interesting
buildings include 18th C
wool merchants' houses.
Local history museum. *ℹ*

Gloucester Farm
Lullington, Frome,
BA11 2PG
☎ (0373) 830293
*230-acre arable and stock
farm. In a quiet unspoilt
village, 3 miles from the
market town of Frome and
within reach of many towns
and country attractions.*
Bedrooms: 2 family rooms.
Bathrooms: 1 public.
Bed & breakfast: £9.50
single, £19 double.
Parking for 3.
Open April-October.
⊛ Ⓤ Ⓥ ⊨ ⊞ ⚱ ⌕ ⚶

Highcroft Farm
West Woodlands, Frome,
BA11 5EQ
☎ (0373) 61941
*5-acre smallholding.
Comfortable, old, stone
farmhouse with pleasant
gardens in country setting.
Close to Longleat, Stourhead
and Bath.*
Bedrooms: 2 double & 1 twin,
1 family room.
Bathrooms: 2 public;
1 private shower.
Bed & breakfast: £8-£9
single, £16-£18 double.
Half board: £13-£15 daily.
Evening meal 6.30pm (l.o.
7pm).
Parking for 14.
⊛ ⚲ Ⓤ ▌ ⊨ ⊞ ⌕ ❈ ⚶

GASTARD

Wiltshire
Map ref 2B2

4m SW. Chippenham

Boyds Farm
Gastard, Corsham,
SN13 9PT
☎ (0249) 713146
*211-acre arable farm. Quiet
country farmhouse, situated
half way between Corsham and
Melksham on the B 3353 road.*
Bedrooms: 1 single, 1 double,
1 family room.
Bathrooms: 2 public.
Bed & breakfast: £10-£10.50
single, £18-£20 double.
Parking for 6.
⊛ ⚲ Ⓤ Ⓥ ⚹ ⊨ Ⓣ ⊞ ⚱
⚶ ▶ ✓ ❈ ⚶ ⊙ᴬᴾ ⊞

GLASTONBURY

Somerset
Map ref 2A2

See also West Pennard.
Old market town
associated with Joseph of
Arimathea and the birth of
English Christianity. Built
around its once-glorious
7th C abbey whose
medieval remains are
said to be the site of King
Arthur's burial, it
prospered from wool until
the 19th C. Glastonbury
Tor with its ancient tower
gives panoramic views
over flat, rural country
rich in remains of Celtic
lake communities. *ℹ*

Cradlebridge Farm
⊛⊛⊛
Glastonbury, BA16 9SD
☎ (0458) 31827

*200-acre dairy farm.
Modernised farmhouse. Quiet
situation and a good touring
area.*
Bedrooms: 1 twin, 2 family
rooms.
Bathrooms: 3 private.
Bed & breakfast: £12.50-£15
single, £25-£30 double.
Half board: from £17.50
daily.
Evening meal 6pm (l.o.
midday).
Parking for 10.
⊛ ⚱ Ⓤ ⊨ Ⓣ ⊞ ⚲ ⚶

Laverley House ᴍ
⊛⊛⊛
West Pennard, Glastonbury,
BA6 8NE
☎ Pilton (074 989) 696
*5-acre soft fruit farm. Listed
grade II Georgian farmhouse
in rural position with views
towards Mendips. On the
A361 4 miles east of
Glastonbury.*
Bedrooms: 2 double, 1 family
room.
Bathrooms: 2 private,
3 public.
Bed & breakfast: £12.50-£16
single, £25-£32 double.
Half board: £20-£23.50 daily,
£126-£148 weekly.
Evening meal 6.30pm (l.o.
9am).
Parking for 12.
⊛ ⚲ ⚓ ⊡ ⚲ Ⓤ Ⓥ ⊨ ⊞
⚱ ⚲ ⚱ ❈ ⚶ ⊞

The Market House Inn
12-14 Magdalene St.,
Glastonbury, BA6 9EH
☎ (0458) 32220
*Located opposite Glastonbury
Abbey ruins. Front bedrooms
overlook ruins and Tor.
Friendly inn with home
cooking.*
Bedrooms: 2 double & 1 twin,
2 family rooms.
Bathrooms: 2 public.
Bed & breakfast: £20 single,
£30 double.
Evening meal 6pm (l.o.
9.30pm).
Parking for 8.
⊛⚲2 ⊡ ⚲ Ⓥ ⊞ ⚷ ❈ ⚶ ⚶
⚶ ⚲ SP

GORRAN

Cornwall
Map ref 1B3

2m SW. Mevagissey

Great Polgrain Farm
Caerhays, Gorran, St.
Austell, PL26 6LZ
☎ Mevagissey (0726) 501269
*230-acre dairy/sheep farm.
Spacious and comfortable
farmhouse on the Roseland
Peninsula. Surrounded by
woodland and only half a mile
from the beach.*
Bedrooms: 1 single, 1 twin,
1 family room.
Bathrooms: 1 public.
Bed & breakfast: £10-£12.50
single, £20-£25 double.
Parking for 4.
Open April-October.
⊛ ⚲ ⚯ Ⓤ ▌ ⚲ ⊞ ⚱ ❈
⚶ ⚶ ⊙ᴬᴾ ⊞

GORRAN HAVEN

Cornwall
Map ref 1B3

3m S. Mevagissey
Once important in the
pilchard fisheries, now a
seaside village gathered
at the mouth of its valley.
A medieval chapel and
Methodist church stand
among the cottages
overlooking the quay and
beautiful unspoilt cliffs
spread south-west of
Dodman Point.

Llawnroc Inn Hotel
⊛⊛⊛
Gorran Haven, St. Austell,
PL26 6NU
☎ Mevagissey (0726) 843461
*Small family-run pub/hotel
with a local inn atmosphere
and fresh, home-cooked food.
All bedrooms face the sea and
have magnificent views.*
Bedrooms: 3 double & 1 twin,
2 family rooms.
Bathrooms: 6 private.
Bed & breakfast: £18-£22
single, £28-£36 double.
Lunch available.
Evening meal 7pm (l.o. 9pm).
Parking for 40.
Credit: Access, Visa, Diners,
Amex.
⊛ ⚱ ⊡ ⊡ ⚯ ▌ Ⓥ ⊨ Ⓣ
⊞ ⚱ ⚷ ⚲ ❈ ⚶ SP

**MAP REFERENCES
APPLY TO THE
COLOUR MAPS
TOWARDS THE END
OF THIS GUIDE.**

**INDIVIDUAL PROPRIETORS HAVE SUPPLIED
ALL DETAILS OF ACCOMMODATION.
ALTHOUGH WE DO CHECK FOR ACCURACY, WE
ADVISE YOU TO CONFIRM PRICES AND OTHER
INFORMATION AT THE TIME OF BOOKING.**

GREAT WISHFORD

Wiltshire
Map ref 2B2

3m N. Wilton

The Old Post House
⊕⊕
South St., Great Wishford,
Salisbury SP2 0NN
☎ (0722) 790211
*A 17th C. house in the much
acclaimed village of Great
Wishford.*
Bedrooms: 1 single, 1 double
& 1 twin, 1 family room.
Bathrooms: 1 private,
2 public.
Bed & breakfast: £14-£18
single, £24-£34 double.
Parking for 6.
⌖2☐♥Ⓤ픽⊙▥Ụ✲
✕♨⊞

GUNNISLAKE

Cornwall
Map ref 1C2

Steep roadside village
with late Georgian houses
built when tin mining
flourished here. One of
the ancient entries into
Cornwall, the Tamar is
still spanned by the 14th
C 'New Bridge'.

Latchley Farmhouse
⟨Listed⟩
Latchley, Gunnislake,
PL18 9AX
☎ Tavistock (0822) 832428
*17th C. farmhouse in mining
village in the Tamar valley.
Signposted from A390
Tavistock to Gunnislake road.*
Bedrooms: 1 single, 1 double
& 1 twin.
Bathrooms: 1 public.
Bed & breakfast: max. £13.50
single, max. £27 double.
Parking for 3.
⌖12☒♥Ⓤ▥▦▦♨✕♨
⊞

GURNEY SLADE

Somerset
Map ref 2B2

4m N. Shepton Mallet

Coombe End
Binegar Lane, Gurney Slade,
Bath, Avon BA3 4TR
☎ Oakhill (0749) 840482
*In a quiet rural village,
personal service and home-
made bread. French spoken,
and spinning demonstrated and
taught.*
Bedrooms: 1 double & 1 twin.

Bathrooms: 1 public.
Bed & breakfast: £9 single,
£18 double.
Half board: £14 daily, £98
weekly.
Evening meal 6pm (l.o. 8pm).
Parking for 3.
⌖⊠♨Ⓤ▮⊙▥▣♨✕♨
⊞ SP

HARBERTON

Devon
Map ref 1D2

2m SW. Totnes
Small village between
southern Dartmoor and
the Dart estuary, noted
for its grand 3-aisled
church. The stone pulpit
and rood screen are fine
examples of late medieval
carving.

Foales-Leigh
Harberton, Totnes, TQ9 7SS
☎ (0803) 862365
*200-acre mixed farm. A Grade
II Listed farmhouse
overlooking traditional
buildings set in a quiet hamlet
three miles from Totnes.*
Bedrooms: 2 double & 2 twin.
Bathrooms: 1 public.
Bed & breakfast: from £9
single, £18 double.
Half board: £14 daily, £98
weekly.
Evening meal 7pm.
Parking for 4.
Open April-October.
⌖♥Ⓤ▣▦⊙▥▣♨♨
Ụ◿✕♨

HARTLAND

Devon
Map ref 1C1

4m W. Clovelly
Hamlet on high, wild
country near Hartland
Point. Just west, the
parish church tower
makes a magnificent
landmark; the light,
unrestored interior holds
one of Devon's finest
rood screens. There are
spectacular cliffs around
Hartland Point and the
lighthouse.

Anchor Inn
⊕
Fore St., Hartland,
EX39 6BD
☎ (023 74) 414
*An attractive 16th C. inn
offering comfortable
accommodation. Family
bookings welcomed.*
Bedrooms: 1 single, 5 double
& 2 twin, 2 family rooms.

Bathrooms: 5 private,
3 public.
Bed & breakfast: £12.50-
£14.50 single, £25-£29 double.
Half board: £17-£19 daily,
£110-£125 weekly.
Lunch available.
Evening meal 7pm (l.o.
9.30pm).
Parking for 21.
⌖♥▮Ⓥ핏⊙▣♨¶⊜
♨✕⊞ SP ⊞

Elmscott Farm
Hartland, Bideford,
EX39 6ES
☎ (023 74) 276
*650-acre mixed farm. In a
coastal setting, quietly situated
bordering Devon and Cornwall.
Signposted from the main A39,
about 4 miles away.*
Bedrooms: 2 double & 1 twin,
1 family room.
Bathrooms: 1 private,
1 public.
Bed & breakfast: £9-£10
single, £18-£20 double.
Half board: £13-£15 daily,
£91-£105 weekly.
Evening meal 6pm.
Parking for 8.
Open April-October.
⌖♥Ⓤ핏⊙▣♨Ụ¶✲
✕♨

Summerwell Farm
Hartland, Bideford,
EX39 6HB
☎ (023 74) 304
*175-acre mixed farm.
Comfortable farmhouse,
attractively furnished and
situated. Close to beaches on
unspoilt north Devon coast.
Traditional English food.*
Bedrooms: 2 single, 1 double
& 1 twin.
Bathrooms: 1 public.
Bed & breakfast: £9-£9.50
single, £18-£19 double.
Half board: £13-£13.50 daily,
£77.50-£80 weekly.
Evening meal 6.30pm (l.o.
7.30pm).
Parking for 6.
Open April-October.
⌖♥Ⓤ▮Ⓥ핏⊙◿✕♨

HATHERLEIGH

Devon
Map ref 1C2

7m NW. Okehampton
Set in pastoral
countryside, small town
with thatched cottages
and a cattle market.
There are trout and
salmon streams close by.

Bridge Inn &
Restaurant ⋔
Bridge St., Hatherleigh,
EX20 3JA
☎ Okehampton
(0837) 810357
*16th C. coaching inn. Chef,
real home-cooked food, special
cooked ham carved at the bar.
Ideal touring centre.*
Bedrooms: 1 single, 1 double
& 1 twin, 1 family room.
Bathrooms: 1 public.
Bed & breakfast: £10.50-
£13.50 single, £19-£22.50
double.
Lunch available.
Evening meal 6.50pm (l.o.
9.30pm).
Parking for 20.
⌖♥▮Ⓥ핏⊙▥¶♨
SP ⊞

HAYLE

Cornwall
Map ref 1B3

Former mining town with
modern light industry on
the Hayle estuary. Most
buildings are Georgian or
early Victorian, with some
Regency houses along
the canal. ⛨

Sandsifter Hotel
⊕⊕⊕
1 Godrevy Towans, Godrevy,
Hayle, TR27 5ED
☎ (0736) 753314
*Comfortable hotel set in over 2
acres of private garden.*
Bedrooms: 2 single, 3 double
& 2 twin, 1 family room.
Bathrooms: 8 private.
Bed & breakfast: £12.50-£20
single, £25-£50 double.
Half board: £17.50-£27 daily,
£122.50-£189 weekly.
Evening meal 6.30pm (l.o.
9pm).
Parking for 100.
⌖8⏣♥Ụ Ⓥ핏⊙▥♨
¶♨Ụ✲✕♨♘ SP

┌─────────────────────────────┐
│ **THERE IS A SPECIAL SECTION IN THIS**
│ **GUIDE LISTING ACCOMMODATION ESPECIALLY**
│ **SUITABLE FOR GROUPS AND YOUNG PEOPLE.**
└─────────────────────────────┘

HEMYOCK

Devon
Map ref 1D2

5m S. Wellington

Brook House
Listed

Hemyock, Cullompton,
EX15 3RG
☎ (0823) 680 811
Small guesthouse, with home comforts, and tea room serving lunches, morning coffee and afternoon teas (cream teas in summer). Coffee and tea in bedrooms on request.
Bedrooms: 2 single, 1 double & 2 twin.
Bathrooms: 2 public.
Bed & breakfast: £8-£8.50 single, £17 double.
Half board: £11.90-£12.50 daily, £79.80-£89 weekly.
Lunch available.
Evening meal 6pm (l.o. 7.50pm).
Parking for 2.
🛇5 🛇 🛇 🅿 🛇 📺 🖥 🛋 ♦ 🗙 🎬 🞓 🞓 🗝

HENSTRIDGE

Somerset
Map ref 2B3

6m S. Wincanton
Village with a rebuilt church containing the Tudor Carent tomb.

Quiet Corner Farm
👑

Henstridge, Templecombe,
BA8 0RA
☎ Stalbridge (0963) 63045
5-acre orchard and grazing farm. Stone farmhouse, part 18th C./Victorian, with a complex of lovely old barns, some converted to holiday cottages. Marvellous views across Blackmoor Vale. In a village with post office, pubs, restaurant and shops.
Bedrooms: 1 double, 1 family room.
Bathrooms: 1 private, 1 public.
Bed & breakfast: £11-£13 single, £20-£24 double.
Evening meal 7pm.
Parking for 8.
🛇5 🛇 🅿 🛇 🅿 📺 🖥 🛋 ∪ 🡒 🞓 ♦ 🗙 🎬 🞓

HENTON

Somerset
Map ref 2A2

Dove Cottage
Henton, Wells, BA5 1PD
☎ Wells (0749) 74604
Friendly Georgian country cottage on the B3139, 3 miles west of Wells. Excellent eating nearby. Near Cheddar, Wookey and Glastonbury.
Bedrooms: 1 single, 2 twin.
Bathrooms: 1 public.
Bed & breakfast: £22 double.
Parking for 3.
🛇 🛇 🅿 🛇 ✕ 🛋 📺 🖥 🛋
🗙 🎬 🞓

HIGHBRIDGE

Somerset
Map ref 1D1

Laurel Farm
Vole Road, Mark,
Highbridge, TA9 4PE
☎ Brent Knoll (0278) 760345
60-acre dairy farm. Spacious listed farmhouse in rural position with lounge/dining room. Large garden and beautiful views.
Bedrooms: 1 double, 1 family room.
Bathrooms: 1 public.
Bed & breakfast: £17 double.
Parking for 4.
🛇 🛇 🅿 🛇 🅿 📺 🖥 🛋 ♦ 🗙
🎬 🞓

Laurel Farm (Puddy) 👑
👑

The Causeway, Mark,
Highbridge, TA9 4PZ
☎ Mark Moor (027 864) 216
120-acre dairy farm. 300-year-old farmhouse with beamed sitting room, log fire, colour TV. Home-produced vegetables, cream cheese and eggs served. Ideal touring centre on the B3139 road between Wells and Burnham-on-Sea.
Bedrooms: 1 single, 3 double & 2 twin, 2 family rooms.
Bathrooms: 2 public.
Bed & breakfast: £9-£10.50 single, £18-£20 double.
Half board: £77-£90 weekly.
Evening meal 6pm.
Parking for 4.
🛇 🛋 🛇 🅿 📺 🖥 🗙 🛋 🞓 🗝
🞓 🎬

New House Farm
👑

Walrow, Highbridge,
TA9 4RA
☎ (0278) 782218

56-acre mixed farm. Large modern farmhouse on the B3139 between Highbridge and Mark. Also, a caravan park for 30 tourers or tents.
Bedrooms: 3 double.
Bathrooms: 2 public.
Bed & breakfast: £10-£15 single, £20 double.
Parking for 3.
🛇12 🛇 🅿 🛇 🅿 📺 🖥 🛋 ♦ ❄
🚐

HINTON CHARTERHOUSE

Avon
Map ref 2B2

Small village in wooded, undulating country south of Bath. Nearby stand the remains of Hinton Priory, founded by the Carthusians in 1232.

Green Lane House 👑
Listed

1 Green La., Hinton
Charterhouse, Bath,
BA3 6BL
☎ Limpley Stoke
(022 122) 3631
Fully renovated, attractive stone house built in 1725, family-run and comfortably furnished. Quiet village in beautiful countryside, convenient for Bath, Bristol and Cotswolds.
Bedrooms: 1 single, 1 double & 2 twin.
Bathrooms: 2 public.
Bed & breakfast: £16-£24 single, £24-£36 double.
Parking for 4.
Open February-November.
Credit: Access, Visa.
🛇 🛇 🅿 🛇 🅿 📺 🖥
🛋 🗙 🎬 🞓

HOLCOMBE

Somerset
Map ref 2B2

4m S. Radstock

Hackmead Farm
Holcombe, Bath, BA3 5EU
☎ Stratton-on-the-Fosse,
(0761) 232207
222-acre dairy farm. In the heart of the Somerset countryside, 20 minutes from Bath, short distance from Wells.
Bedrooms: 1 double, 1 family room.
Bathrooms: 1 public.
Bed & breakfast: £11-£12 single, £20-£22 double.
Parking for 10.
🛇 🛇 🖵 🛇 🅿 🛇 🖥

HOLSWORTHY

Devon
Map ref 1C2

Busy rural town and centre of a large farming community. Market day attracts many visitors.

Aldercott
Pancrasweek, Holsworthy,
EX22 7JN
☎ Bradworthy (040 924) 417
277-acre mixed farm. 17th C. farmhouse in peaceful surroundings. 2 bedrooms have washbasins. Separate dining room. 8 miles from Cornish coast and 3 miles from market town.
Bedrooms: 1 single, 1 double, 1 family room.
Bathrooms: 1 public.
Bed & breakfast: £8 single, £16 double.
Half board: £13 daily, £91 weekly.
Evening meal 6pm (l.o. 6pm).
Parking for 10.
Open April-October.
🛇 🛇 🅿 📺 🗙 🎬

The Barton
Listed

Pancrasweek, Holsworthy,
EX22 7JT
☎ Bridgerule (028 881) 315
140-acre dairy farm. At the Devon/Cornwall border on the A3072, 3.5 miles from Holsworthy and 6 miles from the Cornish coast. Friendly atmosphere and home cooking with home-produced vegetables.
Bedrooms: 2 double & 2 twin, 1 family room.
Bathrooms: 2 public.
Bed & breakfast: £7.50-£8.50 single, £15-£17 double.
Half board: £12.50-£13.50 daily, £87.50-£94.50 weekly.
Evening meal 6pm (l.o. 4pm).
Parking for 5.
Open May-September.
🛇 🛇 🅿 🛇 🅿 📺 🛋 🞓 ∪
🡒 🡒 ✓ ❄ 🎬

Leworthy Farm 👑
👑

Holsworthy, EX22 6SJ
☎ (0409) 253488
240-acre mixed farm. Genuine working farm offering space and comfort in a friendly environment. Ideal touring centre, own fishing, ponies and seasonal entertainment. Mini golf.
Bedrooms: 2 single, 4 double & 2 twin, 4 family rooms.
Bathrooms: 3 private, 2 public.
Bed & breakfast: £12-£15 single, £24-£30 double.

THE SYMBOLS ARE EXPLAINED ON THE FLAP INSIDE THE BACK COVER.

Half board: £20-£23 daily, £120-£140 weekly. Lunch available. Evening meal 6.45pm (l.o. 4pm). Parking for 30.

🐕 ⚒ 🅸 Ⓥ 🖥 📺 ➰ 🍴 🖐 ♿ ☎ ⏱ 🕐 ✦ ❀ 🖐 ⚓ SP Ⓣ

West Coombe Farm
West Coombe, Hollacombe, Holsworthy, EX22 6NP
☎ (0409) 253267
166-acre beef and sheep farm. Ideal centre for touring the moors and 12 miles from the surfing beaches of Bude. Home cooking. Dogs welcome. Rough shooting.
Bedrooms: 1 double & 1 twin, 1 family room.
Bathrooms: 1 public.
Bed & breakfast: £8 single, £16 double.
Half board: £12 daily, £84 weekly.
Evening meal 6.30pm.
Parking for 3.
Open April-October.

🐕 ⚒ 🔳 Ⓥ 🖥 📺 Ⓤ ➰ 🍴 🖐

HOLWELL
Dorset
Map ref 2B3

2m SE. Sherborne

Strawberry Cottage
(Listed)
Packers Hill, Holwell, Sherborne, DT9 5LN
☎ Bishops Caundle
(096 323) 629
Attractive, 16th C., listed thatched cottage in quiet countryside near Hardy's Wessex, Sherborne and within easy reach of coast.
Bedrooms: 1 double & 2 twin.
Bathrooms: 1 public;
1 private shower.
Bed & breakfast: £12-£15 single, £22-£28 double.
Parking for 2.

🐕 10 ⚒ 🔳 📺 🖥 ➰ 🖐 🖐

HONITON
Devon
Map ref 1D2

See also Awliscombe.
Old coaching town in undulating farmland. Formerly famous for lace-making, it is now an antiques trade centre. *ℹ*

Yard Farm
⚅⚅⚅
Upottery, Honiton, EX14 9QP
☎ (040 486) 318

94-acre cattle farm. 17th C. farmhouse with friendly atmosphere and home cooking. 150 yards from the A30 and 3 miles east of Honiton. Use of garden.
Bedrooms: 1 single, 1 double, 1 family room.
Bathrooms: 1 public.
Bed & breakfast: £8.50-£9.50 single, £17-£19 double.
Half board: £13-£14 daily, £80-£90 weekly.
Evening meal 6.30pm (l.o. 5pm).
Parking for 4.

🐕 🔳 📺 🖥 ➰ 🍴 🖐 🖐 🖐

HORTON
Somerset
Map ref 1D2

3m W. Ilminster

Fairfield Farm
⚅⚅⚅
Horton, Ilminster, TA19 9QR
☎ (0460) 52748
67-acre beef and sheep farm. Overlooking the Blackdown Hills, within easy reach of Cricket St. Thomas and both coasts. Home-produced food.
Bedrooms: 2 double & 1 twin.
Bathrooms: 1 public.
Bed & breakfast: £9-£10 single, £18-£20 double.
Half board: £13-£14 daily, £85-£90 weekly.
Evening meal 7pm (l.o. 8pm).
Parking for 4.

🐕 ✿ 🔳 Ⓥ 🖥 📺 🖥 🖐

IDE
Devon
Map ref 1D2

Canns House
Ide, Exeter, EX2 9RU
☎ Exeter (0392) 53016
Spacious and elegantly furnished Georgian house in a charming village, within easy reach of Exeter, Dartmoor and coastal resorts.
Bedrooms: 1 single, 1 double & 1 twin.
Bathrooms: 2 public.
Bed & breakfast: £10 single, £20 double.
Half board: £14-£15 daily, £91-£98 weekly.
Evening meal 6.30pm (l.o. 6.30pm).
Parking for 9.

🐕 1 ⚒ 🔳 🖥 📺 🖥 ➰ 🖐 🖐 SP 🖐

```
PLEASE MENTION
THIS GUIDE WHEN
MAKING A BOOKING.
```

ILFRACOMBE
Devon
Map ref 1C1

Seaside resort of Victorian grandeur set on hillside between cliffs with sandy coves. Earlier a small port and fishing town. On a rock at the mouth of the harbour stands an 18th C lighthouse, built over a medieval chapel. There are fine formal gardens and 2 working mills, restored and open to the public. Museum, donkey rides, Chambercombe Manor, interesting and charming old house nearby. *ℹ*

Sunnymeade Country House Hotel M
⚅⚅⚅
Dean Cross, West Down, Ilfracombe, EX34 8NT
☎ (0271) 63668
Hotel set in over half an acre amid beautiful rolling Devon countryside. Close to beaches and Exmoor. West Down is 4 miles south of Ilfracombe.
Bedrooms: 7 double & 1 twin, 2 family rooms.
Bathrooms: 7 private, 3 public.
Bed & breakfast: £10-£13.50 single, £20-£27 double.
Half board: £15-£20 daily, £90-£120 weekly.
Evening meal 7pm (l.o. 6.30pm).
Parking for 14.
Credit: Access, Visa, Diners, Amex.

🐕 ✦ ✿ 🔳 Ⓥ 🖥 📺 🖥 ➰
❀ 🖐 ♿ SP Ⓣ

ILMINSTER
Somerset
Map ref 1D2

See also Horton.
Former wool town with modern industry set in undulating, pastoral country. Fine market square of mellow ham stone and Elizabethan school house. The 15th C church has a handsome tower and a lofty, light interior with some notable brass memorials. Just north is an arts centre with theatre and art gallery. *ℹ*

Bay House
Bay Hill, Ilminster, TA19 0AT
☎ (0460) 52120

Family-run country guesthouse overlooking rural market town. Large gardens with magnificent views of the Blackdown Hills.
Bedrooms: 1 single, 2 double & 3 twin, 2 family rooms.
Bathrooms: 2 public.
Bed & breakfast: £13-£15 single, £25-£28 double.
Half board: £17.50-£20 daily, £95-£110 weekly.
Evening meal 6pm (l.o. 7.30pm).
Parking for 10.

🐕 🔳 Ⓥ 🖥 📺 🖥 ➰ 🍴 OAP
🖐 Ⓣ

IPPLEPEN
Devon
Map ref 1D2

3m SW Newton Abbot

Bittons
Beech Tree La., Ipplepen, Newton Abbot, TQ12 5TW
☎ (0803) 812489
Delightfully situated, offering comfort and personal attention. Ideal touring centre within easy reach of the sea and moors.
Bedrooms: 1 single, 2 double & 1 twin, 1 family room.
Bathrooms: 2 public.
Bed & breakfast: £9-£10 single, £18-£20 double.
Half board: £15-£16 daily, £105-£112 weekly.
Evening meal 6pm (l.o. 7.30pm).
Parking for 6.

🐕 🔳 🖥 📺 🖥 ➰ ❀ 🖐 🖐

IVYBRIDGE
Devon
Map ref 1C2

Town set in delightful woodlands on the River Erme. Brunel designed the local railway viaduct. *ℹ*

Whiteoaks
Daveys Cross, Ivybridge, PL21 0DW
☎ (0752) 892340
Comfortable country guesthouse with lovely views, on Dartmoor's edge. A warm welcome for all from the resident owners.
Bedrooms: 2 double & 1 twin, 2 family rooms.
Bathrooms: 1 private, 2 public.
Bed & breakfast: £9.50-£12 single, £19-£24 double.
Continued ▶

IVYBRIDGE

Continued

Half board: £13.50-£16 daily, £87.50-£105 weekly.
Evening meal 7pm (l.o. 10.30am).
Parking for 6.

[symbols]

JACOBSTOWE

Devon
Map ref 1C2

4m N. Okehampton
Village in the heart of rural mid-Devon, near the River Okement.

Higher Cadham Farm

Jacobstowe, Okehampton, EX20 3RB
☎ Exbourne (083 785) 647
139-acre mixed farm. 16th C. farmhouse on a typical Devon farm, 5 miles from Dartmoor and within easy reach of coast.
Bedrooms: 1 single, 1 double & 1 twin, 1 family room.
Bathrooms: 1 public.
Bed & breakfast: £8.50-£9 single, £17-£18 double.
Half board: £13-£13.50 daily, max. £85 weekly.
Evening meal 7pm (l.o. 5pm).
Parking for 6.
Open March-November.

[symbols]

KILVE

Somerset
Map ref 1D1

3m NW. Nether Stowey
Old village, once smugglers' haunt, set between gentle slopes of the Quantocks and the sea.

The Old Rectory

Listed

Kilve, Bridgwater, TA5 1DZ
☎ Holford (0278) 74520
200-year-old former rectory in the Quantock village of Kilve on A39. 1 mile from Fossil Beach. 10 miles from Minehead.
Bedrooms: 1 double & 1 twin, 1 family room.
Bathrooms: 1 public.
Bed & breakfast: £19 double.
Half board: from £65 weekly.
Evening meal 6.30pm (l.o. midday).
Parking for 6.
Open April-October.

[symbols]

KINGSBRIDGE

Devon
Map ref 1C3

See also Aveton Gifford, Chillington, Slapton.
Formerly important as a port, now a market town overlooking head of beautiful, wooded estuary winding deep into rural countryside. Summer art exhibitions; William Cookworthy Museum. *i*

Hillside

Ashford, Kingsbridge, TQ7 4NB
☎ (0548) 550752
Modernised country cottage with an acre of orchard garden, in a quiet hamlet just off the Plymouth to Kingsbridge A379. Bedrooms have beautiful views of surrounding countryside.
Bedrooms: 2 double & 1 twin.
Bathrooms: 2 public.
Bed & breakfast: £9-£11 single, £18-£22 double.
Half board: £15-£17 daily.
Evening meal 6.30pm (l.o. 2pm).
Parking for 5.

[symbols]

South Allington House

Listed

Chivelstone, Kingsbridge, TQ7 2NB
☎ (054 851) 272
140-acre mixed farm. Attractive house set in 4 acres with safe play area. Coastal walks leading to safe beaches; sailing, fishing, golf close at hand. South Allington is between Start Point and Prawle Point.
Bedrooms: 2 single, 2 double & 1 twin, 4 family rooms.
Bathrooms: 1 private, 4 public.
Bed & breakfast: max. £11 single, max. £22 double.
Evening meal 7pm.
Parking for 10.

[symbols]

KINGSTON ST MARY

Somerset
Map ref 1D1

3m N. Taunton

Volis Farm

Hestercombe, Kingston St. Mary, Taunton, Somerset. TA2 8HS
☎ (082 345) 545

380-acre dairy/mixed farm. Adjacent to Hestercombe Gardens, 400 feet up on the edge of the Quantock Hills. Tranquillity, magnificent views and a warm welcome. 3 miles from the M5.
Bedrooms: 2 twin, 1 family room.
Bathrooms: 1 public.
Bed & breakfast: £10-£14 single, £20-£28 double.
Parking for 10.
Open February-October.

[symbols]

KINGTON LANGLEY

Wiltshire
Map ref 2B2

2m N. Chippenham

Finnygook

Listed

Days La., Kington Langley, SN15 5PA
☎ Kington Langley (024 975) 272
Modern family home on the edge of a quiet village, less than a mile from the M4 and ideally placed for sightseeing. Information about special activity holidays on request.
Bedrooms: 1 single, 2 double & 1 twin.
Bathrooms: 2 public.
Bed & breakfast: £11-£16 single, £22-£32 double.
Half board: £18-£27 daily, £125-£150 weekly.
Evening meal 6pm (l.o. 8pm).
Parking for 5.

[symbols]

KNOWLE

Devon
Map ref 1C1

5m NW. Barnstaple

Little Orchard

Church Hill La., Knowle, Braunton, EX33 2ND
☎ Braunton (0271) 812359
Just off the A361 within easy reach of north Devon's beaches and moors, offering homely accommodation and plenty of home-cooking. 3 miles from Saunton and 6 miles from Ilfracombe.
Bedrooms: 1 double, 2 family rooms.
Bathrooms: 1 public.
Bed & breakfast: £17-£19 double.
Half board: £12.50-£13.50 daily, £77-£84 weekly.

Evening meal 6.30pm (l.o. 3pm).
Parking for 3.
Open April-October.

[symbols]

LACOCK

Wiltshire
Map ref 2B2

3m S. Chippenham
Village of great charm. Medieval 18th C buildings of stone, brick or timber-frame have jutting storeys, gables, oriel windows. Magnificent church, reflecting former prosperity from wool, has perpendicular fan-vaulted chapel with grand tomb to benefactor who, after Dissolution, bought Augustinian nunnery Lacock Abbey.

Carpenters Arms

Lacock, Chippenham, SN15 2LB
☎ (024 973) 203
Caters for those who enjoy traditional English food and refreshments. Afternoon teas, residents' lounge.
Bedrooms: 3 double.
Bathrooms: 1 public, 2 private showers.
Bed & breakfast: £30-£35 single, £40-£45 double.
Half board: £33-£50 daily.
Lunch available.
Evening meal 7pm (l.o. 10pm).
Parking for 2.
Credit: Access, Visa.

[symbols]

Daisybrook

Forest Lane, Lacock, Chippenham, SN15 2PN
☎ (024 973) 257
On outskirts of National Trust village. 18th C. oak-beamed cottage in picturesque country garden, overlooking open countryside.
Bedrooms: 2 twin.
Bathrooms: 1 public.
Bed & breakfast: max. £25 double.
Parking for 4.

[symbols]

Dalestone House Bed & Breakfast M

Corsham Rd., Lacock, SN15 2LZ
☎ (024 973) 415

1950's house with beautiful views across Lacock to Westbury - on a clear day the famous White Horse can be seen.
Bedrooms: 1 double, 1 family room.
Bathrooms: 2 private.
Bed & breakfast: £18 single, £30-£35 double.
Half board: £28 daily, £196 weekly.
Evening meal 7pm (l.o. 7.30pm).
Parking for 4.
🔣🔣🔣🔣🔣🔣🔣🔣🔣🔣
🔣🔣🔣🔣🔣

Old Rectory
(symbols)
Lacock, Chippenham, SN15 2JZ
☎ (024 973) 335
11-acre mixed farm. As the name implies, shares in the history of Lacock. Located at the approach to the village and set in 7 acres of ground complete with tennis and croquet. Elegant accommodation with private facilities.
Bedrooms: 1 double & 2 twin.
Bathrooms: 3 private, 2 public.
Bed & breakfast: £30 double.
Parking for 6.
🔣🔣🔣🔣🔣🔣🔣🔣🔣🔣
🔣🔣🔣🔣🔣🔣🔣🔣

LAMERTON
Devon
Map ref 1C2

Small village, with a horsebridge dating from 1437, one of the oldest bridges in Devon, spanning the River Tamar.

Langford Farm
Lamerton, Tavistock, PL19 8QQ
☎ Tavistock (0822) 2202
152-acre mixed farm. Tranquil 500-year-old farmhouse approached by long lane of beech trees. Homely, relaxed atmosphere. 2 miles from Tavistock A384.
Bedrooms: 1 single, 2 double, 1 family room.
Bathrooms: 1 public.
Bed & breakfast: £8-£9 single, £16-£17 double.
Parking for 7.
Open April-October.
🔣🔣🔣🔣🔣🔣🔣🔣🔣🔣
🔣🔣

LANDS END
Cornwall

See Porthcurno, Sennen. Zennor.

LAPFORD
Devon
Map ref 1D2

Court Barton
Lapford, Crediton, EX17 6PZ
☎ Lapford (036 35) 441
150-acre mixed stock-rearing & arable farm. 15th C. farmhouse with beams and inglenook fireplace, in a quiet, secluded position on the edge of Lapford village. Half a mile north of A377 Exeter/Barnstaple road.
Bedrooms: 1 double, 2 family rooms.
Bathrooms: 1 public.
Bed & breakfast: from £9.50 single, from £19 double.
Half board: from £14 daily, from £87.50 weekly.
Evening meal 6.30pm (l.o. 7.30pm).
Parking for 3.
Open January-November.
🔣🔣🔣🔣🔣🔣🔣🔣🔣🔣
🔣🔣🔣

LATTON
Wiltshire
Map ref 2B2

Set amid levels of Upper Thames, estate village now owned by co-operative community. Restored Norman church and interesting classic-style wharf owners's house by disused canal.

Little Court
Latton, Swindon SN6 6DP
☎ Swindon (0793) 750 788
Beautiful Cotswold stone house set in lovely gardens with view of Latton Church. Easy access from A419 Swindon-Cirencester road.
Bedrooms: 1 single, 1 double & 1 twin.
Bathrooms: 1 private, 1 public.
Bed & breakfast: £15-£18 single, £36-£40 double.
Half board: £25-£32 daily.
Evening meal 6pm (l.o. 6pm).
Parking for 5.
🔣🔣🔣🔣🔣🔣🔣🔣🔣🔣
🔣🔣🔣🔣🔣🔣

LAUNCESTON
Cornwall
Map ref 1C2

Medieval 'Gateway to Cornwall', county town until 1838, founded by the Normans under their hilltop castle near the original monastic settlement. Today's hilly market town, overlooked by its castle ruin, has a handsome square with Georgian houses and an elaborately-carved granite church. 🄻

Country Friends Restaurant
St Leonards House, Polson, Launceston, PL15 9QU
☎ (0566) 4479
400-year-old Devon longhouse with stone fireplaces, exposed beams and wood burners. Riding holidays available. Ideal touring area.
Bedrooms: 2 twin, 2 family rooms.
Bathrooms: 1 public; 3 private showers.
Bed & breakfast: £12-£13.50 single, £24-£27 double.
Half board: £21-£22.50 daily, £140 weekly.
Evening meal 7.30pm (l.o. 9.30pm).
Parking for 10.
Open January, March-December.
Credit: Access, Visa.
🔣3🔣🔣🔣🔣🔣🔣🔣🔣
🔣🔣🔣

Hurdon Farm
(symbols)
Launceston, PL15 9LS
☎ (0566) 2955
400-acre mixed farm. Fresh farm produce is used for our dinners and soups accompanied by home made rolls. Imaginative starters. Delicious desserts and clotted cream.
Bedrooms: 1 single, 2 double & 2 twin, 1 family room.
Bathrooms: 2 private, 2 public.
Bed & breakfast: £10-£11 single, £20-£22 double.
Half board: £15-£16 daily, £90-£100 weekly.
Evening meal 6.30pm (l.o. 4.30pm).
Parking for 6.
Open April-October.
🔣🔣🔣🔣🔣🔣🔣🔣🔣🔣
🔣🔣🔣

Trethorn Leisure Farm
Kennard House, Launceston, PL15 8QE
☎ (0566) 86324

400-acre dairy farm. Home cooking, freshly baked rolls and home-made biscuits. Leisure farm where caring for animals is actively encouraged.
Bedrooms: 3 double, 3 family rooms.
Bathrooms: 1 public; 4 private showers.
Bed & breakfast: £10-£12 single, £20-£24 double.
Half board: £15-£17 daily, £105-£112 weekly.
Evening meal 7pm (l.o. 7pm).
Parking for 12.
🔣🔣🔣🔣🔣🔣🔣🔣🔣🔣
🔣🔣🔣

LISKEARD
Cornwall
Map ref 1C2

Former stannary town with a livestock market and light industry, situated at the head of a valley running to the Riviera coast. Handsome Georgian and Victorian residences and a fine Victorian Guildhall, reflect the prosperity of the mining boom. The large church has an early 20th C tower and a Norman font.

Tavern An Carow 🅼
😊
Station Rd., Liskeard, PL14 4DA
☎ (0579) 42280
Old postilion inn on edge of Cornish market town. Vegetarian and diabetic diets catered for. Games room.
Bedrooms: 1 single, 2 twin.
Bathrooms: 1 public.
Bed & breakfast: £14 single, £26 double.
Half board: £19.50 daily, £129.67 weekly.
Lunch available.
Evening meal 7pm (l.o. 10pm).
Parking for 10.
🔣🔣🔣🔣🔣🔣🔣🔣

GROUPS, CONSORTIA AND AGENCIES SPECIALISING IN FARM AND COUNTRY HOLIDAYS ARE LISTED IN A SPECIAL SECTION OF THIS GUIDE.

MAP REFERENCES APPLY TO COLOUR MAPS NEAR THE BACK OF THE GUIDE.

LITTLE LANGFORD

Wiltshire
Map ref 2B3

5m NW. Wilton

Little Langford Farmhouse

Little Langford, Salisbury,
SP3 4NR
☎ (0722) 790205
*650-acre dairy and arable
farm. Beautiful Victorian
house with spacious, tastefully
furnished rooms. Lovely
grounds, walks and views.
Excellent touring area -
Stonehenge 6 miles away.
Guests have freedom of the
farm.*
Bedrooms: 2 twin, 1 family
room.
Bathrooms: 2 public.
Bed & breakfast: from £15
single, £25-£27 double.
Parking for 5.

LITTLEHEMPSTON

Devon
Map ref 1D2

2m NE. Totnes
Attractive village in Dart
Valley, whose 15th C
church has a
characteristic Devon
tower and an old screen.
A rare 14th C manor
house lies beside the
church.

Bow Grange Farm
Listed

Littlehempston, Totnes,
TQ9 6NO
☎ Ipplepen (0803) 812390
*250-acre mixed farm. A
family-run farm amongst
rolling Devon countryside. 15
minutes from Torbay and 15
miles from Dartmoor on A381.*
Bedrooms: 2 family rooms.
Bathrooms: 1 public.
Bed & breakfast: £18.50-£20
double.
Evening meal 6.30pm (l.o.
8am).
Parking for 8.
Open April-October.

PLEASE CHECK
PRICES AND OTHER
DETAILS AT THE
TIME OF BOOKING.

LOOE

Cornwall
Map ref 1C3

Small resort developed
around former fishing and
smuggling ports
occupying the deep
estuary of the East and
West Looe rivers. Narrow
winding streets, with old
inns; museums, aquarium
and art gallery are
housed in interesting old
buildings. West Looe has
a medieval seamen's
chapel restored with
timbers from a captured
Spanish ship. Shark
fishing centre, boat trips;
busy harbour. *i*

Coombe Farm ⋔
Listed

Widegates, Looe, PL13 1QN
☎ Widegates (050 34) 223
*10-acre smallholding.
Delightful country house with
superb views to sea. Log fires,
candlelit dining, croquet,
snooker and table tennis.
British Tourist Authority
commended.*
Bedrooms: 1 single, 2 double
& 1 twin, 4 family rooms.
Bathrooms: 3 public.
Bed & breakfast: £12.50-
£18.50 single, £25-£37 double.
Half board: £21-£27 daily,
£140-£180 weekly.
Evening meal 7pm (l.o. 7pm).
Parking for 12.
Open March-October.

Meneglaze Guest House

Shutta, Looe, PL13 1LU
☎ (050 36) 2647
*Family-run guesthouse within
easy reach of town, harbour
and beach. Home cooking,
friendly atmosphere and
personal attention.*
Bedrooms: 3 family rooms.
Bathrooms: 1 public.
Bed & breakfast: £17-£20
double.
Half board: £16-£17.50 daily,
£100-£110 weekly.
Evening meal 7pm (l.o. 6pm).
Parking for 5.
Open April-October.

Pixies Holt ⋔
⌂⌂⌂

Shutta, Looe, PL13 1JD
☎ (050 36) 2726
*Small, friendly and
comfortable. 1.5 acres of
grounds with views over river
and countryside. A few
minutes' walk to picturesque
Looe and beaches.*

Bedrooms: 1 single, 3 double
& 1 twin, 2 family rooms.
Bathrooms: 3 private,
1 public.
Bed & breakfast: £10.50-£16
single, £21-£32 double.
Evening meal 7pm (l.o.
6.30pm).
Parking for 8.
Credit: Access, Visa.

Sea Haze Guest House
Listed

Polperro Rd., Looe,
PL13 2JS
☎ (050 36) 2708
*Bright, clean, comfortable
guesthouse offering personal
attention, friendly atmosphere
and panoramic views. Ideal
touring centre situated between
Looe and Polperro.*
Bedrooms: 1 single, 2 double
& 1 twin, 2 family rooms.
Bathrooms: 2 public.
Bed & breakfast: £17-£20
double.
Parking for 8.
Open April-October.

Ship Inn

Fore Street, East Looe,
PL13 1AD
☎ (050 36) 3124
*An old coaching inn in the
centre of Looe. Ideal for sea
fishing and the beach.*
Bedrooms: 2 single, 2 double
& 2 twin, 2 family rooms.
Bathrooms: 2 public.
Bed & breakfast: £10-£12
single, £20-£22 double.

Stonerock Cottage
⌂⌂

Portuan Rd., Hannafore,
Looe, PL13 2DN
☎ (050 36) 3651
*Modernised, old world cottage
facing south to the Channel.
Ample free parking. 2 minutes
from the beach, shops, tennis
and other amenities.*
Bedrooms: 1 single, 2 double,
2 family rooms.
Bathrooms: 2 public.
Bed & breakfast: £11-£12
single, £22-£24 double.
Parking for 5.

THE SYMBOLS ARE
EXPLAINED ON THE
FLAP INSIDE THE
BACK COVER.

LUDGVAN

Cornwall
Map ref 1B3

2m NE. Penzance

Menwidden Farm
Listed

Ludgvan, Penzance,
TR20 8BN
☎ Penzance (0736) 740415
*40-acre market garden and
dairy farm. Centrally situated
in west Cornwall. Warm
family atmosphere and home
cooking. Right at Browles
crossroads on the A30 from
Hayle, signpost Vellonoweth,
last farm on right.*
Bedrooms: 2 double, 2 family
rooms.
Bathrooms: 1 public.
Bed & breakfast: from £8
single, from £15 double.
Half board: from £10.50
daily, from £70 weekly.
Evening meal 6pm (l.o. 6pm).
Parking for 8.
Open February-November.

LYDFORD

Devon
Map ref 1C2

Former important tin
mining town, a small
village on edge of west
Dartmoor. Remains of
Norman castle which
incarcerated all falling
foul of tinners' notorious
'Lydford Law'. Bridge
crosses River Lyd where
it rushes through a mile-
long gorge of boulders
and trees over pools
rocks and waterfall.

Dartmoor Inn ⋔
⌂⌂⌂

Lydford, Okehampton,
EX20 4AY
☎ (082 282) 221 & 374
*Particularly well suited for
walking, riding and other
country sports and pastimes
including hang gliding. Under
owners supervision.*
Bedrooms: 1 single, 2 double
& 2 twin, 1 family room.
Bathrooms: 4 private,
1 public.
Bed & breakfast: £30-£36
double.
Lunch available.
Evening meal 7pm (l.o.
10pm).
Parking for 50.
Credit: Access, Visa, Diners,
Amex.

Elim
Listed

Lydford, Okehampton,
EX20 4BA
☎ (082 282) 230
*Attractive bungalow on A386,
midway between Okehampton
and Tavistock, in Dartmoor
National Park. Adjacent to
interesting village. Ideal
holiday centre.*
Bedrooms: 1 double & 1 twin.
Bathrooms: 1 public.
Bed & breakfast: £10-£13
single, £14-£17 double.
Parking for 6.

Somerset
Map ref 2A2

Bridgefoot Farm
Lydford-on-Fosse, Somerton,
TA11 7DP
☎ Wheathill (096 324) 571
*17th C. farmhouse with beams,
open fireplace and flagstone
floor in lounge.*
Bedrooms: 1 double & 1 twin,
1 family room.
Bathrooms: 1 public.
Bed & breakfast: from £10
single, from £20 double.
Parking for 3.

Dorset
Map ref 1D2

Pretty historic fishing
town and resort set
against the fossil-rich
cliffs of Lyme Bay. In
medieval times it was an
important port and cloth
centre. The Cobb, a
massive stone
breakwater, shelters the
ancient harbour which is
still lively with boats. *i*

Haye Farm ⋏
Haye La., Lyme Regis,
DT7 3UB
☎ Lyme Regis, (029 74) 2400
*35-acre mixed farm.
Comfortable farmhouse
accommodation, with
spectacular views over glorious
hills and valleys, in an area of
outstanding natural beauty.
Vegetarian and vegan cooking
if preferred.*
Bedrooms: 1 double & 1 twin.
Bathrooms: 1 public.

Bed & breakfast: £10.50-
£11.50 single.
Parking for 8.

Lydwell House
Lyme Rd., Uplyme, Lyme
Regis, DT7 3TJ
☎ (029 74) 3522
*Pleasant, spacious house in
large and lovely gardens. Quiet
village location, 10 minutes'
walk from the sea.*
Bedrooms: 1 single, 2 double
& 1 twin, 1 family room.
Bathrooms: 1 public;
1 private shower.
Bed & breakfast: £9-£9.50
single, £19-£20 double.
Parking for 6.

Norman House
29 Coombe St., Lyme Regis,
DT7 3PP
☎ (029 74) 3191
*16th C. listed building in the
old part of Lyme Regis, a short
walk from the sea and close to
shops and cinema.*
Bedrooms: 3 double & 2 twin.
Bathrooms: 1 private,
1 public.
Bed & breakfast: £9-£10.50
single, £18-£21 double.
Open March-November.

The Red House ⋏
⊜⊜⊜

Sidmouth Rd., Lyme Regis,
DT7 3ES
☎ (029 74) 2055
*Superb coastal views, large
garden, parking.*
Bedrooms: 3 twin.
Bathrooms: 3 private.
Bed & breakfast: £13.50-£27
single, £27-£34 double.
Parking for 4.
Open March-November.

Springfield
⊜⊜

Woodmead Rd., Lyme Regis,
DT7 3LJ
☎ (029 74) 3409
*Elegant Georgian house in
beautiful garden with well-
proportioned, tastefully
decorated rooms, enjoying
magnificent views over sea and
countryside.*
Bedrooms: 1 single, 2 double
& 2 twin, 2 family rooms.
Bathrooms: 1 private,
2 public.

Bed & breakfast: £18-£28
double.
Parking for 9.
Open February-November.

Devon
Map ref 1D2

Village on the Exe estuary
occupying a small river
valley reaching into rural
countryside. Red
sandstone cliffs guard the
harbour, with old lime
kilns and fishermen's
cottages, isolated by the
coastal railway. Seafood,
the 19th C. industry, is still
a local speciality.

Hillside
The Strand, Lympstone,
EX8 5JS
☎ (0395) 266562
*Situated in the heart of this
popular fishing village on the
River Exe. Frequent winners of
the 'Britain in Bloom'
competitions.*
Bedrooms: 1 double, 1 family
room.
Bathrooms: 2 public.
Bed & breakfast: £9 single,
£18 double.

Wiltshire
Map ref 2B2

Overlooking the River
Avon, an old town
dominated by its great
church, once a
Benedictine abbey. The
surviving Norman nave
and porch are noted for
fine sculptures, 12th C
arches and musicians'
gallery. *i*

The Chestnuts
Cleverton, Chippenham,
SN15 5BT
☎ (0666) 823472
*Well-appointed and charming
country cottage, close to
Cotswolds and M4, 3 miles
east of Malmesbury. Private
and peaceful, offering
comfortable living and home
cooking.*
Bedrooms: 1 single, 1 double.
Bathrooms: 1 private,
1 public.
Bed & breakfast: £15-£20
single, £25-£40 double.

Half board: £24.50-£29.50
daily, £150-£175 weekly.
Evening meal 7pm (l.o. 8pm).
Parking for 8.

Oakwood Farm
Listed

Upper Minety, Malmesbury,
SN16 9PY
☎ Malmesbury,
(0666) 860286
*130-acre beef/sheep farm.
Quietly situated family-run
farm in village on edge of
Cotswolds. Excellent touring
base. Near St. Leonards
Church.*
Bedrooms: 2 double & 1 twin.
Bathrooms: 1 public.
Bed & breakfast: £11-£13
single, £20-£22 double.
Half board: £19-£21 daily.
Evening meal 6.30pm (l.o.
10am).
Parking for 5.

Devon
Map ref 1C2

3m S. Moretonhampstead
Scattered village with
white-washed cottages
and a tree-shaded green
set in rugged country on
the eastern edge of
Dartmoor. Becka Brook
with its waterfall flows
through the Bovey Valley
nearby and there are
good moorland walks to
Bowerman's Nose, a
lofty, jutting rock stack.

Barracott
Listed

Manaton, Newton Abbot,
TQ13 9XA
☎ (0647) 22312
*16th C. farmhouse on the edge
of Dartmoor below Easdon
Tor. Sheltered and peaceful
with wide views, ideal for
walking and birdwatching.
Signposted on the B3344.*
Bedrooms: 2 twin.
Bathrooms: 2 private.
Bed & breakfast: £18 single,
£30 double.
Half board: £23.50-£28 daily,
£164.50-£196 weekly.
Evening meal 7pm (l.o.
midday).
Parking for 4.
Open March-November.

**WE ADVISE YOU TO CONFIRM YOUR BOOKING
IN WRITING.**

MANATON

Continued

Moorcrest
Langstone Hill, Manaton,
Newton Abbot, TQ13 9UZ
☎ Manaton (064 722) 407
*Moorcrest is set in 2.5 acres of
garden, situated on Dartmoor.
Walking, riding, golfing and
picnicking available. Relax,
away from the madding crowd.*
Bedrooms: 3 double & 1 twin.
Bathrooms: 1 public.
Bed & breakfast: £8-£10
single, £10-£12 double.
Half board: £13.50-£15.50
daily, max. £73.50 weekly.
Evening meal 7.30pm (l.o.
4pm).
Parking for 3.

MARLBOROUGH

Wiltshire
Map ref 2B2

*See also Avebury,
Ogbourne St. George.*
Important market town, in
a river valley cutting
through chalk downlands.
The broad main street
with colonnaded shops
on one side shows a
medley of building styles,
mainly from the Georgian
period. Lanes wind away
on either side and a
church stands at each
end.

Bayardo Farm
Clatford Bottom,
Marlborough, SN8 4DU
☎ Marlborough (0672) 55225
*255-acre mixed farm. 18th C.
farmhouse with beamed
ceilings and open log fires, in
an area of outstanding natural
beauty. Easy access to
Avebury and Marlborough.
Take the A4 from
Marlborough west, turn left
Clatford and continue straight
for 2 miles, house on sharp
corner.*
Bedrooms: 1 double & 1 twin.
Bathrooms: 1 public.
Bed & breakfast: £22-£26
double.
Half board: £16-£18.50 daily.
Parking for 4.
Open March-October.

**PLEASE MENTION
THIS GUIDE WHEN
MAKING A BOOKING.**

The Cross Keys
High Street, Great Bedwyn,
Marlborough, SN8 3NU
☎ (0672) 870678
*Friendly village inn dating
from early 1600's, close to the
Savernake Forest and the
Kennet and Avon Canal.*
Bedrooms: 1 double & 1 twin,
1 family room.
Bathrooms: 1 public.
Bed & breakfast: £12-£18
single, £24-£35 double.
Half board: £16-£25 daily,
£90-£135 weekly.
Lunch available.
Evening meal 7.30pm (l.o.
10pm).
Parking for 3.
Credit: Access, Visa.

MARTINHOE

Devon
Map ref 1C1

3m W. Lynton

Cherryford
Martinhoe, Woody Bay,
EX31 4QP
☎ Parracombe (059 83) 285
*Relaxing country house in 19
acres of woodland with
beautiful views. Two minutes
from sea. Good walking.*
Bedrooms: 2 double & 1 twin,
2 family rooms.
Bathrooms: 4 private,
1 public.
Bed & breakfast: £7-£12
single, £14-£24 double.
Parking for 6.
Open April-October.

MEAVY

Devon
Map ref 1C2

6m SE. Tavistock
Small village with hump-
back bridge, manor
house and pub sheltering
on the slopes of the
wooded Meavy Valley.
The gnarled oak tree
propped against the
church is said to have
been the site of pagan
rituals. Surrounding
moorlands are scattered
with rough pastures, cliffs
and crags, isolated
woodlands and weird
white cones of the china
clay industry.

Callisham Farm
Meavy, Yelverton, PL20 6PS
☎ Yelverton (0822) 853901

---

*120-acre mixed farm. Lovely
old farmhouse 10 miles from
Plymouth, within Dartmoor
National Park. Clean,
comfortable accommodation in
a homely atmosphere, away
from everything.*
Bedrooms: 2 double, 1 family
room.
Bathrooms: 1 public.
Bed & breakfast: £10-£12
single, max. £18 double.
Half board: max. £100
weekly.
Evening meal 6pm (l.o. 7pm).
Parking for 10.

MEETH

Devon
Map ref 1C2

3m N. Hatherleigh

**The Bull and Dragon
Inn**
Meeth, Okehampton,
EX20 3EP
☎ (0837) 810325
*Thatched, oak-beamed 16th C.
inn with character bedrooms
and new ensuite bathrooms.
Intimate bistro.*
Bedrooms: 2 double.
Bathrooms: 2 private.
Bed & breakfast: £16-£20
single, £30-£35 double.
Lunch available.
Evening meal 7pm (l.o.
10pm).
Parking for 25.

MENHENIOT

Cornwall
Map ref 1C2

3m SE. Liskeard

**San Jose Guest
Bungalow**
Menheniot, Liskeard,
PL14 4QS
☎ (0579) 46525
*Bungalow on edge of village of
Menheniot. Entering from A38,
take second turning left past
church. Sign at top of lane.*
Bedrooms: 2 double.
Bathrooms: 1 public.
Bed & breakfast: £8-£10
single, £16-£18 double.
Half board: £77-£91 weekly.
Parking for 3.
Open April-October.

MERTON

Devon
Map ref 1C2

Pinkhill Farm
Merton, Okehampton,
EX20 3DW
☎ Beaford (080 53) 271
*300-acre mixed farm. Quiet
farm holiday with plenty of
food. Lovely walks by River
Torridge; within easy reach of
coast and moors.*
Bedrooms: 1 double & 1 twin,
1 family room.
Bathrooms: 1 public.
Bed & breakfast: max. £10
single, max. £20 double.
Half board: max. £14 daily,
max. £85 weekly.
Evening meal 6pm (l.o. 8pm).
Parking for 6.
Open April-October.

MEVAGISSEY

Cornwall
Map ref 1B3

Small fishing town, a
favourite with
holidaymakers. Earlier
prosperity came from
pilchard fisheries, boat-
building and smuggling.
By the harbour are fish
cellars, some converted,
and a local history
museum is housed in an
old boat-building shed on
the north quay.
Handsome Methodist
chapel; shark fishing,
sailing.

Auraville
Trevarth, The Drive,
Mevagissey, PL26 6RX
☎ (0726) 843293
*A private residence in quiet
and peaceful surroundings, a
short walk from the harbour.
Central for touring Cornwall.*
Bedrooms: 2 double & 2 twin.
Bathrooms: 2 public.
Bed & breakfast: £8.50-£9
single, £17-£18 double.
Parking for 4.

Steep House
Portmellon Cove,
Mevagissey, St. Austell,
PL26 2PH
☎ (0726) 843732
Telex 45526 YOULDEN
*Comfortable rooms with
panoramic views,
complemented by home-made
food. Panelled dining room,
ample parking, outdoor pool,
winter breaks.*

Bedrooms: 5 double & 1 twin, 1 family room.
Bathrooms: 2 public.
Bed & breakfast: from £13 single, from £21 double.
Half board: from £17 daily, from £115 weekly.
Lunch available.
Evening meal 7pm (l.o. 7pm).
Parking for 7.

Treleaven Farm Guest House M

Mevagissey, St. Austell, PL26 6RZ
☎ (0726) 842413
200-acre mixed farm. Quiet position overlooking Mevagissey, only a few minutes' walk from the harbour.
Bedrooms: 3 double & 2 twin, 1 family room.
Bathrooms: 6 private, 1 public.
Bed & breakfast: £28-£36 double.
Half board: £20-£24 daily, £130-£160 weekly.
Lunch available.
Evening meal 6.30pm (l.o. 8pm).
Parking for 6.
Credit: Access, Visa.

Sherrill Farm M

Milton Abbot, Tavistock, PL19 0QJ
☎ (082 287) 217
200 year old restored farmhouse. Every comfort. In countryside yet easy access north/south coast and Dartmoor. Any diet prepared if sufficient notice is given.
Bedrooms: 1 double, 1 family room.
Bathrooms: 2 private.
Bed & breakfast: from £11.50 single, from £23 double.
Half board: from £19 daily, from £119.25 weekly.
Evening meal 6.30pm (l.o. 9.30pm).
Parking for 6.
Credit: Visa.

MAP REFERENCES APPLY TO COLOUR MAPS NEAR THE BACK OF THE GUIDE.

Victorian resort with spreading sands developed around old, steeply-built fishing port on the coast below Exmoor. Former fishermen's cottages stand beside the 17th C harbour and cobbled streets of thatched cottages climb the hill in steps to the church. Boat trips, steam railway; Hobby Horse festival on 1 May.

Higher Rodhuish Farm
Listed

Rodhuish, Minehead, TA24 6QL
☎ Washford (0984) 40253
Comfortable accommodation with home cooking. Situated in the hamlet of Rodhuish 1.5 miles off the A39.
Bedrooms: 1 double & 1 twin.
Bathrooms: 1 public.
Bed & breakfast: £9.50-£10.50 single, £19-£21 double.
Half board: £14.50-£15.50 daily, £98-£105 weekly.
Evening meal 7.30pm.
Parking for 4.

Hindon Farm

Minehead, TA24 8SM
☎ (0643) 5244
500-acre sheep/mixed farm. In a hidden valley within 3 miles of holiday resort. Log fires. Country pursuits.
Bedrooms: 2 double & 1 twin.
Bathrooms: 2 public.
Bed & breakfast: £10.50-£12.50 single, £21-£25 double.
Half board: £27-£31 daily, £100-£140 weekly.
Evening meal 6pm (l.o. 8pm).
Parking for 6.

Meadow Cottage

Venniford, Tivington, Minehead
☎ (0643) 4063
Listed 16th C. farmhouse standing in 1.5-acre garden with open views of farmlands and Dunkery Beacon. On A39 between Minehead and Porlock. Very peaceful.
Bedrooms: 1 single, 1 double & 1 twin.
Bathrooms: 1 public.

Bed & breakfast: £10.50-£12.50 single, £21-£25 double.
Parking for 4.
Open April-October.

Oakfield

Northfield Rd., Minehead, TA24 5QH
☎ Minehead, (0643) 2594
Family accommodation at the foot of North Hill, a few minutes from the town and seafront. Delightful views. Guests may bring own wine. Non-smokers only.
Bedrooms: 5 single, 4 double & 3 twin, 3 family rooms.
Bathrooms: 3 public.
Bed & breakfast: £9.50-£11 single, £19-£22 double.
Half board: £15.50-£17.50 daily, £98 weekly.
Evening meal 7pm (l.o. 4pm).
Parking for 15.

Attractive South Hams town set in rolling countryside, whose perpendicular church has a rare Devon spire.

Best Park

Mary Cross, Modbury, Ivybridge
☎ (0548) 830776
Converted farm cottage and barn in an acre of garden, 1 mile from Modbury.
Bedrooms: 1 double & 1 twin, 1 family room.
Bathrooms: 1 public.
Bed & breakfast: £9.50-£10.50 single, £19-£21 double.
Half board: £14.50-£16 daily, £91.35-£100.50 weekly.
Evening meal 7pm (l.o. 9am).
Parking for 5.
Open April-October.

THERE IS A SPECIAL SECTION IN THIS GUIDE LISTING ACCOMMODATION ESPECIALLY SUITABLE FOR GROUPS AND YOUNG PEOPLE.

2m SE. Bath
Small village of ancient stone cottages in a deep wooded combe beside a small river, formerly a manor of the Bishops of Bath. Overlooked by Combe Down which commands splendid views. 18th C stone lock-up can be seen in the village, and Midford Castle is close by.

Wheelwrights Arms M

Monkton Combe, Bath, BA2 7HD
☎ Limpley Stoke (022 122) 2287
Ideal centre for sightseeing a short distance from Bath. Guest rooms are in converted 17th C. stables and barn.
Bedrooms: 5 double & 3 twin.
Bathrooms: 8 private.
Bed & breakfast: £36-£38 single, £42-£44 double.
Lunch available.
Evening meal 7.30pm (l.o. 10pm).
Parking for 31.
Credit: Access, Visa.

Small market town with a row of 17th C almshouses standing on the Exeter road. Surrounding moorland is scattered with ancient farmhouses, prehistoric sites.

The Dancing Tree
Listed

8 Cross St
Moretonhampstead, TQ13 8NL
☎ (0647) 40265
Bed and breakfast accommodation with licensed restaurant offering snacks, light lunches and full meals including pizzas and fish and chips.
Bedrooms: 1 single, 1 double & 1 twin, 1 family room.
Bathrooms: 1 public.
Bed & breakfast: £9 single, £18 double.
Lunch available.

Continued ▶

MORETON-HAMPSTEAD

Continued

Evening meal 5.30pm (l.o. 8.30pm).
Open February-November.
☎2 ⚡ Ⓛ ♿ Ⓥ 🖤 📺 📟 🛏 ⚓
🐴 🗻 OAP SP

Great Doccombe Farm
⚘⚘

Doccombe,
Moretonhampstead,
TQ13 8SS
☎ (0647) 40694
8-acre mixed smallholding. Lovely old farmhouse in Dartmoor National Park, 2 miles from Moretonhampstead. Comfortable rooms, home cooking. Ideal for walking or touring moors.
Bedrooms: 1 single, 1 double & 1 twin, 1 family room.
Bathrooms: 2 public.
Bed & breakfast: from £9.50 single, from £19 double.
Half board: from £15.50 daily, from £102 weekly.
Evening meal 6pm.
Parking for 6.
Open March-November.
🐴 ⚡ ♿ Ⓛ 🖤 📺 📟 🛏 ✳
🗻 OAP SP

Great Sloncombe Farm
⚘⚘

Moretonhampstead,
TQ13 8QF
☎ (0647) 40595
170-acre dairy farm. Dating from 13th C. set in peaceful surroundings, rich in wildlife. Homely atmosphere, wholesome farmhouse cooking. Comfortable rooms. Packed lunches available.
Bedrooms: 2 double & 1 twin.
Bathrooms: 2 public.
Bed & breakfast: £10-£11 single, £20-£22 double.
Half board: £15.50-£17 daily.
Evening meal 7pm (l.o. 10pm).
Parking for 3.
🐴 ♿ Ⓛ 🖤 Ⓥ 🖤 📺 ✳ 🗻
📟

White Hart Hotel 🅼
⚘⚘⚘

The Square,
Moretonhampstead,
TQ13 8NF
☎ (0647) 40406
Historic inn, in centre of moorland town. Antiques, log fires, rural bar. A la carte restaurant and bar meals.
Bedrooms: 4 single, 8 double & 8 twin.
Bathrooms: 20 private, 3 public.

Bed & breakfast: from £27.50 single, from £45 double.
Half board: from £35.50 daily.
Lunch available.
Evening meal 7pm (l.o. 8.30pm).
Parking for 10.
Credit: Access, Visa, Diners, Amex.
🐴10 ⓔ 🖤 ♿ 🛏 Ⓥ 🖤 📺
🛏 🗻 🔥 🍴 🗻 OAP ⚓ SP 📟
Ⓣ

Wooston Farm
⚘⚘

Moretonhampstead, Newton Abbot, TQ13 8QA
☎ (0647) 40367
280-acre mixed farm. Situated within Dartmoor National Park above the Teign Valley, amid rolling countryside with scenic views and walks. Packed lunches available if required.
Bedrooms: 2 single, 1 double, 1 family room.
Bathrooms: 1 public.
Bed & breakfast: £8.50-£9.50 single, £17-£19 double.
Half board: £14-£15 daily, £90-£95 weekly.
Evening meal 6pm (l.o. 6.30pm).
Open March-October, December.
🐴 ♿ Ⓛ 🖤 🖤 📺 📟 🗻 🗻

MORTEHOE

Devon
Map ref 1C1

Old coastal village with small, basically Norman church. Wild cliffs, inland combes; sand and surf at Woolacombe.

The Cleeve House 🅼

Mortehoe, Woolacombe,
EX34 7ED
☎ Woolacombe
(0271) 870719
Large Victorian house set in its own grounds, in the old world village of Mortehoe.
Bedrooms: 5 double & 1 twin.
Bathrooms: 4 private, 1 public.
Bed & breakfast: £26-£34 double.
Parking for 9.
Open April-October.
🖤 ♿ Ⓛ 🖤 📺 📟 🛏 ✳ 🐴
🗻 SP

┌─────────────────────────┐
│ **PLEASE CHECK** │
│ **PRICES AND OTHER** │
│ **DETAILS AT THE** │
│ **TIME OF BOOKING.** │
└─────────────────────────┘

MORWENSTOW

Cornwall
Map ref 1C2

6m N. Bude
Scattered parish on the wild north Cornish coast. The church, beautifully situated in a deep combe by the sea, has a fine Norman doorway and 15th C bench-ends. Its unique vicarage was built by the 19th C poet-priest Robert Hawker. There is a memorial to drowned seamen in the churchyard. Nearby are Cornwall's highest cliffs.

Cornakey Farm

Morwenstow, Bude,
EX23 9SS
☎ (028 883) 260
220-acre mixed farm. Convenient coastal walking area with extensive views of sea and cliffs from bedrooms. Home cooking. Pony rides.
Bedrooms: 1 double, 1 family room.
Bathrooms: 1 public.
Bed & breakfast: £8-£9 single, £16-£18 double.
Half board: £11-£12.50 daily, £74-£84 weekly.
Evening meal 6.50pm (l.o. 6.50pm).
Parking for 2.
Open January-November.
🐴 Ⓛ 🖤 🖤 📺 ⚓ 🐴 🗻 SP

MUDDIFORD

Devon
Map ref 1C1

3m N. Barnstaple

Whitehall Farm

Lower Blakewell, Muddiford,
Barnstaple, EX31 4ET
☎ Barnstaple (0271) 42955
70-acre sheep and beef farm. Set in Devonshire countryside, very quiet and peaceful, with outdoor children's play area. Take the A39 Lynton road out of Barnstaple, fork left on to the A3230, turn off main road towards fisheries, continue to end.
Bedrooms: 1 double & 1 twin, 1 family room.
Bathrooms: 1 public.
Bed & breakfast: £10-£15 single, £30-£40 double.
Half board: £15-£20 daily, £85-£100 weekly.
Evening meal 6pm (l.o. 6pm).
Parking for 3.
Open April-October.
🐴 ♿ 🖤 Ⓛ 🛏 🖤 📺 📟 🛏
✳ 🗻 OAP SP

NETTLETON

Wiltshire
Map ref 2B2

7m NW. Chippenham

The Nettleton Arms

Nettleton, Chippenham,
SN14 7NP
☎ (0249) 782783
17th C., Cotswold stone inn close to Castle Combe, Badminton and Bath.
Bedrooms: 1 double & 2 twin, 1 family room.
Bathrooms: 4 private.
Bed & breakfast: £22-£28 single, £35-£42 double.
Parking for 50.
Credit: Access, Visa, Amex.
🐴 ♿ ☎ ⓔ 🖤 ♿ 🛏 Ⓥ 🖤
🍴 ✳ 🗻 🐴 OAP

NEWTON POPPLEFORD

Devon
Map ref 1D2

3m NW. Sidmouth
Interesting riverside village whose 13th C development as an agricultural settlement can still be traced. Today's thatched cottages date from the 17th C, in the centre is a Victorian church.

Charlton House
⚘⚘

High St., Newton Poppleford, Sidmouth,
EX10 0ED
☎ Colaton Raleigh (0395) 68189
Friendly, family-run business, close to coastal resorts. Easy access to motorway and Exeter.
Bedrooms: 1 single, 2 family rooms.
Bathrooms: 1 public.
Bed & breakfast: £10-£12 single, £20-£22 double.
Half board: £16-£18 daily.
Evening meal 6.30pm (l.o. 4.30pm).
Parking for 4.
🐴 ♿ Ⓛ 🛏 Ⓥ 🖤 📺 📟 🛏
🗻 OAP SP

┌─────────────────────────┐
│ **GROUPS, CONSORTIA** │
│ **AND AGENCIES** │
│ **SPECIALISING** │
│ **IN FARM AND** │
│ **COUNTRY HOLIDAYS** │
│ **ARE LISTED IN A** │
│ **SPECIAL SECTION** │
│ **OF THIS GUIDE.** │
└─────────────────────────┘

NORTH BUCKLAND

Devon
Map ref 1C1

5m SW. Ilfracombe

Denham Country House 🏠
😃😃

North Buckland, Braunton,
EX33 1HY
☎ Croyde (0271) 890297
160-acre mixed farm. Family-run farmhouse which invites visiting families to join in the farming activities. Home from home.
Bedrooms: 1 single, 2 double & 1 twin, 3 family rooms.
Bathrooms: 2 public.
Bed & breakfast: from £15 single, from £30 double.
Half board: from £21 daily, from £130 weekly.
Lunch available.
Evening meal 6pm (l.o. 2pm).
Parking for 7.
🛇 🐚 Ⅴ 🗲 📺 🛋 🚲 ⅹⅰ 🐾
ⅅ⅋ ⸤SP⸥

NORTH MOLTON

Devon
Map ref 1C1

3m NE. South Molton
Village on the southern slopes of Exmoor, a centre for local copper mines in the 19th C. A 17th C monument in the church shows the effigies of a mining landlord and his family.

Crangs Heasleigh
Listed

Heasley Mill, South Molton,
EX36 3LE
☎ North Molton
(059 84) 268
180-acre stock farm. 12th C. Devon longhouse within Exmoor National Park. Of special interest are local old mines. Good centre for touring north Devon and Exmoor. Farm food.
Bedrooms: 1 single, 1 double & 1 twin, 1 family room.
Bathrooms: 1 public.
Bed & breakfast: £9-£10 single, £18-£20 double.
Parking for 10.
🛇 🐚 🐾 ⅢⅬ 🗲 📺 Ⅲ 🛋
ⅹⅰ ⅅ⅋ ⸤SP⸥ 🐾

Homedale
😃😃

North Molton, EX36 3HL
☎ (059 84) 206
Comfortable Victorian house in a village 3 miles from South Molton. Easy access to Exmoor.

Bedrooms: 1 single, 1 twin, 1 family room.
Bathrooms: 1 public.
Bed & breakfast: max. £9 single, max. £18 double.
Half board: max. £13.50 daily, max. £85 weekly.
Evening meal 7.30pm (l.o. 6.30pm).
Open March-October.
🛇 🐚 ⅢⅬ 🛋 Ⅴ 🗲 📺 Ⅲ 🛋
ⅹⅰ ⅅ⅋ ⸤SP⸥ 🐾

NORTH PETHERTON

Somerset
Map ref 1D1

3m S. Bridgwater
Small town near the eastern end of the Quantock Hills.

Walnut Tree Inn 🏠
😃😃😃

North Petherton, Bridgwater,
TA6 6QA
☎ (0278) 662255
An 18th C. coaching inn on A38, 1 mile from M5 exit 24. A welcome stopover for businessmen and tourists.
Bedrooms: 2 single, 12 double & 5 twin, 1 family room.
Bathrooms: 20 private.
Bed & breakfast: £35-£42 single, £50-£62 double.
Lunch available.
Evening meal 7pm (l.o. 10pm).
Parking for 80.
Credit: Access, Visa, Diners, Amex.
🛇 🐚 🐾 📞 🖾 🗲 🛋 Ⅴ 🗲
Ⅲ 🛋 🐾 🐚 Ⅴ 🐾 ⅹⅰ 🐾
⸤SP⸥ ⸤T⸥

NORTH TAWTON

Devon
Map ref 1C2

6m NE. Okehampton

Cadditon Farm
😃😃

Bondleigh, North Tawton,
EX20 2AW
☎ (083 782) 450
150-acre dairy farm. Devon thatched farmhouse with inglenook fireplace, offering home comfort and hospitality. Electric blankets in all rooms.
Bedrooms: 1 double, 1 family room.
Bathrooms: 2 public.
Bed & breakfast: £9-£10 single, £18-£20 double.
Half board: £14-£15 daily, from £98 weekly.
Evening meal 6pm (l.o. 7pm).
Parking for 10.
Open March-November.
🛇 🐚 🖾 🐾 ⅢⅬ 🗲 📺 Ⅲ 🛋 🐾
ⅹⅰ 🐾 ⅅ⅋ 🐾

Oaklands Farm
😃😃

North Tawton, EX20 2BQ
☎ (083 782) 340
132-acre mixed farm. Oaklands is centrally situated for north and south Devon coasts and Dartmoor. Cream teas. Very warm welcome.
Bedrooms: 2 double.
Bathrooms: 1 public.
Bed & breakfast: from £8 single, from £16 double.
Half board: from £12.50 daily, from £80 weekly.
Evening meal 6pm (l.o. 8pm).
Parking for 4.
Open April-October.
🛇 🐚 ⅢⅬ 🛋 📺 🛋 ✓ ❄
ⅹⅰ ⅅ⅋

NORTHLEW

Devon
Map ref 1C2

Northcote Farm

Northlew, Okehampton,
EX20 3BT
☎ (0837) 3046
45-acre farm. Peaceful family home in own nature reserve and spacious gardens. Ring for route instructions.
Bedrooms: 3 double & 1 twin.
Bathrooms: 2 private, 1 public.
Bed & breakfast: £13.50-£16.50 single, £19-£25 double.
Half board: £14.50-£22.50 daily, £99-£155 weekly.
Lunch available.
Evening meal 7pm (l.o. 8.30pm).
Parking for 12.
🛇 5 🐚 🖾 🐾 🛋 Ⅴ 🗲 🛋 📺
🛋 🐚 ✓ ✓ ❄ ⅹⅰ 🐾 ⅅ⅋ 🐾
⸤SP⸥ ⸤T⸥

NORTON ST. PHILIP

Somerset
Map ref 2B2

The Plaine
😃😃😃

Norton St. Philip, Bath,
BA3 6LE
☎ Faulkland (037 387) 723
In the heart of a conservation village, facing the famous George Inn, one time headquarters of the Duke of Monmouth. 6 miles from Georgian Bath in unspoilt countryside. Peaceful walks.
Bedrooms: 2 double & 1 twin.
Bathrooms: 1 private, 1 public.
Bed & breakfast: max. £17 single, £30-£36 double.
Parking for 3.
🛇 🐚 🖾 🖾 🐾 ⅢⅬ Ⅴ 🗲 Ⅲ
🛋 ⅹⅰ 🐾 ⅅ⅋ 🐾

OAKFORD

Devon
Map ref 1D1

3m W. Bampton

Harton Farm
Listed

Oakford, Tiverton,
EX16 9HH
☎ (039 85) 209
54-acre mixed farm. Stone farmhouse in secluded position, yet within a quarter of a mile of the A361. Home-baking and home-grown vegetables, dairy produce, pork and lamb.
Bedrooms: 1 double & 2 twin.
Bathrooms: 1 public.
Bed & breakfast: £8-£9 single, £16-£18 double.
Half board: £12-£13 daily, £84 weekly.
Evening meal 7.30pm.
Parking for 6.
🛇 🐚 4 🐚 ⅢⅬ Ⅴ 🗲 📺 🐚 ❄ ⅹⅰ
🐾

Higher Western Restaurant

Oakford, Tiverton, EX16 9JE
☎ Anstey Mills (039 84) 210
Old world residential restaurant, with accent on food at realistic prices using fresh local produce. Good touring base.
Bedrooms: 2 double & 1 twin.
Bathrooms: 3 private, 1 public.
Bed & breakfast: max. £11.50 single, max. £23 double.
Half board: max. £20.50 daily, max. £143.50 weekly.
Lunch available.
Evening meal 7pm (l.o. 10pm).
Parking for 15.
Credit: Access, Visa.
🛇 🐚 🛋 Ⅴ 🗲 Ⅲ 🛋 ❄ ⅹⅰ ⸤SP⸥

OGBOURNE ST. GEORGE

Wiltshire
Map ref 2B2

3m N. Marlborough

Laurel Cottage
😃😃

Southend, Ogbourne St. George, Marlborough,
SN8 1SG
☎ (067 284) 288
16th C. thatched cottage, a fully modernised family home. Low-beamed ceilings and inglenook fireplace.
Bedrooms: 2 double, 1 family room.
Bathrooms: 1 public.
Continued ▶

OGBOURNE ST. GEORGE

Continued

Bed & breakfast: £15-£16
single, £20-£26 double.
Evening meal 6pm.
Parking for 4.
Open April-October.

OKEHAMPTON

Devon
Map ref 1C2

*See also Bridestowe,
Hatherleigh, Jacobstowe,
North Tawton, Sampford
Courtenay, Throwleigh.*
Busy market town near
the high tors of northern
Dartmoor. The Victorian
church, with William
Morris windows and a
15th C tower, stands on
the site of a Saxon
church. A Norman castle
ruin overlooks the river to
the west of the town.

Fowley House
Tavistock Rd., Okehampton,
EX20 4LR
☎ (0837) 2294
*Spacious, well-furnished
Victorian house set well back
in large gardens, overlooking
Dartmoor and the surrounding
countryside. 2 miles west of
Okehampton.*
Bedrooms: 2 double & 1 twin,
1 family room.
Bathrooms: 1 public.
Bed & breakfast: £11.50-
£12.50 single, £23-£25 double.
Half board: £17.50-£18.50
daily, £120-£127 weekly.
Evening meal 7pm (l.o. 6pm).
Parking for 6.
Open April-October.

Hughslade Farm
Okehampton, EX20 4LR
☎ (0837) 2883
*500-acre sheep and cattle
farm. Large family-run
working farm, where the same
family has been offering guest
accommodation for over 30
years. Central for touring
Dartmoor and the coast.*
Bedrooms: 1 single, 2 double
& 2 twin, 1 family room.
Bathrooms: 2 public.
Bed & breakfast: £12.50
single, £20-£25 double.
Half board: max. £18 daily,
max. £95 weekly.

Evening meal 6.30pm (l.o.
5pm).
Parking for 10.

ORCHESTON

Wiltshire
Map ref 2B2

Cozens House Cottage
Orcheston St. Mary,
Salisbury, SP3 4RW
☎ Shrewton (0980) 620257
*Beautifully converted 18th C.
barn set in secluded and
delightful surroundings, 1 mile
from Shrewton off the A360 to
Devizes.*
Bedrooms: 2 twin.
Bathrooms: 1 private,
1 public.
Bed & breakfast: £11.50-
£12.50 single, £23-£25 double.
Parking for 3.
Open April-November.

OSMINGTON

Dorset
Map ref 2B3

Attractive village near the
coast on the road to
Weymouth. Close by on a
hillside is an equestrian
figure of George III,
Weymouth's patron, cut
into the chalk.

Dingle Dell
Church La., Osmington,
Weymouth, DT3 6EW
☎ Preston (Dorset)
(0305) 832378
*Attractive rose-covered house
with charming garden in quiet
location on edge of village.
Large, sunny, well-furnished
rooms with views over
countryside. Local books and
tourist information.*
Bedrooms: 1 double & 1 twin.
Bathrooms: 1 public.
Bed & breakfast: £21-£24
double.
Parking for 3.
Open March-October.

THERE IS A SPECIAL
SECTION IN THIS
GUIDE LISTING
ACCOMMODATION
ESPECIALLY
SUITABLE FOR
GROUPS AND
YOUNG PEOPLE.

OTTERY ST. MARY

Devon
Map ref 1D2

See also Whimple.
Former wool town with
modern light industry set
in rural countryside on the
River Otter. The
Cromwellian commander,
Fairfax, made his
headquarters here briefly
during the Civil War. The
interesting church is built
to cathedral plan, dating
from the 14th C. Rolling
of tar barrels custom on
Bonfire Night.

Heathlands
Higher Metcombe, Ottery St.
Mary, EX11 1SH
☎ (040 481) 4065
*10-acre mixed farm. Spacious,
comfortable country house in
peaceful and secluded
surroundings overlooking Otter
Valley. Working smallholding
with poultry, fruit and
vegetables.*
Bedrooms: 1 single, 2 twin,
1 family room.
Bathrooms: 1 public.
Bed & breakfast: £9.50
single, £19 double.
Parking for 4.
Open April-October.

Home Farm
Listed
Escott, Ottery St. Mary,
EX11 1LU
☎ Honiton (0404) 850241
*300-acre mixed farm. 16th C.
farmhouse with oak beams, in
beautiful parkland near Ottery
St. Mary. 1 mile from A30, 6
miles from coast. Warm
welcome. Own produce.*
Bedrooms: 1 double & 1 twin,
1 family room.
Bathrooms: 2 public.
Bed & breakfast: £19-£21
double.
Half board: from £100
weekly.
Evening meal 7pm (l.o. 7pm).
Parking for 4.
Open April-October.

Pitt Farm
Listed
Ottery St. Mary, EX11 1NL
☎ (040 481) 2439
*190-acre mixed farm.
Thatched 16th C. farmhouse
offering country fare. On
B3176, half a mile off A30 and
within easy reach of all east
Devon coastal resorts.*

Bedrooms: 2 double & 2 twin,
2 family rooms.
Bathrooms: 3 public.
Bed & breakfast: £10-£12
single, £20-£24 double.
Half board: £16.50-£18 daily.
Evening meal 7pm (l.o. 5pm).
Parking for 6.

PAIGNTON

Devon
Map ref 1D2

Lively seaside resort with
a pretty harbour on
Torbay. Bronze Age and
Saxon sites are occupied
by the 15th C church,
which has a Norman door
and font. The beautiful
Chantry Chapel was built
by local landowners the
Kirkhams whose
medieval family home is
open to the public.

Brendoone
3 Mortimer Ave., Paignton,
TQ3 1LR
☎ (0803) 521839
*Small family-run establishment
quietly situated in beautiful
Torbay. Level walk to beaches,
shops and buses.*
Bedrooms: 1 single, 1 double,
1 family room.
Bathrooms: 1 public.
Bed & breakfast: £8-£10
single, £15-£18 double.
Half board: £70-£79 weekly.
Evening meal 6pm (l.o. 6pm).
Parking for 2.
Open February-November.

Marine Guest House
41 Dartmouth Rd., Paignton,
TQ4 5AE
☎ (0803) 552277
*In the heart of Paignton in one
of the finest seafront positions
on the English Riviera.*
Bedrooms: 1 double & 1 twin,
2 family rooms.
Bathrooms: 1 public.
Bed & breakfast: £8-£10
single, £16-£20 double.
Half board: £13-£15 daily,
£75-£95 weekly.
Evening meal 6pm (l.o. 6pm).
Parking for 4.

PLEASE MENTION
THIS GUIDE WHEN
MAKING A BOOKING.

PEASEDOWN ST. JOHN

Avon
Map ref 2B2

2m NE. Radstock

Eastfield Farm Guest House
😊😊

Eastfield, Dunkerton Hill, Peasedown St John, Bath, BA2 8PF
☎ Radstock (0761) 32161
Spacious farmhouse set in 3 acres of garden and paddocks. 5 miles south of Bath overlooking the Cam Valley.
Bedrooms: 1 double & 2 twin.
Bathrooms: 2 public.
Bed & breakfast: £12.50-£15 single, £20-£25 double.
Parking for 5.
🛇 Ⓤ🖰 🛏 �🅣 🎞 ❋ 🗡 🏠

PELYNT

Cornwall
Map ref 1C2

Trenake Farm
😊😊

Pelynt, Looe, PL13 2LT
☎ (0503) 20216
250-acre mixed farm. 14th C. farmhouse, 5 miles from Looe and 3 miles from Talland Bay beach.
Bedrooms: 1 single, 1 double, 1 family room.
Bathrooms: 1 public.
Bed & breakfast: £8.50-£10.50 single, £17-£21 double.
Half board: from £90 weekly.
Parking for 6.
Open April-October.
🛇 ♻ Ⓤ 🛏 ⍥ ⍥ ❋ 🗡 🏠 🏠

> **GROUPS, CONSORTIA AND AGENCIES SPECIALISING IN FARM AND COUNTRY HOLIDAYS ARE LISTED IN A SPECIAL SECTION OF THIS GUIDE.**

> **INDIVIDUAL PROPRIETORS HAVE SUPPLIED ALL DETAILS OF ACCOMMODATION. ALTHOUGH WE DO CHECK FOR ACCURACY, WE ADVISE YOU TO CONFIRM PRICES AND OTHER INFORMATION AT THE TIME OF BOOKING.**

PENDEEN

Cornwall
Map ref 1B3

2m N. St. Just
Small village on the beautiful coast road from Land's End to St. Ives. A romantic landscape of craggy inland cliffs covered with bracken shelving to a rocky shore. There are numerous prehistoric sites, disused tin mines, a mine museum at Geevor and a lighthouse at Pendeen Watch.

Trewellard Manor Farm

Pendeen, Penzance, TR19 7SU
☎ Penzance (0736) 788526
250-acre dairy farm. Friendly and comfortable atmosphere, home cooking and seasonal log fires.
Bedrooms: 2 double & 1 twin.
Bathrooms: 1 public.
Bed & breakfast: £10-£12 single, £20-£24 double.
Evening meal 5.30pm (l.o. 4pm).
Parking for 3.
🛇 🖰 🛏 ⍥ 🎞 ♨ ⍟ ∪ ⍦ 🗡 🏠

PENHALLOW

Cornwall
Map ref 1B3

2m S. Perranporth

Lambourne Castle Farm

Penhallow, Truro, TR4 9LQ
☎ Truro (0872) 572365
62-acre mixed farm. Stone-built farmhouse, tastefully furnished, with plenty of home-produced farmhouse food cooked by the proprietors.
Bedrooms: 1 double & 1 twin, 2 family rooms.
Bathrooms: 1 public.
Bed & breakfast: £8-£9 single, £15-£18 double.
Half board: £11-£13 daily, £75-£87 weekly.
Evening meal 6pm (l.o. 4pm).
Parking for 4.
Open April-October.
🛇4 Ⓤ 🛏 🐾 🗡 🏠

PENZANCE

Cornwall
Map ref 1B3

See also Ludgvan.
Granite-built resort and fishing port on Mount's Bay, with mainly Victorian promenade and some fine Regency terraces. Former prosperity came from tin trade, pilchard fishing and smuggling. Grand Georgian-style church by harbour. Georgian Egyptian building at head of Chapel Street and the municipal Morrab Gardens. ⧉

Con Amore Guest House
😊😊

38 Morrab Rd., Penzance, TR18 4EX
☎ (0736) 63423
Charming, modernised Victorian guesthouse, located 1 minute from South Beach, promenade and tropical gardens.
Bedrooms: 1 single, 3 double & 1 twin, 2 family rooms.
Bathrooms: 2 public; 2 private showers.
Bed & breakfast: £10-£11 single, £18-£22 double.
Credit: Access, Visa.
🛇 🖵 Ⓤ 🛆 🛏 ⍥ 🗡 🏠 🏠

Gray Gables

3 Morrab Rd., Penzance, TR18 4EL
☎ (0736) 65845
Victorian town house central for touring Penwith Peninsula. Overseas visitors especially welcome.
Bedrooms: 1 single, 2 double, 2 family rooms.
Bathrooms: 1 public; 3 private showers.
Bed & breakfast: £8.50 single, £17 double.
Half board: £13 daily, £84 weekly.
Evening meal 7pm (l.o. 5pm).
🛇 🛆 Ⓥ 🛏 ⍥ 🛋 🗡 🏠

Kenegie Home Farm

Gulval, Penzance, TR20 8YN
☎ (0736) 62515
185-acre arable farm. Farmhouse built in 1987. All rooms have views over Mount's Bay. On the B3311, 2.5 miles from Penzance.
Bedrooms: 1 double & 1 twin, 1 family room.
Bathrooms: 1 public.
Bed & breakfast: £10-£14 single, £22-£30 double.

Half board: £17.50-£22.50 daily, £120-£130 weekly.
Evening meal 7pm (l.o. 4pm).
Parking for 6.
Open February-November.
🛇1 🛆 🖵 🛏 Ⓤ 🛏 ⍥ 🎞 🗡 🏠

Lynwood Guest House
😊😊

41 Morrab Rd., Penzance, TR18 4EX
☎ (0736) 65871
Lynwood Guesthouse offers a warm welcome and is situated between promenade and town centre, close to all amenities.
Bedrooms: 1 single, 1 double & 2 twin, 2 family rooms.
Bathrooms: 3 public.
Bed & breakfast: £9.50-£10 single, £18-£19 double.
Credit: Visa.
🛇 🛆 🖵 Ⓤ ♻ 🛏 ⍥ 🎞 🗡 🏠

Union Hotel Ⓜ

Chapel St., Penzance, TR18 4AE
☎ (0736) 62319
16th C. hotel in town centre. Some seaviews. Historic dining room and Georgian theatre. 2 bars. Log fires.
Bedrooms: 3 single, 12 double & 11 twin, 3 family rooms.
Bathrooms: 18 private, 5 public.
Bed & breakfast: £14.50-£19.95 single, £27-£35.90 double.
Half board: £22-£27.45 daily, £141.50-£177.50 weekly.
Lunch available.
Evening meal 6pm (l.o. 8.30pm).
Parking for 20.
Credit: Access, Visa, Amex.
🛇 🛆 ♻ 🛆 Ⓥ 🛏 ⍥ 🎞 🖫 🛋 ♟ ᐅ 🗡 ⍾ ⓢⓟ 🏠 Ⓣ

Yacht Inn

Promenade, Penzance, TR18 4AU
☎ (0736) 62787
On seafront with most rooms offering sea views. Real ale, local seafood a speciality.
Bedrooms: 1 single, 1 double & 1 twin, 1 family room.
Bathrooms: 2 public.
Bed & breakfast: £10-£12 single, £24-£28 double.
Half board: £13.75-£18.90 daily, £97.25-£132.30 weekly.
Lunch available.
Evening meal 7pm (l.o. 9pm).
Parking for 8.
🛇5 ♻ 🛆 Ⓥ 🛏 ⍥ 🎞 🛋 ♟

PERRANPORTH

Cornwall
Map ref 1B2

See also Penhallow.
Small seaside resort
developed around a
former mining village.
Today's attractions
include exciting surf,
rocks, caves and
extensive sand dunes.

Ponsmere Hotel M
😊😊

Ponsmere Rd., Perranporth,
TR6 0BW
☎ (0872) 572225
A family hotel with plenty of
facilities for children, situated
by Perranporth's golden beach.
Well placed for touring
Cornwall.
Bedrooms: 6 single, 13 double
& 10 twin, 47 family rooms.
Bathrooms: 74 private,
3 public.
Bed & breakfast: £14-£19
single, £26-£36 double.
Half board: £20-£25 daily,
£112-£161 weekly.
Lunch available.
Evening meal 6.30pm (l.o.
8pm).
Parking for 80.
Open April-October.
Credit: Access, Visa.
🕙🔥🖃🞏🞏 🗓 V 🚲 📺
🍴 🖵 🖵 🗂 🖼 🛏 🞏 🗭 ⬅ 🏃
🐴 🗂 SP T

PETER TAVY

Devon
Map ref 1C2

5m NE. Tavistock

Churchtown
Listed

Peter Tavy, Tavistock,
PL19 9NN
☎ Mary Tavy (082 281) 477
Large Victorian house in own
grounds on edge of village.
Secluded and quiet with
competition stables attached.
Bedrooms: 2 single, 1 double,
1 family room.
Bathrooms: 1 public.
Bed & breakfast: £8-£9
single, £16-£18 double.
Parking for 6.
🕙 🦯 UL 🞏 U ▶ 🗂

PIDDLETRENTHIDE

Dorset
Map ref 2B3

The Poachers Inn
😊😊😊

Piddletrenthide, Dorchester,
DT2 7QX
☎ (030 04) 358
16th C. listed building with
large riverside garden. Bar
meals and dining room.
Bedrooms: 4 double & 1 twin,
1 family room.
Bathrooms: 6 private.
Bed & breakfast: max. £18
single, max. £29 double.
Lunch available.
Evening meal 6pm (l.o.
10pm).
Parking for 25.
🕙 🦯 🞏 🞏 🗓 🖵 🞏 ➡ 🏃
🌸 🗂 OAP 🞏 🖼

PLYMOUTH

Devon
Map ref 1C2

Devon's largest city,
major port and naval
base, shopping and
tourist centre. Rebuilt
after 1940's bombing
behind old harbour area,
the Barbican. Old
merchants' houses and
inns, customs houses,
Prysten House in
Barbican and ambitious
architecture in modern
centre, with aquarium,
museum and art gallery.
Superb coastal views
over Plymouth Sound
from The Hoe. 🖵

Phantele Guest House
😊😊

176 Devonport Rd., Stoke,
Plymouth, PL1 5RD
☎ (0752) 561506
A small family-run guesthouse
about 2 miles from city centre.
Convenient base for touring.
Close to continental and
Torpoint ferries.
Bedrooms: 2 single, 2 twin,
2 family rooms.
Bathrooms: 2 public.
Bed & breakfast: £8.50-
£10.50 single, £17-£19 double.
Half board: £12-£14 daily,
from £80 weekly.
Evening meal 6pm (l.o. 2pm).
🕙 🞏 🖵 📺 🞏 ➡ 🞏 🗂 OAP
SP

POLBATHIC

Cornwall
Map ref 1C2

6m W. Torpoint

The Copse, Saint
Winnolls
Polbathic, Torpoint,
PL11 3DX
☎ St. Germans (0503) 30205
600-acre mixed farm.
Comfortable farmhouse in
quiet location, midway between
Plymouth and Looe. 2 miles
from beach.
Bedrooms: 2 double & 1 twin.
Bathrooms: 2 public.
Bed & breakfast: £8-£9
single, £16-£18 double.
Half board: £13-£14 daily,
£85-£90 weekly.
Evening meal 7pm (l.o.
8.30pm).
Parking for 3.
Open April-October.
🕙 🞏 🞏 UL 🗶 📺 🞏 ➡ 🌸
🞏 🖼

The Halfway House
Listed

Polbathic, Torpoint,
PL11 3EY
☎ St. Germans (0503) 30202
16th C. coaching inn with real
ales and extensive bar menu.
Candlelit restaurant and beer
garden.
Bedrooms: 1 single, 1 double,
2 family rooms.
Bathrooms: 1 public.
Bed & breakfast: £12.50
single, £25 double.
Lunch available.
Evening meal 6pm (l.o.
10.30pm).
Parking for 12.
🕙 🞏 🗓 V 🞏 🌸 🖼

POLPERRO

Cornwall
Map ref 1C3

Picturesque fishing village
clinging to steep valley
slopes about its harbour.
A river splashes past
cottages and narrow
lanes twist between. The
harbour mouth, guarded
by jagged rocks, is closed
by heavy timbers during
storms.

New House
Talland Hill, Polperro,
PL13 2RX
☎ (0503) 72206
Offering spacious and
comfortable rooms with lovely
garden, harbour and sea views.
Cliff walks and sailing nearby.
Bedrooms: 2 double & 2 twin.

Bathrooms: 1 private,
1 public.
Bed & breakfast: £20-£26
double.
🕙 UL V 🞏 🞏 📺 🖼 🞏 🖼

PORLOCK

Somerset
Map ref 1D1

Village set between steep
Exmoor hills and the sea
at the head of beautiful
Porlock Vale. The narrow
street shows a medley of
building styles. South
westward is Porlock Weir
with its old houses and
tiny harbour and further
along the wooded shingle
shore is Culbone is
England's smallest
medieval church.

The Cleeve
Parsons St., Hawkcombe,
Porlock, TA24 8QW
☎ (0643) 862351
Peacefully sheltered country
house in woodland setting, with
fine views of Porlock and
Exmoor. Comfortably
furnished; relaxed, homely
atmosphere.
Bedrooms: 1 double & 1 twin,
1 family room.
Bathrooms: 2 private,
1 public.
Bed & breakfast: £18-£23
double.
Parking for 6.
Open April-October.
🕙 🞏 UL 🞏 V 🞏 📺 🞏 🌸
🖼

Cloutsham Farm
Porlock
☎ (0643) 862839
230-acre mixed hill farm.
Remote National Trust
farmhouse on Exmoor.
Traditional farmhouse fare, log
fires, ideal for walking and
riding.
Bedrooms: 2 double & 1 twin,
1 family room.
Bathrooms: 1 public;
1 private shower.
Bed & breakfast: £10-£11
single, £20-£22 double.
Half board: £16-£17 daily,
£100-£105 weekly.
Evening meal 7pm (l.o. 8pm).
Parking for 6.
🕙 UL 🞏 V 🞏 📺 🞏 🞏 U
🌸 🞏 🖼

Holmbush
Porlock Hill, Porlock,
TA24 8QH
☎ (0643) 862853

THERE IS A SPECIAL SECTION IN THIS
GUIDE LISTING ACCOMMODATION ESPECIALLY
SUITABLE FOR GROUPS AND YOUNG PEOPLE.

Beautifully converted 18th C. farmhouse in peaceful, idyllic surroundings with magnificent panoramic views. Ideal centre for touring, walking, horseriding and birdwatching.
Bedrooms: 2 double & 1 twin.
Bathrooms: 2 private, 1 public.
Bed & breakfast: £20-£26 double.
Parking for 6.

PORT ISAAC

Cornwall
Map ref 1B2

See also St. Teath.
Old fishing port of whitewashed cottages, twisting stairways and narrow alleys. A stream splashes down through the centre to the harbour. Nearby stands a 19th C folly, Doyden Castle, with a magnificent view of the coast.

Trewetha Farm

Port Isaac, PL29 3RU
☎ (0208) 880256
20-acre smallholding. A 200-year-old farmhouse with poultry, sheep and miniature ponies. Close to beaches and fishing, with views of sea and countryside.
Bedrooms: 2 double, 1 family room.
Bathrooms: 1 public.
Bed & breakfast: £8.25-£8.75 single, £15.50-£16.50 double.
Parking for 6.

PORTHCURNO

Cornwall
Map ref 1B3

3m SE. Land's End
Beautifully-sited village near a beach with white sand and turquoise sea enclosed in granite cliffs. The Minack open air theatre of concrete and granite slabs, perched 200 ft above the sea, has a good view of Treryn Dinas to the east.

Corniche

Trebehor, Porthcurno, Penzance, TR19 6LX
☎ Sennen (0736) 871685

Large dormer bungalow in own grounds. Quiet scenic location, 2 miles from Porthcurno, Minack Theatre, Land's End and Sennen Cove.
Bedrooms: 1 single, 3 double & 1 twin, 1 family room.
Bathrooms: 2 public.
Bed & breakfast: £8.50-£10 single, £17-£20 double.
Half board: £12.50-£14 daily, £84-£98 weekly.
Evening meal 6.30pm (l.o. 3.30pm).
Parking for 8.

POUNDSGATE

Devon
Map ref 1C2

4m NW. Ashburton
Dartmoor village near the Dart Valley. River Dart Country Park is 2 miles to the south east.

New Cott Farm

Poundsgate, Newton Abbot, TQ13 7PD
☎ (036 43) 421
130-acre mixed farm. Own trout fishing and walking, riding, golf and bird watching locally. Friendly relaxed atmosphere, plenty of food, good facilities.
Bedrooms: 2 double & 1 twin, 1 family room.
Bathrooms: 4 private, 1 public.
Bed & breakfast: £23-£25 double.
Half board: £17-£18 daily, £98-£100 weekly.
Evening meal 6.30pm (l.o. 5.30pm).
Parking for 4.

POWERSTOCK

Dorset
Map ref 2A3

4m NE. Bridport
Hilly village of mellow stone houses, overlooked by its church. Partly rebuilt in the 19th C, the church retains a fine Norman chancel arch, gargoyles and 15th C carvings in the south porch.

Powerstock Mill

Powerstock, Bridport, DT6 3SL
☎ (030 885) 213

50-acre dairy farm. Comfortable, old farmhouse nestling in a valley, in an area of outstanding natural beauty. Only four miles away from beautiful coastline.
Bedrooms: 1 single, 2 double & 1 twin.
Bathrooms: 1 public.
Bed & breakfast: £12-£14 single, £24-£28 double.
Parking for 7.
Open January-November.

PRIDDY

Somerset
Map ref 2A2

4m NW. Wells
Village in the Mendips, formerly a lead-mining centre, with old inns dating from the mining era. The area is rich in Bronze Age remains, among them the Priddy nine barrows. There is a sheep fair in the village every August.

Eastwater Cottage

Wells Road, Priddy, Wells, BA5 3AZ
☎ Wells (0749) 76252
200-year-old farmhouse-type cottage in heart of Mendips, in rural setting. Special offer packages available at Christmas and New Year, and special weekends at reduced rates throughout the year.
Bedrooms: 1 double & 1 twin, 1 family room.
Bathrooms: 2 public.
Bed & breakfast: £10-£11 single, £20 double.
Half board: £15-£17 daily.
Lunch available.
Evening meal 6pm (l.o. 6pm).
Parking for 8.

Miners Arms

Priddy, Wells, BA5 3DB
☎ (0749) 870217
Set in the middle of Mendip countryside, with a well-known restaurant and outdoor pool. Children welcome, no age restrictions.
Bedrooms: 1 single, 2 double & 1 twin.
Bathrooms: 1 public.
Bed & breakfast: from £10.50 single, from £19 double.
Half board: £19-£23 daily.
Lunch available.
Evening meal 7pm (l.o. 10pm).

Parking for 30.
Credit: Access, Visa, Diners, Amex.

New Inn

Priddy Green, Priddy, Wells, BA5 3BB
☎ (0749) 76465
Comfortable accommodation and traditional beers in the heart of the Mendips. An excellent centre for walking, riding or driving.
Bedrooms: 3 double & 2 twin, 1 family room.
Bathrooms: 2 public.
Bed & breakfast: from £16.50 single, from £23 double.
Lunch available.
Evening meal 7pm (l.o. 10pm).
Parking for 30.

RADSTOCK

Avon
Map ref 2B2

See also Holcombe.
Thriving small town ideally situated for touring the Mendip Hills.

Midstfields

Listed

Frome Rd., Radstock, Bath BA3 5UD
☎ Bath (0761) 34440
Large country house situated between the cities of Bath and Wells.
Bedrooms: 1 single, 1 twin, 1 family room.
Bathrooms: 1 public.
Bed & breakfast: £10-£12 single, £20-£24 double.
Parking for 4.

The Rookery

Wells Rd., Radstock, Bath, BA3 3RS
☎ (0761) 32626
The Rookery is a homely family-run guesthouse situated between Bath and Wells. Ideal for touring the West Country.
Bedrooms: 2 double & 2 twin, 2 family rooms.
Bathrooms: 4 private, 4 public.
Bed & breakfast: £12-£24 single, £25-£35 double.
Half board: £18-£30 daily.
Lunch available.
Evening meal 6pm (l.o. 9pm).

Continued ▶

RADSTOCK

Continued

Parking for 8.
Credit: Access, Visa.

♿ ⚙ 🏠 ☎ ⚙ 🅿 🔌 Ⓥ ✂ ⤢
📺 🛏 🍺 ♟ Ü ▶ ❄ 🏖 ♿ DAP
🌊 SP 🏥 Ⓣ

REDHILL

Avon
Map ref 2A2

Hailstones Farm

Redhill, Bristol, BS18 7TG
☎ Wrington (0934) 862209
*125-acre mixed farm.
Attractive farmhouse and large
garden with croquet lawn.
Within easy reach of Bath,
Weston and Cheddar.*
Bedrooms: 2 double & 1 twin,
1 family room.
Bathrooms: 1 private,
1 public.
Bed & breakfast: £22-£26
double.
Parking for 6.
Open April-October.

♿ ⚙ ⓊⓁ ✂ 📺 🛏 ❄ 🏖 🏥
SP

ST AGNES

Cornwall
Map ref 1B3

Small town in a once-rich
mining area on the north
coast. Miners' terraced
cottages and granite
houses slope to the
church. Attractive coastal
scenery despite old mine
workings, and St. Agnes
Beacon (National Trust)
offers one of Cornwall's
most extensive views.

Penkerris ⋔
⬤⬤

Penwinnick Rd., St. Agnes,
TR5 0PA
☎ (087 255) 2262
*Enchanting Edwardian
residence in own grounds, just
inside St. Agnes on B3277
road. Large lawn for
relaxation.*
Bedrooms: 1 single, 2 double
& 1 twin, 1 family room.
Bathrooms: 3 public.
Bed & breakfast: £9-£12
single, £17-£20 double.
Half board: £13.50-£15 daily,
from £90 weekly.
Lunch available.
Evening meal 6.30pm (l.o.
6.30pm).
Parking for 8.

♿ ⚙ 🏠 ⚙ 🅿 Ⓥ 🛏 📺 ⤢
❄ 🏖 DAP SP 🏥 Ⓣ

St. Agnes Hotel

St. Agnes, TR5 OQP
☎ (087 255) 2307
*Set in the heart of St.Agnes.
Rich in local history and
renowned for its collection of
nautical treasures and old
photographs.*
Bedrooms: 1 single, 2 double
& 2 twin, 1 family room.
Bathrooms: 2 private,
1 public.
Bed & breakfast: from £14.50
single, £29-£36 double.
Lunch available.
Evening meal 7pm (l.o.
9.30pm).
Parking for 60.
Credit: Access, Visa.

♿ ⚙ 🅿 Ⓥ 🛏 📺 🍺 ♟ ▶
🏖 🏥 Ⓣ

ST BLAZEY

Cornwall
Map ref 1B2

Small market town which
prospered in the mining
and railways boom of the
19th C. The attractive
granite church overlooks
the market house, a
coaching inn and the
charming vicarage of
Pentewan stone in the
town centre. Situated just
north of Par harbour, this
is a convenient base for
visiting the coast.

Nanscawen House
⬤⬤♔

Prideaux Rd., St. Blazey,
Par, PL24 2SR
☎ (072 681) 4488
*Large Georgian house set in 5
acres in the Luxulyan Valley.
Take the A390 and follow
signs to St. Austell. After
crossing railway in St. Blazey,
turn right into Prideaux Road.
Nanscawen is half a mile on
the right.*
Bedrooms: 2 double & 1 twin.
Bathrooms: 1 private,
1 public.
Bed & breakfast: £15-£20
single, £30-£40 double.
Half board: £25.50-£30.50
daily, £178.50-£213.50
weekly.
Evening meal 7.15pm (l.o.
5.30pm).
Parking for 5.
Open March-November.

♿ 12 ⑰ ⚙ ⓊⓁ 🛏 📺 🏖 ⚡
Ü ❄ 🏖 🏥 🏥

ST GENNYS

Cornwall
Map ref 1C2

7m SW. Bude

Treworgie Barton
⬤⬤

Crackington Haven, Bude,
EX23 0NL
☎ (084 03) 233
*200-acre mixed farm. 16th C.
listed farmhouse in secluded
situation with lovely views. 2
miles from sandy surfing
beach.*
Bedrooms: 1 twin, 1 family
room.
Bathrooms: 1 private,
1 public.
Bed & breakfast: £20-£26
double.
Half board: £16.50-£18.50
daily, £110-£120 weekly.
Evening meal 7pm.
Parking for 5.
Open April-September.

♿ 🌊 Ⓥ 🛏 📺 ❄ 🏹 🏖 🏥

ST ISSEY

Cornwall
Map ref 1B2

Trevorrick Farm ⋔

St. Issey, Wadebridge,
PL27 7QH
☎ Rumford (0841) 540574
*11-acre mixed farm.
Delightful, comfortable
farmhouse where quality and
service come first. Located 1
mile from Padstow,
overlooking Little Petherick
Creek and the Camel Estuary.*
Bedrooms: 2 double & 1 twin.
Bathrooms: 2 public.
Bed & breakfast: £12 single,
£24 double.
Lunch available.
Evening meal 7.30pm (l.o.
7.30pm).
Parking for 9.

♿ 🌊 🏖 ⓊⓁ 🛏 Ⓥ 🛏 📺 ⬤
🍽 🛏 ⚙ ❄ 🏹 🏖 🌊 SP 🏥

ST IVES

Cornwall
Map ref 1B3

Old fishing port and
artists' colony and holiday
town with good surfing
beach. Fishermen's
cottages, granite fish
cellars, a sandy harbour
and magnificent
headlands typify a charm
that has survived since
the 19th C pilchard
boom. ⓘ

Craigmeor
⬤⬤

Beach Rd., St. Ives,
TR26 1JY
☎ Penzance (0736) 796611
*Guest house for non-smokers
with uninterrupted sea views
over Porthmeor Beach.
Putting, bowling greens and
coastal footpath. Level
approach from town.*
Bedrooms: 1 single, 2 double
& 1 twin.
Bathrooms: 1 public.
Bed & breakfast: £10-£11
single, £20-£22 double.
Parking for 4.
Open March-October.

♿ 5 ⚙ ⓊⓁ 🏠 Ⓥ ✂ 🛏 📺 🛏
🏥 DAP

Panorama Guest House
Listed

1 Barnoon Ter., St. Ives,
TR26 1JE
☎ Penzance (0736) 795951
*Close to the town centre, with a
magnificent view of harbour,
bay and the island from every
window.*
Bedrooms: 2 double, 3 family
rooms.
Bathrooms: 1 public;
1 private shower.
Bed & breakfast: £20-£22
double.
Open April-October.

♿ 5 ⚙ ⓊⓁ 🛏 📺 🛏 ❄ 🏖

INDIVIDUAL PROPRIETORS HAVE SUPPLIED
ALL DETAILS OF ACCOMMODATION.
ALTHOUGH WE DO CHECK FOR ACCURACY, WE
ADVISE YOU TO CONFIRM PRICES AND OTHER
INFORMATION AT THE TIME OF BOOKING.

THE SYMBOLS ARE
EXPLAINED ON THE
FLAP INSIDE THE
BACK COVER.

GROUPS, CONSORTIA AND AGENCIES
SPECIALISING IN FARM AND COUNTRY
HOLIDAYS ARE LISTED IN A SPECIAL
SECTION OF THIS GUIDE.

ST JUST-IN-ROSELAND

Cornwall
Map ref 1B3

Parish overlooking Carrick Roads on the Roseland Peninsula. The riverside church of St. Just has a beautiful setting under a steep slope of tall trees and sub-tropical shrubs.

Commerrans Farm M

St. Just-in-Roseland, Truro, TR2 5JJ
☎ Portscatho (087 258) 270
61-acre mixed farm. Close to the River Fal, offering a relaxed atmosphere and home cooking. About 4 miles from beaches. Good area for sailing, bird watching and walking.
Bedrooms: 2 double, 1 family room.
Bathrooms: 1 public.
Bed & breakfast: £8.50-£9.50 single, £17-£19 double.
Half board: £87.50-£95 weekly.
Evening meal 6.45pm (l.o. midday).
Parking for 6.
Open April-October.
☎1 ♥ ⑭ Ⓥ ⌕ ⑬ ✿ ⋈

ST MAWES

Cornwall
Map ref 1B3

Small resort and yachting centre in a pretty estuary setting on the Roseland Peninsula. Enclosed by fields and woods of the Percuil River, it is said to be the warmest winter resort in Britain.

Braganza

Listed
Grove Hill, St. Mawes, Truro, TR2 5BJ
☎ (0326) 270281
An elegant Regency house furnished with antiques, overlooking park and harbour. Large garden and parking space. Within walking distance of places to eat.
Bedrooms: 1 single, 4 twin.
Bathrooms: 3 private, 1 public.
Bed & breakfast: £15-£22 single, £30-£34 double.
Parking for 6.
Open April-October.
♥ ⑭ ⌕ ⑬ ⦿ ▦ ✿ ⋈ ⊞

Georgian House

Listed
5 Grove Hill, St Mawes, Truro, TR2 5BJ
☎ (0326) 270707
Refurbished Georgian house with sea views. Grade II listed. Quiet location, centre village, 100 yards from waterfront and ferry to Falmouth.
Bedrooms: 1 double & 1 twin.
Bathrooms: 1 public.
Bed & breakfast: £11-£14 single, £22-£48 double.
Parking for 1.
Open March-October.
☎10 ⚥ ♥ ⑭ ▦ ⦿ ⋈ ⋈

ST TEATH

Cornwall
Map ref 1B2

3m S. Camelford

Treveighan Farm

☎
St. Teath, Bodmin, PL30 3JN
☎ Bodmin (0208) 850286
95-acre dairy farm. In peaceful setting where guests can see all farm activities. Homely atmosphere, tea/coffee facilities, farmhouse fare.
Bedrooms: 1 double, 1 family room.
Bathrooms: 1 public.
Bed & breakfast: max. £10 single, £17-£20 double.
Half board: £13.50-£15 daily, £87.50-£94.50 weekly.
Evening meal 6.30pm (l.o. 9am).
Parking for 4.
Open March-October.
☎ ♥ ⑭ ⌕ ⑬ ⦿ ⋑ ✓ ⋈ ⋈

SALCOMBE

Devon
Map ref 1C3

Sheltered yachting resort of whitewashed houses and narrow streets in a balmy setting on the Kingsbridge estuary. Palm, myrtle and other mediterranean plants flourish, there are sandy bays and creeks for boating. ⓘ

Courtenay House

☎☎
Moult Hill, Salcombe, TQ8 8LF
☎ (054 884) 2761

WE ADVISE YOU TO
CONFIRM YOUR
BOOKING IN WRITING.

Elegant house, beautifully furnished. Bedrooms have sea views, three with balconies. Country house hospitality. Five minutes from beach.
Bedrooms: 1 double & 2 twin, 1 family room.
Bathrooms: 2 public.
Bed & breakfast: £21-£25 single, £30-£35 double.
Half board: £27-£29.50 daily, £182-£196 weekly.
Evening meal 7.30pm (l.o. 8.30pm).
Parking for 7.
☎7 ⑭ Ⓥ ⌕ ⑬ ▦ ⦿ ✿ ⋈ ⋈ ⑰ ⑲

SALISBURY

Wiltshire
Map ref 2B3

See also Alderbury, Barford St. Martin, Little Langford, Shrewton, South Newton, Winterbourne Stoke.
Beautiful city and ancient regional capital set amid water meadows on its medieval plain. Buildings of all periods are dominated by the stately cathedral whose spire is the tallest in England. Built between 1220 and 1258, the cathedral is one of the purest examples of Early English architecture. ⓘ

Beulah

Listed
144 Britford La., Salisbury, SP2 8AL
☎ (0722) 333517
Bungalow in quiet road on outskirts of city. One and a quarter miles from city centre overlooking meadows. Evening meal served on request.
Bedrooms: 2 single, 1 family room.
Bathrooms: 1 public.
Bed & breakfast: £9 single, £18 double.
Parking for 3.
☎2 ⚥ ⦿ ⑭ ⋒ ⌕ ⑬ ▦ ⦿ ⋈ ⋈

Butt of Ale

Sunnyhill Rd., Salisbury, SP1 3QJ
☎ (0722) 27610
Modern inn with 2 bars and garden. Highest pub in Salisbury giving superb views of the cathedral.
Bedrooms: 1 twin, 1 family room.
Bathrooms: 1 public.
Bed & breakfast: £11.50 single, £23 double.

Half board: £16.50-£20 daily, £112-£140 weekly.
Lunch available.
Evening meal 6pm (l.o. 10.30pm).
Parking for 50.
☎ ⦿ ⌗ ③ ▦ ⦿ ⋈

Byways House M

☎☎☎
31 Fowlers Rd., Salisbury, SP1 2QP
☎ (0722) 28364
Victorian house in a quiet area near Salisbury city centre. Modern facilities including some en-suite and ground floor rooms. Ample private parking.
Bedrooms: 4 single, 5 double & 5 twin, 3 family rooms.
Bathrooms: 10 private, 2 public.
Bed & breakfast: £14-£15 single, £28-£32 double.
Parking for 13.
☎ ⚥ ⦿ ⑭ Ⓥ ⌕ ▦ ⦿ ✿ ⋈ ⑰

12 Chiselbury Grove

Harnham, Salisbury
☎ (0722) 337249
In quiet wooded area 10 minutes' walk from town and cathedral. Pretty rooms. Transport to and from station if required.
Bedrooms: 1 double & 1 twin.
Bathrooms: 2 private.
Bed & breakfast: from £22 double.
Parking for 2.
⚥ ⑭ ⑬ ▦ ⋈ ⋈ ⑰ ⑲

Daheim

☎☎
3 Willow Cls., Laverstock, Salisbury, SP1 1QF
☎ (0722) 334536
Modern bungalow in private close, with riverside garden. Transport from station and city centre available. Breakfast a speciality. Sauna. German spoken.
Bedrooms: 1 single, 1 twin.
Bathrooms: 1 public.
Bed & breakfast: £8.50-£10.50 single, £17-£21 double.
Parking for 3.
☎3 ⚥ ⑭ ⓥ ⌕ ⑬ ▦ ⦿ ⋒ ✿ ⋈ ⑰ ⑲

Hayburn Wyke Guest House

72 Castle Rd., Salisbury, SP1 3RL
☎ Salisbury, (0722) 412627
Family-run spacious guesthouse adjacent to Victoria Park. Short walk from the cathedral and city centre.
Bedrooms: 1 single, 3 double & 1 twin, 2 family rooms.
Bathrooms: 1 private, 1 public.

Continued ▶

SALISBURY

Continued

Bed & breakfast: from £15 single, £25-£30 double.
Parking for 6.
🛇6🖵🖵 🛈 V ✕ ▥ ☂
✕ SP ▦

Highfield House
70 London Rd., Salisbury,
SP1 3EX
☎ (0722) 24303
Friendly family-run guesthouse within half a mile of city centre. Homely accommodation. Children of any age especially welcome.
Bedrooms: 1 double & 1 twin,
1 family room.
Bathrooms: 1 private,
2 public.
Bed & breakfast: £10-£15 single, £18-£28 double.
Half board: £14-£19 daily,
£84-£133 weekly.
Evening meal 6pm (l.o. 9pm).
Parking for 2.
🛇 🖻 🖵 🖵 🛈 V ▥ ☂

Holmhurst Guest House
⌂⌂
Downton Rd., Salisbury,
SP2 8AR
☎ (0722) 23164
Pleasant town house, a short walk from Salisbury Cathedral. Riverside and country walks. Easy access to coastal resorts.
Bedrooms: 1 single, 3 double & 3 twin, 1 family room.
Bathrooms: 5 private,
1 public.
Bed & breakfast: £12-£15 single, £20-£24 double.
Parking for 8.
🛇5🖵 UL 🛈 V ✕ ☂ ▥
✕

Kelebrae
⌂⌂
101 Castle Rd., Salisbury,
SP1 3RP
☎ (0722) 333628
A family home, opposite Victoria Park, within walking distance of city centre. Convenient for Stonehenge.
Bedrooms: 2 double.
Bathrooms: 1 public.
Bed & breakfast: £11-£13 single, £22-£24 double.
Parking for 3.
🛇🖵 UL 🛈 ☂ ▥ ☂ ✕ ✕
DAP SP

Leena's Guesthouse
⌂⌂
50 Castle Rd., Salisbury,
SP1 3RL
☎ (0722) 335419

Attractive Edwardian house with friendly family atmosphere and modern facilities. Some ground floor rooms.
Bedrooms: 1 single, 2 double & 2 twin, 1 family room.
Bathrooms: 3 private,
1 public; 1 private shower.
Bed & breakfast: £10-£14 single, £19-£25 double.
Parking for 7.
🛇🖻🖵🖵 UL V 🛈 ☂ ▥
☂ ✕ SP

Stratford Lodge
4 Park La., Castle Rd.,
Salisbury, SP1 3NP
☎ (0722) 25177
Victorian detached residence in quiet road. Attractively furnished with antiques. Imaginative, varied cooking using local and home-grown produce.
Bedrooms: 2 double & 2 twin.
Bathrooms: 4 private.
Bed & breakfast: max. £20 single, max. £32 double.
Half board: from £25 daily,
max. £168 weekly.
Evening meal 6.30pm (l.o. midday).
Parking for 6.
🛇8 🖵 UL V 🛈 ☂ ▥ ☂
❄ ✕ ✕ SP ☂

Wyndham Lodge
51 Wyndham Rd., Salisbury,
SP1 3AB
☎ (0722) 28851
Victorian style house in quiet area and within walking distance of cathedral and museums.
Bedrooms: 1 single, 1 double
& 1 twin.
Bathrooms: 3 private,
1 public.
Bed & breakfast: £12.50-£16 single, £25-£32 double.
Parking for 3.
🖵🖵 UL V ☂ ☂ ✕ ✕

28 Wyndham Rd.
Salisbury, SP1 3AB
☎ (0722) 334138
Central, friendly guesthouse close to swimming pool and fitness centre.
Bedrooms: 1 single, 1 double,
1 family room.
Bathrooms: 1 private,
2 public.
Bed & breakfast: £11-£15 single, £24-£32 double.
Half board: £12.50-£17.50 daily, £77-£110 weekly.
Lunch available.
Evening meal 6.30pm.
🛇🖻🖻🖵🖵 UL V ✕ ▥
☂ ▷ ✕ ✕

SALTASH

Cornwall
Map ref 1C2

Old fishing port with a busy waterfront and much modern development, facing Plymouth across the Tamar estuary. In a square at the top of the town the 17th C pillared Guildhall stands near the parish church, which has granite arcades and medieval carving on the roofs.

The Spaniards Inn ⋔
⌂⌂
Cargreen, Saltash, PL12 6PA
☎ (075 55) 2830
16th C. inn on bank of River Tamar. Restaurant and 3 bars serving real ales and bar snacks lunchtimes and evenings.
Bedrooms: 1 double & 1 twin,
3 family rooms.
Bathrooms: 1 private,
1 public.
Bed & breakfast: £15-£16.50 single, £30-£33 double.
Half board: £22.50-£24 daily,
£157.50-£168 weekly.
Lunch available.
Evening meal 7.30pm (l.o. 9.30pm).
Parking for 60.
🛇🖵 ☂ 🛈 V ♠ ☂ ✕ ✕
DAP SP

SAMPFORD COURTENAY

Devon
Map ref 1C2

5m NE. Okehampton
Picturesque village in gentle, hilly country just north of Dartmoor. Thatched, whitewashed cottages and a 17th C inn, line the village street which climbs to the lichened church.

Higher Town Farm
Listed
Sampford Courtenay,
Okehampton, EX20 2SX
☎ (083 782) 285
15-acre mixed farm. 16th C. farmhouse in good decorative order, set in its own grounds in centre of picturesque village.
Bedrooms: 1 double, 1 family room.
Bathrooms: 1 public.
Bed & breakfast: £8-£12 single, £16-£24 double.
Half board: £15.50-£19.50 daily, £95-£100 weekly.

Evening meal 7pm (l.o. 8pm).
Parking for 4.
Open April-September.
🛇3 ✕ UL 🛈 V ☂ ☂ ▥ ❄
✕ DAP SP

SEATON

Devon
Map ref 1D2

See also Branscombe, Colyton.
Small resort lying near the mouth of the River Axe. A mile-long beach extends to the dramatic cliffs of Beer Head. Annual arts and drama festival. ⓩ

Wayside
⌂⌂
5 Marlpitt La., Seaton,
EX12 2HH
☎ Seaton (0297) 22164
Well-presented, turn-of-century house, some rooms and garden with sea views. Wayside is a non-smoking house.
Bedrooms: 3 double.
Bathrooms: 1 public.
Bed & breakfast: £22-£25 double.
Half board: £18-£19.50 daily.
Evening meal 6.30pm (l.o. 3pm).
Parking for 4.
Open April-October.
🛇10 UL 🛈 🛈 ☂ ▥ ✕
✕

SENNEN

Cornwall
Map ref 1B3

The last village before Land's End. Magnificent beach at Sennen Cove.

The Old Manor Guest House
⌂⌂
Sennen, Lands End,
TR19 7AD
☎ (0736) 871280
On the A30 1 mile from Lands End, very easy to find. Near superb beach. Built of hand-dressed granite for the Squire.
Bedrooms: 4 double & 1 twin,
3 family rooms.
Bathrooms: 2 public;
3 private showers.
Bed & breakfast: £9-£15 single, £19-£28 double.
Half board: £15-£21 daily.
Lunch available.
Evening meal 6.30pm (l.o. 7.30pm).
Parking for 50.
Credit: Access, Visa.
🛇🖻 ☂ ☂ 🛈 🛈 V ☂ ☂
▥ ☂ ✕ ✕ ✕

SHALDON

Devon
Map ref 1D2

Pretty resort facing
Teignmouth from the
south bank of the Teign
estuary. Regency houses
harmonise with others of
later periods; there are
old cottages and narrow
lanes. On the Ness, a
sandstone promontory
nearby, a tunnel built in
the 19th C leads to a
beach revealed at low
tide.

Fonthill
☺☺
Torquay Rd., Shaldon,
TQ14 0AX
☎ (0626) 872344
*Lovely, Georgian, family home
in own grounds overlooking
River Teign. Comfortable
rooms, peaceful, restaurants
nearby.*
Bedrooms: 2 twin, 1 family
room.
Bathrooms: 1 public.
Bed & breakfast: £12.50-
£13.50 single, £25-£27 double.
Parking for 5.
Open March-December.
🛏🚪📺🅅💷📺🍴🅟 ⚹ ✂ 🐾 🏠 🏤

SHEPTON MALLET

Somerset
Map ref 2A2

Important, stone-built
market town beneath the
south west slopes of the
Mendips. Thriving rural
industries include glove
and shoe making,
dairying and cider
making; the remains of a
medieval 'shambles' in
the square dates from the
town's prosperity as a
wool centre. *i*

Raddon House
☺☺
13 Paul St., Shepton Mallet,
BA4 5LD
☎ (0749) 3152
*Lovely Georgian house in
historic town, within easy reach
of Wells, Bath and Bristol.
Comfortable bedrooms.*
Bedrooms: 1 single, 1 double
& 1 twin.
Bathrooms: 2 private.
Bed & breakfast: £13-£14
single, £25-£26 double.
Half board: £20-£22 daily,
£130-£135 weekly.
Evening meal 7.20pm (l.o.
5pm).

Parking for 4.
Open April-December.
🛏🚪📺🅄🅅💷📺💷🍴 ⚹ ✂ 📠 🍴 🆂🅿 🏤 🆃

SHERBORNE

Dorset
Map ref 2B3

*See also Corton Denham,
Henstridge, Holwell.*
Historic town of Ham
stone with busy industries
and an ancient centre. In
Anglo-Saxon times it was
a cathedral city and until
the Dissolution there was
a monastery here. *i*

Meadowcroft
Batcombe Rd., Leigh,
Sherborne, DT9 6JA
☎ Yetminster (0395) 872150
*250-acre dairy farm. Red brick
farmhouse. From Sherborne
take the A352, turn right at
signpost for Leigh. After 4
miles turn right at Give Way
sign. Take next left,
Meadowcroft is three quarters
of a mile on the left. Light
suppers available.*
Bedrooms: 1 double & 1 twin.
Bathrooms: 1 public.
Bed & breakfast: £10 single,
£20 double.
Parking for 1.
🛏🐾📺 🅅💷🍴 🅅📺
💷🚪🕐 ⚹ ✂ 🏠 🏤 📠

SHERSTON

Wiltshire
Map ref 2B2

5m W. Malmesbury

Widleys Farm
☺
Sherston, Malmesbury,
SN16 0PY
☎ (0666) 840213
*300-acre mixed farm. Close to
100 acre arboretum, easily
reached from M4. Central for
Bath, Bristol and Wales via
the Severn Bridge.*
Bedrooms: 1 double & 1 twin,
1 family room.
Bathrooms: 2 public.
Bed & breakfast: £12 single,
£24 double.
Half board: £18 daily, £98
weekly.
Evening meal 6.30pm (l.o.
midday).
Parking for 8.
🛏🚪📺💷📺💷🚪🕐🅿
⚹ ✂ 🏠 🏤

**PLEASE MENTION
THIS GUIDE WHEN
MAKING A BOOKING.**

SHIRWELL

Devon
Map ref 1C1

The Spinney
☺☺
Shirwell, Barnstaple,
EX31 4JR
☎ (0271) 82282
*A former rectory on the A39
Lynton road close to
Barnstaple, within easy reach
of Exmoor and the coast.*
Bedrooms: 1 single, 1 double
& 2 twin.
Bathrooms: 1 public.
Bed & breakfast: £9-£10
single, £18-£20 double.
Half board: £14.50-£15.50
daily, £90-£100 weekly.
Evening meal 7pm (l.o.
5.30pm).
Parking for 12.
🛏🐾📺💷📺🔵💷 ⚹
🏤

Waytown Farm
☺☺
Shirwell, Barnstaple,
EX31 4JN
☎ (0271) 82396
*240-acre mixed farm.
Pleasantly situated 17th C.
farmhouse 3 miles from
Barnstaple. Exmoor and
beaches within easy reach.
Home cooking, relaxed
atmosphere. Access at all
times.*
Bedrooms: 1 double & 1 twin,
1 family room.
Bathrooms: 1 public.
Bed & breakfast: £11-£12
single, £20-£22 double.
Half board: £15-£16 daily,
£91-£98 weekly.
Evening meal 6.30pm (l.o.
4pm).
Parking for 6.
🛏🐾🅄💷📺💷🚪 ✂ 🏠 🏤

SHREWTON

Wiltshire
Map ref 2B3

6m W. Amesbury

The Laurels
Salisbury Rd., Shrewton,
Salisbury, SP3 4EQ
☎ (0980) 620444
*A small country living set in
attractive village, close to
traditional pub, close from
Stonehenge. It is an 18th C.
house with exposed beams and
furnished in character.*
Bedrooms: 1 double & 1 twin.
Bathrooms: 1 public.
Bed & breakfast: £24-£28
double.
Parking for 5.
🐾🅄💷📺💷 ⚹ ✂ 🏠 🏤

Rollestone Manor
Shrewton, Salisbury
☎ (098 062) 620216
*Listed building mentioned in
the Domesday Book. Old oak
beams throughout the house.
Furnished as a family home,
which guests enjoy. Large
garden.*
Bedrooms: 6 double & 3 twin,
2 family rooms.
Bathrooms: 3 public.
Bed & breakfast: £11 single,
£22 double.
Evening meal (l.o. 8pm).
Parking for 6.
🛏🏛🅄🎱🅅🍴📺💷🚪
🏠 🏤

SIDMOUTH

Devon
Map ref 1D2

See also Branscombe.
Charming resort set amid
lofty red cliffs where the
River Sid meets the sea.
The wealth of ornate
Regency or Victorian
villas recalls the time
when this was one of the
south coast's most
exclusive resorts.
Museum; August
International Festival of
Folk Arts. *i*

Lower Pinn Farm
☺☺
Pinn, Sidmouth, EX10 0NN
☎ (039 55) 3733
*200-acre mixed farm. A
family-run farm, 2 miles from
Sidmouth sea front, in a scenic
area.*
Bedrooms: 1 double, 1 family
room.
Bathrooms: 1 public.
Bed & breakfast: £19-£22
double.
Parking for 2.
Open April-October.
🛏🚪🐾🅄💷📺💷🚪 🏠

Sidling Field
105 Peaslands Rd., Sidmouth,
EX10 8XE
☎ (039 55) 3859
*Large bungalow surrounded by
garden, backing on to a small
paddock. On the outskirts of
town, 12 minutes' walk from
the seafront.*
Bedrooms: 1 double & 1 twin.
Bathrooms: 1 public.
Bed & breakfast: £11-£12
single, £19-£20 double.
Parking for 4.
Open February-November.
🛏12🏛♿🐾🅄💷📺💷
🚪 ⚹ ✂ 🏤

SIMONSBATH

Somerset
Map ref 1D1

7m SE. Lynton
Village beside the beautiful River Barle, deep in Exmoor. From the Middle Ages until the 19th C this was stag-hunting country.

Emmetts Grange Farm Guest House ⋀

Simonsbath, Minehead, TA24 7LD
☎ Exford (064 383) 282
1250-acre hill stock farm. Attractive country house on a farm, in a lovely, quiet position 2.5 miles out of Simonsbath on the South Molton road. Specialises in home-cooked food.
Bedrooms: 1 single, 1 double & 2 twin.
Bathrooms: 2 private, 1 public.
Bed & breakfast: £13.50-£16 single, £27-£32 double.
Half board: £23.50-£26 daily, £145-£160 weekly.
Evening meal 8pm (l.o. 6pm).
Parking for 12.
Open March-October.

SLAPTON

Devon
Map ref 1C3

Steeply-built village of narrow, twisting streets lying in a valley near the sea. Interesting buildings include the spired church and a prominent tower and spire just north of the village which formed part of a 14th C chantry college.

Old Walls

Slapton, Kingsbridge, TQ7 2QN
☎ (0548) 580516
Charming, south facing 18th C. house in elevated position, with beamed bedrooms and sunny conservatory. In centre of village, near sea and Slapton Ley Nature Reserve.
Bedrooms: 1 single, 1 double & 2 twin, 1 family room.
Bathrooms: 2 private, 1 public.
Bed & breakfast: £9-£10 single, £18-£20 double.

Half board: £14-£15 daily.
Evening meal 6.50pm (l.o. 6pm).

SOUTH BRENT

Devon
Map ref 1C2

Small town on the southern edge of Dartmoor National Park, just off the A38. Norman to 15th C church with carved Norman font, and the old toll-house in the square still displays toll charges for livestock.

The London Inn

South Brent, TQ10 9DF
☎ (036 47) 3223
Relax in the intimate atmosphere of this superbly situated hostelry, which is close to many beauty spots. Home-cooked food.
Bedrooms: 1 double & 2 twin.
Bathrooms: 2 public.
Bed & breakfast: from £14 single, from £25 double.
Lunch available.
Evening meal 6.30pm (l.o. 10.30pm).
Parking for 30.

SOUTH MOLTON

Devon
Map ref 1C1

See also Ash Mill, Bishop's Nympton, West Anstey, West Buckland.
Busy market town at the mouth of the Yeo Valley near southern Exmoor. Wool, mining and coaching brought prosperity between the Middle Ages and the 19th C and the fine square with Georgian buildings, a Guildhall and Assembly Rooms reflect this former affluence. ⓘ

Bornacott Farm

South Molton, EX36 3EX
☎ North Molton (059 84) 254
220-acre sheep and beef farm. Working family farm on the edge of Exmoor. Visitors are always welcome in the warm and comfortable farmhouse. Home cooking using fresh vegetables from the garden.
Bedrooms: 2 family rooms.
Bathrooms: 1 public.

Bed & breakfast: max. £8.50 single, max. £17 double.
Half board: max. £13 daily, max. £80 weekly.
Evening meal 6.30pm.
Open May-October.

SOUTH NEWTON

Wiltshire
Map ref 2B2

Newton Cottage

South Newton, Salisbury, SP2 0QW
☎ Salisbury (0722) 743111
Typically English thatched cottage built in 1679. Offering hospitality, personal attention and a warm comfortable atmosphere. Chalk stream fly fishing tuition, access to association waters by prior arrangement.
Bedrooms: 1 single, 1 double & 1 twin, 1 family room.
Bathrooms: 2 public.
Bed & breakfast: £11-£15 single, £21-£24 double.
Parking for 4.

SOUTH PETHERTON

Somerset
Map ref 1D1

See also Chiselborough.
Small town with a restored 15th C house, King Ina's Palace. The Roman Fosse Way crosses the River Parrett to the east by way of an old bridge on which there are 2 curious carved figures.

Autumn Dawn

11 Hayes End, South Petherton, TA13 5AG
☎ (0460) 41490
Detached private house with garden at front and rear.
Bedrooms: 2 double & 1 twin.
Bathrooms: 1 private, 1 public.
Bed & breakfast: £10 single, £18-£20 double.
Parking for 3.
Open March-October.

STAPLEFORD

Wiltshire
Map ref 2B2

4m N. Wilton

Elm Tree Cottage

Stapleford, Salisbury, SP3 4LJ
☎ Salisbury (0722) 790507
Character cottage in a picturesque village. Friendly atmosphere. Horse riding and fishing nearby.
Bedrooms: 3 double.
Bathrooms: 1 private, 1 public.
Bed & breakfast: £22-£24.50 double.
Parking for 7.
Open March-October.

STAVERTON

Devon
Map ref 1D2

2m N. Totnes

Sea Trout Inn

Staverton, Totnes, TQ9 6PA
☎ (080 426) 274
Delightful beamed country inn, in attractive village by the River Dart. Good base for walking and touring Dartmoor and South Devon. Vegetarian dishes prepared if required.
Bedrooms: 1 single, 2 double & 2 twin, 1 family room.
Bathrooms: 1 private, 2 public.
Bed & breakfast: £17.50-£25 single, £28-£36 double.
Half board: £22-£25 daily, £135-£148 weekly.
Lunch available.
Evening meal 7pm (l.o. 10pm).
Parking for 70.
Credit: Access, Visa, Diners, Amex.

STOCKLAND

Devon
Map ref 1D2

Kings Arms Inn

Stockland, Honiton, EX14 9BS
☎ (040 488) 361
A traditional country coaching inn, specialising in reasonably priced international cuisine and traditional Sunday lunch. Games room. All bedrooms with TV.
Bedrooms: 2 double & 1 twin.

> **MAP REFERENCES APPLY TO THE COLOUR MAPS TOWARDS THE END OF THIS GUIDE.**

Bathrooms: 3 private.
Bed & breakfast: £20-£30 single, £30-£40 double.
Half board: £30-£40 daily, £190-£250 weekly.
Evening meal 7pm (l.o. 10pm).
Parking for 30.

STOKE ST. GREGORY

Somerset
Map ref 1D1

8m E. Taunton

Parsonage Farm

Listed

Stoke St. Gregory, Taunton, TA3 6ET
☎ Burrowbridge, (082 369) 205
100-acre dairy farm. Large Georgian farmhouse and garden on working farm. On ridge overlooking the Somerset levels. Lovely views, good base for touring. Well-stocked coarse fishing half a mile away.
Bedrooms: 1 double & 2 twin, 1 family room.
Bathrooms: 1 public.
Bed & breakfast: £8.50-£10.50 single, £17-£21 double.
Parking for 6.

SUTTON MONTIS

Somerset
Map ref 2B3

2m SE. Sparkford

Parsonage Farm

Sutton Montis, Yeovil, BA22 7HE
☎ Corton Denham (096 322) 256
100-acre beef farm. 17th C. farmhouse below King Arthur's Cadbury Castle. Unspoilt area and ideal centre for a wide variety of interests. Good local eating places. Babies and toddlers welcome.
Bedrooms: 1 double & 2 twin.
Bathrooms: 2 public.
Bed & breakfast: £9 single, £18 double.
Parking for 4.
Open March-November.

The Red House

Sutton Montis, Yeovil, BA22 7HG
☎ Corton Denham (096 322) 288

Detached country house in its own grounds, with beautiful views of surrounding countryside. Within walking distance of Cadbury Castle. Personal service and a warm welcome.
Bedrooms: 2 single, 1 double & 1 twin.
Bathrooms: 1 public.
Bed & breakfast: from £9 single, from £18 double.
Half board: from £14 daily, from £94 weekly.
Evening meal 6pm (l.o. 6pm).
Parking for 4.

SWINDON

Wiltshire
Map ref 2B2

See also Ashton Keynes.
Wiltshire's industrial and commercial centre, an important railway town in the 19th C, situated just north of the Marlborough Downs. The original market town occupies the slopes of Swindon Hill and the railway village created in the mid-19th C has been preserved. Railway museum, art gallery, theatre. ℹ

Internos

Listed

3 Turnpike Rd., Blunsdon, Swindon, SN2 4EA
☎ (0793) 721496
Detached red brick house off A419, 4 miles north of Swindon and 6 miles from M4 juction 15.
Bedrooms: 1 single, 1 twin, 1 family room.
Bathrooms: 1 public.
Bed & breakfast: £15 single, £28 double.
Parking for 6.

Little Cotmarsh Farm, Cotmarsh

Listed

Broad Town, Wootton Bassett, Swindon, SN4 7RA
☎ Broad Hinton (079 373) 322
108-acre mixed farm. 17th C. farmhouse in the hamlet of Cotmarsh. Within easy reach of Marlborough, Avebury and M4 junction 16.
Bedrooms: 1 double, 1 family room.
Bathrooms: 1 public.
Bed & breakfast: £10 single, £20 double.
Parking for 4.

Relian Guest House

Listed

153 County Rd., Swindon, SN1 2EB
☎ (0793) 21416
Quiet house adjacent to Swindon Town Football Club and near town centre. Close to bus and rail stations. Free car parking.
Bedrooms: 2 single, 2 double & 3 twin, 1 family room.
Bathrooms: 2 public; 2 private showers.
Bed & breakfast: from £15 single, from £28 double.
Parking for 7.
Credit: Amex.

TAUNTON

Somerset
Map ref 1D1

See also Bishop's Lydeard, Combe, Stoke St. Gregory, West Bagborough, West Buckland.
County town well-known for its public schools, sheltered by gentle hill-ranges on the River Tone. Medieval prosperity from wool has continued in marketing and manufacturing and the town retains many fine period buildings. ℹ

Hamilton Guest House

Listed

57 Hamilton Rd., Taunton, TA1 2EL
☎ (0823) 272537
Warm and friendly atmosphere. Home cooking, clean accommodation. Within walking distance of town and close to M5.
Bedrooms: 3 single, 1 twin, 3 family rooms.
Bathrooms: 2 public.
Bed & breakfast: from £11 single, from £22 double.
Half board: from £17 daily.
Evening meal 6pm (l.o. 5pm).
Parking for 7.

The Old Rectory

Clatworthy, Wiveliscombe, Taunton, TA4 2EQ
☎ Wiveliscombe (0984) 23482
Close to Exmoor National Park, reservoir fishing and 10 miles from the coast. Home cooking.
Bedrooms: 1 single, 1 twin, 1 family room.
Bathrooms: 2 public.
Bed & breakfast: from £8.50 single, from £17 double.
Half board: from £14 daily, from £94 weekly.
Parking for 5.
Open April-October.

Prockters Farm

West Monkton, Taunton, TA2 8QN
☎ (0823) 412269
300-acre mixed farm. Family farm, 300-year-old, beamed house, inglenook fireplaces, brass beds, collection of farm antiques. Large garden. Tea and cake on arrival.
Bedrooms: 1 single, 3 double & 2 twin, 1 family room.
Bathrooms: 2 private, 3 public.
Bed & breakfast: £12-£14 single, £24-£26 double.
Evening meal 6pm (l.o. 9pm).
Parking for 6.

Rectory Cottage

Listed

Combe Florey, Taunton, TA4 3JD
☎ (0823) 432349
Character cottage, 6 miles north west of Taunton, within easy reach of Quantock Hills and Exmoor. Comfortable accommodation and home cooking.
Bedrooms: 1 single, 1 twin, 1 family room.
Bathrooms: 1 public.
Bed & breakfast: £10-£12 single, from £20 double.
Half board: from £17 daily, from £110 weekly.
Evening meal 6.30pm (l.o. 8pm).
Parking for 2.

INDIVIDUAL PROPRIETORS HAVE SUPPLIED ALL DETAILS OF ACCOMMODATION. ALTHOUGH WE DO CHECK FOR ACCURACY, WE ADVISE YOU TO CONFIRM PRICES AND OTHER INFORMATION AT THE TIME OF BOOKING.

TAVISTOCK

Devon
Map ref 1C2

See also Peter Tavy.
Old market town beside the River Tavy on the western edge of Dartmoor. Developed around its 10th C abbey, of which some fragments remain, it became a stannary town in 1305 when tin-streaming thrived on the moors. Tavistock Goose Fair, October. *ℹ*

Colcharton

Gulworthy, Tavistock, PL19 8HU
☎ Tavistock, (0822) 613047
150-acre mixed farm. A charming 16th C. farmhouse near moors and within easy reach of many places of interest. Quiet position off main Tavistock/Liskeard road.
Bedrooms: 2 double & 1 twin, 1 family room.
Bathrooms: 2 public.
Bed & breakfast: £11-£12 single, £21-£23 double.
Evening meal 7pm (l.o. 8pm).
Parking for 8.

Wringworthy Farm
Listed

Mary Tavy, Tavistock, PL19 9LT
☎ Mary Tavy (082 281) 434
80-acre dairy farm. Elizabethan farmhouse with modern comforts, in quiet valley near the moors. Within easy reach of sea and well placed for touring.
Bedrooms: 1 double & 1 twin, 1 family room.
Bathrooms: 2 public.
Bed & breakfast: £10-£10.50 single, £20-£21 double.
Half board: £16-£16.50 daily.
Evening meal 7pm (l.o. 9am).
Parking for 3.
Open April-September.

GROUPS, CONSORTIA AND AGENCIES SPECIALISING IN FARM AND COUNTRY HOLIDAYS ARE LISTED IN A SPECIAL SECTION OF THIS GUIDE.

TEIGNMOUTH

Devon
Map ref 1D2

See also Shaldon.
Set on the north bank of the beautiful Teign estuary, busy fishing and shipbuilding port handling timber and locally-quarried ball-clay. A bridge crosses to the pretty town of Shaldon and there are good views of the estuary from here. *ℹ*

Leicester House

Winterbourne Rd., Teignmouth, TQ
☎ (062 67) 3043
Edwardian house overlooking the town, with extensive seaviews. Situated close to the town's amenities. Sunny aspects with a pretty, quiet garden.
Bedrooms: 2 double, 3 family rooms.
Bathrooms: 1 public.
Bed & breakfast: £19 double.
Open April-October.

THROWLEIGH

Devon
Map ref 1C2

6m SE. Okehampton
Charming village below Cawsand Beacon in the Dartmoor National Park, with the Throwleigh stone circle consisting of 6 standing and 36 fallen stones.

Well Farm

Throwleigh, Okehampton, EX20 2JQ
☎ Whiddon Down (064 723) 294
217-acre dairy farm. 16th C. farmhouse in Dartmoor National Park. Ideal situation for walking, riding, fishing, golf, or just relaxing in a family home.
Bedrooms: 1 single, 1 double & 1 twin, 1 family room.
Bathrooms: 2 private, 1 public.
Bed & breakfast: £10-£12 single, £20-£24 double.
Half board: £16-£18 daily, £95-£100 weekly.
Evening meal 8pm (l.o. 6pm).
Parking for 6.

TINTAGEL

Cornwall
Map ref 1B2

See also Treknow.
Coastal village near the legendary home of King Arthur, a lofty headland with the ruin of a Norman castle and traces of a Celtic monastery still visible in the turf.

Castle Villa

Molesworth St., Tintagel, PL34 0BZ
☎ Camelford (0840) 770373
Over 150 years old, Castle Villa is within easy walking distance of the 11th C. church, post office and King Arthur's castle.
Bedrooms: 1 single, 2 double & 1 twin, 1 family room.
Bathrooms: 2 public.
Bed & breakfast: £9.50-£12.50 single, £19-£25 double.
Half board: £17-£20 daily, £115.50-£140 weekly.
Evening meal 6.30pm (l.o. 9.30pm).
Parking for 6.

Ferny Park

Bossiney Hill, Tintagel, PL34 0BB
☎ Camelford (0840) 770523
Comfortable modernised house with pretty garden and stream, on B3263 between Rocky Valley and Bossiney Cove. Ideal for walking, birdwatching and painting. Evening meals available by arrangement.
Bedrooms: 1 double & 1 twin.
Bathrooms: 2 public.
Bed & breakfast: £18-£22 double.
Half board: £15.50-£17.50 daily.
Parking for 3.

Halgabron House

Halgabron, Tintagel, PL34 0BD
☎ Camelford (0840) 770667
Traditional farmhouse dating from 14th C. with sea and coastal views. Adjacent to St. Nectans Glen and Rocky Valley. Non smokers only.
Bedrooms: 2 double & 1 twin, 1 family room.
Bathrooms: 1 public.
Bed & breakfast: £12-£16 single, £22-£30 double.

Half board: £18.50-£23.50 daily, £124-£150 weekly.
Evening meal 7pm (l.o. 1pm).
Parking for 4.

The Old Borough House

Bossiney, Tintagel, PL34 0AY
☎ Camelford (0840) 770475
Charming, licensed 17th C. guesthouse, friendly atmosphere, home cooking, 4 course dinner. Safe bathing at Bossiney Cove, 600 yards away.
Bedrooms: 5 double, 1 family room.
Bathrooms: 2 private, 2 public.
Bed & breakfast: £14-£22 single, £19-£32 double.
Half board: £17.50-£24 daily, £112.50-£153 weekly.
Evening meal 7pm (l.o. 3pm).
Parking for 13.

Rosebud Cottage
Listed

Bossiney, Tintagel, PL34 0AX
☎ Camelford (0840) 770861
Attractive Cornish cottage in a quiet setting with secluded garden. Short walk from the beach along headland and close to Tintagel and Boscastle.
Bedrooms: 2 double, 1 family room.
Bathrooms: 1 public.
Bed & breakfast: £9 single, £18 double.
Half board: £12.50 daily, £87.50 weekly.
Evening meal 7pm (l.o. 7pm).
Parking for 5.

St Adwen

St. Nectan's Glen, Trethevy, Tintagel, PL34 0BE
☎ Camelford (0840) 770450
Nestled in an acre of gardens at the entrance to glen and waterfall. Between Tintagel and Boscastle on the B3263 at Trethevy.
Bedrooms: 1 single, 1 double & 1 twin.
Bathrooms: 2 public.
Bed & breakfast: £9 single, £18 double.
Lunch available.
Parking for 4.
Open April-September.

Trewarmett Lodge Hotel 🏨

Trewarmett, Tintagel,
PL34 0ET
☎ Camelford (0840) 770460
Converted from village pub to family-run hotel and restaurant, providing comfortable, homely accommodation and personal service. Situated in a beautiful area.
Bedrooms: 1 single, 1 double & 2 twin, 2 family rooms.
Bathrooms: 1 private,
2 public.
Bed & breakfast: £15-£17 single, £30-£34 double.
Half board: £21-£24 daily, £140-£148 weekly.
Lunch available.
Evening meal 6.30pm (l.o. 10.30pm).
Parking for 10.
Credit: Access, Visa, Diners.

TIVERTON
Devon
Map ref 1D2

Busy market and textile town, settled since the 9th C, at the meeting of 2 rivers below southern Exmoor. Town houses, Tudor almshouses and parts of the fine church were built by wealthy cloth merchants; a medieval castle is incorporated into a private house and the original building of Blundells school is preserved by the National Trust. ℹ

Little Holwell
Listed

Collipriest, Tiverton,
EX16 1PT
☎ (0884) 258741
Old farmhouse set in rolling countryside 1.5 miles from Tiverton. Quiet and scenic position.
Bedrooms: 1 double & 1 twin, 1 family room.
Bathrooms: 1 public.
Bed & breakfast: £9 single, £18 double.
Half board: £13.50 daily, £75 weekly.
Evening meal 6.30pm.
Parking for 6.

Lower Collipriest Farm

Tiverton, EX16 4PT
☎ (0884) 252321
221-acre dairy and beef farm. Lovely thatched farmhouse in beautiful Exe Valley. Of particular interest to naturalists. Traditional and speciality cooking. Coasts and moors within easy reach.
Brochure available.
Bedrooms: 2 twin.
Bathrooms: 2 private.
Bed & breakfast: max. £18.50 single, max. £37 double.
Half board: max. £21 daily, £130-£140 weekly.
Evening meal 7pm (l.o. midday).
Parking for 4.
Open April-October.

TORQUAY
Devon
Map ref 1D2

Devon's grandest resort, developed from a fishing village. Smart apartments and terraces rise from the sea front and Marine Drive along the headland gives views of beaches and colourful cliffs. ℹ

The Beehive
Steep Hill, Maidencombe,
Torquay, TQ1 4TS
☎ (0803) 314647
In a peaceful valley 4 minutes' walk from the beach, close to Torquay harbour and within easy reach of Dartmoor. All rooms have magnificent sea views.
Bedrooms: 1 single, 2 double & 1 twin.
Bathrooms: 1 private, 1 public.
Bed & breakfast: £10-£12 single, £20-£24 double.
Parking for 7.

Craig Court Hotel

10 Ash Hill Rd., Torquay,
TQ1 3HZ
☎ (0803) 24400
Small hotel situated a short distance from the town centre and the harbour. Quiet location with a lovely garden and choice of menus.
Bedrooms: 2 single, 4 double & 2 twin, 2 family rooms.
Bathrooms: 4 private, 3 public.
Bed & breakfast: £10-£13 single, £20-£26 double.

Half board: £16-£19 daily, £101.50-£122.50 weekly.
Evening meal 6pm (l.o. 6.30pm).
Parking for 10.
Open April-October.

Kirkside Guest House
2 Princes Rd. East, Torquay,
TQ1 1PE
☎ (0803) 23545
Small friendly, family-run accommodation with colour TV in all bedrooms. Keys to rooms provided - access at all times.
Bedrooms: 3 single, 1 double & 1 twin, 1 family room.
Bathrooms: 1 public.
Bed & breakfast: £8-£9 single, £15-£16 double.
Half board: £13-£14 daily, £91-£98 weekly.
Evening meal 6.30pm (l.o. 9am).
Parking for 3.

TORRINGTON
Devon
Map ref 1C1

Perched high above the River Torridge, with a charming market square, Georgian town hall, and a museum. The famous Dartington Crystal Factory, Rosemoor Gardens and Beaford Arts Centre, are all located in the town. ℹ

Flavills Farm
Kingscott, St. Giles in the Wood, Torrington,
EX38 7JW
☎ (080 52) 3250 & 3530
125-acre mixed farm. 15th C. farmhouse in conservation area of picturesque hamlet giving peaceful atmosphere.
Bedrooms: 1 single, 2 double, 1 family room.
Bathrooms: 2 private, 2 public.
Bed & breakfast: £7.50 single, £15 double.
Parking for 12.
Open April-October.

MAP REFERENCES APPLY TO THE COLOUR MAPS TOWARDS THE END OF THIS GUIDE.

TOTNES
Devon
Map ref 1D2

Old market town steeply-built near the head of the Dart estuary. Remains of medieval gateways, a noble church, 16th C Guildhall and medley of period houses recall former wealth from cloth and shipping, continued in rural and water industries. ℹ

Broomborough House Farm
Broomborough Drive
Higher Plymouth Rd.,
Totnes, TQ9 5LU
☎ (0803) 863134
600-acre mixed farm. An elegant mansion 10 minutes' walk from the Elizabethan town of Totnes.
Bedrooms: 1 single, 2 double & 2 twin, 1 family room.
Bathrooms: 4 public.
Bed & breakfast: £13-£14 single, £26-£28 double.
Half board: £20.80-£21.80 daily, £141.50-£145.50 weekly.
Evening meal 6.30pm (l.o. 9am).
Parking for 10.
Open April-October.

Dorsley Park
Listed

Higher Plymouth Rd.,
Totnes, TQ9 6DN
☎ (0803) 863680
23-acre mixed farm. Two 160-year-old stone-built cottages offering comfortable accommodation, in a relaxed and friendly atmosphere. Teas and coffees available in the evening free of charge.
Bedrooms: 1 single, 1 double & 1 twin.
Bathrooms: 2 public.
Bed & breakfast: £9-£10 single, £18-£20 double.
Parking for 5.

Old Forge Guest House 🏨

Seymour Pl., Bridgetown,
Totnes, TQ9 5AW
☎ (0803) 862174
Provides all modern comforts in a delightful 600-year-old stone building.
Bedrooms: 2 double & 2 twin, 4 family rooms.
Bathrooms: 4 private, 1 public.

Continued ▶

TOTNES

Continued

Bed & breakfast: £23.50-£31.50 single, £27-£35 double.
Parking for 10.

🛇 🕭 🕮 💻 🖋 🛈 Ⓥ ✂ 🍴
📺 🎑 🛆 ✿ ✈ 🆂🅿 🎏 Ⓣ

Steam Packet Inn

4 St. Peter's Quay, Totnes,
TQ9 5EW
☎ Torbay (0803) 863880
Old English inn in the historic town of Totnes, right on the edge of the River Dart. Riverside garden and play area for children. We provide pub food all day at reasonable prices.
Bedrooms: 4 double, 1 family room.
Bathrooms: 1 public.
Bed & breakfast: from £14 single, from £26 double.
Lunch available.
Evening meal 6pm (l.o. 9pm).
Parking for 20.
Credit: Visa.

🛇 🖵 🕭 🛈 Ⓥ 🎞 ✿ 🎏

TREKNOW

Cornwall
Map ref 1B2

4m NW. Camelford

Tregosse Guest House

😊😊

Tregosse, Treknow, Tintagel,
PL34 0EP
☎ Camelford (0840) 770482
House situated on cliff alongside National Trust land, with spectacular views. Follow road signs for Treknow. Easy parking.
Bedrooms: 1 single, 2 double & 1 twin.
Bathrooms: 1 public; 2 private showers.
Bed & breakfast: £10-£11 single, £20-£22 double.
Half board: £16-£16.50 daily, £105-£115 weekly.
Lunch available.
Evening meal 6.30pm (l.o. 4pm).
Parking for 8.

🛇 🕭 🕮 🛈 Ⓥ 🍴 📺 ● 🎞
🛆 🎏 ✎ 🆂🅿

TROWBRIDGE

Wiltshire

See West Ashton.

TRULL

Somerset
Map ref 1D1

Higher Dipford Farm

😊😊😊

Dipford, Trull, Taunton,
TA3 7NU
☎ Taunton (0823) 275770 & 283497
120-acre dairy and beef farm. Old Somerset longhouse with inglenook fireplaces. Real farmhouse fare using own produce from the dairy. Fresh salmon a speciality. Friendly atmosphere.
Bedrooms: 3 double & 1 twin, 1 family room.
Bathrooms: 5 private.
Bed & breakfast: £20-£25 single, £40 double.
Half board: £32 daily, £190-£220 weekly.
Lunch available.
Evening meal 6.30pm (l.o. 10pm).
Parking for 10.
Open March-December.

🛇 🕭 🖵 🕭 🕮 🛈 Ⓥ ✂ 🛆
📺 🎞 🛆 ☕ 🕙 🖐 ✎ ✿ ✈
🎏 ✎ 🆂🅿 🎏

The Winchester Arms 😊

Church Road, Trull,
Taunton, TA3 7LG
☎ (0823) 284723
17th C. village inn in pretty, rural village. Restaurant has a la carte menu. Nicely decorated rooms.
Bedrooms: 1 single, 2 double, 1 family room.
Bathrooms: 1 public.
Bed & breakfast: from £12 single, from £22 double.
Lunch available.
Evening meal 7.30pm (l.o. 9.30pm).
Parking for 30.

🛇 🖵 🕮 🛈 Ⓥ 🎞 🛆 ✿ 🎏

TRURO

Cornwall
Map ref 1B3

See also Penhallow. Cornwall's administrative centre and cathedral city, set at the head of Truro River on the Fal estuary. A medieval stannary town, it handled mineral ore from West Cornwall; fine Georgian buildings recall its heyday as a society haunt in the second mining boom. 🅸

Lands Vue Country House 😊

Three Burrows, Truro,
TR4 8JA
☎ (0872) 560242
Offering warm welcome, relaxed atmosphere, peace and quiet and traditional home cooking. Panoramic views. A quarter of a mile off A30.
Bedrooms: 1 single, 1 double & 1 twin, 1 family room.
Bathrooms: 1 public.
Bed & breakfast: £9-£13 single, £18-£26 double.
Half board: £15-£19 daily, £105-£120 weekly.
Evening meal 7pm (l.o. 4pm).
Parking for 4.

🛇 🕮 🕮 🛈 Ⓥ 🍴 📺 🎞 🛆
🍴 🕭 🕙 ✿ 🎏 🆂🅿

Marcorrie Hotel 😊

😊😊

20 Falmouth Rd., Truro,
TR1 2HX
☎ Truro (0872) 77374
Family-run hotel close to the city centre. For business or holiday; central for touring Cornwall.
Bedrooms: 2 single, 3 double & 2 twin, 5 family rooms.
Bathrooms: 6 private, 1 public; 4 private showers.
Bed & breakfast: £14.50-£25 single, £27-£35 double.
Half board: £20.25-£30.75 daily, from £131.75 weekly.
Evening meal 7pm (l.o. 7pm).
Parking for 16.
Credit: Access, Visa.

🛇 🕭 🕮 🖵 🕭 🛈 Ⓥ 🍴 📺
🎞 🛆 🍴 🖐 🕮 🆂🅿 🎏 🆂🅿 Ⓣ

UPLOWMAN

Devon
Map ref 1D2

4m NE. Tiverton

West Pitt Farm

Uplowman, Tiverton,
EX16 7DU
☎ (0884) 820296
33-acre mixed farm. 16th C. farmhouse set in glorious countryside 2 miles from the M5. The guest lounge has inglenook fireplace, bread oven and oak beams. Bedrooms all face south.
Bedrooms: 1 double & 1 twin, 2 family rooms.
Bathrooms: 2 public.
Bed & breakfast: from £11.50 single, from £23 double.
Half board: from £15.50 daily, from £108 weekly.
Evening meal 7pm.
Parking for 6.
Open January-November.

🛇 🕮 🕮 Ⓥ 🛈 🍴 📺 🛆 🕭 🏷
🍴 ✎ ✿ 🎏 🎏

WARMINSTER

Wiltshire
Map ref 2B2

Attractive stone-built town high up to the west of Salisbury Plain. A market town, it originally thrived on cloth and wheat. Many prehistoric camps and barrows nearby, along with Longleat House and Safari Park. 🅸

Otago

😊

3 Portway La., Warminster,
BA12 8RB
☎ (0985) 212182
An attractive quiet house of unusual design and charm, at the edge of the Salisbury Plain. Offering home cooking and comfort.
Bedrooms: 1 single, 2 twin.
Bathrooms: 2 public.
Bed & breakfast: £12-£14 single, £24-£28 double.
Half board: £18-£20 daily, £120-£134 weekly.
Evening meal 6.30pm (l.o. 8pm).
Parking for 3.
Open January-November.

🛇6 🖵 🕭 🕮 🛈 🍴 📺
🎞 🛆 ✿ 🎏

**PLEASE CHECK PRICES AND OTHER DETAILS
AT THE TIME OF BOOKING.**

**THERE IS A SPECIAL SECTION IN THIS
GUIDE LISTING ACCOMMODATION ESPECIALLY
SUITABLE FOR GROUPS AND YOUNG PEOPLE.**

White Lodge
Listed
22 Westbury Rd.,
Warminster, BA12 0AW
☎ (0985) 212378
Small country house in 2 acres of garden, 1 mile from Warminster on the A350. Ample parking.
Bedrooms: 1 single, 1 double & 1 twin, 1 family room.
Bathrooms: 1 private, 1 public.
Bed & breakfast: £11-£14 single, £22-£28 double.
Half board: £16-£19 daily, £96-£114 weekly.
Evening meal 7pm (l.o. 7.30pm).
Parking for 20.
🐾🍴 ⓊⓁ 🅥 🛏 📺 ▥ ⇦ ⌕ ✿ 🏧 🎣 SP

WASHFORD
Somerset
Map ref 1D1

2m SW. Watchet

The Washford Inn
Washford, Watchet,
TA23 0PP
☎ (0984) 40256
On the A39 next to Washford railway station. Perfect for exploring Exmoor, Brendon and Quantock Hills and coastline.
Bedrooms: 5 double & 3 twin.
Bathrooms: 8 private.
Bed & breakfast: £16-£18 single, £32-£36 double.
Lunch available.
Evening meal 6pm (l.o. 9pm).
Parking for 40.
Credit: Access, Visa, Diners, Amex.
🐾 📞 ⌨ 🖂 🎄 SP

GROUPS, CONSORTIA AND AGENCIES SPECIALISING IN FARM AND COUNTRY HOLIDAYS ARE LISTED IN A SPECIAL SECTION OF THIS GUIDE.

INDIVIDUAL PROPRIETORS HAVE SUPPLIED ALL DETAILS OF ACCOMMODATION. ALTHOUGH WE DO CHECK FOR ACCURACY, WE ADVISE YOU TO CONFIRM PRICES AND OTHER INFORMATION AT THE TIME OF BOOKING.

WATCHET
Somerset
Map ref 1D1

Small port on Bridgwater Bay, sheltered by the Quantocks and the Brendon Hills. A thriving paper industry keeps the harbour busy; in the 19th C it handled iron from the Brendon Hills. Cleeve Abbey, a ruined Cistercian monastery, is 3 miles to the south west.

The Haven
59 West Street, Watchet,
TA24 5NX
☎ (0984) 34093
Victorian house close to harbour and town centre. Clifftop location offering views across the Bristol Channel and the Quantocks.
Bedrooms: 1 double & 1 twin.
Bathrooms: 1 public.
Bed & breakfast: £9.50-£11 single, £18-£21 double.
Half board: £14.90-£18.40 daily, £92.30-£116.80 weekly.
Evening meal 7pm (l.o. 9pm).
🐾 ✿ ⓊⓁ 🅘 🅥 📺 ▥ 🖂 🎄 SP

Orchard House
⌂⌂
Roadwater, Watchet,
TA23 0QH
☎ Washford (0984) 41011
A modern comfortable house offering garden with trout stream in a quiet village overlooking the Brendon Hills. Inside Exmoor National Park.
Bedrooms: 3 double & 1 twin.
Bathrooms: 2 public.
Bed & breakfast: £12-£14 single, £24-£28 double.
Half board: £16-£18 daily, £105-£110 weekly.
Evening meal 6.30pm (l.o. 7pm).
Parking for 7.
🐾7 ✿ ⌨ ⓊⓁ 🛏 📺 ▥ ⇦ ♪ ✿ 🎄 🖂 SP

WEDMORE
Somerset
Map ref 1D1

Small stone town dominated by its great cruciform church. To the south, at the village of Meare, remains of a prehistoric lake village have been excavated.

Nut Tree Farm
Stoughton Cross, Wedmore,
BS28 4QP
☎ (0934) 712404
16th C. farmhouse set in peaceful 2 acres. Wholefood or traditional English breakfast. All diets happily catered for. Log fires, woodturning courses.
Bedrooms: 3 double & 1 twin, 1 family room.
Bathrooms: 3 private, 1 public.
Bed & breakfast: £10.50-£12.50 single, £21-£25 double.
Half board: £17-£19.50 daily, £119-£136.50 weekly.
Evening meal 7pm (l.o. 9pm).
Parking for 6.
Credit: Access.
🐾 ✿ ⌨ ⓊⓁ 🅥 ✂ 🛏 📺 ⇦ ✿ 🎄 🖂 DAP

WELLINGTON
Somerset
Map ref 1D1

See also Ashbrittle.
ⓘ

Hangeridge Farm
Wrangway, Wellington,
TA21 9QG
☎ Wellington (082 347) 2339
55-acre mixed farm. 5 minutes' walk from wooded hilly country walks, also close to Wellington Monument. 1 hour drive from West Country coast.
Bedrooms: 2 double, 1 family room.
Bathrooms: 1 public.
Bed & breakfast: £11 single, £21 double.
Half board: £15.50 daily.
Lunch available.
Evening meal 6.30pm.
Parking for 4.
🐾 ⓊⓁ 🅥 ⇦ 📺 ▥ ⇦ ∪ 🎄

Pinksmoor Mill House
⌂⌂⌂
Pinksmoor Farm,
Wellington, TA21 0HD
☎ Greenham (0823) 672361
98-acre dairy/sheep farm. Personal service and home cooking. House adjoins old mill and stream with abundant wildlife and scenic walks. Conservation area. TV available for bedrooms on request.

Bedrooms: 1 double & 1 twin, 1 family room.
Bathrooms: 2 private, 1 public.
Bed & breakfast: £13 single, £23 double.
Half board: £20 daily, £126-£136.50 weekly.
Evening meal 7pm (l.o. 4pm).
Parking for 5.
🐾 ⓊⓁ 🅥 ✂ 🛏 📺 ▥ ⇦ ∪ ⇦ ✿ 🎄 🏧

WELLS
Somerset
Map ref 2A2

See also Coxley, Wookey.
Small city set beneath the southern slopes of the Mendips, dominated by its magnificent cathedral. Built between 1180 and 1424, the cathedral is preserved in much of its original glory and with its ancient precincts forms one of our loveliest and most unified groups of medieval buildings. ⓘ

Bekynton House
⌂⌂⌂
7 St. Thomas St., Wells,
BA5 2UU
☎ Wells (0749) 72222
Comfortable period guesthouse, 3 minutes from cathedral, near city centre. Convenient for Bath, Bristol, Cheddar, Glastonbury and Longleat.
Bedrooms: 1 single, 4 double & 3 twin, 1 family room.
Bathrooms: 3 private, 3 public.
Bed & breakfast: £15-£17 single, £25-£33 double.
Half board: £19.50-£24 daily, £144-£168 weekly.
Evening meal 6.30pm (l.o. 11am).
Parking for 7.
🐾 🛏 ✿ ⓊⓁ 🅘 🅥 ⇦ ▥ ⇦ 🎄 ✿ SP

Burcott Mill
⌂⌂⌂
Burcott, Wells, BA5 1NJ
☎ (0749) 73118
Rural water mill with attached house, set in 1.5 acres. Many animals. Friendly atmosphere and home cooking. Opposite is a good pub.
Bedrooms: 2 single, 2 double & 1 twin, 1 family room.
Bathrooms: 2 private, 1 public; 1 private shower.
Bed & breakfast: £11-£13 single, £22-£26 double.

Continued ▶

WELLS
Continued

Half board: £17-£19 daily, £102-£123 weekly.
Evening meal 6pm (l.o. 4pm).
Parking for 10.

Cross Farm
Yarley, Wells, BA5 1PA
☎ (0749) 78925
17th C. Somerset longhouse, tastefully modernised, offering comfortable facilities.
Bedrooms: 1 double & 1 twin, 1 family room.
Bathrooms: 1 public.
Bed & breakfast: £10 single, £20 double.
Parking for 6.

Littlewell Farm Guest House
Coxley, Wells, BA5 1QP
☎ (0749) 77914
Converted farmhouse with all bedrooms having shower or bathroom en-suite. Coxley is 2 miles south west of Wells.
Bedrooms: 1 single, 2 double & 2 twin.
Bathrooms: 5 private.
Bed & breakfast: £15.50 single, £27-£29 double.
Half board: £24-£26 daily.
Evening meal 7pm.
Parking for 11.

Manor Farm
Listed
Polsham, Wells, BA5 1RP
☎ (0749) 72356
230-acre dairy farm. Centrally situated for Bath and Bristol, midway between Glastonbury and Wells. Eating establishment nearby.
Bedrooms: 1 single, 2 double & 1 twin, 1 family room.
Bathrooms: 1 public.
Bed & breakfast: £10-£12 single, £18-£24 double.
Parking for 12.
Open April-October.

Manor Farm
Old Bristol Rd., Upper Milton, Wells, BA5 3AH
☎ (0749) 73394
130-acre beef farm. Listed Elizabethan manor house on the slopes of the Mendips, 1 mile from Wells.
Bedrooms: 1 double & 1 twin, 1 family room.

Bathrooms: 1 public.
Bed & breakfast: £11 single, £20 double.
Parking for 6.

Tor Guest House
20 Tor St., Wells, BA5 2US
☎ (0749) 72322
Delightful 17th C. building in attractive grounds overlooking the cathedral and Bishops Palace. Comfortable bedrooms. Short walk from the town centre.
Bedrooms: 1 single, 3 double & 3 twin, 2 family rooms.
Bathrooms: 2 private, 2 public.
Bed & breakfast: £12-£15 single, £24-£34 double.
Half board: £20-£23 daily, £125-£145 weekly.
Lunch available.
Evening meal 6.30pm (l.o. 3pm).
Parking for 11.

Trinity Cottage
5 St. Andrew's St., Wells, BA5 2UW
☎ (0749) 73124
Comfortable bed and breakfast 2 minutes from the cathedral.
Bedrooms: 2 double & 3 twin, 1 family room.
Bathrooms: 2 public.
Bed & breakfast: from £11 single, from £22 double.
Parking for 3.

WEST ANSTEY
Devon
Map ref 1C1

4m W. Dulverton

Partridge Arms Farm 🅼
West Anstey, South Molton, EX36 3NU
☎ Anstey Mills (039 84) 217
200-acre mixed farm. Old established family farm. Well placed for touring, walking, riding, fishing, Exmoor National Park, north Devon, west Somerset and coastal resorts.
Bedrooms: 2 single, 2 double & 2 twin, 1 family room.
Bathrooms: 1 private, 3 public.
Bed & breakfast: £9-£10.50 single, £18-£21 double.
Half board: £14-£16 daily, £98-£112 weekly.

Evening meal 6.45pm (l.o. 6pm).
Parking for 10.

WEST ASHTON
Wiltshire
Map ref 2B2

2m SE. Trowbridge

Welam House
Bratton Rd., West Ashton, Trowbridge, BA14 6AZ
☎ (0225) 755908
In a quiet village. Garden of trees and lawn with view of Westbury's White Horse. Well placed for touring.
Bedrooms: 1 single, 1 double & 1 twin, 1 family room.
Bathrooms: 1 private, 2 public.
Bed & breakfast: £10-£11 single, £20-£22 double.
Parking for 6.
Open March-October.

WEST BAGBOROUGH
Somerset
Map ref 1D1

7m NW. Taunton

Higher House 🅼
West Bagborough, Taunton, TA4 3EF
☎ Bishops Lydeard (0823) 432996
Country house nestling on side of Quantock Hills, with superb views. Traditionally furnished, comfortable, friendly atmosphere. 10 miles from the M5. No smoking in dining room.
Bedrooms: 4 double & 3 twin.
Bathrooms: 3 private, 2 public.
Bed & breakfast: £15.50-£18 single, £31-£36 double.
Half board: £25.50-£28 daily, £155-£170 weekly.
Evening meal 7.30pm (l.o. 5pm).
Parking for 13.

WEST BUCKLAND
Devon
Map ref 1C1

5m NW. South Molton

Huxtable Farm
West Buckland, Barnstaple, EX32 0SR
☎ Filleigh (059 86) 254
80-acre sheep farm. Medieval longhouse converted byre, barn and round-house (listed). 4-course candle-lit dinners with home made wine, bread, clotted cream. Own garden and dairy produce. Log fires. Clay pigeon shooting. Games room.
Bedrooms: 1 single, 2 double & 1 twin, 2 family rooms.
Bathrooms: 2 private, 2 public; 2 private showers.
Bed & breakfast: £11-£12 single, £22-£26 double.
Half board: £18-£19 daily, £110-£120 weekly.
Lunch available.
Evening meal 7.30pm (l.o. 6pm).
Parking for 6.

WEST HARPTREE
Avon
Map ref 2A2

Pretty red-stone village, with old manor houses, set under the northern slopes of the Mendips. It is well-placed for exploring the hills or the Somerset coast.

The Farm
West Harptree, Bristol, BS18 6HE
☎ West Harptree (0761) 221348
100-acre dairy farm. Located in the Mendip Hills. Centrally situated for Bath, Bristol, Wells and Cheddar. Complete privacy in a relaxed atmosphere.
Bedrooms: 2 double & 1 twin.
Bathrooms: 1 public.
Bed & breakfast: £10-£12 single, £20-£24 double.
Parking for 5.

INDIVIDUAL PROPRIETORS HAVE SUPPLIED ALL DETAILS OF ACCOMMODATION. ALTHOUGH WE DO CHECK FOR ACCURACY, WE ADVISE YOU TO CONFIRM PRICES AND OTHER INFORMATION AT THE TIME OF BOOKING.

WEST PENNARD

Somerset
Map ref 2A2

Ashcombe Farm M
Steambow, West Pennard,
Glastonbury, BA6 8ND
☎ Pilton (074 989) 734
*Period country house in
Pennard Vale, offering homely
accommodation with four-
poster beds and home cooking.
Excellent touring base near
Wells and Glastonbury.*
Bedrooms: 2 double, 1 family
room.
Bathrooms: 3 private,
1 public.
Bed & breakfast: £19-£24
double.
Evening meal 7pm (l.o. 5pm).
Parking for 10.

WEST STAFFORD

Dorset
Map ref 2B3

3m E. Dorchester

Lower Lewell Farmhouse
⊕⊕
West Stafford, Dorchester,
DT2 8AP
☎ (0305) 67169
*An historic farmhouse in the
beautiful Frome Valley, just
east of Dorchester. Well placed
for exploring the Dorset
countryside and coast.*
Bedrooms: 1 double & 1 twin,
1 family room.
Bathrooms: 1 public.
Bed & breakfast: £12-£13.50
single, £24-£27 double.
Parking for 6.

WESTBURY

Wiltshire

See Erlestoke.

WESTBURY-SUB-MENDIP

Somerset
Map ref 2A2

Stoneleigh House
Roughmoor La., Westbury-
sub-Mendip, Wells,
BA5 1HF
☎ Wells (0749) 870668

**WE ADVISE YOU TO
CONFIRM YOUR
BOOKING IN WRITING.**

---

*Beautiful old farmhouse with
magnificent views across open
country to Glastonbury Tor.
Well-situated for walking and
touring.*
Bedrooms: 2 double.
Bathrooms: 2 private.
Bed & breakfast: £24 double.
Parking for 3.

WESTON-SUPER-MARE

Avon
Map ref 1D1

Large, friendly resort
developed in the 19th C.
Traditional seaside
attractions include
theatres, a dance hall.
The museum shows a
Victorian seaside gallery
and has Iron Age finds
from a hill fort on
Worlebury Hill in Weston
Woods. ℹ

Commodore Hotel M
⬠⬠⬠
Sand Bay, Kewstoke,
Weston-super-Mare,
BS22 9UZ
☎ (0934) 415778
*Traditional hotel facilities with
popular restaurant, lounge bar
and carvery services. Situated
in unspoilt bay close to major
resort amenities.*
Bedrooms: 5 single, 11 double
& 3 twin, 1 family room.
Bathrooms: 20 private,
1 public.
Bed & breakfast: £32-£34
single, £44-£48 double.
Half board: £29-£46.50 daily,
£163-£264.50 weekly.
Lunch available.
Evening meal 6.30pm (l.o.
10pm).
Parking for 80.
Credit: Access, Visa, Diners,
Amex.

Homestead Guest House
⊕
2 Dickenson Rd., Weston-
super-Mare, BS23 1YW
☎ (0934) 26234
*Spacious Edwardian house on
the level and close to sea front,
parks, town and other facilities.*
Bedrooms: 1 single, 2 family
rooms.
Bathrooms: 1 public.
Bed & breakfast: £8-£9
single, £16-£18 double.
Parking for 3.

WEYMOUTH

Dorset
Map ref 2B3

Ancient port and one of
the south's earliest
resorts. Curving beside a
long, sandy beach, the
elegant Georgian
esplanade is graced with
a statue of George III and
a cheerful Victorian
Jubilee clock tower. ℹ

Brookfield
White Horse La., Sutton
Poyntz, Weymouth,
DT3 6LU
☎ (0305) 833674
*Comfortable family home in
attractive rural village. 5 miles
from Dorchester, 3 miles from
Weymouth and 1 mile from
nearest beach.*
Bedrooms: 2 double, 1 family
room.
Bathrooms: 1 public.
Bed & breakfast: £8-£10
single, £20-£25 double.
Parking for 2.
Open May-October.

Green Acre
83 Preston Rd., Preston,
Weymouth, DT3 6PY
☎ Preston (0305) 832047
*Close to Bowleaze Cove at the
east end of Weymouth.
Detached house with wood-
clad gables.*
Bedrooms: 1 single, 3 double
& 1 twin, 2 family rooms.
Bathrooms: 1 private,
2 public.
Bed & breakfast: £8.50-
£10.50 single, £17-£21 double.
Parking for 6.
Open April-October.

Tatton House
⊕⊕
Buckland Ripers, Weymouth,
DT3 4BX
☎ Upwey (030 581) 2840
*440-acre dairy farm. Attractive
Georgian farmhouse, tastefully
modernised with the emphasis
on friendliness and comfort. 3
miles north west of Weymouth.*
Bedrooms: 1 double & 1 twin,
1 family room.
Bathrooms: 1 public.
Bed & breakfast: £22-£24
double.
Parking for 6.
Open March-October.

WHEDDON CROSS

Somerset
Map ref 1D1

*5m SW. Dunster
Crossroads hamlet in the
heart of Exmoor National
Park.*

Little Quarme
Wheddon Cross, Minehead,
TA24 7EA
☎ Timberscombe
(064 384) 249
*15-acre sheep & horses farm.
Lovely old farmhouse in
secluded situation. Sun-lounge,
garden, outstanding views and
stabling available if required.
A quarter of a mile from
Wheddon Cross on Exford
road, B3224.*
Bedrooms: 2 double & 1 twin.
Bathrooms: 2 public.
Bed & breakfast: £10 single,
£20 double.
Parking for 8.

WHIMPLE

Devon
Map ref 1D2

4m NW. Ottery St. Mary

Down House
⊕⊕
Whimple, Exeter, EX5 2QR
☎ (0404) 822860
*5-acre mixed farm. Enjoy
peace and seclusion in this
Edwardian gentleman's
farmhouse and garden. Our
priorities are family
atmosphere, home baking and
personal service.*
Bedrooms: 2 single, 1 double
& 1 twin, 2 family rooms.
Bathrooms: 3 public.
Bed & breakfast: £10-£13.50
single, £20-£27 double.
Half board: £16-£19.50 daily,
£105-£129.50 weekly.
Evening meal 6.30pm (l.o.
5pm).
Parking for 8.
Open February-November.

Keepers Lodge
Strete Raleigh, Whimple
☎ (0404) 822980
*Comfortable home set in 6
acres of grass and trees, with
Dartmoor views. 2.5 miles
from Ottery St. Mary on the
B3174 Exeter road.*
Bedrooms: 1 single, 1 double
& 1 twin, 1 family room.
Bathrooms: 1 private,
2 public.

Continued ▶

WHIMPLE
Continued

Bed & breakfast: £9-£15 single, £18-£24 double.
Half board: £12.50-£18.50 daily.
Evening meal 5.30pm (l.o. 7pm).
Parking for 7.

WHITESTONE
Devon
Map ref 1D2

3m W. Exeter

Rowhorne Farm Guest House

Whitestone, Exeter, EX4 2LQ
☎ Exeter (0392) 74675
103-acre mixed farm. Just outside the city of Exeter in open countryside with extensive views and lovely garden. All visitors made welcome and served with farmhouse-style cooking.
Bedrooms: 1 double, 2 family rooms.
Bathrooms: 2 public.
Bed & breakfast: £9.50 single, £19 double.
Half board: £14 daily, £98 weekly.
Evening meal 7pm (l.o. 4pm).
Parking for 4.

WIDECOMBE-IN-THE-MOOR
Devon
Map ref 1D2

Old village in pastoral country under the high tors of east Dartmoor. The 'Cathedral of the Moor' stands near a tiny square, once used for archery practice, which has a 16th C Church House among other old buildings.

Sheena Tower

Widecombe-in-the-Moor, Newton Abbot, TQ13 7TE
☎ (036 42) 308
Comfortable moorland guesthouse overlooking Widecombe village, offering a relaxed holiday in picturesque surroundings. Well placed for discovering Dartmoor.
Bedrooms: 1 single, 2 double & 1 twin, 2 family rooms.

Bathrooms: 1 private, 2 public.
Bed & breakfast: £9-£10 single, £18-£20 double.
Half board: £15-£16 daily, £101.50-£108.50 weekly.
Evening meal 7.30pm (l.o. 7.30pm).
Parking for 10.

WINCANTON
Somerset

See Charlton Musgrove, Cucklington, Henstridge.

WINSFORD
Somerset
Map ref 1D1

5m N. Dulverton
Small village on the River Exe in splendid walking country under Winsford Hill. On the other side of the hill is a Celtic standing stone, the Caratacus Stone, and nearby across the River Barle stretches an ancient packhorse bridge, Tarr Steps, built of great stone slabs.

Folly
Listed

Winsford, Minehead, TA24 7JL
☎ (064 385) 253
10-acre mixed farm. Countryside accommodation with beautiful views, providing home cooking. Dogs and horses welcome. An ideal 'away from it all' spot, surrounded by moorland.
Bedrooms: 1 double & 1 twin, 1 family room.
Bathrooms: 1 public.
Bed & breakfast: £9.50-£10.50 single, £19 double.
Half board: £14.50-£15.50 daily, £98-£105 weekly.
Evening meal 7pm (l.o. 7pm).
Parking for 6.

Larcombe Foot

Winsford, Minehead, TA24 7HS
☎ (064 385) 306
Comfortable old country house in tranquil, beautiful setting, overlooking River Exe. Lovely walks on doorstep. Ideal for touring.
Bedrooms: 1 single, 1 double & 1 twin.
Bathrooms: 2 private, 1 public.

Bed & breakfast: max. £12 single, max. £24 double.
Parking for 3.
Open April-October.

WINSHAM
Somerset
Map ref 1D2

4m SE. Chard

The Squirrel Inn

Laymore, Winsham, Chard, TA20 4NT
☎ (046 030) 298
Modern country pub with good views. Borders Dorset, Somerset and Devon.
Bedrooms: 1 double & 2 twin.
Bathrooms: 3 private.
Bed & breakfast: £16-£17.50 single, £29-£32 double.
Lunch available.
Evening meal 6pm (l.o. 9.30pm).
Parking for 30.

WINTERBOURNE MONKTON
Wiltshire
Map ref 2B2

1m N. Avebury

New Inn

Winterbourne Monkton, Swindon, SN4 9NW
☎ Avebury (067 23) 240
Small and friendly country pub only 1 mile from Avebury. Games room. Packed lunches prepared if required.
Bedrooms: 1 double & 2 twin.
Bathrooms: 1 private, 1 public.
Bed & breakfast: £22-£25 double.
Lunch available.
Evening meal 6.30pm (l.o. 9.30pm).
Parking for 20.

WINTERBOURNE STOKE
Wiltshire
Map ref 2B3

5m W. Amesbury

Scotland Lodge

Winterbourne Stoke, Salisbury, SP3 4TF
☎ Shrewton (0980) 620943
Private country house offering en-suite bedrooms and self-contained unit; comfortable and ideally situated for touring. Near Stonehenge and Salisbury.
Bedrooms: 1 double & 2 twin, 1 family room.
Bathrooms: 4 private.
Bed & breakfast: £15-£25 single, £25-£35 double.
Parking for 10.

WITHLEIGH
Devon
Map ref 1D2

3m W. Tiverton

Great Bradley Farm
Listed

Withleigh, Tiverton, EX16 8JL
☎ Tiverton (0884) 256946
155-acre dairy farm. Charming 16th C. Devonshire longhouse offering quality accommodation to those seeking peace and quiet and beautiful scenic countryside. Non-smoking establishment.
Bedrooms: 1 double & 1 twin.
Bathrooms: 1 public.
Bed & breakfast: £9.50-£10 single, £19-£20 double.
Half board: £14-£15 daily, £95-£105 weekly.
Evening meal 7pm (l.o. 7.30pm).
Parking for 2.
Open March-October.

THERE IS A SPECIAL SECTION IN THIS GUIDE LISTING ACCOMMODATION ESPECIALLY SUITABLE FOR GROUPS AND YOUNG PEOPLE.

GROUPS, CONSORTIA AND AGENCIES SPECIALISING IN FARM AND COUNTRY HOLIDAYS ARE LISTED IN A SPECIAL SECTION OF THIS GUIDE.

WITHYPOOL

Somerset
Map ref 1D1

Pretty village high on Exmoor near the beautiful River Barle. On Winsford Hill (National Trust) above are Bronze Age barrows known as the Wambarrows.

Royal Oak Inn ♨
😀😀😀😀
Withypool, TA24 7QP
☎ Exford (064 383) 236
17th C. beamed Exmoor inn with open log fires and a great deal of atmosphere and comfort.
Bedrooms: 2 single, 4 double & 1 twin, 1 family room.
Bathrooms: 8 private.
Bed & breakfast: £22-£35 single, £36-£48 double.
Half board: £34-£47 daily, £238-£329 weekly.
Lunch available.
Evening meal 7pm (l.o. 9pm).
Parking for 20.
Credit: Access, Visa, Diners, Amex.
🛇10 ➄ ▨ ® ☐ ❖ ⓘ Ⓥ
⊬ ▥ ▱ ∪ ↗ ▸ ✓ ⌾ SP
⊞

WOODY BAY

Devon
Map ref 1C1

3m W. Lynton
Rocky bay backed by dramatic cliffs thick with oak woods on the western Exmoor coast. To the west over Martinhoe Hill the River Heddon reaches the sea through a steep wooded valley.

Slattenslade
Woody Bay, Parracombe, EX31 4QU
☎ Parracombe (059 83) 250
Overlooking the Bristol Channel. Magnificent scenery. Ideal for families, ramblers and bird watchers. Private lounge/diner, separate front door and own key.
Bedrooms: 1 double & 1 twin.
Bathrooms: 1 public.
Bed & breakfast: £10-£12 single, £20-£24 double.
Half board: £17-£20 daily, £110-£130 weekly.
Evening meal 6pm (l.o. 10am).
Parking for 4.
🛇 ✕ ⓤ Ⓤ ⓘ Ⓥ ⊬ Ⓣ ▱
∪ ❋ ▨ ▤ OAP SP

WOOKEY

Somerset
Map ref 2A2

2m W. Wells
Small village below the southern slopes of the Mendips, near the River Axe. A mile or so north east, the river runs through spectacular limestone caverns at Wookey Hole.

Manor Farm ♨
😀
Worth, Wookey, Wells, BA5 1LW
☎ (0749) 73428
20-acre mixed farm. Friendly accommodation with pony trekking, trout fishing, play area and swimming pool. Farm animals, peaceful fields and a brook to enjoy. Well placed for touring.
Bedrooms: 1 single, 2 double & 1 twin, 3 family rooms.
Bathrooms: 4 public.
Bed & breakfast: £8-£9 single, £16-£18 double.
Half board: £12-£13 daily.
Evening meal 6pm (l.o. midday).
Parking for 14.
🛇 ☐ ❖ ⓤ ▨ ⊬ Ⓣ ▱ ↈ ∪
↗ ▸ ❋ ▨ ⊞

Rushlands Farm
😀
Knowle La., Wookey, Wells, BA5 1LD
☎ Wells (0749) 73181
70-acre livestock farm. Farm with open views, down a lane from the village. There is home cooking and a friendly atmosphere. Central for sightseeing.
Bedrooms: 1 single, 1 double & 1 twin, 2 family rooms.
Bathrooms: 1 public.
Bed & breakfast: £8.75-£9 single, £17.50-£18 double.
Parking for 10.
Open April-October.
⚿ ⓤ Ⓥ ⊬ Ⓣ ▨ ▱ ❖ ⊀
▨

WOOKEY HOLE

Somerset
Map ref 2A2

2m NW. Wells
A series of spectacular limestone caverns on the southern slopes of the Mendips, near the source of the River Axe. The river flows through elaborate formations of stalactites and stalagmites.

The Wookey Hole Inn
Wookey Hole, Wells, BA5 1BP
☎ (0749) 72236
Comfortable Tudor style inn opposite Wookey Hole Caves. Ideal base for touring Somerset and Mendips. Families welcome.
Bedrooms: 1 double & 1 twin.
Bathrooms: 1 public.
Bed & breakfast: £17.50 single, £26-£30 double.
Lunch available.
Evening meal 6.30pm (l.o. 9.30pm).
Parking for 20.
Credit: Access, Visa.
🛇 ☐ ❖ ⓘ Ⓥ ▪ ∪ ▨

WOOLACOMBE

Devon
Map ref 1C1

See also Mortehoe.
Between Morte Point and Baggy Point, Woolacombe and Mortehoe offer 3 miles of the finest sand and surf on this outstanding coastline. Much of the area is owned by the National Trust. ℹ

Manor Farm
Woolacombe, EX34 7HF
☎ (0271) 870472
62-acre dairy farm. Full English breakfast is served. Children are welcome.
Bedrooms: 1 double, 1 family room.
Bathrooms: 1 public.
Bed & breakfast: £8-£8.50 single, £16-£17 double.
Half board: £13.50-£14 daily, £94.50-£98 weekly.
Evening meal 6pm.
Parking for 2.
Open April-October.
🛇 ✕ ⓤ ⓘ ⊬ Ⓣ ❋ ⊀ ▨

WOOLFARDIS-WORTHY

Devon
Map ref 1C1

3m SE. Clovelly

Stroxworthy Farm
Woolsery, Bideford, EX39 5QB
☎ Clovelly (023 73) 333
90-acre dairy farm. Located 4.5 miles from Clovelly, 3 miles south of the A39. Centrally situated, with Dartmoor and Exmoor within 50 miles.
Bedrooms: 2 double & 2 twin, 1 family room.
Bathrooms: 2 private.
Bed & breakfast: max. £25 double.
Half board: max. £18 daily, max. £126 weekly.
Evening meal 6.30pm (l.o. 7.30pm).
Parking for 10.
Open March-October.
🛇5 ▨ ❖ ⓘ ⊬ Ⓣ ▪ ∪ ↗
▸ ▨

WOOTTON BASSETT

Wiltshire
Map ref 2B2

6m W. Swindon
Small hillside town with attractive old buildings and a 13th C church. The church and the half-timbered town hall were both restored in the 19th C and the stocks and ducking pool are preserved.

Fairview Guest House
52 Swindon Rd., Wootton Bassett, Swindon, SN4 8EU
☎ Swindon (0793) 852283
Detached guesthouse close to the M4 junction 16 and major tourist resorts. Motel style annexe with 4 bedrooms.
Bedrooms: 3 single, 2 double & 5 twin, 2 family rooms.
Bathrooms: 4 public.
Bed & breakfast: £13.75-£14.75 single, £27.50-£29.50 double.
Evening meal 6.30pm (l.o. 2pm).
Parking for 15.
🛇 ⚿ ☐ ⓤ ⓘ Ⓥ Ⓣ ▨

The Trotting Horse
😀😀
Bushton, Wootton Bassett, Swindon, SN4 7PX
☎ (0793) 73338
Traditional country pub serving real ale and fresh food, 4 miles from Wootton Bassett.

Continued ▶

PLEASE MENTION THIS GUIDE WHEN MAKING A BOOKING.

WOOTTON BASSETT

Continued

Bedrooms: 1 single, 1 double & 1 twin.
Bathrooms: 3 private.
Bed & breakfast: £20-£25 single, £30-£35 double.
Half board: £26-£31 daily, £150-£185 weekly.
Lunch available.
Evening meal 7pm (l.o. 10pm).
Parking for 65.
Credit: Access, Visa.

YARCOMBE

Devon
Map ref 1D2

5m W. Chard
Tiny village between Honiton and Chard.

Crawley Farm

Yarcombe, Honiton, EX14 9AX
☎ Chard (046 06) 4760
200-acre mixed farm. 17th C. farmhouse with old world charm, set in Yarty Valley. Inglenook fireplace and oak beams. Traditional farmhouse cooking.
Bedrooms: 1 double, 2 family rooms.
Bathrooms: 2 public.
Bed & breakfast: £7.50-£9 single, £15-£18 double.
Half board: £11-£13 daily, from £70 weekly.
Evening meal 5.30pm (l.o. 7pm).
Parking for 6.
Open March-November.

YEOVIL

Somerset
Map ref 2A3

See also Chiselborough.
Lively market town set in dairying country beside the River Yeo, famous for glove making. Interesting parish church, Yeovil Museum at Hendford Manor. *i*

Carents Farm

Yeovil Marsh, Yeovil, BA21 3QE
☎ (0935) 76622
350-acre mixed farm. Set in its own garden, this old 17th C. farmhouse built of local ham stone overlooks peaceful countryside and has inglenooks and oak beams.
Bedrooms: 1 double & 2 twin.
Bathrooms: 1 public.
Bed & breakfast: from £12 single, from £21 double.
Half board: from £17 daily.
Evening meal 7pm (l.o. midday).
Parking for 6.
Open February-November.

Southwoods Guest House

3 Southwoods, Yeovil, BA20 2QQ
☎ (0935) 22178
Tastefully decorated Edwardian house. Friendly atmosphere. Adjoins local wooded beauty spot.
Bedrooms: 1 single, 1 double & 1 twin, 1 family room.
Bathrooms: 1 public.
Bed & breakfast: £10-£12 single, £19-£22 double.
Parking for 3.

Stonecroft Manor Farm
(Listed)

Tintinull, Yeovil, BA22 8PR
☎ Ilchester (0935) 840289
210-acre dairy farm. Large secluded hamstone farmhouse, set in 210 acres of farmland in beautiful open country.
Bedrooms: 1 single, 1 twin, 1 family room.
Bathrooms: 1 public.
Bed & breakfast: £7.50-£10 single, £15-£20 double.
Parking for 4.

ZEALS

Wiltshire
Map ref 2B2

2m W. Mere
Pretty village of thatched cottages set high over the Dorset border. Zeals House dates from the medieval period and has some 19th C. work. The Palladian Stourhead House (National Trust) in its magnificent gardens, lies further north.

Cornerways Cottage

Longcross, Zeals, BA12 6LL
☎ Bourton (0747) 840477
18th C. cottage with original beams. Ideal position for touring Stourhead, Stonehenge, Shaftesbury and other local attractions. Close to A303 midway for London/Devon and Cornwall.
Bedrooms: 1 single, 3 double & 1 twin, 1 family room.
Bathrooms: 1 private, 2 public.
Bed & breakfast: £9-£10 single, £18-£22 double.
Parking for 4.
Open March-November.

Stag Cottage

Fantley La., Zeals, Warminster, BA12 6NA
☎ Bourton(Dorset) (0747) 840458
17th C. thatched and beamed cottage on main A303, 1.5 miles from the National Trust gardens of Stourhead.
Bedrooms: 1 single, 2 double & 1 twin.
Bathrooms: 2 public.
Bed & breakfast: £10.50 single, £20 double.
Parking for 8.

ZENNOR

Cornwall
Map ref 1B3

4m W. St. Ives

Boswednack Manor ♏

Zennor, St. Ives, TR26 3DD
☎ Penzance (0736) 794183
3-acre smallholding. Granite farmhouse with sea and moorland views. Home cooking, peaceful atmosphere. Proprietors are experienced ornithologists and offer various special interest holidays.
Bedrooms: 3 double & 2 twin, 1 family room.
Bathrooms: 2 public.
Bed & breakfast: £9-£10 single, £16-£20 double.
Half board: £13-£14 daily, £91-£98 weekly.
Evening meal 7pm (l.o. 4pm).
Parking for 10.

When enquiring about accommodation you may find it helpful to use the booking enquiry coupons which can be found towards the end of the guide. These should be cut out and mailed direct to the establishments in which you are interested. Remember to include your name and address and please enclose a stamped addressed envelope (or an international reply coupon if writing from outside Britain).

EXMOOR COTTAGES & FARMHOUSES

From the office beside our inn between Exmoor and the sea we can recommend —
- Comfortable Self-Catering Cottages.
- Farmhouse Accommodation with food.
- Spring, Autumn and Winter Weekends.

For free brochure or advice please call anytime —

BEACH & BRACKEN HOLIDAYS
THE WHITE HART INN, BRATTON FLEMING,
BARNSTAPLE, DEVON. EX31 4SA.
TELEPHONE: BRAYFORD (05988) 702

Clennon Valley Hotel

1 Clennon Rise, Paignton, South Devon.
Tel: (0803) 550304

A warm welcome and personal service await you at Clennon Valley Hotel, where the guest is the most important person. All rooms with Private Facilities, Colour TV with Satellite and Video Channels, Direct Dial Telephone, Radio/Alarm, Tea/Coffee Making. Fully Licensed Restaurant, Bar, Dance Floor. Ample Car Parking. With free membership to leisure centre and the new water theme park.

DOCKRELL HOUSE

4 Parkwood Road, Tavistock, Devon PL19 0HQ.
☎ (0882) 614254/614379.

Comfortable rooms, all with shower and colour televisions, some fully en-suite. Off street parking, laundrette and ironing facilities, pay-phone, lounge. Choice of breakfast served in pleasant dining room. Seven rooms in annexe.

English Tourist Board
Listed

Min: £9.20 inclusive of VAT.
Max: £10.35 inclusive of VAT.
20% reduction for children in parents room. Weekly terms.
Dogs welcome.

Jeannie Wilkins & Mike Carter
extend a warm and friendly
welcome at

Hillards

High Street, Curry Rivel, Langport, Somerset TA10 0EY.
☎ (0458) 251737. B&B

Grade II listed of architectural and historical interest. Old world charm — oak & elm panelled walls, beamed ceilings and large open fire places create an intimate and homely atmosphere. Family/TV room — horse brasses adorn the enormous inglenook fireplace and cat baskets fill the hearth. Magnificent oak and elm panelled dining room. Beautiful oak lounge that opens onto a walled garden. Luxurious bedrooms with basin or ensuite facilities. Furnished to a very high standard and centrally heated.

£15-£18 p.p.p.n. Brochure on request.   ETB ♛♛♛   AA Listed.   RAC Highly Acclaimed.

South of England

For military buffs, the South of England tourist region is surely the place to be. Taking in Hampshire, eastern Dorset and the Isle of Wight, the region boasts great natural harbours which have played key roles in England's maritime and military history.

There's plenty of choice if you want to take a look back into this history. Jewel in the crown must be Portsmouth, with its Naval Heritage Area featuring the Royal Naval Museum and such fine ships as HMS Victory, Warrior and Mary Rose at the Naval Base, the D-Day Museum with the Overlord embroidery, the Royal Marines Museum, and old forts such as Spitbank and Widley. Close by is Gosport with the Royal Navy Submarine Museum.

BROWNSEA ISLAND, POOLE HARBOUR

Also on the military theme, Aldershot's Military Museum, Bovington Camp's Tank Museum and the Museum of Army Flying at Middle Wallop are certainly worth a look for an insight into Army history.

More peacefully, the South of England offers a variety of holiday resorts — including the 'Queen of the Coast', Bournemouth — historic towns and cities such as ancient Winchester, and beautiful countryside, including that magnificent 90,000-acre playground, the New Forest.

A short trip across the Solent takes you to another holiday playground — the unique, self-contained and immensely hospitable Isle of Wight.

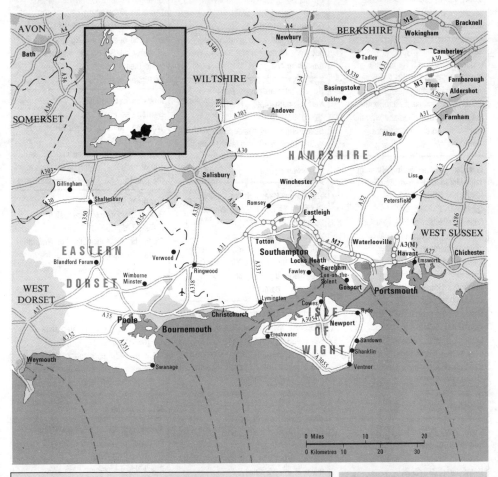

FIND OUT MORE

Further information about holidays and attractions in the South of England tourist region is available from: **Southern Tourist Board**, Town Hall Centre, Leigh Road, Eastleigh, Hampshire SO5 4DE. ☎ (0703) 616027.

These publications are available free from the Southern Tourist Board:
Southern England Holidays '89
Places to Visit '89 (separate brochures covering Hampshire, Dorset, Isle of Wight, Salisbury & District)
Take a Break
Churches and Cathedrals
Events List

Also available are the following Leisure Maps (prices include postage and packing):
Southern England £2.75
Wessex £2.75
Isle of Wight £2.25

WHERE TO GO, WHAT TO SEE

Mid-Hants Railway 'Watercress Line'
Alresford Station, Alresford, Hampshire SP24 9JG ☎ (096 273) 3810/4200
Preserved steam railway operating through attractive Hampshire countryside and passing through famous watercress beds.
Admission charge.

Needles Pleasure Park
Alum Bay, Isle of Wight PO39 0JD
☎ (098 375) 2401 ▶

▶ World-famous coloured sand cliffs. Model railway, studio glassworks, adventure playground.
Admission charge.

New Forest Butterfly Farm
Longdown, Ashurst, Hampshire
S04 4UH ☎ (042 129) 2166
Indoor tropical and British butterfly gardens, exotic insectarium, outdoor dragonfly ponds. Woodland wagon rides, shire horses. Picnic park.
Admission charge.

Beaulieu National Motor Museum
John Montagu Building, Beaulieu, Hampshire S042 7ZN
☎ (0590) 612345
Superb collection of 250 vehicles presenting the story of Britain's motoring heritage.
Admission charge.

Breamore House and Carriage Museum
Breamore, Hampshire SP6 2DF
☎ (0725) 22270
Elizabethan manor house with fine collection of works of art. Carriage museum contains the 'Red Rover', the last stage coach to run from London to Southampton.
Admission charge.

Royal Navy Submarine Museum and HMS Alliance
Haslar Pontoon Road, Gosport, Hampshire PO12 2AB
☎ (0705) 529217
Audio-visual briefing before guided visit to submarine Alliance and tour of Submarine Museum.
Admission charge.

Brownsea Island
Poole Harbour, Dorset BH15 1EE
☎ (0202) 707744
Island of 500 acres of woodland with beaches and glades, nature reserve. Regular boat service from Sandbanks and Poole Harbour.
Admission charge.

Flamingo Park
Oakhill Road, Springvale, Seaview, Isle of Wight PO34 5AP
☎ (0983) 612153
Waterfowl and water gardens with hundreds of tame birds. Shops.
Admission charge.

Royal Victoria Country Park
Netley, Southampton, Hampshire
☎ (0703) 455157
Beautiful grounds beside Southampton Water. Exhibitions, displays, Heritage Centre and shop.
Admission charge.

The Dorset Heavy Horse Centre
Brambles Farm, Verwood, Wimborne, Dorset BH21 5RJ ☎ (0202) 824040
Some of the finest Shire, Clydesdale, Suffolk Punch, Percheron and Ardennes horses in the country. Wagon and farm implements display, picnic area.
Admission charge.

Winchester Cathedral
The Close, Winchester, Hampshire
S023 9LS ☎ (0962) 53137
Norman architecture with various additions to 16th C. Splendid tombs and medieval wall paintings.
Admission free but donations welcomed.

The Hawk Conservancy
Weyhill, Andover, Hampshire SP11 8DY
☎ (026 477) 2252
Specialist birds of prey collection. Birds flown at intervals daily.
Admission charge.

Tank Museum
Bovington Camp, Wareham, Dorset
BH20 6JG ☎ (0929) 462721 Ext. 463
Largest and most comprehensive collection of armoured fighting vehicles in the world. Supporting displays and video theatres.
Admission charge.

Kingston Lacy House, Garden and Park
Wimborne Minster, Dorset BH21 4AE
☎ (0202) 883402
17th C house remodelled in 1835, with one of the finest picture collections in the country.   *Admission charge.*

Stratfield Saye House
Riseley, Basingstoke, Hampshire
RG7 2BT ☎ (0256) 882882
Family home of the Dukes of Wellington containing many mementos of the Iron Duke's military and political career. Unique 18-ton funeral hearse.
Admission charge.

Highclere Castle
Highclere, Nr. Newbury, Berkshire
☎ (0635) 253210
Set in beautiful parkland, castle remodelled by Charles Barry, architect of the Houses of Parliament, in 1839. Home of the Earls of Carnarvon.
Admission charge.

Portsmouth Naval Heritage Centre
Portsmouth, Hampshire
☎ (0705) 839766
Royal Naval Museum, HMS Warrior, HMS Victory and Mary Rose.
Admission charge.

COWES WEEK, ISLE OF WIGHT, 29 JULY – 6 AUGUST

Paul Anscomb

MAKE A DATE FOR...

Wessex Craft Show
Wilton House, Wilton, Salisbury,
Wiltshire *27 – 29 May*

Gold Hill Fair
Gold Hill and High Street, Shaftesbury,
Dorset *2 June*

Andover Festival
Various venues, Andover, Hampshire
1 – 16 July

**New Forest and Hampshire
County Show**
New Park, Brockenhurst, Hampshire
26 – 27 July

Cowes Week
Cowes, Isle of Wight *29 July – 6 August*

Hampshire County Show
Royal Victoria Park, Netley,
Southampton, Hampshire
11 – 13 August

Portsmouth Navy Days
HM Naval Base, Portsmouth, Hampshire
26 – 28 August

Martin Lloyd

Romsey Agricultural and Horse Show
Broadlands Park, Romsey, Hampshire
9 September

Southampton International Boat Show
Mayflower Park, Southampton,
Hampshire *15 – 23 September*

Fireworks Fair
National Motor Museum, Beaulieu,
Hampshire *4 November*

Tourist Information *i*

Tourist and leisure information can be obtained from Tourist Information Centres throughout England. Details of centres in the South of England region are listed below. The symbol 🛏 means that an accommodation booking service is provided. Centres marked with a ✳ are open during the summer months only. In the following pages, towns which have a Tourist Information Centre are indicated with the symbol *i*

Aldershot
Hampshire 🛏
Military Historical Museum,
Queens Avenue
☎ (0252) 20968

Andover
Hampshire 🛏 ✳
Town Mill Car Park, Bridge Street
☎ (0264) 24320

Beaulieu
Hampshire
John Montagu Building
☎ (0590) 612345

Blandford
Dorset 🛏 ✳
Marsh & Ham Car Park,
West Street
☎ (0258) 51989

Bournemouth
Dorset 🛏
Westover Road
☎ (0202) 291715/290883

Christchurch
Dorset 🛏
30 Saxon Square
☎ (0202) 471780

Eastleigh
Hampshire 🛏
Town Hall Centre, Leigh Road
☎ (0703) 614646 ext. 3067

Fareham
Hampshire 🛏
Ferneham Hall, Osborn Road
☎ (0329) 221342

Farnborough
Hampshire 🛏
Divisional Library,
Pinehurst Avenue
☎ (0252) 513838 ext. 24

Fleet
Hampshire 🛏
Ghurka Square, off High Street
☎ (0252) 811151

Gosport
Hampshire 🛏 ✳
Falklands Gardens
☎ (0705) 522944

Havant
Hampshire 🛏 ✳
1 Park Road South
☎ (0705) 480024

Hayling Island
Hampshire 🛏 ✳
Sea Front
☎ (0705) 467111

Isle of Wight:
Cowes 🛏 ✳
8 Fountain Yard
☎ (0983) 291914 ►

▶ **Newport** ⛺
Town Lane Car Park
☎ (0983) 525450

Ryde ⛺ *
Western Esplanade
☎ (0983) 62905

Sandown ⛺
The Esplanade
☎ (0983) 403886

Shanklin ⛺
67a High Street
☎ (0983) 862942

Ventnor ⛺ *
34 High Street
☎ (0983) 853625

Yarmouth ⛺ *
The Quay
☎ (0983) 760015

Lymington
Hampshire ⛺ *
St. Thomas's Car Park

Lyndhurst
Hampshire ⛺ *
Main Car Park
☎ (042 128) 2269

Petersfield
Hampshire
Petersfield Library,
27 The Square
☎ (0730) 63451

Poole
Dorset
Poole Quay ⛺
☎ (0202) 673322
Arndale Centre
(personal callers only)

Portsmouth & Southsea
Hampshire
The Hard ⛺
☎ (0705) 826722/3
Castle Buildings,
Clarence Esplanade ⛺ *
☎ (0705) 754358
Continental Ferry Port, Albert
Johnson Quay, Mile End ⛺ *
☎ (0705) 698111

Ringwood
Hampshire ⛺ *
Furlong Car Park
☎ (0425) 470896

Romsey
Hampshire ⛺ *
Bus Station Car Park,
Broadwater Road
☎ (0794) 512987

St. Leonards
Dorset *
Camper Advisory Service,
St. Leonards Hotel Car Park,
Ringwood Road
☎ (042 54) 70375

Shaftesbury
Dorset
Bell Street
☎ (0747) 3514

Southampton
Hampshire
The Precinct, Above Bar
☎ (0703) 221106
Rownhams Service Area,
M27 Westbound ⛺ *
☎ (0703) 730345

Swanage
Dorset ⛺
The White House, Shore Road
☎ (0929) 422885

Wimborne
Dorset ⛺
The Quarter Jack, Cook Row
☎ (0202) 886116

Winchester
Hampshire ⛺
The Guildhall, The Broadway
☎ (0962) 65406

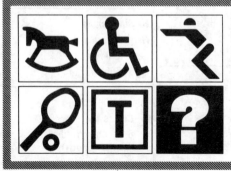

KEY TO SYMBOLS
Open out the flap inside the
back cover of this guide and
the key to symbols will be
easy to use.

Entries in this regional section are listed in alphabetical order of place name, and then in alphabetical order of establishment. County names are not normally repeated in each establishment entry, but please use the full postal address when writing.

The map references refer to the colour maps towards the end of this guide. The first number is the number of the map, and it is followed by the grid reference.

The Crown Classifications are explained on pages 8 and 9, and the key to symbols is on the flap inside the back cover — keep it open for easy reference.

Dorset
Map ref 2B3

3m E. Puddletown

2 Briantspuddle
Dorchester, DT2 7HR
☎ Bere Regis (0929) 471123
Listed 18th C. thatched cottage in secluded garden, 200 yards from centre of pretty village and 3 miles from Bere Regis.
Bedrooms: 1 single, 1 twin.
Bathrooms: 1 public.
Bed & breakfast: £10-£12.50 single, £20-£25 double.
Parking for 2.
🛏4 🎿 ✿ Ⓤ Ⓥ Ⓣⓥ ▲ ✕ 𝄢

Hampshire
Map ref 2C2

Between Old and New Alresford lie the remains of Bishop de Lucy's splendid 12th C reservoir. New Alresford is a pleasant market town and Old Alresford a smaller village with a stream running through the green.

Dean Farm
[Listed]
Kilmeston, Nr. Alresford, SO24 0NL
☎ Bramdean (096 279) 286
200-acre mixed farm. Comfortable, 18th C. farmhouse in Kilmeston, a small and peaceful village one and a half miles off the A272 between Petersfield and Winchester.
Bedrooms: 2 double, 1 family room.
Bathrooms: 1 public.

Bed & breakfast: from £24 double.
Parking for 3.
Open April-November.
🛏10 🎿 Ⓤ ✓ Ⓣⓥ ✿ 𝄢

Hampshire
Map ref 2C2

10m SE. Basingstoke
Pleasant old market town standing on the Pilgrim's Way with some attractive Georgian buildings. The Parish Church still bears the scars of bullet marks, evidence of a bitter struggle between the Roundheads and the Royalists.

Mrs. P.M. Cooper
Long Candovers, Hartley Mauditt, Alton, GU34 3BP
☎ Selborne (042 050) 293
Traditional timber-frame farmhouse, in 3 acre garden and paddocks with sheep and poultry, in an area of outstanding natural beauty. Home baking and fresh produce.
Bedrooms: 1 single, 2 family rooms.
Bathrooms: 1 public.
Bed & breakfast: £12-£18 single, from £24 double.
Half board: £19.50-£25 daily, £125-£160 weekly.
Evening meal 6pm (l.o. 7pm).
Parking for 4.
Open April-October.
🛏 🎿 ✿ Ⓤ 🛉 Ⓥ 𝄢 Ⓣⓥ ●
✿ ✕ 𝄢 𝄢

Glenderry
52 Wellhouse Road, Beech, Alton, GU34 4AG
☎ (0420) 83235
Colonial-style residence set in grounds of three and a half acres with mature trees. Quiet and secluded.
Bedrooms: 1 double, 2 family rooms.

Bathrooms: 1 private, 1 public.
Bed & breakfast: £15-£18 single, £22-£28 double.
Parking for 9.
🛏 🎿 ✿ ✿ Ⓤ 🛉 ✓ 𝄢 Ⓣⓥ
𝄢 ▲ ♪ ✿ ✕ 𝄢

Dorset
Map ref 2B3

3m NW. Milton Abbas
Has a remarkable pub, with a facade like a Victorian railway station and the beer that is served is called Old Ansty Ale.

The Fox ⋔
Ansty, Nr. Dorchester, DT2 7PN
☎ Milton Abbas (0258) 880328
A Victorian traditional inn of Wessex flint and brick, tucked away in the heart of Dorset, with comfortable rooms and bars.
Bedrooms: 5 double, 5 family rooms.
Bathrooms: 10 private, 1 public.
Bed & breakfast: from £24 single, from £36 double.
Lunch available.
Evening meal 7pm (l.o. 10pm).
Parking for 100.
Credit: Access, Visa, Amex.
🛏 ✿ ☎ ☎ ✿ 🛉 Ⓥ 𝄢
𝄢 ▲ 𝄢 ● ✿ 𝄢 𝄢

Hampshire
Map ref 2C3

Small village on the north east edge of the New Forest.

Red Mill House
Southampton Road, Bartley, Southampton, SO4 2NA
☎ (0703) 813032
Bedrooms: 1 double, 1 family room.
Bathrooms: 1 public.
Bed & breakfast: £18-£20 double.
Parking for 2.
Open April-October.
🛏 🎿 Ⓤ 𝄢 ▲ ✕ 𝄢

Hampshire
Map ref 2B3

Seaside village with views of the Isle of Wight. Within easy driving distance of the New Forest.

Laurel Lodge ⋔
😀😀
48 Western Avenue, Barton on Sea, New Milton, BH25 7PZ
☎ New Milton (0425) 618309
Detached chalet bungalow with pleasant gardens. 5 minutes' level walk from cliff top and 2 miles from the New Forest, many beaches and sailing.
Bedrooms: 1 single, 1 double & 1 twin, 1 family room.
Bathrooms: 2 public.
Bed & breakfast: £12.50-£15 single, £22-£26 double.
Half board: £16-£17.50 daily, £110-£120 weekly.
Lunch available.
Evening meal 6pm.
Parking for 4.
🛏 🎿 𝄢 ✿ Ⓤ 🛉 Ⓥ 𝄢 Ⓣⓥ
𝄢 ▲ ✕ 𝄢 ⒹⒶⒻ ✎ Ⓢⓟ

Hampshire
Map ref 2C2

Rapidly developing commercial and industrial centre. The town is surrounded by charming villages and places to visit.

Street Farm House
😀😀
The Street, South Warnborough, Nr. Basingstoke, RG25 1RS
☎ Basingstoke (0256) 862225
1-acre farm. Charming Jacobean farmhouse, offering comfortable facilities. Well situated in a pretty, rural village within easy reach of London, Guildford and the South Coast.
Bedrooms: 2 twin, 1 family room.
Bathrooms: 1 public; 1 private shower.
Bed & breakfast: £13-£18 single, £28-£32 double.
Parking for 9.
🛏 ☎ ✿ Ⓤ 𝄢 🛉 𝄢 Ⓣⓥ 𝄢
▲ ● ✿ 𝄢 𝄢

THERE IS A SPECIAL SECTION IN THIS GUIDE LISTING ACCOMMODATION ESPECIALLY SUITABLE FOR GROUPS AND YOUNG PEOPLE.

BERE REGIS

Dorset
Map ref 2B3

This watercress-growing village was in the Middle Ages famed for its fairs and being a resort of Kings on their way to the south west; its former splendour is well commemorated by its medieval church.

Roke Farmhouse M
Roke Farm, Bere Regis, Wareham, BH20 7JF
☎ (0929) 471451
440-acre sheep/arable farm. Picturesque listed farmhouse, barn and working water wheel in the Isle of Purbeck, close to the beach and Hardy country.
Bedrooms: 1 double & 1 twin, 1 family room.
Bathrooms: 1 private, 1 public.
Bed & breakfast: £10 single, £10-£15 double.
Parking for 10.
♿ ♨ ⓊⓁ ⓉⓋ ▥ ☕ ♪ ❊ ✗
♨ ᴅᴀᴘ ⊞

BISHOPS SUTTON

Hampshire
Map ref 2C2

Village 2 miles south east of New Alresford on the A31.

Tarrenz
Mill Lane, Bishops Sutton, Alresford, SO24 0AA
☎ Alresford (0962) 733694
4.50-acre horticulture/watercress farm. Modern bungalow in country setting, with raspberries and vegetables grown on site.
Bedrooms: 1 twin, 1 family room.
Bathrooms: 1 public.
Bed & breakfast: £11.50 single, £23 double.
Parking for 6.
♿ ♨ ⚬ Ⓠ ♨ ⓊⓁ ⓥ Ⓥ ▥ ☕
❊ ♨

**GROUPS, CONSORTIA
AND AGENCIES
SPECIALISING
IN FARM AND
COUNTRY HOLIDAYS
ARE LISTED IN A
SPECIAL SECTION
OF THIS GUIDE.**

BLANDFORD FORUM

Dorset
Map ref 2B3

Almost completely destroyed by fire in 1731, the town was rebuilt in a handsome Georgian style. The church is large and grand and the town is the hub of a rich farming area. ℹ

Chapel Farm
Listed
Gussage St. Andrew, Blandford, DT11 8DL
☎ Handley (0725) 52267
Farmhouse, 200-400 years old, between Blandford and Salisbury at the village of Cashmoor. In quiet surroundings, with large rooms, four-poster bed and tennis court. Pub nearby.
Bedrooms: 2 double & 1 twin.
Bathrooms: 1 private, 1 public.
Bed & breakfast: £15 single, £35-£40 double.
Half board: £23-£32 daily, £157.50-£224.50 weekly.
Evening meal 7.30pm (l.o. 8.30pm).
♿ ♨ ⚪ ♨ ⓊⓁ ⓲ Ⓥ ⌖ ⓉⓋ
▥ ☕ ♪ ❊ ♨ ⊞

Farnham Farm House
Listed
Farnham, Blandford Forum, DT11 8DG
☎ Tollard Royal (072 56) 254
350-acre arable farm. 19th C. farmhouse in the Cranborne Chase with extensive views to the south, within easy reach of the coast.
Bedrooms: 1 double & 1 twin, 1 family room.
Bathrooms: 1 public.
Bed & breakfast: £12.50-£17.50 single, £25-£30 double.
Parking for 7.
♿ ⚪ ⓊⓁ Ⓥ ⌖ ⓉⓋ ☕ ❊
♨

Longberry Cottage
Piccadilly Lane, Shapwick, Blandford Forum, DT11 9JY
☎ (0258) 857397
18th C. thatched cottage with every comfort. In rural surroundings, 10 minutes from Kingston Lacy and Wimborne Minster. Nearest road B3082.
Bedrooms: 1 double & 1 twin.
Bathrooms: 2 private.
Bed & breakfast: £11 single, £22 double.
Parking for 2.
♿10 ⚪ ⓊⓁ ⓲ ⓉⓋ ▥ ❊ ♨
ᴅᴀᴘ

Meadow House
Tarrant Hinton, Blandford, DT11 8JG
☎ Tarrant Hinton (025 889) 498
Brick and flint farmhouse on historic Cranborne Chase. Double glazed, quiet and comfortable accommodation. Home-produced English breakfast.
Bedrooms: 2 single, 1 double & 2 twin, 2 family rooms.
Bathrooms: 3 public.
Bed & breakfast: £10-£11 single, £20-£22 double.
Parking for 10.
♿ ♨ ⓊⓁ ⓉⓋ ▥ ⌖ ✗ ♨

BOLDRE

Hampshire
Map ref 2C3

Attractive village with pretty views of the river from the bridge. The white plastered church sits on top of a hill.

Orchard House
Battramsley, Boldre, Lymington, SO4 8ND
☎ Lymington (0590) 76686
Quiet, comfortable accommodation set in 2 acres of orchards on the edge of the New Forest.
Bedrooms: 1 single, 2 double & 1 twin.
Bathrooms: 1 private, 1 public.
Bed & breakfast: max. £9.50 single, £22-£26 double.
Parking for 20.
♿6 ⓊⓁ Ⓥ ▥ ❊ ♨

BOURNEMOUTH

Dorset
Map ref 2B3

Seaside town set among the pines with a mild climate, sandy beaches and fine coastal views. The town has wide streets with excellent shops, a pier, a pavilion, museums and conference centre. ℹ

Egerton House Hotel
Listed
385 Holdenhurst Road, Queens Park, Bournemouth, BH8 9AN
☎ (0202) 34024
Tastefully appointed, 8-bedroom family-run hotel, in good position for Bournemouth and Boscombe town centre.
Bedrooms: 2 single, 2 double, 4 family rooms.
Bathrooms: 2 public.

Bed & breakfast: £10-£12 single, £19-£26 double.
Half board: £15-£18 daily, £65-£89 weekly.
Lunch available.
Evening meal 6pm (l.o. 7pm).
Parking for 8.
♿ ♨ ⓲ ⌖ ♨ ⓉⓋ ▥ ☕ ♨ ✗

Mayfield Private Hotel
🅿🅿
46 Frances Road, Bournemouth, BH1 3SA
☎ (0202) 21839
Overlooking public gardens with tennis, bowling and putting greens. Central for sea, shops and main rail/coach stations. Some rooms with shower or toilet/shower.
Bedrooms: 1 single, 4 double & 2 twin, 1 family room.
Bathrooms: 2 private, 2 public; 4 private showers.
Bed & breakfast: £8-£10 single, £16-£20 double.
Half board: £11-£14 daily, £69-£90 weekly.
Evening meal 6pm.
Parking for 5.
Open January-November.
♿6 ♨ ⓲ Ⓥ ▥ ⓉⓋ ▥ ♨ ᴅᴀᴘ
ꜱᴘ

Pinewood Guest House
Listed
197 Holdenhurst Road, Bournemouth, BH8 8DG
☎ (0202) 292684
All rooms are self-contained with every comfort provided, including vanity unit, fitted wardrobes and duvets.
Bedrooms: 1 single, 2 double & 1 twin, 4 family rooms.
Bathrooms: 2 public.
Bed & breakfast: £10-£12 single, £20-£24 double.
Parking for 8.
♿5 ♨ ⓲ Ⓥ ▥ ☕ ✗ ♨

Seabreeze Hotel M
32 St. Catherines Road, Southbourne, Bournemouth, BH6 4AB
☎ (0202) 433888
Victorian residence, family run, with large rooms and sea views. Forecourt parking.
Bedrooms: 2 single, 1 double, 6 family rooms.
Bathrooms: 5 private, 1 public.
Bed & breakfast: £9-£12 single, £18-£24 double.
Half board: £12.50-£15 daily, £75-£105 weekly.
Evening meal 6pm.
Parking for 8.
Credit: Visa.
♿ ♨ ⚪ ⓲ Ⓥ ▥ ⓉⓋ ⵣ ᴅᴀᴘ
⌀ ꜱᴘ

Sunhaven
⚘⚘

39 Southern Road,
Southbourne, Bournemouth,
BH6 3SS
☎ (0202) 427560
150 yards from the cliff zig-zag path and lift leading to sandy beach. Snacks and drinks available on request.
Bedrooms: 1 single, 3 double & 1 twin, 2 family rooms.
Bathrooms: 2 public.
Bed & breakfast: £9-£13.50 single, £18-£27 double.
Parking for 6.
Open March-November.
⛨5 ▦ ▮ Ⅴ ⊨ ⓉⅤ ▦ ☐ ᴅᴀꜰ

Wendover Guest House
Listed

67 Alumhurst Road, Alum
Chine, Bournemouth,
BH4 8HP
☎ (0202) 765924
Family-run guesthouse with home-cooked food and relaxed, friendly atmosphere.
Bedrooms: 1 single, 2 double & 1 twin, 3 family rooms.
Bathrooms: 1 public.
Bed & breakfast: £9-£12.50 single, £18-£25 double.
Half board: £12.50-£16.50 daily.
Evening meal 6pm.
Parking for 4.
Credit: Visa.
⛨3 ⚘ ▮ Ⅴ ⊨ ⓉⅤ ▦ ☐ ᴅᴀꜰ ⚲ ꜱᴘ

BRAMSHAW

Hampshire
Map ref 2C3

5m NW. Lyndhurst
On the northern fringe of the New Forest hidden among the trees. At Nomansland, so called, as it was originally the squatters who built it, red-brick houses sit back from the village green with its cricket pitch.

Parsonage Farm
Bramshaw, Nr. Lyndhurst,
SO43 7JF
☎ Southampton
(0703) 812207
115-acre mixed farm. Farm cottage accommodation with English breakfast in farmhouse. Private coarse fishing available. Close to golf course and forest walks.
Bedrooms: 1 single, 1 double & 1 twin, 1 family room.
Bathrooms: 1 public.

Bed & breakfast: £9.50 single, £19 double.
Parking for 8.
Open March-October.
⛨8 ▦ Ⅿ ⚘ ⚲ ▦ Ⅴ ⊨ ☐ Ｕ ᴊ ▦

BROADSTONE

Dorset
Map ref 2B3

Ashdell
85 Dunyeats Road,
Broadstone, BH18 8AF
☎ (0202) 692032
Secluded, comfortable accommodation with nice garden. In residential area near Wimborne, Poole, beaches and countryside. On bus route.
Bedrooms: 2 twin.
Bathrooms: 1 public.
Bed & breakfast: £10-£12 single, £16-£20 double.
Parking for 3.
⛨8 ▦ ▮ ☐ ▦ ⚲ ▦ ꜱᴘ

BROCKENHURST

Hampshire
Map ref 2C3

Attractive village with thatched cottages and a ford in its main street, well placed for visiting the New Forest.

Caters Cottage
Latchmoor, Brockenhurst,
SO42 7UP
☎ Lymington (0590) 23225
Uniquely secluded, nestling amidst peaceful forest surroundings, offering warm hospitality. The oak-panelled dining room and quaint bedrooms make Caters ideal for the discerning guest.
Bedrooms: 1 single, 1 double & 1 twin.
Bathrooms: 1 public.
Bed & breakfast: £12-£13 single, £23-£24 double.
Parking for 2.
⛨5 ▦ ▦ Ⅴ ⓉⅤ ▦ ❋ ▦ ᴅᴀꜰ ꜱᴘ

Cloud Hotel ⚘
⚘⚘⚘

Meerut Road, Brockenhurst,
SO42 7TW
☎ Lymington (0590) 22165 & 22254
A quiet country hotel overlooking the New Forest, with forest views, home-from-home cooking and comforts. Lunch on Sundays. 4 nights for the price of 3.
Bedrooms: 8 single, 3 double & 4 twin, 4 family rooms.
Bathrooms: 5 public.
Bed & breakfast: £26-£27.50 single, £52-£55 double.

Half board: £38-£40 daily, £180-£188 weekly.
Evening meal 7pm (l.o. 8pm).
Parking for 21.
⛨ ⓒ ▮ Ⅴ ⊨ ⓉⅤ ▦ ⌶ ▦ ᴅᴀꜰ ⚲ ꜱᴘ ▦ Ⓣ

BURLEY

Hampshire
Map ref 2B3

5m SE. Ringwood
Attractive centre from which to explore the south west part of the New Forest. There is an ancient earthwork on Castle Hill near by, which also offers good views.

Bay Tree House ⚘
Listed

1 Clough Lane, Burley, Nr.
Ringwood, BH24 4AE
☎ (042 53) 3215
Bedrooms: 1 single, 1 family room.
Bathrooms: 1 public.
Bed & breakfast: £10-£12 single, £20-£22 double.
Parking for 4.
Open January-November.
⛨ ⓒ ⚲ ▮ ⓉⅤ ▦ ⚲ Ｕ ❋ ✗ ▦

Mrs. A. Clarkson
The Vicarage, Church
Corner, Burley, Ringwood,
BH24 4AP
☎ (042 53) 2303
Very quiet house in lovely part of New Forest, with easy access to A31 and A35. Central for forest and coast, golf and riding.
Bedrooms: 1 double & 1 twin.
Bathrooms: 1 public.
Bed & breakfast: £20-£22 double.
Parking for 3.
⛨ ▦ Ⅴ ✗ ⊨ ⓉⅤ ▦ ⚲ ▦

CADNAM

Hampshire
Map ref 2C3

Village with some attractive cottages and an inn close to the entrance of the M27.

Mrs. Ann M. Dawe
⚘⚘

Budd's Farm, Winsor Road,
Winsor, Cadnam, Nr.
Southampton, SO4 2HN
☎ Southampton
(0703) 812381
200-acre dairy farm. Well-modernised, thatched farmhouse in pretty country garden. Located off A336.
Bedrooms: 1 twin, 1 family room.

Bathrooms: 1 public.
Bed & breakfast: £10-£10.50 single, £20-£21 double.
Parking for 3.
Open April-October.
⛨ ▦ ⊨ ⓉⅤ ▦ ✗ ▦

CHANDLERS FORD

Hampshire
Map ref 2C3

Mrs. J.E. Willis ⚘
68 Shaftesbury Avenue,
Chandlers Ford, Eastleigh,
SO5 3BP
☎ Chandlers Ford
(0703) 262995
Homely accommodation near Winchester, the South Coast and the New Forest - well placed for touring. Home-grown produce in season. Evening snacks. Non-smokers only.
Bedrooms: 1 single, 1 double & 2 twin.
Bathrooms: 1 public.
Bed & breakfast: £11-£12.50 single, £18-£22.50 double.
Half board: £16-£17.50 daily, £112-£120 weekly.
Evening meal 6.30pm (l.o. 8.30pm).
Parking for 5.
⛨10 ▦ ☐ ⚲ ▦ ▮ ⓉⅤ ▦ ⚲ ▮ ✗ ▦ ᴅᴀꜰ ꜱᴘ

CHRISTCHURCH

Dorset
Map ref 2B3

Tranquil town lying between the Avon and Stour just before they converge and flow into Christchurch Harbour. A fine 11th C church and the remains of a Norman castle and house can be seen. 🛈

Tutton's View ⚘
Listed

119 Stanpit, Christchurch,
BH23 3LX
☎ (0202) 471773
Private guest house within easy reach of all amenities. English breakfast.
Bedrooms: 2 double & 1 twin.
Bathrooms: 1 public.
Bed & breakfast: £8.50-£10.50 single, £17-£21 double.
Parking for 4.
⛨ ⚲ ☐ ⚲ ▦ ▮ ⓉⅤ ▦ ⚲ ▦ ᴅᴀꜰ ꜱᴘ

**THE SYMBOLS ARE
EXPLAINED ON THE
FLAP INSIDE THE
BACK COVER.**

COLDEN COMMON

Hampshire
Map ref 2C3

Commons End
Listed
Main Road, Colden
Common, Winchester,
SO21 1RR
☎ Twyford (0962) 713477
*Modern house with large
pleasant garden overlooking
fields. Lunches and dinners
available at nearby village inn.*
Bedrooms: 1 single, 1 family
room.
Bathrooms: 1 public.
Bed & breakfast: £10 single,
£20 double.
Parking for 5.
⌖ ⚲ ♥ 🆄 🛊 Ⅴ ⌷ ⊞
⚓ ❊ 🈺

CORFE CASTLE

Dorset
Map ref 2B3

One of the most
spectacular ruined
castles in Britain. Norman
in origin, the castle was a
Royalist stronghold
during the Civil War and
held out until 1645. The
village had a considerable
marble-carving industry in
the Middle Ages.

Bradle Farmhouse
Listed
Bradle Farm, Church
Knowle, Nr. Corfe Castle,
BH20 5NU
☎ (0929) 480712
*550-acre mixed farm. Built in
1862, set in the heart of
Purbeck, one mile from the
beach and coastal paths. Ideal
for families.*
Bedrooms: 1 double & 1 twin,
1 family room.
Bathrooms: 2 public.
Bed & breakfast: £10-£12
single, £18-£21 double.
Half board: £15-£16 daily,
£92-£100 weekly.
Evening meal 6.30pm (l.o.
8pm).
Parking for 4.
⌖ ⚶ 🆄 🛊 Ⅴ ✂ ⌷ ⊞ ⚓
❊ 🈺 🄟 🆂🅿 🈺

**MAP REFERENCES
APPLY TO THE
COLOUR MAPS
TOWARDS THE END
OF THIS GUIDE.**

CORFE MULLEN

Dorset
Map ref 2B3

Village 3 miles south west
of Wimborne. Church and
mill are of interest.

Highe House
145 Wimborne Road, Corfe
Mullen, Wimborne,
BH21 3DU
☎ Wimborne (0202) 882741
*3-storey Georgian building with
a 2-storey wing.*
Bedrooms: 1 single, 2 double
& 1 twin.
Bathrooms: 1 public.
Bed & breakfast: £11-£13
single, £22-£26 double.
Parking for 1.
⌖ ♥ 🆄 ✂ ⌷ ⊞ 🈺 🈺 🈺

DAMERHAM

Hampshire
Map ref 2B3

The Compasses Inn
Listed
Damerham, Fordingbridge,
SP6 3HQ
☎ Rockbourne (072 53) 231
*Village inn with public bar,
lounge bar and large dining
room, in a rural position
adjoining the village green.
Live jazz on Friday evenings.*
Bedrooms: 1 double & 1 twin,
2 family rooms.
Bathrooms: 1 public.
Bed & breakfast: from £13
single, from £26 double.
Lunch available.
Evening meal 7pm (l.o.
9.30pm).
Parking for 20.
⌖ 🛊 Ⅴ ✂ ⌷ ⚓ ❊ 🈺 🈺
🄟 🆂🅿

DENMEAD

Hampshire
Map ref 2C3

Comparatively modern
town south west of the
original settlement.

Forest Gate
Listed
Hambledon Road, Denmead,
Portsmouth, PO7 6EX
☎ Waterlooville
(0705) 255901
*Georgian house in 2 acre
garden, on main Hambledon
road B2150, halfway between
Denmead and Hambledon.
Dinner by arrangement.*
Bedrooms: 2 twin.
Bathrooms: 1 private,
1 public.

Bed & breakfast: £11.50-
£13.50 single, £23-£27 double.
Half board: £17.50-£19.50
daily, £120-£130 weekly.
Evening meal 7.30pm.
Parking for 4.
⌖ ♥ 🆄 ⌷ ⊞ ⚓ ♫ ❊ 🈺
🈺 🈺

DIBDEN

Hampshire
Map ref 2C3

Small village on the edge
of the New Forest with a
full recreation centre.
Picturesque 13th C
church overlooks
Southampton Water.

Dale Farm Guest
House ⋙
😊
Manor Road, Applemore,
Dibden, Southampton,
SO4 5TJ
☎ Southampton
(0703) 849632
*Friendly, family-run 18th C.
converted farmhouse, in
wooded setting with large
garden. 250 yards from A326,
adjacent to riding stables and
15 minutes from beach.*
Bedrooms: 1 single, 2 double
& 2 twin, 1 family room.
Bathrooms: 1 public;
1 private shower.
Bed & breakfast: £9.50-£12
single, £18-£21 double.
Half board: £14.50-£17.50
daily, £96-£115 weekly.
Evening meal 6pm (l.o.
11am).
Parking for 10.
⌖ ⚲ ♥ 🆄 🛊 Ⅴ ✂ ⌷ ⊞
⚓ ∪ 🅿 ❊ 🈺 🆂🅿 🈺

DROXFORD

Hampshire
Map ref 2C3

Village with numerous
Georgian buildings. Izaak
Walton was a frequent
visitor to the 18th C
rectory now owned by the
National Trust.

The Coach House
Motel ⋙
Listed
Hambledon Road, Droxford,
SO3 1QT
☎ (0489) 877812
*Modern motel accommodation
in area of outstanding beauty,
surrounded by leisure facilities
and adjacent to pub/restaurant.*
Bedrooms: 2 single, 7 double.
Bathrooms: 9 private.
Bed & breakfast: £27.50-
£32.50 single, £37.50-£42.50
double.

Parking for 12.
Credit: Access, Visa, Diners,
Amex.
⌖ ⚲ ♥ 🆄 ⊞ ⚓ ♪ 🈺 ∪
🅿 🈺 🈺

EAST MEON

Hampshire
Map ref 2C3

4m W. Petersfield
Set in one of the prettiest
river valleys in
Hampshire, with quiet
lanes leading over the
downs. The village is
unspoilt and has some
delightful cottages. The
church has a magnificent
black marble font with
scenes from the life of
Adam and Eve.

Dunvegan Cottage
Listed
Frogmore Lane, East Meon,
Nr. Petersfield, GU32 1QJ
☎ (073 087) 213
*Comfortable accommodation,
approximately half a mile
above East Meon along quiet
lane. Offers superb
uninterrupted views over rolling
downland.*
Bedrooms: 1 twin, 1 family
room.
Bathrooms: 1 public.
Bed & breakfast: £12-£15
single, £22-£30 double.
Parking for 4.
Open March-October.
⌖ ⚶ ⚲ ♥ 🆄 🛊 ⌷ ⊞
⚓ ❊ 🈺 🈺

EAST STOUR

Dorset
Map ref 2B3

Village on the A30, 4
miles west of
Shaftesbury.

Hunger Hill Farm
😊
East Stour, Nr. Gillingham,
SP8 5JR
☎ Gillingham (074 76) 2480
*Traditional farmhouse and
buildings set in 2 acres,
supporting small livestock. On
edge of small village near
Shaftesbury, surrounded by
farmland.*
Bedrooms: 1 double & 1 twin,
1 family room.
Bathrooms: 1 public.
Bed & breakfast: from £19
double.
Parking for 6.
Open April-September.
⌖ ♥ 🆄 Ⅴ ⌷ ⊞ ❊ 🈺 🈺

FAIR OAK

Hampshire
Map ref 2C3

*3m E. Eastleigh.
Residential suburb of
Eastleigh.*

Bush Cottage
Botley Road, Fair Oak,
Eastleigh, SO5 7AN
☎ Southampton
(0703) 600356
*17th C. period thatched
cottage which has been fully
modernised. Use of swimming
pool and garden.*
Bedrooms: 1 double, 2 family
rooms.
Bathrooms: 2 public.
Bed & breakfast: £20-£30
double.
Parking for 6.
🛏 🖾 ♿ ♥ Ⓤ Ⓣ ▥ ⚓ ⚲ ❊
✕ 🐾 🏠

FAREHAM

Hampshire
Map ref 2C3

Lies on a quiet backwater
of Portsmouth Harbour.
The High Street is lined
with fine Georgian
buildings. ℹ

St. Ives
76 Portchester Road,
Fareham, PO16 8QJ
☎ (0329) 284974
*Chalet bungalow with garden
for guests' use. On the A27
Fareham to Portsmouth road,
1 mile from Fareham shopping
centre and 7 miles from
continental ferry.*
Bedrooms: 2 double & 2 twin,
1 family room.
Bathrooms: 1 public.
Bed & breakfast: from £9
single, £16-£17 double.
Parking for 6.
🛏 Ⓜ ♿ Ⓤ Ⓣ ⚓ ✕ 🏠

FORDINGBRIDGE

Hampshire
Map ref 2B3

On the north west of the
New Forest. A medieval
bridge crosses the Avon
at this point and gave the
town its name. A good
centre for walking,
exploring and fishing.

Hillbury
2 Fir Tree Hill, Camel Green
Road, Alderholt,
Fordingbridge, SP6 3AY
☎ (0425) 52582

*Quiet situation close to New
Forest. Large garden. Poole,
Salisbury and Bournemouth
within 20 minutes' drive. Easy
access to M27.*
Bedrooms: 1 single, 1 twin,
1 family room.
Bathrooms: 1 private,
1 public.
Bed & breakfast: £9-£10
single, £20-£22 double.
Parking for 4.
Open January-November.
🛏 🖾 ♿ Ⓓ ♥ Ⓤ ✕ ▥ ⚓
🐽 🐾 🏠 ᴰᴬᴾ

Partridge Piece
Ogdens, Fordingbridge,
SP6 2PZ
☎ (0425) 55365
*8-acre smallholding. Attractive
house in heart of New Forest, 3
miles from Fordingbridge.
Superb walking, bird watching
and riding. Catering for horses
and riders a speciality.*
Bedrooms: 1 single, 1 twin.
Bathrooms: 1 private.
Bed & breakfast: £7-£10
single, £20-£24 double.
Parking for 4.
🖾 ♿ Ⓓ ♥ Ⓤ 📞 ✕ ▥ Ʊ
❊ 🏠

The Waverley
⊞⊞
Salisbury Road,
Fordingbridge, SP6 1EX
☎ (0425) 52751
*Detached guesthouse on the
outskirts of the town, close to
the New Forest.*
Bedrooms: 3 single, 4 double
& 2 twin, 1 family room.
Bathrooms: 3 public.
Bed & breakfast: £10.50-
£11.50 single, £21-£23 double.
Half board: from £90 weekly.
Evening meal 7pm (l.o.
10am).
Parking for 9.
Open March-October.
🛏3 Ⓤ Ⓥ ⚓ Ⓣ ✕ 🏠 SP

GILLINGHAM

Dorset
Map ref 2B3

The Stapleton Arms
Buckhorn Weston, Nr.
Gillingham, SP8 5HS
☎ Templecombe
(0963) 70396
*Traditional pub in village
centre, with nice gardens, car
parking, good value pub food
and restaurant. Equidistant
from Gillingham/Wincanton.*
Bedrooms: 2 double & 2 twin.
Bathrooms: 1 private,
1 public.
Bed & breakfast: £15-£17
single, £27-£30 double.

Half board: £25-£35 daily,
£95-£105 weekly.
Lunch available.
Evening meal 6.30pm (l.o.
9.45pm).
Parking for 80.
Credit: Access.
🛏 🖾 ♥ 🛋 Ⓥ ⚓ Ⓣ ▥ ⚓
🔍 ❊ 🏠

GOSPORT

Hampshire
Map ref 2C3

From a tiny fishing
hamlet, Gosport has
grown into an important
centre with many naval
establishments, including
HMS Dolphin, the
submarine base, with the
Naval Submarine
Museum which preserves
HMS Alliance and Holland
I. ℹ

Cherry Trees
Ⓛⁱˢᵗᵉᵈ
15 Linden Grove, Alverstoke,
Gosport, PO12 2ED
☎ (0705) 521543
*Accommodation in family-run,
large Victorian house with
friendly atmosphere. Children
and babies very welcome.*
Bedrooms: 1 single, 1 double
& 1 twin.
Bathrooms: 1 public.
Bed & breakfast: £8-£8.50
single, £16-£17 double.
Half board: £11-£11.50 daily,
£77-£80 weekly.
Parking for 1.
🛏 🖵 ♥ Ⓤ ⚓ Ⓣ ▥ ⚓ ✕
🏠

HAMBLEDON

Hampshire
Map ref 2C3

In a valley surrounded by
wooded downland and
marked by an air of
Georgian prosperity. It
was here that cricket was
given its first proper
rules. The Bat and Ball
Inn at Broadhalfpenny
Down is the cradle of
cricket.

Mornington House
Speltham Hill, Hambledon,
PO7 6RU
☎ (070 132) 704
*18th C. private house with 2
acres of garden and paddock,
in the centre of Hambledon
behind the George Inn.*
Bedrooms: 1 single, 1 twin.

Bathrooms: 1 public.
Bed & breakfast: £12-£14
single, £24-£28 double.
Parking for 6.
🛏 🖾 Ⓤ Ⓣ ▥ ❊ 🐾 🏠

HAVANT

Hampshire
Map ref 2C3

Once a market town
famous for making
parchment. Nearby at
Leigh Park extensive
early 19th C landscape
gardens and parklands
are open to the public.
Right in the centre of the
town stands the
interesting 13th C church
of St. Faith. ℹ

**The Old Mill Guest
House**
Mill Lane, Bedhampton,
Havant, PO9 3JH
☎ (0705) 454948
*Georgian house in large
grounds which incorporate a
lake abundant in wildlife.
Modernised, but still a
comfortable retreat.*
Bedrooms: 2 double & 3 twin.
Bathrooms: 5 private,
1 public.
Bed & breakfast: from £21
single, from £30 double.
Parking for 10.
🛏 Ⓤ Ⓥ ⚓ ▥ ⚓ 📞 ❊
🐾 🏠

HAYLING ISLAND

Hampshire
Map ref 2C3

Small, flat island of
historic interest,
surrounded by natural
harbours and with fine
sandy beaches, linked to
the mainland by a road. ℹ

Brycroft Guest House
206 Havant Road, Hayling
Island, PO11 0LN
☎ Portsmouth (0705) 466185
*Very spacious chalet bungalow
with pretty gardens, in main
road position convenient for
Langstone Harbour. Reduced
rates for children 2-14 years,
babies free.*
Bedrooms: 1 twin, 1 family
room.
Bathrooms: 1 public.
Bed & breakfast: £16-£18.50
single, £22-£25 double.
Parking for 4.
🛏 🖾 Ⓓ 🖵 ♥ Ⓤ Ⓥ Ⓣ ▥
⚓ 🏠 ᴰᴬᴾ SP

HAYLING ISLAND

Continued

Cockle Warren Cottage Hotel M
⊛⊛⊛

36 Seafront, Hayling Island,
PO11 9HL
☎ (0705) 464961
Delightful cottage hotel set in large garden with hens and ducks. Lovely four-poster bedroom suite. Candlelit dinners, log fire in lounge and home-made marmalade.
Bedrooms: 2 double & 1 twin.
Bathrooms: 2 private,
1 public.
Bed & breakfast: £18-£26 single, £30-£44 double.
Half board: £27.50-£34.50 daily, £192.50-£241.50 weekly.
Evening meal 7.30pm (l.o. 4pm).
Parking for 8.

Patch Cottage
15 Seagrove Avenue, Hayling Island, PO11 9EU
☎ (0705) 465338
Large family house and garden, 300 yards from beach.
Bedrooms: 2 double & 1 twin.
Bathrooms: 1 public.
Bed & breakfast: £9-£11 single, £18-£21 double.
Parking for 3.

HIGHCLIFFE

Dorset
Map ref 2B3

3m E. Christchurch
Seaside district of Christchurch some 3 miles to the east. Highcliffe Castle is of interest.

Beverly Glen
1 Stuart Road, Highcliffe, Christchurch, BH23 5JS
☎ (042 52) 3811
Close to the beach, shops and public transport, with the New Forest a short drive away. Home cooking.
Bedrooms: 1 single, 3 double & 1 twin, 1 family room.
Bathrooms: 1 private,
2 public.
Bed & breakfast: £11-£11.50 single, £20-£21 double.
Half board: £16-£16.75 daily, £98.25-£103.25 weekly.
Evening meal 6pm (l.o. 5pm).
Parking for 6.
Credit: Access, Visa.

Lakewood House
1 Lakewood Road, Highcliffe, Christchurch, BH23 5NX
☎ (042 52) 4602
Large, detached house with own secluded garden, in pleasant position within walking distance of beach. Half a mile off A35.
Bedrooms: 1 single, 1 double, 1 family room.
Bathrooms: 2 public.
Bed & breakfast: £10.50-£11.50 single, £18-£21 double.
Parking for 4.

HILL HEAD

Hampshire
Map ref 2C3

3m SW. Fareham

Seven Sevens Hotel
⊛⊛

56 Hill Head Road, Hill Head, Nr. Fareham, PO14 3JL
☎ Stubbington (0329) 662408
Overlooks the Solent towards the Isle of Wight. 1 minute's walk from beach. Close to various tourist attractions of Portsmouth and Winchester.
Bedrooms: 2 double & 3 twin, 1 family room.
Bathrooms: 2 public.
Bed & breakfast: £13.50 single, £22 double.
Parking for 6.

HOLBURY

Hampshire
Map ref 2C3

Bridge House Bed & Breakfast
Bridge House, Ipers Bridge, Holbury, Nr. Southampton, SO4 1HD
☎ Fawley (0703) 894302
Character country house in an acre of delightful gardens, 1.5 miles east of Beaulieu on the Fawley road.
Bedrooms: 1 double & 1 twin, 1 family room.
Bathrooms: 2 public.
Bed & breakfast: £20-£24 double.
Parking for 9.

**PLEASE CHECK
PRICES AND OTHER
DETAILS AT THE
TIME OF BOOKING.**

HOOK

Hampshire
Map ref 2C2

Astride the A30 some 6 miles east of Basingstoke.

Cedar Court
⊛⊛

Reading Road, Hook, Nr. Basingstoke, RG27 9DB
☎ (025 672) 2178
Comfortable ground floor accommodation with delightful gardens. On the B3349 (formerly A32) between the M3 and M4, 1 hour from London and the coast.
Bedrooms: 3 single, 1 double & 1 twin, 1 family room.
Bathrooms: 1 public.
Bed & breakfast: £15-£18 single, £25-£30 double.
Parking for 6.

HORTON HEATH

Hampshire
Map ref 2C3

3m SE. Eastleigh

Sandelwood
Knowle Lane, Horton Heath, Nr. Eastleigh, SO5 7DZ
☎ Southampton (0703) 693726
Quiet country house with easy access to motorway, near Winchester, Southampton, Salisbury and Portsmouth. Family room has large balcony overlooking countryside.
Bedrooms: 1 single, 1 double, 1 family room.
Bathrooms: 1 private,
1 public.
Bed & breakfast: from £10.50 single, from £21 double.
Half board: from £73.50 weekly.
Evening meal 6pm (l.o. 9pm).
Parking for 3.

HYTHE

Hampshire
Map ref 2C3

Changri-La
⊛⊛

12 Ashleigh Close, Hythe, Southampton, SO4 6QP
☎ (0703) 846664
Spacious comfortable home, in unique position on edge of New Forest, a few minutes' drive from Beaulieu and other places of interest.

Bedrooms: 1 single, 1 double & 1 twin.
Bathrooms: 2 public.
Bed & breakfast: £9.50-£11 single, £19-£22 double.
Parking for 3.

IBBERTON

Dorset
Map ref 2B3

Pretty rural village surrounded by open farmland.

Manor House Farm
Ibberton, Blandford Forum, DT11 0EN
☎ Hazelbury Bryan (0258) 817349
250-acre dairy farm. Small 15th C. manor house, now a farmhouse with large garden, in a small, quiet and unspoilt village.
Bedrooms: 2 double & 1 twin.
Bathrooms: 1 public.
Bed & breakfast: £7-£8.50 single, £14-£16.50 double.
Parking for 3.
Open February-November.

ISLE OF WIGHT - BRIGHSTONE

Isle of Wight
Map ref 2C3

Excellent centre for visitors who want somewhere quiet. Calbourne nearby is ideal for picnics and the sea at Chilton Chine has safe bathing at high tide.

Chilton Farm House M
⊛⊛

Chilton Lane, Brighstone, PO30 4DS
☎ (0983) 740338
550-acre mixed farm. Parts of the farmhouse date back to the 17th C. Dinner available by request.
Bedrooms: 1 double & 1 twin, 2 family rooms.
Bathrooms: 4 private.
Bed & breakfast: £11-£12 single, £22-£24 double.
Evening meal 6pm (l.o. 6.30pm).
Parking for 4.

Gillmans
Upper Lane, Brighstone, PO30 4BA
☎ (0983) 740644

The bedroom is in converted stables in the garden of Gillmans, which is a stone-built, thatched cottage. Breakfast is served in Gillmans' beamed dining room.
Bedrooms: 1 double.
Bathrooms: 1 private.
Bed & breakfast: £20 double.
Parking for 2.
Open June-October.

ISLE OF WIGHT-COWES

Isle of Wight
Map ref 2C3

Regular ferry and hovercraft services cross the Solent to Cowes. The town is the headquarters of the Royal Yacht Squadron and Cowes Week is held every August. *i*

Mrs. J. Gibbons
14 Milton Road, Cowes, PO31 7PX
☎ (0983) 295723
Ten minutes' walk from town centre, offering large double room with en-suite shower/wc, and single room.
Bedrooms: 1 single, 1 double.
Bathrooms: 1 private, 1 public.
Bed & breakfast: £9-£14 single, £20-£30 double.
Half board: £16.50-£22.50 daily, £108.50-£150.50 weekly.
Parking for 1.

ISLE OF WIGHT-NEWBRIDGE

Isle of Wight
Map ref 2C3

Small village with thatched stone cottages and mill which still makes stone-ground flour.

Homestead Farmhouse M
Homestead Farm, Newbridge, Yarmouth, PO41 0TZ
☎ Calbourne (098 378) 270
180-acre dairy farm. Ensuite accommodation in new wing of attractive farmhouse in unspoilt West Wight village, tucked between the downs and Solent shores. Ideal for exploring many island beauty spots. Dinner by arrangement.
Bedrooms: 2 family rooms.
Bathrooms: 2 private.

Bed & breakfast: £11-£12 single, £20-£22 double.
Half board: £16-£18 daily, £112-£126 weekly.
Parking for 20.

ISLE OF WIGHT-NITON

Isle of Wight
Map ref 2C3

Part in hollow of the Downs, part along the Undercliff terrace. Once renowned for crabs and for its smuggling activities. Good walking area. St. Catherine's Lighthouse can be visited.

Southcliff M
Sandrock Road, Niton Undercliff, Niton, PO38 2NQ
☎ (0983) 730447
Georgian country house with magnificent sea views in area of natural beauty near St. Catherine's Lighthouse and Marconi's Cottage.
Bedrooms: 2 double & 1 twin.
Bathrooms: 1 public.
Bed & breakfast: £10-£13 single, £20-£26 double.
Parking for 3.

ISLE OF WIGHT-ROOKLEY

Isle of Wight
Map ref 2C3

Small village in centre of Island, once a coaching stage. Rookley Country Park has lakes with wildfowl, adventure playground and amusements.

Barwick M
Rookley Farm Lane, Niton Road, Rookley, PO38 3PA
☎ (0983) 840787
6-acre animal farm. Centrally situated country dwelling 300 yards off main road, with friendly atmosphere and many hand-fed animals.
Bedrooms: 2 double & 1 twin, 3 family rooms.
Bathrooms: 1 private, 2 public.
Bed & breakfast: from £11 single, from £22 double.
Half board: from £17 daily.
Evening meal 6pm (l.o. 6pm).
Parking for 6.

ISLE OF WIGHT-RYDE

Isle of Wight
Map ref 2C3

The island's chief entry port, connected to Portsmouth by ferries and hovercraft. Seven miles of sandy beaches with a half mile pier, esplanade and gardens. *i*

Arlyn House M
59 West Hill Road, Ryde, PO33 1LG
☎ (0983) 67743
Quiet and friendly, 3 minutes from sea, boating lake and swimming pools. Approximately 15 minutes' walk from pier.
Bedrooms: 1 single, 1 double, 1 family room.
Bathrooms: 1 public.
Bed & breakfast: £9-£9.50 single, £18-£19 double.
Open April-November.

Dover Gate Guest House
Listed
23 Dover Street, Ryde, PO33 2AG
☎ (0983) 66587
Small, homely guesthouse, 2 minutes from the Esplanade and sea, and 5 minutes from town centre.
Bedrooms: 1 double & 1 twin, 2 family rooms.
Bathrooms: 2 public.
Bed & breakfast: £10-£12 single, £20-£24 double.

ISLE OF WIGHT-RYDE-WOOTTON

Isle of Wight
Map ref 2C3

Village runs uphill from Wootton Creek, popular with yachtsmen with its sailing school and boat yards.

Ashlake Farmhouse
Ashlake Farm Lane, Wootton Creek, Nr. Ryde, PO33 4LF
☎ (0983) 882124
Lovely 17th C. farmhouse with grounds sloping down to Wootton Creek. Happy, calm atmosphere and friendly service.
Bedrooms: 1 double & 1 twin, 1 family room.
Bathrooms: 2 public.

Bed & breakfast: £10-£15 single, £20-£30 double.
Half board: £12-£20 daily, £70-£90 weekly.
Evening meal 7pm (l.o. 9pm).
Parking for 6.

ISLE OF WIGHT-SANDOWN

Isle of Wight
Map ref 2C3

The 6 miles sweep of Sandown Bay is one of the island's finest stretches, with excellent sands. The pier has a pavilion and sun terrace and the esplanade, amusements, bars, eating-places and gardens. *i*

Cherry Tree Lodge
Newport Road, Apse Heath, Nr. Sandown, PO36 0JR
☎ (0983) 866881
Large country house overlooking farmland, with half an acre of well-kept gardens. 1 mile from lake on A3056. Plans to renovate include some private bathrooms, a licensed bar and colour TVs in all rooms.
Bedrooms: 3 double, 2 family rooms.
Bathrooms: 1 public.
Bed & breakfast: £9-£11 single, £18-£22 double.
Half board: £14-£16 daily, £98-£112 weekly.
Evening meal 6pm (l.o. 3pm).
Parking for 6.
Open April-September.

ISLE OF WIGHT-SHANKLIN

Isle of Wight
Map ref 2C3

Set on a cliff with gentle slopes leading down to the beach, esplanade and marine gardens. The picturesque old thatched village nestles at the end of the wooded chine. *i*

Culham Lodge M
31 Landguard Manor Road, Shanklin, PO37 7HZ
☎ (0983) 862880
Charming hotel in beautiful tree-lined road, with heated swimming pool, solarium, home cooking and personal service.
Bedrooms: 1 single, 6 double & 3 twin.

Continued ▶

ISLE OF WIGHT-SHANKLIN

Continued

Bathrooms: 8 private,
2 public.
Bed & breakfast: £11-£12
single, £22-£24 double.
Half board: £15.50-£16.50
daily, £96-£105 weekly.
Evening meal 6pm (l.o. 4pm).
Parking for 8.
Open April-October.

⌖12 ♨ & ⓊⓁ ⚡ ✿ ✕ Ⓥ ⌗ ⓉⓋ
▥ ♟ ⚹ ✕ ⓓⓐⓟ SP Ⓣ

Loretta House

15 Atherley Road, Shanklin,
PO37 7AT
☎ (0983) 866733
*Small, comfortable guest
house, 3 minutes from sea. All
beds have continental quilts.
Morning tea served. Families
welcome.*
Bedrooms: 1 single, 1 double,
3 family rooms.
Bathrooms: 1 public.
Bed & breakfast: £9.50-
£10.50 single, £19-£21 double.
Evening meal 6pm.

⌖5 ♨ ⓊⓁ ⚡ ⌗ ⓉⓋ ▥ ♟ ✕
⌗ ⓓⓐⓟ

Summercourt Hotel ♏

6 Popham Road, Shanklin,
PO37 6RF
☎ (0983) 863154
*Spacious Tudor house with
large pleasant garden, in a
quiet position in Shanklin Old
Village. Near sea and shops,
adjacent to Rylstone Gardens
and Shanklin Chine.*
Bedrooms: 2 double & 2 twin,
2 family rooms.
Bathrooms: 3 private,
1 public.
Bed & breakfast: £11.50-
£13.50 single, £19-£23 double.
Parking for 6.

⌖2 ♨ ⓊⓁ ⚡ ⌗ ⓉⓋ ▥ ♟ ⌗
ⓓⓐⓟ SP

ISLE OF WIGHT-VENTNOR

Isle of Wight
Map ref 2C3

Town lies at the bottom of
an 800 ft hill and has a
reputation as a winter
holiday and health resort
due to its mild climate.
There is a pier, small
esplanade and Winter
Gardens. ℹ

Hillside Hotel ♏

Mitchell Avenue, Ventnor,
PO38 1DR
☎ (0983) 852271

*Ventnor's only thatched hotel,
built in 1801, in its own 2 acres
of beautifully wooded grounds
overlooking the sea.*
Bedrooms: 1 single, 7 double
& 2 twin, 1 family room.
Bathrooms: 11 private.
Bed & breakfast: £15-£17
single, £30-£34 double.
Half board: £19-£21 daily,
£133-£147 weekly.
Evening meal 6.30pm (l.o.
7.30pm).
Parking for 15.
Credit: Access, Visa.

⌖5 ♨ & ⓊⓁ ⚡ ⌗ Ⓥ ⌗ ▥ ♟
✿ ⌗ ⌗ ⚹ SP ⌗ Ⓣ

ISLE OF WIGHT-WHITWELL

Isle of Wight
Map ref 2C3

West of Ventnor, with
interesting church,
thatched inn and Youth
Hostel. Good walking
area.

Fairmead

12 Strathwell Crescent,
Whitwell, Nr. Ventnor,
PO38 2QZ
☎ Isle of Wight
(0983) 730709
*Bungalow in a rural setting in
the village of Whitwell, which
is 3 miles from Ventnor on the
Godshill to Ventnor road.*
Bedrooms: 1 single, 1 double.
Bathrooms: 1 public.
Bed & breakfast: £8.50-£9
single, £17-£18 double.
Parking for 2.
Open April-October.

⌖6 ♨ & ⓊⓁ ⓉⓋ ▥ ✕ ♟

KIMMERIDGE

Dorset
Map ref 2B3

Kimmeridge Farmhouse

Kimmeridge, Corfe Castle,
Wareham, BH20 5PE
☎ Corfe Castle
(0929) 480990
*750-acre mixed farm. The
farmhouse was built using
Purbeck stone in the 16th C.
and has lovely views of
surrounding countryside and
village.*
Bedrooms: 1 single, 1 double
& 1 twin, 1 family room.
Bathrooms: 2 public.
Bed & breakfast: £9-£12
single, £16-£22 double.
Half board: £14-£17 daily,
£84-£100 weekly.
Evening meal 6.30pm.
Parking for 4.

⌖ ♨ ⚹ & ⓊⓁ ⚡ Ⓥ ⌗ ⓉⓋ ▥
ⓓⓐⓟ SP ⌗

LANGTON MATRAVERS

Dorset
Map ref 2B3

Maycroft

😊

Old Malthouse Lane,
Langton Matravers,
Swanage, BH19 3HH
☎ Swanage (0929) 424305
*Comfortable Victorian home in
quiet position, with magnificent
views of sea and countryside.
Close to all amenities of the
Isle of Purbeck.*
Bedrooms: 1 double & 1 twin.
Bathrooms: 1 public.
Bed & breakfast: £12-£14
single, £20-£25 double.
Parking for 4.

⌗ ♨ ⓊⓁ ▥ ♟ ⌗ ∪ ▶ ✕ ⌗
⌗

LISS

Hampshire
Map ref 2C3

Village including East and
West Liss on the
Hampshire/Sussex
border.

Rose Cottage

Listed

1 The Mead, Liss,
GU33 7DT
☎ (0730) 892378
*A semi-detached, 4-bedroom
house with lounge and dining
area.*
Bedrooms: 1 single, 1 double
& 1 twin.
Bathrooms: 1 public.
Bed & breakfast: max. £10
single, max. £20 double.
Parking for 1.

⌖ ⌗ ⚹ ⓊⓁ Ⓥ ▥ ♟ ✕ ⌗

Mrs. B. Savill

😊

Hill Brow Lodge, Hill Brow,
Liss, GU33 7NY
☎ (0730) 894009
*Large Victorian family house
with relaxed, friendly
atmosphere. Conveniently
situated for coast and
countryside.*
Bedrooms: 2 double & 1 twin.
Bathrooms: 1 public.
Bed & breakfast: £15 single,
£25-£30 double.
Parking for 6.

⌖5 ⌗ ⚹ ⓊⓁ ⚡ ⌗ ⓉⓋ ▥ ♟
✕ ⌗

**THE SYMBOLS ARE
EXPLAINED ON THE
FLAP INSIDE THE
BACK COVER.**

LYMINGTON

Hampshire
Map ref 2C3

Small pleasant town with
bright cottages and
attractive Georgian
houses lying on the edge
of the New Forest with a
ferry service to the Isle of
Wight. A sheltered
harbour makes it a busy
yachting centre. ℹ

Admiral House ♏

5 Stanley Road, Lymington,
SO41 9SJ
☎ (0590) 74339
*House for guests' use alone;
owner resides next door. 200
yards from countryside and
marina. Many pubs and
restaurants nearby.*
Bedrooms: 1 single, 1 twin,
1 family room.
Bathrooms: 1 public.
Bed & breakfast: £9-£10
single, £18-£20 double.

⌖ ⚹ ⓊⓁ ⌗ ⓉⓋ ▥ ∪ ✕
⌗

Altworth ♏

Listed

12 North Close, Lymington,
SO41 9BT
☎ (0590) 74082
*Near centre of town in quiet
residential street, 5 minutes
from bus and railway stations
and close to Isle of Wight
ferry. 30 minutes from
Southampton and
Bournemouth.*
Bedrooms: 1 double, 1 family
room.
Bathrooms: 1 public.
Bed & breakfast: £17 double.
Open April-October.

⌖ ⚹ ⓊⓁ ▥ ✕

Cedars

Listed

2 Linden Way, Highfield,
Lymington, SO41 9JU
☎ (0590) 76468
*Bungalow accommodation in
quiet, secluded area, with
annexed rooms, free access and
ample parking Close to high
street, marinas and ferry.*
Bedrooms: 1 double & 2 twin,
1 family room.
Bathrooms: 2 public.
Bed & breakfast: £22 double.
Parking for 4.

⌖12 ♨ ⌗ ⚹ ⓊⓁ Ⓥ ▥ ♟
✿ ✕ ⌗

Gorse Meadow

Sway Road, Lymington,
SO41 8LR
☎ (0590) 73354

13-acre horse farm. Tranquil setting in 13 acres of park-like grounds, close to Lymington and New Forest.
Bedrooms: 1 double, 2 family rooms.
Bathrooms: 1 private, 1 public.
Bed & breakfast: £27-£34 double.
Half board: £22-£25.50 daily. Evening meal 6.30pm.
Parking for 5.
☎ 🖵 Ⓤ ⌨ Ʊ ❀ ✠ 🏍
⁊

Harts Lane Nurseries
242 Everton Road, Everton, Lymington, SO41 0HE
☎ (0590) 42312
Bungalow set in 3 acres used for horses and nursery. Located half a mile down Everton Road off the A337.
Bedrooms: 1 double, 1 family room.
Bathrooms: 1 public.
Bed & breakfast: £20-£24 double.
Parking for 3.
☎ 🖏 🖵 Ⓤ ⌨ ✠
⁊

Little Orchard
31 Ramley Road, Pennington, Lymington, SO41 8HF
☎ (0590) 73430
Lovely family home with 2 fish ponds and very private, peaceful home. Between sea and forest, just off A337.
Bedrooms: 1 single, 2 double & 1 twin.
Bathrooms: 2 public.
Bed & breakfast: £10 single, £20 double.
Parking for 8.
☎ 🖏 🖵 Ⓤ ⌨ ⌨ ❀ ✠ ⁊

LYNDHURST

Hampshire
Map ref 2C3

The 'capital' of the New Forest, surrounded by attractive woodland scenery and delightful villages. The town is dominated by the Victorian Gothic style church where the original Alice in Wonderland is buried. 🅘

Burton House 🅜
😊🍴
Romsey Road, Lyndhurst, SO43 7AA
☎ (042 128) 2445
Lovely house in half an acre of garden, near the village centre.
Bedrooms: 1 single, 2 double & 1 twin, 2 family rooms.
Bathrooms: 6 private.

Bed & breakfast: £15 single, £22-£28 double.
Parking for 8.
☎ 🖵 Ⓤ ⌨ TV ⌨ ❀ ✠
⁊ DAP

Eyeworth Lodge
Fritham, Nr. Lyndhurst, SO43 7HJ
☎ Southampton (0703) 812256
Large rooms in beautiful character country house in superb, secluded forest opposite Eyeworth Pond. Two-room, private suite with own TV, shower and w.c. Stabling available.
Bedrooms: 3 double, 1 family room.
Bathrooms: 1 private, 1 public.
Bed & breakfast: from £14 single, £20-£28 double.
Parking for 10.
☎ 🖏 Ⓤ Ⓥ ⌨ TV ⌨ ❀
✠ ⁊ DAP SP 🎏

Forest Cottage
Listed
High Street, Lyndhurst, SO43 7BH
☎ (042 128) 3461
300-year-old cottage with great charm, friendly atmosphere and an extensive natural history library with New Forest maps and reference books.
Bedrooms: 1 single, 1 double & 1 twin.
Bathrooms: 1 public.
Bed & breakfast: max. £12 single, £22-£24 double.
Parking for 3.
☎12 Ⓤ 🖊 Ⓥ ⌨ TV ⌨ ❀
✠ ⁊

Margarets Mead Farm
Fritham, Lyndhurst, SO43 7HJ
☎ Southampton (0703) 813388
20-acre mixed farm. .
Bedrooms: 1 double & 1 twin.
Bathrooms: 1 public.
Bed & breakfast: £9-£10 single, £18-£20 double.
Open April-October.
☎3 🖏 Ⓤ ⌨ ⁊

The Stag Hotel 🅜
69 High Street, Lyndhurst, SO43 7BE
☎ (042 128) 3492
Country town hotel, part Georgian and part Victorian.
Bedrooms: 2 double & 2 twin, 4 family rooms.
Bathrooms: 2 public; 4 private showers.
Bed & breakfast: £12-£15 single, £24-£30 double.
Evening meal 7pm (l.o. 9pm).
Parking for 20.
☎ 🖵 Ⓤ ❀ ◉ ⌨ 🍴 ❦ ▶ DAP
🦮 SP

Yew Tree Cottage
Bank, Nr. Lyndhurst, SO43 7FD
☎ Lyndhurst (042 128) 2193
18th C. cottage in idyllic forest setting, 1 mile from Lyndhurst. En-suite accommodation has a private entrance. Breakfast served in picturesque Victorian-style conservatory.
Bedrooms: 1 twin.
Bathrooms: 1 private.
Bed & breakfast: £15 single, £24 double.
Parking for 2.
☎ 🖏 Ⓤ ◉ 🖵 Ⓤ ⌨ 🖵 ❀
⁊ SP

MIDDLE WALLOP

Hampshire
Map ref 2C2

On the main Salisbury to Andover road and between Over and Nether Wallop. The Army Air Corps (Museum) and Training Centre is 2 miles north east.

Turnpike Cottage
Salisbury Road, Middle Wallop, Stockbridge, SO20 8EG
☎ Andover (0264) 781341
17th C. thatched cottage with picturesque gardens. Within easy reach of Salisbury, Stonehenge and historic Winchester.
Bedrooms: 1 single, 1 double & 1 twin, 1 family room.
Bathrooms: 1 private, 1 public.
Bed & breakfast: £21-£25 double.
Evening meal 6pm (l.o. 9.30pm).
Parking for 6.
☎ 🖏 🖵 Ⓤ Ⓤ 🖊 Ⓥ ✂ ⌨
🖵 🖏 ❀ ✠ DAP SP 🎏

MINSTEAD

Hampshire
Map ref 2B3

Cluster of thatched cottages and detached period houses. The church, listed in the Domesday Book, has private boxes - one with its own fireplace.

Acres Down Farm
Listed
Minstead, Nr. Lyndhurst, SO43 7GE
☎ Southampton (0703) 813693

55-acre mixed farm. Working farm in the New Forest with homely atmosphere, in very quiet surroundings opening directly on to open forest. House built in 1868.
Bedrooms: 1 double & 1 twin, 1 family room.
Bathrooms: 1 public.
Bed & breakfast: from £9.50 single, from £19 double.
Parking for 6.
Open April-October.
☎ 🖏 Ⓤ 🖊 Ⓥ TV ✠ ⁊

NETLEY ABBEY

Hampshire
Map ref 2C3

4m SE. Southampton Romantic ruin, set in green lawns against a background of trees on the east bank of Southampton Water. The abbey was built in the 13th C by Cistercian monks from Beaulieu.

Netley Lodge
Netley Lodge Close, Netley Abbey, SO3 5AJ
☎ Southampton (0703) 453296
17th C. lodge set in 10 acres. Ideally located for Hamble and Southampton and within easy reach of Poole, Lymington, Portsmouth, Chichester and Isle of Wight.
Bedrooms: 1 single, 1 twin, 1 family room.
Bathrooms: 1 private, 1 public.
Bed & breakfast: £20-£25 single, £40-£44 double.
Parking for 12.
☎ 🖏 ❀ Ⓤ ⌨ TV ⌨ ❀ ✠
🖏 🎏

NEW FOREST

See Bartley, Barton on Sea, Boldre, Bramshaw, Brockenhurst, Burley, Cadnam, Damerham, Dibden, Fordingbridge, Holbury, Hythe, Lymington, Lyndhurst, Minstead, New Milton, Ringwood, Stoney Cross, Sway, Tiptoe, Woodgreen.

MAP REFERENCES APPLY TO COLOUR MAPS NEAR THE BACK OF THE GUIDE.

NEW MILTON

Hampshire
Map ref 2B3

New Forest residential
town on the main line
railway.

Wheatsheaf Hotel
👑👑

Christchurch Road, New
Milton, BH25 6QJ
☎ (0425) 611082
*18th C. inn with comfortable
rooms, serving freshly-cooked
meals in the bars. 3 miles from
the forest and 1 mile from the
sea.*
Bedrooms: 1 single, 3 double
& 2 twin, 1 family room.
Bathrooms: 2 public.
Bed & breakfast: £8.50-£9.50
single, £17-£19 double.
Evening meal 6pm (l.o.
9.30pm).
Parking for 40.

🛏🖵🛆🗋 📺 ⬛ 🛆 🍽 🐾 ✿
🐍 🏠

OVER WALLOP

Hampshire
Map ref 2C2

5m NW. Stockbridge
Attractive Hampshire
village in the area known
as the Wallops.

Mrs. M.W. Hart
👑

The Driftway, Over Wallop,
Stockbridge, SO20 8JG
☎ Andover (0264) 781255
*Secluded family house in
country, near village of Over
Wallop. Within easy reach of
many places of historic
interest.*
Bedrooms: 2 single, 2 double.
Bathrooms: 2 public.
Bed & breakfast: max. £10
single, max. £20 double.
Parking for 6.
Open April-October.

🛏 ⬛ 🛆 📺 ⬛ 🛆 ✿ 🐾 🏠
SP

OVERTON

Hampshire
Map ref 2C2

Court Farm House

Overton, Basingstoke,
RG25 3HF
☎ Basingstoke (0256) 770250
*416-acre mixed farm. Situated
in centre of village in beautiful
Test Valley, 3 miles from the
M3 junction 8.*
Bedrooms: 1 double & 2 twin.

Bathrooms: 2 public.
Bed & breakfast: from £12.50
single, from £25 double.
Parking for 4.

🛏 🛆 🖵 ⬛ 📺 ⬛ 🍽 🐾 🏠

OWSLEBURY

Hampshire
Map ref 2C3

Small farming village with
Marwell Conservation
Zoo close by.

Mrs. J. Coombe

Yew Tree Cottage,
Baybridge, Owslebury, Nr.
Winchester, SO21 1JN
☎ (096 274) 254
*17th C. thatched cottage with
2 double rooms, suitable for
family or friends. Lovely
garden.*
Bedrooms: 1 double & 1 twin.
Bathrooms: 1 private,
1 public.
Bed & breakfast: £35 double.
Half board: £27.50 daily,
£192.50 weekly.
Evening meal 7pm.
Parking for 3.

🛏 7 🛆 ⬛ 🖵 🛆 ⬛ 🛆 📺
⬛ 🛆 🐾 🏠

Glasspools Farm House

Longwood Estate,
Owslebury, Nr. Winchester,
SO21 1JS
☎ (096 274) 218
*4000-acre arable and sheep
farm. Modern farmhouse set in
an acre of garden, surrounded
by fields and trees.*
Bedrooms: 1 double & 1 twin.
Bathrooms: 1 public.
Bed & breakfast: £10 single,
£20 double.
Half board: £15 daily, £100-
£105 weekly.
Evening meal 6pm (l.o.
10pm).
Parking for 2.

🛏 5 ⬛ 📺 🛆 ⬛ 🛆 ✿ 🐾
🏠

Miss E.A. Lightfoot ♒
Listed

Tayinloan, Owslebury, Nr.
Winchester, SO21 1LP
☎ (096 274) 359
*Private house with extensive
rural views. Non-smokers
preferred.*
Bedrooms: 1 twin, 1 family
room.
Bathrooms: 1 private,
1 public.
Bed & breakfast: £9-£10
single.
Parking for 3.

🛏 ⬛ 🖵 🛆 ⬛ 📺 ⬛ 🐾 🏠

PETERSFIELD

Hampshire
Map ref 2C3

Grew prosperous from
the wool trade and was
famous as a coaching
centre. Its attractive
market square is
dominated by a statue of
William III. Close by is
Petersfield Heath with
numerous ancient
barrows and Butser Hill
with magnificent views.

Mrs. Mary Bray

Nursted Farm, Buriton,
Petersfield, GU31 5RW
☎ (0730) 64278
*406-acre arable/sheep farm.
Late 17th C. farmhouse near
Hampshire/West Sussex
border, 2 miles south of
Petersfield.*
Bedrooms: 3 twin, 1 family
room.
Bathrooms: 2 public.
Bed & breakfast: £10-£11
single, £20-£22 double.
Parking for 4.

🛏 🛆 ⬛ 🛆 📺 ✿ 🐾 🏠

Mrs. P.A. Bushell

Toads Alley, South Lane,
Buriton, Nr. Petersfield,
GU31 5RU
☎ (0730) 63880
*15th C. cottage in quiet
position overlooking fields, 4
miles from Petersfield. Village
shop and 2 village pubs serving
food 2 minutes' walk away.*
Bedrooms: 1 single, 2 twin.
Bathrooms: 2 private,
1 public.
Bed & breakfast: £12-£15
single, £24-£30 double.
Parking for 5.

🛏 🖵 🛆 🛆 📺 ⬛ 🛆
🐾 ✿ 🐾 🏠

Old Bell Cottage

Rogate, Petersfield,
GU31 5EF
☎ Rogate (073 080) 725
*Part of manor house
surrounding a central
courtyard, in lovely Rother
Valley overlooking the South
Downs.*
Bedrooms: 1 twin.
Bathrooms: 1 public.
Bed & breakfast: £9-£10
single, £18-£20 double.
Parking for 1.

🛆 ⬛ ✂ ⬛ 🐾 🏠 DAP SP 🏠

┌─────────────────┐
│ **WE ADVISE YOU TO** │
│ **CONFIRM YOUR** │
│ **BOOKING IN WRITING.** │
└─────────────────┘

Pillmead House
👑👑

North Lane, Buriton, Nr.
Petersfield, GU31 5RS
☎ (0730) 66795
*Family house of character in
terraced gardens providing
good accommodation, with
owner's interest in cooking
reflected in food.*
Bedrooms: 2 twin.
Bathrooms: 2 private.
Bed & breakfast: £15 single,
max. £25 double.
Half board: from £31 daily.
Evening meal 6.30pm (l.o.
8pm).
Parking for 2.

🛏 ⬛ 🖵 🛆 ⬛ 🛆 📺 ⬛
🛆 ✿ 🐾

Mrs. V. Powell-Thomas

Drovers House, Barham
Road, Petersfield,
GU32 3EX
☎ (0730) 67573
*Modern, comfortable family
house with friendly atmosphere,
2 minutes from town centre
and easy to find.*
Bedrooms: 1 single, 3 twin.
Bathrooms: 1 public.
Bed & breakfast: £11 single,
£22 double.
Parking for 1.

🛏 🛆 🛆 🖵 ⬛ 📺 ⬛ 🛆 🐾
🏠

POOLE

Dorset
Map ref 2B3

Tremendous natural
harbour makes Poole a
superb boating centre.
The harbour area is
crowded with historic
buildings including the
15th C Town Cellars
housing a maritime
museum. ℹ

The Inn in the Park ♒
👑👑

26 Pinewood Road,
Branksome Park, Poole,
BH13 6JS
☎ Bournemouth
(0202) 761318
*A small friendly, family-owned
pub with sun terrace, log fire
and easy access to the beach.*
Bedrooms: 3 double & 1 twin,
1 family room.
Bathrooms: 3 private,
1 public.
Bed & breakfast: £20.50-£37
single, £26-£39 double.
Lunch available.
Evening meal 7pm (l.o.
9.30pm).
Parking for 15.

🛏 🖵 🛆 ⬛ 🛆 🐾 🏠

Hampshire
Map ref 2C3

There have been
connections with the
Navy since early times
and the first dock was
built in 1194. HMS
Victory, Nelson's flagship,
is here and Charles
Dickens' former home is
open to the public.
Neighbouring Southsea
has a promenade with
magnificent views of
Spithead. *i*

Fortitude Cottage
Listed

51 Broad Street, Old
Portsmouth, PO1 2JD
☎ (0705) 823748
*Terraced town house 50 yards
from sea, overlooking boat
quay, near continental ferry
port, trains and bus terminus.
German spoken.*
Bedrooms: 1 twin, 1 family
room.
Bathrooms: 1 private,
1 public.
Bed & breakfast: £24-£26
double.

Granada House Hotel
29 Granada Road, Southsea,
PO4 0RD
☎ (0705) 861575
*The hotel offers spacious
bedrooms, large car park and
English or Continental
breakfast.*
Bedrooms: 1 single, 2 double
& 2 twin, 4 family rooms.
Bathrooms: 4 private,
2 public.
Bed & breakfast: from £10
single, from £20 double.
Half board: from £15 daily,
from £105 weekly.
Evening meal 6pm (l.o. 8pm).
Parking for 10.

Hanway Guest House M
Listed

27 Malvern Road, Southsea,
PO5 2LZ
☎ (0705) 731893
*Comfortable, friendly
guesthouse, very close to pier,
rock gardens, shops, D-Day
Museum, Sea Life Centre and
new Pyramids entertainment
complex.*
Bedrooms: 1 single, 2 double
& 3 twin, 1 family room.
Bathrooms: 2 public.
Bed & breakfast: £8-£9
single, £15-£17 double.

Sallyport Hotel M
High Street, Old Portsmouth,
PO1 2LU
☎ (0705) 821860
*A frame-built building with
oak timbers and a unique
cantilevered staircase, the spine
of which is a ship's top spar.*
Bedrooms: 3 single, 4 double
& 3 twin.
Bathrooms: 8 private;
2 private showers.
Bed & breakfast: from £20
single, from £40 double.
Lunch available.
Evening meal 7.30pm (l.o.
9.30pm).
Parking for 30.
Credit: Access, Visa.

Turret Hotel
3 Lennox Mansions, Clarence
Parade, Southsea, PO5 2HZ
☎ (0705) 291810
*On Southsea seafront opposite
the new Pyramids Centre and
the Lady's Mile. Most unusual
building with turret and
marvellous views.*
Bedrooms: 4 single, 7 double
& 2 twin.
Bathrooms: 7 private,
3 public.
Bed & breakfast: £20-£30
single, £40-£50 double.

Hampshire
Map ref 2B3

Market town by the River
Avon comprising old
cottages, many of them
thatched. Although just
outside the New Forest,
there is heath and
woodland near by and it
is a good centre for
horse-riding and
walking. *i*

Apple Tree Cottage
14 College Road, Ringwood,
BH24 1NX
☎ (0425) 476038
*Enjoy vegetarian or traditional
cooking in our pretty Victorian
home. Quiet yet central
location. Non-smokers please
and reductions for children
sharing parents' room.*
Bedrooms: 1 double, 1 family
room.
Bathrooms: 1 public.

Bed & breakfast: £12-£14
single, £24-£28 double.
Half board: £17.50-£19.50
daily, £122.50-£138.50
weekly.
Evening meal 6pm (l.o.
4.30pm).
Parking for 3.

Fraser House
Salisbury Road, Blashford,
Ringwood, BH24 3PB
☎ (042 54) 3581
*Overlooks the Avon Valley on
the edge of the New Forest,
famous for its ponies and
picturesque scenery.
Convenient for south coast
beaches.*
Bedrooms: 2 double & 1 twin.
Bathrooms: 2 public.
Bed & breakfast: from £11.50
single, from £20 double.
Parking for 5.

Hampshire
Map ref 2C2

4m E. Alresford
Village on the Alresford to
Alton Mid Hants Railway.

The Hermitage
Lyeway Lane, Ropley,
Alresford, SO24 0DW
☎ (096 277) 2279
*New house set in small village
with views over farmland. Very
quiet.*
Bedrooms: 1 double.
Bathrooms: 1 private.
Bed & breakfast: £12-£15
single, £20-£25 double.
Parking for 2.

Mrs. A.S. Humphryes
Belmont House, Gilbert
Street, Ropley, Nr. Alresford,
SO24 0BY
☎ (096 277) 2344
*This house dates back to the
19th C. and is situated in a
quiet country lane. Set in a
beautiful garden with rural
views from the house.*
Bedrooms: 1 twin.
Bathrooms: 1 private.
Bed & breakfast: £24-£30
double.

Hampshire
Map ref 2C2

The Bourne Valley
Inn M

St. Mary Bourne, Nr.
Andover, SP11 6BT
☎ (0264) 738361
Bedrooms: 2 single, 5 double
& 4 twin, 1 family room.
Bathrooms: 10 private,
1 public.
Bed & breakfast: £35-£40
single, £40-£50 double.
Half board: £40-£45 daily,
£245-£280 weekly.
Lunch available.
Evening meal 7pm (l.o.
10.30pm).
Parking for 40.
Credit: Access, Visa, Diners.

Hampshire
Map ref 2C3

Dyer's Oak
18 Heathlands, Shedfield,
Southampton, SO3 2JD
☎ Wickham (0329) 833360
*Comfortable accommodation,
200 yards off main road, and
set in open heathland. Ample
parking.*
Bedrooms: 1 single, 1 twin.
Bathrooms: 1 public.
Bed & breakfast: £11-£11.50
single, £22-£23 double.
Half board: £16.50-£17.50
daily, £100-£110 weekly.
Evening meal 7pm (l.o. 9pm).
Parking for 4.

Dorset
Map ref 2B3

Lattemere
Frog Lane, Shroton,
Blandford, DT11 8QL
☎ Child Okeford
(0258) 860115
*Modern house with pleasant
garden in attractive
conservation area village,
between Hambledon Hill and
edge of Cranborne Chase.*
Bedrooms: 1 double & 1 twin.
Bathrooms: 1 public.
Bed & breakfast: £10.50-
£12.50 single, £21-£24 double.
Parking for 3.

GROUPS, CONSORTIA AND AGENCIES
SPECIALISING IN FARM AND COUNTRY
HOLIDAYS ARE LISTED IN A SPECIAL
SECTION OF THIS GUIDE.

SIXPENNY HANDLEY

Dorset
Map ref 2B3

5m NW. Cranborne

The Barleycorn House
Deanland, Sixpenny
Handley, Salisbury, Wiltshire
SP5 5PD
☎ Handley (0725) 52583
*Converted 17th C. inn with
retained period features, in
very quiet, peaceful
surroundings. Home produce
used.*
Bedrooms: 1 single, 2 twin.
Bathrooms: 1 private,
1 public.
Bed & breakfast: £11 single,
£22 double.
Half board: £17.50 daily,
£110 weekly.
Evening meal 6.30pm.
Parking for 3.

Handley Central House
49-53 High Street, Sixpenny
Handley, Salisbury, Wiltshire
SP5 5ND
☎ Handley (0725) 52235
*Just off the A354 in a central
position between Salisbury,
Blandford and Shaftesbury.*
Bedrooms: 2 double & 1 twin.
Bathrooms: 1 public.
Bed & breakfast: £11-£11.50
single.
Half board: £14.50-£15 daily,
£82-£85 weekly.
Parking for 3.

INDIVIDUAL
PROPRIETORS HAVE
SUPPLIED ALL
DETAILS OF
ACCOMMODATION.
ALTHOUGH WE DO
CHECK FOR
ACCURACY, WE
ADVISE YOU TO
CONFIRM PRICES
AND OTHER
INFORMATION AT
THE TIME OF
BOOKING.

SOUTHAMPTON

Hampshire
Map ref 2C3

One of Britain's leading
seaports with a long
history, and now
developed as a major
container port. In the 18th
C it became a fashionable
resort with the assembly
rooms and theatre. The
old Guildhall is now a
museum and the Wool
House a maritime
museum. Sections of the
medieval wall can still be
seen.

Corhampton Lane Farm
Corhampton, Southampton,
SO3 1NB
☎ Droxford (0489) 877506
*600-acre arable farm.
Comfortable, modernised 17th
C. farmhouse on B3035
Bishops Waltham/Corhampton
road. Owner is qualified
Hampshire guide. Evening
meal by prior arrangement.*
Bedrooms: 2 twin.
Bathrooms: 1 private,
1 public.
Bed & breakfast: £12.50-
£14.50 single, £25-£28 double.
Half board: £18.50-£20.50
daily, £118-£125 weekly.
Evening meal 7.30pm (l.o.
8.30pm).
Parking for 3.

Meadowhead
Listed
139 Burgess Road, Bassett,
Southampton, SO1 7AE
☎ (0703) 768069
*Pleasant 5-bedroomed family
house in attractive, quarter of
an acre garden, 2 miles from
the city centre on the edge of
the common.*
Bedrooms: 1 single, 2 twin.
Bathrooms: 1 public.
Bed & breakfast: £10 single,
£20 double.
Parking for 3.
Open July-September.

Montrose
Solomons Lane, Shirrell
Heath, Southampton,
SO3 2HU
☎ Wickham (0329) 833345
*Attractive, comfortable
accommodation in lovely Meon
Valley, equidistant from main
towns and convenient for
continental ferries and
motorway links.*
Bedrooms: 2 double.

Bathrooms: 1 private,
1 public.
Bed & breakfast: £16-£20
single, £25-£30 double.
Parking for 3.

Verulam House
Listed
181 Wilton Road, Shirley,
Southampton, SO1 5HY
☎ (0703) 773293
*Built in 1905. High ceilings,
cornice in downstairs rooms,
large hall and circular landing.
All rooms are comfortably
sized and warm.*
Bedrooms: 1 single, 1 double
& 1 twin.
Bathrooms: 2 public.
Bed & breakfast: £9 single,
£18-£20 double.
Half board: £14 daily, £70
weekly.
Evening meal 7pm (l.o. 7pm).
Parking for 1.

SPARSHOLT

Hampshire
Map ref 2C2

Village in high position on
the downs. Nearby is
Farley Mount Bronze Age
Barrow and Horse
Monument.

Mrs. A. Barker
The Post House, Sparsholt,
Winchester, SO21 2NR
☎ (096 272) 275
*In a delightful village close to
the church. 15 minutes from
Winchester, 20 from Romsey
and 45 from Salisbury.*
Bedrooms: 2 single, 1 double
& 1 twin.
Bathrooms: 2 public.
Bed & breakfast: £10 single,
£20-£22 double.
Parking for 4.

STONEY CROSS

Hampshire
Map ref 2B3

Cartref
Stoney Cross Nr. Lyndhurst,
SO43 7GN
☎ Southampton
(0703) 812140
*Comfortable, family home in
eight acres, with beautiful
views from all rooms and direct
access to forest. Ideal for
walking and riding, and golf
nearby.*
Bedrooms: 1 double & 1 twin,
1 family room.

Bathrooms: 2 public.
Bed & breakfast: max. £12
single, max. £22 double.
Parking for 8.

STURMINSTER NEWTON

Dorset
Map ref 2B3

Every Monday this small
town holds a livestock
market. One of the
bridges over the River
Stour is a fine medieval
example and bears a
plaque declaring that
anyone 'injuring' it will be
deported.

Dorset Cottage
Bagber Lane, Bagber,
Sturminster Newton,
DT10 2HS
☎ (0258) 72861
*18th C. cottage with new
dining room/lounge for guests
and bedrooms in old part of
building. On the A357 between
Sturminster and Sherborne.*
Bedrooms: 1 single, 1 double
& 1 twin.
Bathrooms: 1 public.
Bed & breakfast: £10.50
single, £21 double.
Parking for 4.
Open April-October.

Fiddleford Inn ♠
Fiddleford, Sturminster
Newton, DT10 2BX
☎ (0258) 72489
*A traditional English inn,
specialising in home-made
food, real ale and old fashioned
hospitality. Near 14th C. mill.*
Bedrooms: 1 single, 2 double
& 1 twin.
Bathrooms: 1 private,
2 public.
Bed & breakfast: £15.50-
£18.50 single, £31-£37 double.
Half board: £20.50-£23.50
daily, £129.15-£148.05
weekly.
Evening meal 7pm (l.o.
10pm).
Parking for 40.
Credit: Access, Visa.

Holebrook Farm
Listed
Lydlinch, Sturminster
Newton, DT10 2JB
☎ Hazelbury Bryan
(025 86) 348 & (0258) 817348

126-acre mixed farm. Georgian stone farmhouse with a warm welcome and friendly atmosphere. Also 3 delightful stable annexes with own sitting rooms and shower units. Swimming pool, clay pigeon shooting and fishing available. From April 1989, telephone number will be 0258 817348.
Bedrooms: 1 single, 5 twin.
Bathrooms: 3 private,
1 public.
Bed & breakfast: £22-£24 double.
Half board: £17-£18 daily, £115.50-£119 weekly.
Evening meal 7pm (l.o. 5pm).
Parking for 6.

The Old Bridge Cottage Restaurant M
Listed
The Bridge, Sturminster Newton, DT10 2BS
☎ (0258) 72689
Attractive 17th C. cottage restaurant in the heart of the Blackmore Vale, overlooking the famous medieval bridge and working mill.
Bedrooms: 1 double & 2 twin.
Bathrooms: 1 private,
1 public.
Bed & breakfast: £13.50-£17.50 single, £27-£31 double.
Half board: £27-£35 daily.
Lunch available.
Evening meal 7pm (l.o. 9.30pm).
Parking for 8.
Credit: Access, Visa.

Old Post Office M
Listed
Hinton St. Mary, Sturminster Newton, DT10 1NG
☎ (0258) 72366
An interesting house with a chequered history, now a cosy and friendly guesthouse. Near River Stour, well placed for exploring Dorset's villages and seashore.
Bedrooms: 1 double & 1 twin, 1 family room.
Bathrooms: 1 public.
Bed & breakfast: max. £9.50 single, max. £19 double.
Half board: max. £15.50 daily, max. £110 weekly.
Evening meal 6.30pm (l.o. 9.30am).
Parking for 7.

SUTTON SCOTNEY
Hampshire
Map ref 2C2

Mrs. D. Somerton
Listed
17 Upper Bullington, Sutton Scotney, Nr. Winchester, SO21 3RB
☎ Winchester (0962) 760566
Modernised, warm, comfortable cottage with large, pretty garden, in quiet country lane surrounded by fields. A real home from home.
Bedrooms: 2 twin.
Bathrooms: 2 public.
Bed & breakfast: £15 single, £25 double.
Parking for 7.

SWANAGE
Dorset
Map ref 2B3

Began life as an Anglo-Saxon port, then a quarrying centre of Purbeck Marble. Now the safe, sandy beach set in a sweeping bay and flanked by downs is good walking country making it an ideal resort. ℹ

Leyland
Quarr Farm Lane, Valley Road, Swanage, BH19 3DY
☎ Corfe Castle (0929) 480573
Modern Purbeck stone house surrounded by open countryside. 2.5 miles from Swanage and the ancient village of Corfe Castle.
Bedrooms: 4 double & 1 twin, 2 family rooms.
Bathrooms: 2 public.
Bed & breakfast: £10.50-£12.50 single, £20-£24 double.
Half board: £14.50-£16.50 daily, £90-£110 weekly.
Evening meal 6pm.
Parking for 8.
Open April-October.

THERE IS A SPECIAL
SECTION IN THIS
GUIDE LISTING
ACCOMMODATION
ESPECIALLY
SUITABLE FOR
GROUPS AND
YOUNG PEOPLE.

SWAY
Hampshire
Map ref 2C3

4m NW. Lymington
Small village on the south western edge of the New Forest. It is noted for its 220 ft tower, Peterson's Folly, built in the 1870's by a retired Indian judge to demonstrate the value of concrete as a building material.

Redwing Farm
Pitmore Lane, Sway, Nr. Lymington, SO41 6BW
☎ Lymington (0590) 683319
20-acre animal farm. Redwing Farm has beamed rooms, modern facilities and warm hospitality. Ideal sight-seeing base in the New Forest.
Bedrooms: 1 single, 3 double & 2 twin.
Bathrooms: 2 public.
Bed & breakfast: £9.50-£9.80 single, £19-£19.60 double.
Half board: £14.50-£14.80 daily, £101.50-£103.60 weekly.
Evening meal 7pm (l.o. 8pm).
Parking for 10.

St. Judes M
Middle Road, Sway, Nr. Lymington, SO41 6AT
☎ Lymington (0590) 683525
Converted Methodist chapel with open plan living room, dining room and kitchen. Quiet bedrooms behind, all on ground floor.
Bedrooms: 1 single, 2 double & 1 twin.
Bathrooms: 1 public; 1 private shower.
Bed & breakfast: £11-£11.50 single, £22-£24 double.
Parking for 4.
Open April-October.

String of Horses M
Mead End, Sway, Lymington, SO41 6EH
☎ Lymington (0590) 682631
Unique, secluded hotel set in 4 acres, in the New Forest. Well-appointed bedrooms and fantasy bathrooms with bubble baths.
Bedrooms: 6 double.
Bathrooms: 6 private.
Bed & breakfast: £30-£50 single, £40-£80 double.
Half board: £31.50-£61.50 daily.
Lunch available.

Evening meal 7.30pm (l.o. 10pm).
Parking for 12.
Credit: Access, Visa, Amex.

THREE LEGGED CROSS
Dorset
Map ref 2B3

5m W. Ringwood

Homeacres
Homelands Farm, Three Legged Cross, Wimborne, BH21 6QZ
☎ Verwood (0202) 822422
270-acre mixed farm. Large chalet bungalow of traditional design, with inglenook fireplace in drawing room. Extensive garden, with access to large patio from drawing room.
Bedrooms: 1 single, 2 double, 3 family rooms.
Bathrooms: 3 public.
Bed & breakfast: £12-£15 single, £20-£24 double.
Parking for 7.

TIPTOE
Hampshire
Map ref 2B3

Brockhills Farm
Sway Road, Tiptoe, Nr. Lymington, SO41 6FQ
☎ New Milton (0425) 611280
100-acre mixed farm. Farm run by the same family for 4 generations. Now rearing beef animals and sheep. On the B3055 between St. Andrews Church on the Tiptoe crossroads and the Plough Inn.
Bedrooms: 1 double, 1 family room.
Bathrooms: 1 public.
Bed & breakfast: £9-£10 single, £18-£20 double.
Parking for 1.
Open April-October.

GROUPS, CONSORTIA
AND AGENCIES
SPECIALISING
IN FARM AND
COUNTRY HOLIDAYS
ARE LISTED IN A
SPECIAL SECTION
OF THIS GUIDE.

UPHAM

Hampshire
Map ref 2C3

6m SE. Winchester
Typical Hampshire village
surrounded by farmland.

Mrs. E.A. Clifton

The Old Fir Tree, Upham,
Nr. Southampton, SO3 1JL
☎ Durley (048 96) 306
Former pub set in a very quiet
and attractive village. Lovely
walks can be taken in the
surrounding countryside. Well
placed for Winchester,
Portsmouth, New Forest and
Salisbury.
Bedrooms: 2 single, 2 twin.
Bathrooms: 2 private,
1 public.
Bed & breakfast: £10-£12
single, £20-£24 double.
Half board: £15-£20 daily.
Evening meal 7pm (l.o. 5pm).
Parking for 4.
රු6 ᾧ ᵾ ⅄ ⊤ⓥ 🖽 ▵ ♠ ⅂
❖ ✗ 🐾

WAREHAM

Dorset
Map ref 2B3

This site has been
occupied since pre-
Roman times and has a
turbulent history. In 1762
fire destroyed much of
the town, so the buildings
now are mostly
Georgian. ⅰ

Cherry Bank Guest House

32 Furzebrook Road,
Stoborough, Wareham,
BH20 5AX
☎ (092 95) 2986
Small country guesthouse at
the foot of Purbeck Hills, with
access to heathland.
Bedrooms: 1 single, 1 double
& 1 twin, 1 family room.
Bathrooms: 1 private,
1 public; 1 private shower.
Bed & breakfast: £14-£16
single, £21-£25 double.
Half board: £20-£22 daily.
Evening meal 6pm.
රු ⓂᎷ ᵾ ✿ ᵾ ⅄ ⅂ ⊤ⓥ
▵ ♨ ❖ ✗ 🐾 🖽 ᴰᴬᴾ ꜱᴾ

Greenacres

Coldharbour, Wareham,
BH20 7PA
☎ (092 95) 3821
Large chalet bungalow in
Wareham Forest, half a mile
past the 'Silent Women' pub,
on the right in Bere Road.
Bedrooms: 1 single, 1 double,
1 family room.

Bathrooms: 2 public.
Bed & breakfast: £13-£14
single, £26-£28 double.
Parking for 6.
රු ᾧ 🅰 ᵾ ⅂ ⓥ ⊤ⓥ 🖽 🐾

Hyde Hill

64 Furzebrook Road,
Wareham, BH20 5AX
☎ (092 95) 2392
Friendly guest house on quiet
country road. Pleasant garden
and open heathland to front
and rear. Home cooking.
Bedrooms: 1 single, 1 twin,
2 family rooms.
Bathrooms: 1 private,
2 public.
Bed & breakfast: £10-£11
single, £20-£22 double.
Half board: £14.50-£15.50
daily, from £98 weekly.
Evening meal 6pm (l.o. 4pm).
Parking for 6.
රු ᾧ 🅰 ᵾ ⅂ ⓥ ⅂ ⊤ⓥ 🖽
▵ ❖ ✗ 🐾

The Quay Inn

The Quay, Wareham,
BH20 4LP
☎ (092 95) 2735
18th C. inn on the quay (River
Frome), popular mooring for
visiting yachtsmen, with
uninterrupted views of Purbeck
Hills.
Bedrooms: 1 single, 2 double,
1 family room.
Bathrooms: 1 public.
Bed & breakfast: £16-£20
single, £30-£36 double.
Lunch available.
Evening meal 6pm (l.o.
9.30pm).
Parking for 28.
රු ⅂ ✿ ᵾ ⅂ ⓥ 🖽 ✗ 🐾

WEST LULWORTH

Dorset
Map ref 2B3

Well known for Lulworth
Cove, the almost
landlocked circular bay of
chalk and limestone cliffs.

Bishop's Cottage Hotel
😊😊

West Lulworth, Wareham,
BH20 5RQ
☎ (092 941) 261
Comfortable family hotel close
to, and overlooking Lulworth
Cove. Ideal for seaside and
walking.
Bedrooms: 3 single, 6 double
& 2 twin, 3 family rooms.
Bathrooms: 6 private,
4 public.
Bed & breakfast: £16.50-
£17.50 single, £33-£35 double.
Half board: £24-£25 daily,
£155-£165 weekly.
Lunch available.

Evening meal 7pm (l.o.
10pm).
Open April-November.
Credit: Access, Visa.
රු ᾧ ⓓ ᵾ 🅸 ⓥ ▵ ⊤ⓥ ▵ ♠ ⅂
❖ 🐾 ꜱᴾ 🖽

Lulworth Cove Inn

West Lulworth, Nr.
Wareham, BH20 5RQ
☎ (092 941) 333
Hotel and pub specialising in
home-made and local seafood.
Spectacular view of Lulworth
Cove from restaurant and
bedrooms.
Bedrooms: 6 double & 3 twin,
2 family rooms.
Bathrooms: 5 private,
1 public; 5 private showers.
Bed & breakfast: £13-£17
single, £26-£32 double.
Half board: £18-£22 daily.
Lunch available.
Evening meal 7pm (l.o.
10.30pm).
Parking for 20.
Credit: Access, Visa, C.Bl.,
Diners, Amex.
රු ⅃ ⓓ ⅂ ✿ 🅸 ⓥ ⅂ ⅂
▵ ⅂ ⅁ ꜱᴾ

The Old Barn ⋈

Lulworth Cove, West
Lulworth, Wareham,
BH20 5RL
☎ (092 941) 305
Converted old barn in peaceful,
picturesque coastal village.
Choice of rooms with
continental breakfast or with
catering facilities. Well placed
for touring Dorset.
Bedrooms: 2 single, 5 double
& 3 twin, 4 family rooms.
Bathrooms: 3 public.
Bed & breakfast: £12-£15
single, £24-£30 double.
Parking for 9.
රු ᾧ 🅰 ᵾ ᴄʙ 🖽 ▵ 🐾 ᴰᴬᴾ
ꜱᴾ

WEST STOUR

Dorset
Map ref 2B3

3m SW. Gillingham

The Ship Inn
😊😊😊

West Stour, Nr. Gillingham,
SP8 5RP
☎ (0747) 85640
18th C. mail coach inn with
fine views over the Dorset
countryside. Log fires during
winter and traditional hand-
pumped ales throughout the
year. Central for touring the
West Country. Facilities for
fishing and shooting with local
club.
Bedrooms: 3 double & 3 twin,
1 family room.

Bathrooms: 6 private,
1 public.
Bed & breakfast: £15-£17.50
single, £30-£38 double.
Half board: £21.50-£26 daily,
£105-£120 weekly.
Lunch available.
Evening meal 7.30pm (l.o.
10pm).
Parking for 50.
Credit: Access, Visa.
රු 🅸 ⓥ ⅄ ⅂ ⊤ⓥ ▵ ⅂
ᴾ ❖ ✗ 🖽 ᴰᴬᴾ ⅂ ꜱᴾ 🐾

WIMBORNE

Dorset
Map ref 2B3

Barnsley Farm

Wimborne, BH21 4HZ
☎ Witchampton
(0258) 840296
270-acre mixed farm. 18th C.
farmhouse, recently
refurbished, in quiet, secluded
location. Within easy reach of
Bournemouth and New Forest.
Bedrooms: 2 double & 1 twin.
Bathrooms: 2 public.
Bed & breakfast: from £12
single, from £22 double.
Parking for 6.
Open April-October.
රු10 ᾧ ✿ ᵾ ⅄ ⊤ⓥ 🖽 ❖
✗ 🐾

WIMBORNE MINSTER

Dorset
Map ref 2B3

Market town centred on
the twin-towered Minster
Church of St. Cuthberga
which gave the town the
second part of its name.
Good touring base for the
surrounding countryside,
depicted in the writings of
Thomas Hardy. ⅰ

Ashton Lodge
😊😊

10 Oakley Hill, Wimborne
Minster, BH21 1QH
☎ (0202) 883423
Large, detached, family house,
with attractive gardens and a
relaxed and friendly
atmosphere.
Bedrooms: 1 double & 1 twin,
1 family room.
Bathrooms: 1 private,
3 public.
Bed & breakfast: £9.50-£20
single, £19-£21 double.
Parking for 3.
රු ⅂ ✿ ᵾ 🖽 ⓥ ⅂ ⊤ⓥ 🖽
▵ ✗ 🐾

Granville

54 Wimborne Road West,
Wimborne Minster,
BH21 2DP
☎ (0202) 886735
*Detached, double-fronted
house in country setting, with
sweeping drive, in three
quarters of an acre garden.*
Bedrooms: 1 single, 3 double,
1 family room.
Bathrooms: 2 private,
1 public.
Bed & breakfast: £12-£20
single, £22-£32 double.
Half board: £16-£25 daily.
Evening meal 6pm (l.o. 9pm).
Parking for 11.
🐃 🛁 ⁑ 🖳 UL 🏧 📻 📺
▥ ▵ ❀

Northill House ᴍ
⏣⏣⏣

Horton, Wimborne,
BH21 7HL
☎ Witchampton
(0258) 840407
*A mid-Victorian former
farmhouse, modernised to
provide comfortable bedrooms.
Log fires and cooking using
fresh produce.*
Bedrooms: 5 double & 3 twin,
1 family room.
Bathrooms: 9 private.
Bed & breakfast: £20 single,
£40 double.
Half board: £29 daily,
£182.70 weekly.
Evening meal 7.30pm (l.o.
6.30pm).
Parking for 12.
Open February-December.
Credit: Access, Visa.
🐃 8 📞 ⊕ 🖳 🏧 ▮ ▥ 📻 ▦
▵ ❀ ✗ 🖼 SP

Thorburn House
Listed

2 Oakley Road, Wimborne,
BH21 1QJ
☎ (0202) 883958
*On the Wimborne to Poole
road, well decorated and
furnished, with ample off-street
parking. Homely atmosphere.
Smoking discouraged.*
Bedrooms: 1 single, 1 double
& 1 twin.
Bathrooms: 1 private,
1 public.
Bed & breakfast: £9.50-£15
single, £19-£26 double.
Half board: £66.50 weekly.
Parking for 3.
🐃 3 🔥 ⊕ 🖳 ⁂ 🖳 ▥ ⅍ ▦
▵ ✗ 🖼

Mrs. Laurie Tyzack
Listed

19 The Vineries, Wimborne,
BH21 2PU
☎ (0202) 883180

---

*Comfortable accommodation,
within easy reach of the
Minster. 1 twin-bedded room
en-suite and a second bedroom
with use of bathroom and toilet
adjacent.*
Bedrooms: 2 twin.
Bathrooms: 1 private,
1 public.
Bed & breakfast: £11-£12.50
single, £20-£23 double.
Parking for 2.
Open April-October.
🐃 ⅍ 🖳 🏧 📺 ▥ ✗

WINCHESTER

Hampshire
Map ref 2C2

*See also Sparsholt and
Sutton Scotney.*
King Alfred the Great
made Winchester the
capital of Saxon England.
A magnificent Norman
cathedral, with one of the
longest naves in Europe,
dominates the city. Home
of Winchester College
founded in 1382. ℹ

Aquarius Bed &
Breakfast
Listed

31 Hyde Street, Winchester,
SO23 7DX
☎ (0962) 54729
*Lovely town house within 5
minutes of railway, coach and
bus stations. 10 minutes from
the cathedral, high street and
museums. 2 minutes from the
recreation centre. Evening meal
available on request.*
Bedrooms: 1 single, 1 double
& 1 twin, 1 family room.
Bathrooms: 1 private,
1 public.
Bed & breakfast: £15 single.
🐃 🛁 🖳 ⅍ 🖳 ▮ ▥ 📺 ▥
▵ ⌴ ⤻ ✗ 🖼 ▦

Mrs. A.S. Baird
Listed

Rutland House, 11 Park
Road, Winchester,
SO22 6AA
☎ (0962) 60196
*A personal and warm welcome
is assured in this fine
Edwardian residence,
surrounded by peaceful
gardens with marvellous views.
20 minutes' walk from city
centre. Evening meals available
on request.*
Bedrooms: 1 single, 1 double
& 2 twin.
Bathrooms: 1 private,
2 public.
Bed & breakfast: £14.50-
£16.50 single, £26-£35.50
double.
Half board: £21-£25 daily,
£140-£170 weekly.

Evening meal 6.45pm (l.o.
5pm).
Parking for 4.
🐃 🖳 🖳 ▥ ⅍ 📺 ▥ ▵ ❀
✗ 🖼 SP ▦

Brentwood ᴍ
⏣⏣⏣

178 Stockbridge Road,
Winchester, SO22 6RW
☎ (0962) 53536 & 840427
*Edwardian house with
comfortable, spacious rooms, 5
minutes from centre of
Winchester. Traditional and
continental breakfast, evening
meals by prior arrangement.*
Bedrooms: 1 double & 1 twin,
1 family room.
Bathrooms: 2 public.
Bed & breakfast: £12.50-£15
single, £22-£25 double.
🐃 ⅍ 🖳 ▥ ⅍ 📺 ▥ ▵
✗ 🖼 SP

Mrs. V. Edwards

4 Bereweeke Close,
Winchester, SO22 6AR
☎ (0962) 67242
*Detached house with open
garden, in a quiet area 10
minutes' walk from the railway
station. Family home.*
Bedrooms: 1 single, 1 family
room.
Bathrooms: 1 public.
Bed & breakfast: £10-£15
single, £20-£24 double.
🐃 🛁 ⊕ 🖳 🖳 ▥ ▵ ✗
🖼 SP

Mrs. A.P. Farrell
Listed

5 Ranelagh Road, St. Cross,
Winchester, SO23 9TA
☎ (0962) 69555
*Comfortable Victorian house
close to city centre, St. Cross
Hospital and water meadows.*
Bedrooms: 1 single, 1 double,
1 family room.
Bathrooms: 2 public.
Bed & breakfast: £10-£11
single, £20-£22 double.
🐃 5 ⅍ 🖳 ▮ 📺 ⅍ ✗ 🖼

Mrs. O. Fetherston-
Dilke
⏣⏣

85 Christchurch Road,
Winchester, SO23 9QY
☎ (0962) 68661
*Comfortable, Victorian family
house in St. Cross, Winchester.
Convenient for exploring
Hampshire. Evening meal by
prior arrangement.*
Bedrooms: 1 single, 1 double
& 1 twin.
Bathrooms: 1 public.

Bed & breakfast: £10-£12.50
single, £20-£25 double.
Half board: £16.50-£19 daily.
Evening meal 6pm (l.o. 7pm).
Parking for 3.
🐃 🖳 🖳 ▥ ⅍ ▵ ✗ 🖼

Mrs. J. Gaskell

58 Fairfield Road,
Winchester, SO22 6SG
☎ (0962) 67978
*Victorian terraced town house
with authentic interior. In a
quiet area, 15 minutes' walk
from the cathedral.*
Bedrooms: 1 double.
Bathrooms: 1 public.
Bed & breakfast: from £25
double.
🐃 🖳 ▮ ▥ ▵ ✗ 🖼 SP
▦

Mrs. H. Lawrence
⏣⏣⏣

67 St. Cross Road,
Winchester, SO23 9RE
☎ (0962) 63002
*Close to beautiful St. Cross
Church and water meadows.*
Bedrooms: 1 double, 1 family
room.
Bathrooms: 2 public.
Bed & breakfast: £20-£22
double.
🐃 3 ⊕ 🖳 🖳 ▮ ▥ 📺
▥ ▵

Mrs. Christine
Leonard ᴍ
⏣⏣⏣

Dellbrook, Hubert Road, St.
Cross, Winchester,
SO23 9RG
☎ (0962) 65093
*Comfortable, Edwardian house
in quiet area of Winchester
close to water meadows, golf
and recreation centre. Easy
access to the New Forest, Isle
of Wight and London.*
Bedrooms: 1 twin, 2 family
rooms.
Bathrooms: 1 private,
1 public.
Bed & breakfast: £12-£13.50
single, £24-£27 double.
Half board: £19-£21 daily,
£128-£140 weekly.
Evening meal 6pm (l.o. 1pm).
Parking for 4.
🐃 ⅍ 🖳 ▮ ▥ ⅍ 📺 ▥ ▵
OAP

The Lilacs
Listed

1 Harestock Close, Littleton,
Winchester, SO22 6NP
☎ (0962) 884122
*An attractive Georgian style
family home on Winchester's
northern outskirts, offering
comfortable, clean, friendly
accommodation and country
views.*

Continued ▶

WINCHESTER

Continued

Bedrooms: 1 double, 1 family room.
Bathrooms: 1 public.
Bed & breakfast: £10-£12 single, £18-£20 double.
Parking for 3.

"Markland"

44 St. Cross Road,
Winchester, SO23 9PS
☎ (0962) 54901
Delightful Victorian house, close to cathedral, college, St. Cross Hospital, water meadows and town centre. A warm welcome awaits you.
Bedrooms: 2 double & 2 twin.
Bathrooms: 4 private.
Bed & breakfast: £19-£22 single, £30-£36 double.
Open January-November.
Credit: Access.

The Plough Inn

Main Road, Itchen Abbas,
Nr. Winchester, SO21 1BQ
☎ Itchen Abbas
(096 278) 537
Homely village inn close to the River Itchen, with easy access to New Forest and South Coast resorts.
Bedrooms: 1 double & 2 twin.
Bathrooms: 1 public.
Bed & breakfast: from £17.25 single, from £34.50 double.
Lunch available.
Evening meal 7pm (l.o. 10pm).
Parking for 35.

Stratton House

Stratton Road, St. Giles Hill,
Winchester, SO23 8JQ
☎ (0962) 63919 & 64529
Telex 477379 Winser G
A lovely old Victorian house with an acre of grounds, in an elevated position on St. Giles Hill.
Bedrooms: 1 single, 2 double & 1 twin, 2 family rooms.
Bathrooms: 1 private, 3 public; 2 private showers.
Bed & breakfast: £14-£16 single, £28-£32 double.
Half board: £20-£22 daily, £130-£144 weekly.
Evening meal 6pm (l.o. 4pm).
Parking for 8.

WINFRITH NEWBURGH

Dorset
Map ref 2B3

West Burton Farm

Winfrith, Dorchester,
DT2 8DD
☎ Warmwell (0305) 852956
80-acre dairy/tree & shrub nursery farm. A secluded Queen Anne farmhouse.
Bedrooms: 2 double & 2 twin, 1 family room.
Bathrooms: 2 public.
Bed & breakfast: £22-£28 double.
Half board: £17.50-£20.50 daily, £122.50-£143.50 weekly.
Evening meal 6.30pm.
Parking for 6.

WINTERBORNE STICKLAND

Dorset
Map ref 2B3

3m W. Blandford Forum

Restharrow

North Street, Winterborne
Stickland, Nr. Blandford,
DT11 0NH
☎ Milton Abbas
(0258) 880936
Comfortable accommodation in centre of pretty village in the Winterborne Valley. Well placed for exploring Dorset. Friendly welcome assured.
Bedrooms: 2 double.
Bathrooms: 2 private.
Bed & breakfast: £20-£28 double.
Parking for 3.

WOODGREEN

Hampshire
Map ref 2B3

Typical New Forest village, with brick and thatch cottages surrounded by thick hedges to keep out the cattle and ponies. A reminder of the village's way of life in the 1930's is depicted by murals inside the village hall.

Cottage Crest

Castle Hill, Woodgreen, Nr.
Fordingbridge, SP6 2AY
☎ Downton (0725) 22009

Set high in its own 3.5-acres overlooking the River Avon Valley and adjoining the New Forest. An acre of land reserved for badger colony.
Bedrooms: 1 single, 1 double, 1 family room.
Bathrooms: 3 private.
Bed & breakfast: £11-£13 single, from £22 double.
Parking for 5.

YATELEY

Hampshire
Map ref 2C2

4m W. Camberley
Mainly residential area. 2 miles from Blackbushe Airport.

Beechwood House

Vicarage Road, Yateley
Green, Camberley, Surrey
GU17 7QT
☎ (0252) 872395
Secluded, character house with all comforts, set in a conservation area overlooking farmland.
Bedrooms: 1 double & 1 twin.
Bathrooms: 2 public.
Bed & breakfast: £17 single, £27 double.
Parking for 3.

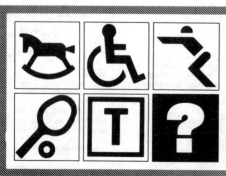

KEY TO SYMBOLS

Open out the flap inside the back cover of this guide and the key to symbols will be easy to use.

CROWN CLASSIFICATIONS

All the establishments displaying a national classification in this guide are inspected regularly. All can be chosen with confidence.

There are six classifications — from Listed to 5 Crowns; each indicates the level of facilities and services provided.

All classified establishments are required to provide a high standard of cleanliness, courtesy and service and to be well maintained. A lower classification does not imply lower standards; although the range of facilities and services may be smaller, they may be provided to a high standard.

You will find a full explanation of the national Crown Classification Scheme towards the end of this guide.

FOLLOW THE SIGN

It leads to over 550 Tourist Information Centres throughout England offering friendly help with accommodation and holiday ideas as well as suggestions of places to visit and things to do.

In your home town there may be a centre which can help you before you set out. If not, why not send for the Directory of Tourist Information Centres in Great Britain? It is available free from English Tourist Board, Department D, Bromells Road, Clapham, London SW4 0BJ.

South East England

England's warmest welcome — that's the proud boast of the South East England tourist region, which encompasses East and West Sussex, Kent and Surrey.

Come for a week, come for a short break or even just for a family day out and you'll find the South East an accommodating sort of place where the 'Welcome' mat is always out.

You can make the most of your time away here, with places to visit and things to do which are thick on the ground, from Surrey to the sea.

Well-loved coastal resorts like Brighton & Hove, Hastings, Worthing, Eastbourne, Folkestone, Ramsgate, Margate and Broadstairs hold the key to the South East's popularity. They sit alongside other coastal towns with various claims to fame, such as Dover and Deal with their mighty castles, Chichester with its yachting and Whitstable of oyster fame.

And backing up the coastal towns you'll discover the best of England's countryside, including the South Downs with its 80-mile South Downs Way, Kent's 'Garden of England', the wilder Romney Marsh and the breezy ridges of the North Downs.

Add in historic houses and glorious gardens, vineyards and vintage trains, animal kingdoms and adventure worlds, castles and collections, and you complete the welcoming picture of the South East.

Paul Anscomb

INTERNATIONAL CLOWNS CONVENTION

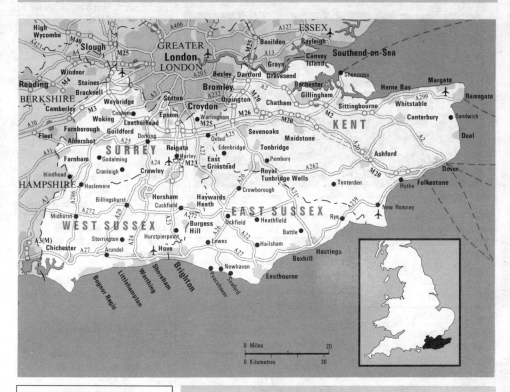

FIND OUT MORE

Further information about holidays and attractions in the South East tourist region is available from:

South East England Tourist Board,
1 Warwick Park, Tunbridge Wells, Kent TN2 5TA. ☎ (0892) 40766.

These publications are available free from the South East England Tourist Board:

South East England '89
Take a Break 1989
Diary of Events
Also available are the following (prices include postage and packing):
Hundreds of Places to Visit in the South East 1989 *(£1.35)*
Leisure Map for South East England *(£2.55)*

WHERE TO GO, WHAT TO SEE

Drusilla's Zoo Park
Alfriston, East Sussex BN26 5QS
☎ (0323) 870234
Small zoo with railway, adventure playland, traditional gardens, pottery, leatherworker, butterfly house, bakery.
Admission charge.

Wildfowl Trust
Mill Road, Arundel, West Sussex BN18 9PB ☎ (0903) 883355
Wildfowl Trust's Reserve in 75 acres of water-meadows. Tame swans, ducks, geese and other rare endangered species. Visitor centre with gallery.
Admission charge.

Whitbread Hop Farm
Beltring, Paddock Wood, Kent TN12 6PY ☎ (0622) 872068
Working hop farm with award-winning museums set in the largest group of Victorian oasts in the world. Museums, rural crafts and agricultural machinery. Famous Whitbread shire horses, children's play area, nature trail.
Admission charge.

Preston Manor
Preston Park, Brighton, East Sussex BN1 6SD ☎ (0273) 603005
Georgian manor house with Edwardian additions. Large collection of furniture, pictures and silver arranged to recall the way of life of a wealthy family.
Admission charge. ▶

PRESTON MANOR, BRIGHTON

Mary Stubberfield

Canterbury Heritage and Poor Priests' Hospital

20 Stour Street, Canterbury, Kent
☎ (0227) 452747
Museum on the city's story set in one of its loveliest buildings.
Admission charge.

Thorpe Park

Staines Road, Chertsey, Surrey
KT16 8PN ☎ (0932) 562633
One of Europe's largest leisure parks with wide variety of entertainments, rides, shows and exhibits.
Admission charge.

Polesden Lacey

Great Bookham, Nr. Dorking, Surrey
RH5 6BD ☎ (0372) 58203
Regency villa featuring interesting collection of 17th and 18th C furniture, portraits and Chinese porcelain. Exquisite grounds and gardens.
Admission charge.

Maison Dieu

Town Hall, Biggin Street, Dover, Kent
☎ (0304) 201200
Once a pilgrims' hostel, dating from 1203. Magnificent interior, stained glass windows depicting local history. Armoury.
Admission free.

Butterfly Centre

Royal Parade, Eastbourne, East Sussex
BN22 7AQ ☎ (0323) 645522
Exhibition of free-flying foreign and indigenous butterflies set in landscaped gardens with waterfalls, fountains and pools.   *Admission charge.*

Firle Place

Firle, Lewes, East Sussex BN8 6LP
☎ (079 159) 335
Tudor house with Georgian additions in Downland park. English and European Old Masters, French and English furniture, notable Sevres porcelain.
Admission charge.

Loseley Park

Guildford, Surrey GU3 1HN
☎ (0483) 571881
Early Elizabethan mansion surrounded by parkland and farm. Period furniture, paintings and unusual chalk fireplace. Farm tours available. Shop.
Admission charge.

St. Clement's Caves

West Hill, Hastings, East Sussex
☎ (0424) 422964
Caves set in West Hill, reputedly connected with coast's 18th C smuggling trade, and supposed to have been used for storing contraband.
Admission free.

Leeds Castle

Maidstone, Kent ME17 1PL
☎ (0622) 65400
Fairy-tale castle, dating from 9th C, in the middle of a lake. Furniture, art, tapestries. Dog collar museum. Parkland gardens, duckery and aviaries, maze and grotto.   *Admission charge.*

The Dickens Centre

Eastgate House, High Street, Rochester, Kent ☎ (0634) 44176
Unique experience of Dickens' life and novels. Life-size models, tableaux, sound and light effects.
Admission charge.

Sheffield Park Gardens

Uckfield, East Sussex TN22 3QX
☎ (0825) 790655
Originally 18th C garden modelled by 'Capability' Brown, with plants and shrubs planted earlier this century making an impressive floral spectacle. Wide variety of unusual and exotic species.   *Admission charge.*

Chatham Historic Dockyard

Church Lane, Chatham, Kent ME4 4TE
☎ (0634) 812551
Britain's most historic dockyard, giving a unique insight into the nation's naval heritage.   *Admission charge.*

MAKE A DATE FOR...

International Clowns Convention

Town Centre, Bognor Regis, West Sussex *7 — 9 April*

Chichester Festival Theatre Season

Chichester Festival Theatre, Chichester, West Sussex *May — October*

Horse racing: The Derby (7 June); Coronation Cup (8 June); International Day (9 June); Oaks Stakes (10 June)

Epsom Racecourse, Epsom, Surrey
7 — 10 June

South of England Show

South of England Showground, Ardingly, West Sussex *8 — 10 June*

Kent County Show

County Showground, Detling, Nr. Maidstone, Kent *13 — 15 July*

London to Brighton Veteran Car Run

Finishes at Madeira Drive, Brighton, East Sussex *5 November* *

* Provisional date only

Tourist and leisure information can be obtained from Tourist Information Centres throughout England. Details of centres in the South East England region are listed below. The symbol 🏠 means that an accommodation booking service is provided. Centres marked with a * are open during the summer months only. In the following pages, towns which have a Tourist Information Centre are indicated with the symbol *i*

Arundel
W. Sussex 🏠
61 High Street
☎ (0903) 882268

Ashford
Kent
Information Kiosk,
Lower High Street
☎ (0233) 37311 ext. 316

Battle
E. Sussex 🏠
88 High Street
☎ (042 46) 3721

Bexhill-on-Sea
E. Sussex 🏠
De La Warr Pavilion, Marina
☎ (0424) 212023

Bognor Regis
W. Sussex 🏠
Belmont Street
☎ (0243) 823140

Brighton
E. Sussex
Marlborough House,
54 Old Steine 🏠
☎ (0273) 23755
Kings Road, Seafront 🏠 *
☎ (0273) 23755

Broadstairs
Kent 🏠
Pierremont Hall, 67 High Street
☎ Thanet (0843) 68399

Canterbury
Kent 🏠
34 St. Margaret's Street
☎ (0227) 766567

Chichester
W. Sussex 🏠
St Peter's Market, West Street
☎ (0243) 775888

Cranbrook
Kent 🏠 *
Vestry Hall, Stone Street
☎ (0580) 712538

Deal
Kent 🏠
Town Hall, High Street
☎ (0304) 369576

Dover
Kent 🏠
Townwall Street
☎ (0304) 205108

Eastbourne
E. Sussex
3 Cornfield Terrace 🏠
☎ (0323) 411400
The Pier, Marine Parade 🏠 *
☎ (0323) 411800

Farnham
Surrey 🏠
Locality Office, South Street
☎ Godalming (048 68) 4104
ext. 543

Farthing Corner (M2)
Kent 🏠
Motorway Service Station,
Farthing Corner, Nr. Gillingham
☎ Medway (0634) 360323

Faversham
Kent
Fleur de Lis Heritage Centre,
13 Preston Street
☎ (0795) 534542

Folkestone
Kent
Harbour Street 🏠
☎ (0303) 58594
Pedestrian Precinct,
Sandgate Road 🏠 *
☎ ((0303) 53840

Gatwick Airport
International Arrivals Concourse
☎ (0293) 560108

Gravesend
Kent 🏠
10 Parrock Street
☎ (0474) 337600

Guildford
Surrey
Civic Hall, London Road
☎ (0483) 575857

Hailsham
E. Sussex 🏠
The Library, Western Road
☎ (0323) 840604

▶

Hastings
E. Sussex
4 Robertson Terrace ᐟ
☎ (0424) 722022
The Fishmarket *
☎ (0424) 721201

Herne Bay
Kent ᐟ
The Bandstand
☎ (0227) 361911

Hove
E. Sussex
Town Hall, Norton Road ᐟ
☎ Brighton (0273) 775400
King Alfred Leisure Centre,
Kingsway ᐟ
☎ Brighton (0273) 720371

Hythe
Kent ᐟ *
Prospect Road Car Park
☎ (0303) 67799

Lewes
E. Sussex ᐟ
32 High Street
☎ (0273) 471600

Littlehampton
W. Sussex ᐟ *
The Windmill Complex, The Green
☎ (0903) 713480

Maidstone
Kent ᐟ
The Gatehouse, Old Palace
Gardens, Mill Street
☎ (0622) 602169 & 673581

Margate
Kent ᐟ
Marine Terrace
☎ Thanet (0843) 220241

New Romney
Kent ᐟ
2 Littlestone Road
☎ (0679) 64044

Peacehaven
E. Sussex
Meridian Centre, Roderick Avenue
☎ (079 14) 2668

Pevensey
E. Sussex ᐟ *
Castle Car Park, High Street
☎ Eastbourne (0323) 761444

Ramsgate
Kent
The Argyle Centre,
Queen Street ᐟ
☎ Thanet (0843) 591086
Ferry Terminal,
Port Ramsgate ᐟ *
☎ Thanet (0843) 589830

Rochester
Kent ᐟ
Eastgate Cottage, High Street
☎ Medway (0634) 43666

Rye
E. Sussex ᐟ
48 Cinque Ports Street
☎ (0797) 222293

Sandwich
Kent ᐟ *
St Peter's Church, Market Street
☎ (0304) 613565

Seaford
E. Sussex ᐟ
Station Approach
☎ (0323) 897426

Sevenoaks
Kent ᐟ
Buckhurst Lane
☎ (0732) 450305

Sheerness
Kent ᐟ
Bridge Road Car Park
(to meet incoming boats only)
☎ (0795) 665324

Shoreham-by-Sea
W. Sussex ᐟ
86 High Street
☎ (0273) 452086

Tenterden
Kent ᐟ
Town Hall, High Street
☎ (058 06) 3572

Tunbridge Wells
Kent ᐟ
Town Hall
☎ (0892) 26121

Walton-on-Thames
Surrey
Town Hall, New Zealand Avenue
☎ (0932) 228844

Whitstable
Kent ᐟ
Horsebridge
☎ (0227) 275482

Worthing
W. Sussex
Town Hall, Chapel Road ᐟ
☎ (0903) 210022
Marine Parade ᐟ
☎ (0903) 210022

Entries in this regional section are listed in alphabetical order of place name, and then in alphabetical order of establishment. County names are not normally repeated in each establishment entry, but please use the full postal address when writing.

The map references refer to the colour maps towards the end of this guide. The first number is the number of the map, and it is followed by the grid reference.

The Crown Classifications are explained on pages 8 and 9, and the key to symbols is on the flap inside the back cover — keep it open for easy reference.

ABINGER HAMMER

Surrey
Map ref 2D2

4m SW. Dorking
Lying in some of the most beautiful wooded land in the country this village is notable for the clock on which the figure of a blacksmith strikes the hours on a bell. The 'Hammer' takes its name from an old forge where cannon balls were made in the 16th C.

Crossways Farm
Raikes La., Abinger Hammer, Nr. Dorking, RH5 6PZ
☎ Dorking (0306) 730173
200-acre arable & beef farm. 17th C. listed farmhouse. Good centre for London, the South East and airports. Large comfortable rooms. Home produce.
Bedrooms: 1 double & 2 twin.
Bathrooms: 1 public.
Bed & breakfast: max. £15 single, max. £22 double.
Half board: max. £16.50 daily, max. £105 weekly.
Evening meal 7pm (l.o. 10am).
Parking for 3.

ALDINGTON

Kent
Map ref 3B4

6m W. Hythe
Once the home of Elizabeth Barton, the 'Holy Maid' or 'Nun of Kent'.

Hogben Farm
Church La., Aldington, Ashford, TN25 7EH
☎ (023 372) 219
3-acre farm. Small 16th C. country house, surrounded by pretty garden and farmland. Convenient for Channel Ports, Canterbury, Rye, Tenterden and Romney Marsh.
Bedrooms: 1 single, 1 double, 1 family room.
Bathrooms: 1 private, 1 public.
Bed & breakfast: £12-£14 single, £24-£28 double.
Half board: £19.50-£21.50 daily.
Parking for 4.

ALFRISTON

E. Sussex
Map ref 2D3

4m NE. Newhaven
Ancient town in the Cuckmere Valley and a former smugglers' haunt. The 14th C Clergy House was the first building to be bought by the National Trust. The spaciousness of the 14th C St. Andrew's Church has earned it the title of 'Cathedral of the South Downs' and the 13th C Star Inn is one of the oldest in England.

Alfriston Wingrove Inn M
High St., Alfriston, BN26 5TD
☎ (0323) 870276
Beside Alfriston village green with breathtaking views, Wingrove is one of the most popular country eating places in Sussex.
Bedrooms: 1 double & 2 twin.
Bathrooms: 3 private.
Bed & breakfast: £21-£26 single, £38-£50 double.
Lunch available.
Evening meal 6.30pm (l.o. 9pm).
Parking for 24.
Credit: Access.

AMBERLEY

W. Sussex
Map ref 2D3

Marsh Acres
South Lane, Houghton, Amberley, Arundel, BN18 9LN
☎ Bury (0798) 831854
Marsh Acres is at the end of a quiet lane with magnificent views of the River Arun, Arundel Park and the South Downs.
Bedrooms: 1 single, 2 twin.
Bathrooms: 1 private, 1 public.
Bed & breakfast: £10.50 single, £21-£25 double.
Parking for 3.

ARDINGLY

W. Sussex
Map ref 2D2

4m N. Haywards Heath
Famous for the South of England Agricultural Showground and public school. Nearby is Wakehurst Place (National Trust), the gardens of which are administered by the Royal Botanic Gardens, Kew.

Ardingly Inn M
Street La., Ardingly, RH17 6UA
☎ (0444) 892214
Free house village inn located in Sussex Weald adjacent to South of England Showground. Close to M23. Gatwick 11 miles.
Bedrooms: 3 double & 3 twin.
Bathrooms: 3 private, 1 public.
Bed & breakfast: £27-£34 single, £34-£42 double.
Lunch available.
Evening meal 7pm (l.o. 10pm).
Parking for 15.
Credit: Access, Visa, Diners, Amex.

ARGOS HILL

E. Sussex
Map ref 2D3

1m N. Mayfield
Hamlet with a post windmill on top of the hill (not open to the public).

Brook Farm
Argos Hill, Salters Green, Mayfield, TN20 6NP
☎ Mayfield (0435) 873269
65-acre beef farm. 15th C. yeoman's cottage with a wealth of oak beams on a family-run beef farm deep in the Sussex countryside.
Bedrooms: 1 single, 2 family rooms.
Bathrooms: 2 public.
Bed & breakfast: £10 single, £20 double.
Half board: £13.50 daily, £94.50 weekly.
Evening meal 7pm (l.o. midday).
Parking for 5.

INDIVIDUAL PROPRIETORS HAVE SUPPLIED ALL DETAILS OF ACCOMMODATION. ALTHOUGH WE DO CHECK FOR ACCURACY, WE ADVISE YOU TO CONFIRM PRICES AND OTHER INFORMATION AT THE TIME OF BOOKING.

THERE IS A SPECIAL SECTION IN THIS GUIDE LISTING ACCOMMODATION ESPECIALLY SUITABLE FOR GROUPS AND YOUNG PEOPLE.

PLEASE MENTION THIS GUIDE WHEN MAKING A BOOKING.

WE ADVISE YOU TO CONFIRM YOUR BOOKING IN WRITING.

ARUNDEL

W. Sussex
Map ref 2D3

Pleasant town on the River Arun, dominated by Arundel Castle, home of the Dukes of Norfolk. There are many 18th C houses and the Toy and Military Museum, Wildfowl Trust Reserve and Heritage Centre. ℹ

Arden Guest House
4 Queens Lane, Arundel, BN18 9JN
☎ (0903) 882544
Comfortable guesthouse close to Arundel Castle and all local facilities.
Bedrooms: 4 double & 3 twin, 1 family room.
Bathrooms: 2 private, 3 public.
Bed & breakfast: £20-£28 double.
Parking for 4.
Open February-December.
⌂2 🍴 ☐ 🌢 ⓉⓋ 🕮 ➡ ✠ 🅗
SP

ASHFORD

Kent

See Mersham

ASHURST

Kent
Map ref 2D2

5m W. Tunbridge Wells
Small hamlet on a hill at the top of which is the church with its unusual weatherboarded bellcote. The Wealdway long-distance footpath passes nearby at Stone Cross.

Manor Court Farm
Listed
Ashurst, Nr. Tunbridge Wells, TN3 9TB
☎ Fordcombe (089 274) 279
350-acre mixed farm. Georgian farmhouse. Guests welcome to explore the farm. Many footpaths and lovely views. Tennis and fishing by arrangement with owner. On the A264, half a mile east of Ashurst village (Tunbridge Wells/East Grinstead road).
Bedrooms: 1 single, 1 twin, 1 family room.
Bathrooms: 2 public.
Bed & breakfast: £12-£15 single, £24-£30 double.
⌂5 🍴 🖭 ☐ 🌢 ⓊⓁ ➡ Ⓣ 🕮
➡ ♨ ✿ 🅗 SP Ⓣ

BARFRESTON

Kent
Map ref 3C4

Church Farm
Barfreston, Nr. Dover, CT15 7JQ
☎ Shepherdswell (0304) 830366
256-acre arable farm. Georgian farmhouse in the hamlet of Barfreston with its beautiful Norman church, 2.5 miles from the A2. Car essential.
Bedrooms: 1 single, 1 double, 1 family room.
Bathrooms: 1 public.
Bed & breakfast: £8-£8.50 single, £16-£17 double.
Parking for 3.
Open April-October.
⌂ 🍴 Ⓤ ⓉⓋ ✠ 🅗 🅗

BATTLE

E. Sussex
Map ref 3B4

See also Robertsbridge. Built on the site of the Battle of Hastings, when William defeated Harold II and so became the Conqueror in 1066. This thriving town contains many old buildings, including the impressive abbey ruins. The Museum deals with history from the Neolithic age and has a fine collection relating to the Sussex iron industry. ℹ

Moonshill Farm ⋒
🛏🛏🛏
The Green, Ninfield, Battle, TN33 9JL
☎ (0424) 892645
10-acre mixed smallholding. Modernised farmhouse in the village centre, in the heart of "1066 country". A warm welcome with Sussex home cooking. Pub opposite.
Bedrooms: 1 single, 1 double & 3 twin.
Bathrooms: 3 private, 1 public.
Bed & breakfast: £10-£12 single, £20-£24 double.
Evening meal 6.30pm.
Parking for 12.
Open January-November.
⌂5 🖭 ☐ ☐ 🌢 Ⓤ ➡ Ⓣ 🕮
➡ ♨ ✿ 🅗 SP Ⓣ

BETHERSDEN

Kent
Map ref 3B4

Typical Wealden village with plenty of weatherboarded houses. Famous in the Middle Ages for its marble used in Canterbury and Rochester Cathedrals.

Odiam Farm
Bethersden, Nr. Ashford, TN26 3HE
☎ High Halden (023 385) 243
38-acre mixed farm. 14th C. with brick and tile outside. Inside are large fireplaces showing lovely old oak beams. Views of the North Downs.
Bedrooms: 2 double, 2 family rooms.
Bathrooms: 1 public; 3 private showers.
Bed & breakfast: £11-£12 single, £22-£24 double.
Half board: £16-£17 daily, £102-£109 weekly.
Evening meal 6.30pm (l.o. 7pm).
Parking for 5.
⌂ 🌢 Ⓤ ➡ ⓉⓋ ◐ 🕮 ➡ ♨ ♫
✿ ✠ 🅗 🅗

Snoad Hill Farm
Listed
Bethersden, Ashford, TN26 3DY
☎ (023 382) 269
250-acre mixed farm. Warm and comfortable, 17th C. farmhouse. One mile from village in quiet countryside. Central for touring historic Kent and Sussex.
Bedrooms: 1 single, 2 double & 2 twin.
Bathrooms: 2 public.
Bed & breakfast: max. £12 single, max. £24 double.
Parking for 7.
🌢 Ⓤ ➡ ⓉⓋ ◐ 🕮 ➡ ♨ ♫
✿ ✠ 🅗 🅗

BEXHILL-ON-SEA

E. Sussex
Map ref 3B4

Popular seaside resort with a gently shelving beach of shingle, with firm sand at low tide. A feature is the De la Warr Pavilion, containing a theatre, ballroom, banqueting suite, restaurant and sun terrace. East of the town, at Little Gally Hill, a submerged forest can be seen at low tide, a land bridge which linked Britain to the Continent 10,000 years ago. ℹ

Buenos Aires
Listed
24 Albany Rd., Bexhill-on-Sea, TN40 1BZ
☎ (0424) 212269
Well-established guesthouse adjacent to seafront, theatre and town centre.
Bedrooms: 1 double & 1 twin, 2 family rooms.
Bathrooms: 1 public.
Bed & breakfast: £12.50 single, £23 double.
Half board: £17 daily.
Evening meal 6pm (l.o. midday).
⌂5 ☐ 🌢 🏦 Ⓥ ➡ Ⓣ 🕮 ➡
✠ 🅗 🅗

Sea Breeze Guest House ⋒
Listed
65 Egerton Road, Bexhill-on-Sea, TN39 3HL
☎ (0424) 225952
Quietly situated, overlooking park and close to seafront, town centre and other amenities. Comfortable accommodation with relaxed atmosphere.
Bedrooms: 1 single, 1 double & 1 twin.
Bathrooms: 1 public.
Bed & breakfast: £9-£10.50 single, £18-£21 double.
Half board: £13-£14.50 daily, £88-£98 weekly.
Lunch available.
Evening meal 6pm (l.o. 7.30pm).
⌂ ☐ 🌢 Ⓤ 🏦 Ⓥ 🕮 ➡ 🅗

GROUPS, CONSORTIA AND AGENCIES SPECIALISING IN FARM AND COUNTRY HOLIDAYS ARE LISTED IN A SPECIAL SECTION OF THIS GUIDE.

THE SYMBOLS ARE EXPLAINED ON THE FLAP INSIDE THE BACK COVER.

BIDDENDEN

Kent
Map ref 3B4

Perfect village with black and white houses, a tithe barn and a pond. Part of the village is grouped round a green with a village sign depicting the famous Biddenden Maids. It was an important centre of the Flemish weaving industry hence the beautiful Old Cloth Hall.

Biddenden Place
Tenterden Rd., Biddenden, Ashford, TN27 8BB
☎ (0580) 291419
Elizabethan building set in 2 acres of formal gardens, with a Grecian styled pavilion overlooking the goldfish pond. Carvery open to the public Fridays and Saturdays.
Bedrooms: 2 single, 2 double & 1 twin, 1 family room.
Bathrooms: 4 private, 1 public.
Bed & breakfast: £12-£15 single, £24-£30 double.
Lunch available.
Evening meal 7pm (l.o. 7.30pm).
Parking for 7.
Credit: Access, Visa.
⛷ ⅏ ⊕ ⊡ ♻ Ⓥ ✕ ▥ ⚓ ❀ ⌱ 🏠

BIRCHINGTON

Kent
Map ref 3C3

Town on the north coast of Kent offering sandy beaches and rock pools. Powell Cotton Museum in nearby Quex Park.

Woodchurch Farmhouse
Woodchurch, Birchington, CT7 0HE
☎ Thanet (0843) 32468
6-acre arable farm. This Elizabethan farmhouse provides a warm welcome and ensures a comfortable stay. An excellent base for exploring south east Kent.
Bedrooms: 1 single, 2 double.
Bathrooms: 1 public.
Bed & breakfast: £9.50 single, £19 double.
Half board: £16 daily, £112 weekly.
Evening meal 7pm.
Parking for 20.
⛷ ⅏ ≅ ♻ ⓊⓁ ▮ Ⓥ ⌱ ⊡ ● ▥ ⚓ ∪ ❀ ✕ ⌱ 🏠

BODIAM

E. Sussex
Map ref 3B4

3m NE. Robertsbridge Small village with a beautifully set 14th C castle (NT) standing in a moat, that was built to resist possible invasion from France. Now a well-preserved ruin with a museum.

Castle Inn
Main Road, Bodiam
TN32 5UB
☎ Staplecross (058 083) 330
Public house/quality restaurant adjacent to the famous Bodiam Castle. Convenient for Tunbridge Wells, Hastings, Rye and Battle.
Bedrooms: 2 single, 1 double & 2 twin, 1 family room.
Bathrooms: 2 public.
Bed & breakfast: from £12 single, from £24 double.
Half board: £16-£25 daily.
Lunch available.
Evening meal 7pm (l.o. 10pm).
Parking for 20.
⛷ 1 ♻ ▮ Ⓥ ⌱ ⊡ ▥ ⚓ ✕ ☒ ⌱

BRASTED

Kent
Map ref 2D2

Holmeside House
High Street., Brasted
☎ Westerham (0959) 64834
Large Victorian house on the A25 opposite The Bull Inn at Brasted, between Sevenoaks and Westerham.
Bedrooms: 2 single, 1 twin, 2 family rooms.
Bathrooms: 2 private, 1 public.
Bed & breakfast: £16-£17 single, £32-£35 double.
Half board: £18.50-£20.50 daily, £129.50-£143.50 weekly.
Parking for 5.
⛷ ⅏ ≅ ♻ ⊡ ⓊⓁ ⌱ ⊡ ▥ ⌱ ⌲ 🏠

**THERE IS A SPECIAL
SECTION IN THIS
GUIDE LISTING
ACCOMMODATION
ESPECIALLY
SUITABLE FOR
GROUPS AND
YOUNG PEOPLE.**

BRIGHTON & HOVE

E. Sussex
Map ref 2D3

First and largest seaside resort in the south east with a host of attractions such as the Royal Pavilion, The Dome, Theatre Royal, Aquarium and Dolphinarium, Volks Railway, Palace Pier, Stanmer Park, Marina, Art Gallery and Museum, Booth Musem, Preston Manor, Conference and Exhibition Centre and 'The Lanes'. Neighbouring Hove is a resort in its own right with interesting Museum of Art and King Alfred's Leisure Centre on the seafront. ⌕

Andorra Hotel Ⓜ
⛺⛺⛺
15-16 Oriental Pl., Brighton, BN1 2LJ
☎ (0273) 725485 & 21787
Try our established, comfortable hotel, with well-appointed bedrooms, smart cocktail bar and home-cooked food.
Bedrooms: 8 single, 5 double & 5 twin, 3 family rooms.
Bathrooms: 10 private, 3 public; 1 private shower.
Bed & breakfast: £14-£22 single, £28-£44 double.
Half board: £20-£28 daily, £140-£196 weekly.
Evening meal 6pm (l.o. 6.30pm).
Credit: Access, Visa.
⛷ ⅏ ≅ ♻ ▮ Ⓥ ⌱ ⊡ ▥ ⚓ ⒹⒶⒻ ⌲ ⌱ 🏠 ⌱

Hotel Brunswick Ⓜ
⛺⛺
69 Brunswick Pl., Hove, BN3 1NE
☎ (0273) 733326/730785
Telex 877159 BHVTXSG
Regency building in quiet residential area of Hove. Short walk from Brunswick lawn, seafront and Brighton centre. Bowling green, tennis courts and golf course nearby.
Bedrooms: 9 single, 4 double & 5 twin, 4 family rooms.
Bathrooms: 2 private, 3 public; 4 private showers.
Bed & breakfast: £19-£23 single, £32-£46 double.
Half board: £28.50-£35.50 daily, £150-£190 weekly.
Evening meal 7pm (l.o. 10pm).
Parking for 6.
Credit: Access, Visa, Diners, Amex.
⛷ ⌱ ♻ ▮ Ⓥ ⌱ ⊡ ▥ ⚓ ⌱ ▮ ✕ ⚓ ☒ ⒹⒶⒻ ⌲ ⌱ 🏠 ⌱

Marina House Hotel Ⓜ
8 Charlotte St., Brighton, BN2 1AG
☎ (0273) 605349
Cosy, well-maintained Regency hotel, offering cleanliness, comfort and hospitality. English breakfast ; candlelit dinners in romantic surroundings, with a wide choice of menu. Near Palace Pier, adjacent to the sea and a few minutes from the marina, Royal Pavilion and all amenities. Flexible breakfast, check-in and check-out times. Secretarial services available.
Bedrooms: 3 single, 5 double & 2 twin, 1 family room.
Bathrooms: 5 private, 1 public; 3 private showers.
Bed & breakfast: £12.50-£15 single, £25-£31 double.
Half board: £19-£21.50 daily, £133-£150 weekly.
Evening meal 7pm (l.o. 4pm).
Credit: Access, Diners.
⛷ ⅏ ⊕ ⊡ ♻ ▮ ⌱ ⌱ ⊡ Ⓥ ▥
⌱ ✕ ⚓ ⒹⒶⒻ ⌲ ⌱ ⌱

St. Mary Farmhouse
⛺⛺
Ridge Rd., Falmer, Brighton BN1 9PL
☎ (0273) 692445
750-acre dairy and arable farm. Modern farmhouse 4 miles from Brighton. Scenic and quiet. Downland walking. Traditional breakfast, home cooking.
Bedrooms: 1 double, 1 family room.
Bathrooms: 1 private, 2 public.
Bed & breakfast: £12-£13.50 single, £24-£27 double.
Half board: £18.50-£20 daily.
Evening meal 6pm (l.o. 8pm).
Parking for 3.
⛷ ⌱ ♻ ▮ ⌱ ⊡ ⌱ ❀ ✕ 🏠

Sillwood Lodge Hotel Ⓜ
6 Sillwood Pl., Brighton, BN1 2LH
☎ (0273) 25493
A clean, comfortable and quiet hotel in a mews just off the sea front, with own car park. Central for all amenities.
Bedrooms: 4 single, 3 double & 3 twin.
Bathrooms: 2 private, 2 public.
Bed & breakfast: £14-£24 single, £26-£40 double.
Half board: £18-£28 daily, £125-£150 weekly.
Evening meal 6pm (l.o. 6pm).
Parking for 6.
⛷ ⊕ ⊡ ♻ ⓊⓁ ⌱ Ⓥ ⌱ ⊡ ▥ ⚓ ⒹⒶⒻ ⌲ 🏠 ⌱

BURWASH

E. Sussex
Map ref 3B4

Village of old houses, many from the Tudor and Stuart periods. One of the old ironmasters' houses is Bateman's (now a museum) which was the home of Rudyard Kipling.

Woodlands Farm

Listed

Heathfield Rd., Burwash, TN19 7LA
☎ (0435) 882794
55-acre mixed farm. Modernised 16th C. farmhouse set away from road, amidst fields and woods. Working farm giving friendly welcome and good fresh food. Near Batemans.
Bedrooms: 2 double & 1 twin.
Bathrooms: 2 public.
Bed & breakfast: £21-£25 double.
Half board: £16.50-£18.50 daily, from £115.50 weekly.
Parking for 4.

BUXTED

E. Sussex
Map ref 2D3

3m NE. Uckfield
Small Wealden village near the towns of Crowborough and Uckfield, within easy reach of the Ashdown Forest.

Buxted Inn

♨♨

High St., Buxted, TN22 4LA
☎ (082 581) 3510
Family-run Victorian inn in the High Weald of East Sussex, within easy reach of Eastbourne and Brighton. Close to Tunbridge Wells and Ashdown Forest. Chef-proprietor.
Bedrooms: 1 single, 1 double & 1 twin, 1 family room.
Bathrooms: 2 public.
Bed & breakfast: £15 single, £28-£30 double.
Half board: £22-£25 daily, from £140 weekly.
Lunch available.
Evening meal 6pm (l.o. 10pm).
Parking for 40.
Credit: Visa, Diners, Amex.

CANTERBURY

Kent
Map ref 3B3

See also Chilham.
The birthplace of English Christianity and a place of pilgrimage since the martyrdom of Thomas Becket in 1170. The seat of the Primate of All England and the site of Canterbury Cathedral. Not to be missed are St. Augustine's Abbey, St. Martin's (the oldest church in England), Royal Museum and Old Weaver's House and the exciting new Pilgrim's Way attraction. At nearby Bekesbourne is Howletts Zoo Park.

Alicante Guest House ⋔

Listed

4 Roper Rd., Canterbury, CT2 7EH
☎ (0227) 66277
Double-fronted Victorian house close to city centre . Plenty of parking spaces opposite. Public telephone in hall for guests only.
Bedrooms: 1 single, 1 double & 1 twin, 3 family rooms.
Bathrooms: 2 public; 1 private shower.
Bed & breakfast: from £12.50 single, from £22 double.

The Bield

2 Canterbury Hill, Tyler Hill, Canterbury CT2 9LS
☎ (0227) 464621
Spacious, modern house in rural setting about 1.5 miles from the city centre, with buses nearby. Fresh, home-cooked food.
Bedrooms: 1 single, 1 double & 1 twin.
Bathrooms: 1 public; 1 private shower.
Bed & breakfast: £12 single, £20-£22 double.
Half board: £16-£18 daily, £98 weekly.
Evening meal 6.30pm.
Parking for 4.
Open March-November.

Broad Street Lodge ⋔

♨♨♨

89 Broad St., Canterbury, CT1 2LU
☎ (0227) 470185

Georgian family residence nestling beside the ancient city wall. 2 minutes' walk from the cathedral.
Bedrooms: 1 twin, 1 family room.
Bathrooms: 2 private.
Bed & breakfast: £28-£40 double.

Castle Court Guest House ⋔

Listed

8 Castle St., Canterbury, CT1 2QF
☎ (0227) 463441
Peaceful central position. Close to Cathedral, shops, gardens and theatre. Car parking nearby and an easy walk to station. TV lounge.
Bedrooms: 4 single, 5 double & 3 twin.
Bathrooms: 2 public.
Bed & breakfast: £12-£14 single, £24-£26 double.
Credit: Access, Visa.

Cathedral Gate Hotel ⋔

36 Burgate, Canterbury, CT1 2HA
☎ (0227) 464381
Central position at main entrance to the cathedral. Car parking nearby. Baby listening service. Old world charm at reasonable prices.
Bedrooms: 5 single, 7 double & 10 twin, 3 family rooms.
Bathrooms: 12 private, 3 public; 2 private showers.
Bed & breakfast: from £16-£32 single, £30-£47.50 double.
Evening meal 7pm (l.o. 9.30pm).
Parking for 12.
Credit: Access, Visa, Diners, Amex.

The Corner House

Listed

113 Whitstable Road, Canterbury, CT2 8EF
☎ (0227) 61352
Just a few minutes' walking distance from city, shops and restaurants. Spacious family house and friendly hospitality.
Bedrooms: 1 double & 1 twin.
Bathrooms: 2 public.
Bed & breakfast: £22-£24 double.
Parking for 4.

Dar-Anne

65 London Road, Canterbury
☎ Canterbury (0227) 60907
Modern 4-bedroomed semi-detached house, set back from the road.
Bedrooms: 1 single, 1 double & 1 twin.
Bathrooms: 1 public.
Bed & breakfast: £9-£12 single, £18-£22 double.
Parking for 3.

Lyon House ⋔

Petham., Canterbury, CT4 5QY
☎ Petham (022 770) 326
18th C. villa in centre of village.
Bedrooms: 2 double & 1 twin, 1 family room.
Bathrooms: 4 private showers.
Bed & breakfast: from £13 single, from £26 double.
Half board: from £17 daily, from £100 weekly.
Evening meal 7.30pm.
Parking for 4.

Maudsley House ⋔

High St., Bridge, Canterbury, CT4 5JZ
☎ (0227) 830751
About 200 years old, with a peg tile roof.
Bedrooms: 1 double & 2 twin, 1 family room.
Bathrooms: 1 private, 1 public.
Bed & breakfast: £10-£13 single, £20-£26 double.
Half board: £15-£19 daily, £95-£120 weekly.
Evening meal 6pm (l.o. 9am).
Parking for 3.

Milton House

9 South Canterbury Rd., Canterbury, CT1 3LH
☎ (0227) 65531
Semi-detached house built 1906. Quiet residential position just off the Dover road. Easy walk to shops and cathedral.
Bedrooms: 1 double & 2 twin.
Bathrooms: 1 public.
Bed & breakfast: £18-£21 double.

Old Rectory

Ashford Road, Chartham, Canterbury, CT4 7HS
☎ (0227) 730075
Former Georgian rectory in rural valley overlooking village. House set in 2 acres on A28 with orchards to side and rear.
Bedrooms: 1 double & 1 twin, 1 family room.

Bathrooms: 1 public.
Bed & breakfast: £25-£32 double.
Parking for 4.
♿ 🍽 📺 ▥ 🏧 ❋ 🛡

The Tanner of Wingham
(symbols)

44 High Street, Wingham, Canterbury CT3 1AB
☎ Canterbury (0227) 720532
Old English tea rooms and licensed restaurant, built in 1620. Oak beamed but with all modern facilities, in a small village.
Bedrooms: 1 double & 2 twin, 1 family room.
Bathrooms: 2 public.
Bed & breakfast: £15 single, £25 double.
Half board: £21.25 daily, £134 weekly.
Lunch available.
Evening meal 7pm (l.o. 10pm).
Parking for 4.
Open March-December.
Credit: Access, Visa, Diners, Amex.
♿ 🍽 🕯 🅥 ▥ 🏧 🐾 🛡

Thanington Hotel M
(symbols)

140 Wincheap, Canterbury, CT1 3RY
☎ (0227) 453227
Low cost accommodation with private car parking and gardens. Close to the cathedral and city centre. Easily located from the main A28 Canterbury/Ashford road.
Bedrooms: 5 double & 3 twin, 2 family rooms.
Bathrooms: 10 private.
Bed & breakfast: £35-£42 single, £42-£48 double.
Parking for 12.
Credit: Access, Visa.
♿🍽🕯 ▢ 🏧 🌀 ▥ 🕯 🅟
📺 ▥ ▣ 🏧 🛡 ❚ SP 🏰 T

Challock House
Listed

Canterbury Road, Challock, Ashford, TN25 4DL
☎ (023 374) 506
Spacious country house, tastefully furnished. Ample courtyard parking. Ideally situated in central Kent on the A252 between Leeds Castle and Canterbury.
Bedrooms: 2 double & 1 twin.
Bathrooms: 2 public.

Bed & breakfast: max. £14 single, max. £25 double.
Parking for 6.
♿5 🏧 🌀 ▥ 🌙 🏧 📺 ▥ 🏧 ❋ 🐾 🛡

Tram Hatch M

Charing Heath, TN27 0BN
☎ Charing (023 371) 3373
14th C. manor house set in 7.5 acres including 2 acres of formal gardens. Original features. Close to Leeds and Chilham Castles.
Bedrooms: 2 double, 1 family room.
Bathrooms: 2 private, 1 public.
Bed & breakfast: £30-£40 double.
Evening meal 7pm (l.o. 9pm).
Parking for 16.
♿5 🍽 🕯 ▢ 🏧 ▥ 📺 ▥ 🏧
🌀 🍴 ⚓ ❋ 🐾 🛡 🐟 🏰

See also Chidham.
The county town of West Sussex with a beautiful Norman cathedral lying beneath the South Downs. Noted for its Georgian architecture but with modern buildings like the Festival Theatre. Surrounded by places of interest like Fishbourne Roman Palace and Weald and Downland open-air museum. ℹ

Whyke House

13 Whyke Lane, Chichester, PO19 2JR
☎ (0243) 788767
Comfortable, quiet house, only three minutes from city centre. Fully-equipped kitchen available.
Bedrooms: 1 double & 1 twin, 1 family room.
Bathrooms: 2 public.
Bed & breakfast: £10.50-£12.50 single, £21-£25 double.
Parking for 3.
♿ 🍽 🏧 🌀 ▥ 🅥 🌙 🏧 📺
▥ 🏧 ❋ 🐾 🛡 🐾

5m SW. Chichester
Small and pretty village on Chichester Harbour.

The Old Rectory
Listed

Chidham, Nr. Chichester, PO18 8TA
☎ Bosham (0243) 572088
Period country house in secluded setting with large garden and swimming pool. Friendly family atmosphere. Interesting area near Chichester harbour.
Bedrooms: 3 twin.
Bathrooms: 1 private, 2 public.
Bed & breakfast: £11-£12 single, £22-£30 double.
Parking for 6.
♿ 🌀 ▥ 🕯 🅥 🏧 📺 ▥ 🏧
🍴 ❋ 🛡

6m SW. Canterbury
An extremely pretty village of mostly Tudor and Jacobean houses. The village rises to the spacious square with the castle and the 15th C church. The grounds of the Jacobean House, laid out by Capability Brown, are open to the public.

Jullieberrie House M

Canterbury Rd., Chilham, CT4 8DX
☎ Canterbury (0227) 730488
Modern house with lovely views over lake and woodland. On the A28 Ashford to Canterbury road, close to Chilham village.
Bedrooms: 2 double & 2 twin.
Bathrooms: 1 private, 1 public.
Bed & breakfast: £15-£20 single, £22-£27 double.
Parking for 4.
♿ 🍽 🌀 ▥ 🕯 ▥ 🏧 🛡

Picturesque village in the Surrey Hills where Lloyd George spent some time. Nearby Frensham Country Park offers many leisure facilities.

Pride of the Valley Restaurant and Hotel M
(symbols)

Tilford Rd., Churt, Farnham, GU10 2LE
☎ Hindhead (042 873) 5799
A family-run hotel and restaurant set among pine trees and bordering on thousands of acres of National Trust woodland and common.
Bedrooms: 2 single, 5 double & 2 twin, 1 family room.
Bathrooms: 10 private, 1 public.
Bed & breakfast: £43-£60 single, £53-£72 double.
Half board: £53-£70 daily, £239-£263 weekly.
Lunch available.
Evening meal 7.30pm (l.o. 10.30pm).
Parking for 50.
Credit: Access, Visa, Diners, Amex.
♿ 🍽 🕯 ▢ 🍽 🌀 🕯 🅥 🏧
▥ 🏧 ⚓ 🍴 🌀 ❋ 🐾 SP 🏰
T

3m NE. Crawley
Residential village on the Surrey/West Sussex border, near Crawley and within easy reach of Gatwick Airport.

Broad Oak
(symbols)

West Park Rd., Copthorne, Nr. Crawley, RH10 3EX
☎ (0342) 714882
Modernised country house built in early 1920s, set in beautiful secluded garden. Courtesy transport provided for Gatwick travellers. Dining-out facilities nearby.
Bedrooms: 1 single, 1 twin, 1 family room.
Bathrooms: 1 public.
Bed & breakfast: max. £18 single, max. £30 double.
Parking for 6.
♿ 🌀 ▥ CB ▥ 📺 ▥ 🏧 🐾
🕯 🍴 ❋ 🏰 T

INDIVIDUAL PROPRIETORS HAVE SUPPLIED ALL DETAILS OF ACCOMMODATION. ALTHOUGH WE DO CHECK FOR ACCURACY, WE ADVISE YOU TO CONFIRM PRICES AND OTHER INFORMATION AT THE TIME OF BOOKING.

COPTHORNE
Continued

Kitsbridge House
Common Rd., Copthorne,
RH10 3PF
☎ Copthorne (0342) 714422
*In the rural village of
Copthorne, 6 minutes from
Gatwick Airport and the
station.*
Bedrooms: 1 single, 1 double
& 1 twin, 1 family room.
Bathrooms: 2 private;
2 private showers.
Bed & breakfast: £22-£24
single, £30-£34 double.
Parking for 9.
🛇 🖛 🗘 ☺ Ⓤ CB ⅢⅢ 🛋 ❋
🕸 🎏 🕮

Oakleigh House
☺☺
West Park Rd., Copthorne,
RH10 3HG
☎ (0342) 712703
*Small country house in
secluded grounds. 5 miles from
Gatwick Airport. Directions on
B2028.*
Bedrooms: 1 single, 1 double,
1 family room.
Bathrooms: 1 private,
1 public; 1 private shower.
Bed & breakfast: £20-£25
single, £30-£35 double.
Parking for 4.
🛇 🖳 🗘 Ⓤ ⅢⅢ ❋ 🕸 🎏 Ⓣ

CRANBROOK
Kent
Map ref 3B4

An old town, a centre for
the weaving industry in
the 15th C. The 72 ft high
Union Mill is a three-
storeyed windmill and still
in working order. ⓘ

The White Horse
High Street, Cranbrook.,
TN17 3EX
☎ Cranbrook (0580) 712615
*Victorian public house and
restaurant in the centre of the
smallest town in Kent, once the
capital of the Weald.*
Bedrooms: 1 double & 1 twin,
1 family room.
Bathrooms: 1 public.
Bed & breakfast: max. £17
single, max. £27 double.
Half board: max. £22 daily.
Lunch available.
Evening meal 6.30pm (l.o.
9.30pm).
Parking for 12.
Credit: Access, Visa.
🛇 🖳 🗘 🛉 ⅢⅢ 🍷 Ⓤ ♪ 🕸
🕮

CRAWLEY
W. Sussex
Map ref 2D2

One of the first new
towns built after World
War II, but it also has
some old buildings. Set in
magnificent wooded
countryside.

Little Foxes Guest House
☺☺
Ifield Rd., Ifield Wood,
Crawley, RH11 0JY
☎ (0293) 552430
*Bungalow in five acres of
grounds. Ten minutes from
Gatwick Airport. Free parking
and transport included.*
Bedrooms: 1 double & 2 twin,
1 family room.
Bathrooms: 2 public;
1 private shower.
Bed & breakfast: £34.50-£46
single, £46-£57.50 double.
Parking for 50.
Credit: Access, Visa, Amex.
🛇 🖛 🖳 🗘 Ⓤ 🚄 Ⓣ ⬤ ⅢⅢ
🛋 ☽ ❋ 🕸 🕮

Radford Farm
Radford Rd., Tinsley Green,
Crawley, RH10 3NW
☎ (0293) 884336
*400-year-old thatched cottage
with pretty bedrooms. 4
minutes from Gatwick and 35
minutes from London Victoria.*
Bedrooms: 1 single, 1 double
& 1 twin.
Bathrooms: 1 public.
Bed & breakfast: £14-£17
single, £23-£28 double.
Evening meal 6pm (l.o. 9pm).
Parking for 3.
🛇 🖳 🗘 ☺ Ⓤ Ⓥ ⅙ 🚄 ⅢⅢ 🛋
❋ 🕸 🕮 Ⓣ

Westoe Guest House ⓜ
128 Malthouse Rd.,
Southgate, Crawley,
RH10 6BH
☎ (0293) 24189
*Quiet, select guesthouse, close
to town centre. Convenient
travelling distance from
Gatwick Airport.*
Bedrooms: 1 single, 2 double
& 2 twin, 1 family room.
Bathrooms: 1 private,
2 public.
Bed & breakfast: £20-£24
single, £30-£38 double.
Parking for 10.
🛇 🖛 🖳 🗘 Ⓤ 🚄 Ⓣ ⅢⅢ 🕸 🕮

**PLEASE CHECK
PRICES AND OTHER
DETAILS AT THE
TIME OF BOOKING.**

CRAWLEY DOWN
W. Sussex
Map ref 2D2

Oak Tree Cottage
☺
Sandhill La., Crawley Down,
Nr.Gatwick, RH10 4LB
☎ Copthorne (0342) 714750
*Modernised cottage in quiet
country lane, with a large
garden. 4 miles north east of
Crawley off B2028. 15 minutes
from Gatwick.*
Bedrooms: 2 twin.
Bathrooms: 1 public.
Bed & breakfast: £18-£20
single, £28-£30 double.
Parking for 5.
🛇 🗘 Ⓓ 🗘 Ⓤ 🛉 Ⓥ 🛋
🕸 🕮 SP

CRUNDALE
Kent
Map ref 3B3

Ripple Farm
Crundale, Nr. Canterbury,
CT4 7EB
☎ (0227) 730748
*15-acre mixed farm. 16th C.
farmhouse in a peaceful setting
overlooking the North Downs.
1 mile from Godmersham
crossroads on the A28.*
Bedrooms: 2 family rooms.
Bathrooms: 1 private,
1 public.
Bed & breakfast: £10.50
single, £21 double.
Parking for 6.
🛇 🗘 ☺ 🛉 Ⓥ ⅙ 🚄 Ⓣ ⅢⅢ
🛋 ☽ ❋ 🕸 🕮

DEAL
Kent
Map ref 3C4

Coastal town and popular
holiday resort. Deal
Castle was built as a fort
and the museum is
devoted to finds
excavated in the area.
Also the Time-ball Tower
museum. Angling
available from both beach
and pier. ⓘ

Finglesham Grange ⓜ
☺☺☺
Finglesham, Nr. Deal,
CT14 ONQ
☎ Sandwich (0304) 611314
*Georgian country house in 4.5
acres of secluded grounds. 4
miles from both Deal and
Sandwich.*
Bedrooms: 1 double & 2 twin.
Bathrooms: 3 private.

Bed & breakfast: £17.50
double.
Half board: £26 daily, £155
weekly.
Parking for 5.
🛇 Ⓤ 🛉 🚄 Ⓣ ⅢⅢ 🛋 ❋ 🕸
DAP 🕮

Sutherland House Guest House ⓜ
☺☺
186 London Rd., Deal,
CT14 9PT
☎ Deal (0304) 362853
*Victorian house, retaining its
character and with decor of the
period, in a quiet residential
area.*
Bedrooms: 3 double & 1 twin,
1 family room.
Bathrooms: 1 public;
5 private showers.
Bed & breakfast: £18.50-£28
single, £28 double.
Half board: £28-£37.50 daily,
£196-£262.50 weekly.
Evening meal 7.30pm (l.o.
3pm).
Parking for 11.
🛇 🖛 🗘 Ⓥ 🚄 Ⓣ ⅢⅢ 🍷 🕸
🕮

DIAL POST
W. Sussex
Map ref 2D2

8m S. Horsham
Small village on the main
road from Horsham to the
coast at Worthing.

Swallows Farm
☺☺
Swallows Lane, Dial Post,
Horsham, RH13 8NN
☎ Partridge Green
(0403) 710385
*210-acre mixed farm. Georgian
farmhouse in the quiet Sussex
countryside half a mile off
A24, within easy reach of
coast, Downs and many places
of historic interest. Gatwick
Airport 16 miles.*
Bedrooms: 2 double & 2 twin.
Bathrooms: 2 public.
Bed & breakfast: £15-£20
single, £24-£26 double.
Half board: £20.50-£27 daily.
Evening meal 6.30pm.
Parking for 4.
Open March-October.
🛇 10 🖳 🗘 ☺ 🚄 Ⓣ ⅢⅢ 🛋
❋ 🕸 🕮 🕮

**THE SYMBOLS ARE
EXPLAINED ON THE
FLAP INSIDE THE
BACK COVER.**

DITCHLING

E. Sussex
Map ref 2D3

8m N. Brighton
Village sited at a crossroads. Ditchling Beacon lies impressively behind the village and was where one of the fires that warned of the Armada was lit. A well known centre for arts and crafts.

The Bull Hotel
😃😃😃

2 High Street, Ditchling, BN6 ASY
☎ (079 18) 3147/2976
Coaching inn of considerable character, with a wealth of oak beams, 3 open log fires and a beer garden.
Bedrooms: 3 double.
Bathrooms: 3 private.
Bed & breakfast: £28.50 single, £38.50 double.
Evening meal 7pm (l.o. 9.30pm).
Parking for 30.
Credit: Access, Visa, Diners, Amex.
🖧 🗗 🗘 ✿ 🛢 💷 🛏 🏆 🏃 🛏 🏠

DORKING

Surrey
Map ref 2D2

See also Abinger Hammer, Holmbury St. Mary.
Ancient market town and a good centre for walking, delightfully set between Box Hill and the Downs.

Steyning Cottage
Horsham Rd., South Holmwood, Dorking, RH5 4NE
☎ (0306) 888481
Detached tile-hung house adjacent to A24, opposite Holmwood Common and within walking distance of Leith Hill. Gatwick Airport approximately 20 minutes away. French spoken.
Bedrooms: 1 single, 2 twin.
Bathrooms: 1 public.
Bed & breakfast: £9-£15 single, £18-£22 double.
Half board: £12.50-£20 daily, £65-£110 weekly.
Lunch available.
Evening meal 7pm (l.o. 8pm).
Parking for 4.
🖧 🔥 💷 🛢 🛏 📺 💷 🛏 🏠

DOVER

Kent
Map ref 3C4

See also Deal, Elham.
Once a Cinque Port now the busiest passenger port in the world. Still a historic town and seaside resort beside the famous White Cliffs. Numerous buildings trace the town's history from the Roman Painted House and lighthouse, Saxon church, Norman castle to the 13th C Maison Dieu and adjacent Victorian "Old Town Gaol". *i*

Bleriot's
Listed

185 Folkestone Road, Dover, CT17 9SJ
☎ (0304) 211394
Four storey, Victorian terraced house.
Bedrooms: 1 double & 2 twin, 1 family room.
Bathrooms: 1 public.
Bed & breakfast: £12-£15 single, £16-£22 double.
Parking for 6.
🖧 💷 💷 🛏 🏠 🅣

Castle Guest House 𝓜
😃😃😃

10 Castle Hill Rd., Dover, CT16 1QW
☎ (0304) 201656
2 minutes away from docks, castle and town centre. Extra local car parking available.
Bedrooms: 4 double & 1 twin, 1 family room.
Bathrooms: 2 private; 4 private showers.
Bed & breakfast: £16-£20 single, £20-£26 double.
Evening meal 6pm (l.o. 5pm).
Parking for 3.
Credit: Visa.
🖧 🗗 🗘 🛢 💷 ✂ 🔥 💷 🛏 🏠 🕱
GAP SP 🏠 🅣

Coldred Court Farm
Church Rd., Coldred, Nr. Dover, CT15 5AQ
☎ Dover (0304) 830816
7-acre mixed farm. 1620 farmhouse full of old world charm, with modern facilities. Situated 1 mile from the A2, 5 minutes from Dover.
Bedrooms: 1 single, 2 double & 1 twin.
Bathrooms: 4 private.
Bed & breakfast: £12-£15 single, £24-£30 double.
Half board: £20-£23 daily, £140-£161 weekly.
Evening meal 6pm (l.o. 9pm).
Parking for 12.
🖧 🗗 🗘 🛢 💷 🔥 📺 🛏 🐾 ✿ 🕱 🏠 🏠

Dell Guest House
😃😃

233 Folkestone Rd., Dover, CT17 9SL
☎ (0304) 202422
Victorian house with modern facilities, convenient for Dover Priory railway station, docks and hoverport. Ideal overnight stay for the Continent.
Bedrooms: 2 single, 1 double & 1 twin, 2 family rooms.
Bathrooms: 2 public.
Bed & breakfast: £8.50-£12 single, £17-£22 double.
Evening meal 6.30pm.
Parking for 6.
🖧 🗘 💷 🔥 📺 💷 🕱 🛏 SP

East Lee Guest House
😃😃😃

108 Maison Dieu Rd., Dover, CT16 1RT
☎ (0304) 210176
Victorian residence furnished in traditional English style. Convenient for town centre, buses, trains and ferries.
Bedrooms: 3 double & 1 twin.
Bathrooms: 4 private, 1 public.
Bed & breakfast: from £20 single, £26-£30 double.
Parking for 4.
Credit: Access, Visa, Diners, Amex.
🖧 🖧 📞 🛢 🗘 💷 Ⅴ ✂ 🔥
📺 💷 🛏 🕱 🏠

Hayesleigh Guest House
😃😃

187 Folkestone Rd., Dover, CT17 9JA
☎ (0304) 203476
Near ferry, hoverport and town centre. Early breakfasts served for those catching early ferries. Reduced rates for children sharing parents' bedrooms.
Bedrooms: 2 double & 1 twin, 2 family rooms.
Bathrooms: 2 public.
Bed & breakfast: £12-£14 single, £20-£24 double.
Parking for 6.
🖧 🖧 💷 🔥 📺 💷 🛏 🕱 🏠

Loddington House Hotel 𝓜
😃😃

14 East Cliff, Dover, CT16 1LX
☎ (0304) 201947
Regency style hotel with panoramic views over harbour and Channel. 5 minutes from ferry.
Bedrooms: 3 double & 2 twin, 1 family room.
Bathrooms: 1 private, 2 public.
Bed & breakfast: £20-£25 single, £28.50-£32 double.

Half board: £25-£30 daily, £160-£175 weekly.
Evening meal 7.30pm (l.o. 9pm).
Parking for 5.
🖧2 🔥 📺 💷 🕱 🛏 SP 🏠

Number One Guest House 𝓜
😃😃😃

1 Castle St., Dover, CT16 1QH
☎ (0304) 202007
Georgian town house, overlooked by the historic castle. Ideally situated for town centre, ferries and hoverport.
Bedrooms: 2 double & 2 twin, 2 family rooms.
Bathrooms: 3 private; 3 private showers.
Bed & breakfast: £24-£30 double.
Parking for 6.
🖧 🖧 🗗 🗘 💷 💷 🛢 🛏 🏠

Tower Guest House 𝓜
😃😃😃

98 Priory Hill, Dover, CT17 0AD
☎ (0304) 208212
Converted water tower in quiet surroundings. Six minutes' drive to docks. Lock-up garages available.
Bedrooms: 1 double & 2 twin, 2 family rooms.
Bathrooms: 3 private, 1 public.
Bed & breakfast: £22-£28 double.
Half board: £20-£22 daily, £140-£154 weekly.
Evening meal 7pm.
Parking for 2.
🖧 🖧 🗗 🗘 💷 💷 🛢 🛏 🏠 SP 🏠 🅣

EAST DEAN

E. Sussex
Map ref 2D3

Pretty village on green near Friston Forest and Birling Gap.

Birling Gap Hotel
😃😃

Seven Sisters, East Dean, Nr. Eastbourne, BN20 0AB
☎ (032 15) 3163 & 3197
Single-storey country hotel with views over sea and South Downs. On Seven Sisters cliffs with access to beach. All rooms on ground floor.
Bedrooms: 2 single, 5 double & 1 twin, 2 family rooms.
Bathrooms: 9 private, 1 public.
Bed & breakfast: £17.25-£23 single, £28.75-£34.50 double.
Lunch available.

Continued ▶

EAST DEAN

Continued

Evening meal 6pm (l.o.
9.30pm).
Parking for 100.
Credit: Access, Visa, Amex.

EAST GRINSTEAD

W. Sussex
Map ref 2D2

*See also Hartfield,
Lingfield.*
A number of fine old
houses stand in the High
Street, one of which is
Sackville College,
founded in 1609.

Cranston House

Cranston Rd., East
Grinstead, RH19 3HW
☎ (0342) 23609
*Detached house in quiet
location near town centre. 15
minutes' drive from Gatwick.*
Bedrooms: 1 double & 1 twin,
1 family room.
Bathrooms: 1 public.
Bed & breakfast: £16-£18
single, £30-£34 double.
Half board: £22-£24 daily,
£133-£140 weekly.
Evening meal 7pm (l.o. 7pm).
Parking for 3.

Victoria

17 Portland Rd., East
Grinstead, RH19 4EB
☎ (0342) 322308
*Homely Victorian guesthouse
in a quiet residential road, in
the centre of town. Close to
shops, restaurants, pubs and
Gatwick Airport.*
Bedrooms: 2 double, 1 family
room.
Bathrooms: 2 public.
Bed & breakfast: from £14
single, from £24 double.
Parking for 3.

EASTBOURNE

E. Sussex
Map ref 3B4

One of the finest, most
elegant resorts on the
south east coast and
beautifully situated beside
Beachy Head. Long
promenade, plenty of
gardens, several theatres,
Towner Art Gallery,
Lifeboat Museum and the
Redoubt housing the
Sussex Combined
Services Museum and
aquarium. ℹ

Bay Lodge Hotel M

61-62 Royal Pde.,
Eastbourne, BN22 7AQ
☎ (0323) 32515
*Small seafront hotel opposite
Redoubt Gardens, close to
bowling greens, sailing clubs
and entertainments. Large sun-
lounge.*
Bedrooms: 3 single, 5 double
& 3 twin, 1 family room.
Bathrooms: 7 private,
2 public.
Bed & breakfast: £13-£19
single, £28.50-£39 double.
Half board: £18-£24 daily,
£96-£140 weekly.
Evening meal 6pm (l.o.
6.30pm).
Parking for 2.
Credit: Access, Visa.

Beachy Rise

Beachy Head Rd.,
Eastbourne, BN20 7QN
☎ (0323) 639171
*In a quiet, select part of
Eastbourne, a few minutes'
walk from sea and glorious
downs. No restrictions, own
keys. Vegetarian cooking a
speciality.*
Bedrooms: 3 double & 1 twin,
2 family rooms.
Bathrooms: 6 private.
Bed & breakfast: £12.50-£20
single, £25-£35 double.
Half board: £17-£25 daily.
Evening meal 6.30pm (l.o.
6pm).
Credit: Access, Visa.

Farrar's Hotel M

Wilmington Gdns.,
Eastbourne, BN21 4JN
☎ (0323) 23737
*Family hotel in quiet square,
200 yards from the seafront,
opposite the Devonshire Park
and Congress Theatre. Send
for brochure giving details of
mini-breaks.*
Bedrooms: 13 single, 8 double
& 18 twin, 5 family rooms.
Bathrooms: 44 private,
3 public.
Bed & breakfast: £20-£28
single, £40-£56 double.
Half board: £26-£36 daily,
£170-£220 weekly.
Lunch available.
Evening meal 6.45pm (l.o.
8pm).
Parking for 26.
Credit: Access, Visa, Amex.

EDBURTON

W. Sussex
Map ref 2D3

4m E. Steyning
Small village at the foot of
Edburton Hill on the
South Downs Way.

Tottington Manor Hotel

Edburton, Nr. Henfield,
BN5 9LJ
☎ Steyning (0903) 815757
*16th C. country manor house
with log fires and oak beams,
set in its own grounds at the
foot of the South Downs.*
Bedrooms: 4 double & 2 twin.
Bathrooms: 6 private.
Bed & breakfast: from £28.50
single, from £44 double.
Half board: from £38 daily.
Lunch available.
Evening meal 7pm (l.o.
10.30pm).
Parking for 60.
Credit: Access, Visa, Diners,
Amex.

ELHAM

Kent
Map ref 3B3

6m NW. Folkestone
In the Nailbourne Valley
on the chalk downlands,
this large village has an
outstanding collection of
old houses. Abbot's
Fireside, built in 1614, has
a timbered upper storey
resting on brackets
carved into figures.

Tye

Collards La., Elham, Nr.
Canterbury, CT4 6UF
☎ (030 384) 271
*Country house, less than a mile
from the village, beautifully
situated on top of a hill with
lovely views and walks. Very
quiet.*
Bedrooms: 2 single, 1 twin,
1 family room.
Bathrooms: 1 public.
Bed & breakfast: £13 single,
£26 double.
Parking for 6.
Open March-November.

ETCHINGHAM

E. Sussex
Map ref 3B4

Pleasant village at the
confluence of the rivers
Rother and Dudwell.

Little Grandturzel Farm

Fontridge Lane, Etchingham,
TN19 7DE
☎ Burwash (0435) 882279
*70-acre grazing and corn farm.
Quiet house, down long drive.
Extensive views of Kipling
Country. Many walks and
places of interest in area.*
Bedrooms: 1 single, 1 double
& 1 twin.
Bathrooms: 1 public.
Bed & breakfast: £12-£16
single, £22-£25 double.
Half board: £17.50-£22.50
daily, £90-£110 weekly.
Evening meal 6pm (l.o. 4pm).
Parking for 4.
Open February-October.

**MAP REFERENCES
APPLY TO COLOUR
MAPS NEAR THE
BACK OF THE GUIDE.**

**GROUPS, CONSORTIA AND AGENCIES
SPECIALISING IN FARM AND COUNTRY
HOLIDAYS ARE LISTED IN A SPECIAL
SECTION OF THIS GUIDE.**

**PLEASE CHECK
PRICES AND OTHER
DETAILS AT THE
TIME OF BOOKING.**

FARNHAM

Surrey
Map ref 2C2

Town noted for its
Georgian houses. Willmer
House (now a museum)
has a facade of cut and
moulded brick with fine
carving and panelling in
the interior. The 12th C
castle has been occupied
by Bishops of both
Winchester and Guildford.

Sycamore
Listed
Sands Rd., The Sands,
Farnham, GU10 1LW
☎ Runfold (025 18) 2117
*240-year-old cottage with its
own pastures where our sheep
graze. The village shop and inn
are nearby.*
Bedrooms: 1 single, 1 twin.
Bathrooms: 1 public.
Bed & breakfast: £12-£16
single, £20-£24 double.
Parking for 2.

FAVERSHAM

Kent
Map ref 3B3

Historic town, once a
port, dating back to
prehistoric times. Abbey
Street has more than 50
listed buildings. Roman
and Anglo-Saxon finds
and other artefacts can be
seen in a museum in the
Maison Dieu at Ospringe.
Fleur de Lis Heritage
Centre. *i*

Frith Farm House
Otterden, Nr. Faversham,
ME13 0DD
☎ Eastling (079 589) 701
*Georgian country house in area
of outstanding natural beauty.*
Bedrooms: 1 double & 1 twin.
Bathrooms: 2 private.
Bed & breakfast: £30-£33
double.
Evening meal 7pm.
Parking for 13.

Homestall Farmhouse
Listed
Homestall Farm, Faversham,
ME13 8UT
☎ (0795) 532152
*250-acre hop, fruit and animal
farm. Georgian farmhouse in
attractive garden. Quiet, yet
convenient for all main routes.
Canterbury 8 miles, Dover 23
miles.*
Bedrooms: 1 double & 2 twin.
Bathrooms: 1 public.
Bed & breakfast: £12 single,
£24 double.
Parking for 8.

Owens Court Farm
Listed
Selling, Faversham,
ME13 9QN
☎ Canterbury (0227) 752247
*270-acre hops and fruit farm.
A charming Georgian
farmhouse surrounded by hop
gardens and orchards. 1.5
miles off the A2, near
Faversham. 9 miles from
Canterbury.*
Bedrooms: 1 single, 1 twin,
1 family room.
Bathrooms: 1 public.
Bed & breakfast: £10-£11
single, £20-£22 double.
Parking for 5.
Open January-August,
October-December.

Queens Head Inn
Listed
111 The Street, Boughton-
under-Blean, Faversham,
ME13 9BH
☎ Canterbury (0227) 751369
*Public house two miles from
Canterbury and Faversham.
Lunches and evening meals.
Weekly rates available.*
Bedrooms: 1 double & 1 twin,
2 family rooms.
Bathrooms: 1 public.
Bed & breakfast: £17.50-£20
single, £27.50-£30 double.
Lunch available.
Evening meal 7pm (l.o.
9.30pm).
Parking for 25.

**INDIVIDUAL PROPRIETORS HAVE SUPPLIED
ALL DETAILS OF ACCOMMODATION.
ALTHOUGH WE DO CHECK FOR ACCURACY, WE
ADVISE YOU TO CONFIRM PRICES AND OTHER
INFORMATION AT THE TIME OF BOOKING.**

FINDON

W. Sussex
Map ref 2D3

4m N. Worthing
Downland village well
known for its annual
sheep fair and its racing
stables. The ancient
landmarks, Cissbury Ring
and Chanctonbury Ring,
and the South Downs
Way, are nearby.

Racehorse Cottage
Nepcote, Findon, BN14 0SN
☎ (090 671) 3783
*Comfortable cottage in historic
downland village, 4 miles from
coast. Excellent walking and
riding. Evening meal with host
family. Visitors met at
Gatwick or Worthing, if
required.*
Bedrooms: 2 twin.
Bathrooms: 1 public.
Bed & breakfast: £14 single,
£22-£24 double.
Half board: £19-£22 daily,
£133-£150 weekly.
Evening meal 7pm (l.o.
8.30pm).
Parking for 2.

FITTLEWORTH

W. Sussex
Map ref 2D3

3m NW. Pulborough
Quiet village that attracts
artists and anglers.
Groups of cottages can
be found beside the
narrow lanes and paths in
the woodlands near to the
River Rother.

Sorrels Farm
Listed
The Fleet, Fittleworth,
RH20 1HU
☎ Fittleworth (079 882) 372
*Situated on A283
Petworth/Pulborough road. 3
miles from Petworth, 2 miles
from Pulborough. Conveniently
situated for many places of
interest.*
Bedrooms: 1 double, 1 family
room.
Bathrooms: 2 private.
Bed & breakfast: £26-£28
double.
Parking for 2.
Open April-October.

FOLKESTONE

Kent
Map ref 3C4

See also Elham.
Popular resort and
important cross-Channel
port. The town has a fine
promenade, the Leas,
from where orchestral
concerts and other
entertainments are
presented. Horse racing
at Westenhanger. *i*

Crete Down
Crete Rd. West, Folkestone,
CT18 7AA
☎ Hawkinge (030 389) 2392
*In a quiet location among hills,
outside the town. Beautiful
views over hills, town and sea.
5 minutes from the town
centre.*
Bedrooms: 1 twin, 1 family
room.
Bathrooms: 1 private,
1 public.
Bed & breakfast: from £20
double.
Half board: from £16 daily,
from £110 weekly.
Evening meal (l.o. 6pm).
Parking for 6.

Grafton Cottage
Sandgate Espl., Folkestone,
CT20 3DP
☎ (0303) 49005
*Regency house built at the end
of the Napoleonic Wars and
sited on the seafront.*
Bedrooms: 2 double & 1 twin,
1 family room.
Bathrooms: 2 private,
3 public.
Bed & breakfast: £18-£22
single, £20-£25 double.

FRITTENDEN

Kent
Map ref 3B4

Quiet village with a
picturesque centre of old
houses, trees and the
little church of St. Mary.
Staplehurst and
Headcorn mainline
railway stations are within
3 miles of the village.

Poplar House
The Green, Frittenden,
TN17 2DG
☎ (058 080) 408
*A 15th C. Kent hall house with
exposed beams, inglenooks and
kingpost, set in 6 acres of land.*

Continued ▶

FRITTENDEN

Continued

Bedrooms: 2 double, 2 family rooms.
Bathrooms: 1 private,
1 public.
Bed & breakfast: from £15 single, from £28 double.
Half board: from £19 daily, from £130 weekly.
Lunch available.
Evening meal 7.30pm (l.o. 9.30pm).
Parking for 10.

GILLINGHAM

Kent
Map ref 3B3

The largest Medway Town, it merges into its neighbour Chatham. *i* (Farthing Corner Services-M2)

Mrs. B. L. Penn

178 Bredhurst Rd., Wigmore, Gillingham, ME8 0QX
☎ Medway (0634) 33267
Private house in quiet residential area. 4 minutes from M2 motorway via the A278.
Bedrooms: 2 twin, 1 family room.
Bathrooms: 2 private, 2 public.
Bed & breakfast: £10-£12 single, £20-£24 double.
Parking for 2.

GOUDHURST

Kent
Map ref 3B4

4m NW. Cranbrook
Village on a hill surmounted by a square towered church with fine views of orchards and hopfields. Achieved prosperity through weaving in the Middle Ages. Finchcocks houses a museum of historical keyboard instruments.

Mrs. J.M. Wickham ♨
Listed

Combourne Farm, Goudhurst, TN17 1LP
☎ (0580) 211382
300-acre hop, fruit and sheep farm. 400-year-old Wealden farmhouse. Ideally placed for visiting Leeds Castle, Chartwell, Sissinghurst Castle. London 1 hour by train. Car essential.

Bedrooms: 2 twin.
Bathrooms: 1 public.
Bed & breakfast: £12.50-£15 single, £25-£30 double.
Lunch available.
Evening meal 7pm (l.o. 10am).
Parking for 6.
Open January-August, October-December.

GUILDFORD

Surrey
Map ref 2D2

See also Abinger Hammer.
Bustling town with many historic monuments, one of which is the Guildhall clock jutting out over the old High Street. The modern cathedral occupies a commanding position on Stag Hill. *i*

Appletrees

Malthouse La., Fox Corner, Worplesdon, Nr. Guildford, GU3 3PS
☎ Worplesdon (0483) 232079
Secluded residence in woodland area away from main road. 4 miles from Guildford and Woking town centres. Easy commuting to London.
Bedrooms: 1 double & 1 twin, 2 family rooms.
Bathrooms: 1 private, 1 public; 3 private showers.
Bed & breakfast: from £16 single, from £26 double.
Parking for 5.

Mr. & Mrs. J.Cook, Beevers Farm

Chinthurst Lane, Bramley, Guildford, GU5 0DR
☎ Guildford (0483) 898764
At Bramley roundabout take Station Road. Over bridge, first left - signposted Shalford. We are third gate on the left. Peaceful. Near village and restaurants. 2 miles from Guildford. Non-smokers only.
Bedrooms: 1 twin, 2 family rooms.
Bathrooms: 2 private, 2 public.
Bed & breakfast: £20-£30 double.
Parking for 10.
Open March-November.

The Old Malt House

Bagshot Rd., Worplesdon, Nr. Guildford, GU3 3PT
☎ Worplesdon (0483) 232152
Old country house in extensive grounds with ancient trees. Easy access to Heathrow, Gatwick and Central London.
Bedrooms: 1 double & 1 twin, 1 family room.
Bathrooms: 2 public.
Bed & breakfast: £16-£18 single, £24-£25 double.
Parking for 4.

HAILSHAM

E. Sussex
Map ref 3B4

See also Herstmonceux.
Has been an important market town since Norman times and still one of the largest markets in Sussex. Two miles west, at Upper Dicker, is Michelham Priory, an Augustinian house founded in 1229.
i

Wilmington House

26 London Rd., Hailsham, BN27 3BW
☎ (0323) 842580
Detached Edwardian house with small front garden. Family home run on those lines, offering warm welcome to guests.
Bedrooms: 2 twin.
Bathrooms: 1 public.
Bed & breakfast: from £11 single, from £22 double.
Parking for 3.

HARTFIELD

E. Sussex
Map ref 2D2

Pleasant village in Ashdown Forest.

Bolebroke Mill ♨

Edenbridge Rd., Hartfield, TN7 4JP
☎ Until April 1989 (089 277) 425 & After April 1989 (0892) 770425
6.5-acre smallholding, beef farm. Domesday watermill in romantic, secluded woodland. Accommodation of great character set around millstones and wheels. Regret stairs unsuitable for small children, the elderly and the disabled.
Bedrooms: 2 double.
Bathrooms: 2 private.

Bed & breakfast: max. £29 single, max. £33 double.
Half board: max. £29.50 daily, max. £189 weekly.
Parking for 16.
Open March-October.

Stairs Farmhouse
Listed

High Street, Hartfield, TN7 4AB
☎ (089 277) 793
80-acre farm. 17th C., modernised farmhouse with various period features, in the centre of a picturesque village. Close to Pooh Bridge and Hever Castle. Views over open countryside. Sells additive-free produce.
Bedrooms: 1 twin, 1 family room.
Bathrooms: 2 public.
Bed & breakfast: £25-£28 double.
Parking for 3.

HASLEMERE

Surrey
Map ref 2C2

Town set in hilly, wooded countryside, much of it in the keeping of the National Trust. Its outstanding attractions are the Educational Museum, the Dolmetsch Workshops and the annual music festival.

Houndless Water

Bell Vale La., Haslemere, GU27 3DJ
☎ (0428) 2591
Traditional tile-hung country house in secluded position, 1 mile south of Haslemere off the A286. On the Surrey/Sussex border in an area of outstanding natural beauty. 1 hour by car from Gatwick and Heathrow Airports and the South Coast. 55 minutes by train from London.
Bedrooms: 1 single, 2 twin.
Bathrooms: 2 public.
Bed & breakfast: £12-£15 single, £20-£30 double.
Half board: £18.50-£22.50 daily, £120-£150 weekly.
Evening meal 7pm (l.o. 9pm).
Parking for 8.
Open January-November.

HASTINGS

E. Sussex
Map ref 3B4

Ancient town which became famous as the base from which William the Conqueror set out to fight the Battle of Hastings. Later became one of the Cinque Ports, now a leading resort. Fishermen's Museum and Hastings Embroidery inspired by the Bayeux Tapestry. *i*

Greensleeves
Vicarage Lane, Westfield, Hastings, TN35 4SD
☎ Hastings (0424) 753196
Comfortable Georgian country house set in beautiful countryside close to many places of historic interest. Also a self-catering cottage adjacent. Large garden.
Bedrooms: 1 double & 1 twin.
Bathrooms: 2 private.
Bed & breakfast: £10-£12 single, £20-£24 double.
Parking for 5.

The Tamar Guest House
7 Devonshire Rd., Hastings, TN34 1NE
☎ (0424) 434076
Overlooks Hastings cricket ground and has fine views of the castle. Few minutes' walk from railway stations, main shops and seafront.
Bedrooms: 2 double & 1 twin, 2 family rooms.
Bathrooms: 2 public.
Bed & breakfast: £9.50-£10.50 single, £18-£20 double.

HAWKHURST

Kent
Map ref 3B4

Village in 3 parts: Gill's Green, Highgate and The Moor. There is a colonnaded shopping centre, large village green, church and inn which is associated with the Hawkhurst smuggling gang.

Conghurst Farm
Conghurst Lane, Hawkhurst, TN18 4RW
☎ (0580) 753331

500-acre arable/sheep farm. Georgian farmhouse on Kent/Sussex border two miles from Hawkhurst, in peaceful countryside.
Bedrooms: 1 double & 2 twin.
Bathrooms: 1 private, 1 public.
Bed & breakfast: £10-£15 single, £22.50-£30 double.
Half board: £15-£22.50 daily, £95-£140 weekly.
Evening meal 7pm (l.o. 7pm).
Open March-November.

Ockley
Heartenoak Rd., Hawkhurst, TN18 4EX
☎ Hawkhurst (058 05) 2290
25-acre mixed farm. Beautiful old farmhouse in idyllic, unspoilt rural location. Lovely garden and swimming pool available for guests' use.
Bedrooms: 1 double & 2 twin.
Bathrooms: 1 private, 1 public.
Bed & breakfast: £12.50-£14 single, £25-£28 double.
Parking for 10.

HEATHFIELD

E. Sussex
Map ref 3B4

Old Heathfield is a pretty village which was one of the major centres of the Sussex iron industry.

Little Stonehurst Farm
Pottens Mill Lane, Broad Oak, Heathfield, East Sussex TN21 8UA
☎ (043 52) 2569
72-acre arable farm. Old family farmhouse in the 'back of beyond'. Reduced rates for children.
Bedrooms: 3 twin.
Bathrooms: 1 public.
Bed & breakfast: from £10.50 single, from £23 double.
Half board: from £16 daily, from £110 weekly.
Evening meal 6.30pm.
Parking for 8.

MAP REFERENCES APPLY TO THE COLOUR MAPS TOWARDS THE END OF THIS GUIDE.

HELLINGLY

E. Sussex
Map ref 2D3

Village on the Cuckmere River.

Blackstock Farm *Listed*
Grove Hill, Hellingly, Nr. Hailsham BN27 4HF
☎ (0323) 844453
220-acre mixed farm. Substantial Victorian farmhouse with commanding views of surrounding countryside. Well placed for access to towns and many tourist attractions.
Bedrooms: 1 double, 1 family room.
Bathrooms: 2 public.
Bed & breakfast: max. £10 single, max. £20 double.
Parking for 8.
Open April-September.

HENFIELD

W. Sussex
Map ref 2D3

See also Wineham.
In flat or gently sloping countryside with views to the Downs. Early English church with a fine perpendicular tower.

Fairmount Private Guest House *Listed*
6 Church Terrace, Henfield, BN15 9PB
☎ Brighton (0273) 493692
Located in an attractive conservation area. Pretty house offering all family comforts in a friendly atmosphere.
Bedrooms: 1 single, 2 double.
Bathrooms: 1 public.
Bed & breakfast: £15 single, £30 double.
Half board: £21 daily, £125 weekly.
Evening meal 7pm (l.o. 9.30pm).
Parking for 1.

Great Wapses Farm
Wineham, Nr. Henfield, BN5 9BJ
☎ (0273) 492544
33-acre mixed farm. Attractive Tudor and Georgian farmhouse in rural, peaceful surroundings with horses, calves and other animals.
Bedrooms: 2 double & 1 twin.
Bathrooms: 3 private.

Bed & breakfast: from £17 single, £25-£27 double.
Parking for 7.

HERSTMONCEUX

E. Sussex
Map ref 3B4

4m E. Hailsham
Pleasant village noted for its woodcrafts but dominated by the beautiful 15th C Herstmonceux Castle and gardens. Now home of the Royal Greenwich Observatory which is open to visitors.

The Stud Farm *Listed*
Bodle Street Green, Herstmonceux, Nr. Hailsham, BN27 4RJ
☎ (0323) 833201
70-acre mixed farm. Upstairs, 2 bedrooms and bathroom let as one unit to party of 2, 3 or 4. Downstairs, twin-bedded room with shower, W.C. and handbasin en suite, sunroom.
Bedrooms: 1 double & 2 twin.
Bathrooms: 2 private, 1 public.
Bed & breakfast: from £15 single, from £24 double.
Half board: from £21.50 daily, £115.50-£129.50 weekly.
Parking for 3.

HOLMBURY ST. MARY

Surrey
Map ref 2D2

4m SW. Dorking
Pleasant valley village with a church which was established in the 1870's when the railway came to Dorking. Magnificent views from Holmbury Hill.

Bulmer Farm
Holmbury St. Mary, Nr. Dorking, RH5 6LG
☎ Dorking (0306) 730210
30-acre cattle and horticulture farm. 17th C. character farmhouse with beams and inglenook fireplace on working family farm in Surrey hills.
Bedrooms: 3 twin.
Bathrooms: 2 public.
Bed & breakfast: from £22 double.
Parking for 10.

HORLEY

Surrey
Map ref 2D2

Town on the London to Brighton road, just north of Gatwick Airport, with an ancient parish church and 15th C inn.

Chithurst Farm

Chithurst Lane, Horne, Horley, RH6 9JU
☎ Smallfield (034 284) 2487
80-acre dairy farm. 16th C. listed farmhouse, recently renovated, with genuine beamed rooms and inglenook fireplaces, set in a quiet country lane.
Bedrooms: 1 single, 1 double, 1 family room.
Bathrooms: 2 public.
Bed & breakfast: £10-£12 single, £22-£25 double.
Parking for 3.
Open February-November.
➣ ⚲ Ⓤ Ⓣ ▱ ❋ ✕ ﬤ 🏠

Prinsted Guest House

Listed

Oldfield Rd., Horley, RH6 7EP
☎ (0293) 785233
Detached, Edwardian guesthouse with spacious accommodation, including large, family rooms. Close to Gatwick and London.
Bedrooms: 1 double & 2 twin, 3 family rooms.
Bathrooms: 3 public.
Bed & breakfast: £20-£28 single, £29-£32 double.
Parking for 10.
Credit: Amex.
➣ ⚲ ⚖ ♡ Ⓤ ▱ Ⓣ ▥ ▱ ✕ ﬤ Ⓣ

Rosemead Guest House

Listed

19 Church Rd., Horley, RH6 7EY
☎ (0293) 784965
Small guesthouse providing cooked breakfast, 5 minutes from Gatwick.
Bedrooms: 2 single, 2 double & 2 twin, 1 family room.
Bathrooms: 2 public.
Bed & breakfast: £18 single, £29 double.
Parking for 8.
➣ ▱ ♡ Ⓤ ▱ Ⓣ ▥ ▱ ﬤ Ⓣ

Springwood Guest House

58 Massetts Road, Horley, RH6 7DS
☎ Horley (0293) 775998
Elegant detached Victorian house in pleasant residential road close to Gatwick Airport. Long-term car parking.

Bedrooms: 2 single, 2 double & 3 twin, 1 family room.
Bathrooms: 2 public.
Bed & breakfast: £16.50-£19 single, £25-£28.50 double.
Parking for 10.
➣ 2 ⚖ ▱ ▥ ▥ ✕ ﬤ

HORSHAM

W. Sussex
Map ref 2D2

Busy town with much modern development but still retaining its old character. The museum is housed in Causeway House and devoted chiefly to local history and the agricultural life of the country.

Brookfield Farm Hotel (NFU) M

Ⓔ Ⓔ Ⓔ

Winterpit Lane, Plummers Plain, Horsham, RH13 6LY
☎ Lower Beeding (040 376) 568 & 645
250-acre mixed farm. In beautiful countryside in a central position, ideal for touring. Convenient for Gatwick Airport - lift service and long term car parking available. Family-run. A warm welcome assured.
Bedrooms: 7 single, 10 double.
Bathrooms: 16 private, 1 public; 1 private shower.
Bed & breakfast: max. £25 single, £35-£50 double.
Half board: £40-£45 daily.
Lunch available.
Evening meal 6.50pm (l.o. 9.50pm).
Parking for 100.
Credit: Access, Visa.
➣ ⚖ ▱ ☎ ⊡ ▱ Ⓥ ▱ Ⓣ ▥ ▱ ✦ ♡ ● Ù ✈ ▶ ❋ ▱ 🅂🅿

Rosedene

Listed

10, North Heath Lane Horsham RH12 4AH
☎ Horsham (0403) 66033
Leafy and attractive location 20 minutes' walk from main line station (Gatwick 20 minutes) and town centre. Bus stop outside.
Bedrooms: 3 single, 2 double & 1 twin.
Bathrooms: 1 public.
Bed & breakfast: £10-£15 single, from £18 double.
Half board: £20-£22 daily, £130-£140 weekly.
Evening meal 6.50pm (l.o. 8.50pm).
Parking for 3.
➣ 6 ⚖ ▱ ♡ Ⓤ ▮ ▱ Ⓣ ▥ ▱ ▶ ✕ ﬤ 🄳🄰🄵 🅂 🅂🅿

Winterpick Corner

Winterpit La., Mannings Heath, Nr. Horsham, RH13 6LZ
☎ (0403) 53882
Secluded country house with wide views overlooking St. Leonard's Forest and Mannings Heath Golf Course. 15 minutes from Gatwick Airport.
Bedrooms: 1 single, 2 double & 1 twin, 1 family room.
Bathrooms: 3 public.
Bed & breakfast: £18 single, £30 double.
Parking for 8.
➣ ♡ Ⓤ ▱ Ⓣ ▥ ▱ ▶ ❋ ✕ ﬤ

HOVE

See Brighton & Hove.

ICKLESHAM

E. Sussex
Map ref 3B4

4m W. Rye
Small village between the ancient towns of Rye and Hastings. The village itself was first recorded in 772 AD.

Oast House Inn

Main Rd., Icklesham, TN36 4BN
☎ Hastings (0424) 814217
Converted oast house built in 1535 during the reign of Henry VIII. Midway between Hastings and Rye on the A259.
Bedrooms: 6 double & 2 twin, 1 family room.
Bathrooms: 9 private.
Bed & breakfast: £25-£26.45 single, £35-£37.90 double.
Evening meal 6.30pm (l.o. 9.30pm).
Parking for 100.
Credit: Visa.
➣ ⚖ ▱ ♡ ▮ ▥ ❋ ✕ ﬤ ▥ 🅂🅿 🏠

THERE IS A SPECIAL SECTION IN THIS GUIDE LISTING ACCOMMODATION ESPECIALLY SUITABLE FOR GROUPS AND YOUNG PEOPLE.

LAMBERHURST

Kent
Map ref 3B4

7m SE. Tunbridge Wells
Long village street passes over the River Teise and has retained much of its ancient character. The Owl House is a small tile-hung, half-timbered house, a former haunt of wool-smugglers, not open to the public. Scotney Castle Gardens are close by.

Furnace Farm

Ⓔ Ⓔ Ⓔ

Furnace La., Lamberhurst, TN3 8LE
☎ (0892) 890788
Separately owned farmhouse on working farm, conveniently sited for touring Kent and East Sussex. London an hour from nearby Frant station.
Bedrooms: 1 double & 2 twin.
Bathrooms: 1 private, 1 public; 1 private shower.
Bed & breakfast: £11.50-£12.50 double.
Half board: £18.50-£19.50 daily, £129.50-£136.50 weekly.
Evening meal 7pm (l.o. midday).
Parking for 6.
Open April-October.
➣ ⚲ ⚖ ♡ ▮ Ⓥ ▱ Ⓣ ▱ ❋ ﬤ 🏠

LAUGHTON

E. Sussex
Map ref 2D3

6m NE. Lewes
Once the home of the Sussex Pelham family, the village has views towards Firle Beacon.

Sargeants Farm

Laughton, BN8 6BX
☎ Halland (082 584) 489
200-acre mixed farm. A delightful farmhouse ideal for walking or quiet holidays. Home-produced food.
Bedrooms: 1 double & 1 twin.
Bathrooms: 1 public.
Bed & breakfast: max. £10 single, max. £20 double.
Half board: max. £15 daily, max. £75 weekly.
Evening meal 6pm (l.o. 8pm).
Parking for 4.
➣ ⚲ ♡ Ⓤ ▮ Ⓥ ✂ ▱ Ⓣ ▥ ▱ Ù ▶ ▶ ✂ ❋ ﬤ 🏠

LENHAM
Kent
Map ref 3B4

9m SE. Maidstone
Shops, inns and houses, many displaying timber-work of the late Middle Ages, surround a square which is the centre of the village. The 14th C parish church has one of the best examples of a Kentish tower.

Dog and Bear Hotel
☺☺☺
The Square, Lenham, Nr Maidstone, ME17 2PG
☎ Maidstone (0622) 858219
15th C. coaching inn - the original stable block has been converted to provide a further 15 double bedrooms and function room.
Bedrooms: 10 double & 7 twin, 2 family rooms.
Bathrooms: 19 private.
Bed & breakfast: from £32 single, from £48 double.
Half board: from £45 daily, from £227 weekly.
Lunch available.
Evening meal 7pm (l.o. 9.30pm).
Parking for 70.
Credit: Access, Visa.
☺ ☎ ▣ ❖ ▤ V ﹏ ▥
▤ ⫯ ✕ ◩ SP ▦

LEWES
E. Sussex
Map ref 2D3

Historic old county town with Norman castle. The steep High Street has mainly Georgian buildings. There is a folk museum at Anne of Cleves House and the archaeological museum is in Barbican House. **ℹ**

The Anchor Inn & Boating
Barcombe, Lewes BN8 5BS
☎ Barcombe (0273) 400414
The Anchor Inn enjoys a totally isolated position on the River Dube and is about 5 miles from Lewes and Glyndebourne.
Bedrooms: 1 single, 3 double & 1 twin.
Bathrooms: 2 private, 2 public; 1 private shower.
Bed & breakfast: £25 single, £38-£47 double.
Half board: £37.50-£40 daily, £200-£225 weekly.

Lunch available.
Evening meal 7pm (l.o. 8pm).
Parking for 50.
▥ ▤ V ▤ ▤ ⫯ 𝄞 U ✧
▶ ✿ ✕ ▦

Dairy Farmhouse
☺☺
Wick St., Firle, Nr. Lewes, BN8 6NB
☎ Glynde (079 159) 280
1600-acre mixed farm. Farmhouse between Lewes and Eastbourne. Homely, relaxed and flexible. Firle Place, Glyndebourne and Charleston Farmhouse are all nearby.
Bedrooms: 1 single, 1 double, 1 family room.
Bathrooms: 1 public.
Bed & breakfast: £12.50 single, £25-£27 double.
Half board: £17.50-£18.50 daily.
Evening meal 5pm (l.o. 9pm).
Parking for 8.
Open April-October.
☺ ☒ ▥ ▤ TV ﹏ ▤ ✿ ▦

Felix Gallery
[Listed]
2 Sun St., Lancaster St., Lewes, BN7 2QB
☎ (0273) 472668
Fully-modernised period cottage with walled garden. In quiet street, 2 minutes' walk from town centre and castle. Easy parking.
Bedrooms: 1 single, 1 twin.
Bathrooms: 1 public.
Bed & breakfast: £13-£15 single, £26-£30 double.
☺4 ▤ ❖ ▥ ▤ V ﹏ ▤ ✕
▦

Millers
☺☺☺
134, High St., Lewes, BN7 1XS
☎ (0273) 475631
Grade II listed 16th C. timber-framed town house with secluded walled garden. Antique furnishing. No smoking.
Bedrooms: 3 double.
Bathrooms: 3 private.
Bed & breakfast: £29-£34 double.
Parking for 1.
▥ ▤ ▥ V ✂ ▤ ﹏ ▤ ✕
▦ ▦

PLEASE CHECK PRICES AND OTHER DETAILS AT THE TIME OF BOOKING.

LINGFIELD
Surrey
Map ref 2D2

3m N. East Grinstead
Wealden village with many buildings dating back to the 15th C. Nearby there is horse racing at Lingfield Park.

The College
College Cl., Lingfield, RH7 6HG
☎ (0342) 834215
Restored former monastery with walled garden terrace. Regency dining room, lounge with inglenook. Close to village centre.
Bedrooms: 1 single, 1 double & 1 twin.
Bathrooms: 1 public.
Bed & breakfast: £16.50-£18.50 single, £30-£34 double.
Half board: £24-£27 daily, £144-£162 weekly.
Evening meal 7pm (l.o. 8pm).
Parking for 4.
▥ ☒ ❖ ▥ ▤ ▤ TV ﹏ ▤
✿ ▦ SP ▦ T

Oaklands
Felcourt, Lingfield, RH7 6NF
☎ (0342) 834705
Spacious country house set in its own grounds, dating from the 16th C. 1 mile from the village of Lingfield, 3 miles from East Grinstead.
Bedrooms: 1 single, 2 double & 2 twin, 1 family room.
Bathrooms: 1 private, 2 public.
Bed & breakfast: £12-£14 single, £24-£28 double.
Half board: £16-£18 daily.
Lunch available.
Evening meal 7pm (l.o. 9pm).
Parking for 6.
▥ ☒ ❖ ▥ ▤ V ✂ ▤ TV
﹏ ▤ ✿ ✕ ▦ ▦

LITTLEBOURNE
Kent
Map ref 3C3

4m E. Canterbury
A group of houses around a large 13th C church with a long 14th C thatched barn, a few oast houses and a white weather-boarded watermill (not open to visitors).

Bow Window Inn **M**
☺☺
48-50 High St., Littlebourne, Nr. Canterbury, CT3 1ST
☎ (0227) 721264

17th C. Grade II listed building with exposed oak beams and inglenook fireplaces. Central village location, 2 miles from Canterbury.
Bedrooms: 1 single, 4 double & 3 twin.
Bathrooms: 8 private.
Bed & breakfast: £30-£35 single, £42-£46 double.
Half board: from £27.50 daily, from £183 weekly.
Lunch available.
Evening meal 7pm (l.o. 9.30pm).
Parking for 20.
Credit: Access, Visa, Diners, Amex.
☺ ▥ ▣ ⫯ ❖ ▤ V ▤ ▥
▤ ⫯ ✕ ◩ SP ▦

LYMINSTER
W. Sussex
Map ref 2D3

Sandfield House
☺☺
Lyminster, BN17 7PG
☎ Littlehampton (0903) 724129
Spacious country style family house in 2 acres. Between Arundel and sea, in area of great natural beauty.
Bedrooms: 1 double & 1 twin.
Bathrooms: 1 public.
Bed & breakfast: £25 double.
Parking for 5.
▥ ▥ ▤ ▤ TV ﹏ ▤ ✿ ✕
▦

LYNSTED
Kent
Map ref 3B3

Village noted for its charming half-timbered houses and cottages, many of which date from the Tudor period.

Forge Cottage
Lynsted, Sittingbourne, ME9 0RH
☎ Teynham (0795) 521273
Historic half-timbered cottage with oak beams and inglenook, in a picturesque village. Walled garden with terraced lawns. Good touring centre.
Bedrooms: 2 double & 1 twin.
Bathrooms: 2 public.
Bed & breakfast: £10-£12 single, £20 double.
☺10 ☒ ❖ ▥ ▤ ▤ TV ﹏
▤ ▦ SP ▦

THE SYMBOLS ARE EXPLAINED ON THE FLAP INSIDE THE BACK COVER.

MAIDSTONE

Kent
Map ref 3B3

See also West Malling.
Busy county town of Kent
on the River Medway has
many interesting features
and is an excellent centre
for excursions. Museum
of Carriages, Chillington
Manor House Museum
and Art Gallery,
Archbishop's Palace,
Allington Castle, Mote
Park. ℹ

30 Bower Mount Rd.

Maidstone, ME16 8AU
☎ (0622) 51928
Spacious Edwardian house in
residential road backing on to
parkland. Convenient for town
centre.
Bedrooms: 2 double.
Bathrooms: 1 public.
Bed & breakfast: £9-£10
single, £18-£20 double.
Parking for 1.
⊗ ▯ ⓤ ▥ ▤ ✕ ㈚

Bydews Place Ⓜ

Farleigh Hill, Maidstone,
ME15 0JB
☎ (0622) 58860
11-acre cattle & horses farm.
Part medieval, Elizabethan
farmhouse 1 mile from
Maidstone. Four poster beds
available. Bird garden. Please,
no smoking.
Bedrooms: 3 double, 1 family
room.
Bathrooms: 1 private,
1 public.
Bed & breakfast: £10-£15
single, £20-£30 double.
Half board: £15-£23 daily,
£100-£155 weekly.
Evening meal 7pm (l.o. 9pm).
Parking for 12.
⊗ ⅋ ⓤ ⅄ ⅊ ⓣⓥ ▥ ▤
❋ ㈚ ㈲

Court Lodge Farm

♔♔♔
The Street, Teston,
Maidstone, ME18 5AQ
☎ (0622) 812570 & 814200
4-acre farm contractor &
arable farm. 16th C.
farmhouse on A26 4 miles
Maidstone. Exposed beams
and inglenook fireplaces. Set in
beautiful garden overlooking
River Medway.
Bedrooms: 1 double & 1 twin,
1 family room.
Bathrooms: 2 private,
1 public.
Bed & breakfast: £10-£18
single, £20-£30 double.

Half board: £19-£28 daily,
from £115 weekly.
Evening meal 6.30pm (l.o.
8am).
Parking for 10.
⊗ 4 ⅊ ⓤ ⓥ ⅄ ⓣⓥ ▥ ▤ ❋
㈚ ㈷ SP ㈲

Fieldings

71 Church Street, Boughton
Monchelsea, Maidstone,
ME17 4HN
☎ Maidstone (0622) 45850
Comfortable modern home with
pretty garden in rural village.
Off the B2163, opposite the
village hall.
Bedrooms: 1 single, 1 twin.
Bathrooms: 1 public.
Bed & breakfast: from £10
single, from £20 double.
Parking for 2.
⊗ ⅍ ▯ ⅊ ⓤ ▥ ▤ ㈚ ㈲

Homestead

Greenhill, Otham,
Maidstone, ME15 8RR
☎ Maidstone (0622) 862234
16th C. beamed farmhouse in
the peaceful village of Otham,
1 mile from Leeds Castle and 3
miles east of Maidstone centre.
Proceed out of Maidstone on
the A20 Ashford road through
Bearsted, turn right on to
Otham Lane. After half a mile
turn left down unpaved drive.
Bedrooms: 1 single, 1 double
& 1 twin.
Bathrooms: 1 public.
Bed & breakfast: £10-£11
single, £20-£22 double.
Parking for 2.
Open April-October.
⊗ ⅍ ⅊ ⓤ ⓣⓥ ▥ ▤ ❋ ㈚

Mannamead

Pilgrims Way, Harrietsham,
Maidstone, ME17 1BT
☎ (0622) 859336
Bungalow on Pilgrims Way
with large garden and ample
parking. Quiet, comfortable
accommodation, only 3 miles
from Leeds Castle.
Bedrooms: 1 single, 1 double
& 1 twin.
Bathrooms: 1 public.
Bed & breakfast: £10-£11
single, £20-£22 double.
Parking for 4.
Open April-October.
⊗ ⅍ ⅍ ⓤ ⓣⓥ ▥ ▤ ❋ ㈚
㈲

Rock House Hotel

♔♔
102 Tonbridge Rd.,
Maidstone, ME16 8SL
☎ (0622) 51616
Family-run guesthouse close to
town centre. Central for
London, Gatwick and Channel
Ports. French and Spanish
spoken.

Bedrooms: 2 single, 4 double
& 3 twin, 1 family room.
Bathrooms: 2 public;
5 private showers.
Bed & breakfast: £21-£24
single, £30-£33 double.
Parking for 7.
Credit: Access, Visa.
⊗ 1 ▯ ⅊ ⓤ ⅄ ⓣⓥ ▥ ▤ ㈚

Roslin Villa

11 St. Michael's Rd.,
Maidstone, ME16 8BS
☎ (0622) 58301
Spacious, Edwardian house in
quiet road, within easy reach of
Maidstone centre.
Bedrooms: 2 double, 2 family
rooms.
Bathrooms: 1 private,
4 public; 2 private showers.
Bed & breakfast: £12-£13
single, £19-£23 double.
Parking for 3.
⊗ 4 ⓤ ▤ î ⓥ ▥ ▤ ❋ ㈚
㈷ ᴰᴬᶠ SP

Veglios Motel

Chatham Road, Sandling,
Maidstone, ME14 3AP
☎ (0622) 55459/673411
Motel in an orchard setting,
conveniently situated for the
M20, M2 and ports.
Bedrooms: 12 single,
10 double & 4 twin, 2 family
rooms.
Bathrooms: 28 private.
Bed & breakfast: £23 single,
£37-£49 double.
Evening meal 7pm (l.o.
10pm).
Parking for 28.
Credit: Access, Visa.
⊗ ⅍ ⅊ ⓓ ▯ ⅊ ▥ ▤ ❋ ㈚

Willington Court Ⓜ

♔♔
Willington St., Maidstone,
ME15 8JW
☎ (0622) 38885
Grade II listed Tudor style
house with carved oak
staircase and large inglenook
fireplace in dining room. TV
lounge. Adjacent to Mote
Park. Friendly atmosphere.
Bedrooms: 2 single, 1 double
& 1 twin, 1 family room.
Bathrooms: 1 public.
Bed & breakfast: £11-£12
single, £22-£24 double.
Parking for 4.
⊗ 7 ⅊ ⓤ ⓥ ⅄ ⅊ ⓣⓥ ▥ ▤
㈚ ㈷ SP ㈲

MARDEN

Kent
Map ref 3B4

10m SE. Tonbridge
The village is believed to
date back to Saxon times,
though today more
modern homes surround
the 13th C church.

Tanner House, Tanner Farm

♔♔♔
Goudhurst Road, Marden.,
TN12 9ND
☎ Maidstone (0622) 831214
210-acre mixed farm. Tudor
farmhouse in centre of
attractive family farm.
Inglenook dining room. Off
B2079. Car essential.
Bedrooms: 1 double & 2 twin.
Bathrooms: 3 private,
1 public.
Bed & breakfast: from £25
single, £30-£32 double.
Half board: from £35 daily,
from £160 weekly.
Evening meal 7.30pm (l.o.
8.30pm).
Parking for 4.
Open February-November.
⊗ ⅍ ⓓ ▯ ⅊ ⓤ î ⅊ ⓣⓥ
▥ ▤ ⅊ ❋ ㈚ ㈚ SP ㈲

MARGATE

Kent
Map ref 3C3

Oldest and most famous
resort in Kent. Many
Regency and Victorian
buildings survive from the
town's early days. There
are 9 miles of sandy
beach. Bembom Brothers
is a 20 acre amusement
park and the Winter
Gardens offers concert
hall entertainment. ℹ

Bridge Hotel Ⓜ

♔♔♔♔
13-15 St. Mildreds Road,
Westgate, Margate, CT8 8RE
☎ Thanet (0843) 31023
Totally rebuilt and refurbished
100-year-old establishment
upgraded to international
standards. Hotel and public
house complete with coffee
shop/restaurant.
Bedrooms: 1 single, 13 double
& 2 twin, 3 family rooms.
Bathrooms: 19 private.
Bed & breakfast: £25-£32
single, £32-£42 double.
Lunch available.

THERE IS A SPECIAL SECTION IN THIS
GUIDE LISTING ACCOMMODATION ESPECIALLY
SUITABLE FOR GROUPS AND YOUNG PEOPLE.

Evening meal 7pm (l.o. 10pm).
Parking for 12.
Credit: Access, Visa.

♿ ☎ Ⓡ 🖳 ⌷ 🕯 Ⓥ ◑ 🛏
🔺 ♻ 🐾 ⛱ SP

5m SE. Tonbridge
Village with Georgian houses, green and pond.

Matfield Court

The Green, Matfield,
TN12 7JX
☎ Brenchley (089 272) 3515
Non-smoking family offer accommodation in large, hospitable home facing south side of village green, backing on to orchard.
Bedrooms: 2 single, 1 twin, 2 family rooms.
Bathrooms: 2 public.
Bed & breakfast: £13.50-£15.50 single, £26-£32 double.
Half board: £20-£26 daily.
Evening meal 7.30pm (l.o. 8pm).
Parking for 6.

♿ 🐾 ♻ Ⓤ🅛 🕯 Ⓥ ✂ ⌷ 🅣🅥
🛏 🔺 ❋ ⛱ 🐾 DAP

8m S. Tunbridge Wells
On a ridge offering wide views of the Sussex Weald. Fire swept through the village in 1389, thus the oldest houses in the Main Street date from the 15th C.

Brook House

Salters Green, Mayfield,
TN20 6NP
☎ Rotherfield (089 285) 2491
Stone cottage in an area of outstanding beauty between Rotherfield and Mayfield.
Bedrooms: 1 double.
Bathrooms: 1 public.
Bed & breakfast: max. £25 double.
Parking for 1.
Open April-October.

♻ Ⓤ🅛 🅣🅥 🛏 ❋ ⛱ 🐾

Huggetts Furnace Farm

Stonehurst Lane Five Ashes,
Mayfield, TN20 6LL
☎ Hadlow Down
(082 585) 220/722

8-acre mixed and pedigree sheep farm. Comfortable medieval farmhouse. Idyllic position off beaten track. All meat and vegetables home produced; heated swimming pool. Lovely walks. Brochure available.
Bedrooms: 1 single, 1 double & 1 twin.
Bathrooms: 2 private, 1 public.
Bed & breakfast: £15 single, £40-£50 double.
Half board: £27.50-£37.50 daily, £192.50-£262.50 weekly.
Evening meal 7pm (l.o. 9pm).
Parking for 8.
Open February-December.

♿ ☎ Ⓤ🅛 🕯 Ⓥ ✂ ⌷ 🅣🅥
🔺 ☎ Ⓤ ♫ ❋ 🐾 ⛱ 🐾 SP
🏠

Rose and Crown Inn

Fletching Street, Mayfield
☎ Mayfield (0435) 872200
Uniquely charming, 500-year-old, Sussex inn with delightfully quaint, beamed bedrooms. On original London-to-coast road.
Bedrooms: 3 double.
Bathrooms: 3 private.
Bed & breakfast: £28 single, £40 double.
Lunch available.
Evening meal 7.15pm (l.o. 9.30pm).
Parking for 35.
Credit: Visa.

⌷ 🕯 🛏 🔺 🐾 ⛱ SP

3m SE. Ashford
Village with Norman church, with 14th C glass. Manor house designed by Robert Adam.

The Corner House
Listed

Church Rd., Mersham, Nr. Ashford, TN25 6NS
☎ Ashford (0233) 36117
Attractive house with large garden in pleasant village. Good centre, 4 miles from Wye, North Downs and Pilgrims Way. Half an hour from Canterbury, coast and ferry ports.
Bedrooms: 1 single, 1 double & 1 twin.
Bathrooms: 2 public.
Bed & breakfast: £10-£12 single, £20-£24 double.
Evening meal 7pm.
Parking for 2.

♿ 🐾 ♻ ⚘ Ⓤ🅛 🕯 🅣🅥 🛏 🔺
🐾

On the outskirts of the town are the remains of Cowdray Park, a substantial 16th C fortified mansion. There is a museum and the public can watch the famous Cowdray Park polo.

Mizzards Farm
⬛⬛⬛

Rogate, Midhurst,
GU31 5HS
☎ Rogate (073 080) 656
13-acre smallholding & sheep farm. 17th C. carefully modernised farmhouse in a peaceful setting by a river, quarter of a mile from the road. Panoramic views. Vaulted dining room with inglenook. No smoking in rooms.
Bedrooms: 1 double & 2 twin.
Bathrooms: 3 private, 2 public.
Bed & breakfast: £30-£36 double.
Parking for 12.

♿ 🐾 4 ⌷ 🖳 Ⓤ🅛 🛏 🔺 ☎ Ⓤ ❋
🐾 ⛱ 🏠

3m W. Folkestone

Beachborough Park ♨
⬛⬛⬛

Newington, Folkestone,
CT18 8BW
☎ (0303) 75432
30-acre livestock farm. Beautiful setting, ideal for sightseeing and convenient for the continent. Very comfortable for active people and those seeking peace and quiet.
Bedrooms: 3 double & 2 twin.
Bathrooms: 5 private.
Bed & breakfast: £25-£30 double.
Half board: £21.50-£25 daily.
Lunch available.
Evening meal 7pm (l.o. 9.30pm).

♿ 🐾 ⚘ Ⓡ 🖳 🕯 Ⓥ ⌷ 🅣🅥
🛏 🔺 ☎ Ⓤ ♫ ♬ ❋ 🐾
DAP 🐾 SP 🏠

┌─────────────────┐
│ **MAP REFERENCES** │
│ **APPLY TO THE** │
│ **COLOUR MAPS** │
│ **TOWARDS THE END** │
│ **OF THIS GUIDE.** │
└─────────────────┘

3m NW. Leatherhead

Apple Tree Cottage

3 Oakshade Rd., Oxshott,
KT22 0LF
☎ (037 284) 2087
Quiet village cottage near lovely Surrey countryside. Easy access to London (30 minutes), historic Guildford, Gatwick and Heathrow.
Bedrooms: 1 single, 1 double & 1 twin, 1 family room.
Bathrooms: 1 public.
Bed & breakfast: £13 single, £28-£30 double.
Half board: £18-£20 daily.
Evening meal 6pm (l.o. 10am).
Parking for 3.

♿ 🐾 Ⓡ ⚘ Ⓤ🅛 🕯 Ⓥ ⌷ 🅣🅥
🛏 🔺 Ⓤ ▶ 🐾 🏠

Pleasant town on the edge of National Trust woodland and at the foot of the North Downs. Chartwell, the former home of Sir Winston Churchill, is close by.

The New Bungalow, Old Hall Farm
⬛⬛

Tandridge La., Oxted,
RH8 9NS
☎ South Godstone
(0342) 892508
44-acre mixed farm. A spacious, modern bungalow set in the centre of a small, mixed farm and reached by a private drive.
Bedrooms: 1 twin, 2 family rooms.
Bathrooms: 1 public.
Bed & breakfast: £11-£13 single, £22-£26 double.
Half board: £16-£18 daily, £105-£119 weekly.
Evening meal 7pm (l.o. midday).
Parking for 5.
Open January-November.

♿ 🐾 🐾 ⚘ Ⓤ🅛 🕯 Ⓥ ✂ ⌷
🅣🅥 🛏 🔺 Ⓤ 🐾 🏠

Mr. and Mrs. C. A. Snell

12 Hoskins Rd., Oxted,
RH8 9HT
☎ (0883) 712700

Continued ▶

┌─────────────────┐
│ **PLEASE MENTION** │
│ **THIS GUIDE WHEN** │
│ **MAKING A BOOKING.** │
└─────────────────┘

OXTED

Continued

Family house in the centre of Oxted. London 40 minutes by train. Gatwick Airport 20 minutes; transport can be provided.
Bedrooms: 1 twin.
Bathrooms: 1 public.
Bed & breakfast: max. £24 double.
Parking for 1.
Open January-September.
🐕 🛏 ♿ UL V ▥ ✕ 🛏

PEASMARSH

E. Sussex
Map ref 3B4

Oak Cottage
Listed

Tanhouse Lane, Peasmarsh, TN31 6UY
☎ (079 721) 229
17th C. cottage with beams and inglenooks; set in colourful gardens. Located in peaceful country lane. Walking distance of good restaurants.
Bedrooms: 2 double.
Bathrooms: 2 public.
Bed & breakfast: from £11 single, £22-£24 double.
Half board: £16-£17 daily, £90-£100.80 weekly.
Parking for 4.
🐕 ⚒ ® ♿ UL 🔋 ▮ V ⤵ TV
▥ 🛎 ❄ ✕ 🛏 SP

PENSHURST

Kent
Map ref 3B4

Village in a hilly wooded setting with Penshurst Place, the ancestral home of the Sidney family since 1552, standing in delightful grounds with a formal Tudor garden.

Swale Cottage
Listed

Old Swaylands Lane, Off Poundsbridge Lane, Penshurst, Nr. Tonbridge, TN11 8AH
☎ Penshurst (0892) 870738
Magnificently converted 18th C. Kentish barn with beautifully furnished rooms. Close to many country houses and gardens. Located near the A26 on the B2176. Half an hour from Gatwick.
Bedrooms: 2 double & 1 twin.
Bathrooms: 3 private, 1 public.

Bed & breakfast: £20-£22 single, £34-£38 double.
Half board: £30-£31 daily.
Parking for 4.
🐕 🛏 ® ♿ 🖥 ▥ UL ▮ ⤵ 🛏 TV ▥
🛎 ❄ ✕ 🛏 SP 🏠

PETHAM

Kent
Map ref 3B4

4m SSW. Canterbury
On the west side of Stone Street amongst wooded chalk hills rising to 440 ft above sea level.

Upper Ansdore

Duckpit Lane, Petham, Canterbury, CT4 5QB
☎ (022 770) 672
4-acre mixed farm. Grade II listed Tudor farmhouse. Secluded, elevated position in the North Downs, overlooking nature reserve. 5 miles south of Canterbury.
Bedrooms: 2 double.
Bathrooms: 1 public.
Bed & breakfast: £24 double.
Parking for 5.
Open April-October.
🐕5 ⚒ ♿ UL ▥ ♨ ❄ ✕ 🛏
🏠

PETWORTH

W. Sussex
Map ref 2D3

Town dominated by Petworth House, the great 17th C mansion, set in 2000 acres of parkland laid out by Capability Brown. The house contains wood-carvings by Grinling Gibbons.

Eastwood Farm

Graffham, Nr. Petworth, GU28 0QF
☎ Graffham (079 86) 317
Country house in 15 acres. Lovely grounds with swimming pool, tennis court and lakes. Ideal for walking, riding and sightseeing.
Bedrooms: 1 single, 1 double & 1 twin.
Bathrooms: 1 public; 1 private shower.
Bed & breakfast: £11-£12.50 single, £20-£25 double.
Parking for 5.
🐕2 ♿ UL V ▥ TV ▥ ▵ ⤴
🐾 ♨ ❄ 🛏 OAP SP

PEVENSEY BAY

E. Sussex
Map ref 3B4

Small but popular resort, with spacious beach, near to the village of Pevensey.

Montana
😎😎

The Promenade, Pevensey Bay, BN24 6HD
☎ Eastbourne (0323) 764651
Quiet seafront position with own beach. Close to amenities. Private parking for cars and small boats. Non smoking.
Bedrooms: 1 single, 2 twin.
Bathrooms: 1 public.
Bed & breakfast: £10-£12 single, £18-£20 double.
Parking for 4.
🐕 ♿ UL ⤴ TV ◐ ▥ ✕ 🛏

REDHILL

Surrey
Map ref 2D2

Part of the borough of Reigate and now the commercial centre. Gatwick Airport is 3 miles to the south.

Beechwood House

39 Hatchlands Rd., Redhill, RH1 6AP
☎ (0737) 61444 & 64277
Victorian house with easy access to all amenities and Gatwick Airport. 10 minutes' walk from mainline station (Victoria 20 minutes).
Bedrooms: 2 single, 1 double & 3 twin, 1 family room.
Bathrooms: 2 public.
Bed & breakfast: £23 single, £30-£32 double.
Parking for 9.
🐕2 ♿ UL V ▥ TV ▥ ❄ ✕
SP

INDIVIDUAL
PROPRIETORS HAVE
SUPPLIED ALL
DETAILS OF
ACCOMMODATION.
ALTHOUGH WE DO
CHECK FOR
ACCURACY, WE
ADVISE YOU TO
CONFIRM PRICES
AND OTHER
INFORMATION AT
THE TIME OF
BOOKING.

ROBERTSBRIDGE

E. Sussex
Map ref 3B4

Small town in well-wooded country near the River Rother, with a number of old timber and boarded houses. An important local industry is the making of Gray-Nicolls cricket bats.

Mrs. M. Hoad

Parsonage Farm, Salehurst, Robertsbridge, TN32 5PJ
☎ (0580) 880446
300-acre mixed and hops farm. 15th C. farmhouse with beams and panelling. Relaxed atmosphere. Within easy reach of South Coast resorts and many places of historic interest and natural beauty.
Bedrooms: 1 single, 1 twin, 1 family room.
Bathrooms: 1 public.
Bed & breakfast: max. £9 single, max. £18 double.
Half board: max. £14 daily, max. £93 weekly.
Evening meal 6.30pm.
Parking for 20.
Open January-August, November-December.
🐕3 ⚒ ♿ UL ▥ ⤵ TV ▥ ✕ 🛏
🏠

ROCHESTER

Kent
Map ref 3B3

Ancient cathedral city on the River Medway. Has many places of interest connected with Charles Dickens (who lived nearby) including the fascinating Dickens Centre. Also massive castle overlooking the river and Guildhall Museum. ✏

Gainsborough Hotel

254 High St., Rochester, ME1 1HY
☎ Medway (0634) 45596
Large owner-run comfortable establishment opposite BR station. Listed Georgian building.
Bedrooms: 4 single, 2 double & 2 twin, 4 family rooms.
Bathrooms: 4 public.
Bed & breakfast: from £10.50 single, from £21 double.
Parking for 3.
🐕2 ⚒ UL V ▥ ⤵ TV ▥ ▵ 🛏

WE ADVISE YOU TO CONFIRM YOUR BOOKING
IN WRITING.

RYE

E. Sussex
Map ref 3B4

Cobbled hilly streets and fine old buildings make Rye, once a Cinque Port, a most picturesque town. Noted for its church with ancient clock, potteries and antique shops, and the Ypres Tower museum. ⓘ

Aviemore Guest House M
☺☺

Fishmarket Rd., Rye, TN31 7LP
☎ (0797) 223052
Owner-run, friendly guesthouse offering a warm welcome and hearty breakfast. Overlooking "Town Salts" and the River Rother. 2 minutes from town centre.
Bedrooms: 1 single, 2 double & 3 twin, 2 family rooms.
Bathrooms: 2 public.
Bed & breakfast: £12-£14 single, £22-£24 double.
Evening meal 7pm (l.o. 11pm).

Little Orchard House M
☺☺☺

West St., Rye, TN31 7ES
☎ (0797) 223831
Elegant Georgian home with panelled rooms, period furnishings and Old English walled garden, at the heart of ancient town. Generous country breakfast.
Bedrooms: 2 double & 1 twin.
Bathrooms: 3 private.
Bed & breakfast: £30-£50 single, £56-£70 double.

The Old Vicarage

Rye Harbour, Rye, TN31 7TT
☎ (0797) 222088
Imposing house with views over nature reserve to sea. Antique furniture, silver and linen. Informal atmosphere. Plenty of parking spaces.
Bedrooms: 1 single, 1 double & 1 twin, 1 family room.
Bathrooms: 1 public.
Bed & breakfast: £12.50-£15 single, £22-£27 double.
Parking for 3.

RYE FOREIGN

E. Sussex
Map ref 3B4

Village set behind the ancient town and port of Rye.

Rumpels Motel M
☺☺☺

Rye Foreign, Nr. Rye, TN31 7SY
☎ Peasmarsh (079 721) 494 & 495
Set in 3 acres of grounds surrounded by beautiful Sussex countryside.
Bedrooms: 3 single, 9 double & 2 twin, 4 family rooms.
Bathrooms: 13 private, 1 public.
Bed & breakfast: £20-£25 single, £30-£35 double.
Lunch available.
Evening meal 7pm (l.o. 9.30pm).
Parking for 54.
Credit: Access, Visa, Amex.

ST NICHOLAS-AT-WADE

Kent
Map ref 3C3

3m SW. Birchington Village in the Isle of Thanet with ancient church built of knapped flint.

Streete Farm House

Court Rd., St. Nicholas-at-Wade, CT7 0NH
☎ Thanet (0843) 47245
120-acre arable and mixed farm. 16th C. farmhouse on the outskirts of the village with original oak-panelled dining room.
Bedrooms: 1 single, 1 twin.
Bathrooms: 1 public.
Bed & breakfast: £9-£10 single, £18-£20 double.
Parking for 3.

SEAFORD

E. Sussex
Map ref 2D3

The town was a bustling port until 1579 when the course of the River Ouse was diverted. The downlands around the town make good walking country, with fine views of the Seven Sisters Cliffs. ⓘ

Fairy Cross Weekend Retreat

Stonewood Close, Seaford, BN25 3UX
☎ Seaford (0323) 896784
Tranquil country house atmosphere and personal service. 1 mile from the sea. Bordering Seven Sisters Country Park. Convenient for Alfriston, Eastbourne, Brighton and many National Trust properties.
Bedrooms: 3 single, 2 twin, 2 family rooms.
Bathrooms: 2 public.
Bed & breakfast: £11-£15 single, £22-£30 double.
Half board: from £17 daily.
Evening meal 7.30pm (l.o. 10.30am).
Parking for 4.

SEVENOAKS

Kent
Map ref 2D2

Set in pleasant wooded country, with a distinctive character and charm. Nearby is Knole, home of the Sackville family and one of the largest houses in England, set in a vast deer park. ⓘ

The Gables
Listed

36 Dartford Rd., Sevenoaks, TN13 3TQ
☎ (0732) 456708
Built in 1870, conveniently situated for local amenities and the frequent rail service to and from London. Non-smokers only.
Bedrooms: 2 single, 1 family room.
Bathrooms: 2 public.
Bed & breakfast: £10-£12 single, £20-£22 double.
Parking for 1.

Moorings Hotel M
☺☺

97 Hitchen Hatch Lane, Sevenoaks, TN13 3BE
☎ (0732) 452589
Bed and breakfast hotel in quiet position near station. London half an hour by train. Knole House and Chartwell nearby.
Bedrooms: 3 single, 1 double & 7 twin, 1 family room.
Bathrooms: 3 private, 2 public; 4 private showers.
Bed & breakfast: £25-£30 single, £32-£42 double.
Parking for 10.
Credit: Visa.

Nearly Corner

Heaverham, Nr Sevenoaks, TN15 6NQ
☎ (0732) 62039
A 15th C. friendly family house in a small peaceful hamlet, just below the North Downs amid farming country. No smoking.
Bedrooms: 1 single, 1 double.
Bathrooms: 2 public.
Bed & breakfast: from £15 single, from £26 double.
Parking for 2.

THERE IS A SPECIAL SECTION IN THIS GUIDE LISTING ACCOMMODATION ESPECIALLY SUITABLE FOR GROUPS AND YOUNG PEOPLE.

GROUPS, CONSORTIA AND AGENCIES SPECIALISING IN FARM AND COUNTRY HOLIDAYS ARE LISTED IN A SPECIAL SECTION OF THIS GUIDE.

MAP REFERENCES APPLY TO THE COLOUR MAPS TOWARDS THE END OF THIS GUIDE.

PLEASE MENTION THIS GUIDE WHEN MAKING A BOOKING.

SITTINGBOURNE
Kent
Map ref 3B3

The town's position and its ample supply of water make it an ideal site for the paper-making industry. Delightful villages and orchards lie round about.

Brusons
Listed

5 London Road, Teynham, Sittingbourne, ME9 9QW
☎ Sittingbourne (0795) 521122
On A2 halfway between Faversham and Sittingbourne. Large Victorian building with three quarters of an acre of garden backing on to orchards. Large rooms, original fireplaces.
Bedrooms: 1 single, 1 twin, 1 family room.
Bathrooms: 1 public.
Bed & breakfast: £10-£12 single, £20-£24 double.
Parking for 6.

SMARDEN
Kent
Map ref 3B4

8m W. Ashford
Pretty village with a number of old well-presented buildings. The 14th C St. Michael's Church, is known as the 'Barn of Kent' because of its 36 ft roof span.

The Flying Horse
Cage Lane, Smarden, TN27 8QD
☎ (023 377) 432
Public house of historic interest. Backs on to village church.
Bedrooms: 1 double & 1 twin.
Bathrooms: 1 public.
Bed & breakfast: £14 single, £28 double.
Half board: £16.50-£24 daily.
Lunch available.
Evening meal 7pm (l.o. 10pm).
Parking for 15.

STAINES
Surrey
Map ref 2D2

Ever since Roman days Staines has been a river crossing of the Thames on the route to the west from London.

The Blue Anchor Inn
13/15 High St., Staines, Middlesex TW18 4QY
☎ (0784) 52622
A 400-year-old market town hotel by the Thames, with public bars. Close to Heathrow Airport, the M3 and M4.
Bedrooms: 3 single, 1 double & 5 twin, 1 family room.
Bathrooms: 2 public.
Bed & breakfast: £21 single, £29 double.
Lunch available.
Evening meal 5.30pm (l.o. 10.30pm).
Parking for 15.
Credit: Access, Visa, Amex.

STEYNING
W. Sussex
Map ref 2D3

The jumble of building styles is typical of this village. Half a mile to the east of the village is Bramber Castle, a ruin now in the care of the National Trust.

Wappingthorn Farm
Horsham Rd., Steyning, BN4 3AA
☎ (0903) 813236
287-acre dairy and horse farm. Lovely views, surrounded by large garden and farmland.
Bedrooms: 1 single, 2 twin, 1 family room.
Bathrooms: 1 public; 2 private showers.
Bed & breakfast: from £12.50 single, from £21 double.
Evening meal 5pm (l.o. 9pm).
Parking for 23.
Open April-October.

TENTERDEN
Kent
Map ref 3B4

See also Wittersham.
Most attractive market town with a broad main street full of 16th C houses and shops. The tower of the 15th C parish church is the finest in Kent.

Collina House Hotel

5 East Hill, Tenterden, TN30 6RL
☎ (058 06) 4852
Edwardian house overlooking orchards and garden, within walking distance of picturesque town. Swiss-trained proprietors offering both English and continental cooking.
Bedrooms: 3 single, 5 family rooms.
Bathrooms: 8 private.
Bed & breakfast: £18.40-£20.70 single, £25.30-£32.20 double.
Half board: £27-£29.30 daily, from £161 weekly.
Evening meal 7pm (l.o. 7.30pm).
Parking for 11.
Credit: Access, Visa, Diners, Amex.

Finchden Manor
Listed

Appledore Rd., Tenterden, TN30 7DD
☎ (058 06) 4719
Early 15th C. manor house, grade II listed, with inglenook fireplaces, panelled rooms and beams. Set in four acres of gardens and grounds.
Bedrooms: 1 single, 3 double.
Bathrooms: 3 private, 1 public.
Bed & breakfast: £14-£16 single, £28-£32 double.
Parking for 4.

London Beach Farm

Ashford Rd., St. Michaels, Tenterden, TN30 6SR
☎ High Halden (023 385) 422
Modern private house surrounded by fields, set well back from main Ashford-Tenterden road. Good touring centre.
Bedrooms: 1 single, 1 double & 1 twin, 1 family room.
Bathrooms: 1 private, 1 public.

Bed & breakfast: £10-£15 single, £20-£28 double.
Half board: £17.50-£21.50 daily, £120-£140 weekly.
Evening meal 6.30pm (l.o. 7.30pm).
Parking for 4.

West Cross House Hotel

2 West Cross, Tenterden, TN30 6JL
☎ (058 06) 2224
Private hotel in fine, spacious Georgian house on wide tree-lined main street of attractive Kent town, convenient for touring.
Bedrooms: 1 single, 2 double & 2 twin, 2 family rooms.
Bathrooms: 2 public.
Bed & breakfast: £12 single, £24-£26 double.
Half board: £19-£22 daily, £126-£146 weekly.
Evening meal 7pm (l.o. 10am).
Parking for 7.
Open March-October.

TONBRIDGE
Kent
Map ref 3B4

Ancient town built on the River Medway, it has a long history of commercial importance and is still a thriving town.

Marchants Barn
Coldharbour Lane, Hildenborough, Nr. Tonbridge, TN11
☎ Hildenborough (0732) 832085
Interesting old beamed house in four acres of beautiful and peaceful gardens. Ideal touring centre and close to buses and trains.
Bedrooms: 1 single, 2 double & 1 twin.
Bathrooms: 2 public.
Bed & breakfast: £13-£16 single, £28-£34 double.
Parking for 20.

INDIVIDUAL PROPRIETORS HAVE SUPPLIED ALL DETAILS OF ACCOMMODATION. ALTHOUGH WE DO CHECK FOR ACCURACY, WE ADVISE YOU TO CONFIRM PRICES AND OTHER INFORMATION AT THE TIME OF BOOKING.

MAP REFERENCES APPLY TO THE COLOUR MAPS TOWARDS THE END OF THIS GUIDE.

TUNBRIDGE WELLS
Kent
Map ref 2D2

See also Ashurst, Hartfield, Penshurst, Wadhurst.
This 'Royal' town became famous as a spa in the 17th C and much of its charm is retained as in the Pantiles, a delightful shaded walk lined with elegant shops. Rich in parks and gardens and a good centre for walks. 🆔

Mrs. A. Kibbey, Birkfield
92 Ravenswood Ave., Tunbridge Wells, TN2 3SJ
☎ (0892) 31776
Warm, friendly atmosphere in quiet, comfortable family house, conveniently situated. Dining room and conservatory overlooking landscaped garden and woods. Full English breakfast.
Bedrooms: 1 single, 1 double & 1 twin.
Bathrooms: 1 public.
Bed & breakfast: £9.50-£10.50 single, £19-£21 double.
Parking for 4.
🛇 ⓊⓁ Ⓥ ⤫ �📺 ▦ ♨ ✠ ⚑

Clarken Guest House
61/63 Frant Road, Tunbridge Wells, TN2 5LH
☎ (0892) 33397
Large Victorian detached house on main Eastbourne/ Hastings road. 5 minutes from mainline station to London. 5 minutes to Pantiles. French spoken.
Bedrooms: 2 single, 5 twin, 2 family rooms.
Bathrooms: 1 private, 4 public.
Bed & breakfast: £12-£18 single, £24-£36 double.
Parking for 8.
🛇 ⚒ ♿ ⓊⓁ Ⓥ 📺 ▦ ♨ ⬥ ⚑ SP

Mrs. R. M. Clowes-Tester
☎
28 Yew Tree Rd., Southborough, Tunbridge Wells, TN4 0BA
☎ (0892) 22860
10 minutes' walk from sports centre and restaurants. Garden, patio, fountain and waterfall fishpool.
Bedrooms: 1 single, 2 double & 1 twin.

Bathrooms: 1 private, 1 public.
Bed & breakfast: from £11 single, from £22 double.
🛇 ▭ ♨ ⓊⓁ 📺 ▦ ♨ ♨ ⚑

Danehurst ♨
✧✧✧
41 Lower Green Rd., Rusthall, Tunbridge Wells
☎ (0892) 27739
Large Victorian family house built in 1902. Meals served in conservatory so guests can appreciate the lovely garden.
Bedrooms: 2 double & 1 twin, 1 family room.
Bathrooms: 3 private, 1 public.
Bed & breakfast: £16-£22 single, £26.50-£30 double.
Parking for 2.
Credit: Access, Visa.
🛇 ⓑ ▭ ♨ ⓊⓁ ⓘ ⤫ ☀ 📺 ▦ ♨ ❊ 🐕

149 Forest Road
Tunbridge Wells, TN2 5EX
☎ Tunbridge Wells
(0892) 30615
Friendly informal atmosphere in very pleasant home with beautiful garden. Private bathroom available. Centrally heated bedrooms with washbasins.
Bedrooms: 2 single, 1 twin.
Bathrooms: 2 public.
Bed & breakfast: £11-£12.50 single, £24-£26 double.
Parking for 2.
Open January-November.
🛇 ⚒ ☀ ⓊⓁ Ⓥ 📺 ▦ ♨ ⟋

10 Modest Corner
Listed
Southborough, Tunbridge Wells, TN4 0LS
☎ (0892) 22450
Located at the back of Southborough Common, on the Weald Way. All guest facilities on ground floor. No passing traffic. Good public transport to Tunbridge Wells and London.
Bedrooms: 2 twin.
Bathrooms: 1 private, 1 public.
Bed & breakfast: £15-£18.50 single, £25-£30 double.
Parking for 2.
🛇 ⚒ ♿ ♨ ⓊⓁ Ⓥ ▦ ♨ ♿
⚑

UCKFIELD
E. Sussex
Map ref 2D3

Once a medieval market town and centre of the iron industry, Uckfield is now a busy country town on the edge of the Ashdown Forest.

The Cottage
High Hurstwood, Uckfield, TN22 4AA
☎ Buxted (082 581) 2279
Attractive 250-year-old cottage set in picturesque valley near Ashdown Forest. Own farm half a mile away.
Bedrooms: 2 single, 1 family room.
Bathrooms: 2 public.
Bed & breakfast: £10 single, £20 double.
Half board: £15 daily, £105 weekly.
Evening meal 6pm (l.o. 8.30pm).
Parking for 4.
🛇 ⚒ ⓑ ♨ ⓊⓁ ⓘ 📺 ▦ ♨
❊ ⚑ ⚑ ⊞

Hooke Hall ♨
✧✧✧
250 High St., Uckfield, TN22 1EN
☎ (0825) 61578
Telex 95228 DPL
Queen Anne town house with rooms on the first floor.
Bedrooms: 1 single, 3 double & 1 twin.
Bathrooms: 2 private, 3 private showers.
Bed & breakfast: £38.50-£55.50 single, £52.50-£77.50 double.
Half board: £56-£73 daily.
Parking for 7.
Credit: Access, Visa, Diners, Amex.
🛇 ⓬ ☎ 📞 ▭ ♨ ⓘ Ⓥ
⤫ ▦ ♨ ⚑ 🐕 ⚑ SP ⊞

WADHURST
E. Sussex
Map ref 3B4

6m SE. Tunbridge Wells
Village in the Sussex Weald. The village sign shows an anvil, recalling the iron industry and also an oast-house showing that this is hop country.

Best Beech Hotel
Mayfield La., Best Beech, Wadhurst, TN5 6JH
☎ (089 288) 2046
Quiet, rural public house set in pretty Sussex countryside and surrounded by beech trees.

Bedrooms: 1 single, 2 double & 1 twin.
Bathrooms: 1 public.
Bed & breakfast: from £14 single, from £25 double.
Lunch available.
Evening meal 7pm (l.o. 9.30pm).
Parking for 30.
🛇 ⚒ ▭ ♨ ⓘ Ⓥ ▦ ♨ ⚑

Cheviots
Listed
Cousley Wood, Wadhurst, TN5 6HD
☎ Wadhurst (089 288) 2952
On B2100 between Lamberhurst and Wadhurst. Comfortable bed and breakfast in modern country house with extensive garden. Home cooking. Convenient base for walking and motoring. Close to Bewl Water.
Bedrooms: 2 single, 2 twin.
Bathrooms: 1 private, 1 public.
Bed & breakfast: £12-£15 single, £24-£30 double.
Half board: £17-£20 daily, £119-£140 weekly.
Parking for 4.
Open February-November.
🛇 ⚒ ♿ Ⓥ ⤫ 📺 ♨
♨ ❊ ⚑ ⚑ ⧉ SP

Kirkstone
✧✧
Mayfield La., Wadhurst, TN5 6HX
☎ (089 288) 3204
Large Victorian house in countryside near Tunbridge Wells. Large garden, fine views.
Bedrooms: 1 double, 1 family room.
Bathrooms: 2 public.
Bed & breakfast: from £12 single, from £24 double.
Parking for 4.
🛇 ⓊⓁ ⓘ ⤫ 📺 ▦ ♨ ❊ ♨ ⚑

Mount Farm
Faircrouch Lane, Wadhurst, East Sussex. TN5 6PT
☎ Wadhurst (082 88) 3152
65-acre sheep farm. Telephone for directions. Very peaceful setting surprisingly close to station and amenities. Prettily furnished in country style.
Bedrooms: 2 double & 1 twin.
Bathrooms: 1 public.
Bed & breakfast: £21-£24 double.
Half board: max. £19 daily, max. £126 weekly.
Evening meal 7pm (l.o. 8pm).
Parking for 3.
🛇 ⚒ ⓑ ⓊⓁ ⓘ Ⓥ ▦ 🐕 ⚑
⊞ SP

THE SYMBOLS ARE EXPLAINED ON THE FLAP INSIDE THE BACK COVER.

WADHURST

Continued

Newbarn
⚒⚒⚒
Wards Lane, Wadhurst,
TN5 6HP
☎ (089 288) 2042
*15-acre sheep farm. 18th C.
secluded farmhouse adjacent to
old farm buildings, barn and
twin oast house. Overlooks
Bewl Water trout fishery;
permits and boats for hire from
house. 3 miles from Ticehurst
and Wadhurst off B2099.*
Bedrooms: 1 single, 2 double
& 1 twin.
Bathrooms: 1 private,
1 public.
Bed & breakfast: £13.50-£15
single, £29-£40 double.
Parking for 10.

WALTHAM

Kent
Map ref 3B4

7m SW. Canterbury
West of Stone Street, the
old Roman road, Waltham
has an old brick and flint
church with an oak-
beamed roof.

Waltham Court Hotel
⚒⚒
Waltham, Nr. Canterbury,
CT4 5RY
☎ Petham (022 770) 413
*Tasteful conversion of an
elegant 18th C. house, set in
idyllic and tranquil
surroundings 10 minutes from
Canterbury.*
Bedrooms: 2 double & 1 twin,
1 family room.
Bathrooms: 4 private
showers.
Bed & breakfast: £20-£25
single, £34-£40 double.
Half board: £27-£33 daily.
Evening meal 7pm (l.o.
9.30pm).
Parking for 30.
Credit: Access, Visa.

WARLINGHAM

Surrey
Map ref 2D2

5m SE. Croydon
Pleasant town separated
by the Green Belt from
the more built-up areas to
the North.

Farleigh Court
⚒⚒
Farleigh Court Rd.,
Warlingham, CR3 9PX
☎ Upper Warlingham
(088 32) 2115
*512-acre dairy & arable farm.
17th C. farmhouse on a busy
working farm with a warm
welcome. Oak beams and log
fires.*
Bedrooms: 2 single, 1 double
& 1 twin.
Bathrooms: 1 public.
Bed & breakfast: £12.50-£14
single, £25-£28 double.
Parking for 8.

WEST CHILTINGTON

W. Sussex
Map ref 2D3

3m E. Pulborough
Well-kept village caught in
the maze of lanes leading
to and from the South
Downs.

New House Farm ⋀
⚒⚒⚒
Broadford Bridge Rd., West
Chiltington, Nr. Pulborough,
RH20 2LA
☎ (079 83) 2215
*50-acre mixed farm. 15th C.
farmhouse with oak beams and
inglenook for log fires. 40
minutes' drive from Gatwick.
Within easy reach of local inns.*
Bedrooms: 1 double & 1 twin,
1 family room.
Bathrooms: 3 private,
1 public.
Bed & breakfast: £32-£36
double.
Parking for 6.
Open January-November.

WEST HORSLEY

Surrey
Map ref 2D2

6m SW. Leatherhead
This affluent area of West
Surrey has long been a
popular location for grand
houses, including
Hatchlands and Clandon
Park, both of which are
close to West Horsley.

Hazelgrove
Epsom Rd., West Horsley,
Nr. Leatherhead, KT24 6AP
☎ East Horsley (048 65) 4467
*A comfortable 1920's family
house pleasantly set within
secluded gardens, close to the
Sheepleas (National Trust
woodlands) and Wisley
Horticultural Gardens.*
Bedrooms: 1 single, 1 double,
1 family room.
Bathrooms: 1 public.
Bed & breakfast: £12.50-£16
single, £24-£30 double.
Parking for 10.
Open April-October.

WEST MALLING

Kent
Map ref 3B3

Became prominent in
Norman times when an
abbey was established
here.

Scott House
37 High St., West Malling,
ME19 6QH
☎ (0732) 841380
*Georgian town house. A family
home from which we run an
antique business as well as bed
and breakfast. No smoking.*
Bedrooms: 1 double & 2 twin.
Bathrooms: 3 private.
Bed & breakfast: max. £27
single, max. £33 double.
Credit: Access.

WINEHAM

W. Sussex
Map ref 2D3

3m NE. Henfield
Hamlet in the Sussex
countryside close to the
All England Showjumping
Course at Hickstead.

Frylands
⚒⚒
Wineham, Nr. Henfield,
BN5 9BP
☎ Partridge Green
(0403) 710214

*250-acre mixed farm. Timber-
framed Tudor farmhouse, well
placed for touring and visiting
the coast. Many places of
interest to be found nearby. 20
minutes from Gatwick. Colour
TV in all bedrooms.*
Bedrooms: 1 double & 1 twin,
1 family room.
Bathrooms: 1 public.
Bed & breakfast: £11-£12
single, £22-£24 double.
Parking for 6.

WINGHAM

Kent
Map ref 3C3

On the A257 halfway
between Sandwich and
Canterbury. The main
street is notable for its
many half-timbered
buildings.

Crockshard Farmhouse
Crockshard La., Wingham,
Nr. Canterbury, CT3 1NY
☎ Canterbury (0227) 720464
*300-acre orchard and pasture
farm. Large Regency
farmhouse and family home in
beautiful countryside with
pleasant gardens and farmyard
animals. 7 miles Canterbury,
13 miles Dover.*
Bedrooms: 1 single, 2 double
& 1 twin, 1 family room.
Bathrooms: 2 public.
Bed & breakfast: £10 single,
£20 double.
Half board: £15 daily, £90
weekly.
Evening meal 6pm (l.o. 8pm).
Parking for 12.

WITTERSHAM

Kent
Map ref 3B4

Village in the Isle of
Oxney with a well-
preserved 18th C post
mill, Stocks Mill, open to
the public.

Knoll House
Wittersham, Nr. Tenterden,
TN30 7HN
☎ (079 77) 258
*In peaceful rural surroundings,
set well back off the road.*
Bedrooms: 2 single, 1 double
& 1 twin.
Bathrooms: 2 public.
Bed & breakfast: £9.50-£11
single, £20-£22 double.
Parking for 4.

INDIVIDUAL PROPRIETORS HAVE SUPPLIED
ALL DETAILS OF ACCOMMODATION.
ALTHOUGH WE DO CHECK FOR ACCURACY, WE
ADVISE YOU TO CONFIRM PRICES AND OTHER
INFORMATION AT THE TIME OF BOOKING.

WORTHING
W. Sussex
Map ref 2D3

See also Findon.
Largest town in West Sussex, a popular seaside resort with extensive sand and shingle beaches. Seafishing is excellent here. The museum contains finds from Cissbury Ring.

Burcott Guest House
6 Windsor Rd., Worthing, BN11 2LX
☎ (0903) 35163
Comfortable accommodation in a quiet position near the sea and amenities. Home cooking with health foods including vegetarian, vegan and meat diets. Peaceful garden. Ideal for holidays and convalescence.
Bedrooms: 3 single, 2 double, 2 family rooms.
Bathrooms: 1 public; 2 private showers.
Bed & breakfast: £12-£13 single, £24-£26 double.
Half board: £18-£19 daily, £110-£120 weekly.

Lunch available.
Evening meal 6pm (l.o. 7pm).
Parking for 4.

Moorings Hotel M
4 Selden Rd., Worthing, BN11 2LL
☎ (0903) 208882
Victorian house, tastefully renovated and retaining many original features. Close to the beach, Beach House Park, Aquarena, children's playground and town centre.
Bedrooms: 2 double & 3 twin, 2 family rooms.
Bathrooms: 3 private, 1 public; 3 private showers.
Bed & breakfast: £11-£15 single, £22-£30 double.
Half board: £16-£20.50 daily, £66-£129 weekly.
Lunch available.
Evening meal 7pm.
Parking for 5.
Credit: Access, Visa.

WYE
Kent
Map ref 3B4

4m NE. Ashford
Well-known for its agricultural and horticultural college. The Olantigh Tower with its imposing front portico is used as a setting for part of the Stour Music Festival held annually in June.

Kings Head M
Church St., Wye, Ashford, TN25 5BM
☎ (0233) 812418
Comfortable old Victorian coaching house, pleasantly decorated, with food at reasonable prices.
Bedrooms: 3 single, 3 double & 1 twin.
Bathrooms: 4 private, 1 public.
Bed & breakfast: £17.25-£21.25 single, £28.75-£34.50 double.
Half board: £22.25-£35 daily, £140.18-£245 weekly.

Lunch available.
Evening meal 7pm (l.o. 10pm).
Credit: Access, Visa.

New Flying Horse Inn M
Upper Bridge St., Wye, TN25 5AN
☎ (0233) 812297
17th C. former coaching inn with oak beams and gleaming brasses. Ideal for touring and walking in Kent countryside and coast.
Bedrooms: 5 double & 4 twin, 1 family room.
Bathrooms: 4 private, 2 public.
Bed & breakfast: £25-£35 single, £35-£45 double.
Half board: £32-£42 daily, £175-£250 weekly.
Lunch available.
Evening meal 6.50pm (l.o. 9.50pm).
Parking for 50.
Credit: Access, Visa, Diners, Amex.

W hen enquiring about accommodation you may find it helpful to use the booking enquiry coupons which can be found towards the end of the guide. These should be cut out and mailed direct to the establishments in which you are interested. Remember to include your name and address and please enclose a stamped addressed envelope (or an international reply coupon if writing from outside Britain).

KEY TO SYMBOLS
Open out the flap inside the back cover of this guide and the key to symbols will be easy to use.

BRIGHTON
Beside the sea~in style

Wherever you're staying in the South of England, don't miss out on Brighton. It offers so much more than the traditional seaside resort. There's history and heritage, and a huge range of sophisticated, up-to-the-minute attractions...all in that stylish setting that first made Brighton famous.

You can visit Brighton any time of the year - there's always something happening at the South Coast's entertainments capital. You'll enjoy excellent shopping, magnificent architecture, an exceptional range of restaurants and a cosmopolitan night-life.

It's all so easy to get to. And it's all in the new Brighton brochure. For your copy, simply 'phone our free, 24-hour Link Line 0800-521711 or write to Room 207, Holiday Bureau, Brighton BN1 1EQ.

Don't miss Brighton - Britain's brightest, most stylish resort.

Angela & Michael Godbold

Danehurst

We claim to treat you as a privileged guest in our home with dedication to high standards and detail

41 LOWER GREEN RD., RUSTHALL
TUNBRIDGE WELLS, KENT, TN4 8TW
Telephone 0892-27739

Southbourne GUEST HOUSE

- Southbourne is a friendly Guest House, catering for small numbers, with personal service
- 1½ miles from Gatwick Airport & M23 ● 23 miles from London or Brighton ● All rooms centrally heated, hot & cold water and tea & coffee making facilities ● Colour TV all rooms (some en-suite) breakfast room (separate tables) ● Guest bath/shower room ● Private car park ● Payphone ● Overnight tariff includes light English breakfast ● OPEN ALL YEAR

34 Massetts Road, Horley, Surrey RH6 7DS
☎ **(0293) 771991 (res.)**
Prop: Mrs. Jean Castellari   ETB 👑

When requesting brochures or further information from advertisers in this guide, you may find it helpful to use the advertisement enquiry coupons which can be found towards the end of the guide. These should be cut out and mailed direct to the companies in which you are interested. Remember to include your name and address and enclose a stamped and addressed envelope or stamps if requested by the advertiser.

English Tourist Board

CROWN CLASSIFICATIONS

All the establishments displaying a national classification in this guide are inspected regularly. All can be chosen with confidence.

There are six classifications — from Listed to 5 Crowns; each indicates the level of facilities and services provided.

All classified establishments are required to provide a high standard of cleanliness, courtesy and service and to be well maintained. A lower classification does not imply lower standards; although the range of facilities and services may be smaller, they may be provided to a high standard.

You will find a full explanation of the national Crown Classification Scheme towards the end of this guide.

The town or village you wish to visit may not have accommodation entirely suited to your needs, but there could be somewhere ideal quite close by. From the colour maps towards the end of this guide you will be able to identify nearby towns and villages with accommodation listed in the guide. You can then use the index to find the relevant page numbers.

FOLLOW THE COUNTRY CODE

♣ Enjoy the countryside and respect its life and work ♣ Guard against all risk of fire ♣ Fasten all gates ♣ Keep your dogs under close control ♣ Keep to public paths across farmland ♣ Use gates and stiles to cross fences, hedges and walls ♣ Leave livestock, crops and machinery alone ♣ Take your litter home ♣ Help to keep all water clean ♣ Protect wildlife, plants and trees ♣ Take special care on country roads ♣ Make no unnecessary noise

This section of the guide lists groups specialising in farm and country based holidays. Mos† offer bed and breakfast accommodation (some with evening meal) and self-catering accommodation.

Each of the groups listed has registered properties with the English Tourist Board.

To obtain further details of individual properties please contact the group(s) direct, indicating the time of year when the accommodation is required and the number of people to be accommodated. You may find the booking enquiry coupons in this guide helpful when making contact.

The cost of sending out brochures is high, and the groups would appreciate written enquiries being accompanied by a stamped and addressed envelope (at least 9in x 4.5in).

The 'b&b' prices shown are per person per night; the self-catering prices are weekly terms per unit.

The symbol 🐄 before the name of a group indicates that it is a member of the Farm Holiday Bureau, set up by the Royal Agricultural Society of England in conjunction with the English Tourist Board.

The symbol T at the end of some of the entries means that accommodation may be booked with the group through a bona fide travel agent.

Tim Britton

MISS PIM
COUNTRY HOTELS Co.

🐄 BEDFORDSHIRE FARM AND COUNTRY HOLIDAYS GROUP

Janet Must, Church Farm, 41 High Street, Roxton, Bedford, Bedfordshire MK44 3EB
🕿 Bedford (0234) 870234 (for North Bedfordshire).
Judy Tookey, Pond Farm, 7 High Street, Pulloxhill, Bedfordshire MK45 5HA
🕿 Flitwick (0525) 712316 (for South Bedfordshire).
Bed and breakfast and self-catering in Bedfordshire and neighbouring counties, in a wide range of farms and country properties.
11 properties offering bed and breakfast; 5 properties offering bed, breakfast and evening meal: £11 – £16 b&b.
4 self-catering units: £70 – £120.

COUNTRY FARM HOLIDAYS

Del Williams, Shaw Mews, Shaw Street, Worcester, Worcestershire WR1 3QQ
🕿 Worcester (0905) 613744 Telex 339176 (FHOLS) Fax (0905) 726677
A large selection of farmhouses throughout England, all offering bed and
breakfast for only £12 per night. Ideal for a go-as-you-please touring holiday. Also a wide range of self-catering properties.
100 properties offering bed and breakfast; 500 properties offering bed, breakfast and evening meal: £12 b&b.
350 self-catering units: low season (November-March) £70 – £100; high season (June-September) £120 – £250.
Short breaks also available. T

🐄 EAST DEVON FARM AND COUNTRY HOLIDAYS

Mrs S. Glanvill, Rydon Farm, Woodbury, Exeter, Devon EX5 1LB
🕿 Woodbury (0395) 32341
Choice of bed and breakfast and self-catering establishments in this beautiful unspoilt area of East Devon. Lovely walks and scenery.
15 properties offering bed and breakfast; 6 properties offering bed, breakfast and evening meal: £9 – £15 b&b.
7 self-catering units: low season from £85; high season £230 maximum.
Short breaks also available.

🐄 HADRIAN'S WALL FARM HOLIDAYS

Mrs Georgina Elwen, New Pallyards Farm, Hethersgill, Carlisle, Cumbria CA6 6HZ
🕿 Nicholforest (022 877) 308
A friendly group of hill sheep/beef farms offering bed and breakfast and self-catering in our beautiful northern borderlands.
12 properties offering bed and breakfast; 11 properties offering bed, breakfast and evening meal: £6.50 – £14.50 b&b.
17 self-catering units: low season (November-May) £65 – £100; high season (June-October) £100 – £258.
Short breaks also available. T

KENT FARM HOLIDAYS GROUP

Mrs D. Day, Great Cheveney Farm, Marden, Kent TN12 9LX

Maidstone (0622) 831207

or Mrs R. Bannock, Court Lodge Farm, The Street, Teston, Maidstone, Kent ME18 5AQ.

Maidstone (0622) 812570

A wide variety of properties providing serviced and self-catering accommodation and a touring caravan and camping park. Many interesting architectural features. Non-smokers welcomed in many establishments.

4 properties offering bed and breakfast; 5 properties offering bed, breakfast and evening meal: £10 – £16 b&b.

39 self-catering units: low season (October-May) £60 – £200; high season (June-September) £120 – £450.

Short breaks also available.

STAFFORDSHIRE'S VALE OF TRENT

Mrs D. E. Morton, Moors Farm & Country Restaurant, Chillington Lane, Codsall, Nr. Wolverhampton, Staffordshire WV8 1QH

Codsall (090 74) 2330

Sample the warm hospitality of farm and country accommodation in Staffordshire's picturesque Vale of Trent.

13 properties offering bed and breakfast; 4 properties offering bed, breakfast and evening meal: £9 – £18 b&b.

8 self-catering units: low season (1 November-end March) £50 – £100; high season (1 April-end October) £100 – £130.

Short breaks also available.

THAMES VALLEY FARM AND COUNTRY HOUSE ACCOMMODATION

Margaret Palmer, Morar Farmhouse, Weald Street, Bampton, Oxfordshire OX8 2HL

Bampton Castle (0993) 850162
Telex 83343 ABTELX Ref MORAR

A group of enthusiastic people providing comfortable, clean accommodation in a friendly family atmosphere. Excellent value for money.

16 properties offering bed and breakfast; 3 properties offering bed, breakfast and evening meal: £11 – £16 b&b.

3 self-catering units: low season £100 – £160; high season £130 – £190.

Short breaks also available.

YORKSHIRE COAST, MOORS AND WOLDS FARM HOLIDAYS

Heather Kelly, The Grange, Glaisdale, Whitby, North Yorkshire

Whitby (0947) 87241

A wide variety of farms offering bed, breakfast and evening meals, and self-catering accommodation, in Yorkshire and Humberside.

4 properties offering bed and breakfast; 8 properties offering bed, breakfast and evening meal: £10 – £15.

12 self-catering units: low season (October-April) £50 – £90; high season (July-September) £65 – £240.

Short breaks also available.

♣ Enjoy the countryside and respect its life and work ♣ Guard against all risk of fire ♣ Fasten all gates ♣ Keep your dogs under close control ♣ Keep to public paths across farmland ♣ Use gates and stiles to cross fences, hedges and walls ♣ Leave livestock, crops and machinery alone ♣ Take your litter home ♣ Help to keep all water clean ♣ Protect wildlife, plants and trees ♣ Take special care on country roads ♣ Make no unnecessary noise

FOLLOW THE COUNTRY CODE

Most of the accommodation establishments listed in this 'Where to Stay' guide are suitable for people who need to 'count the pennies' they spend on places to stay — especially students and the young. However, there are a number which make a point of providing low-cost accommodation, whether for young people or for large groups, whatever their ages.

These establishments range from Youth Hostels, YMCAs and YWCAs through budget and student hotels to the seasonally unused campuses of universities and colleges. Many are listed individually in the pages which follow, but here's a quick guide to what's available and where you can get further information.

YOUTH HOSTELS

The Youth Hostels Association (YHA) provides basic accommodation, usually in single-sex bunk-bedded rooms or dormitories, with self-catering facilities. Most hostels also provide low-cost meals or snacks. At the time of going to press, a night's stay at a Youth Hostel will cost between £1.70 and £7.00.

In spite of the word 'youth' in the name, there is in fact no upper age limit. Indeed, many

Youth Hostels also offer family accommodation, either in self-contained annexes (with kitchen, living room and bathroom) or by letting the smaller, four-to-six bed dormitories as private units.

Groups are very welcome at Youth Hostels, whether for educational or leisure pursuits: some hostels offer field study facilities and many more have classrooms. The YHA also offers a wide range of Adventure Holidays and Special Interest Breaks.

Youth Hostels — from medieval castles to shepherds' huts — can be found all over the country, both in countryside and coastal locations and in towns and cities.

You need to be a member of the YHA in order to take advantage of the facilities. Membership entitles you to use not only the 260 hostels in England and Wales but also the thousands of Youth Hostels in other parts of the British Isles and around the world. Membership costs from just £1.60.

Further information from:
Youth Hostels Association, National Office, Trevelyan House, 8 St Stephen's Hill, St Albans, Hertfordshire AL1 2DY. Tel: (0727) 55215.

YWCA & YMCA

The Young Women's Christian Association, founded in 1855, has grown into the world's largest women's organisation. Among its many activities is the running of over 60 hostels in Britain (known as YWCAs) which offer safe, reasonably priced accommodation, either on a permanent or temporary basis.

Most YWCAs take short-stay visitors only during the summer months when their permanent residents — in many cases, students — are on holiday. However, some of the hostels do accept short-stay visitors all the year round. And although the word 'women' appears in the name of the organisation, many of the residences now take men and boys as well as women and girls.

The Young Men's Christian Association (YMCA), founded in 1844, operates on much the same basis as the YWCA, taking people of both sexes at its residences around the country either on a permanent or short-stay basis.

Further information from:
YWCA HQ, Clarendon House, 52 Cornmarket Street, Oxford OX1 3EJ. Tel: (0865) 726110;
YMCA, National Council, 640 Forest Road, Walthamstow, London E17 3DZ. Tel 01-520 5599.

Tim Britton

UNIVERSITIES & COLLEGES

Accommodation in universities and colleges offers excellent value for money in a choice of dozens of campus locations around England. This type of accommodation is particularly suitable for groups, whether on a leisure trip or participating in a conference or seminar. Beds available at a campus can number up to 4,500 while meeting facilities can extend to 2,000 people and banqueting facilities to 1,500 people.

Most campuses are compact units with the bedrooms, restaurants, bars and meeting rooms all near each other.

Accommodation is mainly in single 'study bedrooms'. There is usually a variety of sports and recreational facilities available on the campus, ranging from football and cricket to boating, golf, trim trails and sauna.

At most universities and colleges, the accommodation is available only during the academic vacation periods (usually July to September and for three-week periods at Christmas and Easter).

Further information from:
British Universities Accommodation Consortium (BUAC), Box No 486, University Park, Nottingham NG7 2RD. Tel: (0602) 504571;
Higher Education Accommodation Consortium

(HEAC), 36 Collegiate Crescent, Sheffield S10 2BP. Tel: (0742) 683759.

OTHER ACCOMMODATION

In addition to the above main providers on a countrywide basis of budget accommodation for young people and groups, there are, of course, the many individual student and budget hotels around England and also such places as outdoor and field study centres. Some of these feature in the following pages but for more information on what is available in a particular area, please contact a local Tourist Information Centre (details of these centres are given in each of the regional introductory pages in this guide).

yha ....the Place to Stay

* Over 260 Youth Hostels throughout England and Wales

* Superb locations - Mountains, coast, cities and countryside

* Unbeatable prices from just £1.70 per overnight

* Special facilities for walkers and cyclists

* Exciting range of Adventure Holidays and Special Interest Breaks

For details of membership and your full colour brochure please contact:
YHA
Trevelyan House
8 St Stephen's Hill
St Albans
Herts AL1 2DY
Tel: (0727) 55215

The entries in this section are listed in alphabetical order of place name, and then in alphabetical order of establishment. County names are not normally repeated in each establishment entry, but please use the full postal address when writing.

The map references refer to the colour maps towards the end of this guide. The first number is the number of the map, and it is followed by the grid reference. London can be found on maps 6 and 7.

The key to symbols is on the flap inside the back cover — keep it open for easy reference.

AMBLESIDE
Cumbria
Map ref 5A3

4m NW. Windermere
At the head of Lake Windermere and surrounded by fells. Good centre for touring, walking and sailing. *i*

Iveing Cottage Holiday House, Y.W.C.A. ♪
Old Lake Rd., Ambleside, LA22
☎ (053 94) 32340
Contact: Mr. I. Coughlin
On the original coaching road from Windermere to Keswick. Ideal for fell-walking, rambling and climbing. Close to centre of village.
Bedrooms: 1 single, 2 twin/double, 7 sleeping 3 or more. Total number of beds 49.
Bathrooms: 7 public.
Bed & breakfast: from £9.
Open February-November.

BARDEN
N. Yorkshire
Map ref 4B1

5m NE. Skipton
Situated in Wharfedale. 17th C Barden Tower which was restored in 1658 by Lady Anne Clifford.

Barden Tower Bunkbarn
Barden, Skipton
Contact: Mr. I.H. Leak, High Gamsworth Cottage, Barden, Skipton, BD23 6DH
☎ Burnsall (075 672) 630
Barden Tower is on the west bank of the River Wharfe, about 3 miles north of Bolton Abbey, on the B6160. 200 years old and built on 2 levels.

Bedrooms: 4 sleeping 3 or more. Total number of beds 20.
Bathrooms: 1 public.
Bed only: from £5.
Open March-December.

BELFORD
Northumberland
Map ref 5B1

Small market town on the old coaching road, close to the coast, the Scottish border and the north east flank of the Cheviots. Mostly built in stone and very peaceful now that the A1 has by-passed the town, Belford makes an ideal centre for excursions to the moors and to the beautiful unspoilt coastline around Holy Island. *i*

Windy Gyle Outdoor Centre "Bearsports Group" ♪
30 West St., Belford, NE70 7QE
☎ (066 83) 289
Contact: Mr. P. Clark
Recently modernised country house offering outdoor activity. Holidays for individuals, families and groups. Long established.
Bedrooms: 6 sleeping 3 or more. Total number of beds 45.
Bathrooms: 2 public.
Bed only: £4-£4.50.
Bed & breakfast: £7-£7.50.
Full board: £60-£65 weekly.

THE SYMBOLS ARE EXPLAINED ON THE FLAP INSIDE THE BACK COVER.

BUDE
Cornwall
Map ref 1C2

Sandy resort on dramatic Atlantic coast. High cliffs give spectacular sea and inland views. Georgian cottages beside canal basin, otherwise 19th and 20th C development. Golf course, cricket pitch, folly, surfing, coarse-fishing and boating. Mother-town Stratton was base of Royalist Sir Bevil Grenville and birthplace of his famous retainer, the 'Cornish Giant', Anthony Payne. *i*

Adventure International ♪
Belle Vue, Bude, EX23 8JP
☎ (0288) 55551/2
Contact: Mr. Paddy Frost
Multi-activity centre. Expert instruction, excellent equipment, superb location, accommodation and food. All ages welcome. Friendly atmosphere.
Min. age 8.
Bedrooms: 18 single, 5 twin/double, 49 sleeping 3 or more. Total number of beds 400.
Bathrooms: 67 private, 2 public.
Full board: £90.85 weekly.

CANTERBURY
Kent
Map ref 3B3

The birthplace of English Christianity and a place of pilgrimage since the martyrdom of Thomas Becket in 1170. The seat of the Primate of All England and the site of Canterbury Cathedral. Not to be missed are St. Augustine's Abbey, St. Martin's (the oldest church in England), Royal Museum and Old Weaver's House and the exciting new Pilgrim's Way attraction. At nearby Bekesbourne is Howletts Zoo Park. *i*

University of Kent at Canterbury ♪
Conference Office, The University, Canterbury, CT2 7NZ
☎ (0227) 69186 Telex 965449
Contact: Mr. P. Jordan

The university, with its fine views of Canterbury, has 4 colleges, each with its own accommodation, catering and meeting rooms.
Min. age 16.
Bedrooms: 1100 single, 100 twin/double. Total number of beds 1300.
Bathrooms: 120 public.
Bed & breakfast: £13.50-£15.
Open January, March-April, July-September, December.

CASTLETON
Derbyshire
Map ref 4B2

5m W. Hathersage
Large village in a spectacular setting with a ruined Norman castle and 4 great show caverns, where the Blue John stone and lead were mined. One cavern offers a mile-long underground boat journey.

Losehill Barn ♪
Peak National Park Centre, Losehill Hall, Castleton, Nr. Sheffield, S30 2WB
☎ Hope Valley (0433) 20373
Contact: Mr. P. Townsend
Modernised Victorian mansion with a comfortable atmosphere, providing accommodation for approximately 60 people in single and twin bedrooms.
Min. age 8.
Bedrooms: 29 single, 20 twin/double. Total number of beds 69.
Bathrooms: 10 public.
Full board: from £139 weekly.

COVENTRY
West Midlands
Map ref 4B3

Modern city with a long history. It has many places of interest including the post-war and ruined medieval cathedrals, art gallery and museums, some 16th C almshouses, St. Mary's Guildhall, Lunt Roman fort and the Belgrade Theatre. *i*

University of Warwick ♪
Gibbet Hill Rd., Coventry, W. Midlands, CV4 7AL
☎ (0203) 523279 Telex 31406
Contact: Mr. D. Wilson
Continued ▶

Modern accommodation on a landscaped campus, set in Warwickshire farmland at the southern boundary of Coventry. Easy access.
Min. age 14.
Bedrooms: 2000 single, 100 twin/double. Total number of beds 2200.
Bathrooms: 250 private, 650 public.
Bed & breakfast: £15.43-£22.43.
Full board: £108-£157 weekly.
Open January, March-April, July-September, December.

Ⓥ ⛽ 📺 ⊞ ☎ ⛵ 🍴 ⊕ ⊘
🐾 🗽 🎿 ♿ ❀ 🎪 Ⓣ

COWLING
N. Yorkshire
Map ref 4B1

5m E. Colne

Ned Nook Field Centre
Keighley Rd., Cowling, Keighley, W. Yorkshire BD22 0AA
Contact: J.F. & J.M. Ackroyd, 233 Keighley Rd., Cowling, Keighley, W. Yorkshire BD22 0AA
☎ Cross Hills (0535) 33888
This centre provides a fulfilling and stimulating residential experience for teacher-organised groups of school children.
For groups only.
Ages 9-13.
Bedrooms: 2 sleeping 3 or more.
Total number of beds 30.
Bathrooms: 2 public.
Full board: max. £80 weekly.

Ⓤ Ⓥ ⛽ ⊞ ☎ ⛵ ♿ 🗽

CREWE
Cheshire
Map ref 4A2

Famous for its railway junction. The railway reached Crewe in 1837 when the Warrington-Birmingham line passed through here transforming this small market town into the first great railway town. ▨

Crewe & Alsager College of Higher Education
Crewe Road, Crewe, CW1 1DU
☎ (0270) 500661 Ext 2005
Contact: Mr. H.G Richardson

Ideal centre for visiting the wide variety of North West countryside and sampling the cultural life of Liverpool and Manchester.
For groups only.
Ages 10-70.
Bedrooms: 280 single. Total number of beds 280.
Bathrooms: 18 public.
Bed only: £6.15-£7.05.
Bed & breakfast: £8.50-£9.55.
Full board: £127.75-£139.30 weekly.
Open April, June-September, December.

Ⓥ ⛽ 📺 ⊞ ☎ ⛵ 🍴 ⊕ ♿
♿ ❀ Ⓣ

DARTINGTON
Devon
Map ref 1D2

Hilltop village in the Dart Valley. The educational and commercial centre, Dartington Hall, occupies a group of 20th C buildings centred on a house built by Richard II's half brother. Gardens, open-air theatre, shop and craft centre all welcome visitors.

The Old Postern Short Course Centre ⓜ
The Old Postern, Dartington, Totnes, TQ9 6EA
☎ (0803) 866051
Contact: Mr. M. Harris
14th C. manor house in private estate, renowned for its arts and theatre programme.
Modern residential accommodation, and access to high quality training equipment and activities.
Min. age 16.
Bedrooms: 20 single, 20 twin/double. Total number of beds 60.
Bathrooms: 12 public.
Bed only: £10-£15.
Bed & breakfast: £15-£20.
Full board: £140-£240 weekly.

Ⓥ ⛽ 📺 ⊞ ☎ ⛵ 🍴 ⊕ ♿
🎿 ❀ 🎪 Ⓣ

GROUPS, CONSORTIA AND AGENCIES SPECIALISING IN FARM AND COUNTRY HOLIDAYS ARE LISTED IN A SPECIAL SECTION OF THIS GUIDE.

DURHAM CITY
Co. Durham
Map ref 5C2

Ancient city with its Norman castle and cathedral set on a bluff high over the Wear, a market and university town and regional centre, spreading beyond the Market Place on both banks of the river. July Miners' Gala is a celebrated Durham tradition. ▨

Durham University Business School ⓜ
Mill Hill Lane, Durham City, DH1 3LB
☎ 091-374 2211
Contact: Mrs. A. Robinson
Modern university complex offering 41 study bedrooms and full conference facilities. Close to the centre of historic Durham with pleasant woodland surroundings.
Min. age 14.
Bedrooms: 39 single, 2 twin/double. Total number of beds 43.
Bathrooms: 2 private, 10 public.
Bed only: £10.50-£12.08.
Bed & breakfast: £13.50-£15.53.

Ⓥ ⛽ 📺 ⊞ ☎ ⛵ 🍴

St. Aidans College ⓜ
Windmill Hill, Durham City, DH1 3LJ
☎ 091-374 3269
Contact: Lt. Cdr. J.C. Bull
A modern college in beautiful landscaped gardens, overlooking the cathedral. Comfortable single and twin-bedded rooms, bar, TV lounge, free tennis and croquet.
Bedrooms: 190 single, 50 twin/double, 50 sleeping 3 or more. Total number of beds 290.
Bathrooms: 2 private, 48 public.
Bed only: £8-£10.
Bed & breakfast: £9-£10.70.
Full board: £104 weekly.
Open January, March-April, July-September, December.

Ⓥ ⛽ 📺 ⊞ ☎ ⛵ 🍴 ⚲ ⊕
🐾 ♿ ❀ 🎪

St. Cuthberts Society
12 South Bailey, Durham City, DH1 3EE
☎ 091-374 3464
Contact: Mrs. H. Bowler
3 old stone houses with riverside gardens, 5 minutes' walk from the city centre and close to the cathedral.
Max. age 60.

Bedrooms: 40 single, 18 twin/double, 6 sleeping 3 or more. Total number of beds 80.
Bathrooms: 15 public.
Bed & breakfast: from £9.10.
Full board: from £118.75 weekly.
Open July-September.

Ⓤ Ⓥ ⛽ 📺 ⊞ ♿ ❀

St. Marys College ⓜ
Elvet Hill Rd., Durham City, DH1 3LR
☎ 091-374 2700
Contact: Mrs. P. Aynesworth
Imposing, stone-built college in beautiful grounds overlooking the cathedral. 7 minutes from the city centre and on a bus route.
Bedrooms: 214 single, 20 twin/double. Total number of beds 254.
Bathrooms: 36 public.
Bed & breakfast: from £11.
Full board: from £125 weekly.
Open March-April, July-October, December-January.

Ⓥ ⛽ 📺 ⊞ ☎ ⛵ 🍴 ⊕ 🐾
♿ ❀

Trevelyan College (Univerisity of Durham) ⓜ
Elvet Hill Road, Durham, DH1 3LN
☎ 091-374 3764 Telex 537351
Contact: Mr. B. Brown
Set in parkland, within 1 mile of the city centre. The college is proud of its service, food and hospitality.
Bedrooms: 208 single, 24 twin/double. Total number of beds 256.
Bathrooms: 47 public.
Bed & breakfast: £10.50-£12.
Full board: £143.50-£154 weekly.
Open January, March-April, July-September.

Ⓥ ⛽ 📺 ⊞ ☎ ⛵ 🍴 ⊕ 🐾
❀ 🎪

INDIVIDUAL PROPRIETORS HAVE SUPPLIED ALL DETAILS OF ACCOMMODATION. ALTHOUGH WE DO CHECK FOR ACCURACY, WE ADVISE YOU TO CONFIRM PRICES AND OTHER INFORMATION AT THE TIME OF BOOKING.

EXETER

Devon
Map ref 1D2

University city rebuilt after 1940s around its venerable cathedral. Suffered Danish raids under Anglo-Saxons but repulsed William I until 1068. Fragments of Roman wall survive; early Norman towers preserved in 13th C cathedral with fine west front. Notable waterfront buildings, Maritime Museum. Guildhall, old inns; Cathedral library, Rougemont House Museum of Costume and Lace, Royal Albert Memorial Museum, Northcott Theatre. 🄸

University of Exeter ♨
Domestic Services Dept., Dept. WTS 89, Devonshire House, Stocker Rd., Exeter, EX4 4PZ
☎ (0392) 211500 Telex 42894
Contact: Miss E.M. Stephenson
Accommodation in university halls on perimeter of attractive estate. Common rooms, licensed bars, function catering, sports facilities and teaching rooms.
Bedrooms: 2000 single, 150 twin/double. Total number of beds 2300.
Bathrooms: 350 public.
Bed & breakfast: £9.95-£17.25.
Full board: from £125 weekly.
Open March-April, July-September, January-December.
🅅 🖼 📺 🖾 🛦 🖪 🍽 🗘 🍴
🔲 🏃 🛪 🐾 ✳ 🅣

INDIVIDUAL
PROPRIETORS HAVE
SUPPLIED ALL
DETAILS OF
ACCOMMODATION.
ALTHOUGH WE DO
CHECK FOR
ACCURACY, WE
ADVISE YOU TO
CONFIRM PRICES
AND OTHER
INFORMATION AT
THE TIME OF
BOOKING.

HASTINGS

E. Sussex
Map ref 3B4

Ancient town which became famous as the base from which William the Conqueror set out to fight the Battle of Hastings. Later became one of the Cinque Ports, now a leading resort. Fishermen's Museum and Hastings Embroidery inspired by the Bayeux Tapestry. 🄸

Hurst Court Residential Centre & Self-Catering Wing ♨
The Ridge, Hastings, TN34 2RA
☎ Hastings (0424) 751400
Contact: Mr. B White
A comfortable, friendly residential centre available to organisations wishing to run residential courses. Separate self-catering unit for groups up to 24. Owned by an independent, self-supporting trust.
For groups only.
Bedrooms: 1 single, 17 twin/double, 2 sleeping 3 or more. Total number of beds 41.
Bathrooms: 6 public.
Full board: £91.88-£146.65 weekly.
🅅 🖼 📺 🖾 🛦 🖪 🍽 🗘 🞉
🍴 🏃 🐾 ✳

Hurst Court Self-Catering Wing ♨
Hurst Court Residential Conf. Centre, The Ridge, Hastings, TN34 2RA
☎ (0424) 751400
Contact: Mr. B. White
A separate unit from the main centre, which accommodates up to 24 persons in bunk beds, with lounge and dining areas, and separate, fully-equipped kitchen.
For groups only.
Bedrooms: 12 twin/double. Total number of beds 24.
Bathrooms: 2 public.
Bed only: from £4.50.
🆄 🖾 🛦 🖪 🞉 🏃 ✳

GROUPS, CONSORTIA
AND AGENCIES
SPECIALISING
IN FARM AND
COUNTRY HOLIDAYS
ARE LISTED IN A
SPECIAL SECTION
OF THIS GUIDE.

HEALEY

N. Yorkshire
Map ref 5C3

3m W. of Masham
Village to the west of the attractive market town of Masham, on the eastern edge of the Yorkshire Dales.

Healey Mill ♨
Healey, Masham, HG4 4LH
☎ Ripon (0765) 89168
Contact: Mrs. H.J. Dawson, Howgrave House, Howgrave, Bedale, DL8 2NS
☎ Melmerby (0765) 84218
Former mill complex tastefully converted into self-catering holiday accommodation, well equipped for groups of up to 25 people. 2 bedrooms have private shower.
For groups only.
Bedrooms: 3 single, 1 twin/double, 3 sleeping 3 or more. Total number of beds 25.
Bathrooms: 4 public.
Bed only: £4-£6.
🆄 🖾 📺 🖾 🛦 🖪 🍽 🍴 🌑 ✳
🎏

ILFRACOMBE

Devon
Map ref 1C1

Seaside resort of Victorian grandeur set on hillside between cliffs with sandy coves. Earlier a small port and fishing town. On a rock at the mouth of the harbour stands an 18th C lighthouse, built over a medieval chapel. There are fine formal gardens and 2 working mills, restored and open to the public. Museum, donkey rides, Chambercombe Manor, interesting and charming old house nearby. 🄸

The Youth Hostel - Ilfracombe
Ashmoor House, 1 Hillsborough Terrace, Ilfracombe, EX34 9NR
☎ (0271) 65337
Contact: Mr and Mrs M. Jenkins
End of fine Georgian listed terrace overlooking splendid harbour. Easy access to sand, sea, burrows, moors, Lundy Island and Wales (by ferry).
Bedrooms: 3 twin/double, 10 sleeping 3 or more. Total number of beds 50.

Bathrooms: 3 public.
Bed only: £2.95-£4.35.
Bed & breakfast: £4.75-£6.15.
Open March-October.
🆄 🅅 📺 🖾 🛦 🍴 🔺 🎏

ILKLEY

W. Yorkshire
Map ref 4B1

This moorland spa town, famous for its ballad, is a lively tourist centre with many hotels and shops. 16th C Manor House, now a museum, displays local prehistoric and Roman relics. Popular walk leads up Heber's Ghyll to mysterious Swastika Stone, White Wells, 18th C plunge baths on Ilkley Moor. 🄸

Bradford & Ilkley Community College
Wells Rd., Ilkley, LS29 9RD
☎ (0943) 609010
Contact: Mrs. R.J. Wilson, Bradford & Ilkley Community College, Margaret McMillan Hall, Easby Rd., Bradford, BD7 1QZ
☎ Bradford (0274) 733291
Ilkley campus is on the edge of Rombalds Moor overlooking the pleasant town of Ilkley and the Wharfe Valley.
For groups only.
Ages 16-70.
Bedrooms: 80 single, 60 twin/double. Total number of beds 210.
Bathrooms: 20 public.
Bed only: £4.75-£8.25.
Bed & breakfast: £7.25-£11.75.
Full board: £103.25-£161 weekly.
Open April, July-August.
🅅 🖼 📺 🖾 🛦 🖪 🍴 🌑 🐾
✳ 🎏

INGLETON

N. Yorkshire
Map ref 5B3

Ingleton is a thriving tourist centre for fell-walkers, climbers and pot-holers. Popular walks up beautiful Twiss Valley to Ingleborough Summit, Whernside and White Scar Caves. 🄸

The Barnstead ♨
Stackstead Farm, Ingleton, Carnforth, Lancashire LA6 3HS
☎ (052 42) 41386
Contact: Jim or Mona Charlton

Continued ▶

Continued

Well-equipped, bunk-style, self-catering accommodation for groups of 2-22 with 4 bedrooms, a communal kitchen and a lounge/dining area. Panoramic views of surrounding limestone countryside. TV point for guests' own use.
Bedrooms: 4 sleeping 3 or more. Total number of beds 22.
Bathrooms: 4 public.
Bed only: £4.50.
🔲 🍴 ▥ �car 🍴 ❄

KINGSTON-UPON-HULL

Humberside
Map ref 4C1

Busy seaport with a modern city centre and deep-sea fishing base at junction of the Rivers Hull and Humber, founded by Cistercian monks in 12th C. Maritime traditions in the town, docks and the museum, and the home of William Wilberforce, the slavery abolitionist, whose house is now a museum. The world's longest single span suspension bridge crosses the Humber 5 miles west. *ℹ*

Cumberbirch Conference Centre, Humberside College of Higher Education
Cottingham Rd., Kingston-upon-Hull, N. Humberside
HU6 7RT
☎ (0482) 41451 & 446707
Telex HUMCOL - G 592717
Contact: Miss Linda Ellis, Conf. Centre Manager
6 halls of residence on 2 very pleasant sites 3 miles from the city centre. Conference centre accommodation also available throughout the year with a variety of meal arrangements, including restaurant and bar complex. Fees negotiable depending on numbers and type of accommodation required.
For groups only.
Min. age 9.
Bedrooms: 466 single, 45 twin/double. Total number of beds 556.
Bathrooms: 127 public.
Bed only: from £8.05.
Bed & breakfast: from £10.06.
Open April, July-September.
🔲 🍴 📺 ▥ 🚃 🚗 🍴 ⊕ 🍷
🔑 ❄

University of Hull 🏠
Conference Office,
Cottingham Rd., Kingston-upon-Hull, N. Humberside
HU6 7RX
☎ (0482) 465947
Telex 592530 UNIHULG
Contact: The Conference Officer
Min. age 10.
Bedrooms: 1270 single, 190 twin/double. Total number of beds 1650.
Bathrooms: 330 public.
Bed & breakfast: from £10.06.
Open January, March-April, July-September, December.
🔲 🍴 📺 ▥ 🚃 🚗 🍴 ⊕ 🍷
🔑 🅣

LEICESTER

Leicestershire
Map ref 4C3

Modern industrial city with a wide variety of attractions including Roman remains, ancient churches, Georgian houses and a Victorian clock tower. There are pedestrianised shopping precincts, an excellent market, several museums, theatres, concert hall and sports and leisure centres. *ℹ*

University of Leicester
University Road, Leicester,
LE1 7RH
☎ (0533) 522423
Telex 347250 LEICUN G
Contact: Mrs. Sue Ingle
Leicester University offers comprehensive accommodation and professional services to conferences and groups in beautiful, peaceful surroundings.
For groups only.
Bedrooms: 1227 single, 161 twin/double, 19 sleeping 3 or more. Total number of beds 1606.
Bathrooms: 250 public.
Bed & breakfast: £12.95-£15.50.
Full board: £90.65-£108.50 weekly.
Open January, March-April, July-September, December.
🔲 🍴 📺 ▥ 🚃 🚗 🍴 ⊕ 🍷
🔑 ❄ 🏠

LONDON

Allen Hall Summer Hostel 🏠
Allen Hall, 28 Beaufort St.,
London SW3 5AA
☎ 01-351 1296 & 01-351 1297

Contact: The Domestic Bursar
Built on the site of the home of St. Thomas More and his family, Allen Hall is a training college for the Catholic priesthood. Open as a hostel when students are on holiday.
Bedrooms: 42 single, 13 twin/double. Total number of beds 68.
Bathrooms: 5 public.
Bed & breakfast: £14.50-£15.
Open July-August.
🔲 🍴 📺 🚗 🍴 🏠

Boka Hotel 🏠
35 Eardley Cres., London
SW5 9JT
☎ 01-373 2844 & 01-370 1388 Telex 269712 GLOBE G
Contact: Mr. Misha
Bedrooms: 10 single, 33 twin/double, 7 sleeping 3 or more. Total number of beds 98.
Bathrooms: 7 private, 10 public.
Bed & breakfast: £11-£22.
🔲 🍴 📺 ▥ 🅣

Campbell House
Taviton St., London
WC1H 0BX
☎ 01-388 0060
Contact: Mr. R.L. Sparvell
Specially reconstructed Georgian housing providing self-catering accommodation in a peaceful, central London location.
Min. age 10.
Bedrooms: 60 single, 40 twin/double. Total number of beds 140.
Bathrooms: 9 public.
Bed only: £9-£11.
Open June-September.
🔲 🍴 📺 ▥ 🚗

Carr-Saunders Hall 🏠
18-24 Fitzroy St., London
W1P 5AE
☎ 01-580 6338
Contact: The Hall Bursar
Modern hall of residence with lift. Central for Oxford Street and the West End.
Bedrooms: 100 single, 12 twin/double. Total number of beds 124.
Bathrooms: 4 private, 35 public.
Bed & breakfast: £12.65-£15.81.
Open March-April, July-September.
🔲 🍴 📺 ▥ 🚗 🚗

Central University of Iowa Hostel
7 Bedford Pl., London
WC1B 5JA
☎ 01-580 1121
Contact: Ms. W. Bristow

An old Georgian house near the British Museum. Closest underground stations are Russell Square and Holborn.
Bedrooms: 1 single, 6 twin/double, 5 sleeping 3 or more. Total number of beds 30.
Bathrooms: 7 public.
Bed only: £12.50-£14.50.
Open May-August.
🔲 🍴 📺 ▥ 🚗 🏠

Crosby Hall
Cheyne Walk, Chelsea,
London SW3 5AZ
☎ 01-352 9663
Contact: Miss. S.E. Willisch
15th C. dining hall overlooking the River Thames The garden opens directly onto the Embankment.
For females only.
Ages 17-80.
Bedrooms: 73 single, 10 twin/double. Total number of beds 93.
Bathrooms: 6 private, 20 public.
Bed & breakfast: £15.87-£21.39.
Full board: £109.14-£127.08 weekly.
🔲 🍴 📺 ▥ 🚗 🍴 🏠

Girls Friendly Society
32 Evelyn Gdns., London
SW7 3BG
☎ 01-370 2121
Contact: Mrs. L. Phelps
The hostel is in a quiet residential road close to all amenities and offers secure accommodation.
For female individuals only.
Min. age 16.
Bedrooms: 9 single, 14 twin/double, 3 sleeping 3 or more. Total number of beds 46.
Bathrooms: 12 public.
Bed & breakfast: £10-£12.
Open March-April, July-September.
🔲 🍴 📺 🚗

Gloucester Court
47 Gloucester Pl., London
W1H 3PD
☎ 01-935 8571 & 8572
Contact: Mrs V.J. Huntington
Min. age 16.
Bedrooms: 1 single, 7 twin/double, 7 sleeping 3 or more. Total number of beds 38.
Bathrooms: 6 private, 3 public.
Bed & breakfast: £10-£16.
🔲 🍴 📺 ▥ 🚗

Halliday Hall ⚠

King's College London
(KQC), 64-67 Clapham
Common S. Side, London,
SW4 8AN
☎ 01-673 2032 Telex 8954102
BBS LON G
Contact: The Conference
Administrator, King's
College London (KQC),
552 Kings Rd., London
SW10 0UA
☎ 01-351 6011
*Private hostel residence in
south London, in large lawned
gardens fronting on to
extensive open grassed areas of
Clapham Common.*
Bedrooms: 22 single,
60 twin/double, 15 sleeping 3
or more. Total number of
beds 202.
Bathrooms: 100 private,
2 public.
Bed & breakfast: £13.20-
£13.75.
Open April, July-September,
December.
Ⓥ 🛏 📺 🖾 ⚍ 🍽 ✺ ♪ ❋
Ⓣ

Ingram Court ⚠

King's College London
(KQC), Chelsea Campus,
552 Kings Rd., London
SW10 0UA
☎ 01-351 2488 Telex 8954102
BBS LON G
Contact: The Conference
Administrator
☎ 01-351 6011
*Study-bedrooms grouped
around a quiet courtyard on a
spacious private campus in the
heart of Chelsea. 6 additional
campus halls of residence in
central London.*
Bedrooms: 107 single,
7 twin/double. Total number
of beds 121.
Bathrooms: 30 public.
Bed & breakfast: £16-£17.50.
Open April, July-September,
December.
Ⓥ 🛏 📺 🖾 ⚍ 🍽 ✺ ♪ ❋
♪ Ⓣ

International Students House ⚠

229 Great Portland St.,
London W1N 5HD
☎ 01-631 3223
Contact: Ms. S. Ballofet
*10 minutes' walk from the
West End and next to Regents
Park. Numerous facilities
available in a modern building.*
Ages 17-50.

THE SYMBOLS ARE
EXPLAINED ON THE
FLAP INSIDE THE
BACK COVER.

Bedrooms: 151 single,
12 sleeping 3 or more. Total
number of beds 295.
Bed & breakfast: £6.85-
£14.25.
🛏 📺 🖾 ⚍ 🍽 ✺ ❋ 🏠
Ⓣ

International Students Hostel

99 Frognal, London
NW3 6XR
☎ 01-794 6893 & 8095
Contact: Sr. P.S. Taylor
*Establishment convenient for
Hampstead Heath.
Underground station nearby.
Budget rates for students.
For females only.*
Min. age 16.
Bedrooms: 17 single,
2 twin/double, 4 sleeping 3 or
more. Total number of
beds 40.
Bathrooms: 14 public.
Bed only: £7-£10.50.
Bed & breakfast: £7.50-£12.
Ⓥ 🛏 📺 🖾 ⚍ 🚗 ✺ 🏠

John Adams Hall ⚠

15-23 Endsleigh St., London
WC1H 0DH
☎ 01-387 4086 & 4796
Contact: Miss. C. Stubbs
*John Adams Hall is an
assembly of Georgian houses;
the hall has retained its old
glory.*
Bedrooms: 126 single,
22 twin/double. Total number
of beds 170.
Bathrooms: 22 public.
Bed & breakfast: £14.95-
£16.67.
Open December-January,
March-April, June-
September.
Ⓥ 🛏 📺 🖾 ⚍ 🍽 ✺ ⚏ 🏠 Ⓣ

Kent House ⚠

325 Green Lanes, London
N4 2ES
☎ 01-802 0800 & 01-341
2105
Contact: The Manager
*Special off-season and weekly
rates for young tourists.
Facilities for self-catering.
Adjacent to Manor House
underground station and
10 minutes from central
London.*
Ages 16-45.
Bedrooms: 3 single,
13 twin/double, 3 sleeping
3 or more. Total number of
beds 34.
Bathrooms: 6 public.
Bed only: £7-£13.
Ⓥ 🛏 📺 🖾 ⚍ 🚗 Ⓣ

King George's House Y.M.C.A. ⚠

Stockwell Rd., London
SW9 9ES
☎ 01-274 7861

Contact: Ms. J. Banks
*Close to the Victoria and
Northern underground lines,
ideal for visitors and also for
those who wish to study and
work in London.*
Ages 18-35.
Bedrooms: 230 single,
15 twin/double, 12 sleeping
3 or more. Total number of
beds 300.
Bathrooms: 30 public.
Bed & breakfast: £12.65-
£15.18.
Ⓥ 🛏 📺 🖾 ⚍ 🍽 ✺ ❋

King's College Hall ⚠

King's College London
(KQC), Champion Hill,
London SE5 8AN
☎ 01-733 2166 Telex 8954102
BBS LON G
Contact: The Conference
Administrator, King's
College London (KQC),
552 Kings Rd., London
SW10 0UA
☎ 01-351 6011
*The hall is 3 miles from
Westminster and the City, set
in pleasant quiet grounds away
from busy roads.*
Bedrooms: 446 single,
4 twin/double. Total number
of beds 454.
Bathrooms: 66 public.
Bed & breakfast: £13.
Open April, July-September,
December.
Ⓥ 🛏 📺 🖾 ⚍ 🍽 ✺ ♪ ❋
✺ Ⓣ

Lightfoot Hall ⚠

King's College London
(KQC), Manresa Road,
London SW3 6LX
☎ 01-351 2488 Telex 8954102
BBS LON G
Contact: The Conference
Administrator, King's
College London (KQC),
552 Kings Rd., London
SW10 0UA
☎ 01-351 6011
*A modern 10-storey building in
the famous King's Road,
Chelsea, in the heart of
London.*
Bedrooms: 186 single. Total
number of beds 186.
Bathrooms: 28 public.
Bed & breakfast: £16-£17.50.
Open April, July-September,
December.
Ⓥ 🛏 📺 🖾 ⚍ 🍽 ✺ Ⓣ

London Friendship Centre

Peace Haven, 3 Creswick
Rd., London W3 9HE
☎ 01-992 0221
Contact: Mr. P. O'Nath
*A comfortable residential
hostel, most suitable for groups
of young people and school
parties.*

Min. age 12.
Bedrooms: 2 single,
6 twin/double, 8 sleeping 3 or
more. Total number of
beds 53.
Bathrooms: 5 public.
Bed & breakfast: £6-£10.50.
Ⓤ Ⓥ 🛏 📺 🖾 ⚍ 🍽 ✺
✺ 🏠

Lords Hotel ⚠

20-22 Leinster Sq., London
W2 4PR
☎ 01-229 8877 Telex 298716
LORDS G
Contact: The Manager
*Bed and breakfast
accommodation in the heart of
London, with residents' bar.*
Bedrooms: 12 single,
22 twin/double, 25 sleeping
3 or more. Total number of
beds 145.
Bathrooms: 7 private,
19 public.
Bed & breakfast: £11-£23.
🛏 📺 🖾 ♪ 🏠 Ⓣ

Malcolm Gavin Hall ⚠

King's College London
(KQC), Beechcroft Rd.,
London SW17 7DS
☎ 01-767 3119 Telex 8954102
BBS LON G
Contact: The Conference
Administrator, King's
College London (KQC),
552 Kings Rd., London
SW10 0UA
☎ 01-351 6011
*A modern residence set in
lawned grounds with ample
parking for coaches and cars.*
Bedrooms: 150 single. Total
number of beds 150.
Bathrooms: 24 public.
Bed & breakfast: £13.
Open April, July-September,
December.
Ⓥ 🛏 📺 🖾 ⚍ 🚗 ✺ Ⓣ

Newham Youth Trust

Newham Youth Lodge, 315
Roman Rd., East Ham,
London E6 3SQ
☎ 01-476 3027
Contact: Mr G.P. Owen
*Short stay hostel dormitory
accommodation for groups of
12 people or more only (no
individuals please). Bookings
especially welcome from
affiliated members of the Trust
and registered youth clubs and
organisations.
For groups only.*
Ages 10-24.
Bedrooms: 2 twin/double,
4 sleeping 3 or more. Total
number of beds 26.
Bathrooms: 3 public.
Bed only: min. £3.
Ⓤ 🖾 🚗 ✺

Northampton Hall, City University ♨

Bunhill Row, London
EC1Y 8LJ
☎ 01-628 6661 & 2953
Contact: Mr. C. Powner, The
Conference Office, The City
University, Northampton
Sq., London EC1V 0HB
☎ 01-253 4399 & 3003
*Opposite the Barbican Arts
Centre, near St. Paul's
Cathedral in the City of
London.*
Min. age 18.
Bedrooms: 488 single,
70 twin/double. Total number
of beds 558.
Bathrooms: 265 public.
Bed & breakfast: £14-£15.
Open July-September.
Ⓥ 🖵 ⓉⓋ 🛏 ⚊ 🚗 🍴

O'Callaghan's

205 Earls Court Rd., London
SW5 9AN
☎ 01-370 3000 & 01-540
5958
Contact: Mr. B.J. Browning
*Central London low budget
guesthouse for tourists and
students. Open all year round.*
Ages 16-60.
Bedrooms: 5 twin/double,
5 sleeping 3 or more. Total
number of beds 24.
Bathrooms: 3 public.
Bed only: £8-£10.
Ⓤ ⓉⓋ ⚊

Passfield Hall ♨

1 Endsleigh Pl., London
WC1H 0PW
☎ 01-387 7743 & 3584
Contact: The Hall Bursar
*University hall of residence
with washbasin in all rooms,
suitable for families. Meals
available. Central for Oxford
Street and the West End.*
Bedrooms: 100 single,
34 twin/double, 10 sleeping
3 or more. Total number of
beds 198.
Bathrooms: 36 public.
Bed & breakfast: £12.30-
£14.84.
Open March-April, July-
September.
Ⓤ Ⓥ 🖵 ⓉⓋ 🛏 ⚊ 🚗 🍴

Queen Elizabeth Hall ♨

King's College London
(KQC), Campden Hill Rd.,
London W8 7AH
☎ 01-937 5411 Telex 8954102
BBS LON G
Contact: The Conference
Administrator, King's
College London (KQC),
552 Kings Rd., London
SW10 0UA

☎ 01-351 6011
*On a self-contained campus
near Kensington High Street
convenient for shopping,
sightseeing and London's
theatres.*
Bedrooms: 50 single,
100 twin/double. Total
number of beds 250.
Bathrooms: 28 public.
Bed & breakfast: £16-£17.50.
Open April, July-September,
December.
Ⓥ 🖵 ⓉⓋ 🛏 ⚊ 🍴 🎣 ♪ ✳
Ⓣ

Queen Mary College, Halls of Residence ♨

98-110 High Rd., South
Woodford, London E18 2QJ
☎ 01-504 9282 Telex 893750
QMC VOL G
Contact: The Conference &
Booking Sec
*The Halls at South Woodford
offer moderately-priced,
university accommodation.
Easy access to the centre of
London by underground.*
Min. age 2.
Bedrooms: 635 single,
38 twin/double. Total number
of beds 711.
Bathrooms: 90 public.
Bed only: max. £8.05.
Bed & breakfast:
max. £11.75.
Full board: max. £140 weekly.
Open March-April, July-
September.
Ⓥ 🖵 ⓉⓋ 🛏 ⚊ 🍴 ☉ ♪
♪ ✳ 🏠 Ⓣ

Rosebery Avenue Hall ♨

90 Rosebery Ave., London
EC1R 4TY
☎ 01-278 3251
Contact: The Hall Bursar
*Modern hall of residence.
Meals available. Convenient
for Oxford Street and the
West End. Lift. Washbasin in
all rooms. TV available
through the winter.*
Bedrooms: 161 single,
16 twin/double. Total number
of beds 193.
Bathrooms: 19 public.
Bed & breakfast: £12.65-
£16.50.
Open March-April, June-
September.
Ⓥ 🖵 🛏 ⚊ 🍴 ♿

Rywin House

36 Christchurch Ave.,
Brondesbury, London
NW6 7BE
☎ 01-459 5434
Contact: Mr. P. Horsley
*In a quiet residential area with
British Rail and London
Transport stations nearby.
Short walk to local tennis
courts.*

Bedrooms: 2 single,
1 twin/double, 6 sleeping 3 or
more. Total number of
beds 23.
Bathrooms: 3 public.
Bed & breakfast: £10.50.
Ⓤ 🖵 ⓉⓋ 🍴

Hotel Saint Simeon ♨

38 Harrington Gdns.,
London SW7 4LT
☎ 01-373 0505 & 4708
Telex 269712 GLOBE G
Contact: Mr. J. Gojkovic
Bedrooms: 5 single,
15 twin/double, 12 sleeping
3 or more. Total number of
beds 83.
Bathrooms: 4 private,
7 public.
Bed & breakfast: £8-£9.
Ⓤ 🖵 ⓉⓋ 🛏 Ⓣ

Sir John Cass Hall

150 Well St., Hackney,
London E9 7LO
☎ 01-533 2529
Contact: Mr. I. McConchie
*Modern purpose-built hall with
comfortable accommodation,
near many tourist attractions
and the City.*
Min. age 16.
Bedrooms: 97 single. Total
number of beds 97.
Bathrooms: 12 public.
Bed & breakfast: £10.50.
Ⓤ Ⓥ 🖵 ⓉⓋ 🛏 ⚊ 🍴

Tent City ♨

Old Oak Common Lane, East
Acton, London W3 7DP
☎ 01-743 5708
Contact: Mr. B. Martin
*A tented hostel in a large park
providing cheap, simple
accommodation for summer
visitors to London.*
Bedrooms: 14 sleeping 3 or
more. Total number of
beds 448.
Bathrooms: 24 public.
Bed only: £3.
Bed & breakfast: £4.
Open June-September.
Ⓤ 🖵 ⚊ ✳

Wellington Hall ♨

King's College London
(KQC), 71 Vincent Square,
London SW1P 2PA
☎ 01-834 3980 Telex 8954102
BBS LON G
Contact: The Conference
Administrator, King's
College London (KQC),
552 Kings Rd., London
SW10 0UA
☎ 01-351 6011
*Delightfully situated in a quiet,
green central London square,
combining modern facilities
with traditional style. 6
additional campus halls of
residence in central London.*

Bedrooms: 39 single,
43 twin/double. Total number
of beds 125.
Bathrooms: 22 public.
Bed & breakfast: £17-£18.
Open April, July-September,
December.
Ⓥ 🖵 ⓉⓋ 🛏 ⚊ 🍴 ☉ ✳ 🏠
Ⓣ

West London Institute of Higher Education

Borough Rd., Isleworth,
Middlesex TW7 5DU
☎ 01-891 0121
Contact: G. Campbell-Smith,
300 St. Margaret's Rd.,
Twickenham, Middlesex
TW1 1PT
☎ 01-891 0121
*Spacious campus close to
Heathrow Airport, within easy
reach of Richmond, Windsor
and central London.
For groups only.*
Min. age 13.
Bedrooms: 86 single,
2 twin/double. Total number
of beds 90.
Bathrooms: 14 public.
Bed & breakfast: £11.20-
£12.30.
Full board: £133.98-£141.68
weekly.
Open March-April, July-
September, December.
Ⓥ 🖵 ⓉⓋ 🛏 ⚊ 🍴 ☉ ♪ ♪
✳ 🏠

West London Institute of Higher Education

300 St. Margaret's Rd.,
Twickenham, Middlesex
TW1 1PT
☎ 01-891 0121
Contact: Miss. P. McGrath
*Pleasant campus on the
Thames near Richmond, within
easy reach of Heathrow
Airport and central London.
For groups only.*
Min. age 13.
Bedrooms: 278 single. Total
number of beds 278.
Bathrooms: 36 public.
Bed & breakfast: £11.20-
£12.30.
Full board: £133.98-
£141.68 weekly.
Open March-April, July-
September, December-
January.
Ⓥ 🖵 ⓉⓋ 🛏 ⚊ 🍴 ♿ ☉ ♪
♪ ✳

> **MAP REFERENCES
> APPLY TO THE
> COLOUR MAPS
> TOWARDS THE END
> OF THIS GUIDE.**

Gtr. Manchester
Map ref 4B1

The industrial capital of the North, second only to London as a commercial, financial, banking and newspaper centre. Victorian architecture, many churches, museums, art galleries, libraries, 15th C cathedral and Bellevue Zoo. New shopping centre at Piccadilly. 🛈

University of Manchester Dept. C328 ♨

Oxford Road, Manchester, M13 9PL
☎ 061-273 1946
Contact: Miss. C.S. Bolton
Accommodation for groups and facilities for conferences and exhibitions in university halls of residence. Small or large groups - long or short stay, flexible arrangements, friendly staff.
For groups only.
Ages 12-70.
Bedrooms: 3200 single, 130 twin/double. Total number of beds 3460.
Bathrooms: 1031 public.
Bed & breakfast: £12.
Full board: £140 weekly.
Open March-April, June-September, December-January.

University of Manchester Sci. & Technology

P.O. Box 88, Sackville Street, Manchester, M60 1QD
☎ 061-236 3311 Ex2812
Telex 666094
Contact: Mr. A.F. Yates
Modern city centre campus within a few hundred yards of main coach and rail links. In addition to student bedrooms, we offer a hotel booking agency with discounted accommodation in city centre hotels.
Bedrooms: 1100 single, 36 twin/double. Total number of beds 1172.
Bathrooms: 300 public.
Bed & breakfast: £11-£14.
Full board: £120-£165 weekly.
Open December-January, March-April, June-September.

NEWCASTLE UPON TYNE

Tyne & Wear
Map ref 5C2

Commercial and cultural centre of the north east, with a large indoor shopping centre, Quayside market, museums and theatres which offer an annual 6 week season by the Royal Shakespeare Company. The Norman castle keep and the town's medieval alleys are near the river with its 6 bridges, old Guildhall and timbered merchants' houses. 🛈

Newcastle Polytechnic ♨

Coach Lane Campus Halls of Residence, Coach Lane, Newcastle upon Tyne, NE7 7XA
☎ 091-232 6002
Contact: Mrs. J. Kendall, Newcastle Upon Tyne Polytechnic, Elison Building, Ellison Place, Newcastle Upon Tyne, Tyne and Wear NE1 8ST
☎ 091-232 6002
Accommodation in modern halls of residence, set in pleasant grounds, 3 miles from the city centre.
Bedrooms: 100 single, 50 twin/double, 44 sleeping 3 or more. Total number of beds 244.
Bathrooms: 44 public.
Bed only: £6-£6.50.
Bed & breakfast: £8.75-£9.25.
Open July-September.

NEWPORT

Shropshire
Map ref 4A3

Small market town on the Shropshire Union Canal, it has a wide high street and its church has some interesting monuments. It is close to Aqualate Mere which is the largest lake in Staffordshire. 🛈

Harper Adams Agricultural College ♨

Newport, TF10 8NB
☎ (0952) 820280
Contact: Mrs. C. Paine
A country estate of 400 acres. Single study bedrooms. Conference, tutorial and sports facilities.
For groups only.

Bedrooms: 210 single. Total number of beds 210.
Bathrooms: 20 public.
Bed only: £8.05-£9.77.
Bed & breakfast: £9.77-£11.50.
Open January-April, July-September.

NORWICH

Norfolk
Map ref 3C1

Beautiful cathedral city and county town on the River Wensum with many fine museums and medieval churches. Norman castle, Guildhall and interesting medieval streets. Good shopping centre and market. 🛈

Norwich City College ♨

Southwell Lodge, Ipswich Rd., Norwich, NR2 2LL
☎ (0603) 618327
Contact: Mr. V.J. Seaman
Halls of residence built in 1972 on a pleasant, landscaped site south of Norwich, within 15 minutes' walk of city centre.
Min. age 18.
Bedrooms: 257 single, 6 twin/double. Total number of beds 269.
Bathrooms: 13 private, 16 public.
Bed & breakfast: £12.55-£15.25.
Open April, July-August.

NOTTINGHAM

Nottinghamshire
Map ref 4C2

Modern city with a wide range of industries including lace. Its castle is now a museum and art gallery with a statue of Robin Hood outside. The many attractions include excellent shopping facilities, theatres, museums, Wollaton Hall and the National Water Sports Centre. 🛈

University of Nottingham ♨

Conference Office, University Park, Nottingham, NG7 2RD
☎ (0602) 420420 Telex 37346
Contact: Ms. J. Lankester
A modern university with fine buildings in 300 acres of parkland, offering all facilities for conferences.
Min. age 17.

Bedrooms: 2600 single, 36 twin/double. Total number of beds 2672.
Bathrooms: 30 private, 1500 public.
Bed only: max. £8.85.
Bed & breakfast: max. £11.79.
Open January, March-April, July-September, December.

OTTERBURN

Northumberland
Map ref 5B1

Small village set at the meeting of the River Rede with Otter Burn, the site of the battle of Otterburn in 1388. A peaceful tradition continues in the sale of Otterburn tweeds in this beautiful region, which is ideal for exploring the border country and the Cheviots. 🛈

Otterburn Hall

Otterburn, NE19 1HE
☎ (0830) 20663
Contact: Mrs. Hardy
Family holiday hotel, conference venue and training establishment in 100 acres. Offering special interest holidays.
Min. age 10.
Bedrooms: 12 single, 36 twin/double. Total number of beds 120.
Bathrooms: 8 public.
Bed & breakfast: £17.25.

OXFORD

Oxfordshire
Map ref 2C1

Beautiful university town with many ancient colleges, some dating from the 13th C, and numerous buildings of historic and architectural interest. The Ashmolean Museum has outstanding collections. There are lovely gardens and meadows with punting on the Cherwell. 🛈

Cheney Hall, Oxford Polytechnic

Cheney Lane, Oxford, OX3 0BD
☎ (0865) 819113 Telex 83147 VIA

Continued ▶

OXFORD

Continued

Contact: Mr. P. Ledger,
Catering, Conference &
Residential Services, Oxford
Polytechnic, Gipsy Lane,
Headington, Oxford
OX3 0BP
☎ (0865) 819100
*Modern 3-storey flats for 8 to
12 persons. Surrounded by
trees in a hillside setting,
adjacent to large car park, with
superb views of Oxford's
dreaming spires.
For groups only.
Min. age 18.*
Bedrooms: 200 single. Total
number of beds 200.
Bathrooms: 18 public.
Bed only: from £7.50.
Open March-April, July-
September.
Ⓥ ⊞ ▥ ♨ ⧗ ♨ ⌇ ✿

SHEFFIELD

S. Yorkshire
Map ref 4B2

Local iron ore and coal
gave Sheffield its
prosperous steel and
cutlery industries. The
modern city centre retains
many interesting buildings
- cathedral, Cutlers' Hall,
Crucible Theatre, Graves
and Mappin Art Galleries
and has an excellent
shopping centre. Ⓘ

Sheffield YMCA
Residential Centre
20 Victoria Rd., Sheffield,
S10 2DL
☎ (0742) 684807
Contact: Residential Officer
*A large sports, social and
residential centre with facilities
for weddings, functions and
conferences. Children aged
between 10 and 18 are
accepted as part of a group.
Ages 18-60.*
Bedrooms: 80 single,
7 twin/double, 5 sleeping 3 or
more. Total number of
beds 124.
Bathrooms: 12 public.
Bed & breakfast: £5.50-£10.
Ⓤ Ⓥ ⊞ Ⓣⓥ ▥ ♨ ⧗ 🍽 ⌇
♨

SOUTHAMPTON

Hampshire
Map ref 2C3

One of Britain's leading
seaports with a long
history, and now
developed as a major
container port. In the 18th
C it became a fashionable
resort with the assembly
rooms and theatre. The
old Guildhall is now a
museum and the Wool
House a maritime
museum. Sections of the
medieval wall can still be
seen. Ⓘ

Southampton YMCA
International Youth
Hotel ♨
Cranbury Place, The Avenue,
Southampton, SO2 0LG
☎ (0703) 221202
Contact: The Executive
Director
*Educational groups welcome
from home and overseas.
Min. age 12.*
Bedrooms: 73 single,
5 twin/double. Total number
of beds 83.
Bathrooms: 15 public.
Bed & breakfast: £8-£10.
Ⓤ ⊞ Ⓣⓥ ▥ 🚐 🍽 ♨

SPARSHOLT

Hampshire
Map ref 2C2

Village in high position on
the downs. Nearby is
Farley Mount Bronze Age
Barrow and Horse
Monument.

Sparsholt College,
Hampshire ♨
Sparsholt, Winchester,
SO21 2NF
☎ (096 272) 441
Contact: Mr. R. Rogers
*The College is set among
rolling countryside with
unspoilt views and provides
accommodation with friendly
service. Ideal for conferences
or group holidays. Additional
accommodation opening in
1989.
Min. age 16.*
Bedrooms: 100 single. Total
number of beds 100.
Bathrooms: 21 public.
Bed & breakfast: from
£13.80.
Open July-September.
⊞ Ⓣⓥ ▥ ♨ 🚐 🍽 ⊙ ♨ ℗
✿ 🎦

STOKE-ON-TRENT

Staffordshire
Map ref 4B2

Famous for its
Wedgwood pottery,
whose factory along with
several other famous
makers can be visited.
The City Museum has
one of the finest pottery
and porcelain collections
in the world. Ⓘ

Stoke-on-Trent & North
Staffordshire YMCA
Edinburgh House, Harding
Rd., Hanley, Stoke-on-Trent,
ST1 3AE
☎ (0782) 202460
Contact: Mrs. M. Allbutt
*Modern YMCA hotel with
extensive facilities in the heart
of the Potteries. Convenient for
Hanley shopping centre.*
Bedrooms: 100 single. Total
number of beds 100.
Bathrooms: 21 public.
Bed & breakfast: £9-£12.
Ⓥ ⊞ Ⓣⓥ ▥ ♨ 🚐 🍽 ☼ ♨
♨ ⌇

WYE

Kent
Map ref 3B4

4m NE. Ashford
Well-known for its
agricultural and
horticultural college. The
Olantigh Tower with its
imposing front portico is
used as a setting for part
of the Stour Music
Festival held annually in
June.

Wye College (University
of London) ♨
Wye, Nr. Ashford,
TN25 5AH
☎ Wye (0233) 812401
Telex 96118
Contact: Mr. P. Belcher
*Close to the A28 between
Ashford and Canterbury, Wye
College offers excellent
conference facilities with
friendly service, in picturesque
surroundings.
For groups only.
Ages 16-70.*
Bedrooms: 146 single,
12 twin/double. Total number
of beds 181.
Bathrooms: 24 public.
Bed & breakfast:
max. £14.40.
Full board: max. £195 weekly.
Open March-April, July-
September.
Ⓥ ⊞ Ⓣⓥ ▥ ♨ 🚐 🍽 ⊙ ⌇
⧗ ℗ ✿ 🎦

YORK

N. Yorkshire
Map ref 4C1

Roman walled city nearly
2000 years old containing
many well preserved
medieval buildings (The
Shambles, Stonegate). Its
Minster has over 100
stained glass windows
spanning 800 years.
Castle Museum contains
city's history and there is
a National Railway
Museum. Many
attractions including a
new Wax Museum, Viking
Centre and York
Dungeon. Ⓘ

Bar Convent Youth
Centre
Blossom St., York, YO2 2AH
☎ (0904) 629359
Contact: Sister M. Agatha &
Miss H. Porthouse
*Accommodation for parties of
school children aged 7-16 with
special rates for accompanying
adults. Open 5pm to 10am.
Evening meal and packed
lunch included. Residents'
lounge and TV available for
use in evenings only.
For groups only.
Ages 7-16.*
Bedrooms: 9 single,
8 twin/double, 3 sleeping 3 or
more. Total number of
beds 46.
Bathrooms: 8 public.
Bed only: £6.25.
Bed & breakfast: £8.
Full board: £87.50 weekly.
Ⓤ Ⓥ Ⓣⓥ ▥ ♨ 🚐 ♨ 🎦

Racecourse Centre
Racing Stables, Dringhouses,
York, YO2 2QG
☎ (0904) 706317
Contact: Mrs. W. Patmore,
David Patmore Ltd., 5 High
Petergate, York, YO1 2EN
☎ (0904) 36553 & 636553
*Single-storey, hostel style
accommodation in a large safe
play area. Dormitories plus
students plus single or twin
rooms for group leaders.
For groups only.*
Bedrooms: 12 single,
8 twin/double, 9 sleeping 3 or
more. Total number of
beds 192.
Bathrooms: 11 public.
Bed only: from £5.75.
Bed & breakfast: from £6.90.
Full board: from £88.55
weekly.
Open March-August.
Ⓤ Ⓥ ⊞ Ⓣⓥ ▥ ♨ 🚐 🍽 ⊙
♨ ✿

PLEASE CHECK PRICES AND OTHER DETAILS
AT THE TIME OF BOOKING.

York Youth Hotel M
11-13 Bishophill Senior,
York, Y01 1EF
☎ (0904) 625904 Telex 57877
YYH
Contact: Maureen Sellers
*Dormitory-style
accommodation in the city
centre. Private rooms, TV
lounge, snack shop, evening
meals, packed lunches, games
room, residential licence, disco
and 24-hour service.*
Min. age 2.
Bedrooms: 7 single,
14 twin/double, 10 sleeping
3 or more. Total number of
beds 120.
Bathrooms: 8 public.
Bed only: £4-£7.
Bed & breakfast: £4.80-£8.80.
Full board: £84 weekly.
Ⓥ ✉ ⓣⓥ ▦ ☎ ▼ ♣ 🏠 Ⓣ

KENT HOUSE

STUDENT RESIDENCE
325 GREEN LANES,
LONDON N4 2ES
Tel. (01) 802 0800, 341 2105

**BUDGET ACCOMMODATION FOR
STUDENTS AND YOUNG TOURISTS**

FROM **£6.50**

★ 10 minutes from centre by underground and within easy reach of all London tourist attractions.
★ Facilities for self catering.
★ No curfew
★ Friendly young atmosphere - ages 16-40
★ Large common room/TV lounge + 2 kitchens for residents' use.
★ Single, double, twin and multi-bedded rooms.
★ Adjacent to Manor House Underground Station (Piccadilly Line) – 20 metres from Green Lanes South exit.

When enquiring about accommodation you may find it helpful to use the booking enquiry coupons which can be found towards the end of the guide. These should be cut out and mailed direct to the establishments in which you are interested. Remember to include your name and address and please enclose a stamped addressed envelope (or an international reply coupon if writing from outside Britain).

CROWN CLASSIFICATIONS

All the establishments displaying a national classification in this guide are inspected regularly. All can be chosen with confidence.

There are six classifications — from Listed to 5 Crowns; each indicates the level of facilities and services provided.

All classified establishments are required to provide a high standard of cleanliness, courtesy and service and to be well maintained. A lower classification does not imply lower standards; although the range of facilities and services may be smaller, they may be provided to a high standard.

You will find a full explanation of the national Crown Classification Scheme towards the end of this guide.

FOLLOW THE SIGN

It leads to over 550 Tourist Information Centres throughout England offering friendly help with accommodation and holiday ideas as well as suggestions of places to visit and things to do.

In your home town there may be a centre which can help you before you set out. If not, why not send for the Directory of Tourist Information Centres in Great Britain? It is available free from English Tourist Board, Department D, Bromells Road, Clapham, London SW4 0BJ.

BOOKING ENQUIRIES

➡ Please complete this coupon and mail it direct to the establishment in which you are interested. Do not send it to the English Tourist Board. Remember to enclose a stamped addressed envelope (or international reply coupon).

➡ Tick as appropriate and complete the reverse side if you are interested in making a booking.

➡ ☐ **Please send me a brochure or further information, and details of prices charged.**

➡ ☐ **Please advise me, as soon as possible, if accommodation is available as detailed overleaf.**

My name is: _____ (BLOCK CAPITALS)

Address: _____

_____

_____

Telephone number: _____ Date: _____

Where to Stay 1989 Farmhouses,
Bed & Breakfast, Inns and Hostels in England

🏵 **English Tourist Board** 👑

➡ Please complete this coupon and mail it direct to the establishment in which you are interested. Do not send it to the English Tourist Board. Remember to enclose a stamped addressed envelope (or international reply coupon).

➡ Tick as appropriate and complete the reverse side if you are interested in making a booking.

➡ ☐ **Please send me a brochure or further information, and details of prices charged.**

➡ ☐ **Please advise me, as soon as possible, if accommodation is available as detailed overleaf.**

My name is: _____ (BLOCK CAPITALS)

Address: _____

_____

_____

Telephone number: _____ Date: _____

Where to Stay 1989 Farmhouses,
Bed & Breakfast, Inns and Hostels in England

🏵 **English Tourist Board** 👑

➡ **Please complete this side if you are interested in making a booking.**

I am interested in booking accommodation for:

_____ adults and _____ children (ages: _____)

(Please give the number of people and the ages of any children)

From (date of arrival): _____ To (date of departure): _____

or alternatively from: _____ to: _____

Accommodation required: _____

Meals required: _____

Other/special requirements: _____

➡ **Please enclose a stamped addressed envelope (or international reply coupon).**

➡ **Please read the 'Further Information' section before confirming any booking.**

➡ **Please complete this side if you are interested in making a booking.**

I am interested in booking accommodation for:

_____ adults and _____ children (ages: _____)

(Please give the number of people and the ages of any children)

From (date of arrival): _____ To (date of departure): _____

or alternatively from: _____ to: _____

Accommodation required: _____

Meals required: _____

Other/special requirements: _____

➡ **Please enclose a stamped addressed envelope (or international reply coupon).**

➡ **Please read the 'Further Information' section before confirming any booking.**

BOOKING ENQUIRIES

COUPONS

BOOKING ENQUIRIES

➡ Please complete this coupon and mail it direct to the establishment in which you are interested. Do not send it to the English Tourist Board. Remember to enclose a stamped addressed envelope (or international reply coupon).

➡ Tick as appropriate and complete the reverse side if you are interested in making a booking.

➡ ☐ **Please send me a brochure or further information, and details of prices charged.**
➡ ☐ **Please advise me, as soon as possible, if accommodation is available as detailed overleaf.**

My name is: (BLOCK CAPITALS)

Address:

Telephone number: Date:

Where to Stay 1989 Farmhouses,
Bed & Breakfast, Inns and Hostels in England

English Tourist Board

➡ Please complete this coupon and mail it direct to the establishment in which you are interested. Do not send it to the English Tourist Board. Remember to enclose a stamped addressed envelope (or international reply coupon).

➡ Tick as appropriate and complete the reverse side if you are interested in making a booking.

➡ ☐ **Please send me a brochure or further information, and details of prices charged.**
➡ ☐ **Please advise me, as soon as possible, if accommodation is available as detailed overleaf.**

My name is: (BLOCK CAPITALS)

Address:

Telephone number: Date:

Where to Stay 1989 Farmhouses,
Bed & Breakfast, Inns and Hostels in England

English Tourist Board

➡ **Please complete this side if you are interested in making a booking.**

I am interested in booking accommodation for:

_____ adults and _____ children (ages: _____)

(Please give the number of people and the ages of any children)

From (date of arrival): _____ To (date of departure): _____

or alternatively from: _____ to: _____

Accommodation required: _____

_____

Meals required: _____

Other/special requirements: _____

➡ **Please enclose a stamped addressed envelope (or international reply coupon).**

➡ **Please read the 'Further Information' section before confirming any booking.**

➡ **Please complete this side if you are interested in making a booking.**

I am interested in booking accommodation for:

_____ adults and _____ children (ages: _____)

(Please give the number of people and the ages of any children)

From (date of arrival): _____ To (date of departure): _____

or alternatively from: _____ to: _____

Accommodation required: _____

_____

Meals required: _____

Other/special requirements: _____

➡ **Please enclose a stamped addressed envelope (or international reply coupon).**

➡ **Please read the 'Further Information' section before confirming any booking.**

BOOKING ENQUIRIES

COUPONS

BOOKING ENQUIRIES

➡ Please complete this coupon and mail it direct to the establishment in which you are interested. Do not send it to the English Tourist Board. Remember to enclose a stamped addressed envelope (or international reply coupon).

➡ Tick as appropriate and complete the reverse side if you are interested in making a booking.

➡ ☐ **Please send me a brochure or further information, and details of prices charged.**

➡ ☐ **Please advise me, as soon as possible, if accommodation is available as detailed overleaf.**

My name is: _____ (BLOCK CAPITALS)

Address: _____

_____

_____

Telephone number: _____ Date: _____

Where to Stay 1989 Farmhouses,
Bed & Breakfast, Inns and Hostels in England

🌸 English Tourist Board 👑

➡ Please complete this coupon and mail it direct to the establishment in which you are interested. Do not send it to the English Tourist Board. Remember to enclose a stamped addressed envelope (or international reply coupon).

➡ Tick as appropriate and complete the reverse side if you are interested in making a booking.

➡ ☐ **Please send me a brochure or further information, and details of prices charged.**

➡ ☐ **Please advise me, as soon as possible, if accommodation is available as detailed overleaf.**

My name is: _____ (BLOCK CAPITALS)

Address: _____

_____

_____

Telephone number: _____ Date: _____

Where to Stay 1989 Farmhouses,
Bed & Breakfast, Inns and Hostels in England

🌸 English Tourist Board 👑

➡ **Please complete this side if you are interested in making a booking.**

I am interested in booking accommodation for:

_____ adults and _____ children (ages: _____)

(Please give the number of people and the ages of any children)

From (date of arrival): _____ To (date of departure): _____

or alternatively from: _____ to: _____

Accommodation required: _____

Meals required: _____

Other/special requirements: _____

➡ **Please enclose a stamped addressed envelope (or international reply coupon).**

➡ **Please read the 'Further Information' section before confirming any booking.**

➡ **Please complete this side if you are interested in making a booking.**

I am interested in booking accommodation for:

_____ adults and _____ children (ages: _____)

(Please give the number of people and the ages of any children)

From (date of arrival): _____ To (date of departure): _____

or alternatively from: _____ to: _____

Accommodation required: _____

Meals required: _____

Other/special requirements: _____

➡ **Please enclose a stamped addressed envelope (or international reply coupon).**

➡ **Please read the 'Further Information' section before confirming any booking.**

BOOKING ENQUIRIES

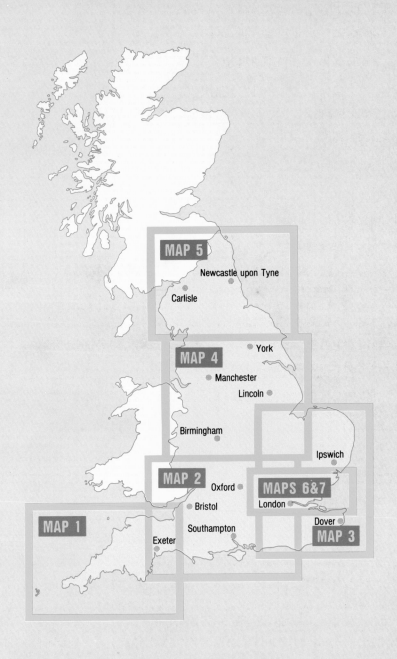

MAP 5

Newcastle upon Tyne

Carlisle

MAP 4

York

Manchester

Lincoln

Birmingham

Ipswich

MAP 2

Oxford

MAPS 6&7

London

Bristol

MAP 1

Dover

Southampton

MAP 3

Exeter

M A P 1

A

B

1

2

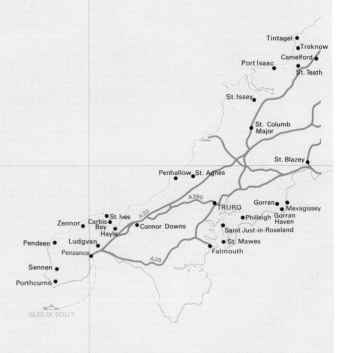

Tintagel
Treknow
Camelford
Port Isaac
St. Teath
St. Issey
St. Columb Major
St. Blazey
Penhallow St. Agnes
Gorran
Mevagissey
A390
TRURO
Philleigh Gorran Haven
Zennor
St. Ives
Carbis Bay
Hayle
Connor Downs
A30
Saint Just-in-Roseland
Pendeen
Ludgvan
St. Mawes
Penzance
Falmouth
Sennen
A39
Porthcurno
3
ISLES OF SCILLY

Based upon Ordnance Survey maps with the permission of The Controller of H.M. Stationery Office, Crown Copyright Reserved.

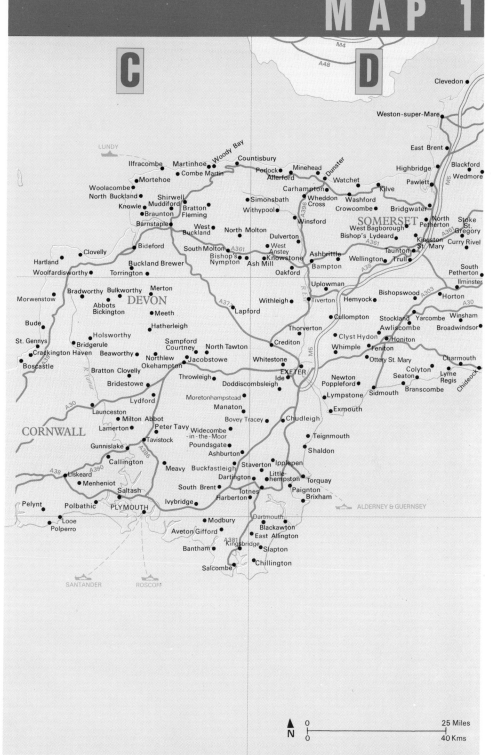

C

D

Clevedon

Weston-super-Mare

East Brent

LUNDY

Ilfracombe   Martinhoe   Woody Bay   Countisbury
Mortehoe   Combe Martin   Porlock   Minehead   Dunster   Highbridge   Blackford
Woolacombe   Shirwell   Allerford   Watchet   Pawlett   Wedmore
North Buckland   Muddiford   Bratton   Simonsbath   Wheddon   Washford   Kilve
Knowle   Braunton   Fleming   Withypool   Cross   Crowcombe   Bridgwater   SOMERSET
Barnstaple   West   North Molton   Winsford   West Bagborough   North   Stoke
Buckland   Dulverton   Bishop's Lydeard   Petherton   St.
Bideford   South Molton   West   Kingston   Gregory   Curry Rivel
Clovelly   Bishop's   Anstey   Ashbrittle   Taunton   St. Mary
Buckland Brewer   Nympton   Knowstone   Wellington   Trull
Hartland   Torrington   Ash Mill   Bampton   South
Woolfardisworthy   Oakford   Petherton

Morwenstow   Bradworthy   Bulkworthy   Merton   Uplowman   Ilminster
DEVON   Withleigh   Tiverton   Hemyock   Bishopswood   Horton
Abbots   Meeth   Lapford   Cullompton   Stockland   Yarcombe   Winsham
Bude   Bickington   Hatherleigh   Thorverton   Awliscombe   Broadwinsor
St. Gennys   Holsworthy   Sampford   North Tawton   Crediton   Clyst Hydon   Honiton   Charmouth
Crackington Haven   Bridgerule   Courtney   Whimple   Feniton   Colyton   Lyme
Boscastle   Beaworthy   Northlew   Jacobstowe   Whitestone   Ottery St. Mary   Seaton   Regis   Chideock
Bratton Clovelly   Okehampton   EXETER   Newton   Branscombe
Bridestowe   Throwleigh   Doddiscombsleigh   Ide   Poppleford   Sidmouth
Lydford   Moretonhampstead   Lympstone
Launceston   Manaton   Exmouth
Milton Abbot   Bovey Tracey   Chudleigh
CORNWALL   Lamerton   Peter Tavy   Teignmouth
Gunnislake   Widecombe   Shaldon
Tavistock   -in-the-Moor
Callington   Poundsgate   Ashburton
Meavy   Buckfastleigh   Staverton   Ipplepen
Liskeard   Dartington   Little-   Torquay
Menheniot   South Brent   hempston   Paignton
Saltash   Totnes   Brixham
Pelynt   Polbathic   Ivybridge   Harberton
PLYMOUTH   ALDERNEY & GUERNSEY
Looe   Modbury   Dartmouth
Polperro   Aveton Gifford   Blackawton
Bantham   Kingsbridge   East Allington
Salcombe   Slapton
Chillington

SANTANDER   ROSCOFF

N
0   25 Miles
0   40 Kms

Produced by E.S.R. Limited, West Byfleet, Surrey

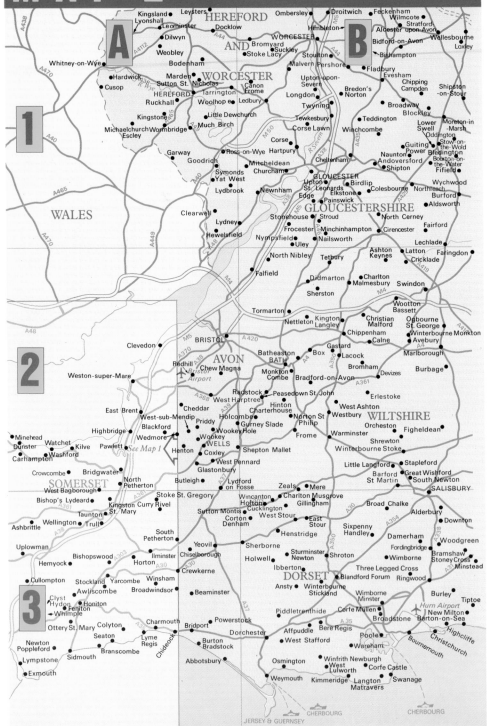

MAP 2

A **B** **1** **2** **3**

Kingsland
Lyonshall
Leysters
Leominster
HEREFORD
Docklow
Ombersley
Droitwich
Feckenham
Wilmcote
Stratford
Alcester upon-Avon
Wellesbourne
Loxley
Himbleton
WORCESTER
Bidford-on-Avon
Bishampton

Whitney-on-Wye
Dilwyn
Weobley
Bodenham
Bromyard
Suckley
Stoke Lacy
Stoulton
Malvern Pershore
Fladbury
Evesham
Chipping
Campden
Shipston
-on-Stour

Hardwick
Cusop
Marden
Sutton St. Nicholas
HEREFORD
Tarrington
Ruckhall
Woolhop e
Canon
Frome
Ledbury
Upton-upon-
Severn
Longdon
Bredon's
Norton
Broadway
Blockley
Teddington
Lower
Swell
Moreton-in
-Marsh
Oddington
Stow-on-
the-Wold

Kingstone
Michaelchurch
Escley
Wormbridge
Little Dewchurch
Much Birch
Twyning
Tewkesbury
Corse Lawn
Winchcombe
Guiting
Power
Naunton
Andoversford
Shipton
Bledington
Bourton-on-
the-Water
Fifield

Garway
Goodrich
Ross-on-Wye
Mitcheldean
Corse
Hartpury
Churcham
Cheltenham
Birdlip
Colesbourne
Northleach
Wychwood
Burford
Aldsworth

Symonds
Yat West
Lydbrook
Newnham
Upton
St. Leonards
Elkstone
Edge
Painswick
GLOUCESTER

WALES
Clearwell
Lydney
Hewelsfield
Stonehouse
Stroud
Frocester
Nympsfield
Uley
Minchinhampton
Nailsworth
North Cerney
Cirencester
Fairford
Lechlade
Latton
Faringdon

North Nibley
Tetbury
Ashton
Keynes
Cricklade

Falfield
Didmarton
Malmesbury
Swindon
Charlton

Sherston
Tormarton
Nettleton
Kington
Langley
Christian
Malford
Wootton
Bassett
Ogbourne
St. George
Winterbourne Monkton
Avebury

Chippenham
Calne
Marlborough
Burbage

Clevedon
BRISTOL
AVON
Batheaston
BATH
Box
Gastard
Lacock
Bromham
Devizes

Redhill
Bristol
Airport
Chew Magna
Monkton
Combe
Bradford-on-Avon
Erlestoke

Weston-super-Mare
Radstock
West Harptree
Peasedown St. John
Hinton
Charterhouse
West Ashton
Westbury
WILTSHIRE

East Brent
Cheddar
West-sub-Mendip
Priddy
Holcombe
Gurney Slade
Norton St
Philip
Warminster
Orcheston
Figheldean

Highbridge
Blackford
Wedmore
Wookey
Wookey Hole
Frome
Shrewton
Winterbourne Stoke

Minehead
Watchet
Dunster
Kilve
Pawlett
See Map 1
WELLS
Coxley
Henton
Shepton Mallet
Little Langford
Stapleford

Carhampton
Washford
West Pennard
Barford
St. Martin
Great Wishford
South Newton

Crowcombe
Bridgwater
Butleigh
Glastonbury
Lydford
on Fosse
Zeals
Mere
Charlton Musgrove
Broad Chalke
SALISBURY

West Bagborough
North
Petherton
Stoke St. Gregory
Wincanton
Holton
Gillingham
Alderbury

Bishop's Lydeard
Curry Rivel
Sutton Montis
Cucklington
West Stour
Sixpenny
Handley
Downton

Kingston
St. Mary
Corton
Denham
East
Stour
Damerham
Woodgreen

Taunton
Trull
South
Petherton
Yeovil
Sherborne
Henstridge
Fordingbridge
Bramshaw
Stoney Cross

Ashbrittle
Wellington
Chiselborough
Holwell
Sturminster
Newton
Shroton
Wimborne
Minstead

Uplowman
Bishopswood
Ilminster
Horton
Crewkerne
Ibberton
Three Legged Cross
Ringwood

Hemyock
Winsham
Blandford Forum
Burley
Tiptoe

Cullompton
Stockland
Yarcombe
Broadwindsor
Beaminster
Ansty
Winterbourne
Stickland
Wimborne
Minster
New Milton
Barton-on-Sea

Awliscombe
Honiton
Corfe Mullen
Broadstone
Hurn Airport

Clyst
Hydon
Whimple
Charmouth
Powerstock
Piddletrenthide
Bere Regis
Poole
Highcliffe
Christchurch

Ottery St. Mary
Colyton
Bridport
Dorchester
Affpuddle
West Stafford
Wareham
Bournemouth

Newton
Poppleford
Seaton
Lyme Regis
Chideock
Burton
Bradstock
Abbotsbury
Osmington
Winfrith Newburgh
West
Lulworth
Corfe Castle
Swanage

Lympstone
Sidmouth
Branscombe
Weymouth
Kimmeridge
Langton
Matravers

Exmouth

DORSET
SOMERSET
GLOUCESTERSHIRE

JERSEY & GUERNSEY
CHERBOURG
CHERBOURG

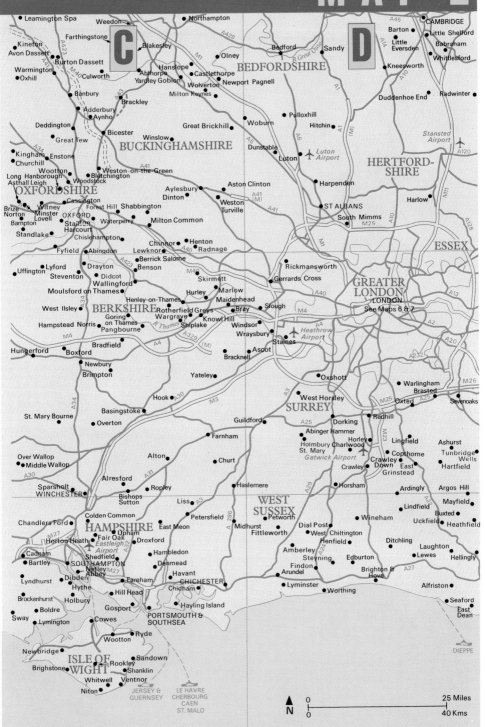

MAP 2

C

Leamington Spa
Weedon
Northampton
CAMBRIDGE
Barton
Little Shelford

D

Kineton
Farthingstone
Blakesley
Bedford
R Great Ouse
Sandy
Little Eversden
Babraham
Avon Dassett
Burton Dassett
Olney
Whittlesford
Warmington
Culworth
Abthorpe
Hanslope
Castlethorpe
Newport Pagnell
Kneesworth
Oxhill
Yardley Gobion
Wolverton
Banbury
Milton Keynes
Duddenhoe End
Radwinter
Adderbury
Brackley
Aynho
Woburn
Pulloxhill
Deddington
Bicester
Great Brickhill
Hitchin
Winslow
Stansted Airport
Great Tew
Dunstable
BUCKINGHAMSHIRE
Luton
Kingham
Enstone
Luton Airport
HERTFORD-SHIRE
Churchill
Weston-on-the-Green
Wootton
Long Hanborough
Bletchington
Aylesbury
Aston Clinton
Harpenden
Asthall Leigh
Woodstock
Dinton
Weston Turville
OXFORDSHIRE
Cassington
Forest Hill
Shabbington
ST ALBANS
Harlow
Brize Norton
Witney
OXFORD
South Mimms
Minster Lovell
Stanton Harcourt
Waterperry
Milton Common
Bampton
Chislehampton
Chinnor
Henton
Standlake
Lewknor
Radnage
Fyfield
Abingdon
Berrick Salome
ESSEX
Uffington
Lyford
Drayton
Benson
Rickmansworth
Steventon
Didcot
Gerrards Cross
Skirmett
GREATER LONDON
Moulsford on Thames
Wallingford
Hurley
Marlow
LONDON
See Maps 6 & 7
West Ilsley
Henley-on-Thames
Maidenhead
Slough
BERKSHIRE
Rotherfield Greys
Bray
Hampstead Norris
Goring on Thames
Wargrave
Knowl Hill
Shiplake
Windsor
Heathrow Airport
Pangbourne
Wraysbury
Staines
Hungerford
Bradfield
Ascot
Boxford
Bracknell
Newbury
Brimpton
Yateley
Oxshott
Warlingham
Brasted
West Horsley
Oxted
Sevenoaks
St. Mary Bourne
Hook
SURREY
Basingstoke
Dorking
Redhill
Overton
Guildford
Abinger Hammer
Lingfield
Farnham
Holmbury Charlwood
St. Mary
Ashurst
Over Wallop
Horley
Copthorne
Tunbridge Wells
Middle Wallop
Alton
Churt
Gatwick Airport
Crawley
Down
East
Hartfield
Alresford
Crawley
Grinstead
Sparsholt
Ropley
Haslemere
Ardingly
Argos Hill
WINCHESTER
Horsham
Lindfield
Mayfield
Bishops Sutton
Liss
WEST SUSSEX
Wineham
Uckfield
Buxted
Chandlers Ford
Colden Common
Petersfield
Petworth
Heathfield
Upham
East Meon
Midhurst
Dial Post
Ditchling
HAMPSHIRE
Fair Oak
Droxford
Fittleworth
West Chiltington
Laughton
Horton Heath
Eastleigh Airport
Hambledon
Amberley
Henfield
Edburton
Lewes
Cadnam
Shedfield
Denmead
Steyning
Hellingly
Bartley
SOUTHAMPTON
Netley Abbey
Havant
Findon
Brighton & Hove
Lyndhurst
Dibden
Fareham
CHICHESTER
Arundel
Dibden
Hythe
Chidham
Lyminster
Worthing
Alfriston
Brockenhurst
Holbury
Hill Head
Hayling Island
Seaford
Sway
Boldre
Gosport
Lymington
Cowes
PORTSMOUTH & SOUTHSEA
East Dean
Ryde
Newbridge
Wootton
DIEPPE
ISLE OF WIGHT
Sandown
Brighstone
Rookley
Shanklin
Whitwell
Ventnor
Niton
JERSEY & GUERNSEY
LE HAVRE
CHERBOURG
CAEN
ST. MALO

0   25 Miles
N
0   40 Kms

Produced by E.S.R. Limited, West Byfleet, Surrey

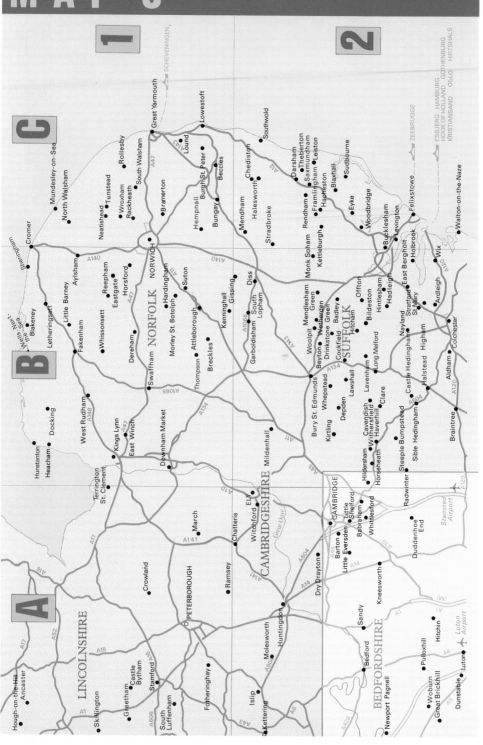

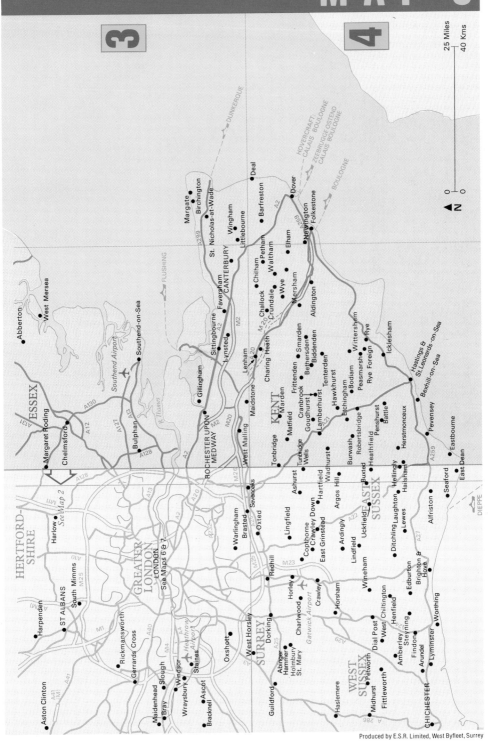

M A P 3

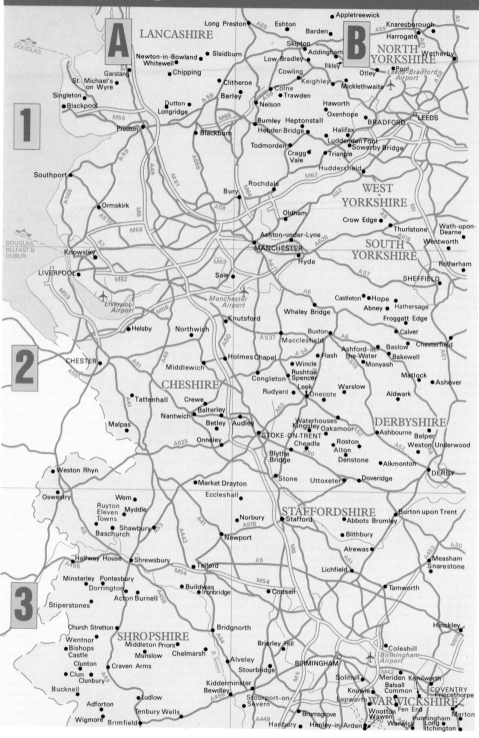

MAP 4

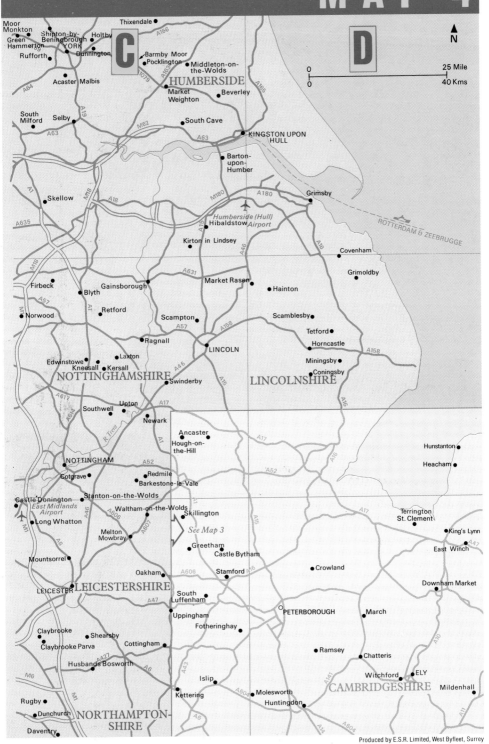

MAP 4

N

0   25 Mile
0   40 Kms

C   **D**

Moor
Monkton
Green   Shipton-by-
Hammerton   Beningbrough   Holtby
   YORK
Rufforth   Dunnington

Thixendale

Barmby Moor
Pocklington   Middleton-on-
       the-Wolds

HUMBERSIDE

Market
Weighton   Beverley

Acaster Malbis

South   Selby
Milford

South Cave

KINGSTON UPON
HULL

Barton-
upon-
Humber

Skellow

Grimsby

ROTTERDAM & ZEEBRUGGE

Humberside (Hull)
Hibaldstow   Airport

Covenham

Kirton in Lindsey

Grimoldby

Firbeck   Gainsborough   Market Rasen
   Blyth

Hainton

Norwood   Retford

Scamblesby

Scampton

Tetford
Ragnall   Horncastle

LINCOLN

Edwinstowe   Laxton
Kneesall   Kersall   Miningsby
NOTTINGHAMSHIRE   Coningsby
Swinderby   ## LINCOLNSHIRE

Upton
Southwell

Newark

Ancaster
Hough-on-
the-Hill

Hunstanton

NOTTINGHAM   Heacham
Cotgrave   Redmile
     Barkestone-le-Vale

Stanton-on-the-Wolds   Terrington
Castle Donington   St. Clement
East Midlands   Waltham-on-the-Wolds
Airport   Skillington   King's Lynn
Long Whatton   *See Map 3*
Melton   East Winch
Mowbray   Greetham
   Castle Bytham
Mountsorrel   Crowland   Downham Market

Oakham   Stamford
LEICESTER ## LEICESTERSHIRE
South   March
Luffenham
Uppingham   PETERBOROUGH

Claybrooke   Shearsby   Fotheringhay
Claybrooke Parva   Cottingham   Ramsey   Chatteris
Husbands Bosworth   Witchford   ELY
   Islip   ## CAMBRIDGESHIRE   Mildenhall
Rugby   Kettering   Molesworth
Dunchurch   Huntingdon
Daventry   ## NORTHAMPTON-
        SHIRE

Produced by E.S.R. Limited, West Byfleet, Surrey

MAP 5

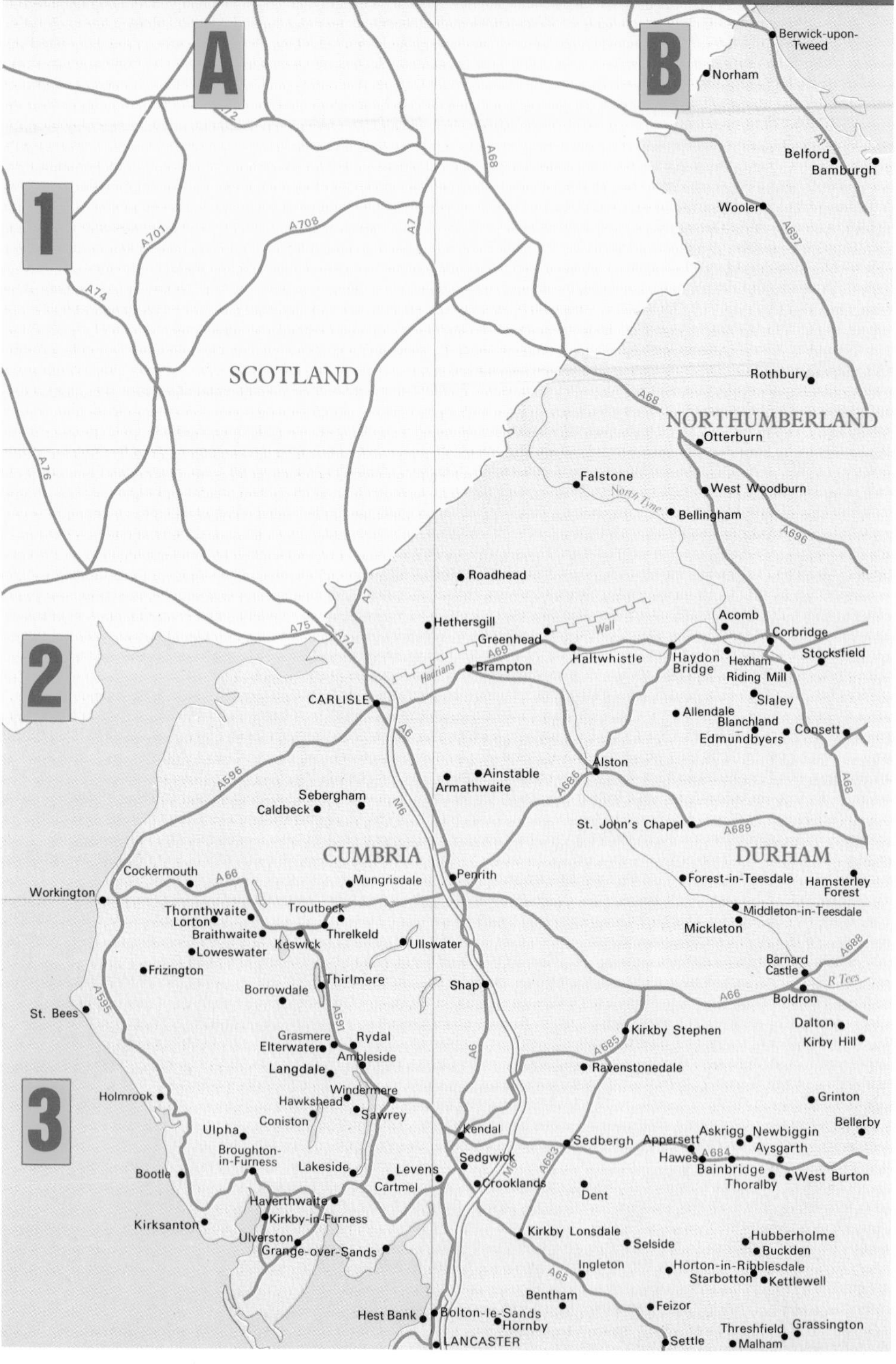

A
B

1

2

3

SCOTLAND

NORTHUMBERLAND

CUMBRIA

DURHAM

Berwick-upon-Tweed
Norham
Belford
Bamburgh
Wooler
Rothbury
Otterburn
Falstone
West Woodburn
Bellingham
North Tyne
Roadhead
Hethersgill
Acomb
Corbridge
Greenhead
Wall
Stocksfield
Haltwhistle
Haydon Bridge
Hexham
Riding Mill
Slaley
Brampton
CARLISLE
Allendale
Blanchland
Consett
Edmundbyers
Alston
Ainstable
Armathwaite
St. John's Chapel
Sebergham
Caldbeck
Penrith
Forest-in-Teesdale
Hamsterley Forest
Cockermouth
Mungrisdale
Middleton-in-Teesdale
Mickleton
Workington
Thornthwaite
Lorton
Troutbeck
Braithwaite
Threlkeld
Keswick
Ullswater
Loweswater
Barnard Castle
R Tees
Frizington
Thirlmere
Shap
Boldron
Borrowdale
Dalton
St. Bees
Kirby Hill
Grasmere
Rydal
Kirkby Stephen
Elterwater
Ambleside
Holmrook
Langdale
Windermere
Ravenstonedale
Grinton
Hawkshead
Sawrey
Bellerby
Ulpha
Coniston
Askrigg
Newbiggin
Broughton-in-Furness
Kendal
Sedbergh
Appersett
Aysgarth
Bootle
Lakeside
Levens
Hawes
Bainbridge
West Burton
Sedgwick
Thoralby
Kirksanton
Haverthwaite
Cartmel
Crooklands
Dent
Kirkby-in-Furness
Kirkby Lonsdale
Hubberholme
Ulverston
Grange-over-Sands
Selside
Buckden
Ingleton
Horton-in-Ribblesdale
Starbotton
Kettlewell
Bentham
Feizor
Hest Bank
Bolton-le-Sands
Threshfield
Grassington
Hornby
LANCASTER
Settle
Malham

MAP 5

C

D

N 0 ————— 25 Miles
   0 ————— 40 Kms

Seahouses
Beadnell
Chathill
Craster
Alnwick Alnmouth
Warkworth Amble-by-the-Sea

Morpeth
Bedlington
Newcastle Airport
Ponteland

BERGEN AND STAVANGER
GOTHENBURG
ESBJERG

TYNE AND
A69 NEWCASTLE UPON TYNE
WEAR

Rowlands Gill Sunderland
Tantobie
Chester-le-Street

Brancepeth
DURHAM A1(M)
Crook
Spennymoor
Bishop Auckland

Heighington

Redcar

A66
CLEVELAND Staithes
Forcett Darlington Ellerby Whitby
A19 A171
Carlton Sleights
Ingleby Grosmont Robin Hood's Bay
Skeeby Greenhow Ravenscar
Richmond Goathland
Hackforth Osmotherley Farndale Rosedale Abbey Cloughton
Scruton NORTH YORKSHIRE
Crakehall Newby Bilsdale West Gillamoor Appleton-le-Moors Scarborough
Spennithorne Wiske Hawnby Kirkbymoorside East Ayton Osgodby
Bedale South Otterington Pickering
Thornton Sutton Helmsley Allerston Snainton
Healey Watlass Thirsk Bank Sproxton East Heslerton
Masham Sowerby Kilburn Ampleforth
Wath Dalton Coxwold
Hutton Conyers Husthwaite Malton Weaverthorpe Flamborough
RIPON Crayke Stittenham Scagglethorpe
Easingwold A64 Sledmere
Pateley Bridge Myton-on-Swale Kirkham
Summer BishopThornton Tollerton A165
Bridge Marton-cum-Grafton Linton-on-Ouse A66

Produced by E.S.R. Limited, West Byfleet, Surrey

MAP 6

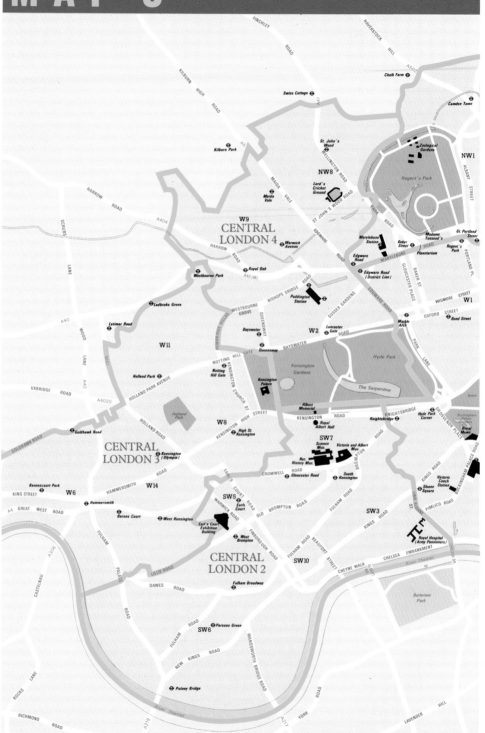

CENTRAL LONDON 4

CENTRAL LONDON 3

CENTRAL LONDON 2

© BTA

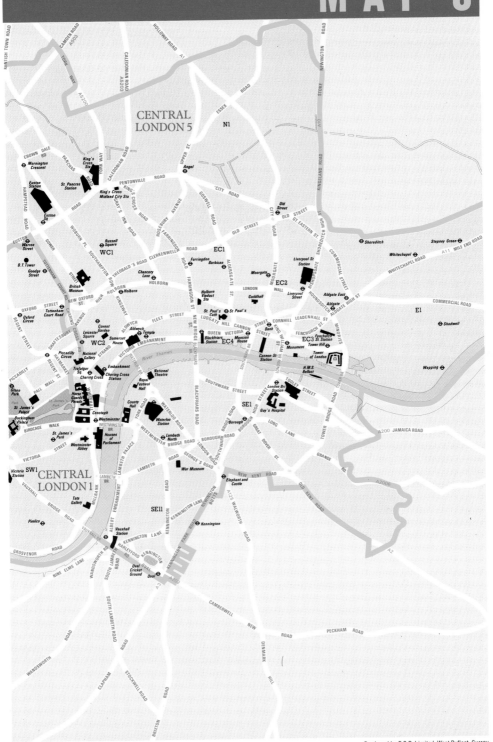

MAP 6

MAP 7

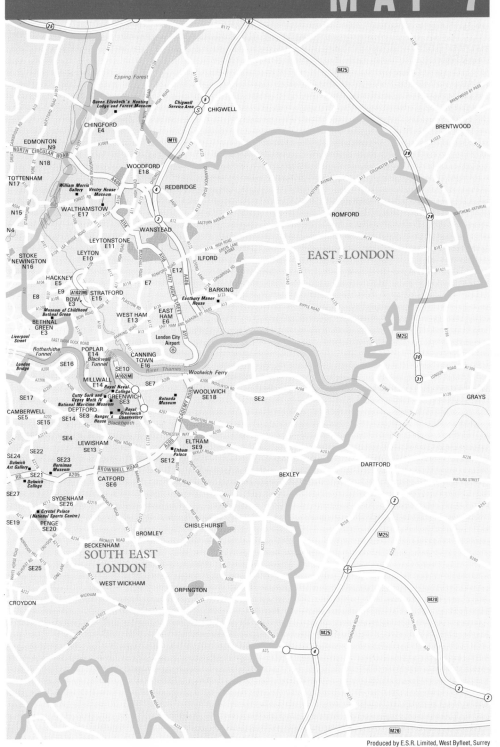

MAP 7

Rickerby Grange

PORTINSCALE, KESWICK, CUMBRIA CA12 5RH.

Quiet location in the pretty village of Portinscale — two minutes A66, five minutes walk via scenic route along public footpath. Ideal base for exploring the lakes by foot or car.

Comfortable accommodation with first class facilities in friendly surroundings and real home cooked meals to satisfy the heartiest of appetites.

Quiet lounge, TV lounge and Bar lounge for guest use. Three ground floor rooms — two with separate patio door entrance. Large private Car Park. AA "Specially Recommended Award 1987", "Selected Award 1988".

For colour brochure telephone Rodney or Margaret Roper on Keswick (0596) 72344.

J O U R N E Y S

TRAIN JOURNEYS THROUGH BRITISH LANDSCAPES

Published by David and Charles in association with the English Tourist Board

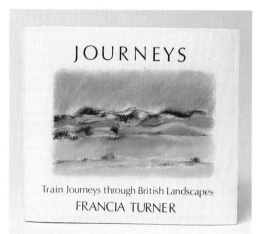

"Whenever I board a train I feel a tremendous enthusiasm in anticipation of the unfolding experience to come", says Francia Turner, artist and writer, who has translated her feelings about train journeys into images and words. Sponsored by British Rail, from Wick to Penzance.

Hardback, price £14.95
Available June 1989 from
all good bookshops.

CROWN CLASSIFICATIONS

All the establishments displaying a national classification in this guide are inspected regularly. All can be chosen with confidence.

There are six classifications — from Listed to 5 Crowns; each indicates the level of facilities and services provided.

All classified establishments are required to provide a high standard of cleanliness, courtesy and service and to be well maintained. A lower classification does not imply lower standards; although the range of facilities and services may be smaller, they may be provided to a high standard.

You will find a full explanation of the national Crown Classification Scheme towards the end of this guide.

♣ Enjoy the countryside and respect its life and work ♣ Guard against all risk of fire ♣ Fasten all gates ♣ Keep your dogs under close control ♣ Keep to public paths across farmland ♣ Use gates and stiles to cross fences, hedges and walls ♣ Leave livestock, crops and machinery alone ♣ Take your litter home ♣ Help to keep all water clean ♣ Protect wildlife, plants and trees ♣ Take special care on country roads ♣ Make no unnecessary noise

FOLLOW THE SIGN

It leads to over 550 Tourist Information Centres throughout England offering friendly help with accommodation and holiday ideas as well as suggestions of places to visit and

things to do. In your home town there may be a centre which can help you before you set out. If not, why not send for the Directory of Tourist Information Centres in Great Britain? It is available free from English Tourist Board, Department D, Bromells Road, Clapham, London SW4 0BJ.

PRICES

The prices appearing in this publication will serve as a general guide, but we strongly advise you to check them at the time of booking. This information was supplied to us by proprietors in the summer of 1988 and changes may have occurred since the guide went to press. Prices are shown in pounds sterling and include Value Added Tax if applicable.

double room price is for two people. If a double room is occupied by one person there is normally a reduction in the quoted tariff, but some establishments may charge the full rate.

2. Half board. Price for room, breakfast and evening meal, per person per day and per person per week.

A number of establishments do not quote or offer an inclusive room and breakfast rate in their published tariff. In such cases the minimum charge for

is to ensure that prospective guests can obtain adequate information about prices before taking up accommodation.

When you arrive it is in your own interests to check prices and what they include.

A reduced price is often quoted for children, especially when sharing a room with their parents. Some establishments, however, charge the full price when a child occupies a room which might otherwise have been let at the full rate to an adult.

The upper age limit for reductions for children may vary according to the establishment and should therefore be checked at the time of booking.

Prices often vary according to the time of year and may be substantially lower outside the peak holiday weeks. Many hotels and other establishments offer special 'package' rates (for example, fully inclusive weekend rates) particularly in the autumn, winter and spring.

Further details of bargain packages can be obtained from the establishments themselves or from the English Tourist Board and England's regional tourist boards. Your local travel agent may also have information about these packages and can help you make bookings.

Establishments which offer a special Christmas/New Year package have been indicated by means of a holly leaf symbol ✳.

Some, but not all, establishments include a service charge in their standard tariff so this should also be checked at the time of booking.

There are many different ways of quoting prices for accommodation and in order to make this as clear as possible and provide a basis for comparison we have adopted a standardised approach.
For example, we show:
1. Bed and breakfast. Price for overnight accommodation with breakfast — single room and double room. The

breakfast has been added to the room charge to arrive at a combined price.

Some establishments provide a continental breakfast only for the room and breakfast tariff and make an extra charge if a full English breakfast is ordered. Establishments which provide a continental breakfast only are indicated by the symbol CB .

There is a statutory requirement for establishments which have at least four bedrooms, or eight beds, to display overnight accommodation charges in the reception area or at the entrance. This

TIPPING

Many establishments now levy a service charge automatically and if so this fact must be stated clearly in the offer of accommodation at the time of booking. If the offer is then accepted by the customer the service charge becomes part of the contract.

At establishments where a service charge of this kind is made there is no need for guests to give tips to the staff unless some particular or exceptional service has been rendered. In the case of meals the usual amount is 10% of the total bill.

CHARGES FOR TELEPHONE CALLS

The provision of a telephone for the use of guests can mean considerable overhead expenses for the management.

There are two ways of covering these costs. The first is by including an amount to defray telephone costs in the quoted tariff for all bedrooms. The second method is to levy a small extra service charge on telephone calls made by guests.

Many proprietors think it is unfair to charge all guests whether or not they use the telephone and so they make a surcharge on calls put through their telephone system. Before making long trunk calls within Britain or calls to places outside Britain, we advise you to check the charges made by the establishment.

MAKING A BOOKING

When enquiring about accommodation, as well as checking prices and other details you will need to state your requirements clearly and precisely — for example:

1. Arrival and departure dates with acceptable alternatives if appropriate.

2. The accommodation you need. For example: double room with twin beds, private bath and toilet.

3. The terms you want. For example: room only; bed & breakfast; bed, breakfast and evening meal (half board); bed, breakfast, lunch and evening meal (full board).

4. If you have children with you give their ages, state whether you would like them to share your room or have an adjacent room and mention any special requirements such as a cot.

5. Tell the management about any particular requirements such as a ground floor room or special diet.

Misunderstandings can occur very easily over the telephone so we recommend that all bookings should be confirmed in writing if time permits.

When first enquiring in writing about a reservation you may find it helpful to use the booking enquiry coupons at the back of this guide which can be cut out and mailed to the establishment(s) of your choice. Remember to include your name and address and please enclose a stamped and addressed envelope or an international reply coupon if writing from outside Britain.

ARRIVING LATE IN THE EVENING

If you will be arriving late in the evening it is advisable to say so at the time of booking; if you are delayed on

your way, a telephone call to inform the management that you will be late might help to avoid problems on arrival.

DEPOSITS AND ADVANCE PAYMENTS

For reservations made weeks or months ahead a deposit is usually payable and the amount will vary according to the length of booking, time of year, number in party and so on. The deposit is then deducted from the total bill at the end of the stay.

More and more establishments, particularly larger hotels in big towns, now require payment for the room on arrival if a prior reservation has not been made — especially when a guest arrives late and/or with little luggage. Regrettably this practice has become necessary because of the number of guests who have left without paying their bills. If you are asked to pay on arrival it may be advisable to see your room first to ensure that it meets your requirements.

CANCELLATIONS

When you accept offered accommodation, on the telephone or in writing, you may be entering into a legally binding contract with the proprietor of the establishment. This means that if you cancel a reservation, fail to take up the accommodation or leave prematurely the proprietor may be entitled to compensation if the accommodation cannot be relet for all or a good part of the booked period. If a deposit has been paid it is likely to be forfeited and an additional payment may be demanded.

However, no such claim can be made by the proprietor until after the booked period, during which time every effort should be made to relet the accommodation. Any circumstances ▶

▶ which might lead to repudiation of a contract may also need to be taken into account and, in the case of a dispute, legal advice should be sought by both parties.

It is therefore in your interest to advise the management immediately if you have to change your travel plans, cancel a booking or leave prematurely.

INSURANCE

Travel and holiday insurance protection policies are available quite cheaply and will safeguard you in the event of your having to cancel or curtail your holiday. Your insurance company or travel agent can advise you further on this. Some hotels also offer insurance schemes.

ADDRESSES

Establishments are listed in this guide under the name of the place where they are situated or, in the case of isolated spots in the countryside, under the nearest village or town. City, town and village names are listed alphabetically within each regional section and for smaller places an indication of their location is also given. For example '5m N. Anytown' means 5 miles North of Anytown.

County names are not normally repeated in the entries for each establishment but you should ensure that you use the full postal address and post code when writing.

TELEPHONE NUMBERS

The telephone number, exchange name (where this differs from the name of the town under which the establishment is listed) and STD code (in brackets) are given immediately below the establishment address in the listings pages of this guide. The STD code applies to calls made anywhere in the UK except for local calls.

MAP REFERENCES

Map references are given against each place name in this guide. These refer to the colour maps which precede these information pages. The first figure is the map number and the second two indicate the grid reference. A number of entries were included just' before the guide went to press and therefore may not appear on the maps.

BATHROOMS

In each accommodation entry we have shown the number of private bathrooms available, the number of public

bathrooms and the number of private showers. 'Private bathroom' means a bath and/or shower plus a WC en suite with the bedroom; 'private shower' means a shower en suite with the bedroom but no WC.

Public bathrooms are normally equipped with a bath and sometimes also a shower attachment. Some establishments, however, have showers only. If the availability of a bath is an important factor, this should be checked before booking.

CREDIT CARDS

We have indicated immediately above the line of symbols at the end of each accommodation entry any credit or charge cards that are accepted by the establishment concerned. However, you are advised to check this at the time you make a booking if you intend to pay by this method. The abbreviations are set out below:

Access	—	Access/Eurocard/Mastercard
Visa	—	Visa/Barclaycard/Trustcard
C.Bl	—	Carte Blanche
Diners	—	Diners
Amex	—	American Express

VALUABLES

Property of value may be deposited for safe-keeping with the proprietor or manager of the establishment who should give you a receipt and who will then generally be liable for the value of the property in the case of loss. For your peace of mind we advise you to adopt this procedure. In establishments which do not accept articles for safe custody, you are advised to keep valuables under your personal supervision.

You may find that proprietors of some establishments disclaim, by notice, liability for property brought on to their premises by a guest; however, if a guest engages overnight accommodation in a hotel the proprietor is only permitted to restrict his liability to the minimum imposed upon him under the Hotel Proprietors Act, 1956. Under this Act, a proprietor of a hotel is liable for the value of the loss or damage to any property (other than a motor car or its contents) of a guest who has engaged overnight

accommodation, but if the proprietor has a notice in the form prescribed by that Act, his liability is limited to the sum of £50 in respect of one article and a total of £100 in the case of any one guest.

These limits do not apply, however, if the guest deposited the property with him for safe-keeping or if the property is lost through the default, neglect or wilful act of the proprietor or his staff.

To be effective, any notice intended to disclaim or restrict liability must be prominently displayed in the reception area of, or in the main entrance to, the premises.

EVENING MEALS

The starting time for the serving of evening meals and the last order time

(l.o.) is shown in each entry. At some smaller establishments you may be asked at breakfast time or midday whether you will require a meal that evening. So, the last order time could read, say, 9.30am or 1.30pm. The abbreviation 24hr. means that a meal of some kind is always available.

WHEN IS THE ESTABLISHMENT OPEN?

Except where an opening period is shown (e.g. Open March-October), the establishment should be open throughout the year.

YOU WANT A 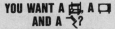, A 🖵 AND A 🎣?

The fold-out flap at the back of this guide shows the symbols which indicate the facilities available at each establishment. If you want, say, a four

poster bed or a swimming pool or you want to be sure that the place you choose will welcome children then fold out the key to symbols so it can be read alongside the entries.

WILL WE BE ABLE TO GET A DRINK?

Alcoholic drinks are available at all types of accommodation listed in this guide unless the symbol UL appears. However, the licence to serve drinks may be restricted, for example to diners only, so you may wish to check this when enquiring about accommodation.

CAN WE TAKE THE DOG WITH US?

Many establishments will accept guests with dogs but we advise you to confirm this at the time of booking when you should also enquire about any extra charges. Some establishments will not accept dogs in any circumstances and these are marked with the symbol 🐕.

Visitors from overseas should not bring pets of any kind into Britain ▶

Cartoons by Tim Britton

▶ unless they are prepared for the animals to go into lengthy quarantine. Owing to the continuing threat of rabies, penalties for ignoring the regulations are extremely severe.

CONFERENCES AND GROUPS

Establishments which can cater for conferences of 10 persons or more have been marked with the symbol ♟. Rates are often negotiable and the price may be affected by a number of factors such as the time of year, number of people and any special requirements stipulated by the organiser.

HOLIDAYS FOR THE PHYSICALLY HANDICAPPED

The symbol ⅙ has been used to indicate establishments which may be suitable for physically handicapped guests. The minimum requirements are:

At least one entrance must have no steps or be equipped with a ramp whose gradient does not exceed 1:12. The entrance door must have a clear opening width of at least 80cm.

Where provided, the following accommodation must either be on the ground floor or accessible by lift (NB where access to a specified area involves step(s), a ramp with a gradient of no more than 1:12 must be provided): — Reception; Restaurant/Dining Room; Lounge; Bar; TV Lounge; public WC; and at least one bedroom served EITHER by a private bath/shower and WC en suite, OR by public facilities on the same floor.

A lift giving access to any of the above must have clear gate opening of at least 80cm; the lift must be at least 140cm deep and 110cm wide.

Doors giving access to any of the above areas (including bath/WC facilities) must have at least 75cm clear opening width.

Tim Britton

In bedrooms, private or public bathrooms and WCs used by disabled people, there must be a clear space immediately adjacent to the bed, bath or WC with a width of at least 75cm. In bedrooms, there must be a turning space of 120cm x 120cm (in bathrooms and WCs: 110cm x 70cm) clear of the line of the doorswing.

Please check the suitability of the establishment at the time of booking and ensure that the management is fully aware of any special requirements.

HOLIDAY CARE SERVICE

For free information and advice on holidays for physically handicapped people and anyone else with special needs contact:
Holiday Care Service
2 Old Bank Chambers, Station Road, Horley, Surrey RH6 9HW
☎ Horley (0293) 774535.

CODE OF CONDUCT

All establishments appearing in this guide are registered with the English Tourist Board and have agreed to observe the following Code of Conduct:
1. To ensure high standards of courtesy and cleanliness; catering and service appropriate to the type of establishment.
2. To describe fairly to all visitors and prospective visitors the amenities, facilities and services provided by the establishment, whether by word of mouth or any other means. To allow visitors to see accommodation, if requested, before booking.
3. To make clear to visitors exactly what is included in all prices quoted for accommodation, meals and refreshments, including service charges, taxes and other surcharges. Details of charges, if any, for heating or for additional services or facilities available should also be made clear. If applicable the establishment should comply with the provisions of the hotel industry's voluntary Code of Booking Practice.
4. To adhere to, and not to exceed, prices current at time of occupation for accommodation or other services.
5. To advise visitors at the time of booking, and subsequently of any change, if the accommodation offered is in an unconnected annexe, or similar, or by boarding out, and to indicate the location of such accommodation and any difference in comfort and amenities from accommodation in the main establishment.
6. To give each visitor, on request, details of payments due and a receipt, if required.
7. To deal promptly and courteously with all enquiries, requests, reservations, correspondence and complaints from visitors.

COMMENTS AND COMPLAINTS

Accommodation establishments have a number of legal and statutory responsibilities towards their customers in areas such as the provision of information on prices, the provision of adequate fire precautions and the safeguarding of valuables. Like other businesses, they must also meet the requirements of the Trade Descriptions Acts 1968 and 1972 when describing and offering accommodation and facilities. When registering with the English Tourist Board establishments declare that they fulfil all applicable statutory obligations.

The establishment descriptions and other details appearing in this guide have been provided by proprietors themselves who have paid for their entries to appear. They have signed a declaration that the information conforms with the requirements of the Trade Descriptions Acts.

Establishments which have a 'Listed' or 'Crown' Classification have been subject to an inspection under the national Crown Classification Scheme.

The English Tourist Board cannot guarantee the accuracy of the information in this guide and accepts no responsibility for any error or misrepresentation. All liability for loss, disappointment, negligence or other damage caused by reliance on the information contained in this guide, or in the event of bankruptcy or liquidation or cessation of trade of any company, individual or firm mentioned, is hereby excluded. Prices and other details should always be carefully checked at the time of booking.

We naturally hope that you will not have any cause for complaint but problems do inevitably occur from time to time. If you are dissatisfied, make your complaint to the management at the time of the incident. This gives the management an opportunity to take action at once to investigate and to put things right without delay. The longer a complaint is left the more difficult it is to deal with effectively.

In certain circumstances the English Tourist Board may look into complaints. However, the Board has no statutory control over registered establishments or their methods of operation and cannot become involved in legal or contractual matters.

We find it very helpful to receive comments about establishments in WHERE TO STAY and suggestions on how to improve the guide. We would like to hear from you. Our address is on page 1.

FOLLOW THE SIGN

It leads to over 550 Tourist Information Centres throughout England offering friendly help with accommodation and holiday ideas as well as suggestions of places to visit and things to do.

In your home town there may be a centre which can help you before you set out. If not, why not send for the Directory of Tourist Information Centres in Great Britain? It is available free from English Tourist Board, Department D, Bromells Road, Clapham, London SW4 0BJ.

The national Crown Classification scheme is simplicity itself.

Before you check into any serviced accommodation, check the display sign outside the premises or in this guide. Instantly, you will know what to expect.

Hotels, guesthouses, motels, inns, farmhouses and bed and breakfast establishments displaying the LISTED or CROWN sign have been checked out by inspectors from the Tourist Boards. Here are some of the other highlights:

* You now have one national classification for serviced accommodation throughout England, Scotland and Wales.

* The system provides you with instant and easy comparison of facilities and services offered.

* You will find it easy to identify and select classified establishments in accommodation guides, advertisements, publicity material and by the signs displayed at the premises.

The classifications that appear in this WHERE TO STAY guide were correct at the time the entries were accepted. All establishments are subject to regular inspection and classifications may be amended from time to time.

LISTED

Establishments displaying the LISTED sign meet the minimum standards required by the national Tourist Boards. They fulfil their statutory obligations, including the requirements of the Fire Precautions Act 1971 (if applicable), the Price Display Order and the provision of public liability insurance.

Buildings, fixtures, furnishings, fittings and decor are maintained in sound and clean condition. In addition, you can expect:

Bedrooms to have...
* Internal lock, bolt or equivalent on bedroom door.
* Reasonable free space for movement and for easy access to beds, doors and drawers.
* A minimum recommended floor area, excluding private bath or shower areas, of: 60sq.ft. single bedrooms, 90sq.ft. double bedrooms, 110sq.ft. twin bedded rooms. Family rooms — 30sq.ft. plus 60sq.ft. for each double bed — plus 40 sq.ft. for each adult single bed — plus 20 sq.ft. for each cot.
* Minimum bed sizes of 6' x 2'6" for single beds and 6' x 4" for double beds.
* Mattresses will be in sound condition and could be spring interior, foam or of similar quality.
* Bedding will be clean and in sufficient quantity with bed linen changed for every new guest and at least once a week.
* Bed linen other than nylon to be available on request and beds will be made daily and bedrooms cleaned daily.
* There will be clean hand towels for every new guest and bath towels available on request. If your room has a washbasin, then soap will be provided.

* There will be adequate ventilation, at least one external window, opaque curtains or blinds.
* Minimum lighting levels of 100 watt in single bedrooms and 150 watt or equivalent in double bedrooms. All bulbs, unless decorative, will be covered or have shades.
* There will be a carpet or bedside rugs or mats. A wardrobe or clothes hanging space (with four or more hangers per person) will be provided.
* Your room will also have a dressing table or equivalent and mirror. There will be a bedside table or equivalent, adequate drawer space, one chair or equivalent, waste paper container, ashtray where smoking permitted, one drinking tumbler per guest and adequate heating according to season.

Bathrooms to have...
* Bath or shower, washbasin and

Cartoons by Tim Britton

CLASSIFICATIONS

mirror (if any bedrooms without wash handbasins), electric razor point and soap.

  * There will be at least one bathroom for every 15 residents and it will be available at all reasonable times.

  * Hot water will be available at reasonable times and the bathroom will be adequately heated.

  * You will not be charged extra for baths or showers.

LISTED establishments will also provide at least one WC, adequately ventilated, for every 12 residents and there will be a sanitary disposal bin and toilet paper in each WC.

Additional benefits include...

Provision of breakfast, with dining/breakfast room unless meals are served only in bedrooms. All public areas will be well lit for safety and comfort. There will be adequate heating in all public areas, according to season. Public areas in the establishment will also be cleaned daily. Furthermore, you will be informed, when checking in, if access to the establishment is restricted during the day or night.

1 CROWN

Serviced accommodation displaying the single CROWN will provide all the minimum standard requirements of a LISTED establishment plus several additional comforts and conveniences.

For instance, you can expect both single and double beds in a 1 CROWN establishment to be larger and nylon bed linen will not be acceptable. There will be washbasins, with hot and cold running water, either in the bedroom or in a private bathroom with fresh soap for every new letting. There will be a light adjacent to or above the washbasin, a 13 amp socket with suitable adaptor, electric razor point or adaptor and a light controlled from the bed.

You will enjoy the comfort of at least one chair or equivalent per guest and a minimum of two in family rooms. There will be no extra charge for room heating and you will have 24 hour access to your room(s).

1 CROWN establishments will provide at least 1 bathroom, with bath or shower, for every 10 residents — and at least 1 bathroom for the sole use of guests. There will be at least one WC for every 8 resident guests.

The lounge area will have an adequate number of chairs and you will have easy access to the lounge at all reasonable hours. There will be a separate reception facility or bell to call for attention. You will have use of a telephone and tourist information should you need any.

2 CROWNS

With every additional CROWN, you can expect better facilities.

For instance, 2 CROWN establishments meet all the criteria of 1 CROWN serviced accommodation and offer several additional comforts and services.

The dining/breakfast room will be separate from the lounge unless meals are served in the rooms. You can enjoy morning tea/coffee in your bedroom on

request. (You may even find your own beverage making facilities in your bedroom.) After a tiring day, you may order a hot beverage in the evening. There may be alarm clocks in bedrooms or else you can request an early morning call. If there is no TV in your room, you can be sure there will be a colour TV in the lounge.

Double beds will have bedside lights or a single bedhead light, in addition to a light controlled from the door. Double beds will have access from both sides and there will be an electric razor point near the mirror.

You can also request assistance with your luggage when you check in and check out.

3 CROWNS

Are you particular about having your own attached bath or shower with WC en suite?

If you are checking into a 3 CROWN establishment, chances are you will get one, as at least 33% of bedrooms in a 3 CROWN establishment must have them. You may also relax in the easy chair provided in your room.

There will be one additional chair if you have booked a twin or double room. There will be a full length mirror, luggage stand and fixed heating ▶

▶ with automatic and individual control.

Should you need any assistance, you can talk to the staff or proprietor who will be available throughout the day. You can catch a quiet moment or two in the lounge which will be separate from the bar or TV lounge.

You can also request a hair dryer, electric iron and ironing board. The establishment will have a pay telephone.

And do you like your shoes to shine before that important business call? Just use the shoe-cleaning facilities provided with the compliments of the establishment.

4 CROWNS

If a 3 CROWN establishment isn't enough, book into a 4 CROWN and enjoy even more facilities.

For instance, 75% of all bedrooms will have a private bath or shower and WC en suite. You can relax in your own room and watch your colour TV or tune into your favourite radio station, and your room telephone will enable you to make external calls.

Lounge service will be available until midnight and you will have 24 hour access to the establishment. So if you're out until the early hours of the morning, you can still get back to your room to catch some sleep and be ready for the next day.

If the establishment has four or more floors, then a passenger lift is

John Hillaby's
WALKING IN BRITAIN

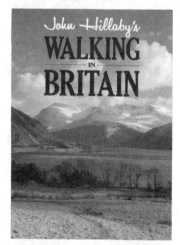

A comprehensive and inspirational guide to the great walks and finest walking country of Britain. With contributions from 20 leading writers and walking enthusiasts such as Hunter Davies, Richard Mabey and Adam Nicolson.

Beautifully illustrated with over 150 colour photographs and stunning watercolours by David Bellamy.

Published in association with the English Tourist Board.

£14.95 Available from all good bookshops

Collins    English Tourist Board

CLASSIFICATIONS

compulsory. The lounge will have writing tables if comparable facilities are not available in rooms.

Finally, there will be additional facilities like message taking, newspapers and toiletries available on request.

And all these services are in addition to what you would otherwise enjoy in a 3 CROWN establishment.

5 CROWNS

If you are about to check into an establishment displaying 5 CROWNS, then you can expect the most of everything. Every facility in a 4 CROWN establishment will be there to enjoy — plus a few more.

Every bedroom, for instance, will have private bath, fixed shower attachment and WC en suite.

There will be a direct dial telephone, writing table, or appropriate alternative, with chair/seat. If your clothes need pressing, you can summon the valet or use the trouser press and also avail yourself of the 24 hour return laundry service (except at weekends).

Room service is assured should you need any and the lounge service is available all night. There will be a night porter at your service as well.

Finally, the establishment will offer one or more suites for bookings.

5 GOLD CROWNS

FIVE GOLD CROWNS is an accolade awarded by the English Tourist Board to distinguish those hotels in England that have attained exceptionally high standards in their provision of facilities and services.

* The facilities indicated under each classification are minimum requirements. Establishments often provide their own additional 'extras' — inside and outside the prices quoted in their tariffs.

• HISTORIC HOUSES ASSOCIATION •

THE COUNTRY HOUSE GUIDE

• FAMILY HOMES IN THE H.H.A. •

Anna Sproule

Fully illustrated with over 100 colour and 150 black and white photographs. Published by Century in association with the English Tourist Board and the Historic Houses Association

Hardback, price £16.95
Available from all good bookshops.

English Tourist Board

FOLLOW THE SIGN

It leads to over 550 Tourist Information Centres throughout England offering friendly help with accommodation and holiday ideas as well as suggestions of places to visit and things to do.

In your home town there may be a centre which can help you before you set out. If not, why not send for the Directory of Tourist Information Centres in Great Britain? It is available free from English Tourist Board, Department D, Bromells Road, Clapham, London SW4 0BJ.

♣ Enjoy the countryside and respect its life and work ♣ Guard against all risk of fire ♣ Fasten all gates ♣ Keep your dogs under close control ♣ Keep to public paths across farmland ♣ Use gates and stiles to cross fences, hedges and walls ♣ Leave livestock, crops and machinery alone ♣ Take your litter home ♣ Help to keep all water clean ♣ Protect wildlife, plants and trees ♣ Take special care on country roads ♣ Make no unnecessary noise

When enquiring about accommodation you may find it helpful to use the booking enquiry coupons which can be found towards the end of the guide. These should be cut out and mailed direct to the establishments in which you are interested. Remember to include your name and address and please enclose a stamped addressed envelope (or an international reply coupon if writing from outside Britain).

COUPONS

➡ Please complete this coupon and mail it direct to the establishment in which you are interested. Do not send it to the English Tourist Board. Remember to enclose a stamped addressed envelope (or international reply coupon).

➡ Tick as appropriate and complete the reverse side if you are interested in making a booking.

➡ ☐ **Please send me a brochure or further information, and details of prices charged.**

➡ ☐ **Please advise me, as soon as possible, if accommodation is available as detailed overleaf.**

My name is: _____ (BLOCK CAPITALS)

Address: _____

_____

_____

Telephone number: _____   Date: _____

Where to Stay 1989 Farmhouses,
Bed & Breakfast, Inns and Hostels in England

English Tourist Board

➡ Please complete this coupon and mail it direct to the establishment in which you are interested. Do not send it to the English Tourist Board. Remember to enclose a stamped addressed envelope (or international reply coupon).

➡ Tick as appropriate and complete the reverse side if you are interested in making a booking.

➡ ☐ **Please send me a brochure or further information, and details of prices charged.**

➡ ☐ **Please advise me, as soon as possible, if accommodation is available as detailed overleaf.**

My name is: _____ (BLOCK CAPITALS)

Address: _____

_____

_____

Telephone number: _____   Date: _____

Where to Stay 1989 Farmhouses,
Bed & Breakfast, Inns and Hostels in England

English Tourist Board

C O U P O N S

➡ **Please complete this side if you are interested in making a booking.**

I am interested in booking accommodation for:

_____ adults and _____ children (ages: _____)

(Please give the number of people and the ages of any children)

From (date of arrival): _____ To (date of departure): _____

or alternatively from: _____ to: _____

Accommodation required: _____

_____

Meals required: _____

Other/special requirements: _____

➡ **Please enclose a stamped addressed envelope (or international reply coupon).**
➡ **Please read the 'Further Information' section before confirming any booking.**

➡ **Please complete this side if you are interested in making a booking.**

I am interested in booking accommodation for:

_____ adults and _____ children (ages: _____)

(Please give the number of people and the ages of any children)

From (date of arrival): _____ To (date of departure): _____

or alternatively from: _____ to: _____

Accommodation required: _____

_____

Meals required: _____

Other/special requirements: _____

➡ **Please enclose a stamped addressed envelope (or international reply coupon).**
➡ **Please read the 'Further Information' section before confirming any booking.**